Numerical Methods and Computer Simulations in Energy Analysis

Numerical Methods and Computer Simulations in Energy Analysis

Editors

Marcin Kamiński
Angel A. Juan

MDPI

Basel • Beijing • Wuhan • Barcelona • Belgrade • Novi Sad • Cluj • Manchester

Editors
Marcin Kamiński
Lodz University of Technology
Lodz, Poland

Angel A. Juan
Universitat Politècnica de València (UPV, Spain)
Alcoy, Spain

Editorial Office
MDPI
St. Alban-Anlage 66
4052 Basel, Switzerland

This is a reprint of articles from the Topic published online in the open access journals *Energies* (ISSN 1996-1073), *Mathematics* (ISSN 2227-7390), and *Sci* (ISSN 2413-4155) (available at: https://www.mdpi.com/topics/numerical_methods).

For citation purposes, cite each article independently as indicated on the article page online and as indicated below:

Lastname, A.A.; Lastname, B.B. Article Title. *Journal Name* **Year**, *Volume Number*, Page Range.

ISBN 978-3-0365-9200-8 (Hbk)
ISBN 978-3-0365-9201-5 (PDF)
doi.org/10.3390/books978-3-0365-9201-5

Cover image courtesy of Marcin Kamiński

Contents

About the Editors

Marcin Kamiński

Marcin Kamiński has been a Full Professor in the Department of Structural Mechanics, Łódź University of Technology, since 2015. He has been the Head of the Discipline Civil Engineering, Geodesy & Transportation in the Faculty of Civil Engineering, Architecture & Environmental Engineering, since 2019. His main research includes the stochastic finite element method, numerical modeling of random composites including homogenization theory, reliability assessment and optimization of civil engineering structures, stochastic ageing processes, and, recently, an application of probabilistic entropy in engineering computations.

He spent a postdoctoral study at Rice University in Houston, USA, and was a visiting professor at Leibniz-Institute of Polymer Research in Dresden, Germany, and also at Politecnico di Milano, Italy. He authored more than 200 research papers in various journals including the *International Journal for Numerical Methods in Engineering, Composite Structures, International Journal of Solids & Structures, and also Computers & Structures*. He published two monographs: "Computational Mechanics of Composite Materials", Springer, 2005; and "The Stochastic Perturbation Method for Computational Mechanics", Wiley, 2013. He serves as the Associate Editor of Mechanics Research Communications and a member of the editorial board in *Acta Mechanica, Computers & Structures, Journal of Composites Science* and *SCI*.

He has been the recipient of fellowships from the Foundation for Polish Science, J. Argyris Award from ECCOMAS and Elsevier, J.T. Oden Scholarship at The University of Texas at Austin, and also some Polish national or academic awards including Bronze Cross of Merit (1998), Silver Cross for the Longstanding Service (2017), Medal of Commission of Education (2022), and also very recently The Research Prize of Ministry of Education & Science in 2023. He has recently been recognized (since 2021) as the World's Top 2% Scientists by Stanford University, CA, USA.

Angel A. Juan

Angel A. Juan is a Full Professor of Data Science and Operations Research at the Universitat Politècnica de València and Invited Professor at University College Dublin. Dr. Juan holds a Ph.D. in Industrial Engineering/Applied Mathematics, an M.S. in Information Systems & Technology, and an M.S. and B.Sc. in Mathematics. He completed a predoctoral internship at Harvard University and has been a Visiting Researcher at the Massachusetts Institute of Technology and the Georgia Institute of Technology, among others.

His main research interests include applications of Data Analytics, Optimization, Simulation, and Artificial Intelligence in Computational Transportation and Logistics, Production and Manufacturing, Computational Finance and Insurance, and Smart Cities. He has published over 150 articles in JCR-indexed journals and more than 325 documents indexed in Scopus. Dr. Juan is or has been Principal Investigator of several R&D projects.

Dr. Juan is one of the founders of the Decision Science Alliance. He is a member of the Mathematics/Business Expert Panels of the Flanders Research Foundation (FWO) and the Agencia Andaluza del Conocimiento (AAC). He has been a Council Member of the INFORMS i-Sim society as well as an Executive Council member of the Spanish Society of Statistics and Operations Research (SEIO).

energies

MDPI

Article

Analysis of Hybrid Hetero-Homo Junction Lead-Free Perovskite Solar Cells by SCAPS Simulator

Marwa. S. Salem [1,2], Ahmed Shaker [3,*], Abdelhalim Zekry [4], Mohamed Abouelatta [4], Adwan Alanazi [5], Mohammad T. Alshammari [5] and Christian Gontand [6,7]

1 Department of Computer Engineering, Computer Science and Engineering College, University of Ha'il, Ha'il 55211, Saudi Arabia; marwa_asu@yahoo.com
2 Department of Electrical Communication and Electronics Systems Engineering, Faculty of Engineering, Modern Science and Arts (MSA) University, Cairo 12566, Egypt
3 Department of Engineering Physics and Mathematics, Faculty of Engineering, Ain Shams University, Cairo 11566, Egypt
4 Department of Electronics and Communications, Faculty of Engineering, Ain Shams University, Cairo 11566, Egypt; aaazekry@hotmail.com (A.Z.); m.abouelatta@eng.asu.edu.eg (M.A.)
5 Department of Computer Science and Information, Computer Science and Engineering College, University of Ha'il, Ha'il 55211, Saudi Arabia; a.alanazi@uoh.edu.sa (A.A.); md.alshammari@uoh.edu.sa (M.T.A.)
6 INSA–Lyon, Villeurbanne, 69621 Lyon, France; christian.gontrand@insa-lyon.fr
7 IEP, Université Euro-Mé Diterrané enne de Fès, INSA-Fès, Fès 30120, Morocco
* Correspondence: ahmed.shaker@eng.asu.edu.eg

Citation: Salem, M.S.; Shaker, A.; Zekry, A.; Abouelatta, M.; Alanazi, A.; Alshammari, M.T.; Gontand, C. Analysis of Hybrid Hetero-Homo Junction Lead-Free Perovskite Solar Cells by SCAPS Simulator. *Energies* **2021**, *14*, 5741. https://doi.org/10.3390/en14185741

Academic Editor: Marcin Kamiński

Received: 17 August 2021
Accepted: 9 September 2021
Published: 12 September 2021

Abstract: In this work, we report on the effect of substituting the active intrinsic i-layer on a conventional pin structure of lead-free perovskite solar cell (PSC) by a homo p-n junction, keeping the thickness of the active layer constant. It is expected that when the active i-layer is substituted by a p-n homo junction, one can increase the collection efficiency of the photo-generated electrons and holes due to the built-in electric field of the homo junction. The impact of the technological and physical device parameters on the performance parameters of the solar cell have been worked out. It was found that p-side thickness must be wider than the n-side, while its acceptor concentration should be slightly lower than the donor concentration of the n-side to achieve maximum efficiency. In addition, different absorber types, namely, i-absorber, n-absorber and p-absorber, are compared to the proposed pn-absorber, showing a performance-boosting effect when using the latter. Moreover, the proposed structure is made without a hole transport layer (HTL) to avoid the organic issues of the HTL materials. The back metal work function, bulk trap density and ETL material are optimized for best performance of the HTL-free structure, giving J_{sc} = 26.48, V_{oc} = 0.948 V, FF = 77.20 and PCE = 19.37% for AM1.5 solar spectra. Such results highlight the prospective of the proposed structure and emphasize the importance of using HTL-free solar cells without deteriorating the efficiency. The solar cell is investigated by using SCAPS simulator.

Keywords: lead-free; perovskite solar cell; homo p-n junction; HTL-free cells; SCAPS simulator

1. Introduction

Among the various new energy technologies, solar power is one of the most favorable technologies [1,2]. In this regard, solar cells which can directly convert the sunlight to electricity are growing rapidly in their use [3,4]. Currently, silicon-based solar cells, utilized in industrial applications, have attained a power conversion efficiency (PCE) of more than 20% [5,6]. Nevertheless, such silicon solar cells require a thicker absorber layer due to the low absorption coefficient of Silicon and so they involve higher manufacturing costs [7,8]. In previous decades, different types of photovoltaic devices were established [9–15]. Perovskite solar cells (PSCs) have experienced speedy development during the last decade because of several advantages, including low density, flexibility and low-cost production [16–20]. Despite the fast growth of the reported PCE of lead-based PSCs from an initial value of 3.8% [21] to values higher than 25% [22], their usage is limited as they are not eco-friendly and cause serious environmental concern.

To avoid the instability and toxicity issues of lead, two principal approaches have been presented in the literature. The first technique is accomplished by mixing other metals with lead, where the metals used in the mixture have lower toxicity. One of the most widely used mixtures is tin-lead alloyed perovskite ($CH_3NH_3Sn_xPb_{1-x}$) [23]. The second methodology is performed by entirely substituting lead with similar metals. As a candidate of the toxic lead, the innocuous Tin is regarded as the most appropriate metal because both metals are in the same group in the periodic table [24]. In this regard, $CH_3NH_3SnI_3$ is considered a promising competitor to replace lead-based PSCs [25]. This material demonstrates a direct band gap of 1.3 eV, which is considered a proper range for the solar cell absorber material [26]. Recently, several groups have effectively fabricated and simulated $CH_3NH_3SnI_3$-based PSCs, which yielded competitive PCEs [27–29]. Further progress in the solar cell efficiency is constrained by the charge carrier recombination, mainly in the absorber layer when utilizing heterojunction-based structures. Recent works have shown that reducing the charge carrier recombination in the absorber layer and at the interfaces between the absorber layer and adjacent layers allows a PCE to get closer to theoretical values [30,31].

In general, a perovskite material could be either a p-type or an n-type via managing the process condition and the ratio of composition stoichiometry [32–35]. Therefore, it is possible to produce a p–n homojunction PSC because of this self-doping property. Homojunction could decrease the defects/traps that operate as recombination centers [36]. Compared to heterojunction PSC, a homojunction cell has an extra built-in electric field that can boost the transport of photoexcited electrons and holes which, in turn, can reduce the recombination losses. Therefore, the homojunction device is extremely attractive for further enhancement of PSCs [36]. Recent research works are concerned with investigating the lead-based homojunction PSCs [35–40]. However, the lead-free homojunction PSCs have not been investigated yet. To our best knowledge, this is the first study to inspect the device characteristics of hybrid hetero-homojunction lead-free PSCs. The design guidelines provided in this work regarding the lead-free homojunction PSCs are completely different from those encountered in the lead-based homojunction cells. This is mainly due to the difference in absorber material properties, especially the energy band gap, as will be seen hereafter.

Moreover, the most widely used hole transport layer (HTL) material in PSCs is based on organics [41–43], which results in instability issues and an overall expensive cost of PSCs. To conquer these concerns, lots of research has focused on the HTL-free PSCs to simplify the cell architecture and reduce the overall production cost [44,45]. However, the lack of the HTL is accompanied by a poorer hole extraction. This weak extraction behavior might limit the cell performance. Therefore, new strategies have to be carried out to unravel this major issue. As a result, designing efficient p–n homojunctions in the HTL-free PSCs could be a useful and favorable approach to further improve the solar cell performance and to decrease the production cost as well.

Numerical simulation is a basic technique by which the feasibility of a novel device can be tested. In addition, the impact of physical and technological parameters on device performance could be easily investigated. In this work, we propose a hybrid hetero-homojunction-based, lead-free PSCs utilizing an n-type $CH_3NH_3SnI_3$/p-type $CH_3NH_3SnI_3$ bilayer as an absorber layer by deploying SCAPS for the numerical analysis. This configuration allows for omitting the HTL layers, making an HTL-free device structure. A thorough investigation of the device working principles along with their underlying physics is performed. Firstly, the simulation model is justified by means of comparing the theoretical performance of a conventional pin lead-free PSC with experimental results. Then, the effect of both absorber (n-type and p-type) thickness and doping concentration is inspected in order to get an optimum value for the PCE. Moreover, the HTL-free configuration is investigated, and the work function of the back contact and defect density of the absorber are studied to determine their influence on the device performance. Based on the presented results, we provide some recommendations and guidance to the design of hetero-homojunction lead-free PSCs, either with or without HTL.

2. Device Structure and Simulation Parameters

2.1. SCAPS Highlight

Numerical simulation was performed in the work by utilizing the SCAPS-1D program [46]. SCAPS (solar cell capacitance simulator) is a one-dimensional simulation program dedicated for various types of solar cells. The program is widely utilized to simulate the device parameters of PSCs and other solar cell structures. Most of the simulation results are consistent with measurements and offer vital indications and predictions for experimental work. Based on SCAPS simulations, one can get cell parameters like dark and illuminated current density vs voltage (J–V) characteristics, quantum efficiency (QE) and energy bands. This can be done by solving the electron (Equation (1)) and hole (Equation (2)) continuity equation coupled with Poisson's equation (Equation (3)), together with the constitutive equations (Equations (4) and (5)),

$$\frac{dJ_n}{dx} = G(x) - U_n \tag{1}$$

$$\frac{dJ_p}{dx} = G(x) - U_p \tag{2}$$

$$\frac{d}{dx}\left(\varepsilon_r\varepsilon_o\frac{d\psi}{dx}\right) = -\frac{q}{\varepsilon}(p - n + N_D^+ - N_A^- + p_t - n_t) \tag{3}$$

$$J_n = -\frac{n\mu_n}{q}\frac{dE_{Fn}}{dx} \tag{4}$$

$$J_p = +\frac{p\mu_p}{q}\frac{dE_{Fp}}{dx} \tag{5}$$

where G denotes the generation rate (cm^{-3}·s^{-1}) and x is the distance along the device. The electron and hole recombination rates (cm^{-3}·s^{-1}) are denoted by U_n and U_p, respectively. ε_r is the dielectric constant, q is electron charge and ψ is the electrostatic potential. N_D^+ and N_A^- are donor and acceptor doping concentration. $p(x)$, n, p_t and n_t represent the free hole, free electrons, trapped electron, and trapped hole concentrations, respectively. The electron and hole mobilities are denoted by μ_n and μ_p while the Fermi level of the electrons and holes are denoted by E_{Fn} and E_{Fp}, respectively.

After applying the appropriate boundary conditions at the contacts and the interfaces, Equations (1)–(5) are transported to a system of coupled differential equations in (ψ, n, p) or (ψ, E_{Fn}, E_{Fp}). SCAPS numerically computes a steady state and a small signal solution of this resulting system. The first step in every calculation is to discretize the structure by a coarse meshing in the middle of a layer. Meanwhile, a finer meshing near the interfaces and contacts are utilized. Further, the mesh can be optimized during the calculations. The system of equations is solved numerically, using a Gummel iteration scheme with Newton-Raphson sub-steps [46].

2.2. Device Model and Parameters

The conventional undoped absorber and proposed hybrid lead-free PCS structures are illustrated in Figure 1a,b, respectively. In Figure 1b, the p-$CH_3NH_3SnI_3$ and n-$CH_3NH_3SnI_3$ are perovskite layers having two different doping types, namely the p-type and n-type regions. In these devices, TCO and Au are front and back electrodes, TiO_2 is used as the electron transporting layer (ETL), and Spiro-OMeTAD is utilized as a hole transporting layer (HTL). Further, Figure 1c presents the energy level diagram of the conventional pin structure and how carriers are transported across the layers.

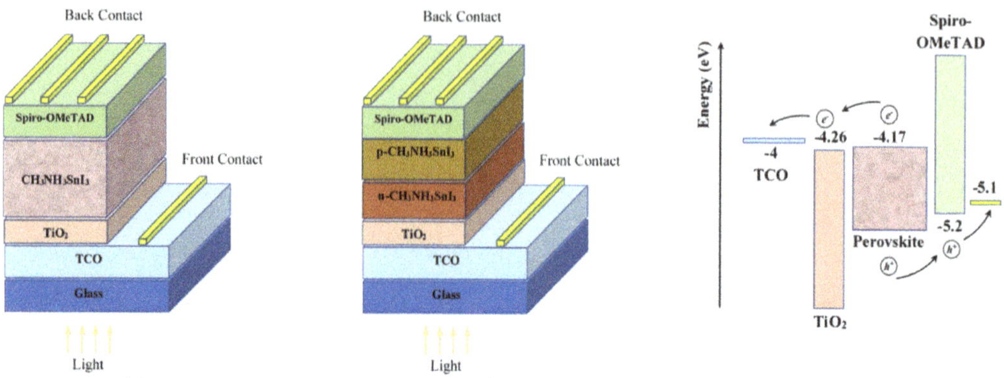

(a) (b) (c)

Figure 1. (**a**) A schematic representation of the conventional pin lead-free PSC, (**b**) the proposed hybrid hetero-homo junction-based structure, (**c**) the energy level diagram of the conventional pin structure showing how carriers are transported across the layers.

In order to validate the SCAPS simulation model, the conventional pin lead-free PSC with the structure of TCO/TiO_2/$CH_3NH_3SnI_3$/Spiro-OMeTAD/Au [47], illustrated in Figure 1a, is simulated. The material parameters for the used layers are given in Table 1, which are derived from some reported experimental and simulated works [27,47–51]. The thickness is denoted by t, the band gap energy is termed E_g while the electron affinity is denoted by χ. The relative dielectric permittivity is ε_r, and conduction and valence band effective density of states are N_c and N_v, respectively. μ_n and μ_p are the electron and hole mobility, respectively. The donor concentration, acceptor concentration and trap density are denoted as N_D, N_A and N_t, respectively. The front and back electrode work functions are 4.4 eV (corresponding to TCO) and 5.4 eV (corresponding to Au), respectively. Other parameters of the front and back metal contacts utilized in SCPAS simulation are presented in Table S1 in the Supplementary Material.

Table 1. Simulation parameters of materials used in simulation of PSC devices.

Parameters	TCO [48]	TiO_2 [48,50]	$CH_3NH_3SnI_3$ [47,49,51]	Spiro-OmeTAD [48]
t (nm)	500	30	350	200
E_g (eV)	3.5	3.2	1.3	3.17
χ (eV)	4	4.26	4.17	2.05
ε_r	9	9	8.2	3
N_c (cm^{-3})	2.2×10^{18}	2×10^{18}	1×10^{18}	2.2×10^{18}
N_v (cm^{-3})	1.8×10^{19}	1.8×10^{19}	1×10^{18}	1.8×10^{19}
μ_n (cm^2/V.s)	20	20	1.6	2×10^{-4}
μ_p (cm^2/V.s)	10	10	1.6	2×10^{-4}
N_D (cm^{-3})	2×10^{19}	1×10^{16}	0	0
N_A (cm^{-3})	0	0	0	2×10^{19}
N_t (cm^{-3})	1×10^{15}	1×10^{15}	5×10^{17}	1×10^{15}

In this simulation study, the defects are situated above the valence band by 0.65 eV (which coincides with the mid gap of the perovskite material under consideration) and put as neutral Gaussian distribution, having a characteristic energy of 0.1 eV. The trap density was found to be 5×10^{17} cm^{-3} for the best fit between experimental results and simulation. The capture cross-section of the electron (σ_n) and hole (σ_p) is 1×10^{-15} cm^2. Very thin interface defect layers (IDLs) are inserted at the TiO_2/$CH_3NH_3SnI_3$ and $CH_3NH_3SnI_3$/Spiro-OMeTAD interfaces to represent the interface carrier recombination.

The physical parameters of the IDLs are as follows. The defect energy (E_t) is located at the mid gap of the perovskite and the defect type is set as neutral single defect with a total density of 10^{17} cm^{-3}. The capture cross-section of the electron and hole is also 1×10^{-15} cm^2, like the bulk traps. A summary of the main defect parameters is presented in Table 2.

Table 2. Defect density parameters in the absorber and at the interfaces.

	ETL/Absorber	Absorber/HTM	$CH_3NH_3SnI_3$
Defect type	Neutral	Neutral	Neutral
σ_n and σ_p (cm^{-2})	1×10^{-15}	1×10^{-15}	2×10^{-14}
Energetic distribution	Single	Single	Gaussian
E_t—E_v	0.6	0.6	0.65
Characteristic energy (eV)	-	-	0.1
Total density (cm^{-3})	1×10^{15}	1×10^{15}	5×10^{17}

Further, Equation (6) is used for the calculations of the absorption coefficients (α) of TCO, ETL, $CH_3NH_3SnI_3$ and HTL materials with a pre-factor (A_α), which is selected to be 10^5 cm^{-1}eV$^{-1/2}$ [52],

$$\alpha(E) = A_\alpha \sqrt{h\nu - E_g} \quad (6)$$

The simulation results are compared vs the reported experimental results [47]. Figure 2 illustrates the illuminated *J–V* curve of the simulated device vs measurements showing a good accuracy. The main parameters are listed in Table 3, indicating an absolute error ($\Delta\xi$) of less than 8% for all parameters. Therefore, the reliability of our simulation model is validated, and further inspections can be done based on this simulation model.

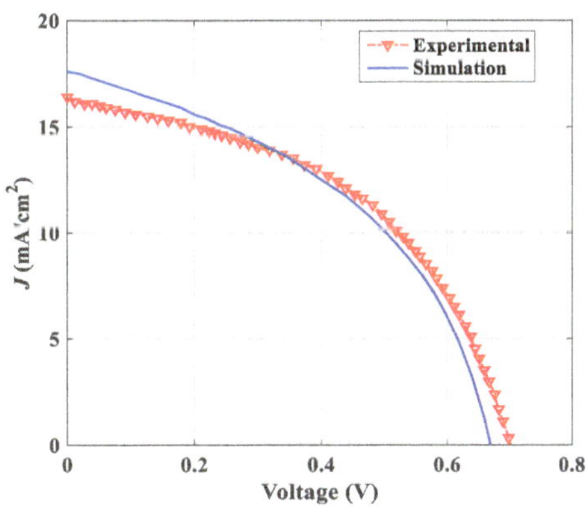

Figure 2. The illuminated *J–V* curve of the simulated device vs measurements.

Table 3. Main performance parameters and absolute error between simulation results compared with measurements.

	J_{sc} (mA/cm^2)	V_{oc} (V)	*FF* (%)	η (%)
Measurements	16.40	0.696	48.00	5.23
Simulation	17.60	0.670	44.20	5.15
$\Delta\xi$	7.32%	3.74%	7.92%	1.53%

3. Results and Discussion

3.1. Design of Hybrid Hetero-Homojucntion Cell

Firstly, we will discuss the main design rule that governs the operation of the p-n homojunction part of the hybrid hetero-homojunction cell. The doping densities of the two regions of a p–n junction must fulfill a condition to ensure that the depletion width is considerably lesser than the absorber layer thickness (t). Therefore, the doping densities must meet the following condition [53],

$$N_{A/D} > \frac{2\varepsilon_0 \varepsilon_r V_{bi}}{qt^2} \quad (7)$$

where V_{bi} is the built-in voltage. Figure 3 shows the variation of the depletion width vs donor or acceptor doping density for two different values of V_{bi}. The horizontal line indicates the perovskite absorber thickness, which is 350 nm in our design. Therefore, the threshold (minimum) doping density depends on the value of V_{bi} and it is in the order of 1×10^{16} cm^{-3}, given the reported experimental thickness of d = 350 nm and ε_r = 8.2 for a typical value of $V_{bi} \sim 1$ V. Our initial design starts by N_D (n-$CH_3NH_3SnI_3$) = N_A (p-$CH_3NH_3SnI_3$) = 1×10^{16} cm^{-3}.

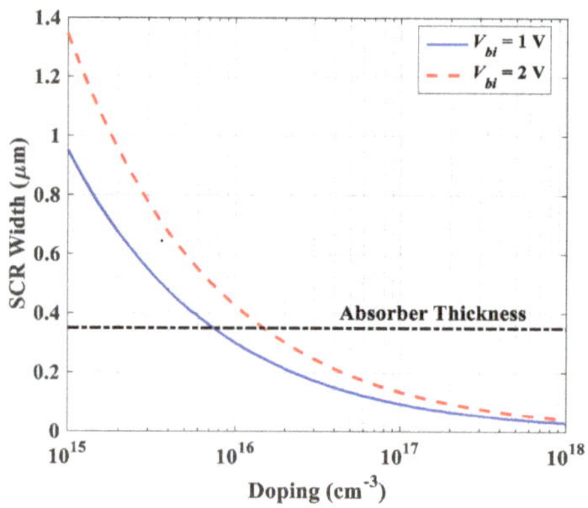

Figure 3. The variation of the depletion width vs donor or acceptor doping density.

3.1.1. Influence of n- and p-Region Thickness

Regarding the hybrid hetero-homojunction lead-free PSC shown in Figure 1b, the whole n-$CH_3NH_3SnI_3$/p-$CH_3NH_3SnI_3$ homojunction functions as the perovskite absorber region. When the cell is illuminated, the photoinduced charge carriers are produced in both the p-type and n-type layers. The variations of the photovoltaic parameters are examined with p-type $CH_3NH_3SnI_3$ layer thickness varying from 0 nm to 350 nm, taking into account that the sum of the n-type and p-type layers is fixed at 350 nm, which is the original, experimentally reported, overall thickness of the absorber layer [47].

The J_{sc}, V_{oc}, FF, and PCE vs. p-layer thickness are given in Figure 4. Referring to the figure, it can be observed that all performance parameters are gradually increasing with the increase of p-$CH_3NH_3SnI_3$ thickness. Beyond a thickness of 300 nm, J_{sc} saturates at a value of about 20 mA/cm^2. The thickness of p-$CH_3NH_3SnI_3$ affects V_{oc} as it increases and then decreases slightly beyond a thickness of 300 nm. FF is increased because the series resistance declines with the decreasing thickness of the n-$CH_3NH_3SnI_3$ layer (as the p-$CH_3NH_3SnI_3$ layer thickness increases). The combination of the J_{sc}, V_{oc} and FF results in the variation trend of PCE shown in the figure. The PCE is first enhanced with increasing the thickness of p-$CH_3NH_3SnI_3$ and then slowly decreases beyond a p-type layer thickness of 300 nm. Accordingly, in the following simulations, we set thicknesses of 300 and 50 nm as optimized values of the p-$CH_3NH_3SnI_3$ and n-$CH_3NH_3SnI_3$ thickness, respectively.

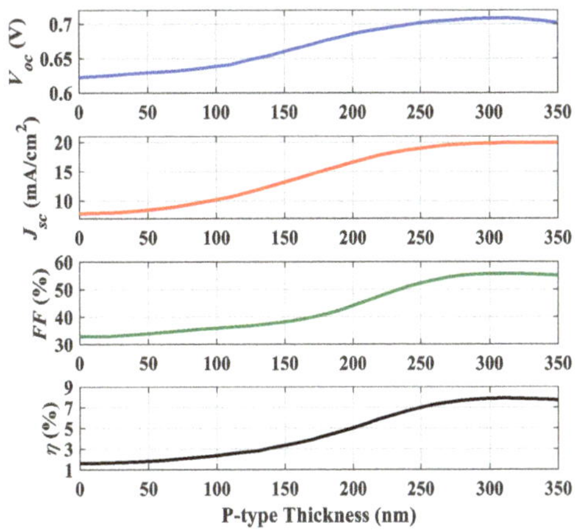

Figure 4. Impact of p-layer thickness on the photovoltaic parameters.

Figure 5 shows the J–V characteristics under illumination (Figure 5a) and the quantum efficiency (Figure 5b) for three selected cases. The first case is the conventional pin structure for which the absorber is intrinsic and the other two cases are for $x_p > x_n$ (taking $x_p = 300$ µm) and $x_n > x_p$ (taking $x_p = 50$ µm) to demonstrate the difference between the impact of n-type and p-type thicknesses on the terminal characteristics compared to the conventional case. The results are confirmed in Figure 4, as both V_{oc} and J_{sc} are degraded when the n-type thickness is higher than the p-type thickness. It was observed that when the p-type thickness is higher, the performance is enhanced over the conventional pin structure.

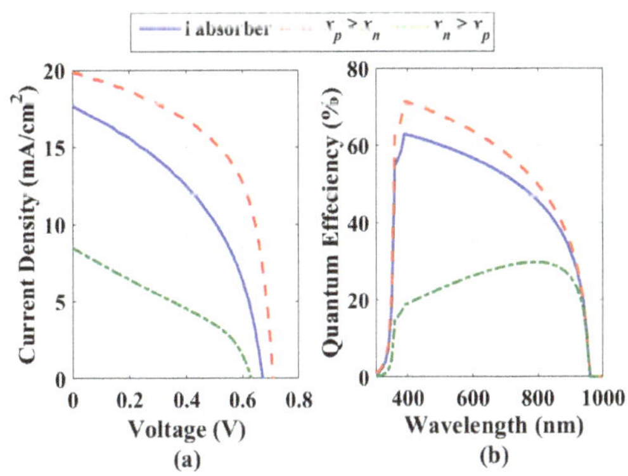

Figure 5. Difference between hetero-homo p-n junction (for $x_n > x_p$ and $x_p > x_n$) vs conventional pin solar cell (**a**) illuminated J–V under AM1.5 and (**b**) quantum efficiency.

To give a physical insight about the dependence of the performance parameters on the thickness of the p- (or n-) layer, we drew the generation and the recombination rates across the device distance at a voltage of 0.5 V, as illustrated in Figure 6. The generation rate is the same for the different cases, as is clear from Figure 6a. It can be seen in Figure 6b that it is better to choose a wider p-layer to suppress the recombination losses. When using a wider n-layer, the recombination increases in the n-layer. Although it is suppressed in the p-layer when compared to the case of intrinsic absorber, the overall recombination losses are higher when the n-layer thickness exceeds the p-layer thickness.

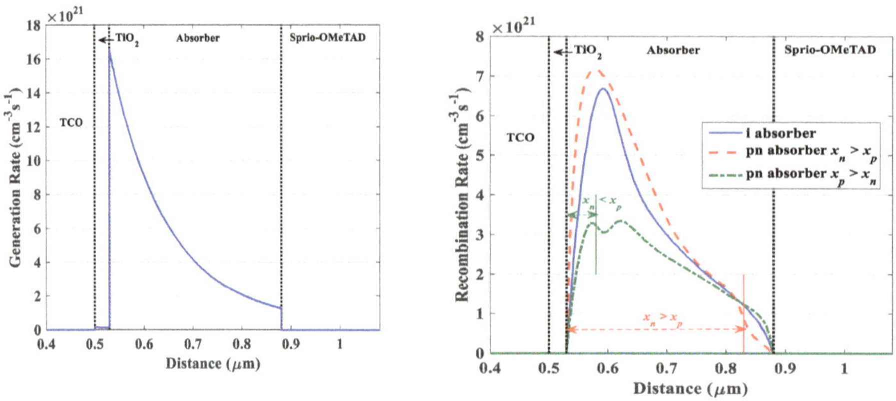

(a) (b)

Figure 6. (**a**) The generation rate and (**b**) recombination rate across the device distance at a voltage of 0.5 V for three distinctive cases of absorber.

In addition, the electric field distribution along the device structure (from ETL to HTL direction) at a voltage of 0.5 V supports the idea of recombination behavior, and this distribution is shown in Figure 7. The field distribution illustrates that the field direction of the case when $x_n > x_p$ is reversed at the absorber/ETL interface, so it is in opposite direction to the two other cases. This field reversal affects the carrier collection and results in an increase in recombination rates and thus a reduction in the current. On the other hand, the field direction of the two other cases is in the proper route at the absorber/ETL interface in such a way as to enhance the electron collection by pushing the electrons from the absorber to the ETL. In addition, it is noted that when $x_p > x_n$, the field has the highest peak value amongst the other cases. This electric field behavior explains the reduction of the recombination rate inside the absorber near the ETL for the case when $x_p > x_n$. It also explains the higher rate near the HTL, as the field for $x_p > x_n$ is reversed which limits the carrier collection which, in turn, slightly increases the recombination rate. However, this reduction in the carrier collection has a minor impact. Further, the electron and hole concentration distributions, which strongly depend on the electric field behavior, are shown in Figure S1 (see Supplementary Material).

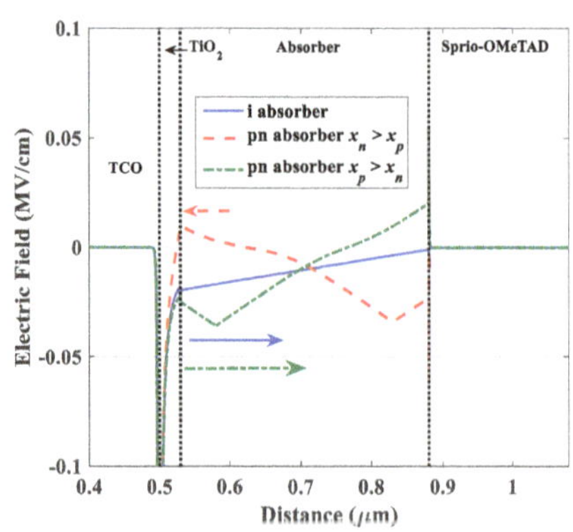

Figure 7. Electric field distribution across the device distance for the three cases of absorbers. The field is calculated at a voltage of 0.5 V. The electric field direction is also indicated in the figure by arrows.

3.1.2. Influence of Perovskite Doping Concentration

In this subsection, the impact of the doping concentrations of the p-type and n-type $CH_3NH_3SnI_3$ films on the performance parameters of the proposed structure is investigated. Figure 8 demonstrates the changes of performance parameters vs both donor concentration N_D of n-$CH_3NH_3SnI_3$ and acceptor concentration N_A of the p-$CH_3NH_3SnI_3$ from 10^{16} to 10^{18} cm^{-3}, with maintaining other material parameters as they are recorded in Table 1.

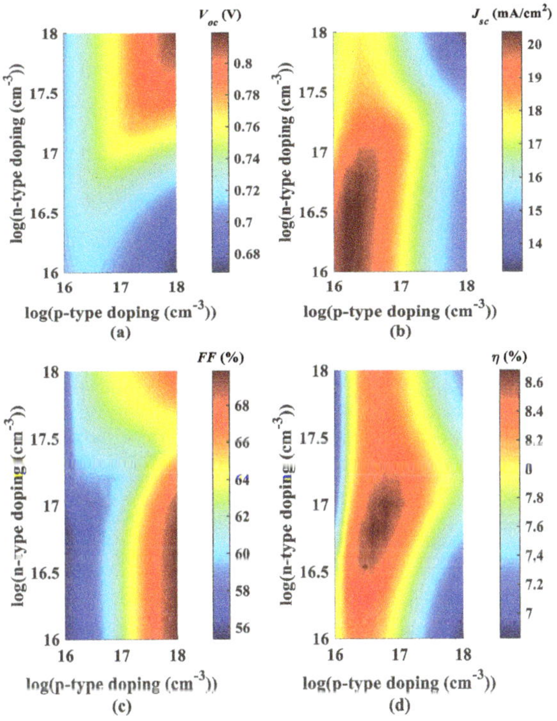

Figure 8. Variations of solar cell performance parameters with the donor concentration N_D of n-$CH_3NH_3SnI_3$ and acceptor concentration N_A of the p-$CH_3NH_3SnI_3$ (**a**) open circuit voltage, (**b**) short-circuit current, (**c**) fill factor and (**d**) efficiency.

It can be seen from Figure 8a that for higher values of N_D (>10^{17} cm^{-3}) in n-$CH_3NH_3SnI_3$, V_{oc} rises with rising N_A in p-$CH_3NH_3SnI_3$, which can be clarified by drawing the energy band diagram, as shown in Figure 9a, at the dark condition, in which N_A in p-$CH_3NH_3SnI_3$ varies (10^{16} and 10^{18} cm^{-3}) and N_D in the n-side is maintained at 3×10^{17} cm^{-3}. We can observe that by increasing N_A, the degree of band bending increases on the n-side, which causes V_{bi} to increase, leading to the rise of V_{oc} [54]. The built-in voltage is calculated from the conduction band (or valence band) energy difference between the n-side and p-side. Meanwhile, for lower values of N_D (<10^{17} cm^{-3}) in n-$CH_3NH_3SnI_3$, the open circuit voltage increases slightly with increasing N_A and then decreases, also marginally, further increasing N_A beyond about 10^{17} cm^{-3}. Therefore, the effect of N_A is minor for lower values of N_D. This can also be attributed to the behavior of V_{bi}, as illustrated in Figure 9b, which shows the energy band diagram (at dark) for two values of N_A (3×10^{16} and 10^{18} cm^{-3}) at a fixed value of $N_D = 3 \times 10^{16}$ cm^{-3}. As can be inferred from the figure, the variation of V_{bi} is insignificant, which reflects on the V_{oc} trivial change.

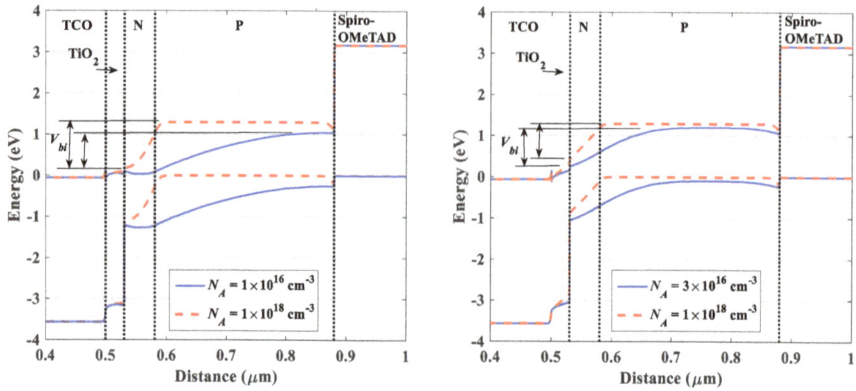

(**a**) (**b**)

Figure 9. The energy band diagrams of the proposed structure at the dark condition for (**a**) N_D in the n-side is maintained at 3×10^{17} cm^{-3}, (**b**) fixed value of $N_D = 3 \times 10^{16}$ cm^{-3}.

Moreover, in Figure 8b, J_{sc} declines with the rise in N_A in p-$CH_3NH_3SnI_3$, as the higher doping concentration results in thinner depletion region width and a broader neutral region, in which the greater bulk recombination takes place and thus reduces the collection chance of photoexcited electrons and holes. In addition, N_D of n-$CH_3NH_3SnI_3$ has a minor influence on the J_{sc}. This is because the n-region has the smallest thickness. Although light is illuminated from the TCO side, the number of photogenerated carriers of the n-$CH_3NH_3SnI_3$ region is considered low when compared to that at the wider p-$CH_3NH_3SnI_3$ region.

Regarding the *FF* in Figure 8c, its variation with doping concentration of n- and p-$CH_3NH_3SnI_3$ is the opposite of that of J_{sc}. The general tendency of rising *FF* with increasing N_A can be noticed, which is nearly independent of the value of N_D. As N_A increases, the resistivity of the layer decreases and hence the series resistance declines, which improves *FF*. This phenomenon can be explained based on the dark characteristics of the cell. As shown in Figure 10a, the dark *J–V* is drawn for three different values of p-side acceptor concentration. Using the *J–V* dark characteristics, the local ideality factor can be extracted, as seen in Figure 10b. The fill factor is directly correlated to the value of the local ideality factor at the maximum power point (MPP) [55,56]. As can be inferred from Figure 10b, the local ideality factor decreases as N_A increases, which proves the enhancement in the fill factor. Further, the corresponding values of the reverse saturation current and ideality factor of the equivalent single diode model are presented in Table S2 (see Supplementary Material).

Finally, in Figure 8d, the PCE is enhanced with moderate N_A values of p-side which are in the order 4×10^{16} to 6×10^{16} cm^{-3}. Higher N_D of n-side values is required to obtain high efficiencies. Values of N_D are in the range of 9×10^{16} to 2×10^{17} cm^{-3}. Therefore, the n-side is suggested to be slightly at a higher doping level than the p-side doping. Hence, in the simulation, the optimized doping concentration of the n-side and the p-side is 10^{17} and 5×10^{16} cm^{-3}, respectively. In this case, the photovoltaic parameters are: $V_{oc} = 0.7513$, $J_{sc} = 19.62$, $FF = 58.72$ and PCE = 8.66%. Based on these reported values, the efficiency of the hybrid cell after a proper choice of the thickness and doping is higher than that of the conventional pin structure by more than 3.5%.

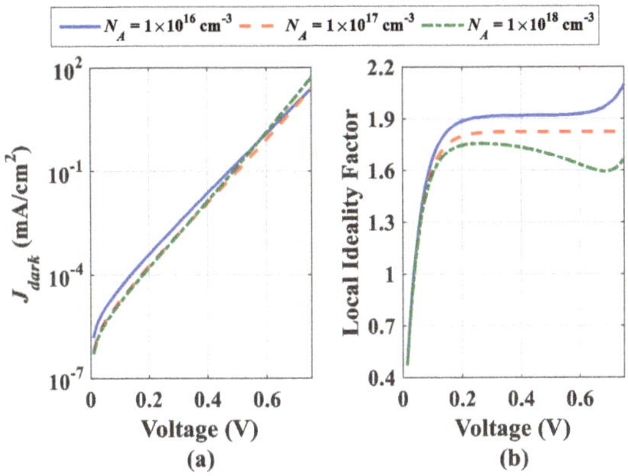

Figure 10. Impact of p-side acceptor concentration. (**a**) The cell dark *J*–*V* characteristics, (**b**) the cell local ideality factor.

3.1.3. Comparison between Absorber Doping Types

In this subsection, we compare four different devices: namely, the reference intrinsic absorber (having a p-type doping concentration of 1×10^{15} cm^{-3}), a single p-layer (concentration of 1×10^{16} cm^{-3}) a single n-layer (concentration of 1×10^{16} cm^{-3}) and a pn-absorber, including the n- and p-layers. The impact of the doping concentration on the efficiency when using a single n-layer and p-layer absorbers is shown in Figure S2 (see Supplementary Material) in which the optimum efficiency occurs near the selected value of 1×10^{16} cm^{-3} for the single p-layer, while the impact of doping on the efficiency of the single n-layer is very weak. The *J*–*V* characteristics under illumination and EQE are presented in Figure 11a,b, respectively, for a series of devices with the differently tuned doping. The performance of the p-absorber cell is higher than that of the intrinsic case. However, the optimized hybrid cell gives a higher performance, indicated by the cell performance presented in Table 4. The situation is different if the n-absorber perovskite is used. Due to the strongly reduced carrier collection, a low J_{sc} of 7.91 mA/cm^2 is obtained and the *FF* is as low as 32.98%. Moreover, the spectral response of the hybrid and single p-layer cells are close (see Figure 11b), while the intrinsic absorber cell is lower. The single n-layer has the lowest EQE, as expected from its low J_{sc}.

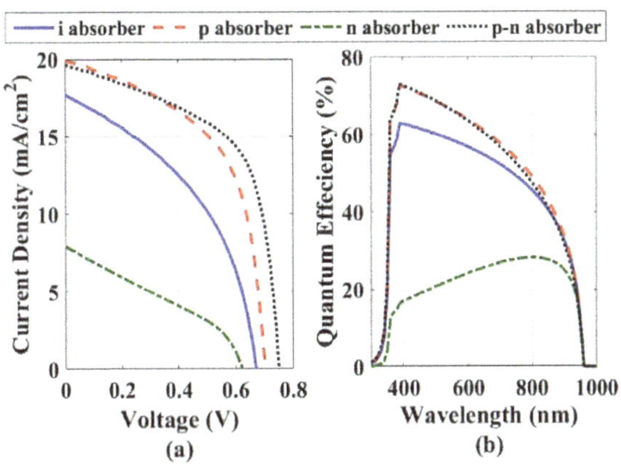

Figure 11. Comparison between different types of absorbers. (**a**) The cell *J*–*V* characteristics under illumination, (**b**) quantum efficiency.

Table 4. Cell performance parameters of the four studied cases of the absorber layer.

	J_{sc} (mA/cm^2)	V_{oc} (V)	FF (%)	η (%)
i absorber	17.60	0.670	44.00	5.15
p absorber	19.91	0.702	55.21	7.72
n absorber	7.91	0.623	32.98	1.63
p-n absorber	19.62	0.751	58.72	8.66

This can be explained by plotting the electric field distribution along the device distance, as previously discussed in Section 3.1.1. The distribution is shown in Figure S3 (see Supplementary Materials) for two cases, namely the short-circuit condition and at a voltage of 0.5 V. The results indicate that the field direction of the n-absorber is reversed, contrary to the other three cases, which results in higher recombination rates due to the poor electrons and hole extraction. The results also indicate that the pn absorber has the highest electric field peak compared to the other cases. To conclude this comparison, the cell containing the perovskite homojunction has a remarkable performance, especially its V_{oc} (0.751 V) and FF (58.72%), which improved significantly compared to those of the other structures, even if J_{sc} is slightly less than the single p-layer case. The overall efficiency indicates the superiority of the hybrid homojunction lead-free cell design which gives 8.66%.

3.2. Design of HTL-Free Hybrid Hetero-Homojunction Cell

In this section, the HTL-free configuration is investigated. A carbon-electrode can be utilized which is considered a good candidate when compared with traditional metal electrodes. The reason is because carbon is air-stable and inert to ion migration [40,57,58]. Figure 12 shows the illuminated J–V (Figure 12a) and quantum efficiency (Figure 12b) of the HTL-free structure, which is shown in the inset of the figure. For such an initial HTL-free configuration, the photovoltaic parameters are V_{oc} = 0.7513 V, J_{sc} = 19.63 mA/cm^2, FF = 58.77% and PCE = 8.67%.

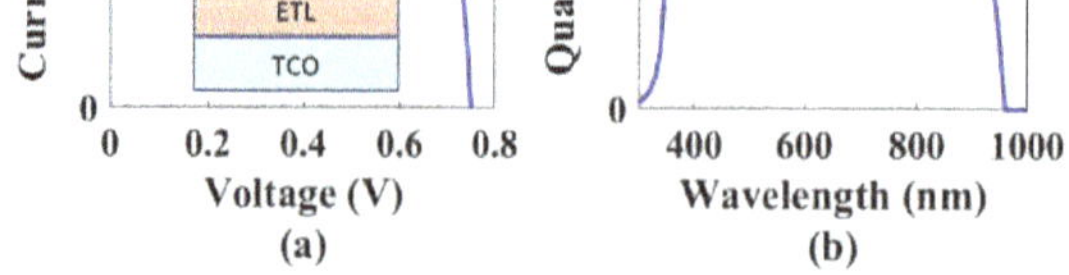

Figure 12. HTL-free structure characteristics: (**a**) the illuminated J–V, (**b**) the quantum efficiency.

The optimization of the performance of our proposed HTL-free p-n homojunction absorber lead-free PSC is carried out in the coming subsections. Firstly, the effect of p-absorber doping variation is illustrated. Secondly, the work function of the different back contact materials is studied to find out its influence on the device performance. Then, the effect of the absorber defect density is investigated. Finally, the impact of different ETL materials is examined and the best ETL material, which gives the optimum performance for the designed HTL-free configuration, is determined.

3.2.1. Influence of Doping

In this subsection, the effect of p-doping variation on the HTL-free configuration is performed for two values of n-doping, namely 1×10^{17} and 1×10^{18} cm^{-3}. Figure 13a shows the influence of such doping variation on the photovoltaic parameters. It is obvious that the optimum p-side doping is a little above 5×10^{16} cm^{-3} (exactly at 6.3×10^{16} cm^{-3}), giving an n-type doping of 1×10^{17} cm^{-3}. In this case, the optimum PCE is 8.69% which indicates a slight enhancement, 0.02%, compared to the starting PCE (8.67%). The variation of the photovoltaic parameters with the p-doping concentration can be explained from the perception of the recombination rate, as shown in Figure 13b, which illustrates the recombination rate across the device distance at the short-circuit condition. As can be seen, the recombination rate increases considerably when N_A is 1×10^{18} cm^{-3}. In addition, for $N_A = 6.3 \times 10^{16}$ cm^{-3}, the recombination rate is decreased near the ETL interface and deep inside the absorber, which implies a higher short-circuit current. Although the rate is higher when moving towards the back contact, this high rate is not effective because the generation rate is minimized since that region is relatively far away from the light source.

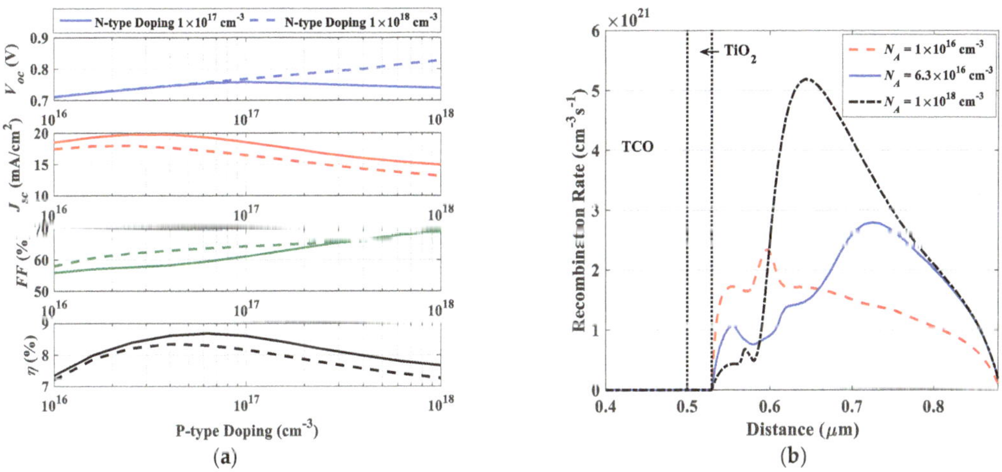

Figure 13. (**a**) Impact of p-layer doping variation on the HTL-free configuration photovoltaic parameters for two values of n-layer doping, and (**b**) recombination rates for three different values of p-layer doping.

3.2.2. Influence of Back Metal Work Function

In this subsection, different metal contacts with distinct work function values are examined. From Figure 14a, it is clear that optimum performance occurs by using the carbon-based contact at 5.4 eV, which also satisfies the flat band condition. For work function values lower than 5.1 eV, the performance is deteriorated. Therefore, it is recommended to use carbon as a back contact metal in the HTL-free architecture. The explanation of the improvement of the open circuit voltage, and hence the efficiency, when increasing the work function could be attributed to the built-in potential enhancement. This can be deduced from the energy band diagram plotted in Figure 14b, in which three different values of work functions are plotted, showing that the highest V_{bi} is obtained when using carbon contact.

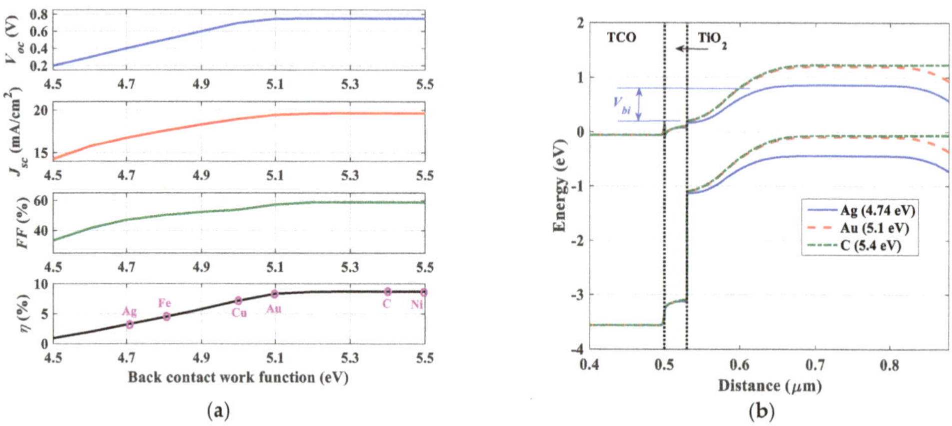

Figure 14. Impact of different metal contacts with distinct work function values on the HTL-free configuration photovoltaic parameters. (**a**) Photovoltaic parameters, and (**b**) energy band diagram drawn at the short-circuit condition for three different metal electrodes (work function values are also indicated).

3.2.3. Influence of Absorber Defect Trap Density and Energy

The photo-excited charge carriers are primarily produced within the absorber region. The existence of defects inside the absorber has a crucial impact, as they result in a nonradiative recombination process which limits the overall solar cell performance. The defect density inside the absorber perovskite films has to be alleviated to reduce carrier recombination losses [59]. Here, we study the impact of reducing the defect density inside the two sides of the absorber. Figure 15 depicts the photovoltaic parameters of the device with various defect density (N_t) in both n-$CH_3NH_3SnI_3$ and p-$CH_3NH_3SnI_3$ (N_t is set equal in the two layers). It is obvious that decreasing defect density beyond 10^{15} cm^{-3} results in a considerable rise in the V_{oc}. The V_{oc} is expressed by [4,5]

$$V_{oc} = n\, V_T \ln\left(1 + \frac{J_{SC}}{J_o}\right) \tag{8}$$

where n is the diode ideality factor and V_T is the thermal voltage. The reverse saturation current density, J_o, is determined by the recombination processes. Hence, V_{oc} measures the recombination losses in the solar cell structure. As the bulk defect in absorber layers functions as nonradiative recombination centers, rising N_t results in increasing the probability of recombination, which causes a decline in V_{oc}. Besides, one can see from Figure 15 that there is almost no impact on J_{sc} when N_t is less than 10^{15} cm^{-3}; however, J_{sc} drops substantially with the further rising of N_t. This can be clarified by the dependence of the hole (electron) diffusion length L_p (L_n) on N_t, which is presented by,

$$L_{n/p} = \sqrt{\frac{\mu_{n/p} kT}{q} \frac{1}{\sigma_{n/p} v_{th} N_t}} \tag{9}$$

Equation (9) describes that the rise of N_t causes a smaller L_p (L_n). For low N_t values, L_p (L_n) is greater than the thickness of the absorber; therefore, N_t has a minor effect on J_{sc}. However, if N_t surpasses 10^{15} cm^{-3}, L_p (L_n) is smaller than the absorber thickness and J_{sc} reduces with further rise of N_t. Furthermore, when $N_t < 10^{15}$ cm^{-3}, the PCE remains almost unaffected. However, the efficiency decreases markedly when $N_t > 10^{15}$ cm^{-3}. Consequently, controlling the N_t below 10^{15} cm^{-3} is essential for accomplishing higher efficiencies. At N_t equals 10^{15} cm^{-3}, an optimized conversion efficiency of 16.57% (at V_{oc} = 0.896 V, J_{sc} = 25.86 mA/cm^2, FF = 71.53%) can be obtained for the proposed HTL-free cell. The enhancement of the parameters according to reducing the trap density could be explained in many aspects, one of which is the recombination rate, as shown in Figure S4 (see Supplementary Material).

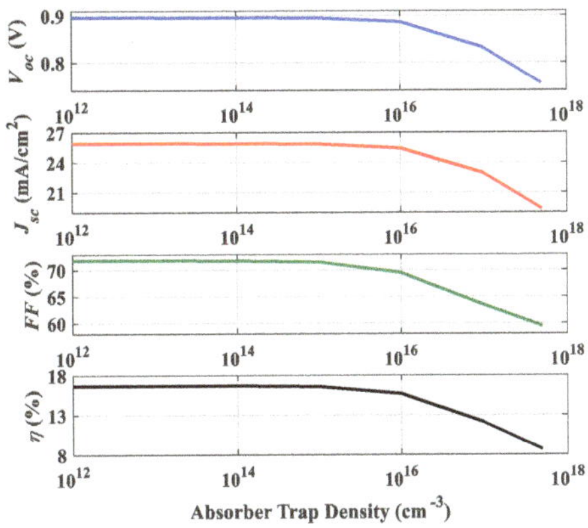

Figure 15. The HTL-free configuration photovoltaic parameters with various defect density (N_t) in both n-$CH_3NH_3SnI_3$ and p-$CH_3NH_3SnI_3$.

Moreover, the influence of the trap energy position with respect to the valence band edge energy E_v was investigated. Figure 16 demonstrates this impact for two different values of N_t. The trap position is varied from 0.1 to 1.2 eV. Regarding the higher value of N_t (5×10^{17} cm^{-3}), the trap energy position has a crucial effect. Generally, the defects with low formation energy produce shallow levels. These levels are close to E_c or E_v and result in long diffusion lengths. This is clear from the figure as the long diffusion length results in a high V_{oc} and, in turn, an enhancement in the overall performance is achieved. On the other hand, when the formation energy is high, the trap energy position is near the mid-gap. These levels are called deep levels and the resulting diffusion length is short, which deteriorates the performance. Regarding the lower value of N_t (10^{15} cm^{-3}), the situation is different. The impact of the trap energy is minor and thus the cell becomes extremely immune to the defect energy position. These results imply the crucial impact of the bulk trap density. Careful manufacturing processes are needed in order to decrease the trap density to boost the cell performance for either deep or shallow levels.

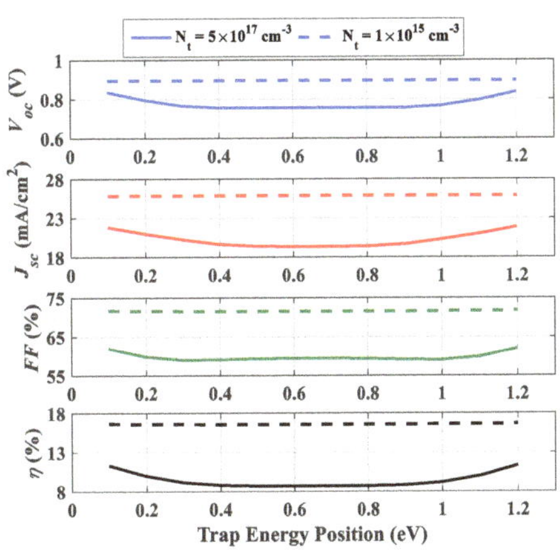

Figure 16. Impact of bulk trap energy position relative to E_v on the photovoltaic parameters of the hetero/homojunction HTL-free solar cell.

3.2.4. ETL Variation

Using TiO_2 as ETL is very popular in normal PSCs. However, other candidates are required to be inspected to see more suitable alternatives to TiO_2. In this subsection, we investigate the influence of changing the conduction band offset (CBO) by varying ETL affinity. The CBO is calculated as,

$$\text{CBO} = \Delta E_c = \chi_{\text{absorber}} - \chi_{\text{ETL}} \tag{10}$$

The simulated ETL affinity is changed in the range of 3.9 eV to 4.26 eV, which gives a CBO in the range of −0.09 to 0.27 eV. Figure 17 shows the variation of the performance parameters vs CBO. As shown in the figure, V_{oc} increases gradually with the increasing of CBO and reaches 0.758 V when CBO is 0.17 eV (which is corresponding to ZnO as ETL). J_{sc} changes slightly and reaches 20.09 mA/cm^2 for the same CBO (0.17 eV). The fill factor (*FF*) increases up to 61.50% and then slightly decreases. The efficiency behavior is the same as the V_{oc} trend. It has an optimum value of 9.35% which occurs when utilizing ZnO as ETL.

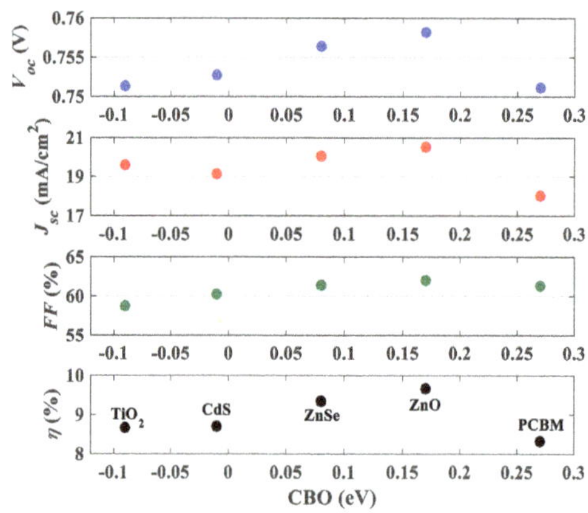

Figure 17. Effect of electron affinity of ETL on PCE.

Figure 18 displays the energy band diagrams of the HTL-free PSC for three cases; namely, when the ETL material is TiO_2 (Figure 18a), ZnO (Figure 18b) and PCBM (Figure 18c). In the first case, the CBO is negative (−0.09 eV), while it is positive for the second case (having 0.17 eV) and the third case (having 0.27 eV). Regarding the first case, a cliff is formed at the ETL/absorber interface which does not hinder the flow of photogenerated electrons toward the front electrode. However, the activation energy for carrier recombination (E_a) becomes lower than the energy gap of the absorber (E_g), where E_a is given by $E_a = E_g - |\text{CBO}|$. For this case, the main recombination mechanism of the solar cell is the interface recombination of $E_a < E_g$ [60,61], and the recombination probability of the electrons at the ETL/absorber interface rises significantly. Therefore, E_a directly links with the open circuit voltage and V_{oc} is, consequently, reduced for negative values of CBO.

On the other hand, when the CBO is positive, a spike is formed at the ETL/absorber interface, as shown in Figure 18b,c. This spike behaves like a barrier against the flow of photogenerated electrons. When CBO is positive, E_a is equal to E_g. When the spike is low enough (Figure 18b), the barrier is not strong and the flow of electrons towards the contact is substantial. However, when the barrier spike is too high (>0.2 eV), as in the third case, the normal flow of photogenerated electrons to PCBM is affected drastically. As a result, the equivalent series resistance of the cell is increased, resulting in *FF* deterioration. As a result, the best choice for the ETL material is ZnO, which gives V_{oc} = 0.757 V, J_{sc} = 20.09 mA/cm^2, *FF* = 61.50%, and PCE = 9.35%. The main parameters of the ETL materials mentioned here are listed in Table S3 (see Supplementary Material).

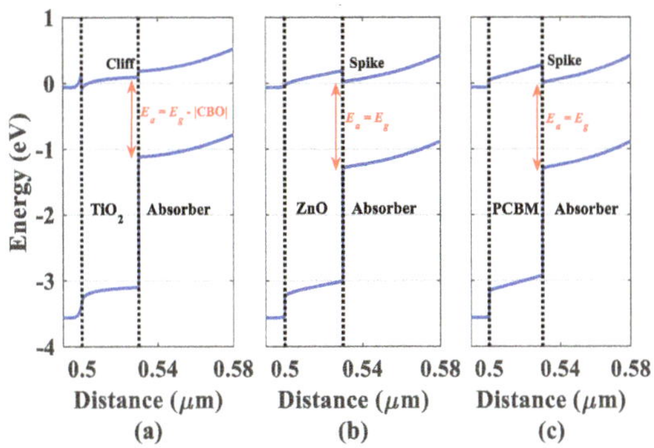

Figure 18. The energy band diagrams of the hybrid hetero-homojunction HTL-free PSC for three cases: (**a**) CBO = −0.09 eV, (**b**) CBO = 0.17 eV and (**c**) CBO = 0.27 eV.

3.3. Comparison of Various Designed Structures

The illuminated *J–V* characteristics and quantum efficiency of optimized HTL-free and other cases of homojunction-based lead-free PSCs are compared in detail in Figure 19. The studied cases are related to the initial hetero-homojunction, while the other four cases are associated with the HTL-free configuration. The first case is the initial homo design, having optimized p-layer thickness and doping. The second case is the HTL-free structure with an optimized doping. The third case is taken for ZnO as an ETL, and the bulk defect density is 5×10^{17} cm^{-3}, while the fourth case is dedicated for TiO_2 as an ETL, and the defect density is 1×10^{15} cm^{-3}. The last case is the final optimized HTL-free structure whose ETL material is ZnO and its defect density is 1×10^{15} cm^{-3}.

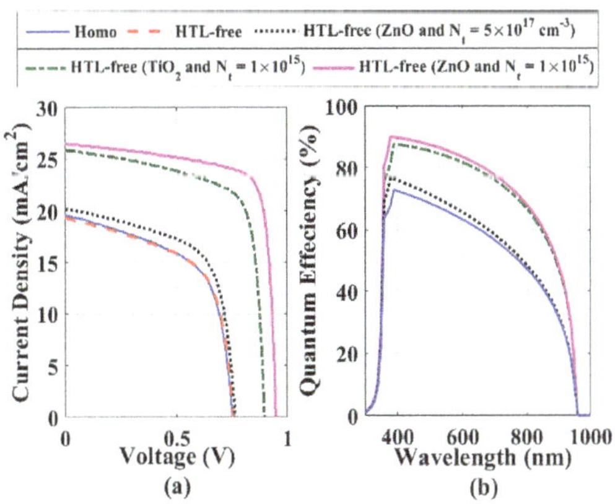

Figure 19. A comparison between (**a**) the illuminated *J–V* characteristics and (**b**) quantum efficiency of optimized HTL-free and other cases of homo-junction-based lead-free PSCs.

Referring to Figure 19, it is clear that our proposed HTL-free cell after optimization has superior photovoltaic properties than the other four candidates. The homojunction-based carbon PSC shows an apparent improvement in V_{oc} owing to the improved V_{bi} inside the perovskite layer caused by homojunction, thus boosting the quantum efficiency (Figure 19b). Table 5 gives the main parameters to compare between the different cases. These results demonstrate that the HTL-free hybrid cell is a better choice compared to the conventional homojunction PSCs.

Table 5. Comparison between five different cases of hybrid hetero-homojunction-based PSCs.

Structure	ETL	HTL	N_t (cm^{-3})	J_{sc} (mA/cm^2)	V_{oc} (V)	*FF* (%)	η (%)
Case 1	TiO_2	Spiro-OMeTAD	5×10^{17}	19.62	0.751	58.71	8.66
Case 2	TiO_2	None	5×10^{17}	19.35	0.756	59.41	8.69
Case 3	ZnO	None	5×10^{17}	20.23	0.764	62.69	9.69
Case 4	TiO_2	None	1×10^{15}	25.86	0.896	71.53	16.57
Case 5	ZnO	None	1×10^{15}	26.48	0.948	77.20	19.37

Finally, we investigate the effect of interface traps, which arise due to the structural mismatch between two dissimilar materials, on the performance of the initial hetero-homojunction (case 1) and the final optimized HTL-free cell (case 5). Figure 20 demonstrates the influence of the interfacial defects of ETL/absorber layer on the device efficiency. Both interface defect density (in the range 10^8–10^{18} cm^{-2}) and defect energy level position (in the range 0.1–1.2 eV relative to E_v of the perovskite) are investigated simultaneously. As displayed, the interface quality of the ETL/absorber layer has a substantial role on the cell performance, especially for the optimized HTL-free cell. The dependency of the efficiency on the interface defect density is more noticeable than the energy level. For both studied cases, the efficiency almost does not change for a given value of interface defect density. Reducing the interface trap density from 1×101^8 to 1×10^8 cm^{-2} results in a rise in the efficiency of about 1% and 2.5% for case 1 and case 5, respectively. This shows that the optimized HTL-free cell is more sensitive to the variations of the trap density than the conventional hetero-homojunction case. Working on methods to reduce the interface trap density, by passivation for instance, draws another promising route to improve the efficiency.

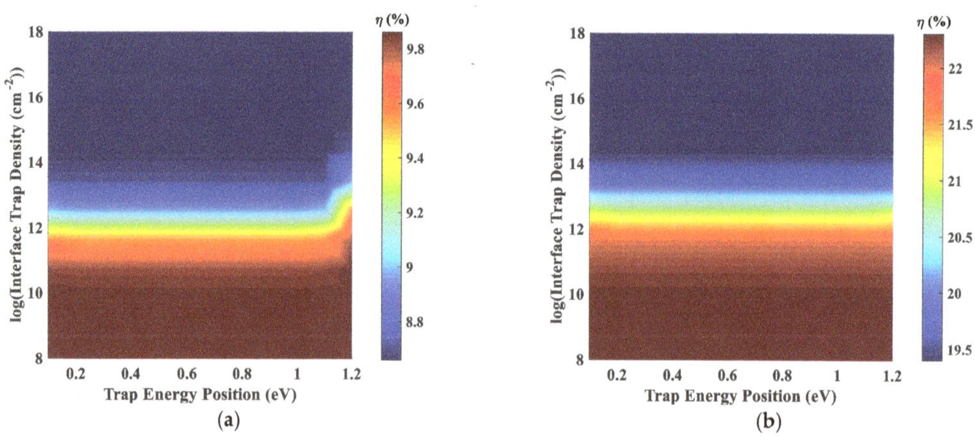

Figure 20. Effect of interfacial trap parameters on the efficiency of (**a**) initial hetero/homojunction solar cell and (**b**) final optimized HTL-free structure.

It should be mentioned here that the realization of the homojunction pn design is feasible and has been demonstrated experimentally. Many techniques have been investigated to attain doped perovskite films [35]. For instance, by control the stoichiometry of the PbI_2/MAI precursor ratio, a p-type $MAPbI_3$ with rich MAI can be obtained while an n-type $MAPbI_3$ with rich PbI_2 can be generated [36]. Besides, the defect-assisted self-doping could offer an opportunity for the deposition of p- or n-type compounds [33]. More intensive research is needed to explore the likelihood of obtaining p- and n-type lead-free perovskite materials in order to fabricate efficient p-n junctions to benefit from enhanced charge separation and limited recombination rates.

4. Conclusions

Although many investigations have been done on the lead-free $CH_3NH_3SnI_3$ solar cells, they suffer from low photovoltaic performance. In this paper, a SCAPS device simulation of a hybrid hetero-homojunction $CH_3NH_3SnI_3$ was performed. The influence of varying the main solar cell parameters on the cell performance was thoroughly investigated. The initial cell was based on an experimental work with a record efficiency of 5.24%. The thickness and doping of both n- and p-side of the cell was investigated to find out the optimum thickness and doping of each layer. It was discovered that the thickness of the p-side should be much more than that of the n-side, taking a fixed overall thickness of the absorber. The optimized doping concentration of the n-side and the p-side was found to be 10^{17} and 5×10^{16} cm^{-3}, respectively. The photovoltaic parameters for the optimized thickness and doping were: V_{oc} = 0.7513, J_{sc} = 19.62, FF = 58.72% and η = 8.66%.

Further, the structure was HTL-free to overcome the organic issues usually encountered with the HTL materials. The HTL-free cell is optimized in terms of doping, work function of the back contact and bulk trap density to obtain the maximum efficiency. Moreover, the impact of different ETL materials was explored. It was observed that positive CBO up to 0.17 eV is adequate to obtain low recombination rates and, consequently, larger open circuit voltage. On the other hand, a negative CBO or a high positive CBO was not beneficial. Optimized photovoltaic parameters could be obtained for the proposed hybrid hetero-homojunction HTL-free cell using a bulk trap density of 1×10^{15} cm^{-3} and utilizing ZnO as an ETL, giving V_{oc} = 0.948 V, J_{sc} = 26.48 mA/cm^2, FF = 77.20 and an efficiency of 19.37%.

The presented study highlights some design rules regarding the hybrid hetero-homojunction lead-free PSCs. For the selected initial cell, whose energy gap was 1.3 eV, the p-layer should be higher than the n-layer thickness. The doping levels could be selected in order to boost the cell performance. Moreover, the appropriate choice of the ETL material for the HTL-free configuration is crucial. Further, optimization of the different technological parameters of the HTL-free cell could lead to a low-cost, high-efficiency lead-free PSC.

Supplementary Materials: The following are available online at https://www.mdpi.com/article/10.3390/en14185741/s1, Figure S1: Electron and hole concentration distribution for three case studies, Figure S1: Impact of doping on the efficiency of the single n-layer and single p-layer, Figure S3: Electric field distribution inside the absorber region for the four cases of absorbers, the filed is calculated at (a) short-circuit condition and (b) V = 0.5 V, Figure S4: Impact of bulk trap density on the recombination rate of the HTL-free configuration, Table S1: The parameters of the front and back metal contacts, Table S2: Reverse saturation and ideality factor of the single diode model for three different values of p-side doping concentration, Table S3: Main parameters of selected materials for ETL.

Author Contributions: Conceptualization, M.S.S. and A.S.; methodology, M.S.S., A.S. and A.Z.; validation and formal analysis, M.A., M.S.S. and M.T.A.; Funding acquisition, M.S.S.; Visualization, A.S., M.T.A. and A.A.; investigation, all authors; writing—original draft preparation, M.S.S., A.S. and A.A.; writing—review and editing, All authors; supervision, M.S.S., A.S., A.Z., M.A., A.A. and M.T.A. All authors have read and agreed to the published version of the manuscript.

Funding: This research was funded by Deanship of Scientific Research at the University of Ha'il, project number RG-20 047.

Institutional Review Board Statement: Not applicable.

Informed Consent Statement: Not applicable.

Data Availability Statement: No new data were created or analyzed in this study. Data sharing is not applicable to this article.

Acknowledgments: The authors would like to thank the Deanship of Scientific Research at the University of Ha'il for their sponsorship to the project number RG-20 047.

Conflicts of Interest: The authors declare no conflict of interest. The funders had no role in the design of the study; in the collection, analyses, or interpretation of data; in the writing of the manuscript, or in the decision to publish the results.

References

1. Reddy, V.S.; Kaushik, S.C.; Ranjan, K.R.; Tyagi, S.K. State-of-the-art of solar thermal power plants. *Renew. Sustain. Energy Rev.* **2019**, *27*, 258–273. [CrossRef]
2. Jäger, K.D.; Isabella, O.; Smets, A.H.; van Swaaij, R.A.; Zeman, M. *Solar Energy: Fundamentals, Technology and Systems*; UIT Cambridge Ltd.: Cambridge, UK, 2016.
3. Ranabhat, K.; Patrikeev, L.; Antal'evna-Revina, A.; Andrianov, K.; Lapshinsky, V.; Sofronova, E. An introduction to solar cell technology. *J. Appl. Eng. Sci.* **2016**, *14*, 481–491. [CrossRef]
4. Luque, A.; Hegedus, S. *Handbook of Photovoltaic Science and Engineering*; John Wiley & Sons Ltd.: Chichester, UK, 2011.
5. Zekry, A.; Shaker, A.; Salem, M. Solar Cells and Arrays: Principles, Analysis, and Design. In *Advances in Renewable Energies and Power Technologies*; Yahyaoui, I., Ed.; Elsevier Science Publishing Co Inc.: Amsterdam, The Netherlands, 2018; Volume 1, pp. 3–56.
6. Masuko, K.; Shigematsu, M.; Hashiguchi, T.; Fujishima, D.; Kai, M.; Yoshimura, N.; Yamaguchi, T.; Ichihashi, Y.; Mishima, T.; Matsubara, N.; et al. Achievement of more than 25% conversion efficiency with crystalline silicon heterojunction solar cell. *IEEE J. Photovolt.* **2014**, *4*, 1433–1435. [CrossRef]
7. Battaglia, C.; Cuevas, A.; De Wolf, S. High-efficiency crystalline silicon solar cells: Status and perspectives. *Energy Environ. Sci.* **2016**, *9*, 1552. [CrossRef]
8. Yin, J.; Lu, X. Theoretical study impurities intermediate band material based on Sn heavily doped ZnO by first principles. *Superlattices Microstruct.* **2020**, *145*, 106608. [CrossRef]
9. Colombo, A.; Dragonetti, C.; Roberto, D.; Ugo, R.; Manfredi, N.; Manca, P.; Abbotto, A.; Giustina, G.D.; Brusatin, G. A carbon doped anatase TiO_2 as a promising semiconducting layer in Ru-dyes based dye-sensitized solar cells. *Inorg. Chim. Acta* **2019**, *489*, 263–268. [CrossRef]
10. Zhang, X.; Liu, F.; Huang, Q.L.; Zhou, G.; Wang, Z.S. Dye-sensitized W-doped TiO_2 solar cells with a tunable conduction band and suppressed charge recombination. *J. Phys. Chem. C* **2011**, *115*, 12665–12671. [CrossRef]
11. Lu, W.H.; Chou, C.S.; Chen, C.Y.; Wu, P. Preparation of Zr-doped mesoporous TiO_2 particles and their applications in the novel working electrode of a dye sensitized solar cell. *Adv. Powder Technol.* **2017**, *28*, 2186–2197. [CrossRef]
12. Xiang, P.; Lv, F.; Xiao, T.; Jiang, L.; Tan, X.; Shu, T. Improved performance of quasi solid-state dye-sensitized solar cells based on iodine-doped TiO_2 spheres photoanodes. *J. Alloy. Compd.* **2018**, *741*, 1142–1147. [CrossRef]
13. Tran, V.A.; Truong, T.T.; Phan, T.A.P.; Nguyen, T.N.; Huynh, T.V.; Agrestic, A.; Pescetelli, S.; Le, T.K.; Carlo, A.D.; Lund, T. Application of nitrogen-doped TiO_2 nano-tubes in dye-sensitized solar cells. *Appl. Surf. Sci.* **2017**, *399*, 515–522. [CrossRef]
14. Ahmad, K.; Ansari, S.N.; Natarajan, K.; Mobin, S.M. A two-step modified deposition method based $(CH_3NH_3)_3Bi_2I_9$ perovskite: Lead free, highly stable and enhanced photovoltaic performance. *ChemElectroChem* **2019**, *6*, 1192–1198. [CrossRef]
15. Ahmad, K.; Mobin, S.M. Graphene oxide based planar heterojunction perovskite solar cell under ambient condition. *New J. Chem.* **2017**, *41*, 14253–14258. [CrossRef]
16. Lee, M.M.; Teuscher, J.; Miyasaka, T.; Murakami, T.N.; Snaith, H.J. Efficient hybrid solar cells based on meso super structured organometal halide perovskites. *Science* **2012**, *338*, 643–647. [CrossRef]
17. Burschka, J.; Pellet, N.; Moon, S.J.; Humphry-Baker, R.; Gao, P.; Nazeeruddin, M.K.; Grätzel, M. Sequential deposition as a route to high-performance perovskite sensitized solar cells. *Nature* **2013**, *499*, 316–319. [CrossRef] [PubMed]
18. Zhou, H.P.; Chen, Q.; Li, G.; Luo, S.; Song, T.B.; Duan, H.S.; Hong, Z.; You, J.; Liu, Y.; Yang, Y. Interface engineering of highly efficient perovskite solar cells. *Science* **2014**, *345*, 542–546. [CrossRef]
19. Mei, A.Y.; Li, X.; Liu, L.F.; Ku, Z.; Liu, T.; Rong, Y.; Xu, M.; Hu, M.; Chen, J.; Yang, Y. A hole-conductor-free, fully printable mesoscopic perovskite solar cell with high stability. *Science* **2014**, *345*, 295–298. [CrossRef]
20. Bai, Y.B.; Wang, Q.Y.; Lv, R.T.; Zhu, H.; Kang, F. Progress on perovskite based solar cells. *Chin. Sci. Bull.* **2016**, *61*, 489–500.
21. Kojima, A.; Teshima, K.; Shirai, Y.; Miyasaka, T. Organometal halide perovskites as visible-light sensitizers for photovoltaic cells. *J. Am. Chem. Soc.* **2009**, *131*, 6050–6051. [CrossRef]
22. Best Research Cell Efficiencies. Available online: https://www.nrel.gov/pv/assets/pdfs/cell-pv-eff-emergingpv.pdf (accessed on 1 July 2021).
23. Ogomi, Y.; Morita, A.; Tsukamoto, S.; Saitho, T.; Fujikawa, N.; Shen, Q.; Toyoda, T.; Yoshino, K.; Pandey, S.S.; Ma, T.; et al. $CH_3NH_3Sn_xPb_{(1-x)}I_3$ perovskite solar cells covering up to 1060 nm. *J. Phys. Chem. Lett.* **2014**, *5*, 1004–1011. [CrossRef]
24. Hao, F.; Stoumpos, C.C.; Chang, R.P.H.; Kanatzidis, M.G. Anomalous band gap behavior in mixed Sn and Pb perovskites enables broadening of absorption spectrum in solar cells. *J. Am. Chem. Soc.* **2014**, *136*, 8094–8099. [CrossRef] [PubMed]
25. Patel, P.K. Device simulation of highly efficient eco-friendly $CH_3NH_3SnI_3$ perovskite solar cell. *Sci. Rep.* **2021**, *11*, 1–11.
26. Eperon, G.E.; Burlakov, V.M.; Docampo, P.; Goriely, A.; Snaith, H.J. Morphological control for high performance, solution-processed planar heterojunction perovskite solar cells. *Adv. Funct. Mater.* **2014**, *24*, 151–157. [CrossRef]
27. Baig, F.; Khattak, Y.H.; Marí, B.; Beg, S.; Ahmed, A.; Khan, K. Efficiency enhancement of $CH_3NH_3SnI_3$ solar cells by device modeling. *J. Electron. Mater.* **2018**, *47*, 5275–5282. [CrossRef]

28. Shi, Z.J.; Guo, J.; Chen, Y.H.; Li, Q.; Pan, Y.; Zhang, H.; Xia, Y.; Huang, W. Lead-free organic-inorganic hybrid perovskites for photovoltaic applications: Recent advances and perspectives. *Adv. Mater.* **2017**, *29*, 1605005–1605032. [CrossRef]
29. Shah, S.A.A.; Sayyad, M.H.; Khan, K.; Guo, K.; Shen, F.; Sun, J.; Tareen, A.K.; Gong, Y.; Guo, Z. Progress towards High-Efficiency and Stable Tin-Based Perovskite Solar Cells. *Energies* **2020**, *13*, 5092. [CrossRef]
30. Zheng, X.; Chen, B.; Dai, J.; Fang, Y.; Bai, Y.; Lin, Y.; Wei, H.; Zeng, X.C.; Huang, J. Defect passivation in hybrid perovskite solar cells using quaternary ammonium halide anions and cations. *Nat. Energy* **2017**, *2*, 1–9. [CrossRef]
31. Jiang, Q.; Zhang, L.; Wang, H.; Yang, X.; Meng, J.; Liu, H.; Yin, Z.; Wu, J.; Zhang, X.; You, J. Enhanced electron extraction using SnO_2 for high-efficiency planar-structure $HC(NH_2)_2PbI_3$-based perovskite solar cells. *Nat. Energy* **2016**, *2*, 1–7. [CrossRef]
32. Frolova, L.A.; Dremova, N.N.; Troshin, P.A. The chemical origin of the p-type and n-type doping effects in the hybrid methylammonium–lead iodide ($MAPbI_3$) perovskite solar cells. *Chem. Commun.* **2015**, *51*, 14917–14920. [CrossRef] [PubMed]
33. Wang, Q.; Shao, Y.; Xie, H.; Lyu, L.; Liu, X.; Gao, Y.; Huang, J. Qualifying composition dependent p and n self-doping in $CH_3NH_3PbI_3$. *Appl. Phys. Lett.* **2014**, *105*, 163508. [CrossRef]
34. Yin, W.J.; Shi, T.; Yan, Y. Unusual defect physics in $CH_3NH_3PbI_3$ perovskite solar cell absorber. *Appl. Phys. Lett.* **2014**, *104*, 063903. [CrossRef]
35. Danekamp, B.; Müller, C.; Sendner, M.; Boix, P.P.; Sessolo, M.; Lovrincic, R.; Bolink, H.J. Perovskite–perovskite homojunctions via compositional doping. *J. Phys. Chem. Lett.* **2018**, *9*, 2770–2775. [CrossRef]
36. Cui, P.; Wei, D.; Ji, J.; Huang, H.; Jia, E.; Dou, S.; Wang, T.; Wang, W.; Li, M. Planar p–n homojunction perovskite solar cells with efficiency exceeding 21.3%. *Nat. Energy* **2019**, *4*, 150–159. [CrossRef]
37. Maram, D.K.; Haghighi, M.; Shekoofa, O.; Habibiyan, H.; Ghafoorifard, H. A modeling study on utilizing ultra-thin inorganic HTLs in inverted p–n homojunction perovskite solar cells. *Sol. Energy* **2021**, *213*, 1–12. [CrossRef]
38. Sengar, B.S.; Garg, V.; Kumar, A.; Dwivedi, P. Numerical Simulation: Design of High-Efficiency Planar p-n Homojunction Perovskite Solar Cells. *IEEE Trans. Electron Devices* **2021**, *68*, 2360–2364. [CrossRef]
39. He, Q.; Gu, H.; Zhang, D.; Fang, G.; Tian, H. Theoretical analysis of effects of doping $MAPbI_3$ into pn homojunction on several types of perovskite solar cells. *Opt. Mater.* **2021**, *121*, 111491. [CrossRef]
40. Lin, L.; Li, P.; Kang, Z.; Xiong, H.; Chen, Y.; Yan, Q.; Qiu, Y. Device Design of Doping-Controlled Homojunction Perovskite Solar Cells Omitting HTL and Exceeding 25% Efficiency. *Adv. Theory Simul.* **2021**, *4*, 2000222. [CrossRef]
41. Zhang, L.; Liu, C.; Zhang, J.; Li, X.; Cheng, C.; Tian, Y.; Jen, A.K.Y.; Xu, B. Intensive exposure of functional rings of a polymeric hole-transporting material enables efficient perovskite solar cells. *Adv. Mater.* **2018**, *30*, 1804028. [CrossRef] [PubMed]
42. Xie, J.; Huang, K.; Yu, X.; Yang, Z.; Xiao, K.; Qiang, Y.; Zhu, X.; Xu, L.; Wang, P.; Cui, C.; et al. Enhanced electronic properties of SnO_2 via electron transfer from graphene quantum dots for efficient perovskite solar cells. *ACS Nano* **2017**, *11*, 9176–9182. [CrossRef] [PubMed]
43. Li, S.; Cao, Y.L.; Li, W.H.; Bo, Z.S. A brief review of hole transporting materials commonly used in perovskite solar cells. *Rare Met.* **2021**, *40*, 2712–2729. [CrossRef]
44. Liao, J.F.; Wu, W.Q.; Jiang, Y.; Zhong, J.X.; Wang, L.; Kuang, D.B. Understanding of carrier dynamics, heterojunction merits and device physics: Towards designing efficient carrier transport layer-free perovskite solar cells. *Chem. Soc. Rev.* **2020**, *49*, 354–381. [CrossRef]
45. Xiao, Y.; Wang, C.; Kondamareddy, K.K.; Liu, P.; Qi, F.; Zhang, H.; Guo, S.; Zhao, X.Z. Enhancing the performance of hole-conductor free carbon-based perovskite solar cells through rutile-phase passivation of anatase TiO_2 scaffold. *J. Power Sources* **2019**, *422*, 138–144. [CrossRef]
46. One Dimensional Solar Cell Simulation Program; SCAPS 3.3.08 Manual. Available online: https://users.elis.ugent.be/elisgroups/solar/projects/scaps/SCAPSinstallatie%202903.html (accessed on 15 August 2021).
47. Hao, F.; Stoumpos, C.C.; Cao, D.H.; Chang, R.P.; Kanatzidis, M.G. Lead-free solid-state organic–inorganic halide perovskite solar cells. *Nat. Photonics* **2014**, *8*, 489–494. [CrossRef]
48. Du, H.J.; Wang, W.C.; Zhu, J.Z. Device simulation of lead-free $CH_3NH_3SnI_3$ perovskite solar cells with high efficiency. *Chin. Phys. B* **2016**, *25*, 108802. [CrossRef]
49. Bansal, S.; Aryal, P. Evaluation of new materials for electron and hole transport layers in perovskite-based solar cells through SCAPS-1D simulations. In Proceedings of the IEEE 43rd Photovoltaic Specialists Conference (PVSC), Portland, OR, USA, 5–10 June 2016; pp. 0747–0750.
50. Mandadapu, U.; Vedanayakam, S.V.; Thyagarajan, K. Simulation and analysis of lead based perovskite solar cell using SCAPS-1D. *Indian J. Sci. Technol.* **2017**, *10*, 65–72. [CrossRef]
51. Noel, N.K.; Stranks, S.D.; Abate, A.; Wehrenfennig, C.; Guarnera, S.; Haghighirad, A.A.; Sadhanala, A.; Eperon, G.E.; Pathak, S.K.; Johnston, M.B.; et al. Lead-free organic–inorganic tin halide perovskites for photovoltaic applications. *Energy Environ. Sci.* **2014**, *7*, 3061–3068. [CrossRef]
52. Salah, M.M.; Hassan, K.M.; Abouelatta, M.; Shaker, A. A comparative study of different ETMs in perovskite solar cell with inorganic copper iodide as HTM. *Optik* **2019**, *178*, 958–963. [CrossRef]
53. Kirchartz, T.; Cahen, D. Minimum doping densities for p–n junctions. *Nat. Energy* **2020**, *5*, 973–975. [CrossRef]
54. Byeon, J.; Kim, J.; Kim, J.Y.; Lee, G.; Bang, K.; Ahn, N.; Choi, M. Charge transport layer-dependent electronic band bending in perovskite solar cells and its correlation to light-induced device degradation. *ACS Energy Lett.* **2020**, *5*, 2580–2589. [CrossRef]

55. Gamal, N.; Sedky, S.H.; Shaker, A.; Fedawy, M. Design of Lead-Free Perovskite Solar Cell using $Zn_{1-x}Mg_xO$ as ETL: SCAPS Device Simulation. *Optik* **2021**, *242*, 167306. [CrossRef]
56. Abdelnaby, M.; Zekry, A.; Elakkad, F.; Ragaie, H. Dependence of dark current on zinc concentration in $Zn_xCd_{1-x}S/ZnTe$ heterojunctions. *Sol. Energy Mater. Sol. Cells* **1993**, *29*, 97–108. [CrossRef]
57. Chen, H.; Yang, S. Carbon-based perovskite solar cells without hole transport materials: The front runner to the market? *Adv. Mater.* **2017**, *29*, 1603994. [CrossRef] [PubMed]
58. López-Vicente, R.; Abad, J.; Padilla, J.; Urbina, A. Assessment of Molecular Additives on the Lifetime of Carbon-Based Mesoporous Perovskite Solar Cells. *Energies* **2021**, *14*, 1947. [CrossRef]
59. Abdelaziz, S.; Zekry, A.; Shaker, A.; Abouelatta, M. Investigating the performance of formamidinium tin-based perovskite solar cell by SCAPS device simulation. *Opt. Mater.* **2020**, *101*, 109738. [CrossRef]
60. Minemoto, T.; Murata, M. Theoretical analysis on effect of band offsets in perovskite solar cells. *Sol. Energy Mater. Sol. Cells* **2015**, *133*, 8–14. [CrossRef]
61. Tanaka, K.; Minemoto, T.; Takakura, H. Analysis of heterointerface recombination by $Zn_{1-x}Mg_xO$ for window layer of Cu (In, Ga) Se_2 solar cells. *Sol. Energy* **2009**, *83*, 477–479. [CrossRef]

energies

MDPI

Article

Healthy and Faulty Experimental Performance of a Typical HVAC System under Italian Climatic Conditions: Artificial Neural Network-Based Model and Fault Impact Assessment

Antonio Rosato [1,*], Francesco Guarino [1], Sergio Sibilio [1], Evgueniy Entchev [2], Massimiliano Masullo [1] and Luigi Maffei [1]

[1] Department of Architecture and Industrial Design, University of Campania Luigi Vanvitelli, Via San Lorenzo 4, 81031 Aversa, Italy; francesco.guarino@unicampania.it (F.G.); sergio.sibilio@unicampania.it (S.S.); massimiliano.masullo@unicampania.it (M.M.); luigi.maffei@unicampania.it (L.M.)

[2] Natural Resources Canada, CanmetENERGY, 1 Haanel Drive, Ottawa, ON K1A 1M1, Canada; evgueniy.entchev@canada.ca

* Correspondence: antonio.rosato@unicampania.it; Tel.: +39-081-501-0845

Citation: Rosato, A.; Guarino, F.; Sibilio, S.; Entchev, E.; Masullo, M.; Maffei, L. Healthy and Faulty Experimental Performance of a Typical HVAC System under Italian Climatic Conditions: Artificial Neural Network-Based Model and Fault Impact Assessment. *Energies* **2021**, *14*, 5362. https://doi.org/10.3390/en14175362

Academic Editor: Chi-Ming Lai

Received: 21 July 2021
Accepted: 25 August 2021
Published: 28 August 2021

Abstract: The heating, ventilation, and air conditioning (HVAC) system serving the test room of the SENS i-Lab of the Department of Architecture and Industrial Design of the University of Campania Luigi Vanvitelli (Aversa, south of Italy) has been experimentally investigated through a series of tests performed during both summer and winter under both normal and faulty scenarios. In particular, five distinct typical faults have been artificially implemented in the HVAC system and analyzed during transient and steady-state operation. An optimal artificial neural network-based system model has been created in the MATLAB platform and verified by contrasting the experimental data with the predictions of twenty-two different neural network architectures. The selected artificial neural network architecture has been coupled with a dynamic simulation model developed by using the TRaNsient SYStems (TRNSYS) software platform with the main aims of (i) making available an experimental dataset characterized by labeled normal and faulty data covering a wide range of operating and climatic conditions; (ii) providing an accurate simulation tool able to generate operation data for assisting further research in fault detection and diagnosis of HVAC units; and (iii) evaluating the impact of selected faults on occupant indoor thermo-hygrometric comfort, temporal trends of key operating system parameters, and electric energy consumptions.

Keywords: HVAC system; air-handling unit; experimental performance; artificial neural network; simulation model; faults' impact assessment

1. Introduction

The building sector contributes to approximately 40% of overall energy demand in industrialized countries, with Heating, Ventilation, and Air Conditioning (HVAC) systems accounting for a large part of this energy consumption [1,2]. Several scientific publications have discussed the application of efficient/innovative technologies [3] and/or optimal control strategies [4] with the aim of reducing the energy demand and related greenhouse gas emissions of HVAC units. However, HVAC systems could be exposed to various abnormal faults during operation as a consequence of a failure of components, lack of correct maintenance, or wrong installation. Each component of HVAC systems can be eventually altered by a fault, where a fault is an anomalous state of the system, i.e., an undesired divergence of at least one of the properties of the HVAC unit with respect to healthy/standard conditions [5]. The faults can involve sensors, devices, equipment, and controllers [5]. A study conducted on more than 55,000 Air Handling Units (AHUs) showed that up to 90% runs with one or multiple faults [6]. Lin et al. [7] underlined that an effective detection of faults in HVAC units could save from 15% to 30% of overall energy required by buildings. In addition, Au-Yong et al. [8] highlighted a relevant impact of poor maintenance of HVAC systems on indoor thermo-hygrometric comfort, identifying several maintenance factors significantly correlated with occupants' satisfaction. This means that adopting a proper maintenance strategy is fundamental. Companies generally adopt a reactive maintenance or a preventive maintenance. Repairs are carried out only in the case of failures when a reactive maintenance is adopted; this approach could be expensive and may cause safety issues. In the case of a preventive maintenance, systems are examined and maintained at given periods (whatever their state is); however, this approach requires identifying a proper maintenance schedule in order to not waste component life that is still profitable as well as avoid safety problems.

1.1. Automated Fault Detection and Diagnosis Methods for HVAC Systems

Critical points of reactive and preventive maintenance approaches underline how "predicting" the faults of HVAC units could be essential. This task could be performed by means of the so-called Automated Fault Detection and Diagnosis (AFDD), which is an automated process of detecting faults and diagnosing the type of problem and/or its location [5,7,9]. It could be adopted to take advantage of potentialities associated to building energy management systems in quasi-real-time by comparing expected behavior with actual performance over a predefined period. AFDD technologies can provide numerous benefits, such as improved operational efficiency, energy savings, reductions of utility costs, as well as reduced equipment downtime [5,7,9]. Although currently underutilized, AFDD products represent one of the most active research areas as well as a very fast-growing market section in the sector of building analytics technologies [10]. The methodologies adopted for carrying out AFDD analyses can be categorized as (i) data-driven-based, (ii) quantitative model-based, and (iii) qualitative model-based [5]. The first category needs pre-labeled operational data acquired from the system under investigation in order to the develop AFDD models; data-driven AFDD approaches achieved promising results thanks to their applicability even in the case of simulation models are challenging to be developed [5,10]. The quantitative model-based approach relates to the methods involving simulation models physically describing the system at different levels of detail. Finally, the qualitative models are based on the knowledge of the system deriving from area expertise.

Nowadays, buildings are equipped with numerous sensors used for their energy management. In addition, innovative devices are allowed to connect occupancy sensors, power meters, and appliances that collect data in order to derive information with the aim of taking data-driven actions. In this context, the integration of artificial intelligence technologies (that highlighted fast advancements in last years), including both unsupervised and supervised algorithms [5,11], is particularly encouraging due to the fact that they could allow to improve self-diagnosis capabilities and optimize energy management systems. In particular, an Artificial Neural Network (ANN) represents a kind of artificial intelligence that simulates the operation of the human brain; it can learn from training data and replicate the trends of data time series, approximating nonlinear relationships between inputs and outputs of advanced energy systems without involving explicit mathematical representations [11]. The data-driven approach integrating artificial intelligence [5,12,13], with respect to the other methods, allows (i) achieving higher accuracy of fault detection and diagnosis; (ii) learning patterns from field data without involving physical models as well as needing an a priori knowledge of connections among faults and associated symptoms; and (iii) performing AFDD analyses considering a restricted number of variables and, therefore, limiting the number of sensors. In more detail, supervised approaches use the domain knowledge with the aim of developing a prediction tool, while the unsupervised methods get out concealed knowledge without a predefined goal [5,12,13]. Supervised models are mainly based on the implementation of residual analyses to perform an AFDD process [5,14,15], where a residual is the difference between the predicted and the experimental values of a specific parameter.

Several studies focusing on supervised techniques for AFDD of HVAC systems are reported in the scientific literature. Piscitelli et al. [5] suggested an innovative AFDD method based on both unsupervised and supervised data-driven approaches by considering the operational data of an AHU recorded during steady-state and transient periods. Dehestani et al. [16] suggested a methodology based on a multi-class support vector machine with the aim of identifying faults related to air dampers and fans of AHUs. A Bayesian network was considered in [17,18] for diagnosing faults associated to air dampers, return fan failure, and cooling coil valve; the network exploited as inputs the residuals derived from a set of statistical models and checking rules. Mulumba et al. [19] suggested a method to predict the occurrence of faults related to return air fan, air dampers, and cooling coil valve by means of a support vector machine combined with an autoregressive model. Yan et al. [20] presented a mixing of two supervised methods to detect blockage of coil valves and air dampers, return air fan failure, and duct leakage; a classification tree has been developed using as inputs both field data and residuals derived from a regression model, while the labels of different faults have been assumed as outputs; the method described in [20] can be helpful in performing AFDD analyses without considering transient operation of HVAC systems. McHugh et al. [21] compared several classification models for AFDD and the classification tree model was identified as the best option for chilled water or steam leakage.

1.2. Novelty and Structure of the Paper

The literature review performed in the previous subsection demonstrates how the scientific community is engaged in the research area of artificial intelligence techniques-based AFDD for HVAC units. According to the authors of [1,7,22], even if AFDD is an effective approach to guarantee an efficient operation of HVAC systems and associated technology is growing, it is still in the initial stage of utilization. This means that additional investigations are still mandatory in order to address several research gaps.

First, the architecture of sensors in HVAC units is usually not designed with AFDD in mind, and therefore some important variables are generally not measured causing a lack of labeled data. Moreover, measurements under faulty conditions are even more challenging to be obtained due to the uncommon faults' occurrence as well as the inconvenience of implementing faults into complex and expensive devices with the purpose of collecting data [23]. In addition, relatively few studies give detailed information on how faults are empirically introduced into an existing HVAC system [5,24]; almost all the works only take into account one HVAC operating mode under different weather scenarios [5,24]. Lin et al. [7] highlighted that there is a need of standard datasets for assessing the accuracy of AFDD methods and future AFDD studies should focus on the expansion of databases as well as their provision for public use. Granderson et al. [25] also underlined that it is unusual to find datasets characterized by labeled data clearly indicating whether they represent faulty, healthy, or simply unusual operating states. Finally, Casillas et al. [26] indicated that one of the most important challenges of researches focusing on AFDD methods is represented by the insufficiency of shared databases to benchmark the performance of algorithms with the aim of assessing improvements and prioritizing future investments in these methods. With reference to this point, it should be highlighted that most of AFDD studies are based on the ASHRAE RP-1312 data set [24] (dated 2011) consisting of measurements recorded every minute from an experimental set-up comprising two AHUs; recently, Piscitelli et al. [5], Yun et al. [27], as well as Fan et al. [28] proposed novel methodologies for performing AFDD analyses of AHUs based on the ASHRAE RP-1312 data set [24]. Therefore, as also suggested by Hu et al. [23], additional researches are required in order to obtain more experimental data under both normal and faulty operation considering the occurrence of a number of different faults upon varying the boundary conditions.

One more research gap associated with the application of AFDD analyses is related to the fact that not many studies quantitatively examine how various faults and fault severities impact energy consumption, user comfort, maintenance cost, and equipment life cycle [6]. This point represents a demanding task taking into account that (i) several faults could have comparable symptoms and (ii) faults of AHUs could interact each other and, therefore, it could be challenging to isolate multiple faults of AHUs [1,24]. According to the authors of [7], additional works better characterizing faults' impact based on field measurements could prove valuable in addressing future developments and implementation attempts of AFDD techniques. Piscitelli et al. [5] also indicated that the majority of AFDD applications are used for detecting and/or diagnosing faults of HVAC units during steady-state operation, and therefore they could not be effectively used with reference to transient periods because they are not fully able to automatically determine the system operation mode and prevent false alarms. In this context, accurate simulation models of HVAC units can provide significant benefits for performing AFDD analyses taking into account that they could help in quantifying faults' impact on both energy demand and occupant comfort and, therefore, supporting corrective actions which can facilitate more reliable commissioning decisions, more efficient system operation, improved indoor conditions, and prolonged equipment service life [29]. However, according to the authors of [30,31], most existing simulation models of HVAC systems assume normal/healthy conditions without any operational faults and do not capture the significant impact of faults on energy consumption and indoor comfort conditions. In addition, Zhang and Hong [31] highlighted that modeling activities of HVAC systems operating under faulty conditions are still insufficient mostly due to the fact that several fault-related researches focus on single subcomponent operation rather than whole system performance and, consequently, they cannot predict the comprehensive faults' impact.

One additional knowledge gap to be underlined relates to the fact that models of HVAC units developed for AFDD purposes should be fully validated via extensive comparisons with experimental data under both faulty and normal conditions as well as different boundary scenarios. However, comparative analyses against field measurements are usually not performed for validation purposes mainly because, as mentioned above, accurate experimental datasets, covering a wide range of operating conditions and including faulty data, are not generally available. For example, Zhang and Hong [31] introduced a methodology for modeling operational faults of HVAC units by using a comprehensive whole-building performance simulation program; impacts of faults with reference to a small-size office building have been investigated in [31], but a validation process against experimental data has not been carried out; similarly, Basarkar et al. [30] assessed the effects of four typical faults on the HVAC unit serving a commercial reference building by means of a simulation program; the results of comparisons between predictions and field measures have not been reported in the paper in order to check the models' accuracy.

In this paper, the operation of the HVAC system assisting the integrated test room of the SENS i-Lab of the Department of Architecture and Industrial Design of the University of Campania Luigi Vanvitelli (located in Aversa, south of Italy) has been experimentally characterized on the basis of a series of tests performed during both summer and winter under both normal and faulty operating conditions (transient and non-transient). In particular, five different typical faults (affecting the supply/return air fans, the valve supplying the heating coil, the valve supplying the cooling coil, and the valve supplying the steam humidifier) have been artificially implemented in the HVAC system and analyzed during transient and steady-state operation. An optimal artificial neural network-based system model has been identified and verified by contrasting the experimental data with the predictions of twenty-two different neural network architectures developed in the MATLAB environment [32]; the selected artificial neural network has been coupled with a dynamic simulation model developed using the TRaNsient SYStems (TRNSYS) software platform (version 17) [33]. The effect of selected faults on occupant indoor comfort, temporal trends of key operating system parameters, as well as electric energy consumptions has been assessed.

This paper addresses several research gaps highlighted by the literature review focusing on AFDD applications to HVAC systems. In fact, the dataset described in this article includes fault free and faulty operational data of a typical HVAC unit, coupled with ground-truth information and the indication of absence or presence of faults. In addition, this dataset covers a wide range of operating scenarios (both transient and steady-state) and weather conditions while encompassing five typical fault types. Moreover, a whole-system simulation model using both MATLAB and TRSNSYS environments has been created and extensively validated by contrasting predicted data with measurements; then, it has been used to discover a number of patterns related to the faulty system operation and assess the impacts of selected typical faults. Both the labeled measured data as well as the developed simulation models will be made available on a public data repository allowing access, consultation, and utilization to readers and organizations for institutional and research purposes.

The paper consists of six main sections. In Section 2, the experimental setup is detailed. Section 3 describes the investigated faults as well as the experimental results of both fault free and faulty tests. A detailed outline of the simulation model is reported in Section 4. An assessment of faults' impact is performed and discussed in Section 5. Finally, the conclusions and future research steps are indicated in Section 6.

2. Description of the Experimental Setup

The SENS i-Lab is a multi-sensorial laboratory of the Department of Architecture and Industrial Design of the University of Campania Luigi Vanvitelli (Aversa, southern Italy, longitude: 14°12′26″ E, latitude: 40°58′21″ N). The SENS i-Lab consists of a human-centered, multi-physical, and multi-purpose test room served by an HVAC system, including a single duct dual-fan constant air volume (CAV) air handling unit, controlling indoor air temperature, indoor air relative humidity, indoor air velocity, and indoor air quality. The test room has a floor area of 16.0 m^2 (its height is 3.6 m) and four vertical walls (without windows and one door); both the ceiling and floor are horizontal. It is installed inside the Department, so that its indoor conditions are not directly affected by external climatic conditions. Table A1 in Appendix A describes the material, thickness, thermal conductivity, conductive thermal resistance of each layer composing the walls, the ceiling, and the floor of the integrated test room.

A CAV AHU is commonly used in buildings; it is more common in existing old buildings or small new buildings, while in new medium/large buildings variable air volume (VAV) AHUs are the common choice of installation. In the case of CAV AHUs, volumetric flow rate of supply air is constant, while its supply temperature and relative humidity are varying. With respect to VAV AHUs, CAV AHUs are easier, cheaper, and quicker to install, but they are less efficient and with higher lifetime running costs. The AHU of the SENS i-Lab consists of these main functional subcomponents: return air fan (RAF); supply air fan (SAF); pre-heating coil (PreHC); post-heating coil (PostHC); cooling coil (CC); steam humidifier (HUM); static cross-flow heat recovery system (HRS); vapor compression air-to-water single-stage electric refrigerating system (RS) connected with the cooling coil; vapor-compression air-to-water single-stage electric heat pump (HP) connected with the pre-heating coil and the post-heating coil; valves (V_{PreHC}, V_{PostHC}, V_{CC}, V_{HUM}) controlling the flow rate of heat carrier fluid entering, respectively, the pre-heating coil, the post-heating coil, the cooling coil and the steam humidifier; return air damper (D_{RA}); outside air damper (D_{OA}); exhaust air damper (D_{EA}); damper of the HRS (D_{HRS}); return air filter (RAFil); outside air filter (OAFil); supply air filter (SAFil). Two 0.08 × 0.18 cm^2 air grilles are mounted on the south-oriented wall at floor level and two 0.08 × 0.18 cm^2 air grilles are mounted on the north-oriented wall at floor level with the aim of extracting air from indoor space to be moved into the AHU; a 0.60 × 0.60 cm^2 swirl diffuser acting as supply air grille is mounted on the ceiling of the test room. Figure 1 reports the scheme of the AHU together with its main components.

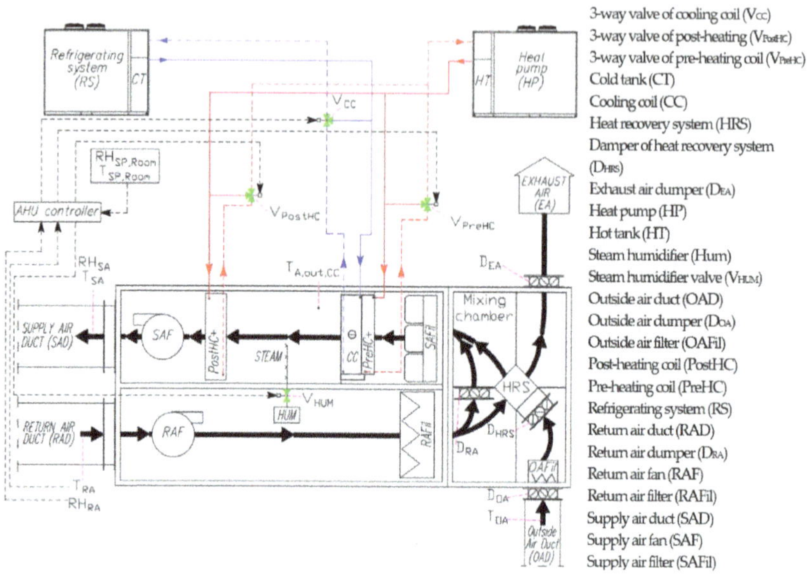

Figure 1. Air handling unit scheme.

Figure A1 of Appendix A shows the floor plan of the test room including the AHU, together with the refrigerating system (RS), the heat pump (HP), as well as the return and supply air ducts. Table 1 indicates the characteristics of the functional components of the HVAC serving the SENS i-Lab. The system fulfills the requirements prescribed by the Ecodesign Directive 1253/2014 [34] introduced by the European Union in order to support the diffusion of energy efficient AHUs. The HVAC unit is equipped with a number of sensors to observe and register the key operating system parameters. The measuring range as well as the accuracy of the sensors are showed in Table 2.

The AHU is operated according to a specific control logic. In particular, the following parameters are manually set (and eventually modified during the test) by the end users: (i) the desired targets of both indoor relative humidity ($RH_{SP,Room}$) and indoor air temperature ($T_{SP,Room}$) to be reached and maintained into the test room; (ii) the deadband DB_T for $T_{SP,Room}$ and the deadband DB_{RH} for $RH_{SP,Room}$; (iii) air flow rate of both the supply air fan (OL_{SAF}) and the return air fan (OL_{RAF}); (iv) opening percentages of the outside air damper (OP_{DOA}), the return air damper (OP_{DRA}), and the exhaust air damper (OP_{DEA}); and (v) activation of the heat recovery system damper (OP_{DHRS}). Flow rate of air moved by the supply air fan can range between 0 (OL_{SAF} = 0%) and 1080 m^3/h (OL_{SAF} = 100%), while flow rate of air moved by the return air fan is between 0 (OL_{RAF} = 0%) and 1460 m^3/h (OL_{RAF} = 100%); the maximum electric consumption of the SAF and RAF are, respectively, 1.22 kW and 0.48 kW. The parameter OP_{DHRS} can be fixed at 100% (no heat recovery) or 0% (heat recovery takes place). The variation range of the parameters OP_{DRA}, OP_{DOA}, and OP_{DEA} is 0 ÷ 100% (100% corresponds to the dampers fully open). Once the previous parameters are manually set by the end-users, opening percentages of the valves (OP_{V_PreHC}, OP_{V_PostHC}, OP_{V_CC} and OP_{V_HUM}) are automatically managed in the range 0 ÷ 100% by proportional-integral-derivative (PID) controllers in order to achieve the indoor desired targets. Opening percentages of the valves are continuously regulated between 0% and 100% as a function of differences between the targets of air temperature and relative humidity into the test room and their current values. In more detail, volumetric flow rate of fluid streaming inside the coils can be modulated between 0 and 0.860 m^3/h, while flow rate of steam mass of the steam humidifier can be varied from 0 up to 5 kg/h.

Table 1. Main AHU components' characteristics.

Supply air fan (SAF)	Maximum number of revolutions per minute (rpm) Nominal velocity of supply air fan (%)	3640 50
Return air fan (RAF)	Maximum number of revolutions per minute (rpm) Nominal velocity of return air fan (%)	3080 50
Cross flow heat recovery system (HRS)	Nominal recovery capacity (kW) Nominal efficiency (%) Nominal pressure drops on external/exhaust air side (kPa)	3.1 74.7 0.047/0.048
Return air filter (RAFil) and outside air filter (OAFil)	Type/Efficiency class	Fluted/G4
Supply air filter (SAFil)	Type/Efficiency class	Rigid pocket/G4
Return air duct (RAD) and supply air duct (SAD)	Diameter (m) Supply/Return length (m) Thermal resistance of insulating material (m^2K/W)	0.25 9.8/16.8 0.25
Pre-heating coil (PreHC)	Nominal heating capacity (kW) Nominal air/fluid volumetric flow rate (m^3/h) Nominal air/fluid pressure drops (kPa)	4.1 600/0.710 0.00321/12.43
Colling coil (CC)	Nominal cooling capacity (kW) Nominal air/fluid volumetric flow rate (m^3/h) Nominal air/fluid pressure drops (kPa)	5.0 600/0.860 0.0178/13.56
Steam humidifier (HUM) [35]	Nominal steam capacity (kg/h) Nominal power (kW)	5.0 3.7
Post-heating coil (PostHC)	Nominal heating capacity (kW) Nominal air/fluid volumetric flow rate (m^3/h) Nominal air/fluid pressure drops (kPa)	5.0 600/0.860 0.0497/20.35
Heat Pump (HP) [36]	Nominal capacity (kW) Nominal input power (kW) Nominal heat carrier fluid volumetric flow rate (m^3/h)	14.0 4.75 2.41
Refrigerating System (RS) [36]	Nominal capacity (kW) Nominal input power (kW) Nominal heat carrier fluid volumetric flow rate (m^3/h)	13.4 4.48 2.31

Table 2. Measuring range and the accuracy of the AHU sensors.

Sensor Model	Monitored Parameter	Measuring Range	Accuracy
Siemens QFM2160 [37]	Return air temperature (T_{RA})	0 ÷ 50 °C	±0.8 °C
	Return air relative humidity (RH_{RA})	0 ÷ 100%	±3%
Siemens QFM2160 [37]	Supply air temperature (T_{SA})	0 ÷ 50 °C	±0.8 °C
	Supply air relative humidity (RH_{SA})	0 ÷ 100%	±3%
Siemens QAM2161.040 [38]	Outside air temperature (T_{OA})	−50 ÷ 50 °C	±0.75 °C
Siemens QAM2161.040 [38]	Cooling coil outlet air temperature ($T_{A,out,CC}$)	−50 ÷ 50 °C	±0.75 °C
TSI 7575, 982 IAQ [39]	Temperature of air around the test room (T_{BEA})	−10 ÷ 60 °C	±0.50 °C
	Relative humidity of air around the test room (RH_{BEA})	5 ÷ 95%	±3%

Table 3 reports the main criteria for activating and deactivating the main functional subsystems of the AHU serving the test room. The pre-heating coil is not included in the table because this subsystem has been kept deactivated during the entire duration of all experimental tests. The post-heating coil is activated when return air temperature becomes not larger than the temperature difference ($T_{SP,Room} - DB_T$), while it is deactivated in the case of T_{RA} assumes a value not lower than the temperature ($T_{SP,Room} + DB_T$). The cooling coil is activated when return air temperature becomes not lower than the temperature ($T_{SP,Room}$ + DB_T), while it is deactivated in the case of T_{RA} assumes a value not larger than the temperature difference ($T_{SP,Room}$ − DB_T). The steam humidifier is activated when return air relative humidity becomes not larger than the air relative humidity difference ($RH_{SP,Room}$ − DB_{RH}), while it is deactivated in the case of RH_{RA} assumes a value not lower than the air relative humidity ($RH_{SP,Room}$ + DB_{RH}). The heat pump is activated when temperature into the hot tank T_{HT} is lower than 44 °C, while it is deactivated in the case of T_{HT} assumes a value not lower than 46 °C. The refrigerating device is activated when the temperature into the cold tank T_{CT} is larger than 8 °C, while it is deactivated in the case that T_{CT} assumes a value not larger than 6 °C. The signals managing the opening percentages of the valves (OP_{V_PreHC}, OP_{V_PostHC}, OP_{V_CC}, and OP_{V_HUM}) are generated by PID controllers. As an alternative to the automatic operation based on PID controllers, the opening percentages of the valves (OP_{V_PreHC}, OP_{V_PostHC}, OP_{V_CC}, and OP_{V_HUM}) can be also forced by the end-users; therefore, the end user is allowed to force component operation/parameters based on specific research purposes.

Table 3. Activation criteria of the AHU's components.

Component of AHU	ON	OFF
Steam humidifier (HUM)	$RH_{RA} \leq (RH_{SP,Room} - DB_{RH})$	$RH_{RA} \geq (RH_{SP,Room} + DB_{RH})$
Cooling coil (CC)	$T_{RA} \geq (T_{SP,Room} + DB_T)$ OR $RH_{RA} \geq (RH_{SP,Room} + DB_{RH})$	$T_{RA} \leq (T_{SP,Room} - DB_T)$ AND $RH_{RA} \leq (RH_{SP,Room} - DB_{RH})$
Post-heating coil (PostHC)	$T_{RA} \leq (T_{SP,Room} - DB_T)$	$T_{RA} \geq (T_{SP,Room} + DB_T)$
Heat Pump (HP) [36]	T_{HT} < 44 °C	$T_{HT} \geq$ 46 °C
Refrigerating System (RS) [36]	T_{CT} > 8 °C	$T_{CT} \leq$ 6 °C

However, alternatively, the end users can also manually force (at the beginning or during the test) the opening percentages of the valves for research purposes (instead of operating according to the automatic control logic).

3. Experimental Tests

A set of 18 fault-free and faulty daily experimental tests has been performed in order to examine the HVAC system operation during transient and steady-state operation under both winter and summer conditions. Tables 4 and 5 describe the operating of the experimental tests under summer and winter conditions, respectively.

Table 4. Operating conditions of the experimental tests under fault free (tests 1–4) and faulty operation (tests 5–9) during summer.

Test n.	$T_{SP,Room}$ (°C)	$RH_{SP,Room}$ (%)	T_{OA} (°C)	OL_{RAF} (%)	OL_{SAF} (%)	OP_{V_PostHC} (%)	OP_{V_CC} (%)	OP_{V_HUM} (%)	Date (dd/mm/yyyy)
1	26	50	20.6 ÷ 26.7	50	50	0 ÷ 100	0 ÷ 100	0 ÷ 100	29/06/2020
2	26	50	29.1 ÷ 35.2	50	50	0 ÷ 100	0 ÷ 100	0 ÷ 100	28/07/2020
3	26	50	25.3 ÷ 32.0	50	50	0 ÷ 100	0 ÷ 100	0 ÷ 100	23/07/2020
4	26	50	28.6 ÷ 35.3	50	50	0 ÷ 100	0 ÷ 100	0 ÷ 100	21/07/2020
5 (fault1)	26	50	30.4 ÷ 34.9	50	20	0 ÷ 100	0 ÷ 100	0 ÷ 100	31/07/2020
6 (fault2)	26	50	32.1 ÷ 38.8	20	50	0 ÷ 100	0 ÷ 100	0 ÷ 100	03/08/2020
7 (fault3)	26	50	33.8 ÷ 38.4	50	50	0	0 ÷ 100	0 ÷ 100	16/09/2020
8 (fault4)	26	50	29.4 ÷ 35.8	50	50	0 ÷ 100	0	0 ÷ 100	16/09/2020
9 (fault5)	26	50	28.7 ÷ 38.2	50	50	0 ÷ 100	0 ÷ 100	0	18/09/2020

Table 5. Operating conditions of the experimental tests under fault free (tests 10–13) and faulty operation (test 14–18) during winter.

Test n.	$T_{SP,Room}$ (°C)	$RH_{SP,Room}$ (%)	T_{OA} (°C)	OL_{RAF} (%)	OL_{SAF} (%)	OP_{V_PostHC} (%)	OP_{V_CC} (%)	OP_{V_HUM} (%)	Date (dd/mm/yyyy)
10	20	50	10.3 ÷ 15.0	50	50	0 ÷ 100	0 ÷ 100	0 ÷ 100	23/12/2020
11	20	50	13.2 ÷ 15.4	50	50	0 ÷ 100	0 ÷ 100	0 ÷ 100	28/12/2020
12	20	50	12.7 ÷ 18.6	50	50	0 ÷ 100	0 ÷ 100	0 ÷ 100	29/12/2020
13	20	50	8.0 ÷ 13.5	50	50	0 ÷ 100	0 ÷ 100	0 ÷ 100	05/01/2021
14 (fault1)	20	50	12.3 ÷ 20.0	50	20	0 ÷ 100	0 ÷ 100	0 ÷ 100	12/01/2021
15 (fault2)	20	50	5.6 ÷ 12.2	20	50	0 ÷ 100	0 ÷ 100	0 ÷ 100	14/01/2021
16 (fault3)	20	50	10.5 ÷ 15.9	50	50	0	0 ÷ 100	0 ÷ 100	28/01/2021
17 (fault4)	20	50	7.8 ÷ 16.8	50	50	0 ÷ 100	0	0 ÷ 100	15/02/2021
18 (fault5)	20	50	9.2 ÷ 13.3	50	50	0 ÷ 100	0 ÷ 100	0	12/02/2021

During all the tests, a number of system parameters have been kept constant: $DB_T = 1$ °C, $DB_{RH} = 5\%$, $OP_{DRA} = 100\%$, $OP_{DOA} = 20\%$, $OP_{DEA} = 20\%$, and $OP_{DHRS} = 100$. In more detail, 8 tests have been performed under fault free conditions (tests n. 1, 2, 3, 4 in Table 4 carried out during summer and tests n. 10, 11, 12, 13 in Table 5 carried out during winter). The remaining 10 tests have been carried out while artificially introducing specific faults (tests n. 5, 6, 7, 8, 9 in Table 4 carried out during summer and tests n. 14, 15, 16, 17, 18 in Table 5 carried out during winter). The experiments have been performed by measuring every minute all the parameters indicated in Table 2. In this study, the recording time step of measured data has been defined according to the experimental approaches adopted in similar works available in the scientific literature. For example, the ASHRAE RP-1312 data set [24] developed for AFDD purposes consists of experimental data recorded every minute from a facility comprising two AHUs; recently, Piscitelli et al. [5], Yun et al. [27], as well as Fan et al. [28] proposed novel methodologies for performing AFDD analyses of AHUs based on this ASHRAE RP-1312 database [24]; Cheng et al. [40] developed a new AFDD method for AHUs using experimental data measured every minute. Therefore, a measurement time step of one minute could be reasonably assumed as acceptable in order to take into account the response time of HVAC components.

Only during the faulty tests, the operation of specific AHU components has been forced to assure user-specified positions in order to artificially simulate the following 5 specific typical faults (named fault 1, 2, 3, 4, 5):

- Fault 1 has been implemented during both the tests n. 5 and n. 14, i.e., the velocity of the supply air fan has been kept at 20% (instead of the nominal value of 50%);
- Fault 2 has been implemented during both the tests n. 6 and n. 15, i.e., the velocity of the return air fan has been kept at 20% (instead of the nominal value of 50%);
- Fault 3 has been implemented during both the tests n. 7 and 16, i.e., the valve managing the flow rate entering the post-heating coil has always been kept closed (instead of allowing its normal operation with an opening percentage in the range 0 ÷ 100% according to the AHU automatic control logic);
- Fault 4 has been implemented during both the tests n. 8 and n. 17, i.e., the valve managing the flow rate entering the cooling coil has always been kept closed (instead of allowing its normal operation with an opening percentage in the range 0 ÷ 100% according to the AHU automatic control logic);
- Fault 5 has been implemented during both the tests n. 9 and n. 18, i.e., opening percentage of the valve managing the flow rate entering the steam humidifier has always been kept closed (instead of allowing its normal operation with an opening percentage in the range 0 ÷ 100% according to the AHU automatic control logic).

In this study, the above-mentioned faults have been introduced at the beginning of the faulty tests and maintained during the entire duration of the experiments (what happens in the case of the faults are shorter has not been investigated).

During the tests n. 1–4 and n. 10–13 (fault free tests), the AHU's components have been operated without any artificial faults.

In both Tables 4 and 5, the parameters characterizing the corresponding faults have been highlighted in red.

Figures 2a–d and 3a–e highlight the experimental trends of return air temperature T_{RA}, supply air temperature T_{SA}, outside air temperature T_{OA}, air temperature around the test room T_{BEA}, return air relative humidity RH_{RA}, supply air relative humidity RH_{SA}, and air relative humidity around the test room RH_{BEA} recorded during the fault free and faulty tests, respectively, performed under summer conditions (detailed in Table 4).

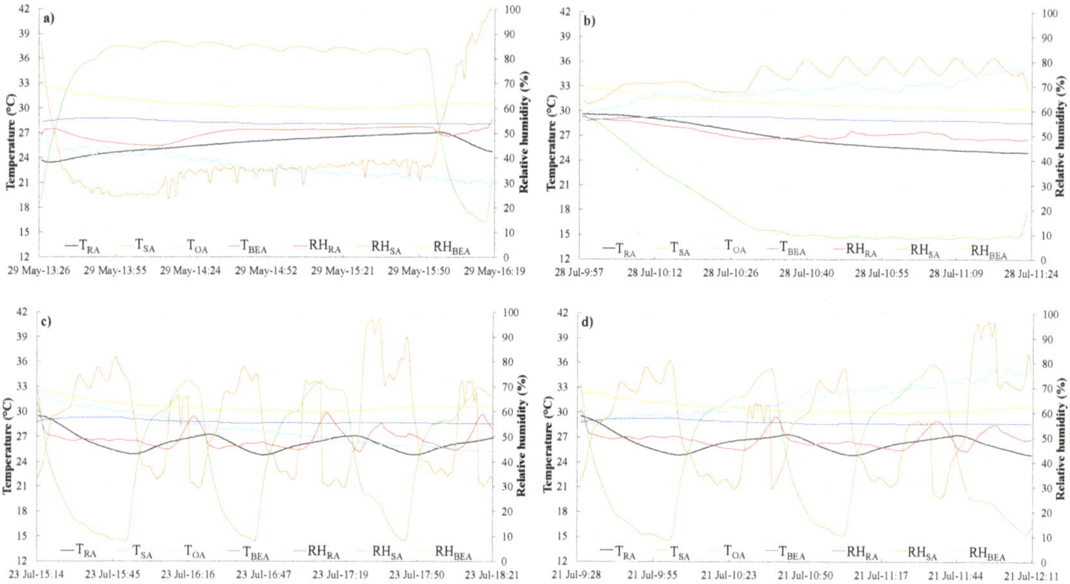

Figure 2. Experimental data measured during the fault free tests under summer conditions: test n. 1 (**a**), test n. 2 (**b**), test n. 3 (**c**), and test n. 4 (**d**).

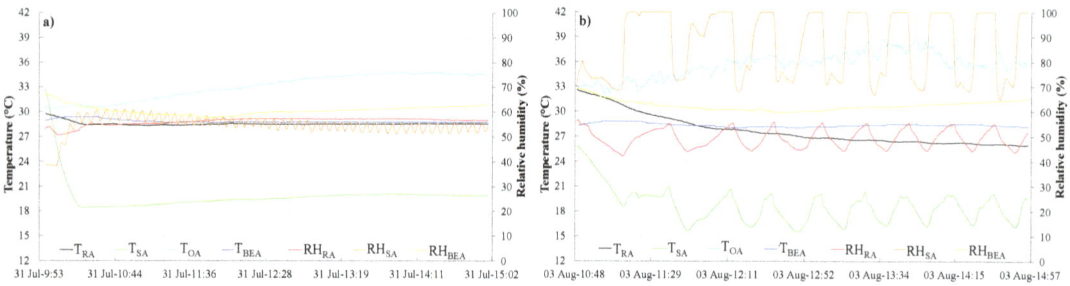

Figure 3. *Cont.*

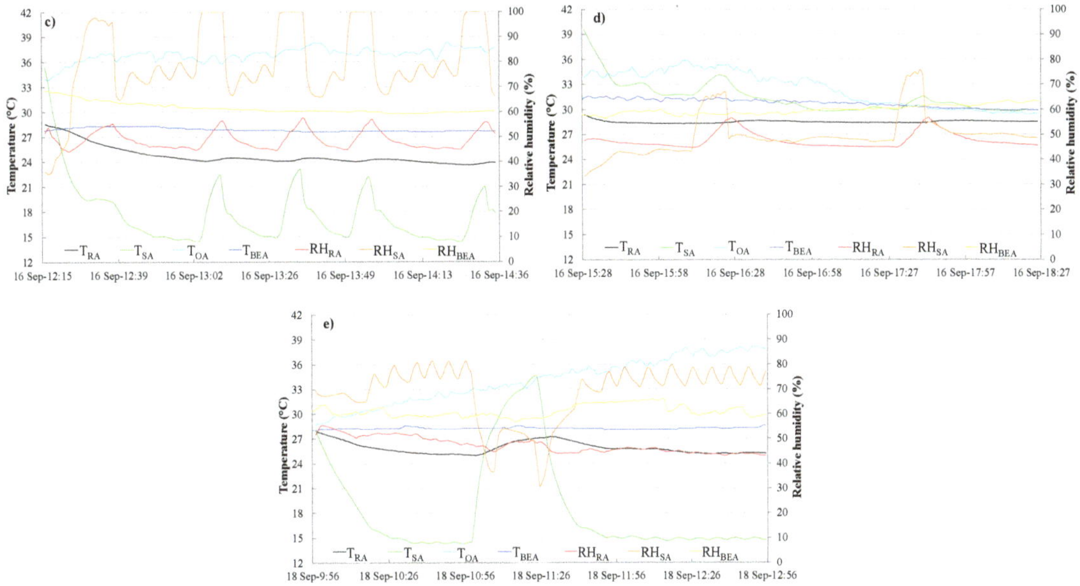

Figure 3. Experimental data measured during the faulty tests under summer conditions: test n. 5 (**a**), test n. 6 (**b**), test n. 7 (**c**), test n. 8 (**d**), and test n. 9 (**e**).

Figure 2a reports the experimental trends of T_{RA}, T_{SA}, T_{OA}, T_{BEA}, RH_{RA}, RH_{SA}, RH_{BEA} during the fault free test n.1; Figure 2b shows the measured parameters T_{RA}, T_{SA}, T_{OA}, T_{BEA}, RH_{RA}, RH_{SA}, RH_{BEA} during the fault free test n.2; Figure 2c indicates the measured data associated to T_{RA}, T_{SA}, T_{OA}, T_{BEA}, RH_{RA}, RH_{SA}, RH_{BEA} during the fault free test n.3; Figure 2d highlights the temporal variation of T_{RA}, T_{SA}, T_{OA}, T_{BEA}, RH_{RA}, RH_{SA}, RH_{BEA} during the fault free test n.4.

Figure 3a reports the experimental trends of T_{RA}, T_{SA}, T_{OA}, T_{BEA}, RH_{RA}, RH_{SA}, RH_{BEA} during the faulty test n.5; Figure 3b shows the measured parameters T_{RA}, T_{SA}, T_{OA}, T_{BEA}, RH_{RA}, RH_{SA}, RH_{BEA} during the faulty test n.6; Figure 3c indicates the measured data associated to T_{RA}, T_{SA}, T_{OA}, T_{BEA}, RH_{RA}, RH_{SA}, RH_{BEA} during the faulty test n.7; Figure 3d highlight the temporal variation of T_{RA}, T_{SA}, T_{OA}, T_{BEA}, RH_{RA}, RH_{SA}, RH_{BEA} during the faulty test n.8; the values of T_{RA}, T_{SA}, T_{OA}, T_{BEA}, RH_{RA}, RH_{SA}, RH_{BEA} recorded during the faulty test n.9 are depicted in Figure 3e.

Figures 4a–d and 5a–e report the experimental trends of T_{RA}, T_{SA}, T_{OA}, T_{BEA}, RH_{RA}, RH_{SA}, RH_{BEA} recorded during the fault free and faulty tests, respectively, performed under winter conditions (detailed in Table 5).

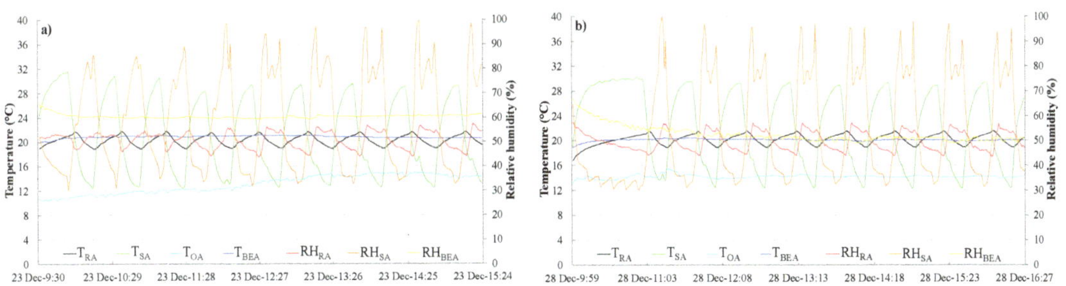

Figure 4. *Cont.*

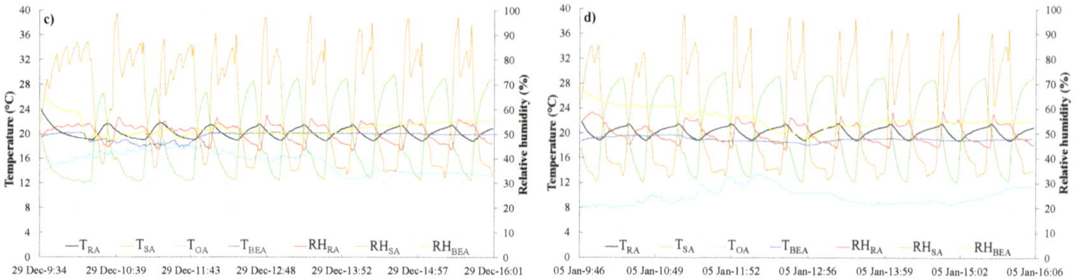

Figure 4. Experimental data measured during the fault free tests under winter conditions: test n. 10 (**a**), test n. 11 (**b**), test n. 12 (**c**), and test n. 13 (**d**).

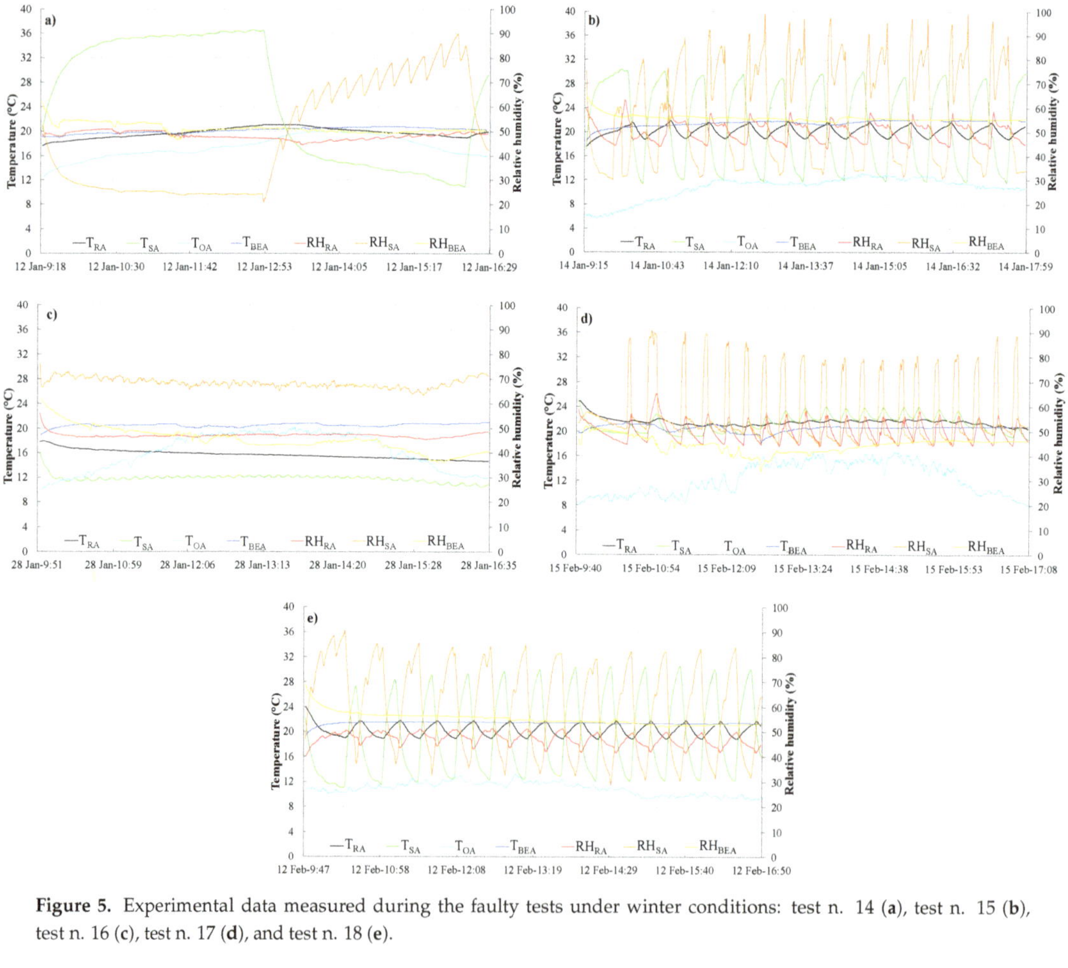

Figure 5. Experimental data measured during the faulty tests under winter conditions: test n. 14 (**a**), test n. 15 (**b**), test n. 16 (**c**), test n. 17 (**d**), and test n. 18 (**e**).

Figure 4a reports the experimental trends of T_{RA}, T_{SA}, T_{OA}, T_{BEA}, RH_{RA}, RH_{SA}, RH_{BEA} during the fault free test n.10; Figure 4b shows the measured parameters T_{RA}, T_{SA}, T_{OA}, T_{BEA}, RH_{RA}, RH_{SA}, RH_{BEA} during the fault free test n.11; Figure 4c indicates the measured data associated to T_{RA}, T_{SA}, T_{OA}, T_{BEA}, RH_{RA}, RH_{SA}, RH_{BEA} during the fault free test n.12;

Figure 4d highlights the temporal variation of T_{RA}, T_{SA}, T_{OA}, T_{BEA}, RH_{RA}, RH_{SA}, RH_{BEA} during the fault free test n.13.

Figure 5a reports the experimental trends of T_{RA}, T_{SA}, T_{OA}, T_{BEA}, RH_{RA}, RH_{SA}, RH_{BEA} during the faulty test n.14; Figure 5b shows the measured parameters T_{RA}, T_{SA}, T_{OA}, T_{BEA}, RH_{RA}, RH_{SA}, RH_{BEA} during the faulty test n.15; Figure 5c indicates the measured data associated to T_{RA}, T_{SA}, T_{OA}, T_{BEA}, RH_{RA}, RH_{SA}, RH_{BEA} during the faulty test n.16; Figure 5d highlight the temporal variation of T_{RA}, T_{SA}, T_{OA}, T_{BEA}, RH_{RA}, RH_{SA}, RH_{BEA} during the faulty test n.17; the values of T_{RA}, T_{SA}, T_{OA}, T_{BEA}, RH_{RA}, RH_{SA}, RH_{BEA} recorded during the faulty test n.18 are depicted in Figure 5e.

Analysis of Experimental Trends

The data acquired during normal and faulty operation tests (and reported in previous section) highlight that the percentages of time with values of indoor air temperature within the given deadband (1 °C) around the user-defined target (setpoint 26/20 °C for summer/winter season) are equal to 69.8%, 57.0%, 71.3%, 69.1%, 0%, 36.1%, 13.4%, 0%,86.6%, 68.3%, 69.6%, 72.5%, 71.4%, 75.4%, 68.7%, 0.0%, 15.7%, and 64.9% for the tests 1–18, respectively. Furthermore, the percentages of time with values of air relative humidity inside the test room within the deadband (5%) around the target (50%) are equal to 98.4%, 84.9%, 83.5%, 88.3%, 16.2%, 80.6%, 88.1%, 90.6%, 65.4%, 84.7%, 80.7%, 87.3%, 81.2%, 49.4%, 82.3%, 99.6%, 80.5%, and 76.0%, during the tests 1–18, respectively. The results of calculation highlight a good capability of the HVAC unit under healthy operation (tests n. 1–4 and 10–13) to accurately control indoor conditions. The previously mentioned percentages are lower than 100% because (a) the initial values of return air temperature and return air relative humidity are in some cases far from target values and (b) during the start-up phases the AHU operates under transient conditions trying to approach the steady-state conditions to achieve the desired targets.

In more detail, Figure 3a–e (associated to the faulty tests performed during summer) highlights the different trends/patterns associated to key operating parameters with respect to the scenarios without faults:

- In Figure 3a (corresponding to the fault 1, i.e., velocity of the supply air fan reduced at 20%), supply air temperature and supply air relative humidity are in a much narrower range as it would expected in the case of reduced supply air flow; in this case, T_{SA} drops to about 18.4 °C and then it remains below 20.5 °C (out of the desired thermal comfort range) during the remaining part of the test, while RH_{SA} is in the range of 51% to 61% with a larger number of oscillations; in addition, it can be noticed that both return air temperature T_{RA} and return air relative humidity RH_{RA} vary much more slowly as a function of time;
- Figure 3b (corresponding to the fault 2, i.e., velocity of the return air fan reduced at 20%) indicates that, as supposed, supply air temperature varies in a smaller range (in this case between 15.5 °C and 21.0 °C) when return air flow rate is reduced;
- In Figure 3c (corresponding to the fault 3, i.e., post-heating coil valve kept fully closed), supply air temperature T_{SA} assumes lower average values, ranging in a narrower interval (in this case between 14.5 °C and 23.0 °C) due to the fact that post-heating coil is not active; as a consequence, return air temperature, after the initial drop from ~28.5 °C down to ~24.0 °C, remains almost constant during the remaining part of the test (with a value smaller than its lower deadband and, therefore, out of desired thermal comfort range); in addition, it should be underlined that average values of supply air relative humidity are greater;
- In Figure 3d (corresponding to the fault 4, i.e., cooling coil valve kept fully closed), supply air temperature is characterized by much larger average values (as it would be expected due to the missing contribution of the cooling coil), with a narrower variation range (in this case between 30.0 °C and 34.0 °C); return air temperature is substantially constant, assuming a value larger than its upper deadband (in this case equal to ~28.5 °C) and, therefore, out of the desired thermal comfort range;

- In Figure 3e (corresponding to the fault 5, i.e., steam humidifier valve kept fully closed), return air relative humidity varies in a narrower range (in this case between 43.0% and 55.5%), highlighting a significantly reduced number of oscillations (as it would be presumed in the case of the humidifier is not active).

Figure 5a–e (associated to the faulty tests performed during winter) allows to underline the different trends/patterns of key operating parameters with respect to the cases without faults:

- In Figure 5a (corresponding to the fault 1, i.e., velocity of the supply air fan reduced at 20%), the supply air temperature and supply air relative humidity are in a wider range, with a much lower number of oscillations; similar trends can be recognized for both return air temperature and return air relative humidity;
- Figure 5b (corresponding to the fault 2, i.e., velocity of the return air fan reduced at 20%) indicates that the impact of a reduced return ai flow rate is almost negligible in terms of supply and return air temperature as well as supply and return air relative humidity;
- In Figure 5c (corresponding to the fault 3, i.e., post-heating coil valve kept fully closed), supply air temperature assumes lower average values (as post-heating coil is not active); in particular, T_{SA} is almost constant (and equal to ~12.0 °C in this case). As a consequence, return air temperature remains almost constant during the test, assuming a value much smaller than its lower deadband and, therefore, out of the desired thermal comfort range. In addition, it should be underlined that average values of supply air relative humidity are greater and included in a narrower range (without significant oscillations); return air relative humidity is almost constant (and equal to about 47% in this case);
- In Figure 5d (corresponding to the fault 4, i.e., cooling coil valve kept fully closed), supply air temperature is characterized by lower average values (as it would be presumed due to the missing contribution of the cooling coil), with a narrower variation range (approximately 19.0–24.0 °C in this case); return air temperature is substantially constant, assuming a value out of desired thermal comfort range (slightly larger than its upper deadband and equal to about 22.0 °C in this case);
- In Figure 5e (corresponding to the fault 5, i.e., steam humidifier valve kept fully closed), return air relative humidity varies in a slightly narrower range (as it would be expected in the case of the humidifier is not active).

4. Simulation Model

In this paper, an artificial neural network (ANN)-based model has been developed in the MATLAB environment. The aim was to predict (i) the supply air temperature, (ii) the supply air relative humidity, (iii) the opening percentage of the valve supplying the post-heating coil, (iv) the opening percentage of cooling coil valve, and (v) the opening percentage of the steam humidifier valve. This ANN has been first validated with measured data and then coupled with a dynamic simulation model developed in TRNSYS environment in order to simulate (i) the return air temperature; (ii) the return air relative humidity; as well as (iii) the electric energy consumptions (not measured) of the heat pump, the refrigerating system, the steam humidifier, the supply air fan, and the return air fan with the aim of rating the effects of the selected faults on both energy consumption as well occupant indoor thermo-hygrometric comfort. The artificial neural network-based model is described in Sections 4.1 and 4.1.1–4.1.3, while the description of the TRNSYS model is reported in Section 4.2.

4.1. Artificial Neural Network-Based Model

In this section, the ANN-based models developed with the aim of simulating the performance of the test room-integrated HVAC system under both normal and faulty scenarios are described.

4.1.1. Artificial Neural Networks' Architecture

ANNs usually consist of three parts: one input layer; one or more hidden layers, and one output layer. All layers include neurons, and each neuron in a given layer is linked to the neurons of previous as well as successive layers. Each link between two neurons is characterized by an adaptable synaptic weight and bias. Three main different functional operations occur in ANNs:

- all the inputs are multiplied by their weights;
- the weighted values are added to the bias in order to form the net inputs;
- the net inputs are passed by means of the transfer function, which generates the outputs.

ANNs are trained by means of a suitable learning method in order to obtain a specific target output from a particular input by regulating the weights and biases. The training process is stopped only when the error between the desired target and the corresponding network output is lower than a given tolerance value or when the maximum number of epochs (given number of iterations) is achieved. A transfer function is a mathematical representation of the relation between inputs and outputs. Transfer functions generally have a sigmoid shape, but they may also assume the form of piecewise linear functions, nonlinear functions, or step functions. One of the most commonly adopted transfer functions for multilayer networks is the hyperbolic tangent sigmoid transfer function (tansig) [32] generating outputs between −1 and 1.

Performance of artificial neural networks is sensitive to both the number of hidden layers as well as the number of neurons in their hidden layers [32]. In particular, networks with more hidden layers require a larger computation time, but their use gives the network more flexibility and could result in resolving challenging tasks more efficiently [32]. Larger numbers of neurons allow the network to figure out more difficult issues; however, they require more computation and they can play a part to "overfitting" (in that case the fitting curve fluctuates wildly among training points, even if these points are well fitted); on the other hand, few neurons can reduce the computation time, but they could also lead to "underfitting".

The MATLAB (The MathWorks Inc., Natick, Massachusetts, USA) Neural Network Toolbox [32] has been used in this work in order to develop and analyze 22 artificial neural network-based simulation models (ANN1-ANN22) of the HVAC system. All the artificial neural networks have been configured with 10 inputs and 5 outputs, varying the number of hidden layers and neurons in each hidden layer. One of the most common issues to be addressed in configuring the architecture of ANNs is connected to the ANNs topology allowing to achieve the requested accuracy and/or minimize the computation time. Several studies [41–46] have determined the number of hidden layers and the number of neurons in the hidden layers by trial and error, employing a grid search technique to find them. A sensitivity analysis has been performed in this study in order to find out the optimal number of hidden layers and neurons in each hidden layer according to the information and approaches reported in the current literature. In particular, several scientific papers investigated the application of ANNs for HVAC systems' modeling [41–43], adopting a number of hidden layers varying from a minimum of 1 [41] up to a maximum of 5 [41–43]. In addition, several formulas are available in the scientific literature [44–46] in order to provide a starting point for determining the optimal number of neurons in each hidden layer of ANNs as a function of (i) number of inputs [44–46], (ii) number of outputs [44], (iii) number of hidden layers [45], and (iv) number of training examples [45,46]; these formulas suggest a number of neurons per hidden layer in the range of 7 to 83 when applied to the ANNs investigated in this paper.

4.1.2. Sensitivity Analysis of Artificial Neural Networks

Table 6 describes the architectures of the 22 ANN-based models investigated in this paper, highlighting both number of hidden layers as well as number of neurons in each hidden layer.

Table 6. Architectures of the investigated ANNs.

ANN ID	Number of Hidden Layers	Number of Neurons in Each Hidden Layer
ANN1	1	10
ANN2	1	20
ANN3	1	30
ANN4	1	40
ANN5	1	50
ANN6	1	60
ANN7	1	70
ANN8	2	10
ANN9	2	20
ANN10	2	30
ANN11	2	40
ANN12	2	50
ANN13	3	10
ANN14	3	20
ANN15	3	30
ANN16	3	40
ANN17	4	10
ANN18	4	20
ANN19	4	30
ANN20	5	10
ANN21	5	20
ANN22	5	30

The following 10 variables have been set as inputs of all ANNs:

1. difference between current return air temperature and related target (ΔT)
2. difference between current return air relative humidity and related target (ΔRH)
3. supply air temperature at previous minute ($T_{SA\text{-}1}$)
4. supply air relative humidity at previous minute ($RH_{SA\text{-}1}$)
5. outside air temperature (T_{OA})
6. opening percentage of the valve managing the flow entering the post-heating coil at previous minute ($OP_{V\_PostHC\text{-}1}$)
7. opening percentage of the valve managing the flow entering the cooling coil at previous minute ($OP_{V\_CC\text{-}1}$)
8. opening percentage of the valve managing the flow entering the steam humidifier at previous minute ($OP_{V\_HUM\text{-}1}$)
9. supply air fan velocity (OL_{SAF})
10. return air fan velocity (OL_{RAF}).

The following five parameters have been set as outputs of all ANNs:

1. supply air temperature (T_{SA})
2. supply air relative humidity (RH_{SA})
3. opening percentage of the post-heating coil valve (OP_{V_PostHC})
4. opening percentage of the cooling coil valve (OP_{V_CC})
5. opening percentage of the steam humidifier valve (OP_{V_HUM}).

Table 7 summarizes the inputs and the outputs used in the artificial neural networks. Each ANN has 1 input layer with 10 neurons and 1 output layer with 5 neurons.

Table 7. Inputs and outputs of the ANNs.

Number of Inputs	Input ID	Number of Outputs	Outputs ID
1	ΔT	1	T_{SA}
2	ΔRH		
3	$T_{SA\text{-}1}$	2	RH_{SA}
4	$RH_{SA\text{-}1}$		
5	T_{OA}	3	OP_{V_PostHC}
6	$OP_{V\_PostHC\text{-}1}$		
7	$OP_{V\_CC\text{-}1}$	4	OP_{V_CC}
8	$OP_{V\_HUM\text{-}1}$		
9	OL_{SAF}	5	OP_{V_HUM}
10	OL_{RAF}		

The hyperbolic tangent sigmoid transfer function (tansig) has been adopted in the hidden and output layers of each ANN. Levenberg–Marquart back-propagation training algorithms (trainlm) have been selected as training function with the aim of updating the weights and biases.

4.1.3. Training, Testing and Validation of ANNs

The experimental data measured during the tests described in Section 3 have been used for training, testing, and validating the ANNs. Two different datasets have been randomly extracted from the entire database (5352 data points in total): the first dataset (3746 points) has been utilized for training purposes, while the second one (1606 points) has been considered for testing and validating the networks. The predictions of the ANN-based models have been compared with the whole experimental dataset (containing all training, testing, and validation points) to evaluate the reliability of the ANNs by means of the metrics reported below (the average error $\overline{\varepsilon}$, the average absolute error $|\overline{\varepsilon}|$, the mean square error MSE, the root mean square error RMSE, and the coefficient of determination R^2):

$$\varepsilon_i = g_{pred,i} - g_{exp,i} \tag{1}$$

$$\overline{\varepsilon} = \sum_{i=1}^{N} \varepsilon_i / N \tag{2}$$

$$|\overline{\varepsilon}| = \sum_{i=1}^{N} |\varepsilon_i| / N \tag{3}$$

$$\text{MSE} = \frac{1}{N}\sum_{i=1}^{N} (\varepsilon_i - \overline{\varepsilon})^2 \tag{4}$$

$$\text{RMSE} = \sqrt{\sum_{i=1}^{N} \frac{(\varepsilon_i - \overline{\varepsilon})^2}{N}} \tag{5}$$

$$R^2 = 1 - \left[\sum_{i=1}^{N} \frac{\left(g_{exp,i} - g_{pred,i}\right)^2}{\left(g_{exp,i} - \overline{g}_{pred,i}\right)^2}\right] \tag{6}$$

where N is the total number of experimental points, while $g_{pred,i}$, $g_{exp,I}$, and $\overline{g}_{pred}$ are, respectively, the predictions at time step i, the measurements at time step i, and the arithmetic mean of the predicted values. Table 8 reports the calculated values of $\overline{\varepsilon}$, $|\overline{\varepsilon}|$, MSE, RMSE, and R^2 associated with the performance of all the ANNs developed in this study, highlighting in green and red, respectively, the best and worst results.

Table 8. Errors between predictions of ANN-based models and measurements.

Errors	ANN Outputs	ANN1	ANN2	ANN3	ANN4	ANN5	ANN6	ANN7	ANN8	ANN9	ANN10	ANN11	ANN12	ANN13	ANN14	ANN15	ANN16	ANN17	ANN18	ANN19	ANN20	ANN21	ANN22
$\overline{\varepsilon}$	T_{SA} (°C)	−0.11	−0.03	0.00	−0.01	−0.01	−0.01	−0.01	0.00	−0.01	0.00	0.05	−0.01	−0.09	0.00	0.01	0.00	0.00	0.04	−0.02	0.02	10.71	−0.01
	RH_{SA} (%)	0.22	−0.02	0.10	0.08	0.04	−0.06	0.04	−0.03	0.06	−0.02	−0.24	0.06	0.18	0.05	0.00	−0.01	−0.04	0.02	−0.05	−0.02	0.01	0.01
	OP_{V_PostHC} (%)	0.00	0.01	0.00	0.01	0.00	0.01	−0.01	−0.01	0.00	0.01	0.00	0.00	0.00	−0.01	−0.01	0.02	0.00	0.01	−0.01	0.00	3.66	−0.01
	OP_{V_CC} (%)	0.00	−0.02	0.00	0.06	0.01	0.04	0.01	−0.02	0.01	0.02	−0.02	−0.01	−0.03	0.00	0.02	0.01	−0.03	0.01	−2.48	0.00	0.02	0.01
	OP_{V_HUM} (%)	0.01	0.00	−0.03	0.04	−0.01	−0.02	−0.02	0.01	−0.01	−0.02	−0.02	−0.02	0.03	−0.03	0.01	0.01	0.07	0.00	0.03	0.03	−0.02	0.01
$\lvert\overline{\varepsilon}\rvert$	T_{SA} (°C)	0.72	0.36	0.36	0.36	0.31	0.26	0.25	0.62	0.41	0.42	0.44	0.34	0.70	0.47	0.43	0.27	0.72	0.46	0.45	0.69	10.71	0.36
	RH_{SA} (%)	2.80	2.00	2.00	1.95	1.80	1.67	1.75	2.32	2.02	1.98	1.99	1.77	2.46	2.13	1.94	1.62	2.26	2.00	1.88	2.57	2.00	1.83
	OP_{V_PostHC} (%)	0.08	0.06	0.08	0.19	0.12	0.10	0.12	0.06	0.06	0.20	0.13	0.11	0.07	0.10	0.13	0.06	0.05	0.11	0.07	0.10	3.66	0.05
	OP_{V_CC} (%)	0.07	0.07	0.06	0.15	0.08	0.09	0.08	0.07	0.07	0.14	0.09	0.10	0.07	0.08	0.11	0.07	0.09	0.08	2.48	0.09	0.12	0.05
	OP_{V_HUM} (%)	0.19	0.13	0.15	0.20	0.15	0.13	0.17	0.13	0.12	0.23	0.15	0.18	0.16	0.17	0.18	0.11	0.16	0.15	0.13	0.16	0.16	0.11
MSE	T_{SA} (°C)	0.81	0.26	0.26	0.28	0.21	0.16	0.14	0.77	0.35	0.38	0.36	0.24	0.94	0.50	0.40	0.16	1.15	0.50	0.44	1.04	6.01	0.27
	RH_{SA} (%)	16.59	10.00	9.86	10.14	9.18	8.05	8.60	13.07	10.13	10.48	9.74	8.73	13.77	11.16	10.17	7.69	13.30	10.17	8.93	15.38	9.48	8.31
	OP_{V_PostHC} (%)	0.49	0.35	0.43	0.82	0.50	0.38	0.51	0.37	0.32	0.81	0.51	0.51	0.42	0.43	0.49	0.36	0.32	0.52	0.38	0.47	36.62	0.28
	OP_{V_CC} (%)	0.41	0.48	0.28	0.75	0.40	0.65	0.39	0.57	0.28	0.57	0.49	0.46	0.59	0.39	0.37	0.41	0.61	0.41	24.83	0.47	0.80	0.33
	OP_{V_HUM} (%)	1.10	0.79	0.82	1.12	0.71	0.72	1.17	0.94	0.68	1.03	0.74	0.75	1.12	0.88	0.94	0.77	1.21	0.75	0.72	1.11	0.78	0.68
RMSE	T_{SA} (°C)	0.89	0.51	0.51	0.53	0.46	0.40	0.38	0.88	0.59	0.61	0.60	0.49	0.97	0.71	0.63	0.40	1.07	0.71	0.66	1.02	7.17	0.52
	RH_{SA}	4.07	3.16	3.14	3.18	3.03	2.84	2.93	3.62	3.18	3.24	3.11	2.95	3.71	3.34	3.19	2.77	3.65	3.19	2.99	3.92	3.08	2.88
	OP_{V_PostHC} (%)	0.70	0.59	0.66	0.90	0.71	0.62	0.71	0.60	0.57	0.90	0.71	0.72	0.65	0.66	0.70	0.60	0.56	0.72	0.62	0.69	4.82	0.53
	OP_{V_CC} (%)	0.64	0.69	0.53	0.86	0.63	0.80	0.63	0.75	0.53	0.75	0.70	0.68	0.76	0.62	0.61	0.64	0.78	0.64	4.32	0.68	0.89	0.57
	OP_{V_HUM} (%)	1.05	0.89	0.90	1.06	0.84	0.85	1.08	0.97	0.83	1.01	0.86	0.86	1.06	0.94	0.97	0.88	1.10	0.87	0.85	1.06	0.88	0.83
R^2	T_{SA} (°C)	0.985	0.995	0.994	0.994	0.996	0.996	0.997	0.980	0.991	0.990	0.991	0.996	0.976	0.987	0.990	0.996	0.967	0.988	0.989	0.978	0.118	0.994
	RH_{SA} (%)	0.955	0.975	0.976	0.975	0.978	0.981	0.979	0.957	0.972	0.974	0.977	0.977	0.963	0.967	0.974	0.982	0.964	0.973	0.976	0.956	0.976	0.980
	OP_{V_PostHC} (%)	0.979	0.989	0.982	0.981	0.982	0.988	0.990	0.987	0.987	0.985	0.980	0.978	0.982	0.981	0.987	0.982	0.987	0.984	0.978	0.984	0.140	0.993
	OP_{V_CC} (%)	0.981	0.986	0.985	0.976	0.975	0.980	0.983	0.979	0.983	0.969	0.984	0.968	0.974	0.977	0.986	0.973	0.962	0.981	0.131	0.971	0.974	0.983
	OP_{V_HUM} (%)	0.965	0.975	0.978	0.972	0.982	0.973	0.977	0.970	0.977	0.957	0.977	0.981	0.961	0.965	0.969	0.970	0.975	0.975	0.966	0.969	0.990	0.981

For each line of Table 8 the green shade has been assigned to the cell corresponding to the best performance (the readers can find more green cells for each line in the cases of more ANNs achieve the same best performance), while the worst results have been highlighted by red shades.

The results reported in this table highlight that:

- the overall minimum value of $\overline{\varepsilon}$ (−2.48%) is obtained in the case of the ANN19 for the parameter OP_{V_CC}; the overall maximum value of $\overline{\varepsilon}$ (10.71 °C) is obtained in the case of the ANN21 for the parameter T_{SA};
- the overall minimum value of $|\overline{\varepsilon}|$ (0.05%) is achieved by the ANN22 for the parameters OP_{V_PostHC} and OP_{V_CC} as well as in the case of the ANN17 for the parameter OP_{V_PostHC}; the overall worst value of $|\overline{\varepsilon}|$ (10.71 °C) is obtained in the case of the ANN21 for the parameter T_{SA};
- the overall minimum value of MSE (0.14 °C) is obtained in the case of the ANN7 for the parameter T_{SA}; the overall maximum value of MSE (36.62%) is obtained in the case of the ANN21 for the parameter OP_{V_PostHC};
- the overall minimum value of RMSE (0.38 °C) is achieved by the ANN7 for the parameter T_{SA}; the overall worst value of RMSE (7.17 °C) is obtained by the ANN21 for the parameter T_{SA};
- with reference to all the ANNs, average values of coefficient of determination R^2 in predicting supply air temperature, supply air relative humidity, opening percentage of the post-heating coil valve, opening percentage of the cooling coil valve, and opening percentage of the humidifier valve are very close to 1 and, respectively, equal to 0.95 °C, 0.97%, 0.95%, 0.94%, and 0.97%; the overall worst value of R^2 (0.118) is obtained in the case of the ANN21 for the parameter T_{SA}; the overall best value of R^2 (0.997) is achieved by the ANN7 for the parameter T_{SA};
- the ANN22 is characterized by 8 green cells in Table 8, i.e., it works better than the other ANNs with reference to 8 lines of this table; the ANNs 3, 9, and 16 denote 5 green cells, while a lower number of green cells can be recognized for the other ANNs; the ANN4 has no green cells, while the ANN with the largest number of red cells (denoting the worst performance) is the ANN21;
- whatever the metric is, the ANN16 is characterized by greater performance in comparison to the ANN22 with reference to the predictions of both supply air temperature

and supply air relative humidity. The percentage difference between the ANN16 and the ANN22 in predicting T_{SA} is 27% in terms of $|\bar{\varepsilon}|$, 40% in terms of MSE, 22% in terms of RMSE, and 0.21% in terms of R^2. The percentage difference between the ANN16 and the ANN22 in predicting RH_{SA} is 11% in terms of $|\bar{\varepsilon}|$, 7% in terms of MSE, 4% in terms of RMSE, and 0.21% in terms of R^2;

- ANN22 provides better results than ANN16 in predicting the opening percentages of the post-heating coil valve, the cooling coil valve as well as the humidifier valve. The maximum percentage difference in terms of $|\bar{\varepsilon}|$ between the ANN22 and the ANN16 in predicting OP_{V_PostHC}, OP_{V_CC} and OP_{V_HUM} is 26%; the maximum percentage difference in terms of MSE between the ANN22 and the ANN16 in predicting OP_{V_PostHC}, OP_{V_CC}, and OP_{V_HUM} is 21%; the maximum percentage difference in terms of RMSE between the ANN22 and the ANN16 in predicting OP_{V_PostHC}, OP_{V_CC} and OP_{V_HUM} is 11%; the maximum difference in terms of R^2 between the ANN22 and the ANN16 in predicting OP_{V_PostHC}, OP_{V_CC}, and OP_{V_HUM} is 1.13%.

Even if the ANN22 performs better than the ANN16 in predicting the opening percentages of the valves, in this paper the ANN16 has been selected in order to obtain improved predictions in terms of supply air temperature as well as supply air relative humidity (that represent the fundamental outputs of AHU operation), while maintaining an adequate accuracy in forecasting the valves operation. The errors reported in Table 8 demonstrate how the ANN16 can be effectively used to generate operation data for assisting further research in fault detection and diagnosis of HVAC units.

Figures 6–9 report the instantaneous errors between the values predicted by the ANN16 and the measured data in terms of (i) supply air temperature (T_{SA}), (ii) supply air relative humidity (RH_{SA}), (iii) opening percentage of the post-heating coil valve (OP_{V_PostHC}), (iv) opening percentage of the cooling coil valve (OP_{V_CC}), and (v) opening percentage of the humidifier valve (OP_{V_HUM}) as a function of time.

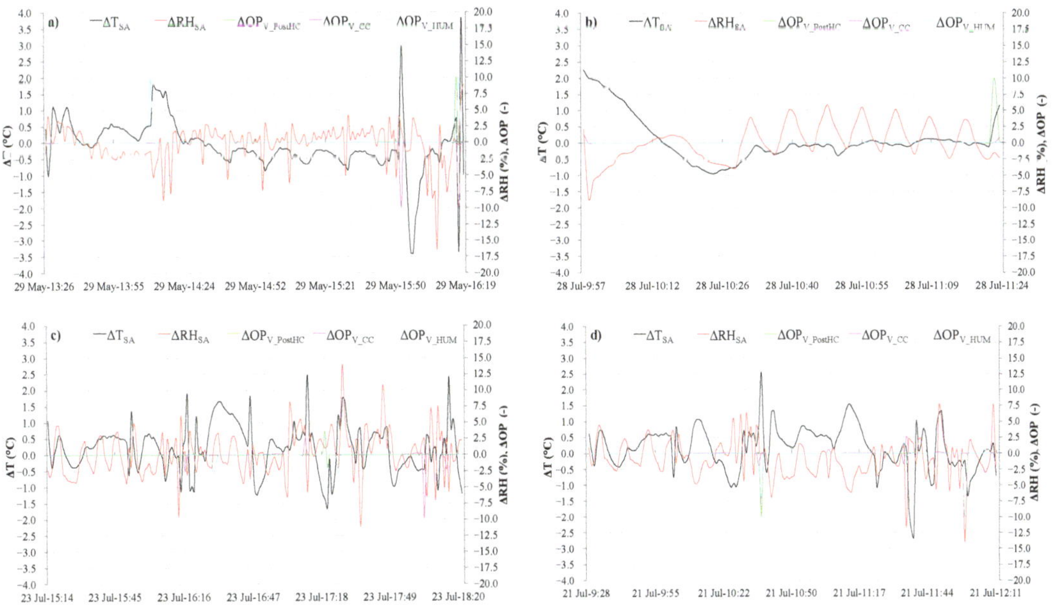

Figure 6. Comparison between ANN16 predicted values and experimental data under fault free tests during summer: test n. 1 (**a**), test n. 2 (**b**), test n. 3 (**c**), and test n. 4 (**d**).

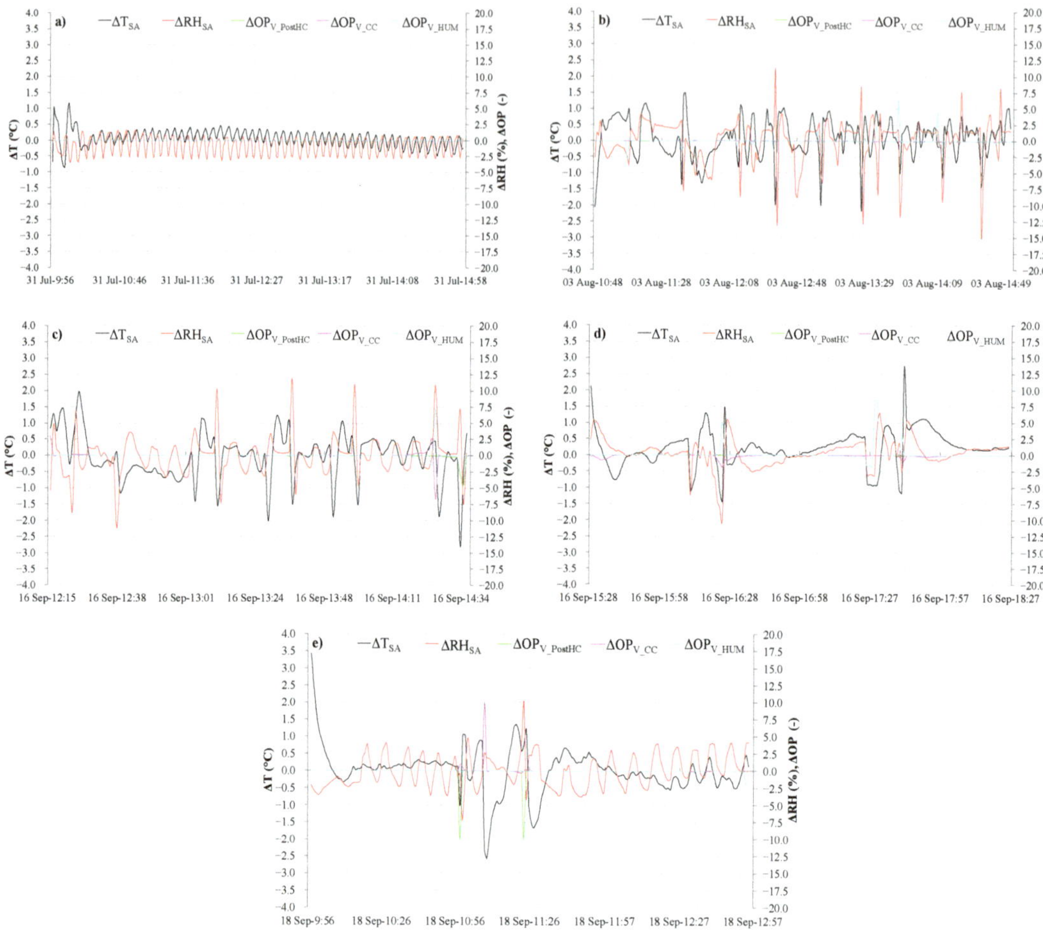

Figure 7. Comparison between ANN16 predicted values and experimental data under faulty tests during summer: test n. 5 (**a**), test n. 6 (**b**), test n. 7 (**c**), test n. 8 (**d**), and test n. 9 (**e**).

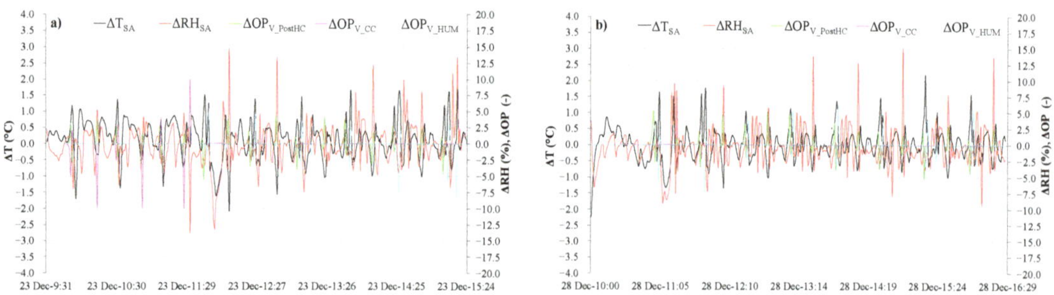

Figure 8. *Cont.*

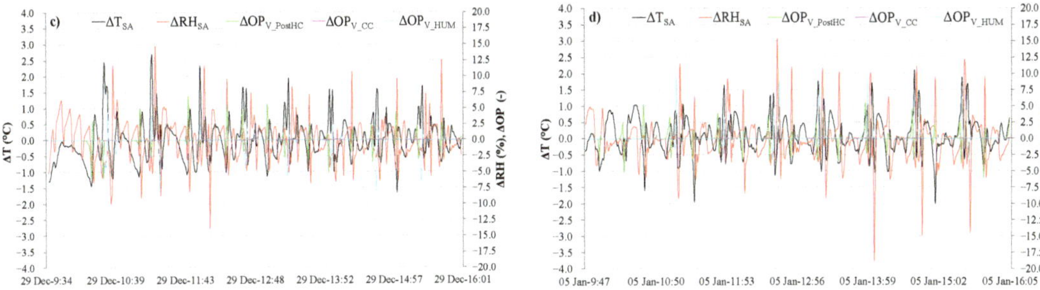

Figure 8. Comparison between ANN16 predicted values and experimental data under fault free tests during winter: test n. 10 (**a**), test n. 11 (**b**), test n. 12 (**c**), and test n. 13 (**d**).

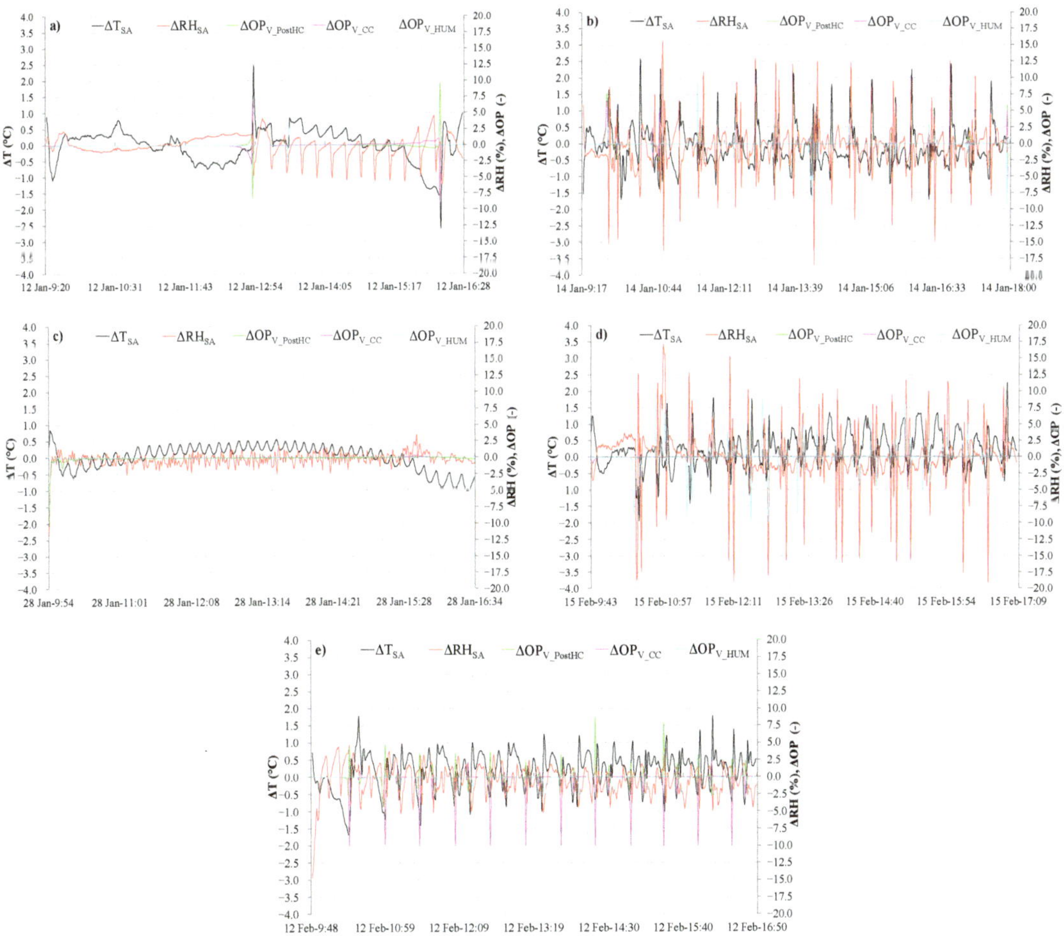

Figure 9. Comparison between ANN16 predicted values and experimental data under faulty tests during winter: test n. 14 (**a**), test n. 15 (**b**), test n. 16 (**c**), test n. 17 (**d**), and test n. 18 (**e**).

In more detail, the following parameters are showed in Figures 6–9:

$$\Delta T_{SA} = T_{SA,pred} - T_{SA,exp} \tag{7}$$

$$\Delta RH_{SA} = RH_{SA,pred} - RH_{SA,exp} \tag{8}$$

$$\Delta OP_{V\_PostHC} = OP_{V\_PostHC,pred} - OP_{V\_PostHC,exp} \tag{9}$$

$$\Delta OP_{V\_CC} = OP_{V\_CC,pred} - OP_{V\_CC,exp} \tag{10}$$

$$\Delta OP_{V\_HUM} = OP_{V\_HUM,pred} - OP_{V\_HUM,exp} \tag{11}$$

where $T_{SA,\,pred}$, $RH_{SA,\,pred}$, $OP_{V\_PostHC,\,pred}$, $OP_{V\_CC,\,pred}$, and $OP_{V\_HUM,\,pred}$ are, respectively, the values predicted by the ANN16, while $T_{SA,\,exp}$, $RH_{SA,\,exp}$, $OP_{V\_PostHC,\,exp}$, $OP_{V\_CC,\,exp}$, and $OP_{V\_HUM,\,exp}$ represent the experimental values.

Figures 6–9 highlight that:

- the minimum value of ΔT_{SA} is −3.41 °C (test n. 1), while its maximum value is 3.80 °C (test n. 1);
- the values of ΔRH_{SA} range from −19.20% (test n. 17) up to 17.03% (test n. 17);
- the parameter ΔOP_{V_PostHC} is in the range −10.05% ÷ 10.12%, where the minimum is achieved during the test n. 4, while the maximum refers to the test n. 2;
- the values of ΔOP_{V_CC} vary from −10.03% (test n. 18) up to 10.09% (test n. 9);
- the values of ΔOP_{V_HUM} range between −9.97% (test n. 4) and 10.11% (test n.17).

In order to better point out the results of comparisons between predicted and experimental values reported in Figures 6–9, the values of the metrics defined by the Equations (1)–(6), calculated for the parameters specified by the Equations (7)–(11), have been summarized in Table 9. For each line of this table, the green shade has been assigned to the cells corresponding to the best performance, while the worst results have been highlighted by red shades.

Table 9. Errors between the ANN16-based model predictions and experimental points.

		Fault Free Tests during Summer				Faulty Tests during Summer					Fault Free Tests during Winter				Faulty Tests during Winter				
Errors	Parameters	Test n. 1	Test n. 2	Test n. 3	Test n. 4	Test n. 5	Test n. 6	Test n. 7	Test n. 8	Test n. 9	Test n. 10	Test n. 11	Test n. 12	Test n. 13	Test n. 14	Test n. 15	Test n. 16	Test n. 17	Test n. 18
	ΔT_{SA} (°C)	−0.10	0.09	0.22	0.17	0.06	0.09	−0.04	0.21	0.01	0.11	−0.01	−0.02	0.07	−0.02	−0.11	0.01	0.22	0.16
	ΔRH_{SA} (%)	−0.18	0.04	0.28	−0.88	−0.87	0.11	0.01	0.33	−0.05	−0.24	−0.43	−0.03	−0.36	−0.08	−0.61	−0.22	−0.02	−0.39
$\bar{\varepsilon}$	ΔOP_{V_PostHC} (%)	0.06	0.11	0.02	−0.06	0.00	−0.01	−0.07	0.00	−0.11	0.01	0.06	0.00	0.02	−0.03	0.05	−0.10	0.00	0.05
	ΔOP_{V_CC} (%)	−0.12	0.03	−0.05	−0.01	0.00	0.01	0.03	−0.10	0.06	−0.06	0.02	0.01	0.01	0.02	0.06	0.02	−0.01	−0.31
	ΔOP_{V_HUM} (%)	0.12	0.00	−0.04	−0.10	0.00	0.03	0.04	0.12	−0.03	−0.07	−0.03	−0.16	0.11	−0.01	−0.04	0.00	−0.01	−0.16
	ΔT_{SA} (°C)	0.55	0.46	0.60	0.56	0.19	0.38	0.53	0.44	0.43	0.47	0.38	0.48	0.43	0.41	0.47	0.30	0.45	0.46
	ΔRH_{SA} (%)	1.97	2.19	2.57	2.40	1.21	11.09	2.12	1.47	1.99	2.24	2.04	2.49	2.32	1.18	2.26	0.70	2.84	1.69
$\lvert\bar{\varepsilon}\rvert$	ΔOP_{V_PostHC} (%)	0.06	0.11	0.04	0.06	0.00	0.00	0.07	0.00	0.11	0.24	0.23	0.26	0.30	0.09	0.12	0.10	0.00	0.25
	ΔOP_{V_CC} (%)	0.12	0.03	0.11	0.07	0.00	0.00	0.13	0.10	0.07	0.18	0.02	0.01	0.01	0.13	0.12	0.02	0.01	0.36
	ΔOP_{V_HUM} (%)	0.12	0.00	0.05	0.13	0.00	0.37	0.07	0.21	0.03	0.19	0.20	0.26	0.22	0.02	0.15	0.00	0.45	0.16
	ΔT_{SA} (°C)	0.71	0.51	0.58	0.51	0.07	0.38	0.52	0.36	0.47	0.36	0.27	0.42	0.32	0.28	0.38	0.14	0.34	0.32
	ΔRH_{SA} (%)	8.59	7.44	11.13	10.23	2.48	11.09	10.08	4.85	6.15	10.50	9.12	11.06	12.27	2.73	13.25	1.08	22.41	5.19
MSE	ΔOP_{V_PostHC} (%)	0.58	1.15	0.09	0.62	0.00	0.00	0.22	0.00	1.18	0.74	0.73	0.99	0.95	0.40	0.43	0.31	0.00	0.87
	ΔOP_{V_CC} (%)	1.16	0.03	0.60	0.13	0.00	0.00	0.47	0.07	0.60	1.33	0.00	0.00	0.00	0.38	0.40	0.00	0.00	3.00
	ΔOP_{V_HUM} (%)	1.16	0.00	0.10	0.95	0.00	0.37	0.42	1.12	0.03	0.85	0.79	1.10	1.38	0.05	0.78	0.00	2.63	0.29
	ΔT_{SA} (°C)	0.84	0.71	0.73	0.70	0.25	0.61	0.72	0.57	0.67	0.59	0.52	0.65	0.56	0.53	0.61	0.37	0.54	0.54
	ΔRH_{SA} (%)	2.93	2.74	3.34	3.09	1.32	3.34	3.19	2.18	2.42	3.24	2.99	3.33	3.49	1.65	3.59	1.02	4.74	2.25
RMSE	ΔOP_{V_PostHC} (%)	0.76	1.07	0.30	0.79	0.00	0.01	0.46	0.01	1.05	0.86	0.85	1.00	0.98	0.63	0.65	0.55	0.01	0.93
	ΔOP_{V_CC} (%)	1.08	0.17	0.78	0.35	0.00	0.01	0.68	0.25	0.75	1.15	0.03	0.02	0.02	0.61	0.63	0.04	0.07	1.71
	ΔOP_{V_HUM} (%)	1.07	0.00	0.32	0.97	0.03	0.61	0.65	1.05	0.17	0.92	0.89	1.04	1.17	0.21	0.89	0.01	1.62	0.51
	ΔT_{SA} (°C)	0.98	0.99	0.99	0.99	0.98	0.85	0.96	0.92	0.99	0.99	0.99	0.99	0.99	1.00	0.99	0.60	0.85	0.99
	ΔRH_{SA} (%)	0.97	0.76	0.97	0.96	0.89	0.92	0.93	0.94	0.96	0.97	0.98	0.97	0.97	1.00	0.97	0.77	0.87	0.98
R^2	ΔOP_{V_PostHC} (%)	0.95	0.49	1.00	0.98	1.00	1.00	1.00	1.00	1.00	0.97	0.97	0.96	0.96	0.98	0.89	1.00	1.00	0.96
	ΔOP_{V_CC} (%)	0.91	1.00	0.95	0.99	1.00	1.00	0.97	1.00	1.00	0.91	1.00	1.00	1.00	0.98	0.90	1.00	1.00	0.88
	ΔOP_{V_HUM} (%)	0.94	1.00	0.99	0.94	1.00	0.98	0.98	0.92	1.00	0.93	0.95	0.92	0.86	1.00	0.94	1.00	0.87	1.00

This table underlines that the ANN16 is able to carefully predict the experimental data measured during summer and winter under both normal and faulty conditions and it provides a rigorous representation of the HVAC system's steady-state and transient operation taking into account that:

- with reference to all the tests, the average values of R^2 in predicting T_{SA}, RH_{SA}, OP_{V_PostHC}, OP_{V_CC} and OP_{V_HUM} are, respectively, 0.95 °C, 0.93%, 0.95%, 0.97%, and 0.96%;
- with reference to the tests n. 1–4 (performed without faults during summer), the values of R^2 are always larger than 0.9 for all the parameters, except the cases of ΔRH_{SA} and ΔOP_{V_PostHC} for the test n. 2;
- with reference to the tests n. 5–9 (performed with faults during summer), the coefficient of determination is always greater than 0.9 for all the parameters, except the cases of ΔRH_{SA} for the test n. 5 (with fault 1) and ΔT_{SA} for the test n. 6 (with fault 2);
- with reference to the tests n. 10–13 (performed without faults during winter), the values of R^2 are always larger than 0.9 for all the parameters, except the case of ΔOP_{V_HUM} for the test n. 13;
- with reference to the tests n. 14–18 (performed with faults during winter), the coefficient of determination is always greater than 0.9 for all the parameters, except (i) the cases of both ΔT_{SA} and ΔRH_{SA} for both the tests n. 16 (fault 3) and n. 17 (fault 4), (ii) the cases of both ΔOP_{V_PostHC} and ΔOP_{V_CC} for the test n. 15 (fault 2), (iii) the case of ΔOP_{V_CC} for the test n. 18 (fault 5) as well as (iv) the case of ΔOP_{HUM} for the test n. 17 (fault 4);
- whatever the test is, the values of $|\overline{\varepsilon}|$ for the parameter ΔT_{SA} are always lower than 0.8 °C (that is the accuracy of the sensor used for measuring T_{SA}), with a minimum of 0.19 °C (test n. 5) up to a maximum of 0.60 °C (test. n. 3);
- the values of $|\overline{\varepsilon}|$ for the parameter ΔRH_{SA} range between a minimum of 0.7% up to a maximum of 11.1% and, therefore, they are always smaller than 3% (that is the accuracy of the sensor used for measuring RH_{SA}), except the only case of the test n. 6 (performed with fault 2 during summer);
- the maximum values of MSE and RMSE with reference to the parameter ΔT_{SA} are, respectively, not larger than 0.71 °C and 0.84 °C (obtained for the test n. 1 performed without faults during summer);
- the maximum values of MSE and RMSE with reference to the parameter ΔRH_{SA} are, respectively, not larger than 22.4% and 4.74% (achieved for the test n. 17 performed with fault 4 during winter);
- the maximum value of MSE with reference to the parameters ΔOP_{V_PostHC}, ΔOP_{V_CC} and ΔOP_{V_HUM} is 3.0%, obtained in the case of the test n. 18 performed with fault 5 during winter;
- the maximum value of RMSE with reference to the parameters ΔOP_{V_PostHC}, ΔOP_{V_CC} and ΔOP_{V_HUM} is 1.7%, achieved in the case of the test n. 18 performed with fault 5 during winter.

4.2. TRNSYS Model

In the dynamic simulation software TRNSYS (version 17) [33], the whole system is first broken up into specific models (named "Types") of each single system component, where each "Type" is represented by a FORTRAN code. The users can assemble the TRNSYS Types by connecting component outputs with component inputs and then specifying the corresponding components' performance parameters. Finally, the software solves the corresponding equations in order to characterize the component/system operation every time step.

In this study, a detailed model in TRNSYS environment has been developed to simulate, using a time step of 1 min (according to the time step of experimental data utilized in this work for training, testing, and validating the ANN-based model), (i) the return air temperature (T_{RA}); (ii) the return air relative humidity (RH_{RA}); as well as the electric energy consumptions (not measured) of (iii) the heat pump (HP), (iv) the refrigerating system (RS), (v) the humidifier (HUM), (vi) the supply air fan (SAF), and (vii) the return air fan (RAF). With reference to the several performance parameters to be specified in the TRNSYS Types used into the simulation model, it can be noticed that, in this study, some of the parameters have been directly identified or calculated based on catalog data; the remaining parameters have been defined based on field measurements.

Table 10 lists the main modeled components and the corresponding TRNSYS Types used in the simulation model.

Table 10. Main simulated components and corresponding types of TRNSYS software.

Simulated Component	TRNSYS Type/Model
Test room	56
Heat pump/Refrigerating system	941
Hot and cold tanks	534
Humidifier	641
HP/RS pump	654
Diverting/mixing valves	647/649
On/Off differential controllers	2
Moist air properties	33e
Integrated test room	56

Figure 10 depicts a screenshot of the TRNSYS model, highlighting the main circuits with different colors. In particular, the circuit of cold fluid supplied by the refrigerating system to the cooling coil is depicted in blue; the circuit of hot fluid supplied by the heat pump to the post-heating coil is indicated in red; finally, the inputs and outputs of the ANN-based model are highlighted in light blue. The other connections of TRNSYS Types are pointed out by dashed black lines.

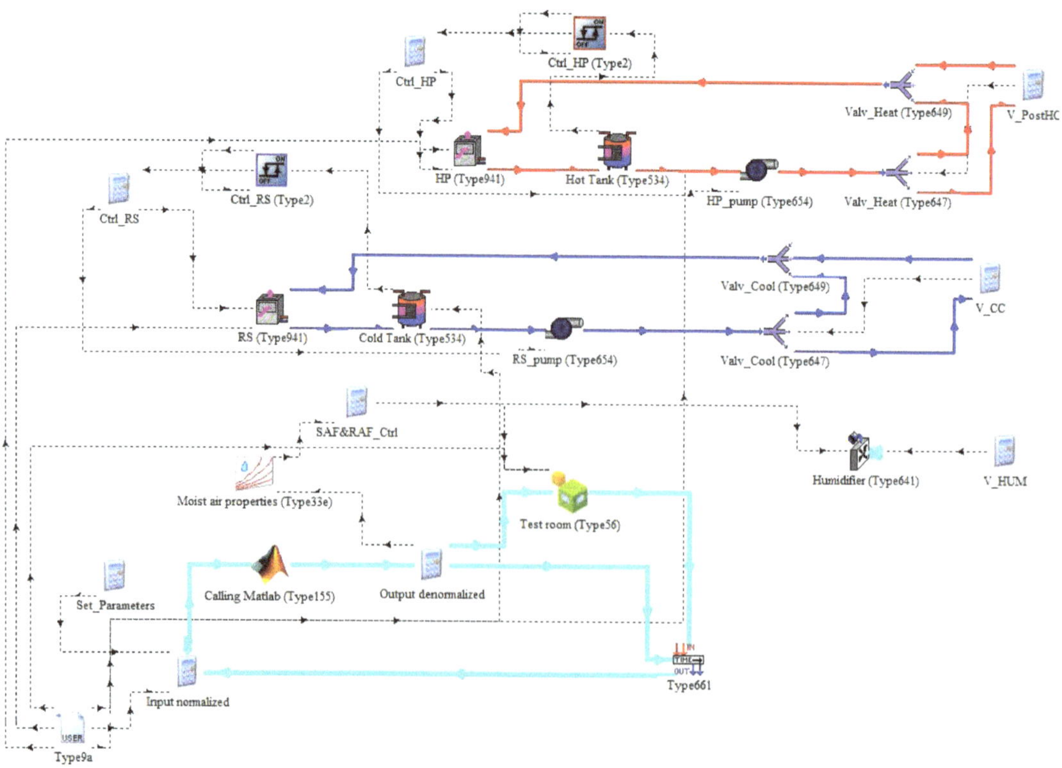

Figure 10. Screenshot of the TRNSYS model.

The TRNSYS model has been coupled with the artificial neural network ANN16 (described in the previous section) via the TRNSYS Type 155.

The ANN16 uses as inputs the 10 variables indicated in the previous section and provides as outputs the 5 parameters specified in the same section.

The Type 155 links ANN16 with both the Type 56 as well as the Type 661. In particular, the Type 155 provides two of the outputs of the ANN16, i.e., the supply air temperature and relative humidity, as inputs to the Type 56. In addition, the Type 155 provides as inputs to the Type 661 all the outputs of the ANN16, i.e., the supply air temperature, the supply air relative humidity, as well as the opening percentages of the valves supplying the humidifier, the pre-heating coil, and the cooling coil. The Type 661 models a "sticky" controller with its outputs assumed equal to the inputs at the earlier time step; the outputs of the Type 661 are then provided as inputs to the Type 155.

A dynamic model of the "building" corresponding to the integrated test room has been developed by means of the Type 56. This model allows calculation of the return air temperature and relative humidity (then assigned as inputs to the Type 661) according to the geometry, thermo-physical properties of walls' layers, air infiltration rate, as well as internal loads/gains. In particular, the geometry and walls' layers have been characterized according to the content of the previous section, while air infiltration rate as well as internal loads/gains are kept equal to zero according to the experimental conditions.

The Type 941 has been considered for simulating the operation of both the refrigerating unit (RS) and the heat pump (HP) of the experimental setup. This Type allows to obtain as outputs (a) the absorbed power and (b) the exiting fluid temperature in the case of (i) the outside air temperature, (ii) the entering fluid temperature, (iii) the fluid flow rate, as well as (iv) the performance maps of the devices are provided as inputs. In this study, the outside temperature has been assumed to be equal to the measured values (the Type 9a has been used for reading data from an external file and making them available to the TRNSYS Types 941), the fluid mass flow rate is set to 2310 kg/h for the refrigerating system and 2410 kg/h for the heat pump according to the manufacturer datasheet [36], and the performance maps suggested by the manufacturer [36] and reported in Figure A2a,b of Appendix A have been provided. In particular, Figure A2a,b, respectively, indicates the coefficient of performance COP of the heap pump (useful thermal power output divided by required electric power input) and the energy efficiency ratio EER of the refrigerating system (useful cooling power output divided by required electric power input) depending on supply fluid temperature and outside air temperature.

Both the heat pump and the refrigerating system are coupled with a 75 L tank that is devoted to storing the hot and cold fluids, respectively. The operations of both hot and cold tanks have been simulated with the Type 534. This Type models a cylindrical vertical tank; it divides the tanks into 10 isothermal temperature layers in order to carefully consider thermal stratification (where the layer n. 1 is positioned on the uppermost portion of the tank and the layer n. 10 is positioned on the lowest part of the tank).

With reference to the modeling of the fans, a specifically devoted data set was gathered from a calibration activity performed by adjusting and maintaining the supply and return fans at various speeds from 10% to 100%. Figure A3 in Appendix A shows the air volumetric flow rate Q_V measured at SENS i-Lab and the power consumption P_{el} suggested by the manufacturer as a function of the fan' velocity OL. In particular, Figure A3a refers to the supply air fan, while Figure A3b is related to the return air fan.

The following equations, interpolating the values reported in Figure A3a,b, have been derived to calculate both the air volumetric flow rate Q_V as well as the power consumption P_{el} of both supply and return air fans as a function of fans' velocity:

$$Q_V{}^{SAF} = -0.00001 \cdot OL_{SAF}{}^3 + 0.0634 \cdot OL_{SAF}{}^2 + 5.1789 \cdot OL_{SAF} + 8.7704 \quad (12)$$

$$P_{el}{}^{SAF} = 0.0003 \cdot OL_{SAF}{}^3 + 0.1068 \cdot OL_{SAF}{}^2 + 0.7383 \cdot OL_{SAF} + 4.9372 \quad (13)$$

$$Q_V{}^{RAF} = 14.491 \cdot OL_{RAF} + 12.352 \quad (14)$$

$$P_{el}^{RAF} = 0.001 \cdot OL_{RAF}^{3} - 0.078 \cdot OL_{RAF}^{2} + 3.120 \cdot OL_{RAF} - 2.102 \quad (15)$$

Equations (12)–(15) have been included in the TRNSYS project via the Type 9a (external file data reader) for calculating the fans' power consumption according to the fans' velocity.

The operation of the adiabatic steam humidifier has been modeled via the Type 641; this model permits the humidifier not to respond instantaneously to the control signal, but to get the steady-state values of both power consumption and gain rate exponentially. In the TRNSYS project, the control signal associated to the opening percentage of the humidifier valve is provided as input to the Type 641 by the ANN16 through the Type 155. Based on catalog data, the humidifier power consumption has been considered equal to the nominal value of 3.7 kW, while the humidifier is activated taking into account that it has been experimentally verified that water flow rate supplied by the humidifier increases from the minimum to the maximum value (5 kg/h) almost instantaneously.

The Type 654 has been used for modeling the single-speed pumps maintaining a constant fluid flow exiting/entering the heat pump and the refrigerating system.

The Type 647 has been used to model the diverting valves that split a liquid inlet flow into two fractional outlet flows, while the Type 649 is adopted to simulate the mixing valves that combine two individual liquid streams into a single outlet.

The moist air properties have been evaluated by means of the Type 33e; this Type takes as inputs the air relative humidity and the air dry bulb temperature and generate the other corresponding air properties as outputs.

In this paper, the Type 2 has been adopted for simulating on/off differential controllers. These devises generate a value in the range between 0 and 1 that is used to deactivate or activate the refrigerating system or the heat pump. In particular, this Type activates the component generating a signal equal to 1 when the observed parameter becomes lower than the user-defined setpoint by a certain value (upper deadband), while it is switched off in the case of the observed parameter approaches the user-defined setpoint within a given limit (lower deadband). The successive value generated by the differential controller is also affected by the value assumed by the control signal used as input at the earlier time step. In this work, the differential controller is operated by connecting the input and output signals in order to give a hysteresis effect. In greater detail, the temperature at node 2 of the tank storing the cold fluid has been assumed as the observed temperature for activating/deactivating the refrigeration unit; with reference to the hot tank, the temperature at node 8 has been adopted as the watched temperature for operating the heat pump. A target temperature of 45 °C was assumed for activating the heap pump, with a turn-on temperature difference of 1 °C and a turn-off temperature difference of −1 °C. A target temperature of 7 °C was defined for activating the refrigeration unit, with a turn-on temperature difference of 1 °C and a turn-off temperature difference of −1 °C. The hot/cold heat carrier fluid is moved by the pumps into the post-heating/cooling coil according to the opening percentage of the corresponding valves defined by the related outputs of the ANN16 via the Type 155. The temperature of the hot heat carrier fluid is assumed to be reduced by 5 °C when flowing into the post-heating coil (before entering the hot tank), while the temperature of the cold heat carrier fluid is assumed as increased by 5 °C when flowing into the cooling coil (before entering the cold tank).

5. Assessment of Faults' Impact

In this section, the experimental performances of the HVAC system operating under faulty conditions (summer tests n. 5–9 of Table 4 and winter tests n. 14–18 of Table 5) have been compared with those predicted by the artificial neural network ANN16 (described in Section 4a), coupled with the TRNSYS model (described in Section 4b), in the cases of the HVAC system is operating under the same boundary conditions without faults. In more detail, the following inputs have been provided to the ANN16 in order to simulate the HVAC performance without faults: (i) return air temperature calculated by the TRNSYS Type 56 as well as target of indoor air temperature equal to 26 °C; (ii) return air relative humidity calculated by the TRNSYS Type 56 as well as target of indoor air relative humidity equal to 50%; (iii) supply air temperature calculated by the ANN16 itself at previous time step; (iv) supply air relative humidity calculated by the ANN16 itself at previous time step; (v) experimental value of outside air temperature; (vi) opening percentage of the valve supplying the post-heating coil calculated by the ANN16 itself at previous time step; (vii) opening percentage of the valve supplying the cooling coil calculated by the ANN16 itself at previous time step; (viii) opening percentage of the valve supplying the humidifier calculated by the ANN16 itself at previous time step; (ix) velocity of supply air fan equal to the nominal value of 50%; and (x) velocity of return air fan equal to the nominal value of 50%.This means that:

- The experimental tests n. 5 and n. 14 (with the fault 1, i.e., with the velocity of the supply air fan kept at 20%) have been compared with the simulation cases where the velocity of supply air fan has been kept at the nominal value of 50%;
- The experimental tests n. 6 and n. 15 (with the fault 2, i.e., the velocity of the return air fan kept at 20%) have been compared with the simulation cases where the velocity of return air fan has been kept at the nominal value of 50%;
- The experimental tests n. 7 and n. 16 (with the fault 3, i.e., the post-heating coil valve kept always closed) have been compared with the simulation cases where the values of OP_{V_PostHC} can vary according to the automatic control logic in the range of 0 to 100;
- The experimental tests n. 8 and n. 17 (with the fault 4, i.e., the cooling coil valve kept always closed) have been compared with the simulation cases where the values of OP_{V_CC} can vary according to the automatic control logic in the range of 0 to 100;
- The experimental tests n. 9 and n. 18 (with the fault 5, i.e., the opening percentage of the steam humidifier valve kept always closed) have been compared with the simulation cases where the values of OP_{V_HUM} can vary according to the automatic control logic in the range of 0 to 100.

Figures 11 and 12 highlight the values of return air temperature (T_{RA}) and return air relative humidity (RH_{RA}) over time, for the cases without faults (predicted values represented by solid lines) and the cases when only one of the 5 above-mentioned faults is occurred (experimental values indicated by dashed lines) with the aim of helping the contrast between normal and faulty scenarios. In particular, Figure 11 refers to the summer tests, while Figure 12 corresponds to the winter tests.

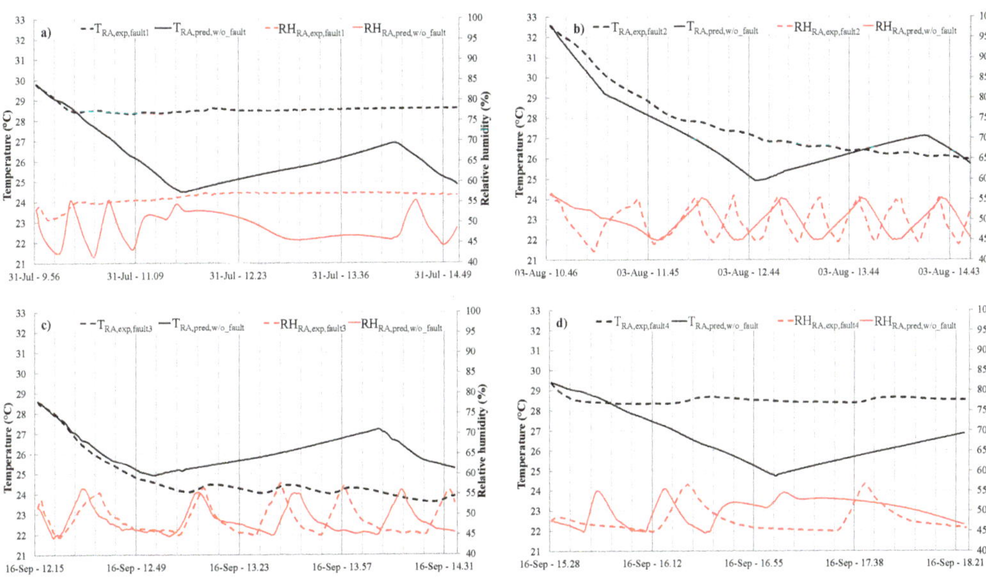

Figure 11. *Cont.*

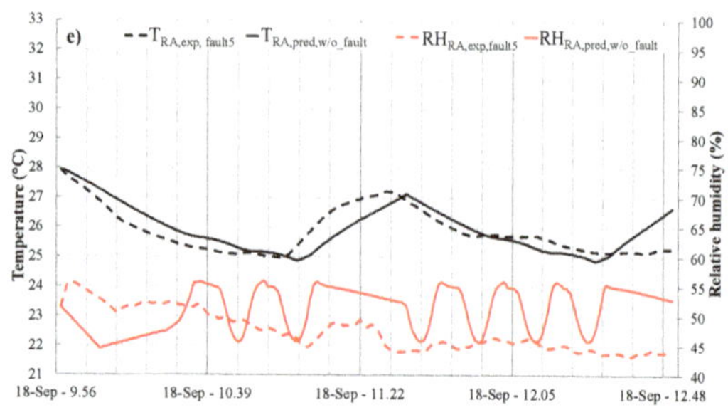

Figure 11. Comparison between experimental faulty operation (dashed lines) and predicted normal operation tests (solid lines) during summer in terms of T_{RA} and RH_{RA}: test n. 5 (**a**), test n. 6 (**b**), test n. 7 (**c**), test n. 8 (**d**), and test n. 9 (**e**).

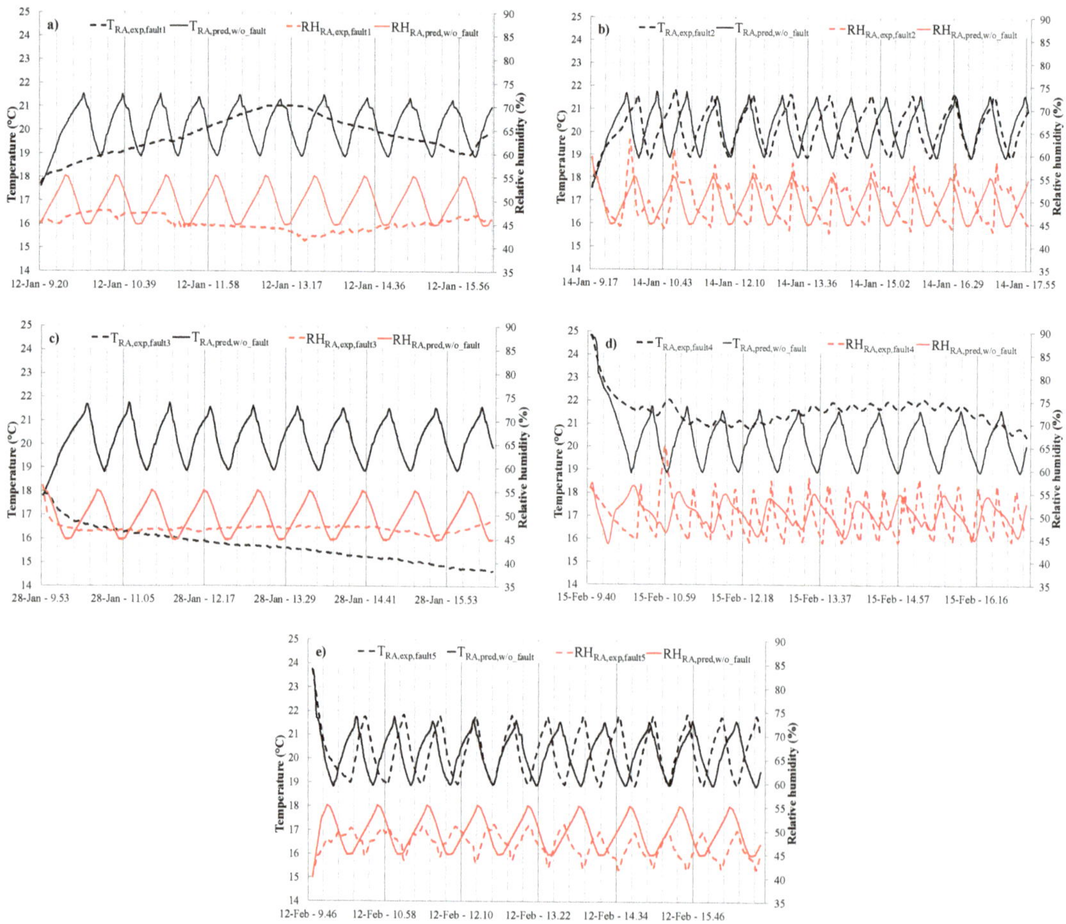

Figure 12. Comparison between experimental faulty operation (dashed lines) and predicted fault free operation tests during winter in terms of T_{RA} and RH_{RA}: test n. 14 (**a**), test n. 15 (**b**), test n. 16 (**c**), test n. 17 (**d**), and test n. 18 (**e**).

These comparisons have been performed in order to assess the impact of each fault on (i) the capability to achieve the desired indoor conditions, (ii) the arithmetic mean and standard deviation of return air temperature and relative humidity, as well as (iii) the electric energy consumptions. In particular, the effects of faults on occupant thermo-hygrometric comfort are reported in Section 5.1.; the faults' impact associated with the trends of return air temperature and relative humidity is described in Section 5.2.; the influence of each fault on electric energy consumptions is indicated in Section 5.3. The discussion about all the results is performed in last Section 5.4.

5.1. Results: Faults' Impact on Thermo-Hygrometric Comfort

Table 11 compares the thermal/hygrometric comfort times (i.e., the percentage of time during with values of indoor air temperature/relative humidity within the given deadbands) of the simulation tests without faults with respect to those associated to the corresponding experimental tests when only one of the five faults (described in the previous Section 3) is occurring.

Table 11. Thermal-hygrometric time with/without faults.

		ID Test	Thermal Comfort Time (%)	Hygrometric Comfort Time (%)
Summer tests	Test 5	With fault 1 (experimental)	0.00	16.17
		Without fault (predicted)	65.79	86.84
		Difference between faulty and healthy operation	−65.79	−70.67
	Test 6	With fault 2 (experimental)	50.61	81.38
		Without fault (predicted)	58.70	88.26
		Difference between faulty and healthy operation	−8.09	−6.88
	Test 7	With fault 3 (experimental)	13.43	88.06
		Without fault (predicted)	81.95	88.72
		Difference between faulty and healthy operation	−68.52	−0.66
	Test 8	With fault 4 (experimental)	0.00	90.59
		Without fault (predicted)	63.31	94.67
		Difference between faulty and healthy operation	−63.31	−4.08
	Test 9	With fault 5 (experimental)	86.59	65.36
		Without fault (predicted)	84.00	81.14
		Difference between faulty and healthy operation	2.59	15.78
Winter tests	Test 14	With fault 1 (experimental)	75.41	49.41
		Without fault (predicted)	76.11	87.35
		Difference between faulty and healthy operation	−0.70	−37.94
	Test 15	With fault 2 (experimental)	68.71	82.34
		Without fault (predicted)	69.23	86.23
		Difference between faulty and healthy operation	−0.52	−3.89
	Test 16	With fault 3 (experimental)	0.00	99.75
		Without fault (predicted)	69.75	86.25
		Difference between faulty and healthy operation	−69.75	13.50
	Test 17	With fault 4 (experimental)	15.73	80.45
		Without fault (predicted)	67.79	95.72
		Difference between faulty and healthy operation	−52.06	−15.27
	Test 18	With fault 5 (experimental)	64.85	22.67
		Without fault (predicted)	70.48	51.03
		Difference between faulty and healthy operation	−5.63	−28.36

5.2. Results: Faults' Impact on Key Operating Parameters

Experimental data under faulty operation and predicted data under fault-free operation were compared by calculating the arithmetic mean μ and the standard deviation σ of (1) return air temperature (T_{RA}) and (2) return air relative humidity (RH_{RA}). The arithmetic mean μ and standard deviation σ have been calculated by means of the following formulas:

$$\mu = \sum_{i=1}^{N} \frac{d_i}{N} \quad (16)$$

$$\sigma = \sqrt{\frac{\sum_{i=1}^{N} (d_i - \mu)^2}{N}} \quad (17)$$

where N is the whole number of points, while d_i is the value at time step i of the above-mentioned parameters. Table 12 compares the arithmetic mean μ and standard deviation σ during tests 5–9 (summer tests) and 14–18 (winter tests).

Table 12. Differences between predicted fault free data and experimental faulty data in terms of T_{RA} and RH_{RA}.

		ID Test	T_{RA} (°C)		RH_{RA} (%)	
			μ	σ	μ	σ
Summer tests	Test 5	With fault 1 (experimental)	28.55	0.22	56.17	1.54
		Without fault (predicted)	26.20	1.28	48.58	3.36
		%D	8.98%	−82.73%	15.64%	−54.25%
	Test 6	With fault 2 (experimental)	27.72	1.78	49.32	3.59
		Without fault (predicted)	27.16	1.79	49.97	3.30
		%D	2.07%	−0.17%	−1.30%	8.75%
	Test 7	With fault 3 (experimental)	24.72	1.20	48.88	3.56
		Without fault (predicted)	26.12	0.84	48.42	3.22
		%D	−5.34%	42.68%	0.96%	10.46%
	Test 8	With fault 4 (experimental)	28.50	0.14	47.77	3.06
		Without fault (predicted)	26.57	1.28	50.13	2.92
		%D	7.24%	−89.05%	−4.69%	4.93%
	Test 9	With fault 5 (experimental)	25.88	0.74	47.50	3.31
		Without fault (predicted)	25.95	0.77	51.15	3.71
		%D	−0.27%	−3.48%	−7.14%	−10.79%
Winter tests	Test 14	With fault 1 (experimental)	19.77	0.80	45.18	1.48
		Without fault (predicted)	20.14	0.84	49.61	3.38
		%D	−1.85%	−4.26%	−8.93%	−56.06%
	Test 15	With fault 2 (experimental)	20.18	0.86	50.12	4.01
		Without fault (predicted)	20.21	0.88	49.70	3.42
		%D	−0.13%	−1.35%	0.85%	17.23%
	Test 16	With fault 3 (experimental)	15.71	0.69	47.22	0.91
		Without fault (predicted)	20.21	0.87	49.67	3.41
		%D	−22.25%	−20.88%	−4.94%	−73.38%
	Test 17	With fault 4 (experimental)	21.55	0.59	49.99	3.95
		Without fault (predicted)	20.38	1.06	50.48	2.76
		%D	5.77%	−44.25%	−0.98%	43.17%
	Test 18	With fault 5 (experimental)	20.30	0.97	47.05	2.41
		Without fault (predicted)	20.25	0.89	49.56	3.46
		%D	0.25%	9.53%	−5.07%	−30.29%

Table 12 also shows the percentage difference (%D) between the values of arithmetic mean and the standard deviation under faulty (predicted values) and fault free operation (experimental values) for each of the above-mentioned parameters. The percentage difference %D has been calculated by means of the following formula:

$$\%D = \frac{(X_{fault,i} - X_{w/o\_fault,i})}{X_{w/o\_fault,i}} \times 100 \quad (18)$$

where X is the arithmetic mean μ or the standard deviation σ of T_{RA} or RH_{RA}.

Table 13 summarizes the comments described above; for each of five typical faults considered and for each of four parameters, a performance index has been assigned with the following signs: "+" indicates that the fault causes substantial positive changes (greater than 20%) of %D; "-" indicates that the fault causes substantial negative changes (greater than −20%) of %D; "0" indicates that the fault causes not substantial changes (between −20% and 20%) of %D.

Table 13. Summary of symptoms associated to the 5 typical faults on T_{RA} and RH_{RA}.

	ID Fault	T_{RA}		RH_{RA}	
		μ	σ	μ	σ
Summer tests	Fault 1 (related to velocity of the supply air fan)	0	-	0	-
	Fault 2 (related to velocity of the return air fan)	0	0	0	0
	Fault 3 (related to the post-heating coil valve)	0	+	0	0
	Fault 4 (related to the cooling coil valve)	0	-	0	0
	Fault 5 (related to the humidifier valve)	0	0	0	0
Winter tests	Fault 1 (related to velocity of the supply air fan)	0	0	0	-
	Fault 2 (related to velocity of the return air fan)	0	0	0	0
	Fault 3 (related to the post-heating coil valve)	-	-	0	-
	Fault 4 (related to the cooling coil valve)	0	-	0	+
	Fault 5 (related to the humidifier valve)	0	0	0	-

5.3. Results: Faults' Impact on Electric Energy Consumption

Table 14 shows the electric energy consumptions of: the heat pump (EE_{HP}), the refrigerating system (EE_{RS}), the humidifier (EE_{HUM}), the supply air fan (EE_{SAF}), the return air fan (EE_{RAF}), and the total electric energy consumption (EE_{TOT}), with and without faults; in particular, the values associated to the faulty tests have been derived as outputs of the TRNSYS model by using the measured data as inputs, while the values associated to the fault free tests have been predicted by the coupling of the ANN16 and the TRNSYS model. Moreover, Table 14 reports the energy percentage difference (EPD) that has been valuated as follows:

$$EPD = \frac{EE_{w/o\_fault,i} - EE_{fault,i}}{EE_{w/o\_fault,i}} \times 100 \quad (19)$$

where $EE_{w/o\_fault,i}$ and $EE_{fault,i}$ are, respectively, the electric energy consumption of AHU component for the case without faults and with one of the above-mentioned faults.

Table 14. Electric energy consumption with and without faults.

		ID Test	Electric Energy Consumption					
			EE_{HP} (kWh)	EE_{RS} (kWh)	EE_{HUM} (kWh)	EE_{SAF} (kWh)	EE_{RAF} (kWh)	EE_{TOT} (kWh)
Summer tests	Test 5	With fault 1 (experimental)	0.28	19.37	0.00	0.17	0.43	20.25
		Without fault (predicted)	9.43	18.99	4.75	1.29	0.43	34.89
		EPD	+97%	−2%	+100%	+87%	0%	+42%
	Test 6	With fault 2 (experimental)	0.29	16.68	9.00	1.04	0.12	27.13
		Without fault (predicted)	5.45	13.88	7.09	1.04	0.35	27.81
		EPD	+95%	−20%	−27%	0%	+66%	+2%
	Test 7	With fault 3 (experimental)	0.22	7.19	2.65	0.56	0.19	10.81
		Without fault (predicted)	4.35	6.91	2.34	0.56	0.19	14.35
		EPD	+95%	−4%	−13%	0%	0%	+25%
	Test 8	With fault 4 (experimental)	0.22	0.99	1.48	0.72	0.24	3.65
		Without fault (predicted)	4.94	10.13	2.96	0.72	0.24	18.99
		EPD	+96%	+90%	+50%	0%	0%	+81%
	Test 9	With fault 5 (experimental)	2.65	8.76	0.00	0.74	0.25	12.40
		Without fault (predicted)	3.90	10.94	3.88	0.74	0.25	19.71
		EPD	+32%	+20%	+100%	0%	0%	+37%
Winter tests	Test 14	With fault 1 (experimental)	13.13	8.49	11.04	0.17	0.61	33.44
		Without fault (predicted)	16.30	13.56	16.16	1.81	0.61	48.44
		EPD	+19%	+37%	+32%	+91%	0%	+31%
	Test 15	With fault 2 (experimental)	28.95	20.23	17.70	2.21	0.25	69.34
		Without fault (predicted)	20.90	21.01	19.36	2.21	0.74	64.22
		EPD	−39%	+4%	+9%	0%	+66%	−8%
	Test 16	With fault 3 (experimental)	0.61	16.27	0.00	1.70	0.57	19.15
		Without fault (predicted)	16.37	12.26	14.00	1.70	0.57	44.90
		EPD	+96%	−33%	+100%	0%	0%	+57%
	Test 17	With fault 4 (experimental)	0.61	0.37	7.65	1.89	0.63	11.15
		Without fault (predicted)	14.85	18.06	9.31	1.89	0.63	44.74
		EPD	+96%	+98%	+18%	0%	0%	+75%
	Test 18	With fault 5 (experimental)	9.05	11.24	0.00	1.78	0.60	22.67
		Without fault (predicted)	16.20	17.10	15.35	1.78	0.60	51.03
		EPD	+44%	+34%	+100%	0%	0%	+56%

5.4. Discussion

With respect to the case without faults, Tables 11 and 14 indicate the effects of the occurrence of fault 1 (velocity of supply air fan kept reduced at 20% instead of the nominal value of 50%):

- During summer (test n. 5) it strongly reduces both the thermal comfort time (66%) and the hygrometric comfort time (71%), while significantly lowering the overall electric energy consumption (42%) thanks to reduced consumption of the heat pump (97%), the steam humidifier (100%), and the supply air fan (87%);
- During winter (test n. 14) it decreases the hygrometric comfort time (38%), without significant variation of the hygrometric comfort time (1%), while considerably lowering the total electric energy consumption (31%) thanks to reduced consumption of the

refrigerating system (37%), the heat pump (19%), the steam humidifier (32%), and the supply air fan (91%).

With respect to the case without fault, Tables 11 and 14 demonstrate the effects of the occurrence of fault 2 (velocity of return air fan kept reduced at 20% instead of the nominal value of 50%):

- During summer (test n. 6) slightly decreases both the thermal comfort time (8%) and the hygrometric comfort time (7%), while slightly reducing the overall electric energy consumption (2%) because of the lower consumption of both the heat pump (95%) and return air fan (66%);
- During winter (test n. 15) slightly decreases the hygrometric comfort time (4%), without relevant variation of the hygrometric comfort time (1%), while increasing the overall electric energy consumption (8%) due to greater consumption of heat pump (39%).

With respect to the case without fault, Tables 11 and 14 show how the occurrence of the fault 3 (the opening percentage of the valve regulating the flow to the post-hating coil kept closed instead of allowing its normal operation in the range of 0 to 100 according to the automatic control logic):

- During summer (test n. 7) strongly reduces the thermal comfort time (69%), without significant variation of the hygrometric comfort time (1%), while lowering the overall electric energy consumption (25%) because of the reduced consumption of the heat pump (95%);
- During winter (test n. 16) strongly reduces the thermal comfort time (70%) and slightly decreases the hygrometric comfort time (14%), while significantly lowering the overall electric energy consumption (57%) because of the reduced consumption of both the heat pump (96%), and the steam humidifier (100%).

With respect to the case without fault, Tables 11 and 14 highlight how the occurrence of the fault 4 (the opening percentage of the valve regulating the flow to the cooling coil kept closed instead of allowing its normal operation in the range of 0 to 100 according to the automatic control logic):

- During summer (test 8) significantly decreases the thermal comfort time (63%) and slightly reduces the hygrometric comfort time (4%), while greatly lowering the overall electric energy demand (81%) because of the reduced consumption of the heat pump (96%), the refrigerating system (90%), and the steam humidifier (50%);
- During winter (test n. 17) significantly decreases the thermal comfort time (52%) and slightly reduces the hygrometric comfort time (15%), while considerably lowering the overall electric energy demand (75%) because of the reduced consumption of the heat pump (96%), the refrigerating system (98%), and the steam humidifier (18%).

With respect to the case without fault, Tables 11 and 14 indicate how the occurrence of the fault 5 (the opening percentage of the valve regulating the flow to the steam humidifier kept closed instead of allowing its normal operation in the range of 0 to 100 according to the automatic control logic):

- During summer (test n. 9) reduces the thermal comfort time by a slight amount (3%) and decreases the hygrometric comfort time (16%), while decreasing the overall electric energy demand (37%) because of the lower consumption of the heat pump (32%), the refrigerating system (20%), and the humidifier (100%);
- During winter (test n. 18) reduces the thermal comfort time by a slight amount (6%) and significantly decreases the hygrometric comfort time (28%), while decreasing the overall electric energy demand (56%) because of the lower consumption of the heat pump (44%), the refrigerating system (34%), and the humidifier (100%).

Table 13 underlines that:

- The fault 1 significantly affects the values of σ for both T_{RA} and RH_{RA} under summer conditions as well as the values of σ for RH_{RA} only under winter conditions;

- The effects of the fault 2 are negligible with reference to the values of both σ and μ for both T_{RA} and RH_{RA} under both summer and winter conditions;
- The fault 3 greatly affects the values of σ for T_{RA} under summer conditions, the values of both σ and μ for T_{RA} under winter conditions, as well as the values of σ for RH_{RA} under winter conditions;
- The impact of the fault 4 is significant with reference to the values of σ for T_{RA} under summer conditions as well as the values of σ for both T_{RA} and RH_{RA} under winter conditions;
- The fault 5 significantly affects only the values of σ associated to RH_{RA} under winter conditions.

6. Conclusions

In this study, a database consisting of experimental measurements of key operating parameters during transient and steady-state operation of a typical HVAC system under both normal and faulty conditions has been obtained with reference to a wide range of summer and winter scenarios. In particular, five different typical faults (affecting the supply air fan, the return air fan, the post-heating coil valve, the cooling coil valve, and the humidifier valve) have been artificially implemented in the HVAC system and analyzed.

An artificial neural network-based model of the HVAC system has also been developed in the MATLAB environment [32] and contrasted with measured data, highlighting that it is able to provide a rigorous characterization of the HVAC system's steady-state and transient performance under both normal and faulty scenarios. In more detail, the model is characterized by average values of coefficient of determination R^2 in predicting supply air temperature, supply air relative humidity, opening percentage of the post-heating coil valve, opening percentage of the cooling coil valve, and opening percentage of the humidifier valve very close to the maximum values and, respectively, equal to 0.95 °C, 0.93%, 0.95%, 0.97%, and 0.96%.

The ANN-based model has also been coupled with a dynamic simulation model developed in TRNSYS environment [33] and then the experimental operation of the HVAC unit without faults has been compared with the predicted performance of the same system while operating with one of the five above-mentioned faults under the same boundary conditions. The results of this analysis highlighted that:

- Fault 3 is associated with the valve supplying the post-heating coil (always kept closed) is the one significantly affecting indoor thermal comfort, with a reduction of about 68% (during summer) and 70% (during winter) with respect to the fault free conditions;
- Fault 1 is associated with the supply air fan (kept at a reduced velocity of 20% instead of the nominal value of 50%) is the one considerably influencing indoor hygrometric comfort, with a reduction of about 71% (during summer) and 38% (during winter) in comparison to the fault free tests;
- Fault 4 is associated with the valve supplying the cooling coil (always kept closed) is the one causing important variation in terms of overall electric energy consumption (81% during summer and 75% during winter) with reference to the fault free scenarios.

In addition, the following results in terms of standard deviation σ and arithmetic mean μ of return air temperature (T_{RA}) and relative humidity (RH_{RA}) have been obtained:

- The fault 1 significantly affects the values of σ for both T_{RA} and RH_{RA} under summer conditions as well as the values of σ for RH_{RA} only under winter conditions;
- The fault 3 greatly affects the values of σ for T_{RA} under summer conditions, the values of both σ and μ for T_{RA} under winter conditions, as well as the values of σ for RH_{RA} under winter conditions;
- The impact of the fault 4 is significant with reference to the values of σ for T_{RA} under summer conditions as well as the values of σ for both T_{RA} and RH_{RA} under winter conditions;

- The fault 5 significantly affects only the values of σ associated to RH_{RA} under winter conditions.

Both the labeled measured data as well as the developed simulation models (together with their learning/validation datasets) will be uploaded in a public data repository and utilization will be permitted to readers for institutional and research purposes. This will allow AFDD developers, AFDD users, and research organizations to (i) explore the symptoms associated to the selected faults on the performance of a typical HVAC system, (ii) exploit the experimentally validated simulation model in order to generate operational data for assisting further research for AFDD of HVAC units, (iii) compare accuracy among AFDD methods, and (iv) identify research gaps to be addressed and future AFDD developments.

The presented experimental database will be extended over time with the aim of investigating a broader range of boundary conditions as well as different fault types. In particular, in the future the authors would like to perform additional tests with the aim of analyzing the effects associated to new faults regarding sensors (e.g., positive and negative offsets in measuring return air relative humidity and temperature), devices (e.g., blockage of air dampers and coil/humidifier valves at different levels), equipment (e.g., complete failure of fans), or controllers (e.g., frozen control signal for coils, dampers, or fans). A measurement time step equal to 1 s will be used during future experiments in order to more carefully take into account the response time of some HVAC components. In addition, the authors will extend the present analysis (where the faults have been introduced at the beginning of the faulty tests and maintained during the entire duration of the experiments) by also considering (i) faults arising suddenly during HVAC operation and remaining at a constant level after occurrence as well as (ii) shorter faulty scenarios where a component is 'sticky' and takes more time to be moved/operated with respect to normal operation. Finally, the authors in the future would like to (i) compare experimental fault free operation against experimental faulty performance of the HVAC system working under same boundary conditions, (ii) refine and improve the simulation model, and (iii) develop and test an innovative method for performing AFDD analyses based on supervised data-driven methods customized on experimental results.

Author Contributions: Conceptualization, A.R., F.G., E.E. and L.M.; methodology, A.R., F.G., M.M., E.E. and L.M.; software, A.R., F.G., S.S., M.M. and E.E.; validation, A.R. and F.G.; formal analysis, A.R., F.G., S.S., M.M., E.E. and L.M.; investigation, A.R., F.G. and M.M.; resources, A.R., S.S., M.M. and L.M.; data curation, A.R., F.G. and M.M.; writing—original draft preparation, A.R., F.G., S.S., M.M., E.E. and L.M.; writing—review and editing, A.R., F.G., S.S., M.M., E.E. and L.M.; visualization, A.R., F.G., S.S., M.M., E.E. and L.M.; supervision, A.R., S.S., M.M., E.E. and L.M.; project administration, A.R. and L.M.; funding acquisition, A.R., M.M. and L.M. All authors have read and agreed to the published version of the manuscript.

Funding: This research received no external funding.

Data Availability Statement: The data presented in this study are available on request from the corresponding author.

Acknowledgments: This work was undertaken as part of the program "PON FSE-FESR Ricerca e Innovazione 2014–2020" of the Italian Ministry of Education, University and Research, Action I.1 "Dottorati Innovativi con caratterizzazione industriale".

Conflicts of Interest: The authors declare no conflict of interest. The funders had no role in the design of the study; in the collection, analyses, or interpretation of data; in the writing of the manuscript; or in the decision to publish the results.

Nomenclature

AFDD	Automatic fault detection and diagnosis
AHU	Air handling unit
ANN	Artificial neural network
CAV	Constant air volume
CC	Cooling coil
COP	Coefficient of performance (-)
CT	Cold tank
DB_{RH}	Deadband of $RH_{SP,Room}$ (%)
DB_T	Deadband of $T_{SP,Room}$ (°C)
D_{EA}	Exhaust air damper
D_{HRS}	Damper of heat recovery system
d_i	Value at time step i
D_{OA}	Outside air damper
D_{RA}	Return air damper
$EE_{fault,i}$	Electric energy consumption of AHU component with fault (kWh)
EE_{HP}	Electric energy consumption of the HP (kWh)
EE_{HUM}	Electric energy consumption of the HUM (kWh)
EER	Energy efficiency ratio (kWh)
EE_{RAF}	Electric energy consumption of the RAF (kWh)
EE_{RS}	Electric energy consumption of the RS (kWh)
EE_{SAF}	Electric energy consumption of the SAF (kWh)
EE_{TOT}	Overall electric energy consumption (kWh)
$EE_{w/o\_fault,i}$	Electric energy consumption of AHU component without faults (kWh)
EPD	Energy percentage difference (%)
$g_{pred,i}$	Predicted value at time step i
$g_{exp,i}$	Measured value at time step i
$\overline{g}_{pred}$	Arithmetic mean of predicted values
HP	Heat pump
HRS	Static cross-flow heat recovery system
HT	Hot tank
HUM	Humidifier
HVAC	Heating, ventilation and air-conditioning
MSE	Mean square error
N	Number of points
OAD	Outside air duct
OAFil	Outside air filter
OL_{RAF}	Velocity of RAF (%)
OL_{SAF}	Velocity of SAF (%)
OP_{DEA}	Opening percentage of D_{EA} (%)
OP_{DHRS}	Opening percentage of D_{HRS} (%)
OP_{DOA}	Opening percentage of D_{OA} (%)
OP_{DRA}	Opening percentage of D_{RA} (%)
OP_{V_CC}	Opening percentage of valve regulating the flow entering CC (%)
OP_{V_CC-1}	Opening percentage of valve regulating the flow entering CC at previous minute (%)
$OP_{V\_CC,pred}$	Predicted opening percentage of valve regulating the flow entering CC (%)
$OP_{V\_CC,exp}$	Experimental opening percentage of valve regulating the flow entering CC (%)
OP_{V_HUM}	Opening percentage of valve regulating the flow entering HUM (%)
OP_{V_HUM-1}	Opening percentage of valve regulating the flow entering HUM at previous minute (%)

$OP_{V\_HUM,pred}$	Predicted opening percentage of valve regulating the flow entering HUM (%)
$OP_{V\_HUM,exp}$	Experimental opening percentage of valve regulating the flow entering HUM (%)
OP_{V_PostHC}	Opening percentage of valve regulating the flow entering PostHC (%)
$OP_{V\_PostHC-1}$	Opening percentage of valve regulating the flow entering the PostHC at previous minute (%)
$OP_{V\_PostHC,pred}$	Predicted opening percentage of valve regulating the flow entering PostHC (%)
$OP_{V\_PostHC,exp}$	Experimental opening percentage of valve regulating the flow entering PostHC (%)
OP_{V_PreHC}	Opening percentage of valve regulating the flow entering PreHC (%)
P_{el}^{RAF}	Power consumption of RAF (W)
P_{el}^{SAF}	Power consumption of SAF (W)
PID	Proportional-integral-derivative
PostHC	Post-heating coil
PreHC	Pre-heating coil
Q_V^{RAF}	Air volumetric flow rate of RAF (m^3/h)
Q_V^{SAF}	Air volumetric flow rate of SAF (m^3/h)
R^2	Coefficient of determination (-)
RAD	Return air duct
RAF	Return air fan
RAFil	Return air filter
RH_{BEA}	Air relative humidity outside the room (%)
RH_{RA}	Return air relative humidity (%)
$RH_{RA,exp,fault}$	Measured return air relative humidity under faulty conditions (%)
$RH_{RA,pred,w/o\_fault}$	Predicted return air relative humidity without faults (%)
RH_{SA}	Supply air relative humidity (%)
RH_{SA-1}	Supply air relative humidity at previous minute (%)
$RH_{SP,Room}$	Target of indoor air relative humidity (%)
RMSE	Root mean square error
RS	Refrigerating unit
SAD	Supply air duct
SAF	Supply air fan
SAFil	Supply air filter
$T_{A,out,CC}$	Air temperature at CC outlet (°C)
T_{BEA}	Air temperature outside the room (°C)
T_{OA}	External air temperature (°C)
T_{RA}	Return air temperature (°C)
$T_{RA,exp,fault}$	Measured return air temperature under faulty conditions (°C)
$T_{RA,pred,w/o\_fault}$	Predicted return air temperature without faults (°C)
T_{SA}	Supply air temperature (°C)
T_{SA-1}	Supply air temperature at previous minute (°C)
$T_{SP,Room}$	Target of indoor air temperature (°C)
VAV	Variable air volume
V_{CC}	3-way valve of CC
V_{HUM}	Valve of HUM
V_{PostHC}	3-way valve of PostHC
V_{PreHC}	3-way valve of PreHC
$X_{fault,i}$	Arithmetic mean or standard deviation with fault
$X_{w/o\_fault,i}$	Arithmetic mean or standard deviation without faults

%D	Percentage difference (%)
ΔRH	Difference between current return air relative humidity and related target (%)
ΔT	Difference between current return air temperature and related target (°C)
Δ_{OPV_CC}	Instantaneous errors between the values predicted by the ANN16 and the measured data in terms of OP_{V_CC} (%)
Δ_{OPV_HUM}	Instantaneous errors between the values predicted by the ANN16 and the measured data in terms of OP_{V_HUM} (%)
Δ_{OPV_PostHC}	Instantaneous errors between the values predicted by the ANN16 and the measured data in terms of OP_{V_PostHC} (%)
Δ_{RHSA}	Instantaneous errors between the values predicted by the ANN16 and the measured data in terms of RH_{SA} (%)
Δ_{TSA}	Instantaneous errors between the values predicted by the ANN16 and the measured data in terms of T_{SA} (°C)
ε_i	Instantaneous error
$\lvert\varepsilon_i\rvert$	Instantaneous absolute error
$\overline{\varepsilon}$	Average error
$\lvert\overline{\varepsilon}\rvert$	Average absolute error
μ	Arithmetic mean
σ	Standard deviation

Appendix A

Table A1. Properties of walls of the test room.

	Material (from Outside to Inside)	Thickness (m)	Thermal Conductivity (W/mK)	Thermal Resistance (m^2K/W)		Heat Transfer Area (m^2)
Ceiling	Plasterboard	0.0125	0.250	0.050	2.023	16.00
	Rock wool	0.0800	0.042	1.905		
	Polyurethane panel	0.0150	0.220	0.068		
Floor	Subfloor	0.1000	1.350	0.074	3.107	16.00
	Tiles	0.0500	2.100	0.024		
	Polystyrene panel	0.0800	0.035	2.286		
	Galvanized steel slab	0.0020	52.000	0.000		
	Tiles	0.0100	1.050	0.010		
West and East oriented vertical walls	Plasterboard	0.0125	0.250	0.050	2.005	14.40
	Rock wool	0.0800	0.042	1.905		
	Radiant panel	0.0150	0.300	0.050		
South and North oriented vertical walls	Plasterboard	0.0125	0.250	0.050	1.998	14.40
	Rock wool	0.0800	0.042	1.905		
	Fiber-cement panel	0.0150	0.350	0.043		
Door	Soft wood	0.0500	0.140	0.357	0.357	1.68

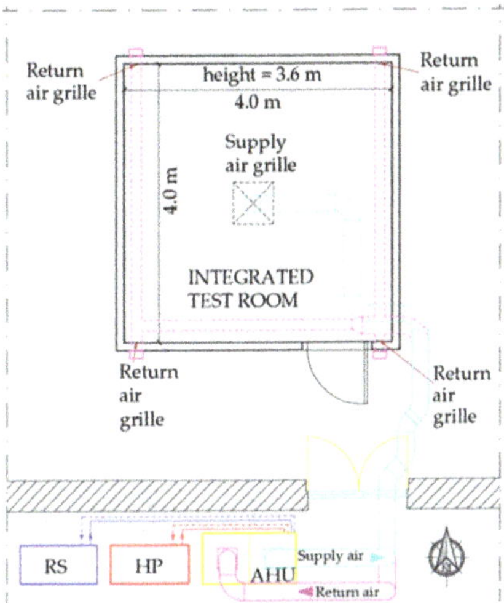

Figure A1. Floor plan of the test room including the AHU.

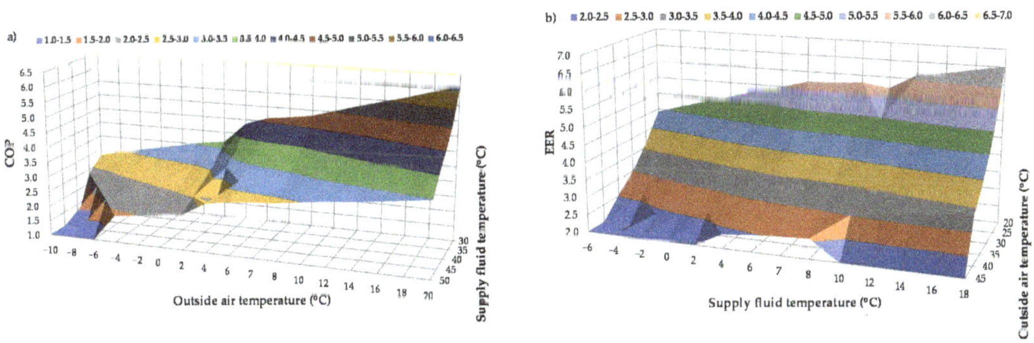

Figure A2. (**a**) COP of the HP and (**b**) EER of the RS upon varying outside air temperature and supply fluid temperature.

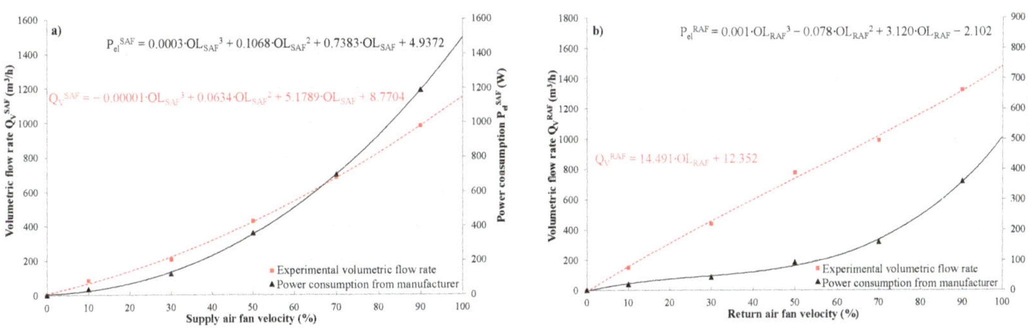

Figure A3. Experimental air volumetric flow rate and power consumption suggested by the manufacturer as a function of fan velocity for the supply air fan (**a**) and the return air fan (**b**).

References

1. Wang, H.; Chen, Y. A robust fault detection and diagnosis strategy for multiple faults of VAV air handling units. *Energy Build.* **2016**, *127*, 442–451. [CrossRef]

2. Lee, K.P.; Wu, B.H.; Peng, S.L. Deep-learning-based fault detection and diagnosis of air-handling units. *Build. Environ.* **2019**, *157*, 24–33. [CrossRef]
3. Schibuola, L.; Scarpa, M.; Tambani, C. Variable speed drive (VSD) technology applied to HVAC systems for energy saving: An experimental investigation. *Energy Procedia* **2018**, *148*, 806–813. [CrossRef]
4. Tang, R.; Wang, S.; Shan, K. Optimal and near-optimal indoor temperature and humidity controls for direct load control and proactive building demand response towards smart grids. *Autom. Construct.* **2018**, *96*, 250–261. [CrossRef]
5. Piscitelli, M.S.; Mazzarelli, D.M.; Capozzoli, A. Enhancing operational performance of AHUs through an advanced fault detection and diagnosis process based on temporal association and decision rules. *Energy Build.* **2020**, *226*, 110369. [CrossRef]
6. Yan, K.; Zhong, C.; Ji, Z.; Huang, J. Semi-supervised learning for early detection and diagnosis of various air handling unit faults. *Energy Build.* **2018**, *181*, 75–83. [CrossRef]
7. Lin, G.; Kramer, H.; Granderson, J. Building fault detection and diagnostics: Achieved savings, and methods to evaluate algorithm performance. *Build. Environ.* **2020**, *168*, 106505. [CrossRef]
8. Au-Yong, C.P.; Ali, A.S.; Ahmad, F. Improving occupants' satisfaction with effective maintenance management of HVAC system in office buildings. *Autom. Constr.* **2014**, *43*, 31–37. [CrossRef]
9. Rosato, A.; Guarino, F.; Filomena, V.; Sibilio, S.; Maffei, L. Experimental calibration and validation of a simulation model for fault detection of HVAC systems and application to a case study. *Energies* **2020**, *13*, 3948. [CrossRef]
10. Granderson, J.; Lin, G.; Singla, R.; Mayhorn, E.; Ehrlich, P.; Vrabie, D.; Franck, S. *Commercial Fault Detection and Diagnostics Tools: What They Offer, How They Differ, and What's Still Needed*; Lawrence Berkeley National Laboratory: Berkeley, CA, USA, 2018. Available online: https://escholarship.org/uc/item/4j72k57p (accessed on 26 August 2021). [CrossRef]
11. Entchev, E.; Yang, L.; Ghorab, M.; Rosato, A.; Sibilio, S. Energy, economic and environmental performance simulation of a hybrid renewable microgeneration system with neural network predictive control. *Alex. Eng. J.* **2018**, *57*, 455–473. [CrossRef]
12. Kim, W.; Katipamula, S. A review of fault detection and diagnostics methods for building systems. *Sci. Technol. Built Environ.* **2018**, *24*, 3–21. [CrossRef]
13. Zhao, Y.; Li, T.; Zhang, X.; Zhang, C. Artificial intelligence-based fault detection and diagnosis methods for building energy systems: Advantages, challenges and the future. *Renew. Sustain. Energy Rev.* **2019**, *109*, 85–101. [CrossRef]
14. Yu, Y.; Woradechjumroen, D.; Yu, D. A review of fault detection and diagnosis methodologies on air-handling units. *Energy Build.* **2014**, *82*, 550–562. [CrossRef]
15. Beghi, A.; Brignoli, R.; Cecchinato, L.; Menegazzo, G.; Rampazzo, M.; Simmini, F. Data-driven Fault Detection and Diagnosis for HVAC water chillers. *Control Eng. Pract.* **2016**, *53*, 79–91. [CrossRef]
16. Dehestani, D.; Eftekhari, F.; Guo, Y.; Ling, S.; Su, S.; Nguyen, H. Online Support Vector Machine Application for Model Based Fault Detection and Isolation of HVAC System. *Int. J. Mach. Learn. Comput.* **2011**, *1*, 66–72. [CrossRef]
17. Zhao, Y.; Wen, J.; Xiao, F.; Yang, X.; Wang, S. Diagnostic Bayesian networks for diagnosing air handling units faults—part I: Faults in dampers, fans, filters and sensors. *Appl. Therm. Eng.* **2017**, *111*, 1272–1286. [CrossRef]
18. Zhao, Y.; Wen, J.; Wang, S. Diagnostic Bayesian networks for diagnosing air handling units faults-Part II: Faults in coils and sensors. *Appl. Therm. Eng.* **2015**, *90*, 145–157. [CrossRef]
19. Mulumba, T.; Afshari, A.; Yan, K.; Shen, W.; Norford, L.K. Robust model-based fault diagnosis for air handling units. *Energy Build.* **2015**, *86*, 698–707. [CrossRef]
20. Yan, R.; Ma, Z.; Zhao, Y.; Kokogiannakis, G. A decision tree based data-driven diagnostic strategy for air handling units. *Energy Build.* **2016**, *133*, 37–45. [CrossRef]
21. Mchugh, M.K. Data-Driven Leakage Detection in Air-Handling Units on a University Campus. In Proceedings of the ASHRAE Annual Conference, Kansas City, MO, USA, 5 March 2019.
22. Du, Z.M.; Jin, X.Q. Detection and diagnosis for multiple faults in VAV systems. *Energy Build.* **2007**, *39*, 923–934. [CrossRef]
23. Hu, R.I.; Granderson, J.; Auslader, D.M.; Agogino, A. Design of machine learning models with domain experts for automated sensor selection for energy fault detection. *Appl. Energy* **2019**, *235*, 117–128. [CrossRef]
24. Wen, J.; Li, S. *ASHRAE RP-1312—Tools for Evaluating Fault Detection and Diagnostic Methods for Air-Handling Units*; American Society of Heating, Refrigeration and Air-Conditioning Engineers: Atlanta, GA, USA, 2012; Available online: https://www.techstreet.com/ashrae/standards/rp-1312-tools-for-evaluating-fault-detection-and-diagnostic-methods-for-air-handling-units?gateway_code=ashrae&product_id=1833299 (accessed on 26 August 2021).
25. Granderson, J.; Lin, G.; Harding, A.; Im, P.; Chen, Y. Building Fault Detection Data to Aid Diagnostic Algorithm Creation and Performance Testing. *Sci. Data* **2020**, *7*, 65. Available online: https://www.nature.com/articles/s41597-020-0398-6.pdf (accessed on 14 August 2021). [CrossRef]
26. Casillas, A.; Lin, G.; Granderson, J. *Curation of Ground-Truth Validated Benchmarking Datasets for Fault Detection & Diagnostics Tools*; Lawrence Berkeley National Laboratory: Berkeley, CA, USA, 2021. Available online: https://eta-publications.lbl.gov/sites/default/files/curation_of_ground-truth_validated_benchmarking_datasets_for_fault_detection_acasillas_0.pdf (accessed on 14 August 2021).
27. Yun, W.S.; Hong, W.H.; Seo, H. A data-driven fault detection and diagnosis scheme for air handling units in building HVAC systems considering undefined states. *J. Build. Eng.* **2021**, *35*, 102111. [CrossRef]
28. Fan, C.; Liu, X.; Xue, P.; Wang, J. Statistical characterization of semi-supervised neural networks for fault detection and diagnosis of air handling units. *Energy Build.* **2021**, *234*, 110733. [CrossRef]

29. Wang, L.; Greenberg, S.; Fiegel, J.; Rubalcava, A.; Earni, S.; Pang, X.; Yin, R.; Woodworth, S.; Hernandez-Maldonado, J. Monitoring-based HVAC commissioning of an existing office building for energy efficiency. *Appl. Energy* **2013**, *102*, 1382–1390. [CrossRef]
30. Basarkar, M. *Modeling and Simulation of Hvac Faults in Energyplus*; Lawrence Berkeley National Laboratory: Berkeley, CA, USA, 2011. Available online: https://escholarship.org/uc/item/9ps43482 (accessed on 14 August 2021).
31. Zhang, R.; Hong, T. Modeling of HVAC operational faults in building performance simulation. *Appl. Energy* **2017**, *202*, 178–188. [CrossRef]
32. MathWorks. Available online: https://it.mathworks.com/products/matlab.html (accessed on 21 July 2021).
33. TRNSYS—Transient System Simulation Tool. Available online: http://www.trnsys.com (accessed on 21 July 2021).
34. COMMISSION REGULATION (EU) No 1253/2014 of 7 July 2014 Implementing Directive 2009/125/EC of the European Parliament and of the Council with Regard to Ecodesign Requirements for Ventilation Units. Available online: https://eur-lex.europa.eu/legal-content/EN/TXT/PDF/?uri=CELEX:32014R1253&from=FR (accessed on 14 August 2021).
35. CAREL Humidifiers Datasheet. Available online: https://www.carel.com/documents/10191/0/%2B030220621/92fca658-a251-49ee-9979-b8829fcba49f?version=1.0 (accessed on 21 July 2021).
36. AERMEC Reversible Air/Water Heat Pump Datasheet. Available online: https://download.aermec.com/docs/schede/ANL-021-203-HP_Y_UN50_03.pdf?r=14395 (accessed on 21 July 2021).
37. SIEMENS Duct Sensors Datasheet. Available online: https://www.downloads.siemens.com/download-center/Download.aspx?pos=download&fct=getasset&id1=24897 (accessed on 21 July 2021).
38. SIEMENS Duct Temperature Sensors Datasheet. Available online: https://www.downloads.siemens.com/download-center/Download.aspx?pos=download&fct=getasset&id1=10859 (accessed on 21 July 2021).
39. TSI Q-TRAK Datasheet. Available online: https://tsi.com/getmedia/d2a8d1d1-7551-47fe-8a0f-3c14b09b494b/7575_QTrak_A4_UK_5001356-web?ext=.pdf (accessed on 21 July 2021).
40. Cheng, F.; Cai, W.; Zhang, X.; Liao, H.; Cui, C. Fault detection and diagnosis for Air Handling Unit based on multiscale convolutional neural networks. *Energy Build.* **2021**, *236*, 110795. [CrossRef]
41. Lee, J.M.; Hong, S.H.; Seob, B.M.; Leec, K.H. Application of artificial neural networks for optimized AHU discharge air temperature set-point and minimized cooling energy in VAV system. *Appl. Therm. Eng.* **2019**, *153*, 726–738. [CrossRef]
42. Jang, J.; Baek, J.; Leigh, S.B. Prediction of optimum heating timing based on artificial neural network by utilizing BEMS data. *J. Build. Eng.* **2019**, *22*, 66–74. [CrossRef]
43. Elnour, M.; Meskin, N.; Al-Naemi, M. Sensor data validation and fault diagnosis using Auto-Associative Neural Network for HVAC systems. *J. Build. Eng.* **2020**, *27*, 100935. [CrossRef]
44. Shibata, K.; Ikeda, Y. Effect of number of hidden neurons on learning in large-scale layered neural networks. In Proceedings of the ICROS-SICE International Joint Conference, Fukuoka, Japan, 18–21 August 2009; pp. 5008–5013.
45. Jinchuan, K.; Xinzhe, L. Empirical analysis of optimal hidden neurons in neural network modeling for stock prediction. In Proceedings of the Pacific-Asia Workshop on Computational Intelligence and Industrial Application, Wuhan, China, 19–20 December 2008; pp. 828–832.
46. Xu, S.; Chen, L. A novel approach for determining the optimal number of hidden layer neurons for FNN's and its application in data mining. In Proceedings of the 5th International Conference on Information Technology and Applications, Cairns, Australia, 23–26 June 2008; pp. 683–686.

energies

MDPI

Article

The Implementation of Multiple Linear Regression for Swimming Pool Facilities: Case Study at Jøa, Norway

Ole Øiene Smedegård [1,2,3,*], Thomas Jonsson [1], Bjørn Aas [3], Jørn Stene [2], Laurent Georges [4] and Salvatore Carlucci [5]

1 Department of Civil and Environmental Engineering, NTNU Norwegian University of Science and Technology, 7491 Trondheim, Norway; thomas.jonsson@ntnu.no
2 COWI AS, 7436 Trondheim, Norway; jost@cowi.com
3 SIAT NTNU—Centre for Sport Facilities and Technology, Department for Civil and Transport Engineering, NTNU Norwegian University of Science and Technology, 7491 Trondheim, Norway; bjorn.aas@ntnu.no
4 Department of Energy and Process Engineering, NTNU Norwegian University of Science and Technology, 7491 Trondheim, Norway; laurent.georges@ntnu.no
5 Energy, Environment and Water Research Center, The Cyprus Institute, Aglantzia 2121, Cyprus; s.carlucci@cyi.ac.cy
* Correspondence: ole.smedegard@ntnu.no

Abstract: This paper presents a statistical model for predicting the time-averaged total power consumption of an indoor swimming facility. The model can be a powerful tool for continuous supervision of the facility's energy performance that can quickly disclose possible operational disruptions/irregularities and thus minimize annual energy use. Multiple linear regression analysis is used to analyze data collected in a swimming facility in Norway. The resolution of the original training dataset was in 1 min time steps and during the investigation was transposed both by time-averaging the data, and by treating part of the dataset exclusively. The statistically significant independent variables were found to be the outdoor dry-bulb temperature and the relative pool usage factor. The model accurately predicted the power consumption in the validation process, and also succeeded in disclosing all the critical operational disruptions in the validation dataset correctly. The model can therefore be applied as a dynamic energy benchmark for fault detection in swimming facilities. The final energy prediction model is relatively simple and can be deployed either in a spreadsheet or in the building automation reporting system, thus the method can contribute instantly to keep the operation of any swimming facility within the optimal individual energy performance range.

Keywords: swimming facilities; energy prediction; fault detection; multiple linear regression analysis

Citation: Smedegård, O.Ø., Jonsson, T.; Aas, B.; Stene, J.; Georges, L.; Carlucci, S. The Implementation of Multiple Linear Regression for Swimming Pool Facilities: Case Study at Jøa, Norway. *Energies* **2021**, *14*, 4825. https://doi.org/10.3390/en14164825

Academic Editor: Marcin Kamiński

Received: 28 June 2021
Accepted: 4 August 2021
Published: 7 August 2021

1. Introduction

1.1. Background

The EU has defined a target for reducing GHG emissions by at least 40% by 2030 compared to 1990 levels [1]. Their long-term goal is defined as "no GHG emissions" by 2050 [2]. Increased energy efficiency in buildings is defined as an important tool for both the short term and long term [3]. One of the "key actions" in the Action Plan related to the 2030 framework is a "renovation wave" of the existing building stock [2].

Within the "renovation wave", the European Commission recommends paying particular attention to energy-reducing refurbishment in types of buildings that support education and public health, such as schools and hospitals [2]. In swimming facilities, which support education and public health, the potential for energy reduction is considerable [4] and the literature associates these facilities with high specific energy use [5] and a large dispersion in energy use. The specific energy use ranges from 400 kWh/(m^2·a) to almost 1600 kWh/(m^2·a) [6–9]. This can be partially explained by the variations in age, technology and the different maintenance routines [7], but the numbers also represent a large energy saving potential [7]. Regarding the building stock of swimming facilities in Norway [6], the overall excessive energy use is estimated to be 28%. This provides a considerable incentive for improvement initiatives.

1.2. Motivation

Since the energy consumption of any building is highly dependent on the operational phase [10], particular attention has to be given to providing optimal operation [11]. Here, both behavioral and operational management are important [12]. It is crucial to emphasize the importance of well-trained and qualified operating personnel [13], especially in buildings with extensive technical installations like swimming facilities [13]. However, this is not always the case [14], and even with skilled operating staff, it is a considerable task to run a facility that has satisfactory performance. In the case of non-skilled operating staff, the performance of the facility is vulnerable if there is improper operation and possible excessive energy use and low indoor environmental quality. The complexity of the operation increases if there are more and more technical components [15]. In addition, during the operation phase, such factors will degrade the building and the technical systems, and the performance of the building will be lower than when it was commissioned [16]. This may lead to a poor indoor environment and increase the energy use. For buildings with extensive technical systems, such as swimming facilities, multiple operational interruptions may conceal other malfunctions and make it difficult for the operating staff to find them. The result is a building with low overall performance compared to the design level. This means that there is a need for strict holistic control and a supervision system for the performance of the building.

Ruparathna et al. [17] proposed a rating system for public buildings based on a level of service (LOS) index. This index is a qualitative measure that is traditionally used to compare the quality of motor vehicle traffic services. When applied to public buildings, the LOS index indicates the level of operational performance provided to building users, society and the environment, based on the assessment of the defined performance indicators in the building. For the operating staff, this kind of rating system can be applied as a useful tool if it is used as a continuous reporting system for the performance of the building. With the implementation of adequate performance indicators, this kind of system will contribute to keeping the technical installations "on track" as a lifetime commissioning system and a tool for fault diagnosis.

For swimming facilities, the number of performance indicators may be considerable and some are impossible to track directly in real time, for example, the level of some airborne disinfection by-products. Ruparathna et al. [17] implemented a set of 22 performance indicators in their case study, including measures like user satisfaction, indoor environmental quality, water quality and energy use, among others. Saleem et al. [18] investigated the choice of performance indicators for aquatic centers in Canada, and proposed a set of 63 indices, including water quality, indoor environmental quality, energy efficiency and user satisfaction.

Energy efficiency is an important aspect in these rating systems and is considered the most important criterion in sustainability rating systems as well as the least achieved [19]. This underlines the importance of a strict system for monitoring the energy performance along with the main functions of the building. Due to the large internal energy flow in swimming facilities, this is even more important because of the increased probability of operational faults and increased energy use.

1.3. Theoretical Background

Continuous assessment of building energy performance is a process of analyzing residuals. Here, the residual is the difference between the monitored energy use and the prediction of the expected energy use of a dynamic benchmarking system. Contrary to "snapshot" rating systems, such as energy labeling of buildings [20] or documentation for fulfilling the passive house standard [21,22], a dynamic benchmarking system depicts the continuous energy performance of the facility.

The prediction of the expected energy use is a complex task which depends on a large set of variables and parameters. The task should preferably be solved in a way which could easily be implemented in existing facilities and control systems. It should also be easy to adapt and be transparent for the operating staff. The importance of easy implementation is related to the increasing climate threat which can also be found in the short-term goal defined as the EU 2030 GHG reduction goal [1].

As they are different from other building types, swimming facilities are characterized by complex energy systems required to maintain appropriate conditions in the swimming hall and pool(s) and provide suitable water quality. Swimming halls are facilities with complex and energy-intensive technical systems [23], with several interacting subsystems. Figure 1 illustrates the extent of the technical systems and how they are connected internally and to external variables. These systems provide functions like fresh air supply, air heating, dehumidification, water heating and water treatment. The thermal and electric power/energy consumption levels of the different systems are logged in the building automation system.

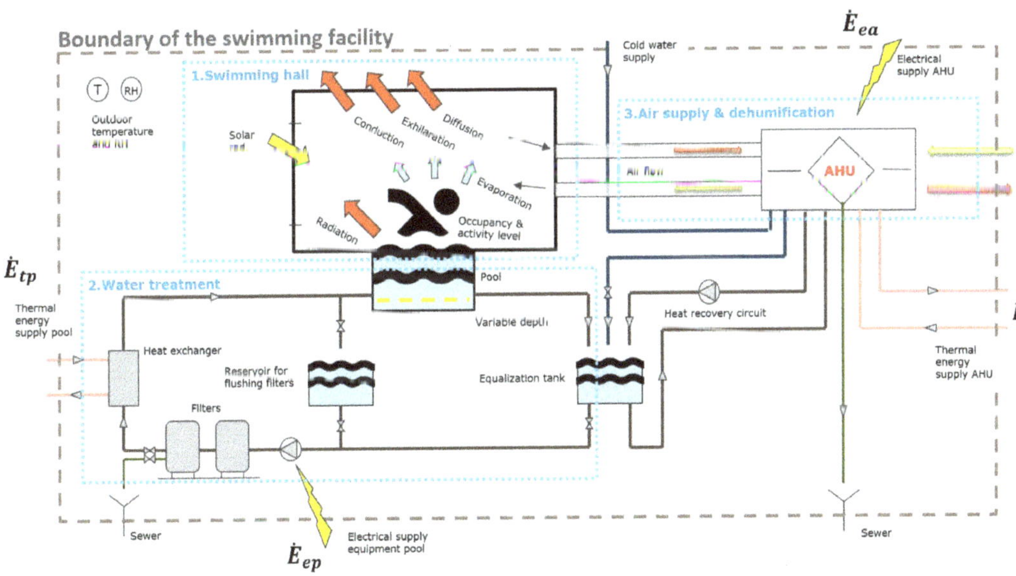

Figure 1. An overview of the extent of the technical systems in a typical swimming pool facility.

The task of predicting the energy use in swimming facilities is complex due to constantly fluctuating variables such as evaporation of water from the pool and surrounding surfaces, the required amount of makeup water and the filter flushing intervals. Energy prediction has been treated in several studies where methods regarding outdoor and indoor swimming facilities have been presented.

1.4. Energy Prediction Methods

The energy prediction methods include physical/engineering methods as well as statistical and artificial intelligence methods [24]. Lu et al. [25] addressed the design and analysis stage and proposed a physical model for a sports facility. Despite the challenge related to the required numbers of parameters, the model performed with a coefficient of correlation (R^2) of 0.934. Westerlund et al. [26] showed that the engineering approach for estimating annual energy use gave satisfactory results in swimming facilities as well.

The results from this study, with a prosaic and simple technical structure, illustrates the importance of heat recovery, where evaporation dominates the energy demand. The same observation was also revealed in the study by Lovell et al. [27] where an engineering model for the prediction of thermal performance for an outdoor Olympic swimming pool in Australia was developed. The model was based on the heat balance and performed with an accuracy of 67% of the predicted heating capacities. This was within a range of ±100 kW, which proved to be the most accurate model compared to other equivalent models. The study confirmed that evaporation dominated the energy demand of an outdoor swimming facility. The same physical and empirical equations are also applied in building performance simulation tools such as TRNSYS [28], ESP-R [29] and IDA ICE [30], among others. Mančić et al. [31] determined the energy losses for a pool hall and pool, and later the optimal configuration of a polygeneration system [32], by modeling the system via physical and empirical equations in TRNSYS. Moreover, Duverge and Rajagopalan [33] investigated the energy and water performance of an aquatic center in Australia. They modeled the facility with the BPS tool EnergyPlus and recommended both solar heating and the use of vacuum filters in their study.

Yuce et al. [34] presented an artificial neural network approach for predicting the energy consumption and thermal comfort in an indoor swimming facility. The prediction was an application for an optimization-based control system for swimming facilities. Kampel et al. [35] proposed a statistical model for predicting the annual energy use of swimming facilities. It was developed through a multiple linear regression (MLR) analysis, and its purpose was to establish a tool for calculating energy performance indicators for the benchmarking of swimming facilities. In addition, the MLR method was also applied in the study by Duverge et al. [36]. One of the outcomes was that the usable floor area and the number of visitors were among the most influential variables for annual energy use.

While the simulation tools based on physical models and artificial neural networks, with different topologies and learning algorithms, can provide useful insights and efficiently predict target values, both frameworks are computationally costly and need case base adaptation. In the context of the practical use and implementation of energy prediction features among existing buildings, MLR has the potential to be in the middle ground with respect to computational cost and the opportunity to adapt it to the different target cases. MLR represents an easy-to-follow statistical method [37] which can explain a dependent variable, using multiple independent variables, but does not require in-depth knowledge of physical processes or training algorithms. It is easy to develop and implement [38] and is widely used in the prediction of energy use. For example, Safa et al. [39] presented a method to predict energy use in office buildings for the purpose of energy auditing. The study showed the capacity of simple models where the final regression model was based on outdoor temperature and occupancy with a monthly resolution. The model performed well with acceptable error, when assessing each of the four buildings in the study individually. Catalina et al. [40] developed a regression model for predicting the monthly space heating demand for residential buildings while another approach developed a generic equation of three variables for predicting the heating demand in apartments blocks [41]. The MLR method has also been applied with success in energy forecasting for swimming pool buildings [38,39].

The objective of this paper is to investigate and propose a method for energy prediction in swimming facilities, based on the MLR method. This approach has considerable potential for reducing the annual energy demand of both existing and new buildings by making the operating staff conscious of the performance of the building in relation to the design level. Buildings are only sustainable if they are operated and maintained properly [15].

2. Method

This study investigates the impact of several independent variables on the energy use of a swimming facility. The analysis has been carried out by applying the multiple linear regression method with the purpose of developing a reliable energy prediction model. Figure 2 illustrates the workflow of the study, where the main topics are identified.

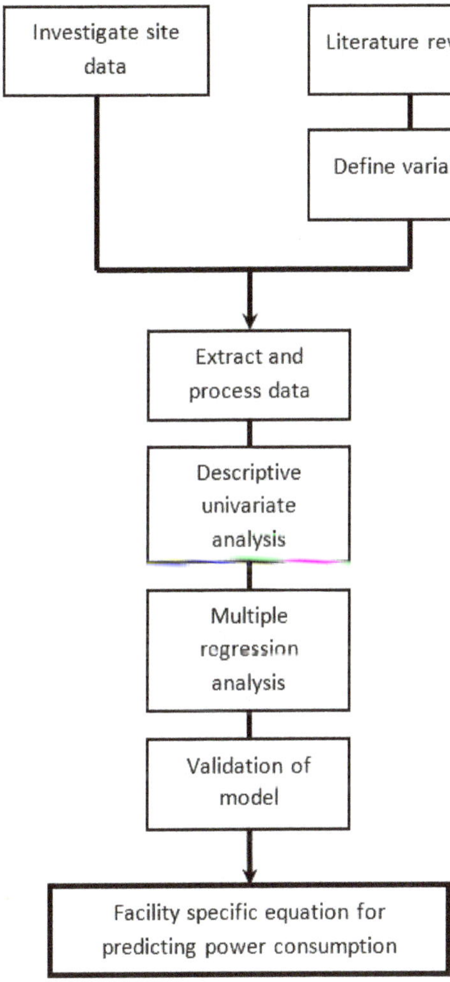

Figure 2. Block diagram representing the workflow of the study.

2.1. The Building

The investigated building is a multi¬purpose sports center located at Jøa, an island in the municipality of Namsos in Norway. It is located at 64.6 N, 11.2 E, 65 m above mean average sea level. It is defined as part of the Marine West Coast climate zone according to the climate zone definition of Köppen and Geiger [42]. The sport center was commissioned in autumn 2016 and contains several facilities besides the swimming pool facility, such as a sports hall, a shooting range, a library, a café, a gym and an outdoor ice rink. Figure 3 shows a photograph of the north-oriented façade for the swimming hall. The swimming hall has a usable area of 266 m² (13.7 m × 9.43 m), including the 8.5 m × 12.5 m swimming pool. Key quantities are presented in Appendix B. This paper investigates only the part of the building with the swimming facilities.

Figure 3. The northern façade of the building.

2.2. The Technical Systems

The swimming facility at Jøa is a state-of-the-art swimming facility which complies with the Norwegian passive house standard [22]. It includes a ventilation heat recovery system equipped with a heat pump, as recommended in the literature [5,43], and conventional water treatment, which research has found to be the most effective water treatment train [44].

2.3. The Dataset

The dataset ranges from November 2017 to June 2019 and is separated into two parts. The training dataset and the validation dataset are, respectively, from November 2017 to June 2018 and September 2018 to June 2019. The size of the datasets was decided based on three main factors: (1) The training dataset should not be too large, due to the purpose of the study; it should be a quick and easy to implement a dynamic energy benchmark for swimming facilities. (2) The validation dataset should be large enough to cover all the seasons and several operation disruptions. (3) It should be preferably based on continuous operation data, without including lockdowns for maintenance.

2.4. The Variables

The objective of the study is to predict the energy use (dependent variable) as a result of several independent variables. The selected independent variables used in this study are listed in Table 1.

The dependent variable was defined by applying the energy conservation Equation (1) at the boundary defining the swimming facility as presented in Figure 1.

$$\frac{dE_{net}}{dt} = \dot{E}_{net} = \dot{E}_{ea} + \dot{E}_{ta} + \dot{E}_{ep} + \dot{E}_{tp} \tag{1}$$

where $\dot{E}_{net}$ is the net delivered energy to the facility, $\dot{E}_{ea}$ is the delivered electricity to the air handling unit, $\dot{E}_{ta}$ is the delivered thermal energy to the air handling unit, $\dot{E}_{ep}$ is the delivered electricity to the pool circuit and $\dot{E}_{tp}$ is the delivered thermal energy to the pool circuit. The units for the variables are given in Table 1.

The independent variables were defined as the meteorological data, ambient air temperature and relative humidity and the usage data. This choice was due to the availability in the respective building and to the known correlation between energy use and outdoor climate [45] and user interference [7,36,45]. In addition, this group of indicators is represented as logged values in conventional building automation systems (BASs). Due to the highly insulated building envelope and the orientation of the façades, the assumption of negligible effects of wind pressure and solar radiation was applied.

The dataset was created by:

1. Extracting historic data from the BAS.
2. Collecting weather data from the national database of the Norwegian Meteorological Institute [46].
3. Digitalizing handwritten occupancy data due to lack of electronic occupancy registration.
4. Calculating new variables based on indirectly monitored data. This is reported for the respective variables in Table 1.

Due to implications within the BAS, extracting data prior November 2017 was not possible. In addition, only a limited part of the variables was logged in June 2018. Table 1 summarizes the variables in the dataset, the units and the origin of the data.

Table 1. The selected variables that have been used in the analysis.

N	Variable	Unit	Type	Source	Comment
$\dot{E}_{ea}$	Electric energy consumption, AHU	$\frac{\text{kWh}}{\text{h}}$	Dependent	BAS	Fans, compressor, pumps and control system
$\dot{E}_{ta}$	Thermal energy consumption, AHU	$\frac{\text{kWh}}{\text{h}}$		BAS	Supplied thermal energy for air heating
$\dot{E}_{ep}$	Electric energy consumption, pool circuit	$\frac{\text{kWh}}{\text{h}}$		BAS	Related to pumps, disinfection, etc.
$\dot{E}_{tp}$	Thermal energy consumption, pool circuit	$\frac{\text{kWh}}{\text{h}}$		BAS	Supplied thermal energy for pool heating
$\dot{E}_{tot}$	Total thermal and electric energy consumption	$\frac{\text{kWh}}{\text{h}}$		Calculated	Summarized load pt. 1–4
T_{out}	Outdoor dry-bulb temperature	°C	Independent	BAS	Measurement from the site
	Moisture content outdoor air	$\frac{\text{g}}{\text{g}}$		Calculated	Meteorological data
	Enthalpy difference indoor/outdoor	$\frac{\text{kJ}}{\text{kg}}$		Calculated	Combining meteorological data and indoor air measurements and by applying the ideal gas law
t_{pu}	Pool usage factor (proportion of time the pool was in use)	-		BAS/ Calculated	Calculated by utilizing water level data in the equalization tank
	Number of adults bathing	adults		Handwritten	Manually digitalized and implemented in the dataset
	Number of children bathing	children		Handwritten	Manually digitalized and implemented in the dataset
Q_w	Water supply flow rate to the pool circuit	$\frac{\text{l}}{\text{s}}$		BAS /Calculated	Calculated by utilizing water level data, flushing reservoir

2.4.1. Cleaning the Dataset

The resolution of the original training dataset was 1 min time steps for all the variables. The dataset was cleaned and preprocessed by detecting and analyzing outliers manually, caused by broken sensors, miscoded values, operation disruption (e.g., unintended operation due to mechanical flaws, software errors or mistakes by the operator), etc. Outlier detection can also be carried out statistically, for example, by using approaches such as standard deviation or the interquartile range [47]. Both techniques identify outliers by comparing each value/measurement to its population. Due to the purpose of this study, outliers are of special interest (fault detection). For the training dataset, operation disruptions were identified and excluded prior to regression analysis, while operation disruption was a part of the validation process.

The process of identifying and categorizing operation disruptions was carried out by an in-depth investigation of the historic data, stored in the BAS and in the dedicated control systems of the air handling unit and heat recovery system.

2.5. *Statistical Methodology*

The choice of the multiple linear regression method was based on its strength as a statistical data handling tool and its simplicity in development, implementation and operation. The latter is crucial if the building owners and the industry are to be able to minimize the energy use, related to undesired operation, over a short period of time. Regarding practical issues, the developers (the engineers) recognize the method in their university education and the operation management can easily evaluate the energy performance in a spreadsheet [41], or it can be easily implemented in any report system, due to its simple algebraic equation.

The dataset was imported and analyzed with IBM SPSS statistical software [48].

2.5.1. Multiple Linear Regression

The MLR method was used to predict the dependent variable y, here the total power consumption, averaged over a certain period. This period was taken to be sufficiently long so that the method only focused on physical effects as processes in the steady state for each time step. The regression equation was trained by the ordinary least square method where the sum of the root square error was minimized. The corresponding regression coefficients, β_0 and β_i, were determined. These comprised the slope coefficient for the independent variables.

$$y_i = \beta_0 + \beta_1 x_1 + \beta_2 x_2 + \ldots + \epsilon \quad (2)$$

where y_i is the dependent variable, β_0 is the intersection with the y-axis when x is zero, β_i is the regression slope coefficient in the linear equation, x_i is the predictor—the independent variable—and ϵ is the error term.

2.5.2. Assumptions

In the development of the model, several assumptions were adopted. The data source was time series data, and, initially, its autoregressive properties or the order of the autoregressive process were not known. These were identified by applying the partial autocorrelation function (PACF), which specifies the number of past lags influencing the dependent variable (i.e., the order of the autoregressive process). The application of the PACF in time series analysis is analogous to deciding the number of independent variables to be included in a multiple linear regression analysis [49]. The dataset was initially investigated for autoregressive properties and reduced by averaging the data and centered in time to eliminate any autoregressive properties in the dependent variable. Each observation in the training dataset was then treated as independent.

2.5.3. Evaluation of the Prediction Model

The "goodness of fit" was evaluated by the coefficient of determination R^2 and the adjusted R^2, which considers the number of explanatory variables and the possibilities of overfitting. R^2 is defined by the relationship between the explained sum of squares and the total sum of squares.

The multiple linear regression equation was validated by analyzing the variance with the F-test. The test operator, F, which is defined by the ratio between the explained sum of squares and the residual sum of squares, was applied to the F-distribution. A significance level of 5% was chosen as the required level.

The coefficients in the equation, the impacts of the independent variables, were evaluated by applying the T-statistic, with the *t*-test, which is similar to the F-test, but which describes the probability of nonlinear correlation by applying the test operator to the T-distribution. The test operator is defined by the relation between the coefficient and its standard error.

The fundamental assumptions for using linear regression were investigated, such as a lack of multicollinearity, no heteroskedasticity, normally distributed residuals and no autocorrelation among the residuals [50], which were fulfilled for each case in the presented analysis. The multicollinearity among the variables was investigated by manually applying the independent variables in a correlation matrix. Potential heteroskedasticity was evaluated visually. The autocorrelation among the residuals was tested with the Durbin–Watson statistic, which assumes a maximum lag of one. The lag of the residuals was investigated by determining the autoregressive process by applying the PACF.

2.5.4. Validation

The prediction model was tested and validated by comparing the prediction and measurement for the whole validation dataset. The criteria for a passed validation process were defined as (1) all the measurements identified as normal operation should be predicted within the prediction interval defined in the training process and (2) all of the operation disruptions should be clearly identified by the validation process.

3. Results and Discussion

3.1. Description—The Training Dataset

The dataset used for training the regression analysis comprises approximately 350,000 observations. Figure 4 shows the collected data for the dependent variable and the total electric and thermal power consumption, plotted together with the outdoor dry-bulb temperature. The average power consumption for the whole dataset is approximately 16 kW and energy supply for the period is 93,000 kWh. The daily average energy use ranges from approximately 190 kWh to nearly 900 kWh, with a corresponding daily average power consumption ranging from approximately 7.9 kW to 37 kW. The registered average diurnal dry-bulb temperature ranges from −11 °C to 20 °C. During this period, nearly 2000 swimmers used the facility, equally divided between adults and youngsters/children.

Figure 4 reveals a seasonal trend, a minor dependency between the energy use and the outdoor temperature, with some spikes in energy use distributed over the period. By visual inspection, it seems that the outdoor temperature variable can explain some of the variations in energy use, but additional variables influenced the variation in daily total energy usage.

3.1.1. The Energy Performance of the Facility

Regarding the energy performance, the swimming facility at Jøa was identified as having an energy performance indicator (EPI) of 44.8 kWh/visitor, calculated over the period of the investigated dataset presented in Figure 4. In comparison, Norwegian swimming facilities are associated with an average EPI for a typical year of approximately 26 kWh/visitor,and a median EPI of approximately 22 kWh/visitor, where the dispersion is reported to range from 10 to 80 kWh/visitor [51]. The EPI has been recommended by Kampel [7] who found that visitors are the single variable that explains most of the variation in the energy performance of swimming facilities [35]. The poor EPI-value of the swimming facility at Jøa can be explained by the low user intensity, on average only 235 visitor/month, compared to Kampel's dataset representing a median annual user intensity of 94,261 visitors (average of 7855 visitors per month). Additionally, the outdoor climate can explain this performance indicator since the data are not climate corrected.

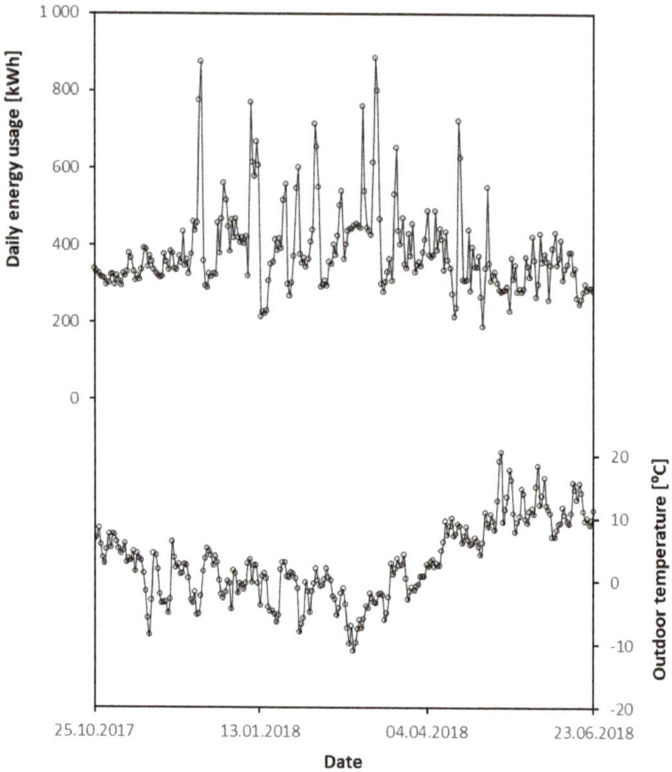

Figure 4. Energy usage for operation of the swimming facility vs. the outdoor temperature, both daily averaged.

3.1.2. Energy Distribution

The delivered energy to the swimming facility is almost evenly divided between electricity and thermal energy. Figure 5 depicts the energy distribution of the building section with the swimming pool. The low thermal energy consumption for the air handling unit (AHU) in comparison with the thermal load of the pool circuit has two major causes. The low overall user intensity for the period of collected data implies that the system operates in air recycling mode (night mode) without fresh air supply for a long period of time, which reduces the air dehumidification and heating demands considerably. Another reason is the operation of the heat recovery system which recovers the latent heat in the exhaust air and supplies heat to the facility, where the order of priority is air heating and pool heating. The building automation system neither collects data regarding the performance of the subsystems nor the thermal efficiency of the heat recovery system.

3.1.3. Time Step Analysis

When treating time series data of energy use in buildings with linear regression, the inertia of the building must be considered due to this impact on the autoregressive process of the variables. This is because the energy use (the dependent variable) is logged with a short time step (1 min). For the swimming pool at Jøa, this impact is partly illustrated using a duration curve depicted in Figure 6, where the data are sorted by decreasing power consumption. The range of outdoor temperatures associated with each step of power demand is wide and can be partly explained by inertia of the building. A short time step resolution will not give any significant correlation, since the process depicted is not steady state. The impact of the time lag can be minimized by averaging the dataset, and thereby reducing the time step resolution (see Section 2.5.2).

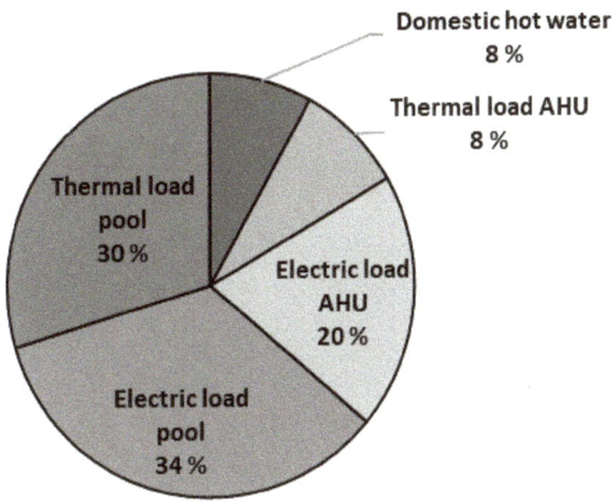

Figure 5. Energy distribution for the swimming facility incl. the energy use for domestic hot water heating.

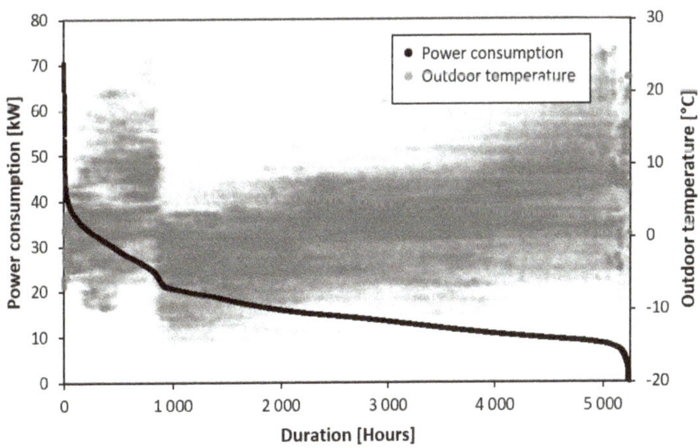

Figure 6. Scatter plot—sorted power consumption presented as a duration curve along with the corresponding outdoor temperature.

Figure 7 illustrates the consequences of averaging the dataset and reducing the time step resolution. The figure presents the dataset with time steps ranging from 1 min to 4 weeks. Both the power consumption and outdoor temperature are presented as time-averaged values centered in time. Firstly, the figure gives an indication of two possible different states in the operation of the facility, represented as a pattern of a divided dataset (clouds of datapoints), for time-step resolution from 1 min up to 60 min. The same can be observed in Figure 6, which represents a pattern of two different duration curves overlapping. Secondly, without considering the significance of the simple linear regressions, a considerable increase in the coefficient of determination, the R^2, is observed when averaging the dataset. This implies that the time step should be maximized in order to obtain the best fitting model if prediction is the main purpose. Concerning the purpose of this study, the time step should correspond to the swimming facility operating staff's requirement to identify and handle possible operational disturbances during a reasonable period of time.

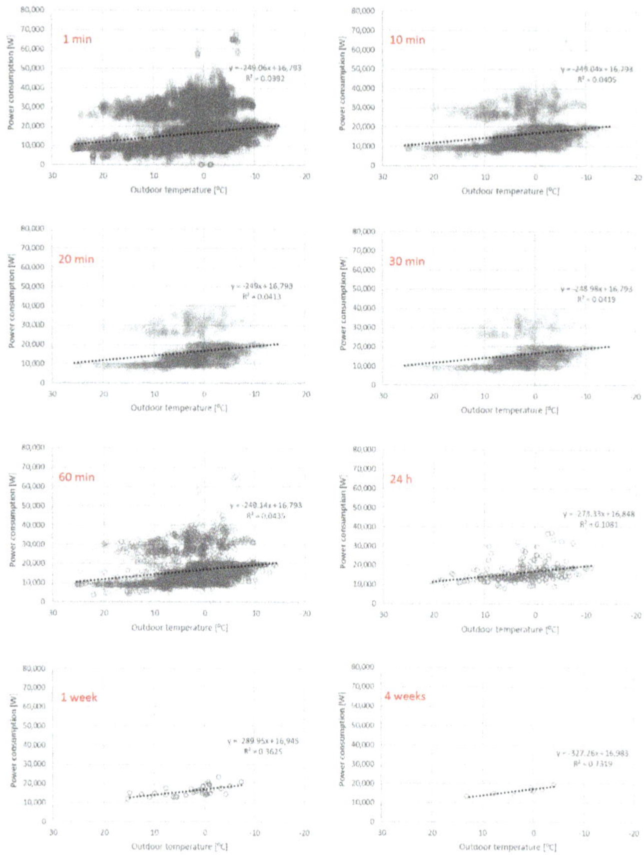

Figure 7. Averaged total power consumption plotted against averaged diurnal outdoor dry-bulb temperature when the dataset is averaged from 1 min to 4 weeks.

3.2. Statistical Analysis—Developing the Model

Since the training dataset consists of operation data from the first period after the building was commissioned, several irregularities may occur. By detecting and excluding observations associated with irregular operation events, the training dataset is optimized to only represent flawless operation. A predictive model trained by this dataset should be able to provide accurate predictions.

By investigating historical operating data from both the BAS and the internal control system of the air handling unit, a major change in operation was found. The consequence of this is illustrated in Figure 8, which depicts the thermal load for the pool heating system, where a change in operation is identified in late March 2018. The reason for the considerable change was issues related to the control of the integrated dehumidification system and the pool temperature, possibly a problem with a mixing valve. However, since this flaw in the operation has implications for both the pool temperature and the heat recovery system, the whole period from 25 October 2017–22 March 2018 must be excluded from the training dataset.

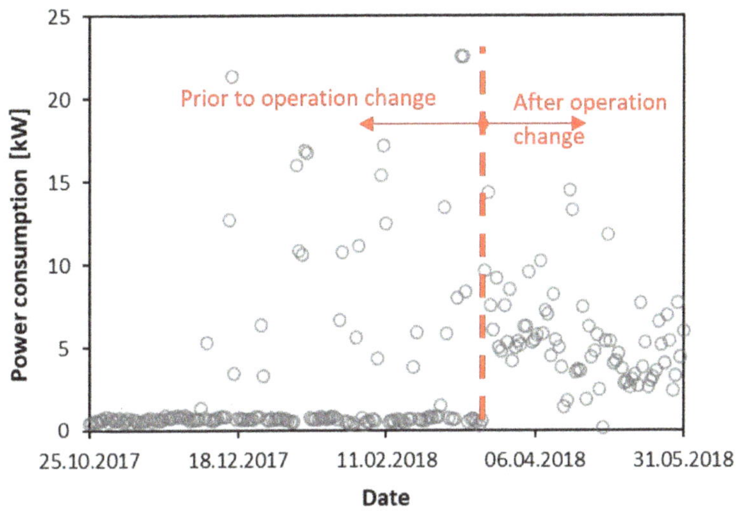

Figure 8. Thermal load for the pool circuit, plotted against the timeline, in averaged 1-day time step resolution.

3.2.1. New Training Dataset

By excluding the period associated with operational irregularities, prior to 22 March 2018, the prediction model was developed. The new training dataset, ranging from 22 March to 24 June 2018, consisted of three-day averaged values, for a total of 29 datapoints. The analysis of the autoregressive properties of the dataset showed no autocorrelation when averaging data for 72 h, or 3 days.

The results of the regression analysis are expressed in Equation (3). The key output from the regression analysis is given in Table 2. Regarding possible problems with overfitting, 15 datapoints per predictor are recommended [52] to obtain reliable fitted regression, which means a maximum of two predictors for a dataset of this size. The two independent variables which are found to explain most of the variance are the outdoor dry-bulb temperature (T_{out}) and the pool usage factor (t_{pu}) (see description of variables in Table 1). This combination has a statistical effect on the energy use, with almost similar impact, and both were identified by a significance level $p < 5\%$. The chosen combination of variables is in accordance with the physics, where the outdoor temperature represents the thermal losses through the envelope and ventilation, and the pool usage represents the water usage and the operation mode of the facility. The number of swimmers was not found to have a statistical effect on the overall power consumption, despite the impact of evaporation on the energy use. This may be explained by the phenomenon of evaporation, which is observed as a step function where a few bathers have a significant impact, but a further increase only gives a small additional contribution to evaporation [53]. However, the combination of weather conditions and usage/occupancy is also found to have a statistically significant effect on energy use in office buildings [38], despite the difference between these building categories.

$$\dot{E}_{tot} = 14,715 - 227.8T_{out} + 24,790t_{pu} \quad (3)$$

where $\dot{E}_{tot}$ is the predicted power consumption [Watt], T_{out} is the outdoor temperature [°C] and t_{pu} is the pool usage factor.

Table 2. Key outputs from the regression analysis.

	Unstandardized Coefficients				
	B	Error	Standardized Coefficients	T	Significance
Constant	14,715	2410.7		16.387	
Outdoor temperature	−227.8	27.2	−0.591	−8.38	0.000
Pool usage	24,790	2607.5	0.671	9.507	0.000

The ability of the model to explain the variance is given by R^2 = 87%. The ability of the prediction model to reproduce the power consumption is illustrated in Figure 9, where the predicted power consumption is plotted along with the training data, the actual power consumption and the corresponding prediction interval. The prediction interval of 95% is the interval where there is 95% confidence of there being an observation within it. It depends on factors like sample size, number of predictors and the significance level. For the range of independent variables given in the training dataset, the mean prediction interval is identified to be ±1.86 kW. Figure 10 shows the linear relationship between the training dataset and the data produced by the prediction model where the Pearson correlation coefficient is 0.93.

Regarding the fundamental assumptions in linear regression, the residuals from the training process, given in Figures 11 and 12, are approximately normally distributed. There are no signs of heteroskedasticity and the residuals are represented with a mean value of approximately 0. The autoregressive process is not found to be on an order higher than 1, but the Durbin–Watson coefficient is approximately 1.4, which possibly indicates some autocorrelation. However, the possible autocorrelation, or the lack of autocorrelation, is not found to be statistically significant. The regression equation is considered to be reliable within the given goodness of fit.

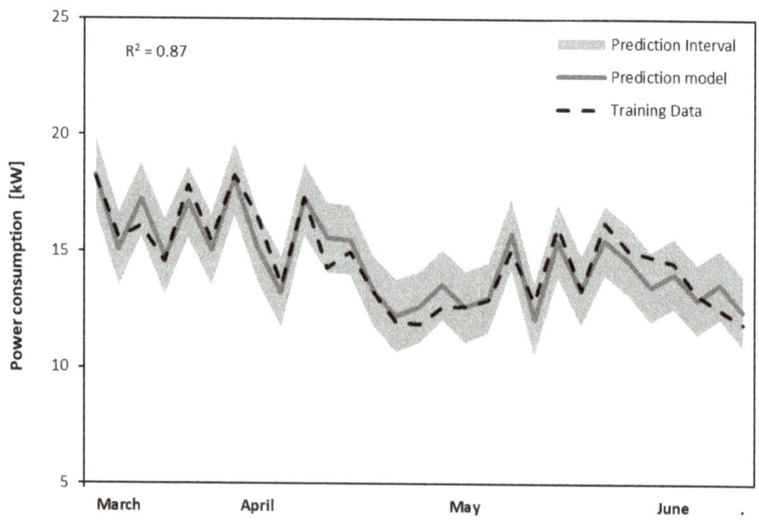

Figure 9. The predicted power consumption plotted against the training data and with the corresponding prediction interval.

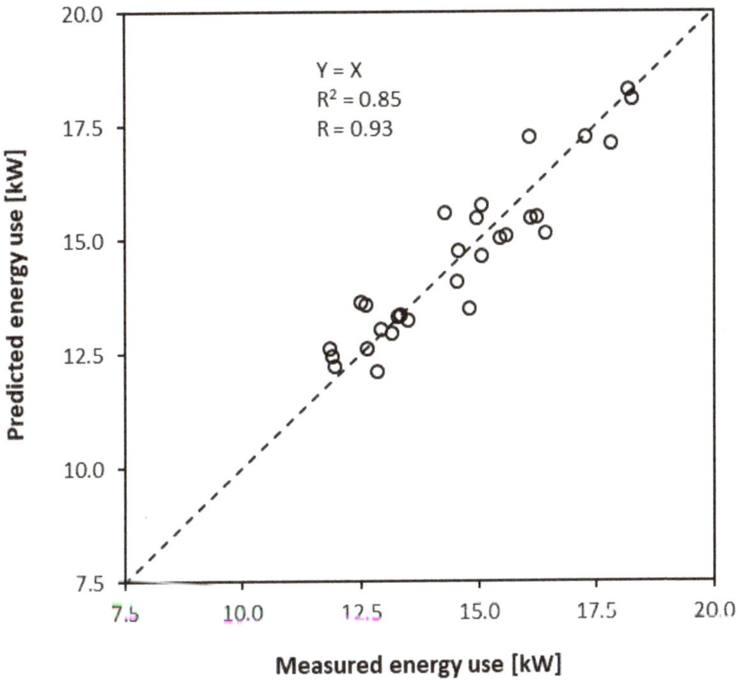

Figure 10. The predicted power consumption plotted against the measured power consumption. The Pearson correlation coefficient is given as the R-coefficient.

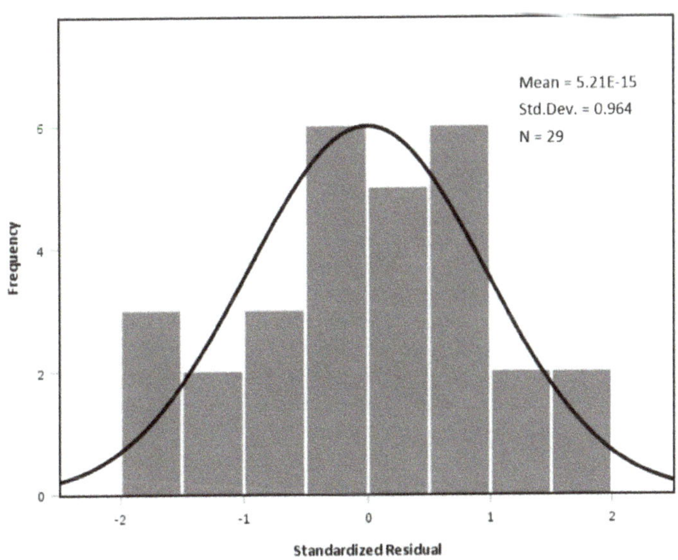

Figure 11. The distribution of the residuals.

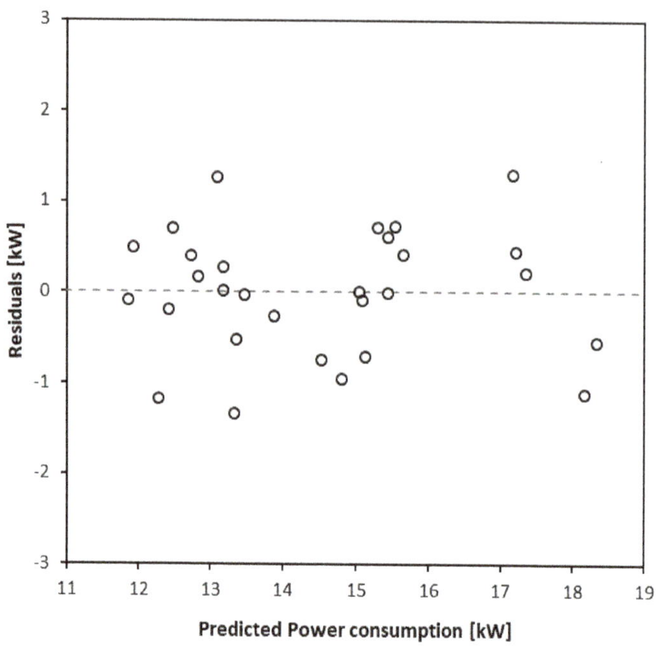

Figure 12. Residuals plotted by power consumption.

3.3. Validation and Application

The validation of the prediction model is illustrated in Figure 13 as a comparison between the predicted and actual data from the validation dataset. The predicted power consumption, including the prediction interval, is the gray shaded area and the measured power consumption is the black line. The numbered red areas are the identified periods with operational disruption, and they include 14 datapoints out of a total of 85 in the validation dataset. The given operation disruptions have been identified as (A) uncontrolled water refill, (B,C) issues with the control system of the water temperature, (D) issues with controlling the indoor environment and water refill system, leading to a consecutive lockdown of the facility and (E) issues related to the control of the air handling unit and the air flow supply. The prediction model identifies all of the disruptions as illustrated. When the facility operates without flaws and faults, the facility performs within the operational baseline provided by the prediction model. Each of the operational disruptions are identified as major deviations from the baseline.

When excluding the data associated with operational disruptions, 14 datapoints in total (approximately 16% of the dataset), the predicted operation fits the actual performance well. Figure 14 illustrates the correlation between the predicted and measured power consumption exclusive of the operation disruptions. The Pearson correlation coefficient is 0.85. However, there are periods where the models seem to consistently over- or underpredict the performance model, and this may have to do with the lack of explanatory variables in the model. However, this deviation is within the prediction interval, which corresponds with no detection of operational disruption for the relevant period. Figures 15 and 16 present the range of the independent variables used in the prediction model. Even though the range of the training dataset was initially significantly reduced to only three months of data (29 datapoints), the dispersion of the variables within this dataset corresponds with the validation dataset.

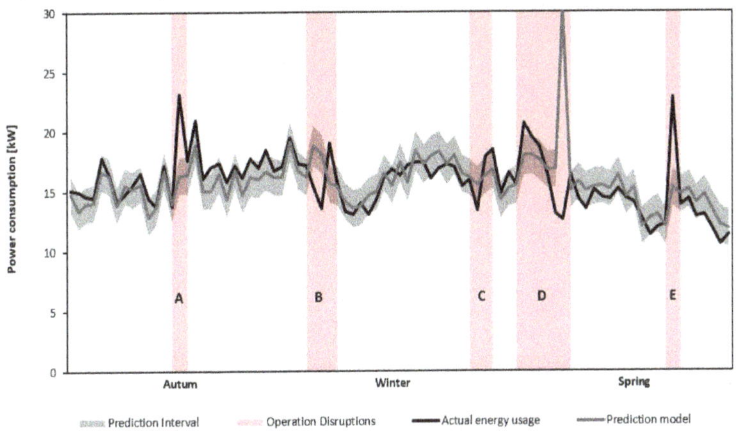

Figure 13. Visual validation of the prediction model from September 2018 to June 2019. The prediction model includes the prediction interval in gray, measured power consumption in black and periods associated with operational disruptions in red (see Appendix A for higher resolution).

In the perspective of applying the presented method to industry, the combination of a short term training dataset and the few predictors makes this method especially useful. This means that a facility can develop a model over a short period of time, with a minimum of sensors. However, the transferability with regard to the choice of independent variables must be further investigated in order to obtain a universal method for industry.

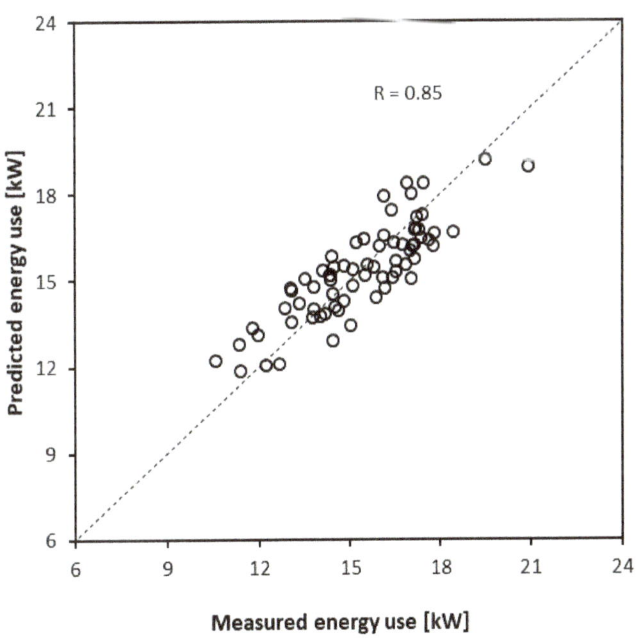

Figure 14. The predicted power consumption plotted against the measured power consumption for the validation dataset. The Pearson correlation coefficient is given as the R-coefficient.

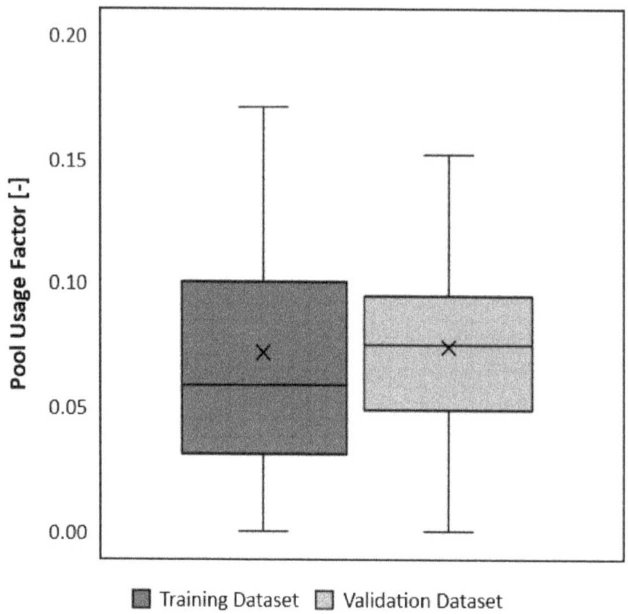

Figure 15. The dispersion of the independent variables in the prediction model, for each dataset used in the analysis.

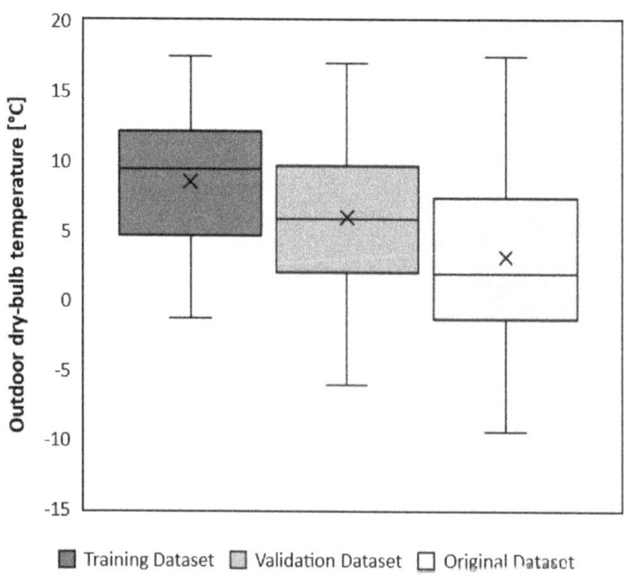

Figure 16. The dispersion of the independent variables in the prediction model, for each dataset used in the analysis.

4. Discussion and Opportunities for Deployment of the Created Model

Due to the importance of focusing on the operating phase when minimizing the environmental impact [10,54], and because operational irregularities are common in buildings [55], an implemented operational tool may have great potential for industry. For swimming facilities, this is especially important since inappropriate operation may also cause problems such as degradation of equipment and the occurrence of the sick building syndrome [56]. When applying the presented method to industry, the combination of a short-term training dataset and a few predictors makes this method especially useful. It means that a facility can develop a personalized model in short period of time with a minimum of sensors. In addition, the final energy prediction model is simple and can be deployed either in a spreadsheet or in the building automation reporting system. This method can therefore contribute instantly to keep the operation of a swimming facility within the optimal and expected individual energy performance range, which is fundamental for achieving the energy target for any building [57]. The MLR method, which is applied in this study, has formerly been recognized for predicting energy use in buildings [39] and has also been applied to determine the parameters of thermal equations for outdoor swimming pools [58]. With respect to the specific case of Jøa, the operational staff have to download the energy usage, the outdoor temperature and the pool usage. The deviation between the prediction and the measured energy use will give the operational staff an alarm if there is a potential flaw in the operation and enable them to detect the fault within a short period of time. However, the transferability with respect to the choice of independent variables must be further investigated in order to obtain a universal method for industry. Additionally, guidelines with respect to the implementation of the model should be provided.

5. Conclusions

This paper presents a model for predicting energy consumption in swimming facilities. The energy prediction model aims to become a dynamic energy benchmark for fault detection in swimming facilities. The investigation has been carried out by using multiple linear regression analysis (MLR) for a specific swimming facility located in Norway. The MLR method has formerly been recognized in predicting energy use in buildings but has also been applied to determine the parameters of thermal equations for outdoor swimming pools. The main findings of this study are:

- The study has shown that it is possible to develop an accurate energy prediction model for swimming facilities with a minimum of variables and datapoints.
- The results from the analysis of the training dataset underlined the importance of investigating the training data prior to training of the model. The original dataset was based on raw data from 7 months of operation after the building was commissioned and approved by the building owner. The modified and preferred dataset was reduced after an in-depth investigation that revealed comprehensive operational disruptions. The final training dataset consisted of only 29 datapoints of 3-day averaged data ranging over a period of 3 months, March to June 2018.
- The statistically significant independent variables were found to be the outdoor dry-bulb temperature and the pool usage factor, which predicted the average power consumption accurately in the validation process. In the validation period from September 2018 to June 2019, the equation correctly identified all the critical operational disruptions.
- The model has been shown to be a suitable tool for helping operating staff in continuous evaluation of the energy performance of a facility and quickly disclosing possible operational disruptions. By identifying possible operational irregularities at an early stage, excessive energy use in operation can be avoided. Operational irregularities occur in a high percentage of new buildings. The importance of focusing on the operating phase and the overall energy consumption is crucial when minimizing the environmental impact. In addition, the knowledge of the energy performance of buildings is fundamental in achieving the energy targets. For swimming facilities,

inappropriate operation of technical installations may also cause problems such as degradation of equipment and the occurrence of sick building syndrome.

- This study only investigated one specific facility and future work should address the robustness of the model and transferability to other swimming facilities.

This study illustrates the strength of multiple regression analysis when applied as a dynamic and continuous energy benchmark. By applying simple input variables, an estimate of the expected power consumption, within an acceptable error range, can be made that reveals potential operational disruptions. The energy prediction model is simple and can be easily implemented in the automation system of a building. The prediction model does not require an operator with an engineering background and may serve as first-line supervision for the use of a dynamic energy benchmark for a facility. By applying this method in existing swimming facilities, the overall energy use may be greatly reduced as it provides the building management with improved knowledge about the energy performance of the building.

Author Contributions: Conceptualization, O.Ø.S.; methodology, O.Ø.S. and T.J.; software, O.Ø.S.; validation, O.Ø.S.; formal analysis, O.Ø.S.; investigation, O.Ø.S.; data curation, O.Ø.S.; writing—original draft preparation, O.Ø.S.; writing—review and editing, O.Ø.S., T.J., B.A., J.S., L.G. and S.C.; visualization, O.Ø.S.; supervision, T.J., B.A., L.G. and S.C.; project administration, O.Ø.S. and J.S. All authors have read and agreed to the published version of the manuscript.

Funding: The project is funded by COWI AS, the Research Council of Norway and COWIFonden.

Institutional Review Board Statement: Not applicable.

Informed Consent Statement: Not applicable.

Data Availability Statement: This data collection campaign was performed within the framework of a PhD study by COWI AS and NTNU SIAT. All the data are privately stored and will not be disclosed until the end of the study.

Acknowledgments: This work is a part of a doctoral project entitled "Optimizing Energy and Climate Systems in Buildings with Swimming Facilities", which is carried out as a cooperation project between the Centre for Sport Facilities and Technology at the Norwegian University of Science and Technology in Trondheim, Norway, and the engineering company COWI AS.

Conflicts of Interest: The authors declare no conflict of interest.

Appendix A

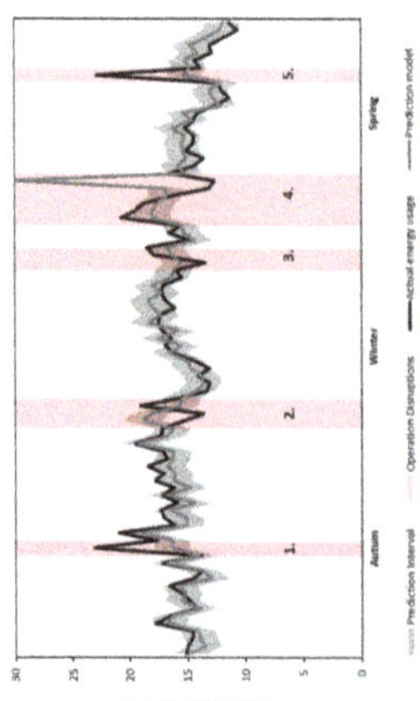

Figure A1. Visual validation of the prediction model from September 2018 to June 2019. The prediction model includes the prediction interval in gray, measured power consumption in black and periods associated with operational disruptions in red.

Appendix B

Subject	Quantity
Window surface area	30 m^2
Water surface	12.5 m × 8.5 m
Useable area	266 m^2
Nominal air flow, air handling unit	11,000 m^3/h
Nominal thermal power, air condenser	26 kW
Nominal thermal power, pool water condenser	34 kW
Nominal water flow circulation pool circuit	60 m^3/h
Rating condition pool circuit	300 visitors/day
Nominal power pool heater	70 kW

References

1. Progress Made in Cutting Emissions. 2020. Available online: https://ec.europa.eu/clima/policies/strategies/progress_en (accessed on 15 April 2021).
2. The European Green Deal. Available online: https://eur-lex.europa.eu/resource.html?uri=cellar:b828d165-1c22-11ea-8c1f-01aa75ed71a1.0002.02/DOC_1&format=PDF (accessed on 21 August 2021).
3. Energy Roadmap. 2050. Available online: https://eur-lex.europa.eu/LexUriServ/LexUriServ.do?uri=COM:2011:0885:FIN:EN:PDF (accessed on 21 August 2021).
4. Ratajczak, K.; Szczechowiak, E. Energy consumption decreasing strategy for indoor swimming pools Decentralized Ventilation system with a heat pump. *Energy Build.* **2020**, *206*, 109574. [CrossRef]
5. Ratajczak, K.; Szczechowiak, E. The Use of a Heat Pump in a Ventilation Unit as an Economical and Ecological Source of Heat for the Ventilation System of an Indoor Swimming Pool Facility. *Energies* **2020**, *13*, 6695. [CrossRef]
6. Kampel, W.; Aas, B.; Bruland, A. Energy-use in Norwegian swimming halls. *Energy Build.* **2013**, *59*, 181–186. [CrossRef]
7. Kampel, W. Energy Efficiency in Swimming Facilities. 2015. Available online: https://ntnuopen.ntnu.no/ntnu-xmlui/handle/11250/2366793 (accessed on 20 November 2020).
8. Røkenes, H. Betraktninger Rundt Svømmehallers Energieffektivitet. Master's Thesis, Norwegian University of Science and Technology, Trondheim. 2011.
9. Swim England. The Use of Energy in Swimming Pools. 2016. Available online: https://www.swimming.org/library/documents/1187/download (accessed on 24 March 2021).
10. Rincón, L.; Castell, A.; Pérez, G.; Solé, C.; Boer, D.; Cabeza, L.F. Evaluation of the environmental impact of experimental buildings with different constructive systems using Material Flow Analysis and Life Cycle Assessment. *Appl. Energy* **2013**, *109*, 544–552. [CrossRef]
11. Catrini, P.; Curto, D.; Franzitta, V.; Cardona, F. Improving energy efficiency of commercial buildings by Combined Heat Cooling and Power plants. *Sustain. Cities Soc.* **2020**, *60*, 102157. [CrossRef]
12. GlobalABC/IEA/UNEP (Global Alliance for Buildings and Construction, International Energy Agency, and the United Nations Environment Programme). *GlobalABC Roadmap for Buildings and Construction: Towards a Zero-Emission, Efficient and Resilient Buildings and Construction Sector*; IEA: Paris, France, 2020.
13. ASHRAE. *Applications Handbook. American Society of Heating, Refrigerating and Air-Conditioning Engineers*; ASHRAE: Atlanta, GA, USA, 2015.
14. Smedegård, O.; Aas, B.; Stene, J.; Georges, L.; Carlucci, S. A Systematic and Data-Driven Literature Review on the Energy and Environmental Performance of Swimming Facilities. Unpublished work, 2021.
15. Djuric, N. Real-Time Supervision of Building HVAC System Performance. 2008. Available online: https://ntnuopen.ntnu.no/ntnu-xmlui/handle/11250/231184 (accessed on 24 November 2020).
16. Nord, N.; Novakovic, V.; Frydenlund, F. *Kontinuerlig Funksjonskontroll for Effektiv Drift av Bygninger*; SINTEF: Oslo, Norway, 2012.
17. Ruparathna, R.; Hewage, K.; Sadiq, R. Developing a level of service (LOS) index for operational management of public buildings. *Sustain. Cities Soc.* **2017**, *34*, 159–173. [CrossRef]
18. Saleem, S.; Haider, H.; Hu, G.; Hewage, K.; Sadiq, R. Performance indicators for aquatic centres in Canada: Identification and selection using fuzzy based methods. *Sci. Total Environ.* **2021**, *751*, 141619. [CrossRef]
19. Berardi, U. Sustainability assessment in the construction sector: Rating systems and rated buildings. *Sustain. Dev.* **2012**, *20*, 411–424. [CrossRef]

20. The Norwegian Ministry of Petroleum and Energy. Energy Labelling Regulations for Buildings. 2010. Available online: https://lovdata.no/dokument/SF/forskrift/2009-12-18-1665 (accessed on 25 November 2020).
21. NS 3700. Criteria for Passive Houses and Low Energy Houses: Residential Buildings (Original: Kriterier for Passivhus og Lavenergihus: Boligbyginger). 2013. Available online: https://www.standard.no/no/nettbutikk/produktkatalogen/Produktpresentasjon/?ProductID=636902 (accessed on 15 November 2020).
22. NS 3701. Criteria for Passive Houses and Low Energy Buildings-Non-Residential Buildings. 2012. Available online: https://www.standard.no/no/Nettbutikk/produktkatalogen/Produktpresentasjon/?ProductID=587802 (accessed on 15 November 2020).
23. Duverge, J.J.; Rajagopalan, P.; Fuller, R. Defining aquatic centres for energy and water benchmarking purposes. *Sustain. Cities Soc.* **2017**, *31*, 51–61. [CrossRef]
24. Zhao, H.X.; Magoulès, F. A review on the prediction of building energy consumption. *Renew. Sustain. Energy Rev.* **2012**, *16*, 3586–3592. [CrossRef]
25. Lu, T.; Lü, X.; Viljanen, M. A new method for modeling energy performance in buildings. *Energy Procedia* **2015**, *75*, 1825–1831. [CrossRef]
26. Westerlund, L.; Dahl, J.; Johansson, L. A theoretical investigation of the heat demand for public baths. *Energy* **1996**, *21*, 731–737. [CrossRef]
27. Lovell, D.; Rickerby, T.; Vandereydt, B.; Do, L.; Wang, X.; Srinivasan, K.; Chua, H. Thermal performance prediction of outdoor swimming pools. *Build. Environ.* **2019**, *160*, 106167. [CrossRef]
28. Klein, S.; Beckman, W.; Mitchell, J.; Duffie, J.; Duffie, N.; Freeman, T.; Braun, J.; Evans, B. *TRNSYS 18. A TRaNsient SYstem Simulation Program*; Standard Component Library 515 Overview; Solar Energy Laboratory, University of Wisconsin-Madison: Madison, WI, USA, 2017; Volume 3, p. 516.
29. Energy Systems Research Unit (ESRU). The ESP-r System for Building Energy Simulation: User Guide Version 10 Series. Available online: www.esru.strath.ac.uk/Documents/ESP-r_userguide.pdf (accessed on 15 April 2021).
30. EQUA Simulation AB. Building Performance—Simulation Software EQUA 2020. Available online: www.equa.se (accessed on 15 April 2021).
31. Mančić, M.V.; Živković, D.S.; Milosavljević, P.M.; Todorović, M.N. Mathematical modelling and simulation of the thermal performance of a solar heated indoor swimming pool. *Therm. Sci.* **2014**, *18*, 999–1010. [CrossRef]
32. Mančić, M.V.; Živković, D.S.; Đorđević, M.L.; Jovanović, M.S.; Rajić, M.N.; Mitrović, D.M. Techno-economic optimization of configuration and capacity of a polygeneration system for the energy demands of a public swimming pool building. *Therm. Sci.* **2018**, *22*, 1535–1549. [CrossRef]
33. Duverge, J.J.; Rajagopalan, P. Assessment of factors influencing the energy and water performance of aquatic centres. *Build. Simul.* **2020**, *13*, 771–786. [CrossRef]
34. Yuce, B.; Li, H.; Rezgui, Y.; Petri, I.; Jayan, B.; Yang, C. Utilizing artificial neural network to predict energy consumption and thermal comfort level: An indoor swimming pool case study. *Energy Build.* **2014**, *80*, 45–56. [CrossRef]
35. Kampel, W.; Carlucci, S.; Aas, B.; Bruland, A. A proposal of energy performance indicators for a reliable benchmark of swimming facilities. *Energy Build.* **2016**, *129*, 186–198. [CrossRef]
36. Duverge, J.J.; Rajagopalan, P.; Fuller, R.; Woo, J. Energy and water benchmarks for aquatic centres in Victoria, Australia. *Energy Build.* **2018**, *177*, 246–256. [CrossRef]
37. Gassar, A.A.A.; Cha, S.H. Energy prediction techniques for large-scale buildings towards a sustainable built environment: A review. *Energy Build.* **2020**, *224*, 110238. [CrossRef]
38. Safa, M.; Safa, M.; Allen, J.; Shahi, A.; Haas, C.T. Improving sustainable office building operation by using historical data and linear models to predict energy usage. *Sustain. Cities Soc.* **2017**, *29*, 107–117. [CrossRef]
39. Safa, M.; Allen, J.; Safa, M. Predicting energy usage using historical data and linear models. In Proceedings of the International Symposium on Automation and Robotics in Construction, Sydney, Australia, 9–11 July 2014 ; IAARC Publications: Sydney, Australia, 2014; Volume 31, p. 1.
40. Catalina, T.; Virgone, J.; Blanco, E. Development and validation of regression models to predict monthly heating demand for residential buildings. *Energy Build.* **2008**, *40*, 1825–1832. [CrossRef]
41. Catalina, T.; Iordache, V.; Caracaleanu, B. Multiple regression model for fast prediction of the heating energy demand. *Energy Build.* **2013**, *57*, 302–312. [CrossRef]
42. Köppen, W.; Geiger, R. *Handbuch der Klimatologie*; Gebrüder Bornträger: Berlin, Germany, 1930.
43. Johansson, L.; Westerlund, L. Energy savings in indoor swimming-pools: Comparison between different heat-recovery systems. *Appl. Energy* **2001**, *70*, 281–303. [CrossRef]
44. Skibinski, B.; Uhlig, S.; Müller, P.; Slavik, I.; Uhl, W. Impact of different combinations of water treatment processes on the concentration of disinfection byproducts and their precursors in swimming pool water. *Environ. Sci. Technol.* **2019**, *53*, 8115–8126. [CrossRef]
45. Novakovic, V.; Hanssen, S.; Thue, J.; Wangensteen, I.; Gjerstad, F. Enøk i bygninger-Effektiv energibruk. *Oslo Gyldendal Undervis.* **2007**, *63* , 327–361.
46. Meteorologisk Institutt. eKlima 2018. Available online: www.eklima.no (accessed on 15 April 2021).
47. Henley, A.; Wolf, D. *Learn Data Analysis with Python*; Lessons in Coding; Apress: New York, NY, USA, 2018.
48. IBM Corp Ibm Statistics. *Statistics for Windows, Version 25.0*; IBM Corp.: Armonk, NY, USA, 2017.

49. Box, G.; Jenkins, G.; Reinsel, G.; Ljung, G. *Time Series Analysis, Control, and Forecasting*; John Wiley & Son: Hoboken, NJ, USA, 2015.
50. Eikemo, T.A.; Clausen, T.H. *Kvantitativ Analyse med SPSS: En Praktisk Innføring i Kvantitative Analyseteknikker*; Tapir Akademisk Forlag: Trondheim, Norway; 2012.
51. NTNU Senter for Idrettsanlegg og Teknologi. Kunnskapsportalen for Idretts- og Nærmiljøanlegg Trondheim. 2020. Available online: https://www.godeidrettsanlegg.no/nyhet/energibruk-i-norske-svommehaller (accessed on 15 April 2021).
52. Harrell, F.E., Jr. *Regression Modeling Strategies: With Applications to Linear Models, Logistic and Ordinal Regression, and Survival Analysis*; Springer: New York, NY, USA, 2015.
53. Hanssen, S.O.; Mathisen, H.M. Evaporation from swimming pools. In Proceedings of the Roomvent '90, Oslo, Norway, 13–15 June 1990.
54. Cornaro, C.; Buratti, C. Energy efficiency in buildings and innovative materials for building construction. *Appl. Sci.* **2020**, *10*, 2866. [CrossRef]
55. Wu, L.; Kaiser, G.; Solomon, D.; Winter, R.; Boulanger, A.; Anderson, R. Improving efficiency and reliability of building systems using machine learning and automated online evaluation. In Proceedings of the 2012 IEEE Long Island Systems, Applications and Technology Conference (LISAT), Farmingdale, NY, USA, 4 May 2012; pp. 1–6.
56. Pietkun-Greber, I.; Suszanowicz, D. The consequences of the inappropriate use of ventilation systems operating in indoor swimming pool conditions-analysis. In Proceedings of the E3S Web of Conferences, EDP Sciences, Krakow, 7–8 June 2018; Volume 45, p. 00064.
57. Ciulla, G.; D'Amico, A. Building energy performance forecasting: A multiple linear regression approach. *Appl. Energy* **2019**, *253*, 113500. [CrossRef]
58. Bataineh, K.M. Transient Analytical Model of a Solar-Assisted Indoor Swimming Pool Heating System. *J. Energy Eng.* **2015**, *141*, 04014048. [CrossRef]

energies

MDPI

Article

Modeling Pollutant Emissions: Influence of Two Heat and Power Plants on Urban Air Quality

Robert Cichowicz * and Maciej Dobrzański

Faculty of Architecture, Civil and Environmental Engineering, Lodz University of Technology, Al. Politechniki 6, 90-924 Lodz, Poland; maciej.dobrzanski@p.lodz.pl
* Correspondence: robert.cichowicz@p.lodz.pl

Abstract: Large industrial plants, power plants, and combined heat and power plants are popularly believed to be the main sources of point emissions, affecting both local and global air quality. This is because these installations emit significant amounts of pollutants at high altitudes every year. In this study, we investigate the impact of two solid fuel (hard coal)-fired CHP plants located within the urban agglomeration on the air quality of the city of Lodz in Poland (Europe). We used an OPA03 computer software to model the spatial distribution of pollutants. The results show that the annual average concentrations of pollutants were highest at an altitude of 25 m above ground level and decreased at lower measurement heights. The concentrations did not exceed permissible levels, reaching only 4% of national and international regulatory limits. We also made field measurements during the winter heating period, using an unmanned aerial vehicle (UAV) equipped with sensors to map the distributions of dust and gas pollutants in the areas with the highest concentrations of emissions from the two heat and power plants. Overall, the field measurements confirmed that it is not high-altitude emissions that have the greatest impact on local air quality.

Keywords: air quality monitoring; SO_2; NO_2; NO_X; PM_{10}; $PM_{2.5}$; outdoor air quality; air flow aerodynamics; air quality modeling

Citation: Cichowicz, R.; Dobrzański, M. Modeling Pollutant Emissions: Influence of Two Heat and Power Plants on Urban Air Quality. *Energies* **2021**, *14*, 5218. https://doi.org/10.3390/en14175218

Academic Editor: Angel A. Juan

Received: 5 August 2021
Accepted: 17 August 2021
Published: 24 August 2021

1. Introduction

Air pollution is caused by the emission of gaseous, liquid, and solid substances in amounts that cause environmental damage, adversely affecting flora and fauna, water, soil, and human health [1]. The main air pollutants include nitrogen compounds (NO, NO_2), carbon compounds (CO, CO_2), sulfur dioxide (SO_2), heavy metals (mercury, nickel, lead, arsenic, cadmium), hydrocarbons, and their derivatives, as well as particulate matter pollutants PM_{10}, $PM_{2.5}$, and $PM_{1.0}$. Particulate matter pollutants have a negative impact on human health, both directly, by penetrating the body causing allergies and lung diseases, and indirectly, by acting as a carrier for heavy metals, microorganisms, and bacteria [2–4]. Therefore, it is important both to monitor the concentrations of pollutants in the air and to effectively control the amounts of pollutants emitted. Unfortunately, the regulations of the European Union set permissible dust concentrations only for the PM_{10} and $PM_{2.5}$ fractions [5]. The permissible level of PM_{10} is 50 $\mu g/m^3$ for the daily average and 40 $\mu g/m^3$ for the annual average. For $PM_{2.5}$, the maximum limit is 25 $\mu g/m^3$ (annual average). According to WHO recommendations from 2005 [6], the average annual concentration of PM_{10} should not exceed 20 $\mu g/m^3$, with a daily average of 50 $\mu g/m^3$, whereas for $PM_{2.5}$, the annual average concentration should not exceed 10 $\mu g/m^3$ with a daily average of 25 $\mu g/m^3$. No limits have been set for the $PM_{1.0}$ fraction, although it is increasingly considered the most dangerous type of PM.

Particulate matter is not the only dangerous type of air pollution, however. Gaseous pollutants such as SO_2, which is highly toxic with a suffocating odor, also pose a problem. Sulfur dioxide has a high specific gravity and relative density, which causes it to slowly spread through the atmosphere. It arises mainly as a result of burning solid and liquid fuels contaminated with sulfur (e.g., hard coal, crude oil) in combustion engines, power plants, and combined heat and power plants [7,8]. The amount of SO_2 introduced into the environment largely depends on the quality of the fuel used. Sulfur compounds contribute to acidification of the environment, which leads to the formation of acid rain, lower soil fertility, inhibition of plant growth, and plant death [9]. Sulphur dioxide pollution is "seasonal", in the sense that higher concentrations are observed during the winter/heating seasons, while in summer/vegetation seasons, there are lower concentrations of SO_2. According to a European Union Directive 2008/50/EC [5], the permissible average daily concentration of SO_2 is 125 $\mu g/m^3$, and the permissible average hourly concentration is 350 $\mu g/m^3$. These levels are the acceptable values for the protection of human health. The WHO [6] sets a much lower limit of 20 $\mu g/m^3$ for the daily average. Unfortunately, the WHO guidelines do not provide a limit value for the annual average of SO_2.

Nitrogen compounds NO_x (NO, NO_2) are another significant threat. These compounds are formed during the combustion of fuels at high temperatures, which leads to the oxidation of nitrogen contained in the fuels and in the atmosphere. The main sources of NO_2 are road transport (so-called "linear emissions") [10–12] and energy and heating systems ("point emissions") [13]. The most dangerous nitrogen compounds are odorless and colorless nitrogen oxides and brown-colored suffocating NO_2. Nitrogen oxides could contribute to photochemical smog and high ozone levels. However, more and more scientific works indicate to the contrary that nitrogen oxides can lead to ozone depletion in the air [14]. Nitrogen dioxide emissions are mainly caused by heavy traffic (linear emissions), as well as by heating systems and the energy sector (point emissions) [12]. The environmental damage caused by NO_x includes eutrophication, which is associated with the degradation of terrestrial and aquatic ecosystems [15]. Nitrous oxides also contribute to the formation of tropospheric ozone [16] and acidification of the environment [17]. According to European standards, the daily average NO_2 limit is 130 $\mu g/m^3$ (these levels are the limit values for the protection of human health) [5]. According to WHO guidelines [6], the permissible average annual NO_2 concentration is 40 $\mu g/m^3$, and the hourly average is 200 $\mu g/m^3$.

The basic method for determining the state of air quality is to measure pollutant concentrations. Stationary ground stations monitor pollutant concentrations in manual daily and automatic continuous systems [18–20]. However, the small number of such stations and the distance between them mean that the data they collect can only be used to evaluate the state of air quality on a global or national scale. It is not possible to assess the impact of individual emitters on the state of local air quality [21,22]. Local analyses are influenced by a number of important factors, such as wind direction and strength, meteorological conditions, topography, and roughness of the terrain [23–25]. To take into account all of these variables in the analysis, it would be necessary to have a complex network of numerous measuring stations located around the area. This is a very time-consuming and costly solution, so computer programs are used to simulate the concentrations and spread of pollutants based on detailed emitter data. Examples of such software include Aero 2010, Emitor, OPA03 [26], AERMOD [27], ENVI-met, and Austal 2000 [28].

Local analysis should also take into account the division of pollutant emissions into so-called "low" and "high" emissions. Low emissions are from pollution sources up to a height of about 40 m from ground level, i.e., from "line emitters" such as communication routes [29], "point emitters" such as the flue gas systems used in small industrial plants and individual households, and "surface emitters" such as densely built-up and inhabited residential quarters with individual heating systems [30]. "High emissions" are mainly produced by large industrial plants, power plants, and combined heat and power plants [31–33].

Here, we analyze an area of the city of Lodz (in the center of Poland, in Central Europe). The main sources of "high" and "point" emissions in Lodz are two coal-fired CHP plants. Despite technological progress and the introduction of substitutes in the form of biomass, hard coal is still the main raw material used to generate energy, with several hundred megagrams being burned each year. As a result, facilities such as combined heat and power plants are popularly considered to be the main emitters of air pollutants. In this study, we set out to determine whether the CHP plants are in fact the largest emitter of pollutants and the extent of their impact on the local environment.

2. Analyzed Objects

We analyzed emissions from the two main combined heat and power plants in the city of Lodz (Figure 1). Lodz is the third largest city in Poland (Central Europe) in terms of the number of inhabitants (area: 293.2 km^2; population density: 2292.2 people/km^2; population: 672,185). In the north-west part of the city, there is a combined heat and power plant designated with the number EC-3 (Figure 2A). This combustion installation includes five coal-fired steam boilers, including one capable of co-firing 20% biomass with hard coal, one steam boiler fired with light fuel oil, and three water boilers fired with heavy oil. The total thermal power is 804 MW, and the electric power is 205.85 MW. To the north and west of EC-3 there are industrial areas, and to the east and south there are single-family and multi-family residential areas. The gross development index in the area ranges from 0.5 to 1.0.

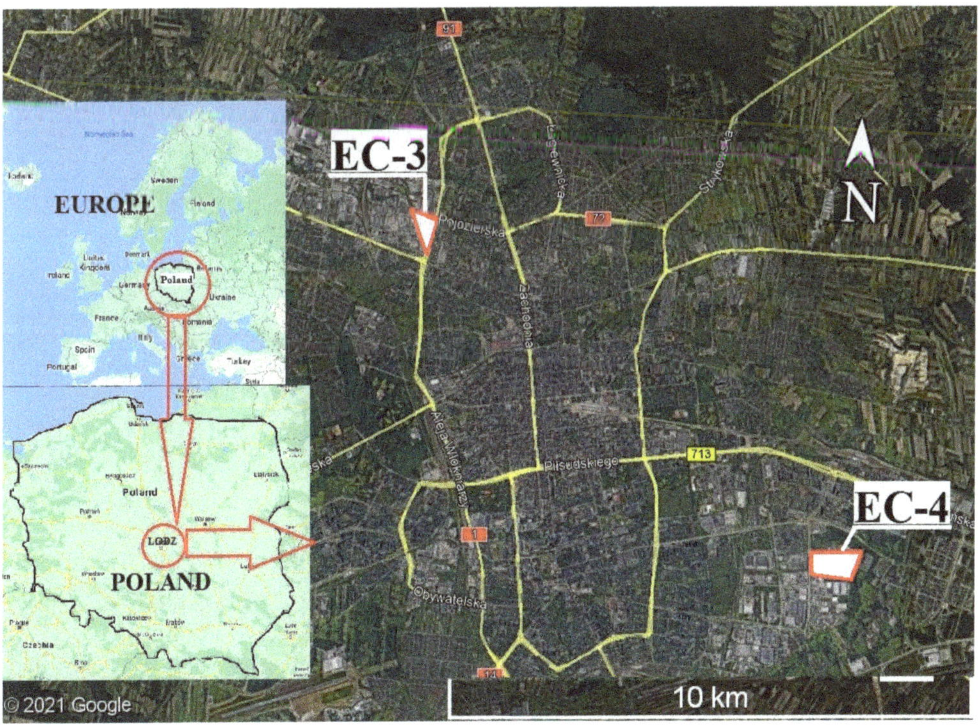

Figure 1. Location of the EC-3 and EC-4 CHP plants in the city of Lodz in Poland, Europe (photo background source: Google Earth Pro).

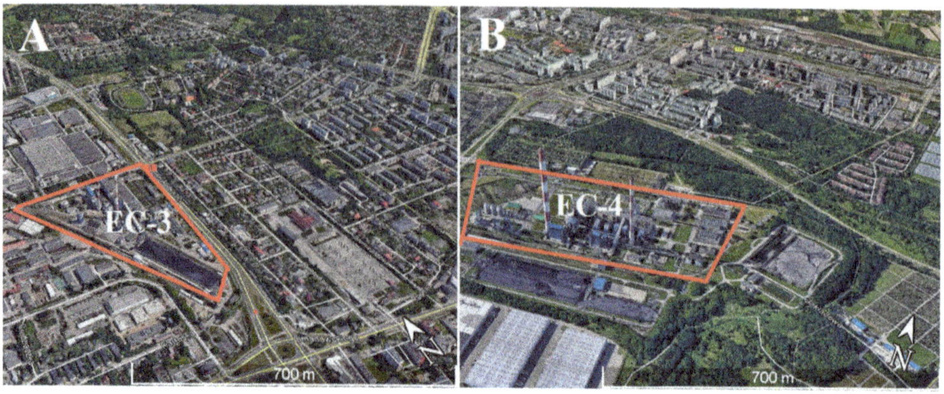

Figure 2. Location and immediate surroundings of the heat and power plant EC-3 (**A**) and EC-4 (**B**) (photo background source: Google Earth Pro).

The second facility is the EC-4 CHP plant in the east of the city (Figure 2B). The EC-4 fuel combustion installation includes two coal-fired steam boilers, one biomass-fired steam boiler, one light fuel oil-fired steam boiler, and three coal-fired water boilers. The total thermal power of EC-4 is 820 MW, and its electric power output is 198 MW. In the immediate vicinity of EC-4 is an industrial and storage district. However, to the north and north-west nearby, there are single-family housing and collective housing areas. Towards the south, there are industrial areas, and towards the east and north-east, there are recreational and leisure areas with high greenery in the form of trees. The gross development index in this area ranges from 0.5 to 1.0. Significant sources of pollution in close proximity to both heat and power plants include busy roads leading to housing estates and out of the city. These line sources contribute to increasing the level of pollution in the area.

3. Methodology

The year 2019 was selected for analysis because it was the most recent before the COVID-19 pandemic, and so, there were no possible changes in pollutant emissions resulting from health restrictions. Detailed, real input data were provided for scientific purposes by Veolia Energia Łódź. OPA03 (Eko-Soft) [34] computer software was used to calculate the concentration of pollutants in the atmospheric air and their spatial dispersion. The program also includes the MAPS module, which is used for graphical interpretation of the results. The OPA03 system can analyze up to 900 point, surface, line, and equivalent emitters. The software enables calculation of boundary dust and gaseous emissions, with the diameter and height of the emitters as variables. The calculations were based on the legal regulation in force in Poland and the European Union [5,35], assuming "limit values" for selected substances in the air, "conditions" for which the reference values are determined (such as pressure and temperature), "periods" for which average reference values are provided, "conditions" for which reference values are considered acceptable, and reference values or "methods of modeling" levels of substances in the air. As part of the analysis, two dust pollutants PM_{10} and $PM_{2.5}$ and two gaseous pollutants sulfur dioxide (SO_2) and nitrogen dioxide (NO_2) were selected. Due to the legal acts in force in Poland based on the regulations of the European Union [5,35], the background of pollutants for emitters higher than 100 m is not determined. In the analyzed cases, the background pollution was not taken into account, due to the fact that all chimneys/emitters are higher than 100 m (for the EC-3 CHP plant the height of the chimney is 120 m, and for the EC-4 CHP plant, the chimneys are 200 m and 250 m high). Pollution from the H120 stack was analyzed for the EC-3. However, for the EC-4 CHP plant, the basic configuration is the H250 chimney and the H200 chimney, to which five boilers are connected.

Data from the "wind rose" for the year 2019 (Figure 3) were entered into the program. In the city of Lodz in 2019, the prevailing winds were from the west (13%), north-west (14%), and south-west (11%), while northerly and southerly winds (about 4%) were much less frequent, and easterly winds were the least frequent (2%). The year 2019 can be considered typical in terms of these meteorological parameters.

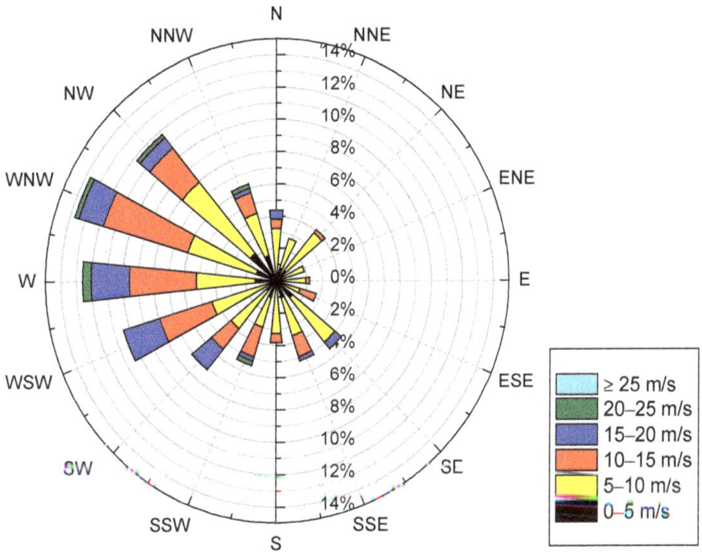

Figure 3. Wind rose for the city of Lodz in 2019 (own study based on data from source: [36]).

To obtain more accurate calculation data, 2019 was divided into three sub-periods: the "summer" period (from April 1 to September 30) and two "winter/heating" periods. In the "1st winter/heating period" (from 1 January to 31 March), the average air temperatures were lower (Table 1) than those in the "2nd winter/heating period" (from 1 October to 31 December). This is a typical phenomenon in the region of Central Europe. As a result, there is greater demand for thermal energy in the period from January to March, which translates into higher pollutant emissions.

Table 1. Average monthly temperatures in 2019 for Lodz (own study based on data from source: [36]).

Month	January	February	March	April	May	June
Temperature [°C]	−1.7	2.6	5.7	10.1	12.4	22.2
Month	**July**	**August**	**September**	**October**	**November**	**December**
Temperature [°C]	18.7	20.2	14.0	10.4	6.2	3.2

Three heights of pollution dispersion were selected for analysis: 1.5, 14, and 25 m. The height of 1.5 m is the minimum measurement height recommended in national regulations based on European Union directives [5,17,35]. The height of 14 m is the height at which anemometers (devices used to measure the speed of movement of gases and liquids) are located. The height of 25 m is the average height of skyscrapers in Lodz.

Field measurements were also made, using an unmanned aerial vehicle (UAV) equipped with mobile measuring equipment [37,38]. The measuring equipment included a laser-scattered (LS) sensor to measure PM_{10}, $PM_{2.5}$, and $PM_{1.0}$ (10,000 particles per second) and electrochemical (EC)-type sensors to measure H_2S (3 ppb–1 ppm), O_2 (0.20–100%), and SO_2 (0.5–2000 ppm). Measurements were made at the heights of 1.5, 14, 25, 30, and 50 m, in those places where the numerical analysis had predicted the highest concentrations of emissions from the two power stations. The field measurements were compared to the results of the numerical analysis.

4. Results and Discussion

The total emissions of pollutants in 2019 were calculated based on measurement data provided by the network heat supplier, Veolia Energia Łódź (Table 2). Despite the comparable power of the two heat and power plants, "EC-4" emitted higher total emissions of pollutants than "EC-3". This was probably caused by the higher fuel consumption of the EC-4 CHP plant, due to the greater demand for power in this area of the city of Lodz.

Table 2. Emission of pollutants from EC-3 and EC-4 in 2019 (own calculations based on data from Veolia Energia Łódź).

	EC-3 CHP Plant			
Emitor:	**Emission [kg]**			
	PM_{10}	**$PM_{2.5}$**	**SO_2**	**NO_2**
H120-K1, K2, K3, K6, K9	11,080.37	4748.73	578,788.3	583,515.8
	EC-4 CHP Plant			
H250-K7	10,645.88	4562.52	228,952.5	300,471.9
H200-K2	4783.52	2050.08	135,430.6	151,654.8
H200-K3	3286.64	1408.56	72,609.9	171,419.2
H200-K4, K5	1267.21	543.09	46,013.7	29,063.1
H200-K6	808.78	346.62	26,176.0	14,290.0

Based on the data in Table 2 and the operating time of individual boilers, the maximum hourly emissions of pollutants (Table 3) from the EC-3 and EC-4 CHP plants in 2019 and the average hourly emissions (Table 4) for selected sub-periods were also calculated. The highest average hourly emissions (kg/h) and maximum hourly emissions occurred in the "1st winter and heating period". Most likely, this was associated with the low atmospheric temperatures (Table 1) and the need to generate more thermal power for residential properties. In the coldest periods, all CHP boilers work to cover the demand for heating. The atmospheric temperatures in the "2nd winter/heating period" were on average 3.9 °C higher, and there was, therefore, a lower demand for thermal energy.

Table 3. Maximum hourly emissions of pollutants for EC-3 and EC-4 CHP plants in 2019 (own calculations based on data from Veolia Energia Łódź).

	EC-3 CHP Plant			
Emitor	**Maximum Hourly Emission [kg/h]**			
H120	PM_{10}	$PM_{2.5}$	SO_2	NO_2
	2.667	1.143	128.81	144.20
	EC-4 CHP Plant			
	PM_{10}	$PM_{2.5}$	SO_2	NO_2
H250-K7	4.760	2.040	103.40	79.30
H200-K2	3.430	1.470	189.90	48.96
H200-K3	0.896	0.384	24.12	34.49
H200-K4, K5	6.286	2.694	122.83	86.70
H200-K6	8.085	3.465	285.95	145.7

Table 4. Average hourly emissions of pollutants for the EC-3 and EC-4 CHP plants, divided into sub-periods (own calculations based on data from Veolia Energia Łódź).

Emitor:	Period:	Average Hour Emission [kg/h]			
		PM_{10}	**$PM_{2.5}$**	**SO_2**	**NO_2**
EC-3 CHP Plant					
H120-K1, K2, K3, K6, K9	Summer period	0.91	0.39	34.65	34.80
	I Winter-heating period	2.317	0.993	113.38	124.37
	II Winter-heating period	1.316	0.564	96.46	87.61
EC-4 CHP Plant					
H250-K7	Summer period	2.31	0.99	45.63	63.50
	I Winter-heating period	2.611	1.119	50.16	62.37
	II Winter-heating period	1.806	0.774	48.14	65.41
H200-K2	Summer period	0.896	0.384	21.27	30.49
	I Winter-heating period	1.302	0.558	26.78	36.6
	II Winter-heating period	0.945	0.405	55.96	37.11
H200-K3	Summer period	0.434	0.186	9.59	21.17
	I Winter-heating period	0.42	0.18	11.44	28.87
	II Winter-heating period	0.553	0.237	10.33	24.88
H200-K4, K5	Summer period	0.931	0.399	38.37	23.31
	I Winter-heating period	2.324	0.996	73.62	45.56
	II Winter-heating period	1.323	0.567	54.85	36.18
H200-K6	Summer period	1.204	0.516	69.36	57.6
	I Winter-heating period	3.206	1.374	87.05	45.3
	II Winter-heating period	1.491	0.639	91.09	54.41

The lowest average hourly emissions (kg/h) occurred in the "summer period", when, due to the higher atmospheric temperatures, the combined heat and power plants needed to generate only enough energy to provide domestic hot water to premises connected to the heating network and to cover demand for electricity and, therefore, burned less fuel. On the other hand, the highest average hourly emissions (kg/h) occurred in the "I winter-heating period", when, due to the lower atmospheric temperatures (Table 1), the combined heat and power plants needed to generate the greatest amount of energy. The permissible emissions of pollutants were not exceeded in any of the sub-periods, thanks to the high quality standards for exhaust gasses maintained by environmental protection devices, such as electrostatic precipitators and flue gas desulphurization installations.

In the next stage of the analysis, we simulated the environmental impact of the CHP plants. The value of the load of imitated pollutants was converted into the concentration of the pollutants in the air. The average annual and maximum hourly concentrations were taken into account for three heights: 1.5 m, 14 m, and 25 m. We also analyzed the spatial dispersion of the selected pollutants in the vicinity of the two CHP plants.

As can be seen from Figures 4 and 5, the EC-4 CHP plant was associated with the highest calculated average annual concentrations of pollutants in the air. This is consistent with the higher emission (kg) of pollutants from EC-4 compared to EC-3. Calculations made using OPA03 software for the EC-4 CHP plant show that the highest calculated annual average concentrations for PM_{10} was still very low, amounting to only about 0.04% of the reference value of 40 $\mu g/m^3$ stipulated in Directive 2008/50/EC [5]. Similar conclusions apply to the annual average concentrations of $PM_{2.5}$, which were also about 0.03% of the reference value of 25 $\mu g/m^3$. Much higher concentrations were calculated for gaseous pollutants than for dust pollutants. The average annual concentration of SO_2 was 4.24% of the reference value of 20 μg/m^3 [6]. The highest average annual concentration of nitrogen compounds, including both NO_2 and NO converted to NO_2, amounted to 1.73% of the reference value (40 μg/m^3). Detailed calculations made using OPA03 software for EC-3 show that the highest of the annual concentrations for PM_{10} and $PM_{2.5}$ were only 0.02 and 0.01% of the permissible values, respectively. As in the case of EC-4, lower concentrations than the permissible values were recorded for gaseous pollutants in EC-3. The average annual concentration of SO_2 reached 2.46% of the limit value and, for NO_2, amounted to 1.17% of the limit value. Generally, the concentrations of pollutants increased at higher altitudes (1.5 m, 14 m, and 25 m). The highest concentrations were recorded primarily at the height of 25 m.

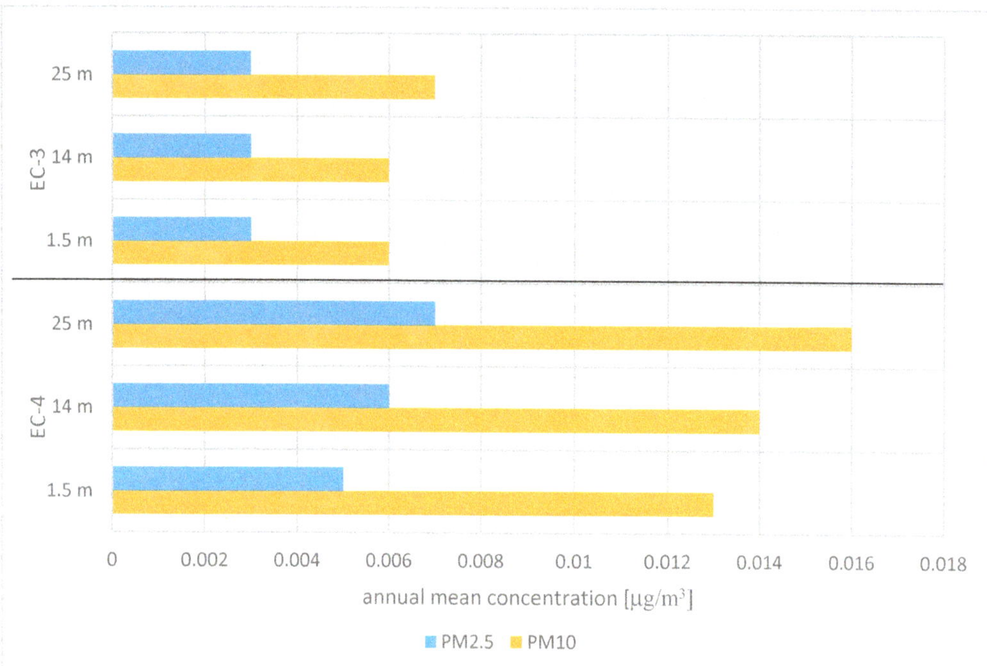

Figure 4. The highest annual average concentration of particulate matter pollutants at the height of 1.5, 14, and 25 m for the EC-3 and EC-4 CHP plants based on the results from OPA03.

Overall, the average annual concentrations of the analyzed pollutants amounted to a maximum of 4% of the relevant permissible values. This is probably due to the flue gas cleaning systems used in both CHP plants, which reduce the emission of pollutants into the atmosphere. Another important parameter in the analysis of the impact of the CHP plant on air quality is the maximum 1 h concentration (Figure 6). In general, the changes in the concentrations of gaseous pollutants that occurred at increasing heights were negligible. In the case of the EC-4 plant, the maximum 1 h concentration of SO_2 was approximately 114.5 μg/m^3, which is approximately 33% of the reference value of 350 μg/m^3. For NO_2, the concentration was about 89.5 μg/m^3, i.e., about 45% of the reference value of 200 μg/m^3. In the case of the EC-3 plant, the values for SO_2 were around 31 μg/m^3, which is about 9% of the reference value (350 μg/m^3). For NO_2, the hourly concentration was about 31.5 μg/m^3, which is about 16% of the reference value (200 μg/m^3).

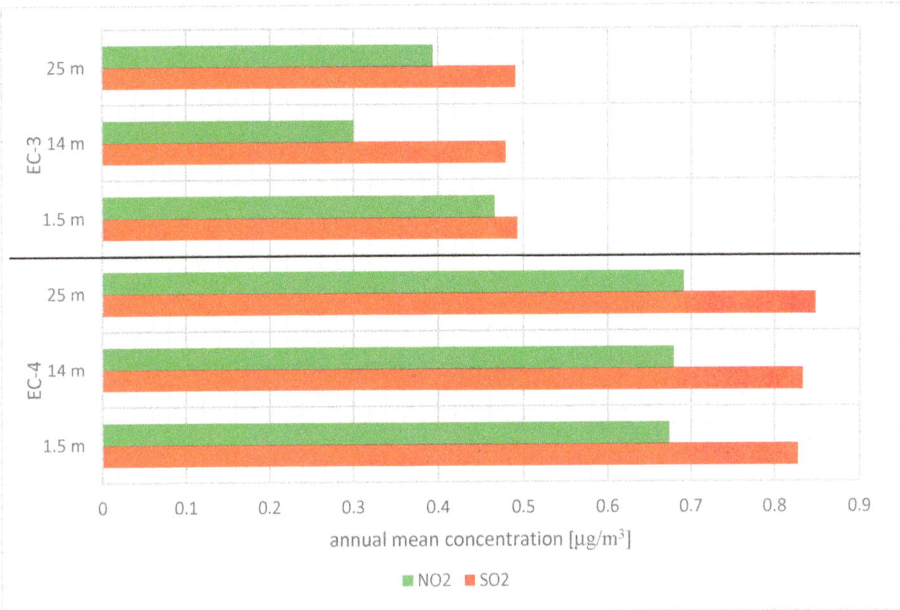

Figure 5. The highest annual average concentration of gaseous pollutants at the height of 1.5, 14, and 25 m for the EC-3 and EC-4 CHP plants based on the results from OPA03.

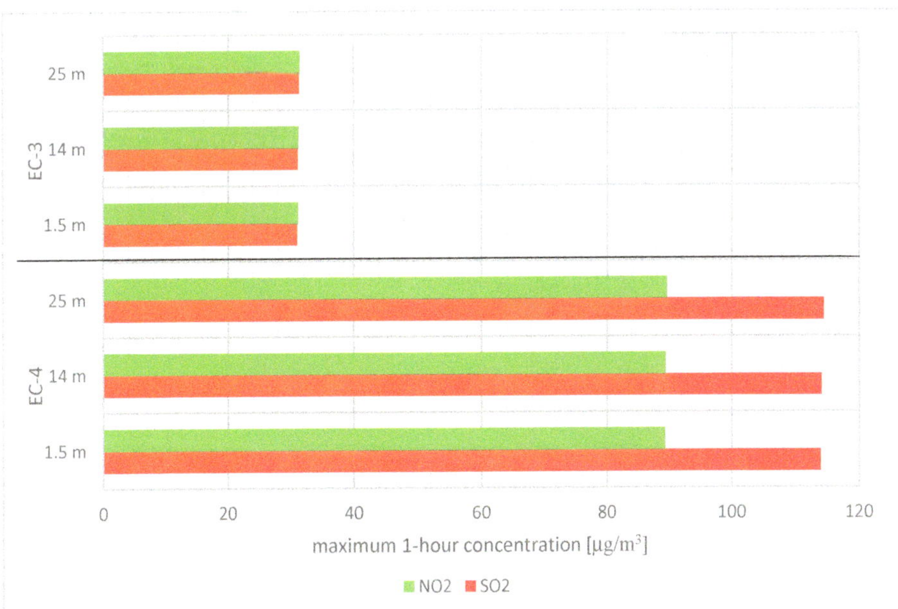

Figure 6. The highest hourly concentration of gaseous pollutants at the height of 1.5 m, 14 m, and 25 m for the EC-3 and EC-4 CHP plants based on the results from OPA03.

To analyze more fully the impact of the heat and power plant on the surroundings, we made dispersion maps. The black points on the maps show the location of the EC-3 and

EC-4 CHP plants and the administrative borders of the city of Lodz. Figure 7 shows the dispersions of SO_2 from the EC-4 plant at heights of 1.5 m, 14 m, and 25 m.

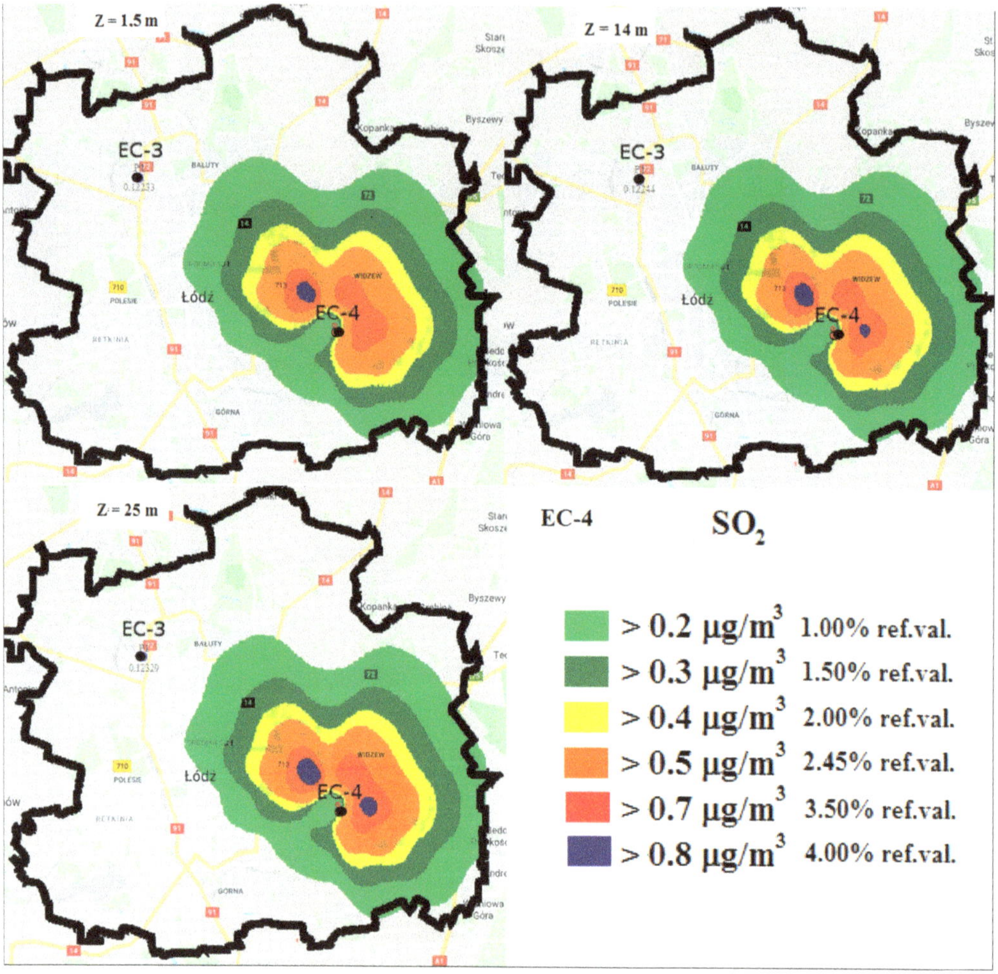

Figure 7. Distribution of annual average SO_2 concentrations of 1.5 m, 14 m, and 25 m surrounded by EC-4 in 2019 based on the results from OPA03.

The values range from 0.2 µg/m^3 to 0.8 µg/m^3, which is between 1% and 4% of the reference value. The area with SO_2 concentrations of 0.8 µg/m^3 doubled as the measurement height increased from 1.5 m to 25 m (Figure 7). The SO_2 pollution from EC-4 spread in accordance with the wind rose shown in Figure 3. The pollution spread mainly towards the north, north-east, and east, i.e., following the prevalent winds for Lodz in 2019. Concentrations of SO_2 above 0.2 µg/m^3 covered about 35% of the area of the city of Lodz.

Figure 8 shows the dispersions of SO_2 pollutants from EC-3 at heights of 1.5, 14, and 25 m. The average annual concentrations range from 0.2 to 0.5 µg/m^3. The area with a concentration of SO_2 equal to or greater than 0.5 µg/m^3 doubled as the measurement height increased from 1.5 m to 14 m. However, at a height of 25 m, it tripled relative to the concentration at 1.5 m. The dispersion of pollutants again coincided with the established wind rose. The impact of pollutants from EC-3 was negligible, amounting to a maximum of 3.4% of the reference value. Hao et al. report similar results [33]. Concentrations of SO_2 from EC-3 above 0.2 μg/m^3 (Figure 8) covered about 13% of the area of the city of Lodz.

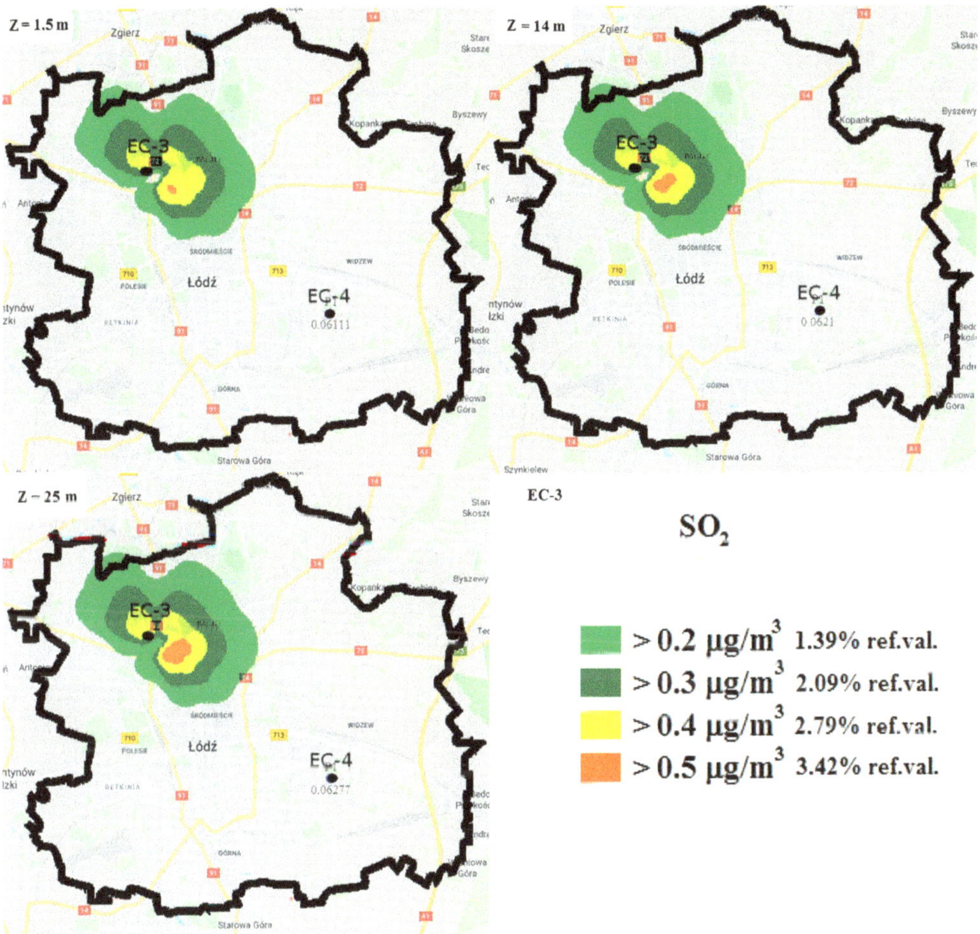

Figure 8. Distribution of annual average SO_2 concentrations at the height of 1.5, 14, and 25 m surrounded by EC-3 in 2019 based on the results from OPA03.

Figure 9 shows an example of the dispersion of NO_2 pollutants from the EC-4 heat and power plant at heights of 1.5, 14, and 25 m. As can be seen, the highest annual average NO_2 concentration is 0.6 μg/m^3. The area with a concentration of 0.6 μg/m, which constitutes 1.5% of the reference value, is 40 μg/m^3. Ghermandi et al. also showed that the limit values were not exceeded during their computer analysis of NO_2 emissions from a CHP plant in San Marino [39]. The dispersion of NO_2 pollutants also coincided with the wind rose for Lodz for 2019.

Figure 10 shows the spatial dispersion of PM_{10} from EC-4. The distribution of pollutants at 1.5 m is shown on the left, and the distribution at 25 m is shown on the right. The concentrations of pollutants are in the range of 0.003–0.015 μg/m^3, which is 0.007–0.03% of the reference value. The highest values of 0.015 μg/m^3 occurred only at a height of 25 m. Of all the pollutants, PM_{10} had the largest area of influence.

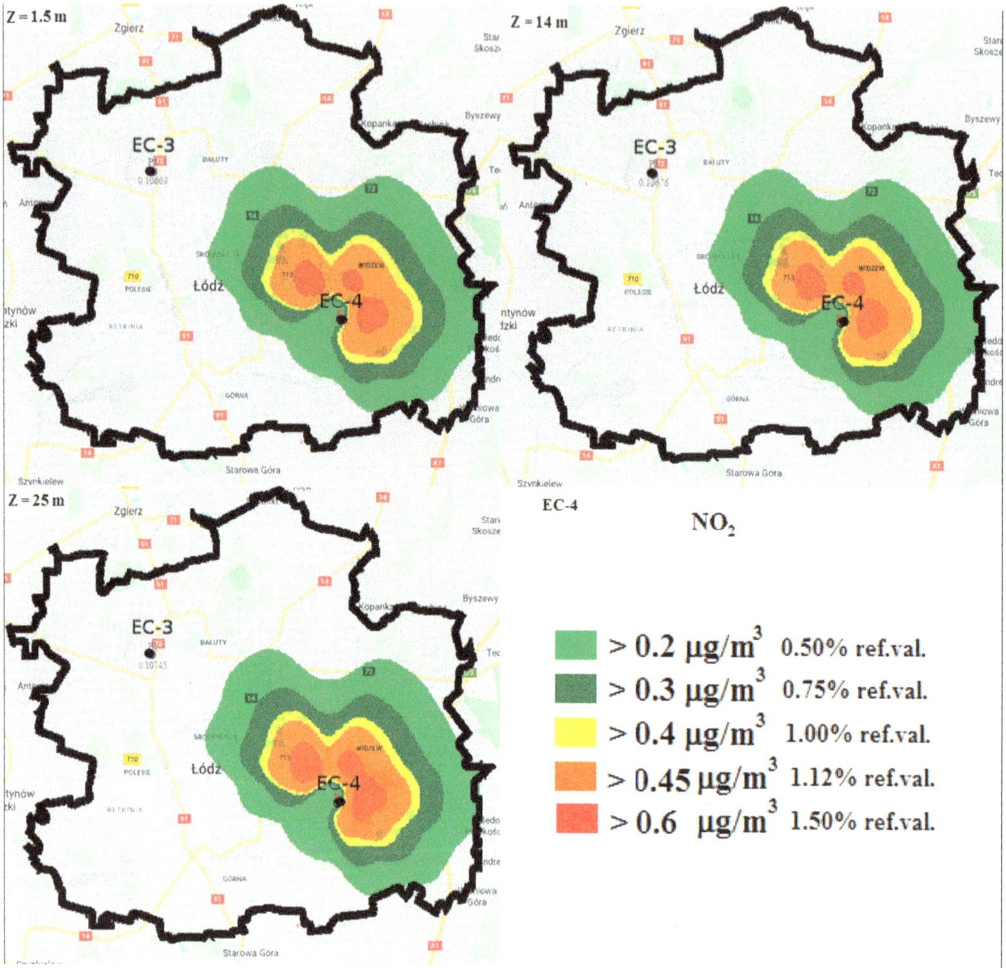

Figure 9. Distribution of annual average NO_2 concentrations at the height of 1.5 m, 14 m, and 25 m surrounded by EC-4 in 2019 based on the results from OPA03.

Summarizing the results of analysis using the OPA03-Maps program, the average annual concentrations range from thousandths of a percent to several percent of the permissible values. This can be attributed to the use of dedusting devices, flue gas denitrification, and desulphurization installations, as well as various types of filters with high dedusting efficiency. Both CHP plants, thus, have a negligible impact on air quality. The highest concentrations of pollutants occurred at a height of 25 m. Due to the movement of air masses, the concentrations of pollutants from the heat and power plants fall significantly as the measuring height reduces. This is very important because, as shown by the pollution dispersion maps, the main areas to which the pollutants are transported by the predominant wind directions are mainly collective and individual residence areas, as well as green areas used by residents for relaxation and recreation.

Field measurements were made with the use of UAV to verify the impact of the CHP plants on air quality. The field measurements were taken during the heating season in the areas with the highest concentrations of pollutants from the heat and power plants, according to the analysis in OPA03. In the case of EC-4, these were two intersections of the main streets in the city, indicated in Figure 11.

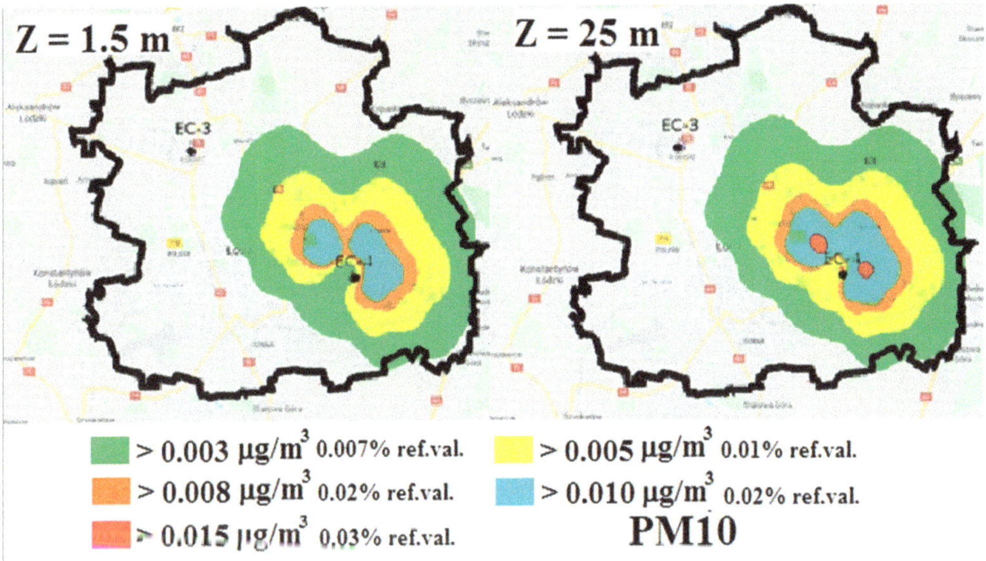

Figure 10. Distribution of annual average concentrations of PM_{10} at the height of 1.5 m and 25 m surrounded by EC-4 in 2019 based on the results from OPA03.

As shown in Figure 11, in location no. 1, located closer to EC-4, the concentration of PM_{10} varied in the range 27.57–84.76 µg/m^3. In location no. 2, the concentration of PM_{10} varied in the range 44.05–80.37 µg/m^3. According to the analysis in OPA03, the highest average annual concentration of PM_{10} particulate pollutants emitted from EC-4 was 0.016 µg/m^3. The concentrations recorded in the field measurements were 5000 times higher. This proves the negligible impact of the EC-4 heat and power plant on air quality. It can be assumed that the high measured concentrations of PM_{10} were caused by "low emissions" from transport and individual heating systems, which in Poland, do not have to meet high standards for exhaust gas treatment, such as those set for municipal heat and power plants. The concentration of SO_2 measured for location no. 1 varied in the range 0.06–0.40 ppm (Figure 12), i.e., about 170–1130 µg/m^3. In location no. 2, the concentration of SO_2 varied in the range 0.15–0.40 ppm (420–1130 µg/m^3). According to the analysis in OPA03, the maximum hourly concentration SO_2 emitted from EC-4 was 115 µg/m^3. This means that the SO_2 concentrations measured in location no. 2 were almost 10 times higher than the emissions from the combined heat and power plant. As in the case of particulate pollutants, this can be explained by "low emissions" providing the dominant share of the total concentration of sulfur dioxide.

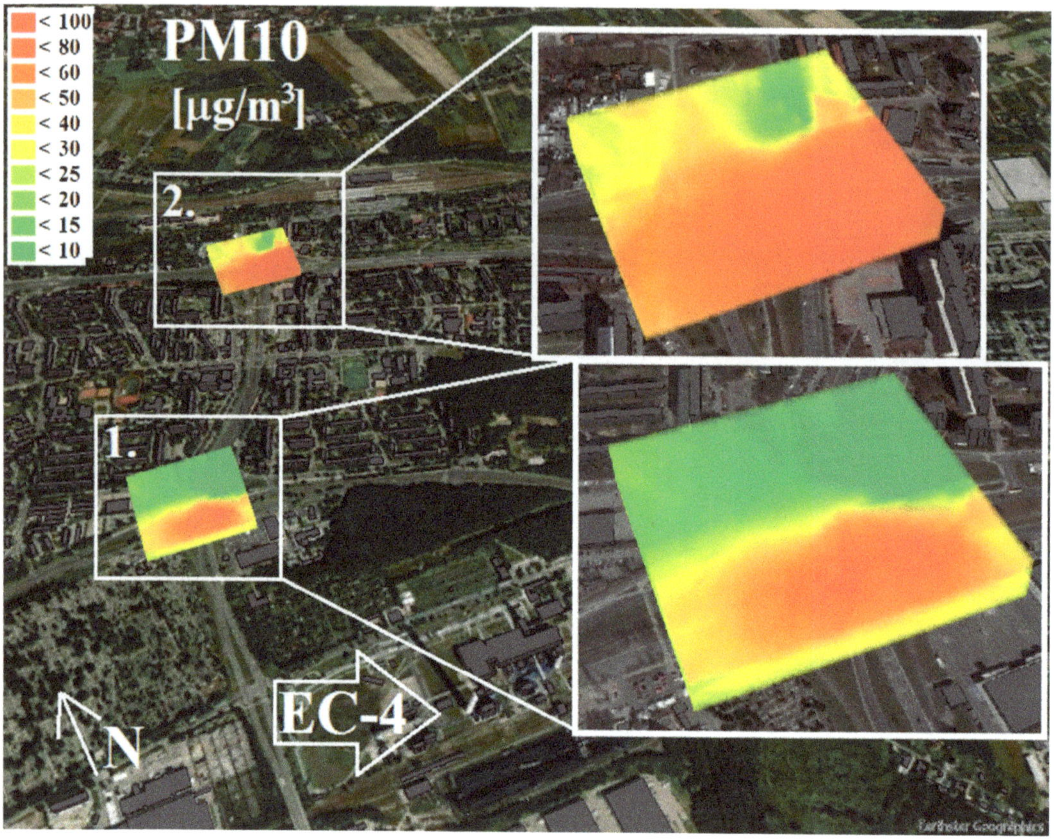

Figure 11. Spatial distribution of PM_{10} concentration for a selected location in the vicinity of EC-4.

Another area we analyzed was at a distance of approx. 1.5 km from the EC-3 heat and power plant (Figures 13 and 14). The concentration of PM_{10} varied spatially in a narrow range, from 13.52 to 38.25 µg/m^3 (Figure 13). The real concentrations were, thus, more than 5000 times higher than the emissions from EC-3 determined on the basis of OPA03 modeling (the highest annual average concentration was 0.007 µg/m^3).

On the other hand, field measurements of the SO_2 concentration (Figure 14) showed variations in the range 0.01–0.14 ppm (about 30–390 µg/m^3). The real concentrations were more than 12 times higher than the maximum hourly value of about 32 µg/m^3 calculated in OPA03. As in the case of EC-4, the EC-3 CHP plant was, therefore, found to emit only a small proportion of the actual concentration of pollutants. This proves that the main sources of the analyzed pollutants were not the CHP plants, but probably "low" and "linear" emissions from transport and individual heating.

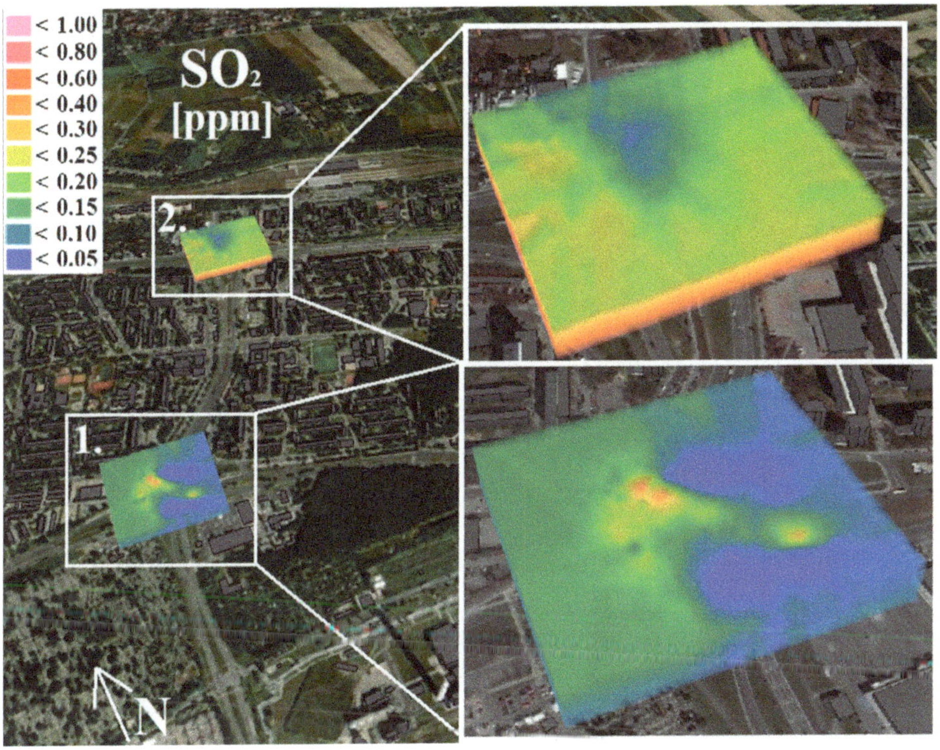

Figure 12. Spatial distribution of SO_2 concentration for a selected location in the vicinity of EC-4.

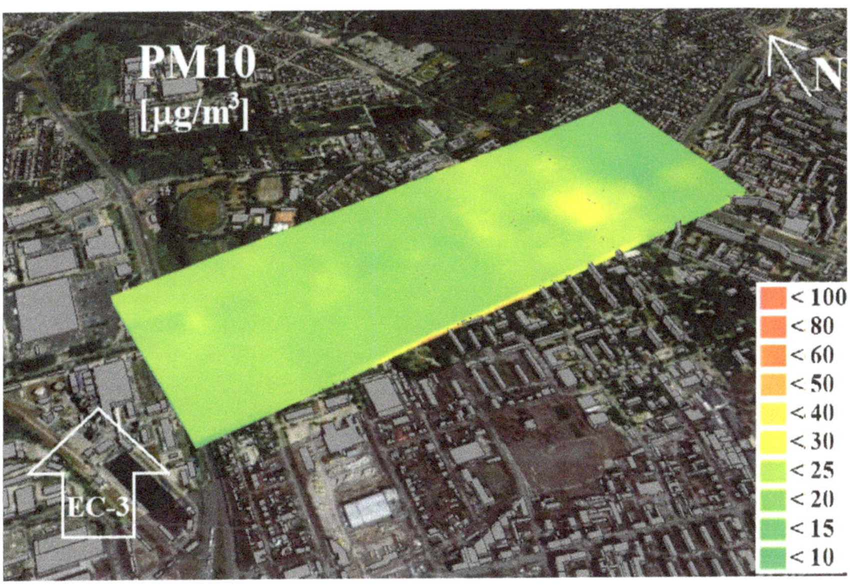

Figure 13. Spatial distribution of PM_{10} concentration for a selected location in the vicinity of EC-3.

Figure 14. Spatial distribution of SO_2 concentration for a selected location in the vicinity of EC-3.

5. Conclusions

Based on our analysis of the dispersion of atmospheric air pollutants in 2019, the concentrations of pollutants from the EC-3 and EC-4 municipal heat and power plants do not exceed the permissible values and do not independently present a threat to human health. Organizational units of Veolia Energia Łódź, which manage facilities including the EC-3 and EC-4 CHP plants, comply with the applicable regulations and implement plans to limit emissions into the air, using desulphurization installations and flue gas cleaning devices. However, field measurements showed that total emissions including other sources, i.e., "linear emissions" in the form of transportation and "low emissions" from home furnaces, do pose a real threat to environmental health and safety, because the concentrations of pollutants exceed permissible levels in the air. In order to improve air quality, it is necessary to act to reduce the amount of pollution emitted from all sources. In particular, it is possible to mention a reduction in the number of vehicles used for public transport or replacing them with electric vehicles and the replacement of individual coal-fired boilers with gas or electric heat sources.

Our numerical analysis in OPA03 software showed that at lower measuring heights, the concentrations of pollutants from EC-3 and EC-4 decreased, and the area with the highest average annual concentrations approximately doubled. However, the field measurements showed that the highest concentrations of the pollutants were recorded close to the ground surface and decreased at higher altitudes. This demonstrates the direct impact of "low emissions" on air quality. Pollutants emitted, for example, from vehicles and individual heating systems, accumulate at the ground surface and, then, through air movement, are lifted to higher parts of the atmosphere. There, there is a gradual dilution/reduction in their concentration by mixing with air. Dispersion maps generated based on the analysis in OPA03 and field measurements confirmed that the spread of pollutants was mostly influenced by wind speed and direction. Another very important factor influencing the condition of atmospheric air is the season. As shown in Table 4, higher emissions of pollutants occur during the winter-heating period. In the "winter/heating period", in addition to sources of air pollution that are active throughout the year, it is necessary to take into account those that are used seasonally, e.g., individual heating systems. In colder weather, there is more demand for heat energy, and therefore, higher levels of pollutants are produced both by CHP plants ("high emissions") and home furnaces ("low emissions").

The combined use of field measurements and computer simulations constitutes a new approach to analyzing air quality, making it possible to select areas for field analysis and to verify the impact of emitters on air quality. This method can be implemented anywhere in the world, in relation to various emitters of air pollutants.

Author Contributions: Conceptualization, R.C. and M.D.; methodology, R.C. and M.D.; software, M.D. and R.C.; writing—original draft, R.C. and M.D., review and editing, R.C. All authors have read and agreed to the published version of the manuscript.

Funding: This study was conducted as part of the research project entitled "Spatial analysis of air pollution changes in the Lodz agglomeration (in Polish: Analiza przestrzenna zmian stanu zanieczyszczenia powietrza w aglomeracji łódzkiej)", which was co-financed by approx. 80% by the Provincial Fund for Environmental Protection and Water Management in Lodz (in Polish: Wojewódzki Fundusz Ochrony Środowiska i Gospodarki Wodnej w Łodzi). 590/BN/D/2018.

Institutional Review Board Statement: Not applicable.

Informed Consent Statement: Not applicable.

Data Availability Statement: Data available on request.

Conflicts of Interest: The authors declare no conflict of interest.

References

1. Yang, G.; Wang, Y.; Zeng, Y.; Gao, G.F.; Liang, X.; Zhou, M.; Wan, X.; Yu, S.; Jiang, Y.; Naghavi, M.; et al. Rapid health transition in China, 1990–2010: Findings from the global burden of disease study 2010. *Lancet* **2013**, *381*, 1987–2015. [CrossRef]
2. Sówka, I.; Kobus, D.; Skotak, K.; Zathey, M.; Merenda, B.; Paciorek, M. Assessment of the health risk related to air pollution in selected polish health resorts. *J. Ecol. Eng.* **2019**, *20*, 132–145. [CrossRef]
3. Pope, C.A. Mortality effects of longer term exposures to fine particulate air pollution: Review of recent epidemiological evidence. *Inhal. Toxicol.* **2007**, *19*, 33–38. [CrossRef] [PubMed]
4. Almeida, S.M.; Pio, C.; Freitas, M.; Reis, M.; Trancoso, M. Source apportionment of fine and coarse particulate matter in a sub-urban area at the Western European Coast. *Atmospheric. Environ.* **2005**, *39*, 3127–3138. [CrossRef]
5. UNION, PEAN. Directive 2008/50/EC of the European Parliament and of the Council of 21 May 2008 on ambient air quality and cleaner air for Europe. *Off. J. Eur. Union* **2008**, *29*, 169–212. Available online: http://data.europa.eu/eli/dir/2008/50/oj (accessed on 12 June 2021).
6. World Health Organization. Who Air Quality Guidelines for Particulate Matter, Ozone, Nitrogen Dioxide and Sulfur Dioxide. Global Update 2005. Summary of Risk Assessment, 2005. Available online: https://www.euro.who.int/en/health-topics/environment-and-health/air-quality/publications/pre2009/air-quality-guidelines.-global-update-2005.-particulate-matter,-ozone,-nitrogen-dioxide-and-sulfur-dioxide (accessed on 12 June 2021).
7. Meng, M.; Zhou, J. Has air pollution emission level in the Beijing–Tianjin–Hebei region peaked? A panel data analysis. *Ecol. Indic.* **2020**, *119*, 106875. [CrossRef]
8. World Health Organization. Review of Evidence on Health Aspects of Air Pollution—REVIHAAP Project. World Health Organization 309. 2013. Available online: http://www.euro.who.int/en/health-topics/environment-and-health/air-quality/publications/2013/review-of-evidence-on-health-aspects-of-air-pollution-revihaap-project-finaltechnical-report (accessed on 2 July 2021).
9. Larssen, S.; Hagen, O.L. Air Quality in Europe, 1993. A Pilot Report. November 1996. European Environment Agency. Available online: https://www.eea.europa.eu/publications/2-9167-057-X (accessed on 12 June 2021).
10. Kousoulidou, M.; Ntziachristos, L.; Mellios, G.; Samaras, Z. Road-transport emission projections to 2020 in European urban environments. *Atmospheric. Environ.* **2008**, *42*, 7465–7475. [CrossRef]
11. Kota, S.; Zhang, H.; Chen, G.; Schade, G.; Ying, Q. Evaluation of on-road vehicle CO and NOx national emission inventories using an urban-scale source-oriented air quality model. *Atmospheric. Environ.* **2014**, *85*, 99–108. [CrossRef]
12. Mohsen, M.; Ahmed, M.B.; Zhou, J.L. Particulate matter concentrations and heavy metal contamination levels in the railway transport system of Sydney, Australia. *Transp. Res. Part D Transp. Environ.* **2018**, *62*, 112–124. [CrossRef]
13. Cichowicz, R.; Wielgosiński, G.; Fetter, W. Effect of wind speed on the level of particulate matter PM10 concentration in atmospheric air during winter season in vicinity of large combustion plant. *J. Atmospheric. Chem.* **2020**, *77*, 35–48. [CrossRef]
14. Cocks, A.T.; Kallend, A.S.; Marsh, A.R.W. Dispersion limitations of oxidation in power plant plumes during long-range transport. *Nat. Cell Biol.* **1983**, *305*, 122–123. [CrossRef]
15. Bednova, O.V.; Kuznetsov, V.A.; Tarasova, N.P. Eutrophication of an urban forest ecosystem: Causes and effects. *Dokl. Earth Sci.* **2018**, *478*, 124–128. [CrossRef]
16. Diamond, M.S.; Wood, R. Limited Regional aerosol and cloud microphysical changes despite unprecedented decline in nitrogen oxide pollution during the February 2020 COVID-19 shutdown in China. *Geophys. Res. Lett.* **2020**, *47*, 2020 088913. [CrossRef]

17. Obolkin, V.; Khodzher, T.; Sorokovikova, L.; Tomberg, I.; Netsvetaeva, O.; Golobokova, L. Effect of long-range transport of sulphur and nitrogen oxides from large coal power plants on acidification of river waters in the Baikal region, East Siberia. *Int. J. Environ. Stud.* **2016**, *73*, 452–461. [CrossRef]
18. Nagl, C.; Spangl, W.; Buxbaum, I. Sampling Points for Air Quality. Representativeness and Comparability of Measurement in Accordance with Directive 2008/50/EC on Ambient Air Quality and Cleaner Air for Europe. Policy Department for Economic, Scientific and Quality of Life Policies, Directorate-General for Internal Policies. PE 631.055-March 2019. Available online: http://www.europarl.europa.eu/RegData/etudes/STUD/2019/631055/IPOL_STU(2019)631055_EN.pdf (accessed on 12 June 2021).
19. Chen, W.; Wang, F.; Xiao, G.; Wu, K.; Zhang, S. Air quality of beijing and impacts of the new ambient air quality standard. *Atmosphere* **2015**, *6*, 1243–1258. [CrossRef]
20. Kuklinska, K.; Wolska, L.; Namiesnik, J. Air quality policy in the U.S. and the EU–A review. *Atmospheric. Pollut. Res.* **2015**, *6*, 129–137. [CrossRef]
21. Atamaleki, A.; Zarandi, S.M.; Fakhri, Y.; Mehrizi, E.A.; Hesam, G.; Faramarzi, M.; Darbandi, M. Estimation of air pollutants emission (PM10, CO, SO_2 and NOx) during development of the industry using AUSTAL 2000 model: A new method for sustainable development. *MethodsX* **2019**, *6*, 1581–1590. [CrossRef]
22. Cichowicz, R.; Dobrzański, M. 3D spatial analysis of particulate matter (PM_{10}, $PM_{2.5}$ and $PM_{1.0}$) and gaseous pollutants (H_2S, SO_2 and VOC) in urban areas surrounding a large heat and power plant. *Energies* **2021**, *14*, 4070. [CrossRef]
23. Keshavarzian, E.; Jin, R.; Dong, K.; Kwok, K.C. Effect of building cross-section shape on air pollutant dispersion around buildings. *Build. Environ.* **2021**, *197*, 107861. [CrossRef]
24. Ramponi, R.; Blocken, B.; De Coo, L.B.; Janssen, W.D. CFD simulation of outdoor ventilation of generic urban configurations with different urban densities and equal and unequal street widths. *Build. Environ.* **2015**, *92*, 152–166. [CrossRef]
25. Yuan, C.; Ng, E.Y.Y. Building porosity for better urban ventilation in high-density cities–A computational parametric study. *Build. Environ.* **2012**, *50*, 176–189. [CrossRef]
26. Łatuszyńska, M.; Strulak-Wójcikiewicz, R. A model for assessing the environmental impact of transport. *Oper. Res. Decis.* **2013**, *23*, 67–80. [CrossRef]
27. Abu-Allaban, M.; Abu-Qdais, H. Impact assessment of ambient air quality by cement industry: A case study in jordan. *Aerosol Air Qual. Res.* **2011**, *11*, 802–810. [CrossRef]
28. Paas, B.; Schneider, C. A comparison of model performance between ENVI-met and Austal2000 for particulate matter. *Atmospheric. Environ.* **2016**, *145*, 392–404. [CrossRef]
29. Ropkins, K.; Beebe, J.; Li, H.; Daham, B.; Tate, J.; Bell, M.; Andrews, G. Real-world vehicle exhaust emissions monitoring: Review and critical discussion. *Crit. Rev. Environ. Sci. Technol.* **2009**, *39*, 79–152. [CrossRef]
30. Gebremedhin, A. Introducing district heating in a norwegian town–potential for reduced local and global emissions. *Appl. Energy* **2012**, *95*, 300–304. [CrossRef]
31. Cichowicz, R.; Dobrzański, M. Spatial analysis (measurements at heights of 10 m and 20 m above ground level) of the concentrations of particulate matter (PM 10, PM 2.5, and PM 1.0) and gaseous pollutants (H_2S) on the university campus: A case study. *Atmosphere* **2021**, *12*, 62. [CrossRef]
32. Lee, H.; Yoo, J.; Kang, M.; Kang, J.; Jung, J.; Oh, K. Evaluation of concentrations and source contribution of PM 10 and SO_2 emitted from industrial complexes in Ulsan, Korea: Interfacing of the WRF–CALPUFF modeling tools. *Atmospheric. Pollut. Res.* **2014**, *5*, 664–676. [CrossRef]
33. Hao, J.; Wang, L.; Shen, M.; Li, L.; Hu, J. Air quality impacts of power plant emissions in Beijing. *Environ. Pollut.* **2007**, *147*, 401–408. [CrossRef]
34. Calculation Software for Pollutant Concentration Analysis. Eko-Soft company from Poland. Available online: http://www.eko-soft.com.pl/sysopa.htm (accessed on 12 June 2021).
35. Polish Legal Act. Rozporządzenie Ministra Środowiska z Dnia 26 Stycznia 2010 r. w Sprawie Wartości Odniesienia Dla Niektórych Substancji W Powietrzu. Available online: http://isap.sejm.gov.pl/isap.nsf/DocDetails.xsp?id=wdu20100160087 (accessed on 12 June 2021).
36. Meteorological Data. Available online: https://danepubliczne.imgw.pl/data/dane_pomiarowo_obserwacyjne/dane_meteorologiczne/miesieczne/synop/2019/ (accessed on 12 June 2021).
37. Jumaah, H.; Kalantar, B.; Halin, A.; Mansor, S.; Ueda, N.; Jumaah, S. Development of UAV-based $PM_{2.5}$ monitoring system. *Drones* **2021**, *5*, 60. [CrossRef]
38. Caillouet, C.; Giroire, F.; Razafindralambo, T. Optimization of mobile sensor coverage with UAVs. In Proceedings of the IEEE INFOCOM 2018-IEEE Conference on Computer Communications, Honolulu, HI, USA, 15–19 April 2018; pp. 622–627.
39. Ghermandi, G.; Fabbi, S.; Arvani, B.; Veratti, G.; Bigi, A.; Teggi, S. Impact assessment of pollutant emissions in the atmosphere from a power plant over a complex terrain and under unsteady winds. *Sustainability* **2017**, *9*, 2076. [CrossRef]

energies

MDPI

Article

A New Measurement of Anisotropic Relative Permeability and Its Application in Numerical Simulation

Congcong Li [1], Shuoliang Wang [1,*], Qing You [1] and Chunlei Yu [2]

[1] Faculty of Engineering, School of Energy, China University of Geosciences, Beijing 100083, China; 3006190054@cugb.edu.cn (C.L.); youqing@cugb.edu.cn (Q.Y.)
[2] Shengli Oilfield Exploration and Development Research Institute, Dongying 257001, China; Yuchunlei.slyt@sinopec.com
* Correspondence: wangshuoliang@cugb.edu.cn; Tel.: +86-13501017546

Abstract: In this paper, we used a self-developed anisotropic cubic core holder to test anisotropic relative permeability by the unsteady-states method, and introduced the anisotropic relative permeability to the traditional numerical simulator. The oil–water two-phase governing equation considering the anisotropic relative permeability is established, and the difference discretization is carried out. We formed a new oil–water two-phase numerical simulation method. It is clear that in a heterogeneous rock with millimeter to centimeter scale laminae, relative permeability is an anisotropic tensor. When the displacement direction is parallel to the bedding, the residual oil saturation is high and the displacement efficiency is low. The greater the angle between the displacement direction and the bedding strike, the lower the residual oil saturation is, the higher the displacement efficiency is, and the relative permeability curve tends towards a rightward shift. The new simulator showed that the anisotropic relative permeability not only affects the breakthrough time and sweep range of water flooding, but also has a significant influence on the overall water cut. The new simulator is validated with the actual oilfield model. It could describe the law of oil–water seepage in an anisotropic reservoir, depict the law of remaining oil distribution of a typical fluvial reservoir, and provide technical support for reasonable injection-production directions.

Keywords: relative permeability; anisotropic; reservoir numerical simulation; heterogeneity; fluvial sandstone reservoir

Citation: Li, C.; Wang, S.; You, Q.; Yu, C. A New Measurement of Anisotropic Relative Permeability and Its Application in Numerical Simulation. *Energies* **2021**, *14*, 4731. https://doi.org/10.3390/en14164731

Academic Editor: Marcin Kamiński

Received: 7 June 2021
Accepted: 2 August 2021
Published: 4 August 2021

1. Introduction

Old oilfields in eastern China have generally entered a dual-high development stage with high water cut and high recovery degree. The hydrodynamic adjustment of "liquid flow steering" has achieved good results in improving recovery. Fluid flow steering changes the flow direction of fluid and makes fluid flow paths more intricate. Fluid seepage laws thus become complicated. At present, relative permeability is isotropic in traditional numerical simulations, which cannot accurately calculate residual oil distribution and cannot describe the deep mechanisms of liquid flow steering.

Relative permeability (the ratio of effective permeability to absolute permeability) is a basic parameter to study the seepage law of multiphase fluid. There are many factors affecting relative permeability, among which the heterogeneous pore structure is of vital importance. It is found that relative permeability will change significantly due to microscopic local pore structure, fluid interaction, and rock–fluid interaction [1–5]. Therefore, the relative permeability must be different when the pore structure of the reservoir is different.

In the past several years, a number of works have been reported on the directional characteristics of pore structures. In fluvial sediments, due to long-term erosion and erosion by water flow, the particles that make up the rock skeleton of the reservoir are often in irregular ellipsoid shapes. In the process of deposition, the skeleton particles are arranged directionally with the transport medium, and the direction of the long axis is consistent with the direction of the flow, while the direction of the short axis is perpendicular to the direction of the flow. The compaction in the diagenetic process also strengthens this directional arrangement, which makes the pore structure directional. Effected by the sedimentary environment and the inherent properties of the reservoir, including the original sedimentary bedding, vertical rhythm, and so on, the pore structure will be obviously different in the plane and vertical, and the fluid flow will have a dominant migration direction [5–11]. Recent theoretical and experimental studies have revealed that permeability is anisotropic [12–16]. Since it is the pore throats that govern the percolation threshold for porous media, permeability anisotropy is the behavior of the anisotropy of pore structure. In other words, the pore structure anisotropy has been widely observed.

Since Corey and Rathjens found that the relative permeability of bedded rocks is directional in 1956, research on anisotropic relative permeability has mainly focused on the following three aspects. Firstly, identification of core scales in the laboratory. It has been shown that relative permeability is related to the particle size of the rock composition of bedding structures (namely pore throat structure) and micro fractures. When driven along the direction of penetrating bedding, the change of rock properties leads to the change of capillary resistance so that the movement of fluid in this direction is blocked, and the oil in the core will be blocked, indicating that the relative permeability is directional. The displacement direction is different, the shape of phase permeability curve is different, the vertical displacement remaining oil is less, and the displacement efficiency is higher [17–24]. Secondly, discovery in numerical simulation. Some numerical simulation studies used pore network models to point out that the relative permeability parallel to the bedding direction is larger than that perpendicular to the bedding direction, and the residual saturation and relative permeability are sensitive to anisotropic correlation. The higher the absolute permeability value is, the greater the relative permeability value is, and the relative permeability is related to pore connectivity and pore inclination angles. The dendritic nature of gas-cluster topology, especially in the presence of other forces, such as gravity or strong viscous pressure gradients, clearly suggests that significant anisotropy may exist in relative permeability due to the balance of forces in the dissolved gas drive process [25–31]. Thirdly, microscopic visual seepage physical simulation. It is indicated that the change of injection-production angle will break the pressure balance of the original seepage field, promote the stripping and seepage of all kinds of remaining oil, and make the remaining oil migrate again, thus changing the microscopic remaining oil type and distribution law. The essence of this change is that the percolation law of the oil and water phases has changed due to different pore structures in different displacement directions [32,33]. Numerical models and physical experiments all prove that like porosity and permeability, relative permeability is a direction-dependent tensor, not a scalar.

Although the anisotropic characteristics of relative permeability were recognized earlier, the related studies focused on its embodiment in microscopic displacement experiments, or the demonstration of the characteristics by numerical simulation. In particular, few studies, to our knowledge, have considered two facts. Firstly, the test of anisotropic relative permeability. At present, most studies tested the anisotropic relative permeability curve by drilling cores in different directions. The testing device and the displacement direction is one-dimensional. However, the three-dimensional flow of fluid in the core is not equal to the simple superposition of three one-dimensional flows. The traditional relative permeability curve testing device cannot increase or change the displacement direction and cannot directly test the anisotropic relative permeability curve. It is quite difficult to test the relative permeability in three directions through one sample, However, the different test results of the same sample are the most comparable; Secondly, the application of anisotropic relative permeability in reservoir numerical simulation is very weak. There is a long way to go to test and apply the anisotropic relative permeability.

In this paper, firstly, the typical fluvial sandstone of the Shihezi fomation outcrop in Jiyang depression of Bohai Bay basin are used to measure the anisotropic relative permeability via a self-developed anisotropic cubic core holder; Secondly, we established a new simulator considering anisotropic relative permeability and compared the calculation results between the new simulator and traditional simulator. Finally, we apply the new simulator to the reservoir numerical simulation of Cheng 4 block in Shengli Oilfield (the reservoir is a typical fluvial sedimentary environment). The production data show that the numerical simulation method considering anisotropic relative permeability can describe the remaining oil distribution more accurately, especially in the situation that the reservoir has entered the development period of ultra-high water cut. In order to precisely apply anisotropic relative permeability to typical fluvial reservoir simulation or fractured reservoir, there is an urgent need for working on the upscaling of anisotropic relative permeability.

2. Experiments

2.1. Sample Preparation and Experimental Apparatus

In this study, fluvial facies sandstone outcrop from Guantao formation was used in this study. We can clearly see that the sample has developed plate-like cross-beds, which are at an angle of 30 degrees with the ground (Figure 1). We define the bedding direction as the x direction, the y direction orthogonal to x, and the z direction perpendicular to the xy plane. The water permeability in the three directions of x, y, and z is 37.87 mD, 20.83 mD and 18.94 mD, respectively, and the porosity is 15.98%. The testing oil is a mixture of crude oil and diesel with a viscosity of 10 mPa·s at 20 °C. The salinity and viscosity of the testing water are 4000 mg/L and 1.0 mPa·s, respectively. The testing fluids are based on the actual reservoir oil and water properties in the Shengli Oilfield.

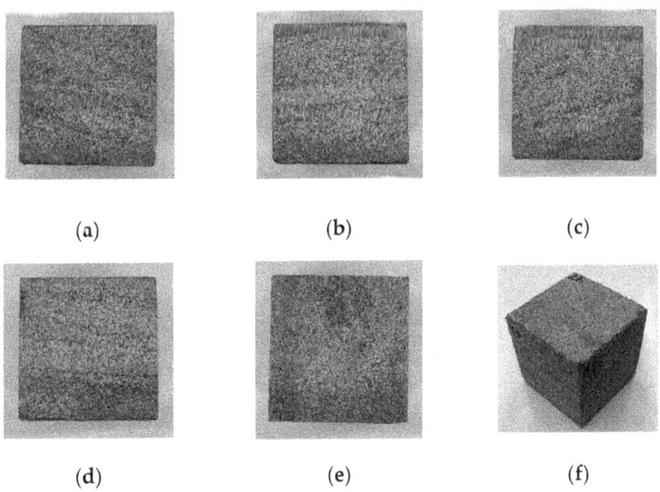

Figure 1. Cores used in our experiment (**a**–**e**) are the 4 side and top photos of the cubic core, (**f**) is the full-view photo of the cubic core.

The experimental apparatus consists of five different parts: injection control system, temperature and pressure control system, core holding system, outlet back pressure control system, and data acquisition system. The schematic representation of the experimental apparatus is shown in Figure 2.

(①—anisotropic cubic core holder; ②—pressure sensor; ③—six-way value; ④- oil–water separator; ⑤—Monitoring camera system; ⑥—value; ⑦—output liquid collector; ⑧—backpressure regulator (BPR); ⑨—confining pressure system; ⑩—water flooding system; ⑪—oil flooding system; ⑫—filter; ⑬—control system).

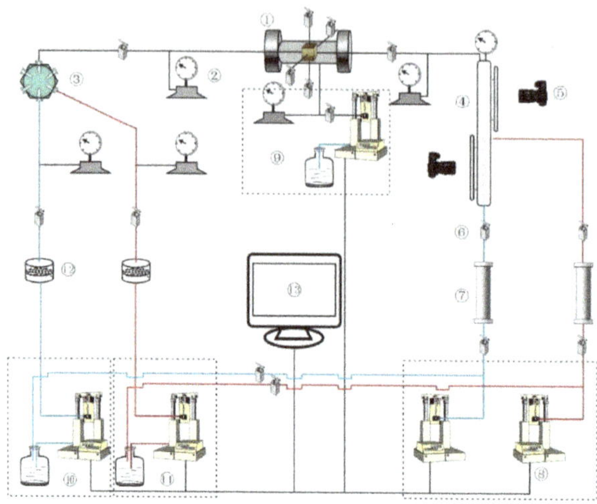

Figure 2. Schematic representation of the experimental apparatus of the anisotropic relative permeability measurement.

2.2. Experimental Process

(1) Use wire cutting technology to cut outcrop rock samples into 50 mm × 50 mm × 50 mm cube core;
(2) Wash the oil, water, salt, soil, and other impurities attached to the cubic core, dry, and weigh the cubic core;
(3) Put the cubic core into a rubber sleeve;
(4) Measure the porosity of the cubic core and test its permeability from three directions of x, y, and z;
(5) Saturate the cubic core with formation water in three directions;
(6) Measure the absolute permeability of water in three directions;
(7) Displace the water in the cubic core with oil along three directions until the irreducible water saturation (record the flow data and time at the outlet; open the outlet plunger and close the inlet; the outlet water cut <0.1%, Additionally, when the number of PV injected is greater than 10 PV, stop the oil saturation process.)
(8) Measure the effective permeability of the oil phase under irreducible water saturation in three directions;
(9) Displace the oil in the sample with water along the x direction, inject at a constant speed, 10 PV (record the flow data and time at the outlet; when the water cut at the outlet is >99.9%, and the injected PV number is greater than 10 PV, stop the water flooding process);
(10) Measure the effective permeability of water under residual oil saturation;
(11) Repeat step 7.
(12) Change the inlet and outlet of the core holder to change the displacement direction;
(13) Repeat steps 9–11 until the relative permeability tests in the three directions of x, y, and z are completed;
(14) Wash, dry, and weigh the sample.
(15) Calculate the relative permeability.

3. Methodology

3.1. Characterization of Anisotropic Relative Permeability

The test process is continuous. After measuring the x direction, the oil is saturated in the x direction, and then the direction is changed to do the water flooding process, so as to ensure that the core porous medium and the oil and water conditions are the same in each test. The main goal of this research is to observe the difference in residual oil saturation after water flooding in different directions. Therefore, minor changes in the irreducible water saturation are ignored.

During the experimental process and numerical simulation research process, we realized that the relative permeability of the XY, XZ, and YZ directions are also important to this experiment. Different inlet and outlet combinations could help to test the relative permeability of the XY, XZ, and YZ directions. For example, if we use the X direction as the injection end, we can use the Y direction or the Z direction as the production end. However, the existing JBN calculation method cannot be used to solve the relative permeability curve of such a combined inject-product method. The automatic history matching method or other methods need to be proposed to solve the relative permeability curve.

In this experiment, the JBN method was used to solve the relative permeability curve. The JBN method is based on the Buckley–Leverett one-dimensional two-phase water flooding front advancement theory, ignoring capillary pressure and gravity, assuming that the two-phase immiscible fluid is incompressible and the oil–water saturation in any cross section of the rock sample is uniform. In the process of water flooding, only when the displacement front breaks through the end, can the relative permeability of the oil and water phase be calculated. For the entire core, the displacement process has a breakthrough time, but for the end face, the flow is pure oil phase before the breakthrough. The saturation in the end face has not changed. After the breakthrough, the process of the end face water saturation from the irreducible water saturation to the maximum water saturation is complete. JBN projects the seepage law of the entire core to the end face. It studies the law of water saturation and oil–water seepage at the end face. The relative permeability calculated by JBN represents the end face, not the entire core.

There is a marked difference between the relative permeability curves derived from the x direction, y direction, and vertical displacements. Different residual oil saturations were obtained for three directions displacements, the residual oil saturation in X direction is 0.56, the residual oil saturation in Y direction is 0.61, the residual oil saturation in Z direction is 0.82. The displacement was more efficient in the vertical than other directions. The greater the angle between the displacement direction and the bedding strike, the lower the residual oil saturation is, the higher the displacement efficiency is, and the relative permeability curve tends towards a rightward shift. The displacement efficiency in the three directions of x, y, and z are 0.664, 0.721, and 0.84, respectively.

3.2. Numerical Simulation with Anisotropic Relative Permeability

According to the experimental results, JBN (calculation of relative permeability from displacement experiments proposed by Johnson, E.F., Bossler, D.P. and Naumann, V.O.) method was used to obtain the relative permeability curves in three directions. The anisotropic relative permeability is applied to the traditional numerical simulator and the traditional numerical simulator is modified.

In this paper, based on the oil–water two-phase black oil model, the isotropic relative permeability in the water phase governing equation and the oil phase governing equation is replaced by the anisotropic relative permeability, and the new oil phase and water phase motion equations are solved by the finite difference method. There are many numerical simulation methods, such as the finite difference method, finite element method, etc. Different solving methods have great influence on the results of fracture–matrix seepage, different mesh sizes, and poor mesh quality. The stochastic perturbation-based finite element approach proposed by Kaminski, M. can even treat uncertainty in inflow or wall boundary conditions, in parameters of the equations, in profile shape, etc. [34]. The model in this paper is relatively simple, so we chose the traditional finite difference method to solve the problem. The assumptions of the numerical simulation model established in this paper are as follows:

(1) There are only two phases, oil and water, in the model.
(2) There is no mass exchange between oil and water.

(3) The fluid flow seepage follows Darcy's law.
(4) Rocks and fluids are slightly compressible.

The oil governing equations used in this study are presented in Appendix A, where the derivation process is discussed.

The fully implicit method is selected to ensure accuracy during the calculation. The heterogeneity of the reservoir is usually strong, and the fluid properties are also complex and diverse. In addition, the time span of historical production data is large, and as a result, the stability and robustness of implicit pressure, explicit saturation (IMPES) implementation are not enough to meet the requirements of reservoir numerical simulation [35]. The fully implicit method is very stable and can solve the problems of non-convergence and computational instability in a heterogeneous model.

4. Numerical Simulation Calculating Results and Discussion

In this study, according to the experimental results, we set up two kinds of numerical simulation models: homogeneous permeability model and heterogeneous permeability model. The numerical simulation calculating results obtained from the new simulator considering anisotropic relative permeability is compared with that from a traditional numerical simulator (isotropic relative permeability). The basic parameters of the numerical simulation model are as shown in Table 1, and the relative permeability curve used in the numerical simulation model is shown in Figure 3.

Table 1. Simulation model parameters.

Grid node	40 × 40 × 1	D_x (m)	10
D_y (m)	10	D_z (m)	10
Top deep (m)	1000	Initial water saturation (f)	0.15
Porosity (f)	0.2	Permeability (10^{-3} μm^2)	50
Water viscosity (mPa·s)	1	Oil viscosity (mPa·s)	10
Exploit scheme	Water flooding	Well pattern	One injection well and one production well

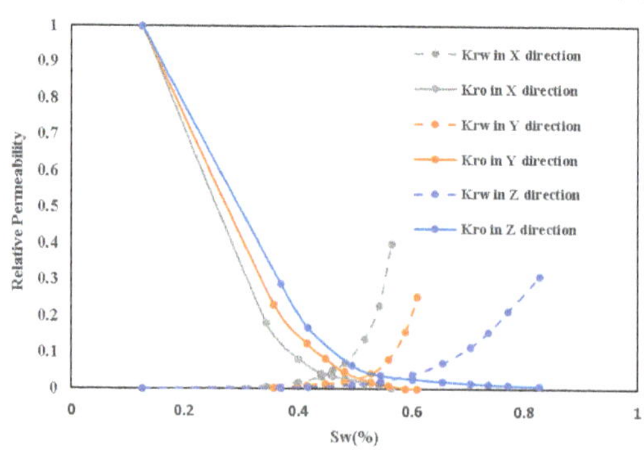

Figure 3. Relative permeability of three directions.

4.1. Effect of Anisotropic Relative Permeability on Pressure Distribution

In order to observe the effect of anisotropic relative permeability on pressure distribution, we made four cases, which are a homogeneous model with isotropic relative permeability (Case A), a homogeneous model with anisotropic relative permeability (Case

B), a heterogeneous model with isotropic relative permeability (Case C), and a heterogeneous model with anisotropic relative permeability (Case D). The pressure distribution results in these four cases are different, and they are very much affected by the heterogeneity of the relative permeability curves, which is different from Gomez-Hernandez's understanding. He proceeded with a derivation of the algorithm used to condition a realization of relative permeability to pressure and saturation data, and he observed that pressures are not very much affected by the heterogeneity of the relative permeability curves [36].

The results show that the pressure distribution uniformity between the injection well and the production well and the tangent of the pressure isoline along the diagonal is perpendicular to the diagonal line in Case A. In Case B, which considers the anisotropic relative permeability, the pressure propagation mode has changed, and the pressure distribution near the injection well and the production well has shifted in the x direction, and the relative permeability in the x direction is higher than that in the y direction. As far as this model is concerned, it seems that the pressure distribution in case A has been twisted counterclockwise. The pressure propagation of Case C is similar to that of Case B, but there is still a difference. The pressure propagation of Case D is also similar to that of Case B and Case C. However, the torsion of pressure distribution is more severe in Case D (Figure 4).

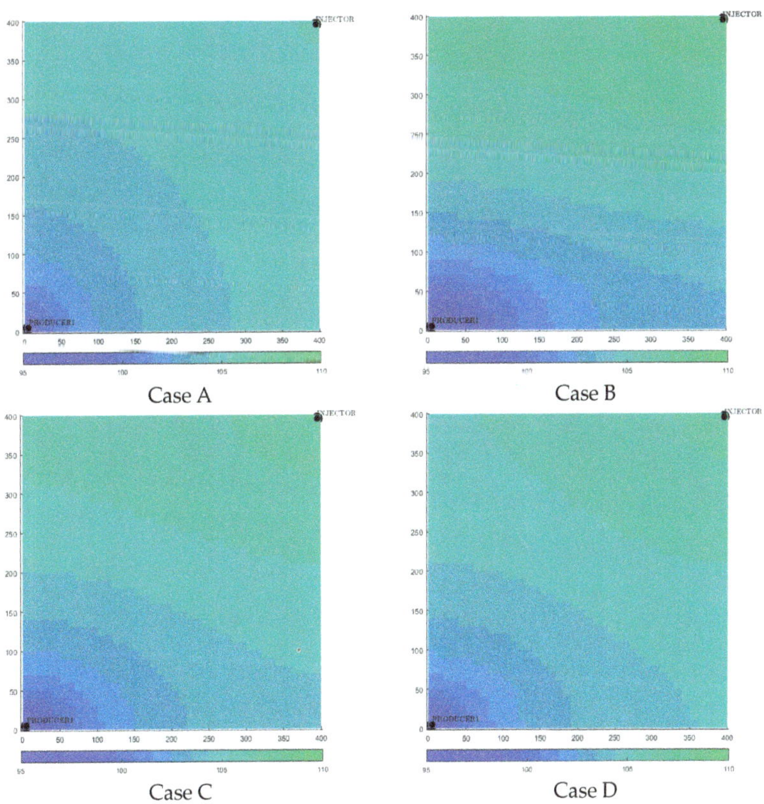

Figure 4. The pressure distribution of the four cases at the 50th time step.

The effective permeability, that is, the product of absolute permeability and relative permeability, determines the flow capacity of one phase in two-phase flow. It is found that both anisotropic absolute permeability and anisotropic relative permeability have an important influence on pressure distribution, and they are not equivalent and cannot be replaced each other, especially since the relative permeability is affected by fluid saturation and at the same time the change of relative permeability is not uniform. Obviously, the pressure propagation shifts to the direction of high relative permeability after considering the anisotropic relative permeability.

4.2. *Effect of Anisotropic Relative Permeability on Remaining Oil Saturation*

In this section, we further study the effect of anisotropic relative permeability on the remaining oil saturation. It is indicated that the water flooding is uniform and the remaining oil is symmetrically distributed along the injection-production wells diagonal line in Case A. The remaining oil of Case A is mainly located near the two sides of the production well and is most enriched at both ends of the diagonal line perpendicular to the injection–production line. The water flooding process obviously shifts to the x direction in Case B, with less remaining oil in the x direction and more remaining oil in the y direction, which is consistent with the experimental results. The result of Case C is not similar to that of Case B. Though the permeability in the x direction is large, there is more remaining oil in the x direction. Case D is the superposition of Case B and Case C, and the process of water flooding obviously shifts in the x direction (Figure 5).

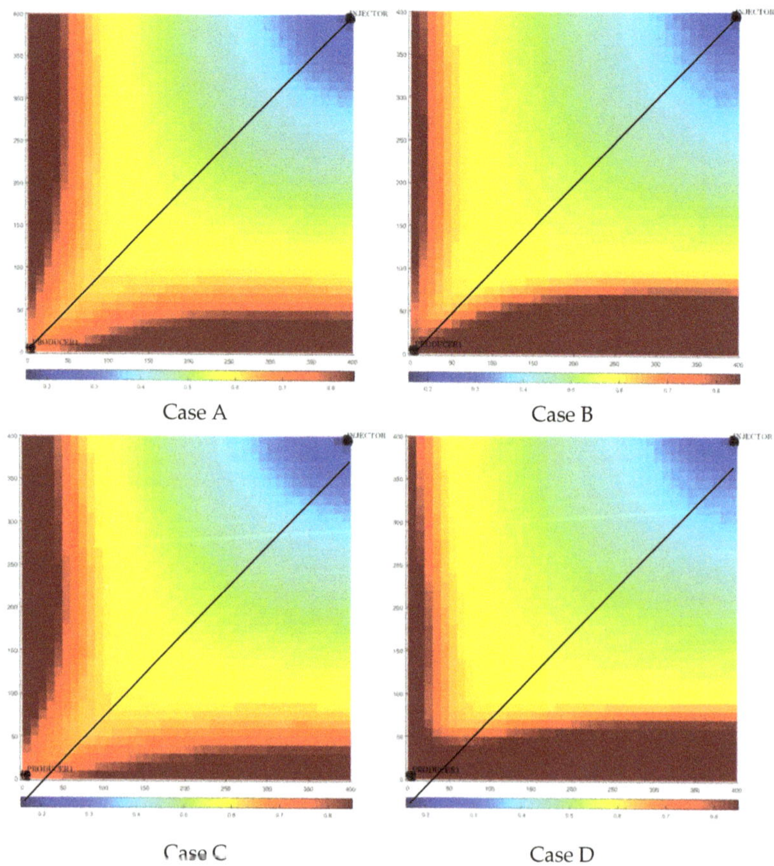

Figure 5. The remaining oil saturation distribution of the four cases at the 50th time step.

The area swept by injection water obviously shifts to the x direction in Case B because the relative permeability in the x direction is greater than that in the y direction. With regard to the phenomenon of Case C, we need to review the pressure distribution characteristics of Case C. Since the pressure at both the injection well and the production well propagates preferentially in the x direction, the injected water flows in the x direction first, and the production well also gives priority to producing oil in the x direction. Therefore, the process of water flooding does not seem to shift blindly to the x direction, but there is an equilibrium point on the injection–production line.

Before the equilibrium point, there is more remaining oil in the y direction, and after the equilibrium point, there is less remaining oil in the y direction. Here, we notice that case B and Case C have similar pressure propagation patterns, and the reason why there is such a big difference in remaining oil saturation is the relative permeability is affected by saturation. The relative permeability in the x direction is larger in Case B, the injected water is rapidly transferred near the production well, and the rapid increase in water saturation makes the flow capacity of water exceed that of oil. As a result, although the relative permeability in the x direction is larger, the movement ability of water in the y direction is higher than that of the oil in the x direction. Therefore, the remaining oil saturation of Case B occurs. However, the evolution of remaining oil saturation of Case C is different from that of Case B because it uses isotropic relative permeability and the absolute permeability is not affected by saturation. From the above analysis, it is not difficult to infer that the influence and mechanism of anisotropic relative permeability and absolute permeability on oil–water two-phase flow are different.

4.3. Effect of Anisotropic Relative Permeability on Water Cut

It is shown that Case A is the first to produce water, followed by Case C, Case B, and Case D, respectively. The reason for the difference can be made clear by comparing the corresponding remaining oil saturation. The flooding process of Case A is uniform, and it is the first to produce water. Most of the remaining oil distributes on both sides of the injection–production line near the production well. The sweep range of Case C is larger than that of Case A, so the time the model begins to produce water is later than in Case A. The flooding degree along the x direction in Case B is higher than Case C, as a result, Case B produces water later than Case C. Case D is affected by both anisotropic relative permeability and absolute permeability, and the degree of water flooding in x direction is the highest so it is the last to see water. However, although the time at which it sees the water is late, once there is a breakthrough, the later the breakthrough, the faster the water cut rises, and the higher the final water cut is (Figure 6).

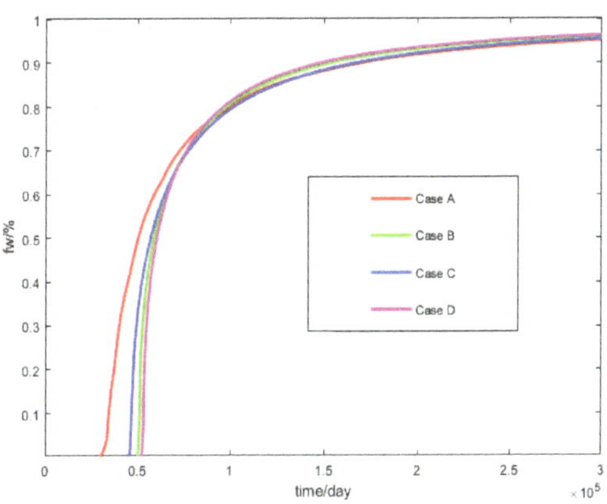

Figure 6. The changing process of water cut of the four cases.

It can be seen from the water cut curves that when the water cut exceed 0.75, the difference between the water cut curves of the four cases is very small, and there is little difference in saturation. However, when the water cut is less than 0.75, there are obvious differences in breakthrough time and the rising speed of water cut. Because of the homogeneity or heterogeneity of the model itself and the relative permeability isotropy or anisotropy, the movement direction and velocity of the displacement fronts of reservoir are sensitive from the beginning of displacement, as described in Section 4.2. Due to the simplicity of the model and well pattern, after breakthrough, the injected water continues to spread to the unused remaining oil area, and the remaining oil is gradually produced. When the water cut reaches a certain value, the difference in saturation and water cut of the four cases gradually decreases.

4.4. Sensitivity of the Measured Anisotropic Relative Permeability Data on the Simulation Model

We tested the relative permeability in three directions, and we call the relative permeability curve in the x direction obtained by the experiment No. 1, the relative permeability curve in the y direction No. 2, and the relative permeability curve in the z direction No. 3. No. 1 and No. 2 relative permeability (the smallest difference), No. 1 and No. 3 relative permeability (the biggest difference), and No. 2 and No. 3 relative permeability (large difference) are applied in the homogeneous model x, y, and z direction, respectively (for the convenience of the description later, we named these three cases low difference, high difference, mid difference). Then, we studied the effect of the difference in anisotropic on the results of the numerical simulation.

The water cut of low difference shows the injected water breakthrough first (waterless oil recovery period is the shortest) with a breakthrough time of 6.3×10^4 days, the water cut rises fastest, the final water cut is the highest, and the daily oil production drops the earliest. The breakthrough time of high difference is later than that of low difference, which is 6.9×10^4 days. The final water cut of high difference case is the lowest. The breakthrough time of mid difference is the latest, which is 7.5×10^4 days. After the breakthrough, the water cut rises rapidly, and at 8.8×10^4 days, the water cut exceeds that of high difference, and the water cut is 68.24%. Accordingly, the daily oil production of high difference decreased earlier than that of mid difference, but the daily oil production of high difference exceeded both at 8.8×10^4 days (Figure 7).

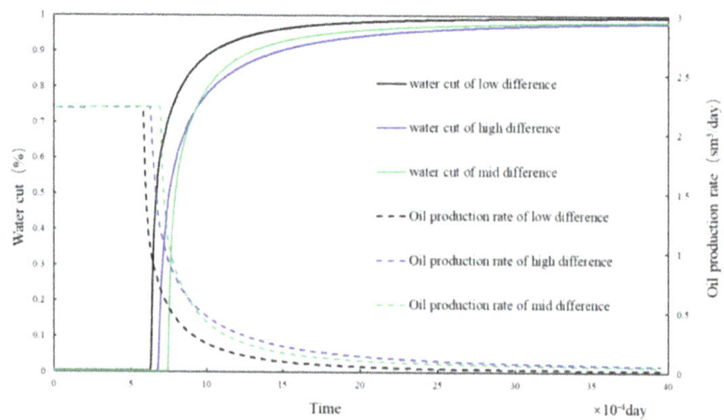

Figure 7. Water cut and daily oil production of different anisotropic relative permeability.

According to the characteristics of the relative permeability curve, the difference of the relative permeability curve between low difference x and y is the smallest, and the difference of residual oil saturation is only 5%. Therefore, the injected water advances uniformly in the x and y direction and breaks through fastest. The difference between the relative permeability curve of high difference x and y is the biggest, and the difference in residual oil saturation is 26%. The displacement efficiency of injected water in the y direction is higher, so the path of injected water to the production well shifts in the y direction, and the path becomes farther, so the breakthrough time is later than low difference. The relative permeability curves of mid difference x and y are quite different, and the difference of residual oil saturation is 21%, but the displacement efficiency in both directions is high, so the injected water breakthrough is the latest. It is precisely because of the high displacement efficiency of mid difference in both directions, once the injected water breaks through, the remaining oil is the least, and the water cut increases rapidly. After the injected water of high difference breakthrough, there is more remaining oil in the x direction, with the continuous increase in injected pv, this part of the remaining oil is gradually drained, resulting in a smaller increase in water cut than the other two cases.

4.5. Actual Model

In this section, we further verify the accuracy of the application of anisotropic relative permeability by comparing the actual production data of the C4N well area in Shengli Oilfield. This well area is a typical fluvial facies sedimentary environment, which belongs to a medium–high permeability reservoir.

In order to apply the anisotropic relative permeability to the actual model more accurately, we carried out a paleomagnetic orientation on the experimental samples (Figure 8). We separated the stable magnetization direction through the high precision magnetometer system in the laboratory and determined the geographic north pole direction of the core. In the paleomagnetic test, the x direction is used as the marking direction. The paleogeographic magnetic declination angle and magnetic inclination angle of the Y direction of the sample are 63.1° and −0.9°, respectively. Two precision parameters K and T95 (the higher the K value, the higher the precision, the smaller the T95, the more reliable the result) are usually used to measure the reliability spectrum degree of the Fisher distribution or the average observation direction of the pole [37–40]. The K value of this paleomagnetic test is 18.7 and T95 is 9.4, which has high reliability (Table 2).

Figure 8. Photo of palaeomagnetic core sample.

Table 2. The results of characteristic remnant magnetization measurements.

Sample Number	Magnetic Declination (°)	Magnetic Inclination (°)	T95	R	K
1	58.1	4.4	8.94	3.03	5.78
2	82.1	−6	5.53	4.24	9.52
Average results of Fisher statistical vector	63.1	−0.9	9.4	1.82	18.7

After that, we established a three-dimensional geological model according to the characteristics of the C4N well area, and the grid system was generated with the north by west 63.1 degrees as the X axis. The C4N well area is in the middle and high water cut stage, when deploying infill wells, and the remaining oil drilling potential will refer to the calculation results of reservoir numerical simulation. We often encounter the deployment of wells in places with high remaining oil saturation, and the drilling and production effect is not necessarily good. In fact, this is due to the inaccurate characterization of remaining oil distribution.

Figures 9 and 10 show the current distribution of remaining oil saturation calculated by traditional relative permeability and anisotropic relative permeability in the Cheng 4 South well area, respectively, as of 1 November 2019. There is a significant difference in remaining oil saturation between the two numerical simulation results. The numerical simulation results considering anisotropic relative permeability show that the sweep range of water is larger and the displacement efficiency in the Y direction (perpendicular to the river flow direction) is higher. There is also a great difference in the average remaining oil saturation obtained by the two algorithms. For example, the average remaining oil saturation of well C13-21 obtained by the numerical simulation algorithm considering anisotropic relative permeability is significantly higher than that of the traditional algorithm. This also explains why well C13-21 has a longer stable production period than other production wells, and the current water cut can still be maintained at 53.7% (Figure 11).

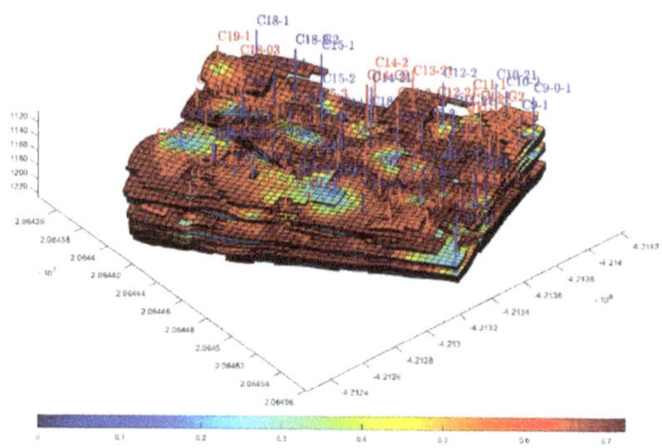

Figure 9. The remaining oil saturation distribution calculated by a traditional simulator.

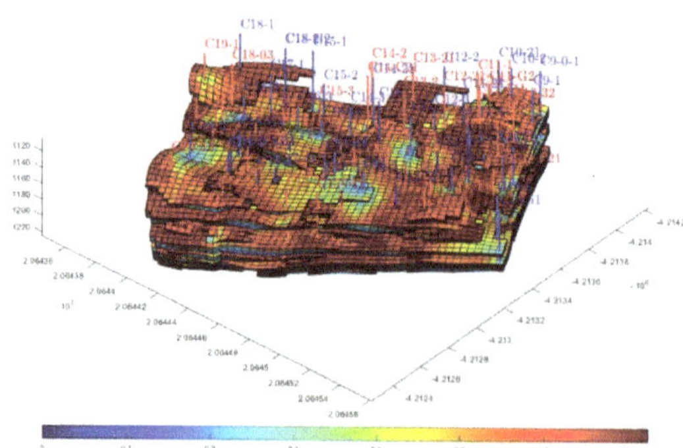

Figure 10. The remaining oil saturation distribution calculated by the new simulator.

Here, we count the first production of producers since 2017. The statistical results are shown in Table 3. Column 5 in Table 3 shows the average production for the first three months. Column 4 in Table 2 shows the average water cut for the first three months. By comparing the results, it can be seen that the numerical simulation algorithm considering anisotropic relative permeability is close to reality. Particularly in the C14-31 and C18-42 wells, when the water cut of these two wells exceeded 98%, though measures of partition were taken, the production effect was still poor and the water cut remained high. The reason is that the traditional numerical simulation results show that there is still some remaining oil in these two wells, but the numerical simulation results considering anisotropic relative permeability show that the contribution of remaining oil considered by the former is actually very small and has been swept in the process of water flooding (Figures 12 and 13).

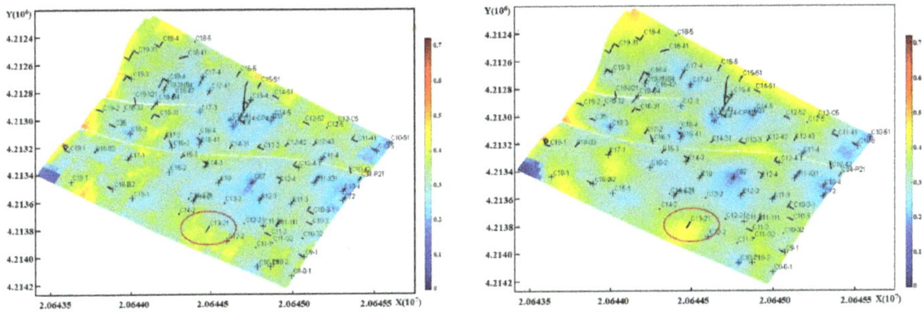

Figure 11. The average remaining oil saturation distribution (the left one is calculated by a traditional simulator, the right one is calculated by the new simulator).

Table 3. The first production of deployed production wells since 2017.

Well Name	Production Date	Permeability	Water Cut (%)	Average Production in the First Three Months (m^3/day)	Average Remaining Oil Saturation of Traditional Simulator	Average Remaining Oil Saturation of New Simulator
C18-3	May 2017	378	53	17.56	0.50	0.49
C19-4	June 2017	523	64.5	13.74	0.59	0.60
C12-1	September 2017	505	48.6	20.53	0.47	0.52
C18-42	April 2018	296	70.4	9.72	0.51	0.37
C16-5	August 2018	448	12.3	22.00	0.57	0.61
C14-31	November 2018	627	63.1	14.70	0.54	0.44
C12.42	April 2019	464	56.7	16.50	0.50	0.47
C13-2	July 2019	838	66.2	13.30	0.44	0.39

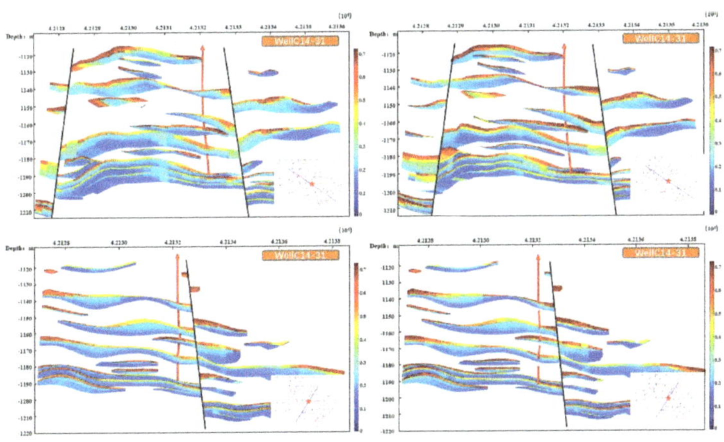

Figure 12. Cross section of remaining oil saturation of well C14-31 (the upper left one and the lower left one are the remaining oil profiles calculated by the numerical simulation method considering anisotropic relative permeability, and the upper right one and lower right one are the results of a traditional simulation).

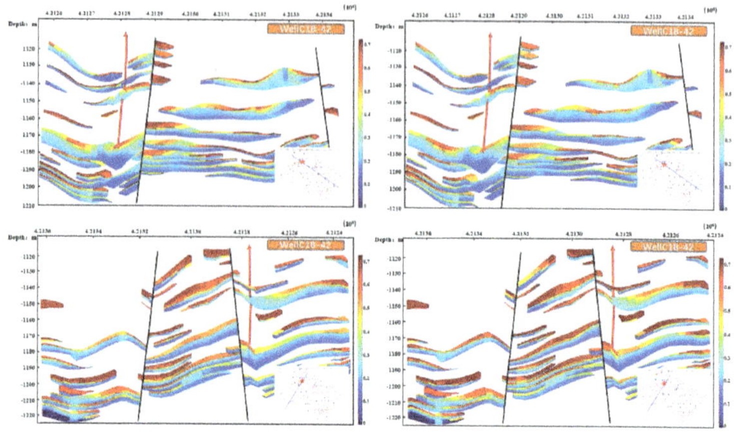

Figure 13. Cross section of remaining oil saturation of well C18-42 (the upper left one and the lower left one are the remaining oil profiles calculated by the numerical simulation method considering anisotropic relative permeability, and the upper right one and lower right one are the results of a traditional simulation).

The coincidence rate between the remaining oil saturation calculated by the traditional relative permeability and the initial production of the oil well is 62.5%, and the coincidence rate between the remaining oil saturation calculated by the anisotropic relative permeability and the initial production of the oil well is 87.5%, which is 25% higher (Table 3). Obviously, the remaining oil saturation calculated by anisotropic relative permeability shows better agreement with the actual situation and can describe the oil–water movement law more accurately.

We compared the change in water cut in the Cheng 4 South well area during the production process. Compared with the water cut calculated by the traditional numerical simulation method, the historical water cut shows a better agreement with that obtained by the numerical simulation algorithm considering anisotropic relative permeability (Figure 14).

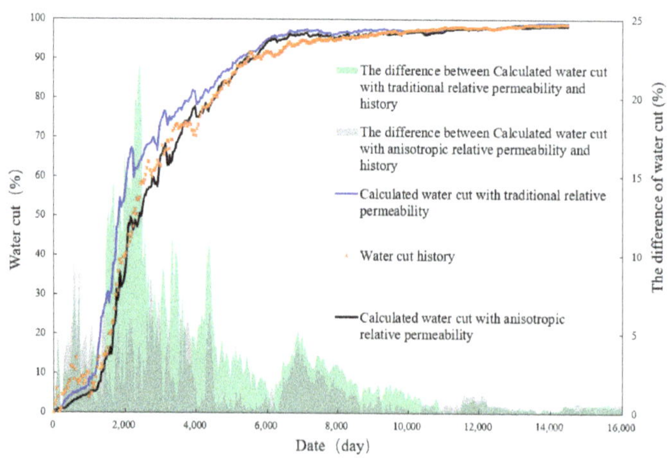

Figure 14. Water cut change with traditional relative permeability and anisotropic relative permeability in the production process of the Cheng 4 South well area.

5. Conclusions

In this paper, the anisotropic relative permeability of typical fluvial sandstone is studied using a self-developed anisotropic cubic core holder by unsteady-states relative permeability experiments. A new numerical simulator considering anisotropic relative permeability is established. The effect of anisotropic relative permeability in the flooding process is analyzed by the new simulator. An actual fluvial facies reservoir of Shengli Oilfield in China is selected as an example to validate the new simulator.

(1) In a heterogeneous rock with millimeter to centimeter scale laminae, relative permeability has directional characteristics. The greater the angle between the displacement direction and the bedding strike, the lower the residual oil saturation is, the higher the displacement efficiency is, and the relative permeability curve tends towards a rightward shift.

(2) Under the condition of anisotropic relative permeability, the pressure propagates more easily in the direction of higher relative permeability, and the fluid saturation changes more in the corresponding direction. The water free oil production period is longer than the calculation results of traditional numerical simulation.

(3) The new simulator shows excellent agreement with the actual oil field data. The coincidence rate between the remaining oil saturation calculated by the new simulator and the initial production of the oil well is 87.5%, which is 25% higher than that of a traditional simulator.

(4) Our work should provide important insights into the importance of anisotropic relative permeability and the application of numerical simulations in actual oil field production predictions.

Author Contributions: Writing—original draft, C.L.; Writing—review & editing, S.W. and Q.Y. Data curation, C.Y. All authors have read and agreed to the published version of the manuscript.

Funding: This research received no external funding.

Acknowledgments: I would like to thank Shuoliang Wang, Chunlei Yu and Qing You for their guidance in the process of writing and revising of this paper.

Conflicts of Interest: The authors declare no conflict of interest.

Nomenclature

μ_w	water vicosity
v_w	injection velocity
ρ_o	oil density
ρ_w	water density
f_w	water cut
λ_w	water mobility
λ_o	oil mobility
A	cross-sectional area
q_t	total volume flow of oil phase and water phase
k_{ro}	oil relative permeability
k_{rw}	water relative permeability
γ_o	oil unit weight
γ_w	water unit weight
K	absolute permeability tensor
μ_o	oil viscosity
P_o	oil phase pressure
P_w	water phase pressure
D	depth
φ	porosity
Δx_i	x-direction grid length
Δy_i	y-direction grid length
Δz_i	z-direction grid length

S_o	oil phase saturation
S_w	water phase saturation
V_{ijk}	volume of the bulk
$K_{rlanisotropic}$	anisotropic relative permeability tensor

Appendix A. The Oil Governing Equations

Oil phase:

$$\nabla \cdot \left[\frac{kk_{roanisotropic}\rho_o}{\mu_o} (\nabla p_o - \gamma_o \nabla D) \right] - q_o = \frac{\partial}{\partial t} (\rho_o \phi S_o) \tag{A1}$$

Water phase:

$$\nabla \cdot \left[\frac{kk_{rwanisotropic}\rho_w}{\mu_w} (\nabla p_w - \gamma_w \nabla D) \right] - q_w = \frac{\partial}{\partial t} (\rho_w \phi S_w) \tag{A2}$$

where: $\gamma_o = \rho_o g$; $\gamma_w = \rho_w g$, $K_{roanisotropic}$ is the oil phase relative permeability, K is the absolute permeability tensor, μ_o, p_o, and γ_o are the viscosity, pressure, and specific gravity of the oil phase, respectively, $K_{rwanisotropic}$ is the water phase relative permeability, μ_w, p_w, and γ_w are the viscosity, pressure, and specific gravity of the water phase, respectively, D is the depth, and ϕ is the porosity.

The results of the experiments in this paper showed that the relative permeability of oil and water is affected by the anisotropy of pore structure. In this paper, the $k_{rlanisotropic}$ in the above formula is written into three relative permeability expressions that vary with different directions when dealing with the anisotropic relative permeability, namely k_{rox}, k_{roy}, and k_{roz}. After the replacement here, the traditional isotropic relative permeability is replaced by the anisotropic relative permeability.

Taking the oil phase as an example, the governing equation is expanded initially into a rectangular coordinate component as follows.

$$\begin{aligned} &\frac{\partial}{\partial x}\left[\frac{\rho_o \cdot k}{\mu_o} \cdot k_{rox}\left(\frac{\partial p_o}{\partial x} - \gamma_o \frac{\partial D}{\partial x}\right)\right] + \frac{\partial}{\partial y}\left[\frac{\rho_o \cdot k}{\mu_o} \cdot k_{roy}\left(\frac{\partial p_o}{\partial y} - \gamma_o \frac{\partial D}{\partial y}\right)\right] \\ &+ \frac{\partial}{\partial z}\left[\frac{\rho_o \cdot k}{\mu_o} \cdot k_{roz}\left(\frac{\partial p_o}{\partial z} - \gamma_o \frac{\partial D}{\partial z}\right)\right] + q_o = \frac{\partial(\phi \rho_o S_o)}{\partial t} \end{aligned} \tag{A3}$$

For $(i,j,k,n+1)$ point, the subscript in the following expression is in an abbreviated form:

$$\begin{aligned} &\frac{\rho_o \cdot k \cdot k_{rox}}{\Delta x_i \cdot \mu_o}\left[\left(\frac{p_{i+1}^{n+1} - p_i^{n+1}}{\Delta x_{i+\frac{1}{2}}} - \gamma_{oi+\frac{1}{2}} \frac{D_{i+1} - D_i}{\Delta x_{i+\frac{1}{2}}}\right) + \left(\frac{p_{i-1}^{n+1} - p_i^{n+1}}{\Delta x_{i-\frac{1}{2}}} - \gamma_{oi-\frac{1}{2}} \frac{D_{i-1} - D_i}{\Delta x_{i-\frac{1}{2}}}\right)\right] \\ &+ \frac{\rho_o \cdot k \cdot k_{roy}}{\Delta y_j \cdot \mu_o}\left[\left(\frac{p_{j+1}^{n+1} - p_j^{n+1}}{\Delta y_{j+\frac{1}{2}}} - \gamma_{oj+\frac{1}{2}} \frac{D_{j+1} - D_j}{\Delta y_{j+\frac{1}{2}}}\right) + \left(\frac{p_{j-1}^{n+1} - p_j^{n+1}}{\Delta x_{j-\frac{1}{2}}} - \gamma_{oj-\frac{1}{2}} \frac{D_{j-1} - D_j}{\Delta x_{j-\frac{1}{2}}}\right)\right] \\ &+ \frac{\rho_o \cdot k \cdot k_{roz}}{\Delta z_k \cdot \mu_o}\left[\left(\frac{p_{k+1}^{n+1} - p_k^{n+1}}{\Delta z_{k+\frac{1}{2}}} - \gamma_{ok+\frac{1}{2}} \frac{D_{k+1} - D_k}{\Delta z_{k+\frac{1}{2}}}\right) + \left(\frac{p_{k-1}^{n+1} - p_k^{n+1}}{\Delta z_{k-\frac{1}{2}}} - \gamma_{ok-\frac{1}{2}} \frac{D_{k-1} - D_k}{\Delta z_{k-\frac{1}{2}}}\right)\right] \\ &+ q_o^{n+1} = \frac{1}{\Delta t}\left[(\phi \rho_o S_o)^{n+1} - (\phi \rho_o S_o)^n\right] \end{aligned} \tag{A4}$$

Multiply both sides by $V_{ijk} = \Delta x_i \Delta y_j \Delta z_k$ and define the following conductivity:

$$\begin{cases} TX_{oianisotropic+\frac{1}{2}} = \frac{V_{ijk}}{\Delta x_i} \frac{\frac{\rho_o \cdot k}{\mu_o} \cdot k_{rox}}{\Delta x_{i+\frac{1}{2}}} = \frac{\Delta y_j \Delta z_k}{\Delta x_{i+\frac{1}{2}}} \frac{\rho_o \cdot k}{\mu_o} \cdot k_{rox}, TX_{oianisotropic-\frac{1}{2}} = \frac{V_{ijk}}{\Delta x_i} \frac{\frac{\rho_o \cdot k}{\mu_o} \cdot k_{rox}}{\Delta x_{i-\frac{1}{2}}} = \frac{\Delta y_j \Delta z_k}{\Delta x_{i-\frac{1}{2}}} \frac{\rho_o \cdot k}{\mu_o} \cdot k_{rox} \\ TY_{ojanisotropic+\frac{1}{2}} = \frac{V_{ijk}}{\Delta y_j} \frac{\frac{\rho_o \cdot k}{\mu_o} \cdot k_{roy}}{\Delta y_{j+\frac{1}{2}}} = \frac{\Delta x_i \Delta z_k}{\Delta y_{j+\frac{1}{2}}} \frac{\rho_o \cdot k}{\mu_o} \cdot k_{roy}, TY_{ojanisotropic-\frac{1}{2}} = \frac{V_{ijk}}{\Delta y_j} \frac{\frac{\rho_o \cdot k}{\mu_o} \cdot k_{roy}}{\Delta y_{j-\frac{1}{2}}} = \frac{\Delta x_i \Delta z_k}{\Delta y_{j-\frac{1}{2}}} \frac{\rho_o \cdot k}{\mu_o} \cdot k_{roy} \\ TZ_{okanisotropic+\frac{1}{2}} = \frac{V_{ijk}}{\Delta z_k} \frac{\frac{\rho_o \cdot k}{\mu_o} \cdot k_{roz}}{\Delta z_{k+\frac{1}{2}}} = \frac{\Delta x_i \Delta y_j}{\Delta z_{k+\frac{1}{2}}} \frac{\rho_o \cdot k}{\mu_o} \cdot k_{roz}, TZ_{okanisotropic-\frac{1}{2}} = \frac{V_{ijk}}{\Delta z_k} \frac{\frac{\rho_o \cdot k}{\mu_o} \cdot k_{roz}}{\Delta z_{i-\frac{1}{2}}} = \frac{\Delta x_i \Delta y_j}{\Delta z_{i-\frac{1}{2}}} \frac{\rho_o \cdot k}{\mu_o} \cdot k_{roz} \end{cases} \tag{A5}$$

The second-order difference operator is defined as follows:

$$\begin{cases} \Delta_x TX_{oanisotropic}\Delta_x P = TX_{oianisotropic+\frac{1}{2}}(p_{i+1}-p_i) + TX_{oianisotropic-\frac{1}{2}}(p_{i-1}-p_i) \\ \Delta_y TY_{oanisotropic}\Delta_y P = TY_{ojanisotropic+\frac{1}{2}}(p_{j+1}-p_j) + TY_{ojanisotropic-\frac{1}{2}}(p_{j-1}-p_j) \\ \Delta_z TZ_{oanisotropic}\Delta_z P = TZ_{okanisotropic+\frac{1}{2}}(p_{k+1}-p_k) + TZ_{okanisotropic-\frac{1}{2}}(p_{k-1}-p_k) \end{cases} \quad (A6)$$

The oil phase governing equation is discretized as a sample in this section, which is shown as follows:

$$\begin{aligned} &\Delta_x TX_{oanisotropic}\Delta_x P^{n+1} + \Delta_y TY_{oanisotropic}\Delta_y P^{n+1} + \Delta_z TZ_{oanisotropic}\Delta_z P^{n+1} - \Delta_x TX_{oanisotropic}\gamma_{og}\Delta_x D \\ &-\Delta_y TY_{oanisotropic}\gamma_{og}\Delta_y D - \Delta_z TZ_{oanisotropic}\gamma_{og}\Delta_z D + q_o^{n+1}V_{ijk} = \frac{V_{ijk}}{\Delta t}\left[(\phi\rho_o S_o)^{n+1} - (\phi\rho_o S_o)^n\right] \end{aligned} \quad (A7)$$

Then, the formula above can be further simplified as follows:

$$\Delta T_{o_{anisotropic}}\Delta P^{n+1} - \Delta T_{o_{anisotropic}}\Delta D + q_o^{n+1}V_{ijk} = \frac{V_{ijk}}{\Delta t}\left[(\phi\rho_o S_o)^{n+1} - (\phi\rho_o S_o)^n\right] \quad (A8)$$

The governing equation of the water phase is expressed with the same format. So far, the anisotropic relative permeability is introduced into the traditional numerical simulation method by dealing with the relative permeability in the traditional oil and water phase governing equation.

References

1. Honarpour, M.M. *Relative Permeability of Petroleum Reservoirs*; The Chemical Rubber Company Press: Boca Raton, FL, USA, 1986.
2. Ramstad, T.; Idowu, N.; Nardi, C.; Øren, P.-E. Relative permeability calculations from two-phase flow simulations directly on digital images of porous rocks. *Transp. Porous Media* **2012**, *94*, 487–504. [CrossRef]
3. Deng, Q. Microscale Occurence and Recovery Mechanism of Remaining Oil in Sazhong Area at Extra-High Water Stage of Daqing Field. Ph.D. Thesis, Northeast Petroleum University, Daqing, China, 2015.
4. Wang, S.; Yu, C.; Sang, G.; Zhao, Q. A new numerical simulator considering the effect of enhanced liquid on relative permeability. *J. Pet. Sci. Eng.* **2019**, *177*, 282–294. [CrossRef]
5. Fang, Y.; Yang, E.; Yin, D.; Gan, Y. Study on distribution characteristics of microscopic residual oil in low permeability reservoirs. *J. Dispers. Sci. Technol.* **2019**, *41*, 575–584. [CrossRef]
6. Hsieh, A.I.; Allen, D.M.; MacEachern, J.A. Upscaling permeability for reservoir-scale modeling in bioturbated, heterogeneous tight siliciclastic reservoirs: Lower Cretaceous Viking Formation, Provost Field, AL, Canada. *Mar. Pet. Geol.* **2017**, *88*, 1032–1046. [CrossRef]
7. Peng, J.; Zhang, J.; Shen, Z.; Ye, J. Effect of grain shape on pore characteristics and permeabilities of coarse-grained soil. *Rock Soil Mech.* **2017**, *41*, 592–600.
8. Sun, D.; Li, A.; Wang, H.; Zhao, W.; Qiao, E.; Long, C. Experiment on anisotropy of permeability with tight sandstone. *Prog. Geophys.* **2012**, *27*, 1101–1106.
9. Zhang, Q.; Sun, W.; Ming, H.; Wang, Q.; Zhang, L. Micro-pore Structure of Diagenetic Facies of Chang 6_3 Reservoir and Distribution of High Quality Reservoir in Banqiao-Heshui Area. *Acta Sedimentol. Sin.* **2016**, *34*, 336–345.
10. Su, Y.; Li, T. Effects studies of areal heterogeneity on oil-water displacement law in extra-low permeability reservoirs. *Pet. Geol. Recov. Effic.* **2009**, *16*, 69–71.
11. Gao, H.; Jiang, H.; Chen, M. Simulation study on the effect of the microscopic parameters of reservoir pore structure on oi-l water relative permeability. *J. Xi'an Shiyou Univ.* **2007**, *22*, 56–59.
12. Hunt, A.; Ewing, R.; Ghanbarian, B. *Percolation Theory for Flow in Porous Media*; Springer: Berlin/Heidelberg, Germany, 2014.
13. Farquharson, J.I.; Wadsworth, F.B. Upscaling permeability in anisotropic volcanic systems. *J. Volcanol. Geotherm. Res.* **2018**, *364*, 35–47. [CrossRef]
14. Sun, F. Analysis of permeability orientation in reservoir. *Fault Block Oil Gas Field* **2007**, *14*, 38–39.
15. Nordlund, M.; Penha, D.J.L.; Stolz, S.; Kuczaj, A.; Winkelmann, C.; Geurts, B.J. A new analytical model for the permeability of anisotropic structured porous media. *Int. J. Eng. Sci.* **2013**, *68*, 38–60. [CrossRef]
16. Li, T.; Li, M.; Jing, X.; Xiao, W.; Cui, Q. Influence mechanism of pore-scale anisotropy and pore distribution heterogeneity on permeability of porous media. *Pet. Explor. Dev.* **2019**, *46*, 569–579. [CrossRef]
17. Corey, A.T.; Rathjens, C. Effect of stratification on relative permeability. *J. Pet. Technol.* **1956**, *8*, 69–71. [CrossRef]
18. Honarpour, M.; Cullick, A.; Saad, N.; Humphreys, N. Effect of rock heterogeneity on relative permeability: Implications for scale-up. *J. Pet. Technol.* **1956**, *47*, 980–986. [CrossRef]
19. Crotti, M.; Rosbaco, J. Relative Permeability Curves: The Influence of Flow Direction and Heterogeneities. In Proceedings of the SPE/DOE Improved Oil Recovery Symposium, Tulsa, OK, USA, 19–22 April 1998.

20. Crotti, M.; Cobeñas, R. Scaling Up of Laboratory Relative Permeability Curves. An Advantageous Approach Based on Realistic Average Water Saturations. In Proceedings of the SPE Latin American and Caribbean Petroleum Engineering Conference, Buenos Aires, Argentina, 25–28 March 2001.
21. Keilegavlen, E.; Nordbotten, J.M.; Stephansen, A. Simulating two-phase flow in porous media with anisotropic relative permeabilities. In Proceedings of the SPE Reservoir Simulation Symposium, The Woodlands, TX, USA, 21–23 February 2011.
22. Krause, M. Modeling and investigation of the influence of capillary heterogeneity on relative permeability. In Proceedings of the SPE Annual Technical Conference and Exhibition, San Antonio, TX, USA, 8–10 October 2012.
23. Krause, M.; Krevor, S.; Benson, S.M. A procedure for the accurate determination of sub-core scale permeability distributions with error quantification. *Transp. Porous Media* **2013**, *98*, 565–588. [CrossRef]
24. Zheng, W.; Liu, Y.; Liu, Y.; Wang, Y.; Ma, J. Anisotropic experiment of microfracture relative permeability. *Fault-Block OilGas Field* **2019**, *26*, 21.
25. Ezeuko, C.C.; McDougall, S.R.; Bondino, I.; Hamon, G. Anisotropic Relative Permeabilities for Characterising Heavy-Oil Depletion Experiment. In Proceedings of the SPE Symposium on Improved Oil Recovery, Tulsa, OK, USA, 20–23 April 2008.
26. Kortekaas, T.F. Water/oil displacement characteristics in crossbedded reservoir zones. *Soc. Pet. Eng. J.* **1985**, *25*, 917–926. [CrossRef]
27. Paterson, L.; Painter, S.; Zhang, X.; Pinczewski, V. Simulating residual saturation and relative permeability in heterogeneous formations. In Proceedings of the SPE Annual Technical Conference and Exhibition, Denver, CO, USA, 6–9 October 1996.
28. Bondino, I.; McDougall, S.R.; Hamon, G. Interpretation of a long core heavy oil depletion experiment using pore network modelling techniques. In Proceedings of the International Symposium of the Society of Core Analysts, Pau, France, 21–24 September 2003.
29. Pergament, A.K.; Tomin, P.Y. The study of relative phase-permeability functions for anisotropic media. *Math. Models Comput. Simul.* **2012**, *4*, 1–9. [CrossRef]
30. Sedaghat, M.H.; Gerke, K.; Azizmohammadi, S.; Matthai, S.K. Simulation-based determination of relative permeability in laminated rocks. *Energy Procedia* **2016**, *97*, 433–439. [CrossRef]
31. Xiu, L.; Liu, S.; Liu, L.; Liu, L.; Zhang, G. Research on Oil Droplets Deformation Flow of Water-flooding Reservoir. *Contemp. Chem. Ind.* **2015**, *44*, 1443–1445.
32. Yin, D.; Fang, Y.; Xin, Y. Study on Microscopic Mechanism of Changing Displacement Direction in Low-Permeability Reservoirs. *Spec. Oil Gas Reserv.* **2017**, *24*, 59.
33. Zhu, W.; Ma, Q.; Li, B.; Liu, Y.; Yue, M. Influence of injection-production angle variation on oil displacement efficiency and microscope remaining oil. *Fault-Block OilGas Field* **2019**, *26*, 220–224.
34. Kaminski, M.; Carey, G. Stochastic perturbation-based finite element approach to fluid flow problems. *Int. J. Numer. Methods HeatFluid Flow* **2005**, *15*, 671–697. [CrossRef]
35. Hustad, O.S.; Browning, D.J. A fully coupled three-phase model for capillary pressure and relative permeability for implicit compositional reservoir simulation. In Proceedings of the SPE/EAGE Reservoir Characterization, Simulation Conference, Abu Dhabi, United Arab Emirates, 19–21 October 2009.
36. Gomez-Hernandez, J.; Guardiola-Albert, C. Inverse Conditional Simulation of Relative Permeabilities. In *Geostatistics Banff 2004*; Springer: Berlin/Heidelberg, Germany, 2004; pp. 325–331.
37. Hailwood, E.A.; Ding, F. Palaeomagnetic reorientation of cores and the magnetic fabric of hydrocarbon reservoir sands. *Geol. Soc. Lond. Spec. Publ.* **1995**, *98*, 245–258. [CrossRef]
38. Hou, S.; Tian, G. Palaeomagnetic Orientation of Cores and Its Applications for Insitu Stress Measurements. *J. Geomech.* **1999**, *5*, 90–96.
39. Dong, P. Numerical Simulation Technolog Orientation Determination of Maximum Horizontal Stress in Reservoir Formation by Paleomagnetic Orientation of Cores. *Chin. J. Rock Mech. Eng.* **2004**, *23*, 2480.
40. Xie, J.; Ge, K.; Xu, H.; Deng, J. Review of Paleomagnetic Core Orientation Method. *Prog. Geophys.* **2020**, *35*, 906–917.

energies

Article

Development of a Low-Cost Data Acquisition System for Very Short-Term Photovoltaic Power Forecasting

Guilherme Fonseca Bassous *, Rodrigo Flora Calili and Carlos Hall Barbosa

Graduate Programme in Metrology, Pontifical Catholic University of Rio de Janeiro—PUC-Rio, Rio de Janeiro 22451-900, Brazil; calili@puc-rio.br (R.F.C.); hall@puc-rio.br (C.H.B.)
* Correspondence: gfbassous@gmail.com

Abstract: The rising adoption of renewable energy sources means we must turn our eyes to limitations in traditional energy systems. Intermittency, if left unaddressed, may lead to several power-quality and energy-efficiency issues. The objective of this work is to develop a working tool to support photovoltaic energy forecast models for real-time operation applications. The current paradigm of intra-hour solar-power forecasting is to use image-based approaches to predict the state of cloud composition for short time horizons. Since the objective of intra-minute forecasting is to address high-frequency intermittency, data must provide information on and surrounding these events. For that purpose, acquisition by exception was chosen as the guiding principle. The system performs power measurements at 1 Hz frequency, and whenever it detects variations over a certain threshold, it saves the data 10 s before and 4 s after the detection point. A multilayer perceptron neural network was used to determine its relevance to the forecasting problem. With a thorough selection of attributes and network structures, the results show very low error with R^2 greater than 0.93 for both input variables tested with a time horizon of 60 s. In conclusion, the data provided by the acquisition system yielded relevant information for forecasts up to 60 s ahead.

Keywords: solar energy; neural networks; sky-camera; forecasting; renewable energy; energy quality; multilayer perceptron; computer vision; short-term forecasting; metrology

Citation: Bassous, G.F.; Calili, R.F.; Barbosa, C.H. Development of a Low-Cost Data Acquisition System for Very Short-Term Photovoltaic Power Forecasting. *Energies* **2021**, *14*, 6075. https://doi.org/10.3390/en14196075

Academic Editors: Marcin Kamiński and Angel A. Juan

Received: 19 August 2021
Accepted: 18 September 2021
Published: 24 September 2021

1. Introduction

In the past few decades, the world has experienced considerable growth in environmental awareness, especially regarding climate changes. This rise, allied with an ever-increasing population and limitations to fossil fuels, stimulates the development of Renewable Energy Systems (RES). To reduce greenhouse gas emissions, energy matrices must be composed of more low-carbon sources as opposed to the current fossil-reliant paradigm. Solar photovoltaic (PV) and wind are the future of energy systems if the world is to meet the goals set by the Paris Agreement [1,2].

In addition to the climate-specific Paris Agreement, the 2030 Agenda for Sustainable Development [3] proposes 17 general sustainable development goals with 169 associated global targets. Of these goals, the access to affordable and reliable renewable energy sources is directly aligned with three goals: 7—to ensure access to affordable, reliable, sustainable and modern energy for all; 9—to build resilient infrastructure, promote inclusive and sustainable industrialization and foster innovation; and 12—to ensure sustainable consumption and production patterns.

However, each of the mentioned energy sources has its own limitations, such as geographical location and unreliability, mostly regarding weather. In the case of solar energy, particularly PV energy conversion to produce electricity, it possesses high variability from various sources (e.g., weather, Earth's rotation and translation movements).

Solar energy's inherent intermittency creates several economical, technical and political barriers against larger penetration [4–6]. Most of the variability components are deterministic in nature, meaning that they can be easily forecasted and addressed, provided that it is technically possible to do so.

One of the most detrimental variability components is the presence of clouds, which filter the solar radiation and decrease the amount of energy available for photovoltaic conversion. Particularly on days with partial cloudiness and fast-moving clouds, the insolation variation in one solar plant output can reach well over 50% in one minute [7,8]. These fast variations in such a short time may cause technical problems in plant and grid operation, such as voltage variations and current harmonics [5,6,9–11]. To address these variations, it is necessary to forecast them. In the work reported in Reference [8], the need for power system operators to be able to address generation and load profiles over short time-scales was stressed due to the stochastic variations caused by fast cloud transients. Numerous methods for short-term insolation or power forecasting exist; however, for plant and grid operation, conventional statistic forecasting methods based on time series are not well suited [12]. The most widely used physical methods for short-term predictions are sky-image based [13].

Tropical countries, in general, boast higher solar photovoltaic potential in comparison with temperate regions, and, in contrast, these countries also possess lower development indexes. That leads to increased difficulty in acquiring specific equipment for conducting research in solar modeling and forecasting, even more so if such equipment is necessary for implementing mitigation strategies. Figure 1 shows the discrepancy in solar resource availability and, in contrast, its utilization. The red scale represents daily average global tilted irradiance (GTI) [14], and the yellow sun symbols represent the installed capacity normalized by a country's area. In some areas, such as Europe and Central America, only the most important solar generators were kept on the map for clearer data representation.

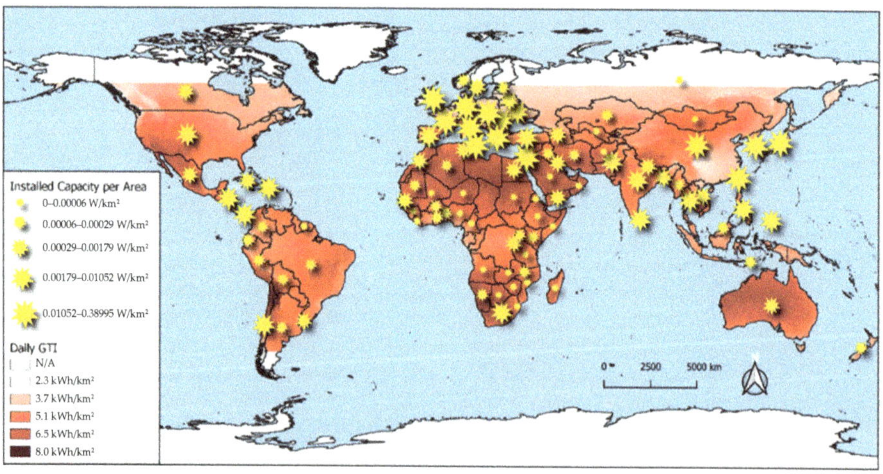

Figure 1. Daily GTI and installed capacity per country [15,16].

The first discrepancy between solar potential and utilization is clearly between African and European countries. Despite having two to three times more average daily global tilted irradiance, most African countries have a couple orders of magnitude less PV installed capacity. Another interesting comparison can be made between Mexico and the United States, because, despite being in the same continent, both have very different development levels, and that is more correlated to the installed capacity than solar resource availability. A similar comparison can be made between Brazil and Uruguay, Morocco and South Africa, and Spain and the United Kingdom. This makes clear the necessity for lower cost equipment, because, by reducing cost barriers, these countries can look to solar energy infrastructure to support their industrial development. Addressing these discrepancies has been recognized as an important step in achieving the sustainable development goals set for 2030 [3,17].

Aside from the solar resource availability, forecasting is essential to energy generation and distribution. As mentioned in Reference [8], system operators need better information about the stochastic behavior of cloud-induced variability, to increase reliability. Several time horizons and resolutions are necessary to meet the demands of each specific aspect in PV energy management. The focus of this work is on very short-term forecasting to bolster PV plant operation capabilities, reliability, grid integration and grid operation in a scenario of high penetration.

In Reference [12], different irradiance forecasting methods are explored with the objective of proposing a small-scale insular grid forecasting system. Small isolated grids have less system inertia, therefore are more susceptible to the negative effects of RES, especially those caused by PV systems. Each different model available has its advantages and disadvantages and, for a holistic forecasting system, different models should be used in parallel.

Persistence and image-based models fit well, for short-term forecasts, in terms of horizon, frequency and spatial resolution. Other statistical models, as named in Reference [12], also encompass various regression models and learning algorithms, such as artificial neural networks (ANN).

In recent years there has been a rise in research work on sky-image based PV or insolation forecasting [18,19]. Sky-image models keep improving the reliability of very short-term forecasting, as shown in Reference [13]. This tendency points towards the superiority of using sky images over what Diagne et al. [12] refer to as statistical models. In the study conducted by Kow et al. [20] it becomes apparent just how powerful sky-image based forecasting can be, achieving a detection rate of over 90% of power fluctuation events and mitigation of almost 80% of power fluctuation events with minimal energy loss.

While being a powerful tool, forecasting alone cannot solve the issues caused by high-frequency variability. However, coupled with other systems, such as energy storage systems and power electronics, especially in progressively smarter grids, forecasting can be a valuable aid in increasing PV penetration [9–11,21–24]. The results presented by Kow et al. [20] depict the beneficial effect that short-term forecasting can have on the operation of PV plants.

As some authors have shown, even lower-cost equipment can yield trustworthy results when comprehensively developed and tested [25]. This serves as encouragement for research institutions in developing and less-developed countries to work on their own equipment to provide their scientific and industrial needs.

Looking at the case for Brazil, which meets the criteria for solar resource abundance and developing economy, increasing accessibility to research equipment aligns with the country's goals set for the UN sustainable development goals prioritized for its 2030 agenda. Oliveira et al. [26] point out that Brazilian relay targets, highly influential as well as dependent within the agenda, can be directly impacted by increased affordability in solar power research. Goals such as resource efficiency, upgraded infrastructure, education and institutional capacity on climate change, and renewable energy depend on other goals, but also impact several others.

Reduction of costs associated with determinant goals such as research and development, innovation and economic growth have a high potential of impacting the relay goals previously mentioned [26]. More specifically, the affordability of newer renewable energy technology and their development align with the following targets: 7.1—"ensure universal access to affordable, reliable and modern energy services"; 7.2—"increase substantially the share of renewable energy in the global energy mix"; 7.3—"double the global rate of improvement in energy efficiency"; 7.b—"expand infrastructure and upgrade technology for supplying modern and sustainable energy services for all in developing countries, in particular least developed countries, small islands developing States and landlocked developing countries [...]"; 9.1—"develop quality, reliable, sustainable and resilient infrastructure, including regional and transborder infrastructure, to support economic development and human well-being, with a focus on affordable and equitable access for all"; 9.2—"promote inclusive and sustainable industrialization [. . .]"; 9.5—enhance scientific research, upgrade the technological capabilities of industrial sectors in all countries in particular developing countries [. . .]"; 12.2—"achieve the sustainable management and efficient use of natural resources"; and 12.a—"support developing countries to strengthen their scientific and technological capacity to move towards more sustainable patterns of consumption and production".

With these possible impacts in mind, the objective of this work is to present and validate a low-cost system for monitoring and modeling short-term variability developed during a Master's course [27].

2. Short-Term Forecasting

As stated in the previous section, accurate very short-term forecasting is the first step in adding reliability to PV plant operation. The first step in forecasting is to build a model that describes the behavior of the studied phenomenon. To that end, many different models can describe or learn the behavior of PV conversion, some more accurately than others. Table 1 presents the terminology regarding forecasting horizons and their applications, based on the concepts used in References [12,28].

Table 1. Forecast horizon categories, granularity and applications.

Category	Time Horizon	Resolution	Applicability
Very short-term	Up to 15 min ahead	Up to 1 min	Plant operation Ramping events Power quality control
Short-term	15 min to 1 h ahead	1 to 5 min	Load following Grid operation planning
Medium-term	1 h to 6 h	Hourly	Load following Grid operation planning
Long-term	One day ahead	Hourly	Unit commitment Transmission scheduling Day ahead markets

Within the statistical category mentioned in Reference [12], persistence models are the best fit for the spatial and temporal requirements of very short-term forecasting for a single PV plant. However, it is a naïve predictor, serving as a baseline for more complex models. It assumes the predicted value $\hat{X}_{t+1}$ to be best described by its value at a previous time X_t. In this case, the modeling and prediction are one and the same; it does not take into consideration the several variables that affect the behavior of real-world PV panels, and that is why it is considered a trivial predictor.

Still, within linear models, the regression models addressed by Diagne et al. [12] use historical data either from irradiance or clear-sky index to make predictions. While better than the previous, naïve predictors in terms of fidelity to the real world, it is still unable to provide forecasts in the required time horizon and resolution. These models, however, fare well from 15 min to hourly forecasts [29]. In the 5 min resolution, results were mixed among the models tested by Reikard [29], but the autoregressive integrated moving average (ARIMA) model started to be outperformed, especially by neural networks. The author also pointed that the ARIMA model exhibited large errors at intermittent intervals, corresponding to the fast cloud transients that deeply impact PV reliability. These intermittent large errors are the events successfully predicted in the work by Kow et al. [20].

Switching over to the non-linear models addressed by Diagne et al. [12], neural-network models attempt to simulate the computational and learning process of the human brain [30]. The complexity, nonlinearity and parallel computational power excel in pattern recognition and perception. The networks are composed of simple processing units commonly referred to as neurons. The network can acquire "knowledge" through a learning process that acts in the interconnection of the neurons, just as synapses would in a biological brain [30].

Neural networks, in their many architectures and sizes, are able to learn from data, in both supervised and non-supervised processes, and apply this knowledge to new data [30]. They are well suited to model complex problems, especially when involving complex relationships between the variables [30], such as forecasting energy conversion dependent on cloud passage, location, time and meteorological variables [31,32].

As mentioned previously, neural networks start faring better against other forecast methods at higher temporal resolution [29]; however, by looking at other studies into the subject, there appears to be a time-resolution limitation in these machine-learning methods for short-term forecasts. Even in the most recent state of the art works with intra-hour forecasting, using time series prediction of irradiance or other atmospheric parameters, the minimum resolution is still 5 min [33,34], which still falls short of the necessary frequency to properly characterize the local solar variability [35]. Still, within the 5 min time horizon, sky images can be used to boost forecasting accuracy when coupled with machine learning models and historic irradiance or power data [36].

The conclusion that can be drawn from the consistent number of time-series models limited to the 5 min time horizon is that the fault is in the type of data used to characterize the relationships involved in the high variability of solar irradiance. As explained before, these models aim to predict the future state of a certain aspect of solar variability. The approaches using cloud tracking in sky images, as proposed by Chow et al. [37] and Kow et al. [20], add components of physical and geometrical modeling of cloud systems. Since the main actor in short-term variability is related to passing clouds, relevant information on their dynamic provides a more comprehensive characterization [38].

The trend in researching sky-based approaches to very short-term solar forecasting began with the work by Chow et al. [37], despite not being the first to approach the subject [38]. The goal behind it is to use physical information from cloud systems, extracted from sky images captured by hemispheric cameras.

Initially, researchers used already existing sky imagers developed for meteorological purposes other than estimating solar quantities [38]. In more recent years, other lower-cost alternatives have been developed for the specific purpose of estimating solar quantities [25,38]. These newer, specific systems are fully programmable and expandable, leaving room for development and expansion, as well as being suitable for use with a plethora of different forecasting models [25,39].

Amongst the already mentioned advantages, specifically designed systems have proven to yield superior results to other non-specific sky imaging systems [25,40,41]. Most likely this superior performance is due to the higher data-acquisition frequency which provides better insight into local short-term solar variability [35]. Another significant difference is that these specific devices do not have a shadow band to occlude the solar disk and part of the circumsolar region. This fact positively impacts the amount of information available for intra-minute forecasts.

Throughout the research process that laid the theoretical foundations of this work, several key works stood out and greatly influenced the work developed here. Table 2 contains these important works in chronological order with their objectives, whether it is forecasting or modeling, and the materials and methods used in the pursuit of these objectives.

Table 2. Important works that shaped this research.

Work	Objective	Materials and Methods
Chow et al. (2011) [37]	Forecast of GHI from 30 s to 5 min ahead	Sky images obtained from a Total Sky Imager (TSI) every 30 s; Clear Sky Library (CSL) + Sunshine Parameter + Red-Blue Ratio (RBR) cloud classification; Cloud tracking through cross-correlationGHI deterministically calculated.
Gohari et al. (2013) [41]	Forecast of Clear Sky Index up to 15 min ahead in 30 s intervals	Comparison between TSI and UCSD-developed USI; Sky images every 30 s + irradiance measurements every second; Geometric cloud tracking; Solar ray tracing.
Chu et al. (2013) [42]	Forecast of 1-min-average DNI 5 min and 10 min ahead	TSI images every 20 s + DNI every 30 s; CLS + RBR adaptive threshold cloud classification; Cloudiness indices from gridded image + time lagged DNI as inputs for NN.
Marquez and Coimbra (2013) [43]	Forecast of 1-min-average DNI 3 min to 15 min ahead	TSI images every minute + 30 s averaged DNI; Cloud tracking, using Particle Image Velocimetry software; Hybrid threshold algorithm for cloud pixel classification; Grid of cloudiness indices used to deterministically calculate DNI.
Quesada-Ruiz et al. (2014) [44]	Forecast of 1-min-average DNI from 3 to 20 min ahead	TSI images every 20 s + 1 min averaged DNI; Hybrid threshold algorithm for cloud pixel classification; Cloud tracking, using grid cloud fraction change; DNI estimation, using grid cloud fraction.
West et al. (2014) [45]	Forecast of DNI from 0 to 20 min ahead in 10 s resolution and updated every 10 s	Sky images from internet protocol (IP) camera + DNI every 10 s; Cloud pixel detection, using NN; Cloud tracking through pixel-wise optical flow; Image regions averaged and total cloudiness as feature to be forecasted and derived into DNI.
Chu et al. (2015a) [46]	Forecast of 10 min ahead GHI and DNI	Images from 2 IP sky cameras every 60 s + irradiance every 30 s; Adaptive threshold cloud detection; Gridded cloudiness + time lagged irradiance as inputs for NN.
Alonso-Montesinos and Battles (2015) [47]	Modeling of GHI, DNI and DIF	TSI images every 60 s + GHI + DNI every 60 s; Correlations of digital image channels to model irradiance.
Alonso-Montesinos et al. (2015) [48]	Forecast of GHI, DNI and DIF from 1 to 180 min, at 15 min resolution	TSI images every 60 s; Cloud tracking, using cloud motion vectors (CMV); Pixel-wise cloud detection;Pixel-wise irradiance, using correlation of digital channel information.
Cazorla et al. (2015) [19]	Methodology for cloud detection	SONA sky imager + GHI + DIF; Multi-exposure (High Dynamic Range—HDR) images every 5 min; Adaptive RBR threshold method for cloud detection.

Table 2. *Cont.*

Work	Objective	Materials and Methods
Chu et al. (2015) [50]	Forecasting of prediction interval for 1-min-average DNI 5, 10, 15 and 20 min ahead	USI images provide parameters for hybrid model; Hybrid estimation/forecast model based on bootstrapped-ANN selected by SVM classifier, using mean RBR, RBR standard deviation and entropy + time-lagged DNI and DIF measurements as inputs; SVM for sky classification and model selection (high vs. low cloud-derived variability).
Chu et al. (2015b) [51]	Forecast of PV power 5, 10 and 15 min ahead	2 TSI providing images every 30 s; 3 methods as inputs for ANN reforecasting (deterministic based on cloud tracking, ARMA and kNN); Preliminary forecast by one of the 3 methods followed by reforecast, using ANN to enhance performance; Genetic algorithm to select ANN inputs; among several time-lagged power measurements and preliminary power forecasts for each of the horizons.
Lipperheide et al. (2015) [52]	Forecast of power ramp events 20 s to 180 s ahead with 20 s resolution	1 Hz power data from PV panels used in 4 different methods; Persistence and ramp persistence forecast based on detection from PV panels within plant; Cloud speed persistence forecast based on cloud motion vectors detected by PV panel power fluctuation;Second-order autoregressive forecast model based on the modified covariance method.
Pedro and Coimbra (2015) [53]	Forecast of GHI and DNI from 5 to 30 min ahead	5-min-averaged irradiance data; IP camera images every 60 s; Digital image channel individual information and relationships' properties, such as mean, standard deviation and entropy; kNN forecast model with images vs. without images vs. persistence.
Xu et al. (2015) [54]	Forecast of GHI from 1 to 15 min ahead	TSI images every 20 s; Complex cloud detection and tracking; Pixel-wise classification using RGB values, RBR and Laplacian of Gaussian (LoG); Cloud-type classification through texture metrics and kNN classifier; Comparison of persistence, linear regression and Support Vector Regression (SVR) with image inputs and NWP variables.
Cervantes et al. (2016) [39]	Forecast of 5 min ahead DNI negative ramp events	Low-cost sky-imager; Cloud detection through RBR; Cloud tracking with optical flow; Shadow mapping, using Cloud Base Height (CBH) data.
Mejia et al. (2016) [55]	Cloud optical depth modeling	2 USI providing images every 30 s; Estimation of irradiance from calibrated pixel values; Usage of deterministic models to obtain optical depth from digital image channels, solar position, pixel position and clear-sky library.

Table 2. *Cont.*

Work	Objective	Materials and Methods
Rana et al. (2016) [56]	Forecast of PV power from 5 to 60 min ahead, with 5 min resolution	5 min power average + meteorological data; Univariate (solely power measurements) vs. multivariate models NN ensemble vs. SVR vs. persistence.
Sanfilippo et al. (2016) [57]	Forecast of 1-min-average clearness index from 1 to 15 min ahead	GHI, DNI and DHI measurements every 60 s; Modeling of solar zenith-independent clearness index; SVR, persistence and autoregressive models of different orders used for forecasting.
Schmidt et al. (2016) [19]	Forecasts of GHI from 15 s to 25 min GHI forecasts in grid form for the surrounding area, updated every 15 s with 15 s resolution	Sky images every 15 s from custom imager + GHI every 1 s from 99 pyranometers + CBH measurements averaged over 10 min; Area of study of 10 km × 12 km; RBR with clear-sky images for cloud pixel classification; SVC cloud type classification from several features;CMV cloud tracking.
Soubdhan et al. (2016) [58]	Forecast of PV power and GHI 1, 5, 10, 30 and 60 min ahead	PV power data every 1 s + percentage cloud cover + ambient temperature + GHI every 1 s; Persistence and smart persistence baselines; Forecasting by Kalman filter with initialized parameters, using expectation-maximization (EM) algorithm vs. autoregressive (AR) estimation; Comparison between with and without exogenous inputs.
Ai et al. (2017) [59]	Forecast of 30-s-average GHI 1, 2, 3 min ahead	Sky images every 30 s from IP camera; SVM-determined clear-sky model; Adaptive threshold cloud detection; Optical flow cloud tracking; GHI deterministically determined, using cloud fraction and clear-sky model.
Blanc et al. (2017) [60]	Forecast of 1-min-average DNI map 15 min ahead with up to 10 m × 10 m spatial resolution	Stereoscopic IP sky cameras providing images every 30 s; CBH estimation from stereography; Cloud-layer CMV for each class of altitude; Estimation of projection-pixel-wise DNI, using beam clear-sky indexes computed per class of cloud combined with physical and geometrical information.
Cheng (2017) [61]	Detection of irradiance ramp down events 5, 10, 15 and 20 min ahead	Sky images every 60 s from Santa Barbara; Instrument Group + 1 min averaged GHI; Cloud detection and tracking through feature point clusters.
Elsinga and Van Sark (2017) [62]	Forecasts of 1 min average GHI from 1 to 30 min ahead for multiple sites	202 rooftop PV systems acting as a sensor grid;PV power data averaged every 1 min from inverter data every 2 s and then converted into GHI; Hourly interpolated ambient temperature deterministically calculated; GHI converted into clearness index Peer-to-Peer (P2P) forecasting method, using correlations between the rooftop PV systems to determine time lag between correlated sites.

Table 2. *Cont.*

Work	Objective	Materials and Methods
Ni et al. (2017) [63]	Forecast of power interval 5 min ahead	Ensemble of single-layer feed-forward NN (weights assigned, using a least-squares method in 1 step); Data from 3 kW micro-grid with 3 PV systems + photosynthetically active radiation + ambient temperature + relative humidity + wind speed + wind direction + GHI and precipitation (all averaged over 5 min).
Richardson et al. (2017) [25]	Forecast of GHI 10 and 15 min ahead	Images from a PiCamera; Cloud detection, using RBR; Optical flow cloud tracking; Ray tracing for GHI forecast, using a fixed ramp rate and clear sky GHI.
Kow et al. (2018) [20]	Forecast of PV power 30 s ahead coupled with mitigation system	GHI every 1 s + ambient temperature every 1 s and PV system modeled power; Self-organizing incremental neural network (M-SOINN) with active learning for forecasting power; Non-supervised method capable of forecasting power output of PV system 30 s ahead.
Kuhn et al. (2018) [64]	Forecast of 1-min-average GHI from 0 to 15 min ahead	Cloud segmentation, detection and georeferencing, using 4 sky cameras (WobaS-4cam) and 4-dimensional CSL; Irradiance maps validated with ground irradiance sensors and shadow camera; GHI and DNI obtained from geo-located shadow map and radiometer measurements at previous time steps.
Bouzgou and Gueymard (2019) [65]	Forecast of GHI from 5 min to 3 h ahead	Mutual information feature selection from time series of recent GHI; Extreme learning machine (ELM) for investigating the relationship between the historical variables and the future value, and also for determining the best combination of variables.
Kumler et al. (2019) [33]	Forecast of GHI 5, 15, 30 and 60 min ahead	Cloud albedo and fraction modeling based on GHI; Cloud optical thickness deterministically calculated; Forecast based on 5 min exponential weighed moving average of cloud fraction, used to determine albedo and GHI.

As seen in Reference [35], data resolutions of 30 s or less are essential for representing local solar variability. Moreover, most of the works presented in Table 2 do not meet this time resolution constraint, and those that do, possess higher cost systems often with multiple cameras and other sensors. As stated in Section 1, this limits the conduction of higher-resolution studies in less-developed countries, due to this fact, the goals of this work were to try and achieve high-resolution data acquisition and modeling, using low-cost equipment.

3. Materials and Methods

This section presents the hardware and methodology used for data collection, as well as the methods used for data analysis.

3.1. Data-Acquisition System

Image-based cloud tracking has become very popular for high-frequency photovoltaic modeling and short-term forecasting [13,37,45,54,66,67]. Cameras have massive variations of price depending on purpose, sensitivity, sturdiness, resolution and other various characteristics. The three main constraints for the camera used in this work were 180-degrees field of view to acquire total-sky images, enough resolution to provide all the information required for modeling the sky and the ability to be controlled by a low-cost embedded system. The system uses an ELP-USBFHD01M-L180 camera, which has a CMOS OV2710 sensor able to provide images with 1920 pixels by 1080 pixels resolution and is controlled directly via USB cable.

A 20 cm by 15 cm, 6 W solar panel was added to the data-acquisition system to provide a solar quantity to develop the image-based model. Power calculations were derived from voltage and current measurements provided by an Adafruit INA219 DC sensor. Another source of data was the panel temperature, provided by a Maxim Integrated DS18B20 temperature sensor attached to the back of the panel. Tying the system together, a Raspberry Pi 3B+ controls the camera and both sensors, synchronizing the data acquisition. Single board computers are ideal for this application due to their price, high tolerance to temperature variations and enough computing power for data acquisition in this scale.

In total, this equipment costs under US$ 100.00, if compared with more traditional sky imagers, such as the Yankee TSI 880, which costs thousands of US dollars, or even some of the lower-cost equipment developed by some research institutions, using IP cameras that can reach hundreds of US dollars [25]. A sky imager expected to be used as part of control strategies for PV plant operation must be low in cost to be commercially attractive for investors.

A 3-dimensional rendering of the equipment is shown in Figure 2.

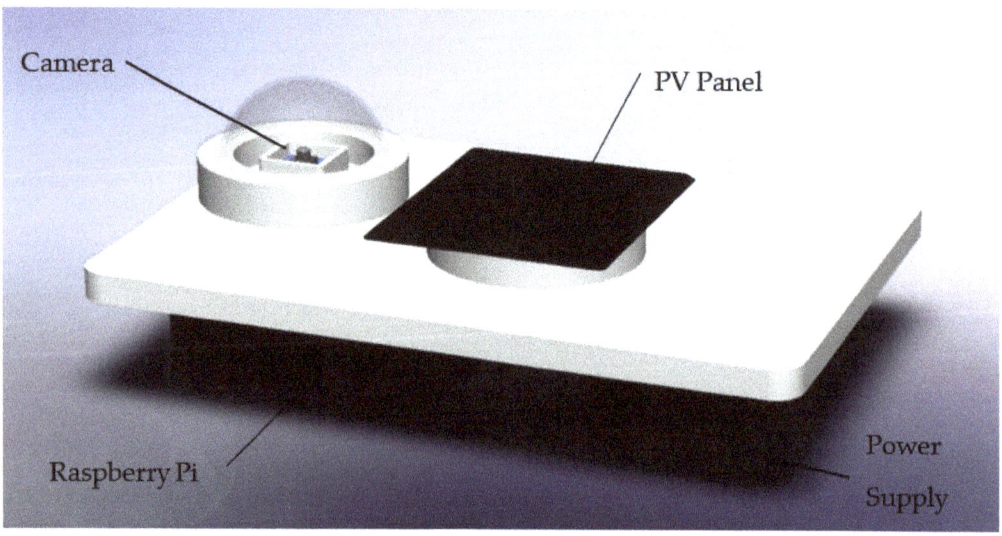

Figure 2. Three-dimensional model of the data-acquisition system.

The image acquisition software was developed using Python 3 with OpenCV 4 in conjunction the "pi_ina219" [68] and "w1thermsensor" [69] libraries for accessing the power and temperature sensors with Python.

To be able to generate power, the PV panel must be in a closed circuit with a load component. The initial goal was to use a ceramic resistor; however, during the testing process, when higher currents were applied to the resistor, it started to overheat, so a dichroic light bulb was used instead.

The thermometer was placed under the PV panel enclosed by the fins from an aluminum heat exchanger pad with the flat part attached to the bottom of the panel. It was then covered by thick dense foam to act as a heat insulator between the thermometer and the environment. Both thermometer and heat exchange pad were assumed to possess higher heat-transfer coefficients than the panel and both have significantly less mass, meaning that they have lower thermal inertia. This causes the thermometer to quickly follow changes in panel temperature, which is a key variable in PV conversion efficiency [70].

As for the INA 219 sensor, it measures both circuit voltage and determines current by measuring voltage across a 0.1 Ω shunt resistor. It is capable of measuring voltages up to 26 V and currents up to 3.2 A at a maximum ADC resolution of 12 bit. Both sensors have well developed Python libraries for use with the Raspberry Pi, which will be presented in the next section, along with all the software components used by the DAS.

Both sensors are supplied by 3.3 V DC provided by the Raspberry Pi's 3V3 pin. The INA 219 communicates, via I2C protocol, with the Pi through the SDA and SCL pins, located on the GPIO2 and GPIO3 pins respectively. Voltage and current are measured between the V_+ connector and ground. The current enters the INA 219 through the V_+ connector, passes through the internal measurement circuit and exits through the V_- connector, then through the dichroic light bulb.

The DS18B20 uses the 1-Wire communication protocol through GPIO4 pin. It requires a pull-up resistor of 10 kΩ to stabilize the signal when not communicating with the Pi. Figure 3 presents the measurement circuit schematics for temperature, voltage and current measurements. The green lines indicate connected terminals, and the camera was not included in this schematic because it uses a simple USB connection.

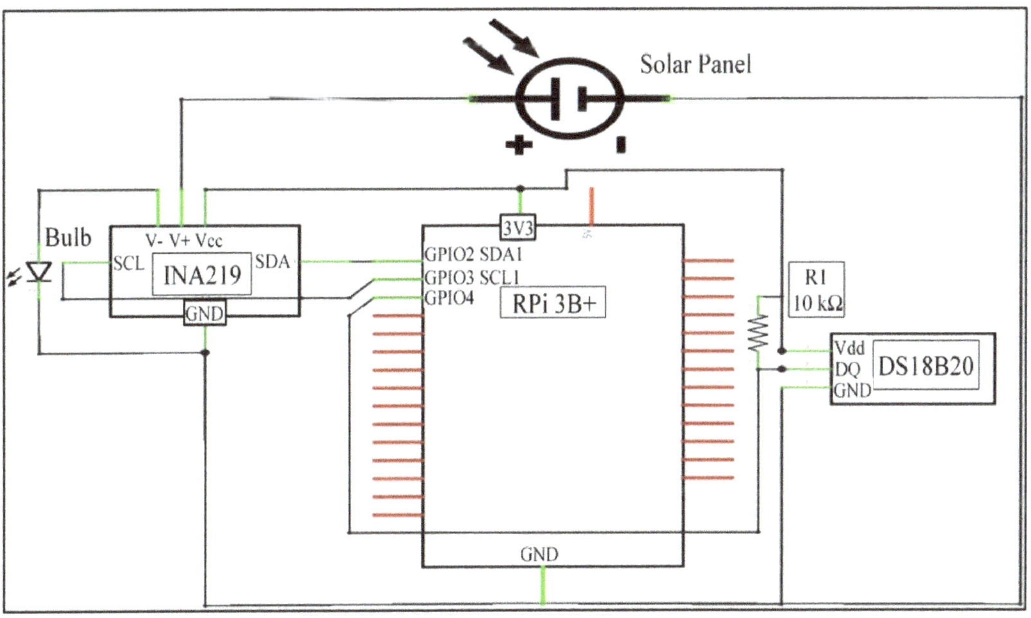

Figure 3. Measurement circuit schematic.

3.2. Acquisition Strategy

Due to the extremely high frequency of variations caused by cloud transients on PV power systems, the acquisition frequency must be high enough to provide information on such variations [7,8,35]. An acquisition frequency of 1 Hz was chosen since it has been shown to provide important information on very short-term solar variability [35]. This approach is important to provide information surrounding fast ramp events; however, it generates so much data not pertaining to such events that it may hinder their study, especially when such a high volume of images must be analyzed.

To focus on the ramp events, the approach used is called acquisition by exception [71]. It consists of monitoring one or more variables of interest and only saving data when an event of interest is detected. In this case, whenever the power measurement would vary beyond a certain threshold, the system would save data pertaining to this event. In practice, the acquisition software continuously acquired data during the daytime at 1 Hz and temporarily stored this information using a queue structure (first in, first out). This queue had a maximum of 10 elements at a given time, and for every iteration where no variation event was detected, the oldest entry was deleted, making room for a new set of measurements. Each element was measured 1 s apart and was comprised of one sky image, one voltage and one current measurement as well as the calculated power from the PV panel.

In order to detect a variation event a moving average of the previous 3 power values—at t_{-3s}, t_{-2s} and t_{-1s}—are calculated and compared with the most recent value, t_0. If there is a variation greater than a certain threshold, either up or down, the program enters the data-saving routine. It keeps acquiring data for 4 more seconds—$t_{+1s} \ldots t_{+4s}$—and then it saves these 15 s worth of data, as well as one temperature measurement representative of this period. This structure of 15 s of measurements is henceforth referred to as an "event". After recording an event, the system goes back into listening mode to detect other variation events.

The reason behind using only one temperature measurement is that, if the system were to include temperature measurements every time step, each iteration would take longer than 1 s, making it impossible to reach the desired 1 Hz acquisition frequency. Upon testing, this did not impact the quality of the data generated, due to the thermal inertia from the panel. Significant changes in panel temperature came at much lower frequencies than 1 Hz. The variation threshold was determined through experimentation and manual analysis of the quantities of interest. Using this strategy, it was possible to acquire data surrounding such ramp events, with images and power measurements taken 10 s before and 4 s after, totaling 15 s of data points per event. In the case of temperature, only one measurement was taken per detected event due to the sampling time from the sensor. Figure 4 presents a flowchart of the decision process and data flow from the data-acquisition system (DAS) software.

3.3. Measured Data

In the end of the data-collection phase, 500 event structures were recorded. Each event instance has 15 s worth of data saved into files: 15 JPG files containing the captured images and one text file containing the rest of the measured data. The text file is structured so every second of the event is one line (separated by a newline character "\n"), and the measured quantities are separated by commas. Table 3 shows an example of the numeric data measured during one event.

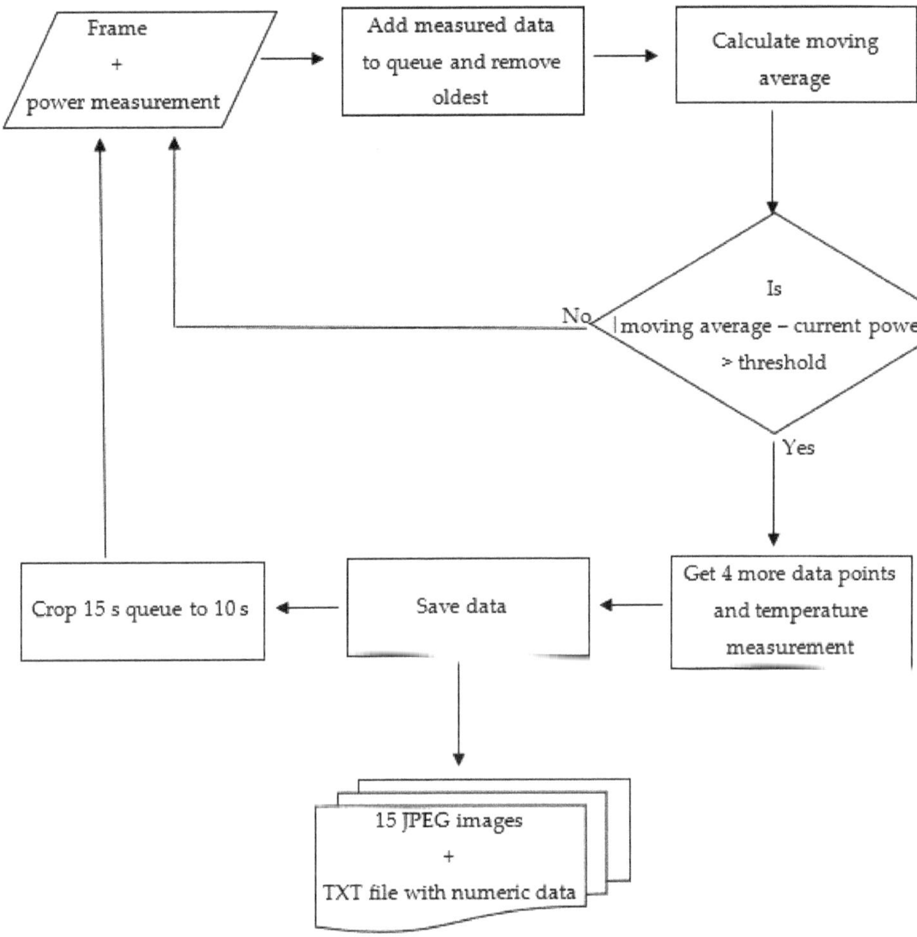

Figure 4. Flowchart of decision process and data flow within DAS software.

The first column contains the time stamps from each measurement point in the event. Each component is separated by an underscore, following the "hh_mm_ss_YYYY_MM_DD" format. The last component is a Boolean value, indicating whether daylight savings time is in effect. This is in local time and is used to determine the solar position angles.

Next are temperature measurements taken once per event, if, as with this example, there is more than one value in one event, it is because events were detected close to one another and some of the time stamps intersect. The negative values were used to represent "no data", and those were replaced by linear interpolations for the data-modeling phase. The last three values are the measured voltage, current and power, respectively. One such file was generated per detected event. As for the captured images, Figure 5 shows two examples of raw images, one from the beginning of the event and the second from the end.

Table 3. Example of numeric data pertaining to one event structure.

Time Stamp	Temperature (°C)	Voltage (V)	Current (A)	Power (W)
12_27_34_2019_03_17_0	48.0	0.241	0.614	0.148
12_27_33_2019_03_17_0	−1000	0.246	0.626	0.154
12_27_32_2019_03_17_0	−1000	0.251	0.632	0.158
12_27_31_2019_03_17_0	−1000	0.247	0.633	0.156
12_27_30_2019_03_17_0	−1000	0.246	0.629	0.155
12_27_29_2019_03_17_0	−1000	0.242	0.621	0.150
12_27_28_2019_03_17_0	−1000	0.236	0.609	0.144
12_27_27_2019_03_17_0	−1000	0.232	0.601	0.139
12_27_26_2019_03_17_0	−1000	0.227	0.595	0.135
12_27_25_2019_03_17_0	−1000	0.226	0.589	0.133
12_27_24_2019_03_17_0	48.0	0.222	0.584	0.130
12_27_23_2019_03_17_0	−1000	0.222	0.581	0.129
12_27_22_2019_03_17_0	−1000	0.217	0.576	0.125
12_27_21_2019_03_17_0	−1000	0.216	0.569	0.123
12_27_20_2019_03_17_0	−1000	0.212	0.561	0.119

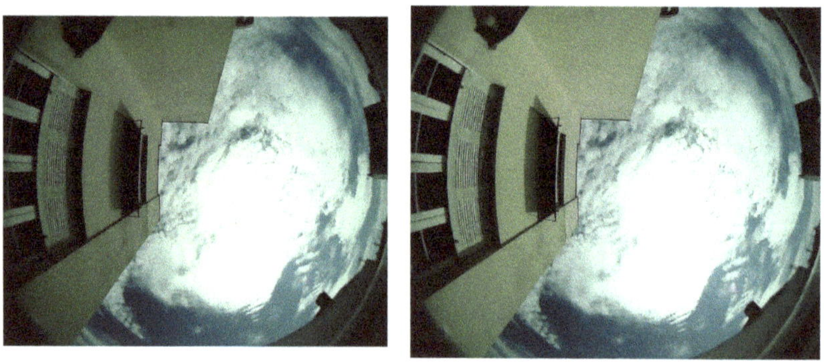

(**a**) (**b**)

Figure 5. Raw image examples from the beginning of an event (**a**) and from the end (**b**).

3.4. Visual Analysis

The first step in analyzing the obtained data was by performing image subtraction to visually assess how much change occurred between different time points. This approach showed no information close to the solar disk because of image saturation, and a neutral density filter was used to try and reduce the saturation problem. This did reduce the saturated area, but there was still no visible information regarding the ramp events. Figure 6 shows the result of the image subtraction with the saturated region highlighted.

In the case of image subtraction, since both images had a similar saturated region, the result after subtraction are black regions in the image. On Figure 6 the rightmost image has a smaller saturated region due to the use of the neutral density filter. Since a visual analysis was not sufficient to determine whether the data obtained were useable for modeling purposes, the next step was to perform a linear correlation analysis from image features and power data.

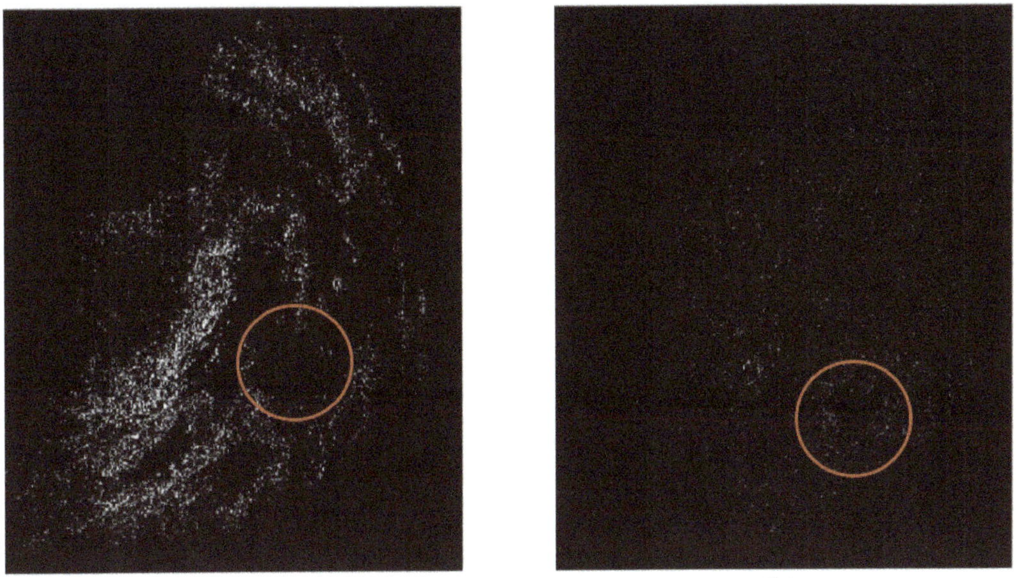

Figure 6. Image subtraction examples with the solar region highlighted. (**a**) Before installing the neutral density filter and (**b**) after installation.

3.5. Correlation Analysis

This goal in this step was not only to determine if there was a linear correlation between image features and the power ramp events, but to determine at which time intervals they were higher. Because of the detection-per ramp event, the data are not contiguous in their entirety; however, during several periods, the variations occurred close enough for the data to overlap and create an almost continuous set of data points.

To unbiasedly determine which time interval would be more adequate for modeling the ramp events, several different values were analyzed. The power variation between points was calculated for each possible pair of data points that fits in the different intervals. Due to the disconnection between the data points, as the intervals grew larger, less points fit in a certain interval, so the maximum interval used was 90 s. The corresponding variable for the correlation analysis is obtained directly from the image. It was obtained by subtracting the corresponding images from each two data points used for calculating the power difference. After subtraction of each digital channel (RGB), the energy (image energy is calculated by summating the individual pixel values in an image or ROI) was calculated for a circular Region of Interest (ROI) around the sun. Different ROI radii (distance in pixels) were used to take into consideration cloud movement (speed) in a given interval (time).

Aside from the power difference and subtracted image energy, the instant power measurements and temperature measurement were also analyzed. In total, 84 combinations of time intervals $\Delta t = \{1; 2; 5; 8; 10; 15; 20; 30; 45; 60; 75; 90\}$ and ROI radii $r = \{25; 50; 75; 100; 150; 200; 250\}$ were analyzed in this step. To be able to present the results in a concise form, each combination of interval and radius was assigned an index that will be used to identify them throughout this work. Table 4 contains the keys to identify the combinations from their respective indexes.

Table 4. Indexes used to identify the combinations of Δt and ROI radius.

ROI Radius (pixels)	Δt (s)											
	1	**2**	**5**	**8**	**10**	**15**	**20**	**30**	**45**	**60**	**75**	**90**
25	1	8	15	22	29	36	43	50	57	64	71	78
50	2	9	16	23	30	37	44	51	58	65	72	79
75	3	10	17	24	31	38	45	52	59	66	73	80
100	4	11	18	25	32	39	46	53	60	67	74	81
150	5	12	19	26	33	40	47	54	61	68	75	82
200	6	13	20	27	34	41	48	55	62	69	76	83
250	7	14	21	28	35	42	49	56	63	70	77	84

Correlation coefficients were calculated for each combination of the target variables (power at t_0, P_0; and power difference between t_0 and $t_{0-\Delta t}$: ΔP) and the aforementioned variables (power at $t_{0-\Delta t}$, P_{-1}; temperature at t_0, T_0; and ROI energy differences between t_0 and $t_{0-\Delta t}$). Correlation coefficients are used to measure linear proportionality between data pairs, which will show if a linear regression model would suffice for this problem.

3.6. Neural Network Modeling

To validate the obtained data, first a baseline regression performance was defined by performing multivariate linear regression to model P_0 and ΔP as a function of P_{-1}, T_0 and the image attribute of the blue channel, previously introduced. Only one color channel was used to prevent a collinearity issue from adversely affecting the model regression. To evaluate the regression performance, the coefficient of determination (R^2) was employed, as it measures how well the model represents the data used for regression.

All attempted linear regressions presented low R^2, despite showing low error, most likely due to the extremely low variation rates in the data presented. This aligns with the information obtained from the correlation analysis, where for shorter time intervals, P_0 and P_{-1} showed high correlation coefficients. This fact does not suffice to produce a good regression model. The other variables were statistically insignificant to the model, despite being relevant in theory. This pointed to the possible suitability of a nonlinear model, and for that step a regression neural network was chosen.

Artificial neural networks aim to mimic a brain's neuronal structure by assigning weights to the individual interconnections between neurons, and thus are capable of solving complex, non-linear problems [30]. Despite the correlation analysis only looking into linear correlation between pairs of variables, most likely there are more complex relationships between these variables, and by increasing size and complexity of a neural network, it should be able to model these relationships.

A multilayer perceptron (MLP) network was used for the purpose of validating the acquired data and selected image features. The network used in this work had fully connected neurons to map underlying relationships between the selected variables. If a certain connection does not prove to be relevant to the problem, the learning process will assign low synaptic weights to them. The selected training algorithm was through feed-forward backpropagation [30].

In it, the function signals resulting of the response of the activation function move forward through the interconnected neurons biased by the synaptic weights until they reach the output layer. The result is compared to a previously known value and the error values are propagated backwards through the network and the synaptic weights are adjusted to minimize the error values. This process may take several iterations depending on the complexity of the model and the network [30].

This process has the potential to overfit the model to the presented data, rendering it unsuitable for interpretingnew data. In order to avoid this, the data provided need to be of sufficient size and pertinent to the problem, a suitable architecture and size of network must be used, the problem must not be complex beyond what the model can handle, and the training process must be stopped before the model is overfitted to the training data. This process may take several iterations depending on the complexity of the model and the network [30].

For the first issue, in the context of this work, the data-acquisition procedure and feature selection were tailored to the problem at hand, so the representativeness of the dataset should be sufficient. As for sample size, the system acquired data for as long as it could, until the camera failed, most likely due to humidity damage to the circuitry or ultraviolet (UV) damage to the camera sensor.

Regarding the second issue, the MLP network was tested with several sizes and architectures to produce the highest accuracy and generalization possible. As for the complexity of the problem, that cannot be changed, but the representativeness of the variables used should provide the network with enough valuable information. Again, that is also a result of the tailoring of the data-acquisition procedures to the very short-term forecast problem.

Finally, regarding overfitting by overtraining, a cross-validation approach [30] was used to the back-propagation learning. This means that the training sample was split into two subsets, one to perform the actual learning with error backpropagation and synaptic weights adjustment, and the other was used to validate the error on a fresh set of data that the model could not have been overfitted to. By comparing the network performance on both subsets, it is clear when the model starts to get overfitted. Whilst the training set would keep reducing errors, the validation set would start to see increasing errors. This would mean that the model was overfitted to the training set and was losing generalization capability.

4. Results

This section presents the results for the data-processing steps introduced previously. To visually aid in the comprehension of the plots, Figure 7 shows how to interpret the x-axis of figures using the aforementioned index.

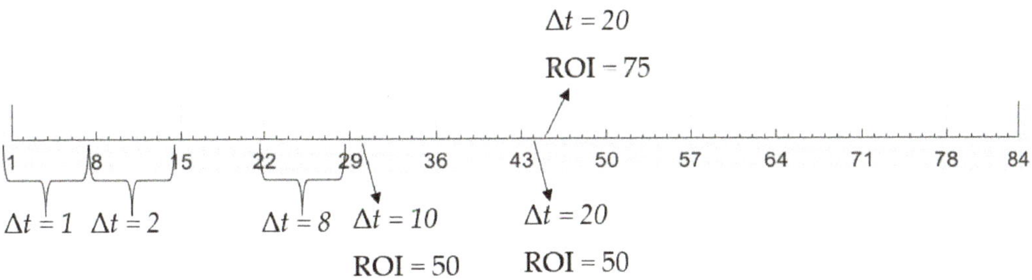

Figure 7. Visual guide to aid in the interpretation of the x-axis of the analysis plots with multiple networks.

Starting with the larger ticks, with the showing indexes, these mark the start of a new Δt value. As for the smaller ticks those correspond to the different ROI radii used within each group of Δt groupings.

4.1. Correlation Analysis

The first set of correlation analysis results, between P_0 and the evaluated variables, is presented in Figure 8.

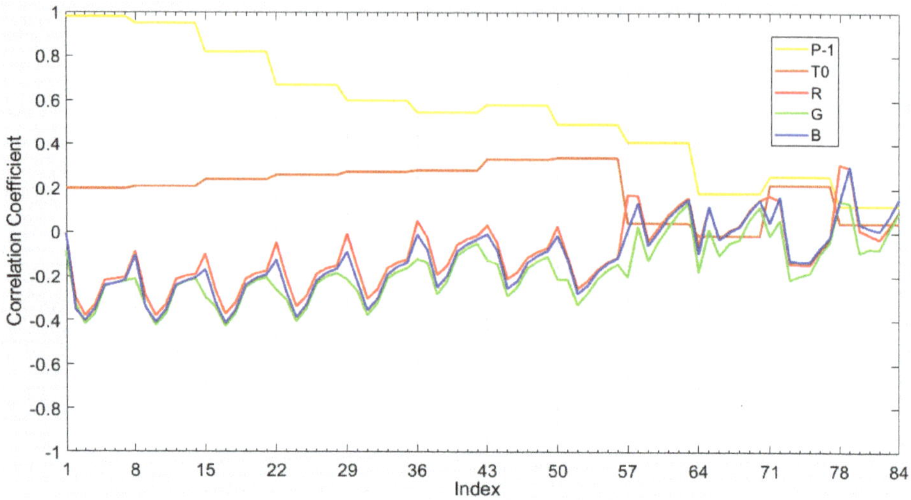

Figure 8. Correlation between P_0 and the evaluated variables.

At shorter time intervals, there is a high correlation between P_0 and P_{-1}; however, as Δt increases, the correlation coefficient approaches zero. Temperature and image attributes present correlation coefficient magnitudes under 0.4, which means that a linear regression model is unsuitable to represent these data. Next, the correlation coefficients between ΔP and the same 5 variables in the previous analysis is presented in Figure 9.

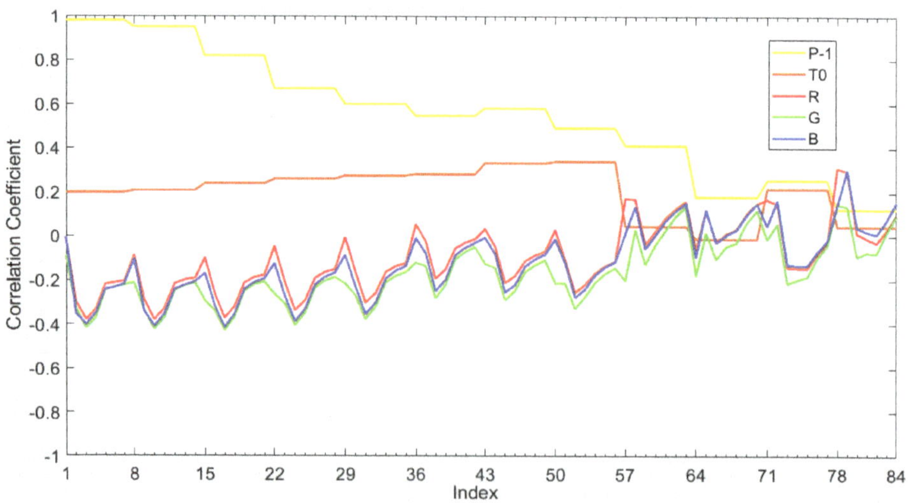

Figure 9. Correlation between ΔP and the evaluated variables.

The results for ΔP present rather different relationships between the chosen variables. As Δt increases the correlation coefficient magnitudes mostly increase as opposed to the results with P_0. In the case of the image attributes, it reaches a value of about 0.7 at 75 s before drastically falling and becoming negative. P_{-1} does correlate better to ΔP than to P_0; however, it is still too low for a proper linear regression model. What these results point out is that a linear model is unsuitable for representing this phenomenon through these data. The next step is to use a nonlinear model to attempt this representation, and the chosen model for that was a MLP (multilayer perceptron) artificial neural network.

4.2. Neural Network Architecture

Different networks with different architectures were trained for each combination of Δt and ROI radius to determine the best architecture for this model. Unlike the default random split employed by the Matlab neural network training tool, for this application an interleaved division algorithm was used to ensure that data from every day were available for training and validation, thus ensuring maximum representativeness. The proportion of training data was 70% of the set and consequently 30% was used for validation. Other splits were preliminarily tested; however, this proportion showed less variation among results when run multiple times. Normalization is an important process for neural network training, framing all values between 0 and 1, so that the gradients applied to the synaptic weights' updates are always decreasing [30].

The Matlab neural network training tool is highly customizable, but some of the default values for data-fitting problems, such as these, were left unchanged: the specific type of backpropagation algorithm, Levenberg–Marquardt; the mean-squared-error performance metric; and the hyperbolic tangent sigmoid (tansig) transfer function for the neurons. This was performed because these default values yielded solid results and were beyond the machine learning scope of this work.

Training was performed for both target variables, P_0 and ΔP, since both had very different behaviors and none were successfully represented by linear models. A diagram of the relationships between the inputs, neurons and modeled variables is presented in Figure 10.

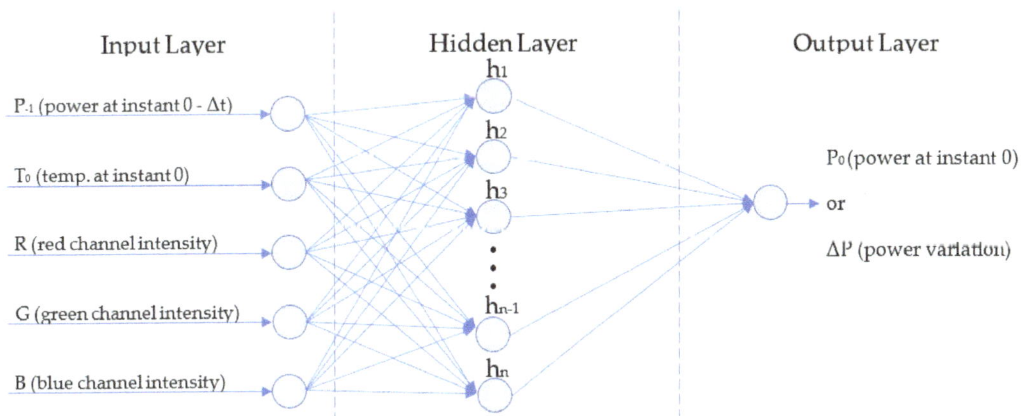

Figure 10. Diagram of inputs, outputs and layers in the tested networks.

First, the P_0 coefficient of determination is presented in Figure 11 for the different architectures and combination of Δt and ROI radius.

The model was trained with all five input variables previously used for the correlation analysis and linear regression (P_{-1}, T_0 and the image attributes from all three channels). Each line on the plot represents a different network architecture, with either one or two hidden layers and several layer sizes listed in the legend. Thicker lines represent networks with two hidden layers.

For the first two Δt values, all plot lines are indistinguishably close and boast good coefficients of determination, this being consistent with the results from the correlation analysis and linear regression. After this point, there is a dip in regression performance consistent with the linear evaluations; it then starts improving again, reaching even higher R^2 than the initial Δt range.

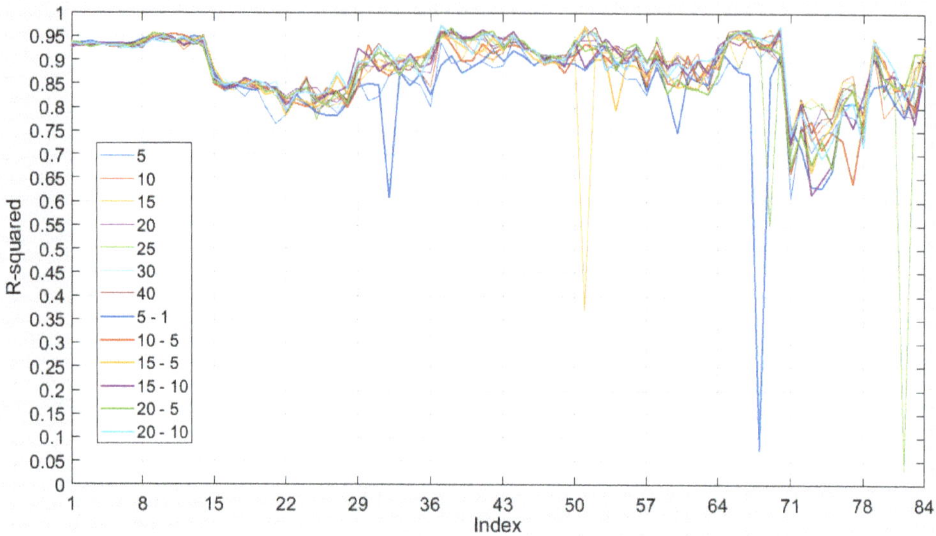

Figure 11. R^2 values for neural network regression models for P_0.

Networks with five neurons on the first hidden layer seem to yield the worst results. Other architectures vary and not one architecture seems significantly better than another. That said, networks with two hidden layers seem to be very similar to one another in most cases, as well as seem to vary less in amplitude than networks with a single hidden layer. The performance starts decreasing again for the last two Δt values, which may be due to a less relevant relationship between input and output or due to less training samples availability. This occurs because the data are not contiguous, and therefore, with larger time intervals, the amount of data points that can be related decreases. These results show that P_0 is more accurately modeled with a nonlinear method, such as neural networks.

The same method, variables and architectures were used for modeling ΔP, and the R^2 values for this step are depicted in Figure 12.

This result showed that, for the first four Δt values, neither a linear nor a non-linear method was capable of properly fitting these data. As of the fifth Δt value, the neural network model starts presenting good R^2, around 0.9. Similar to the previous plot, it is clear that networks with five neurons in the first hidden layer are inferior to the other tested architectures for most data points. After the fifth Δt value, the R^2 behaves similarly in both plots, reaching the highest coefficient of determination for $\Delta t = 60$ s, closely followed by $\Delta t = 15$ s. For both intervals, there are small peaks around ROI radius = 75 and 200 pixels.

One significant difference in both is the lack of the four drastically lower coefficient of determination points in the ΔP models, but that may be due to the lack of outlier analysis prior to model training. Since these regressions were made with all input variables, it was necessary to see if all variables were relevant to represent the target data. For this reason, the same training processes were performed for both target variables but varying the inputs. The chosen architecture was with two hidden layers with 15 and 10 neurons, respectively, which seemed to have some of the highest R^2 values and varied less than others. The inputs used for each model are displayed in Table 5. Each row represents one model, and each column represents one of the five variables. The Xs mark when a variable is used.

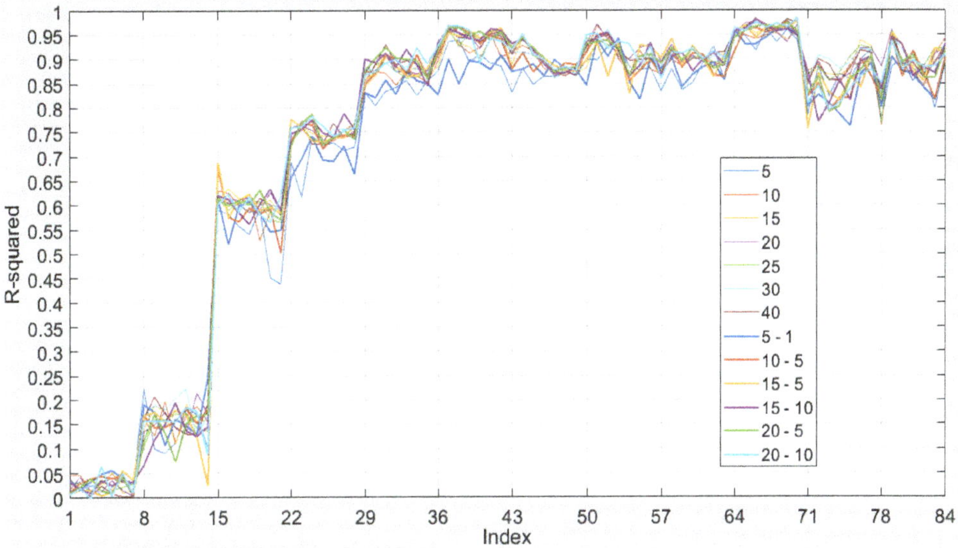

Figure 12. R^2 values for neural network regression models for ΔP.

Table 5. Variables used in the second step of NN modeling.

Model	Variables				
	P_{-1}	T_0	R	G	B
1	X	X	X	X	X
2	X	X	X	X	O
3	X	X	X	O	O
4	X	X	O	O	O
5	X	O	O	O	O
6	O	X	X	X	X
7	X	X	O	X	O
8	X	X	O	O	X
9	X	X	O	X	X
10	X	X	X	O	X
11	X	O	X	X	X

The results from this training with different input variables for target variable ΔP are shown in Figure 13. Each line represents one line on the plot, and to save some room in the legend, the variables P_{-1} (power at instant 0—Δt) and T_0 (temperature at instant zero), were shortened to P and T, respectively. The red, blue, and green channel attributes were represented by R, G and B, respectively. In order to reduce some of the randomness attributed to the initialization of the variables and data division, each network was trained five times, and the best result was selected.

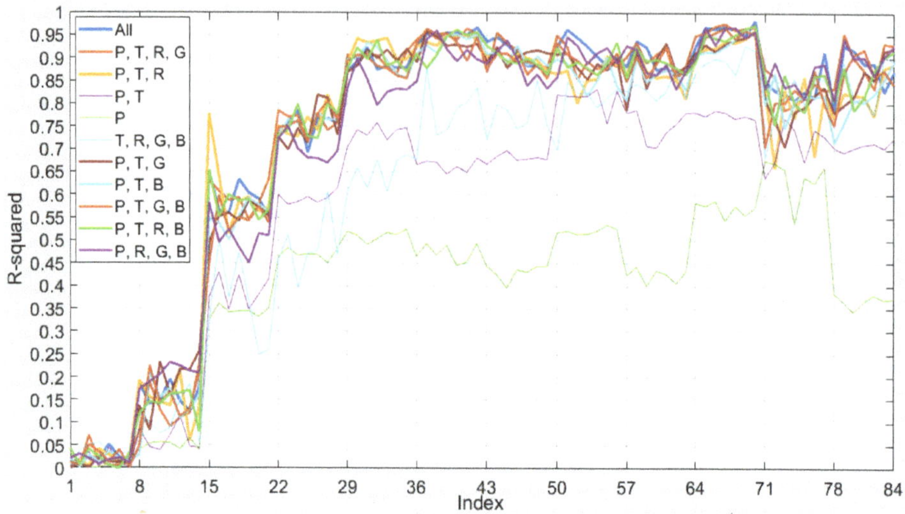

Figure 13. R^2 values for neural network regression models for ΔP with varying input variables.

The first information to stand out in this plot is the three lower performing models with either missing power, temperature or image attributes (P, T or [R, G, B]). The best result was considered to be with all variables, reaching the highest R^2 value (>0.98) and being the best result for several points. This result was achieved for Δt = 60 s and ROI radius = 250 pixels.

The same methodology was applied to training with P_0 as the target, with the same combinations of variables and the results shown in Figure 14.

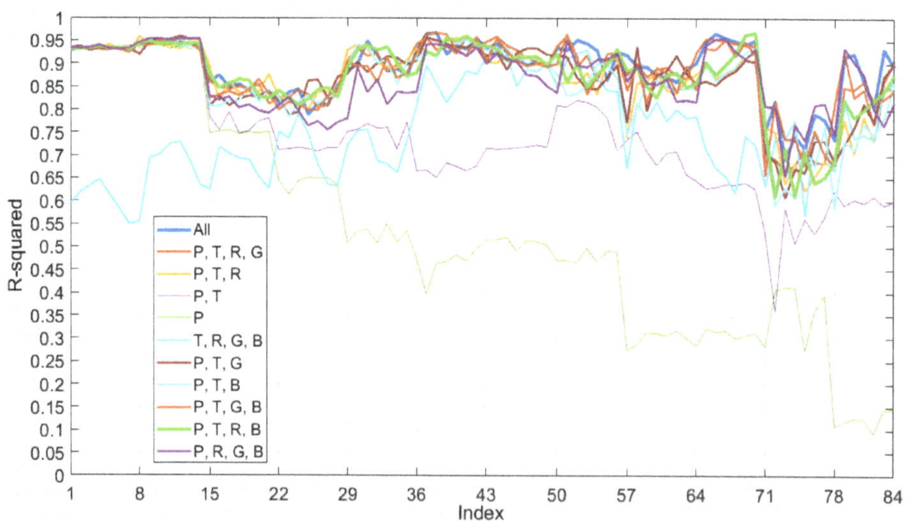

Figure 14. R^2 values for neural network regression models for P_0 with varying input variables.

Similar to Figure 13, the three worst variable selections have either power, temperature or image attribute missing, but in this case, power made a bigger impact. However, as

Δt increases, the importance of P_{-1} decreases, not just linearly as previously thought. Moreover, for P_0 the difference between using two or three image attributes is lower than for ΔP, but with all input variables, the models seem to fare overall slightly better, with ones using just the red and blue channels closely behind. The highest R^2 ($\approx$0.97) is with just red and blue (P, T, R, B) at Δt = 60 s and ROI radius = 250 pixels.

It is safe to say both variables were successfully modeled by using neural networks, especially compared with linear models. For both cases, previous power, temperature and image attributes from image subtraction proved to be important to model the targets.

4.3. Best Neural Network Results

Finally, the selected architecture of two layers with 15 and 10 neurons, respectively, was trained several times, using all five input variables with data from the Δt = 60 s step and ROI radius = 250 pixels to provide further insight on their performance and finish the validation step.

First, the data were tested modeling P_0, using all five input variables. The coefficient of determination obtained was R^2 = 0.94 for the validation process. This means that, when presented with data which were not used to train the network, it still was capable of estimating the output close to the real measured value.

Figure 15 presents the regression plot from this model, the blue line represents the model and the points are the pairs of estimated value versus real value for each input sample.

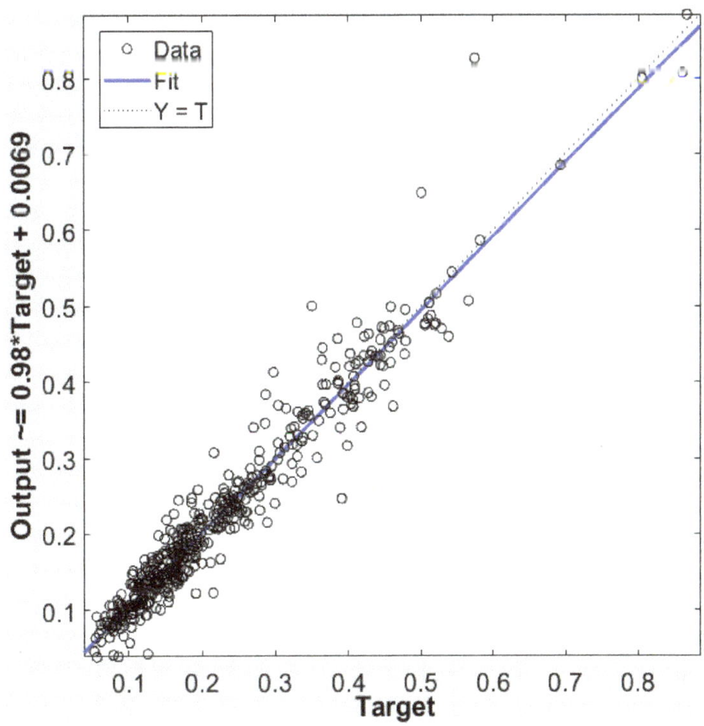

Figure 15. Regression plot for the validation of a NN model of P_0 with Δt = 60 s step and ROI radius = 250 pixels.

In a perfect model, all points would stand on the line, but this result shows a very close representation of the relationship between input variables and the target variable. Next, the same process was applied to modeling ΔP, and the results are presented in Figure 16.

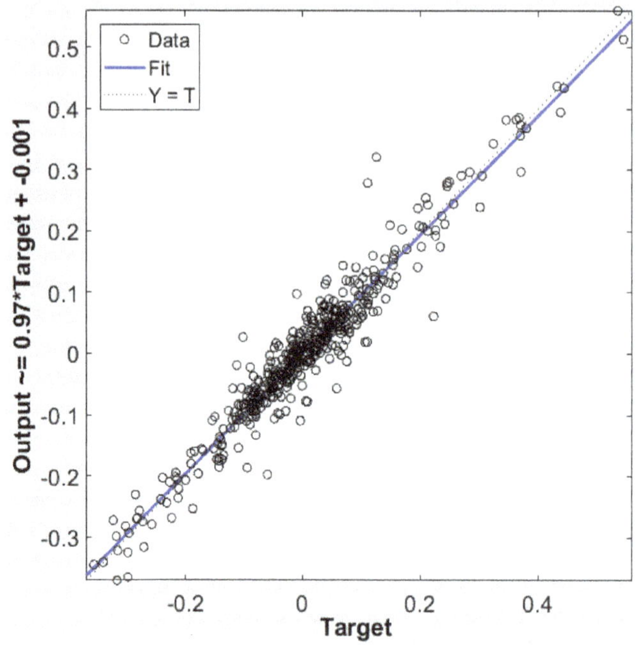

Figure 16. Regression plot for the validation of a NN model of ΔP with Δt = 60 s step and ROI radius = 250 pixels.

In this case, the validation R^2 = 0.93 and the regression plot also show how well the model represents the relationship between input and target variable. It is safe to claim that neural networks are well suited to model this type of data.

4.4. Discussion

When evaluating the obtained results relative to the literature herein presented, the first important point to consider is that the higher frequency of acquisition provided by the current system does offer more, and useful, information for modeling PV generation at a plant level [8,35]. This better resolution, coupled with the acquisition strategy, serves to confirm what other works have shown, that higher resolutions are important for PV forecasting [19,35,51,52,59,60].

The results also show the suitability of neural networks for modeling the relationship between image data and PV power. Its use in applications such as determining cloud albedo [33] or optical depth [55] should aid in forecasting efforts. Due to the low cost of the equipment used and the key information it was able to provide, approaches that employ multiple imagers [51,55,60] should be more easily employed. The combination of high-fidelity regression, high-frequency data and low cost permits not only a higher accessibility for developing countries to endeavor in PV energy research, but also for a more complex and in-depth look into the PV forecast problem.

5. Conclusions

Validation was performed on the data selected during the correlation analysis by using a linear model as the baseline and a neural network regression as a nonlinear model. It was possible to model power variations with up to 60 s intervals based on the data acquired by the developed system. Both the characteristics of the data themselves and of the selected features used for training the neural network were proven relevant to the intra-minute solar forecast problem.

Given the high-accuracy results, the data frequency and chosen variables were deemed relevant for intra-minute forecasting. The acquisition by exception proved to yield data rich in information surrounding solar variability; however, the event structure should be redefined in order to more accurately translate the reality. Since, through the data analysis, a 15 to 60 s horizon was deemed ideal given the available data, and that assumption was validated by the neural network model, an event structure capable of fully encompassing this horizon is recommended. Based on the information provided by this experimental research, an event structure with 90 s prior to the point of detection and 30 s after it should be enough to provide a clearer view on the subject of study.

Through forecasting, renewable energy sources will become more reliable and help steer the energy paradigm into a less fossil-reliant reality. With the coupling of multi-horizon forecasting, power electronics and energy storage systems, RES can lead to a new and clean energy era. To make this happen, more research into forecasting of the solar resource in different temporal and spatial scales is required, as well as the combination of forecasting with energy storage. The recommendations to improve upon the foundation laid by this work are as follows:

- Increase geometrical complexity by using arrays of PV panels, mirroring real-world solar farms;
- Test the system in different seasons and climates;
- Couple the model with a cloud tracking and forecast algorithm to provide power forecasts with the system;
- Model the impact of 60 s ahead forecasts for energy-storage management and PV variability mitigation;
- Test the developed acquisition system with the NN model with entirely new data.

Author Contributions: Conceptualization, G.F.B., R.F.C. and C.H.B.; methodology, G.F.B., R.F.C. and C.H.B.; software, G.F.B.; validation, G.F.B., R.F.C. and C.H.B.; formal analysis, G.F.B., R.F.C. and C.H.B.; investigation, G.F.B.; resources, G.F.B., R.F.C. and C.H.B.; data curation, G.F.B.; writing—original draft preparation, G.F.B.; writing—review and editing, G.F.B., R.F.C. and C.H.B.; visualization, G.F.B., R.F.C. and C.H.B.; supervision, R.F.C. and C.H.B.; project administration, R.F.C. and C.H.B.; funding acquisition, R.F.C. and C.H.B. All authors have read and agreed to the published version of the manuscript.

Funding: The authors thank for the financial support provided by the Brazilian funding agencies CNPq, CAPES, FINEP and FAPERJ. This study was financed in part by the Coordenação de Aperfeiçoamento de Pessoal de Nível Superior—Brasil (CAPES)—Finance Code 001.

Institutional Review Board Statement: Not applicable.

Informed Consent Statement: Not applicable.

Data Availability Statement: The data presented in this study are openly available in Mendeley Data at 10.17632/r83r6g5y6t.1, reference number [72].

Conflicts of Interest: The authors declare no conflict of interest.

References

1. *UNFCCC*; Paris Agreement: Paris, France, 2015.
2. IEA. *World Energy Outlook: Executive Summary*; IEA: Paris, France, 2018.
3. United Nations. *Transforming Our World: The 2030 Agenda for Sustainable Development*; United Nations: New York, NY, USA, 2015.
4. Can Şener, Ş.E.; Sharp, J.L.; Anctil, A. Factors impacting diverging paths of renewable energy: A review. *Renew. Sustain. Energy Rev.* **2018**, *81*, 2335–2342. [CrossRef]
5. Denholm, P.; Margolis, R.M. Evaluating the limits of solar photovoltaics (PV) in traditional electric power systems. *Energy Policy* **2007**, *35*, 2852–2861. [CrossRef]

6. Reddy, S.; Painuly, J.P. Diffusion of renewable energy technologies-barriers and stakeholders' perspectives. *Renew. Energy* **2004**, *29*, 1431–1447. [CrossRef]
7. Dragoon, K.; Schumaker, A. *Solar PV Variability and Grid Integration*; Renewable Northwest Project: Portland, OR, USA, 2010.
8. Mills, A.; Wiser, R. *Implications of Wide-Area Geographic Diversity for Short-Term Variability of Solar Power*; Lawrence Berkeley National Laboratory: Berkley, MI, USA, 2010.
9. Bessa, R.; Moreira, C.; Silva, B.; Matos, M. Handling renewable energy variability and uncertainty in power systems operation. *Wiley Interdiscip. Rev. Energy Environ.* **2014**, *3*, 156–178. [CrossRef]
10. Karimi, M.; Mokhlis, H.; Naidu, K.; Uddin, S.; Bakar, A.H.A. Photovoltaic penetration issues and impacts in distribution network—A review. *Renew. Sustain. Energy Rev.* **2016**, *53*, 594–605. [CrossRef]
11. Liang, X. Emerging Power Quality Challenges Due to Integration of Renewable Energy Sources. *IEEE Trans. Ind. Appl.* **2016**, *53*, 855–866. [CrossRef]
12. Diagne, M.; David, M.; Lauret, P.; Boland, J.; Schmutz, N. Review of solar irradiance forecasting methods and a proposition for small-scale insular grids. *Renew. Sustain. Energy Rev.* **2013**, *27*, 65–76. [CrossRef]
13. Sobri, S.; Koohi-Kamali, S.; Rahim, N.A. Solar photovoltaic generation forecasting methods: A review. *Energy Convers. Manag.* **2018**, *156*, 459–497. [CrossRef]
14. Solargis Methodology—Solar Radiation Modeling. Available online: https://solargis.com/docs/methodology/solar-radiation-modeling (accessed on 16 August 2021).
15. Natural Earth Countries. Available online: http//www.naturalearthdata.com/download/10m/cultural/ne_10m_admin_0_countries.zip (accessed on 4 June 2020).
16. Solargis. Longterm yearly average of global irradiation at optimum tilt. *Global Solar Atlas* **2019**.
17. United Nations. *The Sustainable Development Goals Report*; United Nations: New York, NY, USA, 2021.
18. Barbieri, F.; Rajakaruna, S.; Ghosh, A. Very short-term photovoltaic power forecasting with cloud modeling: A review. *Renew. Sustain. Energy Rev.* **2017**, *75*, 242–263. [CrossRef]
19. Schmidt, T.; Kalisch, J.; Lorenz, E.; Heinemann, D. Evaluating the spatiooral performance of sky-imager-based solar irradiance analysis and forecasts. *Atmos. Chem. Phys.* **2016**, *16*, 3399–3412. [CrossRef]
20. Kow, K.W.; Wong, Y.W.; Rajkumar, R.; Isa, D. An intelligent real-time power management system with active learning prediction engine for PV grid-tied systems. *J. Clean. Prod.* **2018**, *205*, 252–265. [CrossRef]
21. Denholm, P.; Hand, M. Grid flexibility and storage required to achieve very high penetration of variable renewable electricity. *Energy Policy* **2011**, *39*, 1817–1830. [CrossRef]
22. IEC. Electrical Energy Storage—White Paper. *Int. Electrotech. Comm.* **2011**, 1–78. [CrossRef]
23. Petinrin, J.O.; Shaabanb, M. Impact of renewable generation on voltage control in distribution systems. *Renew. Sustain. Energy Rev.* **2016**, *65*, 770–783. [CrossRef]
24. Varma, R.K.; Salehi, R. SSR Mitigation with a New Control of PV Solar Farm as STATCOM (PV-STATCOM). *IEEE Trans. Sustain. Energy* **2017**, *8*, 1473–1483. [CrossRef]
25. Richardson, W.; Krishnaswami, H.; Vega, R.; Cervantes, M. A low cost, edge computing, all-sky imager for cloud tracking and intra-hour irradiance forecasting. *Sustainability* **2017**, *9*, 482. [CrossRef]
26. Oliveira, A.; Calili, R.; Almeida, M.F.; Sousa, M. A Systemic and Contextual Framework to Define a Country's 2030 Agenda from a Foresight Perspective. *Sustainability* **2019**, *11*, 6360. [CrossRef]
27. Bassous, G.F. Development and Validation of a Low-Cost Data Acquisition System for Very Short- Term Photovoltaic Power Forecasting. *PUC-Rio* **2019**. Available online: https://www.maxwell.vrac.puc-rio.br/47953/47953.PDF (accessed on 17 September 2021).
28. Stefferud, K.; Kleissl, J.; Schoene, J. Solar forecasting and variability analyses using sky camera cloud detection and motion vectors. In Proceedings of the 2012 IEEE Power and Energy Society General Meeting, San Diego, CA, USA, 22–26 July 2012. [CrossRef]
29. Reikard, G. Predicting solar radiation at high resolutions: A comparison of time series forecasts. *Sol. Energy* **2009**, *83*, 342–349. [CrossRef]
30. Haykin, S. *Neural Networks and Learning Machines: A Comprehensive Foundation*, 3rd ed.; Prentice Hall: Upper Saddle River, NJ, USA, 2008; ISBN 9780131471399.
31. Raza, M.Q.; Nadarajah, M.; Ekanayake, C. On recent advances in PV output power forecast. *Sol. Energy* **2016**, *136*, 125–144. [CrossRef]
32. Das, U.K.; Tey, K.S.; Seyedmahmoudian, M.; Mekhilef, S.; Idris, M.Y.I.; Van Deventer, W.; Horan, B.; Stojcevski, A. Forecasting of photovoltaic power generation and model optimization: A review. *Renew. Sustain. Energy Rev.* **2018**, *81*, 912–928. [CrossRef]
33. Kumler, A.; Xie, Y.; Zhang, Y. A Physics-based Smart Persistence model for Intra-hour forecasting of solar radiation (PSPI) using GHI measurements and a cloud retrieval technique. *Sol. Energy* **2019**, *177*, 494–500. [CrossRef]
34. Zendehboudi, A.; Baseer, M.A.; Saidur, R. Application of support vector machine models for forecasting solar and wind energy resources: A review. *J. Clean. Prod.* **2018**, *199*, 272–285. [CrossRef]
35. Lave, M.; Reno, M.J.; Broderick, R.J. Characterizing local high-frequency solar variability and its impact to distribution studies. *Sol. Energy* **2015**, *118*, 327–337. [CrossRef]

36. Pedro, H.T.C.; Coimbra, C.F.M.; David, M.; Lauret, P. Assessment of machine learning techniques for deterministic and probabilistic intra-hour solar forecasts. *Renew. Energy* **2018**, *123*, 191–203. [CrossRef]
37. Chow, C.W.; Urquhart, B.; Lave, M.; Dominguez, A.; Kleissl, J.; Shields, J.; Washom, B. Intra-hour forecasting with a total sky imager at the UC San Diego solar energy testbed. *Sol. Energy* **2011**, *85*, 2881–2893. [CrossRef]
38. Yang, D.; Kleissl, J.; Gueymard, C.A.; Pedro, H.T.C.; Coimbra, C.F.M. History and trends in solar irradiance and PV power forecasting: A preliminary assessment and review using text mining. *Sol. Energy* **2018**, *168*, 60–101. [CrossRef]
39. Cervantes, M.; Krishnaswami, H.; Richardson, W.; Vega, R. Utilization of Low Cost, Sky-Imaging Technology for Irradiance Forecasting of Distributed Solar Generation. In Proceedings of the 2016 IEEE Green Technologies Conference (GreenTech), Kansas City, MO, USA, 6–8 April 2016; pp. 142–146. [CrossRef]
40. Urquhart, B.; Kurtz, B.; Dahlin, E.; Ghonima, M.; Shields, J.E.; Kleissl, J. Development of a sky imaging system for short-term solar power forecasting. *Atmos. Meas. Tech.* **2015**, *8*, 875–890. [CrossRef]
41. Gohari, S.M.I.; Urquhart, B.; Yang, H.; Kurtz, B.; Nguyen, D.; Chow, C.W.; Ghonima, M.; Kleissl, J. Comparison of solar power output forecasting performance of the Total Sky Imager and the University of California, San Diego Sky Imager. *Energy Procedia* **2013**, *49*, 2340–2350. [CrossRef]
42. Chu, Y.; Pedro, H.T.C.; Coimbra, C.F.M. Hybrid intra-hour DNI forecasts with sky image processing enhanced by stochastic learning. *Sol. Energy* **2013**, *98*, 592–603. [CrossRef]
43. Marquez, R.; Coimbra, C.F.M. Intra-hour DNI forecasting based on cloud tracking image analysis. *Sol. Energy* **2013**, *91*, 327–336. [CrossRef]
44. Quesada-Ruiz, S.; Chu, Y.; Tovar-Pescador, J.; Pedro, H.T.C.; Coimbra, C.F.M. Cloud-tracking methodology for intra-hour DNI forecasting. *Sol. Energy* **2014**, *102*, 267–275. [CrossRef]
45. West, S.R.; Rowe, D.; Sayeef, S.; Berry, A. Short-term irradiance forecasting using skycams: Motivation and development. *Sol. Energy* **2014**, *110*, 188–207. [CrossRef]
46. Chu, Y.; Pedro, H.T.C.; Li, M.; Coimbra, C.F.M. Real-time forecasting of solar irradiance ramps with smart image processing. *Sol. Energy* **2015**, *114*, 91–104. [CrossRef]
47. Alonso-Montesinos, J.; Batlles, F.J. The use of a sky camera for solar radiation estimation based on digital image processing. *Energy* **2015**, *90*, 377–386. [CrossRef]
48. Alonso-Montesinos, J.; Batlles, F.J.; Portillo, C. Solar irradiance forecasting at one-minute intervals for different sky conditions using sky camera images. *Energy Convers. Manag.* **2015**, *105*, 1166–1177. [CrossRef]
49. Cazorla, A.; Husillos, C.; Antón, M.; Alados-Arboledas, L. Multi-exposure adaptive threshold technique for cloud detection with sky imagers. *Sol. Energy* **2015**, *114*, 268–277. [CrossRef]
50. Chu, Y.; Li, M.; Pedro, H.T.C.; Coimbra, C.F.M. Real-time prediction intervals for intra-hour DNI forecasts. *Renew. Energy* **2015**, *83*, 234–244. [CrossRef]
51. Chu, Y.; Urquhart, B.; Gohari, S.M.I.; Pedro, H.T.C.; Kleissl, J.; Coimbra, C.F.M. Short-term reforecasting of power output from a 48 MWe solar PV plant. *Sol. Energy* **2015**, *112*, 68–77. [CrossRef]
52. Lipperheide, M.; Bosch, J.L.; Kleissl, J. Embedded nowcasting method using cloud speed persistence for a photovoltaic power plant. *Sol. Energy* **2015**, *112*, 232–238. [CrossRef]
53. Pedro, H.T.C.; Coimbra, C.F.M. Nearest-neighbor methodology for prediction of intra-hour global horizontal and direct normal irradiances. *Renew. Energy* **2015**, *80*, 770–782. [CrossRef]
54. Xu, J.; Yoo, S.; Yu, D.; Huang, D.; Heiser, J.; Kalb, P. Solar irradiance forecasting using multi-layer cloud tracking and numerical weather prediction. In Proceedings of the 30th Annual ACM Symposium on Applied Computing—SAC'15, Salamanca, Spain, 13–17 April 2015; ACM Press: New York, NY, USA, 2015; pp. 2225–2230.
55. Mejia, F.A.; Kurtz, B.; Murray, K.; Hinkelman, L.M.; Sengupta, M.; Xie, Y.; Kleissl, J. Coupling sky images with radiative transfer models: A new method to estimate cloud optical depth. *Atmos. Meas. Tech.* **2016**, *9*, 4151–4165. [CrossRef]
56. Rana, M.; Koprinska, I.; Agelidis, V.G. Univariate and multivariate methods for very short-term solar photovoltaic power forecasting. *Energy Convers. Manag.* **2016**, *121*, 380–390. [CrossRef]
57. Sanfilippo, A.; Martin-Pomares, L.; Mohandes, N.; Perez-Astudillo, D.; Bachour, D. An adaptive multi-modeling approach to solar nowcasting. *Sol. Energy* **2016**, *125*, 77–85. [CrossRef]
58. Soubdhan, T.; Ndong, J.; Ould-Baba, H.; Do, M.-T. A robust forecasting framework based on the Kalman filtering approach with a twofold parameter tuning procedure: Application to solar and photovoltaic prediction. *Sol. Energy* **2016**, *131*, 246–259. [CrossRef]
59. Ai, Y.; Peng, Y.; Wei, W. A model of very short-term solar irradiance forecasting based on low-cost sky images. *AIP Conf. Proc.* **2017**, *1839*, 020022. [CrossRef]
60. Blanc, P.; Massip, P.; Kazantzidis, A.; Tzoumanikas, P.; Kuhn, P.; Wilbert, S.; Schüler, D.; Prahl, C. Short-term forecasting of high resolution local DNI maps with multiple fish-eye cameras in stereoscopic mode. *AIP Conf. Proc.* **2017**, *1850*, 140004. [CrossRef]
61. Cheng, H.Y. Cloud tracking using clusters of feature points for accurate solar irradiance nowcasting. *Renew. Energy* **2017**, *104*, 281–289. [CrossRef]
62. Elsinga, B.; van Sark, W.G.J.H.M. Short-term peer-to-peer solar forecasting in a network of photovoltaic systems. *Appl. Energy* **2017**, *206*, 1464–1483. [CrossRef]
63. Ni, Q.; Zhuang, S.; Sheng, H.; Kang, G.; Xiao, J. An ensemble prediction intervals approach for short-term PV power forecasting. *Sol. Energy* **2017**, *155*, 1072–1083. [CrossRef]

64. Kuhn, P.; Nouri, B.; Wilbert, S.; Prahl, C.; Kozonek, N.; Schmidt, T.; Yasser, Z.; Ramirez, L.; Zarzalejo, L.; Meyer, A.; et al. Validation of an all-sky imager–based nowcasting system for industrial PV plants. *Prog. Photovolt. Res. Appl.* **2018**, *26*, 608–621. [CrossRef]
65. Bouzgou, H.; Gueymard, C.A. Fast short-term global solar irradiance forecasting with wrapper mutual information. *Renew. Energy* **2019**, *133*, 1055–1065. [CrossRef]
66. Chow, C.W.; Belongie, S.; Kleissl, J. Cloud motion and stability estimation for intra-hour solar forecasting. *Sol. Energy* **2015**, *115*, 645–655. [CrossRef]
67. Wood-Bradley, P.; Zapata, J.; Pye, J. Cloud tracking with optical flow for short-term solar forecasting. In Proceedings of the 50th Conference of the Australian Solar Energy Society, Melbourne, VIC, Australia, 21–22 August 2012; pp. 2–7.
68. Borrill, C.; Timmons, T.; van Staveren, T.; Kluyver, T.; Bauer, S. pi_ina219. Available online: https://github.com/chrisb2/pi_ina219 (accessed on 24 July 2019).
69. Furrer, T. w1thermsensor. Available online: https://github.com/timofurrer/w1thermsensor (accessed on 24 July 2019).
70. Smets, A.H.; Jäger, K.; Isabella, O.; van Swaaij, R.A.; Zeman, M. *Solar Energy: The Physics and Engineering of Photovoltaic Conversion, Technologies and Systems*, 1st ed.; UIT Cambridge Ltd.: Cambrige, UK, 2016; ISBN 978-1906860325.
71. Amelink, H.; Hoffmann, A.G. Current trends in control centre design. *Int. J. Electr. Power Energy Syst.* **1983**, *5*, 205–211. [CrossRef]
72. Bassous, G.F.; Hall, C.; Calili, R. Sky Images and PV Measurements. Mendeley Data. 2021. Available online: https://data.mendeley.com/datasets/r83r6g5y6t/1 (accessed on 17 September 2021). [CrossRef]

energies

MDPI

Article

Numerical Simulation of Leakage and Diffusion Process of LNG Storage Tanks

Xue Li [1,2], Ning Zhou [1,*], Bing Chen [3], Qian Zhang [1], Vamegh Rasouli [4], Xuanya Liu [5], Weiqiu Huang [1] and Lingchen Kong [6]

1 School of Petroleum Engineering, Changzhou University, Changzhou 213164, China; lix@cczu.edu.cn (X.L.); qzhang@joongsee.com (Q.Z.); hwq213@cczu.edu.cn (W.H.)
2 Jiangsu Key Laboratory of Oil-Gas Storage and Transportation Technology, Changzhou 213164, China
3 Institute of Industrial Safety, China Academy of Safety Science and Technology, Beijing 100012, China; chenb@chinasafety.ac.cn
4 College of Engineering & Mines, University of North Dakota, Grand Forks, ND 58202, USA; vamegh.rasouli@engr.und.edu
5 Tianjin Fire Research Institute of MEM, Tianjin 300381, China; liuxuanya@tfri.com.cn
6 Changzhou Institute of Technology, Changzhou 213032, China; klch-123@126.com
* Correspondence: zhouning@cczu.edu.cn

Abstract: To investigate the evolution process of LNG (Liquefied Natural Gas) liquid pool and gas cloud diffusion, the Realizable *k*-ε model and Eluerian model were used to numerically simulate the liquid phase leakage and diffusion process of LNG storage tanks. The experimental results showed that some LNG flashed and vaporized rapidly to form a combustible cloud during the continuous leakage. The diffusion of the explosive cloud was divided into heavy gas accumulation, entrainment heat transfer, and light gas drift. The vapor cloud gradually separated into two parts from the whole "fan leaf shape". One part was a heavy gas cloud; the other part was a light gas cloud that spread with the wind in the downwind direction. The change of leakage aperture had a greater impact on the whole spill and dispersion process of the storage tank. The increasing leakage aperture would lead to 10.3 times increase in liquid pool area, 78.5% increase in downwind dispersion of methane concentration at 0.5 LFL, 22.6% increase in crosswind dispersion of methane concentration at 0.5 LFL, and 249% increase in flammable vapor cloud volume. Within the variation range of the leakage aperture, the trend of the gas cloud diffusion remained consistent, but the time for the liquid pool to keep stable and the gas cloud to enter the next diffusion stage was delayed. The low-pressure cavity area within 200 m of the leeward surface of the storage tank would accumulate heavy gas for a long time, forming a local high concentration area, which should be an area of focus for alert prediction.

Keywords: LNG leakage and diffusion; combustible cloud; phase change; plume flow; leakage aperture

Citation: Li, X.; Zhou, N.; Chen, B.; Zhang, Q.; Rasouli, V.; Liu, X.; Huang, W.; Kong, L. Numerical Simulation of Leakage and Diffusion Process of LNG Storage Tanks. *Energies* **2021**, *14*, 6282. https://doi.org/10.3390/en14196282

Academic Editor: Marcin Kamiński

Received: 28 July 2021
Accepted: 16 September 2021
Published: 2 October 2021

1. Introduction

LNG is mostly methane with small amounts of ethane, propane, butane and nitrogen, which is expected to be the second-largest energy source in energy composition in 2030 [1]. However, there may be a leak of liquefied natural gas (LNG) in the presence of an ignition source that will cause a fire or explosion in a fully or partially hazardous environment [2].

In view of this, several studies have been published on storage tank accidents [3–6]. Scholars in China and overseas have conducted many studies on the prediction of possible hazards associated with LNG vapor dispersion. Koopman et al. [7] carried out the Burro series of tests in 1980 to observe the diffusion of LNG vapor clouds under different conditions after LNG leaked to the water surface. It was found that the leakage mode of LNG has a certain influence on the vapor cloud diffusion. In 1983, the Coyote series of tests [8] were conducted to study the ignition and flash evaporation processes of LNG, and the rapid phase transition, vapor cloud diffusion and pool fire were all observed in this test. Brown et al. [9] carried out Falcon series of experiments to study the leakage and diffusion of LNG under obstacles. They accurately evaluated the effectiveness of the fence so as to mitigate the harm of LNG gas cloud diffusion.

In addition, several mathematical models have been developed to simulate heavy gas diffusion based on experimental data, such as DEGADIS, SLAB [10], FEM3 [11,12], etc. First of all, field tests can reproduce the actual situation of LNG leakage and diffusion; in addition, the cycle was too long and the repeatability was poor. Therefore, CFD simulation was used as a promising alternative to calculate the diffusion distance of LNG. Giannissi et al. [13] simulated the LNG diffusion under an open and obstructed condition based on Falcon series experiments. It was proved that the leak source model greatly affected LNG diffusion, and the best case to simulate the leakage source was to model the source as having two phases. Vílchez et al. [14] used the DEGADIS model to predict the explosive distances of vapor clouds after LNG leakage and they defined the diffusion safety factor (DSF) to estimate these distances. Li et al. [15] evaluated the effect of safety clearance on the diffusion of cylindrical floating LNG with FLACS software. The results demonstrated that the safety gap increased the size of the gas cloud far from the cylindrical FLNG release position but decreased the size of the gas cloud near the release position.

Zhang et al. [16] studied the process of LNG leakage and diffusion in different wind directions. The results showed that the LNG spread farthest along the horizontal downwind direction. Marsegan et al. [17] carried out a numerical simulation of LNG diffusion under active and passive barriers and found that the active barrier effectively reduced the diffusion area of LNG by accelerating the entrainment between air and gas. Nguyen et al. [18] conducted a liquid pool evaporation experiment with different leak rates on the water surface. They proposed a model to express the function relationship between evaporation rate, leakage rate and time based on the experimental results and one-dimensional heat conduction model. Gopalaswami et al. [19] developed a transient three-dimensional multiphase model in CFX based on the comprehensive test data and numerical simulation data, which was found that wind affected the evaporation and diffusion of LNG by carrying additional heat and unsaturation. Ikealumba et al. [20] studied the effects of atmospheric and ocean stability on LNG diffusion where they found that the instability caused by the waves would aggravate the leakage hazard of LNG ships. Luo et al. [21] proposed an integrated multiphase CFD model to simulate the complete process of LNG leakage on the water surface, concluding that water storage would shorten the horizontal diffusion distance of the gas cloud. Dasgotra et al. [22] simulated the diffusion of heavy gas in natural gas storage facilities. They found that the average diameter of the gas cloud ranged from 0 to 500 m under relatively stable weather conditions. Giannissi et al. [23] investigated the effect of environmental humidity on the diffusion of LNG, and concluded that in the case of high environmental humidity, the explosion distance of gas cloud would be reduced.

The above studies mainly focus on the potential hazards which are associated with LNG leakage and the influence degree of external environmental factors on the dispersion effect of LNG leakage. However, few considerations have been given to phase change. Therefore, in this study, the effect of phase change on dispersion during LNG release is studied to analyze the behavior characteristics of LNG liquid pool expansion and gas cloud diffusion, and the effect of the leaking aperture on the gas cloud diffusion process is also studied.

2. Materials and Methods

2.1. Numerical Model

The homogeneous Eulerian multiphase model [24,25] was adopted to model the phase change process after LNG leaked to the ground. The realizable k-ε model had higher accuracy in concentration distribution than the standard k-ε model by simulating Thorney's heavy gas diffusion (Freon-12) field test [26]. Therefore, the realizable k-ε model was selected for gas diffusion turbulence.

At present, the *k*-ε model is the most widely used turbulence model for the turbulence simulations of wind fields in large structures such as storage tanks. The standard *k*-ε model proposed by Launder and Spalding greatly improves the zero-equation model and one equation model, so it is widely used in engineering flow field calculation and has been well verified in practice. However, the applicability of the standard *k*-ε model for each component of Reynolds stress is not strong. For example, it is assumed that the turbulent viscosity coefficient is isotropic, while the turbulence is anisotropic in the case of curved wall flow, curved streamline flow, or strong swirling flow. Therefore, it is not recommended to use the standard *k*-ε model to calculate the wind field of a storage tank with curved wall flow; otherwise, it will produce a certain degree of distortion in calculation.

The equation of turbulent kinetic energy *k* and dissipation rate ε of the standard *k*-ε model is described as follows.

$$\rho\frac{Dk}{Dt}=\frac{\partial}{\partial x_i}\left[\left(\mu+\frac{\mu_t}{\sigma_k}\right)\frac{\partial k}{\partial x_i}\right]+G_k+G_b-\rho\varepsilon-Y_M \tag{1}$$

$$\rho\frac{D\varepsilon}{Dt}=\frac{\partial}{\partial x_i}\left[\left(\mu+\frac{\mu_t}{\sigma_k}\right)\frac{\partial \varepsilon}{\partial x_i}\right]+C_{1\varepsilon}\frac{\varepsilon}{k}(G_k+C_{3\varepsilon}G_b)-C_{2\varepsilon}\rho\frac{\varepsilon^2}{k} \tag{2}$$

In the above equation, G_k represents the turbulent kinetic energy generated due to the average velocity gradient; G_b refers to the turbulent kinetic energy caused by buoyancy; Y_M refers to the effect of compressible turbulent pulsating expansion on the total dissipation rate.

The coefficient of turbulence viscosity is:

$$\mu_t=\rho C_\mu\frac{k^2}{\varepsilon}$$

In FLUENT, these three parameters $C_{1\varepsilon}$, $C_{2\varepsilon}$, C_μ are the default constant, $C_{1\varepsilon}$ = 1.4, $C_{2\varepsilon}$ = 1.92, and C_μ = 0.09. The turbulent Prandt numbers of turbulent kinetic energy *k* and dissipation rate ε are respectively 1.0 and 1.3.

The transport equation of turbulent kinetic energy *k* and dissipation rate ε is described as follows.

The equation *k*:

$$\rho\frac{Dk}{Dt}=\frac{\partial}{\partial x_j}\left[\left(\mu+\frac{\mu_t}{\sigma_k}\right)\frac{\partial k}{\partial x_j}\right]+G_k+G_b-\rho\varepsilon-Y_M \tag{3}$$

The equation ε:

$$\rho\frac{D\varepsilon}{Dt}=\frac{\partial}{\partial x_j}\left[\left(\mu+\frac{\mu_t}{\sigma_t}\right)\frac{\partial \varepsilon}{\partial x_j}\right]+\rho C_1 S\varepsilon-\rho C_2\frac{\varepsilon^2}{k+\sqrt{v\varepsilon}}+C_{1\varepsilon}\frac{\varepsilon}{k}C_{3\varepsilon}G_b \tag{4}$$

where,

$$C_1=\max\left[0.43,\frac{\eta}{\eta+5}\right]\eta=Sk/\varepsilon=\left(2E_{ij}\cdot E_{ij}\right)^{1/2}\frac{k}{\varepsilon}E_{ij}=\frac{1}{2}\left(\frac{\partial u_i}{\partial x_j}+\frac{\partial u_j}{\partial x_i}\right)$$

In the above equation, *k* is the kinetic energy of turbulence pulsation; ε is the dissipation rate of the turbulent pulsation kinetic energy; G_k is the turbulent kinetic energy caused by the average velocity gradient; G_b is the turbulent kinetic energy caused by buoyancy; Y_M is the effect of compressible turbulent pulsating expansion on the total dissipation rate. C_2 and $C_{1\varepsilon}$ are constant; σ_k and σ_ε is turbulent Prandt numbers of turbulent kinetic energy and dissipation rate, respectively.

In Fluent,

$$C_{1\varepsilon} = 1.44,\ C_{2\varepsilon} = 1.9,\ C_{3\varepsilon} = 0.09,\ C_2 = 1.9,\ \sigma_k = 1.0,\ \sigma_\varepsilon = 1.2.$$

2.2. Parameter Setting

A 16 × 104 m^3 large cylindrical LNG storage tank was chosen for numerical simulation, and its structural dimension are shown in Figure 1. The outer diameter of the tank was 82 m and the height was 50 m. The normal operating pressure of the storage tank was 25 kPa, and the maximum liquid level in the tank was 34.6 m. The origin of the computational domain was located at the center of the bottom of the tank. The coordinate of the leakage hole center point was (41, 10, 0), which was located on the leeward side of the tank. The leakage hole sizes were, respectively, 0.1 m × 0.1 m, 0.13 m × 0.13 m, 0.15 m × 0.15 m, 0.18 m × 0.18 m and 0.2 m × 0.2 m. Considering the calculation accuracy, the computational domain was determined to be 1000 m × 250 m × 500 m in the x, y, and z directions, and the tank that has a blocking rate of 2.78% was placed at a distance of 200 m downwind. The whole computational domain was discretized by the structured grid, and the specific grid division is shown in Figure 2a. In order to adapt to the change of flow field and ensure the accuracy of the solution, the grid around the leakage hole was encrypted by the block method. The independence of the grid and time step had been verified. The total number of cells in the calculation domain was finally determined to be 1,865,345, and the simulation time step was set to 0.1 s.

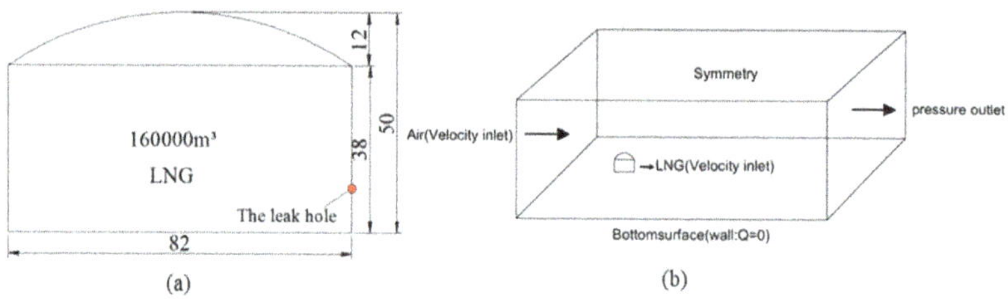

Figure 1. The settings of the large-scale LNG storage tank. (**a**) Geometric schematic of the tank; (**b**) the boundary settings of the tank.

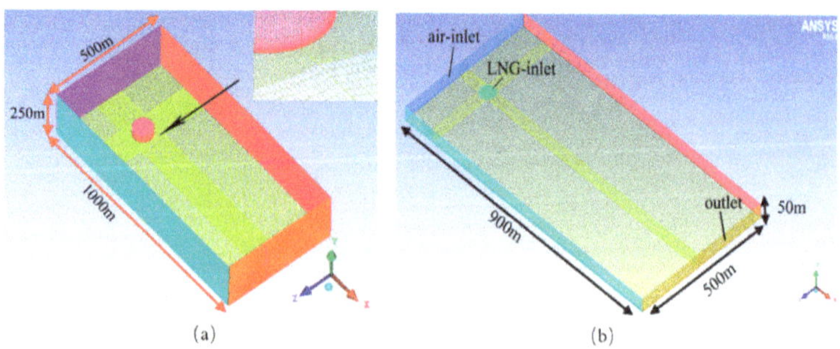

Figure 2. Mesh division in this study. (**a**) The meshing of the computational watershed; (**b**) the meshing of LNG leakage diffusion experiment.

In order to represent the node coordinates more accurately and ensure the convergence of calculation, a double-precision solver and implicit method were used in the calculation. Figure 2b shows the meshing of the LNG leakage diffusion experiment. The calculation domain was established with a size of 900 m × 500 m × 50 m on the x-axis, y-axis, and z-axis, respectively. The x–z plane was placed on the ground, and the y-direction was the vertical height. Furthermore, the wind direction remained unchanged throughout the calculation domain. The boundary conditions on the left and right sides of the calculation domain were the velocity–inlet and the pressure–outlet, respectively. Hexahedral mesh units were used for mesh generation, while the area around the pond was divided into fine meshes. A total of 803,287 cells were used for subsequent simulations.

2.3. Model Validation

In this paper, data from the Burro eight-spill test [27], which was conducted in 1980, was used as the basis of the validation analysis. In the test, LNG was released onto the water surface of a round pond, with 25 gas concentration monitors placed at different heights in the downwind. In addition, the water pond had an average diameter of 58 m, with an average water level about 1.5 m below the surrounding ground level. Based on the Burro series tests, the reliability of the multiphase model was evaluated by comparing the numerical results with the experimental results based on the diffusion range and concentration change of methane.

Figures 3 and 4 show the contour distribution of methane volume fraction after LNG spill 80 s on the x = 57 m and y = 1 m planes, respectively. In Figures 3a,b and 4a,b, the distribution areas of methane with different volume fractions on the horizontal and vertical planes are basically consistent with the experimental data. Figures 3c and 4c show the comparison of the coverage areas of dispersion clouds with different volume concentrations. There is a very good quantitative agreement between the simulation results and the experimental data. Besides, Table 1 shows that the comparison between the calculated and experimental values of maximum volume fraction of methane at different distances in downwind direction. It shows that the calculated maximum volume fraction of methane is lower than that of the experiment; however, in the area away from the leakage source, the calculated maximum volume fraction of methane is higher than that of the experiment. The reason is that the coupled heat transfer between the ground and the LNG vapor cloud is assumed to be constant in the simulation; in fact, the heat produced by ground heat transfer and solar radiation is variable. The error analysis method of the heavy gas diffusion model proposed by Emark et al. [28] is used to analyze the deviation between the simulation result and the test value. The method includes relative deviation (FB), geometric mean deviation (MG), geometric mean-variance (VG), relative mean square error (MRSE), relative mean square error (FAC2) and normalized mean square error (NMSE), which can be used to judge the validity of the numerical model. The deviation between numerical simulation and experimental values is shown in Table 2. It can be seen that all the deviations were within the allowable range of the evaluation parameters. Therefore, the multiphase model is suitable for the study of LNG leakage and diffusion.

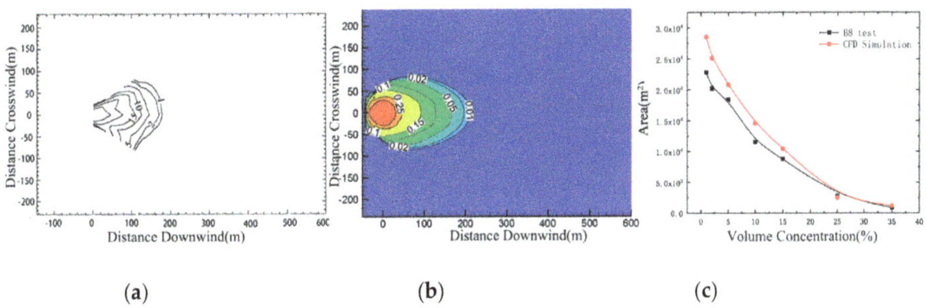

Figure 3. Comparison of experimental and simulated values of methane volume concentration at a vertical height of 1 m. (**a**) Burro eight-test measured value. (**b**) Fluent simulation results. (**c**) Comparison of test and simulation.

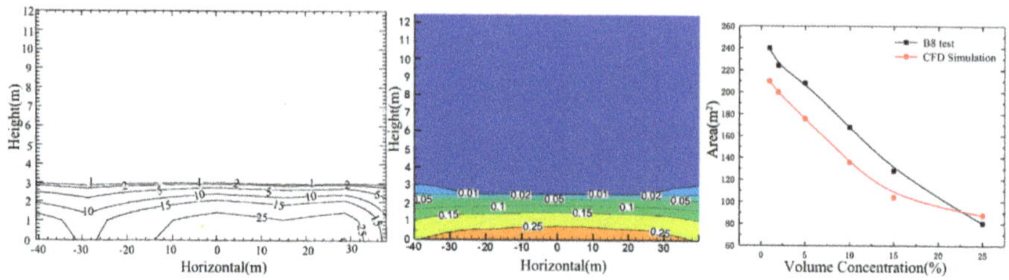

(**a**) (**b**) (**c**)

Figure 4. Comparison between experimental and simulated values of methane volume concentration at 57 m in downwind direction. (**a**) Burro-eight test measured value. (**b**) Fluent simulation results. (**c**) Comparison of test and simulation.

Table 1. Experimental and simulated values of maximum volume fraction of methane at different distances in downwind direction.

Downwind Distance/m	Maximum Methane Volume Fraction at 1 m Height/%	
	Test Measured Value	Fluent Simulation Value
140	16.49	15.4
400	4.25	5.32
800	1.93	2.25

Table 2. The error comparison of simulation results.

Deviation Statistics	FB	MG	VG	MRSE	FAC2	NMSE
Ideal value	0	1	1	0	1	0
Evaluation standard	(−0.4, 0.4)	(0.67 1.50)	<3.3	<2.3	>0.5	<4
Burro 8	−0.18	0.88	1.03	0.04	0.87	0.23

3. Results and Discussions

3.1. The Influence of Wind Field on Leakage and Diffusion of LNG Storage Tank

3.1.1. Numerical Simulation of Wind Field of LNG Storage Tank

The LNG storage tank will obstruct the flow of wind speed and thus affect the diffusion of LNG. In this study, the average wind speed at the height of 10 m is 4 m/s, and the wind speed of the inflow profile is implemented in a user-defined function (UDF) which is embedded in the numerical model as a boundary condition. Figure 5 shows the wind speed distribution in different planes of the calculation domain. As shown in Figure 5a, the wind speed at the boundary of the entire wind field is evenly distributed in the vertical plane of 0 m. The wind speed varied with height, forming gradient wind, which is the same as the wind field distribution law of the real atmospheric environment.

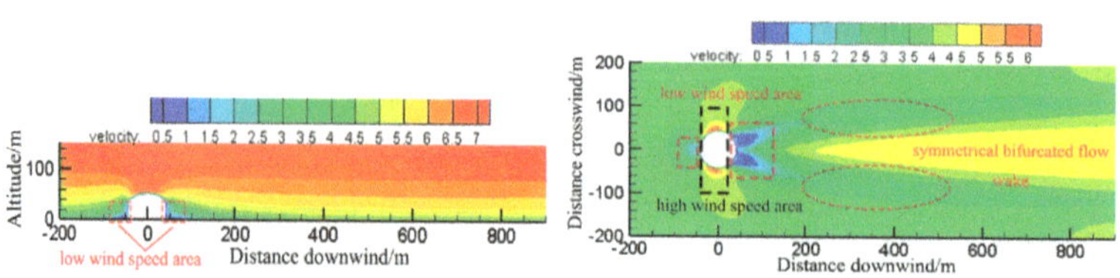

(**a**) Cross wind direction *z*-0 m (**b**) Vertical height *y*-10 m

Figure 5. The wind speed in the calculation area.

However, the atmospheric flow near the storage tank is affected by various factors, resulting in changes in wind speed and direction. When the wind flows from the top and both sides of the storage tank, it causes a high wind speed zone with a speed of 7 m/s on top of the storage tank (shown in the black box, Figure 5 and a low wind speed zone with a speed of less than 1 m/s on both sides of the storage tank (shown in the red box, Figure 5). In Figure 5b, in the area away from the storage tank, the wind keeps up to 4 m/s; however, in the area near the storage tank, the wind speed is reduced because of obstruction. A detention zone is formed on the windward side of the tank due to the obstruction of the tank, so the wind speed decreases sharply. When the wind bypasses both sides of the tank, a certain length of a symmetrical bifurcated flow wake is formed downstream of the tank (shown in the red circle).

Figure 6 shows the distribution of the wind speed streamline near the storage tank. It shows that there are obvious vortices on the windward and leeward sides of the tank. In addition, two symmetrical vortices are formed at 70 m in the x-axis behind the horizontal of the tank after the atmosphere bypasses the tank (Figure 6a). In the process of the wind flowing downstream along both sides of the tank, the wind speed decreases continuously and the wind direction changes, thus producing backflow. When the wind reaches the central axis of the storage tank, the wind speed is close to zero, and a small cavity zone is formed on the back of the storage tank (Figure 6b). However, the vortex and low wind speed areas are very close to the storage tank. When the wind is away from the storage tank, the streamline returns to normal and the wind movement also stabilizes.

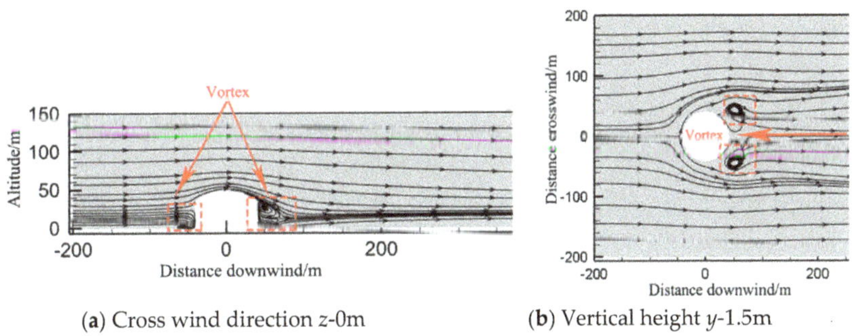

Figure 6. The distribution of wind speed streamlines near the storage tank.

3.1.2. Leakage and Diffusion Process of LNG Storage Tank under Wind Field

The average wind speed was assumed to be 4 m/s, and at the same time LNG was assumed to leak at a rate of 105.5 kg/s for 400 s. The expansion of LNG after leakage is shown in Figure 7. It can be seen that the pressure difference between the inside and outside of the tank causes the LNG to continue to spray from the leakage port to the ground in a parabolic form. The amount of LNG leakage is large, but the heat of the surrounding environment is limited, which makes it difficult to provide enough heat for the entire LNG to vaporize. Therefore, some LNG absorbs heat from the surrounding environment and then evaporates into a low-temperature gas cloud, and others form a liquid pool on the ground. During the landing process, some of the atomized LNG droplets absorb heat from the air and then evaporates into a gas state, resulting in a higher concentration of LNG leaking from the leakage hole and a lower concentration of LNG in the surface liquid pool (Figure 7c). Under the action of initial kinetic energy and gravity, the liquid LNG diffuses around the landing point, which is 7 m away from the storage tank and thus forming a thin "round" liquid pool (Figure 7b).

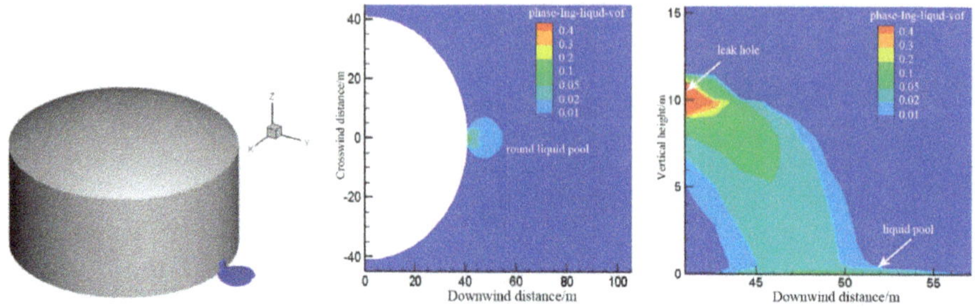

(a) (b) (c)

Figure 7. The distribution of LNG liquid pool. (**a**) Three-dimensional view of the liquid pool; (**b**) expansion of liquid pool at y = 0 m; (**c**) LNG injection at z = 0 m.

Figure 8 is a three-dimensional perspective view of gas clouds, which shows different methane volume fractions at different leakage moments, clearly showing the movement and diffusion process of low-temperature steam cloud containing leaking LNG. At the initial stage of leakage, the density of the low-temperature vapor cloud formed by flash evaporation is greater than that of the surrounding air, resulting in the extremely low gas cloud with methane volume fractions greater than 1%, 5%, and 15%. This phenomenon is also due to gravitational settling. As the leakage time increases to 120 s, the gas cloud with a volume fraction greater than 15% is still close to the ground with a "hole" inside, while the gas cloud with a volume fraction greater than 1% and 5% rises slightly. When the leakage time reaches 320 s, the whole gas cloud presents the phenomenon of "leaf-like bifurcation" on both sides. However, the height of gas clouds with 15% and more than 5% volume fraction is lower, while the height of gas cloud with volume fraction above 1% is relatively high, with a large amount of light methane floating over the tank (shown in the red box). The whole diffusion process fully reflects that LNG accumulates in the form of heavy gas cloud after leakage, mixes with air to absorb and transfer heat, resulting in the gradual narrowing of the difference between gas cloud density and air density. Finally, heavy methane turns into light methane in the periphery of the gas cloud.

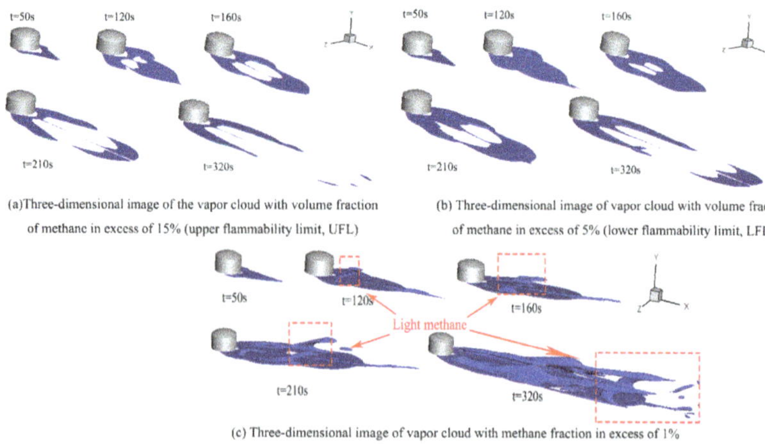

Figure 8. Three-dimensional perspectives of gas clouds with different methane volume concentrations at different leakage moments. (**a**) Three-dimensional image of the vapor cloud with volume fraction of methane in excess of 15%(upper flammability limit, UFL); (**b**) Three-dimensional image of vapor cloud with volume fraction of methane in excess of 5%(lower flammability limit, LFL); (**c**) Three-dimensional image of vapor cloud with methane fraction in excess of 1%.

In order to reveal the spatial distribution characteristics of the LNG vapor cloud near the storage tank, methane concentration contours are selected from the x-y plane, x-z plane, and y-z plane for analysis. Considering that the low height of the gas cloud and bifurcated gas cloud along the z-axis on both sides of the tank, $x = 57$ m, $z = 30$ m and $y = 0.5$ m are selected as the observation surface. Figure 9 shows that the distribution of methane gas cloud concentration is in different planes. As shown in Figure 9a, at the plane $y = 0.5$ m, the overall shape of the gas cloud is "fan-shaped" (shown in white box), accompanied by a cavity with a radius of about 17 m on the back. A high concentration of methane is deposited on both sides of the cloud, while a low concentration of methane is distributed in the middle of the cloud. As the leakage time increases, the low concentration methane in the middle is preferentially diluted by air, resulting in a "hole" in the middle of the gas cloud (shown in white box). As the leak continues for some time, the "hole" area expands from the middle to the tail, and the gas cloud splits into two parts. One part is a heavy gas cloud, which is stacked behind the storage tank in the form of "leaf-like bifurcation" (shown in white box), and the other part is a light gas cloud (shown in a white round frame), spreading further with the wind. During the whole leakage process, the gas cloud gradually develops from a complete "fan shape" to a front-end "leaf-shaped" bifurcation. Due to the disturbance effect of the storage tank on the atmospheric movement, the detention zone and low wind speed region behind the storage tank restrains the downwind expansion in the middle of the gas cloud in some sense. When the low-temperature LNG vapor mixes with the atmosphere, the movement of the vapor cloud also diverges laterally along the streamline development at the back of the tank, resulting in a large amount of methane accumulation on both sides and thus forming a leaf-shaped bifurcation.

In Figure 9b, it can be seen that the gas cloud is divided into different concentration layers along the vertical direction $z = 30$ m, and the methane volume fraction decreases with height. Among them, the methane concentration is high near the ground (shown in white box), and low far away from the ground (shown in white round frame). The reason is that a large amount of highly concentrated methane accumulates near the storage tank during the leakage process, which makes it difficult to dilute and dissipate. However, the heavy methane in the outermost part of the gas cloud continuously absorbs and transfers heat with air in order to form light methane with low concentration and then to spread to higher and farther places. In Figure 9c, the gas cloud after leakage is symmetrically distributed behind the storage tank at 57 m on the x-direction. As the leak progresses, the width and height of the vapor cloud in this area increase slightly. The vapor cloud appears as "low in the middle and high at both ends" (shown in a white circle).

According to the results of numerical simulation and relevant heavy gas diffusion theory [29], the macroscopic diffusion behavior of the LNG vapor cloud could be roughly divided into three stages according to the continuous leakage of the LNG tank studied in this paper.

(1) Initial stage of diffusion (heavy gas accumulation): This stage is a period of heavy gas accumulation and diffusion. As shown in Figure 9, from the beginning of the leakage to 50 s, the vapor cloud is in the shape of "fan leaf", and its internal concentration of the vapor cloud is in an unstable state.

(2) Mid-stage of diffusion (Transitional levitation): This stage is the period of heavy gas transiting to light gas. From 120 s to 160 s, the development of gas cloud is in a neutral state, and the whole gas cloud is still in a "fan leaf shape". The methane concentration inside the gas cloud increases to a peak.

(3) Post-diffusion stage (Light gas drift): this stage is the light gas into passive diffusion. After 210 s of leakage, the development of the vapor cloud is in a stable state, in which case the width of the gas cloud remains unchanged, but the length and height of the vapor cloud slowly increases. As the "hole" area inside the vapor cloud continues to expand, the contact area between the gas cloud and the surrounding air increases, which lead to the rise of temperature and the decrease of methane density at the tail of the gas cloud. Under

the influence of wind, methane in the outermost part of the cloud is diluted the fastest. As a result, the cloud still behaves as "low in the middle and high at both ends".

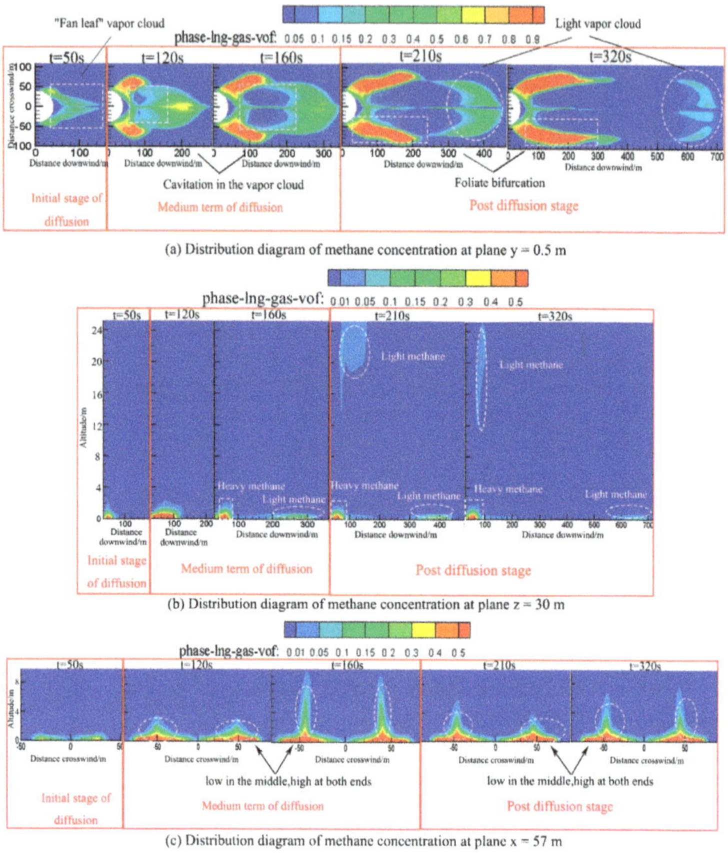

Figure 9. Distribution of methane concentration in different planes. (**a**) Distribution diagram of methane concentration at plane y = 0.5 m; (**b**) Distribution diagram of methane concentration at plane z = 30 m; (**c**) Distribution diagram of methane concentration at plane x = 57 m.

3.2. *Influence of Leakage Aperture on LNG Vapor Cloud Diffusion*

Figure 10 shows the change in the morphology of LNG vapor cloud with time at 0.5 m on the *y*-axis under five leakage apertures. When the leakage lasts for 60 s, which belongs to the initial stage of diffusion, the vapor cloud is in the shape of "fan leaf" with a similar downwind diffusion speed under different leakage aperture. As the leakage aperture increases, the volume concentration of methane in the gas cloud keeps rising, and the width of the gas cloud increases slightly. Compared with the situation at 60 s, the gas cloud has different degrees of holes inside at 180 s, which is at the middle stage of diffusion. However, the area of the hole in the gas cloud decreases with the leakage aperture increasing (shown in the white box). When the leak lasts for 320 s, it reaches the late stage of diffusion, the heavy gas in the vapor cloud is accumulated behind the storage tank in the form of "leaf like bifurcation", while the light gas at the tail of the vapor cloud is diluted with the wind. With the increase of the leakage aperture, the width of the heavy gas cloud becomes larger, and the methane volume concentration of the light gas in the tail increases (shown in white round frame), which makes it more difficult to be diluted. According to the LNG gas cloud diffusion under different leakage conditions, it could be demonstrated that the trend of the LNG vapor diffusion under different leakage apertures has similar characteristics. The change of the leakage aperture size will affect the coverage and concentration of the gas cloud, thus delaying the development of the gas cloud to the next diffusion stage. The motion trajectory of the vapor cloud is still determined by the wind field behind the tank.

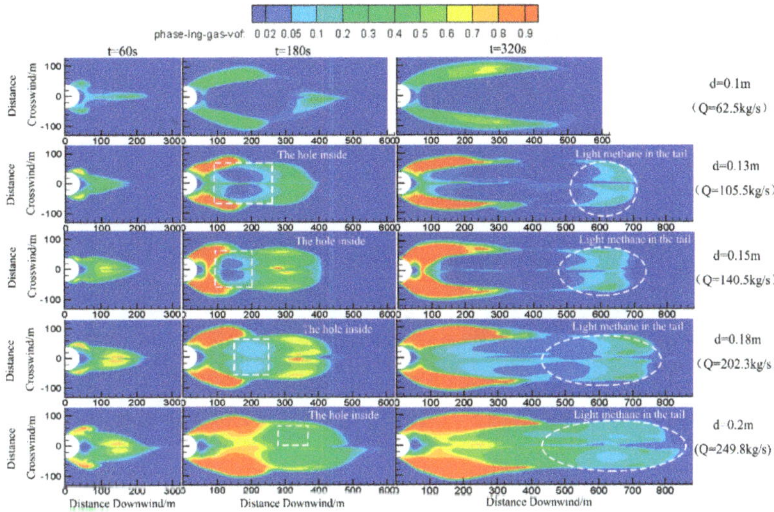

Figure 10. Variation of gas cloud concentration distribution at y = 0.5 m plane under different leakage apertures.

Figure 11 shows the furthest length, maximum width and height of the gas cloud diffusion with 1/2 LFL concentration under different leakage apertures. The increase of the leakage aperture will promote the diffusion speed of the vapor cloud in the downwind direction. As the leakage aperture increases, the maximum explosion range of methane and the volume of flammable clouds increases rapidly. For example, when the leakage aperture increases from 0.1 m to 0.2 m, the maximum diffusion distance of methane 0.5 LFL in Figure 11a increases by 78.5% from 531 m to 948 m, and the volume of flammable vapor cloud in Figure 11c enlarges from 13,563.44 m^3 to 53,642.89 m^3, with a growth rate of 295%. However, there is some difference, as shown in Figure 11b. When the leakage aperture is 0.1 m, the gas cloud with a concentration of 0.5 LFL has the largest width on the z-axis at 243 m. When the leakage aperture increases from 0.13 m to 0.2 m, the largest width of methane 0.5 LFL increases by 22.6% from 194.6 m to 238.6 m. This was because that when the leakage pore size is 0.1 m, due to the small leakage volume, the methane density in the late stage of diffusion is close to the air and the gas cloud diffuses faster in the horizontal direction, resulting in the farthest diffusion distance of the gas cloud along the z-axis. As leakage aperture increases, the leakage and vaporization of LNG increases, and a larger volume of combustible gas clouds increases too. However, the dilution ability of air is limited, and the gas cloud rapidly accumulates and diffuses along the downwind distance, resulting in a larger diffusion distance along the x-axes and z-axes. Therefore, after the LNG leaks, the leakage source should be cut off or blocked in time to reduce the amount of LNG leakage.

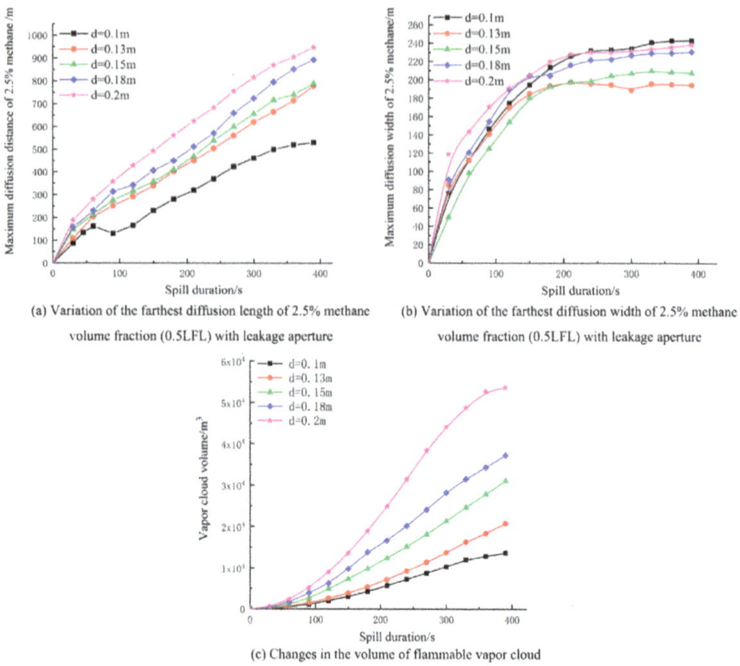

(a) Variation of the farthest diffusion length of 2.5% methane volume fraction (0.5LFL) with leakage aperture

(b) Variation of the farthest diffusion width of 2.5% methane volume fraction (0.5LFL) with leakage aperture

(c) Changes in the volume of flammable vapor cloud

Figure 11. Variation of the farthest moving distance and volume of flammable vapor clouds with leakage time under different leakage apertures. (**a**) Variation of the farthest diffusion length of 2.5% methane volume fraction (0.5 LFL) with leakage aperture; (**b**) Variation of the farthest diffusion width of 2.5% methane volume fraction (0.5 LFL) with leakage aperture; (**c**) Changes in the volume of flammable vapor cloud.

4. Conclusions

With the integrated use of the realizable k-ε turbulence model and the Eluerian model, numerical simulation of the leakage and diffusion process of the LNG storage tank was conducted. The conclusions were drawn as follows.

(a) After the storage tank leaked, LNG was sprayed to the ground to form a circular liquid pool and then continuously exchanged heat with air to evaporate into low-temperature steam. The diameter of the liquid pool increased first and then remained unchanged with the leakage time, and the gas cloud diffusion state was divided into three stages due to the cylindrical turbulence of the tank. In these three stages, the LNG gas cloud experienced heavy gas accumulation, entrainment heat transfer and light gas drift, with the shape gradually developing from a complete "fan blade" to a "leaf bifurcation" of heavy methane at the front end.

(b) The leakage aperture greatly affected the heat transfer between LNG and the surrounding environment. It delayed the development of the liquid pool and gas cloud to a stable state. The increase of leakage aperture quantitatively affected the distribution of vapor clouds across LNG dispersion routes. The liquid pool area was increased by 10.3 times, while the length, width, and volume of the flammable vapor cloud increased by 78.5%, 22.6%, and 249%, respectively. In addition, within the variation range of leakage aperture, there would always be a local high concentration area within 200 m downstream of the storage tank. In the field near the storage tank, the clouds settled and accumulated towards the ground in the state of gas–liquid two-phase flow, and the density of the cloud was gradually lower than the air in the far-field, manifesting as light gas diffusion. This area was characterized by high concentration and long duration of methane, which should be the focus area of alarm prediction.

Author Contributions: Conceptualization, X.L. (Xue Li) and N.Z.; methodology, X.L. (Xuanya Liu); validation, W.H.; formal analysis, Q.Z.; resources, B.C.; data curation, L.K.; writing—original draft preparation, X.L. (Xue Li); writing—review and editing, X.L. (Xue Li), N.Z. and V.R.; project administration, N.Z. All authors have read and agreed to the published version of the manuscript.

Funding: This study was funded by National Key R&D Program of China [No. 2017YFC0805100]; The Natural Science Research Project of Higher Education Institutions of Jiangsu Province [No. 20KJB620004]; Scientific Research Project "Fire Risk Analysis of Petrochemical Enterprises" of Fire Department of Ministry of Public Security [No. 2016JSYJD04]; Tianjin Science and Technology Project [No. 2016ZX-CXSF0080]; Major projects supported by the Natural Science Research of Jiangsu Higher Education Institutions [No. 17KJA440001]; Open Project of Jiangsu Key Laboratory of Oil and Gas Storage and Transportation Technology [No. CDYQCY202104].

Institutional Review Board Statement: Not applicable.

Informed Consent Statement: Not applicable.

Conflicts of Interest: The authors of this study have no conflict of interests or competing interests.

References

1. Eser, P.; Chokani, N.; Abhari, R. Impact of Nord Stream 2 and LNG on gas trade and security of supply in the European gas network of 2030. *Appl. Energy* **2019**, *238*, 816–830. [CrossRef]
2. Zerouali, B.; Hamaidi, B. Predictive analysis for risk of fire and explosion of LNG storage tanks by fuzzy Bayesian network. *Life Cycle Reliab. Saf. Eng.* **2020**, *9*, 319–328. [CrossRef]
3. Zhang, M.; Song, W.; Chen, Z.; Wang, J. Risk assessment for fire and explosion accidents of steel oil tanks using improved AHP based on FTA. *Process Saf. Prog.* **2017**, *35*, 260–269. [CrossRef]
4. Schmidt, M.S. Atmospheric tank failures: Mechanisms and an unexpected case study. *Process Saf. Prog.* **2017**, *36*, 353–361. [CrossRef]
5. Choi, I.H.; Chang, D. Reliability and availability assessment of seabed storage tanks using fault tree analysis. *Ocean Eng.* **2016**, *120*, 1–14. [CrossRef]
6. Necci, A.; Argenti, F.; Landucci, G.; Cozzani, V. Accident scenarios triggered by lightning strike on atmospheric storage tanks. *Reliab. Eng. Syst. Saf.* **2014**, *127*, 30–46. [CrossRef]
7. Koopman, R.P.; Baker, J.; Cederwall, R.T.; Goldwire, H.C., Jr.; Hogan, W.J.; Kamppinen, L.M.; Kiefer, R.D.; McClure, J.W.; McRae, T.G.; Morgan, D.L. *Burro Series Data Report LLNL/NWC 1980 LNG Spill Tests. UCID-19075*; Lawrence Livermore National Laboratory: Livermore, CA, USA, 1982.
8. Ermak, D.L.; Chapman, R.; Goldwire, H.C.; Gouveia, F.J.; Rodean, H.C. *Heavy Gas Dispersion Test Summary Report. ESL-TR-88-22*; Lawrence Livermore National Laboratory: Livermore, CA, USA, 1989.
9. Brown, T.C.; Cederwall, R.T.; Chan, S.T.; Ermak, D.L.; Koopman, R.P.; Lamson, K.C.; McClure, J.W.; Morris, L.K. *Falcon Series Data Report: 1987 LNG Vapor Barrier Verification Field*; Gas Research Institute Report: Chicago, IL, USA, 1990.
10. Siuta, D.; Markowski, A.S.; Mannan, M.S. Uncertainty techniques in liquefied natural gas (LNG) dispersion calculations. *J. Loss Prev. Process. Ind.* **2013**, *26*, 418–426. [CrossRef]
11. Chan, S.T. Numerical simulations of LNG vapor dispersion from a fenced storage area. *J. Hazard. Mater.* **1992**, *30*, 195–224. [CrossRef]
12. Chan, S.T. *Three-Dimensional Model for Simulating Atmospheric Dispersion of Heavy-Gases over Complex Terrain. UCRL-JC-127475*; Lawrence Liver More National Laboratory: Livermore, CA, USA, 1997.
13. Giannissi, S.G.; Venetsanos, A.G.; Markatos, N.; Bartzis, J.G. Numerical simulation of LNG dispersion under two-phase release conditions. *J. Loss Prev. Process Ind.* **2013**, *26*, 245–254. [CrossRef]
14. VílchezJuan, A.; Villafane, D.; Casal, J. A dispersion safety factor for LNG vapor clouds. *J. Hazard. Mater.* **2013**, *246–247*, 181–188. [CrossRef] [PubMed]
15. Li, J.; Ma, G.; Abdel-Jawad, M.; Huang, Z. Gas dispersion risk analysis of safety gap effect on the innovating FLNG vessel with a cylindrical platform. *J. Loss Prev. Process Ind.* **2016**, *40*, 304–316. [CrossRef]
16. Zhang, Q.X.; Liang, D. Numerical simulations of LNG vapor dispersion from LNG jetting in different directions. *Procedia Eng.* **2016**, *135*, 316–321. [CrossRef]
17. Marsegan, C.; Busini, V.; Rota, R. Influence of active mitigation barriers on LNG dispersion. *J. Loss Prev. Process Ind.* **2016**, *44*, 380–389. [CrossRef]
18. Nguyen, L.D.; Kim, M.; Choi, B. An experimental investigation of the evaporation of cryogenic-liquid-pool spreading on concrete ground. *Appl. Therm. Eng.* **2017**, *123*, 196–204. [CrossRef]

19. Gopalaswami, N.; Kakosimos, K.; Zhang, B.; Liu, Z.; Mentzer, R.; Mannan, M.S. Experimental and numerical study of liquefied natural gas (LNG) pool spreading and vaporization on water. *J. Hazard. Mater.* **2017**, *334*, 244–255. [CrossRef] [PubMed]
20. Ikealumba, W.C.; Wu, H. Effect of atmospheric and sea stability on liquefied natural gas (LNG) dispersion: Implications to Australian LNG marine transport. *Fuel* **2017**, *197*, 8–19. [CrossRef]
21. Luo, T.P.; Yu, C.C.; Liu, R.M.; Li, M. Numerical simulation of LNG release and dispersion using a multiphase CFD model. *J. Loss Prev. Process Ind.* **2018**, *56*, 316–327. [CrossRef]
22. Dasgotra, A.; Varun Teja, G.V.V.; Sharma, A.; Mishra, K.B. CFD modeling of large-scale flammable cloud dispersion using FLACS. *J. Loss Prev. Process Ind.* **2018**, *56*, 531–536. [CrossRef]
23. Giannissi, S.G.; Venetsanos, A.G. A comparative CFD assessment study of cryogenic hydrogen and LNG dispersion. *Int. J. Hydrogen Energy* **2018**, *44*, 9018–9030. [CrossRef]
24. Urióstegui-Hernández, A.; Garnica-González, P.; Ramos-Banderas, J.N.; Hernández-Bocanegra, C.A.; Solorio-Díaz, G. Multiphasic Study of Fluid-Dynamics and the Thermal Behavior of a Steel Ladle during Bottom Gas Injection Using the Eulerian Model. *Metals* **2021**, *11*, 1082. [CrossRef]
25. Gallot-Lavallée, S.; Jones, W.P.; Marquis, A.J. Large Eddy Simulation of an Ethanol Spray Flame with Secondary Droplet Breakup. *Flow Turbul. Combust.* **2021**, *107*, 709–743. [CrossRef]
26. Tauseef, S.M.; Rashtchian, D.; Abbasi, S.A. CFD-based simulation of dense gas dispersion in presence of obstacles. *J. Loss Prev. Process Ind.* **2011**, *24*, 371–376. [CrossRef]
27. Kovalets, I.V.; Maderich, V.S. Numerical Simulation of Interaction of the Heavy Gas Cloud with the Atmospheric Surface Layer. *Environ. Fluid Mech.* **2006**, *6*, 313–340. [CrossRef]
28. Sklavounos, S.; Rigas, F. Simulation of coyote series trials-Part I: CFD estimation of non-isothermal LNG releases and comparison with box-model predictions. *Chem. Eng. Sci.* **2006**, *61*, 1434–1443. [CrossRef]
29. Duijm, N.J.; Carissimo, B.; Mercer, A. Development and test of an evaluation protocol for heavy gas dispersion models. *J. Hazard. Mater.* **1997**, *56*, 273–285. [CrossRef]

energies

Article

Airtightness and Heat Energy Loss of Mid-Size Terraced Houses Built of Different Construction Materials

Valdas Paukštys [1,2], Gintaris Cinelis [1,*], Jūratė Mockienė [1] and Mindaugas Daukšys [1]

1 Faculty of Civil Engineering and Architecture, Kaunas University of Technology, Studentų st. 48, 51367 Kaunas, Lithuania; valdas.paukstys@ktu.lt (V.P.); jurate.mockiene@ktu.lt (J.M.); mindaugas.dauksys@ktu.lt (M.D.)
2 Institute of Architecture and Construction, Kaunas University of Technology, Tunelio st. 60, 44405 Kaunas, Lithuania
* Correspondence: gintaris.cinelis@ktu.lt; Tel.: +370-687-98786

Abstract: The European Union has adopted legislation aimed to increase the use of renewable energy and improve the effectiveness of conventional-form energy use. Additional structure insulation helps to decrease heat energy loss. Airtightness of the building envelope (building airtightness) is an additional factor that determines comfortable and energy-saving living environment. The conformity of heat energy loss with the object's design energy class is one of the mandatory indicators used in the obligatory building energy performance certification procedure. Optionally, the objects to be certified are the entire buildings or separate units (flats). There is an issue of concern whether a flat assessed as a separate housing unit would meet the requirements of design energy class depending on the location of the unit in the building. The study is aimed to determine the change in heat loss of end units in terraced houses (townhouses) as a result of various factors, leading to uneven airtightness of the building envelope. The non-destructive assessment of building airtightness was implemented through the combined use of methods, namely Blower Door Test (around 200 measurements) and Infrared Thermography. The hollow clay unit masonry showed ca. 7–11% less airtightness than the sand–lime block masonry structure. The end units were up to 20% less airtight compared to the inside units.

Keywords: airtightness; Blower Door; heat energy loss; thermographic photo research; building energy performance

Citation: Paukštys, V.; Cinelis, G.; Mockienė, J.; Daukšys, M. Airtightness and Heat Energy Loss of Mid-Size Terraced Houses Built of Different Construction Materials. *Energies* **2021**, *14*, 6367. https://doi.org/10.3390/en14196367

Academic Editor: Marcin Kamiński

Received: 3 August 2021
Accepted: 29 September 2021
Published: 5 October 2021

1. Introduction

To fulfil the requirements of the European Energy Performance of Buildings Directive (EPBD) [1,2] related to the reduction of energy consumption by using high-quality materials and implementing efficient solutions for structural connections and joints, the national requirements for thermal properties in building envelope were formulated and building energy efficiency calculation methodology was developed. Many European countries have developed national methodologies for the assessment of building energy efficiency according to DIN 18599 [3] in Germany, DOCET in Italy, CALENER in Spain, etc. [4]. The above-mentioned methods vary depending on the type of buildings, climatic zone, minimal thermal requirements, and certification indexing [4].

The main evaluation criteria used in these methodologies are CO_2 emissions and primary energy or heat energy consumption in buildings. All the methodologies pursue the main aim to reduce energy consumption in buildings. To this end, not only are efficient engineering systems that improve the thermal properties of the building required, but also appropriate technological solutions to assure the high quality of work and good airtightness of the buildings. A properly insulated building together with efficient heating and ventilating systems can save up to 50% of heating energy and assure comfortable conditions in the premises [5,6].

The airtightness of and energy efficiency of the buildings can be determined by different methods [7]: theoretical investigation [8,9], empirical research [10,11], modelling of general building characteristics, or modelling of one component of the building [12]. The analysis of the related literature revealed that building energy performance calculations are precise only if building airtightness is defined by measurements. The measurements help to assess the construction workmanship and define the airtightness level, which is used to calculate the energy consumption of the building according to the 2010/31/EU Directive [2]. The most widely used method of airtightness measurement is the blowing door test method, prescribed by EN ISO 9972 2015 [13,14].

The main index of airtightness used in Lithuania is n_{50}, which indicates the part of internal air volume having changed in one hour at the set pressure of 50 Pa. The measurements of this kind are performed in many countries aiming to assess the general airtightness level of buildings using various criteria like the building type, its height, geometric forms, envelope structure, the ratio of the envelope, the floor area, etc. [15–18].

There are several main ways of air infiltration. One of the reasons is improper structural connections in the building due to using low quality insulation materials or not using them at all. In this case, the outside air penetrates through structural joints. The other path of air leakage is the building construction material. In this case, the air can infiltrate through the voids and cracks of construction elements.

The level of building airtightness can be determined and air infiltration paths in the building envelope can be detected by means of non-destructive tests using an infrared camera and observing the cold air movement in the external structures [19], or measuring the air movement speed near the splits with the anemometer sensors and calculating the approximate area of the split [20], or even measuring the sound of penetrating air.

The research objectives were: (1) experimental assessment of the flat airtightness distribution in terraced houses made of different materials, (2) theoretical heat energy loss calculation and finding out the differences in the heat loss values between the flats in different places in the building plan, (3) assessment of the compliance of flats in different places in the building with the design energy performance class.

2. Literature Review

T. Kalamees [21] conducted laboratory tests of various structural timber framework connections and compared the obtained results with airtightness results of real-built houses. The researchers concluded that it was difficult to ensure the quality of airtightening works on site in the installation of both structural connections and engineering systems (water supply, electricity).

The authors of the paper [22] discussed the airtightness estimation procedure applicable in the design phase. The methodology being in its early phase included quantitative characterization of expected leaks, evaluation of building airtightness in-situ using fan pressurization, component testing for air permeability in laboratory conditions with the completion of air leakage values obtained from the published database, and correction/validation of airtightness values. The investigation of several building parts showed that ventilation ridge was responsible for the highest percentage (61%) of airflow (the air leakage values were as follows: 11.0 $m^3/(h{\cdot}m^2)$ for ventilation ridge, 0.66 $m^3/(h{\cdot}m^2)$ for window frame and connection of steel columns with the floor, and 1.15 $m^3/(h{\cdot}m^2)$ for panel joints).

Another article [23] discusses the air leakage problem, considering the national building energy-related regulations and the methodology of energy performance calculation. The authors investigated the construction type, the age, design details, and retrofitting of the building as airtightness factors and found better quality of newly-built dwellings, good design, high-quality workmanship, and proper quality control during the construction period contribute to energy efficiency of buildings the most. The inclusion of the airtightness factor during the energy performance assessment process could improve the energy consumption by up to 7%.

Another paper [24] presents and discusses the results of measuring the airtightness of 170 single-family houses and 56 apartments. The construction method, insulation materials, joint insulation materials, and the ceiling structure were studied in the research as the factors related to airtightness. Good airtightness of individual houses was reached in all house groups regardless of the choice of structure, number of stories, ventilation system, or technology of construction. This fact pointed out the importance of construction quality.

The research paper [25] includes a proposal for the development of a rough predictive model of the degree of envelope airtightness as a regional tool for energy efficiency assessment and tailored to southern European construction stock. The results were assessed as widely scattered due to the impact of the random component of manual construction. The paper presents the results of statistical analysis and describes the protocol used both for the identification and quantification of air leakage pathways and for construction quality management.

The authors of the paper [26] conducted a study on the relation between the airtightness of a building envelope, air infiltration, and energy use of a typical modern Finnish detached house with an IDA-ICE simulation model also considering the stack-induced infiltration. An adapted model for the rough estimation of the annual air infiltration was determined from the numerical simulation results. The dependency of both the infiltration rate and heat energy use is nearly linear on the building's leakage rate, measured as n_{50}. This research showed that infiltration induces about 15–30% of the energy used for space heating, together with the ventilation in the prototypical detached house.

The authors of the work [27] performed the univariate analysis and multiple linear regression of the Canadian airtightness database to reveal the important trends. Two airtightness model classes with 3 variables and 8 variables (building volume, climate, building age, building height, and insulation levels for basements, walls, roofs, and windows) using two airtightness metrics (ACH and NL) were developed. The models referred to the found half airtightness variation of the building. The study set a feasible lower boundary of perspective models for regression-based airtightness prediction.

Tests were carried out in five flats of the same building in order to characterize the air permeability and to improve the design of buildings [28]. Although the flats tested were of the same size, with the same components, and were erected using the same construction processes, their overall air permeability showed a wide variation. The authors assumed this was mainly due to the change of the width of the gaps around the roller shutter boxes and the gaps in the bottom opening joint of the doors. The quality of windows, entrance doors, and kitchen external doors also had an impact.

The results presented in [29] give some ideas for how to decrease the measurement uncertainty in the blowing door test and to better detect energy and environmental issues in the audits of buildings. The chimney and the windows, without sealing and natural ventilation systems, were discovered to be the critical causes in the building's over-ventilation. The most critical uncertainty contributions were found to be the operative test conditions and metrological performances (e.g., internal–external temperature and the wind velocity difference) of the pressure measuring device.

The research [30] empirically investigated factors that should be considered while using pressure difference measurement values and airflow rate to derive more accurate airtightness values for large buildings. The distribution of vertical pressure across the whole building envelope can differ considerably when the building is pressurized. A method to measure airtightness was proposed where the pressure difference on each level of the building is measured and a medium value of pressure difference is defined.

Two problems related to design solutions of building airtightness were revealed in the work [31]: contemporary airtightness predictive models are too complex to be used for everyday design practice, and existing airtightness predictive models do not meet the needs of contractors and designers. More detailed issues in this context could be addressed: the lack of standardization, including factors classification, parameters definition, their impact quantification and significance assessment, metric analysis, the influence of supervision and workmanship, the classification of the air leakage paths, and research of significant air penetration areas/points.

The air permeability measurement results of 287 post-2006 new-built UK dwellings averaged 5.97 $m^3/(h{\cdot}m^2)$ at 50 Pa were studied in the paper [32]. Relationships between the airtightness and management context, building method, and dwelling type as the influencing factors were investigated. The superior airtightness was achieved in buildings with the self-build procurement route as a result of more innovative construction practice, prefabricated concrete panel systems, etc.; the houses built using site-based labour-intensive methods were the most air leaky. The predictive regression model was developed to predict the potential impacts of the air leakage-related factors of dwellings and improving energy efficiency.

Airtightness testing is described in [33] as a highly informative tool of the dwelling retrofit process. The authors refer to the statement that air infiltration through apertures in the building envelope can make up to one-third of the total heat loss. Particularly in this project, it was possible to reduce the measured air permeability (from 15.57 to 4.74 $m^3/(h{\cdot}m^2)$ @ 50 Pa) during the dwelling retrofit. This improvement was achieved through the use of usual draught-proofing means (a decrease in air permeability more than 30%), close attention to installation detail, workmanship, and sealing of the floor/wall joints at the skirting board connection (air permeability reduction of 3.6 $m^3/(h{\cdot}m^2)$ @ 50 Pa). Airtightness measures alone contributed to around 9% of the forecasted total reduction of heat energy demand. The effectiveness of fabric measures was very good (64% reduction considering the case of the uninsulated house), although the installation of double glazed units combined with the roof and wall insulation showed minimal improvement of airtightness (approximately 1.26 $m^3/(h{\cdot}m^2)$).

The paper [34] investigates the building's airtightness in terms of location and exposure of the building. The authors state that energy-efficient buildings situated in windy areas and at exposed locations could constitute up to 10% of the total heat consumption. The altitude, strength, and speed of the wind have a significant impact on the building by determining the amount of airflow through gaps, cracks, and leaks in the envelope. The possible impact of main parameters of location on the ultimate airtightness of the building envelope was verified while investigating 150 low-energy houses constructed in 2004–2014. The altitude's contribution to airtightness is 0.06%, whereas 99.94% of the airtightness is influenced by other factors.

A statistical method is presented in the work [14] investigating relevant factors related to the airtightness of the dwellings: climate zone, year of construction, and typology. The proposed methodology and its results were compared to the extracted database values. An open to expanding quota sampling scheme consisting of 411 representative cases was built to extrapolate the infiltration rates for Spanish buildings using typical constructive solutions. In the case study, leakage paths were located mainly around shutter boxes, window joints, and frames. The research of the infiltration impact on the ventilation and energy performance of the dwellings has been planned on this basis.

The authors of [35] developed a simplified method to evaluate energy savings from enhanced airtightness. This method was aimed to facilitate the use of energy savings estimates available to building designers and owners and expand the possibilities of the existing governmental online calculator. It expanded the ability to examine energy savings in commercial buildings for all cities in the USA. A simplified approach including energy savings predicting equations was developed to estimate annual and hourly heating energy savings. The equations predicting the percental energy savings for retrofitted buildings only require their expected air leakage rates before the retrofit and after it. Annual energy savings estimated using the online calculator and the proposed approach differed by 15% to 24%.

In the study [36], a model equation was obtained that uses statistical analysis based on empirical models to predict the apartment airtightness of reinforced concrete buildings with the data from 486 units. Two groups of variables were used in the airtightness prediction model equations along with correlation dependence analysis and multiple regression analysis. The model with the area variables was more accurate in predicting airtightness out of the two models. This approach has a limitation because the prediction results may differ depending on the characteristics and the data type collected by various countries. Nevertheless, the methodology presented in this work contributes to similar studies for finding influential variables with better applicability in the future.

The paper [37] investigates the problem of the seeming airtightness of partitions constructed in buildings. The study deals with the wind effect which is the washing reason of fibrous and porous materials of the envelopes. The authors explain how the disintegration of insulation material by forming empty areas determining local discontinuities of material in the envelope reduces thermal resistance. Appropriate areas were proved by the dynamic infrared detection method. The results show that thermal resistance of such envelopes is reduced to 87% with an absence of wind protection. The authors recommend considering the decomposition of this type while calculating the heat transfer coefficient.

In the study [12], an alternative approach was advanced to evaluate the air infiltration rate and air leakage area in building envelope parts such as exterior and interior floors and walls. Physical and acoustical methods were applied in measuring the sound reduction index to determine the leakage area. Therewith, the airflow rate through air leaks was determined using pressure difference over the floor or behind the wall and the values of leakage area. Subsequently, the calculated air infiltration rate also enabled evaluating the convective moisture rate through leaks and heat losses of the building.

The study [38] examined the airtightness performance of container houses and the impact of airtightness on their energy efficiency comparing the measurement and calculation results before and after building treatment. The identified weak places (thermal bridges, air leakages, and condensation) were mainly as junctions of walls, slabs, roof panels, and the edges of the openings. Significant improvement of the airtightness (81%) led to a certain reduction of annual energy demand (9.3%). Airtight joints and thermal brakes are essential for junction details seeking to avoid thermal problems and improve the energy performance of the building.

The authors of the work [39] studied the leakage–infiltration ratio by implementing the tests of more than twenty houses in the UK. The existing rule of thumb of the divide-by-20 (the error of using ranged from 3% to 175%) was revised and a new rule divide-by-37 as a more representative of the leakage–infiltration ratio was proposed. The mismatch of the assessment using the existing Standard Assessment Procedure (SAP) was particularly noticeable after adding the modification factors for local wind and sheltering: the overestimated infiltration rate values reached 500% and more, especially in airtight houses.

In the research [40], the airtightness role in the context of thermal insulation performance of traditional double-glazed air-filled windows was analysed. Tests were conducted in a typical dwelling in the UK by comparing the windows that are fitted with a special transparent cover improving airtightness and standard windows. The average U-value of the window sash with air-filled double-glazing was calculated to be 2.67 $W/m^2 \cdot K$, as it was 1.79 $W/m^2 \cdot K$ for the airtight window sash which resulted in a 33% decrease in heat losses. Windows are still important in the energy demand of buildings, and effective solutions such as retrofitting windows with covers can notably contribute to decreasing the windows-related energy losses in buildings.

Performing Blower Door Tests in large buildings [41] requires airflow rates that are impractical to achieve using available equipment and because of the necessity to test only the individual zones of buildings. The Lstiburek method and the Love and Passmore method were adapted for use in multi-unit high-rise residential buildings. The results showed that neither of the proposed methods could be finally recommended as a replacement for the pressure neutralization method in traditional residential buildings. The first method was unacceptable in the accuracy estimation for exterior boundary leakage (estimation error exceeded 108%). The second method showed a small error of 0.2% for the exterior boundary leakage estimation, though the pressure neutralization method was less sensitive to measurement noise compared to the alternative Lstiburek method. There is still a need for new methods that can accurately represent the external boundary airflow while still being less labour-demanding than the pressure neutralization method.

The paper [42] describes the validation of the new model for prediction of the airtightness of buildings utilising a neural network and using four corrective factors related to the building envelope. The model was obtained based on measurements in the field at 58 units in Croatia. The model, which requires a reduced amount of data and therefore is more economical and faster than the field measurements, was validated both in the local field and outside the native country conditions. The proposed model is supposed to be appropriate for predicting airtightness values at the early design phase, as well as for the planning of regular energy refurbishment of dwellings.

Based on the literature analysis and the use of around 300 dwellings' empirical data the study [43] analysis the relationships between the airtightness of building and eight individual variables. Correlation analyses indicated the significant relationship of the construction method, roof type, year of construction, and construction typology with building airtightness. Regression analysis showed that only the year of construction and the total leakage affect the airtightness. ANOVA tests revealed that both variables have a notable influence on the airtightness, in terms of specific leakage rate. Both variables could hardly help to assess the specific air leakage in advance because the year of construction correlates with many other variables and the building leakages can only be assessed when the construction is over.

The paper [44] concerns measurements of airtightness of 16 single-family houses with natural ventilation built from 1880 to 2007 (the measurement values ranged from 1.1 to 5.8 $L/(s{\cdot}m^2)$ at 50 Pa). The results of the ventilation measurements (from 0.09 to 0.28 $L/(s{\cdot}m^2)$ per heated floor area) did not meet the requirement established in the Danish Building Regulations (0.3 $L/(s{\cdot}m^2)$). The typical places of leaks were identified: the penetrations of electrical installations, exhaust ducts, chimneys, contours of older doors and windows, attic hatches, and connections with wooden ceilings. The findings are relevant for the renovation projects of the older small building stock, especially where mechanical ventilation systems are planned to be installed.

In the article [45], the research of the airtightness level of single-family energy-efficient houses was measured and compared with the requirements of Polish norms and European standards. The different wall structures of the buildings did not significantly affect the level of airtightness (ranged within n_{50} = 0.17 to 5.33 h^{-1}): the buildings with the worst and the best tightness had the same brickwork wall construction. As the reason for the insufficient tightness, the human factor was referred: a lack of experience and inaccurate performance of coatings, not airtight insulating layer, the mistakes made in porous insulation of transition systems, and the leaks of vapour barrier at connections.

The study [46] focused on the infiltration rate prediction of public buildings in China by implementing the in-situ tests and simulating the infiltration rates for 1800 cases. The main factors influencing the air infiltration were described as meteorological parameters, architectural structure, infiltration path characteristics. The construction period was not useable individually as a separate factor: zones that were built later (2007) had even worse airtightness than zones built earlier (1990). The airtightness of public buildings was found to be much worse than that of traditional dwellings. The centralized HVAC system had more elements in the building envelope than the split HVAC system, and the outer windows' airtightness was worse than the wall. For buildings with a mechanical fresh air system, the airtightness needs to be strengthened in order to reduce the impact of air infiltration. The conclusion was that the influence of air infiltration on public buildings should be acknowledged by policymakers in defining more energy-reasoned design standards.

The authors of the research [47] aimed to reveal the impact of local conditions by evaluating relations of infiltration rate and individual location and heat demand of residential buildings. Depending on the airtightness of buildings the differences in energy consumption between two different locations from the same climatic zone were evaluated in a rather wide range (from 70% to 90%) and could reach even 200% considering sheltered environmental conditions. The general conclusion of the research was that the building location and its level of exposure were recommended to be considered in forthcoming airtightness regulations.

While investigating the airtightness through the light concrete chimney elements, T.O. Relander [48] found out that better airtightness results can be achieved if the chimney is installed near the wall or in the wall corner because the external surface of the chimney through which air can penetrate will be reduced. External surface finishing workmanship and the materials used also influence the airtightness.

In the study [49], the energy performance of a school building before major renovation planning was modelled using the energy simulation software IDA ICE. The annual simulation indicated the following renovation measures with the best potential: improved envelope airtightness, changing to energy-efficient windows, new controls of the HVAC system, and improved outer wall thermal insulation.

Some articles have weaker relation to our research because the airtightness problem appears there as one among the other research aspects. The researchers investigate the association of the building envelope tightness, its improvements, and ventilation with relative humidity and air distribution in buildings [50,51], discuss the reasonable building airtightness level to seek for [52], the airtightness and thermal defect detection using thermographic research and image processing [53], the impact of airtightness of window and door openings, more stringent requirements for the products [54,55], point out very contrasting air leakage rates of some structural joints [56], the effect of airtightness when investigating the relation of the energy performance, and the indoor air quality performance [57].

The review of the recent studies helped to shed some light on the research hypothesis and formulate an adequate approach to the problem of airtightness influence on the energy performance of the particularly widely spread type of buildings. What did we expect, what did we find in the publications on the one hand, and what was subsequently visually observed, instrumentally measured, recorded, and computed from the field on the other hand speaking more generally? After the extensive review of research results, one can safely assert that the characteristics of the building airtightness or air permeability have a significant influence on the building's energy behaviour. At the same time, it was evident both from the theoretical review and from the field measurements that the nature of these properties is characterized by a rather wide distribution of the values, despite the same construction and material of the building. One of the main reasons revealed in most of the papers and confirmed in the field is the quality of the workmanship. This generalization led to the idea of limiting the diversity of the workforce on the construction site by choosing for the investigation the buildings constructed only by the same company. Furthermore, previous studies have covered a wide range of technical factors with the discussion about their influence on airtightness (as power supply installation). The analysis of recent studies in this regard helped to focus on the aspects discussed in the next chapters.

The literature review encouraged the formation of the research methodology, as well as the logic of its process. It was apparent that the starting point should be the experimental airtightness measurements of separate flats, as the logical architectural building parts with the aim to check the hypothesis that the flats in different locations of the building could have different airtightness values. The literature provided no definite answer to this question. Airtightness-related heat loss values (expressed in percentage) provided in the papers were presented in a rather wide range (not exact), or the data came from buildings of different structures, materials, and typology. Afterwards, it would be possible to theoretically calculate the heat loss of the flats with their subsequent evaluation of compliance with the design energy performance class. More details about the research process are provided in Section 3.2.

The standard methodology of energy performance calculation was also modified based on the analysis of literature sources in the part of the heat loss differences evaluation between the equal floor area flats situated in different parts of the building. It was appropriate to undervalue the formula member for solar radiation, considering the environmental factors described in Section 3.3 in more detail.

3. Methods

3.1. Buildings under Investigation

Relatively new buildings constructed in the period between 2016 and 2019 were chosen for the research. At this time, the new requirements demanding not lower than class A energy performance for newly designed and built buildings were introduced, and airtightness measurements became mandatory in Lithuania. More than 200 measurements were implemented in this research in sum (Figure 1).

All the buildings and flats were divided into groups using several factors:

- According to the situation of the flat in the building plan: the flats with the end location in the building and the flats with the inside location when they are surrounded by the two adjacent flats.
- According to the floor area of flats: the largest group included the flats with a floor area of 90–120 m^2, the second group of 150 m^2 area, and the largest flats exceeded the floor area of 200 m^2.
- According to the structural material of the walls: the buildings of the first group were constructed of sand–lime blocks, the buildings of the second group had the walls erected of hollow clay masonry units.
- According to the insulation level of structures: one group of the buildings that were designed as class A energy performance housing had the 200–220 mm polystyrene (EPS) insulation layer, the other group of buildings that were declared as the class A+ energy performance dwelling had the 240–260 mm polystyrene (EPS) insulation, and the most energy-efficient buildings of the class A++ were insulated with the 280–310 mm polystyrene (EPS) layer.

The main characteristics of the buildings are provided in Table 1.

Table 1. Properties of buildings.

Construction Type	Location	Average Floor Areas, m^2	Energy Class	Glazed Areas, m^2	Ventilation Type
Hollow clay masonry units	Inside 2 facades	90	A, A+, A++	12.85	Natural
		120	A, A+, A++	17.14	Natural
		150	A, A+, A++	19.64	Natural
		200	A, A+, A++	24.43	Natural
	End 3 facades	90	A, A+, A++	14.35	Natural
		120	A, A+, A++	19.14	Natural
		150	A, A+, A++	21.43	Natural
		200	A, A+, A++	28.57	Natural
Sand–lime blocks	Inside 2 facades	90	A, A+, A++	12.85	Natural
		120	A, A+, A++	17.14	Natural
		150	A, A+, A++	19.64	Natural
		200	A, A+, A++	24.43	Natural
	End 3 facades	90	A, A+, A++	14.35	Natural
		120	A, A+, A++	19.14	Natural
		150	A, A+, A++	21.43	Natural
		200	A, A+, A++	28.57	Natural

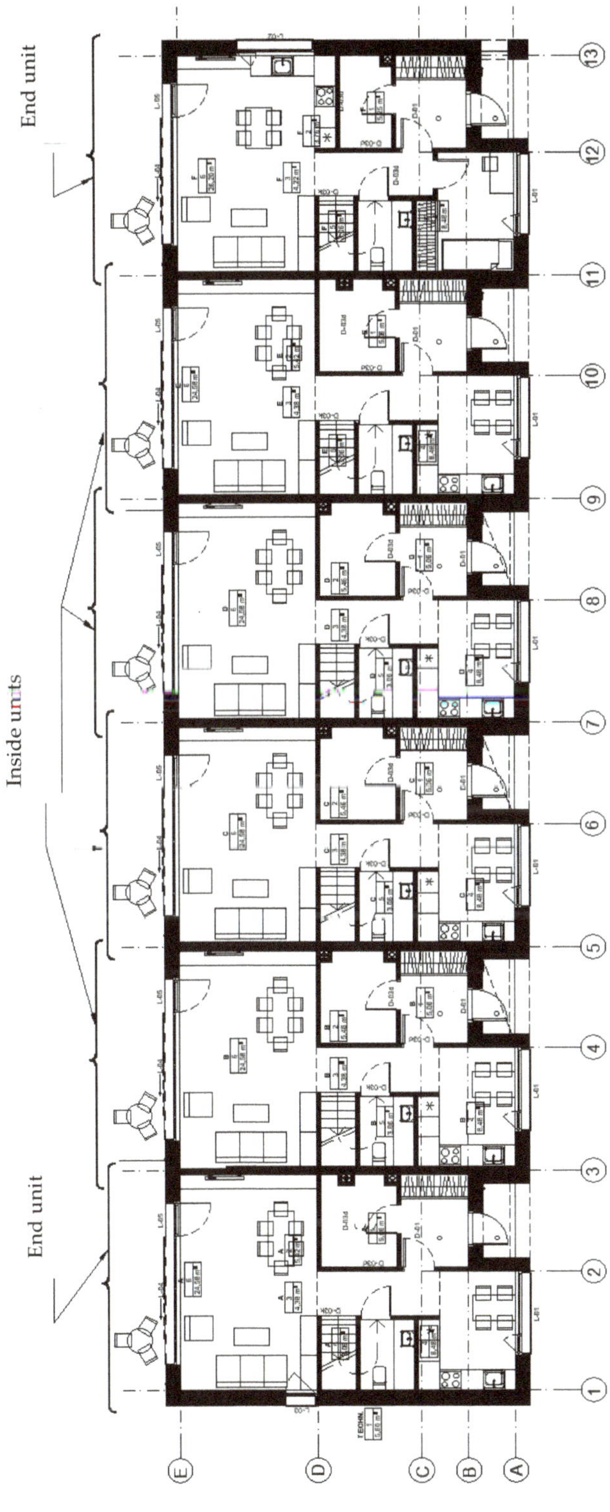

Figure 1. Architectural plan of building with specified types of the flats.

All the buildings were equipped with energy-efficient plastic windows having two insulated glass units (IGU) with selective glass coating. All the windows had appropriate construction inserts positioning window frames in the range of the wall insulation layer and in that way minimizing the linear thermal bridges of the window jambs. The roof load-bearing structures were made of hollow prefabricated reinforced concrete slabs insulated with polystyrene (EPS), the thickness of which was determined by building design energy class. The floor structures consisted of the most commonly applied layers: reinforced concrete, insulation, and damp proofing. All the buildings were two-level houses. Their heights ranged from 6.25 m to 6.35 m, although the internal ceiling height of the premises remained constant at 2.7 m. Therefore, this geometric peculiarity had no significant impact in our opinion neither on heat energy loss nor on the airtightness of the buildings. The buildings chosen for the research had the same engineering system equipment: the heat source was the heat pump with the floor heating system, all the flats had the same natural ventilation system. These choices allowed to eliminate the occurrence of possible airtightness defects in different equipment mounting places or installations, such as intersections of ventilating equipment piping with the walls or different heat sources. To reduce the influence of construction works quality to airtightness measurements as much as possible [21–25,31,33], only the buildings constructed by the same construction enterprise were chosen.

3.2. Measurement Methods

The principal scheme of the whole research process is provided below (Figure 2), followed by a detailed explanation of the steps.

The airtightness measurements were performed in all flats of the terraced houses analysed. The airtightness values of the premises were determined according to the standard measurement method (LST EN 13829). As stated by this method, all windows of the building were fully closed, the natural ventilation channels were properly glued, and all internal doors were opened to let the air inside and distribute easily in the flat. The measurements were implemented using Blower Door Model 4 equipment with the following technical specifications: measurement precision ±3%, measurement uncertainty 8.3%. The obtained results were statistically processed to get the average values for separate building groups and define possible dependencies on the flat location in the building.

There are mandatory requirements for the airtightness value of buildings, and the energy performance class of every newly designed building cannot exceed the predefined value. In case the building does not meet the airtightness requirements, it should be classified as belonging to the lower energy performance class. As the required airtightness cannot be achieved in a smaller part of buildings, the related defects must be recorded and rectified. For this purpose, the infrared (IR) research was performed using the FLIR ThermaCAM B640 infrared camera with measurement precision of 2% or 2 °C. All research was performed in the winter period when the temperature difference between the internal and external air was about 15–20 °C.

To examine the leaks of the building envelopes the infrared camera research was done twice. At the initial stage, there the temperature measurements were obtained on the surface in the natural conditions without creating an additional pressure difference. Afterward, in order to identify the main leakage locations a 50 Pa pressure difference between the outside and inside air in the rooms was created by means of airtightness equipment and the internal wall surface temperature was measured. There was an alteration of the internal surface temperatures compared to assess the tightness of the structures and to find out if the temperature differences are normal. There were two goals to perform the infrared research: first, to identify the problematic places that do not meet the tightness requirements in the buildings, and subsequently to implement corrective actions by repairing the defects and achieving the desired airtightness level, and second, to statistically evaluate the obtained results in order to determine in what type of buildings the most frequent problems were met.

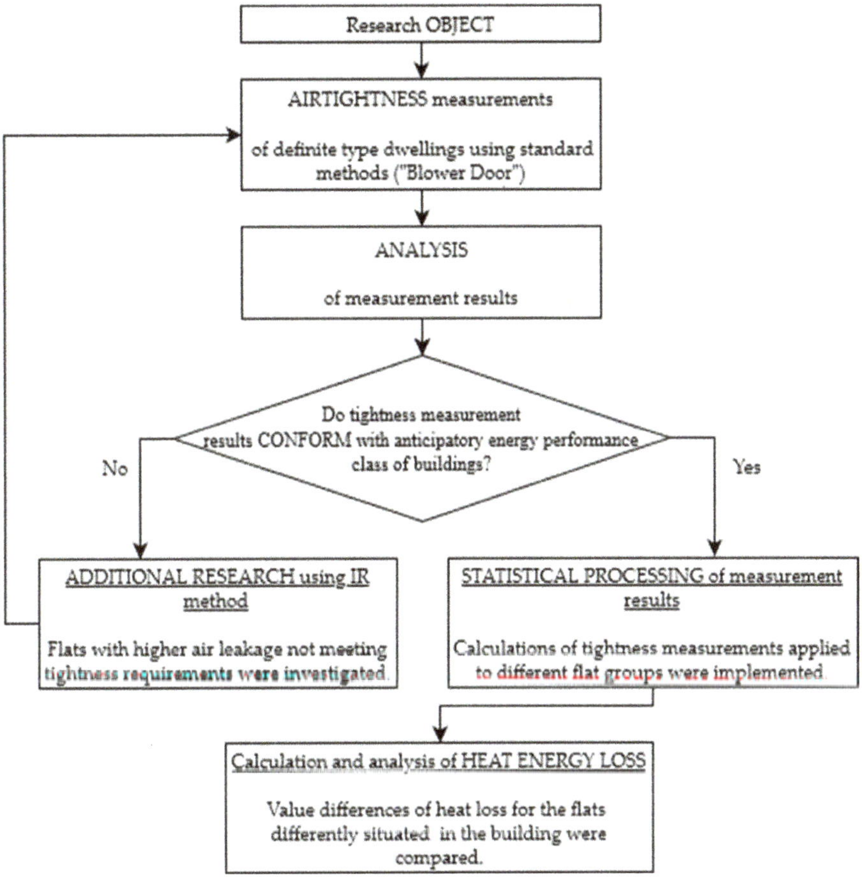

Figure 2. Principal scheme of the research process.

3.3. Building Energy Performance Assessment Methods

The main requirements of building energy performance related to EPBD (European Energy Performance of Buildings Directive) [1,2] are described in Building Technical Regulation STR 2.01.02: 2016 [58]. Using the building energy consumption evaluation methodology with the application of outside temperatures derived from many years of observations, it is accepted that the duration of the heating season exceeds 220 days, the average outside temperature of the heating season is 0.6 °C, and the inside temperature of the premises is 20 °C. The index of total heat energy loss calculated per 1 m^2 heated area of building throughout the year is one of the assessment criteria used in the said methodology. In general, it can be expressed by the following equation:

$$Q_{sum} = \frac{Q_{env} + Q_{vent} + Q_{do} + Q_{inf} - Q_e - Q_i}{\eta_{h.s.}} + Q_E + Q_{h.w.} \quad (1)$$

where: Q_{env} is the calculated heat loss through building envelope for 1 m^2 of heated floor area throughout the year, kWh/m^2·year;

Q_{vent} is the calculated energy consumption for ventilation, kWh/m^2·year;

Q_{do} is the calculated heat loss due to entrance door opening, kWh/m^2·year;

Q_{inf} is the calculated heat loss due to excessive air infiltration through windows and external doors, kWh/m^2·year;

Q_e is the heat gain in the building due to solar radiation, $kWh/m^2{\cdot}year$;
Q_i is the heat gain from internal heat sources, $kWh/m^2{\cdot}year$;
Q_E is the annual electricity consumption, $kWh/m^2{\cdot}year$;
$Q_{h.w.}$ is the annual energy consumption from domestic hot water, kWh/m^2 year;
$\eta_{h.s.}$ is the efficiency coefficient of building heating system, in part of a unit.

The aim was to evaluate the differences between the heat energy loss of the flats located in different parts of the same type buildings. Some of the formula components may be underestimated considering all the flats are operated in equal conditions. These components include heat loss because of external door opening, natural ventilation, electric power, and domestic hot water consumption. Since all the flats are designed with almost identical transparent enclosures, the heat increase resulting from direct solar radiation through the windows can be assessed as being the same.

Minor exceptions can be found in some rear facades of the end units. Because of different architectural solutions, some of these facades have one additional window with an area of around 2 m^2. Therefore, during the thorough investigation of the buildings, some circumstances were found in this particular context of the built environment: most of the facades in question were not fully exposed to solar radiation for a longer time because of their shadowing by existing trees and buildings, most of the walls had East and West orientation, a large part of these windows were equipped with roller shutters, and a number of the flats did not have the additional window at all. Because of these factors substantially diminishing the solar heat energy gains, all end units were considered as solar radiation invariant in this research.

Excluding all these components mentioned above, the difference of the heat energy loss between the flats of different locations may be represented as:

$$Q_{sum(difference)} = Q_{env\ (difference)} + Q_{\inf\ (difference)} \tag{2}$$

where:

$$Q_{env} = \frac{0.001 \cdot t_m \cdot 24}{A_p} \cdot (\theta_{iH} - \theta_{e,m}) \cdot \sum_{x=1}^{n} (A_{env} \cdot U_{env}) \tag{3}$$

and

$$Q_{\inf} = 0.001 \cdot t_m \cdot 24 \cdot \rho_{air} \cdot c_{air} \cdot v_{\inf,m} \cdot (\theta_{iH} - \theta_{e,m}) \tag{4}$$

where:

t_m is the number of days for the appropriate month of the year;
A_p is the heated area of the building, m^2;
θ_{iH} is the internal temperature of the building during the heating season °C;
$\theta_{e,m}$ is the average air temperature of the appropriate month, °C;
A_{env} is the area of the building envelope, m^2;
U_{env} is the U-value of the building envelope, $W/m^2{\cdot}K$;
ρ_{air} is the air density, kg/m^3

$$v_{\inf,m} = 0.25 \cdot n_{50} \cdot \left(0.75 \cdot \frac{\rho_{air}}{2 \cdot 50} \cdot (0.9 \cdot v_{wind,m})^2\right)^n \cdot \frac{V_{p.n_{50}}}{A_p} \tag{5}$$

where:

n_{50} is the air exchange value of the building, h^{-1};
$v_{wind,m}$ is the average wind speed of the month, m/s;
$V_{p.n_{50}}$ is the volume of heated premises of the building, m^3.

4. Results

4.1. Analysis of Building Airtightness

The airtightness of buildings is very much dependent on the quality of construction works and even the small mistakes can lead to significant differences in airtightness;

therefore, the evaluation of airtightness results was based on the comparison of statistical averages of the flats of the same type (Figure 3).

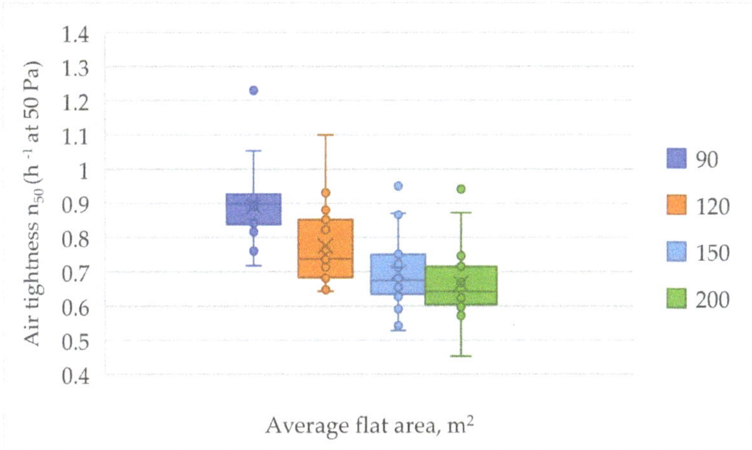

Figure 3. Airtightness measurement distribution for the flats of different floor areas.

The recorded results show that the values of airtightness of the flats with the same floor area can vary in a large range reaching the difference up to two times. The analysis of airtightness values of the flats of different floor areas revealed that the statistic average of results gradually decreases with the increase of the floor area of the flat, but the overall measurement scatter remains almost constant. The comparison of the groups of flats of 90 m^2 and 200 m^2 floor area showed that the average value of airtightness for the flats with larger floor area is 25% smaller. The obtained results can be interpreted as the achievement of better average airtightness measurement result for the flats with a larger floor area and the same time a larger volume. This fact of the better results for larger flats could be explained as a minor defect that has a smaller effect on the general result of the airtightness of the building.

After the study of two material alternatives, such as hollow clay masonry units (also known as ceramic small blocks) (1) and sand–lime blocks (2) used for the construction of external walls, it can be stated that regardless of the floor area, airtightness values for hollow clay masonry walls were higher than the respective values for the more favourable sand–lime block walls. The processed data of the airtightness measurements of the equal-area flats located in different places of the buildings are presented in Table 2. The differences in statistical averages of the measurements reach 7–11%. When interpreting the results, the following reasons can be pointed out regarding this aspect. First, in the case of the structure of hollow clay masonry units, where the bricklaying technology requires only to fill the horizontal seams of the brickwork with the mortar, the air can circulate easier through many empty vertical seams in the wall. Second, in the case of hollow clay units, the air can circulate more freely in the structure because of the internal hollows of the elements. In addition, uncontrollable air can enter the room through the openings made for the installation of electric outlets through the other hollows that were not carefully tightened, and thus increase the air leakage in the building.

Additional information about this issue will also be given in the next chapter which concerns thermographic photo research.

A graphical illustration of the contrast of airtightness distribution data for end and inside units in the buildings with the walls of sand–lime blocks is shown below (Figure 4).

The general analysis and comparison of the data shows that the average values of airtightness in end units are 20% higher than the values in inside units of the same type.

Based on the research results, mathematical dependencies were derived to be used for the forecasting of airtightness values for the flats with various floor areas (Figure 5).

R-squared (R^2) value in both flat location cases is close to 1, which indicates a high predictive quality of these models.

Table 2. Measurement values of the airtightness of the flats.

Construction Type	Flat Location	Average Flat Area, m^2	Max of Airtightness n_{50} (h^{-1} at 50 Pa)	Min of Airtightness n_{50} (h^{-1} at 50 Pa)	Average Value of Airtightness n_{50} (h^{-1} at 50 Pa)
Hollow clay masonry units	Inside	90	1.25	0.71	0.97
		120	1.15	0.62	0.85
		150	1.13	0.49	0.79
		200	1.05	0.49	0.74
	End	90	1.49	0.89	1.10
		120	1.35	0.76	1.03
		150	1.29	0.70	0.97
		200	1.23	0.63	0.93
Sand–lime blocks	Inside	90	1.23	0.72	0.89
		120	1.10	0.64	0.78
		150	0.95	0.53	0.70
		200	0.94	0.45	0.67
	End	90	1.31	0.91	1.04
		120	1.34	0.78	0.97
		150	1.28	0.68	0.91
		200	1.18	0.61	0.85

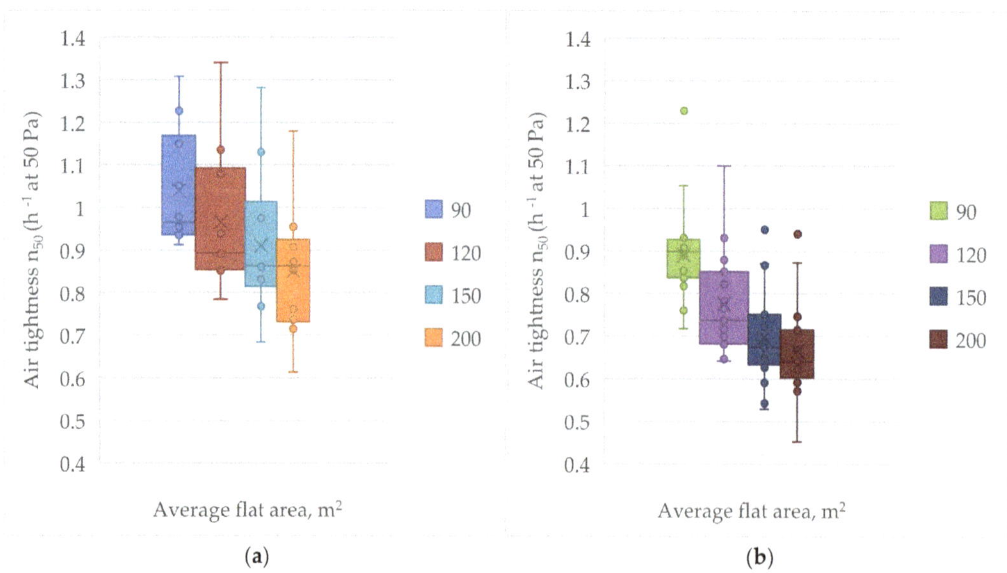

Figure 4. Airtightness of buildings with walls of sand–lime blocks, end units (**a**), and inside units (**b**).

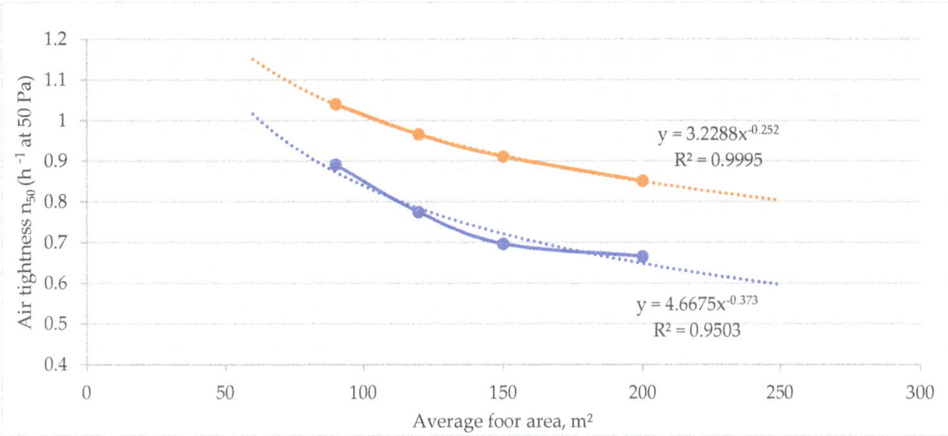

Figure 5. Dependency diagrams of airtightness and floor area for the end (orange) and inside (blue) units in the sand–lime buildings of energy efficiency class A.

The comparison of statistical airtightness measurement data with the main metrics n_{50} (h^{-1}), mainly of small and medium-size low-rise residential buildings along with the national regulation values from various countries, is provided below (Table 3). The juxtaposition of earlier and the newest data show an improvement in airtightness quality in recent years in Lithuania. Another noticeable trend is better airtightness values of Northern European countries and Canada, despite various construction periods of buildings. Airtightness in countries such as the UK and Ireland seems to be worse because of a very broad period of the building samples. Interesting outstanding results were obtained from a study of relatively new Passive House buildings in Germany.

Table 3. Comparison of statistical airtightness measurement data between previous studies and the current research.

Authors/Reference	Country	Construction Period	Airtightness n_{50} (h^{-1}) Mean Values, Standard Devia-tion or Estimated from Snedecor's Rule, Min/Max Values	Limit Airtightness Metrics and Value According to National Regulation	Notes
Kalamees [59]	Estonia	2003–2005	$\bar{x}, \sigma$ 4.9 ± 3.5	q_{50}, <6 (single-family)	Values are based on results provided in the reference
Hamlin and Gusdorf [60]	Canada	1921–1997	$\bar{x}, \sigma_{Sn}$ 3.1 ± 1	No mandatory regulation requirement	Values are based on results provided in the reference
Jokisalo et al. [26]	Finland	Pre-2007	$\bar{x}, \sigma$ 3.7 ± 2.2	q_{50}, <4	Values are based on results provided in the reference
Kalamees [59]	Norway	1984	$\bar{x}, \sigma$ 4.0 Min 3.3 Max 5.4	n_{50}, <1.5	Values are based on results providedin the reference
Alfano et al. [29]	Italy	1810–2010	$\bar{x}, \sigma$ 7.26 ± 4.02 Min 3.2 Max 23.3	No mandatory regulation requirement	Values are based on the measurement data

Table 3. *Cont.*

Authors/Reference	Country	Construction Period	Airtightness n_{50} (h^{-1}) Mean Values, Standard Devia-tion or Estimated from Snedecor's Rule, Min/Max Values	Limit Airtightness Metrics and Value According to National Regulation	Notes
Sfakianaki et al. [16]	Greece	Pre-2007	$\overline{x}, \sigma$ 6.79 ± 3.15 Min 1.87 Max 11.3	No mandatory regulation requirement	Values are based on the measurement data
Sinnot and Dyer [23]	Ireland	1944–2008	$\overline{x}, \sigma$ 9.64 ± 2.9 Min 5.39 Max 14.9	q_{50}, <5	Values are based on the measurement data
Chen et al. [61]	China	1980–1990	$\overline{x}, \sigma$ 9.8 ± 8.11 Min 1.59 Max 27.16		Values are based on the measurement data
Pasos [39]	UK	1900–2012	$\overline{x}, \sigma$ 8.39 ± 3.22 Min 3.51 Max 14.97	q_{50}, <10 Notional recommended value: 5 $m^3/(h{\cdot}m^2)$	Values are based on the measurement data
Kalamees [59]	Sweden	Pre-1978	$\overline{x}, \sigma$ 3.7 ± 0.24	q_{50}, <0.6	Values are based on results providedin the reference
Hasper [62]	Germany	2006–2014	$\overline{x}, \sigma$ 0.50 ± 0.27 Max 1.1 Min 0.18	n_{50} < 0.6 for passive houses and <1.5 as a general value	Values are based on passive buildings measurement data
Sadauskiene et al. [63]	Lithuania Class B	2005–2011	$\overline{x}, \sigma$ 6.24 ± 2.63 Max—11.3 Min—2.19	n_{50} Class B < 1.5; Class A < 1; Class A+ and A++ < 0.6	Values are based on the measurement data
Current research	Lithuania Class A	2016–2019	$\overline{x}, \sigma$ 0.88 ± 0.18 Min 0.618 Max 1.35		Values are based on the measurements of current research
Current research	Lithuania Class A+ and A++	2016–2019	$\overline{x}, \sigma$ 0.62 ± 0.08 Min 0.818 Max 0.479		

Notes: "n_{50}" air change rate at 50 Pa pressure difference, "$\overline{x}$" mean, "σ" standard deviation or "σ_{Sn}" deviation estimated from Snedecor's rule. If any value is not indicated it was not available.

Relatively large standard deviation values of airtightness measurements can be noticed in some lines of the summary above. One of the implicit main reasons for this could be the broad construction period of buildings examined in the studies. The other significant factor is the relatively high airtightness limit value indicated in the regulation or the absence of any definite requirements in some countries. These factors lead to different levels of construction work by different companies and greater inequality of airtightness values.

4.2. Thermographic Photo Research

To determine the reasons for the rather low airtightness of the buildings, thermographic photo research was performed. It revealed the defects related to improper construction works and wrong structural solutions. The most frequently met defects are presented in the diagrams (Figure 6).

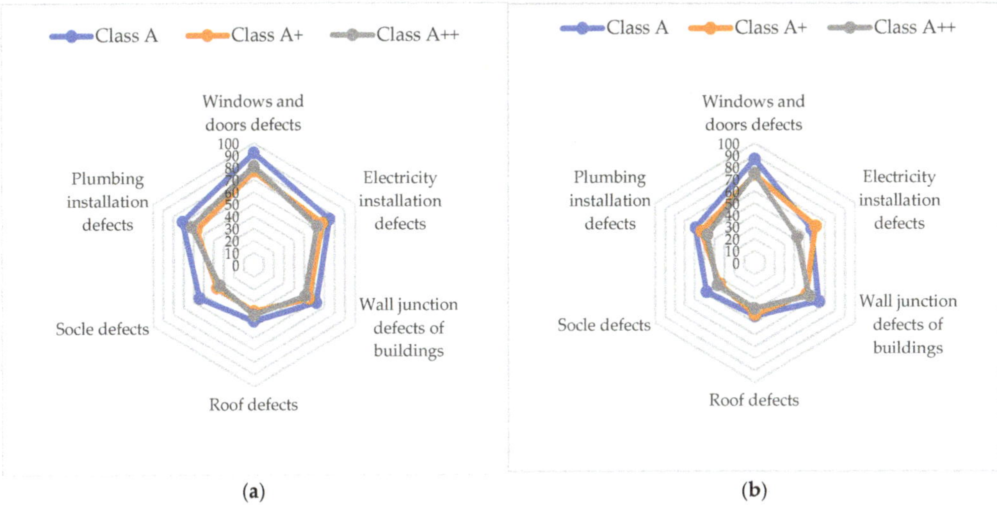

Figure 6. Frequency of defects for hollow clay masonry buildings (**a**) and sand–lime block masonry buildings (**b**).

The analysis of research results showed that the most popular defect type in the buildings can be associated with improper installation of windows and their technical adjustment. During the assessment process of the buildings of the energy class A, the defects of that kind were recorded in 90% of the cases and in 75–80% of A+ and A++ energy class buildings. The most likely reason and explanation of this finding could be the thicker insulation layer of the envelopes and the opening jambs of higher energy class buildings. A thick insulation layer creates a lengthy way between the internal and external surfaces of construction, and thus stronger resistance to the moving airflow.

The joints of external walls with other parts of the building, such as floor or roof structures, can also be described as important and defect-sensitive and adding to the airtightness of entire structure. This factor can be related to the flats at different locations in the building and having different lengths of joints of these types. It also influences the differences in the airtightness measurement values of differently situated flats.

Evaluation of the junctions and details of electric installation and water pipes showed significant differences in recorded results. In structures made of hollow clay masonry units, the risk of defects in the above-mentioned junctions grows up to 30%. In the envelope structure constructed of hollow clay elements, the external layer of the building products is destroyed when electric outlets are installed and cables are routed. In this way, the interlinked hollows of the building envelope through which air can flow easily are reached. Installation and repair of these elements and their junctions must involve careful insulation, otherwise defects cannot be avoided (Figure 7).

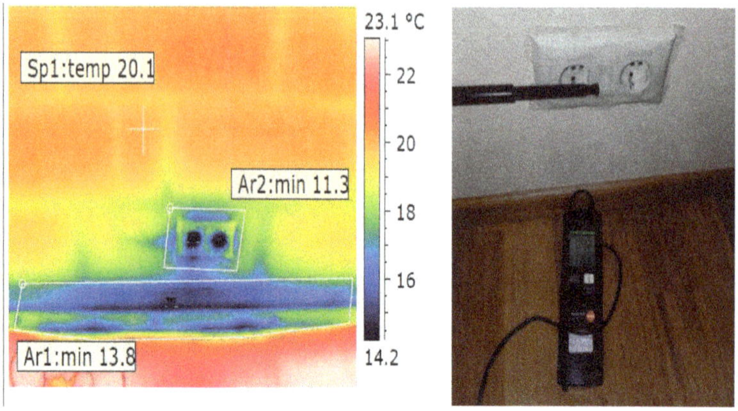

Figure 7. Defects of electric installation influencing the airtightness of construction.

4.3. Analysis of the Heat Loss

Total heat loss through the building envelopes of the flats with different floor areas and various building energy classes calculated per 1 m^2 of the heated floor area expressed in kWh/m^2 per year depending on the location of the flat in the building plan are presented in Table 4.

Table 4. Total heat energy loss kWh per 1 m^2 of the floor area per year of the flats of various size and energy classes, considering where the flat is situated in the building plan.

Average Floor Areas of the Flats, m^2	Energy Class	Average Values of the End Units, Q_{sum} (kWh/m^2·year)	Average Values of the Inside Units, Q_{sum} (kWh/m^2·year)	Difference, $Q_{sum\ diferent}$ (kWh/m^2·year)	Difference, %
90	A	93.21	82.32	10.89	11.7
	A+	83.67	73.99	9.68	11.6
	A++	74.04	65.55	8.49	11.5
120	A	84.27	75.25	9.02	10.7
	A+	75.68	67.59	8.09	10.7
	A++	66.98	59.92	7.06	10.5
150	A	79.94	71.46	8.48	10.6
	A+	71.82	64.18	7.64	10.6
	A++	63.52	56.81	6.71	10.6
200	A	77.77	70.47	7.3	9.4
	A+	69.83	63.29	6.54	9.4
	A++	61.76	55.99	5.77	9.3

The analysis of obtained results revealed that a bigger heated floor area leads to higher values of the total heat loss, regardless of the building energy performance class. The explanation could be that the envelope areas increase together with the floor area of the flats and the heat loss is directly related to the size of the envelope area.

The assessment of the influence of different locations in the building plan of flats with the same floor area showed that the total heat loss through the building envelopes calculated per 1 m^2 of heated floor area and expressed in kWh/(m^2·year) is around 9–12% higher for the end units compared to the middle units (Figure 8). The distance between the chart lines for lower energy performance building of class A (blue colour) is bigger than respective distances for the buildings of higher classes A+ and A++ (red and green colours). Accordingly, the heat loss increases calculated as differences between the values considering air infiltration and despite air infiltration are different: for the class A it makes approximately 12% and for the classes A+ and A++ it makes about 4%. This fact is logical evidence that better thermal insulation of the building contributes to higher airtightness values.

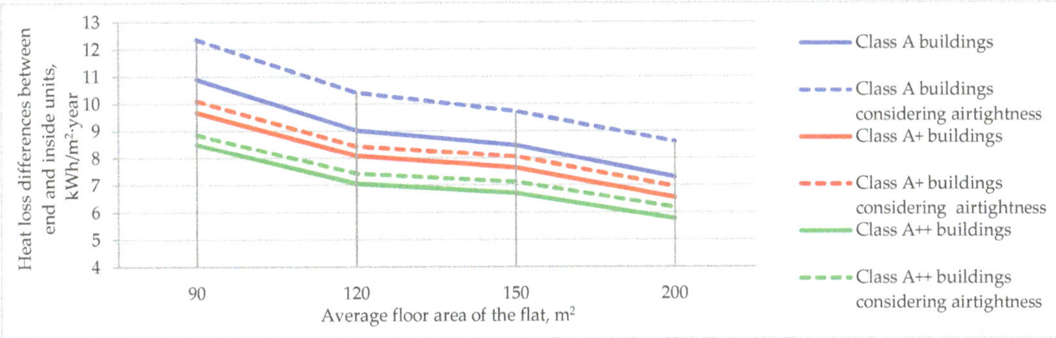

Figure 8. Heat loss differences reflecting the increase of values for end units in comparison with inside units.

The two above-mentioned tendencies remain, regardless of the material of the flat wall structure.

Generally, the total heat loss difference considering air infiltration per 1 m^2 of heated floor area (kWh/(m^2 per year)) between the end units and inside units can exceed 15% because of the different airtightness of these flats.

Currently, the compliance with the allowable value of heat loss is assessed by examining the volume of the entire building in its design stage. The heat loss criterion is difficult to meet in the process of energy certification when there is a need or opportunity to assess individual flats or other logical architectural parts.

Figure 9 shows the average design values of heat energy loss for different flats and their comparison with the corresponding limit values prescribed by the regulation. The dwellings that exceed these limit values should be assigned to a lower energy performance class, i.e., moved one class down in the classification.

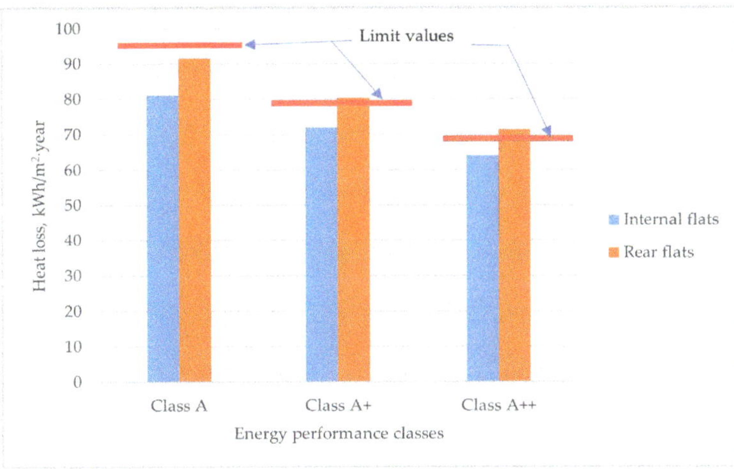

Figure 9. Comparison of heat energy loss values with limit values of different flat types.

The results also show that all inside units of the investigated buildings meet the heat loss requirement, regardless of their design class. Therefore, the assessment of the end units shows that some of them would exceed the allowable limit, which would lead to downshifting their energy class. To avoid these problems, it would be reasonable to plan improvement measures for end units, which include both additional airtightening and thermal insulation, already on the design stage.

5. Conclusions

Airtightness as an important factor, together with other complex design solutions, can reduce heat energy expenses, increase thermal comfort, and ensure a healthy building environment and its longevity. Airtightness as a property is dependent on human factors, technical solutions, and materials, therefore it will differ in every single case.

Only the buildings constructed by the same construction company were investigated in the research. Nevertheless, the difference of airtightness values measured in the flats of the same category was twice as high. Most researchers underline the aspects related to the construction work quality. Therefore, the average values of the entire building group, but not separate measurements, should be used for the assessment of airtightness values of separate building groups.

The average airtightness value differences collating the smallest and the largest flats exceeded approximately 25%. This can be explained by the fact that local air leakages or minor construction defects of larger flats statistically had less influence on the general airtightness, understood as the air exchange speed in the premises.

Evaluating the buildings constructed of different types of brickwork, it is safe to state that the building's airtightness values depend on the material structure of the chosen brickwork as well as on bricklaying technology and proper installation of engineering systems. When the construction of hollow clay masonry units is chosen where the bricklaying technology involves the filling of horizontal brickwork seams with mortar, the air can circulate through many open voids in the wall. The comparison of the hollow clay unit masonry structure with the solid sand–lime block masonry, the seams of which are filled with mortar both vertically and horizontally, revealed the airtightness reduction of ceramic structure around 7–11% on average.

The comparison of the airtightness measurement results for the flats of equal floor area located at different places of the buildings showed up to 20% higher airtightness measurement values for end units than in inside units, which is a significant difference. The reasons for these value differences could be explained by a larger length of structural joints in the end units. The longer structural joints and additional windows in the walls of the end units cause the higher probability of the emergence of defects worsening the general result.

The obtained results show that all the dwellings surveyed did not exceed the allowable heat loss limits when the total heat loss of the inside units was assessed. As for the end units, we see that most of them, especially the ones in the buildings belonging to higher energy classes A+ and A++, exceed the heat loss limits prescribed for these energy classes. In the further process of real estate development and design of terraced houses, they should be assessed not as a single object, but as a whole consisting of separate units, where each unit should meet the heat loss requirements.

Continuing the research, the role of airtightness should be extended to overall building energy performance assessment by combining and incorporating comprehensive experimental test results, database data, and simulation that could lead to more precise and reliable results and give the opportunity to verify them.

Author Contributions: Conceptualization, V.P., G.C., J.M. and M.D.; methodology, V.P. and M.D.; software, V.P., G.C. and J.M.; validation, V.P., G.C. and J.M.; formal analysis, V.P. and G.C.; investigation, V.P.; resources, V.P. and M.D.; data curation, V.P.; writing—original draft preparation, V.P. and G.C.; writing—review and editing, V.P., G.C. and J.M.; visualization, V.P.; supervision, V.P., G.C.

and J.M.; project administration, V.P. All authors have read and agreed to the published version of the manuscript.

Funding: This research received no external funding.

Institutional Review Board Statement: Not applicable.

Informed Consent Statement: Not applicable.

Data Availability Statement: Data sharing not applicable.

Conflicts of Interest: The authors declare no conflict of interest.

References

1. *Directive 2002/91/EC of the European Parliament and of the Council of 16 December 2002 on the Energy Performance of Buildings*; European Parliament: Brussels, Belgium, 2002.
2. *Directive 2010/31/EU of the European Parliament and of the Council of 19 May 2010 on the Energy Performance of Buildings (Recast)*; European Parliament: Brussels, Belgium, 2010.
3. *Energy Efficiency of Buildings—Calculation of the Energy Needs, Delivered Energy and Primary Energy for Heating, Cooling, Ventilation, Domestic Hot Water and Lighting*; DIN V 18599; German Institute for Standardization: Berlin, Germany, 2007.
4. Gonzalez, A.B.R.; Diaz, J.J.V.; Caamano, A.J.; Wilby, M.R. Towards a universal energy efficiency index for buildings. *Energy Build.* **2011**, *43*, 980–987. [CrossRef]
5. Jaraminienė, E. Air Infiltration in Buildings with Uncertainty Analysis. Ph.D. Thesis, Vilnius Gediminas Technical University, Vilnius, Lithuania, 2008. (In Lithuanian).
6. Venckus, N.; Bliūdžius, R.; Endriukaitytė, A.; Parasonis, J. Research of low energy house design and construction opportunities in Lithuania. *Technol. Econ. Dev. Econ.* **2010**, *16*, 541–554. [CrossRef]
7. Relander, T.-O.; Holøs, S.B.; Thue, J.V. Airtightness estimation—A state of the art review and an en route upper limit evaluation principle to increase the chances that wood-frame houses with a vapour- and wind-barrier comply with the airtightness requirements. *Energy Build.* **2012**, *54*, 444–452. [CrossRef]
8. Younes, C.; Shdid, C.A. A methodology for 3-D multiphysics CFD simulation of air leakage in building envelopes. *Energy Build.* **2013**, *65*, 146–158. [CrossRef]
9. Wang, L.; Chen, Q. Validation of a coupled multizone-CFD program for building airflow and contaminant transport simulations. *HVAC R Res.* **2007**, *13*, 267–281. [CrossRef]
10. Chan, W.R.; Joh, J.; Sherman, M.H. Analysis of air leakage measurements of US houses. *Energy Build.* **2013**, *66*, 616–625. [CrossRef]
11. Montoya, M.I.; Pastor, E.; Carrié, F.R.; Guyot, G.; Planas, E. Air leakage in Catalan dwellings: Developing an airtightness model and leakage airflow predictions. *Build. Environ.* **2010**, *45*, 1458–1469. [CrossRef]
12. Hassan, O.A. An alternative method for evaluating the air tightness of building components. *Build. Environ.* **2013**, *67*, 82–86. [CrossRef]
13. International Organization for Standardization (ISO). *EN ISO 9972:2015—Thermal Performance of Buildings–Determination of Air Permeability of Buildings–Fan Pressurization Method*; International Organization for Standardization: Geneva, Switzerland, 2015.
14. Feijó-Muñoz, J.; Poza-Casado, I.; González-Lezcano, R.A.; Pardal, C.; Echarri, V.; De Larriva, R.A.; Fernández-Agüera, J.; Dios-Viéitez, M.J.; Del Campo-Díaz, V.J.; Calderín, M.M.; et al. Methodology for the study of the envelope airtightness of residential buildings in Spain: A case study. *Energies* **2018**, *11*, 704. [CrossRef]
15. Kalamees, T.; Kurnitski, J.; Jokisalo, J.; Eskola, L.; Jokiranta, K.; Vinba, J. Measured and simulated air pressure conditions in Finnish residential buildings. *Build. Serv. Eng. Res. Technol.* **2010**, *31*, 177–190. [CrossRef]
16. Sfakianaki, A.; Pavlou, K.; Santamouris, M.; Livada, I.; Assimakopoulos, M.-N.; Mantas, P.; Christakopoulos, A. Air tightness measurements of residential houses in Athens, Greece. *Build. Environ.* **2008**, *43*, 398–405. [CrossRef]
17. Becker, R. Air leakage of curtain walls—diagnostics and remediation. *J. Build. Phys.* **2010**, *34*, 57–75. [CrossRef]
18. Kovanen, K.A.; Laamanen, J.; Kauppinen, T.; Duanmu, L. Air tightness of new residential buildings in Finland. In Proceedings of the 6th International Symposium on Heating, Ventilating and Air Conditioning, Nanjing, China, 6–9 November 2009; pp. 207–213.
19. Lucchi, E. Non-invasive method for investigating energy and environmental performances in existing buildings. In Proceedings of the 27th Conference on Passive and Low Energy Architecture, Louvain-la-Neuve, Belgium, 13–15 July 2011; pp. 571–576.
20. Lucchi, E.; Pereira, L.D.; Andreotti, M.; Malaguti, R.; Cennamo, D.; Calzolari, M.; Frighi, V. Development of a compatible, low cost and high accurate conservation remote sensing technology for the hygrothermal assessment of historic walls. *Electronics* **2019**, *8*, 643. [CrossRef]
21. Kalamees, T.; Alev, Ü.; Pärnalaas, M. Air leakage levels in timber frame building envelope joints. *Build. Environ.* **2017**, *116*, 121–129. [CrossRef]
22. Pereira, P.F.; Almeida, R.M.S.F.; Ramos, N.M.M.; Sousa, R. Testing for building components contribution to airtightness assessment. In Proceedings of the 35th AIVC Conference Ventilation and airtightness in transforming the building stock to high performance, Poznań, Poland, 24–25 September 2014.

23. Sinnott, D.; Dyer, M. Air-tightness field data for dwellings in Ireland. *Build. Environ.* **2012**, *51*, 269–275. [CrossRef]
24. Vinha, J.; Manelius, E.; Korpi, M.; Salminen, K.; Kurnitski, J.; Kiviste, M.; Laukkarinen, A. Airtightness of residential buildings in Finland. *Build. Environ.* **2015**, *93*, 128–140. [CrossRef]
25. Fernández-Agüera, J.; Domínguez-Amarillo, S.; Sendra, J.J.; Suárez, R. An approach to modelling envelope airtightness in multi-family social housing in Mediterranean Europe based on the situation in Spain. *Energy Build.* **2016**, *128*, 236–253. [CrossRef]
26. Jokisalo, J.; Kurnitski, J.; Korpi, M.; Kalamees, T.; Vinha, J. Building leakage, infiltration, and energy performance analyses for Finnish detached houses. *Build. Environ.* **2009**, *44*, 377–387. [CrossRef]
27. Khemet, B.; Richman, R. A univariate and multiple linear regression analysis on a national fan (de) Pressurization testing database to predict airtightness in houses. *Build. Environ.* **2018**, *146*, 88–97. [CrossRef]
28. Pinto, M.; Viegas, J.; de Freitas, V.P. Air permeability measurements of dwellings and building components in Portugal. *Build. Environ.* **2011**, *46*, 2480–2489. [CrossRef]
29. Alfano, F.D.A.; Dell'Isola, M.; Ficco, G.; Tassini, F. Experimental analysis of air tightness in Mediterranean buildings using the fan pressurization method. *Build. Environ.* **2012**, *53*, 16–25. [CrossRef]
30. Lee, D.-S.; Jeong, J.-W.; Jo, J.-H. Experimental study on airtightness test methods in large buildings; proposal of averaging pressure difference method. *Build. Environ.* **2017**, *122*, 61–71. [CrossRef]
31. Prignon, M.; Van Moeseke, G. Factors influencing airtightness and airtightness predictive models: A literature review. *Energy Build.* **2017**, *146*, 87–97. [CrossRef]
32. Pan, W. Relationships between airtightness and its influencing factors of post-2006 new-build dwellings in the UK. *Build. Environ.* **2010**, *45*, 2387–2399. [CrossRef]
33. Gillott, M.C.; Loveday, D.L.; White, J.; Wood, C.J.; Chmutina, K.; Vadodaria, K. Improving the airtightness in an existing UK dwelling: The challenges, the measures and their effectiveness. *Build. Environ.* **2016**, *95*, 227–239. [CrossRef]
34. Kraus, M.; Charvatova, P. Location as a determinative factor of building airtightness. *Procedia Eng.* **2016**, *161*, 1532–1537. [CrossRef]
35. Bhandari, M.; Hun, D.; Shrestha, S.; Pallin, P.; Lapsa, M. A simplified methodology to estimate energy savings in commercial buildings from improvements in airtightness. *Energies* **2018**, *11*, 3322. [CrossRef]
36. Ji, K.-H.; Shin, H.-K.; Han, S.; Jo, J.-H. A statistical approach for predicting airtightness in residential units of reinforced concrete apartment buildings in Korea. *Energies* **2020**, *13*, 3598. [CrossRef]
37. Wójcik, R.; Kosinski, P. Seeming air tightness of construction partitions. *Energy Procedia* **2015**, *78*, 1519–1524. [CrossRef]
38. Tanyer, A.M.; Tavukcuoglu, A.; Bekboliev, M. Assessing the airtightness performance of container houses in relation to its effect on energy efficiency. *Build. Environ.* **2018**, *134*, 59–73. [CrossRef]
39. Pasos, A.V.; Zheng, X.; Smith, L.; Wood, C. Estimation of the infiltration rate of UK homes with the divide-by-20 rule and its comparison with site measurements. *Build. Environ.* **2020**, *185*, 107275. [CrossRef]
40. Cuce, E. Role of airtightness in energy loss from windows: Experimental results from in-situ tests. *Energy Build.* **2017**, *139*, 449–455. [CrossRef]
41. Fine, J.P.; Gray, J.; Tian, X.; Touchie, M.F. An investigation of alternative methods for determining envelope airtightness from suite-based testing in multi-unit residential buildings. *Energy Build.* **2020**, *214*, 109845. [CrossRef]
42. Krstic, H.; Istoka Otkovic, I.; Todorovic, G. Validation of a model for predicting airtightness of residential units. *Energy Procedia* **2015**, *78*, 1525–1530. [CrossRef]
43. Bramiana, C.N.; Entrop, A.G.; Halman, J.I.M. Relationships between building characteristics and airtightness of Dutch dwellings. *Energy Procedia* **2016**, *96*, 580–591. [CrossRef]
44. Mortensen, L.H.; Bergsøe, N.C. Air tightness measurements in older Danish single-family houses. *Energy Procedia* **2017**, *132*, 825–830. [CrossRef]
45. Miszczuk, A. The level of airtightness in energy-efficient single-family houses in Poland. *Procedia Eng.* **2016**, *153*, 461–466. [CrossRef]
46. Jia, Y.; Duanmu, L.; Liu, Y.; Dong, H. Air infiltration rate of typical zones of public buildings under natural conditions. *Sustain. Cities Soc.* **2020**, *61*, 102290. [CrossRef]
47. Miszczuk, A.; Heim, D. Parametric study of air infiltration in residential buildings—The effect of local conditions on energy demand. *Energies* **2021**, *14*, 127. [CrossRef]
48. Relander, T.-O.; Heiskel, B.; Tyssedal, J.S. The influence of the joint between the basement wall and the wood-frame wall on the airtightness of wood-frame houses. *Energy Build.* **2011**, *43*, 1304–1314. [CrossRef]
49. Englund, J.S.; Cehlin, M.; Akander, J.; Moshfegh, B. Measured and simulated energy use in a secondary school building in Sweden—A case study of validation, airing, and occupancy behaviour. *Energies* **2020**, *13*, 2325. [CrossRef]
50. Prasauskas, T.; Martuzevicius, D.; Kalamees, T.; Kuusk, K.; Leivo, V.; Haverinen-Shaughnessy, U. Effects of energy retrofits on indoor air quality in three Northern European countries. *Energy Procedia* **2016**, *96*, 253–259. [CrossRef]
51. Carlsson, M.; Touchie, M.; Richman, R. Investigating the potential impact of a compartmentalization and ventilation system retrofit strategy on energy use in high-rise residential buildings. *Energy Build.* **2019**, *199*, 20–28. [CrossRef]
52. Papadopoulos, A.M. Forty years of regulations on the thermal performance of the building envelope in Europe: Achievements, perspectives and challenges. *Energy Build.* **2016**, *127*, 942–952. [CrossRef]

53. Cai, W.; Wen, X.; Wang, S.; Wang, L. A real-time detection method of building energy efficiency based on image processing. *J. Vis. Commun. Image R.* **2019**, *60*, 295–304. [CrossRef]
54. Gaglia, A.G.; Dialynas, E.N.; Argiriou, A.A.; Kostopoulou, E.; Tsiamitros, D.; Stimoniaris, D.; Laskos, K.M. Energy performance of European residential buildings: Energy use, technical and environmental characteristics of the Greek residential sector –energy conservation and CO_2 reduction. *Energy Build.* **2019**, *183*, 86–104. [CrossRef]
55. Kim, S.S.; Bae, M.J.; Kim, Y.D. Policies and status of window design for energy efficient buildings. *Procedia Eng.* **2016**, *146*, 155–157. [CrossRef]
56. Alev, U.; Antsov, P.; Kalamees, T. Air leakage of concrete floor and foundation junctions. *Energy Procedia* **2015**, *78*, 2046–2051. [CrossRef]
57. Heibati, S.; Wahid Maref, W.; Saber, H.H. Assessing the energy and indoor air quality performance for a three-story building using an integrated model, part one: The need for integration. *Energies* **2019**, *12*, 4775. [CrossRef]
58. *Design and Certification of Energy Performance of Buildings*; STR 2.01.02:2016; Ministry of Environment of Republic of Lithuania: Vilnius, Lithuania, 2016.
59. Kalamees, T. Air tightness and air leakages of new lightweight single-family detached houses in Estonia. *Build. Environ.* **2007**, *42*, 2369–2377. [CrossRef]
60. Hamlin, T.; Gusdorf, J. *Airtightness and Energy Efficiency of New Conventional and R-2000 Housing in Canada*; The CANMET Energy Technology Centre (CETC), Energy Technology Branch, Natural Resources Canada: Ottawa, ON, Canada, 1997.
61. Chen, S.; Levin, M.D.; Li, H.; Yowargana, P.; Xie, L. Measured air tightness performance of residential buildings in North China and its influence on district space heating energy use. *Energy Build.* **2012**, *51*, 157–164. [CrossRef]
62. Hasper, W.; Kirtschig, T.; Siddall, M.; Johnston, D.; Vallentin, G.; Harvie-Clark, J. Long-term performance of Passive House buildings. *Energy Effic.* **2021**, *14*, 5. [CrossRef]
63. Šadauskienė, J.; Paukštys, V.; Šeduikytė, L.; Banionis, K. Impact of air tightness on the evaluation of building energy performance in Lithuania. *Energies* **2014**, *7*, 4972–4987. [CrossRef]

energies

MDPI

Article

Study on the Efficiency and Dynamic Characteristics of an Energy Harvester Based on Flexible Structure Galloping

Peng Liao [1], Jiyang Fu [1], Wenyong Ma [2], Yuan Cai [1] and Yuncheng He [1,*]

[1] Research Center for Wind Engineering and Engineering Vibration, Guangzhou University, Guangzhou 510006, China; 2111916022@e.gzhu.edu.cn (P.L.); jiyangfu@gzhu.edu.cn (J.F.); 2112016080@e.gzhu.edu.cn (Y.C.)

[2] Innovation Center for Wind Engineering and Wind Energy Technology of Hebei Province, Shijiazhuang 050043, China; mawenyong@126.com

* Correspondence: yuncheng@gzhu.edu.cn

Abstract: According to the engineering phenomenon of the galloping of ice-coated transmission lines at certain wind speeds, this paper proposes a novel type of energy harvester based on the galloping of a flexible structure. It uses the tension generated by the galloping structure to cause periodic strain on the piezoelectric cantilever beam, which is highly efficient for converting wind energy into electricity. On this basis, a physical model of fluid–structure interaction is established, and the Reynolds-averaged Navier–Stokes equation and SST K -ω turbulent model based on ANSYS Fluent are used to carry out a two-dimensional steady computational fluid dynamics (CFD) numerical simulation. First, the CFD technology under different grid densities and time steps is verified. CFD numerical simulation technology is used to simulate the physical model of the energy harvester, and the effect of wind speed on the lateral displacement and aerodynamic force of the flexible structure is analyzed. In addition, this paper also carries out a parameterized study on the influence of the harvester's behavior, through the wind tunnel test, focusing on the voltage and electric power output efficiency. The harvester has a maximum output power of 119.7 μW/mm^3 at the optimal resistance value of 200 KΩ at a wind speed of 10 m/s. The research results provide certain guidance for the design of a high-efficiency harvester with a square aerodynamic shape and a flexible bluff body.

Keywords: galloping; energy harvester; computational fluid dynamics (CFD); numerical simulation

Citation: Liao, P.; Fu, J.; Ma, W.; Cai, Y.; He, Y. Study on the Efficiency and Dynamic Characteristics of an Energy Harvester Based on Flexible Structure Galloping. *Energies* **2021**, *14*, 6548. https://doi.org/10.3390/en14206548

Academic Editor: Sandro Nizetic

Received: 22 September 2021
Accepted: 8 October 2021
Published: 12 October 2021

1. Introduction

In recent years, the environmental problems caused by the burning of fossil fuels such as petroleum and coal have become more and more serious, and fossil energy is increasingly depleted. It is an important research focus to obtain clean and renewable energy from the environment [1]. Previous studies have shown that vortices may be generated alternately from the two side surfaces of a bluff body that is immersed in the flow, which results in the phenomenon of flow-induced motion (FIM) [2]. Although FIM may endanger the safety of structures, it can be potentially exploited for collecting energy from the environment [3]. To this end, various energy harvesters and technologies have been developed. It is also expected that such environmental energy harvesters can be utilized in practices to power micro-electromechanical systems (MEMS) and wireless sensor systems so that a more convenient realization of structural health monitoring, industry sense and detection, military track, and environmental monitoring [4] can be achieved.

In reference to wind energy harvesting techniques, the majority of related harvesters were developed using the principles of vortex-induced vibration (VIV), galloping, flutter, and buffeting, the main forms of wind-induced induced VIV and galloping. For the VIV energy harvester, the flow rate range of high-efficiency power generation requires that the vortex shedding frequency of the harvester is consistent with the natural frequency. Therefore, it is commonly used for fluid energy harvesting. Williamson's team [5,6] conducted a lot of research on cylindrical VIV, identified various branches of the VIV amplitude, and summarized the vortex shedding mode into S and P modes. Ding et al. [7] conducted numerical simulation of VIV for different bluff bodies and studied their energy harvesting efficiency. An et al. [8] analyzed and studied the effect of CFD technology on the plate length of the VIV energy harvester on the flow velocity, dynamics, and performance of the wake structure. Zhang et al. [9] used the two-dimensional Reynolds number method to study the VIV of four staggered cylinders, and conducted a series of numerical simulations for energy harvesting. Akaydin et al. [10] developed a cylindrical bluff body VIV piezoelectric energy harvester. When the flow speed is 1.19 m/s, the harvester with a resonance frequency of 3.14 Hz can output a maximum power of 0.1 mW to an optimized load of 2.46 MΩ. Galloping is a typical self-excited vibration phenomenon caused by aeroelastic instability. It mostly occurs in rectangular, angular, and flexible structures, and is usually characterized by low-frequency and high-amplitude oscillations [11]. Due to the greater vibration and higher output power, this aerodynamic instability may be more suitable for energy harvesting than VIV [12]. Barrero-Gil et al. [13] were first to theoretically analyze the potential of using a single-degree-of-freedom (SDOF) system to harvest energy using lateral gallop. Javed et al. [14] used a distributed parameter pattern to study the influence of various aerodynamic force expressions on galloping. Zhao et al. [15] studied the influence of bluff wind exposure area, load resistance, mass of bluff, and piezoelectric sheet length on the output power of a galloping energy harvester. On the other hand, Hu et al. [16] examined the influence of aerodynamic configuration on wind harvesting performance, and found that the VIV of a cylinder could be transformed into galloping if the cylinder was treated via corner modification techniques. Additionally, Sirohi et al. [17] proposed a harvester based on triangular section rods attached to the cantilever beam.

The results from previous studies have shown that transmission lines can be covered with ice on cold days, and their cross section may change to a non-circular shape [18]. Under certain wind speed and wind attack angles, the incoming flow on both sides of the bluff body can produce vortices and shed backwards, and generate an alternate aerodynamic load, which results in the galloping of the transmission line [19]. Previous studies also showed that the tension of the wire can influence galloping significantly, and greater tensions tends to favor the occurrence of galloping. Meanwhile, many galloping energy harvesters were developed by using columns with a square section, as prisms with a square section have more complex cross-section geometric characteristics compared to cylinders. Since Den Hartog first studied and explained the galloping phenomenon, numerous studies have shown that galloping can be widely observed on bluff bodies with a square section [20,21]. Therefore, the square section is usually preferred for the study of galloping energy harvesters.

In this study, a square section energy harvester based on the galloping principle of an iced transmission line was developed. The performance of the harvester was examined via both experimental tests and CFD simulations. The CFD technique was utilized, since it provides a powerful tool to explore the characteristics of flow motions, and to further understand the working mechanism of the harvester. The remainder of the article is organized as follows: Section 2 introduces the design and modeling of the harvester, Sections 3 and 4 detail the CFD method, and the experimental method, respectively. The specific results are presented and discussed in Section 5, and the main findings and conclusions are summarized in Section 6.

2. Design and Modeling of the Energy Harvester

2.1. Configuration

Figure 1 depicts the setup of the developed harvester. It consists of a flexible structure (i.e., the counterpart of transmission lines with a length of 0.42 m) that aims to receive wind energy from incoming flows, a supporting frame where the flexible structure is fixed, and a wind direction regulator that is mainly composed of a spindle and a deflector. The two ends of the flexible structure are respectively connected with the rigid body of the supporting frame, and the free end of a cantilever beam where a piezoelectric film is adhered. The cantilever beam is made of 0.3 mm × 150 mm stainless steel. The piezoelectric film, i.e., the PVDF (Polyvinylidene Fluoride) film (IPS-17020, ZHINK TECHNOLOGY) has dimensions of 30 mm (length) × 12.1 mm (width) × 0.28 μm (depth), and the density is 1.78 × 103 kg/m^3. The spindle is fixed with the supporting frame and the deflector rigidly. Due to the guiding effects of the deflector, incoming wind flows tend to blow in a direction that is perpendicular to the windward surface of the flexible structure. When the wind speed exceeds a certain value, the flexible structure can vibrate up and down severely, i.e., galloping occurs. The vibrating flexible structure then drives the cantilever and therefore the PVDF film to sway, which fulfills the conversion of wind energy into electricity.

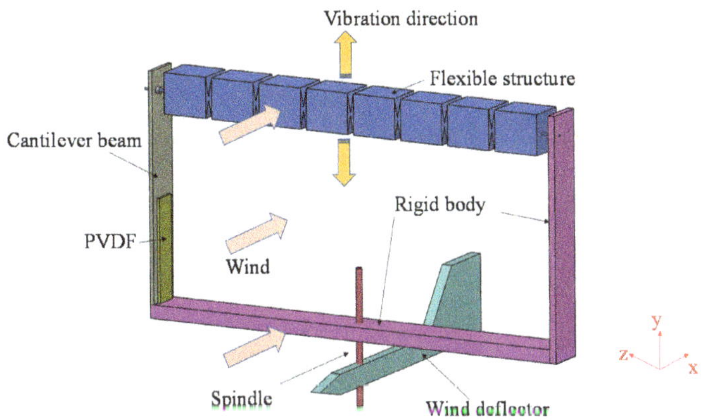

Figure 1. Schematic diagram of energy harvester.

When the energy harvester faces the incoming wind, the flexible bluff body swings around the plane and causes the thin wire to generate tension. The tension at one end of the thin wire directly drives the cantilever beam to produce periodic alternating strain. At the same time, the piezoelectric film is deformed. A certain charge is generated, which effectively converts the flow energy of the air into electric energy. The energy harvester has a simple structure and low manufacturing costs, and is very suitable for the surrounding windy environment all year round. Compared with various forms of energy harvesters, this paper's harvester is not affected by wind direction and is suitable for any wind direction angle. Since the designed energy harvester has excellent parameters, and the critical wind speed generated is small, the flexible structure is prone to galloping and improves the efficiency of energy harvesting.

2.2. CFD Mathematical Model

As shown in Figure 2, the harvester system can be mathematically simplified as a SDOF system. Taking the middle section of the flexible structure as the simulation research object, it is assumed that the wind field is incompressible and the effect of structural torsion and the inverse piezoelectric effect in the system can be reasonably neglected.

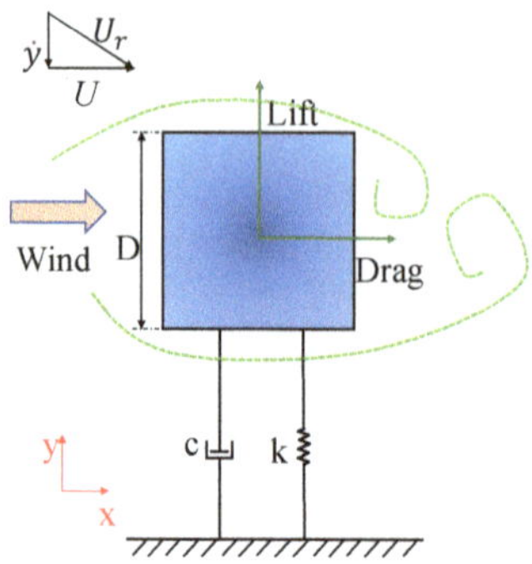

Figure 2. 2-dimensinal dynamic model.

Thus, the dynamics of the harvester body over a unit length can be depicted by [22]:

$$M\ddot{y} + C\dot{y} + Ky = F_y \tag{1}$$

where y denotes the lateral displacement of the square column, M is the mass per length, F_y is the force acting on the square structure in y direction, C is the mechanical damping coefficient, and K is the stiffness of the vibration model.

The details of the equation can be referred to in Barreiro-Gill et al. [23].

According to the quasi-steady theory [24], wind force can be expressed as function of wind velocity U, the characteristic length of the square section D (or the side length in this study) and a dimensionless coefficient, or the lift coefficient C_L in this study:

$$F_y = \frac{1}{2}\rho U^2 D C_L \tag{2}$$

The main parameters involved in this model of harvester are listed in Table 1, where ζ represents the damping ratio, which is defined as $\zeta = C/2\sqrt{MK}$. Note that the values of damping ratio and effective stiffness coefficient can be determined through experiment.

Table 1. Main physical model parameters of the harvester.

Item	Symbol	Value
Mass(g)	M	0.144
Diameter(mm)	D	30
Stiffness (N/m)	K	30.2
Damping ratio	ζ	0.0018
Air density(Kg/m^3)	ρ	1.225
Motion viscosity (m^2·s^{-1})	v	1.41×10^{-6}

2.3. *Piezoelectric Performance Equation*

The energy harvester uses a d_{31} piezoelectric sheet, i.e., the polarization direction is perpendicular to the applied stress direction, and the working mode of the piezoelectric material is the d_{31} mode with the polarized direction parallel to the surface normal. To simplify the analysis, a load resistance (R_L) was attached to the conductive electrode of the PVDF piezoelectric ceramic film. The piezoelectric constitutive relationship can be directly expressed as [25]:

$$D_3 = d_{31}T_1 + \varepsilon_{33}^T E_3 \tag{3}$$

where d_{31} is the piezoelectric charge constant, D_3 is the electric displacement component, T_1 is the stress component, E_3 is the electric field component, and ε_{33}^T is the dielectric constant.

3. CFD Simulation Method

3.1. Numerical Methods

The fluid–structure interaction solution method in conjunction with the weak coupling solution technique were used to numerically calculate the evolutions of wind field over the computational domain and to obtain the aerodynamic force acting on the harvester. The two-dimensional Reynolds number average Navier–Stokes (RANS) equation and the k-ω SST (shear stress transport) turbulent model [26] were used to numerically simulate the flow around a square cross-section. This turbulence model was chosen because, compared to other turbulence models, the k-ω model of SST is a hybrid of the k-ω and k-ε models. It activates the k-ω model near the wall and the k-ε model in free flow. It has better performance when predicting the boundary layer flow of the reverse pressure gradient. Therefore, this paper adopts the SST k-ω turbulence model in CFD simulation.

The interaction effects between the wind flows and the harvester structure were embedded into the CFD to implement the link with the main program. At the same time, the structure dynamic equation was solved and the structure domain calculated, and then the motion lift coefficient and displacement of the structure were obtained. At the same time, the overset grid technology was used to update the grid of the computational domain in real time.

User-defined functions (UDFs) were compiled (in C Language) and embedded into the CFD software to realize the simulation of fluid–structure interaction. In this paper, DEFINE_CG_MOTION was used as the motion function to define the motion mode. The overset grid model was used to define computational grid movement and data exchange. The Newmark-β method was used in UDF (refer to the Appendix A for details). This method is a numerical integration method for solving differential equations. It has been widely used to solve problems with oscillating systems [27].

Based on the basic assumptions of the central difference method, the explicit difference method of dynamic equations was adopted. The basic assumption of the Newmark-β method is that the acceleration changes linearly in each time increment, and the characteristics of the system remain constant during this interval. The equilibrium requirement of the force system acting on the mass at any time is as follows: the Newmark-β method approximates the speed and displacement of the system at time $(t + \Delta t)$ through the following two assumptions:

$$\dot{y}(t+\Delta t) = \dot{y}(t) + (1-\gamma)\Delta t\ddot{y}(t) + \gamma\Delta t\ddot{y}(t+\Delta t) \tag{4}$$

$$y(t+\Delta t) = y(t) + \Delta t\dot{y}(t) + (\frac{1}{2}-\beta)\Delta t^2\ddot{y}(t) + \beta\Delta t^2\ddot{y}(t+\Delta t) \tag{5}$$

The two parameters γ and β in the formula can be selected as required, and different combinations correspond to different processing effects. When $\gamma = \frac{1}{2}$ and $\beta = \frac{1}{2}$, it is the central difference method [28]. Therefore, the acceleration and velocity can be obtained.

$$\ddot{y}(t+\Delta t) = \frac{1}{\beta\Delta t^2}(y(t+\Delta t) - y(t)) - \frac{1}{\beta\Delta t}\dot{y}(t) - (\frac{1}{2\beta} - 1)\ddot{y}(t) \tag{6}$$

$$\dot{y}(t+\Delta t) = \frac{\gamma}{\beta\Delta t}(y(t+\Delta t) - y(t)) + (1 - \frac{\gamma}{\beta})\dot{y}(t) + (1 - \frac{\gamma}{2\beta})\Delta t\ddot{y}(t) \tag{7}$$

The motion of the system at time $t + \Delta t$ can be expressed as:

$$M\ddot{y}(t+\Delta t) + C\dot{y}(t+\Delta t) + Ky(t+\Delta t) = F_y(t+\Delta t) \tag{8}$$

Integrating the above formulas leads to:

$$\widetilde{K}y(t+\Delta t) = \widetilde{F}_y(t+\Delta t) \tag{9}$$

where

$$\widetilde{K} = \frac{1}{\beta \Delta t^2} M + \frac{\gamma}{\beta \Delta t} C + K \quad (10)$$

$$\begin{aligned} \widetilde{F}(t+\Delta t) = & F(t+\Delta t) + M\left[\tfrac{1}{\beta \Delta t^2} y(t) + \tfrac{1}{\beta \Delta t} \dot{y}(t) + (\tfrac{1}{2\beta} - 1)\ddot{y}(t)\right] \\ & + C\left[\tfrac{\gamma}{\beta \Delta t} y(t) + (\tfrac{\gamma}{\beta} - 1)\dot{y}(t) + (\tfrac{\gamma}{2\beta} - 1)\Delta t \ddot{y}(t)\right] \end{aligned} \quad (11)$$

The numerical simulation flowchart is shown in Figure 3.

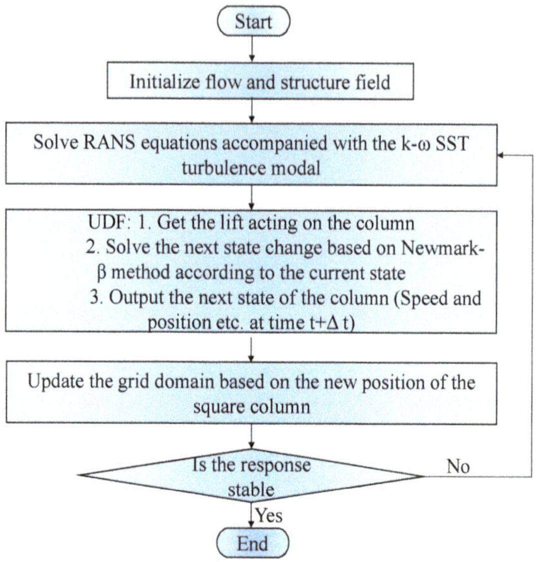

Figure 3. Flowchart of transient numerical simulation.

3.2. *Computational Fluid Domain and Grid*

As shown in Figure 4a, the simulation used a rectangular computational fluid domain. The calculation domain had a width of 20D and a length of 30D. The middle position of the square was 10D away from the inlet. The boundary conditions used included the left speed inlet, the right pressure outlet, and the upper and lower sides' sliding wall surface. The center of the square column was the origin of the coordinate system; x and y respectively represent the along-wind and crosswind directions.

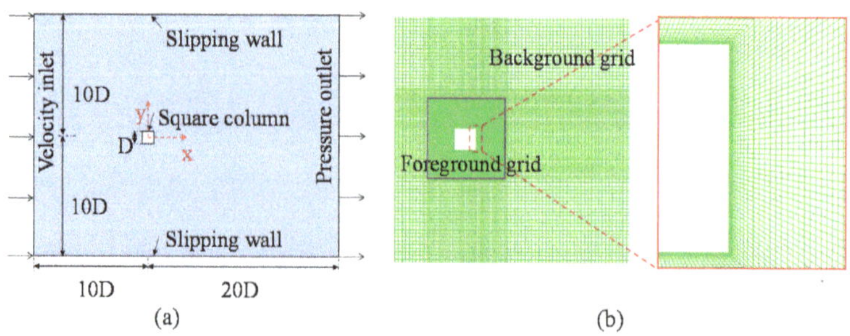

Figure 4. (**a**) Computational fluid domains; (**b**) Computational grid.

The model establishment and grid division were all carried out in the commercial software Ansys ICEM. The grids under different working conditions were all divided by non-uniform structured grids to ensure the accuracy of calculation and save a lot of computing resources. In computational fluid dynamics, the dynamic overset grid method has efficient dynamic grid processing capability and can guarantee the quality of the grid, so it has been widely used in unsteady flow simulation. Therefore, this research used overset grid technology; many concepts related to nested grid computing used today can be traced back to the breakthrough idea of Joseph Steger [29,30]. The overset grid method was used in Fluent; when FIM occurred, the constructed grid oscillated with the square column to ensure that the grid was not updated, which effectively avoided the negative element grid. The square coordinate grid (called the component grid) matched the square cylinder, and the background grid adopted a unified Cartesian grid. Details of the overset grid are shown in Figure 4b.

In order to make the grid height Y+ of the first layer of the wall satisfy the wall function, the height value was determined according to the required Reynolds number [31]. Enough densification was performed close to the wall, and at least 20 layers of wall surface grids were set with a rate of change of 1.2. The Y+ of the wall grids were all around 1.

3.3. Solving Method

The turbulence, pressure, momentum, and other fluid control equations used the second-order upwind spatial discretization algorithm, and the gradient calculation used an algorithm based on a least squares unit [32]. The discretization was performed using the second-order upwind difference scheme, and the transient term was discretized using the second-order backward Euler scheme. The first-order algorithm was used for preliminary calculation and then the second-order algorithm was used to improve the calculation accuracy. All simulation conditions adopted the pressure-velocity (SIMPLEC) coupling method, and the convergence was determined by the size of the residual error of the governing equation [33]. The continuity equation, momentum equation, k equation, and ω of all scale residuals below 1×10^{-5} were used. The equation was used as the convergence criterion, and the corresponding calculation results were observed to be stable, which can be considered reliable results.

3.4. Validation of Numerical Model

To ensure reliability, and that the model used numerical simulation and obtained a convergent and accurate solution within a reasonable calculation time, this paper considers different grid densities and time steps. Tables 2 and 3 list the results of different grid parameters and time steps, in which C_D denotes the mean drag coefficient over the time domain, C_L stands for the root mean square (RMS) of the lift coefficient, and St represents the Strouhal number.

Table 2. Verification of grid density independence (Re = 2.2×10^4).

Grid Density	C_D	C_L	St
Coarse (32,414)	2.20	1.44	0.128
Medium (43,954)	2.25 (2.27%)	1.41 (2.08%)	0.127 (0.78%)
Fine (96,153)	2.26 (2.65%)	1.45 (0.90%)	0.127 (0.78%)

Table 3. Validation of time-step independence (Re = 2.2×10^4).

Time Steps	C_D	C_L	St
0.001	2.25	1.45	0.127
0.0008	2.30 (2.22%)	1.56 (7.59%)	0.129 (1.57%)
0.0006	2.29 (1.78%)	1.66 (14.5%)	0.132 (3.93%)
LES [31]	2.21 (1.78%)	1.71 (17.9%)	0.128 (0.79%)
DNS [32]	2.18 (3.11%)	1.51 (4.14%)	0.132 (3.93%)

As shown in Table 2, the results under the three different grid densities were similar. The scheme with medium grid resolution was adopted in this study so that a balance between computational efficiency and cost could be achieved.

Meanwhile, the transient numerical method was adopted and time-step independent verification was carried out to evaluate the uncertainty of the value. The independence of the time steps was verified by using different time step sizes of 0.0006 s~0.001 s/step for numerical simulation. According to the calculation results for different time steps, a small time step cannot improve the simulation accuracy but takes a long time. Therefore, the time step of 0.0008 s per step was selected. The calculated results of the square at Re = 2.2×10^4 were similar to the results presented by Cao [34] and Trias [35], indicating that the turbulence model adopted can obtain more reliable results.

4. Experimental Method

The experiment was carried out in a subsonic closed recirculation wind tunnel. The design range of the flow velocity at the working section of the tunnel was 1–22 m/s, with the turbulence intensity not exceeding 0.5%. The layout of the experiment is shown in Figure 5. When exploring the influence of the external resistance R_L, the external load resistance of 10 kΩ–1 MΩ was connected in sequence, and the wind tunnel control speed changed in a gradient of 3 m/s–10 m/s. The output voltage was collected and stored by a data acquisition instrument (NI 9234). The highest sampling frequency was 2840 Hz for acquisition, and the acquisition time exceeded 120 s. The voltage and displacement were inputted into labview for visual observation and analysis. The displacement of the transmission-line-like flexible structure was monitored by a laser displacement sensor that was installed on the side wall of the wind tunnel. The output voltage of the harvester was recorded when the vibration of the flexible structure became stable.

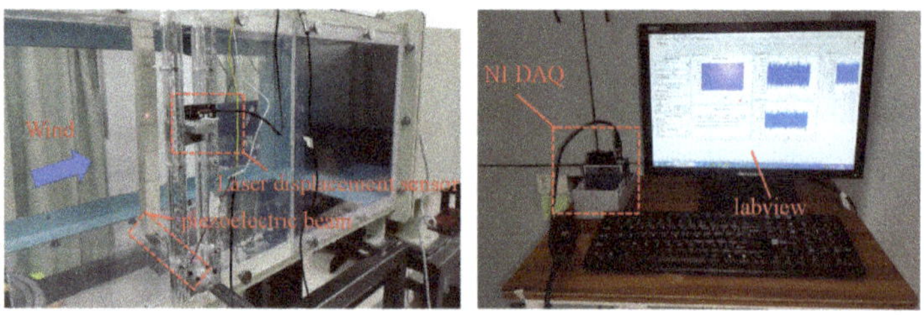

(a) (b)

Figure 5. Experimental setup: (**a**) working section; (**b**) control platform.

5. Results and Discussion

5.1. Performance Analysis of the Harvester

On obtaining the voltage time-history data through wind tunnel experiments, the root mean square (RMS) value of voltage V_{RMS} can be calculated:

$$V_{RMS} = \sqrt{\frac{1}{T_2 - T_1}\int_{T_1}^{T_2} u(t)dt} \tag{12}$$

Accordingly, the mean power P can be obtained as:

$$P = \frac{1}{T_2 - T_1}\int_{T_1}^{T_2} \frac{u(t)^2}{R_L}dt \tag{13}$$

in which T_2 and T_1 are the start and end time during the acquisition period, respectively, R_L is the external load resistance, and $u(t)$ is the instantaneous voltage.

Figure 6 displays the results of the RMS voltage and mean power output by connecting various load resistances from 10 kΩ to 1 MΩ in the PVDF film in the wind speed range of

3–10 m/s. It can be seen in Figure 6a that under the same load resistance, the wind speed continues to increase, and the output RMS voltage has an obvious upward trend. The minimum RMS voltage recorded under a load resistance of 10 kΩ is 350 mV. In addition, the output RMS voltage of this resistance model is relatively small. In the wind speed range of 3–10 m/s, the output RMS voltage steadily increased from 350 mv to 0.14 V. The highest RMS voltage recorded under the load resistance of 1 MΩ was 2.96 V. It can be found from Figure 6b that in the wind speed range of 3–10 m/s, the rising trend of output power was similar to the rising trend of RMS output voltage. When the wind speed was 10 m/s, the maximum load resistance of 200 kΩ in this experiment was 12.1 μW. The results indicate that when the load resistance is constant, as the input air speed increases, the voltage and power between the load resistances increase almost in advance.

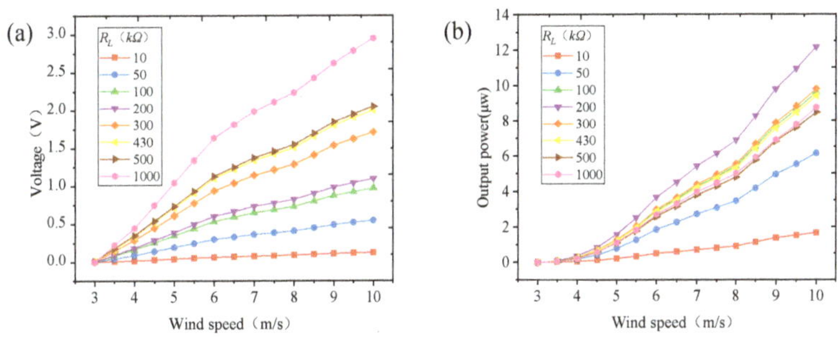

Figure 6. (**a**) Output voltage and (**b**) power with different wind speed.

According to the RMS voltage and output power calculated by Formulas (12) and (13), the power density and voltage density per scanning volume, which are defined as the power value and RMS voltage value divided by the volume of piezoelectric film, were calculated. In the analysis that followed, the load resistance first had to be matched to evaluate the harvesting performance. Figure 7 displays the change of output voltage density and power density with load resistance under different wind speeds. Figure 7a shows that the overall output trend of the measured voltage density increases with the increase of resistance within a certain wind speed range, and the maximum voltage density is 29.1 V/mm^3. Figure 7b shows that within a certain range, the overall output power trend of the measured power density at all wind speeds increases as the resistance increases. The optimal value of the load resistance for different wind speeds is between 100 kΩ and 430 kΩ. Outside this load resistance range, the average power generated is significantly reduced. After intensive testing, it was found that when the load resistance is about 200 kΩ, it provides the highest output average power. Therefore, $R_0 = R_L$ = 200 kΩ is the optimal electrical load resistance, and this result will be used for the efficiency of the energy harvester in the subsequent experimental discussion when the load resistance is 200 KΩ, and the power density is 119.7 μW/mm^3. Previous studies have pointed out that there is an optimal resistance R_0 for the best collection efficiency. Neglecting the effects of damping and dielectric loss, the optimization resistance can be determined as [36]:

$$R_0 = \frac{1}{2\pi f C} \tag{14}$$

where C is the harvester capacitance and f is the vibration frequency.

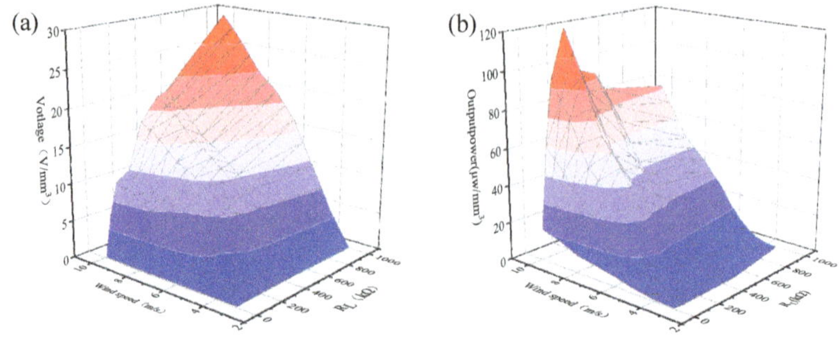

Figure 7. (**a**) Output voltage density and (**b**) power density with different load resistance.

To further explore the working performance of the harvester, it was necessary to analyze the piezoelectric film dynamics characteristics. Figure 8 displays the time history of the output voltage with a load resistance of 300 kΩ at a wind speed of 3–7 m/s. As demonstrated, the voltage signal fluctuates periodically for each case associated with a fixed wind speed, and the amplitude of the voltage increases distinctly as the wind speed increases (from 0.14 V to 1.12 V). Apparently, the periodic variation of output voltage is attributed to the periodic evolution of the strain around the fix end of the cantilever beam. Because the galloping amplitude increases consistently with the increase of wind speed, the strain becomes larger for the cases with stronger incoming wind, which further leads to higher output voltage.

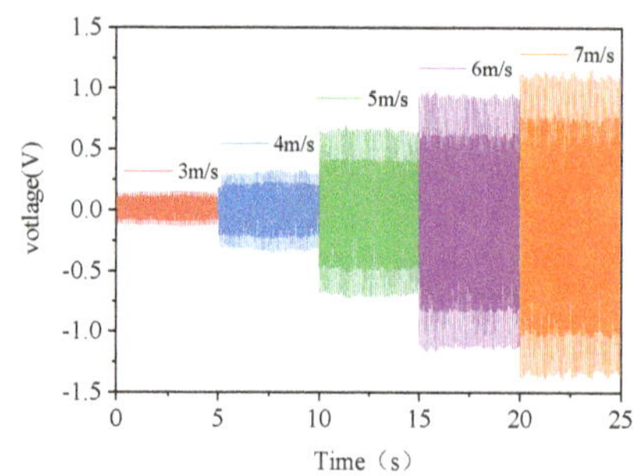

Figure 8. Diagram of Voltage time history (R_L = 100 kΩ).

5.2. *Dynamic Characteristics Analysis*

By calculating the damping coefficient, mass ratio, and Reynolds number selected in this study, it can be found that the value of U_g/U_v is much less than 1, which means that the square column FIM has a strong interaction between VIV and galloping [37]. It can be considered that galloping continuously affects the amplitude and locking area of VIV, and VIV also changes the form of galloping. In order to better understand FIM and flow structure, this paper introduces four kinds representative simulation examples under various Reynolds numbers (Re = 2054/6161/16,430/20,537). This includes four FIM regions: VIV initial branch, VIV upper branch, VIV-galloping transition, and galloping. These vortex patterns, at different Reynolds numbers, are analyzed. In addition, the effects of the amplitude and frequency responses for square columns are discussed as well.

This paper presents the instantaneous vorticity diagram, velocity cloud diagram, and velocity streamline of the square column at different wind speeds (Reynolds number), including the vortex shedding at the highest and lowest points of the structure. In those figures of the vortex pattern, the red vorticity is positive, which means counterclockwise rotation; the blue vorticity is negative, which means clockwise rotation. There are two vortex shedding modes: 2S mode (in one cycle, two vortices shed from opposite sides of the cylinder) and 2P mode (in each cycle, two pairs of vortices shed from each side of the cylinder). As the wind speed changes, the vortex shape can change, and the branch transitions affect each other [27]. In this paper, the vortex shedding mode is studied by observing the instantaneous vorticity contours around the square column oscillator, where the vorticity is defined as $\omega = \partial v/\partial x - \partial u/\partial y$.

When the wind speed is 1 m/s (Re = 2054), the harvester is in the initial branch of VIV. As shown in Figure 9, the 2S model of the vortex shedding mode in the wake can be clearly observed; that is, the positive vortex and the negative vortex separate out during the vibration period. This mode is the classical von Kármán Street. In this range, as Re increases, the size of the vortex is larger than when Re is low, which is consistent with the numerical results given by Ding et al. [27].

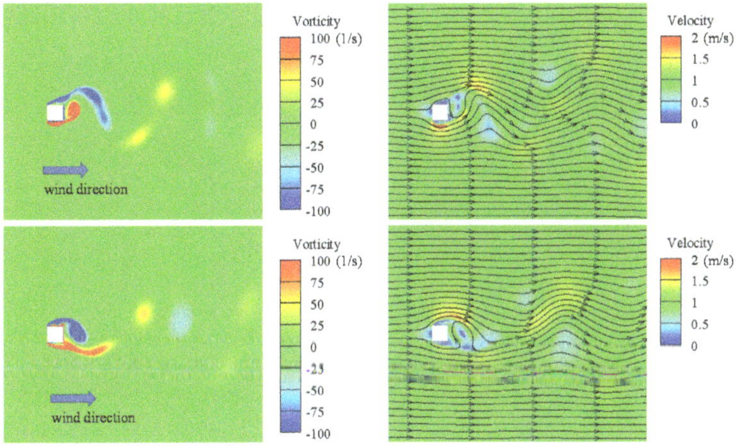

Figure 9. Vortex pattern and Velocity distributions contour (Re = 2054).

As the wind speed increases to 3 m/s (Re = 6161), the number of vortices shed in each oscillation cycle increases. In each oscillation period, 6 vortices shed from the square column and shed in the 2P + 2S mode of two pairs of vortices and one single vortex, as shown in Figure 10. This vortex pattern is known as Quasi-2P, which means two pairs of vortices shedding per cycle.

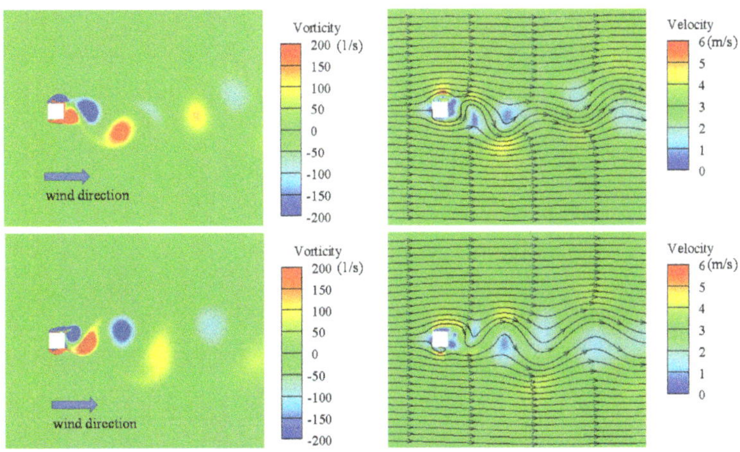

Figure 10. Vortex pattern and velocity distributions contour (Re = 6161).

When the wind speed reaches 8 m/s (Re = 16,430), the vortex pattern in the VIV-galloping transition zone is formed. As shown in Figure 11, ten vortices shed from the square column in an oscillation cycle. According to previous research by Ding [38], a similar near-wake vortex structure was captured as 4P + 2S. There are still many controversies about the identification method of multiple vortices shedding from square columns. At the highest and lowest points of vibration, a single vortex appears first. In the next downward or upward process, a total of two pairs of vortices appear.

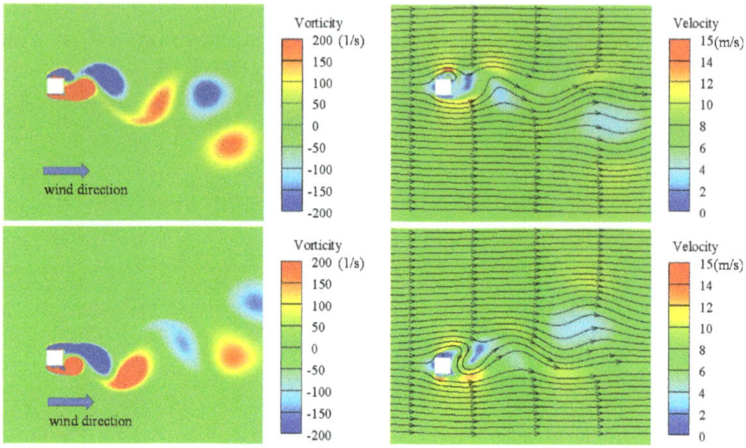

Figure 11. Vortex pattern and Velocity distributions contour (Re = 16,430).

When the wind speed is 10 m/s (Re = 20,537), the FIM of the square column is in the fully developed galloping state zone. As shown in Figure 12, there is a fundamental difference between galloping vibration and VIV. When entering the galloping state, a total of 14 vortices will shed in the manner of 6P + 2S in each oscillation period, two of which are separate vortices. According to the results of previous studies [39], it can be found that the vortex of the square column is at high Reynolds number. The type is np + 2S, where n represents the number of p and increases with the increase of Reynolds number or flow rate. The 2S vortex appears at the highest point and the lowest point of the displacement and falls off respectively.

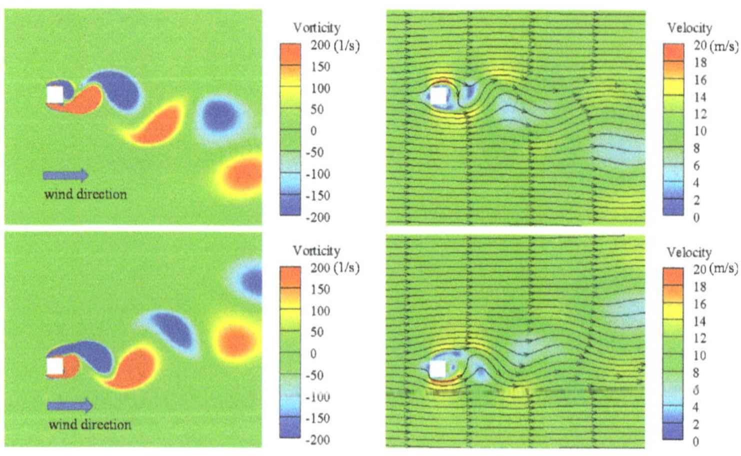

Figure 12. Vortex pattern and Velocity distributions contour (Re = 16,430).

Within a certain wind speed range (as shown in Figures 13–16), the lift coefficient decreases with the increase of wind speed. When the wind speed is relatively small, the lift coefficient becomes a regular oscillation under low Reynolds number [40]. In the initial stage of VIV, comparing the lift coefficient and the displacement graph, the lift coefficient and the displacement performance are highly consistent. The displacement curve and lift coefficient curve are transformed by FFT to obtain the frequency spectrum. In Figure 15b, it can be seen that both the displacement spectrum and lift spectrum have multiple peak frequencies and that they maintain good consistency and their main frequency is close to the natural frequency. When galloping occurs, the dominant frequency of the displacement spectrum decreases, and the lift spectrum frequency is more obviously controlled by the vortex deflation frequency. In Figure 16b, when the square column enters the state of full galloping, it can be found that the proportion of low frequency in the displacement spectrum increases. The increase in its proportion is also an important signal for the full development of galloping. When galloping occurs, the frequency response of the square column is obviously different; its vibration is hardly controlled by the vortex breakaway frequency and the main frequency is always lower than the natural frequency, which also leads to the occurrence of large vibrations.

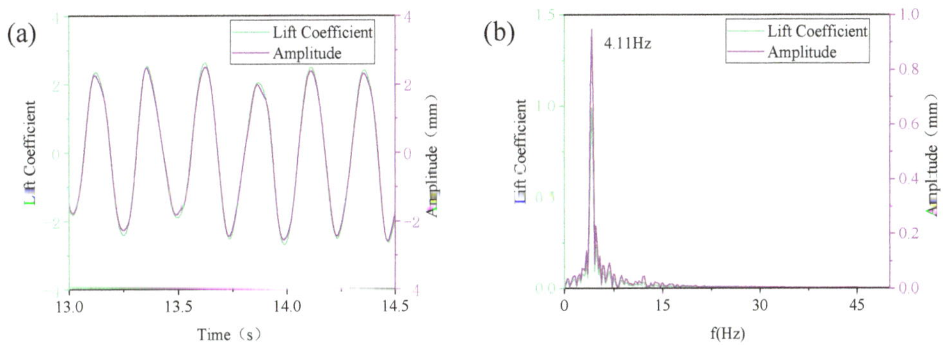

Figure 13. (**a**) Amplitude and lift coefficient versus time; (**b**) Frequency spectrum (Re = 2054).

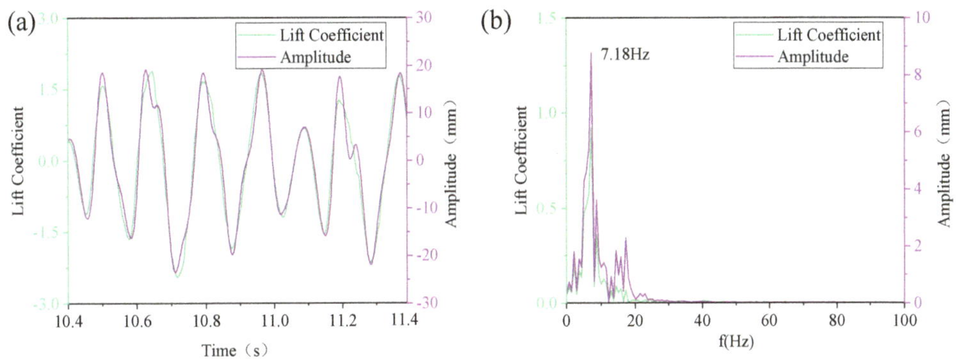

Figure 14. (**a**) Amplitude and lift coefficient versus time; (**b**) Frequency spectrum (Re = 6160).

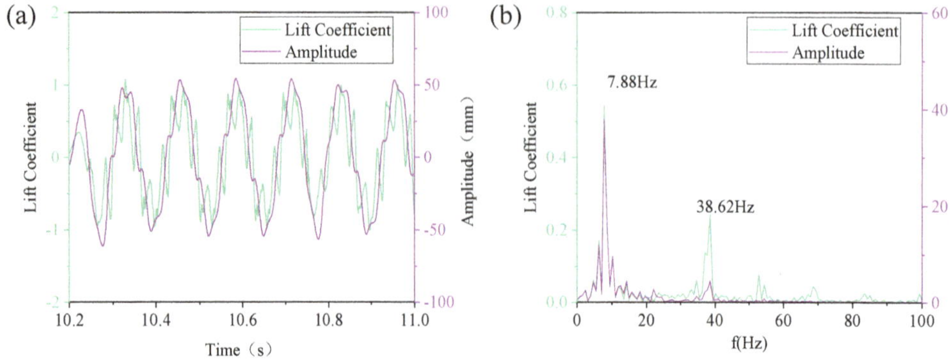

Figure 15. (**a**) Amplitude and lift coefficient versus time; (**b**) Frequency spectrum (Re = 16,430).

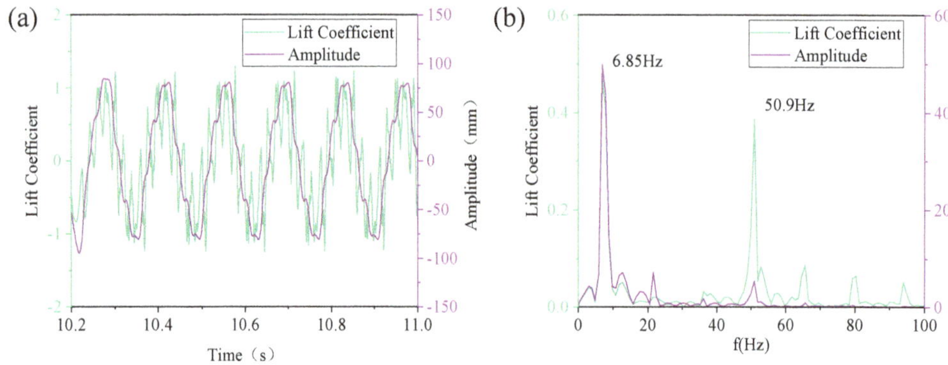

Figure 16. (**a**) Amplitude and lift coefficient versus time; (**b**) Frequency spectrum (Re = 20,538).

Through the numerical simulation results, as the wind speed increases (the Reynolds number also increases), although the lift coefficient decreases, the lift applied to the two sides of the bluff body continues to increase. The maximum displacement of the system also increases, which causes an increase in the instantaneous stress of the piezoelectric thin film. Combined with the results of the output power of the energy harvester, it can be found that when the Reynolds number is low, the bluff body's vibration amplitude and frequency are low, so the harvesting efficiency is at a low level. However, when the incoming wind speed increases and begins to enter the galloping state, the coupling effect of VIV and galloping can accelerate the onset of galloping and increase the displacement response of the bluff body at low and medium wind speeds. After entering full galloping, the amplitude of the entire system will increase significantly, and the output power will be increased. In addition, compared with VIV, the vibration of the square column in the galloping process is unstable, and its amplitude will increase with the increase of the incoming flow velocity. This means that the kinetic energy of the fluid captured by the square column FIM harvesting system will continue to increase with the increase of the incoming wind, and there is no limit [41]. Therefore, it can be seen that the square cylinder has obvious advantages in the application of FIM energy conversion, especially under high Reynolds number. The form of wind-induced vibration is closely related to the damping, elastic stiffness, and mass of energy harvester, which is used as the power source of energy collection. The harvesting efficiency of the flexible structure can be further improved only through analysis of its dynamic characteristics and reasonable design.

6. Conclusions

In this study, a novel type of piezoelectric energy harvester was developed based on the principle of wind-induced galloping. The dynamic model of the fluid–structure interaction system was established, and CFD techniques in conjunction with the Newmark-β method were adopted to obtain corresponding numerical solutions. Wind tunnel tests were also conducted to detail the working performance of the harvester. The main findings and conclusions are summarized below:

1. The flexible structure experienced four FIM stages. The wind speed increased to 8 m/s in the transition zone between vortex-induced resonance and galloping. When the wind speed reached 10 m/s, it started to gallop completely, and the harvester system experienced low-frequency and high-amplitude vibration.
2. Within the studied wind speed range of 3–10 m/s, it was found that as the wind speed increased, the vortex-induced shedding frequency of the flexible structure first increased and then decreased, but the associated displacement increased consistently.
3. When the resistance was constant, the output voltage and power of the harvester increased with the increase of wind speed. When the wind speed was constant, the output voltage increased consistently with increasing resistance. By contrast, the output electric power first increased and then decreased with the resistance, and there was optimal resistance at around 100 kΩ. The maximum output power of the energy harvester was 119.7 $\mu W/mm^3$.

Author Contributions: Formal analysis, P.L.; investigation, P.L.; resources, J.F. and W.M.; data curation, Y.H.; writing—original draft preparation, P.L.; writing—review and editing, Y.C. All authors have read and agreed to the published version of the manuscript.

Funding: The following support is gratefully acknowledged: (a) National Natural Science Foundation of China (11972123), (b) Wind Engineering and Wind Energy Utilization Engineering Technology Innovation Center of Hebei Province (Shijiazhuang Tiedao University) Open Project (ICWEHB202001), (c) Guangzhou University full-time graduate basic innovation project (2020GDJC-M44).

Data Availability Statement: The introduction data supporting this manuscript are from previously reported studies and datasets, which have been cited. The processed data are available from the corresponding author upon request. The test raw data used to support the findings of this study are available from the corresponding author upon request.

Conflicts of Interest: We declare that we do not have any commercial or associated interests that might represent a conflict of interest in connection with the work submitted.

Appendix A

```
#include "udf.h"
#include "stdio.h"
#include "time.h"
#include "stdlib.h"
#include "math.h"
static real speed[ND_ND];
static real weiyi_before[ND_ND],sudu_before[ND_ND],jiasudu_before[ND_ND];
static real speed_nz;
static real weiyi_before_nz,sudu_before_nz,jiasudu_before_nz;
static real number_1 = 0;
static real number_2 = 0;
DEFINE_CG_MOTION(first,dt,vel,omega,time,dtime)
{
  real m[ND_ND],k[ND_ND],zunibi[ND_ND],zunixishu[ND_ND],freq_rad[ND_ND];
  real beta,gama;
  real          k_equ[ND_ND],inertia_equ[ND_ND],damping_equ[ND_ND],force
_equ[ND_ND];
```

```
real code_1,code_2,code_3,code_4,code_5,code_6,code_7;
real weiyi[ND_ND],sudu[ND_ND],jiasudu[ND_ND];
real m_nz,k_nz,zunibi_nz,zunixishu_nz,freq_rad_nz;
real beta_nz,gama_nz;
real k_equ_nz,inertia_equ_nz,damping_equ_nz,force_equ_nz;
real code_1nz,code_2nz,code_3nz,code_4nz,code_5nz,code_6nz,code_7nz;
real weiyi_nz,sudu_nz,jiasudu_nz;
real hezai,force,moment,li[ND_ND],liju[ND_ND];
real cog[ND_ND];
int x, y, z;
#if !RP_NODE
FILE *fp_1;
#endif
#if !RP_HOST
Domain *d;
Thread *t;
face_t f;
cell_t c;
real NV_VEC (A);
d = Get_Domain(1);
t = DT_THREAD(dt);
for(x=0; x<ND_ND; x++)
        {
            cog[x] = DT_CG(dt)[x];
        }
Compute_Force_And_Moment(d, t, cog, li, liju, FALSE);
hezai = li[0];
force = li[1];
moment = liju[2];
#endif
node_to_host_real_4(hezai,force,moment,cog[1]);
if (number_1 == 0)
        {
            weiyi_before[1] = 0;
            sudu_before[1] = 0;
            jiasudu_before[1] = 0;
            weiyi_before[0] = 0;
            sudu_before[0] = 0;
            jiasudu_before[0] = 0;
            weiyi_before_nz = 0;
            sudu_before_nz = 0;
            jiasudu_before_nz = 0;
            number_1 = number_1 + 1;
        }
m[1] = 1; /**the mass of vertical movement, Kg**/
k[1] =1; /**the stiffness of vertical movement, N/m**/
zunixishu[1] =1;
gama = 0.5;
beta = 0.25;
code_1 = gama/(beta*dtime);
code_2 = 1/(beta*dtime*dtime);
code_3 = (1-gama)*dtime;
code_4 = gama/beta;
code_5 = gama*dtime*(0.5-beta)/beta;
```

```
        code_6 = 1/(beta*dtime);
        code_7 = (0.5-beta)/beta;
        k_equ[1] = k[1] + code_1*zunixishu[1] + code_2*m[1];
        inertia_equ[1] = m[1] * (code_2*weiyi_before[1] + code_6*sudu_before[1] +
code_7*jiasudu_before[1]);
        damping_equ[1] = zunixishu[1] * (-1*sudu_before[1] - code_3*jiasudu_before[1] +
code_1*weiyi_before[1] + code_4*sudu_before[1] + code_5*jiasudu_before[1]);
        force_equ[1] = force + inertia_equ[1] + damping_equ[1];
        weiyi[1] = force_equ[1]/k_equ[1];
        sudu[1] = sudu_before[1] + code_3*jiasudu_before[1] + code_1*(weiyi[1]-weiyi_
before[1]) - code_4*sudu_before[1] - code_5*jiasudu_before[1];
        jiasudu[1] = (force - zunixishu[1]*sudu[1] - k[1]*weiyi[1])/m[1];
        weiyi_before[1] = weiyi[1];
        sudu_before[1] = sudu[1];
        jiasudu_before[1] = jiasudu[1];
        speed[1] = sudu[1];
    #if !RP_NODE
        fp_1 = fopen("Fluent_couple.dat","a+");
        fprintf(fp_1, "%.16lf %.16lf %.16lf %.16lf %.16lf %.16lf %.16lf \n", time, hezai, force,
moment, weiyi[1], sudu[1], jiasudu[1]);
        /**1_shijian, 2_zuli, 3_shengli, 4_liju, 5_niuzhuanjiao(hudu), 6_jiaosudu, 7_jiaojia-
sudu, 8_shuxiangweiyi(m), 9_shuxiangsudu, 10_shuxiangjiasudu, 11_zhongxinshuxiang-
weizhi**/
        fclose(fp_1);
        #endif
        host_to_node_real_3(sudu[0],sudu[1],sudu_nz);
        #if !RP_HOST
        NV_S(vel, =, 0.0);
        NV_S(omega, =, 0.0);
        if (!Data_Valid_P())
          return;
        vel[1] = sudu[1];
        #endif
    }
    DEFINE_CG_MOTION(second,dt,vel,omega,time,dtime)
    {
        host_to_node_real_3(speed[0],speed[1], speed_nz);
    #if !RP_HOST
        vel[1] = speed[1];
    #endif
    }
```

References

1. Kabir, E.; Kumar, P.; Kumar, S.; Adelodun, A.A.; Kim, K.-H. Solar energy: Potential and future prospects. *Renew. Sustain. Energy Rev.* **2018**, *82*, 894–900. [CrossRef]
2. Sarpkaya, T. A critical review of the intrinsic nature of vortex-induced vibrations. *J. Fluids Struct.* **2004**, *19*, 389–447. [CrossRef]
3. Wang, J.; Geng, L.; Ding, L.; Zhu, H.; Yurchenko, D. The state-of-the-art review on energy harvesting from flow-induced vibrations. *Appl. Energy* **2020**, *267*, 114902. [CrossRef]
4. Wang, J.; Zhao, G.; Zhang, M.; Zhang, Z. Efficient study of a coarse structure number on the bluff body during the harvesting of wind energy. *Energy Sources Part A Recovery Util. Environ. Eff.* **2018**, *40*, 1788–1797. [CrossRef]
5. Khalak, A.; Williamson, C. Fluid forces and dynamics of a hydroelastic structure with very low mass and damping. *J. Fluids Struct.* **1997**, *11*, 973–982. [CrossRef]
6. Khalak, A.; Williamson, C.H. Motions, forces and mode transitions in vortex-induced vibrations at low mass-damping. *J. Fluids Struct.* **1999**, *13*, 813–851. [CrossRef]

7. An, X.; Song, B.; Tian, W.; Ma, C. Design and CFD simulations of a vortex-induced piezoelectric energy converter (VIPEC) for underwater environment. *Energies* **2018**, *11*, 330. [CrossRef]
8. Zhang, B.; Mao, Z.; Song, B.; Tian, W.; Ding, W. Numerical investigation on VIV energy harvesting of four cylinders in close staggered formation. *Ocean. Eng.* **2018**, *165*, 55–68. [CrossRef]
9. Akaydin, H.; Elvin, N.; Andreopoulos, Y. The performance of a self-excited fluidic energy harvester. *Smart Mater. Struct.* **2012**, *21*, 025007. [CrossRef]
10. Bashir, M.; Rajendran, P.; Khan, S. Energy harvesting from aerodynamic instabilities: Current prospect and future trends. In *IOP Conference Series: Materials Science and Engineering*; IOP Publishing: Bristol, UK, 2018; p. 012054.
11. Jung, H.-J.; Lee, S.-W.; Jang, D.-D. Feasibility study on a new energy harvesting electromagnetic device using aerodynamic instability. *IEEE Trans. Magn.* **2009**, *45*, 4376–4379. [CrossRef]
12. Barrero-Gil, A.; Alonso, G.; Sanz-Andres, A. Energy harvesting from transverse galloping. *J. Sound Vib.* **2010**, *329*, 2873–2883. [CrossRef]
13. Wang, J.; Tang, L.; Zhao, L.; Zhang, Z. Efficiency investigation on energy harvesting from airflows in HVAC system based on galloping of isosceles triangle sectioned bluff bodies. *Energy* **2019**, *172*, 1066–1078. [CrossRef]
14. Javed, U.; Abdelkefi, A. Impacts of the aerodynamic force representation on the stability and performance of a galloping-based energy harvester. *J. Sound Vib.* **2017**, *400*, 213–226. [CrossRef]
15. Zhao, L.; Tang, L.; Yang, Y. Comparison of modeling methods and parametric study for a piezoelectric wind energy harvester. *Smart Mater. Struct.* **2013**, *22*, 125003. [CrossRef]
16. Hu, G.; Tse, K.T.; Kwok, K.C.S.; Song, J.; Lyu, Y. Aerodynamic modification to a circular cylinder to enhance the piezoelectric wind energy harvesting. *Appl. Phys. Lett.* **2016**, *109*, 193902. [CrossRef]
17. Sirohi, J.; Mahadik, R. Piezoelectric wind energy harvester for low-power sensors. *J. Intell. Mater. Syst. Struct.* **2011**, *22*, 2215–2228. [CrossRef]
18. Novak, M. Galloping oscillations of prismatic structures. *J. Eng. Mech. Div.* **1972**, *98*, 27–46. [CrossRef]
19. Ma, G.-M.; Li, Y.-B.; Mao, N.-Q.; Shi, C.; Li, C.-R.; Zhang, B. A fiber Bragg grating-based dynamic tension detection system for overhead transmission line galloping. *Sensors* **2018**, *18*, 365. [CrossRef]
20. Okajima, A. Strouhal numbers of rectangular cylinders. *J. Fluid Mech.* **1982**, *123*, 379–398. [CrossRef]
21. Den Hartog, J.P. *Mechanical Vibrations*; Courier Corporation: Honolulu, HI, USA, 1985.
22. Zhu, M.; Worthington, E.; Njuguna, J. Analyses of power output of piezoelectric energy-harvesting devices directly connected to a load resistor using a coupled piezoelectric-circuit finite element method. *IEEE Trans. Ultrason. Ferroelectr. Freq. Control.* **2009**, *56*, 1309–1317. [CrossRef]
23. Barrero-Gil, A.; Sanz-Andres, A.; Roura, M. Transverse galloping at low Reynolds numbers. *J. Fluids Struct.* **2009**, *25*, 1236–1242. [CrossRef]
24. De Langre, E. *Fluides et Solides*; Editions Ecole Polytechnique: Palaiseau, France, 2001.
25. Priya, S.; Uchino, K.; Viehland, D. *IEEE Standard on Piezoelectricity;* American National Standards Institute: Washington, DC, USA, 1976.
26. Menter, F.R. Two-equation eddy-viscosity turbulence models for engineering applications. *AIAA J.* **1994**, *32*, 1598–1605. [CrossRef]
27. Ding, L.; Zhang, L.; Bernitsas, M.M.; Chang, C.-C. Numerical simulation and experimental validation for energy harvesting of single-cylinder VIVACE converter with passive turbulence control. *Renew. Energy* **2016**, *85*, 1246–1259. [CrossRef]
28. Park, K.; Underwood, P. A variable-step central difference method for structural dynamics analysis—Part 1. Theoretical aspects. *Comput. Methods Appl. Mech. Eng.* **1980**, *22*, 241–258. [CrossRef]
29. Chan, W.M. Overset grid technology development at NASA Ames Research Center. *Comput. Fluids* **2009**, *38*, 496–503. [CrossRef]
30. Shih, T. Overset grids: Fundamental and practical issues. In Proceedings of the 20th AIAA Applied Aerodynamics Conference, St. Louis, MO, USA, 24–26 June 2002; p. 3259.
31. Salim, S.M.; Cheah, S. Wall Y strategy for dealing with wall-bounded turbulent flows. In Proceedings of the International Multiconference of Engineers and Computer Scientists, Hong Kong, China, 18–20 March 2009; pp. 2165–2170.
32. Moukalled, F.; Mangani, L.; Darwish, M. *The Finite Volume Method in Computational Fluid Dynamics;* Springer: Berlin/Heidelberg, Germany, 2016; Volume 113.
33. Patankar, S.V. *Numerical Heat Transfer and Fluid Flow;* CRC Press: Boca Raton, FL, USA, 2018.
34. Cao, Y.; Tamura, T. Large-eddy simulations of flow past a square cylinder using structured and unstructured grids. *Comput. Fluids* **2016**, *137*, 36–54. [CrossRef]
35. Trias, F.; Gorobets, A.; Oliva, A. Turbulent flow around a square cylinder at Reynolds number 22,000: A DNS study. *Comput. Fluids* **2015**, *123*, 87–98. [CrossRef]
36. Li, S.; Lipson, H. Vertical-stalk flapping-leaf generator for wind energy harvesting, Smart materials, adaptive structures and intelligent systems. In Proceedings of the ASME 2009 Conference on Smart Materials, Adaptive Structures and Intelligent Systems, Oxnard, CA, USA, 21–23 September 2009; pp. 611–619.
37. Li, X.; Lyu, Z.; Kou, J.; Zhang, W. Mode competition in galloping of a square cylinder at low Reynolds number. *J. Fluid Mech.* **2019**, *867*, 516–555. [CrossRef]
38. Ding, L.; Zhang, L.; Wu, C.; Mao, X.; Jiang, D. Flow induced motion and energy harvesting of bluff bodies with different cross sections. *Energy Convers. Manag.* **2015**, *91*, 416–426. [CrossRef]

39. Zhang, B.; Mao, Z.; Song, B.; Ding, W.; Tian, W. Numerical investigation on effect of damping-ratio and mass-ratio on energy harnessing of a square cylinder in FIM. *Energy* **2018**, *144*, 218–231. [CrossRef]
40. Sun, H.; Kim, E.S.; Nowakowski, G.; Mauer, E.; Bernitsas, M.M. Effect of mass-ratio, damping, and stiffness on optimal hydrokinetic energy conversion of a single, rough cylinder in flow induced motions. *Renew. Energy* **2016**, *99*, 936–959. [CrossRef]
41. Wang, J.; Sun, S.; Hu, G.; Yang, Y.; Tang, L.; Li, P.; Zhang, G. Exploring the potential benefits of using metasurface for galloping energy harvesting. *Energy Convers. Manag.* **2021**, *243*, 114414. [CrossRef]

energies

Review

Basic Principles, Most Common Computational Tools, and Capabilities for Building Energy and Urban Microclimate Simulations

George M. Stavrakakis [1,2,*], Dimitris Al. Katsaprakakis [1] and Markos Damasiotis [3]

1 Department of Mechanical Engineering, School of Engineering, Hellenic Mediterranean University (HMU), Estavromenos, GR-71410 Heraklion, Greece; dkatsap@hmu.gr
2 MES Energy S.A., 67 Aeolou Str., GR-10559 Athens, Greece
3 Division of Development Programmes, Centre for Renewable Energy Sources and Saving (CRES), 19th km Marathonos Av., GR-19009 Pikermi, Greece; mdamas@cres.gr
* Correspondence: georgstavr@gmail.com; Tel.: +30-69-4646-7937

Abstract: This paper presents basic principles of built-environment physics' modelling, and it reviews common computational tools and capabilities in a scope of practical design approaches for retrofitting purposes. Well-established simulation models and methods, with applications found mainly in the international scientific literature, are described by means of strengths and weaknesses as regards related tools' availability, easiness to use, and reliability towards the determination of the optimal blends of retrofit measures for building energy upgrading and Urban Heat Island (UHI) mitigation. The various characteristics of computational approaches are listed and collated by means of comparison among the principal modelling methods as well as among the respective computational tools that may be used for simulation and decision-making purposes. Insights of coupling between building energy and urban microclimate models are also presented. The main goal was to provide a comprehensive overview of available simulation methods that can be used at the early design stages for planning retrofitting strategies and guiding engineers and technical professionals through the simulation tools' options oriented to the considered case study.

Keywords: building energy performance; urban heat island; building physics; simulation tools

Citation: Stavrakakis, G.M.; Katsaprakakis, D.A.; Damasiotis, M. Basic Principles, Most Common Computational Tools, and Capabilities for Building Energy and Urban Microclimate Simulations. *Energies* **2021**, *14*, 6707. https://doi.org/10.3390/en14206707

Academic Editor: Marcin Kamiński

Received: 29 August 2021
Accepted: 12 October 2021
Published: 15 October 2021

1. Introduction

The building sector in Europe is considered as the largest consumer of energy, using up to 40% of the final energy consumption [1,2]. As reported in the EU directive 2018/844/EU, almost 50% of the Union's final energy consumption is used for heating and cooling, 80% of which is allocated to buildings. This indicates that the achievement of the Union's targets regarding energy efficiency and resilience to climate change depends on the increase of renovation rates of its building stock, in fact, by giving priority to energy efficiency as well as by considering deployment of renewables [3]. According to its (EU) 2019/786 recommendation on building renovation [4], the Commission invites Member States to establish long-term renovation strategies focused on the national building stock, including both public and private buildings, towards highly energy efficient and decarbonized building stock by 2050, also prescribing measures for the cost-effective transformation of existing buildings into nearly zero-energy buildings (the so-called NZEBs). In this framework, it is acknowledged that the design approaches followed in order to achieve the highest possible energy-saving potential require advanced calculation techniques at the design stage, with the highest possible accuracy of predictions. In the context of evaluating building energy performance, many parameters are required, such as the thermo-physical properties of the envelope, indoor–outdoor physical interactions, energy end uses, building systems' operating schedules, etc. Considering all these influencing factors, building energy upgrading is indeed not an easy task. Especially now with more strict regulations and policies, building energy renovation plans require precise estimations of energy indicators, as specific thresholds of these indicators should be satisfied, and at the same time least-cost renovation measures should be identified.

On the other hand, a crucial factor that affects the energy performance of building complexes is the external microclimate, i.e., the microclimatic conditions in the vicinity of buildings determines cooling and heating loads, thus the energy demand and the decision of most appropriate energy-efficiency measures. Especially in densely built environments, the external microclimatic conditions should not be disregarded in the design stage as, indeed, the Urban Heat Island (UHI) effect is ever more intense and impacts many aspects of quality of life in cities, e.g., building energy efficiency, thermal comfort, and indoor and outdoor air quality. Over the last 30 years, heat waves in Europe in combination with the Urban Heat Island (UHI) phenomenon have dramatically deteriorated quality of life in densely built-up Cities, by means of mortality rates due to heat strokes, and of hygiene conditions as well as of the energy demand for cooling purposes. UHI is well documented in terms of its intensity. Indicatively, in Europe, the mean value of recorded maximum UHI intensities ranged between 0.3 °C and 6.8 °C (yielding an average of 2.6 °C), with absolute peaks close to 12 °C [5,6]. Such conditions of unusually high temperatures for long periods favor high energy consumption in buildings. For example, it has been documented that the increase in urban temperature may lead to an average increase of cooling loads from 20% to 45% in the Mediterranean climate [7]. This means that a holistic confrontation over the improvement of building energy performance should not disregard the impact of UHI on energy consumption. Apart from benefiting building energy performance, UHI mitigation projects ensure more comfortable and healthy open spaces for pedestrians.

To deal with the requirements of the latest EU directives as well as of the design challenges, EU Member States have developed their own national methodologies and computational tools (e.g., based on the CEN Standards), aiming to assess building energy performance in the pre-renovation (or pre-construction) and the post-renovation (or post-construction) situations in order to determine renovation measures. However, the available national tools are much more biased to single-building energy simulation, while, concerning the effect of local microclimate, it is often omitted from the numerical-simulation toolboxes used for purposes of compliance with building energy regulations. In current policies and regulatory frameworks, only the general bioclimatic-design principles are adopted regarding urban planning, without addressing the quantification of microclimatic indicators; hence, still no computational tools and/or concrete calculation methodologies are recommended to estimate microclimate and environmental indicators in the study phase specifically for design-for-compliance purposes.

On the other hand, considering the issues raised above, it becomes obvious that in order to comply with the latest energy efficiency policies and much stricter regulations, as well as to obtain sustainably built and urban environments, accurate methods and computational tools to estimate the impact of retrofit options based on the aspects of building and urban physics are required. The use of such methods is considered crucial even in the early study phase, especially for major renovation projects, for the following reasons:

- They assess the pre-renovation situation revealing the energy consumption level of buildings and microclimate conditions of open spaces. This capability contributes to the recognition of vulnerable areas, energy savings potential and, generally, actual needs of the renovation cases under consideration. The provision of such estimations contributes to determining and prioritizing the interventions.
- They can be used to assess the impact of various interventions in a desk-study (fast and with least cost) manner, i.e., computational tools may be executed for various design configurations and calculate the corresponding values of performance indicators (energy indicators for buildings and microclimate indicators for open spaces).
- In a more advanced level aiming at improving estimations' accuracy, many computational tools allow the possibility to conduct coupled simulations in order to account

for the impact of the UHI effect, i.e., of the local microclimate rather than relying on the wider climate zone, on building energy consumption.

- Hourly based calculations prescribed in dynamic simulation tools, provided that occupancy and systems' operation schedules are accessible, allow for energy-behaviour assessments.
- In combination with optimization schemes and algorithms, they support decision making towards the determination of cost-effective renovation measures that ensure minimum requirements of performance indicators, either energy or microclimate ones.

The present paper provides an overview of commercial or freely available computational tools that can be used to assess building energy performance and UHI effect in open spaces. The major categories of physical models are presented, i.e., multi-zonal (also known as nodal models) for building energy performance assessments and field models for UHI assessments. The capabilities of the most popular computational tools of each category are presented together with case studies found in the scientific literature. Furthermore, nodal/field models coupling possibilities to assess UHI effect on building energy consumption are discussed.

2. Physical Models

2.1. Building Thermal-Performance Modelling

Physical models are used to simulate the thermal performance of various buildings with their own special demands and uses, e.g., dwellings, offices, schools, etc. These models involve interpreting of space heating [8], natural ventilation [9], air conditioning systems [10], solar-thermal systems [11], Photovoltaic panels [12], occupants' behaviour [13,14], etc. The physical modelling techniques are based mainly on the solving of heat transfer equations.

To solve such physical problems, numerous simulation software packages are available, many of them also associated by benchmarking activities performed by many authors and researchers. Theoretically, each building software is able to include thermal physical phenomena encountered in buildings. Most computational tools provide the choice to users to select the physical mechanisms and the associated equations required. There are two major building thermal models' categories most commonly used [15] (mainly in the framework of research activities and projects):

- Field models, such as Computational Fluid Dynamics (CFD) models, and
- Multi-zonal or nodal models.

The present paper focuses on the application of the multi-zonal method in case of building energy simulation and provides an extensive presentation of the principles of this method and available computational tools to assess building energy performance. As far as field models are concerned, this paper focuses on their uses for simulating the urban microclimate. Therefore, the overview of field modelling principles and computational tools is restricted herein mainly to open spaces (Section 2.2), while only a short presentation of their uses for indoor airflows and building thermal simulation is provided.

2.1.1. Field Models for Indoor Airflow Assessments

The most complete field modelling approach in building thermal simulation is (so far) the CFD method. This is a "microscopic" approach of heat transfer modelling providing a detailed resolution of the airflow pattern. It is based on the discretization of a building zone into control volumes in the form of structured or unstructured mesh [16]. The CFD approach is essentially based on the solution of the so-called Navier–Stokes equations. A large number of CFD software exists such as Ansys Fluent, Ansys CFX, COMSOL Multi-physics, MIT-CFD, Phoenics, etc., most of them possessing additional capabilities to simulating indoor airflows and building thermal behaviour. They are general-purpose CFD platforms and can be applied to every system involving fluid flow phenomena. The CFD method is mainly employed for its ability to solve for mass, momentum, heat, chemical species, and turbulence parameters' conservation equations. While available software present similar characteristics in terms of the conservation equations solved or on the mathematical formulation of boundary conditions (for example, Dirichlet or Neuman formulations), some of them differ on the equations' discretization method or on the solver used for processing the algebraic system of discretized differential conservation equations. There are three fundamental methods for discretization purposes: The Finite Difference (FDM), the Finite Volume (FVM), and the Finite Element Method (FEM). These methods present different precision and numerical efforts, but they are all based on the discretization of Navier–Stokes equations. On the other hand, the treatment of boundary conditions in these methods is still a key issue in fluid flow numerical simulations depending on the engineering application studied. Indeed, in non-isothermal fluid flows, where design parameters or physical properties have fluctuations, boundary conditions require special treatment. This has led to enhancements of numerical methods, for example, on the basis of fluctuation-based equations, the so-called Stochastic Finite Element Method (SFEM), which was introduced and exercised in benchmark fluid-flow case studies by Kamiński and Carey [17].

The CFD analysis produces a detailed description of the airflow field within indoor environments including velocity vector distribution (magnitude and direction), temperature distribution, chemical species dispersion, etc. The prediction of the aforementioned properties of the flow field is very useful even in the early design stages as it reveals areas with unpleasant droughts and thermal discomfort (refer, for example, to ref. [18]) and areas of pollutants' confinement, for different design alternatives. Hence, it helps the building design practitioner to review and decide the best among the design alternatives. The main disadvantage of the CFD method, however, still is the high computational time required to solve accurately for the conservation equations in full 3D geometries adopting fine meshes respecting the grid-independent solution principle [19] as far as possible. However, given that the airflow in at least 75% of the building volume is almost stagnant (velocity magnitude below 0.5 m/s) [15], it is not always necessary to apply the CFD approach for the entire building but only to certain parts, e.g., within spaces affected by installed Heating Ventilating and Air-Conditioning (HVAC) systems or within naturally ventilated spaces. This allows reducing computational time significantly. For this reason, the CFD is frequently coupled with less time-consuming multi-zonal techniques or other statistical ones. Tan and Glicksman [20] compared the full CFD simulation results with those obtained by the coupling between CFD and a multi-zonal tool for captivating natural ventilation through large openings or an atrium. It was demonstrated that the latter required 10 times less duration of computations until full convergence in relation to the full CFD method, exhibiting similar accuracy. Kato [21] provided an extended review of coupled CFD and zonal or network techniques and applications in building heat-transfer simulations and reported the required theoretical conditions for reliable coupled simulations, balancing fidelity in predictions and reasonable computational times and resources.

2.1.2. The Multi-Zonal (Nodal) Approach

The multi-zonal approach assumes that each building zone is a homogeneous volume with uniform state variables. Thus, each zone is approximated as a node with a unique flow property, e.g., temperature, pressure, pollutant concentration, etc. Generally, a computational node stands for a room, a wall, or the exterior of the building, to which specific loads, such as internal occupancy, equipment gains, heat sources, etc., are allocated. The heat transfer equations are solved for each node and it can be considered as a one-dimensional approach. In international literature, one can find two main methods used for the multi-zonal approach [15]:

- Solution of the state variables transfer equations, and
- Finite difference method.

Most available software is designed based on the former technique. The latter method is applied for nodal approaches through the representation of heat transfer from electrical analogy, which was introduced by Rumaniovski et al. [22]. The usefulness of this method lies in the fact that it drastically simplifies the mathematical representation of the physical problem through the linearization of conservation equations, leading to reduced computational time.

The major advantage of this method is that it describes the behaviour of a building with many zones on a large time scale within modest computational resources. It is a particularly well-adopted technique for energy-consumption estimations and of the dynamic changes of space-averaged temperature into a room. In addition, it is useful to estimate air-change rates and the distribution of airflow properties among different rooms. Ventilation efficiency or pollutant transport in buildings can also be studied by this method [23].

Due to the zero-spatial-gradient assumption regarding the airflow state variables within a node, the multi-zonal method presents the following limitations:

- The study of thermal comfort and air quality in thermal zones is difficult, as the spatial heterogeneity of physical parameters (air velocity, turbulence intensity, relative humidity, temperature, etc.) involved in the conservation equations (heat transfer, mass, momentum, chemical species) is roughly approximated.
- The impact of heating and cooling loads on their close environment is not adequately addressed (for example, a radiator causing buoyant plumes or an air blower causing air drafts).
- It presents significant deviations in airflow predictions, especially in large spaces (e.g., atriums, athletic halls, auditoriums, etc.) where significant non-uniformities of indoor airflow are expected.
- Although it remains a good option to depict the distribution of pollutant concentration between building zones, it prevents the assessment of local effects by a heat or pollutant source within each building zone separately.

According to Kato (2018) [21], one effective way to "heal" the aforementioned limitations is through CFD nodal-coupled simulations. CFD and network-model coupled simulation is particularly useful when ventilation effectiveness of a large indoor space is required to be included in the energy simulation for long-term use. In this case, the nodal model serves as the boundary conditions' generator for the CFD model, which then undertakes the solution of the airflow field within the building zone at each user-defined time step.

One additional limitation acknowledged in the common multi-zonal approach is that the effects of air infiltration through openings, cracks, etc. are not adequately addressed. Indeed, most computational tools for building energy simulation incorporate mainly empirical correlations and default infiltration rates depending on different leakage properties of the building envelope. On the other hand, it is true that air infiltration is a case-sensitive issue, which requires appropriate modelling treatment to account for wind- and/or buoyancy-driven air movement through openings and cracks. It is also true that intervention measures referring to air tightness and consequent infiltration may lead to high amounts of energy savings related to heating/cooling. For instance, simulations of a large number of building types document that reducing air leakage can save 5–40% of heating and cooling energy [24]. An extensive investigation involving real-scale measurements of air leakage in 129 single and multi-family houses in Spain revealed mean air-change rates of 6.1 h^{-1} for single-family dwellings and 7.1 h^{-1} for multi-family housing, which advocate relatively high contributions to the energy consumption of the tested buildings [25]. Considering the fact that air infiltration greatly affects buildings' energy consumption as well as the accuracy of simulation predictions in terms of heating and cooling loads, thus the predicted energy consumption, it deserves a great deal of attention in simulation environments. Han et al. [26] explored different modelling strategies of infiltration rates for an office building and compared their performance in terms of predictions' accuracy. They proposed a coupled approach associated with time-dependent infiltration rates by integrating multi-zone airflow modeling and CFD results into energy simulations. It was demonstrated that the suggested simulation method provides improvement of the accuracy of energy simulations with up to 11% reduction of the root mean square error and of the normalized mean bias error. Prescribing air-tightness interventions, among other envelope interventions, in higher education buildings in Egypt, total energy savings of up to 33% were documented using the multi-zonal simulation approach [27].

2.1.3. Collation of Simulation Methods

The previous paragraphs described the two major methods to deal with building physics' modelling. The CFD method provides a detailed view of the physical mechanisms occurring in building systems. It is particularly adopted to solve for the convective phenomenon that takes place in large building spaces. In such spaces, the convective phenomenon, which causes airflow parameters' non-uniformity, is well analyzed, providing an accurate prediction of the Convective Heat Transfer Coefficient (CHTC) and, thus, of heat transfer. On the contrary, the multi-zonal approach underestimates CHTC and other variables' heterogeneity in these specific cases. However, it should be pointed out that it is difficult to conduct entire building simulations using CFD due to the associated high computational time and resources. Alternatively, coupled CFD with a multi-zonal model can be used.

On the other hand, the multi-zonal method is really well adopted to treat global building physics' resolution, assuming a uniform airflow field in each thermal zone. The main objective of this method is to simplify the algebraic system by linearizing a large part of the governing conservation equations (when it is physically accepted). As a result, the technical complexity is substantially reduced and so is the required time of computations. The multi-zonal method is more appropriate when more "macroscopic" effects are of interest, such as building energy consumption, rather than when the airflow pattern is the main goal. It should be mentioned, however, that the airflow properties' variations significantly affect indoor–outdoor interactions and, in this way, the envelope thermal behaviour as well as air infiltration rates. This causes variations in systems' operation schedules, which, in turn, influence building energy consumption. In this sense, the computational tool or method used to conduct a building energy study requires experience to understand which tool is more appropriate or to know when coupled multizonal/field modelling approaches are required for more accurate and reliable studies. A summary of the capabilities of the methods discussed above is reported in Table 1.

Table 1. Collation of major building physics' simulation methods.

Method	Technical Approach	Application Field	Advantages	Drawbacks
Multi-zonal	A building is discretized into thermal zones, often being rooms. The state variables are considered uniform in each zone.	Estimation of building energy consumption; indoor air temperature; thermal loads; Dynamic change of energy consumption.	Whole building energy simulation over user-defined time periods; reasonable computational time within modest computational resources.	Difficulty to study large volume systems; Unable to study local effects caused by heat or pollutant sources; Rough approximation of air infiltration rates.
CFD	A building zone is further discretized into control volumes.	Contaminant dispersion; Indoor air quality; local thermal comfort; HVAC systems.	Detailed description of the airflow field within large spaces in buildings.	High computational time and resources; modelling complexity; requires advanced knowledge of building physics.

It should be clarified that the techniques described above need input parameters, such as the meteorological data, thermo-physical properties of the building envelope, occupancy parameters, systems' operating schedules, etc. Obviously, all these parameters are interpreted with a degree of uncertainty. In addition to these uncertainties, there are certain assumptions adopted in order to reduce the complexity of building physical mechanisms. The combination of uncertainties in interpreting collected data (physical properties, materials, and occupancy-related) with the adoption of assumptions often leads to discrepancies between the simulated results and reality. The major challenge scientists and engineers currently face is to reduce uncertainties without compromising simulations' time, practicability, and accuracy. One major source of uncertainty in building energy analysis is the end users' behaviour, considering the fact that, ultimately, the building consumes energy in accordance with the habits of occupants over building systems. Hence, it is important to realize that, in view of realistic building energy simulation, the setup of systems' operation schedules should reflect occupants' behaviour as accurately as possible. Motivated by the discrepancy between the measured and the calculated heat consumption of residential buildings, Hansen et al. [28] investigated heat-related habits of occupants, utilizing extensive questionnaire surveys, and correlated practices of adjusting thermostats, clothing conditions, perceived thermal comfort, building envelope, and systems' installations. Their study demonstrated that material arrangements substantially affect occupant expectations and practices, associated with increased indoor temperatures and energy demand. The behavioral effect is evident even in more stable buildings, such as office buildings, as presented by Liu et al. [29]. They conducted a field study in office buildings in the UK and concluded that the adaptive behaviors of occupants showed substantial seasonal and daily variations. It was shown that non-physical parameters such as habit affect the adaptive responses of occupants, sometimes yielding to absurd behavior, which could lead to increased use of energy. The key delivery of the study was the illustration of how occupants would adapt and interact with their built environment, which can be adopted in building retrofitting strategies or in energy management systems for comfortable built environments. The aforementioned studies, but also many others (for example those reported in ref. [30]), suggest that any simulation method, either multi-zonal, CFD, or other, should account for building systems' operation schedules reflecting realistic end users' behaviors. This means that accessibility to building systems' operation schedules is a prerequisite of the computational tool used for energy simulations.

As far as computational time is concerned, several solutions consisting of reducing system size exist in the scientific literature (refer, for example, to refs. [31,32]. Another idea is to reduce the detail of building geometry by merging rooms or merging walls. Such simplifications should speed up significantly the solution process. Generally, an important limitation of the physical formulation is the need for a detailed description of the physical behaviour. Therefore, it implies detailed knowledge of the physical processes, especially of the ones occurring in the interior and the exterior of the building geometry. Within the scope of this paper is to help designers in understanding better the available methods to assess building energy performance and in identifying the most appropriate computational tools in order to balance accuracy and practicability in terms of easiness to use and of calculation time. In the next subsection the most popular and widely used building energy (mainly multi-zonal) simulation tools are described, highlighting their strengths and weaknesses.

2.1.4. Building Energy Simulation Tools

There is indeed a vast amount of available computational tools for building energy simulation purposes. IBPSA-USA has developed and manages the so-called Building Energy Software Tools (BEST) directory [33], which enlists more than 200 building software tools for evaluating building energy performance. The energy tools listed in the directory range from simple databases and spreadsheets to whole building energy simulation programs. In agreement with other review studies [15,34], the current paper focuses on the most popular tools used mainly for whole building energy performance assessments regarding at least commercial and residential buildings. In the following subsections, a short overview of each tool's capabilities is reported, supported by a summary of their characteristics presented in Table 2.

Table 2. Strengths, weaknesses, and special features of computational building energy simulation tools.

Tool	Strengths	Weaknesses	Special Features			Most Common Applications	Availability
			Handling of Climate Conditions	**Handling of Building Systems' Operating Schedules and Occupancy**	**Building Systems**		
Autodesk Green Building Studio (GBS)	>Provision of hourly whole building energy, emissions, and water analysis >Reduces setup and processing time, providing possibilities for extensive tests of design alternatives >Facilitates analysis for LEED compliance	>The level of detail of the resulting DOE-2 and EnergyPlus models implies quite advanced knowledge to understand the outcomes	>Input available data of specific climate zones >User-defined climate data time series	>User-defined schedules	>Common building systems for heating, cooling, Domestic Hot Water (DHW), etc. are easily compiled >Provision of renewable energy potential (solar and wind)	>Whole building thermal performance >Building Information Modelling (BIM) > BIM-LCA coupled simulations >LEED compliance assessments	Subscription web-based service
BEAVER	>Hourly-based whole building energy performance >Calculation of building construction and systems' types to retain desired environmental conditions >Modelling of a wide range of building end uses >ASHRAE-based building load calculation and on-site generation >Numerous options of air handling systems including provisions for modifications >Fast set-up compared to most other similar programs	>Some system types are not included, e.g., chillers and condensers > limited range of window types available for selection >Does not provide environment to analyze building impact on grid >Poor approximation of natural ventilation and daylighting >Limited database of climatic conditions	>Input available data of specific climate zones >User-defined climate data time series (measured or simulated) can be fed	>User-defined schedules may be prepared and fed to the simulation engine	>Detailed representation of heating and cooling systems >Various extra components or operating strategies can be added including Heat Recovery, Preheating Coils, Exhaust Fan, Temperature reset on heating and cooling coils, etc.	>Whole building energy performance >Used mainly for residential buildings energy assessments	Commercial
Bsim	>High flexibility in the assessment of indoor environment and energy performance and in designing HVAC systems >Simultaneous simulation of heat and moisture transfer through building walls >Multi-zone air flow simulations >Graphical user interface >Reliable representation of building systems >User-friendly optimization platform >hybrid system simulation >Flexible compatibility of results' files with other Windows programs	>Cannot simulate all renewable-energy sources >Limited ready-to-use climate data (only for certain regions and Countries)	>It integrates a built-in function for converting text-based time series to the binary format >User-defined climate data time series may be prepared and inserted	>Default library of systems' schedules >User-defined schedules may be prepared and inserted	>Automatic control strategies for each ventilation plant >heating, cooling, and ventilation systems	>Phase Change Materials >Building energy performance >Building hygrothermal performance	Commercial

Table 2. *Cont.*

Tool	Strengths	Weaknesses	Special Features			Most Common Applications	Availability
			Handling of Climate Conditions	Handling of Building Systems' Operating Schedules and Occupancy	Building Systems		
ENER-WIN	>Hourly whole building energy analysis >HVAC loads' calculations >Energy consumption and demand > Life cycle cost analysis >Graphic sketch interface > Libraries for windows, wall materials, profiles, costs, lights, world-wide weather data >Thermal comfort, greenhouse gas emission, and life-cycle cost calculations	>It uses simplified algorithms >Only nine HVAC systems available >Not recommended for HVAC design analysis >Cannot simulate RES technologies	>Hourly weather data generator based on data for 1500 cities worldwide	>Limited interpretation of building systems' schedules' impact on electrical energy use	>Equipment mainly handled as thermal loads	>Large commercial buildings >Economic analysis of building energy systems and emission calculation	Commercial
EnergyPlus	>It includes innovative simulation capabilities including time steps of less than an hour >Simulation modules are integrated with a heat balance-based zone simulation >It facilitates third party interface development for co-simulation purposes >Inclusion of multizone airflow, electricity simulation including fuel cells and other distributed energy systems > Designbuilder: User-friendly graphics interface, CFD module, Optimization module	>Relatively high level of complexity >No grid-integration analysis >Energy simulation and computer skills are required >Building physics' knowledge is a prerequisite >DesignBuilder: Offers a user-friendly interface and well-structured input wizards, which simplify simulation setup	>Extensive library of weather of specific locations >User-defined climate data time series >DesignBuilder: the CFD suite allows for estimating local microclimate effects	>User-defined systems' schedules >DesignBuilder: Vast menu of default occupancy schedules are available according to the building use	>The majority of systems (HVAC, Air handling units and control, DHW, etc.) of various building types can be employed >DesignBuilder: Provides vast lists of building systems, construction materials, and properties	>Whole building energy analysis for various building types >DesignBuilder: Widely used for extensive parametric analysis and optimization of alternative energy-upgrading measures >Proof-of-concept purposes for new technologies	>EnergyPlus: Free >DesignBuilder: Commercial
eQUEST	>User friendly building energy analysis tool >It provides interactive graphics, parametric analysis, and rapid execution >Flexible application to the entire design process, from the conceptual design stage to the final design >It offers detailed analysis throughout the construction documents, commissioning, and post-occupancy phases	>Supports only IP units (no SI units) >Ground-coupling and infiltration/natural ventilation models are simplified and limited >Does not include RES technologies >Does not calculate thermal comfort indices > Weather files	>Library of pre-defined weather data limited for US regions >User-defined climate data time series may be prepared and inserted	>User-defined systems' schedules	>It contains a relatively large database of HVAC systems	>Whole building energy analysis for various building types >It is particularly useful to assess occupants' behaviour in tertiary buildings >Suitable for EPC projects (when calibrated in comparison with actual energy consumption data)	Free

Table 2. *Cont.*

Tool	Strengths	Weaknesses	Special Features			Most Common Applications	Availability
			Handling of Climate Conditions	Handling of Building Systems' Operating Schedules and Occupancy	Building Systems		
ESP-r	>Provision of in-depth appraisal of the factors that influence the energy and environmental performance of buildings >Flexible and powerful enough to simulate many innovative or cutting-edge technologies including daylight exploitation, natural ventilation, combined heat and electricity generation and photovoltaic facades, CFD, multi-gridding, and control system	>It is a general-purpose tool and requires user efforts to set up modelling for certain cases; thus it implies advanced expertise >It is focused mainly on building thermal performance >No automatic optimization is provided >No economic analysis is provided	>User-defined climate data time series	>Limited interference with thermal-related building systems >User-defined schedules may be imported	>Handled mainly as heat sources >Supports simulations for RES technologies (mainly PVs)	>Whole building energy simulation >Used mainly to estimate energy demand >Often used to study behaviour relevant to daylighting >Study of combined heat and power applications	Free
IDA-ICE	>Annual dynamic multi-zone simulation application for indoor climate assessments and energy performance >Early-Stage Building Optimization >Complete energy and design studies >Accessibility to incorporate user-defined models	>Time-consuming calculations due to the employment of the airflow network modelling method, which often requires a large number of zones	>Library of climate data >User-defined climate data time series	>User-defined systems' schedules >Adjustable windows' modelling is also included	>HVAC systems may be analyzed >DHW >Renewable energy systems	>Whole building energy simulation >It is widely used to assess the efficiency of heating systems >PCM applications	Commercial
IESVE	>Provision of in-depth suite of building performance analysis modules >Useful to identify best passive options and renewable energy measures >HVAC system modelling >Natural ventilation modelling >Daylight and shading analysis >CFD analysis	>Energy and building physics' expertise are required >Linux environment is not supported	>Library of climate data included >User-defined climate data time series may be imported	>Menu of default HVAC schedules >User-defined HVAC schedules	>pre-defined HVAC component libraries and Manufacturer properties	>Whole building energy simulation >Often used for assessing renovation projects >Investigation of future-proof energy-upgrading measures	Commercial
SUNREL	>Appropriate for passive solar buildings >Predicts occupant behavior >Includes algorithms for Trombe walls, glazings, controllable window shading, active-charge/ passive-discharge thermal storage, and natural ventilation	>Limited HVAC modelling >Does not calculate thermal comfort indicators >Does not provide RES simulations >Does not model building-to-grid integration	>Available hourly weather data >User-defined hourly weather data may be imported	>User-defined schedules mainly for envelope parameters, such as windows >Occupancy schedules	>In its early versions, HVAC performance was not supported	>Building thermal performance >Shading analysis >Insulation performance analysis >Energy load modelling >Mainly used for single- and multi-family buildings	Free

Table 2. *Cont.*

Tool	Strengths	Weaknesses	Special Features			Most Common Applications	Availability
			Handling of Climate Conditions	Handling of Building Systems' Operating Schedules and Occupancy	Building Systems		
TAS	>Prediction of energy consumption, CO2 emissions, operating costs, and occupant comfort >Building thermal simulation >Plant and systems' operation modelling >Offers comprehensive capabilities for all types of energy modelling >User-defined special building physics' models, such as evaporation and evapotranspiration >Can simulate large and complex buildings	>Energy and building physics' expertise are required >Computer skills are required	>User-specified detailed weather data >Default weather files	>User-defined systems and occupancy schedules>Default schedules based on building type	>HVAC systems with HVAC manufacturers' databases >DHW systems >Daylighting >Renewable energy systems	>Whole building energy analysis >Often used to test planted roofs and walls >Able to test CHP applications in buildings	Commercial
TRNSYS	>Whole building energy analysis >HVAC analysis and customization, multi-zone airflow analyses, electrical power simulation, solar design, building thermal performance, control schemes >It interfaces with various other simulation software such as FLUENT for airflow impact on energy consumption, GenOpt and MATLAB for optimum building control	>Energy and building physics' expertise are required >Fluent computer skills are required in case of co-simulations >Grid interconnection analysis is not included >Direct economic analysis is not included	>User-specified detailed weather data >Extensive Default weather files >Interconnects with CFD tools to account for local microclimate effects	>User-defined systems and occupancy schedules>Default schedules available based on building type	>HVAC systems with manufacturers' databases >DHW systems >Daylighting >Renewable energy systems' databases	>Whole building energy analysis >Often used to test PCM performance >Coupling with CFD tools >Building energy management systems (model-predictive control cases) >HVAC and power systems' analysis >Solar systems design	Commercial

The tools of interest herein are:

- Autodesk Green Building Studio
- BEAVER
- BSim
- ENER-WIN
- Energy plus
- eQUEST
- ESP-r
- IDA Indoor Climate and Energy (IDA-ICE)
- IES Virtual Environment (IESVE)
- SUNREL
- TAS
- TRNSYS

Autodesk Green Building Studio

The Autodesk Green Building Studio is a web-based service that envisages whole building energy, water resources, and CO_2 emission analyses of buildings. The analysis is conducted via the Internet in a personalised web environment. This streamlines the entire setup process and facilitates immediate feedback on design alternatives. Based on the building's basic characteristics, such as size, type, and climate zone, the web-based service defines default values for construction materials and equipment by adopting regional building regulations. Using simple drop-down menus, the user can test different settings of the design, orientation, thermal transmittance, window glazing, or various HVAC systems. The service includes hourly weather data, as well as historical rain data as inputs. It calculates carbon emissions and presents the output in a web browser, for instance, the energy consumption and cost indicators as well as the potential for carbon neutrality. The output also tabulates the consumption of water resources and energy costs, providing an ENERGY-STAR score. Other useful indicators are also calculated such as solar and wind energy potential, LEED daylighting credit, and natural ventilation potential.

Najjar et al. (2017) [35] used the software in the case of a typical multi-storey office building located in Brazil in the framework of Building Information Modelling (BIM)—Life Cycle Analysis (LCA) simulation concept. In their modelling approach they incorporated Green Building Studio (GBS) to assess building energy performance for different construction materials. In a design control volume extending from the extraction of raw materials through construction and operation to disposal and recycling, they demonstrated that most of the negative environmental impacts are occurring during the manufacturing and operation phases. The methodology proposed can successfully determine which building elements have major importance in the LCA at the early design stage, thus providing an adequate decision-making tool for minimizing buildings' environmental impacts throughout the building lifespan. Using Revit, Abanda and Byers [36] developed a house model that was exported into Green Building Studio (GBS) for further calculations. The energy-efficiency potential was explored by means of a parametric analysis for building orientation. GBS is particularly efficient to conduct extensive parametric analyses regarding building energy performance. Indeed, it has been successfully used to study the energy impacts of extensive combinations of envelope and internal configurations, e.g., Window-to-wall ratios, wall and roof construction materials, and HVAC, and of external conditions such as climatic ones, and orientation and building exposure levels (by means of building complexes) [37].

BEAVER

BEAVER [38,39] is a Windows environment for the APEC ESPII Building Energy calculation Program. It provides easy input of data, model set-up, and results' preview. The program computes building energy consumption over a defined period, taking into account climate zone and location, construction materials, and systems' types required to satisfy the desired environmental conditions. It allows parametric analysis regarding building configurations and air conditioning systems. Data input is inserted via windows wizards, which include drop-down menus and entry fields on consecutive screens going through the general Project information to individual space data and building systems, capacities, operating schedules, etc. It includes default air handling systems, primary plant, and control schemes enabling the compilation of a wide range of building services. The Air Handling system type is quite easily prepared through a graphic-based manner of the units' assembly. Various extra components and operation schedules may be imposed referring, for instance, to Heat Recovery, Preheat Coils, Exhaust Fan, Temperature reset on heating and cooling coils, etc.

An extensive application study of BEAVER for assessing building energy performance was presented by ACADS-BSG Pty Ltd. and Elms Consulting Engineers [40]. The software was used to review and provide comments on suitability of the climate zones proposed in terms of the theoretical energy use. It facilitated proposing a representative location within each zone that can be adopted to reflect the thermal resistance of the predefined buildings and define the least number of other locations required to define the thermal-response extremes within each zone. The substrates used for the review of zones were various types of office buildings with and without infiltration conditions. The software was successfully used for the revision of climate zones used as inputs to assess building energy performance.

BSim

BSim [41] envisages user-friendly simulation of energy and hygrothermal simulations of buildings. The software consisted of the following modules: SimView (user interface and graphic model editor), tsbi5 (simultaneous thermal and moisture building simulation tool), XSun (dynamic solar and shadow simulation and visualisation), SimLight (daylight calculation tool), SimDXF (CAD import facility), and SimPV (building-integrated PV system calculation). Furthermore, there are export facilities to external tools: Be06 (Danish compliance checker), Radiance (advanced light simulations), and boundary conditions for CFD simulations and visualisation in tools using DirectX input files. BSim has been used extensively over the past 20 years in Denmark, presenting increased interest abroad, as it provides both energy and moisture analysis [42]. BSim applies the quasi-steady approach in building modelling, and it is often used for phase change materials' modelling using the heat capacity method. The BSim software has been successfully applied for the determination of the effect of the basic heat gains on building energy consumption by Sikula et al. [43] and it was demonstrated that the highest heat gain comes from solar radiation. Model validation procedures showed a deviation of only 8% between the simulated annual energy consumption and the measured one. Applications of the BSim, among other tools, may be also found in a report under the International Energy Agency (IEA) Programme for energy conservation in buildings and Community systems [44]. The software was used mainly to simulate energy performance of typical residences located in different locations (climatic zones) in the pre-renovation situation in order to assess the impact of different climatic conditions on building energy consumption. The high fidelity of BSim simulations is documented by the fact that it has been also used as a generator of reference building energy performance indicators over which other novel energy calculation methods are tested, for example, in the case of a smart glazing facade under different control contexts (night shutter, solar shading, and natural ventilation) [45]. Sorensen et al. [46] used the software to develop an integrated building energy design of a Danish office building, incorporating a Monte Carlo Simulation method, and produced a pool of engineering solutions with enough design freedom for architects. The study explores global design with Monte Carlo Simulations, in order to form feasible solutions for architects and facilitates the collaboration linkages between architects and engineers.

ENER WIN

The ENER-WIN [47] simulates hourly based energy consumption, including annual and monthly averages, peak demand, peak heating and cooling loads, solar-fraction through glazing, daylighting contribution, and life-cycle cost analysis. Design parameters are separately tabulated for each zone, also providing duct sizes and electrical power requirements. The software comprises several modules, i.e., an interface module, a weather-data retrieval module, and a sketching and an energy simulation module. ENER-WIN requires the following inputs: the building type, location and geometry, external ground parameters, operation patterns and loads (e.g., occupancy, lighting, equipment, and domestic hot water), and heating and cooling inputs (ventilation rate and schedules, thermostat settings and heating/cooling equipment types, systems' efficiency and set points).

Using ENERWIN in order to evaluate the reasons for high electrical use in 30 residences in Kuwait allowed for researchers to conclude that annual energy use in residential buildings was directly related to occupants' behavior and that data relating to the type of occupant should be taken into account as accurately as possible [48]. ENER-WIN was applied by Soebarto and Williamson [49] for the development of a multi-criteria decision-making approach based on the "Reference Building" concept. Using the databases of building materials, climate conditions, and systems incorporated in the ENER-WIN tool, they integrated an approach of creating a reference building that satisfies ASHRAE Standard 90.1 [50] requirements. The energy performance of the actual building was evaluated based on the deviations between the actual and reference building and it was concluded that the approach was useful for testing different design strategies. It should be clarified that the referred ASHRAE Standard has been replaced by the latest version 90.1-2019, i.e., the study cited previously is limited only to the older version of the Standard. As indicated by the software vendor [47], the latest Enerwin 2020 version incorporates ASHRAE Standards 90.1-2019.

EnergyPlus

EnergyPlus [51] is a modular-based code that is built upon the well-known models BLAST and DOE-2 [52]. It is a simulation engine that manipulates input and output in text-command formats. A heat-balance engine undertakes the calculation of loads at a user-specified time step, which is then passed to the building systems' simulation module at each time step. The systems' simulation module computes heating and cooling system and electrical system responses. This integrated solution ensures precise space temperature prediction, which is crucial for system design, occupant comfort, and air quality calculations. Integrated simulation provides possibilities to evaluate plausible system controls, moisture transfer through construction elements, radiant heating and cooling systems, and interzone airflow.

Tsikaloudaki et al. (2012) [53] used EnergyPlus to evaluate the cooling performance of a wide variety of geometrical, thermo-physical, and optical properties of windows. The maximum cooling loads were documented when windows' solar transmittance is high and thermal transmittance is low. It was demonstrated that in Mediterranean climates the combined high efficiency of transparent elements and controlled ventilation in office buildings reduce heat losses and ultimately result in higher cooling energy loads. Goia et al. [54] used EnergyPlus to develop a methodology for determining the optimal glazing percentage in a façade unit for low-energy office buildings. The investigation involved three alternative building design versions with different HVACs' efficiency. It was shown that, regardless of the orientation and building façade area, the optimal configuration corresponds to a transparent-area percentage ranging between 35% and 45% of the total façade area. Due to its fully accessible suites, it has been widely used for coupled Building Energy/Computational Fluid Dynamics (BES-CFD) simulations for the quantitative analysis of building energy performance, taking into account the external microclimate conditions, thus accounting better for local environmental effects in the vicinity of the buildings [55–57]. Due to its modular nature, it requires advanced knowledge of building physics as well as high computer skills, especially in case of complex physical systems such as those focusing particularly on indoor–outdoor interactions.

The DesignBuilder software [58] confronts the aforementioned barrier as it essentially represents a user-friendly version (in fact, with elegant graphical interface), including additional modules such as that of CFD computations for both indoor and outdoor airflow simulations. DesignBuilder software stands for a general purpose simulation engine allowing for energy analysis and automatic optimization for various building systems (HVAC, lighting, DHW), RES technologies, and construction materials, calculating additional key performance indicators such as thermal comfort (PMV, PPD), carbon and GHG emissions, and financial analysis. Thus, it serves for holistic decision-making strategies. In the framework of the IMPULSE project (Interreg MED 2014–2021), it has been used to prioritize retrofitting measures towards the gradual energy-upgrading plan for public buildings (in accordance with the EU directive 2012/27/EU) in the Municipality of Heraklion, Greece [59]. Among many applications for both practical and research purposes, it has been used to demonstrate proof of concept regarding energy-upgrading measures, for example, for reflective (cool) materials' applications [60,61]. Specifically, for PCM applications it has become evident that EnergyPlus contains numerical models much more accurate than those of other popular BES tools, such as TRNSYS [62]. The tool has been also used with success to prescribe retrofitting strategies, focused on the building envelope, for higher education buildings in Egypt [27], concluding with useful suggestions for design codes ensuring balance between thermal comfort and energy efficiency.

eQUEST

eQUEST [63] is a user-friendly building energy simulation tool consisting of a building creation wizard, an energy systems' wizard, and a graphical interface module. It incorporates an enhanced DOE-2 simulation program, which performs an hourly based energy simulation based on properties of opaque and glazing construction elements, occupancy patterns, loads, and ventilation. The simulation module also accounts for the performance of conditioning systems, such as fans and chillers, boilers, and other energy-consuming devices. The eQUEST foresees utilities for parametric analysis of alternative designs and viewing of immediate, collated results. It foresees energy-cost estimating, daylighting, and lighting system control as well as quickly imposing energy-efficiency measures (by selecting preferred measures from a list).

Azar and Menasa [13] used eQUEST to conduct a sensitivity analysis on the occupancy behavioral parameters of typical office buildings of different sizes and in different climate zones. Sensitivity levels varied with building size and weather conditions, and the highest sensitivity was observed when altering the "heating temperature set-point" parameter in small-size buildings located in dry climatic conditions. Recently, the software was used to review the effects of thermal and optical properties of electrochromic windows (ECWs) on the energy performance of a typical office building configuration in Korea [64]. Kim et al. [65] demonstrated the flexibility in incorporating user-defined solar models as input conditions into the software towards the estimation of typical office building energy performance. In view of the important need for the lowest possible deviation between simulated and actual energy consumption when it comes to Energy Performance Contracts (EPC), the eQUEST has been already used to calibrate energy simulation results using actual electricity bills and further applied to investigate EPC reliability for an actual office building in Taiwan [66]. The software allows detailed techno-economic assessment of novel technologies in buildings, as demonstrated by Seyednezhad and Najafi [67]. They investigated various operating conditions for a Thermoelectric-based cooling and heating system on an office-type building in Melbourne, FL, USA, and determined the cost, as well as potential savings, for each tested operating condition. Wang et al. [68] used the software to develop a strategic approach on the energy efficient analysis of the water-heating-system retrofit by applying a heat pump system in a university dormitory located in a central part of Taiwan.

ESP-r

ESP-r [69] is a general purpose, multi-domain-building thermal, interzone airflow, intrazone air movement, HVAC systems, and electrical power flow-simulation environment. It supports CFD models for analyzing air quality and comfort calculations. By addressing all design and systems' aspects simultaneously, ESP-r permits the investigation of complex relationships among building form, envelope, airflow, systems, and control. It employs a finite volume conservation approach in which a problem is transformed into a system of algebraic transfer equations of dependent variables (energy, mass, momentum, etc.), which are then integrated at successive time steps with respect to climate, occupant, and control system conditions. It comprises a central Project Manager providing navigation through support databases, a simulator, performance assessment tools, and a variety of third party applications for CAD, visualization, and report generation.

Hoseggen et al. [70] applied ESP-r to conclude whether a double-skin façade should be applied to the east façade of an office building in Trodheim, Norway, towards the reduction of heating demand. The paper also demonstrates how a double-skin façade with controllable windows and hatches for natural ventilation can be implemented in the simulation program. Bourgeois et al. [71] studied the occupancy behavioral patterns on building energy consumption using ESP-r. They demonstrated the implementation and integration of a sub-hourly occupancy-based control model that enabled advanced behavioral models. It was shown that building occupants seeking daylighting can lower the primary energy consumption by more than 40% compared to occupants relying on constant artificial lighting. The software (among others) has been employed to develop guidelines for seasonal energy consumption for heating and ventilation based on short periods of heat demand measurements and to determine the optimal duration of the measurement period [72]. Bonetti and Kokogiannakis [73] revealed a fine performance of the software in the framework of exploring exergy potential of seven different building wall types for utilizing nocturnal ventilation as a passive cooling strategy. Eller et al. [74] used the software to explore the potential of a bio-based phase change material (PCM) applied to construction components regarding the impacts on thermal performance under several climates, and determined the associated potential of energy savings.

IDA-ICE

IDA Indoor Climate and Energy (IDA-ICE) [75] software is a whole year detailed and dynamic multi-zone simulation application for the study of indoor climate and energy. The IDA-ICE user interface is designed to ease the development and simulation of both simple and advanced cases, in a 3D environment, in combination with comprehensive tables, providing the optimal feedback. A simple procedure for calculating and reporting thermal loads and energy demand, together with a built-in version handling system, facilitates comparisons among different systems and results.

IDA physical systems are described using symbolic equations, in either Neutral Model Format (NMF) or Modelica. IDA-ICE offers separated but integrated user interfaces to different user categories, e.g., wizard interfaces for developing the building model, standard interface serving for model setup by means of concepts and objects (such as zones, radiators, and windows), interfaces for advanced users to import, browse, and edit the mathematical formulations, etc.

Salvalai [76] used IDA-ICE as a building energy simulation platform within which a water-to-water heat pump model was implemented. Results obtained were in good agreement with experimental data. Hesaraki and Holmberg [77] also used IDA ICE to investigate the impact of low-energy heating systems in newly built semi-detached dwellings in Stockholm, in relation to the Swedish building regulations. They demonstrated that the installation of heating systems in combination with under-floor and ventilation radiators not only met energy requirements of regulations but also provided thermal comfort. Numerical results were validated with measured data. Rabani et al. [78] used the software to develop a fully integrated BES optimization CFD daylight simulation applied for a generic office building located in Oslo. The proposed model successfully optimized building envelope properties, fenestration parameters, and HVAC systems' set points towards minimization of building energy consumption and acceptable thermal and visual comfort conditions. As far as its accuracy is concerned, very good agreement with internal air temperature has been documented in comparison with measurements obtained at controlled free-floating conditions regarding PCM performance [62]. Recently, IDA-ICE was used for the energy-renovation study of two Danish heritage/historical buildings [79]. Two renovation cases were studied through the available measurement and calculation results before and after renovations and significant energy-saving amounts were demonstrated without compromising the cultural values of buildings.

IESVE

IES Virtual Environment (IESVE) IESVE [80] is an in-depth suite of building performance analysis tools. It allows the design and operation of energy efficient buildings. Whether working on a new building or existing building renovation project, IESVE offers the ability to test different options, identify the optimal passive solutions, compare low-emission and renewable-energy technologies, and formulate conclusions on building energy indicators. It includes numerous utilities providing sustainable analysis compatible with the needs of different design team members and design stages. The main modules included in this software are the following:

- Model, IT geometry creation and editing

- ApacheCalc, loads' analysis
- ApacheSim, thermal
- MacroFlo, natural ventilation
- Apache HVAC, component-based HVAC
- SunCast, shading visualization and analysis
- MicroFlo, 3D CFD
- FlucsPro/Radiance, Lighting design
- DEFT, model optimization
- LifeCycle, life cycle energy and cost analysis
- Simulex, building evacuation

Murray et al. [81] applied IESVE to plan a retrofitting project of a case study building located at Cork University College, for which both modelling and actual interventions were applied. This approach allowed the comparison between simulated and measured data and a good agreement between them was concluded. Ouedraogo et al. [82] used IESVE to investigate the impact of climate change on future trends of electricity demand for air conditioning in public buildings within the period 2010–2080. Their study highlights the fact that the predicted mean temperature using a specific climate-change data scenario will increase by about 2 °C by 2050, yielding to a significant increase in air-conditioning energy consumption for case-study buildings in the Burkina Faso built environment. For this specific region, they concluded that shading devices could reduce the cooling load by 40%; thus, they could play an important role in climate-change resilience strategies for buildings. Recently, the tool was used to investigate the energy-saving potential obtained by the application of bio-based wall construction in rural residential buildings in Northeast China [83]. Interestingly, it was found that reductions of 45.82–201.07 kWh/m^2/year in heating energy demand and more than 40% in coal consumption are possible through the application of bio-based wall constructions.

SUNREL

SUNREL [84] developed by the National Renewable Energy Laboratory (NREL) is an hourly based building energy simulation software oriented to the design of small, energy-efficient buildings where the loads are governed by the dynamic interactions among the building envelope, environment, and occupants. It has a simplified multi-zonal airflow algorithm that can be used to calculate infiltration and natural ventilation. Users can enter the optical interactions of windows with identical layers of clear or tinted glass and no coatings on the layers. Thermal properties are modelled with a fixed U-value and fixed interface coefficients. SUNREL is particularly appropriate for passive solar buildings and incorporates specialized algorithms that treat the physical effects of Trombe walls, glazing, controllable window shading, active-charge/passive-discharge thermal storage, and natural ventilation. The building is represented by a thermal network model solved with forward finite differencing, among other techniques. Additionally, a simple graphical interface allows users to easily provide input and preview the output. Elzafraney et al. [85] used SUNREL to demonstrate the benefit of enhanced concretes containing coarse aggregates of recycled plastics. The tool was used to simulate the thermal and building energy performance of two building configurations with and without polymer aggregates, and it was found that the former one led to a substantial reduction of heating and cooling loads while ensuring thermal comfort.

TAS

TAS [86] simulates the dynamic thermal performance of buildings and their systems. Its prevailing module is the TAS Building Designer, which undertakes dynamic simulation with integrated convective airflow. It has a 3D graphics-based geometry input that includes a CAD link. TAS incorporates an HVAC systems/controls' simulator, which can be directly interconnected with the building simulator. The TAS Ambiens module incorporates a 2D CFD package, which produces space microclimate at a cross-section level. TAS combines dynamic thermal simulation with natural ventilation calculations, which include advanced control functions on aperture opening as well as the ability to simulate mixed mode systems. The software has heating and cooling plant sizing procedures, which include optimum start.

Wong at al. [87] used TAS to investigate the impact of vertical greenery systems on the temperature and energy consumption of buildings. The results revealed a linear correlation between shading coefficient and leaf area, where a lower shading factor leads to a greater thermal insulation. As far as the use of TAS for understanding the influence of different architectural design strategies in energy demand is concerned, Pino et al. [88] demonstrated its efficient use for such purposes, especially for office buildings. Recently, it was employed to compare traditional and contemporary mosque buildings by means of dry bulb air temperature and various thermal loads in Oman [89]. As shown by Salem et al. [90], the software can adequately predict the impacts of both combined heating power (CHP) and combined cooling–heating power (CCHP) in a real-case scenario of a hotel building in the UK, regarding energy efficiency, energy cost, payback, and carbon emissions. In the same study, additional simulations under climate-change projections revealed that a CCHP system outperforms a CHP system. Amirkhani et al. [91] investigated the impact of a Low-emissivity window film on the overall energy consumption of an existing hotel building in the UK using the software, and estimated that by applying the suggested low-e film, savings in heating, cooling, and total energy consumptions may reach 3%, 20%, and 2.7%, respectively.

TRNSYS

TRNSYS (Transient system simulation program) [92] is a program with a modular structure that implements a component-based approach. Its components extend from simulating a single pump or pipe to a multi-zonal building model. Its components assemble in a fully integrated visual interface called TRNSYS Simulation Studio, while building input data are entered through a dedicated visual interface (TRNBuild). The simulation engine then solves the algebraic system of the discretized differential conservation equations consisting of the energy system. HVAC system components are solved simultaneously with heat conservation through the building envelope and the air network at each time step. In addition, the TRNSYS library includes components for solar thermal and photovoltaic systems, low-energy buildings, HVAC systems, renewable energy systems, cogeneration, fuel cells, etc. The modular nature of TRNSYS facilitates the compilation and integration of new mathematical models to the program regarding, for example, walls' boundary conditions, systems' properties, and operation schedules. It presents high flexibility and compatibility with other software (e.g., Matlab/Simulink, Excel/VBA) for co-simulation, optimization, and optimal control purposes. TRNSYS can generate redistributable applications that allow less-skilled users to run simulations and parametric studies. It has been widely used and tested for whole building energy simulations for more than 20 years. It exhibits perhaps the highest sophistication regarding modelling of solar radiation passing through windows since it considers variable optical properties with incidence angle and in terms of treatment of direct and diffuse solar radiation distribution into a zone [62].

Ibanez et al. [93] used TRNSYS to simulate the impact of Phase Change Materials (PCM) integrated into walls, ceiling, and floor of an experimental room built with concrete panels with PCM, on the whole building energy balance. An acceptable agreement between the simulated and experimental results was obtained. Beausoleil-Morrison et al. [94] developed an ESP-r/TRNSYS co-simulator, which was applied for evaluating the performance of a solar-thermal system in a low-energy building. The suggested co-simulation environment proved to be an effective tool for designing solar buildings, particularly when architectural, energy conversion, and storage systems are all integrated. The software has been also used to present and compare a series of passive and active measures for energy upgrading of various building types (educational, museum, sports facility, Municipal Office building, and a residential, detached building) in a typical Mediterranean climate [95]. In such climatic conditions, Pérez-Andreu et al. [96] applied TRNSYS to study the benefits of passive construction measures in a typical Mediterranean dwelling, in terms of energy consumption and thermal comfort, taking into account site wind and occupants' behavioral conditions. Validation and model-calibration processes revealed excellent agreement between simulated and actual (measured) data referring to indoor monthly averaged air temperature and relative humidity.

2.2. Urban Microclimate Modelling

The global trend towards urbanization in parallel with climate-change implications justifies the growing interest in the study of combating adverse effects of extreme microclimate conditions on urban activities relating to building energy consumption and health. The Urban Heat Island (UHI) effect presented evermore high intensities during the last 10 years, which significantly impacted pedestrians' thermal comfort and perception of air quality as well as energy demand of buildings in dense urban environments. Landsberg [97] states that the UHI phenomenon is the most obvious climatic manifestation of urbanization. Indeed, numerous studies in the scientific literature have highlighted the adverse effects of urban extreme microclimates, especially UHI, on building energy demand and consumption as well as thermal comfort and well-being [98–100]. In accordance with the scientific evidence, the European Commission indicated the requirement to account for local climate, especially in developing strategies to meet the Nearly-Zero Energy Building (NZEB) goal (refer, for example, to its 2012 release "Evaluating and Modelling Near-Zero Energy Buildings: are we ready for 2018?" [101]). Considering the latest research findings as well as trends in energy policies that necessitate building energy design with accurately predicted performance indicators, building simulation techniques, taking into account the external microclimate effects, should no longer be considered as "for research purposes only" and move to the practitioner level at the early design stages. Accepting the suggestion that in modern case studies indoor and outdoor physical effects are inseparable, this paper extends the review to include basic computational methods and tools for quantifying urban microclimate effects. The present section reviews the methods and popular computational tools that can be used to quantify the physical variables comprising urban microclimate (mainly by means of its UHI manifestation) in open spaces, such as wind speed, temperature, and relative humidity, including thermal comfort indicators of pedestrians.

The Urban Heat Island effect is related to higher urban temperatures in city centres compared to the surrounding rural or suburban areas [102]. This situation emanates from anthropogenic heat sources, e.g., vehicles, power plants, air-condition units, etc., as well as by other heat stresses produced by the use of ground or building materials of poor thermal behaviour and the lack of heat sinks (e.g., water surfaces) and of vegetation [103]. Fundamental causes of the UHI were indicated by Oke [104] and their relative importance was further validated in numerous follow-up studies:

- Trapping of short- and long-wave radiation in areas between buildings
- Reduced long-wave radiative heat loss due to low sky-view factors
- Increased sensible-heat storage in the construction materials
- Anthropogenic heat released mainly from fuel combustion (domestic heating, vehicles, etc.)
- Reduced evapotranspiration due to limited plantation, which means that energy is converted into sensible rather than latent heat
- Reduced heat displacement due to reduced wind speed

Studies of the UHI are usually focused on the so-called heat island intensity, which is the maximum temperature difference between the city and the surrounding rural or suburban area. The intensity is mainly determined by the heat conservation of the region and is, therefore, subject to diurnal variations and short-term weather conditions [105,106]. There are two major simulation methods often used to assess UHI [107]:

- Energy balance models
- Computational Fluid Dynamics (CFD) models

In the following subsections, the background of the simulation methods and a comparative analysis between them is discussed, while the most popular computational tools of each method are briefly described in terms of their strengths and weaknesses.

2.2.1. Energy Balance Models

The energy-balance (or urban energy-budget) concept was first suggested by Oke [104]. This method adopts the principle of energy conservation for a given control volume, and manipulates the wind-induced phenomena, i.e., turbulence and velocity fields, as simple heat fluxes. These fluxes are generally defined by analytical or empirical equations. In the last two decades the energy-budget concept has been enhanced to the so-called Urban Canopy Model (UCM), which is derived from the energy balance equation for a control volume containing two adjacent buildings. The model considers the energy exchanges between solid surfaces of the domain and the urban canopy and predicts the ambient temperature and solid-surfaces' temperature of the urban fabric components. However, the airflow is decoupled from the temperature field, being treated as a separate input into the control volume. For this purpose, the logarithmic or the power law [16] is widely used in order to represent airflow in the domain of interest. In the UCM approach, all surfaces and control volumes are interconnected by means of an electrical analogue. The energy conservation equation [107] is then applied to each node, thus being discretized to an algebraic system comprised of matrices of temperature and humidity coefficients. An iterative solution of the system provides the temperature and relative humidity distributions throughout the domain. One-layer [108] and multiple-layer [109] schemes depend on the nodes' number on the building walls, while such models can be also developed into one to three dimensions. This approach is fast, in general, as it treats building canopies with a low number of nodes. It provides acceptable predictions but mainly in large-scale cityscapes.

The omission of an air velocity pattern represents the major drawback of UCM models. Indeed, the resolution of the air velocity field facilitates the study of special airflow effects, e.g., eddy circulation and dissipation, wake regions, and turbulence intensity, and of the atmospheric phenomena (e.g., precipitation and stratification), towards the determination of heat fluxes' components. The consequent approximation of heat fluxes using empirical correlations in UCM models rarely captivate the interaction between velocity and temperature fields. Provided that data for three-dimensional geometries of building canopies and urban structures correspond to high computer loads, the urban complex is often represented by homogeneous columns as building boxes. Cityscape geometry is also approximated with coarse grids on ground, roofs, and walls, hence, weakening the reliability of the energy-conservation solution, especially when the focus is on pedestrians' thermal comfort.

2.2.2. Computational Fluid Dynamics

Unlike the energy-balance models, CFD simultaneously solves all the governing equations of airflow within the urban fabric, i.e., conservation equations of mass, momentum, thermal energy, chemical species, and turbulence parameters for single- and multi-phase flow phenomena. As a result, CFD can produce more accurate information about the UHI effect within and above building canopies compared to the energy budget models. Consideration of complex details in addition to complicated atmospheric interactions of the cityscape is, nonetheless, both a computational and theoretical challenge. The former refers to the high number of the computational nodes to simulate the airflow, while the latter is related to the unmatched temporal and spatial resolution of the physical mechanisms occurring within the cityscape. For example, turbulence length scales within and above the canopy differ significantly; thus, they cannot be modelled in the same scale. This suggests the division of the CFD simulation into different scales for UHI studies [107]: Meso-scale and Micro-scale (within the urban canopy).

Meso-scale models present horizontal resolutions ranging from one to several hundreds of kilometres. Vertically, they vary with the depth of the so-called Planetary Boundary Layer (PBL) (the layer between the earth surface and geostrophic wind), i.e., in between 200 m and 2 km [107]. In such models, large-scale interactions under the PBL are analysed, involving treatment of the atmospheric stratification and surface layer. In this approach, the atmospheric stratification is resolved by adopting either the hydrostatic or the non-hydrostatic assumption in the Navier–Stokes equations. The hydrostatic assumption refers to a simplified motion equation in the vertical axis in terms of a balanced correlation between the buoyancy and the pressure term. On the other hand, the non-hydrostatic assumption refers to the full Navier–Stokes equation in the vertical axis. Meteorological schemes mostly use Monin–Obukhov or other similarity schemes to model the surface sublayer [110], and building canopies are simulated by means of aerodynamic roughness. This means meso-scale models manipulate the complex phenomena within the urban canopy only by a roughness value. Consequently, information about variations of dependent variables within the canopy layer is extremely limited. However, this simplification facilitates the understanding of physical phenomena (for instance, surface drag, shear stress) at least within the urban surface layer but above the canopy layer. The precision of meso-scale modelling is strongly dependent on the available land-use parameters. Detailed information of solid surfaces at micro-scale level (e.g., thermo-physical properties, geometry, optical properties) is rarely available for the entire urban area of interest. Even in the contrary case, applying these details to a meso-scale model increases the required computational resources. Since the spatial resolution is in the order of a few kilometres, it is also necessary to assume a meso-scale zone as a homogeneous area and estimate the surface properties with bulk values, e.g., albedo, emissivity, and roughness.

On the other hand, micro-scale CFD resolves the conservation equation inside the canopy layer. In the meso-scale layer, the horizontal spatial quantities are usually accounted for as homogeneous values, while the quantities within the actual geometry are simulated in detail, taking into account surface physical interactions in the micro-scale layer. These interactions are generally represented by the Monin–Obukhov similarity theory to represent the PBL in meso-scale layers. Obviously, it is not realistic to apply micro-scale modelling for an entire city, with all geometric details, due to the high computational cost. Therefore, the common approach is to limit the simulation into a small domain in the magnitude of some blocks of buildings (few hundreds of meters), as done, for example, by Stavrakakis et al. [103]. On the other hand, the treatment of the PBL in a micro-scale model is not as comprehensive as in the meso-scale model, which means that micro-scale modelling does not account for atmospheric interactions such as vertical mixing or Coriolis effect. Observational schemes [107] can significantly improve the aforementioned limitations. However, providing boundary conditions in the micro-scale model is even more complicated than in the meso-scale model. In micro-scale modelling more measurements are necessary due to high fluctuations of airflow quantities near surfaces. Although the assumptions of a homogeneous boundary layer [111] and corresponding boundary conditions [103] may be adopted, these approaches are physically weak considering the stochastic nature of airflow velocity and the variety of height and geometry of buildings. Similar to the meso-scale modelling, the treatment of turbulent closure and radiation significantly affects the precision of the micro-scale model prediction.

As far as turbulence modelling is concerned, many theories have been proposed, such as the Direct Navier–Stokes (DNS) simulation, Large Eddy Simulation (LES), and Reynolds Averaged Navier–Stokes (RANS) [16]. Although the precision can be improved using LES and DNS, the application of these schemes is very demanding in terms of CPU resources. On the other hand, RANS models (such as the Standard k-ε model or its modifications [112]) are widely used for turbulence modelling in UHI studies as their requirements for computational resources are moderate in comparison to LES and DNS. However, it should be mentioned that RANS modelling provides limited representation of physical phenomena such as the so-called "horse-shoe vortex" around buildings [113].

This implies that accurate modelling of turbulence phenomena is still one of the weakest points of RANS modelling. Additionally, the size scale of the case considered substantially affects RANS modelling as it is related to the turbulence-length scale i.e., the size of the large energy-containing eddies in the turbulent layer.

2.2.3. Collation of Urban Microclimate Modelling Methods

Table 3 contrasts the capabilities of UHI study methods by means of the governing equations, limitations, domain-size restrictions, resolution in time and space, and computational cost. It becomes obvious that the meso-scale method is practical when urban surface details are less important, i.e., heat transfer at the urban scale, pollutant dispersion, and thermal comfort are not adequately assessed by this method. On the contrary, for cases that such information is required, meaning that the physical phenomena within the urban canopy are of interest, micro-scale CFD or UCM methods are more useful. It should be pointed out, however, that when CFD models are applied in near real-time and -size manner, small time steps and detailed geometries may be prohibitive due to extremely high computational costs for simulations of whole cityscapes. This implies that major assumptions should often be adopted in order to produce realistic results, at least for practical engineering purposes. The most common assumptions followed when micro-scale CFD models were applied for UHI assessments are:

- Restricted computational domain near the area of interest, i.e., the rest of the actual city is represented by roughness equations only (without detailing building geometries).
- Geometry simplifications in order to avoid high spatial resolution.
- Assume homogeneous boundary layer, ignoring the interactions with PBL (200 m height and above).
- Application of unstructured grids (tetrahedral or polyhedral) in order to avoid dense grid propagation along the Cartesian axis of the domain.

Table 3. Collation of major UHI simulation methods.

Key Feature	UCM	CFD	
		Meso-Scale	Micro-Scale
Governing equations	-Energy balance equation -Empirical velocity equation within the urban canopy -Heat conduction equation on solid surfaces	-Navier–Stokes equations including the Coriolis term with hydrostatic or non-hydrostatic assumption -Monin–Obukhov for ground surface effects -Heat conduction equation for soil	-Momentum equations (Navier–Stokes) -Wall functions representing laminar-turbulent stratification near solid surfaces. -Heat transfer equation near surfaces -Chemical-species conservation equations -Turbulence model
Major limitations	-Decoupled velocity field from hygrothermal effects -Representation of cityscape using arrays of similar buildings -Low resolution of model geometry -Assumes steady-state conditions mainly -Empirical assumptions for convective latent and sensible heat	-Treatment of the urban canopy layer as roughness -Difficult to provide Land-use database (user-defined functions are required) -Turbulent effects not captured	-PBL effects are ignored -Difficult to create database for canopy details (user-defined functions are commonly required) -Precise boundary conditions are required, often produced from external, sophisticated physical models -Homogeneous inflow boundary layer, especially when RANS modelling for turbulence is applied
Maximum size of cityscape domain	Whole City	Whole City	District level
Spatial resolution for grid meshing	1–10 m	1–10 km	0.2–10 m
Temporal resolution (time step)	Hour	Minute	Second
Computational load	Medium	Relatively high	Very high (depending on the turbulence model applied and grid size)

Although these assumptions may cause deviations of predictions in comparison with measurements (if available), it has been extensively demonstrated in simulated, measured data comparative studies in real-scale cases that the produced deviations (even when applying the RANS model) are considered acceptable at least for practical engineering purposes [114–116]. It has been pointed out, however, that it is still a research challenge to bridge the gap between micro-scale and meso-scale modelling techniques [117] towards perhaps integrated models utilizing the respective benefits of high-resolution analysis and large urban scales, in order to achieve more accurate predictions at simulation environments.

2.2.4. Urban Microclimate Simulation Tools

This section summarizes research-based, commercial, or freely available simulation tools of each method discussed above. It is true that today's scientific literature contains a plethora of field modelling tools, which are mainly products of mathematical interpretation of the physical phenomena encountered in the urban environment. Since this paper focuses on the physical analysis within the urban canopy layer, meso-scale models are beyond the scope of this review, and the present section describes energy balance models (UCM mainly) and micro-scale CFD tools (excluding the FEM-based ones, since they are not so commonly used in urban microclimate analyses). Respective common modelling developments and tools used worldwide (but there are many more) are the following [107,118]:

- Energy balance models
  - UHSM
  - TEB
  - SOLWEIG
  - Rayman
- CFD tools
  - ENVI-met
  - ANSYS-Fluent
  - ANSYS-CFX
  - Phoenics

A summary of strengths and weaknesses of simulation tools is provided in Table 4.

Table 4. Strengths, weaknesses, and special features of computational urban microclimate simulation models and tools.

Model or Tool/Method	Strengths	Weaknesses	Special Modelling Features		Most Common Applications	CPU Load	Availability
			Evaporation and Evapotranspiration	Radiation			
UHSM/UCM	>Solution of heat transfer equations at representative heights (ground, building, atmosphere) >Anthropogenic heat >Spatial discretization of equations >Distribution of temperature and relative humidity >Hourly temperature results	>No thermal comfort indicators are incorporated >Very simplified geometry >Wind speed decoupled from heat transfer equations >Simple roughness equation for wind speed >Turbulence is dealt with simple drag equation >High urban physics expertise and computer skills are required >Lack of documentation and tutorials	>Since it is a customized model, User-defined models only are assumed	>Short- and long-wave radiation models are included	>Assessment of UHI intensity and implications by means of physical parameters only (temperature, relative humidity, incident radiation)	Low	Research-based; The user must reproduce the model

Table 4. *Cont.*

Model or Tool/Method	Strengths	Weaknesses	Special Modelling Features		Most Common Applications	CPU Load	Availability
			Evaporation and Evapotranspiration	Radiation			
TEB/UCM	>Full 3D modelling >Solution of heat budget at three surfaces (ground, walls, and roofs) >Turbulent fluxes are simulated in the PBL/Canopy layer interface >Roads of any orientation may be placed >Conduction fluxes through solid surfaces >Monin–Obukhov conditions for the surface layer >Human comfort index included >A comprehensive Building Energy Model (BEM) is included in tool's latest version	>Relatively simplified geometry >Wind speed decoupled from heat transfer equations >High urban physics' expertise and computer skills are required >Scattered documentation and examples (some information included in SURFEX tool documentation)	>Water interception and evaporation as well as snow mantel evolution models are included >User-defined evapotranspiration models for plantations are required	>Short- and long-wave radiation models are included	>Simulation of urban fluxes' impacts on the atmosphere >Investigation of UHI intensity >Co-simulations with future climate forecast models towards the assessment of future urban canopy microclimates >Calculation of building thermal loads, taking into account external microclimate	Medium	Free (open source available in http://redmine.cnrm-game-meteo.fr/projects/teb)
SOLWEIG/UCM	>Modelling of 3D radiation fluxes >Relatively accurate geometry >Solves for mean radiant temperature (thermal comfort) > Interconnected to QGIS open platform > Well-structured documentation and guides >Ability for the user to integrate own models/codes, e.g., boundary conditions	>Velocity pattern decoupled from heat transfer >Turbulence is not modelled >Plantation evapotranspiration is ignored >Relatively high knowledge of urban/building physics is required	>By-default models for Evaporation >Evapotranspiration is not included	>Short- and long-wave radiation models are included >Direct calculation of the mean radiant temperature	>Calculation of mean radiant temperature >Estimate radiant effects of UHI	Medium	Free (Open source)
Rayman/UCM	>Modelling of 3D radiation fluxes >Relatively accurate geometry >Solves for radiant heat fluxes from solid surfaces and from human body >Solves for thermal comfort indicators (PET, SET*, and PMV) > User friendly > Average expertise in urban physics is required	> Velocity pattern decoupled from heat transfer >Turbulence is not modeled >Limited documentation and tutorials	>Evaporation is included >Evapotranspira-tion is ignored	Short- and long-wave radiation models are included	>Calculation of mean radiant temperature >Estimate radiant effects of UHI	Medium	Free
ENVI-met/microscale CFD	>Urban microclimate-dedicated tool >Full 3D simulation >Compilation of prevailing urban physics phenomena >Most reliable thermal comfort models and indices are included >Average expertise in urban physics is required for simple case studies >Compatibility with BES software >Widely used and validated in a plethora of case studies >Excellent documentation and user guides	>Restricted to Cartesian geometries >Structured grids only >Limited turbulence modelling options >Very high CPU load	>Models for evaporation and evapotranspiration of trees are included	>Short- and long-wave radiation models are included >Mean radiant temperature calculation code is included	>Simulation of UHI > Calculation of thermal comfort at pedestrian level >UHI mitigation strategies >Building energy performance when coupled with BES tools	Very high (depend-ing on grid size, time step, physical models, and available CPU resourses)	Commercial (Only its Lite version is still free, but only for limited domain size and reduced out-put/analysis options)

Table 4. *Cont.*

Model or Tool/Method	Strengths	Weaknesses	Special Modelling Features		Most Common Applications	CPU Load	Availability
			Evaporation and Evapotranspiration	Radiation			
ANSYS-Fluent/microscale CFD	>General purpose CFD platform >Many options of turbulence models and radiation models >Flexibility and easiness of grid generation >Parallel-processing supported >User friendly >Extensive documentation with tutorials >Applies the so-called multigrid solver, which means faster convergence compared to other CFD software	>Since it is a general CFD platform, the user has to develop and incorporate user-defined models in terms of boundary conditions; thus, it requires high expertise in urban physics >The high purchase cost limits its use by practitioners >High CPU load >Thermal comfort indicators not included. User-defined functions are required. >No database of vegetation properties	>User-defined models for evaporation and evapotranspiration should be prepared and compiled	>Short- and long-wave radiation models are included >User-defined function for mean radiant temperature is required	>Simulation of UHI >UHI mitigation strategies >Building energy performance when coupled with BES tools	High (depending on grid size, time step, physical models, and available CPU resourses)	Commercial
ANSYS-CFX/microscale CFD	>General-purpose CFD platform >Many options of turbulence models and radiation models >Flexibility and easiness of grid generation >Parallel processing supported >Extensive documentation with tutorials >Particularly useful for wind-comfort assessments	>Since it is a general CFD platform, the user has to develop and incorporate user-defined models in terms of boundary conditions; thus, it requires high expertise in urban physics >Not so extensive verification/validation exists in literature specifically for urban microclimate assessments >High CPU load >Thermal comfort indicators not included. User-defined functions are required. >No database of vegetation properties >Less grid-meshing flexibility compared to Ansys Fluent	>User-defined models for evaporation and evapotranspiration should be prepared and compiled	>Short- and long-wave radiation models are included >User-defined function for mean radiant temperature is required	>Simulation of UHI >UHI mitigation strategies	High (depending on grid size, time step, physical models, and available CPU resourses)	Commercial
Phoenics/microscale CFD	>General purpose CFD platform >Many options of turbulence models and radiation models >Parallel processing supported >Extensive documentation with tutorials >Includes the Foliage module to account for evaporation phenomena from vegetation	>Since it is a general CFD platform, the user has to develop and incorporate user-defined models, thus it requires high expertise in urban physics and computer skills >Thermal comfort indicators not included. User-defined functions are required >Limited flexibility in grid generation (e.g., tetrahedral meshing is not included) >High CPU load	>The Foliage module simulates evaporation from vegetation	>Short- and long-wave radiation models are included	>Simulation of UHI >UHI mitigation strategies	Very high (depending on grid size, time step, physical models, and available CPU resourses)	Commercial

UHSM

The Urban Heat Storage Model (UHSM) enhances the Oke's urban energy balance equation and it was developed by Bonacquisti et al. (2006) [119]. The model is founded on four-equation energy balance at the ground level and building level, namely:

- Energy balance equation at building surfaces
- Energy balance equation at the ground level
- Sensible heat balance equation
- Latent heat balance equation

It involves three simulation sections, i.e., atmospheric layer (maximum height above building heights) and building and ground levels. The aforementioned equations formulate a system of linearized algebraic equations to relate four major unknown variables, i.e., building surface temperature, ground surface temperature, air temperature, and relative humidity. Ground and building aerodynamic roughness are evaluated as function of drag coefficients of soil and of wind speed in the canopy layer. Wind deceleration within the urban canopy was evaluated as a function of buildings' density, drag coefficients, and wind speeds within the atmospheric layer section. Anthropogenic heat is also taken into account, using expressions representing heat releases by buildings (produced mainly by electricity and fuel consumption), by transportation (vehicles exhausts), and by human metabolic rates. The equations are spatially discretized in the domain (sub-domains) and based on the heat storage within the urban canopy an iterative solution procedure is followed towards the calculation of the unknown variables in each sub-domain.

The main data used as inputs in the model are the thermo-physical and optical properties of urban surfaces as well as atmospheric parameters. The main output of the tool is the spatial distribution (in hourly basis) of ground and building surface temperature, air temperature and relative humidity, the mean surface temperature, and mean temperature at the pedestrian level height. The tool was applied by Bonacquisti et al. [119] in the case of Rome, Italy, and air temperature was used as a validation parameter, i.e., it was compared with in situ temperature observations. Using this tool, the same authors concluded UHI intensities (temperature increase compared to rural areas) of 2 °C and 5 °C, for winter and summer, respectively.

TEB

The Town Energy Budget (TEB) tool [120] was developed in the Centre National de Recherches Météorologiques, Toulouse, France, and it was presented by Masson [121]. The TEB tool is canyon-based but generalized to capture large horizontal scales. Due to the complex shape of the cityscape, the urban energy budget is divided into three parts, i.e., for roofs, walls, and roads. The model simulates turbulent fluxes into the atmosphere at the surface of the meso-scale atmospheric model covered by buildings, roads, or any other artificial material. Heat fluxes are computed for each land type by the appropriate scheme, and then they are averaged in the atmospheric model grid mesh, with respect to the proportion occupied by each type. The fluxes calculated are Latent and sensible heat fluxes, upward radiative fluxes, and component momentum fluxes.

Cityscape geometry is normally represented by buildings that have the same dimensions. Buildings are located along identical roads, the lengths of which are considered far greater than their widths. Finally, any road orientation is possible, all existing with the same probability, and this hypothesis allows the computation of averaged imposition parameters for road and wall surfaces. In order to treat the conduction fluxes through solid surfaces, TEB discretizes each surface type into several layers. The equations applied to represent temperature evolution in these layers are based on energy budget considerations and several prognostic equations for the surface layers of roofs, walls, and roads emerge. The set of equations describing heat transfer mechanisms and turbulent fluxes is similar to that of the UHSM tool. The main difference is that the surface layer is represented by the Monin–Obukhov equations. Its latest version includes a Building Energy Model

(BEM) suite mainly for thermal loads' predictions. Ren et al. [122] integrated TEB into a climate change air quality model and demonstrated improvement of predictions of NOx, PM2.5, and ground-level O_3 in four major north American Cities. The tool was used by Reder et al. [123] towards the suggestion of climate resilience strategies and measures by means of UHI mitigation. As documented by Pigeon et al. [124], the software, enhanced with the BEM suite, allows reliable predictions of buildings' heating and cooling demands in comparison with the more detailed model, EnergyPlus, for various building types. Lately, and in view of recent trends referring to assessments of future climate change impacts on the development of energy policies, TEB has gained interest in the prediction of impacts of climate change scenarios on UHI and urban energy performance [125–127].

SOLWEIG

SOLWEIG is a radiation-dedicated module of the Urban Multi-scale Environmental Predictor (UMEP) [128], which was developed by the Earth Sciences Department in Gothenburg University, and it is extensively described by Lindberg et al. [129]. UMEP is a climate service plugin for QGIS. It is an open-source tool and can be used for various applications related to urban metabolism processes such as thermal energy balance, energy consumption, etc. UMEP consists of a coupled modelling system, which combines "state-of-the-art" 1D and 2D models related to the processes essential for scale-independent urban climate estimations. SOLWEIG, together with the energy balance model SUEWS available in the UMEP QGIS plugin, simulates spatial gradients of 3D radiation fluxes and the mean radiant temperature (T_{mrt}); therefore, it is particularly useful for the assessment of thermal comfort indicators in the cityscape. Mean radiant temperature is derived by modelling short- and long wave radiation fluxes in six directions, i.e., upward, downward, and from the four cardinal points (horizon) taking into account angular factors. The model requires a relatively limited number of inputs, such as irradiance components (direct, diffuse radiation), air temperature, relative humidity, urban geometry, and geographical coordinates. The output refers mainly to radiation components' fluxes and T_{mrt} distribution.

The framework theory, based on which the mean radiant temperature is calculated, is that one introduced by Hoppe [130] in which radiation fluxes in all six directions are considered. As an energy balance model, it presents the general shortcomings of this certain family of models; e.g., it disregards the velocity pattern in the domain of interest as well as its fluctuations (turbulence). Another shortcoming is that SOLWEIG does not account for evapotranspiration from vegetation. Lindberg et al. (2008) [129] demonstrated its usefulness by performing mean radiant temperature simulations in an urban area of Gothenburg and validated numerical results through comparisons with field measurements. Using SOLWEIG, Chen et al. [131] investigated the spatial variation of mean radiant temperature in different urban settings in Shanghai towards the detection of "hot-spots" with the highest thermal discomfort within the cityscape. In terms of its accuracy, it has been proven that SOLWEIG is equally useful with the microscale ENVI-met model referring to the modelling of the radiation field; however, it presents higher discrepancies because of its less comprehensive calculation model of diffuse radiation [132]. Hosseini-Haghighi et al. [133] developed a systematic approach to upgrade the outdoor thermal comfort using ArcGIS CityEngine for 3D city modeling and SOLWEIG as the climate assessment model, in view of the warmest forecasted year, 2047. The suggested workflow revealed the heat-stress areas and facilitated the efficient intervention regarding tree placement as a passive strategy for heat mitigation.

Rayman

The Rayman [134] software was developed in the Meteorological Institute of Albert Ludwigs University of Freiburg. The capabilities of the tool are described by Matzarakis et al. [135]. Similarly to SOLWEIG, it is a variant of energy balance models, and it mainly computes radiant heat conservation between human skin and its environment. It focuses on the calculation of the mean radiant temperature towards the prediction of thermal comfort conditions. The most important inputs required are Geographical coordinates, meteorological data (temperature, relative humidity, and cloud covering), personal parameters (clothing and activity level), Geological morphology, and urban features (buildings, trees). The results obtained by the model include, among others, Distribution of mean radiant temperature, radiation fluxes, and thermal comfort indices (PMV and PET). In contrast to SOLWEIG it computes more thermal comfort indicators and comprises a more user-friendly environment. However, it should be mentioned that Rayman disregards evapotranspiration from vegetation, while it treats trees as simple obstacles to radiation fluxes. Wind-induced effects and turbulence flow are also ignored. In comparison to SOLWEIG, RayMan has a higher calculation sensitivity and faster simulation speed, while it achieves the best accuracy at high solar altitudes on clear summer days [132]. Battisti [136] used both Rayman and ENVI-met tools to study the impact of using cool materials enhanced with more vegetation and permeable surfaces and demonstrated dramatic improvements regarding summer thermal comfort. Using both ENVI-met and Rayman, Peng and Jim [137] verified that green-roof cooling effects are not restricted to rooftops but extend to the ground to improve neighborhood microclimate.

ENVI-Met

ENVI-met [138] is a three-dimensional, non-hydrostatic model for simulating a microclimate, especially within the urban canyon, taking into account the physical interactions among solid surfaces (e.g., ground and building surfaces), vegetation, and air. It is based on the theoretical background of Computational Fluid Dynamics. It applies the FDM discretization scheme, and it makes use of advanced numerical algorithms for solving the airflow-governing equations, i.e., conservation of mass, momentum, thermal energy, chemical–species' concentration, and turbulence parameters, as well as particle dispersion.

The main input of the model includes, among others, the properties of the incoming wind of the urban domain (wind speed, direction, temperature, relative humidity), a simplified geometry of the urban domain (since only structured grids and cartesian geometries are supported), thermo-physical properties of ground and building materials and of vegetation, and personal parameters of pedestrians (such as metabolic rates and clothing insulation) when the BIO-met is employed. The simulator then executes an iterative solution procedure and produces Distribution of temperature, relative humidity, pollutant concentration, turbulence parameters, wind speed, and thermal comfort indicators (e.g., mean radiant temperature and PMV modified for outdoor conditions), at different heights throughout the urban area of interest.

The background of the ENVI-met system includes sub-models solving for the following special physical mechanisms:

- Long- and short-wave radiation fluxes, accounting for shading
- Radiation reflection from building facades, ground materials, and vegetation
- Evapotranspiration and sensible heat fluxes from vegetation
- Evaporation from water surfaces
- Chemical–species' propagation
- Particles' dispersion
- Heat and water transfer within soil mass
- Body/skin–airflow interactions (e.g., heat transfer, wettedness effect) towards the calculation of thermal comfort indicators

ENVI-met is a useful micro-scale model for the prediction of UHI effects within the urban canopy with acceptable accuracy provided that the model settings are correctly defined. In the case of complex geometries, radical simplifications may be required (such as building merging) in order to comply with grid-mesh restrictions. In addition, mesh possibilities are limited to structured grids with large grid cells (typical spatial resolution: 0.5–10 m). Hence, the effect of viscous sublayers (near solid surfaces) may be seriously underestimated. Another drawback is that only the Standard k-ε model is available for turbulence modelling. Due to the large number of computational nodes, it presents normally very high CPU time until full convergence.

Wania et al. [139] used the ENVI-met system to study the influence of different vertical and horizontal densities of street vegetation on particle dispersion. It was demonstrated that vegetation reduces wind speed, which limits a canyon's ventilation and, therefore, leads to an increase in particle concentration. Vegetation was also found to reduce wind speed at crown height and to disrupt the flow field in close vicinity of the canopy. Szucs [140] highlighted that comfortable and healthy public open spaces encourage people to spend more time outdoors, socialize, exercise, and participate in re-creational events. In this framework, Szucs (2013) used ENVI-met to examine whether climatic conditions in Dublin boost long-term outdoor activities during summer and investigated the extent to which urban planning and the resulting urban morphology of the built environment influence the microclimate created by means of the wind profile. It was confirmed that areas of limited long-term outdoor activities are subjected to high wind speeds, often at the windward sections and around corners of buildings. Compared to the UCM tools SOLWEIG and Rayman, it presents a much better accuracy in comparison to actual measured data regarding radiation parameters [132]. Wai et al. [141] developed an integrated methodology including both ENVI-met and the Weather Research and Forecast (WRF) to explore the cooling performance of a water-spraying system in a sub-tropical compact and high-rise cityscape in a future-climate summer (2050) condition. It was indicated that the spraying system may provide cooling of 2–3 °C for ambient air temperature at the pedestrian level, improving significantly the thermal comfort conditions. In general, it has been widely used for urban planning purposes combating microclimate extremes worldwide; for example, in MDPI one can find 69 research articles with the keyword "envi-met" in their abstract. It presents good compatibility with BES tools; for example, its interconnection with EnergyPlus is now a well-established method [55,142] towards assessments of local climate impacts on building energy performance, especially when building-envelope measures are tested (green roofs, cool materials, insulation materials, PCMs, etc.).

ANSYS-Fluent

Ansys Fluent [143] is a FVM-based, general-purpose CFD platform that provides comprehensive modelling for a wide range of incompressible, compressible, laminar, and turbulent fluid flow problems, under steady or transient conditions. In the software, a wide range of mathematical models for transport phenomena (e.g., heat transfer, momentum, chemical reactions, etc.) is combined with the ability to model complex geometries with high flexibility in grid meshing. Among a wide variety of applications, the platform has been widely used for assessing microclimate conditions in open spaces. In such cases, Fluent has been frequently used to simulate turbulent airflow within urban canopies. To "relax" modelling complexity of fluid flow and related transport phenomena in porous media (i.e., vegetation), various useful features are provided such as porosity functions and others.

Fluent solves for the majority of physical phenomena encountered in urban systems. In addition to those simulated by ENVI-met, it includes:

- A wide variety of turbulence models (RANS, DNS, and LES) providing the user the opportunity to choose (according to the available computational resources and expertise) among different turbulence models aiming to capture the desirable spectrum of turbulent-length scales.
- A wide variety of two-phase flow models to capture particles dispersion.
- A wide variety of radiation models to simulate short- and long-wave radiation.
- A pluralism of grid-meshing options including structured and unstructured grids to build grids with the minimum computational cost, ensuring adequate resolution of results.
- Access to input user-defined functions.

In general, ANSYS Fluent is the one of the most complete platforms existing in the CFD industry including well-known and the latest developments of fluid flow-related models. In terms of computational requirements, Fluent envisages solutions using multiple parallel processors, thus reducing computational costs. The latter, however, is a matter of the user's desires of resolution level; i.e., if a large urban area with a high level of geometrical detail is considered, then the computational cost can be very high, similarly to the most micro-scale CFD tools. The main limitation of the platform is that, since it is not targeted for specific problems, it requires relatively high expertise on fluid flow and transport phenomena for the user to formulate a specific problem. In this sense, the software does not include evapotranspiration and thermal comfort models, which means that, for microclimate modelling, the user should provide him/herself the models via user-defined functions. Nonetheless, it can be easily used to produce the results of parameters required to compute thermal comfort indicators (wind speed, relative humidity, temperature, turbulence intensity) externally.

Numerous CFD studies of the UHI by using Fluent exist in the scientific literature. For example, Stavrakakis et al. [103] used Fluent for the assessment of thermal and wind comfort of pedestrians in an urban area in Crete, Greece. Special physical models, such as evaporation from water surfaces and evapotranspiration from vegetation as well as thermal comfort indicators, were incorporated and compiled in the CFD platform (through user-defined function) towards the formulation of a holistic model that solves for UHI effect on pedestrians' perception of thermal comfort. The micro-scale model developed was then used to assess the pre-renovation situation and to indicate the optimum interventions including vegetation, shading devices, and cool materials in proper locations of the urban domain. Saneinejad et al. [144] studied the evaporative cooling effect on air temperature and thermal comfort within urban street canyons. They took advantage of Fluent capability to incorporate user-defined physical models and they developed a coupled CFD model that solves for vapour and heat transfer in the air, heat and moisture transfer within the porous building walls, and radiative heat exchange between building walls. The effect of evaporation of building surfaces on temperature was adequately quantified and a substantial impact of this phenomenon on pedestrian thermal comfort was shown. Recently, Fluent was used as a reliable database generator for validating a novel energy balance-based model, undertaking the calculation of spatially averaged air temperature within the urban canopy [145]. In terms of its prediction accuracy regarding urban microclimate assessments in real-scale cases, Antoniou et al. [116] applied CFD unsteady RANS modelling and computed an average absolute difference of 1.35 °C, of 0.57 m/s, and of 2.31 °C regarding air temperature, wind speed, and surface temperatures, respectively. As demonstrated in the international scientific literature, Ansys Fluent is particularly useful to test and verify UHI mitigation strategies in cityscapes provided that the designer is familiar with urban physics and possesses computer skills.

ANSYS-CFX

CFX [146] is a FVM-based, general purpose CFD tool that possesses similar capabilities as the ANSYS-Fluent software reported above, at least for airflows within urban canopies. The main differences are focused on mesh-generation algorithms and solution algorithm as well as differences in functionality and operability of available GUIs related to user's actions during pre- and post-processing. By means of spatial discretization, Fluent uses a cell-centered approach, while CFX uses a vertex-centered approach; hence, Fluent can handle polyhedral mesh and cut-cell meshes, while CFX is limited to the traditional tetra- and hexa-mesh topologies. Concerning the comparison between the results obtained by CFX and Fluent, they present similar accuracy; however, Fluent has presented a slightly better accuracy for incompressible flows, although it requires more computational time to converge. This happens due to the fewer computational nodes in CFX grids in comparison to Fluent grids. Fluent has a more functional pre-processor and, thus, it requires less time to prepare the grid and work on available GUIs. Fluent has post-processing capabilities of its own while CFX needs a dedicated post-processor.

Priyadarsini et al. (2008) [147] used CFX to investigate the UHI effect on temperature rising in the urban canopy in Singapore. They determined the key factors causing the phenomenon and investigated the possibilities of improving heat release rate by optimizing airflow in selected hot spots. The main parameters put to the test were building geometry, materials of façades, and the location of air-conditioning units and their impact on the outdoor air temperature. Although a simple model was used (evapotranspiration from vegetation was ignored), good agreement between the computed and the measured results was obtained. It has been demonstrated that the software is particularly useful for urban morphology optimization in terms of acceptable wind speeds within the urban canopy [148], as well as to verify the performance of several bioclimatic interventions (e.g., cool materials) with respect to the reduction of urban surface temperature on hot summer days [149,150].

Phoenics

Phoenics [151] is a FVM-based, general-purpose CFD platform, which, at least for airflows within the urban canopy, provides similar modelling features and capabilities as CFX and Fluent. As the other CFD programs, Phoenics can solve for the most important conservation equations of mass, momentum, heat, chemical species, and turbulent parameters, towards the provision of results of microclimate parameters such as relative humidity, wind speed, turbulence intensity, and temperature. Similarly to the other CFD platforms, it provides access to the user to incorporate special physical models, such as evapotranspiration from vegetation. A substantial advantage of Phoenics over the other CFD tools is that it provides access to the source Fortran-based code rather than only offering the opportunity to incorporate user-defined models. Like previous tools, it possesses a wide variety of models to simulate turbulence, heat, and radiation transfer and, due to its wide validation, it can be confidently used to study microclimates in urban areas. Since it is not just a microclimate-oriented tool, expertise above average on computing and transport phenomena is required in order to develop a reliable microclimate model. The major difference is that it does not implement tetrahedral grids, and either a Body-Fitted or a hexahedral-unstructured grid option is available for complex geometries. The software includes a plant canopy module called FOLIAGE, which accounts for vegetation evaporation phenomena.

Fintikakis et al. [152] used Phoenics to study the urban microclimatic conditions in the historic centre of Tirana. They developed a microclimate model and incorporated it into the CFD platform towards the estimation of pedestrian thermal comfort in order to decide the best retrofitting measures (e.g., trees' kind and orientation, high albedo ground materials, earth-to-air heat exchangers) that ensure the best comfort conditions in strategic locations of the urban domain. Although a simple model was developed (evapotranspiration and radiation were neglected in the mathematical model and they were imposed as temperature boundary conditions taken from field measurements, instead), it provided adequate results at least for practical design purposes. Maragkogiannis et al. [153] combined Terrestrial Laser Scanners (TLS) and aerial ortho-photography with computational fluid dynamics (CFD) to study the thermal conditions of a public square in Chania, Greece. Yang et al. [154] reported that the software presented good structure for developing modular applications but required powerful computer or cloud computing to speed up simulations.

3. Discussion

3.1. Building Energy/Urban Microclimate-Coupled Simulations

As presented in the above sections, currently there is a tremendous availability of computational tools and methods that can be used to conduct urban energy planning studies, even in completely simulated environments. The obvious opportunity that emerged is the ability to predict the energy performance of a group of buildings, taking into account microclimate variations in the vicinity of buildings, at least at a district level. Apparently, the designer may have all the necessary computer tools to conduct joint simulations of urban microclimate and building(s) energy performance, which, however, requires knowledge of building physics, specifically regarding indoor–outdoor interactions. The main question is how the practitioner can really develop such kind of co-simulations. The answer, of course, simply resides on the energy conservation of the control system building/outdoor space. The energy balance equation for a building may be expressed as follows: The heating/cooling load of the building equals the sum of the internal heat gain from lights, occupants, equipment, the convective heat transfer between building's interior surfaces and internal air, and the convective heat transfer due to air infiltration and the change of energy stored in the internal air. On the other hand, the energy balance equation for building exterior surfaces may be expressed as follows: The conduction heat flux through the wall equals the sum of the transmitted solar radiation, the absorbed solar radiation, the net long-wave radiation heat flux, and the convective heat flux exchanged with the outdoor air.

The above description of the heat exchange between indoor and outdoor spaces reveals the physical influences of the external environment to the internal space and vice versa. These influences may be described as follows:

- The incident solar irradiance on building walls.
- The convective heat flux at the external surfaces, which is represented by the Convective Heat Transfer Coefficient (CHTC) and by temperature differences between the ambient air and external surfaces.
- The intensity of long-wave radiation.
- The heat and water-vapor transfer through infiltration.

Ideally, all the above influences should be adequately captured and participate in appropriate boundary conditions of the building energy simulation (BES) model. The last, however, often present some deficiencies in capturing all the impacts described above, such as the following:

- They disregard the non-uniformity of the CHTC in the vicinity of the building. They rely only on a mean value of CHTC based on climate data time series, usually of the wider climate zone (data from remote meteorological stations).
- Infiltration is handled by empirical formulas rather than a more precise representation (accounting for velocity fluctuations through openings, for example).
- Surrounding trees are treated like simple obstacles on incident radiation rather than contributors of moisture and obstructions to outdoor airflow; thus, CHTC and air infiltration rates are underestimated.
- Evaporative cooling effect emanating from water surfaces is ignored.
- Surrounding buildings' (other than being treated as obstacles on incident radiation) effect on airflow pattern and, therefore, on CHTC is not normally taken into account.
- Outdoor climate data are most commonly taken from default libraries of wide climate zones available in the tools' background, which are, however, different from the actual ones especially during summer season due to the Urban Heat Island effect.

On the other hand, as presented in previous sections, the UCM or CFD tools seem very promising towards the simulation of the urban microclimate. The CFD micro-scale models can simulate physical mechanisms that comprise the urban microclimate and by these means they can quantify all the influences of outdoor physical environment to indoor energy consumption. Consequently, the drawbacks reported above can be eliminated under the perspective of CFD/BES tools' coupling. Indeed, numerous authors in scientific literature succeeded to couple these methods based on information exchanging between the two tools in each given time interval as follows [55–57,155]:

- An initial value of external wall temperature in the CFD model is adopted as a wall boundary condition. Air properties of the incoming wind are taken from the nearest meteorological station and they are set as inflow boundary condition in the CFD model. Boundary conditions for physical features, such as trees and water surfaces, are also set as boundary conditions.

- The CFD model is executed and provides a preliminary prediction of the microclimate in the vicinity of the building(s) of interest, i.e., air temperature, convective heat transfer coefficient, and relative humidity.
- These climate parameters are then passed to the BES tool as climate data (i.e., instead of using the default data from the BES tool libraries) and the BES tool calculates, apart from Energy-related indicators, external walls' temperature.
- The new updated value of building external walls returns to the CFD model as a wall boundary condition, which is executed again towards the update of a microclimate surrounding the building. The updated microclimate is then passed to the BES tool, which is executed again towards the update of the energy-related indicators and the wall temperature.
- And so on.

The iterative process above ends when the wall temperature computed by the BES tool, taking into account its pass from the CFD tool, presents a really small change from one loop to the other (convergence of solution). Then the solution is obtained and the building energy-related indicators are finally calculated.

As stated by Kato [21], the full coupling is practically absurd and sometimes impossible because of its enormous computation amount, especially when similarly small time-step scales over long periods are adopted in the two models. Alternatively, he suggests a coupled CFD network model in building energy (heat) and airflow simulation. However, the suggested approach again requires quite advanced knowledge of transport phenomena and computer skills; hence, again it may be considered difficult to use by practitioners, especially professionals conducting studies for compliance purposes with regulations, e.g., energy audits or energy studies for new or renovated buildings. Focusing on that target audience, an alternative practical, although less accurate, approach (let it be called "semi-coupled approach") would rely on the use of an urban microclimate model responsible for producing local climate data, and then automatically (or manually) passing them as input conditions to the BES tool. Essentially, this semi-coupled approach resides to only insert a weather file to the BES tool, which, instead of a default file of the wider climate zone, is now being produced in a control volume close to the district/building of interest from the micro-climate model. In such an approach, normally a UCM tool is preferred due to its simplicity and fast calculation [156]. To date, the main steps of such semi-coupled approach are the following:

- Incoming-wind properties are taken from the nearest meteorological station or from the weather file of the climate zone and they are set as boundary conditions in the urban microclimate model.
- Appropriate boundary conditions to account for urban physical phenomena, e.g., radiative heat fluxes, evaporation, and evapotranspiration, are set to water and vegetations' surfaces of the microclimate model.
- Estimations of the incident solar radiation on solid surfaces may emerge, utilizing a solar ray tracing model, taking into account albedo and emissivity values of materials.
- The microclimate model is then executed and provides the local microclimate in the vicinity of the building, quartier, or district.
- The microclimate provided by the microclimate model can then be transformed in the format of weather files of the BES tool and compiled in the BES tool.

Obviously, the tactic above is a one-way approach, i.e., the microclimate model is executed first and the climatic conditions that emerged are then passed to the BES tool in the format of the default weather file. It should be mentioned that, since this method treats field and zonal models separately, an average expertise is required by the user in order to obtain correct estimations of initial parameters used as boundary conditions. This means that the user should apply external or incorporated special models that solve for these parameters in order to provide boundary conditions, e.g., a correct "guess" of internal temperature and solution of conduction equations to estimate external surface temperatures, taking into account incident solar radiation. It may be concluded that BES/CFD coupling provides a more accurate prediction of energy-related indicators, hence, a more accurate selection of retrofit measures. Through this coupling procedure it becomes clear that energy-related indicators are only a "symptom" of the mathematical interpretation of building and urban physics and, more specifically, of indoor–outdoor interactions. It should be highlighted, however, that further research is required to confront the challenge of high CPU loads and time required for fully coupled approaches. Fortunately, the dramatic improvement of CPU technologies and resources promises such reliable studies in simulation environments.

3.2. Perspectives on the Use of Advanced Simulation Methods

Provided that the ideal physical model for built environment and energy performance assessment is available, it could be integrated to a decision-making procedure in the context of a retrofitting strategy. Building design optimization is indeed a complex task, since the optimal solution should satisfy many criteria, e.g., energy saving, emissions' avoidance, and cost-efficiency indicators (NPV, payback period, etc.). Scientific research has already presented advanced optimization methods and tools to respond to the aforementioned challenge. For example, Nguyen et al. [157] reviewed simulation-based optimization methods in the building sector. They provided an overview on the subject focusing on discontinuous multi-modal building optimization problems, the performance of optimization algorithms, multi-criteria optimization, surrogate models, stochastic optimization, and the propagation of optimization techniques into real-world design challenges. The paper is recommended as a good source of studies and approaches for building energy optimization. Handling of large databases that emerge by extensive parametric simulation analysis towards the identification of optimal solutions is a cutting-edge issue, especially in the context of recent energy regulations. For example, the EU directive 244/2012/EU suggests the exercise of extensive parametric analysis in the scope of identifying the cost-optimal minimum energy performance requirements of buildings and, furthermore, the identification of the nearly zero energy building (NZEB) levels. Responding to the NZEB challenge, Cao et al. [158] reviewed the feasibility of categorized state-of-the-art technologies, namely, passive energy-saving technologies, energy-efficient building service systems, and Renewable Energy Sources. Based on data derived from international energy reports for the US, China, and the EU, they introduced a ZEB concept.

Although new developments regarding advanced physical modelling have flourished during the last 20 years, it is true that they lack acceptance by the wider engineering and architects' community. An extensive survey presented by Fernandez-Antolin et al. [159] showed that one of the main reasons for limited preference on using advanced simulation tools by recent graduate architects is that they consider them inconvenient and challenging to learn. The study suggests that a key driving force to boost the use of such simulation tools in practice is to integrate related education courses, even at the undergraduate level, e.g., in design courses and in building system courses. In the same study, recommendations to software vendors to improve user-friendliness of the problem setup (geometrical model and input conditions) are also reported. Emphasis on bridging the gap between the use of building energy simulation tools and architectural design is given by researchers of the same team [160]. The study raises the dilemma of suggesting the use of energy simulations in the early design stages and concluded that modern architects should be capable to understand simulated results in the context of suggesting design solutions. To that direction, it is acknowledged that teachers in higher education institutes should bring and exercise advances of simulation tools to the attention of students (future architects and engineers). From the software vendors' side, it is expected that no further increase in cost is presumed in case of providing additional information and guidelines when requested. In addition, the administration of educational institutions should also encourage their use in a constructive way, envisaging subsidies and incentives to boost their adoption, and being responsible for reviewing the projects before granting a license.

The usefulness of utilizing reliable simulation tools in the architectural design stage has been highlighted and demonstrated in many studies (refer, for example, to ref. [161]). In this context, Xie and Gou [162] exploited two case studies (a Sports' Centre and a Hotel) that compare building performance simulation as an early intervention and a late verification tool in the architectural design process, contextualizing the building simulation research in real building practices. In the first case study, a simulation tool was integrated in the early-design stage, while, in the other one, the simulation tool was used at the post-design stage, mainly to verify the results obtained by the suggested architectural design. Through collating technical results with those of designers' perceptions regarding the usefulness of simulation tools via questionnaire surveys, it was concluded that a design team must not only provide quantitative results to obtain accredited building design but also provide documentation of at least two design strategies towards the confirmation of the schematic design. This suggests that the focus of green building rating systems is shifting from simply obtaining accurate quantitative goals for the decision-making process. The present focus is to encourage the selection of multiple design plans and optimize the design solutions.

4. Conclusions

This work intended to inform building designers, engineers, and urban planners on the state of the art regarding tools and methods that may be used in practice in the framework of energy efficiency and climate mitigation and adaptation technical studies. Current energy policies, as regards transition to low-carbon economies in future sustainable Cities, necessitate putting advanced study techniques into practice. The comprehensive overview of tools and methods provided herein may guide the target audience through the ongoing design challenges as well as through practical solutions to respond in their studies. To summarize, the following major conclusions may be drawn:

- Informed decision making on building energy renovation and urban rehabilitation through the reliable quantification of energy, cost, and environmental and comfort indicators is becoming increasingly important, even at practical engineering levels, to meet ambitious goals and trends of policies regarding energy efficiency and climate change resilience.
- To respond in meeting minimum energy performance requirements, especially for nearly zero energy buildings, more accurate building energy performance simulation is required. To that direction, studies in simulation environments should take into account systems' operation schedules, occupancy schedules, and external local microclimate effects.
- A plethora of building energy simulation (BES) tools is available, including powerful tools that are still freely available such as the EnergyPlus and the eQUEST software (among many others).
- Urban microclimate and BES tools presented herein are verified and validated.
- All the UCM models presented herein are freely available (open source).
- A coupled BES/urban microclimate simulation method facilitates more reliable predictions of impacts of external microclimate on buildings' energy performance; hence, it quantifies the energetic impacts of external bioclimatic interventions on buildings.
- Most common BES/CFD-coupled methods refer to:
  - EnergyPlus/Envi-met
  - TRNSYS/Fluent
- Further research is required regarding the reduction of CPU loads and time of coupled building energy and urban microclimate simulations.
- Complexity of physical phenomena in urban planning suggests that the modern designer should acquire know-how in building physics and better computer skills. In parallel, further work by software vendors on improving user friendliness remains a

crucial factor that can boost such simulation approaches and practices from research to practice.

- Higher education institutes play a key role in providing the necessary knowledge and expertise to their students in order to respond to evermore required informed decision making at the design stage. It is admitted that simulation tools and practices should be integrated into educational courses in order to ensure a good readiness level of the modern designer to be able to understand better the impacts of alternative design strategies and to work in teams with other experts, e.g., engineers, building physicists, IT experts, etc.

Author Contributions: Methodology, G.M.S. and M.D.; investigation, G.M.S. and D.A.K.; writing—original draft preparation, G.M.S.; writing—review and editing, D.A.K. and M.D.; supervision, M.D.; project administration, G.M.S. and M.D. All authors have read and agreed to the published version of the manuscript.

Funding: Part of this research was funded by the PROGRAMME MED EUROPEAN TERRITORIAL COOPERATION 2007–2013, project: REPUBLIC-MED, grant number: 1C-MED12-73.

Institutional Review Board Statement: Not applicable.

Informed Consent Statement: Not applicable.

Acknowledgments: Part of the work was conducted in the framework of the lead author's former position as a scientific collaborator in the Centre for Renewable Energy Sources and Saving (CRES) and in the framework of the REPUBLIC-MED (1C-MED12-73) project (project duration: March 2013–June 2015). CRES was the Lead Partner (LP) of the project.

Conflicts of Interest: The authors declare no conflict of interest.

References

1. Directive 2010/31/EU of the European Parliament and of the Council of 19 May 2010 on the energy performance of buildings (recast) L153/13. *Off. J. Eur. Union* **2010**, *3*, 124–146.
2. European Commission–Department. *Energy in Focus, Energy Efficiency in Buildings*; European Commission: Brussels, Belgium, 2020.
3. Directive (EU) 2018/844 of the European Parliament and of the Council of 30 May 2018, amending Directive 2010/31/EU on the energy performance of buildings and Directive 2012/27/EU on energy efficiency L156/75. *Off. J. Eur. Union* **2018**, *156*, 75–91.
4. Commission recommendation (EU) 2019/786 of 8 May 2019 on building renovation. *Off. J. Eur. Union* **2019**, *127*, 34–79.
5. Santamouris, M. Heat Island Research in Europe: The State of the Art. *Adv. Build. Energy Res.* **2007**, *1*, 123–150. [CrossRef]
6. Santamouris, M. Innovating to zero the building sector in Europe: Minimising the energy consumption, eradication of the energy poverty and mitigating the local climate change. *Sol. Energy* **2016**, *128*, 61–94. [CrossRef]
7. Chapter 9: Energy Efficiency in Building Renovation. In *Handbook of Energy Efficiency in Buildings-A Life Cycle Approach*; Asdrubali, F.; Desideri, U. (Eds.) Elsevier: Amsterdam, The Netherlands, 2019; pp. 675–810.
8. Liao, Z.; Dexter, A. A simplified physical model for estimating the average air temperature in multi-zone heating systems. *Build. Environ.* **2004**, *39*, 1013–1022. [CrossRef]
9. Stephan, L.; Bastide, A.; Wurtz, E. Optimizing opening dimensions for naturally ventilated buildings. *Appl. Energy* **2011**, *88*, 2791–2801. [CrossRef]
10. Wang, S. Dynamic simulation of building VAV air-conditioning system and evaluation of EMCS on-line control strategies. *Build. Environ.* **1999**, *34*, 681–705. [CrossRef]
11. Katsaprakakis, D.A. Computational Simulation and Dimensioning of Solar-Combi Systems for Large-Size Sports Facilities: A Case Study for the Pancretan Stadium, Crete, Greece. *Energies* **2020**, *13*, 2285. [CrossRef]
12. *BIPV Design and Performance Modelling: Tools and Methods*; Jakica, N.; Yang, R.J.; Eisenlohr, J. (Eds.) IEA PVPS Task 15, Report IEA-PVPS T15-09: 2019; IEA: Paris, France, 2019; ISBN 978-3-906042-86-2.
13. Azar, E.; Menassa, C.C. A comprehensive analysis of the impact of occupancy parameters in energy simulation of office buildings. *Energy Build.* **2012**, *55*, 841–853. [CrossRef]
14. Azar, E.; O'Brien, W.; Carlucci, S.; Hong, T.; Sonta, A.; Kim, J.; Andargie, M.; Abuimara, T.; El Asmar, M.; Jain, R.K.; et al. Simulation-aided occupant-centric building design: A critical review of tools, methods, and applications. *Energy Build.* **2020**, *224*, 110292. [CrossRef]
15. Foucquier, A.; Robert, S.; Suard, F.; Stéphan, L.; Jay, A. State of the art in building modelling and energy performances prediction: A review. *Renew. Sustain. Energy Rev.* **2013**, *23*, 272–288. [CrossRef]

16. Stavrakakis, G.M.; Stamou, A.I.; Markatos, N.C. Evaluation of thermal comfort in indoor environments using Computational Fluid Dynamics (CFD). In *Indoor Work and Living Environments: Health, Safety and Performance*; Harris, R.G., Moore, D.P., Eds.; Nova Science Publishers Inc.: Hauppauge, NY, USA, 2009; pp. 97–166. ISBN 978-1-61728-521-9.
17. Kaminski, M.; Carey, G.F. Stochastic perturbation-based finite element approach to fluid flow problems. *Int. J. Numer. Methods Heat Fluid Flow* **2005**, *15*, 671–697. [CrossRef]
18. Seong, M.; Lim, C.; Lim, J.; Park, J. A Study on the Status and Thermal Environment Improvement of Ceiling-Embedded Indoor Cooling and Heating Unit. *Sustainability* **2021**, *13*, 10651. [CrossRef]
19. Lee, M.; Park, G.; Park, C.; Kim, C. Improvement of Grid Independence Test for Computational Fluid Dynamics Model of Building Based on Grid Resolution. *Adv. Civ. Eng.* **2020**, *2020*, 1–11. [CrossRef]
20. Tan, G.; Glicksman, L.R. Application of integrating multi-zone model with CFD simulation to natural ventilation prediction. *Energy Build.* **2005**, *37*, 1049–1057. [CrossRef]
21. Kato, S. Review of airflow and transport analysis in building using CFD and network model. *Jpn. Archit. Rev.* **2018**, *1*, 299–309. [CrossRef]
22. Rumianowski, P.; Brau, J.; Roux, J.J. An adapted model for simulation of the interaction between a wall and the building heating system. In Proceedings of the Thermal Performance of the Exterior Envelopes of Buildings IV Conference, Orlando, FL, USA, 4–7 December 1989; pp. 224–233.
23. Chen, Q. Ventilation performance prediction for buildings: A method overview and recent applications. *Build. Environ.* **2009**, *44*, 848–858. [CrossRef]
24. *Technology Roadmap-Energy Efficient Building Envelopes*; OECD/IEA Report; OECD/IEA: Paris, France, 2013.
25. Feijó-Muñoz, J.; González-Lezcano, R.A.; Poza-Casado, I.; Padilla-Marcos, M.Á.; Meiss, A. Airtightness of residential buildings in the Continental area of Spain. *Build. Environ.* **2019**, *148*, 299–308. [CrossRef]
26. Han, G.; Srebric, J.; Enache-Pommer, E. Different modeling strategies of infiltration rates for an office building to improve accuracy of building energy simulations. *Energy Build.* **2015**, *86*, 288–295. [CrossRef]
27. El-Darwish, I.; Gomaa, M. Retrofitting strategy for building envelopes to achieve energy efficiency. *Alex. Eng. J.* **2017**, *56*, 579–589. [CrossRef]
28. Hansen, A.R.; Gram-Hanssen, K.; Knudsen, H.N. How building design and technologies influence heat-related habits. *Build. Res. Inf.* **2017**, *46*, 83–98. [CrossRef]
29. Liu, J.; Yao, R.; McCloy, R. An investigation of thermal comfort adaptation behaviour in office buildings in the UK. *Indoor Built Environ.* **2013**, *23*, 675–691. [CrossRef]
30. Tuniki, H.P.; Jurelionis, A.; Fokaides, P. A review on the approaches in analysing energy-related occupant behaviour research. *J. Build. Eng.* **2021**, *40*, 102630. [CrossRef]
31. Goyal, S.; Barooah, P. A method for model-reduction of non-linear thermal dynamics of multi-zone buildings. *Energy Build.* **2012**, *47*, 332–340. [CrossRef]
32. Hazyuk, I.; Ghiaus, C.; Penhouet, D. Optimal temperature control of intermittently heated buildings using Model Predictive Control: Part I—Building modeling. *Build. Environ.* **2012**, *51*, 379–387. [CrossRef]
33. BEST Directory. Available online: https://www.buildingenergysoftwaretools.com (accessed on 26 August 2021).
34. Al Ka'bi, A.H. Comparison of energy simulation applications used in green building. *Ann. Telecommun.* **2020**, *75*, 271–290. [CrossRef]
35. Najjar, M.; Figueiredo, K.; Palumbo, M.; Haddad, A. Integration of BIM and LCA: Evaluating the environmental impacts of building materials at an early stage of designing a typical office building. *J. Build. Eng.* **2017**, *14*, 115–126. [CrossRef]
36. Abanda, F.; Byers, L. An investigation of the impact of building orientation on energy consumption in a domestic building using emerging BIM (Building Information Modelling). *Energy* **2016**, *97*, 517–527. [CrossRef]
37. Singh, P.; Sadhu, A. Multicomponent energy assessment of buildings using building information modeling. *Sustain. Cities Soc.* **2019**, *49*, 101603. [CrossRef]
38. BEAVER. Available online: https://www.acadsbsg.com.au/beaver/ (accessed on 26 August 2021).
39. Mahmud, K.; Amin, U.; Hossain, J.; Ravishankar, J. Computational tools for design, analysis, and management of residential energy systems. *Appl. Energy* **2018**, *221*, 535–556. [CrossRef]
40. ACADS-BSG Pty Ltd.; Elms Consulting Engineers. *ABCB Energy Modelling of Office Buildings for Climate Zoning*; ABCB: Canberra, ACT, Australia, 2002.
41. BSim. Available online: https://sbi.dk/bsim/Pages/About-BSim.aspx (accessed on 26 August 2021).
42. Rose, J.; Lahme, A.; Christensen, N.U.; Heiselberg, P.; Hansen, M.; Grau, K. Numerical method for calculating latent heat storage in constructions containing phase change material. In Proceedings of the 11th International IBPSA Conference, Glasgow, UK, 27–30 July 2009.
43. Sikula, O.; Plášek, J.; Hirs, J. Numerical Simulation of the Effect of Heat Gains in the Heating Season. *Energy Procedia* **2012**, *14*, 906–912. [CrossRef]
44. Zweifel, G. *Prefabricated Systems for Low Energy Renovation of Residential Buildings*; Retrofit simulation report-IEA ECBCS Annex 50; Energy Conservation in Buildings and Community Systems Programme, March 2011; EMPA: Dübendorf, Switzerland, 2011.
45. Liu, M.; Wittchen, K.B.; Heiselberg, P.K. Development of a simplified method for intelligent glazed façade design under different control strategies and verified by building simulation tool BSim. *Build. Environ.* **2014**, *74*, 31–38. [CrossRef]

46. Sørensen, M.J.; Myhre, S.H.; Hansen, K.K.; Silkjær, M.H.; Marszal-Pomianowska, A.J.; Liu, L. Integrated Building Energy Design of a Danish Office Building Based on Monte Carlo Simulation Method. *Energy Procedia* **2017**, *132*, 93–98. [CrossRef]
47. Energy Simulation Software for Aiding Building Design. Available online: http://pages.suddenlink.net/enerwin/ (accessed on 26 August 2021).
48. Al-Mumin, A.; Khattab, O.; Sridhar, G. Occupants' behavior and activity patterns influencing the energy consumption in the Kuwaiti residences. *Energy Build.* **2003**, *35*, 549–559. [CrossRef]
49. Soebarto, V.; Williamson, T. Multi-criteria assessment of building performance: Theory and implementation. *Build. Environ.* **2001**, *36*, 681–690. [CrossRef]
50. *ASHRAE Standard 90.1. Energy Efficient Design of New Buildings Except Low-Rise Residential Buildings*; American Society of Heating Refrigerating and Air-Conditioning Engineers, Inc.: Atlanta, GA, USA, 1989.
51. EnergyPlus. Available online: https://energyplus.net/ (accessed on 26 August 2020).
52. Crawley, D.B.; Hand, J.W.; Kummert, M.; Griffith, B.T. Contrasting the capabilities of building energy performance simulation programs. *Build. Environ.* **2008**, *43*, 661–673. [CrossRef]
53. Tsikaloudaki, K.; Laskos, K.; Theodosiou, T.; Bikas, D. Assessing cooling energy performance of windows for office buildings in the Mediterranean zone. *Energy Build.* **2012**, *49*, 192–199. [CrossRef]
54. Goia, F.; Haase, M.; Perino, M. Optimizing the configuration of a façade module for office buildings by means of integrated thermal and lighting simulations in a total energy perspective. *Appl. Energy* **2013**, *108*, 515–527. [CrossRef]
55. Yang, X.; Zhao, L.; Bruse, M.; Meng, Q. An integrated simulation method for building energy performance assessment in urban environments. *Energy Build.* **2012**, *54*, 243–251. [CrossRef]
56. Shen, P.; Wang, Z. How neighborhood form influences building energy use in winter design condition: Case study of Chicago using CFD coupled simulation. *J. Clean. Prod.* **2020**, *261*, 121094. [CrossRef]
57. Zhang, R.; Mirzaei, P.A.; Jones, B. Development of a dynamic external CFD and BES coupling framework for application of urban neighbourhoods energy modelling. *Build. Environ.* **2018**, *146*, 37–49. [CrossRef]
58. Design Builder. Available online: https://designbuilder.co.uk (accessed on 26 August 2021).
59. Simulated Results and Hierarchy of Retrofitting Measures–Heraklion (Report D3.4.1, Project IMPULSE-Interreg MED, Project Ref.: 1MED15_2.1_M2_178). Available online: https://impulse.interreg-med.eu/what-we-achieve/deliverable-database/detail/?tx_elibrary_pi1%5Blivrable%5D=3167&tx_elibrary_pi1%5Baction%5D=show&tx_elibrary_pi1%5Bcontroller%5D=Frontend%5CLivrable&cHash=691291ce60531eb9a0aba6e6b1e51766 (accessed on 14 October 2021).
60. Stavrakakis, G.; Androutsopoulos, A.; Vyörykkä, J. Experimental and numerical assessment of cool-roof impact on thermal and energy performance of a school building in Greece. *Energy Build.* **2016**, *130*, 64–84. [CrossRef]
61. Androutsopoulos, A.; Stavrakakis, G.; Damasiotis, M. Cool Roof Impacts on a School-building Thermal and Energy Performance in Athens, Greece. *Procedia Environ. Sci.* **2017**, *38*, 178–186. [CrossRef]
62. Mazzeo, D.; Romagnoni, P.; Matera, N.; Oliveti, G.; Cornaro, C.; De Santoli, L. Accuracy of the Most Popular Building Performance Simulation Tools: Experimental Comparison for A Conventional and A PCM-Based Test Box. In Proceedings of the Building Simulation 2019: 16th Conference of IBPSA, Rome, Italy, 2–4 September 2020.
63. Hirsch, J.J. Associates in Collaboration with Lawrence Berkeley National Laboratory. eQUEST. Available online: https://www.doe2.com/equest/ (accessed on 26 August 2021).
64. Park, B.R.; Hong, J.; Choi, E.J.; Choi, Y.J.; Lee, C.; Moon, J.W. Improvement in Energy Performance of Building Envelope Incorporating Electrochromic Windows (ECWs). *Energies* **2019**, *12*, 1181. [CrossRef]
65. Kim, K.H.; Oh, J.K.-W.; Jeong, W. Study on Solar Radiation Models in South Korea for Improving Office Building Energy Performance Analysis. *Sustainability* **2016**, *8*, 589. [CrossRef]
66. Ke, M.-T.; Yeh, C.-H.; Jian, J.-T. Analysis of building energy consumption parameters and energy savings measurement and verification by applying eQUEST software. *Energy Build.* **2013**, *61*, 100–107. [CrossRef]
67. Seyednezhad, M.; Najafi, H. Solar-Powered Thermoelectric-Based Cooling and Heating System for Building Applications: A Parametric Study. *Energies* **2021**, *14*, 5573. [CrossRef]
68. Wang, F.; Lin, H.; Tsai, M. Energy Efficient Approaches by Retrofitting Heat Pumps Water Heating System for a University Dormitory. *Buildings* **2021**, *11*, 356. [CrossRef]
69. ESP-r. Available online: http://www.esru.strath.ac.uk/Courseware/ESP-r (accessed on 26 August 2021).
70. Høseggen, R.; Wachenfeldt, B.; Hanssen, S. Building simulation as an assisting tool in decision making. *Energy Build.* **2008**, *40*, 821–827. [CrossRef]
71. Bourgeois, D.; Reinhart, C.; Macdonald, I. Adding advanced behavioural models in whole building energy simulation: A study on the total energy impact of manual and automated lighting control. *Energy Build.* **2006**, *38*, 814–823. [CrossRef]
72. Ferdyn-Grygierek, J.; Bartosz, D.; Specjał, A.; Grygierek, K. Analysis of Accuracy Determination of the Seasonal Heat Demand in Buildings Based on Short Measurement Periods. *Energies* **2018**, *11*, 2734. [CrossRef]
73. Bonetti, V.; Kokogiannakis, G. Dynamic Exergy Analysis for the Thermal Storage Optimization of the Building Envelope. *Energies* **2017**, *10*, 95. [CrossRef]
74. Eller, C.; Rida, M.; Boudier, K.; Otoni, C.; Celani, G.; Labaki, L.; Hoffmann, S. Climate-Based Analysis for the Potential Use of Coconut Oil as Phase Change Material in Buildings. *Sustainability* **2021**, *13*, 10731. [CrossRef]

75. EQUA. IDA ICE—IDA Indoor Climate and Energy. Available online: https://www.equa.se/en/ida-ice (accessed on 26 August 2021).
76. Salvalai, G. Implementation and validation of simplified heat pump model in IDA-ICE energy simulation environment. *Energy Build.* **2012**, *49*, 132–141. [CrossRef]
77. Hesaraki, A.; Holmberg, S. Energy performance of low temperature heating systems in five new-built Swedish dwellings: A case study using simulations and on-site measurements. *Build. Environ.* **2013**, *64*, 85–93. [CrossRef]
78. Rabani, M.; Madessa, H.B.; Nord, N. Building Retrofitting through Coupling of Building Energy Simulation-Optimization Tool with CFD and Daylight Programs. *Energies* **2021**, *14*, 2180. [CrossRef]
79. Rose, J.; Thomsen, K.E. Comprehensive Energy Renovation of Two Danish Heritage Buildings within IEA SHC Task 59. *Heritage* **2021**, *4*, 155. [CrossRef]
80. IESVE. Available online: https://www.iesve.com (accessed on 26 August 2021).
81. Murray, S.N.; Rocher, B.; Sullivan, D.O. Static Simulation: A sufficient modelling technique for retrofit analysis. *Energy Build.* **2012**, *47*, 113–121. [CrossRef]
82. Ouedraogo, B.; Levermore, G.; Parkinson, J. Future energy demand for public buildings in the context of climate change for Burkina Faso. *Build. Environ.* **2012**, *49*, 270–282. [CrossRef]
83. Yin, X.; Yu, J.; Dong, Q.; Jia, Y.; Sun, C. Energy Sustainability of Rural Residential Buildings with Bio-Based Building Fabric in Northeast China. *Energies* **2020**, *13*, 5806. [CrossRef]
84. SUNREL. Available online: https://www.nrel.gov/buildings/sunrel.html (accessed on 26 August 2021).
85. Elzafraney, M.; Soroushian, P.; Deru, M. Development of Energy-Efficient Concrete Buildings Using Recycled Plastic Aggregates. *J. Arch. Eng.* **2005**, *11*, 122–130. [CrossRef]
86. Tas. Available online: https://www.edsl.net (accessed on 26 August 2021).
87. Wong, N.H.; Tan, A.Y.K.; Tan, P.Y.; Wong, N.C. Energy simulation of vertical greenery systems. *Energy Build.* **2009**, *41*, 1401–1408. [CrossRef]
88. Pino, A.; Bustamante, W.; Escobar, R.; Pino, F.E. Thermal and lighting behavior of office buildings in Santiago of Chile. *Energy Build.* **2012**, *47*, 441–449. [CrossRef]
89. Al Rasbi, H.; Gadi, M. Energy Modelling of Traditional and Contemporary Mosque Buildings in Oman. *Buildings* **2021**, *11*, 314. [CrossRef]
90. Salem, R.; Bahadori-Jahromi, A.; Mylona, A.; Godfrey, P.; Cook, D. Comparison and Evaluation of the Potential Energy, Carbon Emissions, and Financial Impacts from the Incorporation of CHP and CCHP Systems in Existing UK Hotel Buildings. *Energies* **2018**, *11*, 1219. [CrossRef]
91. Amirkhani, S.; Bahadori-Jahromi, A.; Mylona, A.; Godfrey, P.; Cook, D. Impact of Low-E Window Films on Energy Consumption and CO_2 Emissions of an Existing UK Hotel Building. *Sustainability* **2019**, *11*, 4265. [CrossRef]
92. Transient System Simulation Tool. Available online: http://trnsys.com (accessed on 26 August 2021).
93. Ibáñez, M.; Lázaro, A.; Zalba, B.; Cabeza, L.F. An approach to the simulation of PCMs in building applications using TRNSYS. *Appl. Therm. Eng.* **2005**, *25*, 1796–1807. [CrossRef]
94. Beausoleil-Morrison, I.; Kummert, M.; Macdonald, F.; Jost, R.; McDowell, T.; Ferguson, A. Demonstration of the new ESP-r and TRNSYS co-simulator for modelling solar buildings. *Energy Procedia* **2012**, *30*, 505–514. [CrossRef]
95. Katsaprakakis, D.A.; Zidianakis, G.; Yiannakoudakis, Y.; Manioudakis, E.; Dakanali, I.; Kanouras, S. Working on Buildings' Energy Performance Upgrade in Mediterranean Climate. *Energies* **2020**, *13*, 2159. [CrossRef]
96. Pérez-Andreu, V.; Aparicio-Fernández, C.; Vivancos, J.-L.; Cárcel-Carrasco, J. Experimental Data and Simulations of Performance and Thermal Comfort in a Typical Mediterranean House. *Energies* **2021**, *14*, 3311. [CrossRef]
97. Landsberg, H.E. *The Urban Climate*; Academic Press Inc.: New York, NY, USA, 1981.
98. Su, M.A.; Ngarambe, J.; Santamouris, M.; Yun, G.Y. Empirical evidence on the impact of urbanoverheating on building cooling and heatingenergy consumption. *iScience* **2021**, *24*, 10249. [CrossRef]
99. Li, X.; Zhou, Y.; Yu, S.; Jia, G.; Li, H.; Li, W. Urban heat island impacts on building energy consumption: A review of approaches and findings. *Energy* **2019**, *174*, 407–419. [CrossRef]
100. Santamouris, M. On the energy impact of urban heat island and global warming on buildings. *Energy Build.* **2014**, *82*, 100–113. [CrossRef]
101. Bloem, J.J.; Strachan, P. *Evaluating and Modelling Near-Zero Energy Buildings; Are We Ready for 2018?* European Commission, JRC-Institute for Energy and Transport: Petten, The Netherlands, 2012.
102. Santamouris, M.; Synnefa, A.; Karlessi, T. Using advanced cool materials in the urban built environment to mitigate heat islands and improve thermal comfort conditions. *Sol. Energy* **2011**, *85*, 3085–3102. [CrossRef]
103. Stavrakakis, G.; Tzanaki, E.; Genetzaki, V.; Anagnostakis, G.; Galetakis, G.; Grigorakis, E. A computational methodology for effective bioclimatic-design applications in the urban environment. *Sustain. Cities Soc.* **2012**, *4*, 41–57. [CrossRef]
104. Oke, T.R. The energetic basis of the urban heat island. *Q. J. Roy. Meteorol. Soc.* **1982**, *108*, 1–24. [CrossRef]
105. Santamouris, M. *Energy and Climate in the Urban Built Environment*; James & James Ltd.: London, UK, 2001.
106. Moonen, P.; Defraeye, T.; Dorer, V.; Blocken, B.; Carmeliet, J. Urban Physics: Effect of the micro-climate on comfort, health and energy demand. *Front. Arch. Res.* **2012**, *1*, 197–228. [CrossRef]

107. Mirzaei, P.A.; Haghighat, F. Approaches to study Urban Heat Island–Abilities and limitations. *Build. Environ.* **2010**, *45*, 2192–2201. [CrossRef]
108. Kusaka, H.; Kondo, H.; Kikegawa, Y.; Kimura, F. A Simple Single-Layer Urban Canopy Model for Atmospheric Models: Comparison with Multi-Layer and Slab Models. *Bound. Layer Meteorol.* **2001**, *101*, 329–358. [CrossRef]
109. Kondo, H.; Genchi, Y.; Kikegawa, Y.; Ohashi, Y.; Yoshikado, H.; Komiyama, H. Development of a Multi-Layer Urban Canopy Model for the Analysis of Energy Consumption in a Big City: Structure of the Urban Canopy Model and its Basic Performance. *Bound. Layer Meteorol.* **2005**, *116*, 395–421. [CrossRef]
110. Yamada, T.; Bunker, S. Development of a Nested Grid, Second Moment Turbulence Closure Model and Application to the 1982 ASCOT Brush Creek Data Simulation. *J. Appl. Meteorol.* **1988**, *27*, 562–578. [CrossRef]
111. Richards, P.; Hoxey, R. Appropriate boundary conditions for computational wind engineering models using the k-ε turbulence model. *Comput. Wind. Eng.* **1993**, *46*, 145–153. [CrossRef]
112. Stavrakakis, G.M.; Tomazinakis, N.; Markatos, N. Modified "closure" constants of the Standard k–ε turbulence model for the prediction of wind-induced natural ventilation. *Build. Serv. Eng. Res. Technol.* **2011**, *33*, 241–261. [CrossRef]
113. Shah, K.B.; Ferziger, J.H. A fluid mechanicians view of wind engineering: Large eddy simulation of flow past a cubic obstacle. *J. Wind. Eng. Ind. Aerodyn.* **1997**, *67-68*, 211–224. [CrossRef]
114. Stavrakakis, G.; Koukou, M.; Vrachopoulos, M.; Markatos, N. Natural cross-ventilation in buildings: Building-scale experiments, numerical simulation and thermal comfort evaluation. *Energy Build.* **2008**, *40*, 1666–1681. [CrossRef]
115. Brozovsky, J.; Simonsen, A.; Gaitani, N. Validation of a CFD model for the evaluation of urban microclimate at high latitudes: A case study in Trondheim, Norway. *Build. Environ.* **2021**, *205*, 108175. [CrossRef]
116. Antoniou, N.; Montazeri, H.; Neophytou, M.; Blocken, B. CFD simulation of urban microclimate: Validation using high-resolution field measurements. *Sci. Total. Environ.* **2019**, *695*, 133743. [CrossRef] [PubMed]
117. Mirzaei, P.A. Recent challenges in modeling of urban heat island. *Sustain. Cities Soc.* **2015**, *19*, 200–206. [CrossRef]
118. Pignatta, G.; Lim, N.; Mughal, M.O.; Acero, J.A. *Tools for Cooling Singapore: A Guide of 24 Simulation Tools to Assess Urban Heat Island and Outdoor Thermal Comfort*; ETH: Zurich, Switzerland, 2018.
119. Bonacquisti, V.; Casale, G.; Palmieri, S.; Siani, A. A canopy layer model and its application to Rome. *Sci. Total. Environ.* **2006**, *364*, 1–13. [CrossRef]
120. TEB. Available online: https://www.umr-cnrm.fr/spip.php?article199&lang=en (accessed on 26 August 2021).
121. Masson, V. A Physically-Based Scheme For The Urban Energy Budget In Atmospheric Models. *Bound. Layer Meteorol.* **2000**, *94*, 357–397. [CrossRef]
122. Ren, S.; Stroud, C.; Belair, S.; Leroyer, S.; Munoz-Alpizar, R.; Moran, M.; Zhang, J.; Akingunola, A.; Makar, P. Impact of Urbanization on the Predictions of Urban Meteorology and Air Pollutants over Four Major North American Cities. *Atmosphere* **2020**, *11*, 969. [CrossRef]
123. Reder, A.; Rianna, G.; Mercogliano, P.; Castellari, S. Parametric investigation of Urban Heat Island dynamics through TEB 1D model for a case study: Assessment of adaptation measures. *Sustain. Cities Soc.* **2018**, *39*, 662–673. [CrossRef]
124. Pigeon, G.; Zibouche, K.; Bueno, B.; Le Bras, J.; Masson, V. Improving the capabilities of the Town Energy Balance model with up-to-date building energy simulation algorithms: An application to a set of representative buildings in Paris. *Energy Build.* **2014**, *76*, 1–14. [CrossRef]
125. Meyer, D.; Schoetter, R.; Riechert, M.; Verrelle, A.; Tewari, M.; Dudhia, J.; Masson, V.; Van Reeuwijk, M.; Grimmond, S. WRF-TEB: Implementation and Evaluation of the Coupled Weather Research and Forecasting (WRF) and Town Energy Balance (TEB) Model. *J. Adv. Model. Earth Syst.* **2020**, *12*, e2019MS001961. [CrossRef]
126. Nogueira, M.; Lima, D.C.A.; Soares, P.M.M. An integrated approach to project the future urban climate response: Changes to Lisbon's urban heat island and temperature extremes. *Urban Clim.* **2020**, *34*, 100683. [CrossRef]
127. Roberge, F.; Sushama, L. Urban heat island in current and future climates for the island of Montreal. *Sustain. Cities Soc.* **2018**, *40*, 501–512. [CrossRef]
128. UMEP Manual. Available online: https://umep-docs.readthedocs.io/en/latest (accessed on 26 August 2021).
129. Lindberg, F.; Holmer, B.; Thorsson, S. SOLWEIG 1.0–Modelling spatial variations of 3D radiant fluxes and mean radiant temperature in complex urban settings. *Int. J. Biometeorol.* **2008**, *52*, 697–713. [CrossRef]
130. Höppe, P. A new procedure to determine the mean radiant temperature outdoors. *Wetter Leben* **1992**, *44*, 147–151.
131. Chen, L.; Yu, B.; Yang, F.; Mayer, H. Intra-urban differences of mean radiant temperature in different urban settings in Shanghai and implications for heat stress under heat waves: A GIS-based approach. *Energy Build.* **2016**, *130*, 829–842. [CrossRef]
132. Liu, D.; Hu, S.; Liu, J. Contrasting the performance capabilities of urban radiation field between three microclimate simulation tools. *Build. Environ.* **2020**, *175*, 106789. [CrossRef]
133. HosseiniHaghighi, S.; Izadi, F.; Padsala, R.; Eicker, U. Using Climate-Sensitive 3D City Modeling to Analyze Outdoor Thermal Comfort in Urban Areas. *ISPRS Int. J. Geo-Inform.* **2020**, *9*, 688. [CrossRef]
134. Rayman. Available online: https://www.urbanclimate.net/rayman/index.htm (accessed on 26 August 2021).
135. Matzarakis, A.; Rutz, F.; Mayer, H. Modelling radiation fluxes in simple and complex environments: Basics of the RayMan model. *Int. J. Biometeorol.* **2010**, *54*, 131–139. [CrossRef] [PubMed]
136. Battisti, A. Bioclimatic Architecture and Urban Morphology. Studies on Intermediate Urban Open Spaces. *Energies* **2020**, *13*, 5819. [CrossRef]

137. Peng, L.L.; Jim, C. Green-Roof Effects on Neighborhood Microclimate and Human Thermal Sensation. *Energies* **2013**, *6*, 598–618. [CrossRef]
138. ENVI-Met Homepage. Available online: http://www.envi-met.com (accessed on 26 August 2011).
139. Wania, A.; Bruse, M.; Blond, N.; Weber, C. Analysing the influence of different street vegetation on traffic-induced particle dispersion using microscale simulations. *J. Environ. Manag.* **2012**, *94*, 91–101. [CrossRef] [PubMed]
140. Szűcs, Á. Wind comfort in a public urban space—Case study within Dublin Docklands. *Front. Arch. Res.* **2013**, *2*, 50–66. [CrossRef]
141. Wai, K.-M.; Xiao, L.; Tan, T. Improvement of the Outdoor Thermal Comfort by Water Spraying in a High-Density Urban Environment under the Influence of a Future (2050) Climate. *Sustainability* **2021**, *13*, 7811. [CrossRef]
142. Morakinyo, T.E.; Dahanayake, K.; Ng, E.Y.Y.; Chow, C.L. Temperature and cooling demand reduction by green-roof types in different climates and urban densities: A co-simulation parametric study. *Energy Build.* **2017**, *145*, 226–237. [CrossRef]
143. Ansys Fluent. Fluid Simulation Software. Available online: https://www.ansys.com/products/fluids/ansys-fluent (accessed on 27 August 2021).
144. Saneinejad, S.; Moonen, P.; Defraeye, T.; Derome, D.; Carmeliet, J. Coupled CFD, radiation and porous media transport model for evaluating evaporative cooling in an urban environment. *J. Wind. Eng. Ind. Aerodyn.* **2012**, *104–106*, 455–463. [CrossRef]
145. Yuan, C.; Adelia, A.S.; Mei, S.; He, W.; Li, X.-X.; Norford, L. Mitigating intensity of urban heat island by better understanding on urban morphology and anthropogenic heat dispersion. *Build. Environ.* **2020**, *176*, 106876. [CrossRef]
146. Ansys CFX. Available online: https://www.ansys.com/products/fluids/ansys-cfx (accessed on 27 August 2021).
147. Priyadarsini, R.; Hien, W.N.; David, C.K.W. Microclimatic modeling of the urban thermal environment of Singapore to mitigate urban heat island. *Sol. Energy* **2008**, *82*, 727–745. [CrossRef]
148. Taleb, H.; Musleh, M.A. Applying urban parametric design optimisation processes to a hot climate: Case study of the UAE. *Sustain. Cities Soc.* **2015**, *14*, 236–253. [CrossRef]
149. Dimoudi, A.; Zoras, S.; Kantzioura, A.; Stogiannou, X.; Kosmopoulos, P.; Pallas, C. Use of cool materials and other bioclimatic interventions in outdoor places in order to mitigate the urban heat island in a medium size city in Greece. *Sustain. Cities Soc.* **2014**, *13*, 89–96. [CrossRef]
150. Georgakis, C.; Zoras, S.; Santamouris, M. Studying the effect of "cool" coatings in street urban canyons and its potential as a heat island mitigation technique. *Sustain. Cities Soc.* **2014**, *13*, 20–31. [CrossRef]
151. CHAM. Available online: https://www.cham.co.uk (accessed on 27 August 2021).
152. Fintikakis, N.; Gaitani, N.; Santamouris, M.; Assimakopoulos, M.; Assimakopoulos, D.; Fintikaki, M.; Albanis, G.; Papadimitriou, K.; Chryssochoides, E.; Katopodi, K.; et al. Bioclimatic design of open public spaces in the historic centre of Tirana, Albania. *Sustain. Cities Soc.* **2011**, *1*, 54–62. [CrossRef]
153. Maragkogiannis, K.; Kolokotsa, D.; Maravelakis, E.; Konstantaras, A. Combining terrestrial laser scanning and computational fluid dynamics for the study of the urban thermal environment. *Sustain. Cities Soc.* **2014**, *13*, 207–216. [CrossRef]
154. Yang, Y.; Gatto, E.; Gao, Z.; Buccolieri, R.; Morakinyo, T.E.; Lan, H. The "plant evaluation model" for the assessment of the impact of vegetation on outdoor microclimate in the urban environment. *Build. Environ.* **2019**, *159*, 106151. [CrossRef]
155. Bouyer, J.; Inard, C.; Musy, M. Microclimatic coupling as a solution to improve building energy simulation in an urban context. *Energy Build.* **2011**, *43*, 1549–1559. [CrossRef]
156. Lauzet, N.; Rodler, A.; Musy, M.; Azam, M.-H.; Guernouti, S.; Mauree, D.; Colinart, T. How building energy models take the local climate into account in an urban context—A review. *Renew. Sustain. Energy Rev.* **2019**, *116*, 109390. [CrossRef]
157. Nguyen, A.-T.; Reiter, S.; Rigo, P. A review on simulation-based optimization methods applied to building performance analysis. *Appl. Energy* **2014**, *113*, 1043–1058. [CrossRef]
158. Cao, X.; Dai, X.; Liu, J. Building energy-consumption status worldwide and the state-of-the-art technologies for zero-energy buildings during the past decade. *Energy Build.* **2016**, *128*, 198–213. [CrossRef]
159. Fernandez-Antolin, M.-M.; Del-Río, J.-M.; Gonzalo, F.D.A.; Gonzalez-Lezcano, R.-A. The Relationship between the Use of Building Performance Simulation Tools by Recent Graduate Architects and the Deficiencies in Architectural Education. *Energies* **2020**, *13*, 1134. [CrossRef]
160. Fernandez-Antolin, M.-M.; Del Río, J.M.; Gonzalez-Lezcano, R.-A. Building performance simulation tools as part of architectural design: Breaking the gap through software simulation. *Int. J. Technol. Des. Educ.* **2021**, 1–19. [CrossRef]
161. Gaspari, J.; Fabbri, K.; Cancellari, T.; Corazzi, G.; Vodola, V. The use of building performance simulation to support architectural design: A case study. *Energy Procedia* **2017**, *122*, 205–210. [CrossRef]
162. Xie, X.; Gou, Z. Building performance simulation as an early intervention or late verification in architectural design: Same performance outcome but different design solutions. *J. Green Build.* **2017**, *12*, 45–61. [CrossRef]

energies

MDPI

Article

Small-Scale Solar Photovoltaic Power Prediction for Residential Load in Saudi Arabia Using Machine Learning

Mohamed Mohana [1,*], Abdelaziz Salah Saidi [2,3], Salem Alelyani [1,4], Mohammed J. Alshayeb [5], Suhail Basha [6] and Ali Eisa Anqi [6]

1 Center for Artificial Intelligence (CAI), King Khalid University, Abha 61421, Saudi Arabia; s.alelyani@kku.edu.sa
2 Department of Electrical Engineering, College of Engineering, King Khalid University, Abha 61411, Saudi Arabia; asaidi@kku.edu.sa
3 Laboratoire des Systèmes Electriques, Ecole Nationale d'Ingénieurs de Tunis, Université de Tunis El Manar, Tunis 1002, Tunisia
4 College of Computer Science, King Khalid University, Abha 61421, Saudi Arabia
5 Department of Architecture and Planning, College of Engineering, King Khalid University, Abha 61411, Saudi Arabia; malshayeb@kku.edu.sa
6 Department of Mechanical Engineering, College of Engineering, King Khalid University, Abha 61421, Saudi Arabia; spsyed@kku.edu.sa (S.B.); aanqi@kku.edu.sa (A.E.A.)
* Correspondence: mmuhanna@kku.edu.sa

Citation: Mohana, M.; Saidi, A.S.; Alelyani, S.; Alshayeb, M.J.; Basha, S.; Anqi, A.E. Small-Scale Solar Photovoltaic Power Prediction for Residential Load in Saudi Arabia Using Machine Learning. *Energies* **2021**, *14*, 6759. https://doi.org/10.3390/en14206759

Academic Editor: Antonino Laudani

Received: 24 August 2021
Accepted: 13 October 2021
Published: 17 October 2021

Abstract: Photovoltaic (PV) systems have become one of the most promising alternative energy sources, as they transform the sun's energy into electricity. This can frequently be achieved without causing any potential harm to the environment. Although their usage in residential places and building sectors has notably increased, PV systems are regarded as unpredictable, changeable, and irregular power sources. This is because, in line with the system's geographic region, the power output depends to a certain extent on the atmospheric environment, which can vary drastically. Therefore, artificial intelligence (AI)-based approaches are extensively employed to examine the effects of climate change on solar power. Then, the most optimal AI algorithm is used to predict the generated power. In this study, we used machine learning (ML)-based algorithms to predict the generated power of a PV system for residential buildings. Using a PV system, Pyranometers, and weather station data amassed from a station at King Khalid University, Abha (Saudi Arabia) with a residential setting, we conducted several experiments to evaluate the predictability of various well-known ML algorithms from the generated power. A backward feature-elimination technique was applied to find the most relevant set of features. Among all the ML prediction models used in the work, the deep-learning-based model provided the minimum errors with the minimum set of features (approximately seven features). When the feature set is greater than ten features, the polynomial regression model shows the best prediction, with minimal errors. Comparing all the prediction models, the highest errors were associated with the linear regression model. In general, it was observed that with a small number of features, the prediction models could minimize the generated power prediction's mean squared error value to approximately 0.15.

Keywords: solar photovoltaic; power prediction; residential load; environmental parameters; machine learning models; ensemble models; artificial neural networks; correlation; backward feature elimination

1. Introduction

The building sector consumes about one-fifth of the total energy worldwide. The world energy demand for buildings is projected to increase from 81 quadrillion Btu in 2010 to approximately 131 quadrillion Btu by 2040 [1–3]. Buildings in the United States (US), including commercial and residential, accounted for about 28% of total US end-use energy consumption in 2019 [4]. Fossil fuels, the primary energy source, accounted for about

80% of US energy production in the last decade [5]. The combustion of fossil fuels to generate electricity was reported to be the largest single source of carbon dioxide (CO_2) emissions in the US in 2013. It has accounted for about 37% of total CO_2 emissions and 31% of total greenhouse gas emissions in the country [6]. Renewable energy sources are one of the critical sources of reductions in CO_2 emissions. The 2030 challenge requires the global architecture and building communities to design carbon-neutral buildings by 2030 [7]. Moreover, in Saudi Arabia, within five years (2011–2016), the electricity consumption increased from 219.66 terawatts to 287.44 terawatts, i.e., 30% [2,3,8]. In the field of renewable energy technologies, photovoltaic (PV) devices have been extensively adopted in the last decade. The global installed PV capacity increased from 1 gigawatt (GW) in 2000 to 177 GW in 2014, and reached about 633 GW in 2019 [8]. In the US, the installed PV capacity increased from around 2 GW in 2010 to over 88 GW in 2020 [9]. The US market continued this rapid expansion in 2014, with an estimated 6.2 GW added to the grid, raising the total capacity to approximately 19 GW [5]. The demand for PV technology is anticipated to grow over the next few years. A number of countries have set a percentage target for a renewable energy source of the total electricity supply at the national or state levels. In 2015, 38 out of 50 states in the US introduced renewable portfolio standards (RPSs), which require electric utility and other retail electric providers to supply a predetermined minimum percentage of customer demand with eligible renewable electricity sources, thereby creating specific standards for solar energy [10].

In Saudi Arabia, several programs focus on increasing the use of renewable energy. In its National Transformation Program, Saudi Arabia recently set an ambitious target to migrate from oil dependency and divert oil and gas exploration to various higher-value uses [11,12]. As part of its Vision 2030, the country is required to produce 40% of its energy from renewable sources [13]. Due to the availability of solar radiation throughout the year, Saudi Arabia is one of the prime locations for harnessing solar energy [14]. The accuracy of predicting the amount of energy produced by the solar PV system is imperative for appraising the capacity of the PV system, calculating incentives, and obtaining a more accurate forecasting of the investment's feasibility. Several studies in the literature have suggested simulation, modeling, and prediction-based methods for estimating the amount of energy produced by PV systems [15–19].

In this paper, the power generation data were extracted from the polycrystalline PV system at King Khalid University (KKU) in Abha city (one of the coldest cities in Saudi Arabia, with heavy rains and fog). They are correlated with the solar irradiance and other parameters, measured for the same period by the weather station, to develop a model using artificial intelligence (AI) techniques, namely, least absolute shrinkage and selection operator (LASSO), random forest (RF), linear regression (LR), polynomial regression (PR), extreme gradient boosting (XGBoost), support vector machine (SVM), and deep learning (DL), to predict the amount of energy produced by the PV system. The contribution of this work was to study the most compelling features that can be used to predict the solar panel's generated power for the building sector using the backward feature elimination method, which shows an accurate prediction of power with fewer features. The method of backward feature elimination helps to indicate that fewer features can achieve similar results.

2. Literature Review

Numerous studies have developed different forecasting models to estimate the energy output of renewable energy systems. The studies, however, differ with regard to the crucial variables that are to be predicted. Brahimi [20], proposed an artificial neural network (ANN)-based method to forecast the daily wind speed in a number of locations in Saudi Arabia. The weather data were collected from multiple local meteorological measurement stations operated by King Abdullah City for Atomic and Renewable Energy (K.A.CARE.). For this research work, five machine learning (ML) algorithms were developed and compared with each other, including ANN, SVM, random tree, RF, and RepTree. The proposed model was a feed-forward neural network (NN) model that applied a back-propagation algorithm with the administered learning technique. The similarity between predicted and actual data from meteorological stations exhibited a reasonably satisfactory agreement [20]. A study [4] analyzed various ML methods to predict the output power for uniform solar panels. The researchers used a distributed RF regression algorithm and independent variables, namely, the latitude, wind speed, month, time, cloud ceiling, ambient temperature, pressure and humidity. Another study [6] predicted the short-term, next-day global horizontal irradiance using the earlier day's meteorological and solar radiation observations. The models used for this investigation were based on computational intelligence methods of automated-design fuzzy logic systems. Fuzzy c-means clustering (FCM) and simulated annealing (SA) algorithms were utilized in fuzzy logic systems for optimization. The FCM model achieved 79.75% accuracy, and the agreement increased to 88.22% upon using the SA model. A research work conducted by [21] used ANNs to investigate the correlation between irradiance and PV output power. The model was designed for real-time prediction of the power produced the next day. The PV power output data used for the AI model were extracted from an installed PV system. The research findings revealed that ML algorithms exhibit a marked capacity for predicting power production based on various weather conditions and measures. The model helps in the management of energy flows and the optimization of PV plants' integration into power systems. In another study [22], different NN-based techniques were compared with the results procured by the simulation of a moderate manufacturing plant in the UK to forecast energy use and workshop conditions for manufacturing facilities based on output plans, environmental conditions, and the thermal characteristics of the factory building, along with building activity and usage, by comparing two deep neural networks (DNNs), namely feed-forward and recurrent. The recurrent (feed-forward) model can forecast building electricity with a precision of 96.82% (92.4%), workshop air temperatures with a precision of 99.40% (99.5%), and humidity with a precision of 57.60% (64.8%). Coupling modeling techniques with ML algorithms makes it possible to forecast and maximize energy consumption in the industrial industry using a low-cost, non-intrusive approach. Kharlova et al. [23] discussed the end-to-end forecasting of PV power output by introducing a monitored deep learning model. The suggested framework leverages numerical estimates of the weather's historical and high-resolution calculations to predict a binned probability distribution, rather than the prognostic variable's predicted values, over the prognostic time intervals. The suggested sequence-to-sequence model with focus achieved a 48.1% accuracy by root mean square error (RMSE) score on the test range, outperforming the best previously reported ability scores for a day-ahead forecast of 42.5–46.0% by a large margin [24,25]. Rajabalizadeh's study took a PV housing unit in Swanson, New Zealand. The copula method was used to model the stochastic association structure between meteorological variables, such as air temperature, wind speed, and solar radiation. The Clayton copula method was used to estimate a small-scale PV system's output power. The prediction error was crucial and, under all weather situations, copula increased forecasting results. The approach discussed in this report is expected to be sufficient for the control of energy in a smart home. As the model is easy to operate and precise, it will be accessible to residences [26]. The solar PV system was installed on the roof of the Faculty of Electrical engineering, Universiti Tun Hussein Onn Malaysia. The maximal PV output capacity on the roof will then be predicted by using the estimation process and the ANN. The experimental results have validated that ANN is capable of estimating PV performance similar to the approximation process [27]. In this research work, a microgrid residential model was developed in San Diego, California, in 2016. To verify the model precision, the solar irradiance and solar energy generated in the residential microgrid, those expected for 2017, were used in NN-based model. The two metrics used to calculate and compare the model's precision were mean absolute percentage error (MAPE) and mean squared error (MSE). The NN-based model was observed to be effective [28]. Another research work conducted by [10] developed an AI model that improved an ANN with tapped delay lines, built for one-day-ahead forecasting. The model achieved a seasonal mean absolute error that ranged between 12.2%

and 26.0% in different seasons around the year. The inputs of the model were the irradiation and the sampling hours. Monteiro et al. [29] developed models that could predict PV power using numerically predicted weather data and previous hourly values for PV electric power productions. The developed models, the analytical PV power forecasting model and multilayer perceptron PV forecasting model, achieved an RMSE between 11.95% and 12.10%. Wei [30] investigated the southern climate of Taiwan in 2016 to predict the power generation for the building roofs. This study was divided into three phases; the first phase used BP3 solar panels installed on the rooftops of buildings. The most effective model with regard to results is BP380(183.5 KWh/m^2-y), BP3125(182.2 KWh/m^2-y) with the performance of power conversion is 12.4%, 12.3%, respectively. In the second phase, a surface solar radiation measurement analysis was conducted to simulate meteorological instability during hourly PV generation; the results obtained by a DNN method are compared with backpropagation NN (BPN) and an LR model. In the third phase, a BP3125 panel was used for both the second and third phases, and DNN attained the minimum MAEs and RMSEs among the three models at lead times of 1 h, 3 h, 6 h, and 12 h, demonstrating its adequate predictive precision. The approach was validated as sufficient for evaluating the power-generation performance of a roof PV system. According to this paper, a centralized grid unit is constructed to which PV panels are installed on rooftops with an energy storage system, i.e., battery, under the power purchase agreement (PPA) scheme. The system's economic stability relies solely on the quality of the data. Therefore, AI techniques can be used to adequately forecast and control grid load in real-time via PV. This is beneficial for almost all the players concerned, i.e., the solar lease firm, the grid provider, and the end-users [31].

It has been asserted in the extant literature that the models that use numerically predicted weather data do not consider the effect of cloud cover and cloud formation when initializing [32]. Pelland et al. [33] used sky imaging and satellite data to predict the PV energy output. Another study [34] developed a model that predicts the global horizontal radiation for the next day in several weather stations in Saudi Arabia. Although these systems are primarily run and have proven remarkably helpful, they are referred to as unpredictable, uncontrollable, and non-scheduled power source systems. This is because, in line with the system's geographic region, a certain kind of power output is contingent on the atmospheric environment.

3. Experimental Settings

3.1. Site and Instruments

This study was conducted at KKU, located in Abha, Asir, Saudi Arabia. Saudi Arabia is part of the northern hemisphere, centered in West Asia. The country is divided into 13 administrative regions. Abha is the capital of the Asir region, situated 2200 m above sea level in the southwestern part of Saudi Arabia. Its coordinates are 18°13′14.40″ N and 42°30′15.59″ E. The solar PV system was installed on a south-facing rooftop at a tilt angle of 22° with the parking lots of the KKU campus, as shown in Figures 1 and 2. For research purposes, it was installed in November 2018 in the College of Engineering, far away from the harsh weather conditions of the marine environment. The selected parameters for the tilt and azimuth angle for the system are shown in Table 1. The parameters were selected in accordance with the actual values of the existing system.

Table 1. Orientation Parameters Selected In the PV System.

Tilt angle	22°
Azimuth angle	−21°
Field type	Fixed tilted plane

Figure 1. Geographical Location of Abha.

Figure 2. The Installed solar PV system at KKU.

As presented in Table 2, the solar PV system comprises 20 modules of type KS-240PC with one TRIO-5.8-TL-OUTD-400 inverter of 5.8 kW rating. The 20 modules are distributed in a total area of 33.2 m^2 over one string of the maximum power point tracker (MPPT) for maximum installation flexibility for optimal energy production. This inverter includes two MPPTs and integrates power control, monitoring functionalities, and environmental sensor inputs without the need for any external components. The total installed PV power is 4.80 kWp. The PV array parameters considered here have the following manufacturer parameters. The inverter's nominal ac power is 5.22 kW and the maximum ac power is 5.8 kVA, as the name indicates. The maximum efficiency is 98% at a voltage level of 175 V. The maximum efficiency is set as 97.5% according to the European efficiency, the average operating efficiency over a yearly power distribution corresponding to the middle-Europe climate. The inverter has two MPPT inputs, which make it possible to connect strings with different panels to one inverter. The nominal power of the two strings connected to the inverter is 4.6 kW ac, which fits well with the inverter's nominal power.

Table 2. PV Array Parameters and Characteristics.

Mechanical Characteristics	
Model	KS-240PC
Solar cells	Polycrystalline silicon 156 × 156 mm
No. of cells	60 (6 × 10)
Dimensions	1663 mm × 998 mm × 35 mm
Weight	23.5 kg
Front glass	4.0 mm tempered glass
Frame	Anodized aluminum alloy
Cell area	2.9 m^2
PV module Electrical Characteristics (STC) STC: Standard test condition; 1000 W/m^2, 25 °C, AM 1.5	
Optimum operating voltage (Vmp) (V)	30.12
Optimum operating current (Imp) (A)	8.21
Open circuit voltage (Voc) (V)	37.94
Short circuit current (Isc) A)	8.69
Maximum power @ STC (Pmax) (W)	240 W
Module efficiency	14.8%
Operating module temperature	−40 °C to +85 °C
Maximum system voltage	1000 V DC (IEC)/600 V DC (UL)
Maximum series fuse rating	20 A
Power tolerance	0/+5%
Temperature Characteristics NOCT: Nominal operating cell temperature, Irradiance level 800 W/m^2, Spectrum AM 1.5, Wind velocity 1 m/s, Ambient temperature 20 °C	
Nominal operating cell temperature (NOCT)	45 °C ± 2 °C
Temperature coefficient of Pmax	−0.44%/°C
Temperature coefficient of Voc	−0.33%/°C
Temperature coefficient of Isc	−0.055%/°C

Radiation measurements were performed by a Pyranometer (Py), as shown in Figure 3). This is a solar irradiance sensor designed to measure the global solar irradiances, which is the amount of solar energy per unit area per unit time incident on a specific orientation surface emanating from a hemispherical field of view.The global solar irradiance includes both direct and diffuse sunlight, and, in some cases, specular reflections of sunlight. Nothwithstanding this, the weather station mentioned in Section 3.2 includes a built-in Py. We observed the SR20-T2 Py to be more precise than the weather station built-in Py, where we validated our reading via the PVsyst software [35]. The Py's specifications are summarized in Table 3.

Table 3. SR20-T2 Py Specifications.

Spectral range (20% points)	285 to 3000 10^{-9} m
Calibration uncertainty	<1.2% (k = 2)
Rated operating temperature range	−40 to +80 °C
Sensitivity	7 to 25 10^{-6} V/(W/m^2)
Impedance	20 to 200
Maximum operational irradiance	2000 W/m^2
Response time (95%)	4.5 s
Temperature response	<±1% (−10 to +40 °C) and <±0.4% (−30 to +50 °C) with correction in data processing

Figure 3. SR20-T2 Py.

3.2. Weather Station

Figure 4 shows the weather station used in this study, Davis Vantage Pro2, made in the USA. It continuously collects and transmits weather data. It is equipped with several sensors for different parameters such as temperature, pressure, rainfall, solar radiation. The weather station was assembled with the console and the sensor suit. This console and the sensor unit are dual-powered, and have an inbuilt battery and AC-power supply connected as a backup. The sensor suite is succinctly described in Table 4, and the console equipment that displays the pertinent data is presented in Table 5. The maximum capacity of the anemometer is 322 kph (wind speed). This makes the weather station more durable and sensitive to the lightest breeze. The weather station was installed on the rooftop of KKU.

Figure 4. Rooftop Weather Station.

Table 4. The Sensor Suite Consistency.

SI No.	Parameter	Type of Sensor Used
1	Temperature sensor	PN junction silicon diode
2	Wind speed sensor	Solid state magnetic sensor
3	Wind direction sensor	Wind vane with potentiometer
4	Rain collector	Tipping spoon type of Tipping bucket, 0.01″ per tip (0.2 mm with metric rain adapter)
5	Relative humidity sensor	Film capacitor element
6	Housing material	UV-resistance, ABS, Polypropylene

Table 5. Console Output.

Sl No.	Parameter	Resolution	Range	Accuracy
1	Barometric pressure	0.01″ Hg, 0.1 mm Hg, 0.1 hPa/mb	16.00″ to 32.50″ Hg, 410 to 820 mm Hg, 540 to 1100 hPa/mb	±0.03″ Hg (±0.8 mm Hg, ±1.0 hPa/mb) (at room temperature)
2	Clock	1 min	12 or 24 h format	±8 s/month
3	Dew point	1 °F or 1 °C. °C is converted from °F rounded to the nearest 1 °C	−105° to +130 °F (−76° to +54 °C)	±3 °F (±1.5 °C) (typical)
4	Evapotranspiration	0.01″ or 0.1 mm	Daily to 32.67″ (832.1 mm); Monthly Yearly to 199.99″ (1999.9 mm)	Greater of 0.01″ (0.25 mm) or ±5%
5	Forecast	Barometric Reading Trend, Wind Speed Direction, Rainfall, Temperature, Humidity, Latitude Longitude, Time of Year	—	——
6	Heat Index	1 °F or 1 °C. °C is converted from °F rounded to the nearest 1 °C	−40° to +165 °F (−40° to +74 °C)	±3 °F (±1.5 °C) (typical)
7	Humidity	1%	1 to 100% RH	±3% (0 to 90% RH), ±4% (90 to 100% RH)
8	Moon phase	1/8 (12.5%) of a lunar cycle, 1/4 (25%) of lighted face on console	New moon, Waxing crescent, First quarter, Waxing gibbous, Full moon, Waning gibbous, Last quarter, Waning crescent	±38 min

Table 5. *Cont.*

Sl No.	Parameter	Resolution	Range	Accuracy
9	Rainfall	0.01″ or 0.2 mm (1 mm at totals ≥2000 mm)	0 to 199.99″ (0 to 6553 mm)	For rain rates up to 2/h (50 mm/h): ±4% of total or +0.01″ (0.2 mm) (0.01″ = one tip of the bucket), whichever is greater. For rain rates from 2/h (50 mm/h) to 4/h (100 mm/h): ±4% of total or +0.01″ (0.25 mm) (0.01″ = one tip of the bucket), whichever is greater
10	Rain rate	0.01″ or 0.1 mm	0, 0.04/h (1 mm/h) to 96/h (0 to 2438 mm/h)	±5% for rates less than 5″ per hour (127 mm/h)
11	Solar radiation	1 W/m^2	0 to 1800 W/m^2	±5% of full scale
12	Sunrise and sunset	1 min	Depends	±1 min
13	Temperature	0.1 °F or 1 °F or 0.1 °C or 1 °C (user-selectable) °C is converted from °F rounded to the nearest 1 °C	+32° to +140°F (0° to +60 °C)	±1 °F (±0.5 °C)
14	Temperature humidity Sun wind index	0.1 °F or 1 °F or 0.1 °C or 1 °C (user selectable) °C Is converted from °F rounded to the nearest 1 °C	−90° to +165 °F (−68° to +74 °C)	±4 °F (±2 °C) (typical)
15	Ultra violet (UV) radiation dose	0.1 MEDs to 19.9 MEDs; 1 MED above 19.9 MEDS	0 to 199 MEDs	±5% of daily total
16	UV radiation index	0.1 Index	0 to 16 Index	±5% of full scale
17	Wind direction	16 points (22.5°) on compass rose, 1° in numeric display	0°–360°	±3°
18	Wind speed	1 mph, 1 km/h, 0.4 m/s, or 1 knot (user-selectable). Measured in mph, other units are converted from mph and rounded to the nearest 1 km/h, 0.1 m/s, or 1 knot.	1 to 200 mph, 1 to 173 knots, 0.5 to 89 m/s, 1 to 322 km/h	±2 mph (2 kts, 3 km/h, 1 m/s) or ±5%, whichever is greater

4. Methodology

The methodology that was adopted to build an ideal ML model for Abha's PV power prediction involved four general phases: (1) data collection and presentation, (2) data preparation (to obtain the data in a suitable format for analysis, exploration, and understanding the data to identify and extract the features required for the model), (3) feature selection and model building (to select the appropriate algorithm and prepare a training and testing dataset), (4) and model evaluation (to observe the final score of the model for the unseen dataset).

4.1. Data Collection and Presentation

As illustrated in the first part of Figure 5, the power generation data extracted from the polycrystalline PV systems placed at KKU are associated with four primary data sources measured over the same period of time. Weather station sensors (WS) were located near the station to measure various parameters, namely ambient temperature (Ta), relative humidity (RH), wind speed (W), wind direction (WD), solar irradiation (SR), and precipitation (R), where solar irradiance was found to be more accurate using the Py sensor. The computed parameters from the WS and Py were also considered. The latter included the solar PV system inverters (N) and panel sensors (PVSR). The four sources of data were utilized together to conduct our experiment. However, the collected data were for December 2019 until February 2020, between the autumn and the winter seasons. During this time, data were acquired and tabulated from sunrise to sunset at an interval of each five minutes for the parameters of low and high temperatures, average temperature, humidity, wind speed, and solar radiations. This differentiated cloudy days, clear-sky days, and mix days. Eventually, about 5000 samples were collected, with different data types such as integer, float, and object. The generated power statistical summary is presented in Table 6.

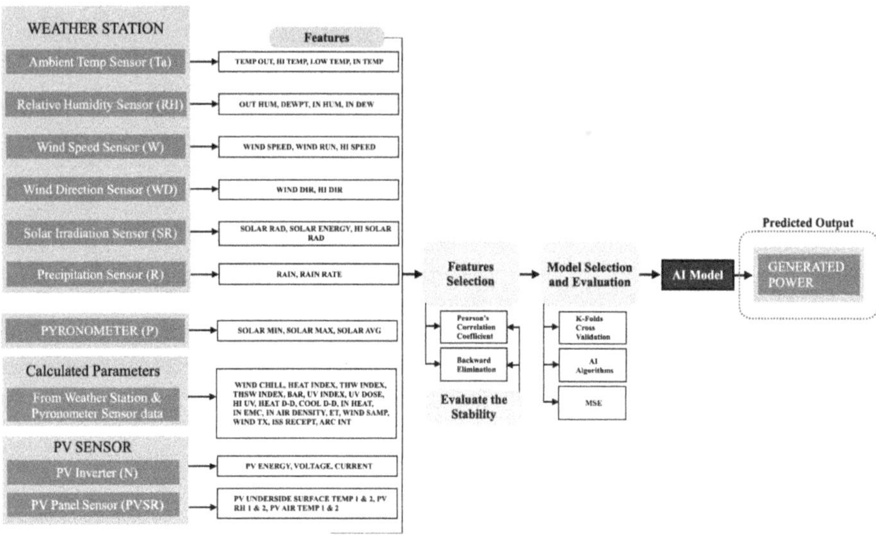

Figure 5. Block Diagram of the System.

Table 6. Statistical Summary for The Generated Power (W).

	Generated Power	Scaled Generated Power
Count	5402	5402
Mean	2336.47108	0
Standard deviation	1569.29464	1
Minimum	0	−1.489
25%	796.435	−0.98145
50%	2460.935	0.07932
75%	3873.59	0.97959
Maximum	5828.5	2.22543

Eventually, the collected dataset represented the sensors readings, assuming $\mathbf{A} = \{\mathbf{a_1}, \mathbf{a_2}, \mathbf{a_3}, \ldots, \mathbf{a_m}\}$ to be the dataset $n - by - m$ matrix, where $n = 5402$ is the number of the observations collected from each sensor and the vector $\mathbf{a_i}$ is the ith observation with $m = 42$ attributes, and the generated power $\mathbf{p}$ is the target of these features.

4.2. Data Preparation

In general, data need to be pre-processed so that they have a proper format, and are free of irregularities such as missing values, outliers, and inaccurate data values. Missing values are typical in any dataset. They may have occurred during data collection or possibly due to sensor-connecting issues. However, they must be considered by dropping their rows, estimating their values or replacing them. In our case, the data had less than 1% missing values in the total dataset; thus, eliminating these missing values was imperative. Outliers and noisy data emerge due to data entering/transmission errors. We discovered one outlier for "PV Energy", which we handled by smoothing its value.

Data scaling is typically required because many ML algorithms perform more accurately and converge faster when attributes are on a moderately similar scale and close to normally distributed. In this work, standardization (see Equation (1)) was applied to rescale data to have a mean $\mu_{(\mathbf{A},\mathbf{p})}$ of zero and a standard deviation $\sigma_{(\mathbf{A},\mathbf{p})}$ of one, where the scaled **p** is shown in Table 6.

$$(a,p)_{scaled} = \frac{((a,p)_i - \mu_{(\mathbf{A},\mathbf{p})})}{\sigma_{(\mathbf{A},\mathbf{p})}} \tag{1}$$

4.3. Feature Selection

Feature selection is one of the core concepts in ML and profoundly affects the model's performance. Its principal objective is to select the feature set with minimum cardinality while maximizing the learning performance. We believe that, when predicting generated power in the PV system, not every feature equally contributes to the prediction performance. Features can be relevant, partially relevant, or even irrelevant. Feature selection algorithms aim to assign weight to each feature according to its pertinence. As illustrated in Figure 5, in this study, we applied two approaches to score each feature, namely, Pearson's correlation coefficient [36] (see Equation (2)) and Information Gain [37] (see Equation (3)). The former measures the amount of correlation between each variable and the target, while the latter quantifies the amount of information provided to the class by evaluating the impurity level of each variable using the entropy $H(\cdot)$ with respect to the target.

$$r_{a,p} = \frac{\sum_{i=1}^{n}(a_i - \bar{a})(p_i - \bar{p})}{\sqrt{\sum_{i=1}^{n}(a_i - \bar{a})^2}\sqrt{\sum_{i=1}^{n}(p_i - \bar{p})^2}} \tag{2}$$

$$IG(p,a) = H(p) - \sum_{v \in Values(A)} \frac{|p_v|}{|p|} H(p_v) \tag{3}$$

The relevant attributes should be sasigned a greater scoring than less relevant attributes. In Equation (2), features were selected by correlating all input sensor parameters with PV-generated power **p**. Pearson's Correlation Coefficient Equation (2) was used to evaluate the correlation between the sensor parameters and PV-generated power, where n is the observation size, a_i and p_i are the single observation points indexed with i, and $\bar{a}$ is the observation mean. A positive and negative correlation score would suggest higher prediction accuracy because an increase in one value of the attribute increases/decreases the generated power value. Meanwhile, zero correlation coefficient indicates no relation. Nevertheless, Figure 6 indicates the amount of correlation of each attribute with the generated power. The Solar Average has the most crucial positive correlation (+ve) with 88%, although the Out Humidity has the most significant negative correlation (−ve) with about −42%. Meanwhile, the rain rate, rain and arc exhibited zero correlation. Furthermore, profound/redundant features that are directly affected by the generated power have been dropped, such as Voltage, Current, PV Energy, and Solar Energy, where the number of attributes were reduced to $m = 38$.

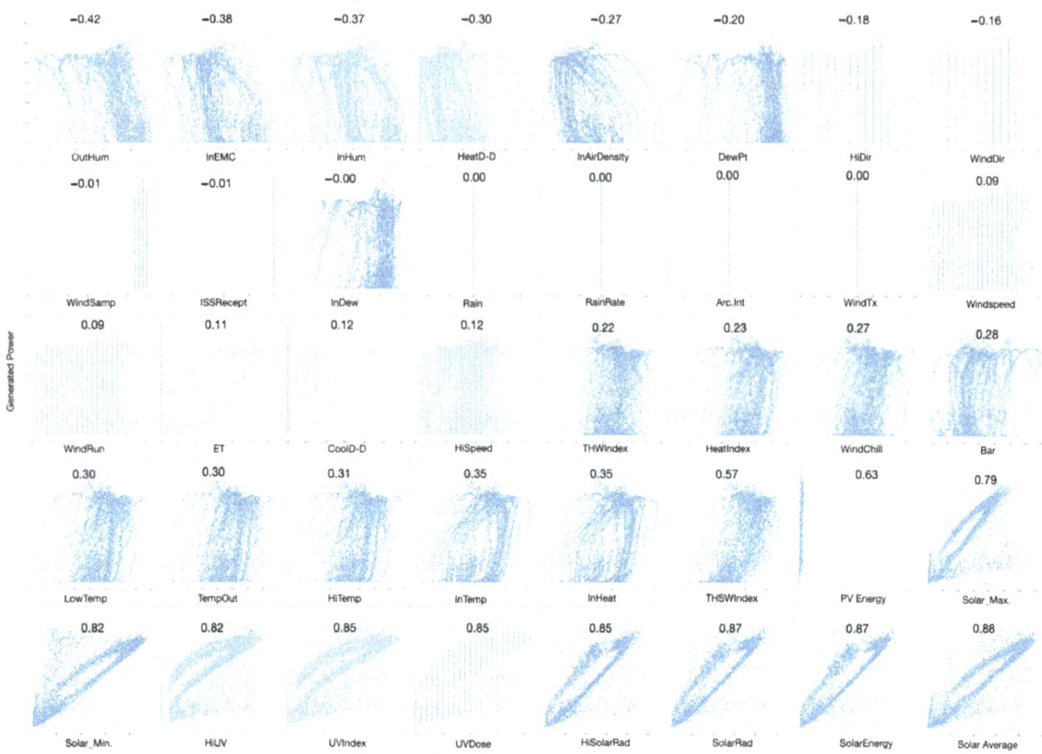

Figure 6. Correlation Plots.

To evaluate the similarity between two ranked sets of features r represented by $r_{a,p}$ and $\bar{r}$ represented by $IG(p,a)$), Spearman's rank correlation coefficient [38] (see Equation (4)) was used to assess the significance of the relationship between them.

$$S_R(r,\bar{r}) = 1 - 6\sum_i \frac{(r_i - \bar{r}_i)^2}{m(m^2-1)} \tag{4}$$

Spearman's rank correlation coefficient resulted in a range of [−1,1]. The maximum value was reached when the two ranks were equivalent, while the minimum was reached when they were precisely in reverse order and zero meaned no correlation between r and $\bar{r}$. However, after we measured the stability of the two sets of features, we observed them to be stable with the value 0.96. In Figure 7, we show the comparison of two ranked feature lists, where the x-axis and the y-axis represent the Pearson's correlation coefficient and information gain for features, respectively. Moreover, the linear line shows the stability between them.

Backward elimination was applied after Pearson's correlation coefficient was calculated, which selected the most appropriate attributes. We started with a complete set of attributes and then recursively removed one attribute after each iteration. The eliminated attribute is the attribute with the lowest absolute correlation coefficient $|r_{a,p}|$. At each iteration, we evaluated the loss using the remaining set of features. The backward elimination criterion was applied from the lowest correlated attribute to the highest, one until only one attribute remained.

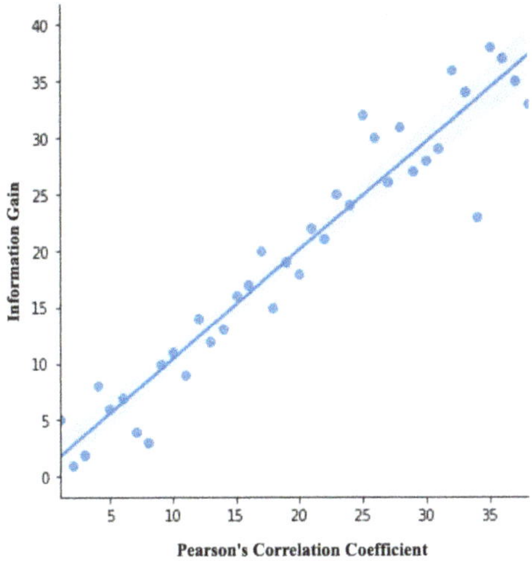

Figure 7. Spearman's Rank Correlation Coefficient.

4.4. Model Selection and Evaluation

The selection of appropriate ML algorithms to predict the amount of power generated $\hat{\mathbf{p}}$ based on the sensors' readings was challenging, because each ML model performs differently on the same dataset according to the model's nature. A number of ML models need to be trained and tested to select the optimal or superior one. Nonetheless, prior to the training, the dataset needs to be divided into a training set, to build up a model by extracting the features and train them to fit the model, and a testing set, to validate the built model by predicting the outcome of the unseen data. There are numerous methods of splitting the dataset, such as hold-out and cross-validation. As illustrated in the first part of Figure 5, in this experiment, we used k-fold cross-validation with $k = 10$. It is known for its ability to reduce overfitting while improving generalizability power. Moreover, cross-validation is known to have a better bias-variance trade-off. Therefore, the models are expected to perform equally well for the unseen data and the training data.

Many classical and modern regression and prediction models were examined in this study to estimate the generated power from the PV system. These include LASSO, RF, LR, PR, XGBoost, SVM, and DL.

The LR model [39] (see Equation (5)) is one of the simplest ML models used to find a linear relationship between the generated power $\mathbf{p}$ and the input parameters $\mathbf{A}$. Taking $\mathbf{y}$ as the response value that lies in the best-fit regression plane, the intercept b in Equation (6) is the reference position of the plane, and $\mathbf{x_m}$ is the m predictor variable from the most effective attributes. $w_1, \ldots, w_m$ in Equation (7) are the parameters of slope coefficients. The response variable is the generated power $\mathbf{p}$, and the predictor variables are selected from the most effective attributes $\mathbf{A}$ variables. Nevertheless, Equation (5) can present all the datapoints as a matrix (see (8)). Next, PR [40] (see Equation (9)) is a well-known algorithm, applied when the data are correlated, but the relationships are non-linear. This is a particular case of LR because we created polynomial attributes to fit the polynomial equation, where the dth power is the PR degree. LASSO [41] is also a type of LR model trained with an L1 regularizer in the loss function $J(w)_{L1} = \frac{1}{n}\sum_{i=1}^{n}(f_w(x)_i - y_i) + \lambda\sum_{j=1}^{n}|w_j|$, to reduce overfitting, which applies shrinkage. Shrinkage is where data values are shrunk toward a central point, where λ denotes the amount of shrinkage. However, it is well-suited for data that show high multi-collinearity levels and fewer parameters.

$$y \leftarrow f_w(x) = b_n + w_1x_1 + \ldots + w_mx_m \tag{5}$$

$$b_n = \frac{(\sum_{i=1}^{n} y_i)(\sum_{i=1}^{n} x_i^2) - (\sum_{i=1}^{n} x_i)(\sum_{i=1}^{n} x_i y_i)}{n(\sum_{i=1}^{n} x_i^2) - (\sum_{i=1}^{n} x_i)^2} \tag{6}$$

$$w_m = \frac{n(\sum_{i=1}^{m} x_i y_i)(\sum_{i=1}^{m} x_i^2) - (\sum_{i=1}^{m} x_i)(\sum_{i=1}^{m} y_i)}{n(\sum_{i=1}^{m} x_i^2) - (\sum_{i=1}^{m} x_i)^2} \tag{7}$$

$$\begin{pmatrix} y_1 \\ y_2 \\ \vdots \\ y_n \end{pmatrix} = \begin{pmatrix} b_1 \\ b_2 \\ \vdots \\ b_n \end{pmatrix} + \begin{pmatrix} w_1 \\ w_2 \\ \vdots \\ w_m \end{pmatrix} \begin{pmatrix} x_1 & x_2 & \cdots & x_m \end{pmatrix} \tag{8}$$

$$y = b + w_1 x_1 + w_2 x_1^2 + \ldots + w_d x_1^d \tag{9}$$

An RF [42] is an ensemble of randomized regression trees that combine predictions from multiple ML algorithms to make more accurate predictions and control overfitting. XGBoost [43] has evolved as one of the most famous ML algorithms in recent years. It relates to a family of boosting algorithms named the gradient boosting decision tree (GBDT), a sequential technique that operates on the principle of an ensemble as it combines a set of weak learners and delivers an increased prediction accuracy. The most prominent difference between XGBoost and GBDT is that the former uses advanced regularization, such as L1 (LASSO) and L2 (Ridge), which is faster and has less chance of overfitting. An SVM [44] (see Equation (10)) performs a non-linear mapping of the training data to a higher-dimension space over a kernel function ϕ. It is possible to perform an LR where the kernel selection defines a more or less efficient model. The radial basis function (RBF) $e^{-\gamma\|x-y\|^2}$, as the kernel function, is used as a mapping function.

$$f_w(x) = \sum_{i=1}^{n} w_i^T \phi(x^i) + b \tag{10}$$

NNs [45,46] have been extensively applied to solve numerous challenging AI problems. They surpass the traditional ML models by dint of their non-linearity, variable synergies, and customizability. The process of building an NN starts with the perceptron. In simple and straightforward terms, the perceptron receives inputs, multiplies them by some weights, and then carries them into an activation function such as a rectified linear unit (ReLU) to generate an output. NNs are designed by adding these perceptron layers together, in what is known as a multi-layer perceptron model. There are three layers of an NN: input, hidden, and output. The input layer immediately receives the data, whereas the output layer produces the required output. The layers in between are called hidden layers, and are where the intermediate computation takes place.

Model evaluation is a critical ML task. It helps to quantify and validate the model's performance, makes it easy to present the model to others, and ultimately selects the most suitable model. There are various evaluation metrics; however, only a few of these are applicable to regression. In this work, the most common metric used for regression tasks (MSE) is applied to compare the models' results. MSE (see Equation (11)) is the average of the squared difference between the predicted power $\hat{\mathbf{p}}$ and the actual power $\mathbf{p}$. This penalizes large errors and is more convenient for optimization, as it is differentiable and has a convex shape.

$$MSE = \frac{1}{n} \sum_{i=1}^{n} (\hat{p}_i - p_i)^2 \tag{11}$$

Figure 5 schematically presents the overall AI system and methodology used in the research and delineates all the steps from data collection until the computation of predicted power.

5. Results and Discussion

As noted previously and depicted in Figure 7, the two feature-scoring approaches generated very similar results. Therefore, the learning performance was almost equivalent using both approaches. We omitted the results of the information gain to reduce duplication.

The results of the prediction error, illustrated in Figure 8, reveal that all prediction models behave in a similar manner. The DL-based model gave the minimum error with the minimum set of features (approximately seven features). The DL error was steady, with almost over all feature sets' cardinalities ranging from almost two features up to the full cardinality. Thus, it can be concluded that, when using only a few features or looking for a very stable prediction regardless of the features, DL is preferable.

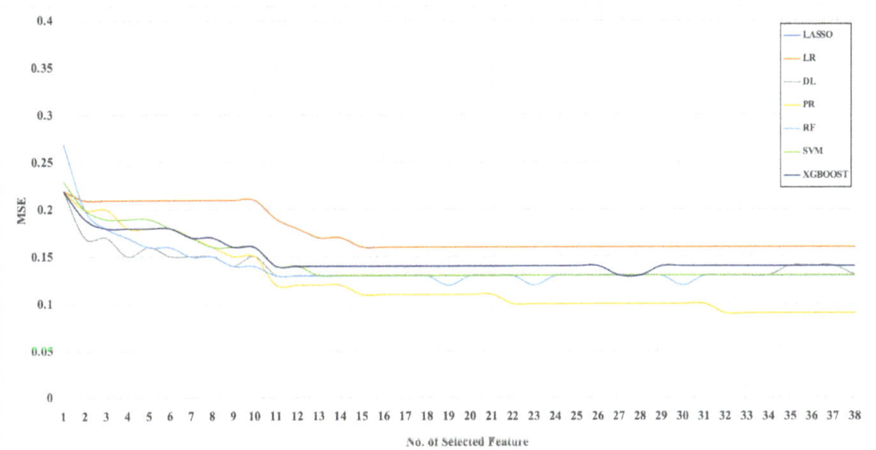

Figure 8. Results attained with various ML techniques.

In contrast, PR's prediction was the best when the feature set was greater than 10 features. This illustrates the advantageous properties of PR in the extraction of marginally useful knowledge, even from extremely irrelevant features. MSE kept steadily reducing after adding more features. With regard to MSE, PR is the most optimal choice in this case, as it had the lowest value.

As expected, LR had the highest error associated, with erros found over various selected cardinalities. LR is not capable of modeling non-linear relationships. The generated power is nonlinear in this problem. Thus, LR is not a suitable and adequate fit for the model.

LASSO, XGBOOST, SVM, and RF behaved in a similar manner. RF was the worst in terms of MSE in the cases with a single feature. This is intuitive, due to the nature of the algorithm. To build more decision trees, RF requires more features. Thus, one feature was not sufficient to extract sufficient and relevant knowledge in this case. However, SVM was extremely steady after selecting 13 features. This is due to the fundamental nature of SVM, which works by selecting a set of support vectors to maximize the margin. These support vectors are the same beyond the thirteenth feature. This is another way of indicating the proper number of selected features.

Figure 9 illustrates the actual active power versus the predicted one from December 2019 to February 2020 using a PR model. Thus, we can observe that the model can reasonably predict the generated power. However, there are still obstacles to some predictions, due to sudden voltage dips in the original dataset. The latter occured because we applied a transient three-phase voltage dip to gauge the performance of the system under study. The active power output from the whole PV system before the fault was 4000 W. After the occurrence of a fault, a transient peak of 5800 W was instantly observed for the active power generation. Within a short interval, and according to the Saudi grid code [47], the transient was cleared. The solar PV system controller action was sustained to cope with the fault, after which the power oscillations were damped out and the system restored to its regular operation. Therefore, immediately after the fault was cleared, the solar PV system entered a voltage regulation mode [48,49], and the active power generated at the solar PV terminals started to reach the rated values. **p** output's mirrored characteristics are a sign of the controlled converter action, which is only limited by the converter's nominal current rating.

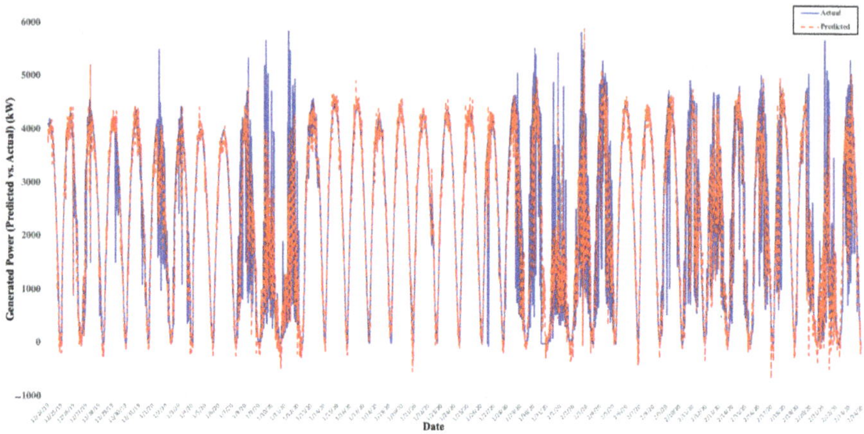

Figure 9. Results.

6. Conclusions and Future Work

In this paper, seven well-known machine learning algorithms were successfully applied to solar PV system data from Abha (Saudi Arabia) to predict the generated power. The prediction error of the algorithms was relatively low. This indicates that we can confidently evaluate the feasibility of installing solar PV systems in residential buildings using only a small set of weather station data. Although the algorithms behaved similarly, the Deep Learning technique gave the minimum error with the minimum set of selected features. However, Polynomial Regression produced the best prediction performance when we incorporated more features.

Author Contributions: Conceptualization, M.M., S.A. and A.S.S.; methodology, M.M. and S.A.; software, M.M.; validation, A.S.S., M.J.A. and S.B.; formal analysis, M.M. and S.A.; investigation, M.M.; resources, S.A. and A.E.A.; data curation, M.M. and A.E.A.; writing—original draft preparation, M.M.; writing—review and editing, M.M., A.S.S., S.A., M.J.A. and S.B.; visualization, M.M. and S.B.; supervision, S.A.; project administration, M.M., S.A. and A.S.S.; funding acquisition, S.A. All authors have read and agreed to the published version of the manuscript.

Funding: This research is financially supported by the Deanship of Scientific Research at King Khalid University under research grant number (RGP1/207/42).

Institutional Review Board Statement: Not applicable.

Informed Consent Statement: Not applicable.

Data Availability Statement: Not applicable.

Acknowledgments: This work would not have been possible without the financial support offered by King Khalid University. We would like to express our deepest gratitude to their generous support.

Conflicts of Interest: The authors declare no conflict of interest.

References

1. Newell, R.; Raimi, D.; Aldana, G. Global Energy Outlook 2019: The Next Generation of Energy. Available online: https://www.rff.org/publications/reports/global-energy-outlook-2019/ (accessed on 11 October 2020).
2. Capuano, L. *International Energy Outlook 2018 (IEO2018)*; US Energy Information Administration (EIA): Washington, DC, USA, 2018; Volume 2018, p. 21.
3. Khan, M.M.A.; Asif, M.; Stach, E. Rooftop PV potential in the residential sector of the Kingdom of Saudi Arabia. *Buildings* **2017**, *7*, 46. [CrossRef]
4. EIA. FREQUENTLY ASKED QUESTIONS (FAQ). 2020. Available online: https://www.eia.gov/tools/faqs/faq.php?id=86&t=1 (accessed on 24 December 2020).
5. U.S. Energy Information Administration. Total Energy Monthly Data. 2020. Available online: https://www.eia.gov/totalenergy/data/monthly/pdf/mer.pdf (accessed on 24 December 2020).
6. Almaraashi, M. Short-term prediction of solar energy in Saudi Arabia using automated-design fuzzy logic systems. *PLoS ONE* **2017**, *12*, e0182429. [CrossRef] [PubMed]
7. Mazria, E.; Kershner, K. Meeting the 2030 challenge through building codes. *Architecture* **2008**, *2030* Available online: https://sallan.org/pdf-docs/2030Challenge_Codes_WP-1.pdf (accessed 24 December 2020)
8. REN21, Global Status Report. Renewable Energy Policy Network for the 21st Century. 2020. Available online: https://www.ren21.net/wp-content/uploads/2019/05/gsr_2020_full_report_en.pdf (accessed on 24 December 2020).
9. SEIA. U.S. Solar Market Insight. 2020. Available online: https://www.seia.org/us-solar-market-insight#:~:text=The%20U.S.%20installed%203.8%20gigawatts,power%2016.4%20million%20American%20homes (accessed on 24 December 2020).
10. Cococcioni, M.; D'Andrea, E.; Lazzerini, B. One day-ahead forecasting of energy production in solar photovoltaic installations: An empirical study. *Intell. Decis. Technol.* **2012**, *6*, 197–210. [CrossRef]
11. IRENA. Energy Profile Saudi Arabia. 2020. Available online: https://www.irena.org/IRENADocuments/Statistical_Profiles/Middle%20East/Saudi%20Arabia_Middle%20East_RE_SP.pdf (accessed on 24 December 2020).
12. Amran, Y.A.; Amran, Y.M.; Alyousef, R.; Alabduljabbar, H. Renewable and sustainable energy production in Saudi Arabia according to Saudi Vision 2030; Current status and future prospects. *J. Clean. Prod.* **2020**, *247*, 119602. [CrossRef]
13. Care, K. *Building the Renewable Energy Sector in Saudi Arabia*; International Renewable Energy Agency: Abu Dhabi, United Arab Emirates, 2012. Available online: https://www.irena.org/-/media/Files/IRENA/Agency/Events/2012/Sep/5/5_Ibrahim_Babelli.pdf (accessed on 24 December 2020).
14. Pazheri, F. Solar power potential in Saudi Arabia. *Int. J. Eng. Res. Appl.* **2014**, *4*, 171–174.
15. Saber, E.M.; Lee, S.E.; Manthapuri, S.; Yi, W.; Deb, C. PV (photovoltaics) performance evaluation and simulation-based energy yield prediction for tropical buildings. *Energy* **2014**, *71*, 588–595. [CrossRef]
16. Chowdhury, S.; Taylor, G.; Chowdhury, S.; Saha, A.; Song, Y. Modelling, simulation and performance analysis of a PV array in an embedded environment. In Proceedings of the IEEE 2007 42nd International Universities Power Engineering Conference, Brighton, UK, 4–6 September 2007; pp. 781–785.
17. Chouder, A.; Silvestre, S.; Sadaoui, N.; Rahmani, L. Modeling and simulation of a grid connected PV system based on the evaluation of main PV module parameters. *Simul. Model. Pract. Theory* **2012**, *20*, 46–58. [CrossRef]
18. Al-Dahidi, S.; Ayadi, O.; Adeeb, J.; Louzazni, M.; Hemidat, S.; Saidan, M.; Al-Zu'bi, S.; Nelles, M.; Hamdan, M.A.; Brawiesh, A.K.; et al. Assessment of Artificial Neural Networks Learning Algorithms and Training Datasets for Solar Photovoltaic Power Production Prediction. *Front. Energy Res.* **2019**, *7*, 130. [CrossRef]
19. Pasion, C.; Wagner, T.; Koschnick, C.; Schuldt, S.; Williams, J.; Hallinan, K. Machine Learning Modeling of Horizontal Photovoltaics Using Weather and Location Data. *Energies* **2020**, *13*, 2570. [CrossRef]
20. Brahimi, T. Using Artificial Intelligence to Predict Wind Speed for Energy Application in Saudi Arabia. *Energies* **2019**, *12*, 4669. [CrossRef]
21. Alomari, M.H.; Adeeb, J.; Younis, O. Solar photovoltaic power forecasting in jordan using artificial neural networks. *Int. J. Electr. Comput. Eng. (IJECE)* **2018**, *8*, 497. [CrossRef]
22. Mawson, V.J.; Hughes, B.R. Deep learning techniques for energy forecasting and condition monitoring in the manufacturing sector. *Energy Build.* **2020**, *217*, 109966. [CrossRef]
23. Kharlova, E.; May, D.; Musilek, P. Forecasting Photovoltaic Power Production using a Deep Learning Sequence to Sequence Model with Attention. In Proceedings of the IEEE 2020 International Joint Conference on Neural Networks (IJCNN), Glasgow, UK, 19–24 July 2020; pp. 1–7.
24. Antonanzas, J.; Osorio, N.; Escobar, R.; Urraca, R.; Martinez-de Pison, F.J.; Antonanzas-Torres, F. Review of photovoltaic power forecasting. *Sol. Energy* **2016**, *136*, 78–111. [CrossRef]
25. Pierro, M.; Bucci, F.; De Felice, M.; Maggioni, E.; Moser, D.; Perotto, A.; Spada, F.; Cornaro, C. Multi-Model Ensemble for day ahead prediction of photovoltaic power generation. *Sol. Energy* **2016**, *134*, 132–146. [CrossRef]
26. Rajabalizadeh, S.; Tafreshi, S.M.M. A Practicable Copula-Based Approach for Power Forecasting of Small-Scale Photovoltaic Systems. *IEEE Syst. J.* **2020**, *14*, 4911–4918. [CrossRef]
27. Wee, Y.N.; Nor, A.F.M. Prediction of Rooftop Photovoltaic Power Generation Using Artificial Neural Network. In Proceedings of the 2020 IEEE Student Conference on Research and Development (SCOReD), Johor, Malaysia, 27–29 September 2020; pp. 346–351.

28. Sabzehgar, R.; Amirhosseini, D.Z.; Rasouli, M. Solar power forecast for a residential smart microgrid based on numerical weather predictions using artificial intelligence methods. *J. Build. Eng.* **2020**, *32*, 101629. [CrossRef]
29. Monteiro, C.; Fernandez-Jimenez, L.A.; Ramirez-Rosado, I.J.; Muñoz-Jimenez, A.; Lara-Santillan, P.M. Short-term forecasting models for photovoltaic plants: Analytical versus soft-computing techniques. *Math. Probl. Eng.* **2013**, *2013*, 767284. [CrossRef]
30. Wei, C.C. Evaluation of Photovoltaic Power Generation by Using Deep Learning in Solar Panels Installed in Buildings. *Energies* **2019**, *12*, 3564. [CrossRef]
31. Amarawardhana, K.N.; Jayasinghe, S.D.; Shahnia, F. Grid-interactive rooftop photovoltaic clusters with third-party ownership. *Int. J. Smart Grid Clean Energy* **2020**, *9*, 102–111. [CrossRef]
32. Tuohy, A.; Zack, J.; Haupt, S.E.; Sharp, J.; Ahlstrom, M.; Dise, S.; Grimit, E.; Mohrlen, C.; Lange, M.; Casado, M.G.; et al. Solar forecasting: Methods, challenges, and performance. *IEEE Power Energy Mag.* **2015**, *13*, 50–59. [CrossRef]
33. Pelland, S.; Remund, J.; Kleissl, J.; Oozeki, T.; De Brabandere, K. Photovoltaic and solar forecasting: State of the art. *IEA PVPS Task* **2013**, *14*, 1–36.
34. Awan, A.B.; Zubair, M.; Abokhalil, A.G. Solar energy resource analysis and evaluation of photovoltaic system performance in various regions of Saudi Arabia. *Sustainability* **2018**, *10*, 1129. [CrossRef]
35. Kandasamy, C.; Prabu, P.; Niruba, K. Solar potential assessment using PVSYST software. In Proceedings of the 2013 IEEE International Conference on Green Computing, Communication and Conservation of Energy (ICGCE), Chennai, India, 12–14 December 2013; pp. 667–672.
36. Lee Rodgers, J.; Nicewander, W.A. Thirteen ways to look at the correlation coefficient. *Am. Stat.* **1988**, *42*, 59–66. [CrossRef]
37. Cover, T.M.; Thomas, J.A. Entropy, relative entropy and mutual information. *Elem. Inf. Theory* **1991**, *2*, 12–13.
38. Kalousis, A.; Prados, J.; Hilario, M. Stability of feature selection algorithms: A study on high-dimensional spaces. *Knowl. Inf. Syst.* **2007**, *12*, 95–116. [CrossRef]
39. Chung, C.J.F.; Fabbri, A.G.; Van Westen, C.J. Multivariate regression analysis for landslide hazard zonation. In *Geographical Information Systems in Assessing Natural Hazards*; Springer: Berlin/Heidelberg, Germany, 1995; pp. 107–133.
40. Ostertagová, E. Modelling using polynomial regression. *Procedia Eng.* **2012**, *48*, 500–506. [CrossRef]
41. Xu, H.; Caramanis, C.; Mannor, S. Robust regression and lasso. *IEEE Trans. Inf. Theory* **2010**, *56*, 3561–3574. [CrossRef]
42. Liaw, A.; Wiener, M. Classification and regression by randomForest. *R News* **2002**, *2*, 18–22.
43. Chen, T.; Guestrin, C. XGBoost: A Scalable Tree Boosting System. Available online: https://dl.acm.org/doi/abs/10.1145/2939672.2939785 (accessed on 24 December 2020).
44. Chang, C.C.; Lin, C.J. Training v-support vector regression: Theory and algorithms. *Neural Comput.* **2002**, *14*, 1959–1977. [CrossRef]
45. Specht, D.F. A general regression neural network. *IEEE Trans. Neural Netw.* **1991**, *2*, 568–576. [CrossRef] [PubMed]
46. Hopfield, J.J. Artificial neural networks. *IEEE CIrcuits Devices Mag.* **1988**, *4*, 3–10. [CrossRef]
47. Sa, N.G. The Saudi Arabian Grid Code, Electronic Update as of February 2020. 2020. Available online: https://www.ecra.gov.sa/ar-sa/ECRARegulations/Codes/Documents/SAGC%20Electronic%20Update.pdf (accessed on 24 December 2020).
48. Saidi, A.S. Impact of large photovoltaic power penetration on the voltage regulation and dynamic performance of the Tunisian power system. *Energy Explor. Exploit.* **2020**, *38*, 1774–1809. [CrossRef]
49. Saidi, A.S. Investigation of Structural Voltage Stability in Tunisian Distribution Networks Integrating Large-Scale Solar Photovoltaic Power Plant. *Int. J. Bifurc. Chaos* **2020**, *30*, 2050259. [CrossRef]

energies

MDPI

Article

Modeling, Simulation, and Analysis of a Variable-Length Pendulum Water Pump

Godiya Yakubu *, Paweł Olejnik and Jan Awrejcewicz

Department of Automation, Biomechanics and Mechatronics, Faculty of Mechanical Engineering, Lodz University of Technology, 1/15 Stefanowski Str., 90-924 Lodz, Poland; pawel.olejnik@p.lodz.pl (P.O.); jan.awrejcewicz@p.lodz.pl (J.A.)

* Correspondence: godiya.yakubu@dokt.p.lodz.pl

Abstract: Due to the long-term problem of electricity and potable water in most developing and undeveloped countries, predominantly rural areas, a novelty of the pendulum water pump, which uses a vertically excited parametric pendulum with variable-length using a sinusoidal excitation as a vibrating machine, is presented. With this, more oscillations can be achieved, reducing human effort further and having high output than the existing pendulum water pump with the conventional pendulum. The pendulum, lever, and piston assembly are modeled by a separate dynamical system and then joined into the many degrees-of-freedom dynamical systems. The present work includes friction while studying the system dynamics and then simulated to verify the system's harmonic response. The study showed the effect of the pendulum length variability on the whole system's performance. The vertically excited parametric pendulum with variable length in the system is established, giving faster and longer oscillations than the pendulum with constant length. Hence, more and richer dynamics are achieved. A quasi-periodicity behavior is noticed in the system even after 50 s of simulation time; this can be compensated when a regular external forcing is applied. Furthermore, the lever and piston oscillations show a transient behavior before it finally reaches a stable behavior.

Keywords: pendulum water pump; piston assembling; harmonic response; variable length pendulum; excited parametric pendulum

Citation: Yakubu, G.; Olejnik, P.; Awrejcewicz, J. Modeling, Simulation, and Analysis of a Variable-Length Pendulum Water Pump. *Energies* **2021**, *14*, 8064. https://doi.org/10.3390/en14238064

Academic Editor: Helena M. Ramos

Received: 29 September 2021
Accepted: 26 November 2021
Published: 2 December 2021

1. Introduction

According to Canada's government, about 40% of the world population does not have a pleasing way of getting sanitary water, which is hugely affected by the developing countries where up to 80% of illness in such areas is caused by inadequate water and sanitation [1]. Furthermore, Ref. [2] shows that more than a billion people in developing countries have insufficient clean water due to deprivation, change in climate, and bad governance. This leads to several issues such as under supply of drinking water, deficient structure to get water supply, swamp, droughts, and contamination of rivers as well as large dams [2]. In addition, people entail good water for livelihood, essential care, farming or agriculture, manufacturing, and trade. According to the 2019 UN World Development report, stated about four billion people, which is virtually two-thirds of the world population, encounter severe water scarcity at least one month in a year [2].

With the long-term problem of electricity and potable water in most developing and underdeveloped countries, especially in rural areas, more research needs to be done in areas that can positively affect their lives. One such area is the availability and accessibility of water for domestic, agricultural, and even industrial uses. There is a need to modify the existing water pump, such as the conventional hand water pumps. These rural dwellers can access good water even without electricity for the pumping (for some types of pumps). A pendulum can be used to provide the initial force for the pumping process in a reciprocating water pump [3,4]. With this principle, more water liters can be pumped with little effort since more energy can be overcome by small or little effort on the pendulum, thereby increasing the whole system's efficiency [5].

The importance of pendulum water pumps is that they significantly reduce to a minimum the human strain, making the water pumps easy to operate [6,7]. The pendulum is occasionally pushed with little effort, even with the fingers. It keeps the pumping continuous, unlike an ordinary hand pump, which always requires a load with significant steps [8]. A normal person can only make use of the hand pump for a few minutes. When pressed, water stops pumping. The situation is different from the pendulum water pump, i.e., a little pressure is needed to push the pendulum to keep changing and keep it oscillating for several hours without getting tired.

In [9], authors presented a three-dimensional model and a fabricated water hand pump with a pendulum. The pendulum's energy was analyzed based on the pendulum's kinetic and potential energy without further algorithms. In addition, 1200 L per hour of water discharge were observed using the pump with a pendulum. We noted that system dynamics need to be studied deeper to improve system efficiency and control for better performance and other research purposes.

In [8], a design, as well as the development of a pendulum-operated water pump, are presented. The mode of operation of the pendulum-operated water pump is based on defining the functions of all parts separately, but a mathematical model is not presented.

A fabricated set-up of an analytical design of a pendulum hand pump using Creo is covered by [6]. The design calculations were performed manually. The analyses show that the set-up has 70% efficiency at the initial angle of the pendulum, 39% efficiency when the pendulum is at 60° with the lever, and 25.5% efficiency when the pendulum angle is at 0 or 90° with the lever. Similarly, experimental statistics from a test rig, including validation of the dual-medium pressurizer's energy transmission strategy, are considered in [10]. An onshore pendulum's wave energy converter test rig was built for validation. It uses a hydraulic cylinder as a replacement for the wave that deploys a force on the pendulum. The overall result of the simulation shows a similar response to the experimental results.

In [11], authors designed and fabricated a pendulum hand pump. Parts of the functions were stated, the advantages and disadvantages of the pendulum pumps, the working principle, and its applications. The equations of motion need to be derived and solved numerically to allow further analysis to achieve better system performance. A kinematic approach in the theoretical analysis of a pendulum hand pump dynamics is presented in [5] where a nonlinear pendulum model is used to power the lever and the piston model for the applied excitation force to the pendulum. It is observed that satisfactory results are obtained where the frequency of excitation is greater than the pendulum's natural frequency of the model. In [5], we find the equation of the pendulum model as follows:

$$\ddot{\varphi} + \frac{g}{l}\sin\varphi = f(t), \tag{1}$$

and the equation of the lever and piston as below

$$\ddot{x} = \frac{3}{m}\left(f_1(t)\frac{l_1}{l_2} - b\dot{x} - kx\right), \tag{2}$$

where: φ—pendulum's angular displacement, g—acceleration due to gravity, l—length of the pendulum, $f(t)$—input force from the pendulum model given as $f(t) = f_0\cos(\omega t)$; f_0—forcing excitation amplitude, ω—excitation frequency, m—the mass of the lever and piston model, k—spring constant, b—viscous damping constant, l_1—distance from the input force and the lever point of pivot, P, l_2—distance from point k and P, and $f_1(t) = \sin\varphi$. Integrating numerically, Equation (7) yields the piston displacement, x. Using the same parameters presented in [5] ($l = 3$ m, $\omega = 5$ rad/s, $f_0 = 3$ m, $l_1 = 0.4$ m, $l_2 = 0.6$ m, $l_3 = \frac{1}{3}l_2$, $k = 5\,\mathrm{N{\cdot}m^{-1}}$, $b = 1\,\mathrm{N{\cdot}s{\cdot}m^{-1}}$, $m = 4$ kg), we use the proposed numerical approach of our modified system to solve Equations (1) and (2), and we have the numerical solution as shown in Figures 1 and 2, which is very similar to the ones presented in [5].

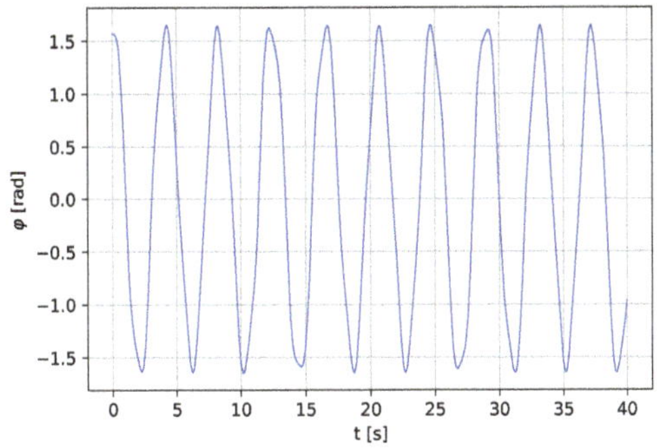

Figure 1. Angular displacement of the Pendulum in Equation (1).

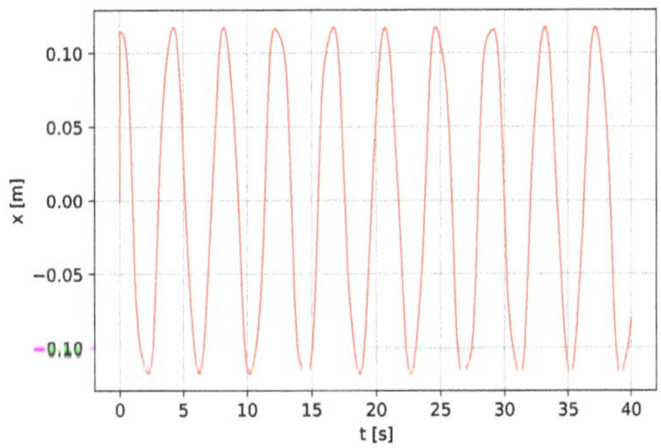

Figure 2. Linear displacement of the Piston in Equation (2).

The study needs a pivotal and in-depth analysis of fluid mechanics, and the pendulum's length can also affect the system's performance.

To further reduce the human effort, we proposed to use a pendulum with a variable-length model instead of the conventional pendulum. This modification would give a faster and longer oscillation, which will, in turn, result in more rapid pumping of fluid since the variable-length pendulum can undergo a quicker and longer oscillation, as presented by the following authors: Ref. [12] derived the differential equations of dynamics for both the first and the second mutation from the sum of kinetic and potential energy for a rigid pendulum's two and three degrees of freedom. It was observed that a successive expansion in the forms of representation of the energy is introduced. The largest Lyapunov exponent was used to classify the system based on computational analysis. The phase planes and the Poincaré maps show some homogeneous dynamic patterns, such as quasi-periodic and chaotic motions. Refs. [13,14], the Euler–Lagrange equation, and the Rayleigh dissipation function are used to derive the equation for a three-degree of freedom pendulum system. The numerical results reveal that a variable-length spring pendulum hung from the occasionally forced slider can demonstrate quasi-periodicity and chaotic motions in a resonance condition. Furthermore, near the resonance, linking bodies on the system dynamics could lead to unforeseeable dynamical comportment.

Krasilnkov presents in [15] the variable-length pendulum harmonic oscillations, which depend on the length of the pendulum. Lyapunov exponents, bifurcation diagrams, and the Poincaré maps situated on phase plane diagrams were used to inspect the system behavior. It was concluded that the system exhibited chaotic properties in the domain of higher-level stability. A control scheme for a vertically excited parametric pendulum with variable length is presented in [16]. It offers two energy sources: a vibrating machine and sea waves simulated by a stochastic process [16]. For the pendulum to be controlled, a telescopic adjustment of the pendulum length [16] is used during the motion. The numerical results show favorable terms for energy harvesting. Steady revolutions can be attained irrespective of the forcing factors and for all established initial conditions. It is concluded that it is hard to attain stable rotation due to the high reliance of the dynamical system on parameters that causes the forcing and the initial conditions. However, the controlled pendulum can reach stable rotations if the threshold velocity is sufficiently selected to modulate the control operation.

In this work, we present the following:

- The mathematical model and simulation results of the variable-length pendulum water pump were performed. The equations were solved using the Runge–Kutta method with 5th order adaptive step size.
  A vertically excited parametric pendulum with variable length [16] is used instead of the conventional pendulum with constant length, minimizing human effort with increasing output of water or liquid from the pump outlet.
- With the variable-length pendulum, more and richer dynamics can be achieved flexibly, giving more and faster oscillations and providing long-lasting energy for the fluid pumping—thus drastically reducing the human effort required for pumping and saving time.

The presented work is practical and valuable because it shows the most responsible mechanism for obtaining the minimum effort to swing the pendulum as well as provides a methodology that guarantees relatively fast and long-lasting oscillations, as stated in the problem definition below. First, the three-dimensional model is introduced. Next, the components are listed, stating the functions of each part of the system. Finally, the system's working principle is supported by mathematical modeling, results of numerical simulations covered by essential conclusions.

2. Problem Definition and Modeling

The rural area dwellers can use the pendulum water pump for farming and irrigation, water-wells, and can also be used for fire extinguishing both in rural areas and in cities. It can also be used for drainage to control liquid (water) levels in a protected area. Other areas of application include: sewage, chemical industries, medical fields, steel mills, etc. [8]. It is useful and practical for older people and children who can operate it easily, since it only requires minimum effort to swing the pendulum. Furthermore, the oscillating nature of the pendulum and maintenance do not require special training or skills to perform the task with hand or agility. Below, based on mathematical analysis and numerical simulation, we show that an initial force could be only required and then maintained for pumping the water. Based on the existing literature (to the best of our knowledge), none have used the pendulum with variable length. In our work, a vertically excited parametric pendulum with variable length [16] is used instead of the conventional pendulum, giving richer swinging dynamics in the entire mechanical coupling.

2.1. A Three-Dimensional Model

The proposed system comprises three main parts: the pendulum, the lever, and the reciprocating pump assembly containing the piston and the pushrod. Other parts include bracket foundation link, pivot point, frame, support at the frame, delivery pipe, and suction pipe. Figure 3 shows the three-dimensional physical model with the various parts of the system. The pendulum's angular motion is transmitted into the to-and-from motion of the piston through the lever and the pushrod [2].

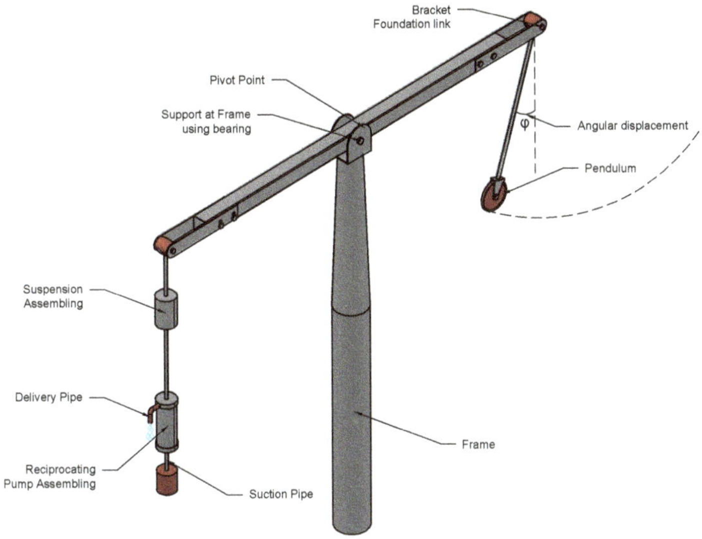

Figure 3. Configuration of the three-dimensional model of the investigated system.

The system input is from the pendulum where an initial force is applied. The lever and the spring act as a transmitter that transmits the energy to the piston (system output), where the pumping of the liquid takes place.

2.2. Components of the System

We modify the existing pendulum water pump to achieve a maximum effect by using a vertically excited parametric pendulum with variable length instead of the conventional pendulum. Each component is briefly described below:

Frame: the rigid part serving as a support where the whole system assembly is mounted.

The parametric pendulum with variable length: Ref. [16], the required energy source for commencing the action of pumping by oscillating. (Detailed in Section 3.1, case II).

Bracket: a connection between the pendulum and lever and also between the lever and the piston.

Pivot point: also called the fulcrum, it is the part where the lever turns. It plays a central role in the lever system, and the lever's power is supplied between the pivot point and the pendulum.

Bearing: to reduce rotational friction and support axial loads.

The rod: held up by double support bearing one on each side of the lever that forms the lever's fulcrum. The coupling of the lever crested on the bearing lever rotates with the use of thrashing. A different support bearing is utilized at the pendulum's bracket, allowing for the pendulum's motion.

Delivery pipe: it connects the pump's cylinder with the exit. The liquid is dispatched to the preferred exit point along this delivery pipe.

Suction pipe: it connects the origin of liquid to the reciprocating pump's cylinder. This pipe sucks the liquid from the source to the cylinder.

Reciprocating pump assembling: convert the mechanical energy into hydraulic energy by sucking the liquid into a cylinder. A piston is reciprocating, which uses thrust on the liquid and increases its hydraulic energy [17].

2.3. The Working Principle

The system free energy is based on the phenomenon of an oscillating pendulum-lever system. The pendulum pump's purpose is the oscillation of the body pendulum controlled with a small pressure hand. Change of the inertial forces causes the fluctuation of the lever attached to the pump piston connected to a spring and a damper. The oscillations of the pendulum serve as the model's input [18]. These oscillations bring about the swinging to and fro of the lever about its turning position; the lever is attached at one end to the pump's rod and brings about the lever movement. For water to flow from the pump, the pendulum does not need to be balanced. Instead, the piston starts oscillating based on gravitational potential, and water begins to come out through the delivery pipe continuously. The pendulum is to be pushed occasionally in other to maintain the continuous flow of water. The pendulum water pump works efficiently with 90° amplitude regardless of the pendulum's size [6]. The foot valve opens at the piston's upstroke, and suction brings water into the pump's upper part (head) from the suction pump. The piston's valve opens up and permits water to spout upward above the piston on the piston's following downstroke. On the subsequent piston's upstroke, water is propelled over the exit [19]. The system does not require fuel or electricity for its operation. Therefore, it is user-friendly and cannot cause global warming.

3. Mathematical Modeling

The complete system is made up of three parts: the pendulum, lever, and piston. These are modeled separately and connected through the bracket, where forces are transferred from one part to another. The motion of one makes the subsequent part move. As the pendulum is set to motion, it transfers the force to actuate the lever. The lever motion is imparted to the piston. The motion equation is established from Newton's second law of motion, i.e., $F = ma$ since a force initiates the motion.

3.1. The Pendulum

Two cases are presented below in deriving the equations of motion of the pendulum. Case I follows the standard models using Newton's second law of motion to derive the pendulum with constant length equations. The works existing in literature use this type of pendulum to act as the system inputs. In Case II of the present work, we used a vertically excited parametric pendulum with variable length as the system input. Hence, more frequent and faster oscillations can be achieved. In this case, the Euler–Lagrange equation is utilized to obtain the governing equations.

Case I: The energy needed for starting the pumping process is initiated by swinging the pendulum with minimum effort [20,21]. The pendulum model showing the free body diagram is shown in Figure 4, and its equation of motion is derived below. The force response does not transmit a moment around the position 0, where the rotation takes place. Therefore, the sum of the moments is 0 about the attachment point.

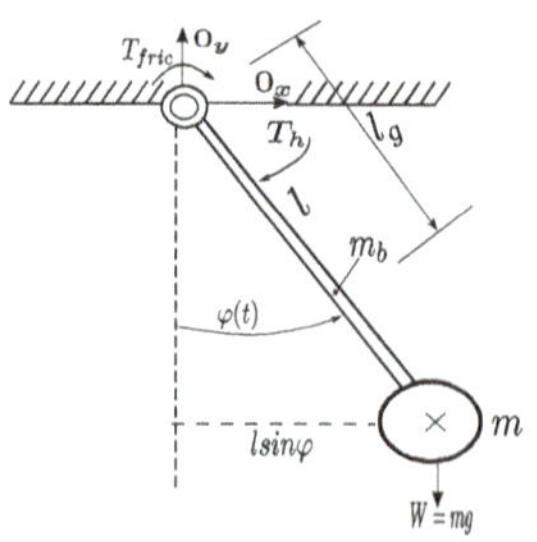

Figure 4. The pendulum free body diagram.

Summing all moments of forces, the following equation is found:

$$\sum M_t = I_0\ddot{\varphi}, \tag{3}$$

$$\sum M_t = -(m + m_b)gl\sin\varphi - T_v + T_h, \tag{4}$$

where: m_b—pendulum's bar mass (kg), m—the pendulum body mass (kg), l—length to the pivot of mass of the end weight (m), T_v—moment of viscous friction force (N·m), T_h—excitation moment (N·m), φ—pendulum angular displacement (rad), I_0—mass moment of inertia (kg·m^2), and g—acceleration due to gravity (m/s^2).

Simplifications: (i) the pendulum mass is concentrated in the center point of the end mass; (ii) $\sin\varphi \approx \varphi$, so we assume small angles of rotation in this case.

The mass moment of inertia I_0 is given as:

$$I_0 \approx (m + m_b)l^2, \tag{5}$$

For a more accurate approach, we consider the body's relative mass of the system to be situated at the system's pivot of mass, which is:

$$l_g = \frac{(ml + 0.5m_b l)}{(m + m_b)}, \tag{6}$$

so the mass moment of inertia yields:

$$I_0 = \frac{m_b l^2}{3} + ml^2. \tag{7}$$

The moment of viscous friction $T_v = b\dot{\varphi}$, where b (N·s·m^{-1}) states the coefficient of viscous damping.

Equation (4) becomes:

$$-(m + m_b)gl_g \sin\varphi - b\dot{\varphi} + T_h = I_0\ddot{\varphi}, \tag{8}$$

and at the assumed simplifications:

$$\ddot{\varphi} + \frac{b}{I_0}\dot{\varphi} + \frac{(m + m_b)gl_g\varphi}{I_0} = T_h, \tag{9}$$

where: $T_h = f_0 \cos\omega t$, f_0—amplitude of forcing excitation (N·m).

The linearized method has the configuration of a typical unconstrained differential equation of the second-order. Complementing Equation (9) to a canonical form, one finds

$$\ddot{\varphi} + 2\zeta\omega_n\dot{\varphi} + \omega_n^2\varphi = T_h, \tag{10}$$

where ω_n is the excitation frequency (rad·s^{-1}), ζ is the damping coefficient (N·s·m^{-1}), $2\zeta\omega_n = \frac{b}{I_0}$, $\omega_n^2 = \frac{(m+m_b)gl_g\varphi}{I_0}$. Later, we will show how numerous variables of the system affect the independent response of the pendulum coupling. For the simplified pendulum having its mass concentrated at its end, we find:

$$\omega_n \approx \sqrt{\frac{g}{l}}. \tag{11}$$

Case II: As shown in Figure 5, Lagrange's equation is utilized to derive the governing equation of the vertically excited parametric pendulum with variable length [16] using the sine function as input for the angular position [16].

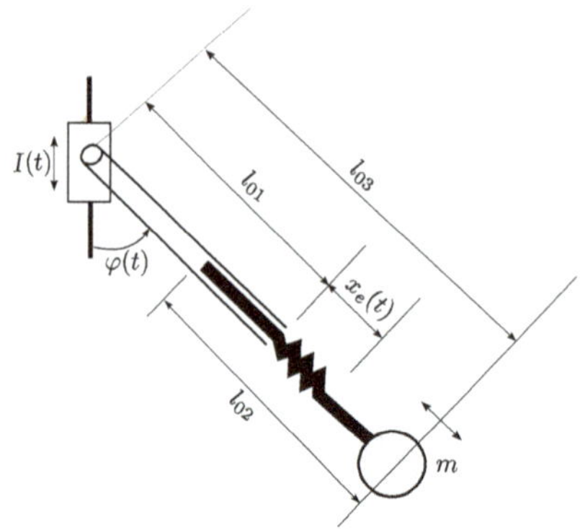

Figure 5. Schematic diagram of the vertical parametric pendulum with variable-length.

It is possible to remodel the overall length of the pendulum l_{03} by readjusting the location of the telescopic bar, l_{02}. As the bar is recanted, the original length of the pendulum l_{01} ($l_{03} = l_{01}$) is regained. The centre of rotation is stimulated vertically as a result of excised motion $I = I(t)$. Using the Euler–Lagrange equation in two degrees of freedom, the unconventional system is expressed in Equation (12)

$$\frac{d}{dt}\left(\frac{\partial L}{\partial \dot{q}}\right) - \frac{\partial L}{\partial q} + \frac{\partial D}{\partial \dot{q}} = 0, \tag{12}$$

where: $\varphi(t)$—angular displacement defined from the downward inclination point, E_k—kinetic energy equation of the system, E_p—potential energy, and D—dissipative energy of the system:

$$\begin{aligned} E_k =& \frac{1}{2}m\Big((\dot{x}_e(t)\sin\varphi(t) + \cos\varphi(t)(l_{01} + l_{02} + x_e)\dot{\varphi}(t))^2 + \\ & (-f_0\omega\sin(\omega t) + \dot{x}_e(t)\cos\varphi(t) - \sin\varphi(t)(l_{01} + l_{02} + x_e)\dot{\varphi}(t))^2\Big), \end{aligned} \tag{13}$$

$$E_p = \frac{1}{2}kx_e^2(t) - gm(f_0\cos(\omega t) + \cos\varphi(t)(l_{01} + l_{02} + x_e(t))), \tag{14}$$

$$D = \frac{1}{2}c_p\dot{\varphi}^2(t). \tag{15}$$

where: m—the mass of the pendulum body (a bob), k—spring stiffness, c_p—viscous damping coefficient of the pendulum. Putting Equations (13)–(15) into Equation (12) and carrying out the analogous derivatives, the equation of motion is obtained as presented in Equations (16) and (17):

$$\begin{aligned} \ddot{\varphi} =& \left(\frac{1}{m(l_{01} + l_{02} + x_e)(l_{01} + l_{02} + x_e)}\right)\Big(-m(l_{01} + l_{02})\Big(g + f_0\omega^2\cos(\omega t)\Big)\sin\varphi(t) - \\ & c_p\dot{\varphi}(t) - mx_e(t)\Big(g + f_0\omega^2\cos(\omega t)\sin\varphi(t)\Big) - m(l_{01} + l_{02} + x_e(t))(2\dot{x}_e(t)\dot{\varphi}(t))\Big), \end{aligned} \tag{16}$$

$$\begin{aligned} \ddot{x}_e(t) =& g\cos\varphi(t) + f_0\omega^2\cos(\omega t)\cos\varphi(t) - \frac{kx_e(t)}{m} - \frac{c\dot{x}_e(t)}{m} + l_{01}\dot{\varphi}^2(t) + \\ & l_{02}\dot{\varphi}^2(t) + x_e(t)\dot{\varphi}^2(t). \end{aligned} \tag{17}$$

The motion considered here is the enforce motion existing as a sinusoidal wave of the conformation $I(t) = f_0\cos(\omega t)$, where f_0 is the excitation amplitude.

The above equation regains the established governing equation of the vertical parametric pendulum when l_{03} is varied due to the extension x_e. It is assumed that an external force causes the excitation. Thus, we assumed the almost ideal case where an external force could partially compensate for dissipation of mechanical energy through a frictional contact from the human effort [16,22].

3.2. The Lever

The lever amplifies the pendulum force and transmits the force to the piston through the bracket foundation link. To understand the lever model fully, we start with a simple model, as can be seen in Figure 6, which shows the lever with the pivot in the middle of the lever or center of gravity (CG), assuming that the CG is at the middle of the lever, that is, l_1 is equal to l_2. Figure 7 represents the lever component showing the pendulum's connection and then to the piston through two different bracket foundation links, respectively. From Newton's second law, the equation of motion of the lever is obtained, where φ is denoted as the input for the lever model, which is the output from the pendulum model.

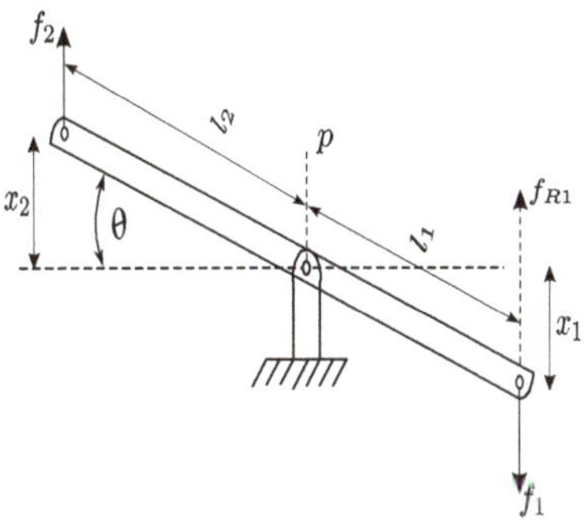

Figure 6. Schematic diagram of the lever device.

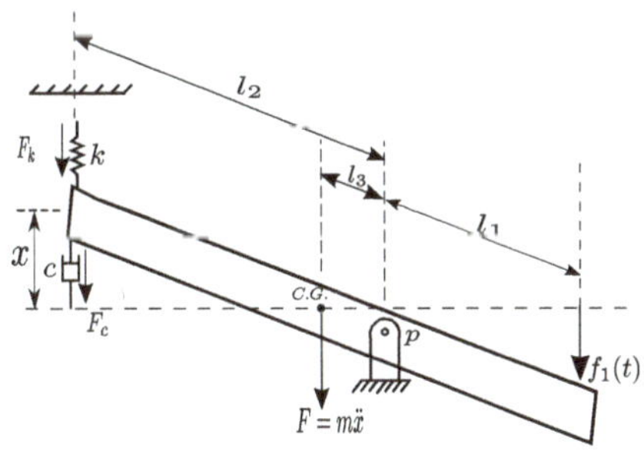

Figure 7. Schematic diagram of the lever device and connecting components like spring and damper.

Analyzing Figure 6, one writes: $x_1 = l_1 \sin\varphi$, $x_2 = l_2 \sin\varphi$ and $\frac{x_1}{x_2} = \frac{l_1}{l_2} = L$. In addition, $\frac{v_1}{v_2} = \frac{l_1}{l_2}$ states a ratio of lever arms: where l_1—distance from f_1 and position p, l_2—distance from f_2 and position p, x_1 and x_2 are the displacements at both ends of the lever. With small-angle approximation and the motion at the lever end to be purely translational in 'x' direction, the relationship between the forces and displacements is carried out by summing the torques T around the pivot point (about fulcrum), i.e.,

$$\sum_{ccw} T_{ccw} - \sum_{cw} T_{cw} = 0, \tag{18}$$

where the subscript ccw—counter-clockwise direction, and cw—clockwise direction. With the relations: $f_1 l_1 - f_2 l_2 = 0$ (balance of momentums), $f_1 l_1 = f_2 l_2$ or $\frac{f_1}{f_2} = \frac{l_2}{l_1} = \frac{1}{L}$ (conservation of power in levers, see [23]); f_1 and f_2 (N) are the forces on both ends of the lever.

It can be noted that the force relationship with the velocity relationship is given as $\frac{v_1}{v_2} = \frac{l_1}{l_2} = L$.

Therefore,

$$\frac{v_1}{v_2} \cdot \frac{f_1}{f_2} = \frac{l_1}{l_2} \cdot \frac{l_2}{l_1} = 1, \tag{19}$$

where we find that the power is preserved if $v_1 f_1 = v_2 f_2$, so it is the same on both sides of the lever.

In Figure 7, one observes that the lever arms are unequal; one side will experience a higher force and velocity than the other side. We assume some definitions $F_k = -kx$, $F_c = -cx$, $F = m\ddot{x}$, and $l_3 = \frac{1}{3}l_2$, which is the distance from CG to p, k stiffness of the stiffness ($\text{N}\cdot\text{m}^{-1}$), and c—viscous damping coefficient ($\text{N}\cdot\text{s}\cdot\text{m}^{-1}$).

Using Newton's second law, the lever governing equation is obtained as follows:

$$m_l \ddot{x} l_3 + c\dot{x} l_2 + kx l_2 = f_1(t) l_1, \tag{20}$$

where m_l—is the total mass of the lever, x—is the displacement of the lever. $f_1(t) = \sin\varphi$.

3.3. Piston Model

According to [20,24], piston has a reverse effect on the lever, and it damps oscillations of the pump. Damping of the lever motion causes damping of the pendulum, but the force damping the pendulum is less than the work of force that dampens the lever. Figure 8 shows a schematic diagram of the piston. An analysis leads to the equations of motion, as it is shown below.

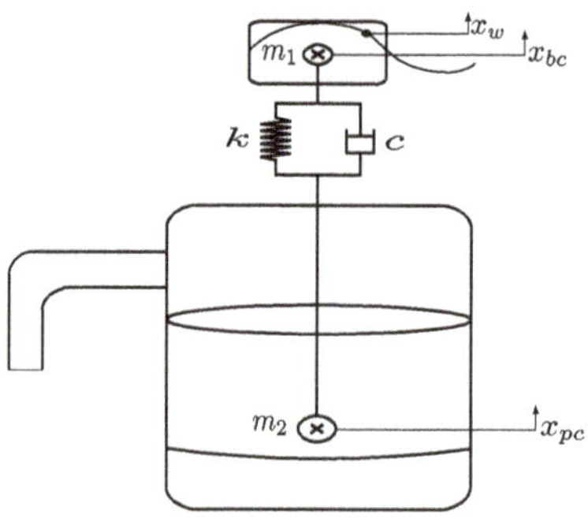

Figure 8. Schematic diagram of the piston.

We introduce the following denotations for the masses (kg): m_1—buoy mass, m_2—piston model mass (total), m_3—mass of the rod, m_4—mass of the piston, m_5—mass of the pumped fluid, together with the two relations $m_2 = m_3 + m_4 + m_5$ in the upstroke and $m_2 = m_3 + m_4$ in the down stream. Therefore, the mass m_2 changes in time t as it moves upward and downward. In addition, the mass m_2 is different in the upstroke due to the pumping processes of the fluid. Ref. [25] delivers a mathematical representation of the dynamical motion of the piston given in a state-space representation as it follows:

$$\dot{q} = Aq + f, \quad \text{for } q(0) = q_0. \tag{21}$$

The state vector is presented as:

$$q = \left[x_{bc}\ \dot{x}_{bc}\ x_{pc}\ \dot{x}_{pc}\ p_{ur}\ p_{lr}\right]^T, \tag{22}$$

where: x_{bc}—position of the buoy's center of mass (m), $\dot{x}_{bc}$—buoy velocity ($\text{m}\cdot\text{s}^{-1}$), x_{pc}—position of the piston center (m), $\dot{x}_{pc}$—piston velocity ($\text{m}\cdot\text{s}^{-1}$), p_{ur}—upper reservoir pressure (Pa), p_{lr}—lower reservoir pressure (Pa).

The governing equations are given in Equations (23) and (24):

$$m_1\ddot{x}_{bc} + c(\dot{x}_{bc} - \dot{x}_{pc}) + k(x_{bc} - x_{pc} - l_R) = F_{bc} - m_1 g, \tag{23}$$

where: l_R—length of the rod (m), F_{bc}—force of the buoy's center of mass (N).

We get the second-order differential equation of dynamics of the piston:

$$m_2\ddot{x}_{pc} + c(\dot{x}_{pc} - \dot{x}_{bc}) + k(x_{pc} - x_{bc} - l_R) = -A_c(p_{ur} - p_{lr}) - m_2 g - F_f, \tag{24}$$

where:

$$x_{bc} = \frac{L_r + 0.5H_b - (m_1 + m_4 + \rho A_c(L_c + H_u))}{\left(S_b\rho_{sw} - \frac{H_w}{2}\right)}, \tag{25}$$

$$x_{pc} = \frac{0.5H_b - (m_1 + m_4 + \rho A_c(L_c + H_u))}{\left(S_b\rho_{sw} - \frac{H_w}{2}\right)}. \tag{26}$$

Continuing, the pumping force is found in the following form:

$$F_p = -A_c p_{lr} + \rho(l_c + L_u)A_{ur}(\ddot{z}_p + g) + \rho A_c \dot{z}_p^2, \tag{27}$$

where area of the piston $A_c = \pi R_p{}^2$ (m^2), z_p—piston displacement about a zero mean, A_{ur}—area of the upper reservoir (m^2), F_f—initial approximation of the friction in the contact between the piston and the cylinder given as $-B\dot{x}_{pc}$, $B = \frac{\mu}{S_p}2\pi R_p H_p$—cylinder damping coefficient ($N \cdot s \cdot m^{-1}$), S_p—separation of piston and cylinder (m), R_p—radius of the piston (m), and H_p—height of the piston (m).

The amount of water pumped by the piston in every upstroke is the water in the cylinder, and the water inside the upper reservoir. Because of this, the fluid mass has to be modified as follows:

$$m_5 = \rho\left(l_c + \frac{p_{ur}}{\rho g}\right)A_c, \tag{28}$$

where: ρ—density of the fluid ($kg \cdot m^{-3}$), g—gravitational acceleration ($m \cdot s^{-2}$), and l_c—length of the cylinder (m).

The buoyancy force depending on the buoy X_{bc} and the position of the wave x_w is given in the form [25]:

$$F_{bc} = \left(x_w - x_{bc} + \frac{1}{2}H_b\right)S_b\rho_{sw}g, \tag{29}$$

where: H_b—height of the buoy (m), S_b—surface of the buoy, ρ_{sw}—reservoir fluid density ($kg \cdot m^{-3}$) and x_w—definition of wave used for the simulation is given:

$$x_w = L_r + \frac{H_w}{2}\sin\left(\frac{2\pi}{T_w}t - \frac{\pi}{2}\right), \tag{30}$$

where: H_w—wave height (m), T_w—wave period (s).

4. Numerical Results and Discussion

The numerical solutions of the system governing equations are solved using the Runge–Kutta method with adaptive step-size, with a simulation time step size of 0.003 s for case I and 0.005 s for case II. The initial condition for the pendulum angle $\varphi(0)$ is 0.5π radians for both case I and case II, with a time scale of 30 s and 50 s for the case I and case II, respectively.

Case I: Water pump pendulum with constant length. We start with the pendulum displacement, then the lever displacement, and finish at the piston's displacement. Finally, various parameters that determine the pendulum pump's output discharge are analyzed, and the numerical results are presented in Figures 9–11 for the pendulum, lever, and piston displacement, respectively. Parameters analysis includes the pendulum's mass, angle of suspension, and the pendulum's length. Therefore, we present only the results with the parameters that show good system responses.

For the pendulum displacement, the computations are performed using the below stated parameter values: $l = 0.5$ m, $M = 0.38$ kg, $m = 0.095$ kg, $f_0 = 0.005$ N, $\omega = 5$ rad·s^{-1}, $g = 9.81$ m·s^{-2}, $b = 0.003$ N·s·m^{-1}. The period of rotational motion depends on the length of the pendulum. The length is varied at a point in time until the desired periods are obtained. As shown in Figure 9, amplitude of the total energy decreases with time due to damped oscillations. Therefore, the pendulum has to be push occasionally for a continuous fluid flow.

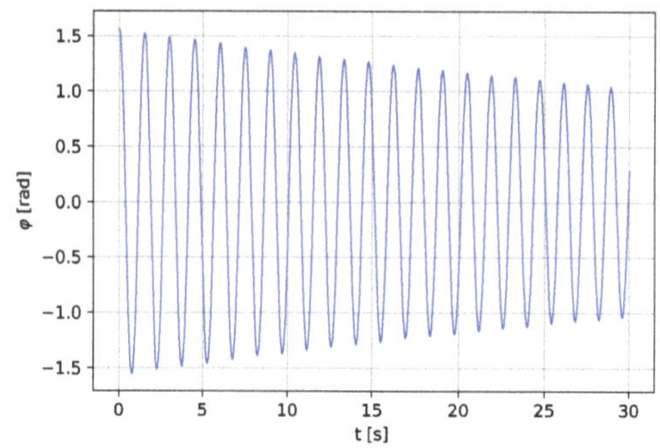

Figure 9. Angular displacement $\varphi(t)$ of the pendulum for $l = 0.5$ m, $b = 0.003$ N·s·m^{-1}.

Simulation of the lever displacement is shown in Figure 10, using the following parameter values: $m_l = 2.0$ kg $c = 1.0$ N·s·m^{-1}, $k = 5.0$ N·m^{-1}, $l_1 = 0.4$ m, $l_2 = 0.6$ m, $l_3 = \frac{1}{3}l_2$, $f_1(t) = \sin\varphi$, where φ—the pendulum angular displacement (rad) is the pendulum system input. The results show that the total energy gradually decreases with time.

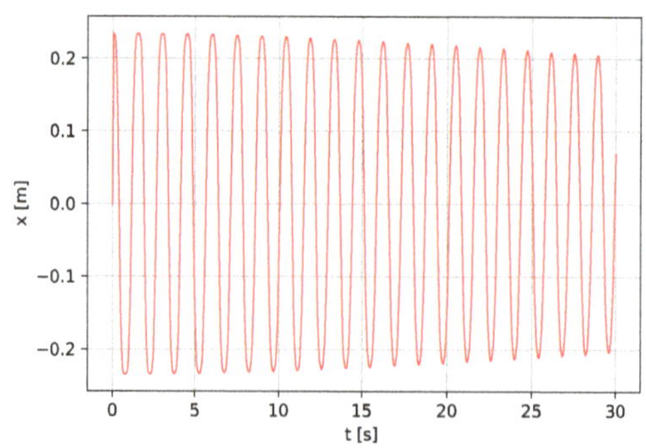

Figure 10. Linear displacement $x(t)$ of the lever for $l = 0.5$ m, $b = 0.003$ N·s·m^{-1}.

An analysis of the piston is presented. Some studies of fluid mechanics are also included in the piston analysis for optimal pump performance. The linear displacement of the piston is shown in Figure 11 with the values of the parameters as $m_1 = 10$ kg, $g = 9.81$ m·s^{-2}, $c = 1.0$ N·s·m^{-1}, $k = 50.0$ N·m^{-1}, $l_R = 4$ m, $g = 9.81$ m·s^{-2}, $B = 1.25915$ N·s·m^{-1}, $m_2 = 6.0242$ kg, $\rho = 1000$ kg·m^{-2}, $\rho_{sw} = 1030$ kg·m^{-2} $A_{ur} = 4$ m^2, $A_{lr} = 4$ m^2, $s_b = 2$ m, $H_b = 2$ m, $T_w = 10$ s, $H_w = 4$ m, $L_c = 10$ m, $z_p = 0$ m, $H_p = 2$ m, $L_r = 2$ m $z_p = 0$ m, $R_p = 0.05$ m^2. The same values for the spring constant, k, and the viscous damping constant, c, was used because of the same connection. It can be observed that the response of the piston is similar to the lever displacement. However, the displacement is not as much as that of the lever because of higher piston mass and other considered factors, overall pump parameters, and fluid analysis.

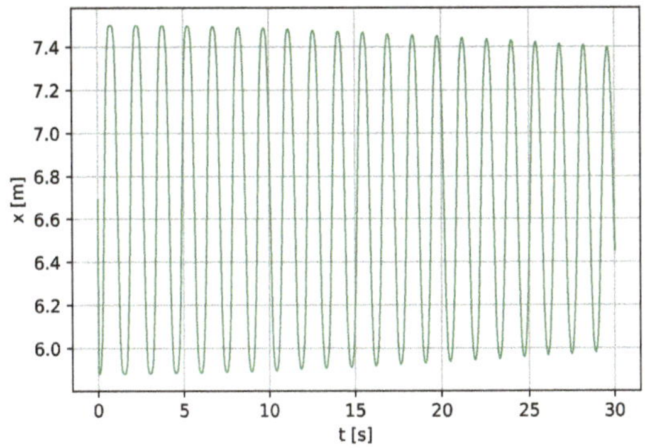

Figure 11. Linear displacement x_{pc} of the piston $l = 0.5$ m, $b = 0.003$ N·s·m^{-1}.

The analysis for different lengths is carried out for a deeper understanding of the relation between pendulum length and output of the system, which was not addressed in [5]. Changing the right-hand side pendulum length alone, i.e., without changing initial parameters of other parts, affects performance of the whole system. Therefore, the efficiency of the pumping depends on the length of the right-hand side pendulum. As can be seen in Figures 12–14, the system becomes more stable, but with a reduced number of oscillation periods for the whole system when the parameter value l is changed from 0.5 to 1.2 m.

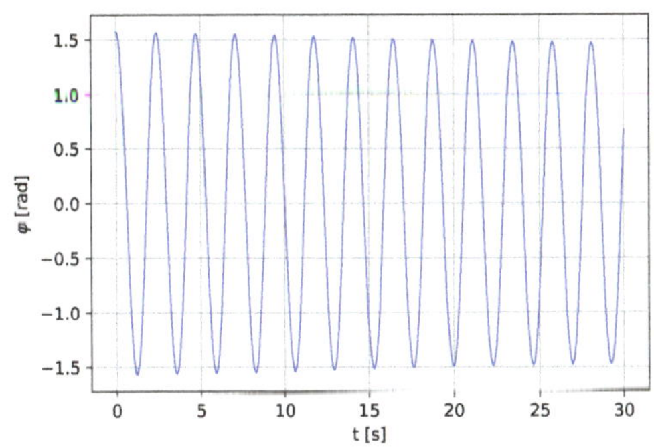

Figure 12. Linear displacement $\varphi(t)$ of the pendulum (continued) for $l = 1.2$ m, $b = 0.003$ N·s·m^{-1}.

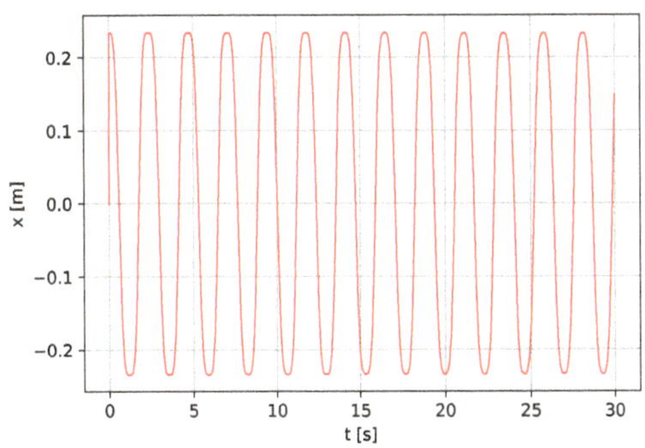

Figure 13. Linear displacement $x(t)$ of the lever (continued) for $l = 1.2$ m, $b = 0.003$ N·s·m^{-1}.

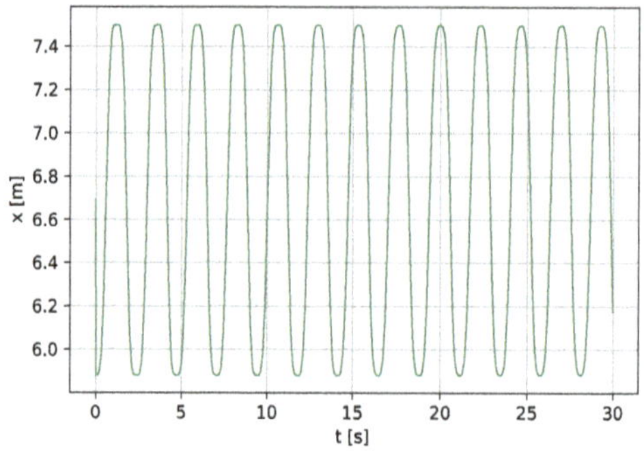

Figure 14. Linear displacement x_{pc} of the piston (continued) for $b = 0.003$ N·s·m^{-1}.

The simulation results shown in Figures 9–14 have been compared with the result delivered by [5]. It has proved that our model follows a more realistic trend because it includes friction and the effect of excitation force on the response of the investigated system. Furthermore, the presented system in case I is more stable than one in [5], as shown in Figures 1, 2 and 12–14. The obtained results clearly show how the pendulum's length plays a critical role in the overall system stability.

In addition, further analysis of Case I of the pendulum model is carried out by increasing the viscous damping with other parameters left unchanged. When the viscous damping b is increased to 0.3 N·s·m^{-1} with the same length $l = 1.2$ m, the time response of the system decreases and vanishes within a few seconds, as shown in Figures 15–17. Providing some technical recommendations, the value of b should be minimum for the system to be more stable and oscillate for a more extended period. Therefore, the value of the pendulum length, l, and the viscous damping, b, are to be selected with care as they have more effect on the system performance.

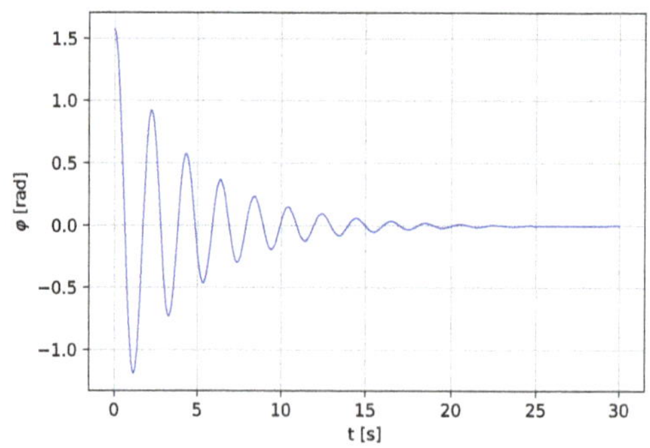

Figure 15. Linear displacement $\varphi(t)$ of the pendulum (continued) for $l = 1.2$ m, $b = 0.3$ N·s·m^{-1}.

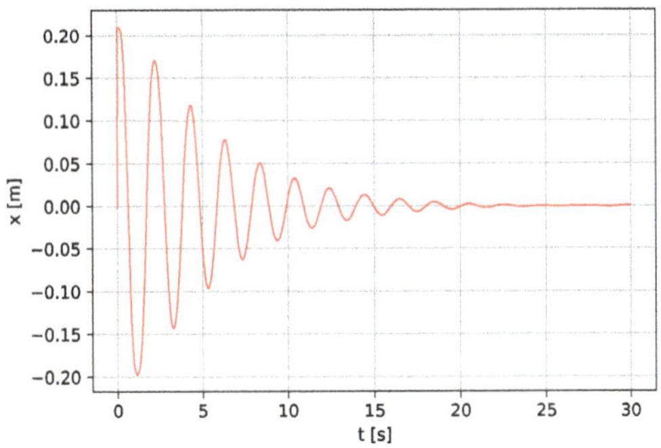

Figure 16. Linear displacement $x(t)$ of the lever (continued) for $l = 1.2$ m, $b = 0.3$ N·s·m^{-1}.

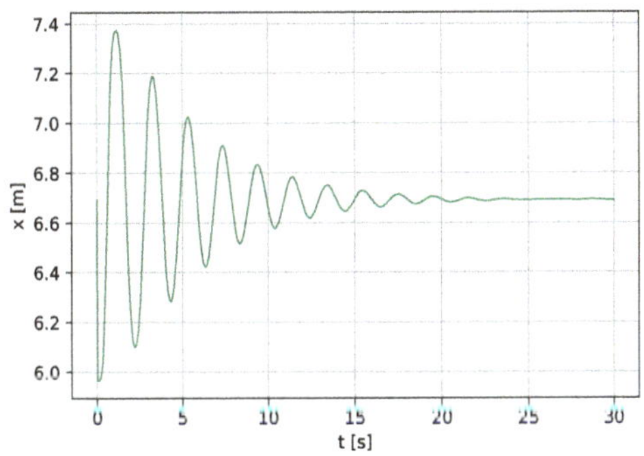

Figure 17. Linear displacement x_{pc} of the piston (continued) for $l = 1.2$ m, $b = 0.3$ N·s·m^{-1}.

Case II: Water pump pendulum with a vertically excited parametric pendulum with variable length [16] is used instead of the conventional pendulum. Figures 18–20 show the simulation results for the whole system when this type of pendulum with variable length is used with the following parameter values: $l_{01} = l_{02} = 4$ m, $m = 5$ kg, $x_e = 1.5$ m, $f_0 = 10$ N, $\omega = 0.5$ rad·s^{-1}, $g = 9.81$ m·s^{-2}, $c_p = 0.1$ N·s·m^{-1}. The parameters' values of the lever and the piston remain unchanged. With $c_p = 1$ N·s·m^{-1} and $\omega = 0.4$ rad·s^{-1}, Figures 21–23 are obtained, which shows more stable oscillation of the variable-length pendulum with more stability of the lever and the piston model as a result of the effect of increasing damping.

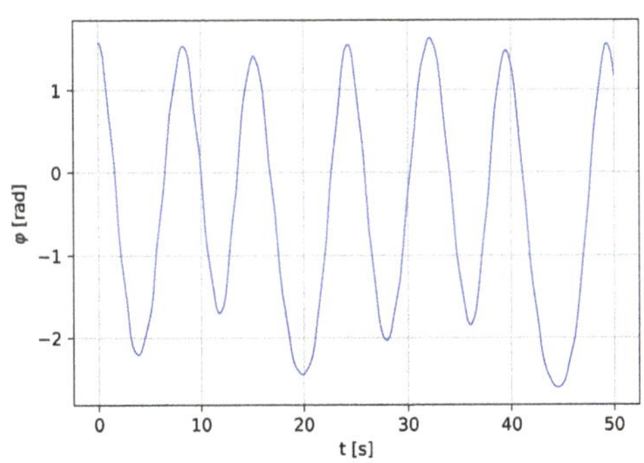

Figure 18. Angular displacement $\varphi(t)$ of the pendulum (Case II—a variable length concept of the pendulum pump) for $c_p = 0.1$ N·s·m^{-1}, $\omega = 0.5$ rad·s^{-1}.

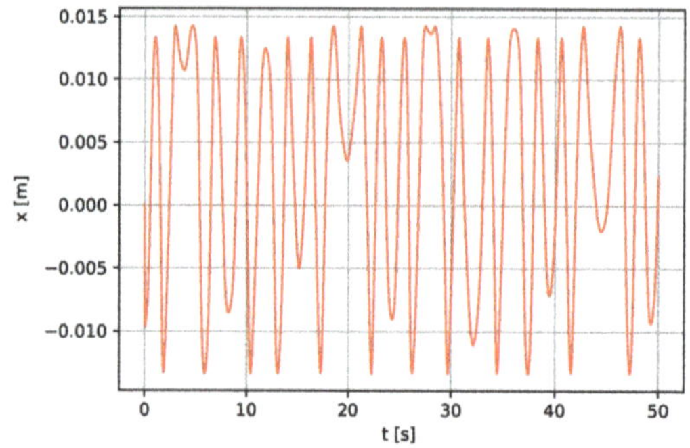

Figure 19. Linear displacement $x(t)$ of the lever (Case II—a variable length concept of the pendulum pump) for $c_p = 0.1$ N·s·m^{-1}, $\omega = 0.5$ rad·s^{-1}.

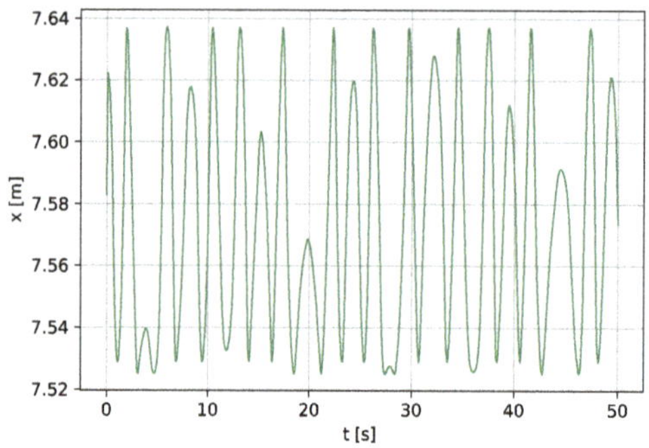

Figure 20. Linear displacement $x_{pc}(t)$ of the piston (Case II—a variable length concept of the pendulum pump) for $c_p = 0.1$ N·s·m^{-1}, $\omega = 0.5$ rad·s^{-1}.

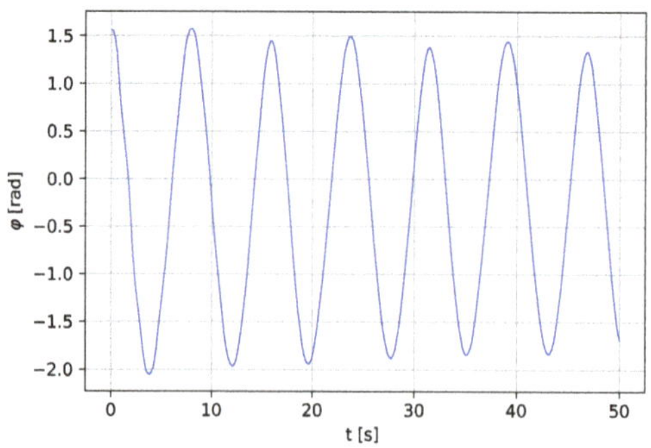

Figure 21. Angular displacement $\varphi(t)$ of the pendulum (Case II—a variable length concept of the pendulum pump) for $c_p = 1$ N·s·m^{-1}, $\omega = 0.4$ rad·s^{-1}.

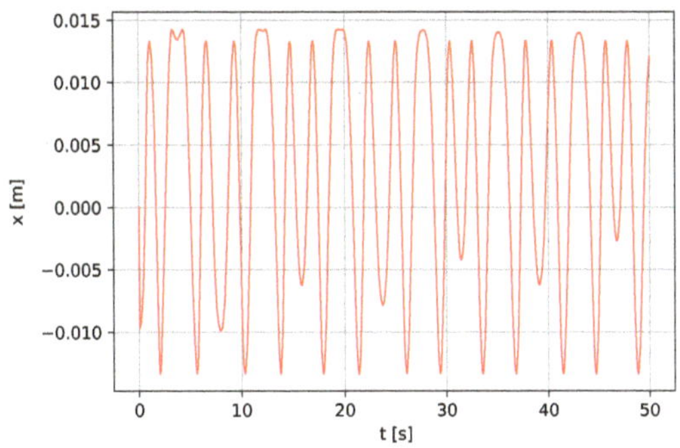

Figure 22. Linear displacement $x(t)$ of the lever (Case II—a variable length concept of the pendulum pump) for $c_p = 1$ N·s·m^{-1}, $\omega = 0.4$ rad·s^{-1}.

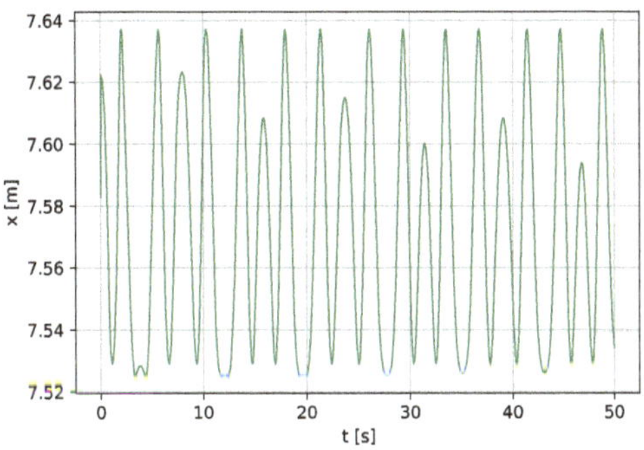

Figure 23. Linear displacement $x_{pr}(t)$ of the piston (Case II—a variable length concept of the pendulum pump) for $c_p = 1$ N·s·m^{-1}, $\omega = 0.4$ rad·s^{-1}.

Figures 18–23 show the time histories of the pendulum, lever, and piston, respectively. Some irregularity and quasi-periodicity are reported, and the behavior does not settle even after 50 s of simulation time. The pattern of recurrence does not lend to precise measurement. However, the oscillations can occur regularly when a regular external forcing forces them. In other words, the quasi-periodicity behavior can be compensated when a regular external forcing is applied to the system.

5. Conclusions

A nonlinear model of a pendulum is used to power the model of the piston through the lever. The system's dynamic response is analyzed, and the presented results show the system's effectiveness after a series of simulations at various parameter values. The numerical results show a good response of the scenario through the power transient from the pendulum to the piston. In addition, the system's response depends on the length of the pendulum that can be manipulated to achieve better performance. The presented results also show that the system can transfer energy with little human effort to do heavy work since the piston's mass is much bigger than the combined mass of the pendulum and the lever. A novelty is presented where a vertically excited pendulum with variable length is used instead of the conventional pendulum with constant length. In the proposed model, the system response shows a quasi-periodicity behavior and does not settle even after 50 s of simulation time. However, the quasi-periodicity behavior can be compensated when a regular external forcing is applied to the system. No control algorithm is included since the aim is to operate a system in rural and urban areas without electricity. However, the system can be constructed to include a control algorithm and transformed into a mechatronics system for any laboratories and industrial uses. Synchronization of the pendulum pump and the human body could be considered a problem of biomechanics. Lastly, further dynamical analysis can be performed to investigate the system's behavior more, and more studies on fluid mechanics will add value to the overall system operation.

Author Contributions: Conceptualization, G.Y. and P.O.; Data curation, P.O. and J.A.; Formal analysis, G.Y. and P.O.; Funding acquisition, J.A.; Investigation, G.Y.; Methodology, G.Y.; Project administration, G.Y.; Resources, G.Y. and J.A.; Software, G.Y.; Supervision, P.O. and J.A.; Validation, G.Y. and P.O.; Visualization, G.Y.; Writing—original draft, G.Y. and P.O.; Writing—review and editing, G.Y. All authors have read and agreed to the published version of the manuscript.

Funding: This research was funded by Narodowe Centrum Nauki Grant No. 2019/35/B/ST8/00980 (NCN Poland).

Institutional Review Board Statement: Not applicable.

Informed Consent Statement: Not applicable.

Data Availability Statement: Not applicable.

Acknowledgments: The first author Godiya Yakubu is the Doctoral Candidate in the Interdisciplinary Doctoral School at the Lodz University of Technology, Poland.

Conflicts of Interest: The authors declare that they have no conflict of interest.

Abbreviations

The following abbreviations are used in this manuscript:

m_b	pendulum bar mass, kg
m	pendulum end weight mass, kg
l	length to end weight center of mass, m
φ	pendulum angular displacement, rad
g	acceleration due to gravity, m·s^{-2}
I_0	mass moment of inertia, kg·m^2
T_v	viscous friction, N
b	viscous damping, N·s·m^{-1}
T_h	excitation force, N
l_{01}	pendulum natural length, m
l_{02}	length of the telescopic rod, m
l_{03}	total length of the pendulum, m
x_e	extension of the variable length pendulum
ω_n	excitation frequency, rad·s^{-1}
f_0	forcing excitation amplitude, N
ζ	damping coefficient, N·s·m^{-1}
L	ratio of lever arm
f_1, f_2	forces on both end of the lever, N
m_l	overall mass of the lever, kg
k	stiffness of the spring, N·m^{-1}
c	viscous damping coefficient, N·s·m^{-1}
m_1	buoy mass, kg
m_2	piston model mass (overall), kg
m_3	rod's mass, kg
m_4	piston's mass, kg
m_5	mass of the pumped fluid, kg
x_{bc}	position of the buoy's center of mass, m
$\dot{x}_{bc}$	buoy velocity, m·s^{-1}
x_{pc}	position of the piston center, m
$\dot{x}_{pc}$	piston velocity, m·s^{-1}
p_{ur}	upper reservoir pressure, Pa
p_{lr}	lower reservoir pressure, Pa
l_R	length of the rod, m
F_{bc}	force of the buoy's center of mass, N

H_w	wave height, m
T_w	wave period, s
x_w	wave definition
ζ	damping coefficient,
A_c	area of the piston, m^2
z_p	piston displacement about a zero mean, m
A_{ur}	area of the upper reservoir, m^2
F_f	initial approximation of the friction between the piston and the cylinder wall, N
B	cylinder damping coefficient, $N{\cdot}s{\cdot}m^{-1}$
S_p	separation of piston-cylinder, m
R_p	radius of the piston, m^2
H_p	height of the piston, m
ρ	fluid density, $kg{\cdot}m^{-2}$
l_c	length of the cylinder, m
E_k	kinetic energy of the parametric pendulum, J
E_p	potential energy of the parametric pendulum, J
D	dissipative energy of the parametric pendulum, J

References

1. Government of Canada. Water in Developing Countries. 2021. Available online: https://www.international.gc.ca/world-monde/issues_development-enjeux_developpement/environmental_protection-protection_environnement/water-eau.aspx?lang=eng (accessed on 31 March 2021).
2. Bain, R.E.S.; Gundry, S.W.; A., W.J.; Yang, H.; S., P.; Bartram, J.K. Accounting for water quality in monitoring access to safe drinking-water as part of the Millennium Development Goals: Lessons from five countries. *Bull. World Health Organ.* **2012**, *90*, 228–235. [CrossRef] [PubMed]
3. Nikhade, G.R.; Patil, R.; Bansal, S.P. Two-stage oscillator mechanism for operating a reciprocating pump. *Asian J. Sci. Technol.* **2013**, *4*, 37–31.
4. Cavalheiro, M. Pendulum pump. *Natl. J. Energy* **2001**, *1*, 156.
5. Memon, M.A.; Nizamani, A.R.; Hussain, A.; Rajper, M.L.; Kumar, B.; Ali, Z. Mathematical Modeling of Pendulum Hand Pump. *Stud. Res. Pap. Conf.* **2015**, *2*, 245–249.
6. Vigithra, R.; Ajith, V.; JayaKrishna, B.R.; Ajithkumar, R.; Dinesh, S. Design and Fabrication of Pendulum Hand Water Pump. *J. Innov. Res. Dev.* **2016**, *1*, 71–75.
7. Okoronkwo, C.A.; Ezurike, B.O.; Uche, R.; Igbokwe, J.O.; Oguoma, O.N. Design of a hand water pump using a quick-return crank mechanism. *Afr. J. Sci. Technol. Innov. Dev.* **2016**, *8*, 292–298. [CrossRef]
8. Shelar, P.B.; Kambale, A.D.; Patil, A.N.; Khandare, R.M.; Sachane, A.H.; Gavali, S.S. Design and Development of Pendulum Operated Water Pump. *Int. Res. J. Eng. Technol. (IRJET)* **2018**, *5*, 1387–1389.
9. Apparao, D.; Sagar, Y. Design and Development of Hand Water Pump with a Pendulum. *Int. J. Eng. Manag. Res.* **2017**, *5*, 357–361.
10. Manoj, C.; Manjunath, T.N.; Raghavendra, G.; Ramakrishna, G.P. Design and Fabrication of Pendulum Operated Pump. *Int. J. Sci. Adv. Res. Technol.* **2018**, *4*, 611–614.
11. Rajendra, T.N.; Rajendra, S.N.; Dattatraya, K.D.; Satish, A.L.; Patwari, A. Pendulum operated hand pump. *Int. Res. J. Eng. Technol. (IRJET)* **2019**, *6*, 2740–2743.
12. Śmiechowicz, W.; Loup, T.; Olejnik, P. Lyapunov Exponents of Early Stage Dynamics of Parametric Mutations of a Rigid Pendulum with Harmonic Excitation. *Math. Comput. Appl.* **2019**, *24*, 90. [CrossRef]
13. Pietrzak, P.; Ogińska, M.; Krasuski, T.; Figueiredo, K.; Olejnik, P. Near the resonance behavior of a periodically forced partially dissipative three-degrees-of-freedom mechanical system. *Lat. Am. J. Sci. Struct.* **2018**, *15*. [CrossRef]
14. Olejnik, P.; Fečkan, M.; Awrejcewicz, J. Analytical and numerical study on a parametric pendulum with the step-wave modulation of length and forcing. *Int. J. Struct. Stab. Dyn.* **2018**, *19*, 1941006. [CrossRef]
15. Krasilnikov, P.; Gurina, T.; Svetlova, V. Bifurcation study of a chaotic model variable-length pendulum on a vibrating base. *Int. J. Non-Linear Mech.* **2018**, *105*, 88–98. [CrossRef]
16. Reguera, F.; Dotti, F.E.; Machado, S.P. Rotation control of a parametrically excited pendulum by adjusting its length. *Mech. Res. Commun.* **2016**, *72*, 74–80. [CrossRef]
17. Reciprocating Pump—Components, Working and Uses. Available online: https://theconstructor.org/practical-guide/reciprocating-pump-components-working-uses/2914/ (accessed on 15 April 2021).
18. Rath, K.C.; Samanta, P.K.; Kanhara, D.K. A brief study on Pendulum based Pump. *Int. J. Mod. Trends Eng. Res. (IJMTER)* **2016**, *3*, 57–62.
19. Gowrishankar, K.; Gobinath, M.; Gani, R. Single Acting Piston Pump Using Oscillating Motion. *Int. J. Res. Mech. Eng. Technol.* **2015**, *5*, 27–29.
20. Anand, A.; Jhakal, D.; Sharma, R.; Deshbhratar, R. Fabrication of Pendulum Pump. *Int. J. Sci. Eng. Res.* **2017**, *8*, 68–70.

21. Singh, R.; Kumar, V. Swing up and Stabilization of Rotary Inverted Pendulum using TS Fuzzy. *Int. J. Sci. Res. Eng. Technol.* **2014**, *2*, 753–759.
22. Cliffort, M. J. Bishop, S.R. Rotating periodic orbit of the parametrically excited pendulum. *Phys. Lett. A* **1995**, *201*, 191–196. [CrossRef]
23. Schlaudt, O. Hölder, Mach, and the Law of the Lever: A Case of Well-founded Non-controversy. *Philos. Sci.* **2013**, *17*, 93–116. [CrossRef]
24. Jong, K.L.; Jun, K.J.; Jang-Bom, C.; Jin-Woo, L. Mathematical modeling of reciprocating pump. *J. Mech. Sci. Technol.* **2015**, *29*, 3141–3151.
25. Galván, G.B. Nonlinear Control Design for Wave Energy Converter. Master's Thesis, University of Groningen, Groningen, The Netherlands, 2014; pp. 1–76.

energies

MDPI

Article

Application of Artificial Neural Networks in the Urban Building Energy Modelling of Polish Residential Building Stock

Marcin Zygmunt * and Dariusz Gawin

Department of Building Material Physics and Sustainable Design, Technical University of Lodz, 93-590 Lodz, Poland; dariusz.gawin@p.lodz.pl

* Correspondence: marcin.zygmunt@p.lodz.pl

Abstract: The development of energy-efficient buildings and sustainable energy supply systems is an obligatory undertaking towards a more sustainable future. To protect the natural environment, the modernization of urban infrastructure is indisputably important, possible to achieve considering numerous buildings as a group, i.e., Building Energy Cluster (BEC). The urban planning process evaluates multiple complex criteria to select the most profitable scenario in terms of energy consumption, environmental protection, or financial profitability. Thus, Urban Building Energy Modelling (UBEM) is presently a popular approach applied for studies towards the development of sustainable cities. Today's UBEM tools use various calculation methods and approaches, as well as include different assumptions and limitations. While there are several popular and valuable software for UBEM, there is still no such tool for analyses of the Polish residential stock. In this work an overview on the home-developed tool called TEAC, focusing on its' mathematical model and use of Artificial Neural Networks (ANN). An exemplary application of the TEAC software is also presented.

Keywords: urban building energy modeling; Artificial Neural Network; energy clusters; Energy Flexible Building Clusters; energy efficiency; environmental impact

Citation: Zygmunt, M.; Gawin, D. Application of Artificial Neural Networks in the Urban Building Energy Modelling of Polish Residential Building Stock. *Energies* **2021**, *14*, 8285. https://doi.org/10.3390/en14248285

Academic Editors: Jaroslaw Krzywanski, Marcin Kamiński and Angel A. Juan

Received: 22 November 2021
Accepted: 7 December 2021
Published: 9 December 2021

1. Introduction

Cities around the globe are growing rapidly, following the rising population. According to the United Nations [1], approx. 55% of the world population currently lives in urban areas, and it is foreseen to double the number of residents by 2050 [2]. Further cities development is causing a rising negative impact on the natural environment. Thus, it is necessary to manage cities effectively, heading towards urban sustainability. In general, modern urban development should promote energy-efficient cities which respect the natural environment and provide high-quality life conditions for residents [3]. The above mentioned is valid for both existing and new urban areas; present cities should be managed in a better, more effective way, while new ones should be correctly designed [4]. Urban modelling is a comprehensive subject, including three main areas: land use and transportation model, Urban Energy System Modelling (UESM) [5] and Urban Building Energy Modelling (UBEM). The UBEM is a concept allowing us to validate possible scenarios of cities development towards their sustainability.

Nowadays, building energy analyses are performed using computational software, allowing for comprehensive studies of a single building. Out of numerous available tools [6], the *Energy Plus* is one of the most universal and popular software for various energy-related studies of a singular building [7]. A study focused on the energy behavior of a single building is called Building Energy Modelling (BEM). It is a well-known issue, already performed by academics all over the world; the overview of some popular BEM codes can be found in [8]. On the other hand, the UBEM allows aggregating the energy-related results of singular buildings to the urban scale, including some complex phenomena occurring in urban environments. Therefore, energy-related analyses of city districts should be performed using specialized UBEM software. According to [9], those tools are the most appropriate approach for analyzing building stocks at a large scale. Each of the UBEM tools has specific fields of applications, as well as they were developed with different assumptions and constraints. Presently, the most popular UBEM software are *CitySim* [10], *Urban Modelling Interface*—UMI [11], *City Building Energy Saver*—CityBES [12] and *City Energy Analyst*—CEA [13]; the capabilities of some UBEM tools are overviewed in [14]. Some interesting analyses can be found in [15–21], where various issues of the UBEM were examined, i.e., city-scale energy planning, renewable energy sources (RES) application, Building Energy Cluster (BEC) modelling or Urban Heat Island (UHI) impact.

The UBEM model can be focused on buildings modelling at an urban scale with different scopes. Some UBEM tools were developed in order to deal with a single and specific aspect, e.g., to optimize daylighting [22] or to provide energy savings derived by buildings [23], while others are more complex in order to examine more comprehensive issues. The UBEM can be categorized into two main approaches (see Figure 1), accordingly top-down and bottom-up methods [14,24]. Generally speaking, the top-down approach is based on the estimation of energy consumption from data of a larger scale (e.g., residential sector), while the bottom-up approach uses calculated energy consumption of individual or group of buildings to aggregate then the results to the urban scale. Out of the literature review, the bottom-up approach is presently a much more popular method of the UBEM.

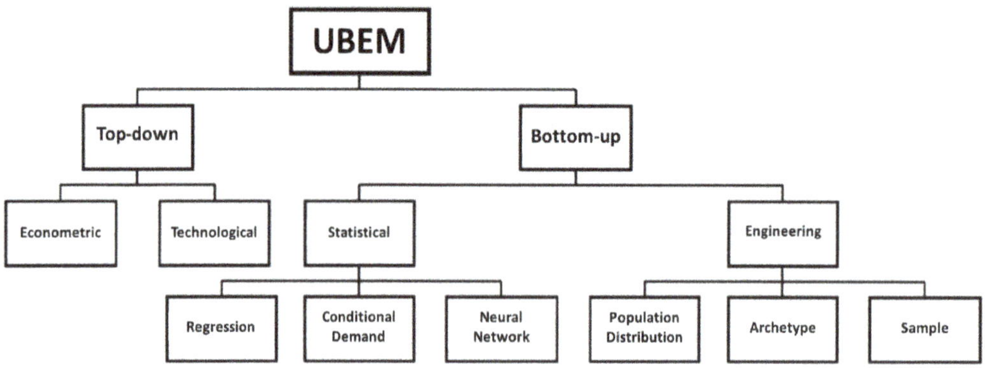

Figure 1. Schematic of the UBEM techniques [25].

The top-down approach assumes the group of buildings as an energy sink, without investigating individual end-uses, based on widely available aggregated data and historic records. Two types of top-down approaches are specified, accordingly econometric or technological. The popularity of the applications of the top-down methods increases whenever the global crisis occurs, such as the one at the end of the 1970s. Some exemplary UBEM analyses using the top-down approach can be found in [26–29].

The bottom-up approach uses data from a small scale (i.e., a single building) for examining the energy consumption at a larger scale (i.e., for a whole region). Usually, the input data for the bottom-up models include parameters such as building geometry and envelope structure, equipment and appliances, exterior and interior climate conditions, occupancy and working schedules. Those detailed parameters are then furtherly used to analyze a whole residential area—it is the biggest advantage of the bottom-up approach. There are two types of bottom-up approaches, accordingly statistical and engineering studies [30]. The statistical approach can be focusing on regression [31,32], conditional demand analysis (CDA) [33,34] or Artificial Neural Network (ANN) approaches [35,36]. On the other hand, the engineering approach might be specified using population distribution [37,38], archetypes [39,40] or sample [41] techniques. The state-of-the-art review on the available bottom-up approaches of the UBEM can be found in [42,43].

Despite the fact, that UBEM became a popular trend for engineers and researchers all over the world, there is no such software available to analyze Polish residential building stock. Therefore, a multi-criteria computer analytic tool called TEAC (*Tool for Energy Efficiency Analyses of an Energy Cluster*), which allows to perform energy, environmental and economic analyses of the Polish household sector was developed. The TEAC software uses a hybrid approach of the UBEM, combining both top-down and bottom-up techniques. The goal of this work is to present the mathematical approaches defining the TEAC software. In this paper, an overview of the method applied for the ANN training process is discussed. Moreover, most of the applied dependencies, expressing considered phenomena of urban-scale areas, are presented. The ANNs application was proven to be useful and efficient for various UBEM analyses, in particular as a main part of the TEAC software. The TEAC software is comprehensively described in [25], while some of its' applications can be found in [44–46]. The analyses described in this paper present exemplary results for a simple neighborhood, considered as BEC. The results are based on the overall energy demand of the cluster, allowing for some further analyses, e.g., the environmental impact of the examined neighborhood or economic profitability of the proposed modernizations. Due to the application of the ANN (and the TEAC software in general), it is possible to perform such comprehensive analyses without the time consuming detailed energy modelling of individual buildings.

2. TEAC Software Concept

A brief concept of the TEAC software is described in this section. The TEAC software is a tool for various UBEM analyses of Polish single-family stocks. It is based on a hybrid approach of UBEM: both top-down and bottom-up methods are included. As a basis for the TEAC software some economic and market-derived drivers were used (econometric model), the ANN was implemented for energy demand predictions (neural network model) as well as a data of representative single-family houses of Poland was used (archetype model). A sequence chart of the TEAC software development is shown in Figure 2. The whole process can be divided into two stages, where the first one includes the software development, while the second one responds to the application phase (marked with a blue outline).

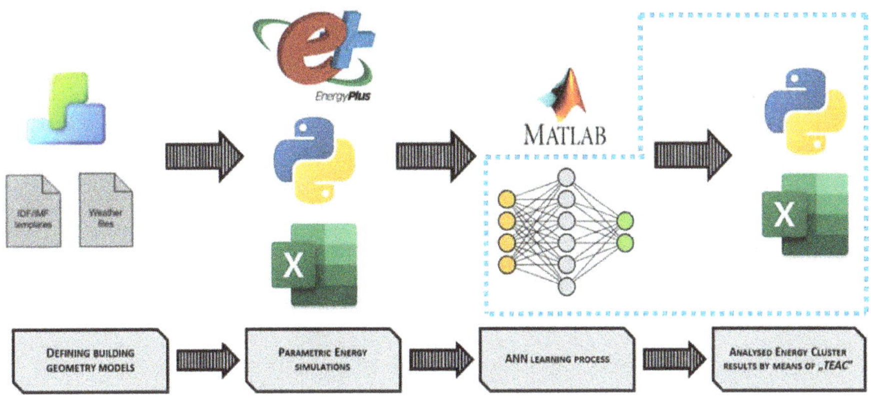

Figure 2. The schematic concept of the TEAC software.

The procedure is developed for the Representative Single-Family Houses (RSFH) of Poland, and those seven buildings were defined by means of the *Design Builder* software [47]. The process was performed to obtain input files (IDF-format), which then are used for parametric simulations performed by means of the *Energy Plus* software. The simulations were automatized by the code written in *Python* programming language and all their results were collected in the csv-files. The performed parametric simulations included the following variables: weather data (air temperature and total solar radiation), building geometry data (area, volume, windows area, U-values of building enclosure), ventilation and infiltration rates, heating system data (type and efficiency), as well as built environment information (building orientation and its' closest surrounding). In total, 358,400 parametric simulations were performed, and their gathered results (expressing the heating demand) were used in the ANN training process. The application of ANN was performed using the *MATLAB* software [48]; it is furtherly described in Section 3. The obtained code was rewritten in the *Phyton* language, allowing to predict the heating demand of an examined neighborhood. Also, some additional modules were defined using the *Python* language, allowing for various energy-, environmental-, and economic-related analyses of the built area. In general, the TEAC software consists of four main modules, while the 3rd module consists of seven submodules. The final analyses of the considered area are performed based on the predicted heating demands, built environment data, as well as some precalculated energy-related data. The results can be presented by means of Urban Energy Maps (UEM) [49], various types of graphs, e.g., Load Duration Curves (LDC), or tabular summaries. The developed software can be used by various authorities in order to improve the local energy efficiency. The comprehensive description of the TEAC software can be found in [43].

3. Mathematical Model

City-scale analyses are characterized by huge complexity, thus present UBEM tools usually require significant computational resources. Then, various assumptions are necessary to simplify the examined issue at an urban scale. Therefore, selecting the appropriate methods is required for valid calculations. In this section, the TEAC software is described, especially its' mathematical model and applied methodologies. Out of all modules of the TEAC software, the ANN application is the most important one—it is detailly presented in this section.

Whenever research is focused on the energy consumption at a building-level or whole city-scale, numerous variables are involved. Those variables usually interact with each other in a not fully understood way, as well as some of them (e.g., outdoor climate conditions) are highly unpredictable. Those types of problems are most appropriate for Artificial Intelligence (AI) applications, which are based on some input-output parameters and functional relationships between them. In general, Artificial Neural Networks (ANNs) can be classified into two main groups: Feed Forward Neural Network (FFNN) and Feed Backward Neural Network (FBNN); the comprehensive classification of the ANNs can be found in [50]. The ANNs have proven to be universal approximators in various fields of application—state-of-the-art overviews can be found in [50–52]. The ANNs are successfully applied for energy loads forecast at the building-scale [53,54], as well as urban-scale [34,55].

The structure of the defined ANN was investigated, in order to provide the best data regression with a reasonably short calculation time for the analyzed issue. Following the procedure published in [56], the different number of neurons within a single hidden layer was examined; the analysis started with 2 and ended with 24 neurons. The final structure of the applied network includes 14 input neurons, 12 neurons within a single hidden layer and one output neuron (see Figure 3). The output expresses the heating demand, while the inputs parameters define: the analysis timestep period (assigned as TP), outdoor temperature (DBT), total solar radiation (ITH), building heating area (A_0), building volume (V_0), total windows area (A_{win}), air-change rate (n_{tot}), U-values of exterior walls (U_{wall}), roofs (U_{roof}), ground floors (U_{floor}) and windows (U_{win}), heating system efficiency (H_{COP}), as well as building orientation (OV) and closest surrounding (SV) variant.

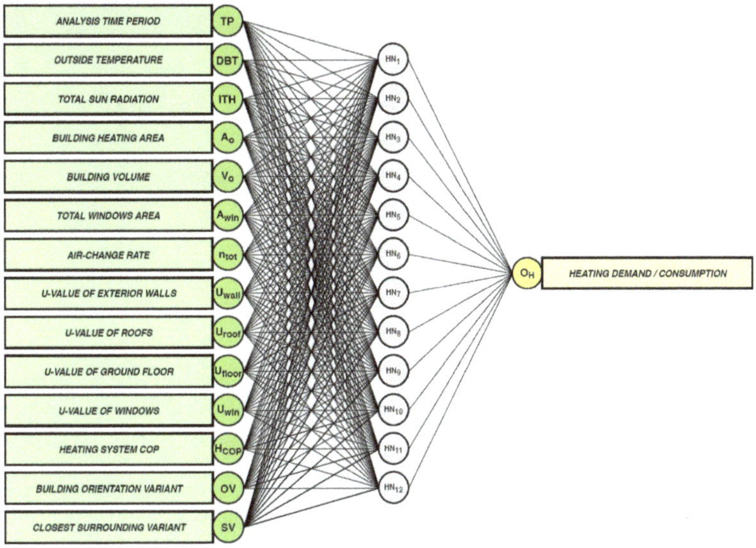

Figure 3. The structure of the defined ANN.

The ANN module in the TEAC software is based on the network trained using the Levenberg-Marquardt method [57–59]. The L-M method was developed in the early 1960s' for solving nonlinear problems. During the definition process, also Bayesian Regularization [60] and Conjugate Gradient [61] methods were examined, but the L-M network was characterized by the best accuracy of predictions. The L-M method is based on a gradient vector and a Jacobian matrix—it might be considered as a combination of two minimization approaches, accordingly the Gauss-Newton [62] and the gradient descent [63] methods. The L-M method works more like a gradient-descent method when the parameters are far from their optimal value, while when the parameters are close to their optimal value it acts more like the Gauss-Newton method. Due to the fact, that the L-M method is a hybrid approach, it can be used to trade off the best features of different algorithms to solve a variety of problems. The L-M algorithm is particularly effective in solving non-linear equations; thus, it was effective for heating demand predictions of an urban area. Further below, for the convenience of the reader, the L-M method is briefly explained.

If the fitting model is a function $\hat{y}(t_i; p)$ of an independent variables t_i, and a vector of parameters p of data points $(t_i; y_i)$, minimize the sum of the weighted squares of the errors, as follows:

$$X^2(p) = \sum_{i=1}^{m} \left[\frac{y(t_i - \hat{y}(t_i;p))}{\sigma_{y,i}} \right] \quad (1)$$

where $\sigma_{y,i}$ is the measured error for datum $y(t_i)$. Equation (1) can be rewritten using the weighting matrix W, as follows:

$$X^2(p) = (y - \hat{y}(p))^T W (y - \hat{y}(p)) \quad (2)$$

$$X^2(p) = y^T W y - 2y^T W \hat{y} + \hat{y}^T W \hat{y} \quad (3)$$

If the function $\hat{y}(t_i; p)$ is nonlinear in the model of parameters p, then the minimization of the $X^2(p)$ is carried out iteratively.

Using the Gradient Decent Method for a minimalization task, the objective function can be expressed with the following equation:

$$\frac{\partial}{\partial p}X^2 = 2(y - \hat{y}(p))^T W \frac{\partial}{\partial p}(y - \hat{y}(p)) \tag{4}$$

$$\frac{\partial}{\partial p}X^2 = -2(y - \hat{y}(p))^T W \left| \frac{\partial \hat{y}(p)}{\partial p} \right| \tag{5}$$

where the $\left| \frac{\partial \hat{y}(p)}{\partial p} \right|$ is the Jacobian matrix, assigned as J; thus:

$$\frac{\partial}{\partial p}X^2 = -2(y - \hat{y}(p))^T W J \tag{6}$$

Finally, the parameter update h_{GD} (for the gradient descent method), which represents the movement of the parameters in the direction of steepest descent is expressed as follows:

$$h_{GD} = \alpha J^T W (y - \hat{y}) \tag{7}$$

where α is a positive scalar determining the length of the steps in the steepest descent direction.

The Gauss-Newton method is used for minimizing a sum-of-squares objective function. Typically, it is much faster than gradient descent methods for moderately sized problems. Let us assume, that the function may be locally approximated using the first-order Taylor series, as follows:

$$\hat{y}(p + h) \approx \hat{y}(p) + \left| \frac{\partial \hat{y}(p)}{\partial p} \right| h = \hat{y}(p) + Jh \tag{8}$$

using the approximation $\hat{y}(p + h) \approx \hat{y}(p) + Jh$ into Equation (3):

$$X^2(p + h) \approx y^T W y + \hat{y}^T W \hat{y} - 2y^T W \hat{y} - 2(y - \hat{y})^T W J h + h^T J^T W J h \tag{9}$$

which can be rewritten as a normal equation for the Gauss-Newton formula:

$$\left[J^T W J \right] h_{GN} = J^T W (y - \hat{y}) \tag{10}$$

It is important to mention, that for both, the gradient descent and Gauss-Newton methods, the right-hand side vectors in normal equations, accordingly Equations (7) and (10), are identical.

Therefore, the L-M algorithm adaptively varies the parameters between the gradient descent and the Gauss-Newton methods. The L-M formula can be expressed as follows:

$$\left| J^T W J + \lambda I \right| h_{GN} = J^T W (y - \hat{y}) \tag{11}$$

where λ is the damping parameter, I is the identity matrix and the h_{LM} is the parameter update for the L-M method. If the values of λ are normalized to the values of $J^T W J$, then the L-M formula for non-linear least squares looks as follows:

$$\left[J^T W J + \lambda diag\left(J^T W J \right) \right] h_{GN} = J^T W (y - \hat{y}) \tag{12}$$

The L-M method is used to solve some non-linear least squares problems. In the TEAC software, the L-M algorithm was used during the ANN training process, allowing for heating demand predictions. The heating demand of a building is a complex and multilayered issue, for analyses of which the L-M method is appropriate.

Validation of the Defined ANN

The data used for the ANN training process were divided into three groups of samples: training, validation and testing sets, in constant shares of respectively 70, 15 and 15%. Training data, which is unknown for the network, is used to test the predefined network (adjusted according to its error) and measure its' performance. Three networks were trained, for monthly, daily and hourly predictions. In Figure 4 the training results are shown; the graph shows a regression plot for the test group of samples. A good match was observed for hourly study, where the correlation coefficient (R) equals 0.9083, while for daily and monthly studies R equals 0.9958 and 0.9838 accordingly.

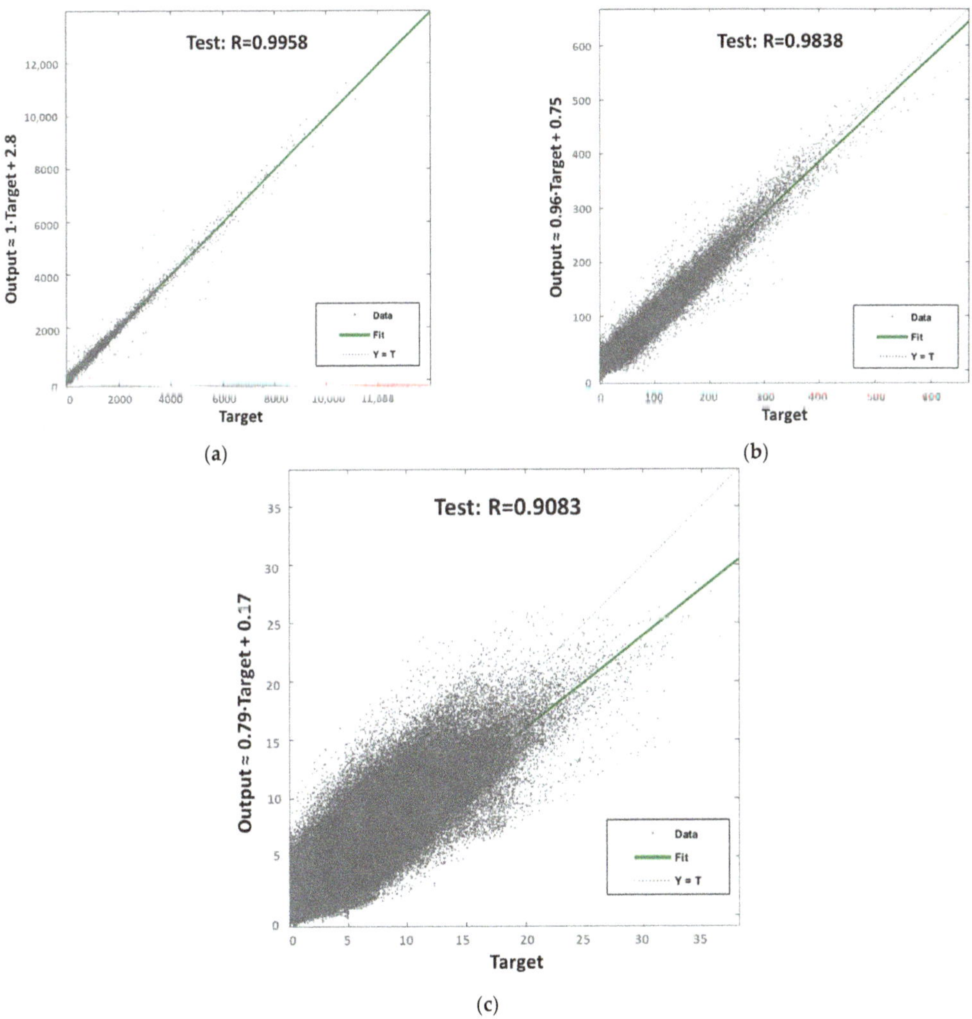

Figure 4. Regression plots for the test data of the ANN analysis for different calculation periods: (**a**) hourly, (**b**) daily and (**c**) monthly.

The definition of ρ for a population of random variables (X,Y) can be described as follows:

$$\rho_{X,Y} = \frac{cov(X,Y)}{\sigma_X \sigma_Y} \tag{13}$$

where cov is the covariance, σ_X is the standard deviation of X and σ_Y is the standard deviation of Y. Using relationship (14),

$$cov(X,Y) = E[(X-\mu_X)(Y-\mu_Y)] \tag{14}$$

Equation (13) can be rewritten as follows:

$$\rho_{X,Y} = \frac{E[XY]-E[X]E[Y]}{\sqrt{E[X^2]-(E[X])^2}\sqrt{E[Y^2]-(E[Y])^2}} \tag{15}$$

where E is the expectation, μ_X is the mean of X and μ_Y is the mean of Y.

Finally, when applied to a sample, the R is commonly represented by r_{XY}, and for a given paired data (x_n, y_n) is defined as:

$$r_{XY} = \frac{\sum_{i=1}^{n}\left(x_i-\bar{x}\right)\left(y_i-\bar{y}\right)}{\sqrt{\sum_{i=1}^{n}\left(x_i-\bar{x}\right)^2}\sqrt{\sum_{i=1}^{n}\left(y_i-\bar{y}\right)^2}} \tag{16}$$

The predefined ANN is a key module of the TEAC software. It allows to predict a heating demand of the examined region, consisting of RSFH of Poland. Due to the application of AI, it is possible to predict the heating demand of an urban area almost effortless, using only a sequence of data lines, describing the analyzed neighborhood. Then, the obtained heating demand, simultaneously with the electricity demand, are furtherly used as a basis for further analysis of the cluster. Also, it is important to mention, that heating demand is the main component of the whole energy consumption of the reference residential buildings in Poland. Thus, predicting heating demand (obtained using the data describing the built environment of the examined cluster) by means of the ANN is huge facilitation for those types of study.

An exemplary line for a single building is presented below. Each color represents one group of parameters, accordingly: orange—calculation step, green—localization (exterior climate), blue—building location, black—building enclosure variant, and yellow—heating system variant. The definition can be performed using some keywords (first line) or using the actual values describing the building. The TEAC software is using the building's coordinates in order to load the analyzed object parameters (buildings placement is defined earlier in 1st module of the software). In order to perform urban-scale analyses, all buildings within the examined region must be described using the mentioned formula in the exact order. Using that type of data, the heating demand predictions of the whole urban-scale region can be performed. The whole process is described in detail in [43].

{*hourly*, *Lodz*, *1_1*, *base*, *base*}

$\{TP, DBT, ITH, A_0, V_0, A_{win}, n_{tot}, U_{wall}, U_{roof}, U_{floor}, U_{win}, H_{COP}, OV, SV\}$

{1, −4.30, 0.00, 134.31, 330.80, 23.10, 0.60, 1.18, 0.65, 1.75, 2.75, 0.59, 225, 6}

Some validation of the predefined ANN was made in order to check the capability and accuracy of the network for heating demand predictions of the Polish single-family sector. The validation of the trained ANN was performed comparing the predicted values with the results obtained using the *Energy Plus* software. The used temperature range and variety of values within that assortment seem sufficient to perform accurate predictions for various localizations (outdoor climates). Here, an examination of the weather parameters (thus different building locations), particularly the outdoor temperature values, is presented, for scenarios before and after building retrofitting. The performed validations can be seen in Figure 5, for Extreme Winter Week (EWW) periods, for better results legibility. The EWW is the coldest week of the year for the examined locations. The validation was performed for cities Czestochowa and Olsztyn, which were not used as input data during ANN training.

In both cases, very good prediction accuracy was obtained, despite the fact, that the used weather data was unknown for the network. The network is also capable to predict the trend of heating demands. An interesting fact is that the predictions are almost perfectly in the most meaningful moments (peaks), while some differences are observed for very low demands (lower than 0.5 kW).

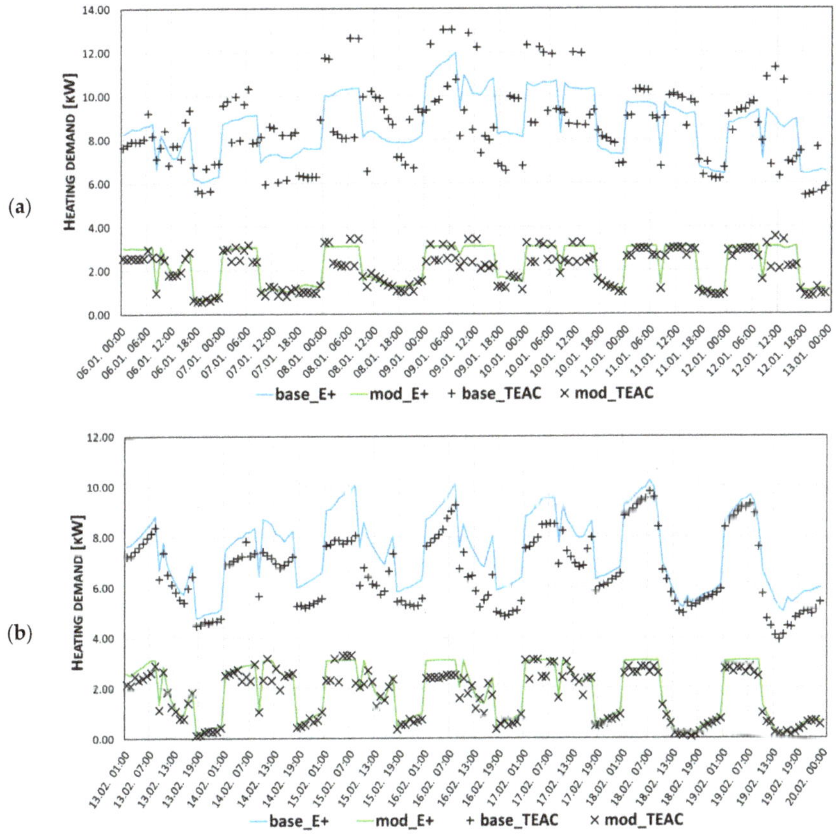

Figure 5. Comparison of heating demands obtained using the *Energy Plus* (solid lines) and the ANN pre-dictions (markers) for Czestochowa (**a**) and Olsztyn (**b**).

A short collation out of the preformed validation is presented in Table 1. It can be seen, that annual heating demand (HC_A) is predicted with a high accuracy—the difference is less than 9% compared to the *Energy Plus* outputs. Similar outputs are observed for the predicted heating demand during EWW periods (HC_{EWW}). The accuracy of peak demands (HD_{max}) varied from approx. 2% up to 14%, nevertheless, the higher differences are usually observed for the modernized buildings, for which peak demands are overall low. Based on the performed validation it can be concluded, that the defined network is an effective tool for the heating demand predictions for Polish climate conditions. In practice, the trained network is capable to perform heating demand predictions regardless of the analyzed building location, aside from extremely harsh places in terms of their climates, such as for example Zakopane city.

Table 1. Comparison of the results obtained by means of the *Energy Plus* (E+) and the TEAC software.

		Base Variant			Modernized Variant		
		E+	**TEAC**	**Rel. Diff.**	**E+**	**TEAC**	**Rel. Diff.**
Czesto-chowa	HD_{max} [kW]	11.98	13.03	8.76%	3.11	3.55	14.15%
	HC_{EWW} [kWh]	1489.34	1480.53	−0.59%	366.58	331.39	−9.60%
	HC_A [kWh/a]	23,593.90	25,661.56	8.75%	4423.06	4794.51	8.40%
Olsztyn	HD_{max} [kW]	11.82	11.30	−4.40%	3.22	3.29	2.17%
	HC_{EWW} [kWh]	1235.38	1102.17	−10.78%	298.51	261.58	−12.37%
	HC_A [kWh/a]	27,149.09	25,961.23	−4.38%	5622.02	5957.98	5.98%

Symbols used: HD_{max}—maximal heating demand; HC_{EWW}—heating demand for EWW period; HC_A—annual heating demand; Rel. Diff.—relative difference.

4. An Exemplary Application of the TEAC Software

It is possible to analyze the actual residential neighborhood using the TEAC software. In this example, the part of the *Smulsko* neighborhood, located in Lodz (Poland), is examined. The neighborhood is analyzed as an Energy Cluster (EC), and due to the fact, that the analysis is focused on the buildings, the area might be considered as a BEC [21]. The area is defined based on the satellite image shown in Figure 6. That image was adjusted (rotated by 45 degrees counter-clockwise) to the predefined grid used by the TEAC software, where each cell represents a parcel for only one house. The built environment is defined by overlapping the grid with the satellite image; whenever a building image fits within a cell, thus the parcel was considered as occupied. The building placement is done following the statistical data (assuming a share of the Polish RSFH) [64] and rotating each house randomly. The schema of the examined BEC is shown in Figure 7; it is a square-based zone, 23 by 23 parcels, consisting of 202 houses (each color represents a different RSFH).

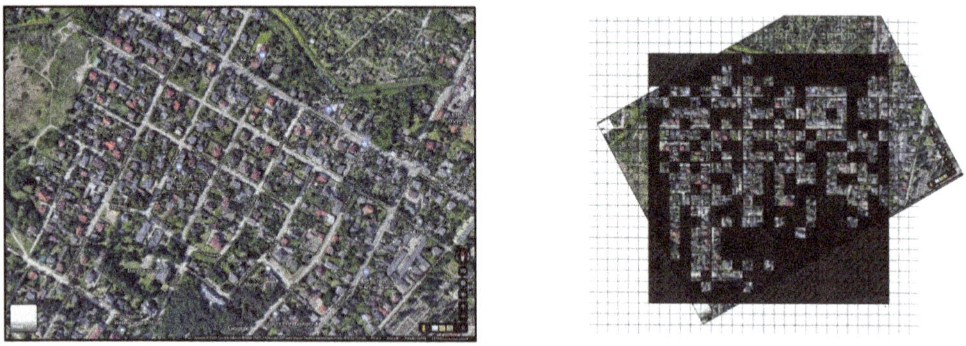

Figure 6. The satellite image of the *Smulsko* cluster (on **left**, source: [65]) and its adjustment schema (on **right**).

In this case, deep buildings thermal modernization is analyzed, concerning their full electrification. The refurbishment assumes building enclosures retrofitting to the actual energy-efficiency standards, following the Polish regulations. The modernization also includes heating system upgrades, from standard stoves to highly efficient heat pumps. Moreover, in all buildings, the lighting systems are modernized with LEDs. Also, Renewable Energy Sources (RES) are applied by means of photovoltaic (PV) systems mounted on the appropriate roof slopes, avoiding surfaces oriented North, North-East, and North-West. The Isometric Radiation Model (IRM) was used in order to calculate the solar outputs; it is comprehensively described in [66]. Finally, some smart-metering techniques are applied for the examined BEC. All the proposed modernizations follow the smart-city concept; thus, the examined neighborhood might be considered as the Energy Flexible Building Cluster (EFBC) [20]. The TEAC software is capable to analyze a single-family house neighborhood as an EFBC, considering various energy-, economic- and environmental-related issues; some of the available outputs are presented.

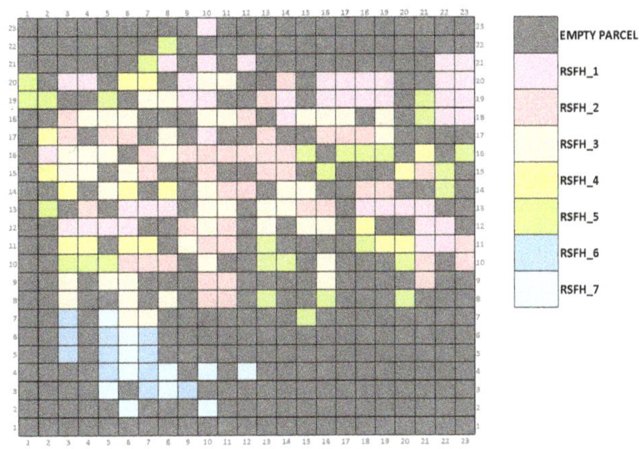

Figure 7. The final schema of the *Smulsko* cluster for the analysis in the TEAC software.

The default outputs using the TEAC software are maps, which might present various results, i.e., heating and electrical energy demands, greenhouse gasses (GHG) emission, RES potential or economic indexes (presenting the modernization or operation costs). It should be repeated, that all the results are obtained based on the predicted heating demand (out of the ANN usage), as well as the electricity consumption for the predefined scenarios. As an example, a comparison of CO_2 emissions before and after modernization is shown in Figure 8. Maps allow us to validate the proposed modernizations for the whole area, as well as for some smaller parts of the neighborhood. On the other hand, maps can be also used to select the most appropriate region for modernization.

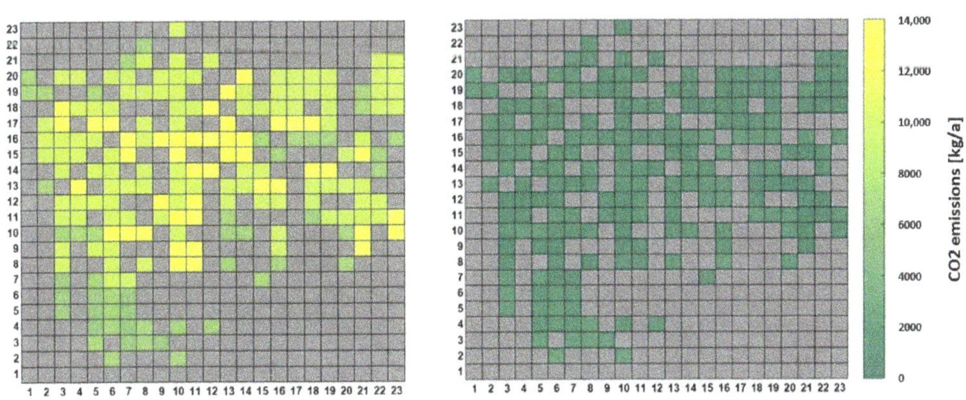

Figure 8. CO_2 emission maps for the *Smulsko* cluster before (on **left**) and after (on **right**) modernization.

A short summary of the analysis results is shown in Table 2, where both examined variants, before (V0) and after (V1) deep retrofitting, are compared. All of the results are obtained out of the TEAC software. In the modernized scenario, only electricity is used, supported by renewables. The heating demand is significantly reduced (by approx. 95%), same as the electricity consumption (63%). The peak demands are also significantly lower, accordingly by 94.6% and 40.5%. Out of the obtained results ones for heating purposes are more important, due to the fact, that heating, in general, is a dominant demand for Polish residential buildings (especially single-family houses). The total amount of 640.40 MWh electricity is produced out of 4443.45 m^2 of PVs, allowing for energy independence (zeroth demand) for more than a quarter of the year (approx. 2450 h). The proposed modernization is also highly pro-ecological—the GHG emissions are significantly reduced (in the range of 82–92%) in the examined cluster. Finally, some economic aspects are presented. The building's deep retrofitting costs slightly over 15 M PLN, and those actions will be profitable after 14–18 years, depending on the calculation method, where the longest time is the most likely, calculated using the Life Cycle Cost (LCC) approach. The whole PV installation costs approx. 3.72 M PLN and due to electricity consumption savings, its payoffs after approx. 9.3 years. Furthermore, using the EC concept it is possible to recon the whole neighborhood as a unity, not as numerous singular buildings. That approach allows to generate some additional savings out of the cluster operating, without (or with minimal) initial costs. Those annual savings, for the modernized scenario, are as high as 62 k PLN, which is a 24% reduction. In Figure 9 a comparison of electricity Load Duration Curves (LDC) is presented. It is evident, that the proposed modernization improved the safety of the local grid: the electricity demand is more uniform, peak demands are lower, as well as some temporal energy-independency (marked as a green box) is observed. The analysis performed using the LDC is an extremely valuable approach in terms of verifying the modernizations validity.

Table 2. An energy-related summary for the *Smulsko* cluster.

	HC_A [MWh/a]	EC_A [MWh/a]	CO_2 [t/a]	SO_2 [t/a]	NO_x [t/a]	$PM_{2.5}$ [t/a]	PM_{10} [t/a]
V0	4913.76	1895.19	2032.16	27.21	1.72	5.63	7.27
V1	256.33	701.13	272.89	4.99	0.23	0.47	0.61

Symbols used: V0—base scenario; V1—modernized scenario; HC_A—annual heating demand; EC_A—annual electricity demand.

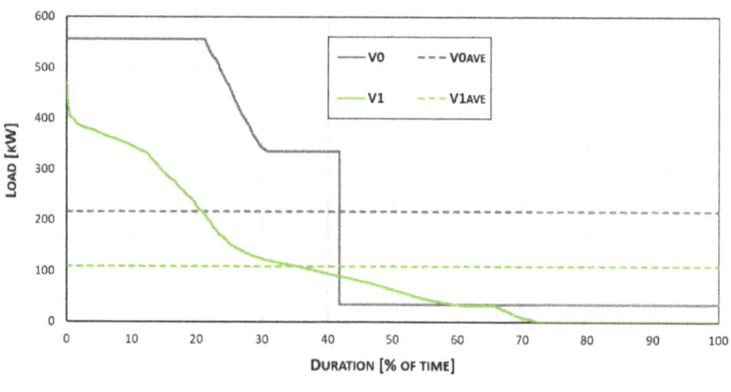

Figure 9. Comparison of the electricity LDCs for the *Smulsko* cluster.

5. Conclusions

This paper presented an application of the ANN trained using the L-M method, for analyzing various issues referring to UBEM. The analysis was performed by means of the TEAC software—a home-developed research computational tool for UBEM of the Polish residential sector. The L-M method was used for the ANN training process. The purpose of the AI application was to define a network, capable to predict the heating demand of the neighborhood of a single-family house in Poland, with sufficiently high accuracy, compared with the *Energy Plus* software outputs. The L-M method was the most accurate (for the examined purpose) out of all examined ones, which was discussed in this paper. The high accuracy was obtained, not only for the total values, i.e., annual heating demand but also for much more detailed results, i.e., peak demands. Thus, the applied method allows not only predicting the accurate values of heating demand (see Table 1), but also its time evolution and characteristics (see Figure 5). Moreover, due to the ANN application, the total computational time of the performed analysis was much shorter comparing with the traditional approaches. The computing time of annual energy demand for a single house is reduced out of approx. 20 s (using the *Energy Plus* software) to approx. 2 s only (by means of the TEAC software). Additionally, the required computational resources are also significantly lesser.

The TEAC software is a useful tool for UBEM of the Polish residential sector. It focuses on the single-family houses sector, due to its impact on the national energy profile. The Polish single-family houses sector is characterized by a huge potential for the overall improvement of energy efficiency, which might be validated using the TEAC software. The tool is using the EC concept, in order to maximize the energy-, economic- and environmental-related profits in the examined region. The TEAC software can be used for various analyses of actual residential areas, as shown in the example discussed in this paper. The developed tool might be used by the local authorities to perform urban-scale management, as well as academics for various UBEM analyses. Further development of the TEAC software is planned (e.g., the addition of GUI), in order to make the TEAC software available as a user-friendly web application.

Author Contributions: M.Z. and D.G. were involved in defining the aim of the paper. M.Z. developed the TEAC software. M.Z performed numerical analyses and prepared results. M.Z. and D.G. analyzed the results and performed writing and editing. All authors have read and agreed to the published version of the manuscript.

Funding: This research received funding of the Faculty of Civil Engineering, Architecture and Environmental Engineering at the Lodz University of Technology—scholarship for young scientists in years 2019 and 2020.

Conflicts of Interest: The authors declare no conflict of interest.

References

1. The United Nations. Available online: https://www.un.org/en/ (accessed on 29 October 2021).
2. The Our World in Data. Available online: https://ourworldindata.org (accessed on 29 October 2021).
3. Sokol, J.; Cerezo Davila, C.; Reinhart, C.F. Validation of a Bayesian-based method for defining residential archetypes in urban building energy models. *Energy Build.* **2017**, *134*, 11–24. [CrossRef]
4. Castaldo, V.L.; Pisello, A.L.; Piselli, C.; Fabiani, C.; Cotana, F.; Santamouris, M. How outdoor microclimate mitigation affects building thermal-energy performance: A new design-stage method for energy saving in residential near-zero energy settlements in Italy. *Renew. Energy* **2018**, *127*, 920–935.
5. Allegrini, J.; Orehounig, K.; Evins, R. A review of modelling approaches and tools for the simulation of district-scale energy systems. *Renew. Sust. Energ. Rev.* **2015**, *52*, 1391–1404. [CrossRef]
6. Crawley, D.B.; Hand, J.W.; Kummert, M.; Griffith, B.T. Contrasting the capabilities of building energy performance simulation programs. *Build. Environ.* **2008**, *43*, 661–673.
7. Crawley, D.B.; Lawrie, L.K.; Winkelmann, F.C.; Buhl, W.F.; Huang, Y.J.; Pedersen, C.O.; Stand, R.K.; Liesen, R.J.; Fisher, D.E.; Witte, M.J.; et al. Energy Plus: Creating a new-generation building energy simulation program. *Energy Build.* **2001**, *33*, 319–331. [CrossRef]
8. The BEST Directory–Building Energy Software Tools. Available online: https://www.buildingenergysoftwaretools.com (accessed on 29 October 2021).
9. Nagpal, S.; Reinhart, C.F. A comparison of two modeling approaches for establishing and implementing energy use reduction targets for a university campus. *Energy Build.* **2018**, *173*, 103–116. [CrossRef]
10. The CitySim Software. Available online: https://www.epfl.ch/labs/leso/transfer/software/citysim/ (accessed on 29 October 2021).
11. The Urban Modeling Interface. Available online: https://web.mit.edu/sustainabledesignlab/projects/umi/index.html (accessed on 29 October 2021).
12. The City Building Energy Saver (CityBES) Software. Available online: https://citybes.lbl.gov (accessed on 29 October 2021).
13. The City Energy Analyst (CEA) Software. Available online: https://cityenergyanalyst.com (accessed on 29 October 2021).
14. Ferrando, M.; Causone, F. An overview of urban building energy modelling (UBEM) tools. *J. Build. Perform. Simul.* **2020**, *16*, 3452–3459.
15. Chen, Y.; Hong, T.; Piette, M.A. Automatic generation and simulation of urban building energy models based on city dataset for city-scale building retrofit analysis. *Appl. Energy* **2017**, *205*, 323–335. [CrossRef]

16. Guen, M.; Mosca, L.; Perera, A.T.D.; Coccolo, S.; Mohajer, N.; Scartezzini, J.-L. Improving the energy sustainability of a Swiss village through building renovation and renewable energy integration. *Energy Build.* **2018**, *158*, 906–923. [CrossRef]
17. Ma, R.; Ren, B.; Zhao, D.; Chen, J.; Lu, Y. Modelling urban energy dynamics under clustered urban heat Island effect with local-weather extended distributed adjacency blocks. *Sustain. Cities Soc.* **2020**, *56*, 1452. [CrossRef]
18. Mastrucci, A.; Baume, O.; Stazi, F.; Leopold, U. Estimating energy savings for the residential building stock of an entire city: A GIS-based statistical downscaling approach applied to Rotterdam. *Energy Build.* **2014**, *14*, 358–367. [CrossRef]
19. Sola, A.; Corchero, C.; Salom, J.; Sanmarti, M. Simulation Tools to Build Urban-Scale Energy Models: A Review. *Energies* **2018**, *11*, 3269. [CrossRef]
20. Vigna, I.; Pernetti, R.; Pasut, W.; Lollini, R. New domain for promoting energy efficiency: Energy Flexible Building Cluster. *Sustain. Cities Soc.* **2018**, *38*, 526–533. [CrossRef]
21. Zhang, X.; Lovati, M.; Vigna, I.; Widen, J.; Han, M.; Gal, C.; Feng, T. A review of urban energy systems at building cluster level incorporating renewable-energy-source (RES) envelope solutions. *Appl. Energy* **2018**, *230*, 1034–1056. [CrossRef]
22. Dogan, T.; Reinhart, C.F.; Michalatos, P. Urban daylight simulation calculating the daylit area of urban design. *SimBuild* **2012**, *5*, 613–620.
23. Dall, G.; Galante, A.; Pasetti, G. A methodology for evaluating the potential energy savings of retrofitting residential building stocks. *Sustain. Cities Soc.* **2012**, *4*, 12–21. [CrossRef]
24. Swan, L.G.; Ugursal, V.I. Modeling of end-use energy consumption in the residential sector: A review of modeling techniques. *Renew. Sust. Energ. Rev.* **2009**, *13*, 1819–1835. [CrossRef]
25. Zygmunt, M. Urban-Scale Energy Modelling of Some Residential Energy Flexible Buildings Clusters in Poland. Ph.D. Thesis, Lodz University of Technology, Lodz, Poland, 2021.
26. Bentzen, J.; Engsted, T. A revival of the autoregressive distributed lag model in estimating energy demand relationships. *Energy* **2001**, *26*, 45–55. [CrossRef]
27. O'Neal, D.L.; Hirst, E. An energy use model of the residential sector. *IEEE Int. Conf. Syst. Man Cybern.* **1980**, *10*, 749–755.
28. Saha, G.P.; Stephenson, J. A model of residential energy use in New Zealand. *Energy* **1980**, *5*, 167–175. [CrossRef]
29. Siller, T.; Kost, M.; Imboden, D. Long-term energy savings and greenhouse gas emission reductions in the Swiss residential sector. *Energy Policy* **2007**, *35*, 529–539. [CrossRef]
30. Larsen, B.M.; Nesbakken, R. Household electricity end-use consumption: Results from econometric and engineering models. *Energy Econ.* **2004**, *26*, 179–200. [CrossRef]
31. Raffio, G.; Isambert, O.; Mertz, G.; Schreier, C.; Kissock, K. Targeting residential energy assistance. *Proc. Int. Conf. Energy Sustain.* **2007**, *11*, 489–495.
32. Tonn, B.E.; White, D.L. Residential electricity use, wood use, and indoor temperature: An econometric model. *Energy Syst. Policy* **1988**, *12*, 151–165.
33. Caves, D.W.; Herriges, J.A.; Train, K.E.; Windle, R. A Bayesian approach to combining conditional demand and engineering models of electricity usage. *Rev. Econ. Stat.* **1987**, *69*, 438–448. [CrossRef]
34. LaFrance, G.; Perron, D. Evolution of residential electricity demand by end-use in Quebec 1979–1989: A conditional demand analysis. *Energy Stud. Rev.* **1994**, *6*, 164–173. [CrossRef]
35. Aydinalp, M.; Ugursal, V.I.; Fung, A. Modeling of the space and domestic hot-water heating energy-consumption in the residential sector using neural networks. *Appl. Energy* **2004**, *79*, 159–178. [CrossRef]
36. Mihalakakou, G.; Santamouris, M.; Tsangrassoulis, A. On the energy consumption in residential buildings. *Energy Build.* **2002**, *34*, 727–736. [CrossRef]
37. Jaccard, M.; Baille, A. CO_2 emission reduction costs in the residential sector: Behavioral parameters in a bottom-up simulation model. *Energy* **1996**, *17*, 107–135. [CrossRef]
38. Kadian, R.; Dahiya, R.P.; Garg, H.P. Energy-related emissions and mitigation opportunities from the household sector in Delhi. *Energy Policy* **2007**, *35*, 6195–6211. [CrossRef]
39. Shimoda, Y.; Fujii, T.; Morikawa, M.; Mizuno, M. Residential end-use energy simulation at city scale. *Build. Environ.* **2004**, *39*, 959–967. [CrossRef]
40. Yao, R.; Steemers, K. A method of formulating energy load profile for domestic buildings in the UK. *Energy Build.* **2005**, *37*, 663–671. [CrossRef]
41. Farahbakhsh, H.; Ugursal, V.I.; Fung, A. A residential end-use energy consumption model for Canada. *Int. J. Energy Res.* **1998**, *22*, 1133–1143. [CrossRef]
42. Ferrando, M.; Causone, F.; Hong, T.; Chen, Y. Urban building energy modeling (UBEM) tools: A state-of-the-art review of bottom-up physics-based approaches. *Sustain. Cities Soc.* **2020**, *62*, 102408. [CrossRef]
43. Kavgic, M.; Mavrogianni, A.; Mumovic, D.; Summerfield, A.; Stevanovic, Z.; Djurovic-Petrovic, M. A review of bottom-up building stock models for energy consumption in the residential sector. *Build. Environ.* **2010**, *45*, 1683–1697. [CrossRef]
44. Zygmunt, M.; Gawin, D. Application of ANN for analysing a neighbourhood of single-family houses constituting an Energy Cluster. *MATEC Web Conf.* **2019**, *12*, 282. [CrossRef]
45. Zygmunt, M.; Gawin, D. Potential of Renewable Energy Sources usage in an energy demand of a single-family houses neighbourhood, constituting an Energy Cluster—A case study. *E3S Web Conf.* **2020**, *12*, 172. [CrossRef]

46. Zygmunt, M.; Gawin, D. Application of the TEAC software for analysis of Energy Flexible Building Clusters—A case study. *J. Phys. Conf. Ser.* **2021**, *2069*, 012226. [CrossRef]
47. The DesignBuilder Software. Available online: https://designbuilder.co.uk (accessed on 29 October 2021).
48. The MATLAB Software. Available online: https://www.mathworks.com (accessed on 29 October 2021).
49. Ascione, F.; De Masi, R.F.; Rossi, F.; Fistola, R.; Sasso, M.; Vanoli, G.P. Analysis and diagnosis of the energy performance of buildings and districts: Methodology, validation and development of Urban Energy Maps. *Cities* **2013**, *35*, 270–283. [CrossRef]
50. Abiodun, I.O.; Jantan, A.; Omolara, E.A.; Dada, V.K.; Mohamed, A.N.; Arshad, H. State-of-the-art in artificial neural network applications: A survey. *Heliyon* **2018**, *4*, 1245. [CrossRef] [PubMed]
51. Foucquier, A.; Robert, S.; Suard, F.; Stephan, L.; Jay, A. State of the art in building modeling and energy performances predicitons: A review. *Renew. Sust. Energ. Rev.* **2013**, *23*, 272–288. [CrossRef]
52. Kalogirou, S.A. Artificial neural network in energy applications in buildings. *Int. J. Low-Carbon Technol.* **2006**, *1*, 201–216. [CrossRef]
53. AlFuhaid, S.A.; El-Sayed, A.M.; Mahmoud, S.M. Cascaded artificial neural networks for short-term load forecasting. *IEEE Trans. Power Syst.* **1997**, *12*, 1524–1529. [CrossRef]
54. Hernandez, L.; Baladron, C.; Aguiar, M.J.; Carro, B.; Sanchez-Esguevillas, J.A.; Lloret, J. Short-Term Load Forecasting for Microgrids Based on Artificial Neural Network. *Energies* **2013**, *6*, 1385–1408. [CrossRef]
55. Aydinalp, M.; Ugursal, V.I.; Fung, A. Modeling of the appliance, lighting, and space cooling energy consumptions in the residential sector using neural networks. *Appl. Energy* **2002**, *72*, 87–110. [CrossRef]
56. Stathakis, D. How many hidden layers and nodes? *Int. J. Remote Sens.* **2008**, *30*, 2133–2147. [CrossRef]
57. Gavin, H.P. The Lavenberg-Marquardt method for nonlinear least squares curve-fitting problems. *Comput. Sci.* **2013**, *112*, 3521.
58. Levenberg, K. A method for the solution of certain non-linear problem in least squares. *Q. Appl. Math.* **1944**, *2*, 164–168. [CrossRef]
59. Marquardt, D. An Algorithm for Least-Squares Estimation of Nonlinear Parameters. *J. Soc. Ind. Appl. Math.* **1963**, *11*, 431–441. [CrossRef]
60. Aggarwal, K.K.; Yogesh, S.; Chandra, P.; Manimala, P. Bayesian Regularization in a Neural Network Model to Estimate Lines of Code Using Function Points. *Comput. Sci.* **2005**, *1*, 505–509. [CrossRef]
61. Nazareth, J.L. Conjugate gradient method. *Wiley Interdiscip. Rev. Comput. Stat.* **2009**, *1*, 348–353. [CrossRef]
62. Wang, Y. Gauss-Newton method. *Wiley Interdiscip. Rev. Comput. Stat.* **2012**, *4*, 415–420. [CrossRef]
63. Fliege, J.; Vaz, A.I.F.; Vicente, L.N. Complexity of gradient descent for multiobjective optimization. *Optim. Methods Softw.* **2019**, *34*, 949–959. [CrossRef]
64. The Statistics Poland. Available online: https://stat.gov.pl/en/ (accessed on 29 October 2021).
65. The Google Maps. Available online: www.google.pl/maps/ (accessed on 29 October 2021).
66. Chwieduk, D. Solar Energy in Buildings. In *Thermal Balance for Efficient Heating and Cooling*, 1st ed.; Academic Press: London, UK, 2014.

energies

MDPI

Article

Comparing 2D and 3D Solar Radiation Modeling in Urban Areas

Štefan Kolečanský *, Jaroslav Hofierka , Jozef Bogľarský and Jozef Šupinský

Institute of Geography, Faculty of Science, Pavol Jozef Šafárik University in Košice, Šrobárova 2, 04154 Košice, Slovakia; jaroslav.hofierka@upjs.sk (J.H.); jozef.boglarsky@student.upjs.sk (J.B.); jozef.supinsky@upjs.sk (J.Š.)

* Correspondence: stefan.kolecansky@student.upjs.sk; Tel.: +421-55-234-2352

Abstract: The use of solar radiation in the urban environment is becoming increasingly important for the sustainable development of cities and human societies. Several factors influence the distribution of solar radiation in urban areas, including urban morphology and the physical properties of urban materials. Most of these factors can be modeled with a relatively high accuracy using 2D and 3D solar radiation models. In this paper, the r.sun and v.sun solar radiation models are used to calculate solar radiation for the city of Košice in Eastern Slovakia to assess the accuracy of both approaches for vertical surfaces frequently found in urban areas. The results were validated by pyranometer measurements. The results showed relatively good estimates by the 3D v.sun model and poor estimates by the 2D r.sun model. This can be attributed to an improper representation of vertical surfaces by a digital surface model, which has a strong impact on solar resource assessments. We found that 3D city models prepared in level of detail 2 (LoD2) are not always adequate in case of complex buildings with morphological structures, such as terraces. These cast shadows on facades especially when solar altitude is high and, thus, assessments, even by a 3D model, are inaccurate.

Keywords: 3D city model; renewable energy; solar radiation; urban solar radiation model

Citation: Kolečanský, Š.; Hofierka, J.; Bogľarský, J.; Šupinský, J. Comparing 2D and 3D Solar Radiation Modeling in Urban Areas. *Energies* **2021**, *14*, 8364. https://doi.org/10.3390/en14248364

Academic Editor: Marcin Kamiński

Received: 10 November 2021
Accepted: 9 December 2021
Published: 11 December 2021

1. Introduction

The majority of the human population is located in cities, where, in developed countries, about 80% of the population lives [1]. This contributes to problems associated with dense urban areas, such as urban heat island effects, which ultimately lead to a higher energy demand, but also to higher production of unwanted exhalants and emissions. Moreover, the use of solar energy helps to mitigate various environmental problems and improve the quality of life in the cities. Solar thermal or photovoltaic applications are very common around the world and have become an important factor in the overall energy production mix in many countries. Therefore, it is increasingly important to know the solar resource potential of urban areas.

Solar radiation in urban areas is a key input factor in many urban energy models and sustainable city designs. Examples include thermal and photovoltaic applications, passive heating systems, or urban microclimate designs [2–4]. The implementation of distributed photovoltaic systems transforms the urban environment from a place of energy consumption to a place of energy production. Distributed solar systems are scalable at a micro-scale and open up new investment opportunities for electricity production within the city, allowing consumers to become producers. The changes, associated with rapidly expanding solar benefits in cities, are expected to have disruptive impacts on urban electricity infrastructures and related institutions, and will require tools to evaluate and plan for future changes.

The increasing availability of three-dimensional (3D) city models and high-resolution geospatial data stimulated solar resource assessments for urban areas [2,5–7]. Currently, there are several well-developed models of solar radiation distribution, such as the r.sun model by Hofierka and Šúri [8], the Solar Analyst model in the ArcGIS program [9], the Perez model [10], the SORAM model [11], SURFSUN3D [12], and the SOL model [6], often used for solar radiation assessments in urban areas. Hofierka and Zlocha [5] developed v.sun, a 3D version of the r.sun model for 3D city models. Freitas et al. [6] pointed out that 3D solar radiation modeling that includes vertical surfaces, such as facades, is very time consuming if applied to large cities. The data must include topologically correct 3D vector data that usually require manual editing and verification of 3D polygon orientation represented by a normal vector. A frequent solution to the problem is the use of a high-resolution digital surface model (DSM) approximating vertical surfaces, such as facades, by quasi-vertical surfaces [13]. This introduces an error in solar radiation estimates for vertical surfaces. To date, no in-depth analysis has been published that assesses whether this approximation is acceptable.

Nevertheless, the previously predominant two-dimensional (2D) solar radiation models, such as the r.sun model [8], are gradually being augmented by 3D solar radiation models that allow a better representation of vertical surfaces (building facades) while facilitating interactive assessment of PV potential in complex urban environments [12,14–16]. Technological advances provide new opportunities for complex 3D approaches in solar modeling [17].

The main objective of this study is to compare the results of 2D r.sun and 3D v.sun solar radiation models implemented in GRASS GIS [18] with field measurements by a pyranometer for the city of Košice in eastern Slovakia to demonstrate the applicability of 2D vs. 3D approaches in assessing the solar resource potential in urban areas. Therefore, five locations are selected with morphologically diverse buildings still typical for this urban area. The measurements and solar radiation modeling were carried out during a typical summer day (23 June 2021) for three different time moments. The solar radiation values were calculated for the time of measurements using the r.sun and v.sun modules integrated in the open-source GRASS GIS software. By comparing the r.sun and v.sun models with the measurements, we demonstrate the accuracy of the models specifically for selected building facades.

2. Methods and Data

Most GIS-based solar radiation models provide estimates of solar radiation over large areas using digital terrain models (DTMs) and selected atmospheric and land cover parameters derived from ground-based or satellite-based data [19–22]. These topographic solar radiation models can only be used for 2D surfaces, such as land surfaces or rooftops. There are 2 models implemented in GRASS GIS that are based on the same fundamental basis of solar radiation, but they work differently with the geometric representation of the Earth's surface. The r.sun model is for 2D surfaces, such as terrain or roofs, represented by rasters, while v.sun is for 3D city models represented by 3D vectors [5].

The solar radiation methodology used in the r.sun and v.sun models is based on the European Solar Radiation Atlas (ESRA) methodology [23,24] and described in [8] and [5]. The calculation of the direct (beam) component of solar radiation on surfaces for clear-sky atmospheric conditions B (W/m^2) is quite straightforward:

$$B = G_0 exp\{-0.8662 T_{LK} m \delta_R(m)\} \sin \delta_{exp} \tag{1}$$

where G_0 is the normal extra-terrestrial irradiance outside the atmosphere (W/m^2), T_{LK} is the air mass 2 Linke atmospheric turbidity factor (-), m is the relative optical air mass (-), $\delta_R(m)$ the Rayleigh optical thickness at air mass m (-), and δ_{exp} is the solar incidence angle measured between the sun and a surface.

The diffuse component implemented in this model is empirically derived from European climate conditions. The model for estimating the clear-sky diffuse irradiance on a surface D [W/m^2] is defined by the following equation [25]:

$$D = G_0 T_n(T_{LK}) F_d(h_0) \{F(\gamma_N)(1 - K_b) + K_b \sin \delta_{exp} / \sin h_0\} \tag{2}$$

where $T_n(T_{LK})$ is a diffuse transmission function dependent on the Linke turbidity factor T_{LK}, $F_d(h_0)$ is a diffuse solar altitude function dependent on the solar altitude h_0, $F(\gamma_N)$ is a function accounting for the diffuse sky irradiance dependent on surface inclination γ_N, and K_b is a measure of the amount of beam irradiance available. For surfaces in a shadow, we assume $\delta_{exp} = 0$ and $K_b = 0$.

The ground reflected clear-sky irradiance received on a surface R (W/m^2) is proportional to the total horizontal irradiance, which is a sum of beam and diffuse irradiance on a horizontal surface, mean ground albedo, and a fraction of the ground viewed by a surface [26]. The reflected radiation contributes to total radiation only by several percents in open areas and depends strongly on the reflectance of surrounding surfaces [8].

2.1. The r.sun Solar Radiation Model

The r.sun model implemented in the open GRASS GIS environment is one of the commonly used GIS-based solar radiation models [18]. The r.sun model is based on a comprehensive methodology for spatially and temporally distributed solar radiation and irradiance calculations developed by Hofierka and Šúri [8]. The model can calculate direct (beam), diffuse, and reflected solar radiation components of the total solar radiation for a specific location on land surface, given day, latitude, and atmospheric conditions. The module is designed to meet the needs of users in different scientific fields, such as environmental sciences, photovoltaics, agriculture, or forestry. Its applications range from local to regional scales. Another typical feature of this module is that it considers the shadow effect of local topography, which can be switched on and off according to the type and need of a given calculation. Solar irradiation maps are calculated by integrating the corresponding irradiances in selected time steps between the sunrise and sunset times for a given day.

The r.sun module works in two modes. In the first mode, it calculates the angle of incidence of solar radiation (expressed in degrees) and the solar irradiance values (W/m^2) for the set local time. In the second mode, the daily solar irradiation amounts are calculated for the set day. By scripting, these two modes can be used separately or in combination to provide estimates for any desired time interval [27].

Together with the r.sun model, the PVGIS online tool was developed to assess the photovoltaic potential of chosen locations within the regions of Europe and Africa [28]. The r.sun model was also used in the assessments of photovoltaic potential in urban areas [2]. The most commonly investigated surfaces include roofs of buildings. Thus, we can determine, for example, the photovoltaic potential for installing PV systems on these rooftops [2].

The basic input parameters of the r.sun model include a DSM and raster maps of slope steepness, aspect, and land surface albedo, as well as Linke's turbidity coefficient. Another input parameter is the specific hour of the day and day of the year for which calculations of global solar radiation, or its individual components, will be performed.

The advantages of this model according to Šúri et al. [27] are as follows:

- Full integration with GRASS GIS;
- Calculations can be performed in sunny weather or during the day;
- Input and output data can be processed by other tools in the GRASS GIS environment;
- The data are obtained from meteorological and satellite stations;
- Memory management and code optimization allows to use high-resolution data from a local to global level.

The growing trend of solar applications in urban areas requires the use of the most efficient models that can evaluate the solar potential of each surface. Therefore, it is important to evaluate the complex morphology of urban areas using models that exploit 3D environments. While the r.sun model can be applied to 2D surfaces in the form of rooftops, the v.sun model has been developed to detect the solar potential of vertical surfaces and facades [5].

2.2. The v.sun Solar Radiation Model

The v.sun model is essentially a 3D variant of the r.sun model that can also calculate direct, diffuse, and reflected solar radiation for a given day, latitude and surface, and atmospheric conditions. It is implemented in the GRASS GIS environment and is based on practically the same radiation methodology as the r.sun model. The difference, however, is that the v.sun model uses a new vector-voxel calculation procedure for complex 3D urban surfaces [5].

Buildings and urban areas are represented by 3D vectors in the form of polygons when using the v.sun model in 3D urban models. A typical simple digital representation of buildings is a box model. Although the calculation of the incident solar radiation for each polygon may seem simple, the shading effect of neighboring buildings must also be taken into account. This is why it is important in the v.sun model to take into account the variations in solar incidence and to divide each polygon into smaller segments. By segmenting the polygons in the next step, we are able to determine a more accurate estimate of the solar potential of polygonal areas thanks to voxels [5].

The v.sun model estimates direct, diffuse, and reflected radiation during clear-sky conditions. As solar radiation passes through the atmosphere, airflow and atmospheric cloudiness are taken into account, which can change the nature of the radiation. Similar to r.sun, the calculation works in two modes. The first mode is used to compute solar irradiances (in W/m^2) for 3D polygonal data. The second mode aims to use the 3D vector data to determine the daily solar irradiation (in W/m^2) over the time span of a particular day within the year. The advantage of these modes is that they can work alone or in combination to estimate the solar radiation impact at different time intervals.

The fundamental difference between the v.sun and r.sun module is in the geometry. While v.sun uses a complete or full 3D model of the city (roofs as well as vertical surfaces, such as facades, are taken into account), r.sun is a 2D (for a given x,y position, only one elevation value is possible). Thus, the r.sun model is more suitable for modeling the distribution of solar radiation for roofs and areas outside buildings.

The preparation of the input data of the v.sun model is quite complicated in terms of structure and topology. The orientation of the polygons (surface normals) must be outwards, and the vertices in all polygons must be ordered in the same manner clockwise or counterclockwise. The accuracy of the calculations depends on the size of the polygons that can be controled by a parameter [5].

2.3. Study Area and Data

Our study area is located in the central part of the city of Košice (Figure 1). The city of Košice is the second largest city in Slovakia with a population of approximately 240,000 inhabitants and an area of 242.77 km^2. It is part of an agglomeration with more than 367,000 inhabitants and the Košice-Prešov agglomeration with 555,800 inhabitants is one of the largest urbanized areas in Slovakia. The city of Košice is a typical example of an urban area in a temperate climate in Central Europe. The eastern part of Slovakia, where the city of Košice is also located, is characterized by warm and relatively dry summers and cold, slightly humid winters, with average daily temperatures ranging from −2 °C in January to 21 °C in July. The average annual number of clear-sky and overcast days for the city Košice is 48 and 126, respectively [29]. Based also on this factor, an area of 4 km^2 was selected, where different types of buildings are located, from administrative to residential buildings.

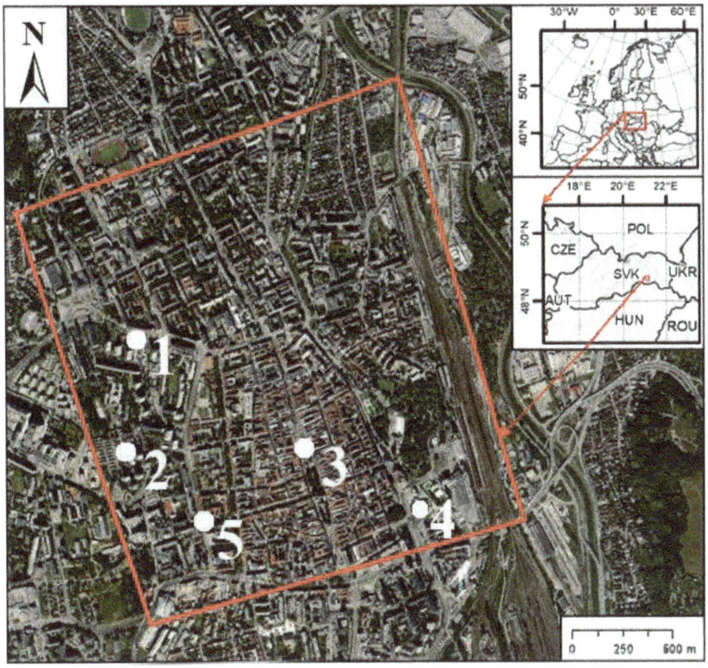

Figure 1. Location of the study area in the city of Košice, Slovakia.

The geometric 3D model of the city of Košice was derived from photogrammetric data collected by PHOTOMAP, s.r.o. company Košice. The model represents a level of detail 2 (LoD2) [30], which means that the model contains information about the basic geometry of buildings, including roofs. The 3D model itself was processed by combining data from aerial surveying and airborne laser scanning. The aerial survey imagery was photogrammetrically mapped in the PHOTOMOD software and the aerial laser scanning data were vectorized in the Ustation software. The 3D city model is stored in a shapefile vector format and consists of 61,766 polygons. A DTM with a cell size of 0.2 m was derived from LIDAR (light detection and ranging) data collected in late summer 2016 using the LEICA ALS70 airborne laser scanner.

Pyranometer MS-60 [31,32] produced by the EKO-INSTRUMENTS company was used to measure solar irradiances. The pyranometer's response time is 95% less than 18 s; the measured irradiance values are in the range of 0–2000 W/m^2; and maximum measuring error is +/−18 W/m^2. Measurements were taken at selected locations around 9:00 a.m., 12:00 p.m., and 4:00 p.m., local time. Two minute measurements at five s intervals were taken at the given location, then the values were averaged.

2.4. Calculation of Solar Radiation

Urban zones can be distinguished on the basis of their morphological and functional characteristics, which are often associated with specific socio-demographic and cultural features [33]. These factors play an important role in the use of solar energy, so it is important to analyze the different aspects of solar radiation distribution in urban environments. Based on these factors, 5 locations in the city of Košice were selected to demonstrate the use of the r.sun and v.sun modules, and then these locations were compared with the data from the pyranometer measurements (Figure 2). These include two buildings in the city centre (the State Theatre and the Greek-Catholic Church) and three buildings from the wider city centre of Košice, namely the Municipal Swimming Pool, the apartment house, and the residential house. The actual measurements were carried out on the selected vertical facades of the buildings. We opted for south-facing facades at the selected locations in most cases; in one case, it was the east-facing facade. Subsequently, the measured values were compared with the calculated irradiance values by the v.sun and r.sun models. In case of the v.sun model, it can be easily identified as an attribute value for the specific polygon representing the facade. In case of the r.sun model, the identification of the site on the steeply inclined surface approximating the facade is more complicated, essentially it is a matter of a specific cell identification within the DSM. The positions of pyranometer measurements were measured by the global navigation satellite system (GNSS) using the Topcon HiPER HR. The point measurements were performed for 30 s using the real-time kinematic (RTK) positioning via weighted averaging with an overall accuracy of the fixed solution between 1 and 2 cm.

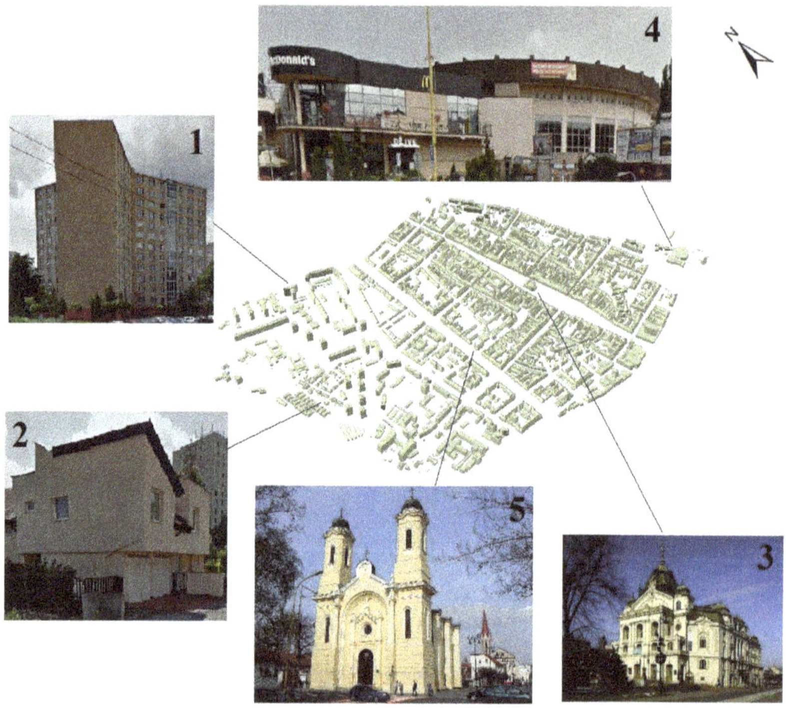

Figure 2. Positions of the selected locations in the city of Košice: Apartment house, Československá Street (**1**); Residential house, Muránska Street (**2**); State Theatre, Hlavná Street (**3**); Municipal swimming pool, Protifašistických bojovníkov Street (**4**); and Greek-Catholic Church of the Nativity of the Virgin Mary, Moyzesova Street (**5**).

3. Results

The selected buildings have different architectures and different types of facades. We selected four south-facing and one east-facing facade. The day during which the measurements took place represents a typical summer day (23 June 2021). The measurements took place at approximately 9:00 a.m., 12:00 p.m., and 4:00 p.m., local time. Since we only had one pyranometer, we had to conduct the actual measurement between 8:30 a.m. and 9:30 a.m., since it was not possible to be at all selected locations at the same time. This was also performed for the 12:00 p.m. and 4:00 p.m. measurements. The exact times of measurements were recorded by the pyranometer. We then computed irradiances by solar models for these exact times of measurements. Using the r.sun module, we calculated raster maps for the selected time horizons for the center of the city of Košice, which are shown in Figure 3. The calculation of solar radiation by the r.sun model is based on the DSM representing terrain and buildings. The facades are only approximated by steeply inclined surfaces. To compare the model with pyranometer measurements for the selected locations, we used their GNSS positions and identified raster cells containing the modeled solar irradiance values. The 3D distribution of solar irradiance by the v.sun model is shown in Figure 4. The model calculates solar irradiance only for polygons of the 3D city model. This means that it is much easier to identify solar irradiance for a particular facade represented by a polygon than by raster cells.

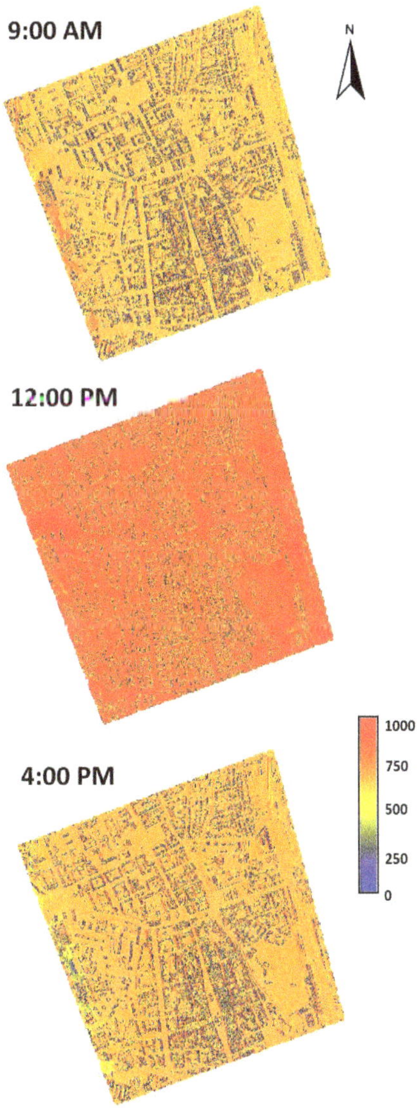

Figure 3. Solar irradiance from the r.sun model in the city center of Košice on 23 June 2021 (W/m^2).

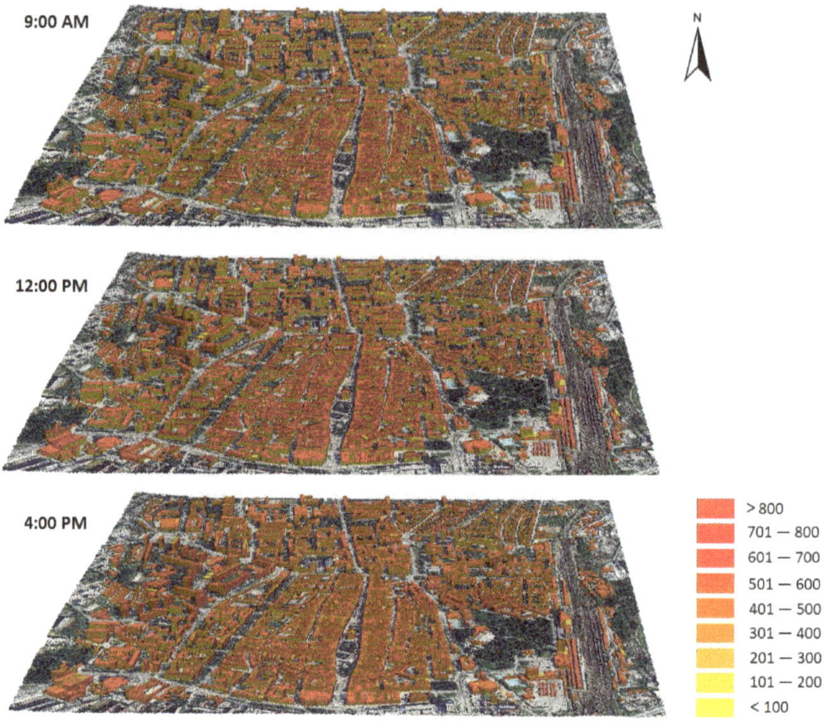

Figure 4. Solar irradiance from the v.sun model in the city center of Košice on 23 June 2021 (W/m^2).

Since the real time of measurement is always recorded by the instrument, we could use the solar radiation models for these exact times to ensure the correct comparison between the values. In the following subsections, we present the results for the particular locations.

3.1. Apartment House

The first location is situated in the wider center of Košice in Československá street-apartment house (Figures 1 and 2). The facade faces the east. At 8:26 a.m., we recorded a value of 663 W/m^2, which is the highest value of all measured objects at that time (Table 1). This is evidently due to the fact that the facade itself is oriented to the east, so solar irradiance is higher than in other south-facing facades or even on horizontal surfaces. The v.sun model gave us a value of 581 W/m^2 (Figure 5A), and the r.sun model calculated a value of 40 W/m^2. The value from the r.sun model was read on a nearly perpendicular building facade represented by a high-resolution DSM. However, the facade approximation in this relatively tall building, apparently, led to geometric deformations that prevented a correct calculation of solar irradiance. Figure 5A shows that in the morning facades receive more solar irradiance than flat, horizontal rooftops.

Table 1. Solar irradiance at the apartment house in Československá street in W/m^2 on 23 June 2021.

Time	Pyranometer	v.sun	r.sun	Position
8:26 a.m.	673	581	40	east
11:25 a.m.	249	396	46	east
3:13 p.m.	72	180	952	east

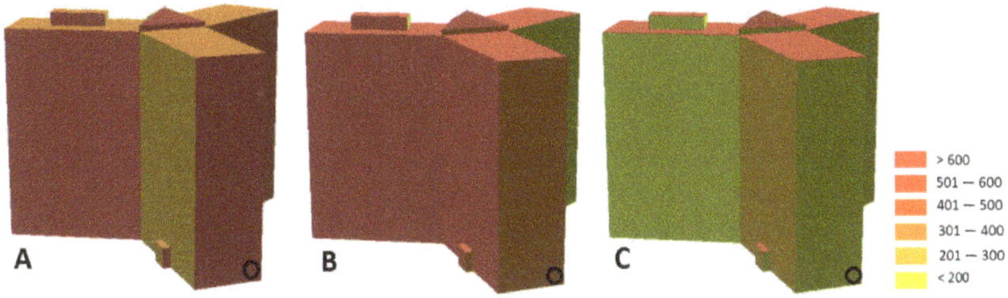

Figure 5. Solar irradiance at the apartment house from the v.sun model on 23 June 2021 (W/m^2) at (**A**) 8:26 a.m., (**B**) 11:25 a.m., and (**C**) 3:13 p.m. The black circle represents the measurement location.

At 11:25 a.m., the measured facade value dropped to 249 W/m^2 compared to the morning measurement. A similar decrease can be observed in the v.sun value (396 W/m^2). This decrease in solar irradiance is due to its facade orientation. The r.sun value still shows a low value due to an improper geometric representation of the facade by the particular raster cell. Figure 5B clearly shows that, at this time, solar irradiance is the highest at the rooftops as well as south-facing facades.

At 3:13 p.m., we recorded a value of only 72 W/m^2. This indicates that the site was already shaded. With the v.sun model, we recorded a value of 180 W/m^2, and r.sun calculated a value of 952 W/m^2. The v.sun model probably records a small amount of beam irradiance, whilst the r.sun model shows a completely opposite value to the morning and noon values and confirms the problem with the accuracy of geometric representation of the facade. At this time, the rooftops receive a relatively large amount of solar irradiance (Figure 5C).

3.2. Residential House

The second analyzed location is a residential house in Muránska Street. It is a classic two-story house in the wider center of Košice. In this case, we selected a south-facing facade. The value measured by the pyranometer at 8:39 a.m. is 458 W/m^2 (Table 2), which is more than 200 W/m^2 less compared to the previous location (Table 1). In the morning, east-facing facades receive more solar irradiance than south-facing facades. We recorded a value of 372 W/m^2 with the v.sun model and 574 W/m^2 with the r.sun model (Figure 6A). Both values vary from the measured value, but they are still reasonable.

Table 2. Solar irradiance at the residential house in Muránska street in W/m^2 on 23 June 2021.

Time	Pyranometer	v.sun	r.sun	Position
8:39 a.m.	458	372	574	south
11:34 a.m.	549	514	903	south
3:59 p.m.	188	164	709	south

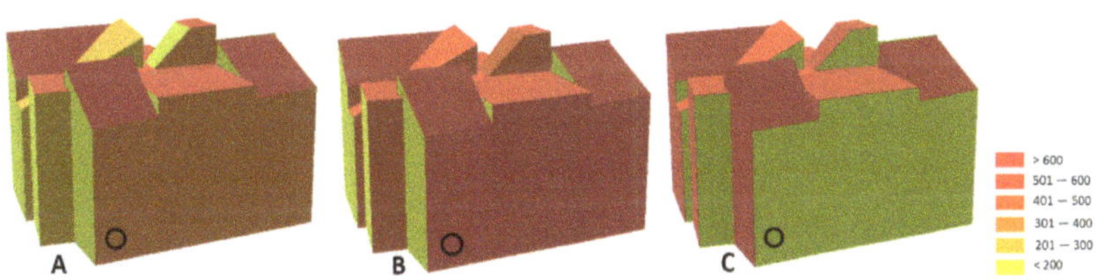

Figure 6. Solar irradiance at the residential house from the v.sun model on 23 June 2021 (W/m^2) at (**A**) 8:39 a.m., (**B**) 11:34 a.m., and (**C**) 3:59 p.m. The black circle represents the measurement location.

The value recorded by the pyranometer at 11:34 a.m. is slightly higher (549 W/m^2) than that recorded in the morning. In June, during the noon, the sun altitude is high, so the solar incidence angle is lower for facades than for rooftops, leading to lower solar irradiance values (Figure 6). Both the v.sun and r.sun models also show maximal values, albeit the v.sun estimate is very close to the measured value (514 W/m^2). At 3:59 p.m., the value recorded by the pyranometer (188 W/m^2) was significantly lower than that recorded in the morning, and a similar value was predicted by the v.sun model (164 W/m^2). The r.sun prediction is almost four times higher than the actual value (709 W/m^2).

3.3. State Theatre

The third location in our study is the State Theatre right in the center of the city of Košice on Hlavná Street. It is a building constructed in the Neo-Baroque style, which corresponds to its rather structured and complicated architecture (Figure 7). The value measured by the pyranometer at 8:57 a.m. was 413 W/m^2, which is almost 260 W/m^2 less compared to the first location facing to the east (apartment building), but similar to the residential house. The recorded value was quite accurately modeled by both models: v.sun (317 W/m^2) and r.sun (456 W/m^2) (Table 3).

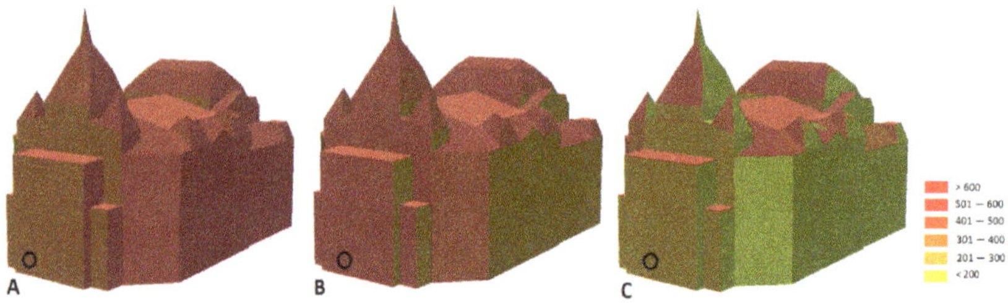

Figure 7. Solar irradiance at the State Theatre on 23 June 2021 (W/m^2) at (**A**) 8:57 a.m., (**B**) 11:50 a.m., and (**C**) 3:31 p.m. The black circle represents the measurement location.

Table 3. Solar irradiance at the State Theatre in W/m^2 on 23 June 2021.

Time	Pyranometer	v.sun	r.sun	Position
8:57 a.m.	413	317	456	south
11:50 a.m.	505	503	688	south
3:31 p.m.	87	293	287	south

The value recorded by the pyranometer at 11:50 a.m. is 505 W/m^2. This can also be attributed to the architecture of the building mentioned above, but also to the position of the Sun in the sky at that moment in time. The v.sun model showed almost an identical value. From this point of view, we can conclude that the comparison of the results is very accurate at this point in time at this location.

The measurement at 3:31 p.m. recorded a value of 87 W/m^2. The v.sun model calculated a significantly higher value (293 W/m^2) as did the r.sun model (287 W/m^2). This can be explained by the fact that, during the measurement at the given place at 3:31 p.m., the sun was slightly shaded by a cloud.

3.4. Municipal Swimming Pool

The fourth location that we will compare is the Municipal Swimming Pool in the Protifašistických bojovníkov Street. The building itself is a morphologically complex structure made up of the swimming pool itself, but also other institutions that are housed there. The measurement at 9:19 a.m. showed a value of 502 W/m^2; the r.sun and v.sun models showed slightly different values (579 W/m^2 and 386 W/m^2, respectively), which can be considered acceptable (Figure 8) (Table 4).

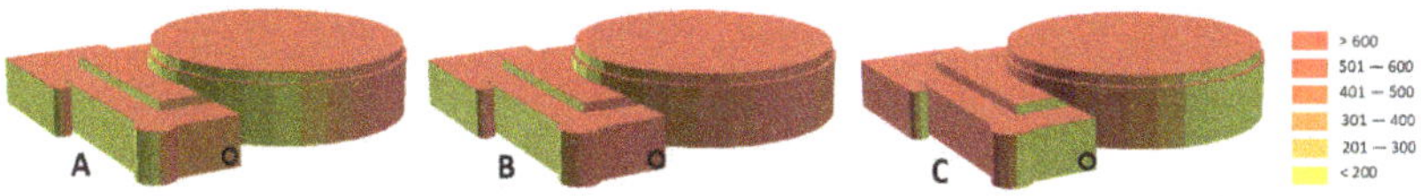

Figure 8. Solar irradiance at the Municipal Swimming Pool on 23 June 2021 (W/m^2) at (**A**) 9:19 a.m., (**B**) 12:09 p.m., and (**C**) 3:47 p.m. The black circle represents the measurement location.

Table 4. Solar irradiance at the Municipal Swimming Pool in W/m^2 on 23 June 2021.

Time	Pyranometer	v.sun	r.sun	Position
9:19 a.m.	502	386	579	south
12:09 p.m.	155	513	819	south
3:47 p.m.	97	170	760	south

The measurement recorded at 12:09 p.m. is much lower (155 W/m^2) and in comparison to predicted values by the v.sun and r.sun models (513 W/m^2 and 819 W/m^2, respectively). However, this fact has a logical explanation. During the actual measurement at that time, we noticed that there was a terrace above the measured facade (Figure 9), which caused a shadow at the time of the measurement since the solar altitude was very high. However, the terrace is not present in our 3D city model and DSM, so the solar radiation models do not reflect this fact in the results. At 3:47 p.m., we have already measured a slightly lower value at this location than at noon (97 W/m^2); a similar value was calculated by the v.sun (170 W/m^2). The r.sun model again predicted a very high value (760 W/m^2), probably due to a DSM distortion at this site.

Figure 9. Location of the terrace on the Municipal Swimming Pool building: (**A**) real state of the building with terrace (white rectangle); (**B**) geometric 3D model, missing the terrace (white rectangle). The black circle represents themeasurement location.

3.5. Greek-Catholic Church

The last location we have consiidered in this article is the Greek-Catholic Church of the Nativity of the Virgin Mary in Moyzesova Street. We also focused on the south-facing facade of the building. At 8:50 a.m., we measured 348 W/m^2; v.sun (Figure 10) calculated a value slightly lower (237 W/m^2) (Table 5). With the r.sun model, we again recorded a significantly higher value, due to the aforementioned facade representation issues.

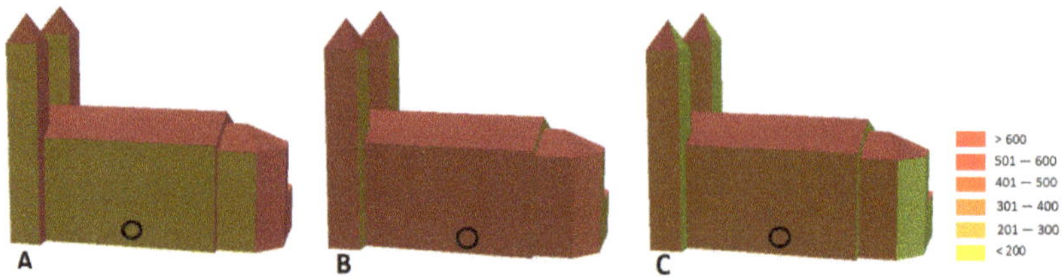

Figure 10. Solar irradiance at Greek Church on 23 June 2021 (W/m^2) at (**A**) 8:50 a.m., (**B**) 11:44 a.m., and (**C**) 3:25 p.m. The black circle represents the measurement location.

Table 5. Solar irradiance at Greek-Catholic Church in W/m^2 on 23 June 2021.

Time	Pyranometer	v.sun	r.sun	Position
8:50 a.m.	348	237	645	south
11:44 a.m.	534	483	771	south
3:25 p.m.	313	357	202	south

At 11:44 a.m., the pyranometer recorded value of 534 W/m^2. The r.sun and v.sun models also recorded similar values, which were increased compared to the morning measurement. The value recorded at 3:25 p.m. by the pyranometer (313 W/m^2) is approximated by the v.sun model with a value of 357 W/m^2 and 202 W/m^2 by the r.sun model. This lower value by r.sun is clearly also affected by a geometric distortion of the DSM.

4. Discussion

The modeling and use of solar radiation in urban environments are an important area of study in various scientific fields and disciplines, especially for solar resource assessments, such as photovoltaic and thermal applications, as well as urban heat island effects. Over the last decade, several studies have focused on this matter [34–36]. In this study, we focused on the accuracy of 2D (r.sun) and 3D (v.sun) solar radiation models for facades in built-up areas in comparison with field measurements using a pyranometer.

We selected five different buildings in locations in the wider center of Košice, which are shown in Figures 1 and 2. The measurements were carried out during a typical summer day (23 June 2021) for morning, noon, and afternoon time horizons, using the EKO-INSTRUMENTS MS-60 pyranometer during 2 min measurements in 5 s interval. The averaged value for each location was used in a comparison with the predicted values by the r.sun and v.sun models.

The results showed relatively large differences in the measured and predicted values of solar irradiance. The mean error and mean absolute error of all predictions are −22 W/m^2 and 103 W/m^2 for v.sun, respectively, and −219 W/m^2 and 345 W/m^2 for r.sun, respectively. Evidently, the 3D v.sun solar radiation model predicted solar irradiances on vertical surfaces with much better accuracy. The 2D r.sun solar radiation model failed to accurately predict solar irradiances in most cases, mostly due to an improper geometric representation of facades by a DSM. High sensitivity of the solar radiation model to input parameters, such as slope steepness or aspect, explains poor results of the model. Nevertheless, the model can provide acceptable results for rooftops and areas between the buildings. However, our results clearly show that a DSM does not provide a sufficiently accurate approximation of vertical surfaces in urban areas to estimate their solar resource potential with an acceptable accuracy.

This study also showed that the morphological complexity of buildings can affect the solar assessments, even in a 3D approach, because currently many 3D city models are available in a LoD2 accuracy with missing morphological structures, such as terraces, casting shadows, especially when solar elevation is high (Figure 9).

It should be noted that this analysis was carried out for selected buildings only and we did not include a complex analysis of shadows cast by neighboring buildings nor trees. This could affect some of the predicted values, especially in the morning and afternoon that have lower solar elevations.

In the manner of every other model, the r.sun/v.sun models have their advantages and disadvantages. The v.sun module can compute a 3D solar radiation for buildings represented by a 3D city model, but the disadvantage is its complicated preparation in terms of structure and topology. Another disadvantage is that it cannot account for vegetation, and this is an area for future improvements. The advantage of the r.sun model is a very simple preparation of input data for raster map calculations, which is easier and faster than for the v.sun model. To conclude, the r.sun solar radiation model should be only used for 2D surfaces, such as roofs and areas between buildings, while the v.sun solar radiation model is more appropriate for buildings, including facades, or other vertical surfaces represented by 3D polygons.

5. Conclusions

Solar energy is one of the most important renewable sources of energy. Therefore, it is desirable to model solar radiation in detail, especially in urban areas. There are currently several models that seek to model more accurately the distribution of solar radiation. Such models include r.sun and v.sun, which we analyzed in our study. They have the advantage of choosing parameters for spatial modeling, while working with spatially differentiated input and output data in raster/vector format. Both models use the same solar radiation component; however, they treat the geometry of input data differently. The results of both models were validated by in situ pyranometer measurements. The comparison of the results of individual models and measurements took place in locations that represent a typical urban environment in the study area. In addition to apartment buildings, with a relatively simple surface geometry, there are often historic buildings in the center with a more complex morphology of facades. By selecting different types of structures, we identified the shortcomings of individual models as well as input data.

The comparison of models and in situ measurements showed relatively good estimates by the 3D v.sun model and poor estimates by the 2D r.sun model. This can be attributed to an improper geometric representation of vertical surfaces by a DSM, which has a strong impact on solar resource assessments of the model. We also found that the LoD2 3D city models can be problematic in case of complex buildings with morphological structures, such as terraces. These cast shadows on facades especially when solar altitude is high and thus assessments even by the 3D model are inaccurate.

Nevertheless, both solar radiation models can be used effectively for solar resource assessments when used properly. The drawback of the v.sun model is that it does not provide estimates of solar radiation for urban greenery, which is often important part of urban areas. Our results also showed that the r.sun model is not able to accurately represent the spatial distribution of solar radiation on vertical surfaces, but its simplicity and speed provide a major advantage in modeling horizontal surfaces, such as roofs of buildings. The vector solar model v.sun proved to be a more suitable alternative for use in a 3D environment, based on its vector-voxel approach and its ability to model even vertical surfaces.

Our analysis can be helpful for solar resource assessments in urban areas using these solar radiation models or other solar radiation models with implemented similar methodology based on DSM and 3D city models. We see a great potential in integration with other areas of research and industry, for example for thermal and photovoltaic applications. We also envisage the use of these models in urban planning, and also in addressing the issue of urban heat islands.

Author Contributions: Conceptualization, Š.K. and J.H.; methodology, Š.K. and J.H.; software, Š.K., J.H., J.B. and J.Š.; validation, Š.K., J.H. and J.Š.; formal analysis, Š.K., J.H., J.B. and J.Š.; investigation, Š.K., J.H., J.B. and J.Š.; writing—original draft preparation, Š.K. and J.H.; visualization, Š.K.; supervision, J.H.; project administration, J.H.; funding acquisition, J.H. All authors have read and agreed to the published version of the manuscript.

Funding: The research was funded by the Slovak Research and Development Agency (APVV) under the contract No. APVV-18-0044 and by the Scientific Grant Agency of the Ministry of Education, Science, Research, and Sport of the Slovak Republic and the Slovak Academy of Sciences (VEGA), under the contract No. 1/0300/19.

Institutional Review Board Statement: Not applicable.

Informed Consent Statement: Not applicable.

Data Availability Statement: The data presented in this study are available on request from the corresponding author. The data are not publicly available due to privacy reasons.

Conflicts of Interest: The authors declare no conflict of interest. The funders had no role in the design of the study; in the collection, analyses, or interpretation of data; in the writing of the manuscript; or in the decision to publish the results.

References

1. Chen, M.; Zhang, H.; Liu, W.; Zhang, W. The global pattern of urbanization and economic growth: Evidence from the last three decades. *PLoS ONE* **2014**, *9*, e103799. [CrossRef] [PubMed]
2. Hofierka, J.; Kaňuk, J. Assessment of photovoltaic potential in urban areas using open-source solar radiation tools. *Renew. Energy* **2009**, *34*, 2206–2214. [CrossRef]
3. Ratti, C.; Baker, N. Energy consumption and urban texture. *Energy Build.* **2005**, *37*, 762–776. [CrossRef]
4. Lindberg, F.; Grimmond, C. The influence of vegetation and buildings morphology on shadow patterns and mean radiant temperatures in urban areas: Model development and evaluation. *Theor. Appl. Climatol.* **2011**, *105*, 1–13. [CrossRef]
5. Hofierka, J.; Zlocha, M. A new 3D Solar Radiation Model for 3D City Models. *Trans. GIS* **2012**, *16*, 681–690. [CrossRef]
6. Freitas, S.; Catita, C.; Redweik, P.; Brito, M.C. Modelling solar potential in the urban environment: State-of-the-art review. *Renew. Sustain. Energy Rev.* **2015**, *41*, 915–931. [CrossRef]
7. Biljecki, F.; Stoter, J.; LeDoux, H.; Zlatanova, S.; Çöltekin, A. Applications of 3D City Models: State of the Art Review. *ISPRS Int. J. Geo Inf.* **2015**, *4*, 2842. [CrossRef]
8. Hofierka, J.; Šúri, M. A new GIS—Based solar radiation model and its application to photovoltaic assessments. *Trans. GIS* **2004**, *8*, 175–190.
9. Chow, A.; Fung, A.S.; Li, S. GIS modeling of solar neighborhood potential at a fine spatiotemporal resolution. *Buildings* **2014**, *4*, 195. [CrossRef]
10. Cheng, L.; Zhang, F.; Li, S.; Mao, J.; Xu, M.; Ju, W.; Liu, X.; Wu, J.; Min, K.; Zhang, X.; et al. Solar energy potential of urban buildings in 10 cities of China. *Energy* **2020**, *196*, 117038. [CrossRef]
11. Erdély, R.; Wang, Y.; Guo, W.; Hanna, E.; Colantuono, G. Three-Dimensional Solar Radiation Model (SORAM) and its application to 3-D urban planning. *Sol. Energy* **2014**, *101*, 63–73. [CrossRef]
12. Liang, J.; Gong, J.; Zhou, J.; Ibrahim, A.N.; Li, M. An open-source 3D solar radiation model integrated with a 3D Geographic Information System. *Environ. Model. Softw.* **2014**, *64*, 94–101. [CrossRef]
13. Redweik, P.; Catita, C.; Brito, M.C. Solar energy potential on roofs and facades in an urban landscape. *Sol. Energy* **2013**, *97*, 332-341. [CrossRef]
14. Ranalli, J.; Calvert, K.; Boz, M.B.; Brownson, J.R.S. Toward comprehensive solar energy mapping systems for urban electricity system planning and development. *Electr. J.* **2018**, *31*, 8–15. [CrossRef]
15. Huld, T. PVMAPS: Software tools and data for the estimation of solar radiation and photovoltaic module performance over large geographical areas. *Sol. Energy* **2017**, *142*, 171–181. [CrossRef]
16. Hofierka, J.; Kaňuk, J. Aplikácie 3D modelov miest v geografickom výskume. *Geogr. Cassoviensis* **2010**, *4*, 69–72.
17. Carneiro, C.; Morello, E.; Ratti, C.; Golay, F. Solar radiation over the urban texture: LIDAR data and image processing techniques for environmental analysis at city scale. In *3D Geo-Information Sciences*; Springer: Berlin/Heidelberg, Germany, 2009; pp. 319–340.
18. Neteler, M.; Mitasova, H. *Open Source GIS: A GRASS GIS Approach*, 3rd ed.; Springer: Boston, MA, USA, 2008; p. 406.
19. Hetrick, W.; Rich, P.M.; Barnes, F.J.; Weiss, S.B. GIS-based solar radiation flux models. *Am. Soc. Photogramm. Remote. Sens. Tech. Pap.* **1993**, *3*, 132–143.
20. Dubayah, R.; Rich, P. Topographic solar radiation models for GIS. *Int. J. Geogr. Inf. Syst.* **1995**, *9*, 405–413. [CrossRef]
21. Kumar, L.; Skidmore, A.K.; Knowles, E. Modeling topographic variation in solar radiation in a GIS environment. *Int. J. Geogr. Inf. Sci.* **1997**, *11*, 475–497. [CrossRef]
22. Wilson, P.; Gallant, J. Secondary topographic attributes. In *Terrain Analysis. Principles and Application*; Wiley: New York, NY, USA, 2000; pp. 87–132.
23. Rigollier, C.; Bauer, O.; Wald, O. On the clear sky model of the ESRA—European Solar Radiation Atlas—With respect to the Heliostat method. *Sol. Energy* **2000**, *68*, 33–48. [CrossRef]

24. Scharmer, K.; Greif, J. *The European Solar Radiation Atlas. Vol. 2: Database and Exploitation Software*; Presses de l´Ecole des Miner: Paris, France, 2000.
25. Muneer, T. Solar radiation model for Europe. *Build. Serv. Eng. Res. Technol.* **1990**, *11*, 153–163. [CrossRef]
26. Muneer, T. *Solar Radiation and Daylight Models for Energy Efficient Design of Buildings*; Architectural Press: Oxford, UK, 1997.
27. Šúri, M.; Huld, T.; Hofierka, J. Digital terrain modeling: Development and application in a policy support environment. In *Lecture Notes in Geoinformation and Cartography*, 1st ed.; Peckham, R.J., Jordan, G., Eds.; Springer: Berlin/Heidelberg, Germany, 2007; pp. 259–273.
28. Huld, T.; Műller, R.; Gambardella, A. A new solar radiation database for estimating PV performance in Europe and Africa. *Sol. Energy* **2012**, *86*, 1803–1815. [CrossRef]
29. Bochníček, O.; Hrušková, K. *Klimatický Atlas Slovenska*; Slovenský Hydrometeorologický Ústav: Bratislava, Slovakia, 2015; p. 132.
30. Biljecki, F.; Ledoux, H.; Stoter, J. An improved LOD specification for 3D building models. *Comput. Environ. Urban Syst.* **2016**, *59*, 25–37. [CrossRef]
31. Guo, W.; Cheng, B.; Wang, C.; Tang, X. Tree planting indices and their effect on summer park thermal environment: A case study of a subtropical satellite city, China. *Indoor Built Environ.* **2020**. [CrossRef]
32. Lee, D.S.; Jo, J.H. Application of simple sky and building models for the evaluation of solar irradiance distribution at indoor locations in buildings. *Build. Environ.* **2021**, *197*, 107840. [CrossRef]
33. Matlovič, R. *Geografia Priestorovej Štruktúry Mesta*; University of Prešov: Prešov, Slovakia, 1998.
34. Okumus, D.E.; Terzi, F. Evaluating the role of urban fabric on surface urban heat island: The case of Istanbul. *Sustain. Cities Soc.* **2021**, *73*, 103128. [CrossRef]
35. Halder, B.; Bandyopadhyay, J.; Banik, P. Monitoring the effect of urban development on urban heat island basedon remote sensing and geospatial approach in Kolkata and adjacent areas, India. *Sustain. Cities Soc.* **2021**, *74*, 103186. [CrossRef]
36. Huang, X.; Song, J.; Wang, C.; Chui, T.F.M.; Chan, P.W. The synergistic effect of urban heat and moisture islands in a compact high-rise city. *Build. Environ.* **2021**, *205*, 108274. [CrossRef]

energies

MDPI

Article

Numerical Analysis of Heat Transfer Performances of Ionic Liquid and Ionanofluids with Temperature-Dependent Thermophysical Properties

Amra Hasečić [1,*], Jaber Hmoud Almutairi [2], Siniša Bikić [3] and Ejub Džaferović [1]

1 Faculty of Mechanical Engineering, University of Sarajevo, 71000 Sarajevo, Bosnia and Herzegovina; dzaferovic@mef.unsa.ba
2 The Public Authority for Applied Education and Training, College of Technological Studies, Shuwaikh 70654, Kuwait; jh.almutairi@paaet.edu.kw
3 Faculty of Technical Sciences, University of Novi Sad, 21000 Novi Sad, Serbia; bika@uns.ac.rs
* Correspondence: hasecic@mef.unsa.ba; Tel.: +387-33-729-825

Abstract: The heat transfer performances of ionic liquids [C_4mpyrr][NTf_2] and ionanofluids with Al_2O_3 nanoparticles under a laminar flow regime, and with constant heat flux on the tube wall is numerically modeled and analyzed for three values of initial/inlet temperature and for two Reynolds numbers. Heat transfer characteristics were considered by analyzing the temperature distribution along the upper wall, as well as by analyzing the Nusselt number and heat transfer coefficient. The results obtained numerically were validated using Shah's equation for ionic liquid. Thermophysical properties were temperature-dependent, and obtained by curve-fitting the experimental values of the thermophysical properties. Furthermore, the same set of results was calculated for the ionic liquid and ionanofluids with constant thermophysical properties. It is concluded that the assumption that thermophysical properties are constant has a significant influence on the heat transfer performance parameters of both ionic liquid and ionanofluids, and therefore such assumptions should not be made in research.

Keywords: ionanofluids; computational fluid dynamics; heat transfer; Nusselt number; temperature-dependent properties

Citation: Hasečić, A.; Almutairi, J.H.; Bikić, S.; Džaferović, E. Numerical Analysis of Heat Transfer Performances of Ionic Liquid and Ionanofluids with Temperature-Dependent Thermophysical Properties. *Energies* **2021**, *14*, 8420. https://doi.org/10.3390/en14248420

Academic Editor: Kamel Hooman

Received: 5 October 2021
Accepted: 17 November 2021
Published: 14 December 2021

1. Introduction

Nanofluids are a mixture of base fluid and small nanoparticles up to 100 nm size. It is proven that nanofluids have better thermal properties than the base fluids [1], therefore, in the last two decades, a substantial amount of research has been conducted related to the nanofluids and their application to the solar systems and other heat exchange devices. A major part of those research studies was focused on the thermophysical properties and heat transfer of nanofluids where the base fluid was water and ethylene-glycol, with nanoparticles with different oxides (Al_2O_3, TiO_2, CuO, etc). Ribeiro et al. [2] introduced ionanofluids, the suspension of nanoparticles in ionic liquids as a new class of nanofluids. One of the first experimental investigations of ionanofluids was done by Altin et al. [3], who analysed the rheological properties of the suspensions of the nanoparticles in the ionic liquids. Following this, Wang et al. [4] and Altamash et al. [5] also experimentally analyzed the rheological properties of ionanofluids. They concluded that ionanofluids show non-Newtonian flow behavior. When it comes to the thermophysical properties of the ionanofluids, Nieto de Castro et al. [6] were among the first who conducted experimental investigations into the thermophysical properties of ionanofluids. They studied the thermal properties of imidazolium and pyrrolidinium and higher wall carbon nanoparticles, and concluded that nanoparticles cause improvement in the thermal conductivity and heat capacity of ionanofluids compared to the base fluids. Ionanofluids are mainly analyzed in respect to their thermophysical properties. The analyses were experimentally conducted by Fox et al. [7], Bridges et al. [8], Titan et al. [9–13] and Bhattacharjee et al. [14], while Minea et al. [15] gave a comparison of thermal conductivity for different ionanofluids. Fox et al. [7] experimentally investigated the influence of alumina nanoparticles on the thermophysical characteristics of ionanofluids, and showed that fibrously shaped Al2O3 nanoparticles show a greater improvement in thermal conductivity. Bridges et al. [8] showed that the increased heat capacity of ionic fluids was improved with alumina particles without a detrimental effect on thermal stability. Titan et al. [9–13] showed that an increased heat transfer coefficient of forced convection and a deterioration in the natural heat transfer of a nanoionic fluid relative to an ionic fluid, as well as showing that there are significant improvements in the thermophysical characteristics of ionanofluids compared to the base ionic fluids. Besides the thermophysical properties, they also analyzed the rheological behavior of the ionanofluids and concluded that ionanofluids show non-Newtonian flow behavior.

As it can be seen from the literature overview, the experimental investigations of ionanofluids are rare in comparison to the published experimental investigations of the nanofluids. When it comes to the analyses of ionanofluids by using computational fluid dynamics, to the authors best knowledge there are only few studies available [16–23], whereas Said [24] analyzed the use of adaptive neuro fussy interface systems to predict the thermal conductivity and viscosity of ionanofluids. Computational fluid dynamic analyses of ionanofluids are mainly focused on the heat transfer performances.

Minea et al. [16] numerically analyzed heat transfer in a square enclosure filled with ionic liquid nanofluid. Although they stated that the thermophysical properties are temperature dependent, it can be concluded that they are only a function of initial temperature. Chereches et al. [17,18] numerically analyzed heat transfer behavior of ionanofluids in laminar flow for different Reynolds numbers and one initial temperature for case without [17] and with [18] insulation over the pipe walls. Titan et al. [19] investigated the natural convection heat transfer of Al_2O_3 nanoparticle enhanced N-butyl-N-methylpyrrolidinium bis {(trifluoromethyl)sulfonyl} imide ([C_4mpyrr][NTf_2]) ionic liquid. The heat transfer performance of ionanofluids was also numerically analyzed by Prasad et al. [20] and Rupesh et al. [21]. Prasad et al. [20] analyzed the heat transfer in a 2-D flat plate, whereas Rupesh et al. [21] analyzed the heat transfer performance of ionanofluids around a circular cylinder. The most recent numerical investigations of the heat transfer behavior of particle suspension in ionic liquids were done by Shah et al. [22] and Bouchta et al. [23].

Although it has been shown that ionanofluids flow behavior corresponds to non-Newtonian flow, the assumption of Newtonian fluid was made in many studies [3–5,9–13]. In most numerical research a single-phase assumption was made, whereas the properties of ionanofluids are calculated as the properties of a mixture and a function of the weight percent of nanoparticles and base liquid. Furthermore, the studies all assumed that the properties are constant and related only to the initial and boundary conditions.

In this research, a numerical analysis of steady, laminar forced convection flow of Al_2O_3 nanoparticles in ([C_4mpyrr][NTf_2]) ionanofluids in a straight tube with constant heat flux on the tube wall for different Reynolds numbers and different values of initial and inlet temperature is presented. The heat transfer characteristic of the ionic liquid and ionanofluids for different weight percentages were analyzed and compared. The geometry was chosen due to its common application in solar collectors. The main contribution of this research is that this is, to the authors best knowledge, the first research on heat transfer characteristics of ionanofluids in which the thermophysical properties are temperature related and described in corresponding equations and implemented in such form. Moreover, the results are compared with results obtained for constant thermophysical properties for different initial temperature values. Although the term constant thermophysical properties is used, it must be emphasized that the thermophysical properties are a function of the initial/inlet temperature and therefore are constant for the same initial/inlet temperature.

2. Materials and Methods

The mathematical model can be summarized in the following governing and constitutive equations:

Continuity equation

$$\frac{d}{dt}\int_V \rho dV + \int_s \rho \boldsymbol{v} \cdot d\boldsymbol{s} = 0 \quad (1)$$

where ρ is density and $\boldsymbol{v}$ is the velocity vector.

Momentum equation

$$\frac{d}{dt}\int_V \rho \boldsymbol{v} dV + \int_s \rho \boldsymbol{v}\boldsymbol{v} \cdot d\boldsymbol{s} = \int_s \boldsymbol{T} \cdot d\boldsymbol{s} + \int_V \boldsymbol{f}_b dV \quad (2)$$

where $\boldsymbol{T}$ the Cauchy stress tensor and $\boldsymbol{f}_b$ is the resultant body force.

Thermal energy equation

$$\frac{d}{dt}\int_V \rho c_v T dV + \int_s \rho c_p T \boldsymbol{v} \cdot d\boldsymbol{s} = -\int_s \boldsymbol{q} \cdot d\boldsymbol{s} + \int_V (\boldsymbol{T} : \text{grad}\boldsymbol{v}) dV \quad (3)$$

where c_p is the specific heat, T is the temperature and $\boldsymbol{q}$ is the heat flux vector.

Stoke's law

$$\boldsymbol{T} = 2\mu\dot{\boldsymbol{D}} - \frac{2}{3}\mu div\boldsymbol{v}\boldsymbol{I} - P\boldsymbol{I} \quad (4)$$

where

$$\dot{\boldsymbol{D}} = \frac{1}{2}[\text{grad}\boldsymbol{v} + (\text{grad}\boldsymbol{v})^{\mathrm{T}}] \quad (5)$$

is the rate of strain tensor, μ is the dynamic viscosity, p is the pressure and $\boldsymbol{I}$ is the unit tensor.

Fourier's law

$$\boldsymbol{q} = -k\,\text{grad}T \quad (6)$$

where k is thermal conductivity.

Thermophysical properties of ionic liquid and ionanofluids.

Relationships for thermophysical properties (density, thermal conductivity, viscosity and specific heat) of ionanofluids [C_4mpyrr][NTf_2] with the Al_2O_3 nanoparticles used in this study are obtained by curve-fitting the experimental results from the literature [22] and are given in the Table 1. Additionally, relationships for certain properties, such as density, were already given by Titan [22] and are used as such.

Table 1. Equations used for predicting the thermophysical properties for different weight percent wt%.

Thermophysical Property	Base Liquid	0.5 wt%	1.0 wt%	2.5 wt%
Density, $[1000\ \text{kg}\cdot\text{m}^{-3}]$	$-7.77\cdot10^{-4}T + 1.6129$ [22]	$-0.0008T + 1.6324$	$-0.00087T + 1.665$	$-0.001T + 1.722$
Viscosity, [Pa·s]	$8\cdot10^{23}T^{-10.15}$	$3\cdot10^{22}T^{-9.544}$	$2\cdot10^{27}T^{-11.46}$	$3\cdot10^{28}T^{-11.93}$
Heat capacity, $[\text{kJ}\cdot\text{kg}^{-1}\cdot\text{K}^{-1}]$	$-3\cdot10^{-6}T^2 + 0.0048T + 0.3941$	$0.0016T + 1.7234$	$-6\cdot10^{-6}T^2 + 0.0076T + 0.1891$	$-8\cdot10^{-6}T^2 + 0.01T + 0.2965$
Thermal cond., $[\text{W}\cdot\text{m}^{-1}\cdot\text{K}^{-1}]$	$-6\cdot10^{-5}T + 0.1398$ [22]	$-0.01 \ln T + 0.1826$	$-0.008 \ln T + 0.1748$	$-0.007 \ln T + 0.1745$

The curve-fits are applied to the experimental values of the thermophysical properties obtained by Titan [22], and the results are presented in Figure 1.

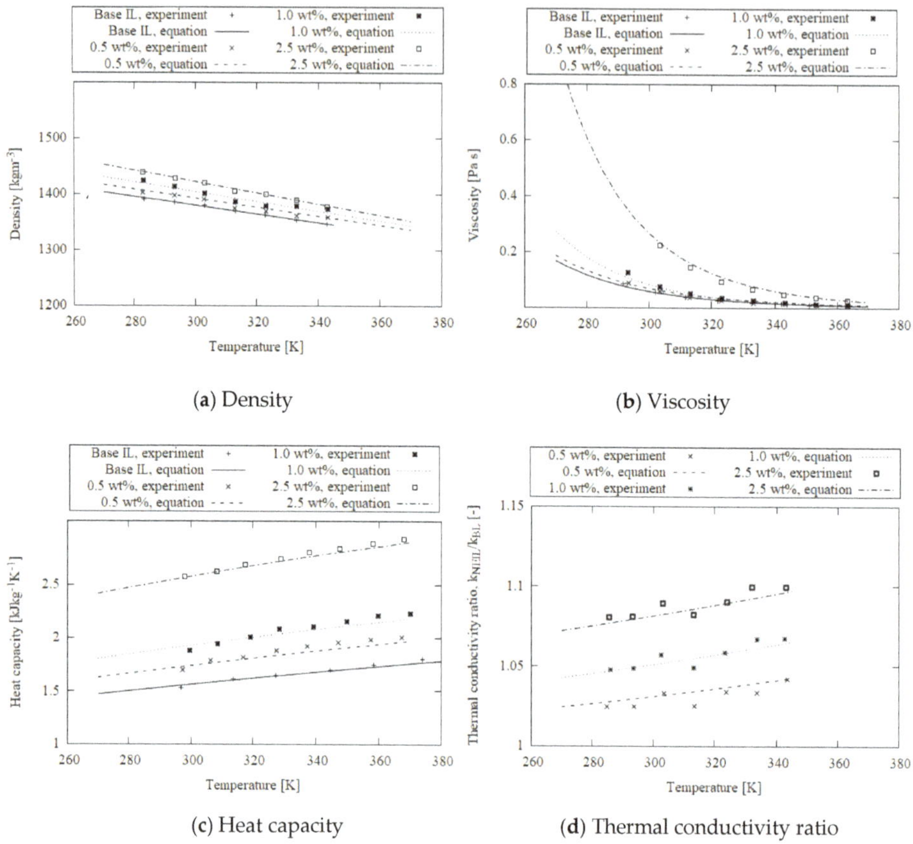

Figure 1. Comparison of the predicted values for thermophysical properties using equations from Table 1 with measured data obtained by [22].

As it can be seen from Figure 1, the temperature variations of density (Figure 1a), viscosity (Figure 1b), heat capacity (Figure 1c) and ratio of thermal conductivity of base liquid and corresponding ionanofluids (Figure 1d) were compared with experimental results obtained by Titan [22]. The comparison was made for the base liquid as well as for ionanofluids with concentrations of 0.5, 1.0 and 2.5 wt% (weight percent). The square of correlation factor (R^2) for density was above 0.95, for viscosity above 0.99, for heat capacity above 0.98 and for the ratio of thermal conductivity above 0.8, regardless of weight percent.

The numerical method employed for modeling the flow and heat transfer of ionic liquid and ionanofluids was the finite volume method. The methodology closely follows the one presented in [23,24].

3. Results

The steady-state flow of ionic liquid [C_4mpyrr][NTf_2] and ionanofluids with Al_2O_3 nanoparticles through the horizontal straight tube of 1.75 m length and 0.014 m diameter was analyzed with convective heat transfer included. The geometry of the problem can be seen from Figure 2. The case study was analyzed for initial temperatures $T_{in1} = 293$ K, $T_{in2} = 303$ K and $T_{in3} = 335$ K, for two Reynolds number values (100 and 512), and for three values of weight percentage (0.5 wt%, 1.0 wt% and 2.5 wt%). Additionally, the heat transfer characteristics of pure ionic liquid was also analyzed. The wall heat flux was constant q = 13 kW·m^{-2}. At the outlet, the pressure was set to 0 Pa. For the purpose of set up, the inlet boundary conditions uniform velocity profile was used.

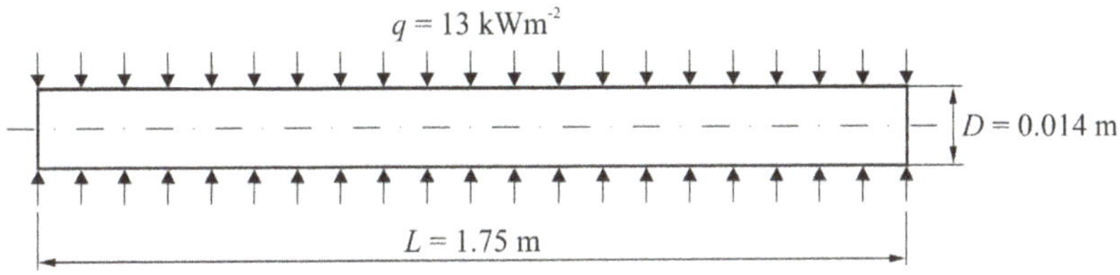

Figure 2. Geometry and boundary conditions.

The effects of natural convection were neglected. Due to computational efficiency, fluid flow was analyzed through a part of the tube in the shape of a longitudinal wedge with an angle of 5° as it can be seen from Figure 3.

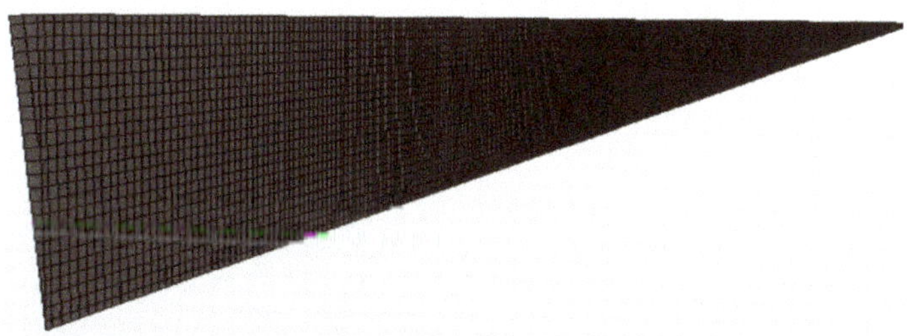

Figure 3. Geometry and mesh of longitudinal wedge with angle of 5°.

The heat transfer characteristics of the ionic liquid and corresponding ionanofluids were investigated by analyzing the heat transfer coefficient and Nusselt number. Additionally, the temperature profile for each case is presented.

The heat transfer coefficient and Nusselt number were calculated using the following equations:

$$h_{IL/NEIL} = \frac{q}{(T_{wall} - T_{in})}, \left[\mathrm{W{\cdot}m^{-2}{\cdot}K^{-1}}\right] \tag{7}$$

$$Nu_{IL/NEIL} = h_{IL/NEIL}\frac{D}{k_{IL/NEIL}} \; [-] \tag{8}$$

where

q $\left[\mathrm{W{\cdot}m^{-2}}\right]$ is heat flux through the shell of the tube given as the boundary condition

T_{wall} [K] is temperature of the tube shell

T_{in} [K] is initial (reference) temperature

$h_{IL/NEIL}$ $\left[\mathrm{W{\cdot}m^{-2}{\cdot}K^{-1}}\right]$ is the heat transfer coefficient of the ionic liquid (IL) or ionanofluids (NEIL)

D [m] is diameter of the tube

$k_{IL/NEIL}$ $\left[\mathrm{W{\cdot}m^{-1}{\cdot}K^{-1}}\right]$ is the thermal conductivity of the ionic liquid (IL) or ionanofluids (NEIL)

The validation of the presented model along with the grid refinement was done for the ionic liquid [C_4mpyrr][NTf_2] and the results were compared with results obtained by using the Shah's equation. The grid sensitivity study was performed for four different values of base cell sizes. The characteristics of the analyzed grids are given in Table 2.

Table 2. Grid characteristics for grid sensitivity study.

Grid	Characteristic Cell Size [mm]	Number of Cells
1	2.4	46,688
2	1.2	198,356
3	0.6	1,353,488
4	0.3	8,493,674

The results for each grid, and the results obtained by using Shah's equation, can be seen from Figure 4. It can be seen from Figure 4 that as the grid is systematically refined, the results approach the results obtained from the Shah's equations.

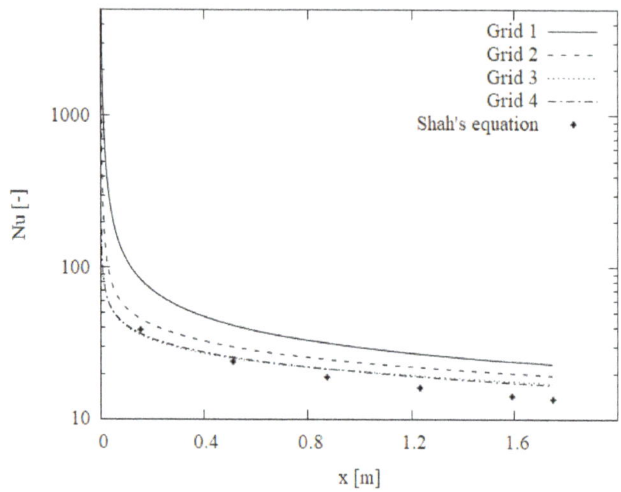

Figure 4. Grid sensitivity study and model validation.

Furthermore, one can conclude that for grid 3 (base cell size of 0.6 mm), the obtained results are grid independent since for further refinement the results remain the same. Hence, the numerical study was performed for grid 3, with a base cell size of 0.6 mm.

Over 40 numerical simulations were performed in order to compare temperature profiles and hence heat transfer characteristics (heat transfer coefficient and Nusselt number) for ionic liquid and ionanofluids with temperature-dependent thermophysical properties and with constant thermophysical properties. For better presentation of the findings, the results were compared in accordance with different perspectives, i.e., in accordance with the weight percent, Reynold numbers, initial temperatures, and/or in accordance with the temperature/dependency of thermophysical properties.

4. Discussion

Figure 5 presents the temperature distribution along the top wall, T_{wall}, at Re = 100 and Re = 500 and 0.5 $\leq$ wt% $\leq$ 2.5 for fluids with constant thermophysical properties, whereas Figure 6 presents the temperature distribution along the top wall, T_{wall}, at Re = 100 and Re = 500 and 0.5 $\leq$ wt% $\leq$ 2.5 for fluids with temperature-dependent thermophysical properties in accordance with Table 1.

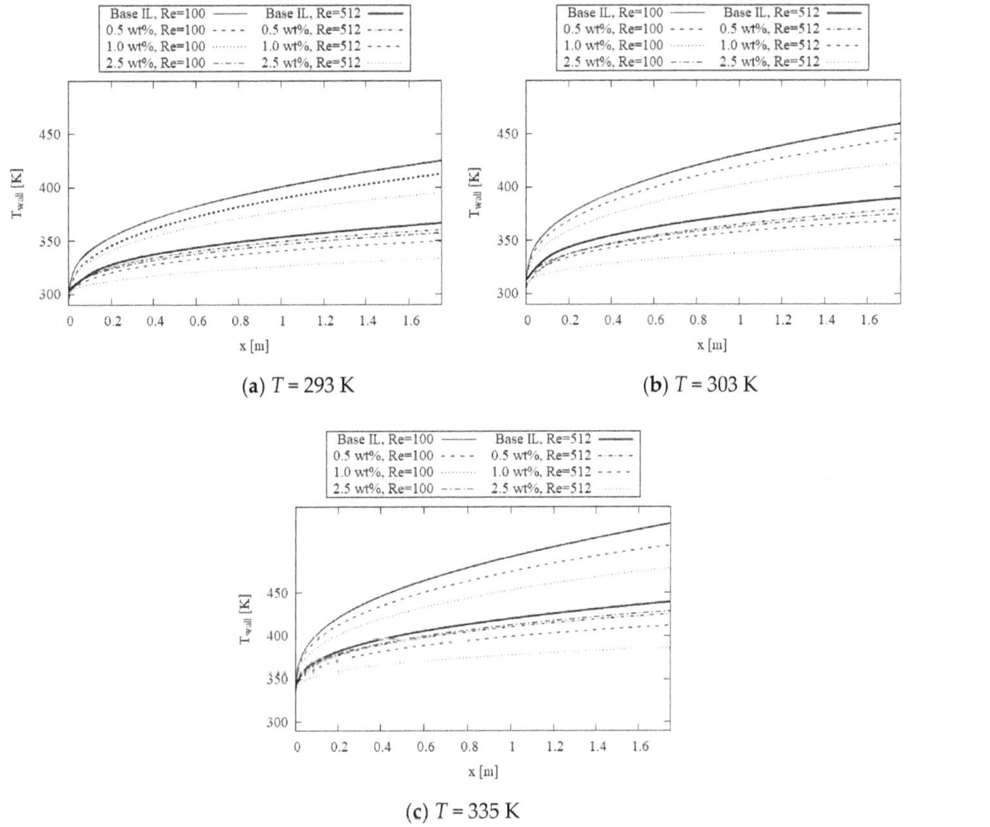

Figure 5. Temperature profile for Re = 100 and Re = 512 for 0.5 $\leq$ wt% $\leq$ 2.5 and constant thermophysical properties.

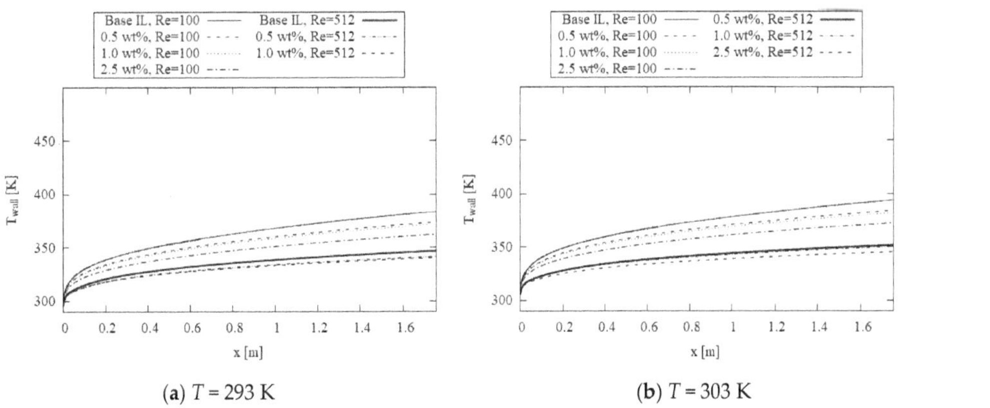

Figure 6. *Cont.*

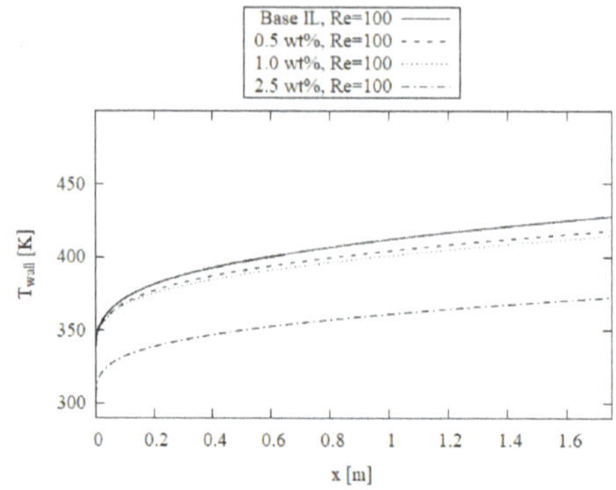

(c) T = 335 K

Figure 6. Temperature profile for Re = 100 and Re = 512 for 0.5 $\leq$ wt% $\leq$ 2.5 and temperature-dependent thermophysical properties.

It can be seen from the Figures 5 and 6 that the temperature at x = 0 m is same as the inlet temperature, and in the developing region (up to x = 0.4 m) the immediate increase is noticeable. Following the gradual linear increase in the developed region due to the constant heat flux applied to the wall surface, the temperature at the upper wall reaches the maximum value at the outlet (x = 1.75 m).

Furthermore, for both constant and temperature-dependent thermophysical properties, the increase in the weight percent of nanoparticles results in lower temperature profiles of the upper wall. One can conclude that the increase in the weight percent of nanoparticles results in more heat transfer from the wall to the fluid regardless of the temperature-dependency of the thermophysical properties. The same can be concluded for the influence of the Reynold's number; the increase in the Reynold's number results in an increase in heat transfer from the wall to the fluid for ionic liquid and ionanofluids for constant and temperature-dependent thermophysical properties.

To better understand the influence of the temperature-dependency of the thermophysical properties of the ionic liquid and ionanofluids on the temperature profile, Figure 7 presents the temperature distributions on the upper wall for Re = 100, inlet temperatures T = 293 K, T = 303 K and T = 335 K and wt% of 0, 0.5 and 1.0 for both constant and temperature-dependent thermophysical properties.

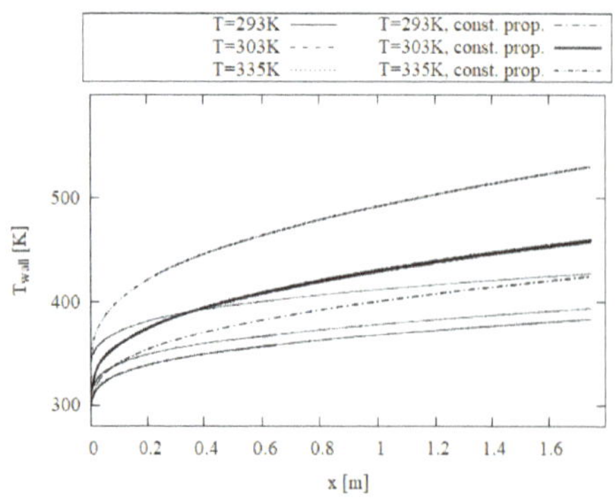

(a) Base IL

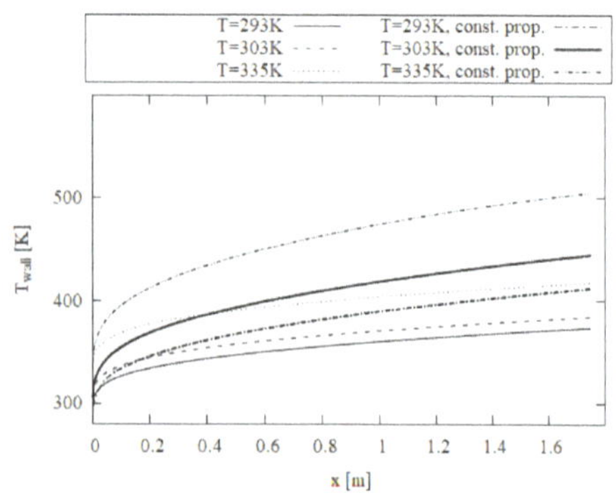

(b) 0.5 wt%

Figure 7. *Cont.*

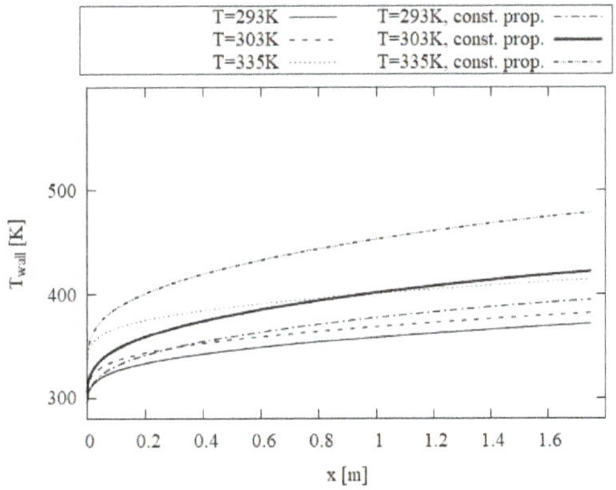

(**c**) 1.0 wt%

Figure 7. Temperature profiles comparison for ionic liquid and ionanofluids with and without constant thermophysical properties for $Re = 100$.

When analyzing the temperature profile on the upper wall for ionanofluids with and without constant properties for constant weight percent and Reynolds number, and with variable inlet temperatures, it can be concluded that the temperature profile is higher when the assumption of constant thermophysical properties is made, regardless of the weight percent or the inlet temperature. Therefore, it can be concluded that the temperature-dependent thermophysical properties of ionanofluids cause better heat transfer from the wall of the tube to the fluid.

Heat transfer performances of ionic liquid and ionanofluids for different weight percent were analyzed through the heat transfer coefficient (Equation (7)) and Nusselt number (Equation (8)). Figure 8 presents the heat transfer coefficient along the tube for ionic liquid, and ionanofluids of 0.5 wt%, 1.0 wt% and 2.5 wt%, and for Reynolds numbers of 100 and 512, for reference temperatures $T = 293$ K, $T = 303$ K and $T = 335$ K.

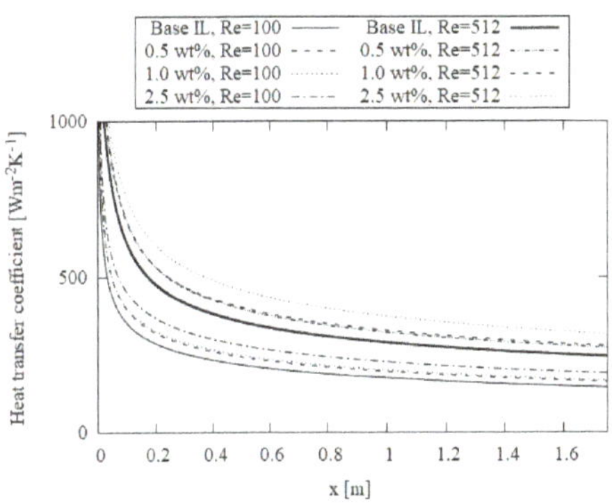

(**a**) $T = 293$ K

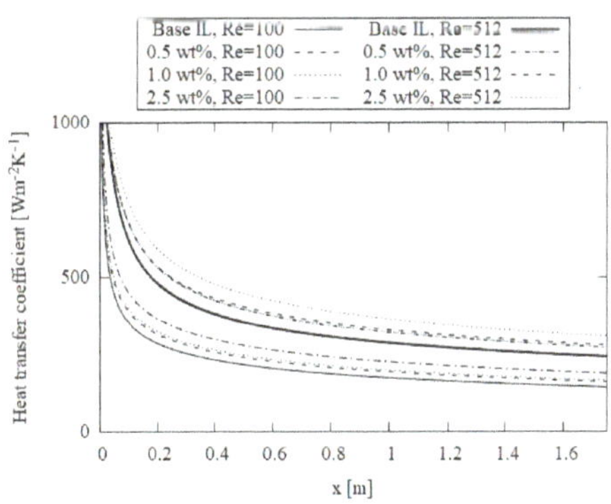

(**b**) $T = 303$ K

Figure 8. *Cont.*

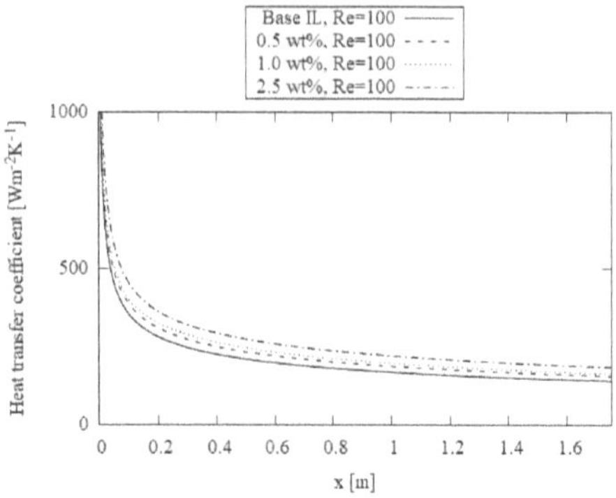

(c) T = 335 K

Figure 8. Heat transfer coefficient for 0.5 $\leq$ wt% $\leq$ 2.5 and Re = 100 and Re = 512.

It is shown in Figure 8 that the increase in the Reynolds number, as well as the increase in the nanoparticle weight percent, causes an increase in the heat transfer coefficient, meaning that the heat transfer is higher for higher values of wt% and Re. The same conclusion can be made for each inlet temperature. Furthermore, it is noticeable that the heat transfer coefficient has the highest values at the inlet of the tube, leading to the exponential decrease in the developing region (up to x = 0.4 m). Following this, the values of the heat transfer coefficient gradually decrease in a linear manner when progressing towards the outlet of the tube where the heat transfer coefficient has the minimum value.

Moreover, in this study, the influence of the assumption of the constant thermophysical properties on the heat transfer performances for ionic liquid and ionanofluids was analyzed. Therefore, Figure 9 presents the Nusselt number values along the tube for both ionanofluids with temperature-dependent thermophysical properties and for ionanofluids with constant thermophysical properties. Analysis was undertaken at a constant weight percentage, so that the influence of the assumption could be analyzed for different inlet temperatures and Reynolds numbers.

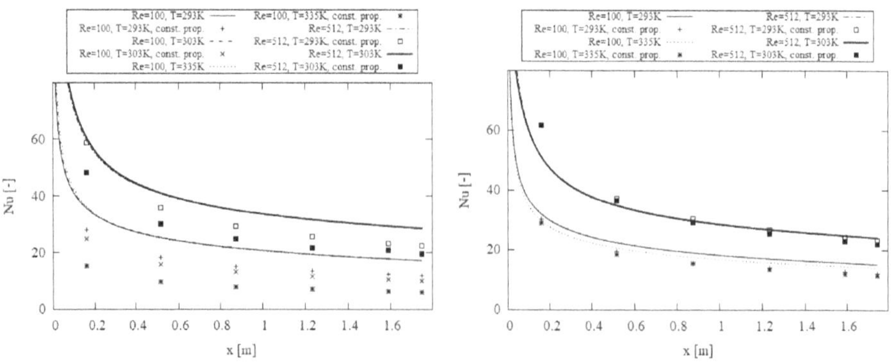

(a) Base IL

(b) 0.5 wt%

Figure 9. *Cont.*

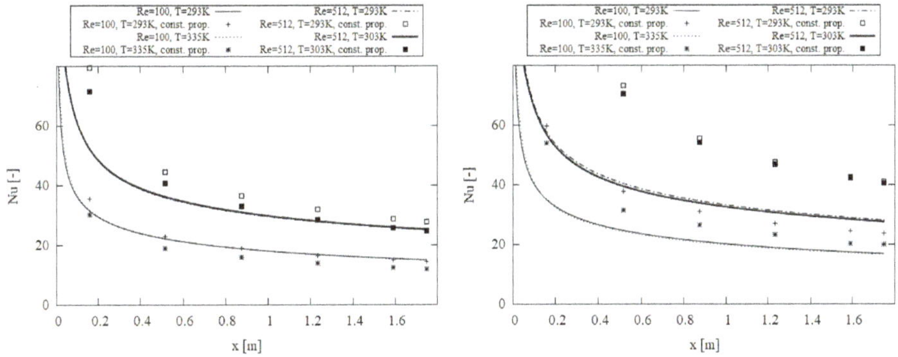

(**c**) 1.0 wt% (**d**) 2.5 wt%

Figure 9. Nusselt number for ionanofluids with and without constant thermal properties for different temperature values and different Reynold numbers.

When analyzing Figure 9, one can conclude that the assumption of the constant thermophysical properties of both ionic liquid and ionanofluids has a great influence on the Nusselt number. The influence is more significant as the weight percent increases. The greatest difference between the results for constant and variable thermophysical properties is for the weight percentage of 2.5%, where significant divergence is noticeable for the Nusselt number, both for $Re = 100$ and $Re = 512$, as well as for each inlet temperature. When analyzing curves for the temperature dependent thermophysical properties (Figure 1) it can be seen that, for wt% 2.5, the viscosity exponentially decreases, resulting in a significant difference in the viscosity values for different temperatures. The Nusselt number values for constant thermophysical properties for $Re = 512$ and $T = 293$ K correspond to the Nusselt number values obtained by Chereches et al. [17].

For better understanding of the heat transfer performances of ionic liquids and ionanofluids, the heat transfer coefficient was analyzed and compared in accordance of weight percent for ionic liquid and ionanofluids, with and without constant properties for $Re = 100$ (Figure 10) and $Re = 512$ (Figure 11).

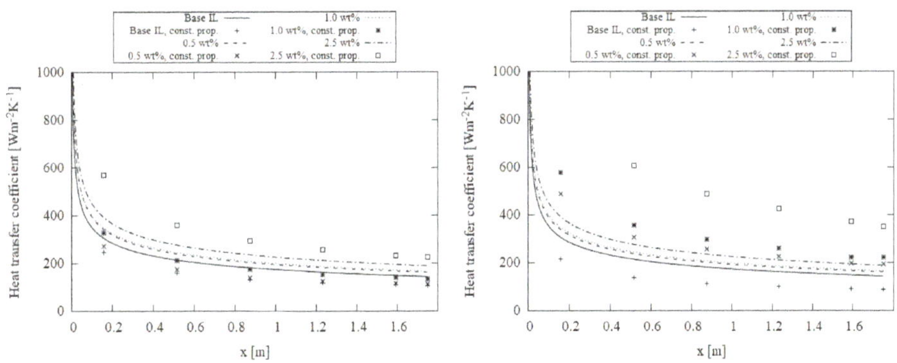

(**a**) $T = 293$ K (**b**) $T = 303$ K

Figure 10. *Cont.*

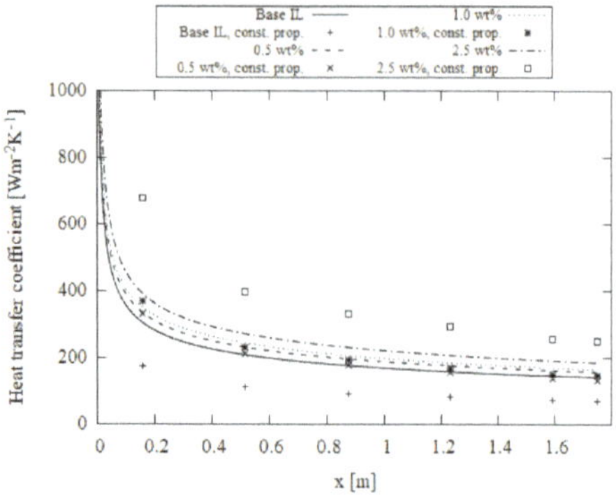

(**c**) $T = 335$ K

Figure 10. Heat transfer coefficient of ionic liquid and ionanofluids with and without constant thermal properties for $0.5 \leq$ wt% ≤ 2.5 and $Re = 100$.

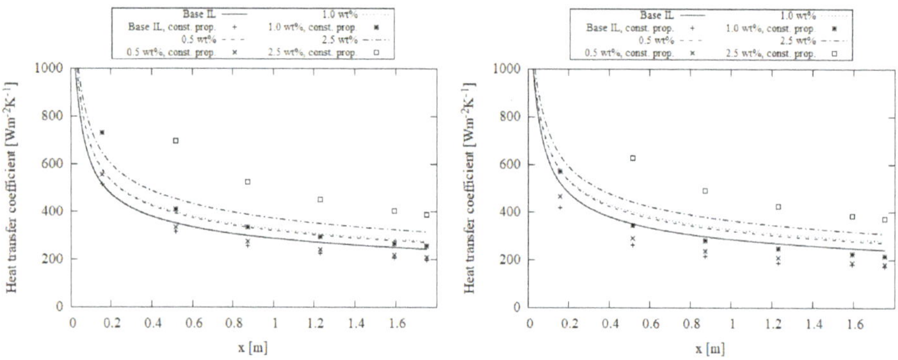

(**a**) T = 293K (**b**) T = 303K

Figure 11. Heat transfer coefficient of ionic liquid and ionanofluids with and without constant thermal properties for $0.5 \leq$ wt% ≤ 2.5 and $Re = 512$.

The heat transfer coefficient increases as the weight percent of ionanofluids increase, and it has the lowest value for ionic liquid for both $Re = 100$ and $Re = 512$, regardless of inlet temperature. Furthermore, it is noticeable from Figures 10 and 11 that the assumption of the constant thermophysical properties has the greatest influence on the heat transfer performances of the observed ionanofluids. The greatest influence is for those with a weight percent of 2.5%. It can also be seen from Figures 10 and 11 that for ionic liquids and ionanofluids with constant thermophysical properties, the heat transfer coefficient is higher or lower (depending on the weight percent and inlet temperature), which can mislead a conclusion that the heat transfer performances are better or worse than they really are.

5. Conclusions

This paper presents a numerical investigation of the forced heat transfer of a ionic liquid [C_4mpyrr][NTf_2] and ionanofluids with Al_2O_3 nanoparticles through a straight tube. Geometric and physical models were defined that adequately describe the problems, as well as the numerical grid on which the simulations were performed in the STAR-CCM + 2019.2 software. Numerical research was undertaken with the following approximations: the effects of natural convection were neglected, and fluid flow through a part of the tube in the shape of a longitudinal wedge with angle of 5° was analyzed. Thermophysical properties of the analyzed ionic liquid and ionanofluids were assumed to be a function of temperature. The adequate equations for each thermophysical property were gained via curve-fitting the experimental values with square of correlation factors above 0.95 for density relations, 0.99 for viscosity relations, 0.98 for heat capacity relations and for a ratio of thermal conductivity above 0.8, regardless of weight percent. In order to obtain grid independent solutions, a grid sensitivity study was performed, and the model was validated with the results of Shah's equation. The presented analysis of the obtained results of the Nusselt number and the heat transfer coefficient of the ionic and nanoionic liquid shows the change in the considered parameters along the tube for different wt% and different Reynolds numbers. During the analysis of the numerical results of the Nusselt numbers and the heat transfer coefficient of both the ionic and nanoionic liquid, a decrease in the Nusselt numbers and the heat transfer coefficient with a decrease of a wt% was found. Moreover, it is concluded that an increase in the Reynolds number results in an increase in both heat transfer coefficient and Nusselt number. The Nusselt number and the heat transfer coefficient of the ionic and nanoionic liquid decrease exponentially along the tube for any case under consideration. The results were compared against the results related to the ionic liquid and ionanofluids with constant thermophysical properties. It is concluded that the assumption that thermophysical properties are constant has a significant influence on the heat transfer performance parameters of both ionic liquid and ionanofluids, and therefore such assumptions should not be made in research.

Author Contributions: Conceptualization, A.H. and J.H.A.; methodology, A.H.; software, A.H. and J.H.A.; validation, A.H., S.B. and E.D.; formal analysis, J.H.A.; investigation, A.H. and J.H.A.; resources, J.H.A.; writing—original draft preparation, A.H.; writing—review and editing, S.B. and E.D.; visualization, J.H.A.; supervision, E.D.; project administration, A.H.; funding acquisition, A.H. All authors have read and agreed to the published version of the manuscript.

Funding: This research was funded by Canton Sarajevo, Ministry for Science, Higher Education and Youth, grant number 27-02-11-4375-6/21. The APC was funded with that grant

Institutional Review Board Statement: Not applicable.

Informed Consent Statement: Not applicable.

Data Availability Statement: Not applicable.

Conflicts of Interest: The authors declare no conflict of interest.

References

1. Choi, S.U.S. Enhancing thermal conductivity of fluids with nanoparticles. In Proceedings of the International Mechanical Engineering Congress and Exhibition, San Francisco, CA, USA, 12–17 November 1995.
2. Ribeiro, A.P.C.; Lourenco, M.J.V.; de Castro, C.A.N. Thermal conductivity of ionanofluids. In Proceedings of the 17th Symposium on Thermophysical Properties, Boulder, CO, USA, 21–26 June 2009.
3. Altin, E.; Gradl, J.; Peukert, W. First studies on the rheological behavior of suspensions in ionic liquids. *Chem. Eng. Technol.* **2006**, *29*, 1347–1354. [CrossRef]
4. Wang, B.; Wang, X.; Lou, W.; Hao, J. Rheological and tribological properties of ionic liquid-based nanofluids containing functionalized multi-walled carbon nanotubes. *J. Phys. Chem. C* **2010**, *114*, 8749–8754. [CrossRef]
5. Altamash, T.; Atilhan, M.; Aliyan, A.; Ullah, R.; Nasser, M.; Aparicio, S. Rheological, thermodynamic, and gas solubility properties of phenylacetic acid-based deep eutectic solvents. *Chem. Eng. Technol.* **2017**, *40*, 778–790. [CrossRef]
6. De Castro, C.A.N.; Lourenco, M.J.V.; Ribeiro, A.P.C.; Langa, E.; Vieira, S.I.C. Thermal properties of ionic liquids and ionanofluids of imidaziolium and pyrrolidinium liquids. *J. Chem. Eng. Data* **2010**, *55*, 653–661. [CrossRef]
7. Fox, E.B.; Bridges, N.J.; Visser, A.E.; Amoroso, J.W. Thermophyiscal properties of nanoparticle-enhanced ionic liquids (NEILs) as advanced heat-transfer fluid. *Energy Fuels* **2013**, *6*, 3385–3393. [CrossRef]
8. Bridges, N.J.; Visser, A.E.; Fox, E.B. Potential of nanoparticle-enhanced ionic liquids (NEILs) as advanced heat-transfer fluid. *Energy Fuels* **2011**, *10*, 4862–4864. [CrossRef]
9. Titan, P.C.; Morshed, A.K.M.M.; Fox, E.B.; Khan, J.A. Effect of nanoparticle dispersion on thermophysical properties of ionic liquids for its potential application in solar collector. *Procedia Eng.* **2014**, *90*, 643–648.

10. Titan, P.C. Investigation of Thermal Performance of Nanopatricle Enhanced Ionic Liquids (NEILs) for Solar Collector Applications. Ph.D. Thesis, Scholar Commons, University of South Carolina, Columbia, SC, USA, 2014.
11. Titan, P.C.; Morshed, A.K.M.M.; Fox, E.B.; Khan, J.A. Thermal performance of Al_2O_3 Nanoparticle Enhanced Ionic Liquids (NEILs) for Concentrated Solar Power (CSP) applications. *Int. J. Heat Mass Transf.* **2015**, *85*, 585–594.
12. Titan, P.C.; Morshed, A.K.M.M.; Khan, J.M.; Fox, E.B. Experimental investigation of natural convection heat transfer of Al2O3 Nanoparticle Enhanced Ionic Liquids (NEILs). *Int. J. Heat Mass Transf.* **2015**, *83*, 753–761.
13. Titan, P.C.; Morshed, A.K.M.M.; Fox, E.B.; Khan, J.A. Enhanced thermophysical properties of NEILs as heat transfer fluids for solar thermal applications. *Appl. Therm. Eng.* **2017**, *110*, 1–9.
14. Bhattacharjee, A.; Luis, A.; Santos, J.H.; Lopes-da-Silva, J.A.; Freire, M.G.; Carvalho, P.J.; Coutinho, J.A.P. Thermophysical properties of sulfonium-and ammonium-based ionic liquids. *Fluid Phase Equlib.* **2014**, *381*, 36–45. [CrossRef]
15. Minea, A.A.; Moldoveanu, M.G.; Dodun, O. Thermal conductivity enhancement by adding nanoparticles to ionic liquids. *Sol. State Phenom.* **2017**, *261*, 121–126. [CrossRef]
16. Minea, A.A.; El-Maghlany, W.M. Natural convection heat transfer utilizing ionic nanofluids with temperature-dependent thermophysical properties. *Chem. Eng. Sci.* **2017**, *174*, 13–24. [CrossRef]
17. Chereches, E.I.; Sharma, K.V.; Minea, A.A. A numerical approach in describing ionanofluids behavior in laminar and turbulent flow. *Continuum Mech. Thermodyn.* **2018**, *30*, 657–666. [CrossRef]
18. Chereches, E.I.; Chereches, M.; Alexandru, A.; Dima, A.; Minea, A.A. Nanoparticles in ionic liquids: Numerical evaluation of heat transfer behavior in laminar flow. *Heat Transf. Eng.* **2020**, *42*, 1625–1634. [CrossRef]
19. Titan, P.C.; Morshed, A.K.M.M.; Khan, J.A. Numerical investigation of natural convection of nanoparticle enhanced ionic liquids (NEILs) in enclosure heated from below. *AIP Conf. Proc.* **2016**, *1754*, 050019.
20. Prasad, S.S.; Selvakumar, R.D. Heat transfer performance of Al_2O_3—([C_4mim][NTf_2]) nano-suspension in a 2-D channel for application in a flat plate solar collector. *IOP Conf. Ser. Mater. Sci. Eng.* **2019**, *577*, 012006. [CrossRef]
21. Rupesh, S.; Selvakumar, R.D. Heat transfer performance of nano-suspension of Al_2O_3 in ([C_4mim][NTf_2]) ionic liquid around a circular cylinder. *IOP Conf. Ser. Mater. Sci. Eng.* **2019**, *577*, 012004. [CrossRef]
22. Shah, R.A.; Ullah, H.; Khan, M.S.; Khan, A. Parametric analysis of the heat transfer behavior of the nano-particle ionic-liquid flow between concentric cylinders. *Adv. Mech. Eng.* **2021**, *13*, 1–14. [CrossRef]
23. Bouchta, S.; Feddaoui, M.; Dayf, A. Numerical simulation of free convection in a partially heated three-dimensional enclosure filled with ionanofluid ([C_4mim][NTf_2]-Cu). *Math. Prob. Eng.* **2021**, *2021*, 6696119. [CrossRef]
24. Sadi, M. Prediction of thermal conductivity and viscosity of ionic liquid-based nanofluids using adaptive neuro fuzzy interface system. *Heat Transf. Eng.* **2017**, *38*, 1561–1572. [CrossRef]

energies

MDPI

Article

A Multimodal Improved Particle Swarm Optimization for High Dimensional Problems in Electromagnetic Devices

Rehan Ali Khan [1], Shiyou Yang [1,*], Shafiullah Khan [2], Shah Fahad [1] and Kalimullah [1]

[1] College of Electrical Engineering, Zhejiang University, Hangzhou 310027, China; rehan@zju.edu.cn (R.A.K.); pirfahad@zju.edu.cn (S.F.); kalim125@zju.edu.cn (K.)

[2] Department of Electronics, Islamia College University, Peshawar 25000, Pakistan; shafielectron@yahoo.com

* Correspondence: eesyyang@zju.edu.cn

Abstract: Particle Swarm Optimization (PSO) is a member of the swarm intelligence-based on a metaheuristic approach which is inspired by the natural deeds of bird flocking and fish schooling. In comparison to other traditional methods, the model of PSO is widely recognized as a simple algorithm and easy to implement. However, the traditional PSO's have two primary issues: premature convergence and loss of diversity. These problems arise at the latter stages of the evolution process when dealing with high-dimensional, complex and electromagnetic inverse problems. To address these types of issues in the PSO approach, we proposed an Improved PSO (IPSO) which employs a dynamic control parameter as well as an adaptive mutation mechanism. The main proposal of the novel adaptive mutation operator is to prevent the diversity loss of the optimization process while the dynamic factor comprises the balance between exploration and exploitation in the search domain. The experimental outcomes achieved by solving complicated and extremely high-dimensional optimization problems were also validated on superconducting magnetic energy storage devices (SMES). According to numerical and experimental analysis, the IPSO delivers a better optimal solution than the other solutions described, particularly in the early computational evaluation of the generation.

Keywords: inverse problem; energy storage device; global optimization; PSO; adaptive mutation operator

Citation: Khan, R.A.; Yang, S.; Khan, S.; Fahad, S.; Kalimullah. A Multimodal Improved Particle Swarm Optimization for High Dimensional Problems in Electromagnetic Devices. *Energies* **2021**, *14*, 8575. https://doi.org/10.3390/en14248575

Academic Editors: Marcin Kamiński and Angel A. Juan

Received: 25 November 2021
Accepted: 9 December 2021
Published: 20 December 2021

1. Introduction

Recently, inverse problems, or real world design problems, have been recognized as an active research topic in the fields of academia and engineering sciences, and the optimal solution to such kinds of problems is difficult and hard due to the presence of multimodal cost functions. Because traditional optimization methods are incapable of resolving inverse or real-world problems, a wealth of studies has consequently contributed to the development of nature-inspired algorithmic models, to improve computational capabilities and diversity of the search space in engineering complex and complicated problems. At the same time, researchers have tried to design various nature-inspired algorithmic models in the state of the art to enhance the computational capabilities as well as increase the diversity of search space in engineering optimization problems.

In this modern world of optimization, when one wishes to solve the engineering optimization problems arising from electromagnetics, more devotion will be paid to optimization techniques. From the previous work, we knew that the optimization problems have more minima and one optimum solution, while the current existence of the stochastic algorithm will try to reach the global optimum region or space. One of these methods' limitations is that they have a slow rate of convergence or require additional computational modifications. In order to relieve unnecessary computational engagement and develop a robust method for the case study, such techniques play an imperative role in improving and makes the algorithms more efficient while building a decent balance between clarity, reliability, and computational performance.

There are a series of metaheuristic algorithms in order to finds the global best solution of inverse problems, but still, there is no evolutionary method to solve most of multimodal optimization problems. Thus, many efforts of the scientist and researchers have been made to optimize the general structure of the algorithm to resolve real-world engineering optimization problems. In this regard, various algorithms have been developed as reported in the following paragraph.

In the field of engineering, a variety of optimal optimization algorithms are used, including ant colony optimization, differential evolution, glowworm swarm optimization, artificial bee colony, genetic algorithm, cuckoo search algorithm, and particle swarm optimization. Among all these methods, PSO is the most recent and simple algorithm [1]. In the search process of the PSO, each candidate shares information with other candidates to expand the search area or space [2]. The PSO optimization algorithm aims to iteratively optimize an issue, starting with a set or population of candidate solutions, referred to as a swarm of particles in this perspective, in which each particle knows both the global best position within the swarm (and its resultant worth in the perspective of the problematic), as well as its personal best position (and its fitness cost) revealed so far during the search [3]. The particles travel randomly in the search space in an iterative process until the entire swarm converges to the global minima.

The PSO comprises three parameters: one control parameter and two learning parameters. Each parameter plays a significant role in the search process. The constant cognitive c_1, and the social constant c_2, give experiences to the personal *pbest* and global best *gbest*. The inertia weight balances the exploration and exploitation search domain [4].

The fundamental equations for updating position and velocity in a PSO are:

$$V_i^k = wV_i^k + c_1 r_1.(pbest_i^k - X_i^k) + c_2 r_2.(gbest^k - X_i^k) \quad (1)$$

$$X_i^k = X_i^k + V_i^k \quad (2)$$

where i denotes the ith particle, k is the generation number, v_k^i is the ith particle's velocity, and X_k^i is its position. For the learning parameters, the cognitive constant represented by c_1 and the social constant by c_2, c_1 attempting to bring the particle into P_{best} where c_2 pushing the particle into g_{best}, and r_1 and r_2 are random values ranging from 0 to 1.

Many researchers and scientists developed various formulations and strategies for the basic three parameters that were explained and described in [5]. When solving a high-dimensional optimization issue, the basic PSO converges early because the parameters are inappropriately chosen and the mutation operators are incapable to optimize the problems. Researchers have recently modified the traditional PSO by adding mutation operators, hybridization with other algorithms, changing the topological structure, and introducing new inertia weight approaches for various problems and produced better results.

In order to control the premature convergence, many researchers have used different mutation operators to make the optimal algorithm more robust and improve the capability of exploration and exploitation searches of the particles. However, most of the strategies are problem-oriented; for example, student "T" mutation is used in local search, but it may fail if the distance between the current search and the optimal position is too wide [6]. The literature illustrates that the performance of a PSO is related to three basic parameters, i.e., inertia weight w, cognitive constant c_1, and social constant c_2. However, in the basic PSO, the values of w, c_1, and c_2 are not appropriately designed to keep a decent balance between local and global search. Consequently, the values of the parameters must be correctly adjusted. A new concept known as the smart particle swarm optimization (SPSO) process is applied in [7] to address the aforementioned problems. The smart particle is based on the convergence factor (CF) technique, which combines memory of particle positions, the second stage is for comparison, and finally the leader declaration, to find the best optimal solution. Furthermore, some researchers have worked on energy system management and design algorithms for the purpose of developing smart artificial intelligence [8–13].

In this paper, a new approach is proposed that is focused on dynamic inertia weight with novel mathematical equations and mutation mechanisms. The mutation process is followed by the personal best particle and global best particles by a unique design roulette wheel selection method to overcome the premature convergence problem by developing proper stability between the exploration and exploitation search.

The remaining of this paper is organized as: the related work of the research is reviewed in Section 2; The novel IPSO is described in Section 3; The numerical results analysis are given in Section 4; A discussion is presented in Section 5; The application of the work is reported in Section 6; and the conclusion is given in Section 7.

2. The Related Work

The previous literature work is mainly categorized into the following four categories.

2.1. Proper Adjustment of Parameters

Researchers have modified the basic three PSO parameters to achieve a decent balance between exploration and exploitation search. Eberhart and Shi first used an inertia weight in the PSO algorithm to control the searching capabilities of the particles [4].

The velocity equation is modified after the incorporation of the inertia weight w:

$$V_i^k = wV_i^k + c_1r_1(pbest_i^k - X_i^k) + c_2r_2(gbest_i^k - X_i^k) \quad (3)$$

To control the diversity of the population and improve the performance of PSO, the authors presented a tactic where the inertia weight can be determined based on Euclidean distance [14]. In [15], an updated version of PSO that sought to solve the drawbacks of traditional PSO in perspective of photovoltaics (PV) parameter estimation has been reported. In this work two ways for controlling the inertia weight and an acceleration coefficients are designed to improve the performance of PSO and to ensure an adequate balance between local and global search, a sine chaotic inertia weight mechanism is first used. Thus, in search of an optimal solution, a tangent chaotic technique is used to steer acceleration coefficients. In [16], an improved multi-strategy particle swarm optimization (IMPSO) approach is described. It proposes to optimize the structure and parameters for better mapping the highly nonlinear characteristics of railway traction braking employing multi-strategy evolution methods with a nonlinear decreasing inertia weight to enhance the global optimizing performance of particle swarms. In the PSO velocity update equation, an adaptive inertia weight factor (AIWF) is added. The main feature is that, unlike a traditional PSO, where the inertia weight is held constant during optimization, the weights are attuned adaptively built on the particle's feat rate in reaching the optimum solution [17].

2.2. Mutation Methods

Many scholars have been working to update the traditional PSO by introducing mutation operators to preserve the diversity of the population and solve the problem of premature convergence. Some of the updated mutation mechanisms are reviewed in the following paragraph. An adaptive mutation strategy is described using the extended non-uniform mutation operator, in which adaptive mutation is used to help trapped particles and extract them from local optima [18]. The hybridizing inertia weight modification tactic, based on new particle diversity and adaptive mutation strategy, has been used to escape local algorithm convergence in complex networks [19]. In [20], they applied different mutation operators on particles in instruction to increase the search capability of particles and avoid them stagnating. In [21], the author proposes a novel idea using an adaptive mutation-selection strategy to conduct local pursuit of the global optimal particle in the up-to-date population, which could help to improve the exploratory potential of the search domain and speed up the convergence speed of the candidates. In [22], the work's aim is to find the best solution with a combination of stochastic methods and PSO with an adaptive cauchy mutation method to design the new algorithm. In [23], the author presents a multiple scale self-adaptive cooperative mutation strategy-based particle swarm optimization algorithm (MSCPSO) to address the two fundamental drawbacks of PSO. To improve the capability of sufficiently searching the whole solution space, we use multi-scale Gaussian mutations with varying standard deviations in the suggested approach. Equations (4) and (5) are the mathematical representation:

$$G_d(t) = G_d(t-1) + \sum_{i=1}^{N} c_{id}(t) \tag{4}$$

in which

$$c_{id}(t) = \begin{cases} 0, & v_{id}(t) > T_d \\ 1, & v_{id}(t) < T_d \end{cases}$$

if $G_d(t) > k_1$ then

$$G_d(t) = 0; \;\; T_d = \frac{T_d}{k_2} \tag{5}$$

In [24], the authors proposed a novel approach to the learning parameters. According to this idea, the two learning variables are dynamically modified in order to affect the particles escaping from a local optimum and converge to the global optimal solution. In [25], the application of Cauchy mutation and Gaussian mutation in the modified PSO is investigated. The major aim is to obtain greater convergence and obtain the best results in the solutions of various real-world problems. In the domain of swarm intelligence, the PSO serves as a basis. The proposed PSO used an improved weight factor compared to the traditional PSO to achieve better convergence.

2.3. Topological Structure

When dealing with complex and high-dimensional optimization problems, researchers are currently working on changing the topological structure of particle swarm optimization to escape the issue of premature convergence. In [26], an example-based learning PSO has been reported to improve swarm and convergence speed diversity. According to the ELPSO idea, many global best particles are set as examples to participate in the velocity update equation, selecting from the current best candidates instead of the *gbest* particle. The proposed work mathematically is shown as:

$$V_i^k = wV_i^k + c_1 rand1_i^k(pbest_{r_i}^k - X_i^k) + c_2 rand2_i^k(gbest_{r_i}^k - X_i^k) \tag{6}$$

In [27], instead of *pbest* and *gbest* particles, only the "historical best info" has been used in the conventional PSO velocity update equation to maintain the population diversification. In [28], the exact particles location and position were described and explained for the purpose of adjusting the balance for exploration and exploitation in the search process and is mathematically expressed as:

$$X_i^{k+1} = (1-\beta(t))p_i^k + \beta(t)p_g^r + \alpha(t)R_i^k \tag{7}$$

In [29], an advanced particle swarm optimization algorithm (APSO) approach is presented. The algorithm uses an improved velocity to modify the equation to ensure that the particles reach the best solution speedily as compared to traditional PSO. In [30], PSO with combined Local and global expanding neighborhood topology (PSOLGENT) is proposed that employs a novel expanding neighborhood topology. In [31], a local search strategy was developed where every candidate tries to reach a better position during the search process and then tries to get the best in the whole swarm.

2.4. Hybridization

Researchers also modified the PSO algorithm by combining it with other optimizers for the purpose of enhancing the performance and expanding the search ability of the particles during the evolution process. According to recent research work, when PSO integrates with other evolutionary operators such as crossover, selection, and mutation, the efficiency of the PSO improves and the PSO is strengthened in terms of robustness, stability, and convergence rate. In [32], the genetic algorithm (GA) is used to amend the decision vectors using genetic operators, while the PSO is used to boost vector position. In [33], the PSO algorithm is paired with the sine cosine algorithm (SCA) and levy flight distribution. According to the SCA algorithm, the updating solution is based on the sine and cosine functions, while levy flight is a random walk that uses the levy distribution to produce search steps and then uses big spikes to search the exploration space more effectively. A new hybrid algorithm is proposed that combines the exploitation capabilities of the PSO with the integration of the exploration capabilities of the grey wolf optimizer (GWO). On the basis of the idea, it combines two methods by substituting a particle from the PSO with a low probability for a partially better particle from the GWO [34]. The hybridization method of PSO and differential evolution (DE) has been reported in [35]. The main idea of the proposal is to control diversity and keep a good balance between the local and global searches of the candidates.

Indeed, PSO has been widely used in large areas of research such as in the application of face recognition systems [36], artificial neural network [37], Internet of Things [38], reliability engineering [39], power-system [40], indoor navigation [41], control-systems [42], EEG signals [43], deep-learning [44], wireless sensor networks [45], cloud computing [46], energy grid [47], Image segmentation [48], and electromagnetics [49,50].

3. The Proposed Work

As explained previously, the traditional PSO algorithm is facing challenges. The main challenge in the PSO process is premature convergence and lack of diversity problems due to unbalance between exploration and exploitation searches of the particles. The PSO technique demands significant testing in order to establish the right parameters required to address the aforementioned difficulties. Therefore, we developed a novel strategy for the control parameter and presented a modified mutation mechanism for the personal best and global best particles.

In the traditional PSOs, the inertia weight value is constant in the search process, so the particles are unable to find the best solution. On the other hand, many researchers are practices the maximum and minimum inertia weight values for exploration and exploitation searches respectively. As the values of inertia weight have an imperative role in a dynamic environment, to solve real world problems in a dynamic environment, we developed a novel strategy for the inertia weight which will try to maintain the best balance between exploration and exploitation search of the candidates in the PSO process. Based on global best function particle values, the inertia weight value is frequently changed during the development process. In the search procedure, the proposed inertia weight strategy is important and works with the current mutation mechanism, and this process mathematically stated as:

$$w_i = \frac{G_{best_{value}}}{M_g} \tag{8}$$

where w is inertia weight, i denotes the ith particle, G_{best} value is the best objective function value of global best particle and M_g represents the maximum number of generation.

Furthermore, because of the presence of static fitness, the traditional PSO technique experiences a lack of diversity problem in the early phases of the evolution process for global best particle *gbest* and personal best particles *pbest*. During the search process, all the particles follow the *gbest* particle, it may be possible that if the *gbest* does not know the best solution, then all the particles are trapped in a local optimal region. During the optimization process, the difference between the global best particle and the current particle is so small due to the increasing number of generations that it causes the particles to become static or stagnant, and as a consequence, the particle velocity is approaching zero, which causes the algorithm to prematurely convergence.

To tackle the aforementioned issues and difficulties in the conventional PSO algorithm, we introduced a new mechanism and strategy that chooses a different mutation operator based on the selection ratio. The mutation operators are accompanied by personal best particles and global best particle for the purpose of enhancing the performance of the PSO process as well as preserving the diversity of the swarm. The proposed adaptive mutation operators are mathematically expressed by:

$$Q_1 = pbest^1_{ij} = pbest_{ij} + Rly_{ij} \tag{9}$$

$$Q_2 = gbest^1_j = g_{best_j} + Rly_j \tag{10}$$

$$Q_3 = pbest^1_{ij} = pbest_{ij} + std_{ij} \tag{11}$$

$$Q_4 = gbest^1_j = gbest_j + std_j \tag{12}$$

$$Q_5 = pbest^1_{ij} = pbest_{ij} + gama_{ij} \tag{13}$$

$$Q_6 = gbest^1_j = gbest_j + gama_j \tag{14}$$

The inspiration of the mutation operators is described in the following paragraph.

The basic PSO is inspired by the flocking of birds or school fishes, such as the birds flying in the air randomly, and the learning rate of each particle in the PSO process is randomized as well. Also, during the motion of birds, the wings of birds play an imperative role in order to continue flight. At the same time, the wings of the birds need randomized energy for their flight to spend more time in the air. Consequently, in the flying mode, the wings of birds are tired due to the presence of less energy during a long journey, and as a consequence, the birds are unable to explore more search space. Viewing the same procedure in the PSO process, where the two particles play a primary role during the search procedure, if the values of personal best and global best particles (energy of the given particles) are less or reduced during the passing of computational time, the velocity of the particles approaches zero, and as a result, the algorithm converges prematurely. In order to avoid this kind of issue, we conducted the mutation operators on particles with the purpose of improving the searching process of the PSO process and enabling the personal and global best particle to explore more optima space. Thus, the novel mutation operators generate random numbers that will provide more energy to the particles and explore more space regions in the evolution process.

In the PSO optimization process, each mutation operator plays a key role in the proposed strategy and has a self-determining selection ratio. The optimum proposed ratios of Q_1 and Q_2 denoted by X, Q_3 and Q_4 by Y and Q_5 and Q_6 by Z respectively. Where X, Y and Z are all set to 0.3 during the initial phases of the optimization process, which ensures that each mutation is chosen an equal number of times. The mutation ratio is updated during the search process depending on the previous mutation operator success rate to summarize the information gained from the history of the objective function. Explicitly, the following updated equations for the novel mutation of mechanism as:

$$X = l + (l - 3l)\frac{out_{Rly}}{out_n} \tag{15}$$

$$Y = l + (l - 3l)\frac{out_{std}}{out_n} \tag{16}$$

$$Z = l + (l - 3l)\frac{out_{gama}}{out_n} \tag{17}$$

The number of successful mutations of unique mutation operators in the primary mutation operations is represented by probability (out) in the above equation. The minimum ratio of each mutation operator is predefined by a constant l, and its value is set to 0.04. Furthermore, during the evolution process the values of X, Y and Z are updated after every generation. The selection process of the best mutation is adapted to the roulette wheel selection method on the basis of the selection ratio of mutation operators, as the roulette wheel selection mechanism is such that the ratio of mutation operators having a longer stay (high selection ratio) will be chosen with a high probability.

4. Numerical Results Analysis

The proposed Improved PSO has been compared to five other well-known optimal algorithms on ten mathematical test functions having dimensions 100. The details are given as under:

- A Particle swarm optimization with adaptive mutation for multimodal optimization (AMPSO) [20].
- A modified PSO algorithm with dynamic parameters for solving complex engineering design problem (MPSOED) [24].
- Analysis of gaussian & cauchy mutations in modified particle swarm optimization algorithm (GCMPSO) [25].
- Global Particle Swarm Optimization for High Dimension Numerical Functions Analysis (GPSO) [27].
- Modified particle swarm optimization algorithm for scheduling renewable generation (MPSO) [51].
- Modified particle swarm optimization with effective guides (MPSOEG) [52].

For the current research work, we use mathematical test functions for the purpose to evaluate the novel method as well as other algorithms, as the said benchmark problems are popular in the field of engineering and are normally considered benchmark problems. In this paper, we employed ten mathematical functions to examine the effectiveness of particle swarm optimization with parameter adjustment. All these are unimodal and multimodal to validate the proposed IPSO algorithm's performance, and the results are compared to the various PSO variants such as, GPSO, AMPSO, MPSO, MPSOED, GCMPSO and MPSOEG, in tabulated data and plots of various methods indicated from 1~10. Table 1 shows these test functions along with the search space in which they are commonly optimized.

Table 1. High Dimensional Classical Benchmark Functions.

Function's Name	Mathematical Definition	Range
Rastrigin	$f_1(x) = \frac{1}{4000}\sum_{i=1}^{n} z_i^2 - \prod_{i=1}^{n} cos\left(\frac{z_i}{\sqrt{i}}\right) + 1$	$[-600, 600]^D$
De Jong's	$f_2(x) = \sum_{i=1}^{n} ix_i^2$	$[-5.12, 5.12]^D$
Bent Cigar	$f_3(x) = x_i^2 + 1^{60}\sum_{i=2}^{n} x_i^2$	$[-100, 100]^D$
Step	$f_4(x) = \sum_{i=1}^{D} (x_i + 0.5)^2$	$[-100, 100]^D$
Quartic	$f_5(x) = \sum_{i=1}^{n} x_i^4 + random(0.1)$	$[-1.28, 1.28]^D$
Sphare	$f_6(x) = \sum_{i=1}^{n} x_i^2$	$[-100, 100]^D$
Schwefel's Problem 1.2	$f_7(x) = \sum_{i=1}^{D}\left(\sum_{I=1}^{n} z_i\right)^2 + f_{bias_1}, z = x - 0$ and $f_{bias_1} = 450$	$[-100, 100]^D$
HappyCat	$f_8(x) = \left\lvert\sum_{i=1}^{n} x_i^2 - n\right\rvert^{\frac{1}{4}} + \frac{(0.5\sum_{i=1}^{n} x_i^2 + \sum_{i=1}^{n} x_i)}{n} + 0.5$	$[-100, 100]^D$
Alpine1	$f_9(x) = \sum_{i=1}^{n} \lvert xsin(x_i) + 0.1x_i\rvert$	$[-10,10]^D$
Griewank	$f_{10}(x) = \frac{1}{4000}\sum_{i=1}^{n} z_i^2 - \prod_{i=1}^{n} cos\left(\frac{z_i}{\sqrt{i}}\right) + 1 + f_{bias_2},$ $z = x - 0$ and $f_{bias_2} = -180$	$[-100, 100]^D$

"D" means search space Dimension.

To judge a proper comparison among the various methods while analyzing the factual analysis of these optimization functions, we employed the same parameter values for all algorithms in the computational testing. The maximum generation was set to 2000 and the dimension to 100. In 60 trial runs, Table 2 records and reports the best values while the worst, mean, variance solution values for are available in Appendix A.

Table 2. Statistical Analysis of the Best Objective Function Values for 100 Dimensions Benchmark Problems.

Function	IPSO	GPSO	AMPSO	MPSOED	MPSO	GCMPSO	MPSOEG
f_1	−14.30	−3.10	−4.00	−2.60	−1.70	−5.40	−7.35
f_2	−99.00	−2.80	−5.80	−22.00	−10.80	−26.10	−16.94
f_3	−32.30	−10.30	−14.60	−7.68	−7.96	−15.20	−4.65
f_4	−75.46	−14.50	−9.70	−17.28	−39.22	−26.30	−24.38
f_5	−60.70	−26.71	−16.30	−47.93	−12.04	−26.70	−19.15
f_6	−11.30	−2.80	−3.30	−7.48	−5.20	−2.20	−5.30
f_7	−95.00	−72.00	−29.00	−32.40	−28.40	−46.20	−22.49
f_8	−1.50	0.20	1.20	1.50	0.40	−0.40	−0.90
f_9	−19.12	−3.80	−1.50	−7.00	−7.50	−4.80	−7.73
f_{10}	−31.80	−18.10	−10.90	−10.80	−7.80	−21.30	−4.90

5. Discussion

On the basis of these comparable data metrics, we claim that our proposed approach (IPSO) performs better as compared to the well-known other algorithms and strategies. The following are the most complicated benchmark problems that are chosen for the validation to recheck the performance of various algorithms. Consequently, the best objective function values for various techniques and our proposed algorithm are indicated in Table 2, while worst, mean and variance results are tabulated in the Appendix A.

Consider the test function, namely the "Rastrigin function", which is a complex multimodal function with a single global optimal solution and multiple local minima. According to tabulation results, we know that our new approach surpasses other methods such as GPSO, AMPSO, MPSO, MPSOED, GCMPSO, and MPSOEG. The test results of Rastrigin function shows that our proposed method performed well as compared to other ones, so it comes in the first category.

To recheck the stability and power of our proposed PSO, we validated the test function, i.e., the "Alpine 1" test function. The Alpine is also a complicated and complex multimodal function, having many local minima and one global optimal solution, while having the range between [−10, 10]. The tabulation value of Alpine function indicates that our algorithms gives minimum result as compared to others. We conclude that our novel approach shows outclassed results on Alpine function as compared to other algorithms.

Similarly, if we check the results of our modified PSO (IPSO) on sphere function, which is unimodal and complex, the global optimal solution of the sphere function is zero and having the range of the search space is [−10, 10]. The tabulation results shows that our modified PSO optimized the said function.

In addition, our modified method produced the top results on the HappyCat benchmark function. The HappyCat function is frequently used to validate the algorithms, due to the presence of so many local minima and complicated structures. If we observe the results of the Quartic function, it shows that our modified approach also gave the top results as compared to the other ones. In summary, the Schwefel's Problem 1.2 function and De Jong's, Bent Cigar, Step, Quartic, Alpine1, and Griewank were all these complex and complicated optimization problems that are commonly used to validate algorithms. In short, our novel IPSO shows good results for most optimization problems as compared to other well-known modified algorithms.

The convergence curve based on test functions f_1, f_5 and f_7 is represented in Figures 1–3 respectively, while the curves for $f_2, f_3, f_4, f_6, f_8, f_9$ and f_{10} are availble in appendix shows the convergence characteristics for various algorithms. Viewing the critical study of test function f_1 we notice that our approach finds the required solution space after 500 generations and other methods such as AMPSO, GPSO, MPSOED, and GCMPSO perform badly, which indicates their low performance and robustness.

From the study of second test function plots, we understand the low performance of other comparable methods and the efficacy of our proposed approach, as in the whole search process, other well-defined methods could not converge to a global region, while our novel modified approach finds the main region after 2000 generations. Similarly, our observation on the third function f_3 plot is reported as the said idea converged before 600 generation, while other algorithms never found the optimal solution of the said algorithms.

If we observe the plot of the sixth test function, we conclude that MPSO performs a little bit better than AMPSO and while the IPSO (proposed approach) performs outclass as compared to all other algorithms, which shows its stability and maturity. So, from the plots, it is obvious that the novel algorithm shows the best performance.

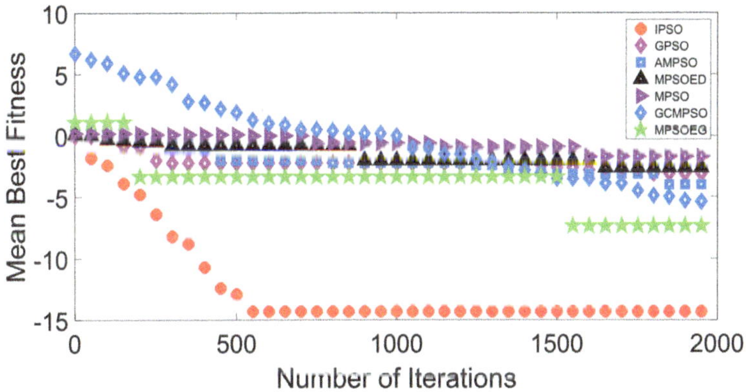

Figure 1. Algorithms convergence plots on f_1.

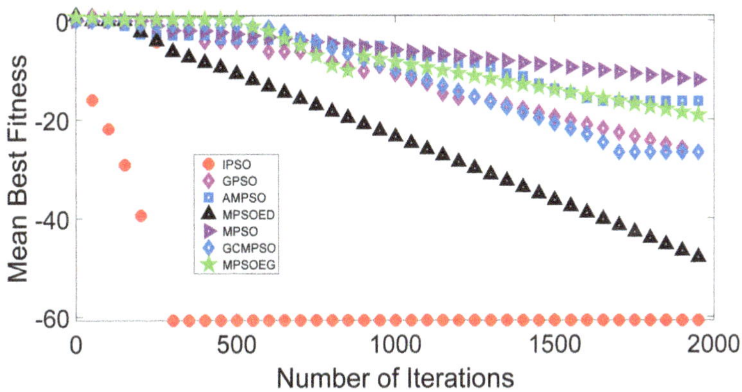

Figure 2. Algorithms convergence plots on f_5.

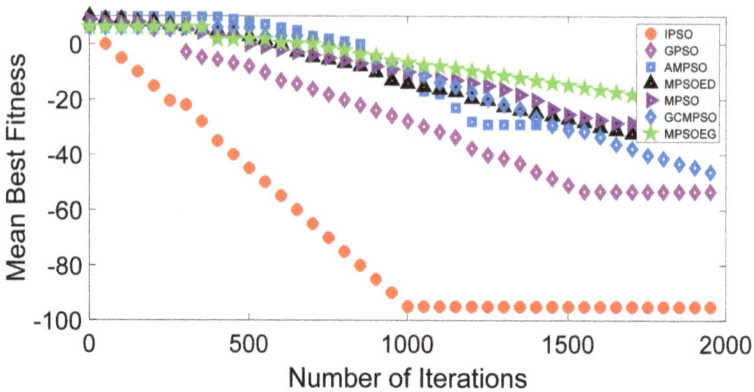

Figure 3. Algorithms convergence plots on f_7.

In this article, we employ the logarithm values of the objective function for comparison. From the graphical results of the test functions, the proposed IPSO converges to the global optimal region faster than the GPSO, AMPSO, MPSO, MPSOED, GCMPSO, and MPSOEG. The reasons are (1) the proposed novel adaptive mutation operator has prevented the diversity loss of the optimization process, (2) the proposed dynamic factor comprises the balance between exploration and exploitation in the search domain. Thus, we conclude from the plots that the suggested approach convergence plots for various test functions proves its superiority compared with others. From the convergence trajectories, it is clear that the novel technique is more efficient, stable and robust. Viewing the numerical results, the proposed IPSO's final solution has significantly greater quality as compared to the others, namely "GPSO", "AMPSO", "MPSO", "MPSOED", "GCMPSO" and "MPSOEG".

6. Application

For better performance analysis of our proposed approach, we choose an engineering electromagnetic device i.e., "TEAM workshop problem 22 (SMES)" as another case study. The optimal design of a SMES device is a popular problem in computational electromagnetics, and it is the 22_{nd} benchmark problem for testing electromagnetic analysis methods (TEAM 22) [53]. The SMES device stores energy in the form of magnetic fields which is generated from the superconducting coils. The TEAM workshop problem 22, is also known as an optimization case of the SMES that has been adapted as a magneto-statics benchmark problem. The following diagram of TEAM 22's design goal, as illustrated in Figure 4, is that the main idea of the problem is to keep the stored energy as close as 180 M Joule, while minimizing the magnetic stray field observed on lines a and b. The first coil is charged to store energy, and the second should be built to reduce the first coil's high magnetic stray. In addition, to maintain the superconductivity of the inside and outside coils, the quenching condition should not be violated. As, the manufacturing tolerance in geometric variables (e.g., R_2, d_2 and h_2 in Figure 4), as well as perturbation compensation of the current controller, can lead to a faulty device.

According to the design procedure of the problem, it incorporates three parameters related to the creation of SMES [54,55].

$$\begin{cases} min\, f = B_{stray}^2/B_{norm}^2 + \left|Energy - E_{ref}\right|/E_{ref} \\ s.t\ \ (J_i < -6.4\left|(B_{max})i + 54)(A/mm^2)(i = 1,2)\right. \end{cases} \tag{18}$$

Obviously, this SMES device is a single objective function design problem, but it actually combines two objective functions to integrate magnetically stored energy in a couple of coils $W_m, W_{erf} = 180$, M Joule, $N = 22$, and $B_{norm} = 3m\, Tesla$.

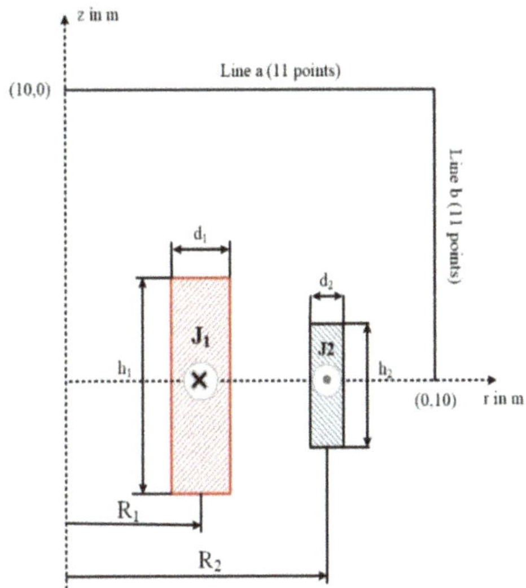

Figure 4. Schematic diagram of SMES device.

The mathematical equation for the stray magnetic field as follows:

$$OF = \frac{B^2_{stray}}{B^2_{ref}} + \frac{\left\| w_m - w_{m.ref} \right\|}{w_{m.ref}} \tag{19}$$

$$B^2_{stray} = \frac{\sum_{i=1}^{N} B^2_{stray.i}}{N} \tag{20}$$

The finite element method is applied to calculate the performance parameters in the above two equations in current research work. When a magnetic field is created, it is essential to keep the physical condition of coils in order to guarantee superconductivity within the solenoids.

Because the current density is 22.5 A/mm^2 then B_{max} must be less than 4.92.

$$J_i < (-6.4|(B_{max})_i| + 54)\left(\frac{A}{mm^2}\right) \tag{21}$$

where, J_1, indicates the coil's current density, and B_{max}, represents the maximum magnetic flux density of the i_{th} coil, while i, denotes the coil's number.

The inner solenoid is fixed in this electromagnetic problem, optimization of SMES device is; $r_1 = 2$ m, $d_1 = 0.27$ m and $\frac{h_1}{2} = 0.8$ m, whereas the outer-solenoid geometrical dimensions is $0.6 \leq r_2 \leq 3.4$ m and $0.1 \leq r_2 \leq 0.4$ m are optimized.

The super conducting magnetic energy storage device conveys currents in opposing directions, associated with radius, height, thickness, and search space of the stray field, as demonstrated in Table 3. For the sake of fair comparison, we set all of the parameters to the same values for IPSO, GPSO, AMPSO, MPSO, MPSOED, GCMPSO, and MPSOEG, and the average value of the objective function was reported in Table 3. The results demonstrate that the novel IPSO recorded output is superior to those of the others.

To synthesize a magnetic field with a desired distribution, appropriately designed current-carrying coils can be used. There are several applications in biomedical engineering: a uniform magnetic field is the background of nuclear magnetic resonance spectroscopy, and a linear profile of the field is required for magnetic resonance imaging. Furthermore, in magneto-fluid hyperthermia (MFH), field uniformity aids in the uniform dispersion of heat generated in the nano-particle fluid that was previously injected into the target region, such as a tumor mass being treated. As a result, major practical applications influenced the concept behind this benchmark problem.

Table 3. Results Comparison of IPSO with other variants on TEAM Workshop Problem 22.

Algorithm	R_2	$h_2/2$	d_2	Objective Function Fitness
IPSO	2.9918	0.2028	0.2939	0.0717
GPSO	2.9713	0.2037	0.3192	0.1287
AMPSO	3.0017	0.6000	0.3201	0.1136
MPSO	3.0084	0.8265	0.2786	0.1356
MPSOED	2.8464	0.5729	0.3382	0.1123
GCMPSO	2.6050	0.2040	0.1000	0.1210
MPSOEG	3.1103	0.7325	0.2731	0.0821

7. Conclusions

PSO is a relatively new metaheuristic for global optimization of a multimodal objective function with continuous variables, and has been recognized a standard global optimizer. Although a wealth of efforts have been devoted to improve its convergence speed, solution quality, and algorithm stability, the performance of the existing PSOs are still unsatisfactory. For example, a premature convergence and the loss of diversity are two challenging issues to be addressed for existing PSOs. In this respect, a novel adaptive mutation operator is designed to ensure the diversity of particles in the optimization process, and a dynamic factor is proposed to ensure a good balance between exploration and exploitation searches. The numerical results on mathematical test problems and an engineering application prototype have validated the effectiveness of the proposed PSO algorithm. Consequently, the present work provides a feasible global optimizer for optimizations of multimodal functions with continuous variables.

In future study, we would really want to analyze the convergence problem using a hybrid optimization algorithm (PSO & ABC) and introducing novel formulations for the cognitive and social components, designing novel selection methods for the leader particle, and creating new equations for the personal best particle using the idea of neighborhood. At the same time, we may choose other case studies such as, solenoid problems, as well as using some novel shifted or rotated mathematical test functions.

Author Contributions: Conceptualization, R.A.K. and S.Y.; methodology, software and validation, R.A.K. formal analysis, investigation and resources, S.F.; writing—original draft preparation, R.A.K.; writing—review and editing, S.K.; visualization, K.; supervision, S.Y. All authors have read and agreed to the published version of the manuscript.

Funding: This research received no external funding.

Institutional Review Board Statement: Not available.

Informed Consent Statement: All authors agree.

Data Availability Statement: The data that support the study's findings, such as numerical simulation, model, or code generated or used during the study, are available upon request from the journal and the corresponding author.

Acknowledgments: Thanks to the China Scholarship Council, Zhejiang University, Hangzhou, China (www.zju.edu.cn, accessed on 5 December 2021) and the University of Science & Technology Bannu, Pakistan (www.ustb.edu.pk, accessed on 5 December 2021) for providing us great research environment during this work.

Conflicts of Interest: The corresponding author declares that there is no contradiction on behalf of all authors.

Abbreviations

PSO	Particle Swarm Optimization
IPSO	Improved Particle Swarm Optimization
C_1	Cognitive Constant
C_2	Social Constant
pbest	Personal Best
gbest	Global Best
W	Inertia Weight
SPSO	Smart Particle Swarm Optimization
CF	Convergence Factor
AIWF	Adaptive Inertia Weight Factor
GA	Genetic Algorithm
SCA	Sine Cosine Algorithm
GWO	Grey Wolf Optimizer
DE	Differential Evolution
PV	Photovoltaics
Mg	Maximum Generation
Rly	Rayleigh's method
Std	Students
Out	Outcome
Q	Mutation Operator
SMES	Super Conducting Magnetic Storage System
TEAM	Testing Electromagnetic Analysis Method
W_m	Magnetic Energy
OF	Objective Function
Ji	Current Coil Density
B_{max}	Maximum Magnetic Flux

Appendix A

Performance Comparison based on Worst, Mean and Variance.

	f_1 Rastrigin						
	IPSO	GPSO	AMPSO	MPSOED	MPSO	GCMPSO	MPSOEG
Worst	0.00	0.00	0.20	0.10	0.20	6.70	1.10
Mean	−12.18	−2.14	−2.10	−1.49	−0.62	−0.21	−3.80
Variance	4.14	0.77	1.13	0.84	0.68	3.45	2.35
	f_2 De Jong's						
	IPSO	GPSO	AMPSO	MPSOED	MPSO	GCMPSO	MPSOEG
Worst	1.00	1.00	0.00	0.00	0.00	16.90	1.20
Mean	−50.64	−1.25	−3.22	−14.41	−7.09	−10.70	−9.77
Variance	30.13	1.08	1.87	7.44	3.59	12.08	6.63
	f_3 Bent Cigar						
	IPSO	GPSO	AMPSO	MPSOED	MPSO	GCMPSO	MPSOEG
Worst	0.00	1.00	1.80	1.70	1.10	0.00	2.60
Mean	−27.01	−7.32	−7.37	−5.69	−3.24	−8.02	−1.01
Variance	10.12	2.92	6.22	3.02	2.84	5.93	2.20
	f_4 Step						
	IPSO	GPSO	AMPSO	MPSOED	MPSO	GCMPSO	MPSOEG
Worst	−1.00	0.90	1.10	1.80	1.70	1.01	0.10
Mean	−45.65	−5.65	−3.79	−7.13	−15.65	−9.95	−11.49
Variance	26.14	5.12	3.75	6.10	12.91	8.78	7.70

	IPSO	GPSO	AMPSO	MPSOED	MPSO	GCMPSO	MPSOEG
			f_5 Quartic				
	IPSO	GPSO	AMPSO	MPSOED	MPSO	GCMPSO	MPSOEG
Worst	0.00	1.00	0.00	1.00	0.00	0.00	0.75
Mean	−54.37	−11.58	−7.79	−22.93	−5.77	−11.18	−8.16
Variance	16.18	8.70	5.52	14.99	3.76	10.00	6.71
			f_6 Sphare				
	IPSO	GPSO	AMPSO	MPSOED	MPSO	GCMPSO	MPSOEG
Worst	0.80	0.90	1.60	0.80	1.00	1.41	0.93
Mean	−5.55	−1.09	−1.18	−2.85	−2.90	−0.82	−3.73
Variance	3.90	1.05	1.43	2.67	2.62	0.90	2.09
			f_7 Schwefel's Problem 1.2				
	IPSO	GPSO	AMPSO	MPSOED	MPSO	GCMPSO	MPSOEG
Worst	5.90	8.30	10.00	10.10	8.90	6.00	6.11
Mean	−68.62	−62.69	−10.44	−12.20	−10.38	−12.75	−6.26
Variance	33.84	21.23	17.25	15.15	13.06	18.28	9.42
			f_8 HappyCat				
	IPSO	GPSO	AMPSO	MPSOED	MPSO	GCMPSO	MPSOEG
Worst	1.90	2.40	2.30	2.50	2.60	8.00	1.19
Mean	−0.75	0.60	1.46	1.88	1.17	1.77	−0.44
Variance	1.17	0.43	0.21	0.29	0.40	1.34	0.71
			f_9 Alpine1				
	IPSO	GPSO	AMPSO	MPSOED	MPSO	GCMPSO	MPSOEG
Worst	0.00	3.20	2.90	0.90	3.00	2.90	3.30
Mean	−14.57	−2.28	1.74	−4.37	−1.34	−0.28	−1.69
Variance	6.33	1.70	1.25	2.62	4.15	2.43	4.20
			f_{10} Griewank				
	IPSO	GPSO	AMPSO	MPSOED	MPSO	GCMPSO	MPSOEG
Worst	0.00	0.90	1.10	1.00	2.00	1.60	1.10
Mean	−17.02	−8.47	−5.60	−7.01	−2.50	−13.59	−2.35
Variance	10.86	6.17	4.14	4.68	3.27	7.94	2.17

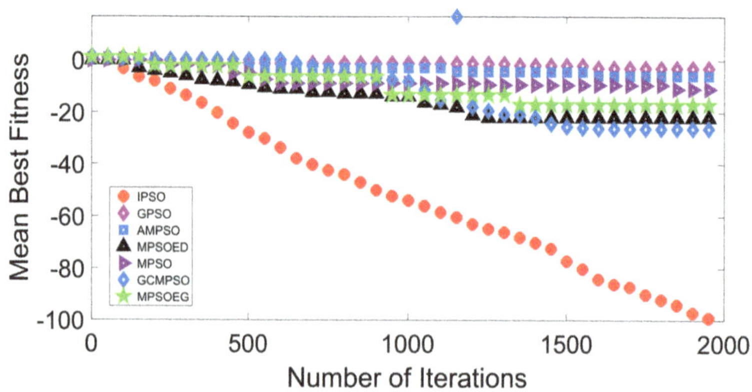

Figure A1. Algorithms' convergence plots on f_2.

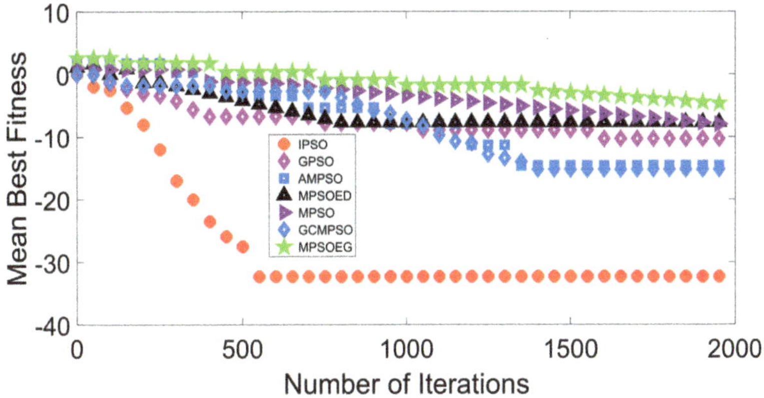

Figure A2. Algorithms' convergence plots on f_3.

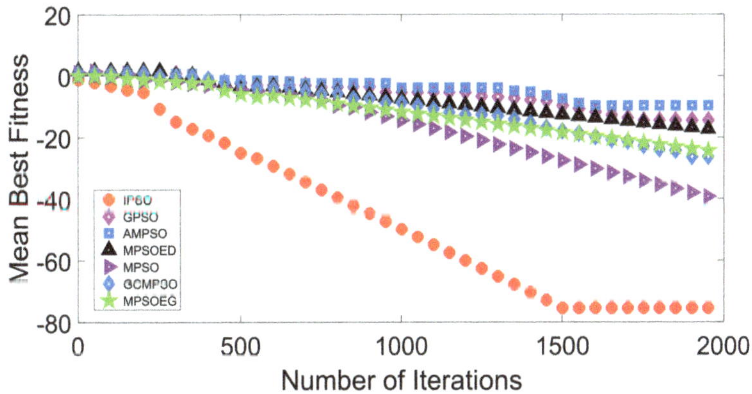

Figure A3. Algorithms' convergence plots on f_4.

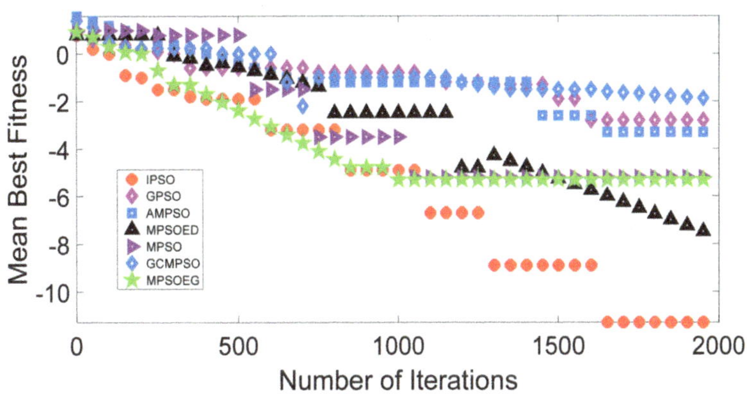

Figure A4. Algorithms' convergence plots on f_6.

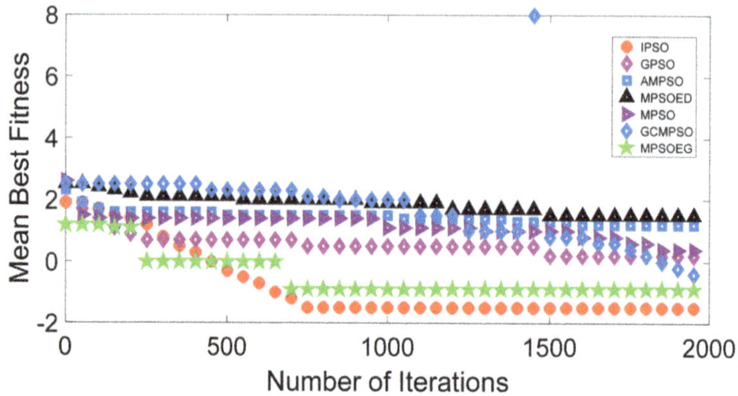

Figure A5. Algorithms' convergence plots on f_8.

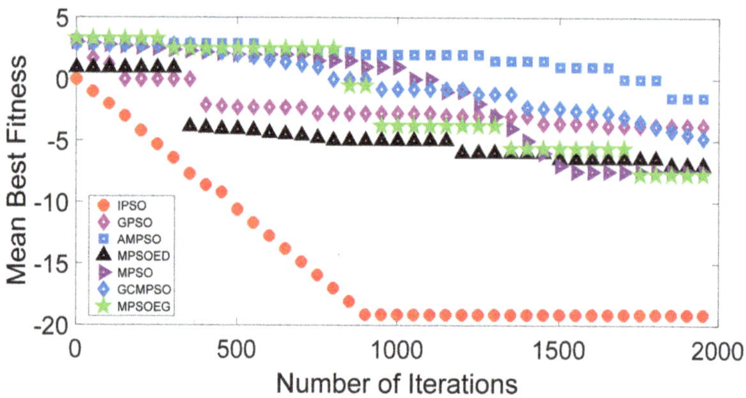

Figure A6. Algorithms' convergence plots on f_9.

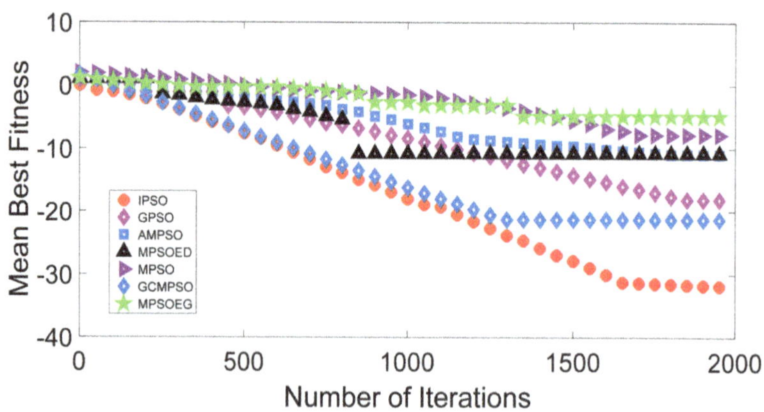

Figure A7. Algorithms' convergence plots on f_{10}.

Discription of Mathematical Test Function

Rastrigin is a multimodal function and is challenging to solve because it contains several local minima regions where an optimization algorithm with limited exploratory power is likely to become trapped. The function's lone globally optimal solution, 0, is located within the domain of $[-5.12, 5.12]$ at f (x^*) = [0, 0, . . . , 0].

The step mathematical test function is one of the more complicated and complex problems due to the lack of suitable direction. The minimum value is fixed at zero. The search region of said benchmark problem is $[-100, 100]$, and the shape of the given benchmark problem is flat.

Researchers are using the Quartic function as a benchmark problem due to its unimodal quality. Its global point is zero and the space of its search is mentioned and presented between the values of $[-1.28]$ and [1.28].

The test function, namely "Sphere," is a unimodal and continuous function, and the solution of such types of problems is easy. The search domain should be mentioned in the brackets $[-5.12, 5.12]$. The zero is the minimum value of the given sphere function where the value is derived by the computational scientist and the research optimization school.

Griewank is the mathematical test function that is used in the field of engineering design for the validation of computational techniques. The mentioned problem is complex and multimodal, and its feasible range of function is $[-100, 100]$. The scientist has already discovered that the global optimal solution to the aforementioned benchmark problem is zero.

The Alpine 1 function is a mathematical test function used to validate computing strategies in the field of engineering optimization. This function is Multimodal and Continuous with a $-10 \leq xi \leq 10$ constraint. The origin is the location of the global minimum, where x = (0, 0) and f(x) = 0.

References

1. Wahab, M.N.A.; Nefti-Meziani, S.; Atyabi, A. A Comprehensive Review of Swarm Optimization Algorithms. *PLoS ONE* **2015**, *10*, e0122827. [CrossRef]
2. Kennedy, J.; Eberhart, R.C. Particle Swarm Optimization. In Proceedings of the ICNN'95—International Conference on Neural Networks, Perth, Australia, 27 November–1 December 1995; pp. 1942–1948.
3. Freitas, D.; Lopes, L.G.; Morgado-Dias, F. Particle Swarm Optimization: A Historical Review up to the Current Developments. *Entropy* **2020**, *22*, 362. [CrossRef]
4. Eberhart, R.C.; Shi, Y. Tracking and Optimizing Dynamic Systems with Particle Swarms. In Proceedings of the Congress on Evolutionary Computation, Seoul, Korea, 27–30 May 2001; pp. 94–100.
5. Banks, A.; Vincent, J.; Anyakoha, C. A Review of Particle Swarm Optimization. Part II: Hybridisation, Combinatorial, Multicriteria and Constrained Optimization, and Indicative Applications. *Nat. Comput.* **2008**, *7*, 109–124. [CrossRef]
6. Imran, M.; Hashim, R.; Khalid, N.E.A. An Overview of Particle Swarm Optimization Variants. *Procedia Eng.* **2013**, *53*, 491–496. [CrossRef]
7. Khan, R.A.; Yang, S.; Fahad, S.; Khan, S.U.; Kalimullah. A Modified Particle Swarm Optimization with a Smart Particle for Inverse Problems in Electromagnetic Devices. *IEEE Access* **2021**, *9*, 99932–99943. [CrossRef]
8. Eysenck, G. Sensor-Based Big Data Applications and Computationally Networked Urbanism in Smart Energy Management Systems. *Geopolit. Hist. Int. Relat.* **2020**, *12*, 52–58.
9. Konecny, V.; Barnett, C.; Poliak, M. Sensing and Computing Technologies, Intelligent Vehicular Networks, and Big Data-Driven Algorithmic Decision-Making in Smart Sustainable Urbanism. In *Contemporary Readings in Law and Social Justice*; Addleton Academic Publishers: New York, NY, USA, 2021; Volume 13, pp. 30–39.
10. Harrower, K. Networked and Integrated Urban Technologies in Sustainable Smart Energy Systems. *Geopolit. Hist. Int. Relat.* **2020**, *12*, 45–51.
11. Nica, E.; Stehel, V. Internet of Things Sensing Networks, Artificial Intelligence-Based Decision-Making Algorithms, and Real-Time Process Monitoring in Sustainable Industry 4.0. *J. Self Gov. Manag. Econ.* **2021**, *9*, 35–47.
12. Valderrama Bento da Silva, P.H.; Camponogara, E.; Seman, L.O.; Villarrubia González, G.; Reis Quietinho Leithardt, V. Decompositions for MPC of Linear Dynamic Systems with Activation Constraints. *Energies* **2020**, *13*, 5744. [CrossRef]
13. Sun, L.; You, F. Machine Learning and Data-driven Techniques for the Control of Smart Power Generation Systems: An Uncertainty Handling Perspective. *Engineering* **2021**, *7*, 1239–1247. [CrossRef]
14. Du, C.; Yin, Z.G.; Zhang, Y.P.; Liu, J.; Sun, X.D.; Zhong, Y.R. Research on Active Disturbance Rejection Control with Parameter Autotune Mechanism for Induction Motors Based on Adaptive Particle Swarm Optimization Algorithm with Dynamic Inertia Weight. *IEEE Trans. Power Electr.* **2019**, *34*, 2841–2855. [CrossRef]

15. Kiani, A.T.; Nadeem, M.F.; Ahmed, A.; Khan, I.A.; Alkhammash, H.I.; Sajjad, I.A.; Hussain, B. An Improved Particle Swarm Optimization with Chaotic Inertia Weight and Acceleration Coefficients for Optimal Extraction of PV Models Parameters. *Energies* **2021**, *14*, 2980. [CrossRef]
16. Kong, X.; Zhang, T. Non-Singular Fast Terminal Sliding Mode Control of High-Speed Train Network System Based on Improved Particle Swarm Optimization Algorithm. *Symmetry* **2020**, *12*, 205. [CrossRef]
17. Kumar, E.V.; Raaja, G.S.; Jerome, J. Adaptive PSO for Optimal LQR Tracking Control of 2 DOF Laboratory Helicopter. *Appl. Soft Comput.* **2016**, *41*, 77–90. [CrossRef]
18. Cui, Q.; Li, Q.; Li, G.; Li, Z.; Han, X.; Lee, H.P.; Liang, Y.; Wang, B.; Jiang, J.; Wu, C. Globally-Optimal Prediction-Based Adaptive Mutation Particle Swarm Optimization. *Inf. Sci.* **2017**, *418–419*, 186–217. [CrossRef]
19. Li, X.; Wu, X.; Xu, S.; Qing, S.; Chang, P.C. A Novel Complex Network Community Detection Approach using Discrete Particle Swarm Optimization with Particle Diversity and Mutation. *Appl. Soft Comput.* **2019**, *81*, 105476. [CrossRef]
20. Wang, H.; Wang, W.; Wu, Z. Particle Swarm Optimization with Adaptive Mutation for Multimodal Optimization. *Appl. Math. Comput.* **2013**, *221*, 296–305. [CrossRef]
21. Dong, W.Y.; Kang, L.L.; Zhang, W.S. Opposition-Based Particle Swarm Optimization with Adaptive Mutation Strategy. *Soft Comput.* **2017**, *21*, 5081–5090. [CrossRef]
22. Zou, Y.; Liu, P.X.; Li, C.; Cheng, Q. Collision Detection for Virtual Environment using Particle Swarm Optimization with Adaptive Cauchy Mutation. *Cluster Comput.* **2017**, *20*, 1765–1774. [CrossRef]
23. Tao, X.; Guo, W.; Li, Q.; Ren, C.; Liu, R. Multiple Scale Self-Adaptive Cooperation Mutation Strategy-Based Particle Swarm Optimization. *Appl. Soft Comput.* **2020**, *89*, 1568–4946. [CrossRef]
24. Khan, S.; Kamran, M.; Rehman, O.U.; Liu, L.; Yang, S. A Modified PSO Algorithm with Dynamic Parameters for Solving Complex Engineering Design Problem. *Int. J. Comput. Math.* **2017**, *95*, 2308–2329. [CrossRef]
25. Sarangi, A.; Samal, S.; Sarangi, S.K. Analysis of Gaussian & Cauchy Mutations in Modified Particle Swarm Optimization Algorithm. In Proceedings of the 5th International Conference on Advanced Computing & Communication Systems (ICACCS), Coimbatore, India, 15–16 March 2019; pp. 463–467.
26. Huang, H.; Qin, H.; Hao, Z.; Lim, A. Example-Based Learning Particle Swarm Optimization for Continuous Optimization. *Inf. Sci.* **2012**, *182*, 125–138. [CrossRef]
27. Jamian, J.J.; Abdullah, M.N.; Mokhlis, H.; Mustafa, M.W.; Bakar, A.H.A. Global Particle Swarm Optimization for High Dimension Numerical Functions Analysis. *J. Appl. Math.* **2014**, *2014*, 329193. [CrossRef]
28. Guedria, N.B. Improved Accelerated PSO Algorithm for Mechanical Engineering Optimization Problems. *Appl. Soft Comput.* **2016**, *40*, 455–467. [CrossRef]
29. Ali, K.T.; Ling, H.S.; Mohan, S.A. Advanced Particle Swarm Optimization Algorithm with Improved Velocity Update Strategy. In Proceedings of the 2018 IEEE International Conference on Systems, Man and Cybernetics (SMC), Miyazaki, Japan, 7–10 October 2018; pp. 3944–3949.
30. Marinakis, Y.; Migdalas, A.; Sifaleras, A. A Hybrid Particle Swarm Optimization-Variable Neighborhood Search algorithm for Constrained Shortest Path problems. *Eur. J. Oper. Res.* **2017**, *261*, 819–834. [CrossRef]
31. Ding, J.; Liu, J.; Chowdhury, K.R.; Zhang, W.; Hu, Q.; Lei, J. A Particle Swarm Optimization using Local Stochastic Search and Enhancing Diversity for Continuous Optimization. *Neurocomputing* **2014**, *137*, 261–267. [CrossRef]
32. Garg, H. A Hybrid GSA-GA Algorithm for Constrained Optimization Problems. *Inf. Sci.* **2019**, *478*, 499–523. [CrossRef]
33. Chegini, S.N.; Bagheri, A.; Najafi, F. PSOSCALF: A new Hybrid PSO based on Sine Cosine algorithm and Levy Flight for Solving Optimization Problems. *Appl. Soft Comput.* **2018**, *73*, 697–726. [CrossRef]
34. Senel, F.A.; Gökçe, F.; Yüksel, A.S.; Yigit, T. A Novel Hybrid PSO–GWO Algorithm for Optimization Problems. *Eng. Comput.* **2019**, *35*, 1359–1373. [CrossRef]
35. Tang, B.; Xiang, K.; Pang, M. An Integrated Particle Swarm Optimization Approach Hybridizing a New Self-Adaptive Particle Swarm Optimization with a Modified Differential Evolution. *Neural Comput. Appl.* **2018**, *32*, 4849–4883. [CrossRef]
36. Hermosilla, G.; Rojas, M.; Mendoza, J.; Farias, G.; Pizarro, F.T.; Martin, C.S.; Vera, E. Particle Swarm Optimization for the Fusion of Thermal and Visible Descriptors in Face Recognition Systems. *IEEE Access* **2018**, *6*, 42800–42811. [CrossRef]
37. Shariati, M.; Mafipour, M.S.; Mehrabi, P.; Bahadori, A.; Zandi, Y.; Salih, M.N.A.; Nguyen, H.; Dou, J.; Song, X.; Poi-Ngian, S. Application of a Hybrid Artificial Neural Network-Particle Swarm Optimization (ANN-PSO) Model in Behavior Prediction of Channel Shear Connectors Embedded in Normal and High-Strength Concrete. *Appl. Sci.* **2019**, *9*, 5534. [CrossRef]
38. Liu, J.; Yang, D.; Lian, M.; Li, M. Research on Intrusion Detection Based on Particle Swarm Optimization in IoT. *IEEE Access* **2021**, *9*, 38254–38268. [CrossRef]
39. Bai, B.; Guo, Z.; Zhou, C.; Zhang, W.; Zhang, J. Application of adaptive reliability importance sampling-based extended domain PSO on single mode failure in reliability engineering. *Inf. Sci.* **2021**, *546*, 42–59. [CrossRef]
40. Hantash, N.; Khatib, T.; Khammash, M. An Improved Particle Swarm Optimization Algorithm for Optimal Allocation of Distributed Generation Units in Radial Power Systems. *Appl. Comput. Intell. Soft Comput.* **2020**, *2020*, 8824988.
41. Sun, D.; Wei, E.; Ma, Z.; Wu, C.; Xu, S. Optimized CNNs to Indoor Localization through BLE Sensors Using Improved PSO. *Sensors* **2021**, *21*, 1995. [CrossRef]
42. Wu, T.Z.; Shi, X.; Liao, L.; Zhou, C.J.; Zhou, H.; Su, Y.H. A Capacity Configuration Control Strategy to Alleviate Power Fluctuation of Hybrid Energy Storage System Based on Improved Particle Swarm Optimization. *Energies* **2019**, *12*, 642. [CrossRef]

43. Arican, M.; Polat, K. Binary Particle Swarm Optimization (BPSO) Based Channel Selection in the EEG Signals and its Application to Speller Systems. *J. Artif. Intell. Syst.* **2020**, *2*, 27–37. [CrossRef]
44. Rajagopal, A.; Joshi, G.P.; Ramachandran, A.; Subhalakshmi, R.T.; Khari, M.; Jha, S.; Shankar, K.; You, J. A Deep Learning Model Based on Multi-Objective Particle Swarm Optimization for Scene Classification in Unmanned Aerial Vehicles. *IEEE Access* **2020**, *8*, 135383–135393. [CrossRef]
45. Edla, D.R.; Kongara, M.C.; Cheruku, R. A PSO Based Routing with Novel Fitness Function for Improving Lifetime of WSNs. *Wirel. Pers. Commun.* **2019**, *104*, 73–89. [CrossRef]
46. Farid, M.; Latip, R.; Hussin, M.; Abdul Hamid, N.A.W. A Survey on QoS Requirements Based on Particle Swarm Optimization Scheduling Techniques for Workflow Scheduling in Cloud Computing. *Symmetry* **2020**, *12*, 551. [CrossRef]
47. Azab, M. Multi-Objective Design Approach of Passive Filters for Single-Phase Distributed Energy Grid Integration Systems using Particle Swarm Optimization. *Energy Rep.* **2020**, *6*, 157–172. [CrossRef]
48. Farshi, T.R.; Drake, J.H.; Ozcan, E. A Multimodal Particle Swarm Optimization-Based Approach for Image Segmentation. *Expert Syst. Appl.* **2020**, *149*, 13. [CrossRef]
49. Khan, S.U.; Yang, S.; Wang, L.; Liu, L. A Modified Particle Swarm Optimization Algorithm for Global Optimizations of Inverse Problems. *IEEE Trans. Magn.* **2015**, *52*, 1–4. [CrossRef]
50. Fahad, S.; Yang, S.; Khan, R.A.; Khan, S.; Khan, S.A. A Multimodal Smart Quantum Particle Swarm Optimization for Electromagnetic Design Optimization Problems. *Energies* **2021**, *14*, 4613. [CrossRef]
51. Gholami, K.; Dehnavi, E. A Modified Particle Swarm Optimization Algorithm for Scheduling Renewable Generation in a Micro-Grid under Load Uncertainty. *Appl. Soft Comput.* **2019**, *78*, 496–514. [CrossRef]
52. Karim, A.A.; Isa, N.A.M.; Lim, W.H. Modified Particle Swarm Optimization with Effective Guides. *IEEE Access* **2020**, *8*, 188699–188725. [CrossRef]
53. Alotto, P.; Baumgartner, U.; Freschi, F. SMES Optimization Benchmark: TEAM Workshop Problem 22. COMPUMAG TEAM Workshop 2008; pp. 1–4. Available online: http://www.compumag.org/jsite/images/stories/TEAM/problem22.pdf (accessed on 8 September 2021).
54. Di Barba, P.; Mognaschi, M.E.; Lowther, D.A.; Sykulski, J.K. A Benchmark TEAM Problem for Multi-Objective Pareto Optimization of Electromagnetic Devices. *IEEE Trans. Magn.* **2018**, *54*, 1–4. [CrossRef]
55. Li, Y.; Lei, G.; Bramerdorfer, G.; Peng, S.; Sun, X.; Zhu, J. Machine Learning for Design Optimization of Electromagnetic Devices: Recent Developments and Future Directions. *Appl. Sci.* **2021**, *11*, 1627. [CrossRef]

energies

Article

Residential Short-Term Load Forecasting during Atypical Consumption Behavior

Cristina Hora, Florin Ciprian Dan *, Gabriel Bendea and Calin Secui

Faculty of Energy Engineering and Industrial Management (ROMANIA), University of Oradea, 410087 Oradea, Romania; chora@uoradea.ro (C.H.); gbendea@uoradea.ro (G.B.); csecui@uoradea.ro (C.S.)
* Correspondence: florin.dan@uoradea.ro; Tel.: +40-7-4263-3462

Abstract: Short-term load forecasting (STLF) is a fundamental tool for power networks' proper functionality. As large consumers need to provide their own STLF, the residential consumers are the ones that need to be monitored and forecasted by the power network. There is a huge bibliography on all types of residential load forecast in which researchers have struggled to reach smaller forecasting errors. Regarding atypical consumption, we could see few titles before the coronavirus pandemic (COVID-19) restrictions, and afterwards all titles referred to the case of COVID-19. The purpose of this study was to identify, among the most used STLF methods—linear regression (LR), autoregressive integrated moving average (ARIMA) and artificial neural network (ANN)—the one that had the best response in atypical consumption behavior and to state the best action to be taken during atypical consumption behavior on the residential side. The original contribution of this paper regards the forecasting of loads that do not have reference historic data. As the most recent available scenario, we evaluated our forecast with respect to the database of consumption behavior altered by different COVID-19 pandemic restrictions and the cause and effect of the factors influencing residential consumption, both in urban and rural areas. To estimate and validate the results of the forecasts, multiyear hourly residential consumption databases were used. The main findings were related to the huge forecasting errors that were generated, three times higher, if the forecasting algorithm was not set up for atypical consumption. Among the forecasting algorithms deployed, the best results were generated by ANN, followed by ARIMA and LR. We concluded that the forecasting methods deployed retained their hierarchy and accuracy in forecasting error during atypical consumer behavior, similar to forecasting in normal conditions, if a trigger/alarm mechanism was in place and there was sufficient time to adapt/deploy the forecasting algorithm. All results are meant to be used as best practices during power load uncertainty and atypical consumption behavior.

Keywords: short term load forecast; atypical consumption behavior; load profile; COVID 19; power load uncertainty

Citation: Hora, C.; Dan, F.C.; Bendea, G.; Secui, C. Residential Short-Term Load Forecasting during Atypical Consumption Behavior. *Energies* **2022**, *15*, 291. https://doi.org/10.3390/en15010291

Academic Editors: Marcin Kamiński and Angel A. Juan

Received: 2 December 2021
Accepted: 28 December 2021
Published: 1 January 2022

1. Introduction

In residential short-term load forecasting (STLF), future power consumption is projected by applying a preestablished relationship between power load and its influence factors, or by dynamically assessing historical data and adapting the correlation of the influence factor—namely, time and/or weather—with the load [1]. Defining this relationship is a two-part process: (a) identifying the correlation between power consumption and factors that influence that consumption, (b) quantifying the effect on consumption by using a suitable technique to estimate each factor. In order for this analysis to generate results that could be easily multiplied, a good understanding of the consumer to be analyzed is required [2]. A prerequisite for developing an accurate forecasting model under atypical consumption behavior or power load uncertainty is a trigger that announces the decision factors for atypical consumption behavior to occur. This knowledge concerning the behavior of the load curve is determined by correlation between the influence factors, consumer data and statistical analysis of past consumption [3–7].

Papers from a literature review address the issue of the methodology used to model the first COVID-19 lockdown effects on power load. In [3] we can see a comparison of convolutional neural network (CNN)-based model forecasting with multiple linear regression (MLR) and an unknown forecasting method used by the system operator (SOM) using a Romanian database of all consumers. We can see in [3] that CNN was the most accurate method used for the COVID-19 database, with a median mean absolute percentage error (MAPE) of 1.0007% relative to 1.0692% for MLR and 1.1552% for SOM. In addition, we can see in [3] that the CNN method had higher maximum errors than the SOM. A database of New York (NY) consumption for the same atypical COVID-19 lockdown consumption event was analyzed in [4] by deploying three forecasting methods, namely Fully Connected Deep Neural Network (FCDNN), Long Short-Term Memory (LSTM), and Gated Recurrent Unit (GRU), along with Auto-Regressive Integrated Moving Average (ARIMA) which did not produce meaningful results on their database and therefore was not considered. The MAPE results in [4] were best in GRU with 4.04%, followed by FCDNN with 4.08% and lastly LDTM with 4.26%, all under the 5.35% benchmark for the NY database. The Jordanian National Electric Power Company (NEPCO) power database was used in [5] to evaluate, also during the COVID-19 lockdown period, the forecast efficiency of Autoregressive Integrated Moving Average with Exogenous (ARIMAX) and Artificial Neural Network (ANN). The daily forecast accuracy was also evaluated with MAPE and had better results with ARIMAX (5.5%) than with ANN (5.8%). Covering the largest US deregulated wholesale electricity market—Pennsylvania, New Jersey, Maryland (PJM)—[6] assessed forecasting under uncertainty in the pre-COVID-19 era by using a Gaussian process and obtaining an efficiency between 2.21% and 3.20% MAPE. Even though the atypical consumption was not related to COVID-19, the methodology used was suitable for any power load uncertainty related to an unforeseen event. Paper [7] assessed national European databases from France and Italy, and was the first study applying the lessons learned from the previous COVID-19 affected power load databases. The forecasting methods used in [7], covering data both from a pre-COVID-19 database and collected during lockdown and post-lockdown recovery, included ARIMA, Generalized Additive Models (GAM), Kalman Filtering and a combination of the first two methods (GAM+ARIMA). During the first lockdown the MAPE results were high, ranging from 4.28% for the GAM+ARIMA model through 4.81% for Kalman static filtering and 4.83% for GAM to 5.44% for the ARIMA model. All papers addressing the issue of forecasting under atypical consumption used methods that were altered by the operator to address the changing consumption profile. This limitation offered us a chance to focus on the consumer profile rather than on the historic trend, giving the forecasting methodology a flexibility in tackling unforeseen power consumption events.

The modeled characteristics of the consumer to be analyzed [1] are an essential indicator of the health of the forecast, seen even more during unpredictable power load events, as the previous research states [3–7]. Power consumers absorbing load in similar socio-economic and weather/climate areas usually have similar consumer behavior, and consumption forecast models developed for a type of consumer can easily be adapted for forecasting the consumption of other consumers in the same conditions. The main aim of the work was to identify the best load forecasting methods, of the ones applied, that gave us the smallest forecasting errors in atypical consumption behavior.

Part of an already ongoing COVID-19 pandemic, the first confirmed cases to reach Romania were on 26 February 2020. Following a rather similar European pattern the pandemic evolved and the first load curve-impacting pandemic-related legal measures were deployed on 16 March 2020, when the Romanian president decreed that a state of emergency should be implemented in Romania for a period of 30 days. Growing numbers of new COVID-19 confirmed cases in Romania led to the government announcing Military Ordinance No. 3 on 24 March 2020, instituting a national lockdown. These unprecedented restrictions were enforced by the support of military personnel, police and Gendarmerie [8–12]. People were not allowed to leave their homes or households, although some exceptions (work, buying food or medicine etc.) were allowed. Older people (over 65) were allowed to leave their homes only in the time interval of 11 a.m. to 1 p.m. This rule was applied to 16.4% of the rural population in Bihor County [13], for whom this restriction was assessed as an influence factor. On 14 May 2020 the state of emergency was lifted and replaced with a state of alert, meaning a decrease in the lockdown measures. A second wave of COVID-19 infections led to a partial lockdown on 9 November 2020. A third wave meant a milder lockdown with reduced restriction rules on 9 March 2021, and mainly local quarantines for the affected locations [8–12]. Urban or rural residential consumers included in the database were not affected by local lockdowns.

In order to validate the results of this study, we used a large multiyear database containing hourly consumption [14] separated into residential urban and residential rural consumers in Bihor County, Romania. The advantages of this database are that it contains a huge number of consumers (households) and that the residential consumers are the ones that have the best correlation to the consumption influence factors, e.g., weather. Previous research was conducted [3–7] mainly on national or international databases containing all consumption, including residential, commercial, industrial, transport, etc. This means that the nonresidential consumers, which have the obligation to forecast their own consumption, accounted for more than half of the power consumption forecasted.

By addressing only forecasting for residential consumers, we mitigate the risk of low efficiency STLF in the area in which the power networks are most vulnerable from the financial point of view and from the stability point of view.

The main contributions of this paper can be summarized as follows:

- Identify the profile of Bihor County's urban and rural residential consumers relative to other EU residential profiles
- Evaluate the efficiency of STLF methods during COVID-19 lockdowns in different scenarios
- Compare the STLF results for residential Bihor County consumers with previous research on STLF under uncertainty.

The rest of the paper is structured as follows: Section 2 describes the database used to test and validate the three STLF methods, presenting also the particularities. In Section 3 the Methodology used is presented, mainly the STLF algorithms and succession of steps, as shown in Figure 1. Case analysis and results are presented in Section 4. Section 5 covers a discussion of the findings and state of the research, and finally conclusions and future research best practices are covered in Section 6.

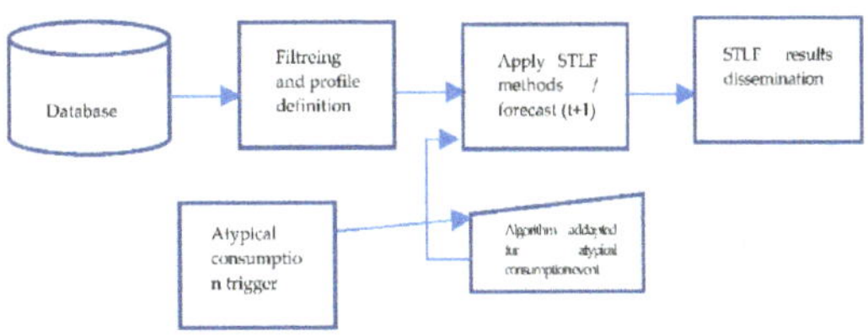

Figure 1. Flowchart of STLF in atypical consumption behavior.

2. Database Presentation

The database is a representative sample of both rural (7k households) and urban consumers (23k households). The database is a multiannual (2019–2021) recording of hourly energy use and is provided as Supplementary Material to this manuscript. Due to the volume of information to disseminate in this paper, we approach all the specifications and particularities of the database that are essential to this research. The urban households are located in cities in Bihor County, Romania, in the second climatological area, with an annual average temperature of 11.6 °C [15]. We present three charts specific to the yearly average urban database. Figure 2 shows the yearly consumption relative to 2020, the year for which we have the atypical consumption behavior that we targeted in our

STLF deployment. Figure 3 shows the weekday consumption and Figure 4 the seasonal profile consumption. For profiling reasons, Figure 2 presents only 2020 data, but Figures 3 and 4 statistically address all three years covered by the database. The rural households are located in Bihor County, Romania, in the third climatological area, with an annual average temperature of 9.6 °C [16]. In Figure 5 we can see a representative chart of the 2020 yearly consumption segmented into weekly loads starting on Sundays. Figures 6 and 7 show the statistics of the specific consumption of the rural household over weekdays and over each season.

Although weekly patterns are rare in nature, they are common in human activities, which is why we chose a 3D yearly chart; this chart contains essential information for classifying the consumption pattern.

The weekday pattern for urban residential consumers in Bihor County (RBCR) was relatively similar to the weekday patterns in Ireland, Hungary, Italy and UK, with the caveat that the household electric energy consumption was different [17]. With regard to the daily high peaks, the urban RBCR consumer was closer to the consumer profile from Hungary and Italy than that from Ireland and the UK [17].

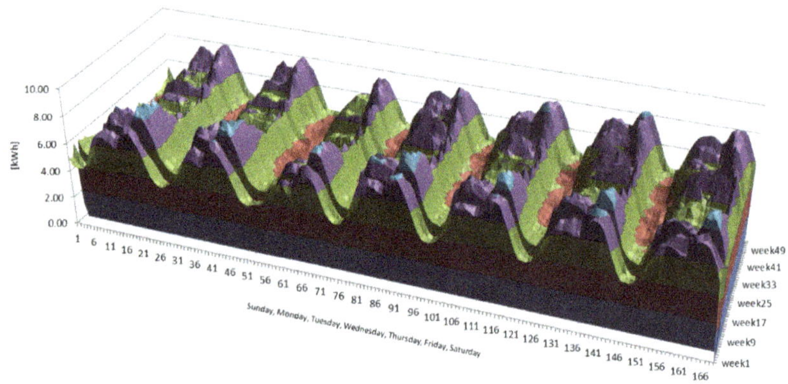

Figure 2. Weekly load curve in 2020 for urban consumers.

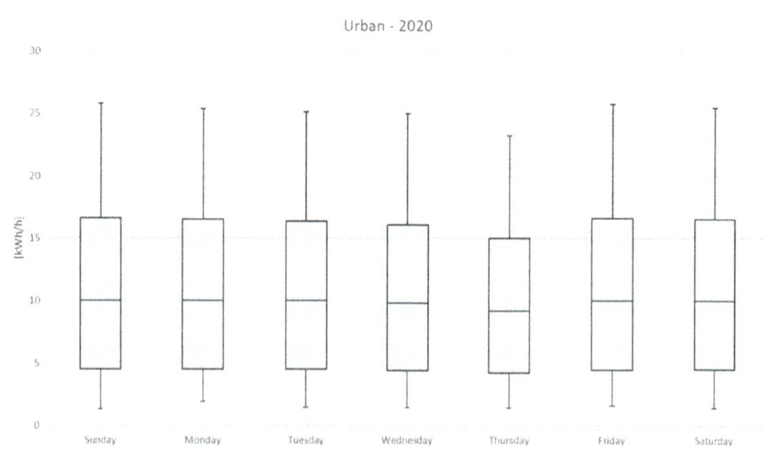

Figure 3. Box and whiskers plots for days of the week in 2020 (urban).

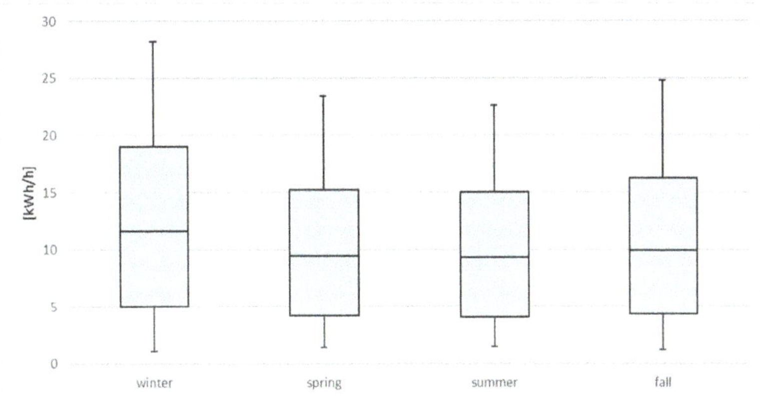

Figure 4. Box and whiskers plots for hourly consumption in each season in 2020 (urban).

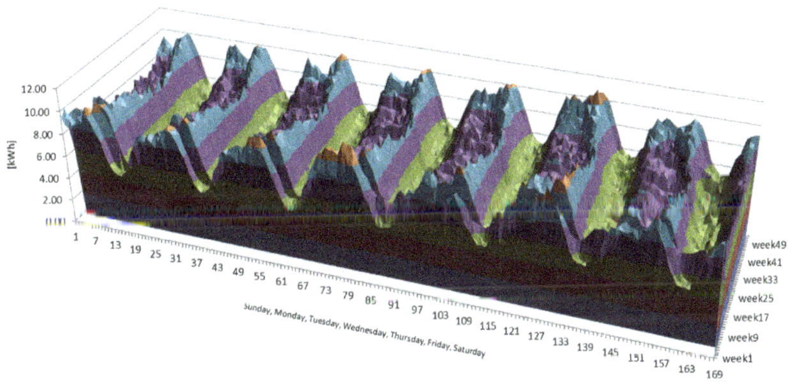

Figure 5. Weekly load curve in 2020 for rural consumers.

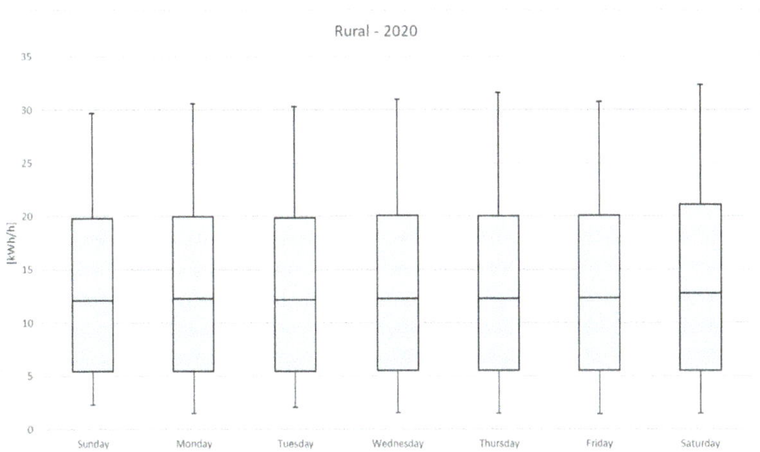

Figure 6. Box and whiskers plots for days of the week in 2020 (rural).

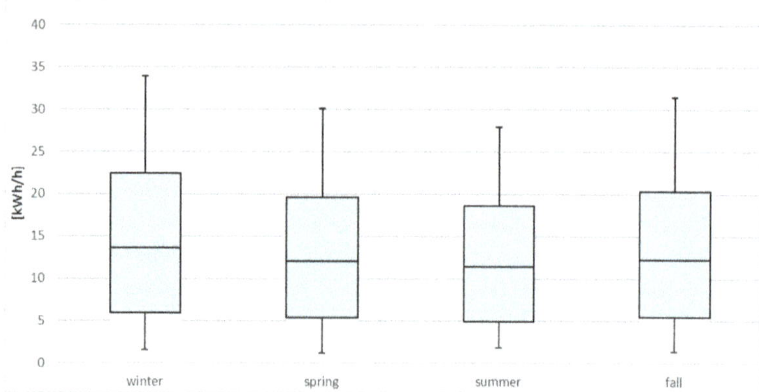

Figure 7. Box and whiskers plots for hourly consumption in each season in 2020 (rural).

In comparing the weekday consumption for rural and urban RBCR, the differences were due to the specific activities that take place in rural areas (Figure 8). While the urban consumption on weekdays (Monday to Friday) showed a bell shape, the rural chart showed a flattened reversed bell. While the most active days in terms of electric energy consumption seemed to take place on Wednesdays in the urban areas, in the rural ones the highest consumption was associated with Fridays [14].

Figure 8. Rural vs. urban weekly consumption patterns.

The weekend daily consumption pattern was relatively similar for urban and rural consumers in the regard that the consumption was lower on Saturday and higher on Sunday. The increase in Sunday consumption was bigger for the urban RBCRs. The same load profile was seen in all other countries' consumers that were analyzed [17] with a higher consumption on Sunday vs. Saturday [14].

A particularity of the rural RCBR is that it stands out of the large EU patterns identified in previous studies [17], with less consumption on Saturday relative to Friday. This particularity could be a good asset in forecasting and deploying power network resources.

With regard to the meteorological season's consumption pattern, we can see that the county is similar to the other EU countries covered so far in previous studies [17] with a good correlation with the day degree influence factor. The seasonal consumption pattern was more closely related to that of Italy and Hungary than that of Ireland and the UK [14].

The gap in summer consumption in seasonal analysis was steeper for the rural RBCR consumers (Figure 9). We associate this finding with a poor penetration of air-conditioning cooling devices in rural areas. In addition, in comparison to previous studies [17], we can see that this consumption was increased in the winter not due to electrical heating but mainly to the lower availability of natural light and the movement of activities indoors.

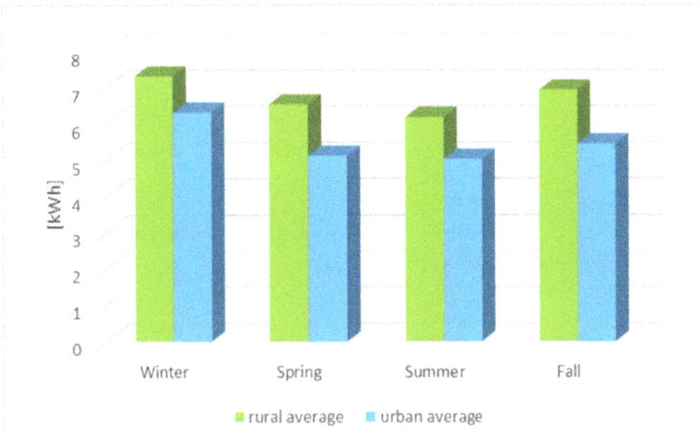

Figure 9. Rural vs. urban meteorological season consumption patterns.

The differences in consumption patterns could be connected to energy-related education levels [18] and with poor market availability of smart meters and hourly billing for RBCRs.

In previous research [2] we found that identifying, analyzing and clustering consumer types can have a very good outcome in modeling and forecasting short-term and medium-term power consumption. These findings have implications in assessing and developing commercial electric energy prices.

The database used in this study was extracted from a public national database [19]

3. Methodology

Although most of the research on load forecasting is on advance forecasting techniques, decision-making revolves around classical forecasting methods: moving average, linear regression and multiple linear regression [20]. We assess three methods of forecasting for atypical consumption behavior: linear regression (LR), autoregressive integrated moving average (ARIMA) and Artificial Neural Network (ANN). Previous estimations performed with fuzzy forecasting methods gave high errors [21], so we did not include fuzzy forecasting in this study.

The first steps were digesting the database and preparing it for deeper understanding and ease of mathematical modeling. Influence factor databases were also added and filtered, including the weather database and the weekly and daily databases containing socio-cultural and economic activity milestones. The database was a fixed one, and none of the methods used was trained to update in real time with an expanding database.

3.1. Database Filtering for Outlier Values and Noise Removal

A relatively simple filter to remove outlier values was constructed. The limit of the outlier value was stated at six times the mean value. First, 25 outlier values in each database were double-checked and manually confirmed [14,22,23].

$$\varepsilon(x) = \overline{x}\ of\ x_0;\ if\ \varepsilon(x) \geq\leq \varepsilon\ (6m),\ x = m \tag{1}$$

where:

x is the actual value,
m is the mean value.

3.2. Correlation of Database Values with the Exterior Influence Factors

We used a standard correlation model for a yearly database [2]:

$$r = Correl(x, y) = \frac{\sum_{0}^{i=8760}(x_i - \overline{x})(y_i - \overline{y})}{\sqrt{\sum_{0}^{i=8760}(x_i - \overline{x})^2(y_i - \overline{y})^2}} \tag{2}$$

where x is the actual power database value and $\overline{x}$ is the average of similar temporal values, e.g., same time interval of the same day of the week in the same season; y is the actual meteorological/daylight database value and $\overline{y}$ is the average of similar temporal values.

3.3. Linear Regression

The first forecasting in each line of estimation was carried out with the industry's most commonly used method [20]:

$$\hat{y}(t) = a_0 + \sum_{i=1}^{n} a_i x_i(t) + r(t) \tag{3}$$

where:

$y(t)$ is value at time t to be forecasted;
$x1(t)$ represents the influence factors;
$r(t)$ is the residual load at t;
a_i is the regression parameter.

3.4. Autoregressive Integrated Moving Average

Having a proven higher efficiency in forecasting data highly related with human activities and behavior [24,25], we used as the second forecasting method the ARIMA technique:

$$X_t - \alpha_1 X_{t-1} - \cdots - \alpha_{p'} X_{t-p'} = \varepsilon_t + \theta_1 X\varepsilon_{t-1} + \cdots + \theta_q X\varepsilon_{t-q} \tag{4}$$

where:

X_t represents the time series data;
α_i represents the parameters of the autoregressive part of the model;
θ_i represents the parameters of the moving average part;
ε_t is the error term.

3.5. Artificial Neural Network

Available on a large scale and easy to train and use, the ANN method is the first weapon of choice after regression techniques. We used a multilevel ANN (feed forward) including gradient descent and backpropagation algorithms by minimizing error with a non-Euclidean-type function. Multilevel feed forward networks are trained via supervised methods involving the use of training instances of the form (X^p, t^p)

$X^p = (X^p{}_1, X^p{}_2, \ldots, X^p{}_N)$ is the input vector for the training p;
$t^p = (t^p{}_1, t^p{}_2, \ldots, t^p{}_M)$ is the desired output vector for p;
N is the number of input units of the network;
M is the number of output units.

If $F(X)$ is the function processing the problem as per input X:

$$t^p = F(X^p) \tag{5}$$

then the output by processing the input data using neural network is defined by:

$$O^p = (O^p{}_1, O^p{}_2, \ldots, O^p{}_M) \tag{6}$$

where O^p is the result of processing of the input, X^p, by using the function $Fw(w;X^p)$ network applied as an approximation of $F(X)$, so:

$$O^p = Fw(w;X^p) \tag{7}$$

The error recorded during processing through the network of the input vector X^p—i.e., the measured error in a unit of output U_j—defined by e_j^p is expressed as the difference between desired and actual output achieved:

$$e_j{}^p = t_j{}^p - O_j{}^p \tag{8}$$

Error E^p, recorded during the processing through the network of the input vector X^p and established across the whole neural network, is obtained by combining the error e_j^p based on a relationship of the form:

$$E^p = \sum_{j=1}^{M} f\left(e_j^p\right) \tag{9}$$

For error calculation the E^p error and zero based log sigmoid function are used:

$$f(x) = \frac{e^{a+bx}}{1+e^{a+bx}} \tag{10}$$

3.6. Forecasting Error Assesing with Mean Absolute Percentage Error (MAPE)

Usually, the assessment of forecasting errors is conducted with two or three indicators, such as Mean Absolute Error (MAE) and MAPE of Root Mean Square Error (RMSE), but taking into consideration that the average values for rural and urban consumption per household differed significantly [14] we used only the MAPE to evaluate forecasting method accuracy.

$$MAPE = \frac{1}{N}\sum_{i=1}^{N}\frac{\left|P_i - \overline{P}_i\right|}{P_i}100\% \tag{11}$$

where P_i is the power value at time I, $\overline{P}_i$ is the forecasted power value for time i and N is the number of the forecasted value.

3.7. Trigger/Alarm for Atypical Consumption Behavior in Near Future

An unpredictable and unexpected event that is related to human behavior as consumption has very limited available information that can be used in forecasting [26,27].

We assume that such an event will not be visible prior to occurrence in available databases. Therefore, we must rely on big data analytics [28] and identify a threshold using methods other than the Twitter analytics proposed in [28] that can raise the alarm for the next STLF. Behind every forecast, there is a human operator that makes sure the database is delivered correctly, and this method would first check the assumptions that are made. Knowing that all human activities are subject to error, we must try to deploy an automatic trigger that raises an alarm based on an explosion of breaking news, such that the human operator could address this alarm and decide if action is needed or if the forecast should be deployed as before [29,30].

3.8. Steps to Identify the Best Forecasting Method under Atypical Consumer Behavior

The recommended way to address a forecast, and afterwards forecast under atypical behavior, is stated hereunder:

1. Database presentation, including specific, known influence factors;
2. Database filtering, denoising and outlier value removal;
3. Identification of sensitivity of consumer behavior to influence factors (weather, socio-economic activities, etc.) by correlation;
4. Deploying multiple forecasting algorithms and identifying the most accurate one for the specific database;
5. Setting up a trigger/alarm for future atypical consumption behavior;
6. Deploying forecasting methods adapted for the atypical event;
7. Identifying best practices and disseminating them.

All these steps should take into consideration that each database has its particularities, and these steps should address each and every one of them, e.g.: one deployment for weekdays and a separate one for weekend days, separate deployments for winter and summer, etc.

4. Case Analysis

Applying the steps mentioned in Section 3.8, the returned results were as follows:

1. The few outlier values identified were removed by the filtering algorithm.
2. The database had high fidelity and we encountered few outlier values, under 0.02% (0 or close to 0, or unusually high, more than six times the load peak value);
3. We assessed the correlation between the influence factors, mainly weather and socio-cultural events, and consumption among rural consumers to be $r = -0.2797$ versus that among urban consumers, $r = -0.2651$;
4. In order to validate the correlation results we clustered the database by weekdays, one profile for each weekday, to identify characteristics and compare with similar consumption in the EU [17]. Clustering was also performed for meteorological seasons for the above-mentioned comparison;
5. The overall short-term load forecast (STLF) was performed over 2020 day by day, using the above-mentioned algorithms, and the results are described in the box and whiskers BW charts in Figure 10 for rural and Figure 11 for urban consumers. This forecast was carried out not taking into consideration the influence of the COVID-19 restrictions and lockdowns, just the usual influence factors and historic data.

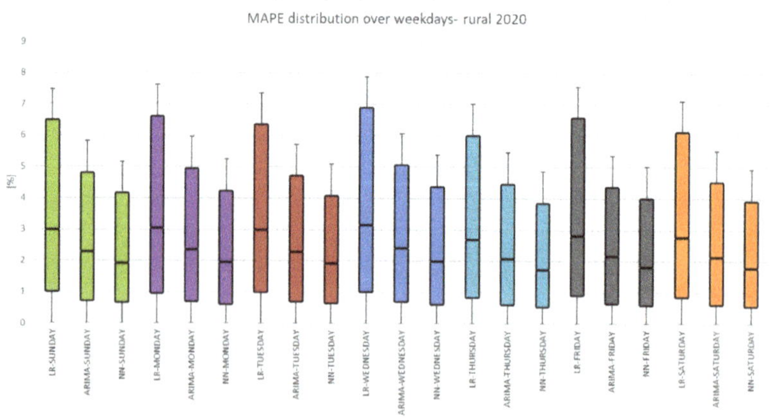

Figure 10. Overall forecasting results for rural consumers in 2020.

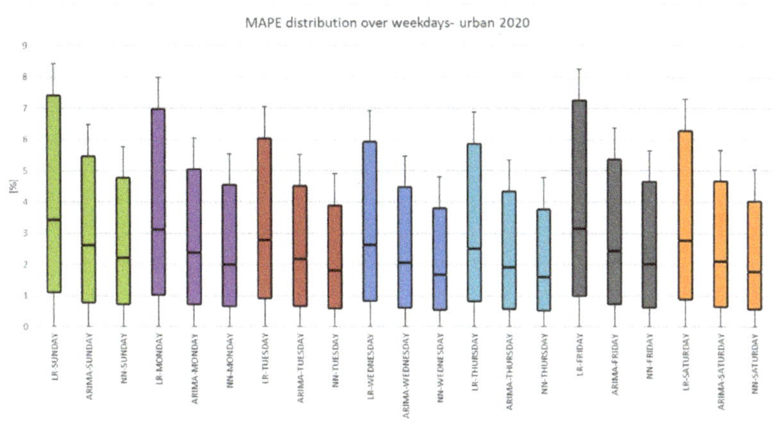

Figure 11. Overall forecasting results for urban consumers in 2020.

6. Examining the forecast for the first day of lockdown without any correction to the algorithm, we encountered very high values of MAPE, as shown in Table 1 and in Figures 12 and 13. Using the atypical consumer behavior alarm trigger, we could increase the forecast accuracy by altering the algorithm, as shown in Table 2, by adding weekend parameters—a combination of morning Saturday and afternoon Sunday—for the first weekday of lockdown; the first day of the lockdown in Bihor County, Romania, was a Tuesday, and as we say in Eastern Europe, Tuesday—three times bad luck [31]. This day provided a mix of bad luck and opportunity for power market participants and for the power grid operating personnel;
7. The effects of the second and subsequent lockdowns did not have such a big impact on the forecast accuracy relative to the preceding history of power load; the MAPE results were almost similar to a common forecast.

Table 1. MAPE results using the unaltered STLF algorithm.

STLF 24 March	MAPE LR [%]	MAPE ARIMA [%]	MAPE NN [%]
RURAL	4.6343	3.5849	2.9351
URBAN	5.3092	4.2102	3.3686

Table 2. MAPE results using the adapted STLF algorithm (TRIGGER ON).

STLF 24 March	MAPE LR [%]	MAPE ARIMA [%]	MAPE NN [%]
RURAL	1.7462	1.3848	1.1217
URBAN	1.7405	1.3802	1.1180

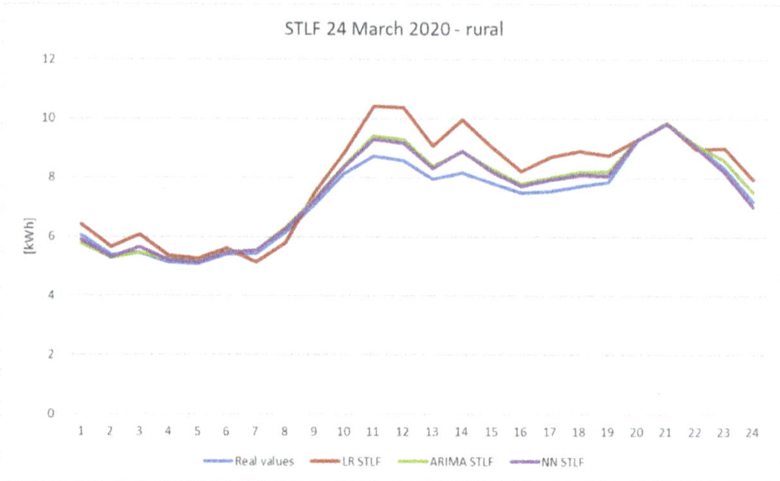

Figure 12. STLF results for 24th March 2020—rural consumers without the adapted algorithm.

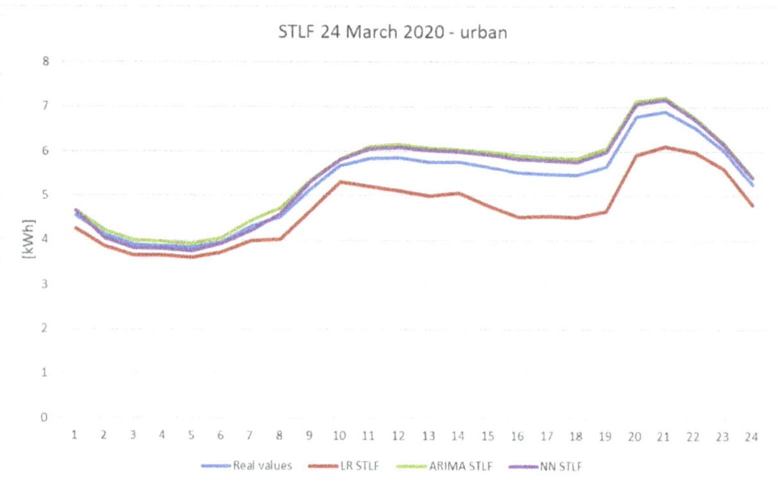

Figure 13. STLF results for 24th March 2020—urban consumers without the adapted algorithm.

5. Discussion

As all the STLF literature states, a deep understanding of the consumers analyzed or of the database modeled is critical in forecasting under atypical consumer behavior [18,32] or under power load black swan events [26].

The analyzed database was composed of multiyear data from rural (7k households) and urban consumers (23k households) in Bihor County, Romania and we managed to identify the social, economic and weather influence factors. The database contained nonresidential consumers at levels that did not influence the residential patterns, including small and medium enterprises (SME).

During this study, we found large gaps between the unaltered STLF algorithm and algorithms adapted to atypical consumption or unforeseen events

Previous studies [3–7] focused on algorithms for predicting outcomes with no historical database for a comparable situation. We tried to highlight the fact that for each unforeseen power load event or atypical behavior pattern, we should adapt the algorithm individually for each scenario. If for COVID-19 lockdown there was an easy fix, as the weekend historical consumption could be easily applied to all of the methods proposed, for other unforeseen events that cause atypical consumption behavior we need to identify scenarios and trends.

We plan to broaden our area of research by covering power load consumption unforeseen events at different layers of social, educational and economic levels and by analyzing different databases that encountered unforeseen events, e.g., the February 2021 Texas blackout, February 2014 Ukraine War, February 2020 market crash, 2021 global and European energy crisis, etc. As future research projects we aim to identify historical power load data that are related to unforeseen events and use them as a load forecast "library" for atypical consumption behavior as a cause of such events.

Regardless of the future conditions and state of the pandemic, its impact should be further studied in regard to the medium- and long-term load forecast (MTLF and LTLF), as COVID-19 more significantly affected other social and economic areas that have a relatively large impact on power consumption. Only working from home and online education, which prior to COVID-19 were merely exceptional cases, will become standard activities that might have a major impact on residential load consumption.

6. Conclusions

The three methods applied were deployed in a short period of time. The hardware configuration of the machine that generated the forecasts included 8 GB RAM, 500 GB SSD and an i5 Intel Processor. The LR and ARIMA methods were easy to use and adjust and could be modeled and tuned in Excel [14] (Microsoft Office 2019). For the ANN method R Statistics software's CRAN package was used. All analyzed methods output a good response to the influence factors with a retardation of one measurement or production data. We are certain that if a database of meteorological data collected from the immediate vicinity were available, we could increase the forecasting methods' accuracies by at least 0.5% (MAPE) for standard consumption data. The ANN method results, for this particular database, did not significantly improve after 100 epochs during the training process. The best results were obtained with seven hidden layers and 10 neurons in each hidden layer.

As we had available multiple metrics to evaluate our forecast, we used only MAPE because there was a significant difference between rural and urban household consumption (kWh) with an approximately 20% larger consumption in rural households.

The high reduction in MAPE of residential consumption on the first day of lockdown in Bihor County, Romania when the algorithm was adapted for the atypical consumption justifies the importance of this study; we had an overall MAPE = 4.0071% compared to the adapted algorithm MAPE = 1.4152%. This almost 3% difference in accuracy could have major economic effects on participants on the energy market. In [3] the results from the same country, but including a database that also contained commercial and industrial consumers, were relatively similar (MAPE) for the model adapted for pandemic effects, but our unadapted forecast method had a 2% to 3% higher MAPE. We conclude that residential consumers are highly sensitive to unforeseen events. We intend to focus our future research on a trigger algorithm that could automatically flag unforeseen events and atypical consumption behavior. This future focus may cover an algorithm for identifying an increase in information shared via social media related to energy consumption and its impact on the load curve, and use this to define the trigger to flag atypical or unforeseen power load consumption events. Also we intend to identify the influence of the level of education [33] and energy education in the power consumption response to atypical events.

Supplementary Materials: The following supporting information can be downloaded at: https://www.mdpi.com/article/10.3390/en15010291/s1.

Author Contributions: Conceptualization, F.C.D. and C.H.; methodology, F.C.D. and C.S.; software, F.C.D.; validation, C.H. and G.B.; formal analysis, C.S.; investigation, F.C.D.; resources, C.H.; data curation, F.C.D.; writing—original draft preparation, F.C.D.; visualization, C.H., G.B. and C.S.; supervision, C.H.; funding acquisition, C.H. All authors have read and agreed to the published version of the manuscript.

Funding: This research received no external funding.

Institutional Review Board Statement: Not applicable.

Informed Consent Statement: Not applicable.

Data Availability Statement: Not applicable.

Acknowledgments: Not applicable.

Conflicts of Interest: The authors declare no conflict of interest.

Abbreviations

ANN	artificial neural network
ARIMA	autoregressive integrated moving average
ARIMAX	Autoregressive Integrated Moving Average with Exogenous
CNN	convolutional neural network
EU	European Union
FCDNN	Fully Connected Deep Neural Network
GAM	Generalized Additive Models
GRU	Gated Recurrent Unit
LR	linear regression
LSTM	Long Short-Term Memory
LTLF	long-term load forecast
MAE	Mean Absolute Error
MAPE	Mean Absolute Percentage Error
MLR	multiple linear regression
MTLF	medium-term load forecast
NEPCO	National Electric Power Company
NY	New York
PJM	Pennsylvania, New Jersey, Maryland
RCBR	residential consumers in Bihor County, Romania
RMSE	Root Mean Square Error
SME	small and medium enterprise
SOM	system operator method
STLF	Short-term load forecasting
UK	United Kingdom
US	United States

References

1. Felea, I.; Goude, Y.; Dan, F. Electric energy forecast for the industrial consumers using neural network. *J. Sustain. Energy* **2011**, *2*, 89–94.
2. Felea, I.; Dan, F.; Dzitac, S. Consumers load profile classification corelated to the electric energy forecast. *Proc. Rom. Acad. Ser. A* **2011**, *13*, 80–88.
3. Tudose, A.M.; Picioroaga, I.I.; Sidea, D.O.; Bulac, C.; Boicea, V.A. Short-Term Load Forecasting Using Convolutional Neural Networks in COVID-19 Context: The Romanian Case Study. *Energies* **2021**, *14*, 4046. [CrossRef]
4. Wang, Z.; Hao, W. *Improving Load Forecast in Energy Markets during COVID-19*; Association for Computing Machinery: New York, NY, USA, 2021. [CrossRef]
5. Alasali, F.; Nusair, K.; Alhmoud, L.; Zarour, E. Impact of the COVID-19 Pandemic on Electricity Demand and Load Forecasting. *Sustainability* **2021**, *13*, 1435. [CrossRef]
6. Kozak, D.; Holladay, S.; Fasshauer, G. Intraday Load Forecasts with Uncertainty. *Energies* **2019**, *12*, 1833. [CrossRef]
7. Obst, D.; Vilmarest, J.; Goude, Y. Adaptive Methods for Short-Term Electricity Load Forecasting During COVID-19 Lockdown in France. *IEEE Trans. Power Syst.* **2021**, *36*, 4754–4763. [CrossRef]

8. COVID-19 Pandemic in Romania. Available online: https://en.wikipedia.org/wiki/COVID-19_pandemic_in_Romania (accessed on 21 November 2021).
9. Romania Announces Nationwide Lockdown Measures to Limit Spread of COVID-19. Available online: https://www.garda.com/crisis24/news-alerts/326626/romania-government-announces-lockdown-measures-on-march-25-update-2 (accessed on 21 November 2021).
10. Press Releases—Health Ministry—Bihor County Public Health Department. Available online: http://www.dspbihor.gov.ro/comunicatedepresa2020.html (accessed on 21 November 2021).
11. Press Releases—Bihor County Prefect Institution—Internal Affairs Ministry. Available online: https://bh.prefectura.mai.gov.ro/category/comunicate-de-presa/ (accessed on 21 November 2021).
12. One Corovanirus, 28 States: A Comparison of Anti-Covid-19 Measures Decided in Each EU Member State. Available online: https://cursdeguvernare.ro/tari-diferite-restrictii-diferite-o-comparatie-a-masurilor-anti-covid-19-decise-in-fiecare-stat-membru-ue.html (accessed on 21 November 2021).
13. Bihor County Population Assessment at 1 January 2020—INS—BIHOR County Statistics Department. Available online: https://bihor.insse.ro/wp-content/uploads/2020/05/Populatia-BH-la-1-ianuarie-2020.pdf (accessed on 21 November 2021).
14. Dan, F.C.; Hora, C.; Gligor, E.; Majoros, N.T. Identification of Load Profiles for Rural and Urban Consumers in Bihor County, Romania. In *Proceedings of the National Technical Scientific Conference, "Modern Technologies for the 3rd Millenium"*, 20th ed.; Editografica: Bologna, Italy, 2021.
15. Dumiter, A.F. Climate and Topoclimates of ORADEA. Ph.D. Thesis, University of Oradea, Oradea, Romania, 2007.
16. National Technical Standard: Order No. 386/2016 for Modification and Completing of Technical Reglementation "Normative Regarding the Thermotechnical Calculation of the Construction Elements of the Buildings", Indicative C 107-2005. Available online: http://www.stim.ugal.ro/crios/Support/IEACA/Anexe/C107-1-3-2005.pdf (accessed on 21 November 2021).
17. Kmetty, Z. Load Profile Classification, WP4—Classification of EU Residential Energy Consumers. *Technical Public Report*, January 2016. [CrossRef]
18. Kiss, J.F. Educational Policies in Relation to Society. *Stud. Teach. J. Teach. Train. Educ. Res.* **2020**, *1*, 43–50.
19. Transelectrica—Consumption Chart. Available online: https://www.transelectrica.ro/en/widget/web/tel/sen-grafic/-/SENGrafic_WAR_SENGraficportlet (accessed on 21 November 2021).
20. Top Four Types of Forecasting Methods. Available online: https://corporatefinanceinstitute.com/resources/knowledge/modeling/forecasting-methods/ (accessed on 21 November 2021).
21. Dan, F.C.; Hora, C.; Bendea, G. Short-Term Forecasting of Wind Power Generation. In Proceedings of the 2021 10th International Conference on ENERGY and ENVIRONMENT (CIEM), Bucharest, Romania, 14–15 October 2021.
22. Xiong, H.; Pandey, G.; Steinbach, M.; Kumar, V. Enhancing data analysis with noise removal. *IEEE Trans. Knowl. Data Eng.* **2006**, *18*, 304–319. [CrossRef]
23. Guo, G.; Wand, H.; Bell, D. Data Reduction and Noise Filtering for Predicting Times Series. In Proceedings of the Advances in Web-Age Information Management, Third International Conference, Beijing, China, 11–13 August 2002. [CrossRef]
24. Sabry, M.; Badra, N. Comparison Between Regression and Arima Models in Forecasting Traffic Volume. *Aust. J. Basic Appl. Sci.* **2007**, *1*, 126–136.
25. ARIMA Compared to Linear Regression, Introduction to Trading, Machine Learning & GCP, Online Video Course. Available online: https://www.coursera.org/lecture/introduction-trading-machine-learning-gcp/arima-compared-to-linear-regression-ZxJ11 (accessed on 21 November 2021).
26. Taleb, N.N. *The Black Swan: The Impact of the Highly Improbable*, 2nd ed.; Random House: New York, NY, USA, 2007.
27. Tan, L. *The Mandelbrot Set, Theme and Variations*; Cambridge University Press: Cambridge, UK, 2000; ISBN 978-0-521-77476-5.
28. Ali, Y. A Proposed Framework for Predicting Emergency Events Using Big Data Analytics. Ph.D. Thesis, Helwan University, Cairo, Egypt, 2021.
29. Lazer, D.; Baum, M.; Grinberg, N.; Friedland, L.; Joseph, K. Combating Fake News: An Agenda for Research and Action, Harvard Kennedy School, Northeastern University, 2017, US. Available online: https://apo.org.au/sites/default/files/resource-files/2017-05/apo-nid76233.pdf (accessed on 21 November 2021).
30. Conneau, A.; Schwenk, H.; Barrault, L.; Lecun, Y. Very Deep Convolutional Networks for Text Classification. *arXiv* **2016**, arXiv:1606.01781. Available online: https://arxiv.org/pdf/1606.01781.pdf (accessed on 21 November 2021).
31. Tuesday 13: Romania Tops Europe's Superstition Charts. Available online: https://www.romania-insider.com/tuesday-13-unlucky-for-some (accessed on 21 November 2021).
32. Blaga, A.C.; Gligor, E. Monoagent heating systems for solitary consumers. *J. Appl. Eng. Sci.* **2011**, *2*, 36–42.
33. Dan B.A.; Kovàcs, K.E. *The Link between Experiential Pedagogy and Community Schools in Community Building and Social Innovation*; Boros, J., Kozma, T., Markus, E., Eds.; Debrecen University Press: Debrecen, Hungary, 2021; pp. 12–25. ISBN 978-963-318-943-6.

energies

MDPI

Article

Applicability of Different Double-Layer Models for the Performance Assessment of the Capacitive Energy Extraction Based on Double Layer Expansion (CDLE) Technique

Zhi Zou [1], Longcheng Liu [1,2], Shuo Meng [2], Xiaolei Bian [1] and Yongmei Li [3,*]

[1] Department of Chemical Engineering and Technology, Royal Institute of Technology, 10044 Stockholm, Sweden; zhizou@kth.se (Z.Z.); lliu@ket.kth.se (L.L.); xiaoleib@kth.se (X.B.)
[2] School of Nuclear Science and Technology, University of South China, Hengyang 421001, China; shuom@usc.edu.cn
[3] School of Resource & Environment and Safety Engineering, University of South China, Hengyang 421001, China
* Correspondence: lymusa8866@163.com

Abstract: Capacitive energy extraction based on double layer expansion (CDLE) is a renewable method of harvesting energy from the salinity difference between seawater and freshwater. It is based on the change in properties of the electric double layer (EDL) formed at the electrode surface when the concentration of the solution is changed. Many theoretical models have been developed to describe the structural and thermodynamic properties of the EDL at equilibrium, e.g., the Gouy–Chapman–Stern (GCS), Modified Poisson–Boltzmann–Stern (MPBS), modified Donnan (mD) and improved modified Donnan (i-mD) models. To evaluate the applicability of these models, especially the rationality and the physical interpretation of the parameters that were used in these models, a series of single-pass and full-cycle experiments were performed. The experimental results were compared with the numerical simulations of different EDL models. The analysis suggested that, with optimized parameters, all the EDL models we examined can well explain the equilibrium charge–voltage relation of the single-pass experiment. The GCS and MPBS models involve, however, the use of physically unreasonable parameter values. By comparison, the i-mD model is the most recommended one because of its accuracy in the results and the meaning of the parameters. Nonetheless, the i-mD model alone failed to simulate the energy production of the full-cycle CDLE experiments. Future research regarding the i-mD model is required to understand the process of the CDLE technique better.

Keywords: CapMix; CDLE; electric double layer; salinity difference energy; modified Donnan

Citation: Zou, Z.; Liu, L.; Meng, S.; Bian, X.; Li, Y. Applicability of Different Double-Layer Models for the Performance Assessment of the Capacitive Energy Extraction Based on Double Layer Expansion (CDLE) Technique. *Energies* **2021**, *14*, 5828. https://doi.org/10.3390/en14185828

Academic Editor: Marcin Kamiński

Received: 16 August 2021
Accepted: 12 September 2021
Published: 15 September 2021

1. Introduction

The rapid economic development has led to increasingly serious conflict between resources and the environment, which forced the world to search for sustainable and green energy to substitute traditional energy [1–3]. One promising and reliable opinion is to extract energy from the salinity difference between seawater and freshwater. It is based firmly on the fact that when two solutions with different salinity are mixed, the entropy of the system will increase, which can be captured and converted into electrical energy [4]. Theoretically, about 2.5 MJ of free energy could be generated by controlled mixing of 1 m^3 river water with a large amount of seawater. The global potential for energy extraction from the world coast would, then, reach 2 TW of power, which satisfies around 20% of the world's energy demand [5,6].

By considering the tremendous amount of energy available from salinity difference, some techniques were proposed to harvest this energy. The pressure-retarded osmosis (PRO) [7,8] and reverse electrodialysis (RED) [9] are two advanced techniques and have been demonstrated at a pilot scale [7,10]. In PRO, the seawater and freshwater are separated by a semi-permeable membrane, which drives water from the freshwater to permeate into the more concentrated seawater due to the difference in osmotic pressure. The expanding volume of the seawater can be depressurized through a hydroturbine to generate electricity. In RED, the solutions with different salt concentrations flow alternately in compartments, which are separated by a stack of positively and negatively charged ion-exchange membrane. The ion diffusion across the membranes generates a current that can be extracted [10,11]. Up to now, the highest reported power density for PRO and RED are around 10 and 1 W/m^2, respectively [12]. Although significant progress has been made in both PRO and RED, the drawbacks of these techniques are also obvious, including the high cost and short lifetime of membranes, as well as the use of additional converters (hydroturbine in PRO) for effectively producing electricity. These drawbacks hampered the commercialization of both PRO and RED techniques and drive researchers to develop new technologies, such as Capacitive mixing (CapMix).

The so-called CapMix is an innovative technology that was recently introduced for extracting energy from salinity differences. It is the common name for several electrode-based technologies [13–16], including Capacitive energy extraction based on Double Layer Expansion (CDLE), Capacitive energy extraction based on Donnan Potential (CDP) and Soft Electrode technique (SE). In CDLE, the porous electrodes are first charged in salty water by an external power source and then discharged in fresh water; this process leads to an electrical double layer (EDL) expansion and results in an increase in electric potential. In CDP, the porous electrodes are covered by ion-exchange membranes, which only allow anion or cation to pass through and thus generates a Donnan potential difference across the membrane. In the SE technique, instead of using membranes in CDP, the electrodes are made of an activated carbon core together with a polyelectrolyte layer, either cationic or anionic. The major disadvantage of CapMix is the intermittent power production as well as the low power density, and the largest reported power density for CDLE, CDP and SE are 35, 105 and 50 mW/m^2, respectively.

Among the techniques of the CapMix family, CDLE is the earliest technique that was first proposed and implemented experimentally by Brogioli [13] in 2009. It is the simplest one in terms of structure, composed of two electrodes that are parallel to each other and a spacer serving as a channel for water flowing through the cell without the use of ion-exchange membranes. The performance of the CDLE technique is dependent on the properties of the electrodes, cell structure as well as operation method. In the study of material properties, Iglesias et al. [17] investigated the effect of carbon wettability and pore size distribution on the performance of CDLE and found that electrodes with hydrophilized material improve the energy production of CDLE. They also concluded that activated carbon with a predominant pore population in the 1 nm region gives an optimum result. In another study about the effects of pore sizes of the porous electrode, Nasir et al. [18] also suggested that the optimum average pore diameter of electrodes for CDLE is about 1 nm. Furthermore, Iglesias et al. [19] investigated the possibility of stacking individual CDLE cells in series to increase energy production. They found that multiple cells in series might increase the potential rise and that such an increase is limited and cannot compensate for the increase in internal resistance. The influence of the operation conditions, such as the flow velocity and the solution temperature, on the performance of CDLE, was also investigated. It was reported that a higher flow rate might lead to an improvement in the power production of CDLE [18] and that by controlled mixing solutions with different temperatures, the potential rise can be maximized, and thus the energy production can be increased [20].

By following experimental works, theoretical studies were also conducted over the years to provide a platform for identifying the influences of different parameters on the CDLE process. The theoretical models in CDLE focus mainly on the description of thermodynamic properties of EDL as well as the transport of ions inside the porous electrode. Among different equilibrium models, the Gouy–Chapman–Stern (GCS) model has been widely used to simulate the thermodynamic CDLE cycle [18,21–23]. This model is simple but does not account for the effects of EDL overlap and the finite size of the ions. To remedy this problem, Jiménez et al. [24] developed a modified Possion–Boltzmann–Stern (MPBS) model and applied it to predict the maximum energy production of CDLE. It was also extended to consider the influences of multi-ionic solutions and cylindrical pores, suggesting that the presence of multivalent ions would reduce the net energy gain in a CDLE cycle [25].

The model for the description of EDL at equilibrium alone cannot be applied to describe the dynamic behavior of CDLE cells. It should, in principle, be coupled with ionic and current transport models to give a fully quantitative description of the complex mechanisms affecting the performance of the CDLE as performed by Rica et al. [26,27]. The dynamic model originally proposed by Rica et al. [27] was based on a 1D theory that was developed by Biesheuvel and Bazant [28] with the use of the GCS model. It was later found that by using a modified Donnan (mD) model instead, the kinetics of ionic transport and adsorption in the CDLE could be better described in the cases where the EDLs are overlapped within the micropores of the electrodes.

For whatever purpose, an accurate description of the structural and the thermodynamic properties of the EDL at equilibrium is essential in understanding the behavior of CDLE cells. In the literature, however, the use of different EDL models in the study of CDLE is somehow arbitrary without giving a detailed discussion on the applicability of the models, especially the rationality and the physical interpretation of the relevant parameters contained in the models, even though these models have been successfully applied in many works [19,22,23]. However, the physical meaning behind the parameters is important for better understand the thermodynamic properties of the EDLs. Mainly, for this reason, we strive to highlight the physical differences between some commonly used EDL models and then evaluate the applicability of different EDL models for the performance assessment of the CDLE technique.

The remainder of this contribution is organized as follows. In the next section, a brief description is provided of the experiment setup and the operation scheme. Then, a detailed elaboration of different EDL models is made in Section 3. The comparison between the experimental results with the simulations of different EDL models is then presented in Section 4, followed by physical interpretations of the parameters used in the models and a discussion on the models' applicability. The contribution ends with concluding remarks.

2. Materials and Methods

In order to investigate the performance of the CDLE cells and also explore the applicability of different EDL models in the description of CDLE behaviors, a series of experiments were made using the setup shown in Figure 1.

2.1. Materials

The slurry of activated carbon was made by mixing commercial activated carbon power (YP-50F, Kuraray Chemical Company, Tokyo, Japan) with a polyvinylidene fluoride binder (Kynar HSV 900 PVDF, Arkema, France) at a ratio of 90:10 wt%. The mixture was dispersed in N-methylpyrrolidone (NMP, 99%, Sigma Aldrich, Milwaukee WI, USA) and was stirred for 12 h to form a homogeneous slurry. It was then cast on a titanium plate and dried in an oven at 80 °C for 2 h to form the carbon sheet electrode. Each electrode had a size of 30 mm × 60 mm and a total weight of about 0.08 g.

The structure of raw activated carbon and the fabricated electrode was both determined by the nitrogen adsorption/desorption isotherm (Micromeritics ASAP 2000) that was based on the Brunauer–Emmett–Teller (BET) method. The average pore diameter and pore volume were estimated by the Barrett–Joyner–Halenda (BJH) method and t-plot method, respectively. The experimental results are listed in Table 1; note that the pore thickness (H_p) is defined as the ratio of the micropores' volume (V_{micro}) to the microporous area (S_{micro}) [28]. As seen in Table 1, there are reductions in some structural parameters of the fabricated electrode (including the specific surface area, micropore surface area, total volume and micropore volume) compared to the same parameters of raw activated carbon. The reason for this may be attributed to the PVDF binder in the fabricated electrode. Nevertheless, there is not much difference in the average pore diameter between activated carbon and fabricated electrode.

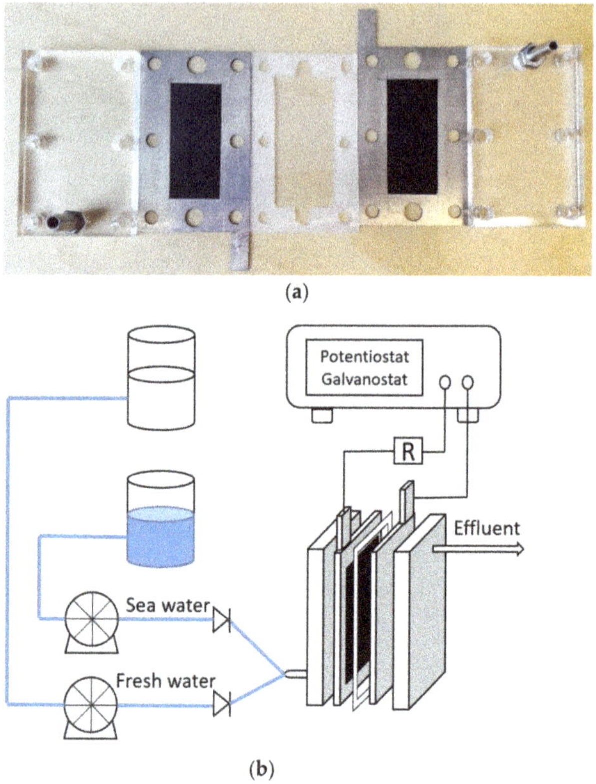

Figure 1. (**a**) Photograph of the CDLE cell, from left to right: acrylic plate, titanium current collector with electrode, silica gel tablet, titanium current collector with electrode, acrylic plate. (**b**) Schematic of the CDLE experiment setup.

Table 1. The specific surface area (S_{BET}), microporous surface area measurement (S_{micro}), total volume of pores (V_{tot}), volume of micropores (V_{micro}), characteristic pore thickness (H_p) and average pore diameter (D_{BJH}) results of activated carbon and electrode.

Materials	S_{BET} **(m²/g)**	S_{micro} **(m²/g)**	V_{tot} **(cm³/g)**	V_{micro} **(cm³/g)**	H_p **(nm)**	D_{BJH} **(nm)**
Raw Activated Carbon	1659.457	1176.362	0.835	0.502	0.427	3.805
Fabricated Electrode	1272.124	906.254	0.649	0.387	0.427	4.043

With the fabricated electrodes, the CDLE cell was also self-made. As illustrated in Figure 1 for the structure and component, it was composed of two rectangular acrylic plates, one pair of activated carbon electrodes, one pair of titanium current collectors and a hollow silica gel tablet with a thickness of 0.5 mm that form a flow channel between two electrodes.

2.2. Operations

Our experiments consist of two parts: (i) a single-pass experiment with a constant voltage charge and (ii) a full-cycle experiment.

As schematically shown in Figure 1b, the experimental setup consists of two containers for fresh and seawater, respectively, two peristaltic pumps (BT100J-1A, HUIYU WEIYE Fluid Equipment Co., Ltd., Beijing, China), a CDLE cell and a potentiostat (PGSTAT30, Metrohm Autolab, Utrecht, The Netherlands) that is used to maintain a constant voltage between the electrodes and measure the change in current.

Before each experiment, the electrodes were short-circuited to ensure that no external charge was left on the electrodes, and the cell was fully flushed by deionized water until the effluent conductivity reached a stable value. The details of the two sets of experiments are summarized in what follows.

(i) Single-pass experiment: The experiments were performed in a single pass mode to investigate the amount of total charge stored on activated electrodes at equilibrium, using NaCl solution with a concentration of 5, 20, 100, 200 and 600 mM, respectively. It consists of two steps. In the charge step, a fixed electrical voltage (0.1 to 1.0 V) was applied to the cell when the feed solution was continuously passing through the cells. The charged positive and negative ions in the solution were then adsorbed into the EDL that was formed near the electrode surface, and as a result of the movement of charged ions, an electric current was generated. This step continued until an equilibrium state was reached. The total electrode charge per mass Q (C/g) can, therefore, be calculated by integrating the electric current I over the charging time t(s) and then divided by the mass of total electrodes in the cell m_{elec}, as [29]:

$$Q = \frac{\int I dt}{m_{elec}} \tag{1}$$

Following the charge step, a zero voltage is immediately applied over a sufficiently long time to remove any ions adsorbed in the electrodes.

To illustrate how the current varies with time in the charge and discharge steps, we show in Figure 2 the current profiles obtained at $V_{ext} = 0.2$, 0.6 and 1.0 V with a solution concentration of 600 mM. It is seen clearly that the current I dropped quickly at the initial stage of charging. After around 100 s, the electrodes were nearly saturated with charged ions as the electric current I of the circuit has reached a stable value that closes to zero. At this moment, the cell could be deemed to reach an equilibrium state.

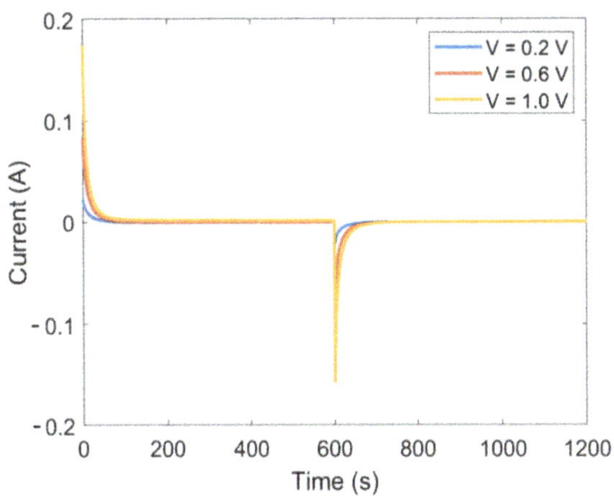

Figure 2. Electrical current as a function of time during the charging and discharging step. The applied voltage $V = 0.2$, 0.6 and 1.0 V, solution concentration $c = 600$ mM.

The small electric current at the end of the charging step is known as the leakage current I_{lea}, and it should be subtracted from the measured current I_{mea} to give the net current $I = I_{mea} - I_{lea}$, used in calculating the electrode charge Q at equilibrium in Equation (1).

(ii) Full-cycle experiment: in this set of experiments, we used 20 mM and 600 mM NaCl solutions as the freshwater and seawater, respectively. These solutions were supplied intermittently to the CDLE cell by a peristaltic pump at a flow rate of 10 mL/min. To harvest the energy, we connect an external resistance R_{ext} = 100 Ω to the cell. As a result, the voltage across the cell can be calculated by: $V = V_{ext} - I{\cdot}R_{ext}$.

A complete cycle CDLE process consists of four steps (Figure 3). In step 1, the circuit was closed, and the cell, immersed with seawater, was charged by a fixed voltage V_{ext} (0.2 to 0.9 V) until the cell potential V becomes equal to V_{ext}. This is followed by step 2, the circuit was opened, and the freshwater was pumped into the cell to replace the seawater until the cell potential increased to a stable value (V_{fresh}). Then in Step 3, the circuit was closed, and the cell was discharged at the same external voltage V_{ext} as it in Step 1, this step continued until the cell potential V decreases to the V_{ext}. Finally in Step 4, the freshwater in the cell was replaced by the seawater until the cell potential V declined to a stable value (V_{salt}). The surface area enclosed in the cycle in Figure 3 represents, therefore, the extracted energy, i.e.,

$$W = \oint V(Q)dQ. \tag{2}$$

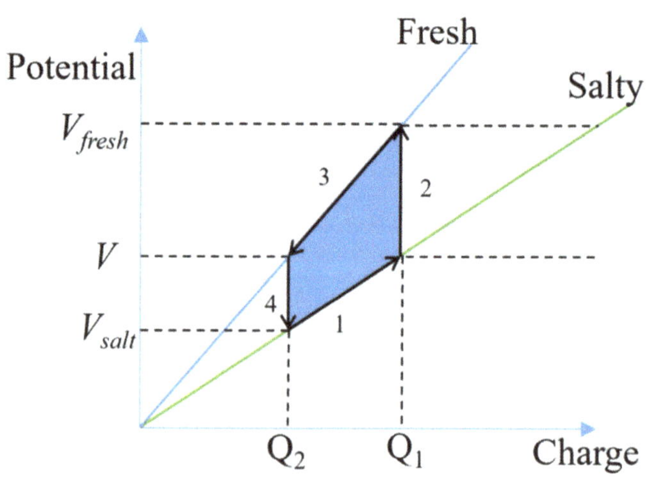

Figure 3. Schematic of the relation between the cell potential and the electrode charge at one CDLE cycle.

The corresponding $V - t$ profile is exemplified in Figure 4a for the case of $V_{ext} = 0.2$ V, which shows that the equilibrium cell potential can only reach 0.185 V due to the use of a large external resistance load in the circuit. The result with respect to the $Q - V$ cycle is shown in Figure 4b, which mimics closely the theoretical plot in Figure 3 and therefore suggests the success of our experiments.

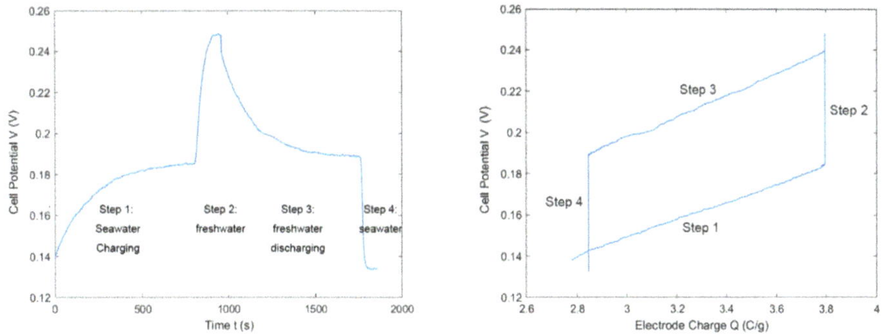

(a) (b)

Figure 4. A full CDLE cycle at the applied voltage V_{ext} = 0.2V, R_{ext} = 100 Ω, c_{fresh} = 20 mM, c_{sea} = 600 mM. (**a**) Cell potential V as a function of time t; (**b**) cell potential V as a function of electrode charge Q.

3. Theory of Electrical Double Layers

The mechanism behind CDLE is the formation of EDL near the electrode surface and the change in the properties of EDL when the concentration of the solution is changed. Therefore, a proper description of the structural and thermodynamic properties of EDLs at equilibrium is of great importance for understanding the performance of the CDLE technique. For this reason, we may start with a summary of the basic assumptions and simplifications about activated carbon electrodes when applying different EDL models. These include [30–33]:

(i) the electrodes are symmetric, meaning that the applied voltage is equally distributed over each electrode and the adsorption amount of the anion in the anode is equal to that of cation in cathode;

(ii) The electric potential of the anode is opposite to that of the cathode in sign but is equal in magnitude;

(iii) the adsorbed ions are positioned only on the surface of electrode particles, meaning that they cannot become part of the electrode matrix.

With these common considerations, different EDL models have been developed over the years to remedy the inherent defects of the Poisson–Boltzmann theory, as shown schematically in Figure 5 and detailed in what follows for the GCS, MPBS and mD models, respectively.

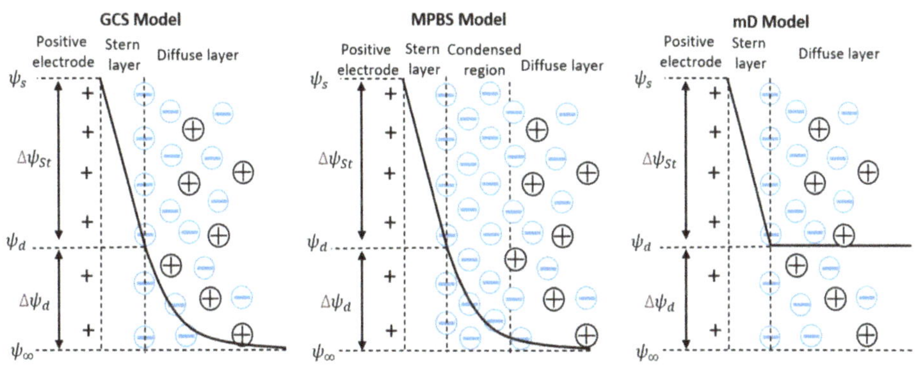

Figure 5. Schematic view of GCS, MPBS and mD models.

3.1. Gouy–Chapmann–Stern Model

The GCS model is the simplest extension of the PB theory in accounting for the effect of the finite size of ions. As illustrated Figure 5, it conceptualizes the structure of EDLs near the electrode surface as being composed of two layers: (i) a compact Stern layer where the ions are immobile and strongly adsorbed to the electrode surface, with a thickness corresponding to the closest approach of hydrated ions to the electrode surface; (ii) a diffuse layer where thermal motion causes the ions to be spread out in space.

It follows that no free charges exist in the Stern layer, while the distribution of ions in the diffuse layer can still be described by the Boltzmann equation, i.e.,

$$n_i = n_{i,\infty} \exp\left(-\frac{z_i e \psi}{k_B T}\right) \tag{3}$$

where ψ is the electric potential (V), $n_{i,\infty}$ is number density ($1/\text{m}^3$) of the ith species at the bulk solution, e is the elementary charge (C), z_i is the valence of the ith species and k_B is the Boltzmann constant (J/K), respectively.

The distribution of electric potential can, therefore, be described by the Poisson equation as

$$\nabla \times (\varepsilon_0 \varepsilon_r \nabla \psi) = -e \sum\nolimits_i z_i n_i \tag{4}$$

where ε_0 and ε_r are the free space permittivity and the relative permittivity of the electrolyte solutions, ∇ is the divergence operator.

As a result, the GCS model can be expressed as:

$$\nabla^2 \psi = \begin{cases} 0 & \text{in Stern layer} \\ -\frac{e}{\varepsilon_0 \varepsilon_r} \sum z_i n_{i,\infty} \exp\left(-\frac{z_i e \psi}{k_B T}\right) & \text{in Difuse layer} \end{cases} \tag{5}$$

subject to the following boundary conditions:

$$\psi|_{x=0} = \psi_s \tag{6}$$

$$\psi|_{x=\delta^-} = \psi|_{x=\delta^+} \tag{7}$$

$$\left.\frac{d\psi}{dx}\right|_{x=\delta^-} = \left.\frac{d\psi}{dx}\right|_{x=\delta^+} \tag{8}$$

$$\psi|_{x\to\infty} = 0 \tag{9}$$

where x is the normal distance from the electrode surface, δ is the thickness of the Stern layer and ψ_s is the surface potential, ∇^2 is the Laplace operator.

The GCS model, as given above, is quite general in that it can be applied to electrode particles with any geometry immersed in any electrolyte solution and can readily be solved numerically to obtain the relation between the surface potential ψ_s and the surface charge σ_s. When used in practice, however, it is commonly assumed that the particle is of planar geometry and that the electrolyte is symmetric. For this special case, the analytical solution to the GCS model can be obtained to give the profile of electric potential ψ as a function of x,

$$\psi = \begin{cases} \psi_s - \Delta\psi_{St} \times x/\delta & \text{in Stern layer} \\ \frac{4k_B T}{e} \tan\text{h}^{-1}\left(\frac{e\Delta\psi_d}{k_B T}\right) exp\left(\frac{x-\delta}{\lambda_D}\right) & \text{in Diffuse layer} \end{cases} \tag{10}$$

with the Debye length λ_D given by:

$$\lambda_D = \sqrt{\frac{\varepsilon_0 \varepsilon_r k_B T}{2e^2 n_{i,\infty}}} \tag{11}$$

where $\Delta\psi_{St}$ is the electric potential drop across the Stern layer, $\Delta\psi_{St} = \psi_s - \psi_d$, $\Delta\psi_d$ is the electric potential difference across the diffuse layer, $\Delta\psi_d = \psi_d - \psi_\infty$ and ψ_d and ψ_∞ are the electric potential at the outer Stern plane and in the bulk solution, respectively.

It follows from Gauss' law that the surface charge σ_s can be related to both $\Delta\psi_{St}$ and $\Delta\psi_d$ as

$$\sigma_s = -\varepsilon_0\varepsilon_r\left(\frac{d\psi}{dx}\right)\bigg|_{x=0} = -\varepsilon_0\varepsilon_r\frac{\Delta\psi_{St}}{\delta} = \sqrt{8n_\infty\varepsilon_0\varepsilon_r k_B T}\sin h\left(\frac{ze\Delta\psi_d}{2k_B T}\right) \tag{12}$$

The total differential capacitance of the double layer, C, can then be given by

$$\frac{1}{C} = \frac{1}{C_{St}} + \frac{1}{C_d} \tag{13}$$

where C_{st} and C_d are the differential capacitances to the Stern layer and the diffuse layer, respectively, with

$$C_{St} = -\frac{d\sigma_s}{d\Delta\psi_{St}} = \frac{\varepsilon_0\varepsilon_r}{\delta} \tag{14}$$

and

$$C_d = -\frac{d\sigma_s}{d\Delta\psi_d} = \frac{\varepsilon_0\varepsilon_r}{\lambda_D}\cos h\left(\frac{ze\Delta\psi_d}{2k_B T}\right) \tag{15}$$

As a result, the surface charge density σ_s from Equation (12) can also be written as a product of $\Delta\psi_{St}$ and C_{St}, i.e.,

$$\sigma_s = -\Delta\psi_{St} \times C_{St} \tag{16}$$

3.2. Modified Poisson–Boltzmann–Stern Model

The GCS model accounts for the effect of the finite size of ions only in the Stern layer but treats the ions in the diffuse layer still as point-charges. In the case of high ion concentration and high surface potential, however, the interfacial region can be largely enriched in counterions to the extent that the point charge hypothesis for the EDL structure leads to unrealistically high counterion concentrations in the vicinity of the solid/solution interface [34]. This fact means a non-negligible role of the size of the ions, even in the diffuse layer, and therefore, as illustrated in Figure 5, a maximum ion concentration must exist corresponding to the closed packing of ions. As a result, the model for the diffuse layer should properly be modified to address the non-ideal behavior of ions therein. This leads Bikerman [34–36] to arrive at, by means of the approximate "free volume" approach:

$$n_i = \frac{n_{i,\infty}\exp\left(-\frac{z_i e\psi}{k_B T}\right)}{1 + \nu\sum_k n_{k,\infty}\left[\exp\left(-\frac{z_k e\psi}{k_B T}\right) - 1\right]} \tag{17}$$

where ν has the meaning of average excluded volume per ion.

When combined with the Poisson equation and consideration of a Stern layer, the MPBS model can be written for a (z:z) symmetric electrolyte as,

$$\nabla^2\psi = \begin{cases} 0 & \text{in Stern layer} \\ -\frac{e}{\varepsilon_0\varepsilon_r}\frac{2zn_\infty\sin h\left(\frac{ze\psi}{k_B T}\right)}{1+2\nu\sin h^2\left(\frac{ze\psi}{2k_B T}\right)} & \text{in Diffuse layer} \end{cases} \tag{18}$$

with

$$\nu = 2d^3 n_\infty \tag{19}$$

where d is the spacing of counterions near a highly charged surface, and it is unnecessarily the diameter of the counterions. One may think of it as a cutoff [36] for the unphysical divergences of PB theory and could include at least a solvation shell (ion–ion correlations could effectively increase it further).

Equation (18) should also be subject to the same boundary conditions of Equations (6)–(9) as the GCS model, and therefore it is also convenient to be solved numerically. However, for a planer electrode surface, an analytical solution to the surface charge density σ_s is available for a symmetric electrolyte and it can be written as,

$$\sigma_s = -2zen_\infty\lambda_D\sqrt{\frac{2}{v}\ln\left[1+2v\sinh^2\left(\frac{ze\Delta\psi_d}{2k_BT}\right)\right]} \tag{20}$$

The relation between σ_s and $\Delta\psi_{St}$, as given in Equation (16), also holds in the MPBS model.

3.3. Modified Donnan Model

When dealing with the experimental results of CDLE processes, the application [28] of both GCS and MPBS models implicitly assume that the characteristic pore thickness is much larger than the Debye screening length so that the pore space is mostly filled with quasi-neutral electrolyte, exchanging ions with a charged, thin double-layer "skin" on the electrode matrix. This is, however, far from realistic because the activated carbon particles are themselves porous, presenting a very large specific surface inside the small micropores (≤2 nm). Therefore, as schematically shown in Figure 6, the free space between different carbon particles filled with electroneutral solution constitutes a macro-porosity that serves as a path for salt and charge transport, whereas the micropores store ionic charge in their EDLs. This fact implies that both GCS and MPBS descriptions of the EDL are not valid inside the micropores of activated carbon particles, which have a size comparable to the EDL thickness and even to that of hydrated ions, leading to EDLs overlap and other complications, such as the observed exceptionally large values of the capacitance.

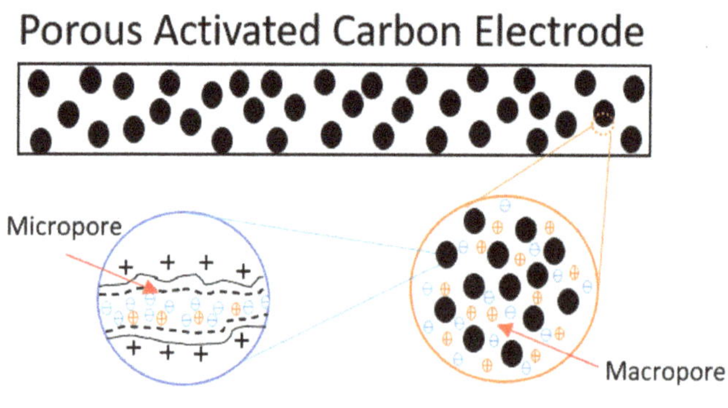

Figure 6. Schematic view of the structure of porous electrode.

To tackle this problem, Biesheuvel et al. [37] combined a modified Donnan description of the diffuse layer together with a charge-free Stern layer to determine the voltage drop at the carbon/solution interface inside the micropores. The main assumption of the mD approach is that the diffuse layer potential inside the micropores is constant, as illustrated in Figure 5, and it is controlled by the concentration of ions in the macropores of the electrode matrix, i.e., one can write [37]

$$n_{i,mi} = n_{i,\infty}\exp\left(-\frac{z_ie\Delta\psi_d}{k_BT}+\mu_{att}\right) \tag{21}$$

where the subscript "mi" emphasizes that it applies only to micropores, $\Delta\psi_d$ is now known as the Donnan potential and μ_{att} is an excess chemical potential that quantifies the chemical attraction between ions and carbon material of the electrodes [37].

This allows one to introduce the concept of volumetric charge density as the number of charges removed from solution per unit micropore volume, and in the case of a symmetric binary $z:z$ electrolyte, it is given by [31]

$$\rho = -2zen_{\infty}\exp(\mu_{att}) \times \sinh\left(\frac{ze\Delta\psi_{\rm d}}{k_BT}\right) \tag{22}$$

and

$$\rho = -C_{St,vol}\Delta\psi_{St} \tag{23}$$

where $C_{St,vol}$ is the volumetric capacitance (F/m^3) of the Stern layer, and it was suggested to be quantified empirically by [38,39]

$$C_{St,vol} = C_{St,vol,0} + \alpha \times \left(\frac{\rho}{F}\right)^2 \tag{24}$$

with both $C_{St,vol,0}$ and α (F·m^3/mol^2) being determined by fitting the mD model to the experimental data.

One key of the mD model is to describe the excess chemical potential properly, μ_{att}. For simplicity, it was generally taken as a constant irrespective of the specific type of ions [30,38]. Although this assumption makes the mD model works well for some cases, it cannot describe the experimental data in a range of bulk salt concentrations simultaneously [37]. An improved modified Donnan model (i-mD model) was developed [39] to rectify this problem by relating μ_{att} with the micropore total ion concentration $c_{ions,mi}$, based on the theory of image forces, to give

$$\mu_{att} = \frac{E}{c_{ions,mi}} \tag{25}$$

with the energy parameter (kT mol/m^3), E, defined as

$$E = z^2 \times k_BT \times \lambda_B \times d_p^{-4} \tag{26}$$

where λ_B is the Bjerrum length, $\lambda_B = e^2/4\pi\varepsilon_0\varepsilon_r k_BT$, at which the bare Coulomb energy of a pair of ions is balanced by thermal energy ($\lambda_B = 0.72$ nm in water at room temperature), and d_p is the size of micropore.

3.4. Booth Correction of Dielectric Permittivity

In most applications of the GCS and MPBS models, the solvent dielectric permittivity was assumed to be a constant or was treated as a fitting parameter. However, it is known that with the increase in the electric field, the relative permittivity of solvent ε_r shows a decreasing trend. The reason for this is that under a large electric field condition, electrolyte molecules become highly oriented, which results in poor capability of providing polarization [40]. To account for this effect of dielectric saturation into EDL models, Booth [41,42] derived the following equations to calculate the relative electrolyte permittivity under the local electric field condition as:

$$\varepsilon_r(E) = \begin{cases} m^2 + \left(\varepsilon_r(0) - m^2\right)\frac{3}{\beta E}\left[\coth(\beta E) - \frac{1}{\beta E}\right] & \text{for } E \geq 10^7\ \text{V/m} \\ \varepsilon_r(0) & \text{for } E < 10^7\ \text{V/m} \end{cases} \tag{27}$$

with

$$\beta = \frac{5\mu}{2k_BT}\left(m^2 + 2\right) \tag{28}$$

where $E = |-\nabla\psi|$ is the norm of the local electrical field vector, $\varepsilon_r(0)$ is the relative permittivity at zero electric field, m is the index of refraction of the electrolyte at zero electric field frequency, μ is the dipole moment of the solvent molecule, and in the case of water, $\mu = 1.85$ D (Debye).

For aqueous binary symmetric electrolytes at room temperature ($T = 298$ K), one may set [40,43]: $\varepsilon_r(0) = 78.5$, $m = 1.33$ and $\beta = 1.41 \times 10^{-8}$ m/V. The result for the relative permittivity as a function of the electric field is shown in Figure 7. It suggests that ε_r may change significantly from 78.5 in the bulk solution to 1.79 near the electrode surface in the cases where the electric field is very strong.

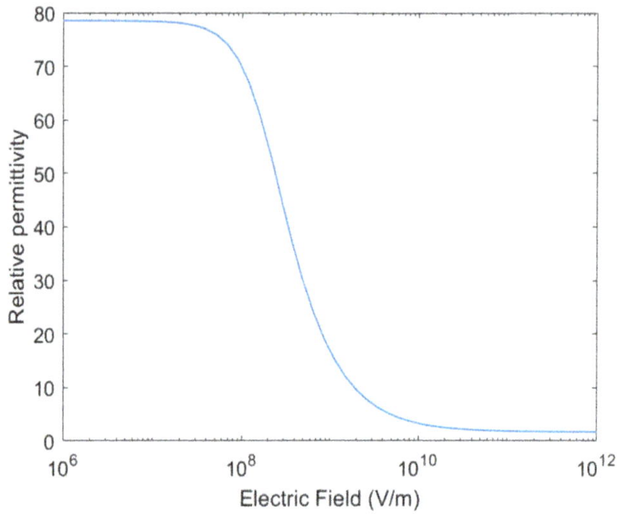

Figure 7. The relative permittivity $\varepsilon_r(E)$ as a function of electric field.

The importance of the Booth correction of dielectric permittivity is, therefore, that it may be used to account for the non-ideal behavior (or excess chemical potential) of ions in EDLs in a different way than MPBS and mD models and that it can be combined with either GCS or MPBS model for the performance assessment of CapMix processes.

4. Experimental Results and Model Applications

The key property of the CDLE cells is the dependence of the equilibrium electrode charge Q on the applied voltage V under different electrolyte concentrations, also known as the Q–V curves. The applicability of different EDL models can, therefore, be justified by comparing the simulated Q–V curves with the results of single-pass experiments.

4.1. Gouy–Chapmann–Stern Model

As discussed above, the GCS model is usually applied to the cases where the Debye screening length of the EDL, λ_D, is much less than the characteristic pore thickness H_p so that a planer electrode surface could effectively be defined. As a result, Q (C/g) can simply be evaluated by multiplying σ_s with the specific electrode area S_{eff} (m^2/g) as:

$$Q = \frac{1}{2}\sigma_s \times S_{eff} \tag{29}$$

The corresponding voltage drop across the cell can, by assuming it to be evenly distributed on the two electrodes, relate to $\Delta\psi_{St}$ and $\Delta\psi_d$ directly as:

$$V = 2(\Delta\psi_{St} + \Delta\psi_d) \tag{30}$$

With these definitions, the GCS model can readily be applied to the CDLE cell to obtain the Q–V curves under different electrolyte concentrations. Since it is commonly assumed in the GCS model that $\varepsilon_r = \varepsilon_r(0)$, the unknown parameters of the specific system only involve C_{st} and S_{eff}. As a result, we may fix $\varepsilon_r = 78.5$ at T = 298 K and evaluate C_{st} and S_{eff} simultaneously by fitting the simulated Q–V curves to the measured data over all the NaCl concentrations of interest by using a nonlinear least square algorithm, supplemented with suitable lower and upper bounds. The result gives C_{St} = 0.131 F/m^2 and S_{eff} = 619.46 m^2/g. At first glance, a good agreement between the calculated and measured Q–V curves, as shown in Figure 8 and the fact that S_{eff} = 619.46 m^2/g is comparable with the findings of reported results [19,22,23] seems to substantiate the rationale of C_{st} and S_{eff} values. However, further analysis suggests that C_{St} = 0.131 F/m^2 corresponds to a Stern layer thickness of 5.3 nm. This is far greater than the hydrated radius [44] of Na+ ions and is therefore unreasonable, meaning that an arbitrary setting of C_{St} = 0.1 F/m^2, as shown by previous work [21,22], is also problematic.

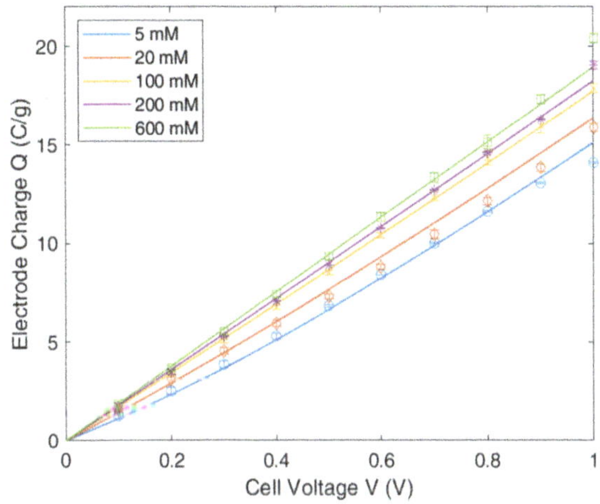

Figure 8. Equilibrium electrode charge Q versus applied voltage V for different values of NaCl solution. Lines refer to the results of GCS model (C_{St} = 0.131 F/m^2, S_{eff} = 619.46 m^2/g, ε_r = 78.5), marks refer to the experiment data and error bars of the experimental data are indicated by horizontal lines through the marked data points.

On the other hand, it is noted from Table 1. that the characteristic pore thickness H_p is on the order of magnitude of 0.43 nm, whereas the Debye screening length of the EDL is about 0.4 nm at a bulk concentration of 600 mM. This suggests that H_p is always smaller than λ_D in all the cases studied, and therefore violates the assumption of thin double-layer "skin" on the electrode matrix. As a result, the GCS model is deemed to be not applicable, especially when the NaCl concentration is small.

If combined with Booth correction of dielectric permittivity, the GCS model gives even worse agreement, as shown in Figure 9, with δ = 4.2 nm and S_{eff} = 540.25 m^2/g. This suggests that accounting for the variation of ε_r with the electric field does not remedy the inherent problem of the GCS model, still making the parameters physically meaningless, and therefore should also be abandoned in the interpretation of the experimental results.

4.2. Modified Poisson–Boltzmann–Stern Model

The MPBS model bears the same conceptualization on the EDL geometry as the GCS model but accounts for the effect of finite-size of ions. We can, therefore, still use Equations (29) and (30) to calculate Q and V in the simulations. As shown in Figure 10, the agreement between the calculated and measured Q–V curves is nearly the same as the GCS model does, with C_{St} = 0.141 F/m^2 and S_{eff} = 580.88 m^2/g when ε_r is fixed at 78.5. The minor difference between the C_{St} value of the two models also suggests that the MPBS model breaks down in the regime of experimental interest.

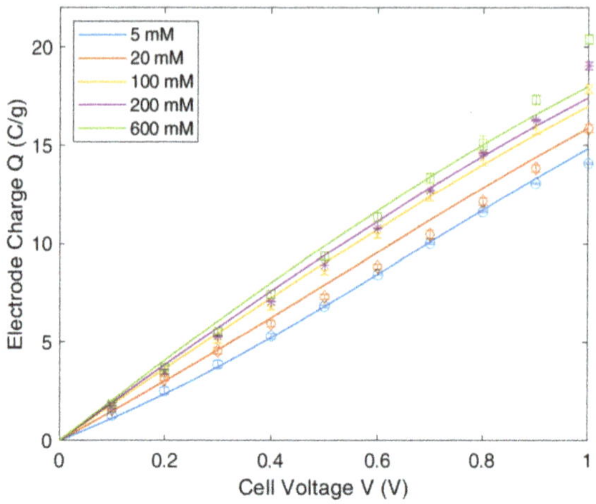

Figure 9. Equilibrium electrode charge Q versus applied voltage V for different values of NaCl solution. Lines refer to the results of the GCS model with Booth correction ($\delta = 4.2$ nm, $S_{eff} = 540.25\ \text{m}^2/\text{g}$), marks refer to the experiment data and error bars of the experimental data are indicated by horizontal lines through the marked data points.

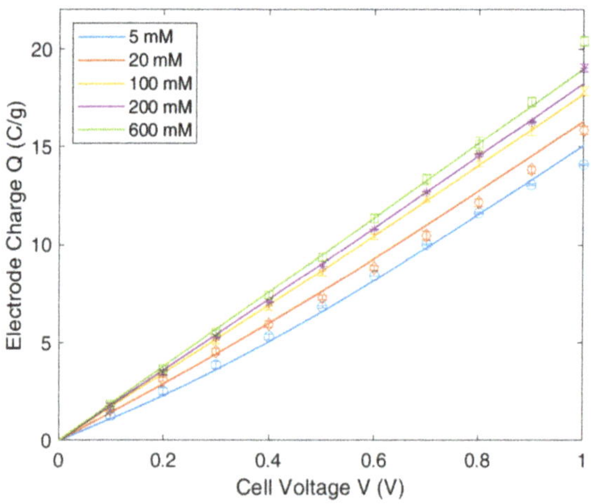

Figure 10. Equilibrium electrode charge Q versus applied voltage V for different values of NaCl solution. Lines refer to the results of MPBS model ($C_{St} = 0.141\ \text{F/m}^2$, $S_{eff} = 580.88\ \text{m}^2/\text{g}$, $\varepsilon_r = 78.5$, $d = 0.75$ nm), marks refer to the experiment data and error bars of the experimental data are indicated by horizontal lines through the marked data points.

Not surprisingly, when combined with Booth correction, the MPBS model does not move the needle at all. It gives $\delta = 7.3$ nm, $S_{eff} = 857.79\ \text{m}^2/\text{g}$ and the spacing of counterions $d = 1.42$ nm, with an acceptable agreement between the calculated and measured Q–V curves, as shown in Figure 11. As a result, accounting for the variation of ε_r with the electric field in the MPBS model does not help to rectify the problems associated with the model in the cases where the assumption of thin double-layer "skin" on the electrode matrix is not valid.

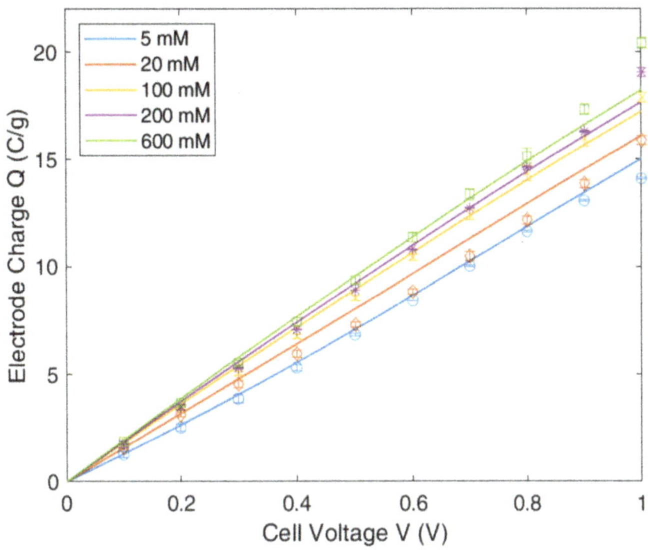

Figure 11. Equilibrium electrode charge Q versus applied voltage V for different values of NaCl solution. Lines refer to the results of MPBS model with Booth correction (δ = 7.3 nm, S_{eff} = 857.79 m^2/g, d = 1.42 nm), marks refer to the experiment data and error bars of the experimental data are indicated by horizontal lines through the marked data points.

4.3. Modified Donnan Model

In contrast to the GCS and MPBS models, the mD model considers that the micropores of activated carbon particles have a size comparable to the EDL thickness and even to that of hydrated ions, leading to EDLs overlap and a constant diffuse layer potential. The total charge in electrode at equilibrium can, therefore, be calculated as:

$$Q = -\frac{1}{2} \times \rho \times v_{mi} \tag{31}$$

where v_{mi} is the micropore volume per unit electrode mass (cm^3/g).

Using this expression for Q and Equation (30) for V, the Q–V curves of the CDLE cell under different electrolyte concentrations can conveniently be obtained in the mD model. The unknown parameters involved are, however, version-dependent. In the standard mD model [29,30,38,39,45], where μ_{att} is taken as a constant, the optimal values of μ_{att}, v_{micro}, $C_{St,vol,0}$ and α are all in need of determination from the procedure of fitting the simulated Q–V curves to the measured data over all the NaCl concentrations of interest. The result shows when a nonlinear least square algorithm is used, μ_{att} = 1.18, v_{mi} = 0.35 cm^3/g, α = 10.5 $F{\cdot}m^3/mol^2$ and $C_{St,vol,0}$ = 2.1 × 108 F/m^3. These values are in line with those suggested by other works [30,38,45], with a good agreement between the simulated and measured Q–V curves as a result, as shown in Figure 12.

The fact of v_{mi} = 0.35 cm^3/g suggests that about 90% of the micropore space is available for counterion adsorption. This is deemed to be much more reasonable than the result (~70%) of the GCS and MPBS models imply. On the other hand, $C_{St,vol,0}$ = 2.1 × 10^8 F/m^3 is equivalent to ε_r = ~7.29 given a Stern layer thickness on the order of magnitude of hydrated ions of Na+. This is also reasonable, as Booth correction of dielectric permittivity (see Figure 7) suggests. Therefore, the mD model is physically much more plausible than both GCS and MPBS models.

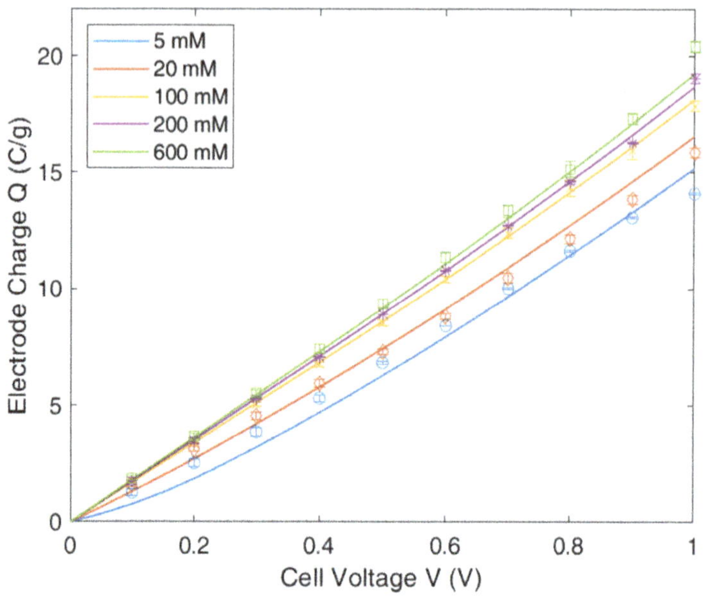

Figure 12. Equilibrium electrode charge Q versus applied voltage V for different values of NaCl solution. Lines refer to the results of mD model (a = 10.5 F·m^3/mol^2, $C_{St,vol,0}$ = 2.1 × 10^8 F/m^3, μ_{att} = 1.18, v_{mi} = 0.35 cm^3/g), marks refer to the experiment data and error bars of the experimental data are indicated by horizontal lines through the marked data points.

In the improved mD (i-mD) model [39], the excess chemical potential, μ_{att} is related to the total concentration of all ions in the micropores as given in Equation (25). The energy parameter E should now be determined a priori, instead of μ_{att}. Using the same fitting procedure as discussed above, we found that the optimal values of the fitting parameters are: E = 436.7 kT mol/m^3, $C_{St,vol,0}$ = 2.06 × 108 F/m^3, α = 13.6 F·m^3/mol^2 and v_{mi} = 0.364 cm^3/g. The value of v_{mi} = 0.364 cm^3/g suggests that the availability of micropore volume for storing the counterions is ~94%. $C_{St,vol,0}$ = 2.06 × 10^8 F/m^3 corresponding to ε_r = ~7.17 also implies a reasonable Stern layer thickness. The difference between mD and i-mD models is, therefore, mainly on the $C_{St,vol,0}$ values. As shown in Figure 13, the decrease of $C_{St,vol}$ with increasing volume charge in both mD models follow essentially the same pattern. As a result, ε_r also decreases but only slightly. It becomes ~6.77 and ~6.49 at $\rho = 1.2\times10^8$ C/m^3 in the mD and i-mD model, respectively.

With the optimal parameters, it is seen from Figure 14 that the simulated Q–V curves by i-mD model agrees almost entirely with the experimental data, much better than the results of the other models (see Figures 7–12).

To facilitate the comparison of different EDL models, we summarize in Table 2. the physical parameters involved in the models and the optimal values obtained from the fitting procedures. As discussed above, the parameter values of both mD and i-mD models are not only reasonable but also roughly the same. However, as clearly seen from the results shown in Figures 12 and 14, the i-mD model is superior to the mD model in reproducing the dependence of Q on V under different electrolyte concentrations.

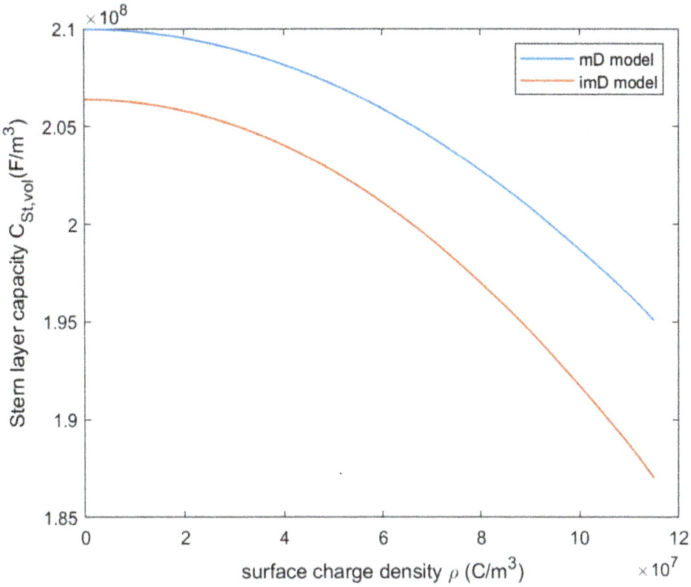

Figure 13. Stern layer capacity $C_{St,vol}$ as a function of surface charge density ρ.

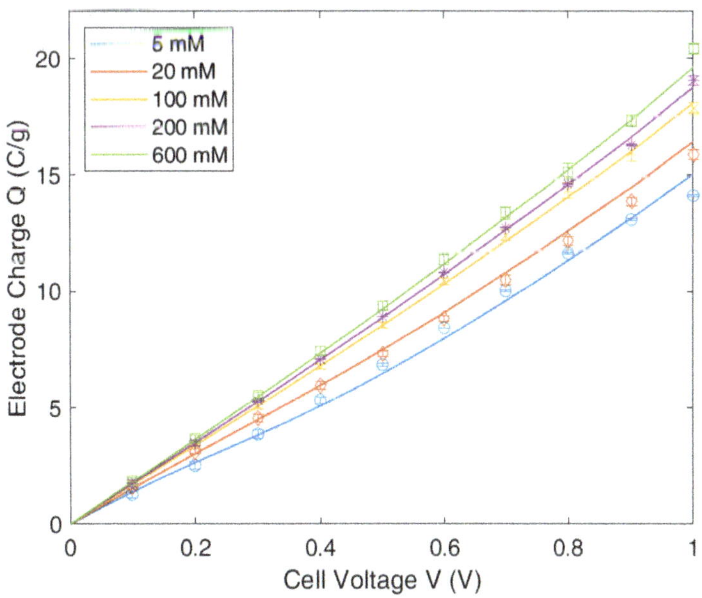

Figure 14. Equilibrium electrode charge Q versus applied voltage V for different values of NaCl solution. Lines refer to the results of i-mD model (a = 13.6 F·m^3/mol^2, $C_{St,vol,0}$ = 2.06 × 10^8 F/m^3, E = 436.7 kT mol/m^3, v_{mi} = 0.36 cm^3/g), marks refer to the experiment data and error bars of the experimental data are indicated by horizontal lines through the marked data points.

Table 2. Optimal parameters values for different theoretical models in the present paper.

Models	Parameters					
	C_{st} (F/m^2)	S_{eff} (m^2/g)	δ (nm)	ε_r	d (nm)	
GCS	0.131	619.46	5.3	78.5	-	
GCS—B *	1.0–1.15	540.25	4.19	68.5–78.5	-	
MPBS	0.141	580.88	4.92	78.5	0.75	
MPBS—B *	0.09–0.095	857.79	7.29	74.6–78.5	1.42	
	$C_{st,vol,0}$ (F/m^3)	α (Fm^3/mol^2)	$C_{st,vol}$ (F/m^3)	μ_{att}	E (kT mol/m^3)	v_{mi} (cm^3/g)
mD	2.1×10^8	10.48	$(2.1–2.24) \times 10^8$	1.18	-	0.35
i-mD	2.06×10^8	13.65	$(2.06–2.23) \times 10^8$	0.23–2.76	436.7	0.367

*: with Booth correction.

By contrast, the optimal parameters of the GCS and the MPBS models are physically unreasonable, especially about the Stern layer thickness. As seen in Table 2, even the minimum d value of 4.19 nm is still far greater than the hydrated radius [44] of Na^+ ions, in contradiction with the physical explanation of the Stern layer. It is mainly this finding that makes us believe the applicability of the GCS and MPBS models is questionable.

4.4. Full CDLE Experiment

The extracted energy per gram W in our CDEL experiment is 0.1 to 0.15 J/g at an applied voltage ranging from 0.3 to 0.8 V, which is comparable to the relevant reported energy production of other works, i.e., the W ranged from 0.2 to 0.6 J/g at an applied voltage ranging from 0.3 to 0.7 V is reported by D. Brogioli et al. [22], and $W \approx 0.11$ to 0.22 J/g at V_{ext} = 0.4 V reported by Nasir et al. [18]. The reason for the difference in energy production might be attributed to the different CDLE cell design and electrode materials. Note that the results of Q vs. V obtained in single-pass experiments clearly show that, for a fixed value of Q, the reduction in the electrolyte concentration results in higher cell potential. This allows us to extract energy by intermittently exchange seawater and freshwater thorough a CDLE cell. In addition, one may expect that, in a full CDLE cycle, the potential rise ΔV at sept 2 and the energy extracted should both increase monotonically with the applied voltage V_{ext}, if the kinetics of the full CDLE cycle is solely controlled by the diffusion of ions within the porous electrodes. However, this not the case. As shown in Figure 15, the experimental results suggest a parabolic curve for both ΔV and W. The potential rise ΔV increases monotonically until it reaches a maximum value at V_{ext} = 0.6 V and then followed with a progressive decay with further increase in V_{ext}. Correspondingly, the energy extracted, W, achieves a maximum value at V_{ext} = 0.6 V. This phenomenon was also observed by Jiménez et al. [24] and Iglesias et al. [17] and explained qualitatively by the MPBS model assuming a spherical geometry of solid carbon particles [24]. Our findings do not, however, support the use of such an MPBS model because the results of single-pass experiments, as shown in Figure 14, clearly indicate that both ΔV and W should monotonically increase with an increase in the applied voltage. The large deviation between experimental data and theoretical prediction at higher applied voltage suggested that using only the equilibrium double layer model itself is not sufficient to describe the performance of a full CDLE cell. An advanced model as the one developed by Rica et al. [27] is then required to include the effect of advection, mass transfer at the electrode/solution interface, ionic diffusion through the electrodes and build-up of EDLs at the micropore space, etc. This work is now undertaken and will be discussed in detail in the near future.

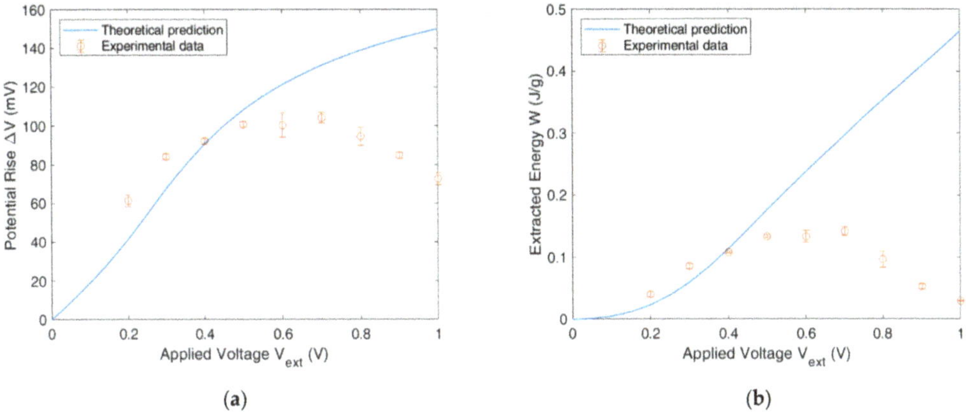

Figure 15. (**a**) Potential rise ΔV in step 2 of CDLE process as a function of cell voltage. (**b**) Extracted energy of one CDLE cycle at different cell voltage. R_{ext} = 100 Ω, c_{fresh} = 20 mM, c_{sea} = 600 mM. The line refers to the theoretical prediction by i-mD model, marks refer to the experiment data and error bars of the experimental data are indicated by horizontal lines through the marked data points.

5. Conclusions

In this study, a series of single-pass and full-cycle experiments were performed for a self-made CDLE cell in order to exploit its potential to harvest energy from an intermittent exchange of seawater and freshwater. The focus is, however, on the analysis of different EDL models in describing the structural and thermodynamic properties of EDLs at the micropore scale at equilibrium. The results suggest that both GCS and MPBS models involve physically unmeaningful parameters, despite their ability to well reproduce the Q–V curves (the key performance of the CDLE cell) at different NaCl concentrations. The reason is, perhaps, that both models were applied on the assumption of thin EDLs, which is unreasonable since $\lambda_D \gtrsim H_p$ in all the cases of interest. By contrast, both the mD and i-mD models consider the strong overlap of EDLs within the micropores of the electrodes, making the diffuse potential constant. As a result, the non-ideal properties of the EDLs were well accounted for with only a few parameters that are physically interpretable. In particular, the i-mD model considers the excess chemical potential as a function of the total concentration of NaCl within the micropores instead of a constant value. This makes i-mD model superior to mD model in describing the performance of the CDLE cell at equilibrium, and therefore should be recommended to be used in the first place.

However, when applied for practical use, it was found that the theoretical calculation of the i-mD model alone gives inconsistent results with the data of the full-cycle CDLE experiments about the dependence of ΔV and W on the applied voltage. The model and the single-pass experimental results suggest that both ΔV and W should increase monotonically with the applied voltage, in contrast to a parabolic behavior that was found experimentally with a maximum of W located at V_{ext} = 0.6 V. The reason for this difference may be attributed to the higher current leakage and the effect of ion size at larger applied voltage [18,24,25]. However, to understand the performance of the full-cycle CDLE cells better, an advanced model is expected to include the effect of advection, mass transfer at the electrode/solution interface, ionic diffusion through the electrodes and i-mD description of EDLs at the micropore space, etc. Thus, the knowledge we obtained from this study provides important guidance towards the application of EDL models in CDLE technology.

Author Contributions: Writing—original draft preparation, Z.Z.; writing—review and editing, L.L.; methodology, Z.Z.; data curation, X.B.; simulation, S.M.; supervision, Y.L. All authors have read and agreed to the published version of the manuscript.

Funding: This research was funded by Swedish Energy Agency (Energimyndigheten), Sweden, project number 44606-1.

Institutional Review Board Statement: Not applicable.

Informed Consent Statement: Not applicable.

Data Availability Statement: Not applicable.

Acknowledgments: Zhi Zou acknowledges the financial support from China Scholarship Council (CSC).

Conflicts of Interest: The authors declare no conflict of interest.

Nomenclature

CapMix	Capacitive mixing
CDP	Capacitive energy extraction based on Donnan Potential
CDLE	Capacitive energy extraction based on Double Layer Expansion
SE	Soft Electrode
EDL	Electric double layer
PB	Poisson Boltzmann
GCS	Gouy–Chapman–Stern
MPBS	Modified Poisson–Boltzmann–Stern
mD	modified Donnan
S_{BET}	Specific surface area
S_{micro}	Microporous surface area measurement
V_{tot}	Total volume of pores
H_p	Pore thickness
D_{BJH}	Average pore diameter
Q	Equilibrium electrode charge per mass, C/g
I	Electric current, A
I_{mea}	Measured current, A
I_{lea}	Leakage current, A
m_{elec}	Mass of total electrodes, g
V_{ext}	Applied voltage, V
V	Cell potential, V
$\times V$	Potential increase due to the double layer expansion, V
R_{ext}	External resistance, Ω
W	Extracted energy, J/g
c	Electrolyte concentration, mm
c_{fresh}	Electrolyte concentration of freshwater, mol/m^3
c_{sea}	Electrolyte concentration of seawater, mol/m^3
$c_{ions,mi}$	micropore total ion concentration, mol/m^3
n_i	number concentration of the ith species in diffuse layer, 1/m^3
$n_{i,\infty}$	number concentration of the ith species at the bulk solution, 1/m^3
$n_{i,mi}$	number concentration of ith species in the micropores of the electrode, 1/m^3
e	elementary charge, C
z_i	valence of the ith species
k_B	Boltzmann constant, J/K
ε_0	free space permittivity, F/m
ε_r	relative permittivity of the electrolyte solutions
ψ	electric potential, V
ψ_s	surface potential, V
$\Delta\psi_{St}$	electric potential drop across the stern layer, V
$\Delta\psi_d$	electric potential difference across the diffuse layer, V

σ_s	surface charge density, C/m^2
C	total differential capacitance of the double layer
C_{st}	differential capacitances of the stern layer, F/m^2
C_d	differential capacitances of the diffuse layer, F/m^2
v	average excluded volume per ion, m^3
d	spacing of counterions near a highly charged surface, m
λ_D	Debye length, m
λ_B	Bjerrum length, m
ρ	volumetric charge density, C/m^3
μ_{att}	excess chemical potential, kT
$C_{St,vol}$	volumetric capacitance of the Stern layer, F/m^3
$C_{St,vol,0}$	volumetric capacitance of the Stern layer (low charge limit), F/m^3
α	Parameter to describe nonlinear part of Stern capacity, $F{\cdot}m^3/mol^2$
E	energy parameter, kT mol/m^3
d_p	size of micropore, m
m	index of refraction of the electrolyte at zero electric field frequency
μ	dipole moment of the solvent molecule and in the case of water, D(Debye)
S_{eff}	effective specific electrode area, m^2/g

References

1. Shirzad, M.; Karimi, M.; Abolghasemi, H. Polymer inclusion membranes with dinonylnaphthalene sulfonic acid as ion carrier for Co(II) transport from model solutions. *Desalin. Water Treat.* **2019**, *144*, 185–200. [CrossRef]
2. De Medeiros, A.D.M.; da Silva, C.J.G.; de Amorim, J.D.P.; do Nascimento, H.A.; Converti, A.; Costa, A.F.D.; Sarubbo, L.A. Biocellulose for Treatment of Wastewaters Generated by Energy Consuming Industries: A Review. *Energies* **2021**, *14*, 5066. [CrossRef]
3. Ozcan, H.G.; Hepbasli, A.; Abusoglu, A.; Anvari-Moghaddam, A. Advanced Exergy Analysis of Waste-Based District Heating Options through Case Studies. *Energies* **2021**, *14*, 4766. [CrossRef]
4. Pattle, R. Production of electric power by mixing fresh and salt water in the hydroelectric pile. *Nature* **1954**, *174*, 660. [CrossRef]
5. Boon, N.; van Roij, R. 'Blue energy' from ion adsorption and electrode charging in sea and river water. *Mol. Phys.* **2011**, *109*, 1229–1241. [CrossRef]
6. Post, J.W.; Hamelers, H.V.M.; Buisman, C.J.N. Energy recovery from controlled mixing salt and fresh water with a reverse electrodialysis system. *Environ. Sci. Technol.* **2008**, *42*, 5785–5790. [CrossRef]
7. Achilli, A.; Childress, A.E. Pressure retarded osmosis: From the vision of Sidney Loeb to the first prototype installation. *Desalination* **2010**, *261*, 205–211. [CrossRef]
8. Loeb, S. Osmotic Power-Plants. *Science* **1975**, *189*, 654–655. [CrossRef]
9. Weinstein, J.N.; Leitz, F.B. Electric power from differences in salinity: The dialytic battery. *Science* **1976**, *191*, 557–559. [CrossRef]
10. Yip, N.Y.; Elimelech, M. Comparison of energy efficiency and power density in pressure retarded osmosis and reverse electrodialysis. *Environ. Sci. Technol.* **2014**, *48*, 11002–11012. [CrossRef]
11. Yip, N.Y.; Brogioli, D.; Hamelers, H.V.M.; Nijmeijer, K. Salinity Gradients for Sustainable Energy: Primer, Progress, and Prospects. *Environ. Sci. Technol.* **2016**, *50*, 12072–12094. [CrossRef] [PubMed]
12. Kim, T.; Rahimi, M.; Logan, B.E.; Gorski, C.A. Harvesting Energy from Salinity Differences Using Battery Electrodes in a Concentration Flow Cell. *Environ. Sci. Technol.* **2016**, *50*, 9791–9797. [CrossRef]
13. Brogioli, D. Extracting Renewable Energy from a Salinity Difference Using a Capacitor. *Phys. Rev. Lett.* **2009**, *103*, 058501. [CrossRef]
14. Sales, B.B.; Saakes, M.; Post, J.W.; Buisman, C.J.N.; Biesheuvel, P.M.; Hamelers, H.V.M. Direct Power Production from a Water Salinity Difference in a Membrane-Modified Supercapacitor Flow Cell. *Environ. Sci. Technol.* **2010**, *44*, 5661–5665. [CrossRef] [PubMed]
15. La Mantia, F.; Pasta, M.; Deshazer, H.D.; Logan, B.E.; Cui, Y. Batteries for Efficient Energy Extraction from a Water Salinity Difference. *Nano Lett.* **2011**, *11*, 1810–1813. [CrossRef]
16. Ahualli, S.; Jimenez, M.L.; Fernandez, M.M.; Iglesias, G.; Brogioli, D.; Delgado, A.V. Polyelectrolyte-coated carbons used in the generation of blue energy from salinity differences. *Phys. Chem. Chem. Phys.* **2014**, *16*, 25241–25246. [CrossRef] [PubMed]
17. Iglesias, G.R.; Fernandez, M.M.; Ahualli, S.; Jimenez, M.L.; Kozynchenko, O.P.; Delgado, A.V. Materials selection for optimum energy production by double layer expansion methods. *J. Power Sources* **2014**, *261*, 371–377. [CrossRef]
18. Nasir, M.; Nakanishi, Y.; Patmonoaji, A.; Suekane, T. Effects of porous electrode pore size and operating flow rate on the energy production of capacitive energy extraction. *Renew. Energy* **2020**, *155*, 278–285. [CrossRef]
19. Iglesias, G.R.; Ahualli, S.; Fernandez, M.M.; Jimenez, M.L.; Delgado, A.V. Stacking of capacitive cells for electrical energy production by salinity exchange. *J. Power Sources* **2016**, *318*, 283–290. [CrossRef]
20. Ahualli, S.; Fernandez, M.M.; Iglesias, G.; Delgado, A.V.; Jimenez, M.L. Temperature Effects on Energy Production by Salinity Exchange. *Environ. Sci. Technol.* **2014**, *48*, 12378–12385. [CrossRef] [PubMed]

21. Zhao, R.; Biesheuvel, P.M.; Miedema, H.; Bruning, H.; van der Wal, A. Charge Efficiency: A Functional Tool to Probe the Double-Layer Structure Inside of Porous Electrodes and Application in the Modeling of Capacitive Deionization. *J. Phys. Chem. Lett.* **2010**, *1*, 205–210. [CrossRef]
22. Brogioli, D.; Zhao, R.; Biesheuvel, P.M. A prototype cell for extracting energy from a water salinity difference by means of double layer expansion in nanoporous carbon electrodes. *Energy Environ. Sci.* **2011**, *4*, 772–777. [CrossRef]
23. Brogioli, D.; Ziano, R.; Rica, R.A.; Salerno, D.; Kozynchenko, O.; Hamelers, H.V.M.; Mantegazza, F. Exploiting the spontaneous potential of the electrodes used in the capacitive mixing technique for the extraction of energy from salinity difference. *Energy Environ. Sci.* **2012**, *5*, 9870–9880. [CrossRef]
24. Jimenez, M.L.; Fernandez, M.M.; Ahualli, S.; Iglesias, G.; Delgado, A.V. Predictions of the maximum energy extracted from salinity exchange inside porous electrodes. *J. Colloid Interface Sci.* **2013**, *402*, 340–349. [CrossRef]
25. Fernandez, M.M.; Ahualli, S.; Iglesias, G.R.; Gonzalez-Caballero, F.; Delgado, A.V.; Jimenez, M.L. Multi-ionic effects on energy production based on double layer expansion by salinity exchange. *J. Colloid Interface Sci.* **2015**, *446*, 335–344. [CrossRef]
26. Rica, R.A.; Ziano, R.; Salerno, D.; Mantegazza, F.; Bazant, M.Z.; Brogioli, D. Electro-diffusion of ions in porous electrodes for capacitive extraction of renewable energy from salinity differences. *Electrochim. Acta* **2013**, *92*, 304–314. [CrossRef]
27. Rica, R.A.; Brogioli, D.; Ziano, R.; Salerno, D.; Mantegazza, F. Ions Transport and Adsorption Mechanisms in Porous Electrodes During Capacitive-Mixing Double Layer Expansion (CDLE). *J. Phys. Chem. C* **2012**, *116*, 16934–16938. [CrossRef]
28. Biesheuvel, P.M.; Bazant, M.Z. Nonlinear dynamics of capacitive charging and desalination by porous electrodes. *Phys. Rev. E* **2010**, *81*, 031502. [CrossRef]
29. Porada, S.; Bryjak, M.; van der Wal, A.; Biesheuvel, P.M. Effect of electrode thickness variation on operation of capacitive deionization. *Electrochim. Acta* **2012**, *75*, 148–156. [CrossRef]
30. Porada, S.; Borchardt, L.; Oschatz, M.; Bryjak, M.; Atchison, J.S.; Keesman, K.J.; Kaskel, S.; Biesheuvel, P.M.; Presser, V. Direct prediction of the desalination performance of porous carbon electrodes for capacitive deionization. *Energy Environ. Sci.* **2013**, *6*, 3700–3712. [CrossRef]
31. Porada, S.; Zhao, R.; van der Wal, A.; Presser, V.; Biesheuvel, P.M. Review on the science and technology of water desalination by capacitive deionization. *Prog. Mater. Sci.* **2013**, *58*, 1388–1442. [CrossRef]
32. Bazant, M.Z.; Chu, K.T.; Bayly, B.J. Current-voltage relations for electrochemical thin films. *Siam J. Appl. Math.* **2005**, *65*, 1463–1484. [CrossRef]
33. Wang, H.N.; Varghese, J.; Pilon, L. Simulation of electric double layer capacitors with mesoporous electrodes: Effects of morphology and electrolyte permittivity. *Electrochim. Acta* **2011**, *56*, 6189–6197. [CrossRef]
34. Biesheuvel, P.M. Thermodynamic cycle analysis for capacitive deionization. *J. Colloid Interface Sci.* **2009**, *332*, 258–264. [CrossRef]
35. Biesheuvel, P.M.; van Soestbergen, M. Counterion volume effects in mixed electrical double layers. *J. Colloid Interface Sci.* **2007**, *316*, 490–499. [CrossRef] [PubMed]
36. Kilic, M.S.; Bazant, M.Z.; Ajdari, A. Steric effects in the dynamics of electrolytes at large applied voltages. I. Double-layer charging. *Phys. Rev. E* **2007**, *75*, 021502. [CrossRef]
37. Biesheuvel, P.M.; Zhao, R.; Porada, S.; van der Wal, A. Theory of membrane capacitive deionization including the effect of the electrode pore space. *J. Colloid Interface Sci.* **2011**, *360*, 239–248. [CrossRef]
38. Porada, S.; Weinstein, L.; Dash, R.; van der Wal, A.; Bryjak, M.; Gogotsi, Y.; Biesheuvel, P.M. Water Desalination Using Capacitive Deionization with Microporous Carbon Electrodes. *ACS Appl. Mater. Inter.* **2012**, *4*, 1194–1199. [CrossRef]
39. Biesheuvel, P.M.; Porada, S.; Levi, M.; Bazant, M.Z. Attractive forces in microporous carbon electrodes for capacitive deionization. *J. Solid State Electr.* **2014**, *18*, 1365–1376. [CrossRef]
40. Wang, H.N.; Pilon, L. Accurate Simulations of Electric Double Layer Capacitance of Ultramicroelectrodes. *J. Phys. Chem. C* **2011**, *115*, 16711–16719. [CrossRef]
41. Booth, F. The dielectric constant of water and the saturation effect. *J. Chem. Phys.* **1951**, *19*, 391–394. [CrossRef]
42. Booth, F. Dielectric constant of polar liquids at high field strengths. *J. Chem. Phys.* **1955**, *23*, 453–457. [CrossRef]
43. Basu, S.; Sharma, M.M. Effect of Dielectric Saturation on Disjoining Pressure in Thin-Films of Aqueous-Electrolytes. *J. Colloid Interface Sci.* **1994**, *165*, 355–366. [CrossRef]
44. Tansel, B.; Sager, J.; Rector, T.; Garland, J.; Strayer, R.F.; Levine, L.F.; Roberts, M.; Hummerick, M.; Bauer, J. Significance of hydrated radius and hydration shells on ionic permeability during nanofiltration in dead end and cross flow modes. *Sep. Purif. Technol.* **2006**, *51*, 40–47. [CrossRef]
45. Zhao, R.; van Soestbergen, M.; Rijnaarts, H.H.M.; van der Wal, A.; Bazant, M.Z.; Biesheuvel, P.M. Time-dependent ion selectivity in capacitive charging of porous electrodes. *J. Colloid Interface Sci.* **2012**, *384*, 38–44. [CrossRef]

energies

MDPI

Article

Wind Speed Forecasts of a Mesoscale Ensemble for Large-Scale Wind Farms in Northern China: Downscaling Effect of Global Model Forecasts

Jianqiu Shi [1,2], Yubao Liu [1,2,3,*], Yang Li [1,2], Yuewei Liu [3], Gregory Roux [3], Lan Shi [4] and Xiaowei Fan [5,*]

1 Key Laboratory for Aerosol-Cloud-Precipition of China Meteorological Administration, Nanjing University of Information Science and Technology, Nanjing 210044, China; 20191203019@nuist.edu.cn (J.S.); yangli@nuist.edu.cn (Y.L.)
2 Precision Regional Earth Modeling and Information Center, Nanjing University of Information Science and Technology, Nanjing 210044, China
3 National Center for Atmospheric Research, Boulder, CO 80307, USA; yueliu@ucar.edu (Y.L.); roux@ucar.edu (G.R.)
4 Inner-Mongolia Meteorological Bureau, Huhhot 010051, China; shilan608993@cma.cn
5 Electric Power Dispatch Center, Jibei Electric Power Company, Beijing 100054, China
* Correspondence: ybliu@nuist.edu.cn (Y.L.); fan.xiaowei@jibei.sgcc.com.cn (X.F.)

Abstract: To facilitate wind power integration for the electric power grid operated by the Inner Mongolia Electric Power Corporation—a major electric power grid in China—a high-resolution (of 2.7 km grid intervals) mesoscale ensemble prediction system was developed that forecasts winds for 130 wind farms in the Inner Mongolia Autonomous Region. The ensemble system contains 39 forecasting members that are divided into 3 groups; each group is composed of the NCAR (National Center for Atmospheric Research) real-time four-dimensional data assimilation and forecasting model (RTFDDA) with 13 physical perturbation members, but driven by the forecasts of the GFS (Global Forecast System), GEM (Global Environmental Multiscale Model), and GEOS (Goddard Earth Observing System), respectively. The hub-height wind predictions of these three sub-ensemble groups at selected wind turbines across the region were verified against the hub-height wind measurements. The forecast performance and variations with lead time, wind regimes, and diurnal and regional changes were analyzed. The results show that the GFS group outperformed the other two groups with respect to correlation coefficient and mean absolute error. The GFS group had the most accurate forecasts in ~59% of sites, while the GEOS and GEM groups only performed the best on 34% and 2% of occasions, respectively. The wind forecasts were most accurate for wind speeds ranging from 3 to 12 m/s, but with an overestimation for low speeds and an underestimation for high speeds. The GEOS-driven members obtained the least bias error among the three groups. All members performed rather accurately in daytime, but evidently overestimated the winds during nighttime. The GFS group possessed the fewest diurnal errors, and the bias of the GEM group grew significantly during nighttime. The wind speed forecast errors of all three ensemble members increased with the forecast lead time, with the average absolute error increasing by ~0.3 m/s per day during the first 72 h of forecasts.

Keywords: mesoscale ensemble system; wind power prediction; wind speed; diurnal variation; global forecast downscaling

Citation: Shi, J.; Liu, Y.; Li, Y.; Liu, Y.; Roux, G.; Shi, L.; Fan, X. Wind Speed Forecasts of a Mesoscale Ensemble for Large-Scale Wind Farms in Northern China: Downscaling Effect of Global Model Forecasts. *Energies* **2022**, *15*, 896. https://doi.org/10.3390/en15030896

Academic Editors: Marcin Kamiński and Andrés Elías Feijóo Lorenzo

Received: 7 December 2021
Accepted: 25 January 2022
Published: 26 January 2022

1. Introduction

Wind energy, with its vast availability, cleanliness, and renewability, is growing rapidly in the energy share, and plays an increasingly important role in the electric energy sector [1]. However, the intermittent and volatile nature of wind speeds poses a great challenge to the grid-connected transmission of wind power output, threatening the security of the grid system and sometimes leading to massive wind abandonment [2]. Reliable wind power forecasting is urgently needed for timely and accurate dispatch of power resources [3,4]. Wind speed forecasting methods include statistical approaches, machine learning methods [5–11], and numerical weather prediction [12]. There have been many works on wind prediction reported in the past two decades, especially over the last few years. However, most of these works are on the refinement of statistical and AI approaches [13–18]; there have been very few studies examining and analyzing the errors of numerical weather models. As a matter of fact, for wind forecasts beyond ~1 h, numerical weather prediction models become essential and fundamental. Improving the performance and capability of numerical weather prediction models and machine learning post-processing for wind farm weather prediction is therefore critical.

The performance of numerical weather models relies greatly on model resolutions [19] and regional climates [20], topography [21], underlying land-surface and soil properties [20], weather measurements [22] and data assimilation schemes for model initiation [23], as well as the lateral boundary conditions for limited-area models [24]. For these reasons, many studies and energy forecasting firms use an ensemble of global and regional NWP outputs to reduce forecast errors [25,26].

There are three main error sources in numerical weather forecasting: uncertainties in initial values [27], approximation of the dynamical and physical models [28], and the intrinsic unpredictability of atmospheric motions [29]. Ensemble numerical weather prediction methods [30,31] have been used to improve the accuracy and reliability of weather forecasts through probabilistic forecasts. Probabilistic forecasts and uncertainty quantification are beginning to take the place of single numerical forecasts in the wind energy industry. An ensemble forecast system can simulate the impact of the uncertainties of initial and boundary conditions derived from different global model forecasts, atmospheric physical parameterization schemes, and data assimilation modules. Perturbation members of a mesoscale ensemble forecast system include sub-grid energy stochastic perturbation members, physical parameterization perturbation members, initial and boundary value perturbation members, and some others. Analyzing the error characteristics of ensemble forecast members is important for exploring the value of ensemble forecast outputs and improving the ensemble forecast system.

With respect to model forecast verification, several researchers have explored the effects of model physical processes on wind speed forecasting [32–36]. Different physical parameterization schemes often present different forecast capabilities under different meteorological conditions or regimes [24,37,38], different geographical regions [39–42], and/or different topographic environments [43]. In responding to atmospheric long- and short-wave radiative forcing, model forecast errors often exhibit diurnal and seasonal variations [44–47]. Some other researchers focused on revising model forecast results through post-processing by using statistical and machine learning methods [48]. However, the errors of the model initial and boundary conditions derived from different global model background fields are often large [49,50], but very little attention has been paid to this issue [51]. In fact, we could not find any report investigating the impact of model initial and boundary conditions of the wind farm wind forecasting based on a 2–4 km grid high-resolution ensemble numerical weather prediction model.

The wind energy density in the Inner Mongolia Autonomous Region, China, is outstanding—over 400 W/m^2 in some regions [52]. In 2019, wind power generation in Inner Mongolia was 66.6 billion kWh, accounting for ~16.4% of China's total wind power generation in the same period (China National Energy Administration). In response to the demand for wind power integration in Inner Mongolia, the Inner Mongolia Electric Power Company (IMEPC) has developed a mesoscale ensemble numerical weather prediction system that is composed of 39 perturbed WRF (Weather Research and Forecasting) forecast members. The system is constructed with multiple global models of forcing, multiple physical parameterization schemes, and stochastic kinetic energy perturbations. The 39 forecast members contain three subgroups of 13 physical perturbation members, driven by the forecasts of the GFS (Global Forecast System), GEM (Global Environmental Multiscale Model), and GEOS (Goddard Earth Observing System), respectively.

This paper evaluates the output of the IMEPC mesoscale ensemble prediction system, focusing on its hub-height wind prediction for the wind farms distributed across the Inner Mongolia Autonomous Region during the spring of 2020. The model performance of three sub-ensemble groups driven by the forecasts of the GFS, GEOS, and GEM global models was studied, and the variations in the forecast errors with forecast lead time, wind speed regimes, diurnal forcing, and regional changes were analyzed. The findings of this study provide guidance for the proper use of the ensemble prediction system at the wind farms, and for the development of model forecast post-processing capabilities by the IMEPC. Our results also support modelers to improve the ensemble model system by adjusting the ensemble members according to the error properties of the ensemble members driven by different global model forecasts.

The remainder of this paper is organized as follows: Section 2 describes the observations in the study area and the setup of the ensemble forecast system used for the numerical experiments. Section 3 presents the results of the wind speed forecast error analysis. Section 4 presents the conclusions from these analyses. Finally, Section 5 discusses the limitations of the present work, and describes the outlook for the future.

2. Data and Meteorology

2.1. Ensemble Numerical Weather Prediction System

The IMEPC's WRF-based ensemble weather forecasting system produces wind power forecasts over 100 wind farms distributed across the Inner Mongolia Autonomous Region. This system was jointly developed by the Inner Mongolia Meteorological Bureau, the US National Center for Atmospheric Research (NCAR), and Nanjing University of Information Science and Technology (NUIST); it started real-time operational forecasting in late 2019. The system uses the forecasts of the GEOS (USA), GEM (Canada), and GFS (USA) to derive the initial and boundary conditions to drive the WRF forecast members. The system is configured with 10 physical parameterization schemes, including 9 boundary layer schemes and 1 radiation scheme, and 3 stochastic kinetic energy backward feedback dynamical perturbation (SKEP) schemes, making up the 13 perturbation members that are driven by initial and boundary conditions derived from the global model forecasts of the GFS, GEM, and GEOS, respectively. The system constitutes a total of 39 ensemble forecast members.

The details of the 13 WRF members are listed in Table 1. Each member runs with the WRF real-time four-dimensional data assimilation system (WRF-RTFDDA) [23,53–55]. The operational ensemble forecast system runs with 3-hour data assimilation and forecast cycles, and each cycle produces 72-hour forecasts at a temporal resolution of 15 min. The system assimilates the observations of the hub-height wind speed (the wind turbine wind speed) and meteorological tower weather observations of the wind farms in the region, along with various conventional weather observations [56–58].

The ensemble model contains three forecast domains (Figure 1). Domain 2 and Domain 3 cover the central and western plateau regions of the Inner Mongolia Autonomous Region (40~45° N, 105~120° E), at 2.7 km grid intervals. Domains 2 and 3 are embedded in a coarser grid domain (Domain 1) with a grid size of 13.5 km. Most of the wind farms studied in this paper are located in Domains 2 and 3, featuring complex terrain including stratified high plains, stony hills, terraces, foothills, and inter-hill lowlands. The wind farms are mostly built around four major mountain ranges, including Langshan Mountain (LS), Seertengshan Mountain (SRTS), Ural Mountain (ULS), and Daqingshan Mountain (DQS), along with fan sites located near the Yinshan Mountains (YS), a low plain area to the south of the Hetao Plain (HTPY), and a high plain area near the Xilin Gol League (XLGL) (Figure 1b).

Table 1. Mesoscale ensemble prediction member names and parameterization scheme configuration.

Member Name	Member Perturbations
CTRL	YSU PBL [59]
BOU	BouLac PBL [60]
MYNN2	MYNN 2.5 level TKE scheme [61]
MYJ	Mellor–Yamada–Janjic TKE PBL scheme [62]
SHS	Shin–Hong 'scale-aware' PBL scheme [63]
TEMF	TEMF (Total Energy Mass Flux) scheme [64]
UNW	UW boundary layer scheme from CAM5 [65]
GBM	Grenier–Bretherton–McCaa scheme [66]
QNS	Eddy-diffusivity mass flux, quasi-normal scale elimination PBL [67]
SKEBA	Stochastic kinetic energy backscatter scheme A
SKEBB	Stochastic kinetic energy backscatter scheme B
SKEBC	Stochastic kinetic energy backscatter scheme C
RRMG	Morrison Microphysics + Mellor–Yamada–Janjic PBL scheme

2.2. The Observations and Forecasts

Verification statistics of the ensemble forecasts were calculated based on 411 representative wind turbine sites selected from 130 wind farms, with 1–4 wind turbine sites per wind farm, depending on the wind farm's size. The wind turbine sites are mainly distributed in central Inner Mongolia (Figure 1b). The analysis period was from 1 March to 15 April 2020. Wind speeds at the hub height of the wind turbines, ~50–80 m high from the ground, were retrieved from the SCADA (Supervisory Control and Data Acquisition System) of the wind turbines and averaged to 15-minute windows. To maintain the data continuity, for periods with less than an hour of missing data, a linear interpolation was used to fill in the gaps. For computing the verification statistics, forecasts of the ensemble numerical weather prediction were interpolated to the location and hub height of the selected turbines through a bilinear interpolation method, forming observation and forecast-matched pairs for direct comparison. With 411 wind turbines, 45 days, 72 h of forecasts per day at 15 min intervals, and 39 ensemble members, there were a total of 207,735,840 data samples processed in the verification computation.

To analyze the regional differences in the model forecasts, the wind farms were divided into seven sub-areas according to the distribution of wind farm clusters and topographic characteristics. These areas are marked in the cyan boxes in Figure 2. The wind farm sites in Area 1 are located on the northern slope of Langshan Mountain. The sites in Area 2 are mostly concentrated between Langshan Mountain and Seertengshan Mountain. Area 3 is over the southern part of the Loop Plain to the north of the mountain. Area 4 is between Seertengshan Mountain and Ural Mountain, and some of the turbine sites are close to the local mountain peaks. Area 5 is in the eastern part of Ural Mountain, with higher elevation. Area 6 is located in the relatively more complex area of Daqingshan Mountain to the west of Ural Mountain, with lower elevation, and the turbine sites are more dispersed. Finally, Area 7 is characterized by a high plain area with a flattering topography near the Xilin Gol League. The numbers of stations in these sub-areas are 22, 61, 13, 131, 72, 72, and 40, respectively.

2.3. Evaluation Metrics

The statistical verification of the ensemble forecasts includes calculation of systematic error (BIAS), mean absolute error (MAE), and correlation coefficient (CC) for all selected wind turbine sites and the wind turbine sites in each sub-area. The ensemble wind speed forecast performance is assessed by examining both individual metrics and their combinations. The three statistical variables are calculated based on the hub-height observed (X_o) and forecast (X_f) 15-minute mean wind speed pairs.

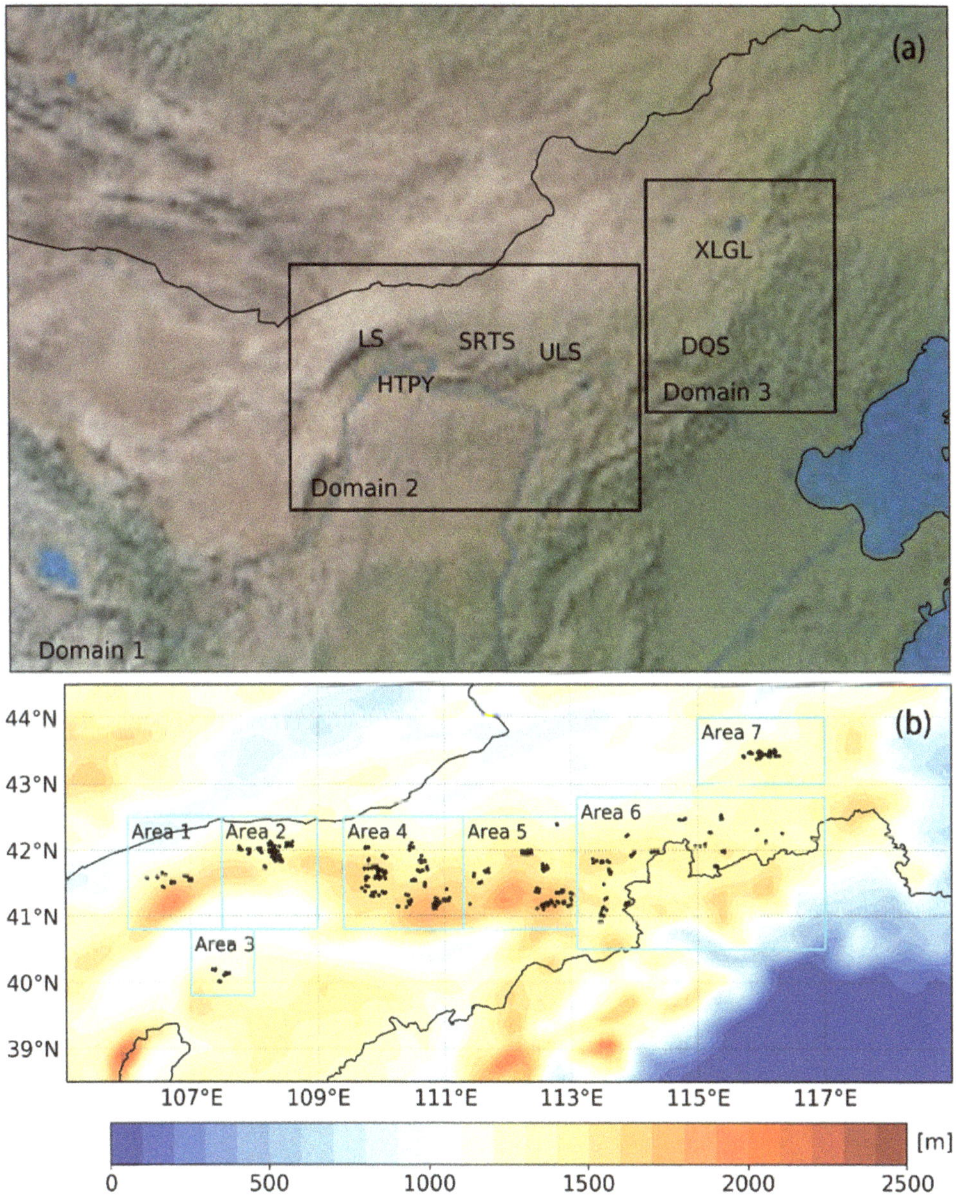

Figure 1. (**a**) Schematic diagram of the ensemble prediction domains for wind farms in the Inner Mongolia Autonomous Region. The horizontal resolution of the coarse-grid simulation domain is 13.5 km, and the horizontal resolution of the two-nested fine-grid simulation domain is 2.7 km. The colored background is the terrain. (**b**) Topography (color filled map) and distribution of test stations (black dots) in the study area. The black line in (**b**) marks the provincial boundary of the Inner Mongolia Autonomous Region, while Areas 1–7 mark the seven subregions enclosed by cyan-colored rectangles.

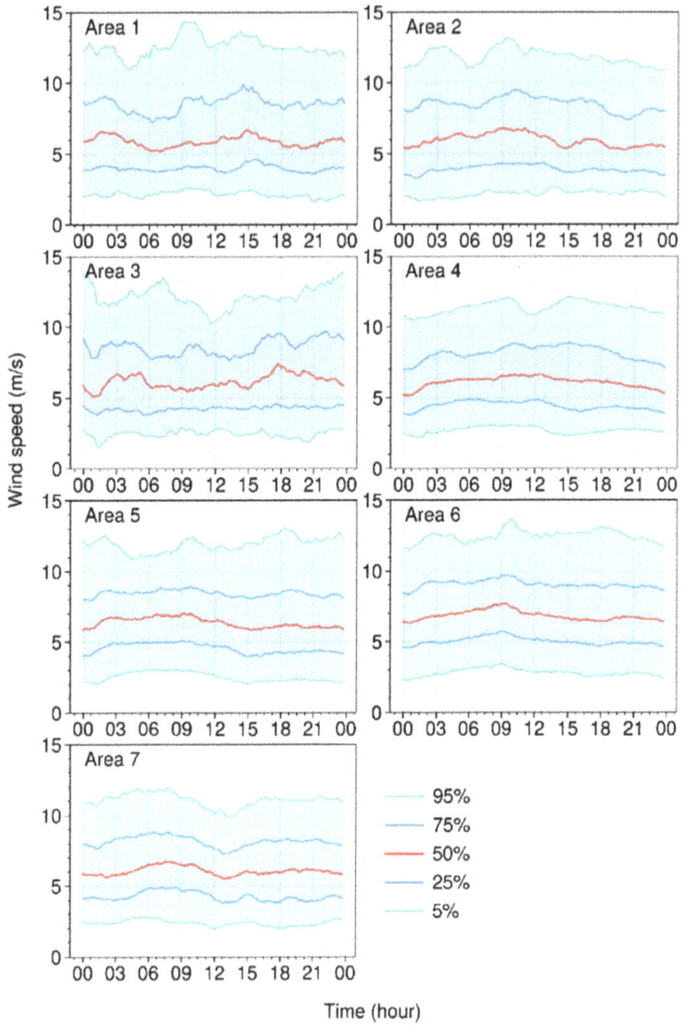

Figure 2. Diurnal variation in the observed wind speeds for the seven sub-areas. The red line is the median value, dark blue is 25–75%, and the light blue zone (including dark blue zone) is 5–95%. The x-axis represents the time (UTC).

3. Statistical Verification Results

3.1. Characteristics of the Winds in the Region

Figure 2 shows the diurnal variation in wind speed observations averaged at all wind turbine sites over the study area, as well as those in the seven sub-areas given in Figure 1. The wind speed over the whole region (Figure 2) exhibits evident diurnal variations, with errors gradually increasing during daytime (from 00:00 to 09:00 UTC, i.e., 08:00–17:00 LST). The median wind speed maximizes between 09:00 UTC and 10:00 UTC (~6.8 m/s), and then starts to decrease in the nighttime. The 25 and 75% sub-quartile wind speeds are 4.2 and 8.2 m/s, respectively; ~5% of the wind speeds are greater than 12 m/s, and ~5% of the wind speeds are less than 2 m/s.

Although the median wind speeds in all seven sub-areas are close (~6 m/s), the diurnal variations in the wind speeds in these regions are quite large. Area 1 possesses a high peak wind speed at 02:00 UTC and 15:00 UTC, and is also prone to greater wind speeds during the day–night transition. The median wind speed in Area 2 tends to slowly increase during daytime, with two local maxima at 03:00 UTC and 09:00 UTC, respectively. The wind speed in Area 3 is higher at night, with a peak median wind speed at 18:00 UTC.

Wind farms in Areas 4, 5, and 6 are in complex mountainous terrain, where winds increase until 09:00–10:00 UTC during the daytime, and show a decreasing trend at night. Finally, Area 7 is in a high plain region, and the diurnal variation in its wind speed is relatively flat, with a small peak in the afternoon, a small trough in the evening, and then a gradual rebound at night.

3.2. Overall Performance of the Wind Forecasts

To compare the forecasts of the ensemble members driven by the initial and boundary conditions derived from the three global model forecasts (GFS, GEOS, and GEM), we first calculated the error metrics of each ensemble member, and then averaged the errors of the 13 members within each subgroup. The average error for each sub-group is computed as follows:

$$\mathrm{x_m} = \frac{1}{13}\sum_{i=1}^{13} x_i \tag{1}$$

where x_i (m/s) represents the error metrics of the forecast of the ith ensemble member. With verification done for 0–24 h forecasts for the 45 days for all 411 wind turbines, the total number of data samples used in computing the statistical verification in each cell of the Table 2 was 23,081,760.

Table 2. Statistical verification of all stations for the GFS, GEOS, and GEM groups (45 days).

	GEOS Group				GEM Group				GFS Group			
	Mean	Max	Median	Min	Mean	Max	Median	Min	Mean	Max	Median	Min
CC	0.68	0.66	0.62	0.58	0.64	0.63	0.58	0.53	0.70	0.67	0.65	0.61
BIAS (m/s)	+0.56	+0.75	+0.60	−0.05	+0.76	+0.91	+0.79	+0.15	+0.67	+0.91	+0.69	+0.04
MAE (m/s)	1.84	2.13	2.06	1.86	1.99	2.32	2.15	1.99	1.81	2.10	2.03	1.80

The overall performance of the three groups of global model forecast members, along with the CC, BIAS, and MAE of the 0–24-hour wind turbine hub-height wind forecasts of all members of the three groups, are calculated and shown in the 'mean' column in Table 2. The CC and MAE of the wind forecasts of the GFS group are better than those of the GEOS group, and both are better than those of the GEM group. In contrast, the BIAS in the GEOS group is smaller than that in the GFS group. The GEM group has the worst scores for all three metrics. The minimum, maximum, and median of correlation coefficients, mean errors, and mean absolute errors of 13 member predictions (13 outcomes for each background field) versus observations are shown in the 'min', 'max', and 'median' columns, respectively, in Table 2. Ensemble average forecasts outperformed the best members. Overall, the GFS group was better than GEOS, and GEM was the worst, which is statistically significant (with all at a confidence level above 98%).

To assess the overall performance of the members driven by the three global model forecasts, the statistical metrics of the three group ensemble forecasts were ranked from the best to the worst for each wind turbine site. The number of stations that performed the best and worst by each ensemble group was counted, as shown in Table 3, along with their proportion to the total turbine sites. The performance of the three ensemble forecast groups varies with the geographic setting of the turbines, as well as the local regional weather and climate characteristics. The statistical verification metrics were calculated separately for each site.

Table 3. Ranking statistics of wind speed forecast errors for the three ensemble forecast groups driven by the GFS, GEOS, and GEM model forecasts.

	GEOS Group		GEM Group		GFS Group	
	NBPS */R *	NWPS */R	NBPS/R	NWPS/R	NBPS/R	NWPS/R
CC	141/34.3%	81/19.7%	8/1.9%	318/77.4%	262/63.7%	12/2.9%
BIAS	315/76.6%	28/6.8%	27/6.6%	315/76.6%	69/16.8%	68/16.5%
MAE	152/37.0%	47/11.4%	9/2.2%	355/86.4%	241/58.6%	9/2.2%

* NBPS: # of best performing stations; NWPS: # of worst performing stations; R: ratio with reference to the total.

Among the three forecast groups, the GFS groups performed the best at ~59–64% of the total sites in terms of CC and MAE, the GEOS group achieved ~34–37%, and the GEM group performed the best for the remaining ~2%. Conversely, from the perspective of the worst performance of the forecasts, the GEM group underperformed at ~77–86% of sites, the GEOS group at ~11–20%, and the GFS group at only ~2–3%. It is interesting to point out that the GEOS group performed the best (~77% of sites) in terms of BIAS, and had relatively more cases with larger positive and negative deviations.

Figure 3 shows the distribution of the turbine sites colored for the predominant best performing ensemble group in terms of the mean CC, BIAS, and MAE among the three ensemble forecast member groups driven by the GFS, GEOS, and GEM global model forecasts. In general, the sites that achieved the best CC and the best MAE coincide. Nevertheless, for BIAS, the GEOS group performed the best at the most turbine sites.

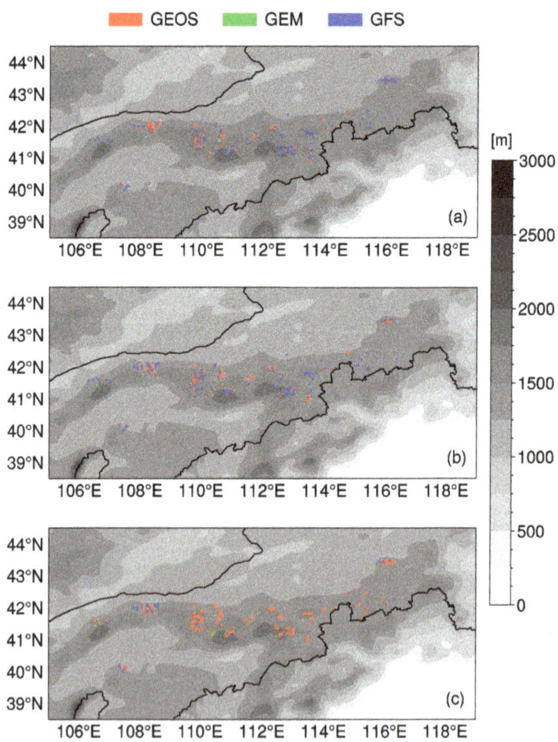

Figure 3. Distribution of the sites colored for the dominant best performing ensemble groups driven by the GFS, GEOS, and GEM forecasts: (**a**) correlation coefficients, (**b**) mean absolute errors, and (**c**) biases.

3.3. Variations of Forecast Errors with Wind Regimes

Wind power generation is proportional to the cubic wind speed [68]. Therefore, it is important to evaluate the model performance in different ranges of wind speeds. Herein, the wind speed is divided into bins of 3 m/s from 0 to 21 m/s, and the forecast errors for each wind speed bin are computed and shown in Figure 4.

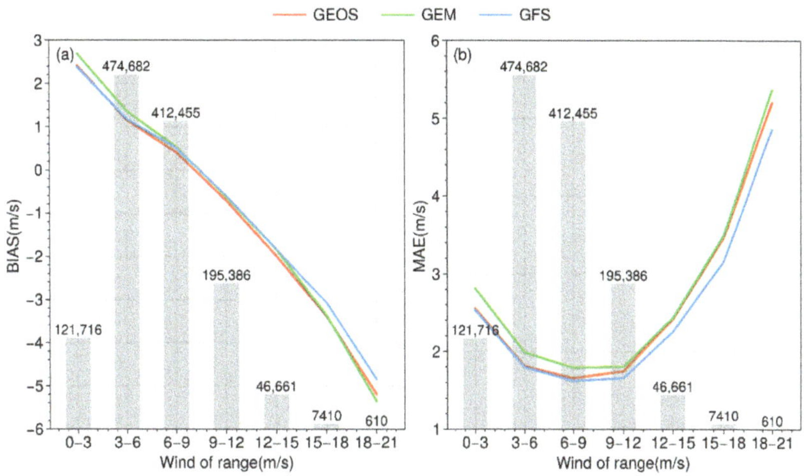

Figure 4. (**a**) BIAS and (**b**) MAE of the wind forecasts of the ensemble groups driven by the GFS, GEOS, and GEM. The line charts are the error statistics, and the histograms correspond to the number of data samples.

The winds in the region are mostly 3–12 m/s (Figure 4). The wind forecast bias of all three groups is similar. The wind forecast bias is negatively correlated with the observed wind speeds, with a nearly linear relationship. For the weak wind conditions of 0–3 m/s, the wind speed is overestimated by 2 m/s. In the bin of 3–9 m/s, the bias gradually decreases to 0, and then the negative bias gradually increases with the wind speed. For winds over 15 m/s, the negative bias reaches 4–5 m/s. The MAE of the wind forecast of the three groups is around 2 m/s in the wind speed range of 3–12 m/s. The overestimation of wind speed in the low-wind-speed range (0–3 m/s) and the underestimation of wind speed in the high-wind-speed range lead to larger MAE for the weak and strong wind ranges.

For the winds in the range of 0–6 m/s, the forecast errors of the GFS and GEOS groups are basically the same, and both are better than the GEM group. For strong winds over 12 m/s, the forecast errors of the GEOS and GEM groups are very similar, and worse than the GFS group. The overestimation of wind speeds in the low-wind-speed range and the underestimation of wind speeds in the high-wind-speed range are smaller for the GFS group than for the other two groups.

3.4. Diurnal Variation in Wind Forecast Errors

Figure 5 presents the diurnal variation of the mean observations, and the forecasts and MAE of the wind speed for the ensemble groups driven by the GFS, GEOS, and GEM forecasts. During daytime (00:00–09:00 UTC), the mean wind speed increases from 6 m/s to 7 m/s from morning to evening. Overall, the bias of the wind forecasts of all three groups is small. The GEOS group shows a bias close to zero, the GEM group has a weak negative deviation, and the GFS group has a bias that gradually increases from a negative deviation of ~0.1 m/s to a positive deviation of 0.2 m/s.

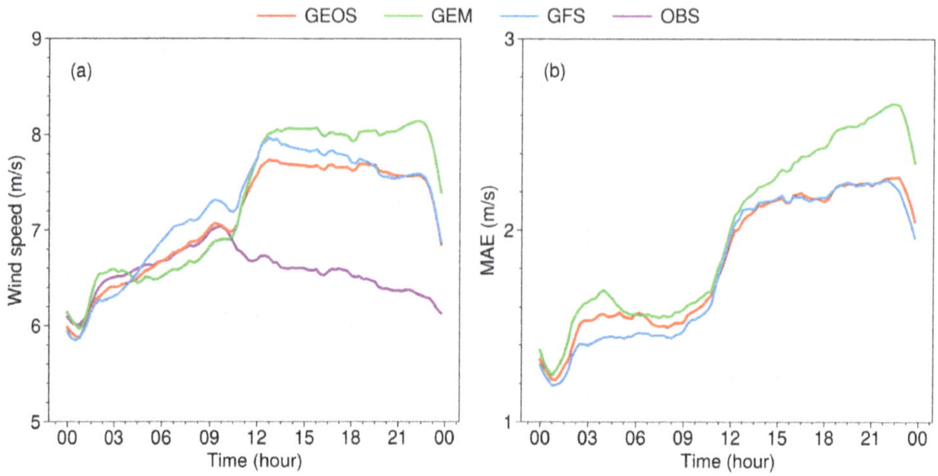

Figure 5. (**a**) Diurnal variation in wind speed observations and forecasts, and (**b**) MAE of the ensemble groups driven by the GFS, GEOS, and GEM. The x-axis represents the time (UTC).

At ~11:00 UTC, the wind forecasts of all three ensemble groups experience a sharp increase toward a positive deviation. Within half an hour, the bias of the wind forecasts of the GEOS, GFS, and GEM groups increases to ~0.9, 1.1, and 1.3 m/s, respectively. Subsequently, at night, the mean wind speed gradually weakens and the mean bias of the wind speed forecasting of the GFS group remains roughly unchanged, but the mean deviation in the GEOS and GEM groups continues to increase. By 23:00 UTC, the positive wind forecast biases of all three groups decrease rapidly as the boundary layer starts to grow after sunrise.

The GEM ensemble group possesses the largest MAE of the wind forecasts during daytime, followed by the GEOS group, while the MAE of the GFS group is the lowest. After a brief increase, MAE stabilizes at ~1.5 m/s between 03:00 and 11:00 UTC. After sunset (11:00–13:00 UTC), the MAE of all three groups increases to ~2.2 m/s. After nightfall, the MAE of the wind speed forecast of the GEM group continues to increase significantly, to 2.7 m/s, while that of the GEOS and GFS groups only increases to 2.3 m/s. Finally, after sunrise at 22:00 UTC, the MAE of all three groups decreases rapidly. Overall, the MAE of the GFS group was smaller than that of the other two groups, and the MAE of the GEM group was the largest for both nighttime and daytime. The MAE of the GEOS group during nighttime is similar to that of the GFS group.

To further compare the distribution of the wind forecast errors of the three ensemble groups and their diurnal variations, the forecast deviations of each ensemble member were analyzed for four day-periods: daytime (00:00–10:00 UTC), sunset (10:00–12:00 UTC), nighttime (12:00–22:00 UTC), and sunrise (22:00–00:00 UTC); the results are summarized in Figure 6.

The error distributions of the wind forecasts of all three groups are quite wide. The forecast members of the GFS group have relatively smaller variance (i.e., smaller dispersion) than the other two groups. In contrast, the forecast members of the GEM group have relatively larger variance and median bias. During the daytime and sunset periods, the error distributions of the three ensemble groups are relatively similar, and the numbers of samples with positive and negative deviations are close. However, during the night and sunrise phases, most of the model forecasts in all groups overestimate the wind speed, and the positive deviations of the GEM group are significantly larger than those of the GFS and GEOS groups.

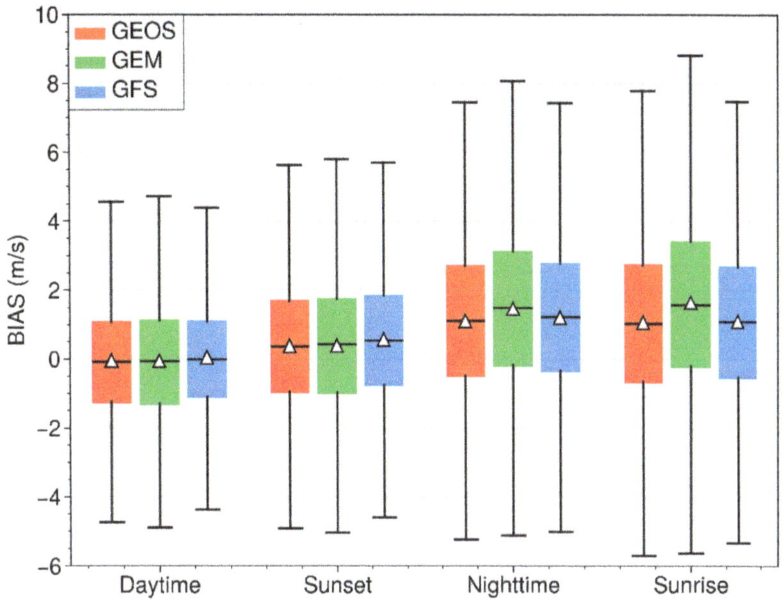

Figure 6. Boxplots of the wind forecast bias distributions for the ensemble groups driven by the GFS, GEOS, and GEM forecasts for daytime (00:00–10:00 UTC), sunset (10:00–12:00 UTC), nighttime (12:00–22:00 UTC), and sunrise (22:00–00:00 UTC). The black horizontal line marks the median bias, while the white triangle represents the mean bias.

3.5. Forecast Errors in Seven Regions

The previous analysis indicates that the ensemble members driven by the three global model forecasts perform differently at different sites (Figure 3). To further investigate the regional differences in these ensemble groups, the wind farms in the study area were divided into seven sub-areas, according to geographical location, from west to east (see Figure 1). As shown in Figure 1, the wind farms are mainly built along the narrow mountain ridges that span the Inner Mongolia region. Based on the topography and wind farm distribution in the seven areas, they can be divided into four main types:

(a) The wind farms located on the northern slope of a mountain, with another mountain tens of kilometers to its northwest (Areas 1 and 3);
(b) The wind farms located on valley passes or leeward slopes of mountains. (Areas 2, 4, and 5);
(c) The wind farms located over relatively low terrain (Area 6);
(d) The wind farms located over flat terrain away from significant mountains (Area 7).

Figure 7 demonstrates that (1) the diurnal variation in the average wind speed and the forecast bias of the three ensemble groups in the four representative areas are quite different, (2) the trend of the wind speed forecast bias of the three ensemble groups is consistent, and (3) the average bias of the wind speed forecasting of all three ensemble groups is negatively correlated with the magnitude of the wind speed, i.e., the higher the wind speed, the smaller the bias.

Area 1 (Figure 7) is located on the north slope of a mountain. The wind in this region displays a very complex diurnal evolution, and the bias of the wind forecasts of all three ensemble groups presents similar, negatively correlated evolution of the mean wind speed. Among the three ensemble groups, the GEOS group has the smallest bias in the daytime and the largest late at night. The GEM group possesses the largest bias during most times, except for a 2-hour period around 18:00 UTC.

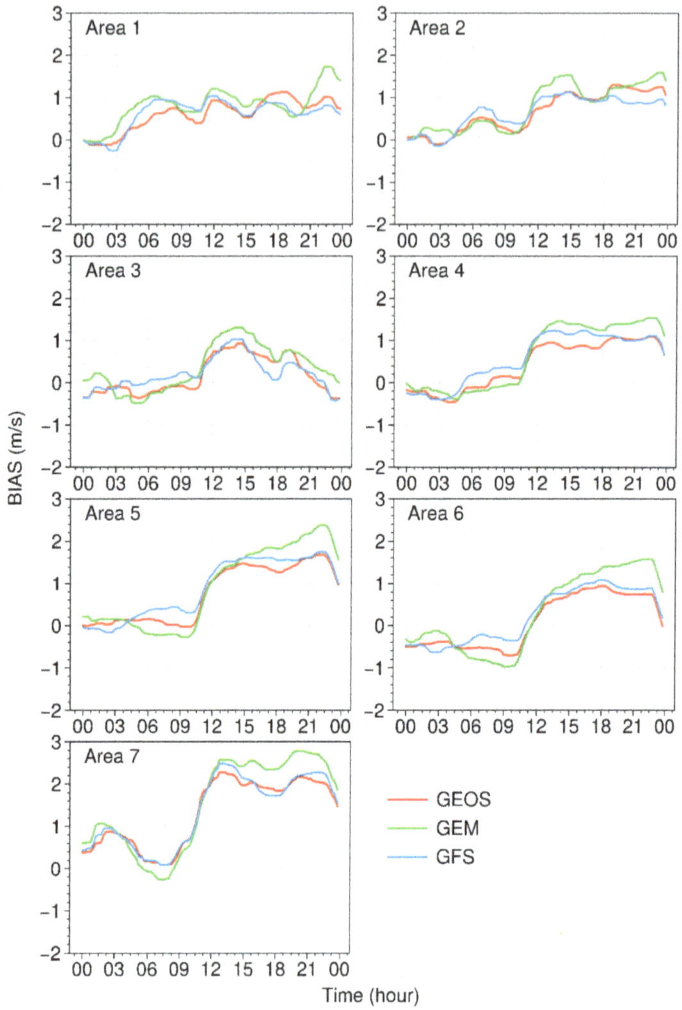

Figure 7. The BIAS of the wind forecasts of the three ensemble groups in the seven sub-areas. The x-axis represents the time (UTC).

Area 3 (Figure 7) is on the southern slope of the Hetao Plain, with a relatively low altitude. This area is affected by the prevailing westerly and northwesterly winds. Blocked by the Langshan Mountain tens of kilometers away to the northwest, the wind speed is smaller during the daytime and higher at nighttime compared to other areas, and the area is prone to strong winds. The nighttime wind speeds in this area gradually increase from 6.1 m/s at sunset to 7.1 m/s before sunrise, and a peak occurs at night (18:00 UTC). The bias of the wind speed forecasting of the three ensemble groups is small during daytime, at close to 0 for the GFS group, and with slight negative bias for the GEOS and GEM groups. In the evening, with the adjustment with the atmospheric boundary layer, the wind speed forecasts of the three ensemble groups grow rapidly to positive bias, reaching a maximum at ~13:00 UTC, and then gradually decreasing. The wind forecast biases of the GFS and GEOS groups are close, but the forecast bias of the GEM group has a much larger amplitude of diurnal variations, with a positive bias 0.3–0.4 m/s larger than that of the GFS group at night. It should be noted that the CC of the sites in Areas 1 and 3 is high (0.7~0.85).

The diurnal variations in the average wind speed and the wind forecast verification in Areas 2, 4, 5, and 6 are relatively similar. Unlike Area 3, the wind speed in these areas is characterized by high wind speeds during daytime, gradually strengthening after sunrise, reaching a peak around 9:00 UTC, and then decreasing to a minimum in the early morning. The bias of the wind speed forecasting of the three ensemble groups exhibits a very similar diurnal trend, with very little bias during daytime and a stable positive deviation of ~1.4 m/s at night. The GEOS group has a higher percentage of superior forecasts in Areas 2 and 4, mainly in the middle of the pass and on the northern slopes of the mountains in Area 4. The GFS group dominates better forecasts on the high slopes. The western part of Area 6, which is on the eastern part of the mountain peak, is a leeward slope where the forecast errors—mainly with negative bias—are relatively larger.

Area 7 (Figure 7) is a high plain characterized by flat terrain. The wind speed is characterized by a peak wind speed in the afternoon (08:00 UTC) and a shallow trough in the evening at 13:00 UTC. The wind speed forecasts of the three ensemble groups possess an obvious positive bias, except for the enhanced wind speed period in the afternoon (06:00–09:00 UTC), when the bias is smaller. The biases of the wind speed forecasts of the GFS and GEOS groups in this area are generally close to one another throughout the day, at ~0.5 m/s during daytime and close to 1.5 m/s at night. The GEM group underestimates the wind speed during daytime and overestimates the wind speed during nighttime, both of which errors are significantly larger than those of the GFS and GEOS groups. On average, the GFS group performs the best in this area, with a high CC of ~0.75.

3.6. Growth of Forecast Errors with Lead Time

The 0–72 h forecasts of the ensemble groups driven by the GFS, GEOS, and GEM were examined to analyze the growth of the wind forecast errors with the forecast length (Figure 8). The MAE of the wind speed forecasts of the three ensemble member groups increases with the forecast length at a rate of ~0.4 m/s per day for the 3 days (Figure 8a). The MAEs of the wind speed forecasts of the GFS and GEOS groups are rather close to one another, while the GFS group has a slight advantage. The wind speed errors of the GEM group grow faster at nighttime, resulting in MAE of 0.4 m/s and 0.6 m/s more than the other two groups on the first and second days, respectively.

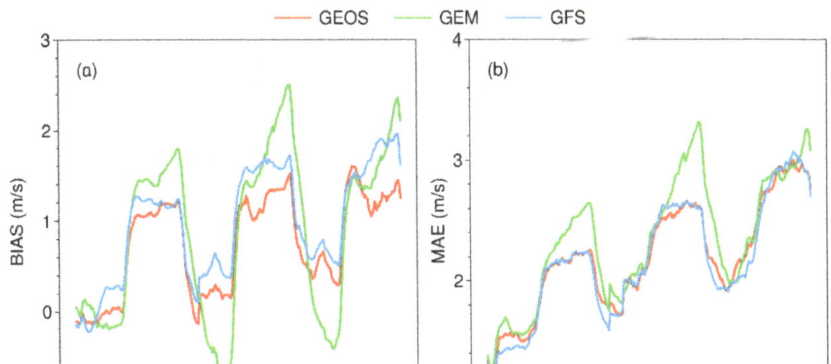

Figure 8. Variation in wind speed forecast errors with forecast time for the ensemble groups driven by the three global model forecasts: (**a**) BIAS and (**b**) MAE. The x-axis represents the time (hours).

Comparing Figure 8a,b, we can see that the large MAE of the wind forecasts at night was mainly due to the systematic overestimation of the nighttime wind speeds by the model. It is interesting to note that although the MAE of wind forecasts of the GFS and

GEOS groups is relatively close, the bias of the wind speed forecasts of the GEOS group is significantly better than that of the GFS group. Figure 8 shows more clearly that the mean wind forecast error of the GEM group has a large diurnal variation, with a large overestimation of positive wind bias in the nighttime and negative bias in the daytime.

4. Summary and Conclusions

In this paper, statistical verification of a mesoscale ensemble numerical weather prediction system was conducted for hub-height wind prediction at 411 wind turbines representing ~130 wind farms. The ensemble system contains 39 forecast members, and is divided into 3 groups driven by the US GFS and GEOS and the Canadian GEM global weather model forecasts. Each group contains the same set of 13 physical perturbations. The verification period was from 1 March to 15 April 2020. This paper analyzes the error characteristics of the mean wind forecasts of the three ensemble groups and compares their performance. The error statistics (CC, BIAS, and MAE) of the wind forecasts—including the diurnal variability, differences in seven geographical regions, dependence on wind speed regimes, and growth by forecast time—are analyzed. The main conclusions of this study are as follows.

(1) Among the ensemble groups driven by the GFS, GEOS, and GEM global weather model forecasts, the GFS group significantly outperformed the other two groups with respect to the CC and MAE of the wind forecasts, with 59–64% of the turbines performing best. The GEM group was poorer overall, with only 2% of turbines achieving the best prediction. The wind forecast MAE of the GEOS group was similar to that of the GFS group, but the GEOS group tended to perform better in terms of BIAS. In the GEOS group, there were some larger positive and negative biases that offset one another, resulting in a smaller overall bias;

(2) All three ensemble groups overestimated the low wind speed (0–3 m/s) and underestimated the high wind speed. All three groups had better forecasts for the wind speeds ranging from 3 to 12 m/s, and the errors of the GFS and GEOS groups were similar. For wind speeds greater than 12 m/s, the GFS group outperformed the GEOS group, and the GEM group had the largest error. The average deviation of the wind forecasts from the observations increased approximately linearly with the magnitude of wind speeds, reaching more than −4 m/s for the cases of strong winds over 15 m/s;

(3) The wind speed forecasts of all three ensemble groups exhibited similar diurnal variation in each of the seven subregions. The wind forecast bias was generally small during daytime but overestimated by 1–1.5 m/s at night. The GFS group had the best performance, the GEOS group was slightly worse, and the GEM group significantly underestimated the wind speed during daytime. The GEOS group had more accurate wind speed forecasts than the GFS group in nighttime in several complex terrain areas;

(4) The errors of the wind forecasts of the three ensemble groups increased with forecast lead time, with a growth rate of ~0.3 m/s for the 3-day forecast period. The nighttime MAE was 0.6–0.5 m/s higher than that in the daytime. The MAEs of wind forecasts of the GFS and GEOS groups were relatively close to one another, and the GFS group had a slight advantage. The wind speed forecast errors of the GEM group grew much faster at night, and its biases were ~0.4–0.6 m/s larger than those of the other two groups. The large MAE of the GEM group wind forecast during nighttime was mainly due to the systematic overestimation of wind speed at night;

(5) Based on the results of this study, the ensemble outputs should first be processed to remove the bias of the three subgroups separately before they are combined for deriving probabilistic wind power forecast products. The model post-processing should be done for each region, as best as possible, for each wind turbine site independently, in order to deal with the unique forecast error properties of the ensembles in different regions. Model developers should devote their attention to mitigating the trend of the wind forecast bias growth with wind speeds.

5. Discussion

It should be noted that the performance of numerical weather models is highly reliant on model resolution [18], regional climate [19], topography [20], underlying land-surface and soil properties [19], weather measurements [21] and data assimilation schemes for model initiation [23], as well as the lateral boundary conditions for limited-area models [24]. The ensemble forecasts overestimate wind speeds. Similar results have also been reported in several previous studies using the WRF model over different global regions [24,36,38]. Although several studies have tried to identify the physical reasons for this, they have not reached a consensus on the issue. From the dynamical point of view, the height and roughness of the subsurface may not be sufficiently considered in the WRF model [69,70], and from the thermodynamic point of view, the WRF model may misestimate the cloudiness, making it difficult to predict the long- and short-wave radiation accurately, and resulting in the misestimation of near-surface wind speed [71–73]. Our results show that, driven by different global model forecasts, the BIAS properties of the WRF forecasts differ, but the overall BIAS trends are the same for all subregions in the studied domain.

This study focused on the wind forecast error characteristics of the Inner Mongolia mesoscale ensemble forecasting system with respect to the impact of the ensemble members driven by different global numerical weather prediction model forecasts. Our findings provide a basis for developing a statistical post-processing of the ensemble forecasts to improve wind and power forecasting for the wind farms, and for further improvement of the forecast capability of the WRF models in the future.

However, the present study was based on only 45 days of wind prediction data in the spring of 2020, making it insufficient to describe the year-round forecast error pattern. We are collecting more data to expand this work to a full-year period, and studying the seasonal variation patterns of wind forecast error statistics. Furthermore, this ensemble forecast system contains 10 perturbed members of the varying atmospheric boundary layer parameterization scheme. We are currently analyzing and comparing the error characteristics of the wind forecasts using these different atmospheric boundary layer parameterization schemes; the results will be reported in a separate paper.

Author Contributions: Conceptualization, J.S., Y.L. (Yubao Liu) and X.F.; methodology, Y.L. (Yubao Liu) and Y.L. (Yang Li); software, J.S.; validation, L.S. and X.F.; formal analysis, J.S.; investigation and resources, Y.L. (Yuewei Liu); data curation, J.S., L.S. and G.R.; writing—original draft preparation, J.S.; writing—review and editing, Y.L. (Yubao Liu) and Y.L. (Yang Li); visualization, J.S. and Y.L. (Yang Li); funding acquisition, Y.L. (Yubao Liu) and X.F. All authors have read and agreed to the published version of the manuscript.

Funding: This research was funded by the Jibei Electric Power Company (Grant #520120210003), the Inner Mongolia Electric Power Company, and the Northwest Region Weather Modification Capability Development Program, RQC19081 and RQC-19176.

Institutional Review Board Statement: Not applicable.

Informed Consent Statement: Not applicable.

Data Availability Statement: Not applicable.

Acknowledgments: We give thanks to the Inner Mongolia Meteorological Bureau, the US National Center for Atmospheric Research (NCAR), and Nanjing University of Information Science and Technology (NUIST) for data and computing support.

Conflicts of Interest: The authors declare no conflict of interest.

References

1. Yu, L.; Zhong, S.; Bian, X.; Heilman, W. Climatology and Trend of Wind Power Resources in China and Its Surrounding Regions: A Revisit Using Climate Forecast System Reanalysis Data. *Int. J. Climatol.* **2016**, *36*, 2173–2188. [CrossRef]
2. Makarov, Y.V.; Loutan, C.; Ma, J.; Mello, P.D. Operational impacts of wind generation on California power systems. *IEEE Trans. Power Syst.* **2009**, *24*, 1039–1050. [CrossRef]

3. Georgilakis, P.S. Technical challenges associated with the integration of wind power into power systems. *Renew. Sustain. Energy Rev.* **2008**, *12*, 852–863. [CrossRef]
4. Smith, J.C.; Milligan, M.R.; DeMeo, E.A.; Parsons, B. Utility wind integration and operating impact state of the art. *IEEE Trans. Power Syst.* **2007**, *22*, 900–908. [CrossRef]
5. Shen, X.; Zhou, C.; Fu, X. Study of Time and Meteorological Characteristics of Wind Speed Correlation in Flat Terrains Based on Operation Data. *Energies* **2018**, *11*, 219. [CrossRef]
6. Zhang, S.; Liu, Y.; Wang, J.; Wang, C. Research on Combined Model Based on Multi-Objective Optimization and Application in Wind Speed Forecast. *Appl. Sci.* **2019**, *9*, 423. [CrossRef]
7. Geng, D.; Zhang, H.; Wu, H. Short-Term Wind Speed Prediction Based on Principal Component Analysis and LSTM. *Appl. Sci.* **2020**, *10*, 4416. [CrossRef]
8. Emeksiz, C.; Tan, M. Multi-step wind speed forecasting and Hurst analysis using novel hybrid secondary decomposition approach. *Energy* **2022**, *238*, 121764. [CrossRef]
9. Jiang, P.; Liu, Z.; Niu, X.; Zhang, L. A combined forecasting system based on statistical method, artificial neural networks, and deep learning methods for short-term wind speed forecasting. *Energy* **2021**, *217*, 119361. [CrossRef]
10. Neshat, M.; Nezhad, M.M.; Abbasnejad, E.; Mirjalili, S.; Tjernberg, L.B.; Garcia, D.A.; Alexander, B.; Wagner, M. A deep learning-based evolutionary model for short-term wind speed forecasting: A case study of the Lillgrund offshore wind farm. *Energy Convers. Manag.* **2021**, *236*, 114002. [CrossRef]
11. Li, D.; Jiang, F.; Chen, M.; Qian, T. Multi-step-ahead wind speed forecasting based on a hybrid decomposition method and temporal convolutional networks. *Energy* **2022**, *238*, 121981. [CrossRef]
12. Bauer, P.; Thorpe, A.; Brunet, G. The Quiet Revolution of Numerical Weather Prediction. *Nature* **2015**, *525*, 47–55. [CrossRef] [PubMed]
13. Alharbi, F.R.; Csala, D. Wind Speed and Solar Irradiance Prediction Using a Bidirectional Long Short-Term Memory Model Based on Neural Networks. *Energies* **2021**, *14*, 6501. [CrossRef]
14. Chen, Q.; Chen, Y.; Bai, X. Deterministic and Interval Wind Speed Prediction Method in Offshore Wind Farm Considering the Randomness of Wind. *Energies* **2020**, *13*, 5595. [CrossRef]
15. Bai, Y.; Tang, L.; Fan, M.; Ma, X.; Yang, Y. Fuzzy First-Order Transition-Rules-Trained Hybrid Forecasting System for Short-Term Wind Speed Forecasts. *Energies* **2020**, *13*, 3332. [CrossRef]
16. Zhao, X.; Wei, H.; Li, C.; Zhang, K. A Hybrid Nonlinear Forecasting Strategy for Short-Term Wind Speed. *Energies* **2020**, *13*, 1596. [CrossRef]
17. Brahimi, T. Using Artificial Intelligence to Predict Wind Speed for Energy Application in Saudi Arabia. *Energies* **2019**, *12*, 4669. [CrossRef]
18. Ren, Y.; Li, H.; Lin, H.-C. Optimization of Feedforward Neural Networks Using an Improved Flower Pollination Algorithm for Short-Term Wind Speed Prediction. *Energies* **2019**, *12*, 4126. [CrossRef]
19. Luo, N.; Guo, Y. Impact of Model Resolution on the Simulation of Precipitation Extremes over China. *Sustainability* **2022**, *14*, 25. [CrossRef]
20. Zhang, M.; Tölle, M.H.; Hartmann, E.; Xoplaki, E.; Luterbacher, J. A Sensitivity Assessment of COSMO-CLM to Different Land Cover Schemes in Convection-Permitting Climate Simulations over Europe. *Atmosphere* **2021**, *12*, 1595. [CrossRef]
21. Zhang, C.; He, J.; Lai, X.; Liu, Y.; Che, H.; Gong, S. The Impact of the Variation in Weather and Season on WRF Dynamical Downscaling in the Pearl River Delta Region. *Atmosphere* **2021**, *12*, 409. [CrossRef]
22. Suh, M.S.; Oh, S.G. Impacts of Boundary Conditions on the Simulation of Atmospheric Fields Using RegCM4 over CORDEX East Asia. *Atmosphere* **2015**, *6*, 783–804. [CrossRef]
23. Liu, Y.; Warner, T.T.; Bowers, J.F.; Carson, L.P.; Chen, F.; Clough, C.A.; Davis, C.A.; Egeland, C.H.; Halvorson, S.F.; Huck, T.W., Jr.; et al. The Operational Mesogamma-Scale Analysis and Forecast System of the US Army Test and Evaluation Command. Part I: Overview of the Modeling System, the Forecast Products, and How the Products are Used. *J. Appl. Meteorol. Climatol.* **2008**, *47*, 1077–1092. [CrossRef]
24. Draxl, C.; Hahmann, A.N.; Peña, A.; Giebel, G. Evaluating Winds and Vertical Wind Shear from Weather Research and Forecasting Model Forecasts Using Seven Planetary Boundary Layer Schemes. *Wind Energy* **2014**, *17*, 39–55. [CrossRef]
25. Li, S.; Wang, Y.; Yuan, H.; Song, J.; Xu, X. Ensemble mean forecast skill and applications with the T213 ensemble prediction system. *Adv. Atmos. Sci.* **2016**, *33*, 1297–1305. [CrossRef]
26. Dube, A.; Ashrit, R.; Singh, H.; Arora, K.; Iyengar, G.; Rajagopal, E.N. Evaluating the performance of two global ensemble forecasting systems in predicting rainfall over India during the southwest monsoons. *Meteorol. Appl.* **2017**, *24*, 230–238. [CrossRef]
27. Rabier, F.; Klinker, E.; Courtier, P.; Hollingsworth, A. Sensitivity of Forecast Error to Initial Conditions. *Q. J. R. Meteorol. Soc.* **1996**, *122*, 121–150. [CrossRef]
28. Buizza, R.; Miller, M.; Palmer, T.N. Stochastic Representation of Model Uncertainties in the ECMWF Ensemble Prediction System. *Q. J. R. Meteorol. Soc.* **1999**, *125*, 2887–2908. [CrossRef]
29. Lorenz, E.N. Deterministic Nonperiodic Flow. *J. Atmos. Sci.* **1963**, *20*, 130–141. [CrossRef]
30. Leith, C.E. Theoretical skill of Monte Carlo Forecasts. *Mon. Weather Rev.* **1974**, *102*, 409–418. [CrossRef]
31. Du, J.; Mullen, S.L.; Sanders, F. Short-Range Ensemble Forecasting of Quantitative Precipitation. *Mon. Weather Rev.* **1997**, *125*, 2427–2459. [CrossRef]

32. Baldauf, M.; Seifert, A.; Foerstner, J.; Majewski, D.; Raschendorfer, M.; Reinhardt, T. Operational Convective-Scale Numerical Weather Prediction with the Cosmo Model: Description and Sensitivities. *Mon. Weather Rev.* **2011**, *139*, 3887–3905. [CrossRef]
33. Eckel, F.A.; Mass, C.F. Aspects of Effective Mesoscale, Short-Range Ensemble Forecasting. *Weather Forecast* **2005**, *20*, 328–350. [CrossRef]
34. Han, J.; Pan, H. Revision of Convection and Vertical Diffusion Schemes in the NCEP Global Forecast System. *Weather Forecast* **2011**, *26*, 520–533. [CrossRef]
35. Pinson, P.; Hagedorn, R. Verification of the ECMWF Ensemble Forecasts of Wind Speed against Analyses and Observations. *Meteorol. Appl.* **2012**, *19*, 484–500. [CrossRef]
36. Xie, B.; Fung, J.C.H.; Chan, A.; Lau, A. Evaluation of Nonlocal and Local Planetary Boundary Layer Schemes in the WRF Model. *J. Geophys. Res. Atmos.* **2012**, *117*, 1–26. [CrossRef]
37. Mass, C.F.; Warner, M.D.; Steed, R. Strong Westerly Wind Events in the Strait of Juan de Fuca. *Weather Forecast* **2014**, *29*, 445–465. [CrossRef]
38. Zhang, D.; Zheng, W. Diurnal Cycles of Surface Winds and Temperatures as Simulated by Five Boundary Layer Parameterizations. *J. Appl. Meteorol. Climatol.* **2004**, *43*, 157–169. [CrossRef]
39. Ancell, B.C.; Mass, C.F.; Hakim, G.J. Evaluation of Surface Analyses and Forecasts with a Multiscale Ensemble Kalman Filter in Regions of Complex Terrain. *Mon. Weather Rev.* **2011**, *139*, 2008–2024. [CrossRef]
40. Carvalho, D.; Rocha, A.; Gómez-Gesteira, M.; Santos, C. A Sensitivity Study of the WRF Model in Wind Simulation for an Area of High Wind Energy. *Environ. Model. Softw.* **2012**, *33*, 23–34. [CrossRef]
41. Coniglio, M.C.; Correia, J., Jr.; Marsh, P.T.; Kong, F. Verification of Convection-Allowing WRF Model Forecasts of the Planetary Boundary Layer Using Sounding Observations. *Weather Forecast* **2013**, *28*, 842–862. [CrossRef]
42. Serafin, S.; Adler, B.; Cuxart, J.; De Wekker, S.F.J.; Gohm, A.; Grisogono, B.; Kalthoff, N.; Kirshbaum, D.J.; Rotach, M.W.; Schmidli, J.; et al. Exchange Processes in the Atmospheric Boundary Layer over Mountainous Terrain. *Atmosphere* **2018**, *9*, 102. [CrossRef]
43. Rife, D.L.; Davis, C.A. Verification of Temporal Variations in Mesoscale Numerical Wind Forecasts. *Mon. Weather Rev.* **2005**, *133*, 3368–3381. [CrossRef]
44. Brewer, M.C.; Mass, C.F. Simulation of Summer Diurnal Circulations over the Northwest United States. *Weather Forecast* **2014**, *29*, 1208–1228. [CrossRef]
45. Brewer, M.C.; Mass, C.F. Projected Changes in Western U.S. Large-Scale Summer Synoptic Circulations and Variability in CMIP5 Models. *J. Clim.* **2016**, *29*, 5965–5978. [CrossRef]
46. Warner, M.D.; Mass, C.F. Changes in the Climatology, Structure, and Seasonality of Northeast Pacific Atmospheric Rivers in CMIP5 Climate Simulations. *J. Hydrometeorol.* **2017**, *18*, 2121–2141. [CrossRef]
47. Weber, N.J.; Mass, C.F. Evaluating the Subseasonal to Seasonal CFSv2 Forecast Skill with an Emphasis on Tropical Convection. *Mon. Weather Rev.* **2017**, *146*, 3795–3815. [CrossRef]
48. Xu, W.; Ning, L.; Luo, Y. Wind Speed Forecast Based on Post-Processing of Numerical Weather Predictions Using a Gradient Boosting Decision Tree Algorithm. *Atmosphere* **2020**, *11*, 738. [CrossRef]
49. Fernández-González, S.; Sastre, M.; Valero, F.; Merino, A.; García-Ortega, E.; Sánchez, J.L.; Lorenzana, J.; Martín, M.L. Characterization of Spread in a Mesoscale Ensemble Prediction System: Multiphysics versus Initial Conditions. *Meteorol. Z.* **2018**, *28*, 59–67. [CrossRef]
50. Mass, C.F.; David, O. The Northern California Wildfires of October 8–9, 2017: The Role of a Major Downslope Windstorm Event. *Bull. Am. Meteorol. Soc.* **2019**, *100*, 235–256. [CrossRef]
51. Zhang, T.; Zhao, C.; Gong, C.; Pu, Z. Simulation of Wind Speed Based on Different Driving Datasets and Parameterization Schemes Near Dunhuang Wind Farms in Northwest of China. *Atmosphere* **2020**, *11*, 647. [CrossRef]
52. Gao, Y.; Ma, S.; Wang, T.; Wang, T.; Gong, Y.; Peng, F.; Tsunekawa, A. Assessing the wind energy potential of China in considering its variability/intermittency. *Energy Convers. Manag.* **2020**, *226*, 113580. [CrossRef]
53. Knievel, J.C.; Liu, Y.; Hopson, T.M.; Shaw, J.S.; Halvorson, S.F.; Fisher, H.H.; Roux, G.; Sheu, R.-S.; Pan, L.; Wu, W.; et al. Mesoscale Ensemble Weather Prediction at U.S. Army Dugway Proving Ground, Utah. *Weather Forecast* **2017**, *32*, 2195–2216. [CrossRef]
54. Kosovic, B.; Haupt, S.E.; Adriaansen, D.; Alessandrini, S.; Wiener, G.; Delle Monache, L.; Liu, Y.; Linden, S.; Jensen, T.; Cheng, W.; et al. A Comprehensive Wind Power Forecasting System Integrating Artificial Intelligence and Numerical Weather Prediction. *Engergies* **2020**, *13*, 1372. [CrossRef]
55. Pan, L.; Liu, Y.; Roux, G.; Cheng, W.; Liu, Y.; Hu, J.; Jin, S.; Feng, S.; Du, J.; Peng, L. Seasonal Variation of the Surface Wind Forcast Performance of the High-Resolution WRF-RTFDDA System over China. *Atmos. Res.* **2021**, *259*, 105673. [CrossRef]
56. Mahoney, W.P.; Parks, K.; Wiener, G.; Liu, Y.; Myers, W.; Sun, J.; Monache, L.-D.; Hopson, T.; Johnson, D.; Haupt, S.E. A Wind Power Forecasting System to Optimize Grid Integration. *IEEE Trans. Sustain. Energy* **2012**, *3*, 670–682. [CrossRef]
57. Cheng, W.Y.Y.; Liu, Y.; Liu, Y.W.; Zhang, Y.; Mahoney, W.P.; Warner, T.T. The Impact of Model Physics on Numerical Wind Forecasts. *Renew. Energy* **2013**, *55*, 347–356. [CrossRef]
58. Cheng, W.Y.Y.; Liu, Y.; Bourgeois, A.; Wu, Y.; Haupt, S.E. Short-Term Wind Forecast of a Data Assimilation/Weather Forecasting System with Wind Turbine Anemometer Measurement Assimilation. *Renew. Energy* **2017**, *107*, 340–351. [CrossRef]
59. Hong, S.-Y.; Noh, Y.; Dudhia, J. A New Vertical Diffusion Package with an Explicit Treatment of Entrainment Processes. *Mon. Weather Rev.* **2006**, *134*, 2318–2341. [CrossRef]

60. Bougeault, P.; Lacarrere, P. Parameterization of Orography-Induced Turbulence in a Mesobeta—Scale Model. *Mon. Weather Rev.* **1989**, *117*, 1872–1890. [CrossRef]
61. Nakanishi, M.; Niino, H. An Improved Mellor-Yamada Level 3 Model: Its Numerical Stability and Application to a Regional. *Bound. Layer Meteorol.* **2006**, *119*, 397–407. [CrossRef]
62. Janjić, Z.I. The Step-Mountain Eta Coordinate Model: Further Developments of the Convection, Viscous Sublayer, and Turbulence. *Mon. Weather Rev.* **1994**, *122*, 927–945. [CrossRef]
63. Shin, H.H.; Hong, S.Y. Representation of the Subgrid-Scale Turbulent Transport in Convective Boundary Layers at Gray-Zone Resolutions. *Mon. Weather Rev.* **2015**, *143*, 250–271. [CrossRef]
64. Angevine, W.M.; Jiang, H.; Mauritsen, T. Performance of an Eddy Diffusivity-Mass Flux Scheme for Shallow Cumulus Boundary Layers. *Mon. Weather Rev.* **2010**, *138*, 2895–2912. [CrossRef]
65. Bretherton, C.S.; Park, S. A New Moist Turbulence Parameterization in the Community Atmosphere Model. *J. Clim.* **2009**, *22*, 3422–3448. [CrossRef]
66. Grenier, H.; Bretherton, C.S. A Moist PBL Parameterization for Large-Scale Models and Its Application to Subtropical Cloud. *Mon. Weather Rev.* **2001**, *129*, 357–377. [CrossRef]
67. Sukoriansky, S.; Perov, V.; Galperin, B. Application of a New Spectral Model of Stratified Turbulence to the Atmospheric Boundary Layer over Sea Ice. *Bound. Layer Meteorol.* **2005**, *117*, 231–257. [CrossRef]
68. Sedaghat, A.; Hassanzadeh, A.; Jamali, J.; Mostafaeipour, A.; Chen, W. Determination of rated wind speed for maximum annual energy production of variable speed wind turbines. *Appl. Energy* **2017**, *205*, 781–789. [CrossRef]
69. Hahmann, A.N.; Lennard, C.; Badger, J.; Vincent, C.L.; Kelly, M.C.; Volker, P.J.; Argent, B.; Refslund, J. Mesoscale modeling for the Wind Atlas of South Africa (WASA) project. *DTU Wind Energy* **2014**, *50*, 80.
70. Floors, R.; Vincent, C.L.; Gryning, S.E.; Peña, A.; Batchvarova, E. The wind profile in the coastal boundary layer: Wind lidar measurements and numerical modelling. *Bound.-Layer Meteorol.* **2013**, *147*, 469–491. [CrossRef]
71. Ruiz-Arias, J.A.; Arbizu-Barrena, C.; Santos-Alamillos, F.J.; Tovar-Pescador, J.; Pozo-Vázquez, D. Assessing the surface solar radiation budget in the WRF model: A spatiotemporal analysis of the bias and its causes. *Mon. Weather Rev.* **2016**, *144*, 703–711. [CrossRef]
72. Mahrt, L. The early evening boundary layer transition. *Q. J. R. Meteorol. Soc.* **1981**, *107*, 329–343. [CrossRef]
73. Varquez, A.C.G.; Nakayoshi, M.; Makabe, T.; Kanda, M. WRF Application of High Resolution Urban Surface Parameters on Some Major Cities of Japan. *J. Jpn. Soc. Civil Eng. Ser. B1 Hydraul. Eng.* **2014**, *170*, I_175–I_180. [CrossRef]

Σ mathematics MDPI

Article

Convergence Investigation of XFEM Enrichment Schemes for Modeling Cohesive Cracks

Guangzhong Liu [1,*], Jiamin Guo [1] and Yan Bao [2]

[1] School of Ocean Science and Engineering, Shanghai Maritime University, Shanghai 200120, China; jmguo@shmtu.edu.cn
[2] Department of Civil Engineering, School of Naval Architecture, Ocean and Civil Engineering, Shanghai Jiao Tong University, Shanghai 200240, China; ybao@sjtu.edu.cn
* Correspondence: to gzliu@shmtu.edu.cn

Abstract: When simulating cohesive cracks in the XFEM framework, specific enrichment schemes are designed for the non-singular near-tip field and an iteration procedure is used to solve the nonlinearity problem. This paper focuses on convergence and accuracy analysis of XFEM enrichment schemes for cohesive cracks. Four different kinds of enrichment schemes were manufactured based on the development of XFEM. A double-cantilever beam specimen under an opening load was simulated by Matlab programming, assuming both linear and exponential constitutive models. The displacement and load factors were solved simultaneously by the Newton–Raphson iterative procedure. Finally, based on a linear or an exponential constitutive law, the influences of variations in these enrichment schemes, including (i) specialized tip branch functions and (ii) corrected approximations for blending elements, were determined and some conclusions were drawn.

Keywords: cohesive cracks; convergence rate; enrichment schemes; XFEM

Citation: Liu, G.; Guo, J.; Bao, Y. Convergence Investigation of XFEM Enrichment Schemes for Modeling Cohesive Cracks. *Mathematics* **2022**, *10*, 383. https://doi.org/10.3390/math10030383

Academic Editor: Marcin Kamiński

Received: 15 December 2021
Accepted: 18 January 2022
Published: 26 January 2022

1. Introduction

In quasi-brittle materials, such as geomaterials and concrete, the fracture behavior is quite different from that of brittle materials. A fracture process zone (FPZ) of negligible size develops at the crack front due to plasticity or micro-cracking [1]. The assumption of linear elastic fracture mechanics (LEFM) is quite restrictive for certain types of failure, where the nonlinear zone ahead of the crack tip is negligible in comparison with the dimension of the crack. Employing LEFM may produce dangerous results for fracture propagation in quasi-brittle materials [2]. Therefore, cohesive crack models have been developed to analyze metal materials. Hillerborg et al. [3] introduced fracture energy into the cohesive crack model and proposed various traction–separation relations for concrete. The cohesive crack models have been extensively used in studies on the FPZ and nonlinear failure in engineering structures.

Within the FPZ ahead of the crack tip, although damage develops to a certain degree, cohesive stress can still be transferred. In the cohesive model, the nonlinear FPZ, where degradation or damage mechanisms occur as a result of micro-cracking or micro-voids, ahead of the crack tip is lumped into a discrete line [4,5]. This stress-softening type of behavior in the FPZ is represented by a cohesive constitutive relation [6]. The FPZ is characterized by two crack tips: a mathematical (or fictitious) crack tip and a physical one. As shown in Figure 1, at the mathematical tip, the crack opening is zero and the cohesive traction equals the tensile strength of the material, while, at the real crack tip, the crack opening equals the critical crack opening and the cohesive traction is zero. The crack smoothly closes from the physical tip to the fictitious tip, and the drawback of infinite stress due to the LEFM theory is avoided [7].

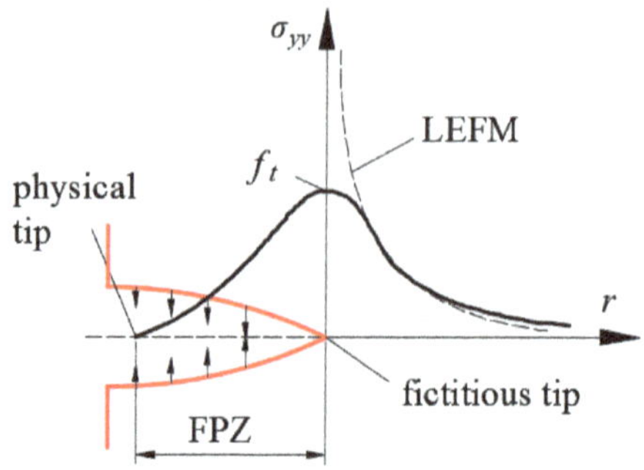

Figure 1. The stress profiles around the fracture process zone.

Over the last two decades, the methodological development of the extended finite element method (XFEM) has led to a phenomenal increase in applications. In the XFEM framework, localized phenomena are modeled by incorporating a priori knowledge about the solution into the FEM approximation using a partition of the unity property. The fracture propagation can be handled even on a structured mesh by dynamically adjusting the pre-selected local approximation spaces in the problem domain. To incorporate a local approximation space, specialized enrichment functions and corresponding degrees of freedom are added onto local existing FE nodes. In contrast to FEM, it relaxes mesh constraints such as mesh conformance to physical discontinuities, mesh refinement around the crack tip, and burdensome adaptive remeshing whenever the crack grows. Various enrichment schemes have been specialized to apply the XFEM in modeling discontinuity problems, such as bi-material [8,9], three-dimensional crack [10,11], inclusion and void [12], microcrack [13,14], two-phase flow [15,16], and frictional contact [17,18] problems. These applications have reached a high degree of robustness and are now being incorporated into general software such as LS-DYNA and ABAQUS.

For linear elastic fracture simulation, two types of enrichment functions are required [19,20]: (i) heaviside functions, which model the jump in the displacement field across the crack surface; and (ii) tip branch functions, which are derived from the theoretical solution of the displacement field in the neighborhood of the crack tip, to capture the singularity. The XFEM provides higher numerical accuracy than FEM without any significant mesh refinement. However, the convergence rate with respect to the mesh parameter h is not improved, because the enriched zone becomes smaller as the mesh is refined [21]. On the other hand, researchers [22] have found that the parasitic terms presented in the blending elements may drastically reduce the convergence rate of XFEM approximations. However, the influence of the parasitic terms cannot easily be predicted [23]; for some enrichments or problems, such as bi-material structures, they may reduce the convergence rate, while for others, such as strong discontinuities, they may only increase the absolute error while keeping the convergence rate unchanged. In order to reach the optimal convergence rate, special treatments to blending elements have been proposed, such as coupling enriched and standard regions [24], hierarchical shape functions [25], the enhanced strain technique [26], and the corrected XFEM [23]. Among these techniques, the corrected XFEM may be the easiest to implement while producing the optimal result.

For cohesive crack simulation, enrichment schemes used for traction-free cracks are no longer suitable. This is because, in the cohesive crack model, the singularity of the crack tip field vanishes. The XFEM enriches the standard local FE approximations with prior known information about the problem. The cohesive crack model abandons the singularity of the crack tip stress field, which is an unrealistic assumption of LEFM. Therefore, new enrichment functions have to be designed in the XFEM framework to simulate the true asymptotic field for the cohesive crack model [2]. To date, various enrichment schemes have been developed for modeling cohesive cracks. Originally, only a heaviside function was employed. Because the singularity vanishes in the near-tip field, the heaviside function can be suitable for the entire crack, including the crack tip. This approach is used by Wells and Sluys [27]. However, if only the heaviside function is applied to all nodes, the crack is restricted to ending at the element edges to ensure that the jump in the displacement field at the mathematical crack tip equals zero. The approaches given in Duarte et al. [28] and Zi and Belytschko [29] overcome this deficiency by modification of the shape functions within the tip element, so that the crack tip can lie within the element. Mariani and Perego [30] proposed enrichment functions as a product of the heaviside function and ramp functions. Some references provide special tip branch functions for cohesive cracks. Moës and Belytschko [31] suggest the following tip branch function: $\phi(r,\theta) = r^k \sin\frac{\theta}{2}$, with k being either 1, 1.5, or 2. Other enrichment functions based on analytical considerations are given by Cox [32]. Meschke and Dumstorff [33] use four tip branch functions similar to those for traction-free cracks, only replacing $\sqrt{r}$ with r, e.g., $\phi_\alpha(r,\theta) = \{r\sin\frac{\theta}{2}, r\cos\frac{\theta}{2}, r\sin\frac{\theta}{2}\sin\theta, r\cos\frac{\theta}{2}\sin\theta\}$. With the employment of tip branch functions, the crack can end arbitrarily within the element. However, a loss of the partition of unity in the blending elements may lead to a reduction in accuracy. Convergence and accuracy studies of these enrichment schemes are needed for a suitable choice.

As far as convergence rates are concerned, when numerically simulating traction-free crack by the XFEM, the factors that influence the convergence rate include the enrichment zone size [21], the shape function polynomial order [24], the special treatment of the blending elements, and the choice of enrichment functions. V. Gupta et al. [34] studied the influence of enrichment zone size on convergence rate and found that, for traction-free crack simulation, the convergence rate is controlled by the stress gradient outside the enrichment zone and the error is caused by the blending element. When it comes to the cohesive crack problem, the smoother stress gradient and the nonlinearity of the governing equation make the accuracy and convergence properties new problems that require study.

In this paper, we focus on investigating the accuracy and convergence properties of different enrichment schemes for cohesive crack simulation. A numerical simulation was conducted on a double-cantilever beam specimen, assuming a linear or an exponential constitutive law, in order to provide useful information for the choice of enrichment scheme for cohesive crack simulation. The enrichment schemes we considered can briefly be stated as follows.

(i) XFEM-h. Only the heaviside function is used, with a small modification of the shape functions in the tip element.
(ii) XFEM-s. Both the heaviside function and the tip branch function $\phi(r,\theta) = r\sin\frac{\theta}{2}$ are used.
(iii) XFEM-c1. Only $\phi(r,\theta) = r\sin\frac{\theta}{2}$ is used as the tip branch function, and a corrected approximation for $\phi(r,\theta) = r\sin\frac{\theta}{2}$ is used in the blending elements.
(iv) XFEM-c2. Both $\phi(r,\theta) = r\sin\frac{\theta}{2}$ and $\phi(r,\theta) = r\cos\frac{\theta}{2}$ are used as tip branch functions in addition to a corrected approximation for these two tip branch functions in blending elements.

The remainder of this paper is organized as follows. A description of the cohesive crack problem domain and the XFEM formulation for the cohesive crack problem are provided in Section 2. Information on these four enrichment schemes is provided in Section 3. Section 4 presents the Newton iterative algorithm for solving the nonlinear problem. In Section 5, numerical results of convergence and accuracy studies on these enrichment schemes for different cohesive constitutive models are presented. The effect of variations in these enrichment schemes is investigated. Finally, our main conclusions are summarized as Section 5.

2. XFEM Formulation for Cohesive Crack Problems

2.1. Model Problem Definition

Consider a two-dimensional domain Ω crossed by a cohesive discontinuity, as shown in Figure 2. The strong form of the equilibrium equation of this body can be expressed as

$$\nabla \cdot \sigma + b = 0 \text{in } \Omega \tag{1}$$

where ∇ is the gradient operator, σ is the Cauchy stress, and b is the body force. The behavior of the bulk material is assumed to be linearly elastic, and the constitutive relation is defined as $\sigma = D \cdot \varepsilon$. The essential and natural boundary conditions are presented as follows

$$\begin{aligned} u = \overline{u} \quad & \text{on} \quad \Gamma_u \\ \sigma \cdot n_\Gamma = \overline{t} \quad & \text{on} \quad \Gamma_t \\ \sigma \cdot n_{\Gamma d} = f^c \quad & \text{on} \quad \Gamma_c \end{aligned} \tag{2}$$

where n_Γ is the outward unit normal vector to the external boundary Γ, $\overline{t}$ is the prescribed load vector on the boundary Γt, $\overline{u}$ is the the prescribed displacement on the boundary Γ_u, and f^c is the cohesive traction transferred across the Γc, which is related to the displacement gap ω across the discontinuity according to the stress softening model.

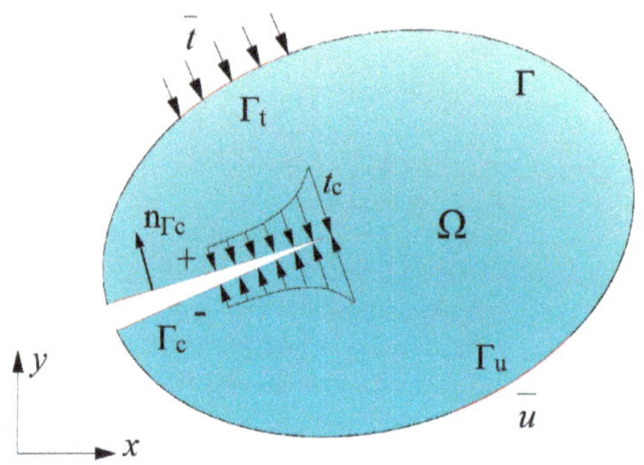

Figure 2. A two-dimensional domain containing a cohesive discontinuity Γc.

2.2. Discretization of Governing Equations

In the XFEM, the displacement discontinuity can be directly embedded by introducing additional degrees of freedom onto existing nodes whose supports are intersected by discontinuities. Comprehensive overviews of the XFEM have been given by numerous studies [35–37].

The generalized form of the XFEM approximation of the displacement field can be written as

$$u^h(x) = \sum_A N_i(x) \cdot u_i + \sum_J N_j(x) \cdot \phi_j(x) \cdot a_j \tag{3}$$

In the above function, the standard FE approximation $\sum_A N_i(x) \cdot u_i$ represents the continuous part of the displacement field, while the second term represents the discontinuous part, where u_i and a_j are standard and enriched DOFs, respectively, $\phi_j(x)$ are the enrichment functions, which take different forms for specific kinds of discontinuity problems, A denotes the set of all nodes, and J denotes the pre-selected set of local nodes associated with discontinuities.

The weak form of the governing partial differential equation can be derived from the principle of virtual work and the Galerkin procedure. When the cohesive crack model is assumed, the cohesive traction fc that transferred is a function of the crack opening ω. The weak form of the equilibrium equation can be expressed as:

$$W^{int} = W^{ext} + W^{coh} \tag{4}$$

Or

$$\int_{\Omega} \sigma \cdot \delta\varepsilon \, \mathrm{d}\Omega = \int_{\Omega} b \cdot \delta u \, \mathrm{d}\Omega + \int_{\Gamma_t} \bar{t} \cdot \delta u \, \mathrm{d}\Gamma + \int_{\Gamma_t} f^c \cdot (\delta u^{+} - \delta u^{-}) \, \mathrm{d}\Gamma \tag{5}$$

Discretization of Equation (5) in the XFEM framework results in:

$$Kq = \lambda f^{ext} + f^{coh} \tag{6}$$

where q is the generalized nodal displacement vector, $q^e = [\; u_i^e \quad a_i^e \;]$ for each element, and λ is the load factor.

The stiffness matrix K is composed of

$$K = \begin{bmatrix} K^{uu} & K^{ua} \\ K^{ua} & K^{aa} \end{bmatrix} \tag{7}$$

With

$$\begin{gathered} K^{uu} = \int_{\Omega} (B^u)^T DB^u \mathrm{d}\Omega \\ K^{ua} = \int_{\Omega_{\mathrm{enr}}} (B^a)^T DB^u \mathrm{d}\Omega \\ K^{aa} = \int_{\Omega_{\mathrm{enr}}} (B^a)^T DB^a \mathrm{d}\Omega + \int_{\Gamma_c} N^T T^c N \mathrm{d}\Gamma \end{gathered} \tag{8}$$

where T_c is the tangential modulus matrix of the cohesive crack determined by the cohesive crack behavior and is obtained from the relation $T^c = \frac{\partial f^{coh}(\omega)}{\partial \omega}$. The external nodal force f_{ext} and the cohesive nodal force f_{coh} can be obtained as

$$\begin{aligned} f^{ext} &= \lambda \int_{\Gamma_t} N^T \bar{t} \mathrm{d}\Gamma + \int_{\Omega} N^T b \mathrm{d}\Omega \\ f^{coh} &= -\int_{\Gamma_c} \sigma_y(\omega)(N_+^T - N_-^T) \, \mathrm{d}\Gamma \end{aligned} \tag{9}$$

where the crack opening displacement ω can be given by

$$\omega = \vec{n} \cdot (u^+ - u^-) = \vec{n} \cdot 2\sum_i N_i a_i \tag{10}$$

It can be observed from the Equations (8) and (9) that the cohesive behavior has a direct effect on both the stiffness matrix K and the nodal force vector f_{coh}. The relation between the cohesive force and the crack opening makes the problem nonlinear.

The four enrichment schemes we examined are designed to consider the effect of their variations, including the employment of tip branch functions and a corrected approximation in blending elements. These four schemes are denoted XFEM-h, XFEM-s, XFEM-c1, and XFEM-c2, and detailed as follows.

2.3. XFEM-h

Because the singularity of the displacement field around the crack tip vanishes, a heaviside function is suitable for the entire crack, including the crack tip. In this scheme, the approximation of the displacement field can be written as

$$u^h(x) = \sum_{i \in A} N_i(x) \cdot u_i + \sum_{j \in J} N_j(x) \cdot [H(x) - H(x_j)] \cdot a_j \tag{11}$$

where $H(x)$ is the heaviside function, which takes +1 on one side of the crack and -1 on the other side, and J is the set of nodes whose supports are fully cut by the crack, which is depicted in Figure 3a.

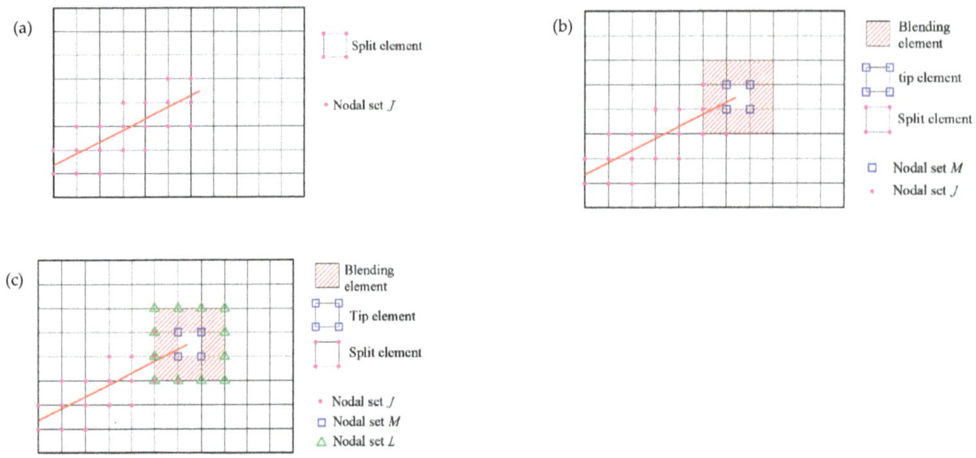

Figure 3. Node subsets and element types in different enrichment schemes. (**a**) XFEM-h; (**b**) XFEM-s; (**c**) XFEM-c1; and XFEM-c2.

In order to make the displacement gap vanish to zero at the crack tip within the tip element, we extended the method proposed by Zi and Belytschko [29] to quadrilateral elements. Specifically, for the tip element, the modified shape function $\overline{N}_j(x)$ was used instead of the standard shape function $N_j(x)$. As shown in Figure 4, if the crack intersects with boundary 14 within the tip element, we make a straight line through the crack tip point and intersect the element boundary at points 5 and 6. Then, the shape function $\overline{N}_j(x)$ used for the tip element is actually the standard shape function of virtual element 1564. Since nodes 1 and 4 are enriched, the discontinuous part of the displacement can be written as

$$u_{disc} = a_1\overline{N}_1(x^*)[H(x^*) - H(x_1)] + a_4\overline{N}_4(x^*)[H(x^*) - H(x_4)] \tag{12}$$

where x^* are the coordinates of virtual element 1564.

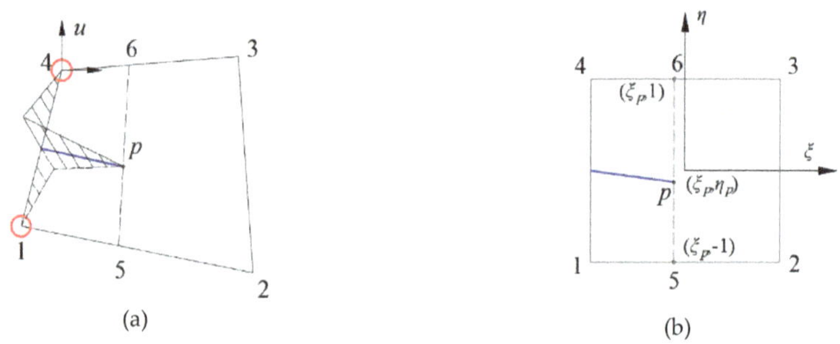

Figure 4. Approximation of the displacement field in the tip element. (**a**) The crack intersecting with boundary 14; (**b**) the corresponding parent element.

Since this scheme treats the entire domain with the heaviside function only, the blending with the unenriched subdomain does not occur, which implies that the PU holds in the entire domain.

2.4. XFEM-s

Another way to allow the crack tip to be located arbitrarily is to employ branch functions. For traction-free cracks, the branch functions are chosen based on the analytical solution of the displacement field in the vicinity of the crack tip, that is $\phi_\alpha(r,\theta) = \{\sqrt{r}\sin\frac{\theta}{2},$

$\sqrt{r}\cos\frac{\theta}{2}$, $\sqrt{r}\sin\frac{\theta}{2}\sin\theta$, $\sqrt{r}\cos\frac{\theta}{2}\sin\theta\}$. However, the combination of these functions does not produce the non-singular stress field at the tip of the cohesive crack. On the basis of the analytical solution of the cohesive crack problem, some researchers proposed that only one non-singular enrichment function be used for the two-dimensional cohesive crack tip, which takes the following form.

$$\phi(r,\theta) = r\sin\frac{\theta}{2},\ \text{or}\ r^{3/2}\sin\frac{\theta}{2},\ \text{or}\ r^{2}\sin\frac{\theta}{2} \tag{13}$$

Others proposed that four branch functions be used to enrich the tip element, which is

$$\{\phi_\alpha(r,\theta)\} = \{\ r\sin\tfrac{\theta}{2}\quad r\cos\tfrac{\theta}{2}\quad r\sin\tfrac{\theta}{2}\sin\theta\quad r\cos\tfrac{\theta}{2}\sin\theta\ \} \tag{14}$$

In this enrichment scheme, $r\sin\frac{\theta}{2}$ is used as a branch function, which is presented in Figure 5a. It is obvious that this branch function is suitable for capturing the displacement gap at the crack tip.

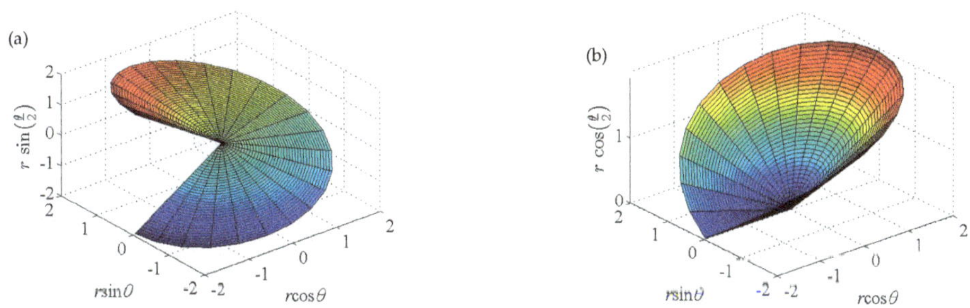

Figure 5. Tip branch functions for cohesive cracks. (**a**) $\phi(r,\theta) = r\sin\frac{\theta}{2}$ and (**b**) $\phi(r,\theta) = r\cos\frac{\theta}{2}$.

In this scheme, the XFEM approximation of the displacement field can be expressed as

$$\begin{aligned} u^h(x) = & \sum_{i\in I} N_i(x)\cdot u_i + \sum_{j\in J} N_j(x)\ [H(x) - H(x_j)]\cdot a_j \\ & + \sum_{k\in M} N_k(x)\cdot[\phi(x) - \phi(x_k)]\cdot b_k \end{aligned} \tag{15}$$

As marked in Figure 3b, J is the set of nodes whose supports are intersected with the crack, and M is the set of nodes whose supports contain the crack tip. If a node simultaneously belongs to J and M, then it belongs to M.

2.5. XFEM-c1 and XFEM-c2

When branch functions are used in conjunction with a heaviside function, the partition of the unity property does not hold in the blending elements. As shown in Figure 3, in blending elements only some of the nodes are enriched, which means that $\sum_k N_k(x) \neq 1$. In addition, the branch function is not a piecewise constant function like the heaviside function, so the parasitic terms resulting from $\sum_k N_k(x)\phi(x)$ do not vanish at the edges of the tip element. The presentation of parasitic terms in blending elements can reduce the convergence rate and accuracy [38]. Fries T.P. [23] proposed a corrected approximation in which all nodes in blending elements are enriched and the enrichment functions are modified, solving the problem most efficiently. The approximation of the displacement field of the corrected XFEM can be written as:

$$\begin{aligned} u^h(x) = & \sum_{i\in I} N_i(x)\cdot u_i + \sum_{j\in J} N_j(x)\cdot[H(x) - H(x_j)]\cdot a_j \\ & + \sum_{k\in M\cup L} N_k(x)\cdot R(x)\cdot\sum_{\alpha}[\phi_\alpha(x) - \phi_\alpha(x_k)]\cdot b_k^\alpha \end{aligned} \tag{16}$$

where L is the set of second-layer nodes around the tip element, as marked with triangles in Figure 3c. In this scheme, the set of nodes L is also enriched with branch functions and additional DOFs b_k^{α}. $R(x)$ is a ramp function, which is defined as follows and depicted in Figure 6.

$$R(x) = \sum_{k \in M} N_k(x) \tag{17}$$

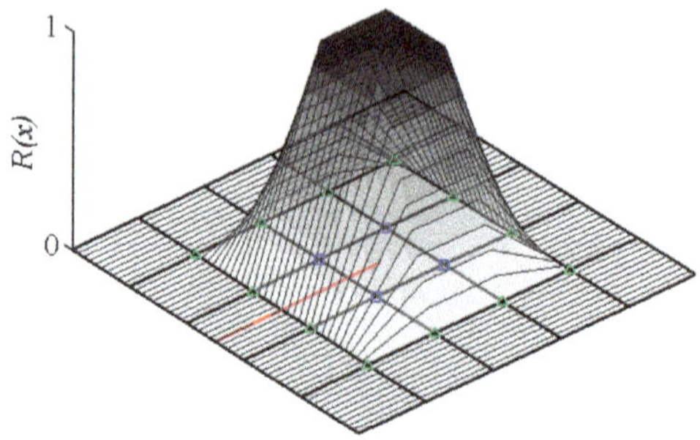

Figure 6. The value of $R(x)$ on a discretized mesh.

It can be seen in Figure 6, within the tip element, that we have $R(x) = 1$, while within the blending element, the ramp function varies continuously and deceases to zero at the element edges. After this modification, the PU holds everywhere in the domain. Improved convergence rates were verified in applications to bi-material problems, while in other applications only the error level was reduced.

In order to investigate the effect of an additional singular branch function in Equation (14), only $r \sin \frac{\theta}{2}$ was employed in XFEM-c1, while both $r \sin \frac{\theta}{2}$ and $r \cos \frac{\theta}{2}$ were employed in XFEM-c2. It can be seen from their plots in Figure 5 that the branch function $r \cos \frac{\theta}{2}$ can help to capture the stress gradient at the rear of the crack tip. In both schemes, a corrected approximation in blending elements is used to eliminate the negative influence of parasitic terms.

3. Nonlinear Algorithm

In order to guarantee the smooth closing of the crack as required by the definition of the cohesive crack model, one more condition is required. This condition is usually referred to as the zero stress intensity factor condition. It is assumed that the crack propagates under the mode I loading condition, so only the mode I stress intensity factor (SIF) is taken into account, i.e.,

$$K_{\mathrm{Itip}} = 0 \tag{18}$$

where K_{Itip} is the mode I SIF calculated at the crack tip. In FEM-based methods, the SIF can be obtained by means of the domain integration method.

A SIF at the crack tip equal to zero implies that the stress component normal to the crack tip is finite [39]. Alternatively, smooth closure can also be guaranteed by a stress condition, where the stress projection in the normal direction n_Γ of the crack is equal to the tensile strength of the material, i.e.,

$$n_\Gamma{}^{\mathrm{T}} \cdot \sigma_{\mathrm{tip}} \cdot n_\Gamma = f_t \tag{19}$$

where σ_{tip} is the stress at the crack tip and f_t is the tensile strength of the material. The zero SIF condition and the stress condition can be used interchangeably, but the stress condition is simpler to implement; therefore, it was adopted in this paper.

The discretized form of the stress condition can be written as

$$M^{\mathrm{T}} \cdot C \cdot B \cdot q = S \cdot q = f_t \tag{20}$$

where $S = M^T \cdot D \cdot B$ is the operator by which the stress at the crack tip is calculated, and $M = n_\Gamma \otimes n_\Gamma$ is the Voigt notation.

It is obvious that in the equilibrium condition (Equation (6)), as the cohesive force depends on the crack opening ω, the problem is nonlinear. The scheme recommended in [29] was employed, we combined Equation (6) and Equation (20), and q and λ were solved simultaneously by the Newton–Raphson iterative procedure. The residual vector of the governing equation is given by

$$r = \left\{ \begin{array}{c} K \cdot q - \lambda f^{ext} - f^{coh}(q) \\ f_t - Sq \end{array} \right\} \tag{21}$$

where the independent unknowns are q and λ. The Jacobian matrix is

$$\Lambda = \left[\begin{array}{cc} K - \frac{\partial f^{coh}(q)}{\partial q} & -f^{ext} \\ -S & 0 \end{array} \right] \tag{22}$$

where $\frac{\partial f^{coh}(q)}{\partial q}$ is the additional stiffness term effective on the crack surface in the FPZ, which can be obtained by

$$\frac{\partial f^{coh}(q)}{\partial q} = -2 \int_{\Gamma_c} \frac{\partial \sigma_y(\omega)}{\partial \omega} N^T \cdot n \cdot n^T \cdot \mathrm{N} d\Gamma \tag{23}$$

At the ith iteration, the increments in independent variables obtained from Equations (21) and (22) are

$$\left\{ \begin{array}{c} \Delta q \\ \Delta \lambda \end{array} \right\}^i = -\left(\Lambda^{i-1}\right)^{-1} \cdot r^{i-1} \tag{24}$$

4. Numerical Study

In this study, a double-cantilever-beam (DCB) specimen containing a level cohesive crack was numerically simulated by the above four different enrichment schemes in order to examine their accuracy and convergence performance. This configuration was taken from the literature [29]. The boundary conditions and dimensions of this case study are provided as a sketch in Figure 7. Uniformly distributed forces were applied on the left side of the beam, and the plane stress condition was assumed to hold. The Young's modulus was 36.5 GPa and the Poisson's ratio was 0.18, which are the material properties of common concrete.

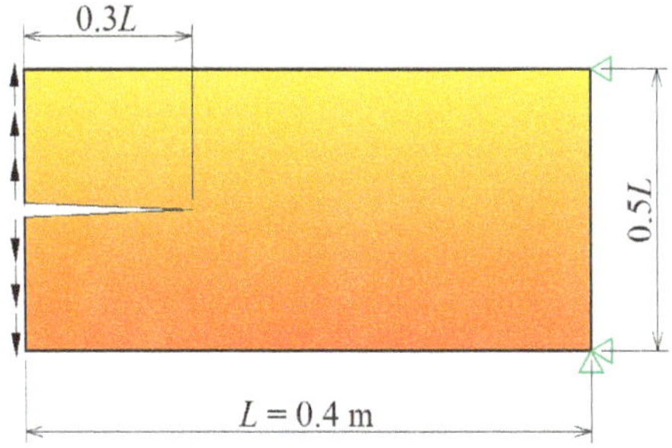

Figure 7. A sketch of the dimensions and boundary conditions of the double-cantilever beam.

Six finite element meshes were used in the convergence studies (17 × 9, 31 × 15, 61 × 31, 121 × 61, 301 × 151, and 601 × 301 grids of quadrilateral elements). The meshes were created by making the element length in the x and y directions approximately equal, with the number of elements being odd, such that the crack tip lies within an element. The mesh size h was represented by the square root of the area of an element.

4.1. Linear Softening Model

For the cases with a linear softening model, the cohesive force can be expressed as

$$\begin{cases} f^c = f_t\left(1 - \frac{\omega}{\omega_c}\right) & 0 \leq \omega \leq \omega_c \\ f^c = 0 & \omega > \omega_c \end{cases} \tag{25}$$

In this paper, the material properties of common concrete were used, where the tensile strength $f_t = 3.18$ MPa and the critical crack opening $\omega_c = 0.0314$ mm. The fracture energy was $E_f = 0.5 f_t \omega_c = 50$ N/m. The plot of this softening model is provided in Figure 8.

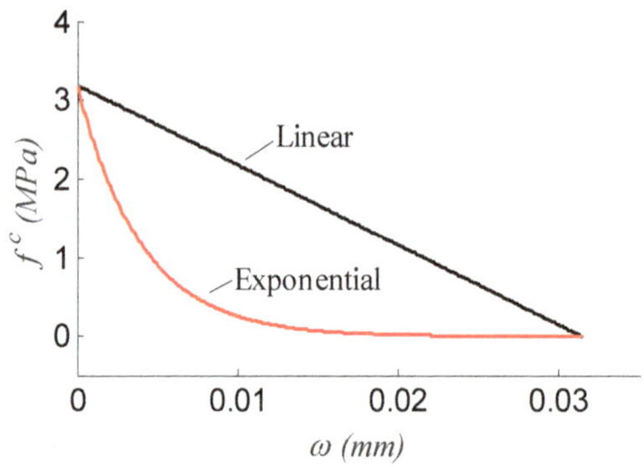

Figure 8. Linear and exponential softening models in terms of the traction–separation relation.

Due to the nonlinearity of the problem, an explicit analytical solution for the displacement field around the crack tip is not available. In order to evaluate the relative error level for different mesh densities, we took the results obtained by the finest meshes with each enrichment scheme as reference exact solutions. The h-version convergence rate of the finite element method was quantified by means of the relative error in the $L2$-norm, which was calculated by the following equations.

$$E_u = \frac{\left\| u - u^{ref} \right\|_{L2}}{\left\| u^{ref} \right\|_{L2}} \tag{26}$$

$$\|u\|_{L2} = \sqrt{\int_{\Omega \backslash \Gamma_c} (u_1)^2 + (u_2)^2 \mathrm{d}\Omega} \tag{27}$$

where the superscript *ref* denotes a reference solution.

In Figure 9, the deformed geometry of the cohesive crack problem is compared with that of the traction-free crack problem when the same load factor is applied. When a cohesive force exists between crack faces, the crack closes smoothly from the physical tip to the fictitious tip. The Contour plots of σ_{yy} for the cohesive crack problem and the traction-free crack problem are provided in Figure 10. It can be seen that, in the cohesive crack model, a stress concentration appears ahead of the crack tip, which is the fracture process zone (FPZ), rather than at the back of the crack tip, which is the case for the traction-free crack problem. The stress gradient at the crack tip is much smaller compared with the case with the traction-free crack. The stress at the crack tip in Figure 10b is finite, and equal to material tensile strength. This means that the cohesive crack model abandons the unrealistic assumption in the LEFM that the stress at the crack tip is infinite, which can be seen in Figure 10a.

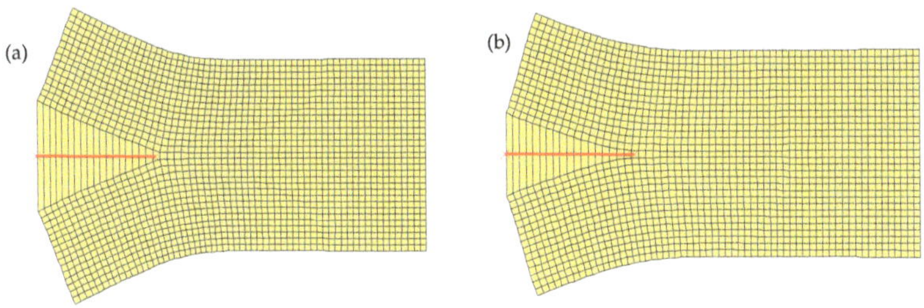

Figure 9. Deformed geometries of the beam with (**a**) a traction-free crack and (**b**) a cohesive crack.

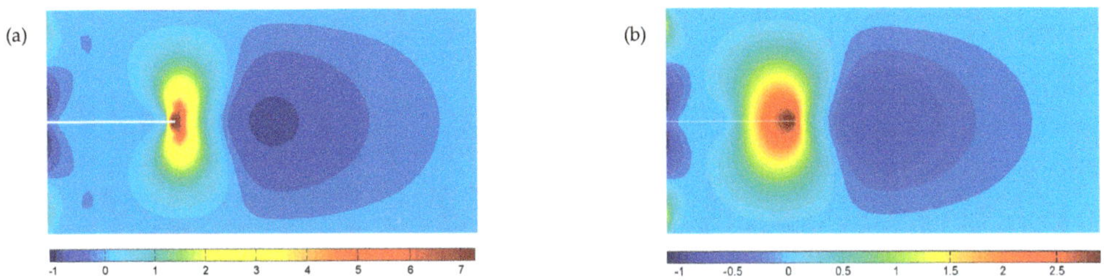

Figure 10. Contour plot of σ_{yy} for (**a**) the traction-free crack problem and (**b**) the cohesive crack problem (unit: Mpa).

The stress σ_{yy} along the axis of symmetry is plotted in Figure 11. The stress profiles obtained by different enrichment schemes are difficult to distinguish from one another. They also show an obvious FPZ ahead of the crack tip, and the stress σ_{yy} is equal to the tensile strength at the crack tip. In contrast, a stress singularity appears around the crack tip in the traction-free crack problem.

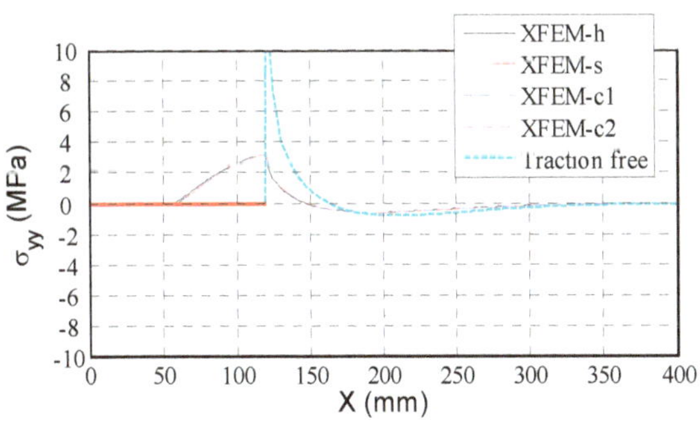

Figure 11. Stress profiles of σ_{yy} obtained by different enrichment schemes for the linear softening model.

Figure 12 shows the relative error in the *L*2-norm plotted against the inverse of the element size h, which is taken as the square root of the area of the element. The rates of convergence were obtained by means of polynomial curve fitting of those data points. It is interesting that, as the linear softening model is considered, with the employment of the branch function $r \sin \frac{\theta}{2}$, XFEM-s, XFEM-c1, and XFEM-c2 achieve a better convergence rate of more than 1, compared with the 0.7 obtained by XFEM-h. The employment of the additional branch function $r \cos \frac{\theta}{2}$ results in a similar convergence rate but a higher accuracy.

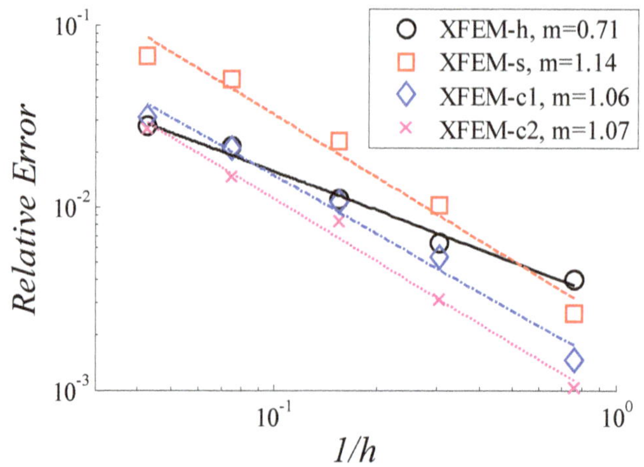

Figure 12. Convergence rate plot for the cohesive crack problem with the linear softening model (m is the convergence rate).

As far as accuracy is concerned, the XFEM-s scheme provides less accuracy for cohesive crack problems, especially when coarse meshes are used. It can be seen from the above stress contour plot in Figure 10 that the singularity vanishes at the crack tip, and only a finite stress gradient exists. If the parasitic terms resulting from the branch function are not corrected, it can reduce the accuracy severely for the case of cohesive cracks. With the corrected approximation for blending elements as in XFEM-c1 and XFEM-c2, the error level is improved by around 2 times, while the convergence rate remains almost the same, which is similar to the case of strong discontinuities.

4.2. Exponential Softening Model

Because of its simplicity, the linear softening model is frequently used; however, for certain brittle materials, a nonlinear softening model may be more accurate. When the cohesive traction–displacement relation changes, the stress gradient around the crack tip differs, and that may affect the convergence rates of enrichment schemes. The same DCB specimen was used for the numerical study of convergence rates. The cohesive force and displacement gap relation can be expressed as

$$f^c = f_t \cdot \exp(-\frac{f_t}{E_f} \cdot \omega) \tag{28}$$

The tensile strength was the same as f_t = 3.18 MPa, and the fracture energy was made to be smaller than E_f = 12.5 N/m to increase the gradient of the cohesive force. The linear and exponential softening models used in this study are depicted in Figure 8. It can be seen from the profile that they will result in a similar FPZ length, but different stress gradients.

The stress σ_{yy} along the symmetric line produced by different enrichment schemes is provided in Figure 13, as well as a comparison of the two cohesive constitutive models. Likewise, the stress profiles produced by these enrichment schemes are hard to distinguish from one another. It can be seen from Figure 13 b that, when the traction–separation relation changes, although the cohesive force remains equal to the tensile strength at the crack tip, the stress gradient differs in the FPZ, and does not make much difference at the back of the crack tip.

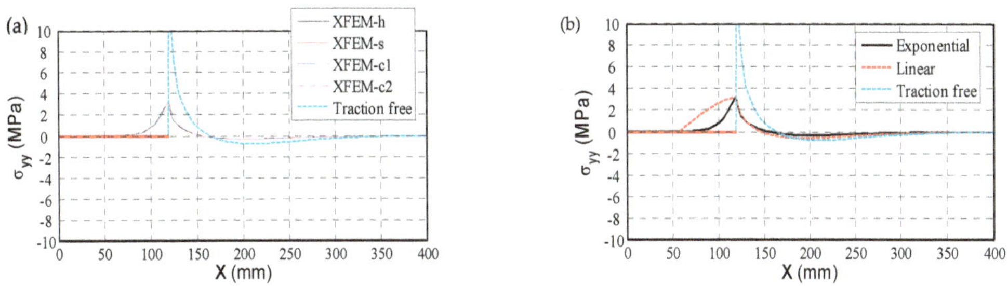

Figure 13. (**a**) Stress profiles of σ_{yy} obtained by different enrichment schemes for the exponential softening model and (**b**) a comparison of different cohesive constitutive models.

Figure 14 shows the convergence rates of these enrichment schemes when the exponential softening model is inserted. Likewise, the enrichment schemes with tip branch functions exhibit a higher convergence rate. The employment of the tip branch function $r\cos\frac{\theta}{2}$ increases both the convergence rate and accuracy substantially. However, especially when coarse meshes are used, these enrichment schemes achieve lower accuracy than XFEM-h in terms of error level. In comparison with the cases of the linear constitutive law, the difference between the convergence rates of these enrichment schemes is more pronounced for the cases of the exponential constitutive law.

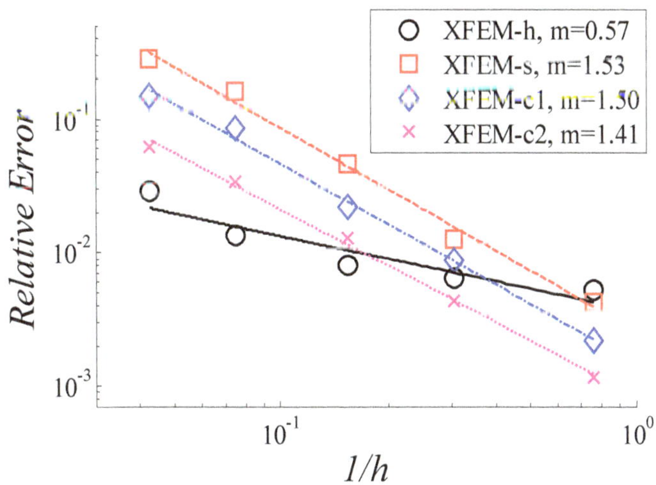

Figure 14. Plot of the convergence rate for the cohesive crack problem with the exponential softening law (m is the convergence rate).

4.3. Mixed-Mode Crack Problem

In this case, a plate with an inclined cohesive crack was analyzed using all four enrichment schemes in order to investigate their convergence properites in depth. The boundary conditions are shown in the sketch in Figure 15. The dimensions of the plate are 200 by 400 mm, with a thickness of 20 mm. The inclined crack is located at [0 150; 100 200]. A uniformly distributed tensile force f_{ext} = 1 Mpa was applied on the top edge with the plane stress condition. All the material properties and softening laws were the same as in previous cases.

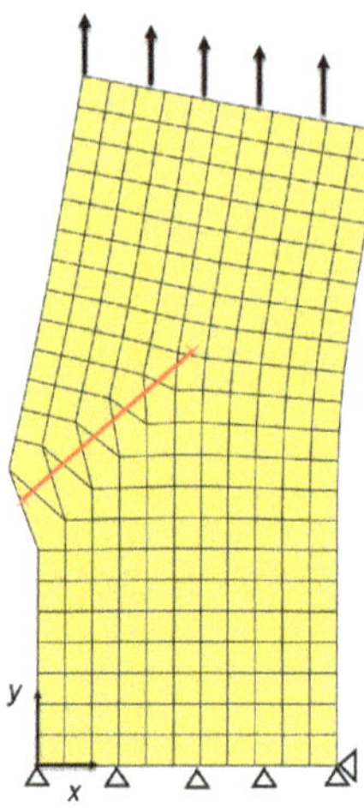

Figure 15. Boundary conditions of a plate containing an inclined crack.

The convergence rates of these enrichment schemes are provided in Figure 16. They follow similar tendencies. The enrichment schemes with tip branch functions have similar convergence properties, while the corrected approximation and additional tip branch functions can increase the accuracy.

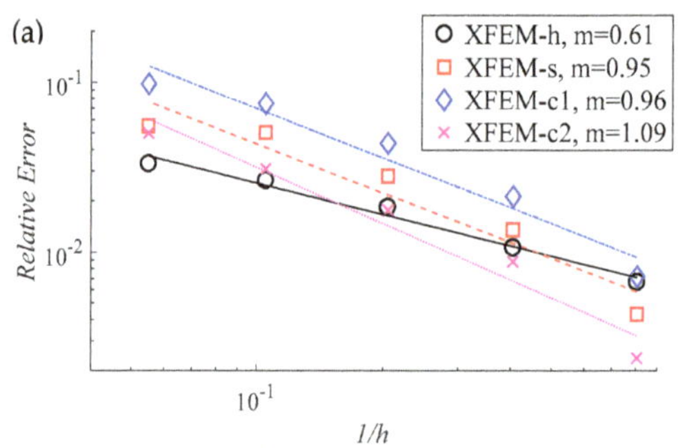

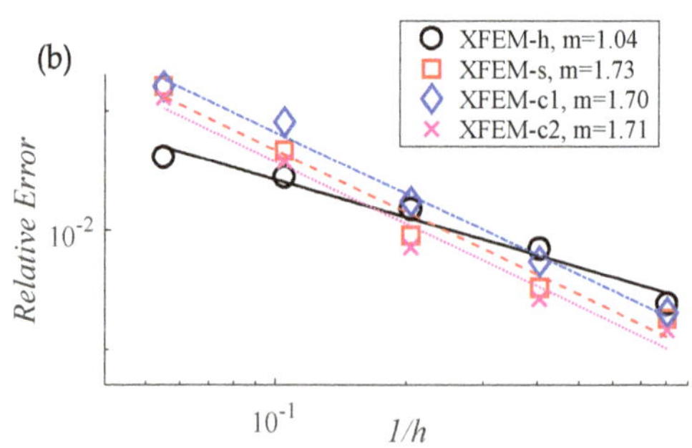

Figure 16. Plots of the convergence rate for the mixed-mode crack problem with (**a**) the linear softening law and (**b**) the exponential softening law (m is the convergence rate).

5. Conclusions

The present work focuses on investigating the convergence properties and accuracy of different enrichment schemes in the XFEM for modeling the cohesive crack problem. Four kinds of enrichment schemes for cohesive cracks were manufactured to examine the influences of their variations on convergence performance and accuracy level. The convergence study was conducted on a double-cantilever beam specimen with both the pure mode I problem and the mixed-mode problem, and cases of linear and exponential constitutive laws were considered. On the basis of the simulation results, our main conclusions are as follows.

1. When both linear and exponential constitutive laws are assumed, the enrichment schemes with tip branch functions achieve a higher convergence rate than XFEM-h; however, they have lower accuracy in terms of the absolute error value.
2. In the case of the cohesive crack simulation, the corrected approximation for blending elements did not change the convergence rate much, but the error level improved substantially, which is similar to the case of traction-free cracks. The enrichment schemes with tip branch functions have similar convergence properties, while the corrected approximation and additional tip branch functions can increase the accuracy.
3. As far as accuracy is concerned, the enrichment schemes with tip branch functions perform worse than XFEM-h when coarse meshes are used. If the parasitic terms resulting from the branch function are not corrected, it can reduce the accuracy severely for the simulation of cohesive cracks.
4. The traction–displacement relation can also affect the convergence properties of these enrichment schemes. In the case of the exponential constitutive law, the difference between the convergence rates of these enrichment schemes is more pronounced.

Author Contributions: Methodology, G.L.; software, G.L.; validation, G.L., J.G. and Y.B.; writing original draft preparation, J.G. and Y.B.; writing—review and editing, G.L. All authors have read and agreed to the published version of the manuscript.

Funding: This study was funded by the National Natural Science Foundation of China (Nos. 51909153, 51108259, and 11772193). And The APC was funded by the National Natural Science Foundation of China (No. 51909153).

Institutional Review Board Statement: Not applicable.

Informed Consent Statement: Not applicable

Data Availability Statement: Not applicable.

Conflicts of Interest: The authors declare no conflict of interest.

Nomenclature

E_f	Fracture Energy
K_{Itip}	Mode I stress intensity factor
f^c, f^{coh}	Cohesive traction
$R(x)$	Ramp function
$\phi(x)$	Enrichment function
ω_c	Critical crack opening

References

1. Liu, G.; Zhou, D.; Bao, Y.; Ma, J.; Han, Z. Multiscale simulation of major crack/minor cracks interplay with the corrected XFEM. *Arch. Civ. Mech. Eng.* **2017**, *17*, 410–418. [CrossRef]
2. Karihaloo, B.L.; Xiao, Q.Z. Asymptotic fields at the tip of a cohesive crack. *Int. J. Fract.* **2008**, *150*, 55–74. [CrossRef]
3. Hillerborg, A.; Modéer, M.; Petersson, P.-E. Analysis of crack formation and crack growth in concrete by means of fracture mechanics and finite elements. *Cem. Concr. Res.* **1976**, *6*, 773–781. [CrossRef]
4. Liu, G.; Zhou, D.; Bao, Y.; Ma, J.; Han, Z. Multiscale analysis of interaction between macro crack and microdefects by using multiscale projection method. *Theor. Appl. Fract. Mech.* **2017**, *90*, 65–74. [CrossRef]

5. Xu, Y.; Yuan, H. On damage accumulations in the cyclic cohesive zone model for XFEM analysis of mixed-mode fatigue crack growth. *Comput. Mater. Sci.* **2009**, *46*, 579–585. [CrossRef]
6. Combescure, A.; Coret, M.; Elguedj, T.; Cazes, F.; Haboussa, D. Cohesive laws X-FEM association for simulation of damage fracture transition and tensile shear switch in dynamic crack propagation. *Procedia IUTAM* **2012**, *3*, 274–291. [CrossRef]
7. Xiao, Q.; Karihaloo, B.L. Asymptotic fields at frictionless and frictional cohesive crack tips in quasibrittle materials. *J. Mech. Mater. Struct.* **2006**, *1*, 881–910. [CrossRef]
8. Yi, G.; Yu, T.; Bui, T.Q.; Tanaka, S. Bi-material V-notched SIFs analysis by XFEM and conservative integral approach. *Comput. Struct.* **2018**, *196*, 217–232. [CrossRef]
9. Kumar, S.; Bhardwaj, G. A new enrichment scheme in XFEM to model crack growth behavior in ductile materials. *Theor. Appl. Fract. Mech.* **2018**, *96*, 296–307. [CrossRef]
10. Jiang, Y.; Li, E. XFEM with Smoothing Technique for Static Fracture Mechanics in Three-Dimension. *Int. J. Comput. Methods* **2016**, 13. [CrossRef]
11. Chadaram, S.; Yadav, S.K. A XFEM approach for the three-dimensional cracks in piezoelectric material using interaction integral. *Eng. Fract. Mech.* **2020**, *239*, 107322. [CrossRef]
12. Wang, Z.; Yu, T.; Bui, T.Q.; Trinh, N.A.; Luong, N.T.H.; Duc, N.D.; Doan, D.H. Numerical modeling of 3-D inclusions and voids by a novel adaptive XFEM. *Adv. Eng. Softw.* **2016**, *102*, 105–122. [CrossRef]
13. Liu, G.; Zhou, D.; Guo, J.; Bao, Y.; Han, Z.; Lu, J. Numerical simulation of fatigue crack propagation interacting with micro-defects using multiscale XFEM. *Int. J. Fatigue* **2018**, *109*, 70–82. [CrossRef]
14. Loehnert, S.; Belytschko, T. Crack shielding and amplification due to multiple microcracks interacting with a macrocrack. *Int. J. Fract.* **2007**, *145*, 1–8. [CrossRef]
15. Luege, M.; Lucero, J.; Torrijos, C.; Orlando, A. Coupled mechanical and fluid flow analysis in fractured saturated porous media using the XFEM. *Appl. Math. Model.* **2016**, *40*, 4480–4504. [CrossRef]
16. Moeeni, M.A.; Hosseini, M.S.; Aghjeh, M.K.R.; Mostafaiyan, M. Numerical study on the effect of rheological parameters on the droplet deformation process in Newtonian and non-Newtonian two-phase systems using extended finite element method. *Prog. Comput. Fluid Dyn.* **2020**, *20*, 143–155. [CrossRef]
17. Fang, H.; Zhang, D.; Zhou, M.; Fang, Q.; Wen, M.; Hu, X. A virtual interface-coupled extended finite element method for three-dimensional contact problems. *Int. J. Numer. Methods Eng.* **2021**, *122*, 386–402. [CrossRef]
18. Zhou, X.-P.; Chen, J.-W.; Berto, F. XFEM based node scheme for the frictional contact crack problem. *Comput. Struct.* **2020**, *231*, 106221. [CrossRef]
19. Belytschko, T.; Black, T. Elastic crack growth in finite elements with minimal remeshing. *Int. J. Numer. Methods Eng.* **1999**, *45*, 601–620. [CrossRef]
20. Moës, N.; Dolbow, J.; Belytschko, T. A finite element method for crack growth without remeshing. *Int. J. Numer. Methods Eng.* **1999**, *46*, 131–150. [CrossRef]
21. Béchet, E.; Minnebo, H.; Moës, N.; Burgardt, B. Improved implementation and robustness study of the X-FEM for stress analysis around cracks. *Int. J. Numer. Methods Eng.* **2005**, *64*, 1033–1056. [CrossRef]
22. Stazi, F.; Budyn, E.; Chessa, J.; Belytschko, T. An extended finite element method with higher-order elements for crack problems with curvature. *Comput. Mech.* **2003**, *31*, 38–48. [CrossRef]
23. Fries, T. A corrected XFEM approximation without problems in blending elements. *Int. J. Numer. Methods Eng.* **2008**, *75*, 503–532. [CrossRef]
24. Laborde, P.; Pommier, J.; Renard, Y.; Salaün, M. High-order extended finite element method for cracked domains. *Int. J. Numer. Methods Eng.* **2005**, *64*, 354–381. [CrossRef]
25. Tarancón, J.E.; Vercher, A.; Giner, E.; Fuenmayor, F. Enhanced blending elements for XFEM applied to linear elastic fracture mechanics. *Int. J. Numer. Methods Eng.* **2009**, *77*, 126–148. [CrossRef]
26. Gracie, R.; Wang, H.; Belytschko, T. Blending in the extended finite element method by discontinuous Galerkin and assumed strain methods. *Int. J. Numer. Methods Eng.* **2008**, *74*, 1645–1669. [CrossRef]
27. Wells, G.; Sluys, L. A new method for modelling cohesive cracks using finite elements. *Int. J. Numer. Methods Eng.* **2001**, *50*, 2667–2682. [CrossRef]
28. Duarte, C.; Babuška, I.; Oden, J. Generalized finite element methods for three-dimensional structural mechanics problems. *Comput. Struct.* **2000**, *77*, 215–232. [CrossRef]
29. Zi, G.; Belytschko, T. New crack-tip elements for XFEM and applications to cohesive cracks. *Int. J. Numer. Methods Eng.* **2003**, *57*, 2221–2240. [CrossRef]
30. Mariani, S.; Perego, U. Extended finite element method for quasi-brittle fracture. *Int. J. Numer. Methods Eng.* **2003**, *58*, 103–126. [CrossRef]
31. Moes, N.; Belytschko, T. Extended finite element method for cohesive crack growth. *Eng. Fract. Mech.* **2002**, *69*, 813–833. [CrossRef]
32. Cox, J.V. An extended finite element method with analytical enrichment for cohesive crack modeling. *Int. J. Numer. Methods Eng.* **2009**, *78*, 48–83. [CrossRef]
33. Meschke, G.; Dumstorff, P. Energy-based modeling of cohesive and cohesionless cracks via X-FEM. *Comput. Methods Appl. Mech. Eng.* **2007**, *196*, 2338–2357.

34. Gupta, V.; Duarte, C.A. On the enrichment zone size for optimal convergence rate of the Generalized/Extended Finite Element Method. *Comput. Math. Appl.* **2016**, *72*, 481–493. [CrossRef]
35. Fries, T.-P.; Belytschko, T. The extended/generalized finite element method: An overview of the method and its applications. *Int. J. Numer. Methods Eng.* **2010**, *84*, 253–304. [CrossRef]
36. Belytschko, T.; Gracie, R.; Ventura, G. A review of extended/generalized finite element methods for material modelling. *Model. Simul. Mater. Sci. Eng.* **2009**, *17*, 043001. [CrossRef]
37. Khoei, A.R. *Extended Finite Element Method: Theory and Applications*; SPi Publisher Services: Pondicherry, India, 2015.
38. Chessa, J.; Wang, H.; Belytschko, T. On the construction of blending elements for local partition of unity enriched finite elements. *Int. J. Numer. Methods Eng.* **2003**, *57*, 1015–1038. [CrossRef]
39. Xu, Y.; Yuan, H. Applications of normal stress dominated cohesive zone models for mixed-mode crack simulation based on extended finite element methods. *Eng. Fract. Mech.* **2011**, *78*, 544–558. [CrossRef]

energies

Article

Numerical Investigation of the Sensitivity of the Acoustic Power Level to Changes in Selected Design Parameters of an Axial Fan

Dawid Romik *,† **and Ireneusz Czajka** †

Department of Power Systems and Environmental Protection Facilities, Faculty of Mechanical Engineering and Robotics, AGH University of Science and Technology, Mickiewicz 30 Av., 30-059 Krakow, Poland; iczajka@agh.edu.pl
* Correspondence: dromik@agh.edu.pl
† These authors contributed equally to this work.

Abstract: The noise generated by different types of fans used in the turbomachinery industry is a topic that has been studied for many years. However, researchers are still looking for a universal solution to reduce noise while maintaining the performance of these machines. This paper, as a contribution to the research, presents the results of numerical investigations of an axial fan installed in a pipeline with a circular cross-section. In particular, the focus was on investigating the sensitivity of the sound power level to changes in selected design and operational parameters of this fan. The simulation studies used the unsteady Reynolds-averaged Navier–Stokes (URANS) approach and the Ffowcs Williams–Hawkings (FW-H) analogy implemented in Ansys Fluent.

Keywords: axial fan; CFD; URANS; fan noise; aeroacoustics; sensitivity

Citation: Romik, D.; Czajka, I. Numerical Investigation of the Sensitivity of the Acoustic Power Level to Changes in Selected Design Parameters of an Axial Fan. *Energies* **2022**, *15*, 1357. https://doi.org/10.3390/en15041357

Academic Editors: Marcin Kamiński and Davide Astolfi

Received: 30 November 2021
Accepted: 7 February 2022
Published: 14 February 2022

1. Introduction

Axial fans typically work in very turbulent flow conditions, e.g., because of their installations in pipelines, behind radiators, etc. This results in very unstable aerodynamic forces on the impeller blades, which in turn cause excessive sound radiation. Noise from flow machines consists of tonal noise, as a result of the interactions among the turbine blades and stationary housing components or guide vanes and broadband noise resulting from the acoustic signal generated by strong turbulent structures occurring in the flow. The most modern aeroacoustic computational methods enable increasingly reliable predictions of the generated noise. They usually require specific information about the transient flow field, obtained by simulation using computational fluid dynamics methods.

The most accurate of these methods, a direct numerical simulation (DNS), could solve the Navier–Stokes equation with no simplifications and could predict the unsteady flow and the associated acoustic field. Unfortunately, DNS is not feasible for a complex geometry, such as a fan, due to the enormous computational costs. Finding a non-stationary flow field with less effort requires modelling of at least part of the of the turbulent fluctuation [1]. Two different ways are currently used to reduce computational costs. The first is time averaging, which is known as the unsteady Reynolds-averaged Navier–Stokes (URANS) simulation (URANS), the second is a spatial filtering of the full Navier–Stokes equations, called large eddy simulation (LES).

In the case of URANS, the reduction of calculation costs is enormous but the cost is a large level of approximation. All random turbulent fluctuations are modeled, so only tonal sources of rotating machine sounds can be predicted. LES solves large turbulent structures, and only small eddies are modeled, but the computational costs are still high. Since this paper contains a very large number of numerical calculations that involve long-term calculations, the authors decided to use the URANS method in the simulations carried out. The relevance of this decision is confirmed by Kissner et al. [2], who show that this way of modelling allows for satisfying accuracy to be achieved.

Solving aeroacoustics problems requires even more computational efforts. In addition to determining the sound sources, it is important to determine how the sound wave propagates. Assuming that the energy difference of the flow and the acoustic wave is sufficiently large, one can focus on the one-way coupling between the fluid flow and the acoustic signal generated. This line of reasoning led Lighthill to develop the aeroacoustic analogy named after him.

Lighthill [3–5] first made a formulation of the acoustic analogy for jet noise in 1952, which demonstrated that the flow mechanisms that were responsible for sound radiation could be expressed in terms of the quadrupole source. Curle [6] extended Lighthill's analogy to the fluid–structure interaction and implemented an extra acoustic source produced from the reaction force that was exerted on the fluids surrounding the body that did not move. FW-H [7,8] generalized Curle's analogy and extended the analogy to a moving structure. The FW-H equation splits up the aeroacoustic source into three different kinds of source: monopoles, dipoles, and quadrupoles.

The general theory of Lighthill introduced by FW-H, which takes into account the motion of a body as a potential source, has been used in many noise studies of rotating machines, i.e., turbines, fans, helicopters, etc. The FW-H analogy also takes surface sources into account, which makes it possible to determine noise from sources other than the quadrupole sources proposed by Lighthill. Schmitz and Yu [9] proved that, at a low Mach number, the volume integral makes no significant contribution to the noise generated by a hovering helicopter rotor. For a given range of speeds, the rotor is a surface of monopole and dipole sources and their contributions depend on factors, i.e., geometry, speed, and forces acting on the surface.

Brentner and Farassat [10], present a comprehensive review of the mathematical basis of the FW-H equation, comparing integral formulas and sufficiently powerful numerical methods applied to helicopter noise. They found that the contribution of the volume integral is small for subsonic flows, but gives a larger result for supersonic and transonic flows. In addition, they found that, by applying a permeable FW-H surface, instead of to the body surface, this would allow quadrupole sources to be included.

Konstantinov et al. [11] showed results of URANS, Delayed Detached Eddy Simulation (DDES), and LES flow and noise distributions in the test cabin segment. Compared to the FW-H mathematical model and the hybrid approach of solving the wave equation, including non-reflecting boundary conditions, a small influence on the sound pressure level from the imperfect boundary condition in the LES was shown.

Sundström et al. [12] used the LES method to investigate which acoustic sources predominated in low mass flux flows. They found that blade forces resulting from varying wall pressures are the main sources of generated noise at low mass flux flows. It turned out that sound sources coming from forces on blades (dipoles), were much larger than quadrupole sources, especially in subsonic flows. Comparing these two sound sources, one can see the relation $W_d : Wq \sim 1 : M^2$ can be observed. Moreover, it can be concluded that monopole sources have a greater influence on the generated noise in sonic flows.

In a study by Al-Am et al. [13], the LES approach was used to numerically calculate the influence of selected parameters on the noise generated around a flat plate. Noise generated at the trailing edge and noise of turbulent nature was investigated. The flow character and geometry were chosen to correspond to the Amiet model. It is shown that the adopted model gives very good noise calculations in agreement with the analytical model and DNS calculations. Moreover, regarding the ACAT1 fan noise test [2], RANS-based analytical methods are commonly used to predict broadband fan noise. The accuracy of the aerodynamic noise results obtained in post-processing calculations depends not only on the choice of acoustic model itself, but to a large extent on the turbulent model adopted, which has a significant influence on the nature of the flow and which in turn affects the fan broadband noise. In continuation of this work, [14] focused on the importance of acoustic models. Twelve different models were investigated and several different solvers were used to solve them. Both models—based on acoustic analogies and those using direct methods—were compared. The methods used are distinguished by the turbulence models, the applied boundary conditions related to the propagation of the acoustic wave and the noise from the rotor blade phenomena. It turns out that at low frequencies, the differences in the generated noises are quite large, while at higher frequencies, the sound power level is within ±3 dB. Furthermore, it is proven that by increasing the rotational speed, the generated acoustic power is similar for different models.

Biedermann et al. in their study [15], provided detailed information on the broadband noise reduction possibilities of a low pressure axial fan with serrations on the leading edges. For the area of instability under partial load conditions, it is proposed that the dominant noise reduction mechanisms are dependent on aerodynamic effects related to the serrated geometry at the leading edge, which results in a reduction of the dominant low and medium frequency noise levels. It was also shown [16] that under the same operating conditions, the sound pressure levels at the two measurement points of the radial fan increases by approximately 5.8% and 2.8%, when the ambient pressure increases from 50 kPa to 100 kPa. As the ambient pressure increases, the fan sound pressure level shows an approximate logarithmic increase trend. It is worth mentioning that researchers [17] have attempted various techniques to identify the source of the sound, i.e., isocontours of the dilatation field, which revealed sources of acoustic scale disturbance, and may be the cause of the noise, a dynamic mode decomposition for the pressure upstream and downstream of the fan blade, which shows several strong fashions around the first three blade frequencies, and finally the acoustic analogy of FW-H, which showed a difference of about 5 dB between the blade tip and the lower parts of the blade in a specific frequency range. These results are consistent with the expectations that higher flow velocities would yield higher acoustic pressures.

The effect of the blade curvature on the generated noise was also investigated [18,19], in relation to the classic Amiet formulation. It has been proven that a curved blade causes a reduction in noise; this effect is particularly noticeable at the blade tip. Significant differences were also observed regarding noise generation at the leading and trailing edges of the blade, where the former is globally dominant but takes on values close to the latter at around 3.75 kHz and higher [20,21]. Similarly, other researchers confirm this relationship that the pressure fluctuation of the radial fan was smallest when the blade outlet angle was smaller, and it was also shown that a corresponding increase in the blade outlet angle reduced the amplitude of the pressure fluctuation in the blade pass frequency and its harmonics, which is conducive to reducing rotor noise [22]. In [23], it was shown that, on the upstream side on the blade walls, the sound pressure level was higher than on the downstream side. This was due to the separation of the boundary layer at the leading edge with increasing radial velocity near the ring, resulting in a low frequency noise. The leading edge therefore turned out to be the dominant dipole source generating tonal noise in contrast to the other rotor elements. The issues of stream separation at too low of a rotational speed of the rotor are also discussed [24], where under rotating stall conditions the fluctuation of the sound pressure amplitude becomes much greater than under other conditions, and the fluctuation of the sound pressure level is greater at a low frequency under stall conditions than under normal operating conditions.

The sensitivity analysis consists of examining how a given model depends on the parameters entering into it. By testing the sensitivity, you can determine which input variables have the greatest impact on a given output, and in this way, areas that require more attention may be identified [25]. Sensitivity analysis is a concept used in various engineering fields, i.e., acoustics, material science, environmental protection, etc. [26–28].

In the above works, different types of fans have been studied, both in terms of increasing their efficiency and reducing noise emissions, which proves the relevance of the issue. Researchers are still looking for a compromise to design these machines in such a way that they achieve the greatest efficiency with the least possible noise emissions. The authors of this paper, in previous studies [29–31], also discussed the influence of design parameters on the noise generated and the efficiency of different types of fans.

The research carried out in this work focuses on the sensitivity of the generated noise to changes in the design parameters of the fan rather than on the determination of the exact value of the acoustic power level.

2. Numerical Simulations

2.1. Research Object

The numerical study was carried out on an axial fan (see Figure 1) with a diameter of 220 mm and a rotational speed of 3000 revolutions per minute, installed in a pipe of a circular cross-section with a diameter of 230 mm. The rotor has six blades on a hub with a diameter of 100 mm and a length of 200 mm at an angle of 20°. For such an assumed rotational speed, the fan achieves a volume flow rate of 750 $m^3 \cdot h^{-1}$.

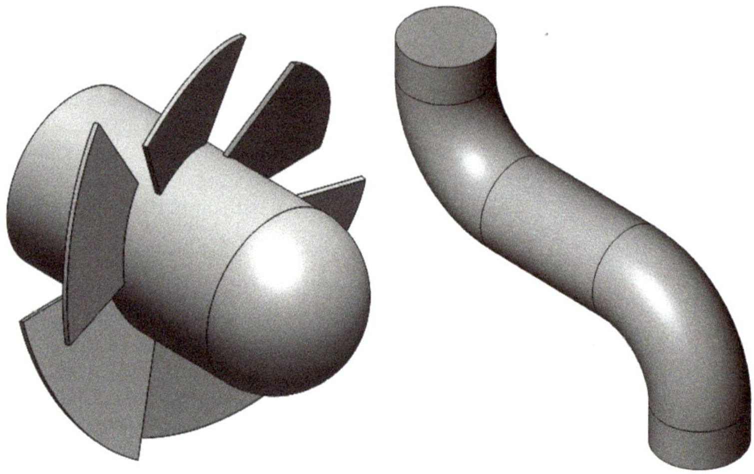

(a) (b)

Figure 1. Geometrical model of the fan: (**a**) rotor, (**b**) pipeline.

The numerical model was a computational grid consisting of 2,120,050 cells, in which the Navier–Stokes equations were solved using the finite volume method. The main fan parameters are shown in Table 1.

Table 1. Parameters of the axial fan.

Parameter	Symbol	Unit	Value
Rotational speed	n	$r \cdot min^{-1}$	3000
Number of blade	z	-	6
Rotor diameter	D	mm	220
Hub diameter	D_h	mm	100
Hub length	H_l	mm	200
Inlet/outlet diameter	D_i/D_o	mm	230
Inlet/outlet length	L_i/L_o	mm	100
Blade angle	θ	°	20

In the model, two characteristic zones can be identified: a rotating zone in which the rotor is located and a stationary zone representing a curved pipeline. The geometric model does not include the fan fixing elements inside the pipeline. To simplify the model, steering systems and airflow straightening elements were also omitted. Marked in Figure 2, distances L_p and L_t are equal to each other and are 70.16 mm. Inlet straight sections L_i and outlet L_o of the pipeline are equal and amount to 100 mm.

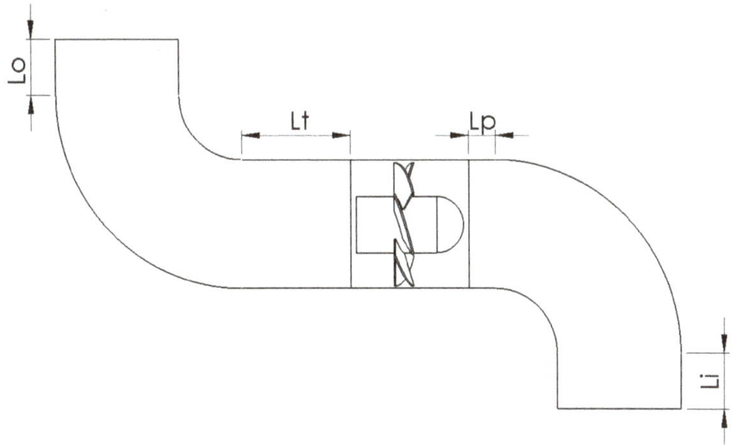

Figure 2. Diagram of built-in fan.

The geometric model of the rotor was made in SolidWorks and then adapted to the ICEM CFD environment. The ICEM CFD program was used to create a orthogonal computational mesh based on a multi-block structure grids topology. In the areas close to the leading and trailing edges, vortices were created due to the separation of the boundary layer, which is why the computational grid was appropriately compacted at these points in order to solve the flow with greater precision. In addition, a wall layer was modeled to provide a parameter $y^+ < 5$. In order to analyze the validity of the model performed, an analysis of the independence of the results from the calculation grid was performed. The mesh used (see Figure 3) allowed for results of sufficient accuracy to be obtained in a reasonable time.

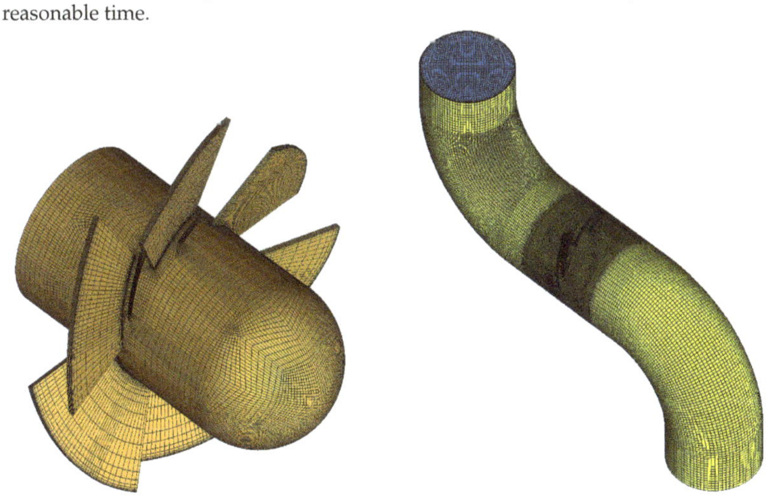

(a) (b)

Figure 3. Fan computational grid: (**a**) rotor mesh, (**b**) pipeline mesh.

2.2. Mathematical Model

The first and very important step in the simulation is to locate the sources that can be used to calculate the generated noise. This can be achieved using appropriate computational fluid dynamics techniques. In this field, the basic equations are based on the Navier–Stokes equations derived from the conservation of mass (continuity equation), conservation of momentum, and conservation of energy.

The continuity equation can be written for fluids as:

$$\rho \frac{\partial u_i}{\partial x_i} = 0 \tag{1}$$

where ρ is the density of the fluid, t is the time, components of the velocity vector $\mathbf{u}$ in the coordinate system, and x_i coordinates in the Cartesian system. The momentum equation is written as:

$$\rho \frac{\partial u_i}{\partial t} + \rho \frac{\partial u_i u_j}{\partial x_j} = -\frac{\partial p}{\partial x_i} + \frac{\partial \tau_{ij}}{\partial x_j}, \tag{2}$$

where p is the pressure and τ_{ij} are viscous stresses. Equation (2) is derived by applying Newton's second law of dynamics, which relates the forces acting on a fluid volume to its acceleration.

Turbulence model $k - \omega$ is one of the most popular models, which shows the phenomena of turbulent flow. It belongs to a family of models in which all turbulence effects are modeled. This is a two equation model. This means that the transport equations are solved to include phenomena, such as convection and turbulent energy dissipation. The variables considered in the equation are the turbulent kinetic energy k, representing the turbulence energy, and the specific turbulent dispersion coefficient $omega$, denoting the dispersion rate of the turbulence kinetic energy. Variable ω is also known as the turbulence scale. The standard $k - omega$ model works well for low Reynolds number flows where the boundary layer is appropriately sized and the viscous sublayer is well separated. Thus, the standard model $k - \omega$ is best suited for modelling the boundary layer. Other advantages include excellent performance in complex near-wall flows with adverse pressure gradients and separation, e.g., in rotating machinery. The model also predicts excessive and early vortex separations.

Model $k - \omega$ SST is a model that offers the strengths of the $k - \epsilon$ proposed by Launder and Spalding [32] and model $k - \omega$ proposed by Wilcox [33], and provides an additional component to limit the overproduction of turbulent kinetic energy in areas of high pressure gradients (stagnation points, areas of separation vortex near wall layer). Menter [34] examining models $k - \epsilon$ and $k - \omega$, and observed that the first handles turbulence well in free and shear layers and shows negligible sensitivity to inlet boundary conditions for quantities describing turbulent flow. This is a desirable quality because these quantities are often not exactly known in practical calculations. However, the $k - \omega$ model better models turbulent flow in the boundary layer but is more sensitive in free flow.

The sound pressure level (SPL) was determined using the FW-H analogy. This model is based on the Lighthill analogy and allows noise to be determined by equivalent acoustic sources. Ansys Fluent uses these equations to determine the sound pressure at a given distance from a sound source by an integral over the surface containing those sources. The FW-H equation is a non-homogeneous wave equation [7,35], which can be derived by combining the continuity and Navier–Stokes equations. It can be written as

$$\begin{aligned} \frac{1}{a_0^2} \frac{\partial^2 p'}{\partial t^2} - \nabla^2 p' = & \frac{\partial^2}{\partial x_i \partial x_j} \{ T_{ij} H(f) \} \\ & - \frac{\partial}{\partial x_i} \{ | P_{ij} n_j + \rho u_i (u_n - v_n) | \delta(f) \} \\ & + \frac{\partial}{\partial t} \{ | \rho_0 v_n + \rho (u_n - v_n) | \delta(f) \} \end{aligned} \tag{3}$$

where u_i—air velocity in the direction of x_i, v_i—surface velocity in the direction of x_i, u_n—air velocity normal to the surface $f = 0$, $\delta(f)$—Dirac delta, v_n—velocity of the surface normal to the surface, $H(f)$—Heaviside function, p'—sound pressure in the far field $(p' - p_0)$, n_i—normal vector pointing to the external area $(f > 0)$, a_0—speed of sound in the far field, Pij—compressive stress tensor, T_{ij}—Lighthill stress tensor.

To solve Equation (3), the Green's function must be used to the open area. The complete solution involves the calculation of surface and volume integrals, the first representing monopole, dipole, and partially quadrupole acoustic sources, and the second representing quadrupole sources in the area outside of the source surface. The volume integral becomes negligible when the Mach number value of the flow is small and the source area covers the source area. In Ansys Fluent, choosing a source on a solid surface-like rotor, the volume integrals are neglected, then the equation takes the following form:

$$p' = (\vec{x}, t) = p'_T(\vec{x}, t) p'_L(\vec{x}, t) \tag{4}$$

$$\begin{aligned} 4\pi p'_T(\vec{x}, t) &= \int_{f=0} \left[\frac{\rho_0 (\dot{U}_n + U_{\dot{n}})}{r(1 - M_r)^2} \right] dS \\ &+ \int_{f=0} \left[\frac{\rho_0 U_n \{ r\dot{M}_r + a_0 (M_r - M^2) \}}{r^2 (1 - M_r)^3} \right] dS \end{aligned} \tag{5}$$

$$\begin{aligned} 4\pi p'_L(\vec{x}, t) &= \frac{1}{a_0} \int_{f=0} \left[\frac{\dot{L}_r}{r(1 - M_r)^2} \right] dS \\ &+ \int_{f=0} \left[\frac{L_r - L_M}{r^2 (1 - M_r)^2} \right] dS \\ &+ \frac{1}{a_0} \int_{f=0} \left[\frac{L_r \{ r\dot{M}_r + a_0 (M_r - M^2) \}}{r^2 (1 - M_r)^3} \right] dS \end{aligned} \tag{6}$$

where

$$U_i = v_i + \frac{\rho}{\rho_0} (u_i - v_i) \tag{7}$$

$$L_i = P_{ij} \hat{n}_j + \rho u_i (u_n - v_n) \tag{8}$$

The contribution of quadrupole terms (volume integrals) in the FW-H analogy is proportional to the square of the Mach number (M^2). In the analyzed system, the Mach number reaches values below 0.1, which means that the volume integrals can be omitted. Considering the time t and a distance to the observer r, the integral equation takes into account the delay due to the distance from the source to the receiver, according to the following formula:

$$\tau = t - \frac{r}{a_0} \tag{9}$$

$$\begin{aligned} &M_r = M_i r_i \quad \dot{M}_r = \tfrac{\partial M_i}{\partial \tau} r_i \\ &Q_n = Q_i \hat{n}_i \quad \dot{Q}_n = \tfrac{\partial Q_i}{\partial \tau} \hat{n}_i \quad Q_{\dot{n}} = Q_i \tfrac{\partial \hat{n}_i}{\partial \tau} \\ &L_i = L_i j \hat{n}_i \quad \dot{L}_r = \tfrac{\partial L_i}{\partial r} \hat{r}_i \quad L_r = L_i \hat{r}_i \quad L_M = L_i M_i \end{aligned} \tag{10}$$

where $\vec{n}, \vec{r}$—unit vectors of radiation and normal to the wall, M—Mach number of the surface source velocity component along the direction of the radiation vector.

2.3. Boundary Conditions and Solver Settings

The calculations started by simulating free flow, i.e., forced only by a rotating impeller at 3000 r·min^{-1} around the X axis. For this purpose, boundary conditions of 0 Pa corresponding to atmospheric pressure were applied at the inlet and outlet, respectively. To reduce calculation time, the strategy involves running the simulation at a steady state (MRF) for about 500 iterations until the solution converges below 10^{-4} and then take the results as initial conditions for the unsteady simulation (sliding mesh) with a time step of $5.5 \cdot 10^{-5}$ s, which corresponds to 360 time steps per rotation of the rotor. Since the Mach number value was approximately 0.1, the flow was assumed to be incompressible, reducing the computational resources required and the computation time. The calculation used the FW-H equation implemented in Ansys Fluent based on Lighthill's acoustic analogy. The rotor and the pipeline walls are indicated as sources of sound (control surface). As receivers, 510 points were selected and placed on a sphere with a radius of 3 m where the acoustic pressure was computed (Figure 4).

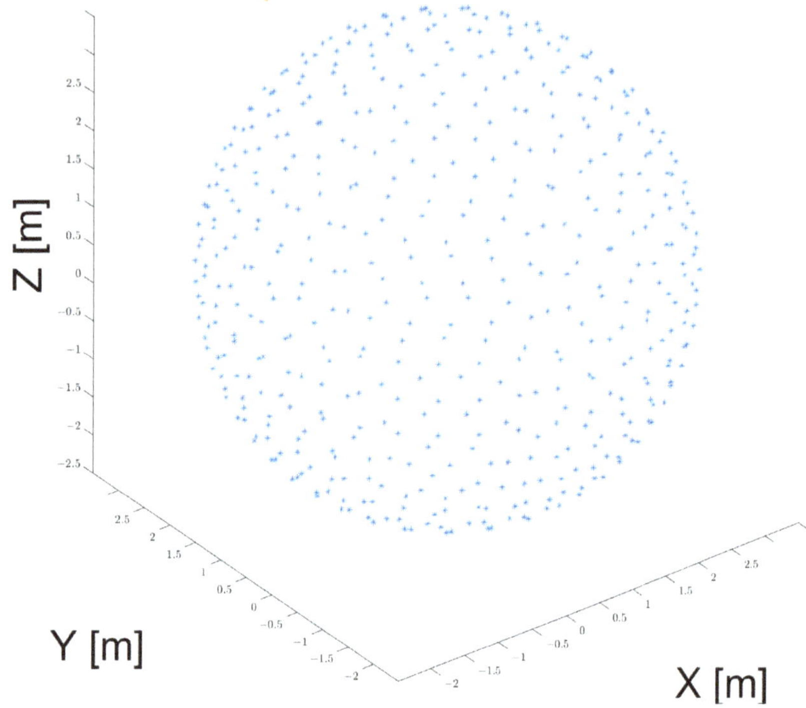

Figure 4. Receivers distribution.

The resulting sound pressure obtained in the time domain was subjected to Fourier analysis. The boundary conditions are shown in Table 2.

Table 2. Boundary Conditions.

Boundary Condition	Symbol	Unit	Value/Zone
Operating pressure	P_{atm}	Pa	101,325
Inlet pressure	P_i	Pa	0
Outlet pressure	P_o	Pa	0
Mesh motion	n	$r \cdot min^{-1}$	3000
Interface	-	-	rotor/duct contact area
Wall	-	-	rotor/duct walls
Time step	t	s	$5.5 \cdot 10^{-5}$

To obtain the fan characteristics, calculations were performed for 20 various volume flow rate values in the range of $0.0997 \div 0.1994$ $m^3 \cdot s^{-1}$, of which the points marked $1 \div 4$ turned out to be a stall range, while the range $5 \div 20$ determined the operating range of the fan. In order to improve the readability of the presented graphs, we decided not to include characteristic points from the stall range on the graphs. Table 3 shows the calculation points and the corresponding percentage of unthrottled flow.

Table 3. Measurement points.

Nr	Volume Flow Rate (m^3/s)	Percentage (%)	Nr	Volume Flow Rate (m^3/s)	Percentage (%)
1	0.0997	50.00	11	0.1770	88.75
2	0.1097	55.00	12	0.1795	90.00
3	0.1196	60.00	13	0.1820	91.25
4	0.1246	62.50	14	0.1845	92.50
5	0.1595	80.00	15	0.1869	93.75
6	0.1645	82.50	16	0.1894	95.00
7	0.1670	83.75	17	0.1919	96.25
8	0.1695	85.00	18	0.1944	97.50
9	0.1720	86.25	19	0.1969	98.75
10	0.1744	87.50	20	0.1994	100.00

A pressure-based coupled algorithm was used to perform the calculations. The pressure-based solver uses an algorithm called the projection method, which solves the continuity and momentum equations [36]. The equation of momentum is calculated by the second-order upwind scheme [37].

3. Results

3.1. Fan Characteristics

The numerical calculations were completed after 7200 time steps, which corresponds to 20 rotations of the rotor. The flow is established after approximately 1000 steps. The total pressure increase Δp was used as a criterion for flow stabilization. The velocity contours of the resolved flow are shown in Figure 5.

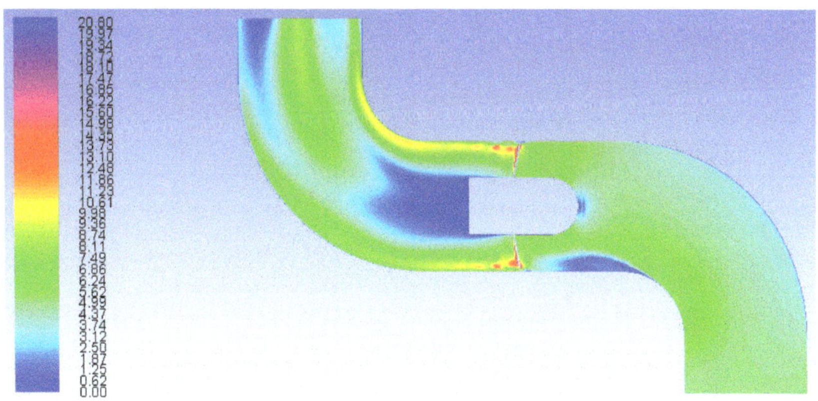

Figure 5. Velocity contours of resolved flow.

On the basis of the obtained results, the basic parameters of the fan were calculated to determine its characteristics. The formula was used to calculate the mechanical power

$$N_m = M\omega \tag{11}$$

where M is the torque on the rotor expressed in [Nm] and ω is the angular velocity expressed in [rad·s^{-1}]. The effective power was calculated as

$$N_u = \Delta p \dot{V} \tag{12}$$

where Δp is the pressure increase and $\dot{V}$ is the volume flow rate behind the rotor. Due to the low compression, the compressibility of the medium is not taken into account. The efficiency was calculated according to the equation

$$\eta = \frac{N_u}{N_m} \tag{13}$$

In Figure 6, it can be seen that points $1 \div 4$ present a pressure increase significantly different from the rest of the measurement points and reach $\Delta p = 185.2 \div 215.7$ Pa and their amplitude is approximately approximately 20 Pa, while the amplitude at the points $5 \div 20$ is only 2 Pa. The results of the calculations of pressure increase and efficiency are shown in Figure 7.

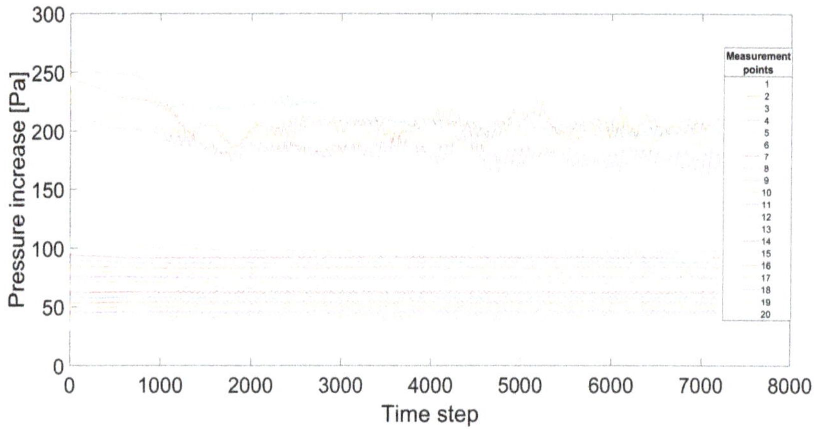

Figure 6. Pressure increase.

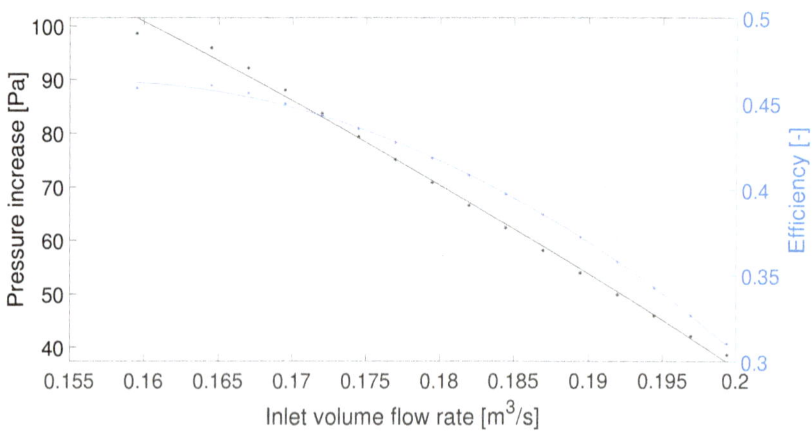

Figure 7. Pressure increase and efficiency characteristics.

3.2. Aerodynamic Noise Characteristics

The acoustic power of the fan during its operational conditions was determined. Therefore, distributions of the fluid pressure and velocity around the fan in the duct in successive moments was calculated. Next, the FW-H analogy was used to determine the sound pressure values in points on the sphere around the fan. In this case, reflections from walls of the duct were not taken into account because the radiated power is a parameter of the acoustic source. At low sound pressures and the assumption of unidirectional coupling between the flow and the acoustic field, the reflections do not have much of an impact on the power of the source itself. The considerable size of the sphere was necessary to be able to treat the acoustic wave as locally plane in the receivers. Using the FW-H analogy, a time domain acoustic signal was obtained on the surface of a sphere of radius $R = 3$ m. On this area, 510 receivers were placed in which the acoustic signal was obtained. Sound pressures were determined at the measurement points, from which the sound intensity was calculated assuming that the wave was locally flat. The integral of the intensity along the surface of the sphere gives the sound power value. The acoustic pressure was determined in each of the receivers, and assuming a locally plane wave, on this basis the sound intensity was calculated. The receivers on the sphere were evenly distributed and each was assigned to a sphere surface element. Integration was performed using the rectangle rule (the value of the intensity in the receiver multiplied by the surface element assigned to a given node) [38]

$$SWL = 10\log_{10}\left(\frac{P}{P_0}\right) \tag{14}$$

where P_0 is the reference power equal to $10^{-12}W$ and P is the power of sound expressed by the formula

$$P = \oint_A I dA = \oint_A \frac{p^2}{\rho_0 c} dA \approx \frac{\sum_i A_i p_i^2}{\rho_0 c} \tag{15}$$

where A is the surface area, p_{rms} is the root mean square of the sound pressure, $\rho = 1.1225\ \mathrm{kg/m^3}$ is the density of air, $c = 340\ \mathrm{m/s}$ is the speed of sound. On the basis of the calculated values of the sound pressure, calculations were carried out to obtain the sound pressure level.

$$SPL = 20\log_{10}\left(\frac{p_{rms}}{p_{ref}}\right) \tag{16}$$

In addition, a Fourier analysis was carried out to verify the blade pass frequency calculated from the relationship

$$BPF = \frac{RPM \times z}{60} \tag{17}$$

where p_{ref} is the reference pressure equal to $2 \cdot 10^{-5}$ Pa. The results are shown in Figure 8, showing the blade pass frequency of 300 Hz and its harmonics.

The results obtained are compared with the fan characteristics in Figure 9. From the results obtained, it can be concluded there is a significant increase in the sound power level in the stall area compared to the working area, which is up to 10 dB. In the operating area, the sound power level is in the range 79.3 ÷ 90.9 dB (see Table 4) and can be approximated by a parabola with a local minimum. In experimental work [39], a similar character of sound power level was obtained.

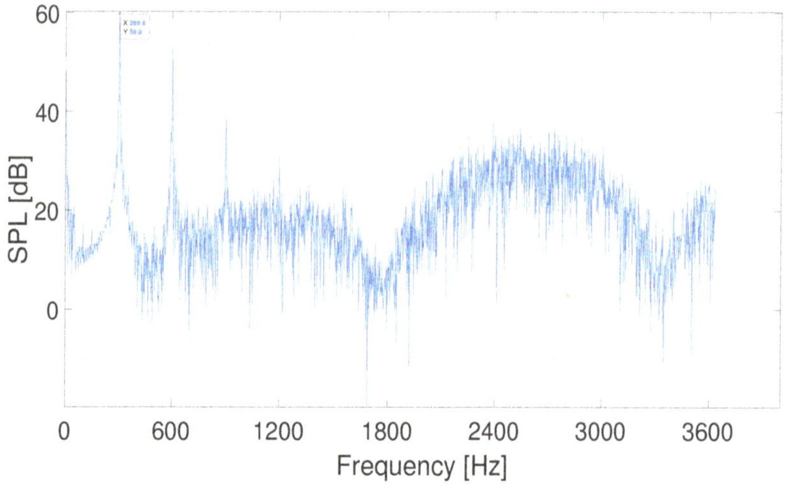

Figure 8. FFT of acoustic signal.

Table 4. SWL results.

Nr	SWL [dB]	Nr	SWL [dB]
1	88.47	11	79.39
2	89.96	12	79.32
3	90.88	13	79.30
4	90.80	14	79.33
5	80.18	15	79.49
6	79.87	16	79.59
7	79.70	17	79.73
8	79.63	18	79.83
9	79.55	19	79.90
10	79.48	20	79.95

From the resulting sound pressure level distribution shown in Figure 10, it can be seen that there are negligible differences in cases 5–20. A common feature of all cases is a higher sound pressure level on the upstream side and around the X axis at the height of the blades. In cases 1–4, the sound pressure level is much higher than in the other cases, and it is related to greater pressure fluctuation in the stall area.

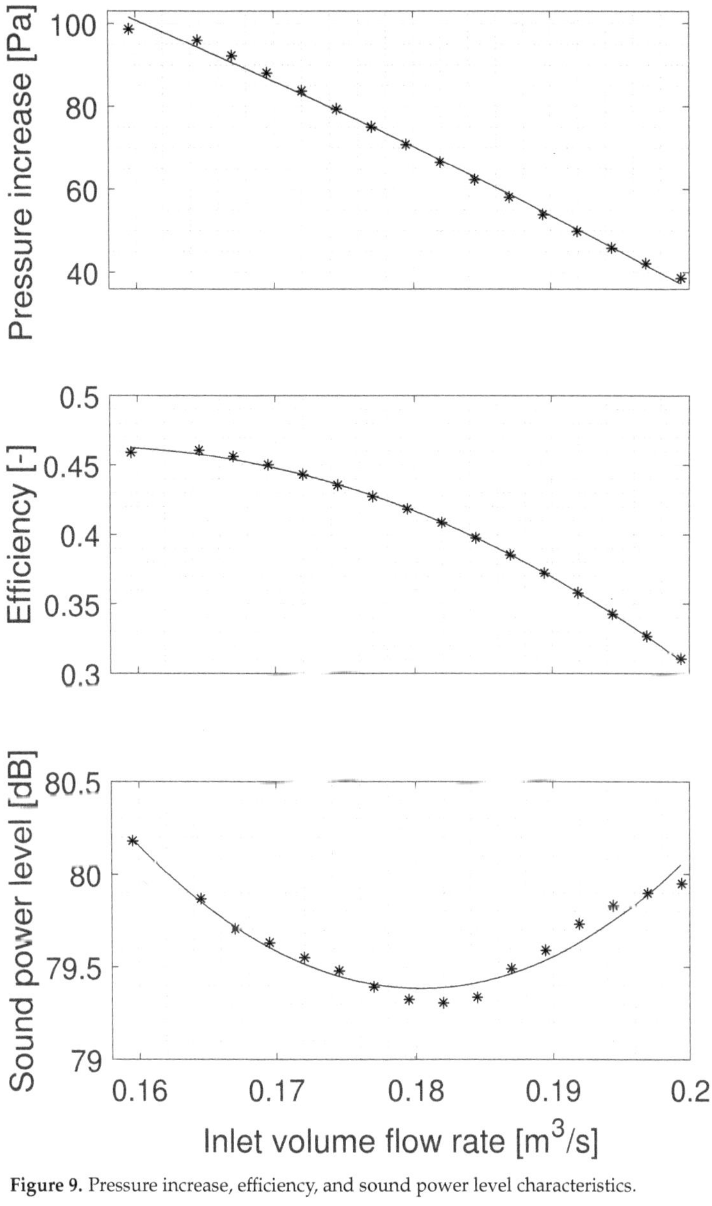

Figure 9. Pressure increase, efficiency, and sound power level characteristics.

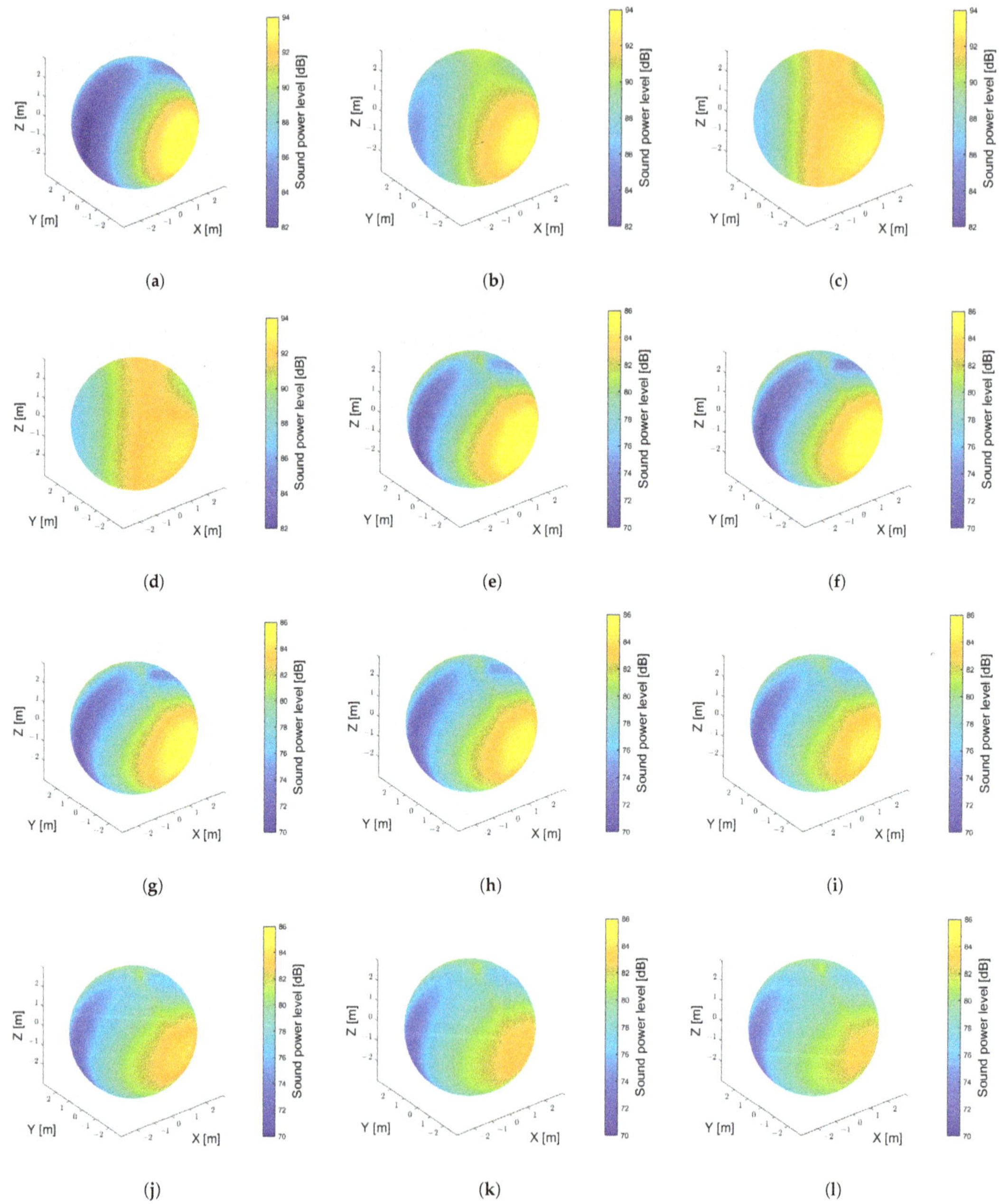

Figure 10. *Cont.*

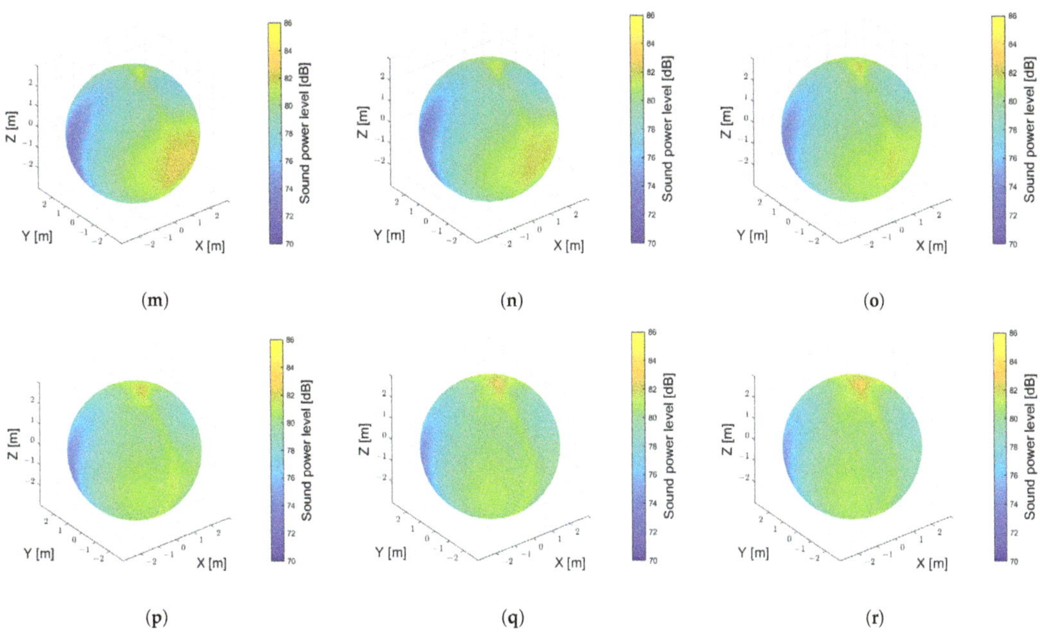

Figure 10. Sound power level distribution: (**a**–**r**) are the measurement points 1–18.

3.3. Sensitivity of the Fan Parameters to the Change of the Blade Angle

The study investigated the sensitivity of the fan characteristics to a change in the blade angle. For this purpose, we carried out additional numerical calculations for the blade angle $\theta = 21^\circ$ (Figure 11).

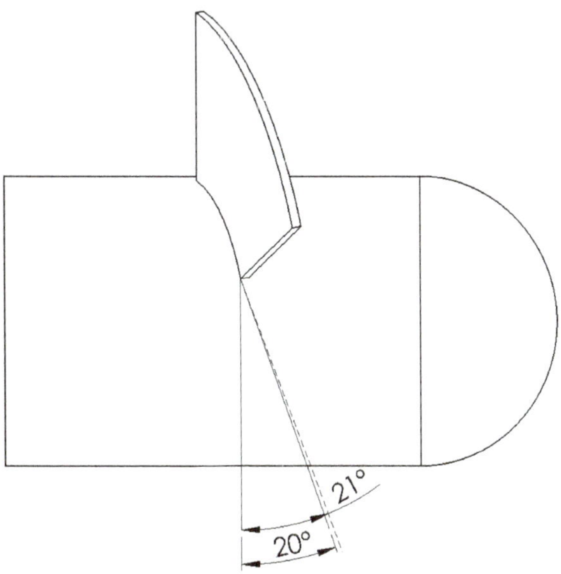

Figure 11. Geometry of the model with marked angles $\theta = 20^\circ$ and $\theta = 21^\circ$.

The sensitivity of a characteristic function to changes in a design parameter can be defined as the partial derivative of the function describing that characteristic, with respect to that parameter. The sensitivity coefficients, in normalized form, can be found as

$$S_x^y = \frac{\partial y_i / y_i}{\partial x_j / x_j} \tag{18}$$

where S_x^y is the normalized sensitivity coefficient, y_i is model dependent variable and x_j is input parameter.

$$S_\theta^{\Delta p} = \frac{\partial p / p}{\partial \theta / \theta} \approx \frac{\Delta p / p}{\Delta \theta / \theta} = 0.2416 \tag{19}$$

$$S_\theta^{\eta} = \frac{\partial \eta / \eta}{\partial \theta / \theta} \approx \frac{\Delta \eta / \eta}{\Delta \theta / \theta} = 0.1042 \tag{20}$$

$$S_\theta^{SWL} = \frac{\partial SWL / SWL}{\partial \theta / \theta} \approx \frac{\Delta SWL / SWL}{\Delta \theta / \theta} = -5.9558 \cdot 10^{-5} \tag{21}$$

The values from points $8 \div 16$, which constitute the work area, were used for the calculations. Two single $(*)$ symbols define the beginning of a new stall zone (see Figure 12).

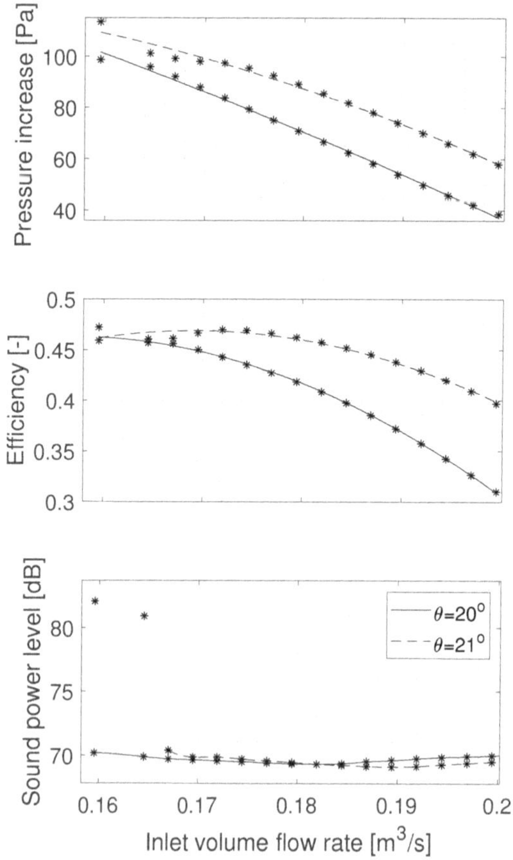

Figure 12. Pressure increase, efficiency, and sound power level characteristics for blade angles 20° and 21°.

4. Conclusions

Computer simulations using CFD techniques were carried out to investigate the noise generated by the axial fan. The URANS time-averaging method and the FW-H analogy implemented in Ansys Fluent were used in the calculations. Using these methods, the sound pressure was calculated on a sphere with a radius of 3 m from the sound source, from which the acoustic characteristics were determined and an FFT analysis was performed. The analysis was carried out for twenty characteristic points for two different blade angles. The main conclusions of the numerical analysis are presented below.

On the basis of the torque and total pressure increase analysis, the stall area can be verified for the operating points $1 \div 4$ and normal work in points $5 \div 20$. In the stall region, the total pressure increase is $\Delta p = 185.2 \div 215.7$ Pa, while in the normal operating area, it is $79.8 \div 99.8$ Pa.

Fourier analysis, calculated using the FW-H acoustic analogy of the acoustic pressure, made it possible to determine the blade pass frequency equal to 300 Hz and its harmonics, which allows to confirm the accuracy of the numerical simulations.

As expected, the determined characteristics show that the fan efficiency increases with increasing total pressure increase.

The difference in the indicated sound power level in the test area is just 1 dB. However, attention should be paid to the obtained characteristics of the sound power level, which in the studied area has a local minimum, which encourages additional considerations on determining the optimal operating point for which the emitted noise is the lowest.

The determined sound power level on a sphere with a radius of 3 m from the noise source indicates higher emission from the upstream, which may be caused by turbulent flow caused by the curved pipeline. The common feature of the presented results is a greater level of generated noise around the X axis at the height of the blades.

From the simulations carried out for a variable blade angle, it can be seen that, for angle $\theta = 21^\circ$ at certain points of the characteristic curve, the fan efficiency increases from 2% to 8%. A sound power level at an angle of $\theta = 21^\circ$ emits 1 dB less at certain points than for angle $\theta = 20^\circ$.

For blade angle $\theta = 21^\circ$, the characteristic point that defines the stall zone has moved, and for this, the angle is located between the points $1 \div 6$.

The generated noise is influenced by many more design and operational parameters of the axial fan. The aim of the article was to show the change in the angle of the rotor blades in the entire exploitation area, i.e., with a variable flow rate. The calculations consist of examining more than 20 measurement points for one parameter change, which require a lot of computational time, but they are planned for the second part of the research. Further experiments on the real object will be aimed at verifying the numerical model and extending the research with parameters influencing the generated noise.

Author Contributions: Conceptualization, D.R. and I.C.; methodology, I.C.; software, D.R.; validation, I.C., D.R.; formal analysis, D.R.; investigation, D.R.; resources, D.R.; data curation, D.R.; writing—original draft preparation, D.R. and I.C.; writing—review and editing, D.R. and I.C.; visualization, D.R.; supervision, I.C.; project administration, I.C. All authors have read and agreed to the published version of the manuscript.

Funding: This research received no external funding.

Institutional Review Board Statement: Not applicable.

Informed Consent Statement: Not applicable.

Data Availability Statement: Data sharing not applicable.

Acknowledgments: This research was supported in part by PLGrid Infrastructure.
This research was supported by national subvention no. 16.16.130.942.

Conflicts of Interest: The authors declare no conflict of interest.

Abbreviations

The following abbreviations are used in this manuscript:

BPF	blade pass frequency
CFD	computational fluid dynamics
DDES	delayed detached eddy simulations
DNS	direct numerical simulations
FFT	fast Fourier transform
FW-H	Ffowcs Williams and Hawkings analogy
MRF	multiple reference frame
LES	large eddy simulation
SST	shear stress transport
URANS	unsteady Reynolds-averaged Navier–Stokes

References

1. Czajka, I. *Modeling of Acoustic Phenomena in Aerodynamic Flows; Volume 365, Dissertations, Monographs*; AGH: Krakow, Poland, 2019.
2. Kissner, C.; Guérin, S.; Seeler, P.; Billson, M.; Chaitanya, P.; Carrasco Laraña, P.; de Laborderie, H.; François, B.; Lefarth, K.; Lewis, D.; et al. ACAT1 Benchmark of RANS-Informed Analytical Methods for Fan Broadband Noise Prediction—Part I—Influence of the RANS Simulation. *Acoustics* **2020**, *2*, 539–578. [CrossRef]
3. Lighthill, M.J. On sound generated aerodynamically I. General theory. *Proc. R. Soc. Lond. Ser. A Math. Phys. Sci.* **1952**, *211*, 564–587. [CrossRef]
4. Lighthill, M.J. On sound generated aerodynamically II. Turbulence as a source of sound. *Proc. R. Soc. Lond. Ser. A Math. Phys. Sci.* **1954**, *222*, 1–32. [CrossRef]
5. Lighthil, M.J. Jet Noise. *AIAA J.* **1963**, *1*, 1507–1517. [CrossRef]
6. Curle, N. The influence of solid boundaries upon aerodynamic sound. *Proc. R. Soc. Lond. Ser. A Math. Phys. Sci.* **1955**, *231*, 505–514. [CrossRef]
7. Williams, J.F.; Hawkings, D.L. Sound generation by turbulence and surfaces in arbitrary motion. *Philos. Trans. R. Soc. Lond. Ser. A Math. Phys. Sci.* **1969**, pp. 321–342. [CrossRef]
8. Williams, J.F.; Hawkings, D. Theory relating to the noise of rotating machinery. *J. Sound Vib.* **1969**, *10*, 10–21. [CrossRef]
9. Schmitz, F.; Yu, Y. *Transonic Rotor Noise: Theoretical and Experimental Comparisons*; National Aeroacoustics and Space Administration: Washington, DC, USA, 1982; pp. 319–330.
10. Brentner, K.S.; Farassat, F. Modeling aerodynamically generated sound of helicopter rotors. *Prog. Aerosp. Sci.* **2003**, *39*, 83–120. [CrossRef]
11. Konstantinov, M.; Wagner, C. *Numerical Simulation of the Sound Generation and the Sound Propagation from Air Intakes in an Aircraft Cabin*; New results in numerical and experimental fluid mechanics XI; Springer: Cham, Switzerland, 2018. [CrossRef]
12. Sundström, E.; Semlitsch, B.; Mihăescu, M. Acoustic signature of flow instabilities in radial compressors. *J. Sound Vib.* **2018**, *434*, 221–236. [CrossRef]
13. Al-Am, J.; Clair, V.; Giauque, A.; Boudet, J.; Gea-Aguilera, F. A Parametric Study on the LES Numerical Setup to Investigate Fan/OGV Broadband Noise. *Int. J. Turbomach. Propuls. Power* **2021**, *6*, 12. [CrossRef]
14. Guérin, S.; Kissner, C.; Seeler, P.; Blázquez, R.; Carrasco Laraña, P.; de Laborderie, H.; Lewis, D.; Chaitanya, P.; Polacsek, C.; Thisse, J. ACAT1 Benchmark of RANS-Informed Analytical Methods for Fan Broadband Noise Prediction: Part II—Influence of the Acoustic Models. *Acoustics* **2020**, *2*, 617–649. [CrossRef]
15. Biedermann, T.M.; Czeckay, P.; Hintzen, N.; Kameier, F.; Paschereit, C.O. Applicability of Aeroacoustic Scaling Laws of Leading Edge Serrations for Rotating Applications. *Acoustics* **2020**, *2*, 579–594. [CrossRef]
16. Zhang, X.; Zhang, Y.; Lu, C. Flow and Noise Characteristics of Centrifugal Fan in Low Pressure Environment. *Processes* **2020**, *8*, 985. [CrossRef]
17. Kholodov, P.; Moreau, S. Identification of Noise Sources in a Realistic Turbofan Rotor Using Large Eddy Simulation. *Acoustics* **2020**, *2*, 691–706. [CrossRef]
18. Zarri, A.; Christophe, J.; Moreau, S.; Schram, C. Influence of Swept Blades on Low-Order Acoustic Prediction for Axial Fans. *Acoustics* **2020**, *2*, 812–832. [CrossRef]
19. Zarri, A.; Christophe, J.; Schram, C.F. Low-Order Aeroacoustic Prediction of Low-Speed Axial Fan Noise. In Proceedings of the 25th AIAA/CEAS Aeroacoustics Conference, Delft, The Netherlands, 20–23 May 2019; p. 2760. [CrossRef]
20. Herold, G.; Zenger, F.; Sarradj, E. Influence of blade skew on axial fan component noise. *Int. J. Aeroacoustics* **2017**, *16*, 418–430. [CrossRef]
21. Sanjosé, M.; Moreau, S. Fast and accurate analytical modeling of broadband noise for a low-speed fan. *J. Acoust. Soc. Am.* **2018**, *143*, 3103–3113. [CrossRef] [PubMed]
22. Ding, H.; Chang, T.; Lin, F. The Influence of the Blade Outlet Angle on the Flow Field and Pressure Pulsation in a Centrifugal Fan. *Processes* **2020**, *8*, 1422. [CrossRef]

23. Mo, J.o.; Choi, J.h. Numerical Investigation of Unsteady Flow and Aerodynamic Noise Characteristics of an Automotive Axial Cooling Fan. *Appl. Sci.* **2020**, *10*, 5432. [CrossRef]
24. Zhang, L.; Yan, C.; He, R.; Li, K.; Zhang, Q. Numerical Study on the Acoustic Characteristics of an Axial Fan under Rotating Stall Condition. *Energies* **2017**, *10*, 1945. [CrossRef]
25. Chan, K.; Saltelli, A.; Scott, E.M. *Sensitivity Analysis*; Wiley: Chichester, UK, 2000.
26. Klieber, M.; Antunez, H.; Hien, T.; Kowalczyk, P. *Parameter Sensitivity in Nonlinear Mechanics*; Wiley: Chichester, UK, 1997.
27. MRÓZ, Z.; HAFTKA, R.T. Sensitivity of buckling loads and vibration frequencies of plates. *Stud. Appl. Mech.* **1988**, *19*, 255–266.
28. Zheng, C.; Zhao, W.; Gao, H.; Du, L.; Zhang, Y.; Bi, C. Sensitivity analysis of acoustic eigenfrequencies by using a boundary element method. *J. Acoust. Soc. Am.* **2021**, *149*, 2027–2039. [CrossRef] [PubMed]
29. Romik, D.; Czajka, I.; Suder-Dębska, K. *Numerical Investigations of the Design Parameters' Influence on the Noise of Radial Fan;* Polish Acoustical Society, Department of Krakow: Krakow, Poland 2019; pp. 133–149.
30. Romik, D.; Czajka, I. *On the Modelling of the Aeroacoustics Phenomena Generated by Axial Fan*; AGH: Krakow, Poland 2019; pp. 122–131.
31. Romik, D.; Czajka, I. *Influence of Turbulence Models on Numerical Investigation of Axial Fans Efficiency*; Department of Power Systems and Environmental Protection Facilities, Faculty of Mechanical Engineering and Robotics, AGH: Krakow, Poland, 2019; pp. 71–79.
32. Launder, B.E.; Spalding, D.B. *Lectures in Mathematical Models of Turbulence*; Launder, B.E., Spalding, D.B., Eds.; Academic Press: London, UK; New York, NY, USA, 1972; p. 7, 169p.
33. Wilcox, D.C. *Turbulence Modeling for CFD*; DCW Industries La Canada: La Canada, CA, USA, 1998; Volume 2.
34. Menter, F.R. Two-equation eddy-viscosity turbulence models for engineering applications. *AIAA J.* **1994**, *32*, 1598–1605. [CrossRef]
35. Brentner, K.S.; Farassat, F. Analytical comparison of the acoustic analogy and Kirchhoff formulation for moving surfaces. *AIAA J.* **1998**, *36*, 1379–1386. [CrossRef]
36. Chima, R.; Liou, M. Comparison of the AUSM(+) and H-CUSP Schemes for Turbomachinery Applications. In Proceedings of the Computational Fluid Dynamics Conference, Orlando, FL, USA, 23–26 June 2003. [CrossRef]
37. Barth, T.; Jespersen, D. The design and application of upwind schemes on unstructured meshes. In Proceedings of the 27th Aerospace Sciences Meeting, Reno, NV, USA, 9–12 January 1989. [CrossRef]
38. McAlpine, A. Aeroacoustics of Low Mach Number Flows: Fundamentals, Analysis and Measurement S. Glegg and W. Devenport Academic Press, Elsevier, The Boulevard, Langford Lane, OX5 1GB, Kidlington, Oxford, UK. xiii; 537pp. 2017. Illustrated. £97. ISBN 978-0-12-809651-2. *Aeronaut. J.* **2018**, *122*, 2030–2032. [CrossRef]
39. Fortuna, S.; Czajka, I. Experimental Verification of Selected Equations Describing the Sound Power Level in Fans. *Turbomachinery* **2010**, *nr 138*, 21–32.

mathematics

Article

A Combined Experimental-Numerical Investigation of the Thermal Efficiency of the Vessel in Domestic Induction Systems

Belén Bonet-Sánchez [1], Iulen Cabeza-Gil [1,*], Begoña Calvo [1,2], Jorge Grasa [1,2], Carlos Franco [3], Sergio Llorente [3] and Miguel A. Martínez [1,2]

1 Aragón Institute of Engineering Research (i3A), University of Zaragoza, 50009 Zaragoza, Spain; bbonet11@gmail.com (B.B.-S.); bcalvo@unizar.es (B.C.); jgrasa@unizar.es (J.G.); miguelam@unizar.es (M.A.M.)
2 Centro de Investigación Biomédica en Red en Bioingenieria, Biomateriales y Nanomedicina (CIBER-BBN), 50018 Zaragoza, Spain
3 BSH Home Appliances Group, 50080 Zaragoza, Spain; carlos.franco@bshg.com (C.F.); sergio.llorente@bshg.com (S.L.)
* Correspondence: iulen@unizar.es

Abstract: New studies are emerging to reduce energy costs and become a more sustainable society. One of the processes where the greatest savings can be made is in cooking, due to its large-scale global use. In this vein, this study aims to analyse the influence of the vessel in the thermal efficiency at the cooking process. For that purpose, a numerical model of a cooking vessel was designed and validated with three different experimental heating tests. One of the key factors of the process is the contact between the vessel and the glass, therefore, two new approaches to model the thermal contact between the vessel and the cooktop were explored. Once the numerical models were calibrated, a full factorial analysis was performed to quantify the influence of the key parameters of the vessel in the heating process during cooking (thermal conductivity, specific heat, convection and radiation coefficients, and vessel concavity). Two of the most influential parameters in the heating process are the conductivity and the thermal contact between the vessel and the glass. Higher cooking efficiency can be achieved both with a low thermal conductivity vessel and with a high concavity, i.e., increasing the isolation between the vessel and the glass.

Keywords: heat transfer; thermal distribution; cooking; finite element analysis; household domestic appliances

Citation: Bonet-Sánchez, B.; Cabeza-Gil, I.; Calvo, B.; Grasa, J.; Franco, C.; Llorente, S.; Martínez, M.A. A Combined Experimental-Numerical Investigation of the Thermal Efficiency of the Vessel in Domestic Induction Systems. *Mathematics* **2022**, *10*, 802. https://doi.org/10.3390/math10050802

Academic Editor: James M. Buick

Received: 11 February 2022
Accepted: 28 February 2022
Published: 3 March 2022

1. Introduction

Domestic cooking appliances have significantly evolved towards a more user-friendly and efficient use during the last decades due to the importance of cooking in our daily life [1]. One of the most important elements of the cooking process is the vessel; however, its influence on the energy efficiency has not yet been widely discussed in literature, in contrast to other domestic appliances such as gas burners and induction systems [2–4].

There are few studies about the vessel influence during cooking related to thermal efficiency and bottom temperature homogenisation. Cadavid et al. [5] analysed the thermal efficiency of a pot on an electric stove using numerical simulations. Villacis et al. [4] experimentally evaluated the energy efficiency of different materials for cookware used in induction systems. Hannani et al. [6] analysed the thermal efficiency of some cookings pots using a combined experimental and neural network method. Sedighi and Dardashti [7] reported that both multilayer plates and some thermal properties, such as thermal conductivity, provide a more uniform temperature profile. Ayata et al. [8] trained a neural network to find a solution to the nonregular distribution of temperature using the most efficient thickness distribution, and Karunanithy and Shafer [9] studied the efficiency of different saucepans on various cooktops and agreed that the surface finish of the pan base significantly affects the cooking efficiency.

There is no study that delves into all factors involved in the properties of cooking vessels, probably due to the difficulty of conducting these tests experimentally [4]. To address this need, we have developed high-fidelity simulations with the finite element method (FEM) and designed a full factorial analysis to study the effect of the main parameters of the vessel. The finite element (FE) model was based on a previous study [10], used to analyse the thermal distribution on the bottom of a pan depending on the meat size and position in the pan.

One of the main limitations of the FE model developed at [10] was the assumption of a constant thermal conductance between the cooking vessel and the glass. The micro-concavity of the vessel and the thermal-deformation of the vessel during the heating makes very complex to model accurately this thermal contact conductance. To address this issue, we explored two novel approaches: (I) including a layer of stratified air between the pan and the glass and (II) setting a variable thermal contact conductance in the interaction between the vessel and the glass along the radius, hereinafter referred to as Model I and Model II, respectively, see Figure 1a.

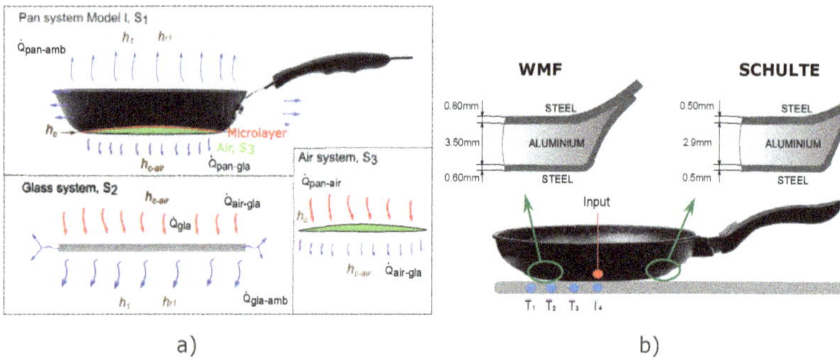

Figure 1. (**a**) Representation of the systems that form Model I (S_1 and S_2 are the same for Model II). S_1 corresponds to the system of the solid/pan, S_2 corresponds to the glass and S_3 corresponds to the air. The input heat is shown as red arrows, while outgoing heat is shown by blue arrows. $\dot{Q}_{pan-air}$ and $\dot{Q}_{air-glass}$ corresponds only to Model I. (**b**) Distribution of thermocouples in the vessel and the glass. The thermocouple (red) placed at the centre is used as input for the PI control (T_{sensor}). Blue thermocouples are placed below the glass.

The first goal of this paper was to study how the bottom of the pan affects the cooking and in detail, the influence of the contact between the vessel base and glass. For that purpose, three FE models were calibrated independently based on experimental heating tests in three different solids: two multilayer frying pans from the Würtembergische Metallwarenfabrik (WMF) and Schulte brands and a steel plate (which was used as a flat sample). Once a high-fidelity numerical model was achieved, the key parameters of the vessel were analysed through a full factorial analysis.

This paper is organised as follows. We first describe the experimental set-up in Section 2.1: the cooktop, the three vessels under investigation and the PI control algorithm used to control the temperature of the vessel. The proposed FE models and the design of the experiments (DoE) to analyse the key parameters of the vessels under heating are explained in Sections 2.2 and 2.3, respectively. This is followed by the results and discussion of the study and, finally, the main conclusions obtained are presented.

2. Materials & Methods

2.1. Experimental Set-Up

The experimental heating tests consisted of heating a vessel to 200 °C for 1800 s on an induction cooktop prototype from BSH Home Appliances. The inductor used in the experiments generates a power distribution resembling a ring, which is assumed to be rotationally symmetric; see Figure 1 in Cabeza-Gil et al. [10]. The applied power turns into heat in a steel microlayer of 100 μm, which is placed at the bottom of the vessel, by means of the dissipation of the eddy current density induced [11]. The power density was controlled with a PI algorithm, whose input is a thermocouple, hereinafter referred to as T_{sensor}, which was located at the centre of the cookware surface for all vessels [12]. To measure the thermal footprint in the glass, four thermocouples were placed under the glass at a radius of 7.00, 5.00, 2.00 cm and at the centre, T_1, T_2, T_3 and T_4, respectively, see Figure 1b.

Three different solids (two vessels and a steel plate) with different concavities, see Figure 2, were heated: a multilayer WMF pan with a diameter of 21 cm and a thickness of 4.9 mm (red line); a multilayer Schulte pan, model Industar, with a diameter of 20 cm and a thickness of 3.9 mm (green line); and a circular steel plate, which was specifically used in this study since its base surface is practically flat, with a diameter of 20 cm and a thickness of 6 mm (blue line). The multilayer pans consisted of three layers: steel, aluminium and steel, from bottom to top. The WMF has an aluminium volume percentage of 71.43%, while the Schulte pan has an aluminium volume percentage of 74.36%. The concavity of each vessel was measured with a Faro Prime robot with an accuracy of ±27.00 μm (see Figure 2). The emissivity (ϵ) of each vessel under investigation was measured with a thermal emissometer, model TIR 100-2 from Inglas, along the whole spectrum.

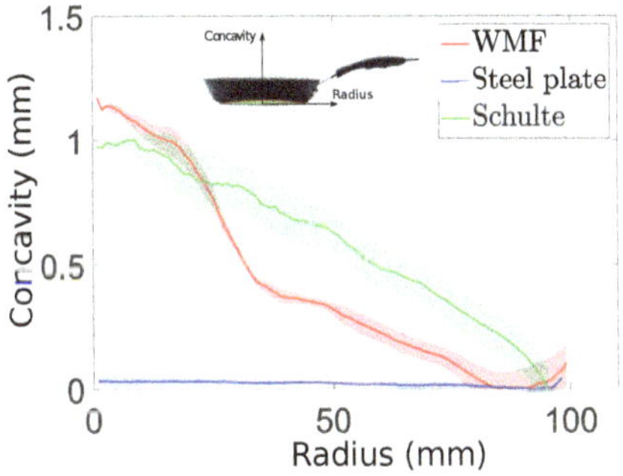

Figure 2. The mean and deviation concavity for each solid under investigation are depicted. The red line corresponds to the WMF, the green line to the Schulte and the blue line to the steel plate. The axis x = 0 is placed at the lowest geometric point of the vessel located in the periphery.

A computer to which the experimental setup was connected calculated the supplied power required and provided it to achieve the target temperature (200 °C) by means of the PI controller [12]. The tests for each sample were carried out three times. The software used to supply the power and to register all temperatures of the thermocouples was MATLAB R2020a.

2.2. Model Description

2.2.1. Heat Transfer Model

Two different FE models were developed to simulate the heating process of the vessels depending on how the heat transfer between the vessel and the glass was modelled. Both models were divided into two coupled systems, the vessel (S_1) and the glass surface (S_2). A new solid domain, a layer of air (S_3), was included in Model I to simulate the thermal contact between the vessel and the glass. In Model II, this thermal contact was modelled through a variable thermal contact conductance.

In S_1, $\dot{Q}_{pan}$ represents the heat rate generated in the ferromagnetic microlayer of the pan from the induction cooking hob. $\dot{Q}_{pan-amb}$ indicates the convective and radiative heat losses from the pan to the ambient environment, modelled by h_1 and h_{r1}, respectively, which are the heat transfer convective and radiation coefficients. Heat losses between the pan and the glass are different in each model because of the presence of air. In Model I,

$\dot{Q}_{pan-air}$ depicts the heat losses to the air between the pan and the glass. In S_2, $\dot{Q}_{air-gla}$ represents the conductive heat transfer between the air and the glass and $\dot{Q}_{pan-gla}$ between the pan and the glass. In Model II, without the layer of air, $\dot{Q}_{pan-gla}$ depicts the conductive heat transfer between the pan and the glass. $\dot{Q}_{gla}$ is the heat absorbed by the glass, and $\dot{Q}_{gla-amb}$ are the convective and radiative losses from the glass to the ambient environment, which are also modelled as h_1 and h_{r1}, respectively.

The governing equations of the systems are described in Cabeza-Gil et al. [10], which come from the local heat transfer equation (Equation (1)) [13,14].

$$\begin{cases} (a)\ P = \rho_{SM} c_{e\text{-}SM} \frac{\partial T_{SM}}{\partial t} - k_{SM} \nabla^2 T_{SM}, \Rightarrow \text{ SM}, \\ (b)\ 0 = \rho_{SD} c_{e\text{-}SD} \frac{\partial T_{SD}}{\partial t} - k_{SD} \nabla^2 T_{SD}, \Rightarrow \text{ SD}. \end{cases} \tag{1}$$

The domain of Equation (1a) is the steel microlayer (SM) of the vessel where the electromagnetic power is supplied, being P the volumetric power density generated by the induction heat source. Equation (1b) refers to the remaining part of the solid domain (SD). The terms ρ_{SD}, c_{e-SD}, and k_{SD} are the density, the specific heat capacity and the thermal conductivity of the solid material (steel or aluminium), respectively. T_{SM} and T_{SD} are the corresponding temperature at some determined point in the volume domain.

Regarding the boundary conditions of the system, Equations (2) and (3) refer to the convection and radiation heat losses to the ambient environment, respectively.

$$-\lambda_i \frac{\partial T_i}{\partial n} = h_i (T_i - T_{amb}), \tag{2}$$

$$h_i = h_i^{conv} + h_i^r = h_i^{conv} + \sigma\epsilon(T_i^2 + T_{amb}^2)(T_i + T_{amb}), \tag{3}$$

where the subscript i refers to outer surface of the vessel or the glass and $\frac{\partial T_i}{\partial n}$ is the partial T-derivative normal to the reference surface. h_i includes both the convective and radiative contributions, i.e., h_i^{conv} and h_i^r are the convective and radiative heat transfer coefficients, respectively. σ is the Stefan–Boltzmann constant, ϵ is the emissivity of the pan and T_{amb} is the ambient temperature.

Thermal conduction was differently modelled for Model I and Model II. In Model I, the conduction heat losses were modelled through Equation (4) from the vessel to the air (h_c^{va}) and from the air to the glass (h_c^{ag}):

$$-\lambda_v \frac{\partial T_v}{\partial n} = h_c^{va}(T_v - T_a), \quad -\lambda_a \frac{\partial T_a}{\partial n} = h_c^{ag}(T_a - T_g), \tag{4}$$

where λ_v and λ_a are the thermal conductivity of vessel and air. T_v, T_a and T_g are the respective temperatures at the vessel, air and glass surfaces. h_c^{va} is the thermal contact conductance to be evaluated between the vessel and the air, and h_c^{ag} is the thermal conductance between the air and the glass. A perfect thermal contact between the vessel and the air surface, and the air and the glass surface, was considered.

For the Model II, an iterative analysis was performed in the three samples under investigation to determine the relationship between the air gap and the thermal conductance coefficient along the radius, see Equation (5):

$$Q_c = \int_0^R \int_0^{2\pi} h_c^{vg}(r) \cdot \Delta T(r) \cdot r \cdot dr \cdot d\theta, \tag{5}$$

where Q_c refers to the heat loss at the contact between the pan and the glass, $h_c^{vg}(r)$ corresponds to the thermal conductance coefficient depending on the radius between the vessel and the glass, and $\Delta T(r)$ is the difference in the surface temperatures in the volume domain.

2.2.2. Finite Element Model

The FE model developed in this study is shown in Figure 3, and it is based on the study developed by Cabeza-Gil et al. [10]. The vessel geometry and the inclusion of the layer of air were different depending on the FE model analysed. Model I includes an air layer between the solid and the glass whereas Model II includes a variable thermal contact conductance. Both FE models consisted of a vitroceramic circular glass with a 200 mm radius × 4 mm thickness and the corresponding vessel previously described in Section 2.1. Due to the rotational symmetry, a quarter of the model was designed.

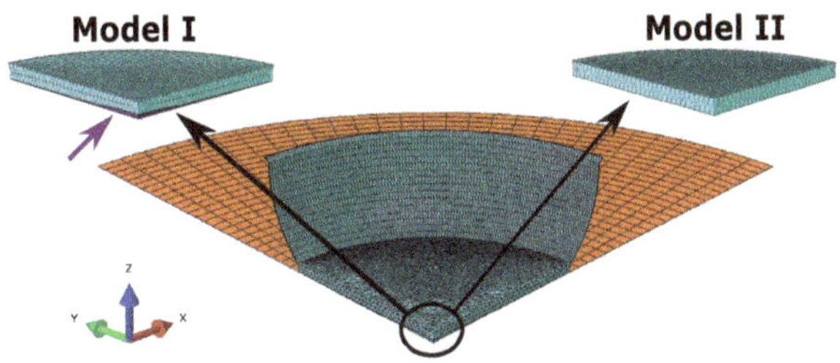

Figure 3. Vitroceramic glass is represented in orange, and the multilayer round WMF pan is represented in blue. Model I is modelled with the air (purple instance) between the glass and the pan, while Model II replaces the air by modelling the interaction between the vessel and glass by a variable thermal conductance coefficient along the radius.

The commercial software Abaqus v.6.14 was used to generate the model mesh and perform the simulations. The glass was considered a shell, which was meshed with 1408 quadratic 4-node quadrilateral (DS4) and 32 3-node linear triangular (DS3) heat transfer shell elements, while the vessel (WMF, Schulte pan and steel plate) was considered a 3D solid, which was meshed with approximately 35,000 (depending on the solid) 10-node quadratic heat transfer tetrahedral elements (DC3D10); see Figure 3. For the Model I, the layer of air was approximately modelled with 200 DC3D10 elements.

The power density distribution generated by the induction system was numerically computed in an electromagnetic FE model [15,16]. The power-density field from the FE model was mapped using an in-house subroutine, which was written in MATLAB 2020a, onto the FE mesh to perform the thermal analysis. The power supplied was calculated using PI control, which is a temperature-level control, and it was added through the URDFIL and DFLUX subroutines. This control reproduces the control implemented in the experimental heating tests by determining the power supplied from the previous time increment ($\Delta t = 1$ s) of the temperature sensor. The target temperature in the control was 200 °C, and the maximum power applied was limited to 2200 W, as in the experimental tests.

The whole model was at ambient temperature ($T_{amb} = 23$ °C) as initial condition. The boundaries conditions applied to the model are described in Section 2.2.1. Briefly, convection and radiation heat losses were imposed to all external surfaces of the model. For Model I, the heat conduction between the vessel and the air, and the air and the glass, was considered through a thermal contact conductance. Whereas for Model II, the heat conduction between the vessel and the glass surfaces was considered through a variable thermal contact conductance depending on the position ($h_c^{vg}(r)$. Convective and conductance parameters used in the computational models were obtained individually for each vessel after an optimisation process by fitting the experimental tests with the numerical tests. In each vessel, the same convective parameter was applied for all external surfaces. The coefficients of the glass were the same for all simulations. The thermal air properties [14] used in the study are shown in Table 1.

Table 1. Properties of air (Model I) modelled based on temperature as a continuum between the vessel and the pan [12].

Temperature (K)	Density (kg/m^3)	Conductivity (W/mK)	Specific Heat (kJ/kgK)	Expansion Coefficient (-)
300	1.16	0.026	1.007	
350	0.99	0.030	1.009	
400	0.87	0.034	1.014	
450	0.77	0.037	1.021	0.0037
500	0.69	0.041	1.030	
550	0.63	0.044	1.040	
600	0.58	0.047	1.051	

2.2.3. Finite Element Method Discretization

The weak form of Equation (1a) can be written as:

$$\int_{\Omega} P\delta T d\Omega = \int_{\Omega} \rho c_e \frac{\partial T}{\partial t} \delta T d\Omega - \int_{\Omega} k \nabla^2 T \delta T d\Omega \tag{6}$$

being Ω the solid domain and δT the virtual temperature. The application of classical differentiation rules to the last term of Equation (6) leads to the following statement:

$$\int_{\Omega} P\delta T d\Omega = \int_{\Omega} \rho c_e \frac{\partial T}{\partial t} \delta T \, d\Omega + \int_{\Omega} \nabla \delta T \, k \nabla T d\Omega - \int_{\partial\Omega} k \nabla T \delta T \, d(\partial\Omega) \tag{7}$$

The FEM discretization procedure starts from the following approximation of the temperature function:

$$T(x,y,z) = N_\alpha T_\alpha, \text{ being } \alpha = 1, \ldots, n \tag{8}$$

where $T(x,y,z)$, the temperature in the Cartesian coordinates, is represented by N_α, the shape functions, and T_α, the nodal temperatures. n is the total number of degrees of freedom of the model. Following the usual approximation of FEM, the virtual temperature (δT) is identified as the shape functions, $\delta T = N_\beta$. The matrix form of Equation (7) is represented as follows:

$$Q_\alpha^{(e)} = \int_{\Omega^{(e)}} P N_\beta d\Omega + \int_{\partial\Omega^{(e)}} k \nabla T N_\beta \, d(\partial\Omega) \tag{9}$$

$$K_{\alpha\beta}^{(e)} = \int_{\Omega^{(e)}} (k_x N_{\alpha,x} N_{\beta,x} + k_y N_{\alpha,y} N_{\beta,y} + k_z N_{\alpha,z} N_{\beta,z}) d\Omega \tag{10}$$

$$M_{\alpha\beta}^{(e)} = \int_{\Omega^{(e)}} \rho c_e N_\alpha N_\beta d\Omega \tag{11}$$

The assemblage and condensation procedures for the system matrices and vectors lead to the well-known final system of algebraic equations, which has been solved implicitly through the trapezoidal rule for time integration in Abaqus. The initial and boundary conditions needed to solve the equations system are described in Section 2.2.1.

$$M_{\alpha\beta} \frac{\partial T_\beta}{\partial t} + K_{\alpha\beta} T_\beta = Q_\alpha \tag{12}$$

2.3. *Design of the Experiment*

The influence of the key parameters of the model, the conductivity (k), specific heat (c_e), emissivity (ϵ), and concavity (Con) of the vessel, and the convective coefficients of the vessel (h_v^{conv}) and the glass (h_g^{conv}) in the cooking process were analysed following the DoE methodology by a full factorial analysis [17]. The simulations consisted in heating the vessel during 1800 s as in the experimental tests. A screening analysis was performed to observe the influence of each variable and decide the levels of the DoE. Based on this analysis, an intermediate value was selected for the conductivity, specific heat and concavity, whereas the remaining terms (emissivity and convective coefficients of the vessel and the glass) had two levels, resulting in 243 simulations (i.e., $3^3 \times 3^2 = 243$ simulations), see Table 2.

Table 2. Values of the analysed parameters for each level. Conductivity, specific heat and concavity have three levels, whereas both convective parameters and emissivity have only two. The steel density was considered constant with a value of 7900 kg/m^3.

Process Parameters	Low Level	Intermediate Level	Maximum Level
k (W/mK)	49	142	235
c_e (J/kgK)	300	420	540
Con	Scenario #A	Scenario #B	Scenario #C
h_v^{conv} (W/m^{2}K)	3	-	9
h_g^{conv} (W/m^{2}K)	3	-	9
ϵ	0.3	-	0.9

The maximum and minimum levels of the conductivity and the specific heat were chosen based on the properties of aluminium and steel [18]. The parameters affecting three heat losses (ϵ, h_v, h_g) were chosen according to values reported in the literature [10,11].

To analyse the influence of concavity, three different scenarios, see Figure 4, were considered. The red line was considered the reference case (from the WMF pan), hereinafter referred to as scenario #B. Two more scenarios where the concavity was increased by 1.5 times and decreased by 0.5 times were introduced (scenario #A and scenario #C, respectively).

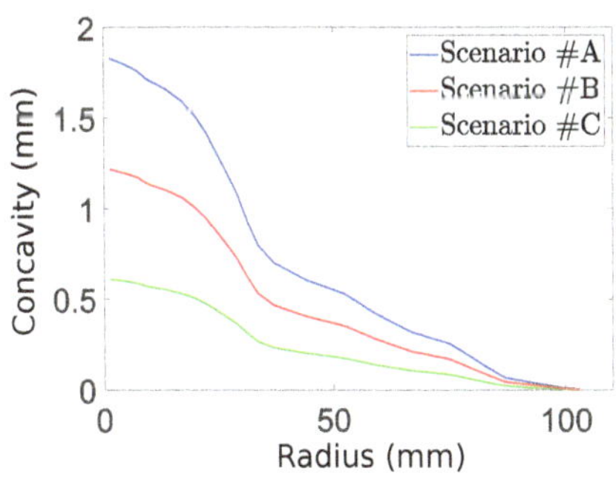

Figure 4. Concavities of the three different scenarios. Scenario #A (blue line) corresponds to a larger concavity compared to scenario #B, the concavity measured to the WMF pan with the robot (red line). Scenario #C (green line) corresponds to a flatter concavity compared to scenario #B.

The effect of the key parameters in the heating process were analysed measuring different factors of the cooking process: time to reach steady state (t_{st}), supplied energy during the cooking (E_{in}), maximum temperature of the sensor (T_s) and temperature homogenisation at the bottom along the radius after 1 min from the start (H_r):

$$H_r = 1 - \frac{1}{S_p} \int_0^{2\pi} \int_0^{r_{ext}} \frac{\mid \bar{T} - T(r,\theta) \mid}{\bar{T}} \cdot r \cdot dr \cdot d\theta, \tag{13}$$

where H_r refers to the temperature homogenisation along the radius in the second 60 of the cooking, S_p is the cookware surface of the pan, r is the radius of the pan, $\bar{T}$ is the mean temperature of the nodes selected in the cookware surface and $T(r,\theta)$ is the temperature in each node.

3. Results & Discussion

3.1. Experimental-Numerical Calibration of the Heat Loss Coefficients

The heat loss coefficients for the five calibrated models are presented in Table 3. Only the WMF and Schulte pans were developed in Model I because the steel plate is flat (Figure 2) and there is no layer of air to be modelled. Convective coefficients were optimised to reduce the mean absolute error (MAE) between the experimental and numerical temperatures. We obtained a convective coefficient of 8.0 W/m^2K, similar to Sanz-Serrano et al. [11], which obtained a convective coefficient of 9.5 W/m^2K using the difference finite method.

Table 3. Heat loss coefficients: convective coefficients (h_v^{conv} and h_g^{conv}), thermal conductance coefficients (h_c^{vg}, h_c^{va} and h_c^{ag}) and emissivity coefficient (ϵ) for the five FE models, the two with the layer of air (Model I) and the three with the non-linear thermal conductance along the radius (Model II).

	Model I		**Model II**		
	WMF	**Schulte**	**WMF**	**Schulte**	**Steel Plate**
h_v^{conv} (W/m^2K)	4	6	5.5	7	8
h_g^{conv} (W/m^2K)	4	4	5.5	5.5	4
h_c^{vg} (W/m^2K)	-	-	h_c^{vg}(r)	h_c^{vg}(r)	h_c^{vg}(r)
h_c^{va} (W/m^2K)	3000	3000	-	-	-
h_c^{ag} (W/m^2K)	3000	3000	-	-	-
ϵ	0.95	0.87	0.95	0.87	0.4

3.1.1. Model I: Modelling the Layer of Air between the Vessel and the Pan

Figure 5a,b show the WMF and Shulte heating processes, respectively. The dotted lines indicate the values obtained from the experimental tests whilst the continuous lines represent the computational results (see Figure 1b for the location of the thermal sensors). Shaded areas in the experimental tests are the standard deviations. Both numerical results of the surface thermocouples are within the experimental deviation.

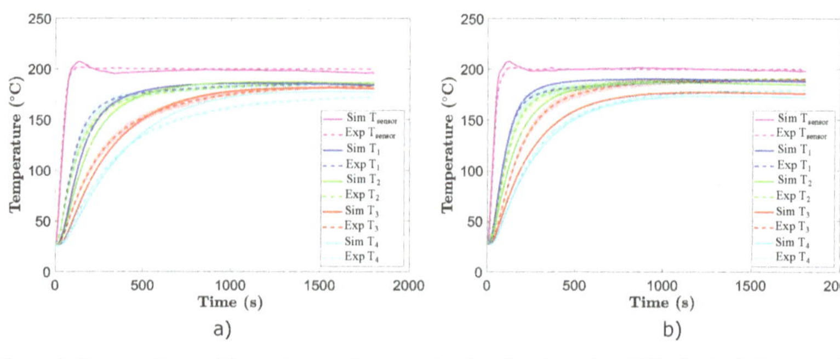

Figure 5. Temperatures of the surface and area under the glass from 0 to 1800 s for both the experimental test (dotted lines) and computational simulations (continuous lines) in Model I. (**a**) corresponds to the WMF pan and (**b**) to the Schulte pan.

The fitting between experimental and numerical results is good, although the experimental glass temperatures of the WMF pan heat up slightly faster than the simulated temperatures in the transient state (0–200 s). The temperatures in the steady state are practically the same. Table 4 shows the MAEs between the numerical and experimental temperatures. The thermocouple placed in the centre (T_4) presented the highest error, 6.75 °C.

Table 4. MAE of the three models with Model I. T_{sensor}, T_1, T_2, T_3 and T_4 are the thermocouples in Figure 1b. The units are °C.

	T_{sensor}	T_1	T_2	T_3	T_4
WMF	2.63	4.63	5.36	3.33	6.75
Schulte	1.33	2.93	4.94	13.27	3.31

On the other hand, during the whole heating process in the Schulte (Figure 5b), both the experimental and simulated results are similar (all MAEs are under 5 °C) except for T_3, which differs more from the experimental temperature (MAE of 13.27 °C). A misalignment of the thermal sensor or the vessel in the experimental tests might be one factor. This area has the largest concavity deviation and small variations can significantly influence the thermal contact conductance and thus the temperature.

3.1.2. Model II: Fitting of the Nonlinear Thermal Conductance along the Radius

The equation that relates the thermal conductance coefficient and the air gap for the pans (WMF and Schulte) is shown in Figure 6. An iterative inverse analysis, such as in Paesa et al. [19], was performed, and it included several simulations of WMF with different variable thermal conductances along the radius. The optimal result was correlated with the concavity of the pan (see Figure 2), and thus, the following relationship, see Figure 6, was achieved. The WMF pan was used as reference vessel and the parameter fitting were also employed later for the Schulte pan simulations.

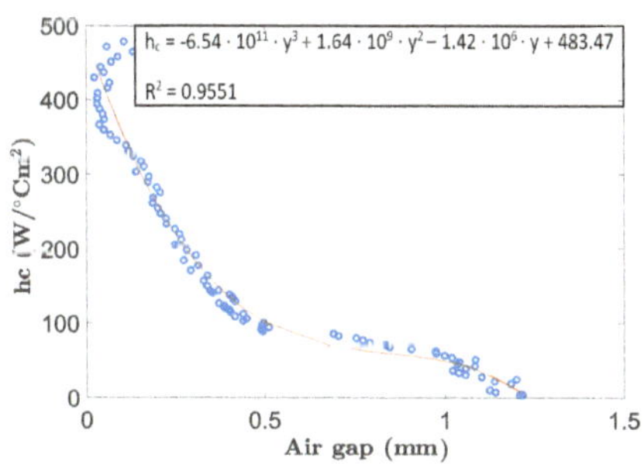

Figure 6. Relation between the thermal conductance coefficient and the air gap. The relation and its equation, where y is the distance between the glass and the base of the pan, are shown graphically. The R-squared value of the regression model is also presented.

The results of the simulations are shown in Figure 7. The surface thermocouples of WMF and Schulte present very low MAEs of 3.09 °C and 1.80 °C, respectively (see Table 5).

Table 5. MAE of the two models modelled with Model II. T_{sensor}, T_1, T_2, T_3 and T_4 are the thermocouples in Figure 1b. The units are °C.

	T_{sensor}	T_1	T_2	T_3	T_4
WMF	3.09	9.45	6.69	3.77	5.65
Schulte	1.8	2.48	12.17	15.01	4.48
Steel plate	2.76	4.55	1.7	0.89	5.39

Regarding the glass thermocouples in the WMF (see Figure 7a), the experimental temperatures are slightly higher than the numerical temperatures in the transient state (approximately 0–200 s). For the Schulte pan, the experimental values are moderately higher than the simulated one during the whole cooking (see Figure 7b).

The heat conduction between the steel plate and the glass was initially considered as perfect as the plate is completely flat; however, the numerical results did not fit the experimental results. Thus, a thermomechanical analysis was performed to observe if there was a significant thermal deformation during the cooking that produced an input of air between the plate and the glass. It was noted that the concavity changes with increasing distance between the base vessel and the glass up to an axial displacement of 120 μm (see Supplemental Data). Thus, h_c^{vg} was modelled as piecewise as follows due to the thermomechanical analysis: from the centre until a radius of 10 cm is 50 W/m^{2}K; from 20 to 50 cm of radii, 150 W/m^{2}K; and the rest of the pan, 500 W/m^{2}K. With this assumption, There was a clear correlation between the experimental and numerical temperatures, see Figure 7c.

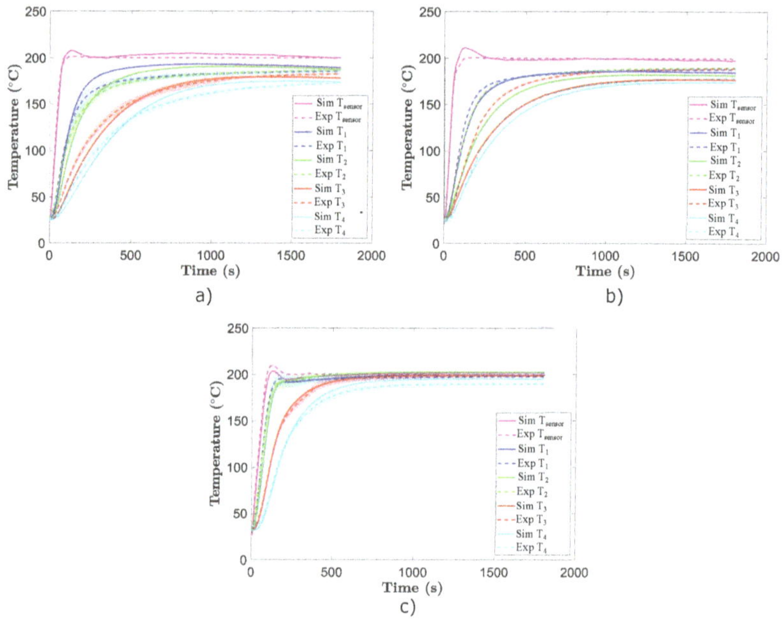

Figure 7. Temperatures of the surface and under the glass (see Figure 1b for location of the temperature sensors) from 0 to 1800 s for both experimental tests (dotted lines) and computational simulations (continuous lines) in Model II: (**a**) WMF pan, (**b**) Schulte pan and (**c**) steel plate.

3.1.3. Comparative between Model I and Model II

Both Model I and Model II show a good agreement with the experimental results. Overall, the results obtained for both the WMF and Schulte pans for Model II are slightly worse than those for Model I (see Tables 4 and 5). If the concavity of the vessel is known, Model I might provide more accurate results. On the other side, Model II is indispensable for simulations where the concavity of the vessel is not known. However, it contains the tedious work of obtaining the variable thermal contact conductance by an inverse analysis.

3.1.4. Heat Flux Analysis

The inbound energies, which are referred to as supplied power, and outbound energies, which are referred to as heat losses, of the WMF (using the Model II approach) are shown in Figure 8. The red dotted line represents the introduced power, the coloured areas refer to the heat losses during cooking, and the dotted and continuous green lines depict the experimental and simulation temperatures of the sensor, respectively. At the beginning of cooking, all the power is used as heat to warm up the vessel. When the temperature of the sensor reaches the target (200 °C), the power decreases and maintains a constant value. The power of the steady state (approximately 400–1800 s) is converted into heat losses, mostly convection and radiation losses from the walls and the upper surface of the base (in yellow and orange).

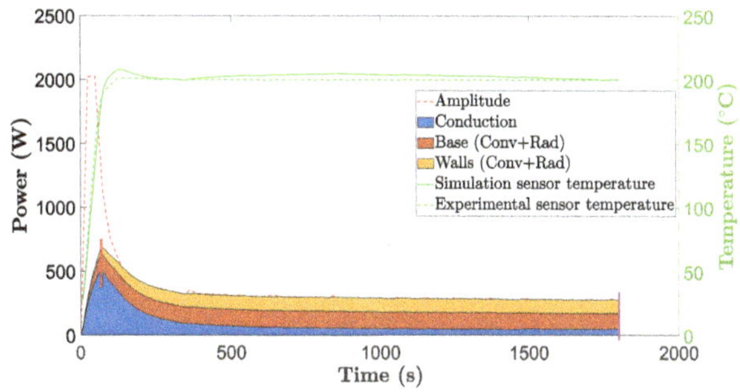

Figure 8. Representation of the heat losses of computational Model II of the WMF (coloured areas), the amplitude of the power density introduced (red dotted line) and the experimental and simulation sensor temperatures (dotted and continuous green lines, respectively). The blue area corresponds to conduction losses between the base of the pan and the glass. The orange and yellow areas indicate the convection and radiation losses in the base and walls of the pan, respectively.

The inbound and outbound energies of the Schulte and steel plate models are shown in the Supplemental Data. The heat losses of the three models at their maximum power level and at the end of cooking (red and pink line markers in Figure 8) are shown in Table 6. In the transient state, conduction losses to the glass prevail above convection and radiation losses. However, in the steady state, convection losses become higher than the remaining ones. The results are consistent with Cabeza-Gil et al. [10] and Cadavid et al. [5].

Table 6. Conduction, radiation and convection losses in the three vessels under investigation. The Schulte pan, that has the biggest concavity, presents the lowest conductivity losses during the transient state.

	Maximum Level			End of the Cooking		
	WMF	**Schulte**	**Steel Plate**	**WMF**	**Schulte**	**Steel Plate**
Conduction (W)	496.7	122.4	546.6	49.6	14.9	46.8
Convection (W)	104.9	65.1	53.5	153.1	111.0	65.1
Radiation (W)	77.8	71.2	32.76	77.8	71.2	32.7

The efficiency of the pans is calculated during the first 400 s as the energy used to heat up the vessel divided by the supplied energy as in Karunanithy and Shafer [9]. The efficiencies of the WMF, Schulte and steel plate are 79.95%, 82.5% and 74.18%, respectively. These values are consistent with those in Karunanithy and Shafer [9] and Villacis et al. [4], although the experimental setups were different and the experimental calculations can lead to some errors due to the approximation of the average temperature of the vessel. The energy necessary to heat up the solids during the 1800 s heating tests was 0.56 kWh, 0.38 kWh and 0.28 kWh for the WMF, Schulte and steel plate, respectively. These measurements were calculated as the temporal integration of the power supplied in the microsteel layer of the vessel.

3.2. Design of Experiments (DoE)

In this section, the effects of the key parameters in the cooking and pan heating, namely, conductivity (k), specific heat (c_e), emissivity (ϵ), concavity (Con) of the vessel, and convective coefficients of the vessel (h_v^{conv}) and the glass (h_g^{conv}), are presented. The main responses in the heating tests, the time to reach steady state t_{st}, the introduced energy E_{in} and the homogenisation along the radius in the second 60 of the cooking H_r, are shown through the main effects plots (see Figure 9). All results were supported by a Pareto analysis (see Supplemental Data).

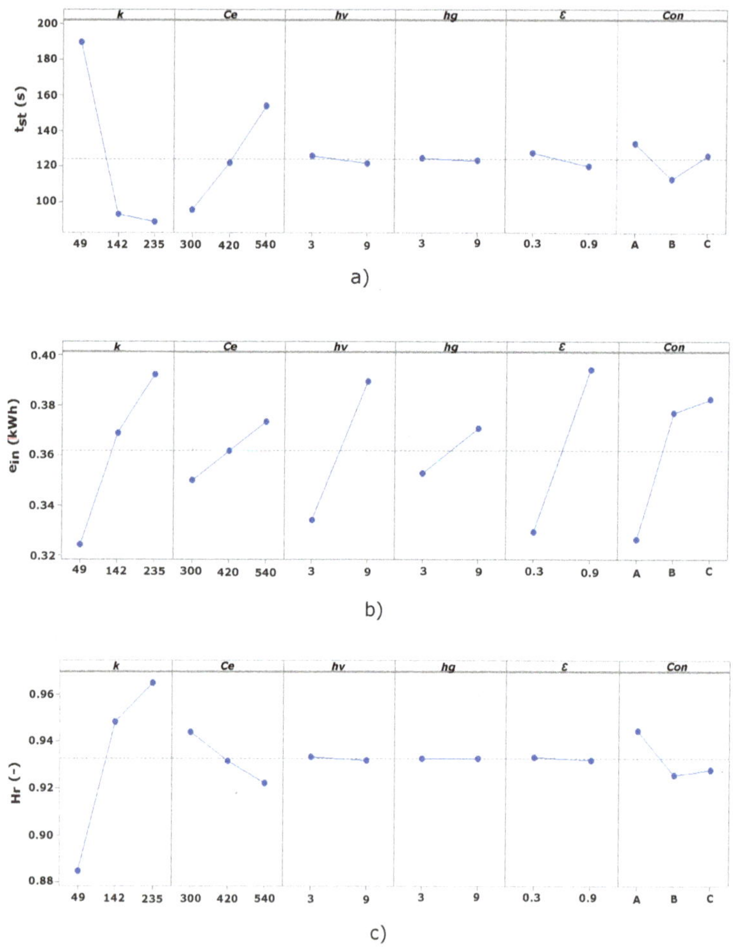

Figure 9. Main effects plot of conductivity (k), specific heat (c_e), pan and glass convective coefficients (h_v and (h_g)), emissivity (ϵ) and concavity (Con) for the responses: time to reach the steady state (**a**), supplied energy (**b**) and temperature homogenisation along the radius in the second 60 of the cooking (**c**). The units of the parameters are conductivity (W/mK); specific heat (J/kgK); convective coefficients (W/m^{2}K); emissivity (-); and concavity (-).

Regarding the time to reach the steady state, as shown in Figure 9a, conductivity has the highest influence [20], and as it increases, the time to achieve the steady state decreases. Specific heat also influences t_{st}, and as it increases, more time is needed to heat the vessel. The rest of the parameters have little influence.

The most influential parameters in the supplied energy (Figure 9b) are the conductivity, vessel convective coefficient, emissivity and concavity. These results are consistent with Villacis et al. [4], Cadavid et al. [5], Newborough et al. [21] and Karunanithy and Shafer [9], who found that the efficiency of the pan depends on the pan composition and external surface emissivity.

We performed another analysis decreasing the cooking time to 400 s (see Supplemental Data), where the influence of the specific heat was not as high as expected. The effect of the supplied energy on the variable parameters was similar to that of the total lost energy during the whole cooking period (t = 1800 s); see Supplemental Data.

Lastly, concerning the temperature homogenisation along the radius after 1 min of cooking (Figure 9c), both convective coefficients and emissivity have no influence at all. The most important parameter is the conductivity, which is directly correlated with the temperature homogenisation.

3.3. *Influence of the Vessel Concavity*

To better explain the effect of the vessel concavity, three heating scenarios were performed as examples with consistency in all of them, which means that they all have the same parameters except for concavity, which varied according to the levels in Table 2, which are represented in Figure 2.

The heat losses, amplitude of the power density and sensor temperature of the three cases are shown in Figure 10. Figure 10a corresponds to the highest concavity case, followed by Figure 10b,c with the lowest concavity. The conduction losses for the highest concavity case are minimum, which makes an overheating of the temperature sensor (because the sensor is placed at the center [10]). For the lowest concavity case, the conduction losses are the main losses at the beginning of the heating. After reaching the highest heat losses, the losses decrease rapidly as the glass has been heated; therefore, the temperature of the sensor decreases slowly because the pan loses less heat.

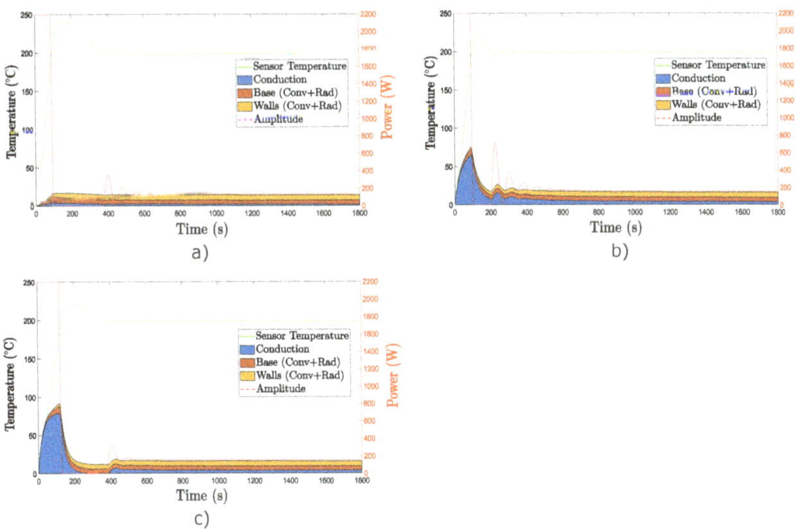

Figure 10. Temperature of the sensor (green continuous line), amplitude of the power density (red dotted line) and losses (coloured areas) of three WMF pans that only differ on its concavity, case #A (**a**), case #B (**b**) and case #C (**c**) (see Figure 4). The yellow area represents convective and radiation losses of the walls, the orange area represents convective and radiation losses of the base of the pan, and the blue area represents conduction losses to the glass.

4. Conclusions

This study explored two novel approaches to model the thermal contact between the vessel and the cooktop, and thus achieving more realistic simulations. Once the numerical model was optimised, a design of experiments was performed to analyse the influence of the main parameters of the vessel during the cooking. The main conclusions of the study are as follows:

- The conductivity is the governing factor of the effect of the vessel in the cooking. When the vessel conductivity is high, it achieves the steady state and a better temperature homogeneity sooner. In contrast, the supplied energy is considerably higher. Thus, manufacturers should reach a compromise between being more energy effective and achieving a homogeneous temperature in the cooking surface in the shortest possible time.
- A more concave cooking vessel is more efficient, as the air layer between the pan base and the glass acts as insulation, reducing the heat losses of the vessel to the glass. The air gap should not be sufficiently large, as the magnetic field could lose efficiency.
- More than 80% of the heat losses during the transient state are due to the heat losses from the vessel to the glass.
- The main heat losses in the steady state are due to the convection and radiation.
- Both numerical approaches (Model I, including a layer of air and Model II, adding a variable thermal contact conductance) lead to similar results with MAEs lower than 5 K for the temperatures in the vessel and the glass. Model II adds the complexity of calibrating the variable thermal contact conductance.

Supplementary Materials: The following supporting information can be downloaded at: https://www.mdpi.com/article/10.3390/math10050802/s1, Figure S1: Profile of the steel plate modelled with the thermo-mechanical analysis. The magnitude are the displacements and it is measured in m; Figure S2: Maximum, minimum and mean temperature of a model made 100% of steel and another made 100% of aluminium along the whole cooking; Figure S3: Main effects plot of steel conductivity, steel specific heat, pan and glass convective coefficients, emissivity and concavity for the: (a) maximum sensor temperature, (b) supplied energy in a cooking time of 400 s and (c) total lost energy during the whole cooking. The units of the parameters are: conductivity (W/mK); specific heat (J/kgK); convective coefficients (W/m^{2}K); emissivity (-); Figure S4: Pareto analysis of the importance of the ouputs studied in DoE: time to reach to stationary state (a), supplied energy (b), homogenisation along the radius in the second 60 of the cooking (c) and maximum sensor temperature (d); Figure S5: Representation of the losses of a computational simplify model of: (a) Schulte and (b) steel plate (coloured areas) and the amplitude of the power density introduced (red dotted line). Blue area corresponds to conduction losses between the base of the pan and the glass. Orange and yellow area indicate the convection and radiation losses in the base and in the walls of the pan respectively.

Author Contributions: Conceptualization, S.L. and M.A.M.; methodology, M.A.M. and I.C.-G.; software, B.B.-S., I.C.-G. and J.G.; formal analysis, I.C.-G.; investigation, B.B.-S.; writing—original draft preparation, B.B.-S.; writing—review and editing, I.C.-G., B.C., J.G., C.F. and M.A.M.; supervision, B.C., J.G., C.F., S.L. and M.A.M.; project administration, B.C.; funding, B.C. and S.L. All authors have read and agreed to the published version of the manuscript.

Funding: This work was funded by the Spanish Ministry of Science, Innovation and Universities RETOS-COLABORATION 2017 programme (project RTC-2017-5965-6, ARQUE) and co-financed by ERDF and BSH Home Appliances Group. The Department of Industry and Innovation (Government of Aragon) provided funding through research group grant no. T24-20R (co-financed by ERDF).

Institutional Review Board Statement: Not applicable.

Informed Consent Statement: Not applicable.

Data Availability Statement: Not applicable.

Conflicts of Interest: The authors declare no conflict of interest.

References

1. Acero, J.; Burdio, J.; Barragan, L.; Navarro, D.; Alonso, R.; Ramon, J.; Monterde, F.; Hernandez, P.; Llorente, S.; Garde, I. Domestic Induction Appliances. *IEEE Ind. Appl. Mag.* **2010**, *16*, 39–47. [CrossRef]
2. Borg, S.; Kelly, N. The effect of appliance energy efficiency improvements on domestic electric loads in European households. *Energy Build.* **2011**, *43*, 2240–2250. [CrossRef]
3. Yohanis, Y.G. Domestic energy use and householders' energy behaviour. *Energy Policy* **2012**, *41*, 654–665. [CrossRef]
4. Villacís, S.; Martínez, J.; Riofrío, A.; Carrión, D.; Orozco, M.; Vaca, D. Energy Efficiency Analysis of Different Materials for Cookware Commonly Used in Induction Cookers. *Energy Procedia* **2015**, *75*, 925–930. [CrossRef]
5. Cadavid, F.J.; Cadavid, Y.; Amell, A.A.; Arrieta, A.E.; Echavarría, J.D. Numerical and experimental methodology to measure the thermal efficiency of pots on electrical stoves. *Energy* **2014**, *73*, 258–263. [CrossRef]
6. Hannani, S.; Hessari, E.; Fardadi, M.; Jeddi, M. Mathematical modeling of cooking pots' thermal efficiency using a combined experimental and neural network method. *Energy* **2006**, *31*, 2969–2985. [CrossRef]
7. Sedighi, M.; Dardashti, B. Finite element analysis of heat transfer in multi-layer cooking pots with emphasis on layer number. *Int. J. Automot. Mech. Eng.* **2015**, *11*, 2253–2261. [CrossRef]
8. Ayata, T.; Çavuşoğlu, A.; Arcaklioğlu, E. Predictions of temperature distributions on layered metal plates using artificial neural networks. *Energy Convers. Manag.* **2006**, *47*, 2361–2370. [CrossRef]
9. Karunanithy, C.; Shafer, K. Heat transfer characteristics and cooking efficiency of different sauce pans on various cooktops. *Appl. Therm. Eng.* **2016**, *93*, 1202–1215. [CrossRef]
10. Cabeza-Gil, I.; Calvo, B.; Grasa, J.; Franco, C.; Llorente, S.; Martínez, M. Thermal analysis of a cooking pan with a power control induction system. *Appl. Therm. Eng.* **2020**, *180*, 115789. [CrossRef]
11. Sanz-Serrano, F.; Sagues, C.; Llorente, S. Inverse modeling of pan heating in domestic cookers. *Appl. Therm. Eng.* **2016**, *92*, 137–148. [CrossRef]
12. Ogata, K. *Modern Control Engineering*; Prentice Hall: Hoboken, NJ, USA , 2010.
13. Hewitt, G.F.; Shires, G.L.; Bott, T.R. *Process Heat Transfer*; BHB: USA, 1994. Available online: https://www.begellhouse.com/ebook_platform/monograph/book/7daba87f6fb65d65.html (accessed on 10 February 2022).
14. Incropera, F.P.; DeWitt, D.P. *Fundamentals of Heat and Mass Transfer*, 8th ed.; John Wiley & Sons, Inc.: New York, NY, USA, 2017.
15. Acero, J.; Carretero, C.; Lope, I.; Alonso, R.; Burdio, J.M. FEA-Based Model of Elliptic Coils of Rectangular Cross Section. *IEEE Trans. Magn.* **2014**, *50*, 1–7. [CrossRef]
16. Lope, I.; Acero, J.; Carretero, C. Analysis and Optimization of the Efficiency of Induction Heating Applications with Litz-Wire Planar and Solenoidal Coils. *IEEE Trans. Power Electron.* **2016**, *31*, 5089–5101. [CrossRef]
17. Weissman, S.A.; Anderson, N.G. Design of experiments (DoE) and process optimization. A review of recent publications. *Org. Process. Res. Dev.* **2015**, *19*, 1605–1633. [CrossRef]
18. Seli, H.; Ismail, A.I.M.; Rachman, E.; Ahmad, Z.A. Mechanical evaluation and thermal modelling of friction welding of mild steel and aluminium. *J. Mater. Process. Technol.* **2010**, *210*, 1209–1216. [CrossRef]
19. Paesa, D.; Llorente, S.; Sagues, C.; Aldana, O. Adaptive Observers Applied to Pan Temperature Control of Induction Hobs. *IEEE Trans. Ind. Appl.* **2009**, *45*, 1116–1125. [CrossRef]
20. Lawless, Z.D.; Hobbs, M.L.; Kaneshige, M.J. Thermal conductivity of energetic materials. *J. Energ. Mater.* **2020**, *38*, 214–239. [CrossRef]
21. Newborough, M.; Probert, S.; Newman, M. Thermal performances of induction, halogen and conventional electric catering hobs. *Appl. Energy* **1990**, *37*, 37–71. [CrossRef]

energies

MDPI

Article

Numerical Study of Heat Transfer in a Gun Barrel Made of Selected Steels

Mateusz Zieliński *, Piotr Koniorczyk, Zbigniew Surma, Janusz Zmywaczyk and Marek Preiskorn

Faculty of Mechatronics, Armament and Aerospace, Military University of Technology, ul. gen. S. Kaliskiego 2, 00-908 Warsaw, Poland; piotr.koniorczyk@wat.edu.pl (P.K.); zbigniew.surma@wat.edu.pl (Z.S.); janusz.zmywaczyk@wat.edu.pl (J.Z.); marek.preiskorn@wat.edu.pl (M.P.)

* Correspondence: mateusz.zielinski@wat.edu.pl; Tel.: +48-261-839-647

Abstract: The results of numerical simulations of transient heat transfer in the barrel wall of a 35 mm caliber cannon for a single shot and the sequences of seven shots and sixty shots for chosen barrel steels are presented. It was assumed that the cannon barrel was made of one of the three types of steel: 38HMJ (1.8509), 30HN2MFA and DUPLEX (1.4462). To model the thermal phenomena in the barrel, the barrel wall material was assumed to be homogeneous and the inner surface of the barrel had no protective chromium or nitride layer. The calculations were made for temperature-dependent thermophysical parameters, i.e., thermal conductivity, specific heat and thermal expansion (in the range from RT up to 1000 °C) of the selected barrel steels. A barrel with a total length of 3150 mm was divided into 6 zones ($i = 1, \ldots, 6$) and in each of them, the heat flux density was calculated as a function of time $\dot{q}_i(t)$ on the inner surface of the barrel. Using lumped parameter methods, an internal ballistic code was developed to compute in each zone the heat transfer coefficient as a function of time $h_i(t)$ and bore gas temperature as a function of time $T_g(t)$ to the cannon barrel for given ammunition parameters. A calculation time equaling 100 ms per single shot was assumed. The results of the calculations were obtained using FEM implemented in COMSOL Multiphysics ver. 5.6 software.

Keywords: anti-aircraft cannon barrel; modeling; heat transfer; numerical simulation; temperature field

Citation: Zieliński, M.; Koniorczyk, P.; Surma, Z.; Zmywaczyk, J.; Preiskorn, M. Numerical Study of Heat Transfer in a Gun Barrel Made of Selected Steels. *Energies* **2022**, *15*, 1868. https://doi.org/10.3390/en15051868

Academic Editor: Dmitry Eskin

Received: 13 January 2022
Accepted: 25 February 2022
Published: 3 March 2022

1. Introduction

It is well known that modern anti-aircraft artillery systems consist of a number of guns, some of which fire at the designated target, while the remaining guns follow the target without firing a shot. This is due to the timing of the single cannon being fired, which is chosen because the high temperatures in the barrel prevent the gun from being fired. In the case of overheating the barrel of one of the guns, it loses its ability to fire. Shooting is then taken over by the other guns that track the target on standby mode. It is also possible to fire all battery guns at once. Low barrel life is a bottleneck that limits the improvement of the weapon's performance for a long time. Many years of research have shown that the erosion of the internal bore is a direct cause that affects the service life of the barrel. The erosion of the inner surface of the barrel is caused by the action of heat, chemistry and mechanics, with heat playing a leading role [1–8]. Although the mechanism of gun barrel wear is not fully understood, it is known that wear is very closely related to the maximum temperature of the bore surface [9]. Usually, when designing the firing cycle, it is essential to maintain the temperature below 800 °C, established by the manufacturer as a maximum temperature when testing the gun barrel's life [9,10]. The maximum temperature limit of the barrel bore in operation is dictated by the thermophysical properties of the steel grade of the barrel. In the steel grades under consideration in our paper, a temperature above 800 °C causes allotropic changes connected with the reconstruction of the crystal lattice of the alloy [11,12]. The kinetics of change is well described by the dilatometric curve characteristics for the individual steel grades [11–13]. The effect of temperature on the barrel bore alters the volume of the surface layer, giving rise to a typical mesh of cracks. This affects the flaking off of the protective coating on the inner surface of the barrel. In older technological processes, the protective coating consists of electroplated chromium. Currently, this process is being replaced by nitriding. In any case, the protective coating is corroded by the structural transformations in the steel layer, which are directly related to the phase transition between ferrite and austenite [3,12,14]. At present, research is being conducted on the implementation of new steel grades with a higher allotropic transition temperature into the production of gun barrels [12]. It is about shifting the ferrite–austenite phase transition towards a higher temperature or using steels in which this transition does not take place [11]. When calculating the heat transfer in the barrel, constant values of thermal conductivity, specific heat and the density of the barrel material are often taken [9,14,15]. Many publications believe that the thermal properties of the gun barrel material are temperature dependent [16–20]. As a rule, the temperature dependence of the barrel material density is neglected due to small changes [16]. It is very important to correctly introduce the thermophysical properties of new steel grades as input data for the heat transfer calculations in the barrel. We consider a phase change only in relation to the thermal conductivity. However, in the literature, one can find papers in which the thermal effect of the phase transformation has been included twice, i.e., in thermal conductivity and specific heat, which seems to be an erroneous [16]. Thermal diffusivity a, thermal conductivity k, specific heat c_p and density ρ are related to the expression $a = k/(\rho \cdot c_p)$. Each of these thermophysical parameters can be determined on separate measuring stations or, for example, the thermal conductivity can be calculated from the expression $k = a \cdot \rho \cdot c_p$. The phase transformation is visible in each thermophysical parameter. Thus, when calculating the thermal conductivity k in the phase transition region from formula $k = a \cdot \rho \cdot c_p$, this effect will be taken into account both in thermal diffusivity and in specific heat. This means that the phase change effect and the associated enthalpy will be accounted for twice. As a rule, we consider the phase transition effect in thermal conductivity characteristic [21]. During the continuous firing of artillery, the inner wall of the barrel will experience a continuous rise of temperature. On each curve of the barrel temperature increase during the shot we can distinguish the so-called highest peak temperature and lowest temperature of the peak base, which is in fact the inner wall temperature of the barrel. In order to reach the temperature of 800 °C of the inner barrel surface, it is often necessary to carry out numerical simulations of the heat transfer in the barrel after firing several dozen shots [14,18,19].

Over the years, numerous research groups have carried out a series of tests to determine the temperature field of the gun barrel. These calculations are becoming more and more accurate and verifiable in experimental research [1,15,22,23]. However, it is often important to simulate heat transfer throughout the barrel, not just a fragment of it. In order to avoid very time-consuming calculations, the barrel can be divided into sectors. In this paper an initial boundary value problem (IBVP) of heat transfer in the barrel wall of a 35 mm caliber cannon was solved for the single shot and the sequence of seven shots for chosen barrel steels. For calculation purposes, the barrel with a total length of 3150 mm has been divided into six zones S1 to S6—Figure 1. The heat transfer coefficient was calculated as a function of the time $h_i(t)$ in the six cross-sections P1 to P6 on the inner surface of the barrel: P1: z = 216 mm, P2: z = 385 mm, P3: z = 535 mm, P4: z = 880 mm, P5: z = 2081 mm, P6: z=2980 mm and the gas temperature as a function of time $T_g(t)$. The functions $h_i(t)$ in cross-sections P1 to P6 are valid in the zones S1 to S6. Additionally, the S0 zone of the cannon breech was distinguished in the range from 0 to 216 mm, for which—at the present stage of the research—the same function $h_i(t)$ was assigned as for the S1 zone. The calculations were carried out considering the temperature-dependent thermophysical parameters in the model, i.e., thermal conductivity, specific heat and thermal expansion (in the range from RT to 1000 °C). In 2020, the authors of this study tested the thermophysical properties of selected barrel steels, i.e., 38HMJ (1.8509), 30HN2MFA and DUPLEX (1.4462) (in the range from RT to 1000 °C) [12]. In this study, particular attention was paid to the correct introduction of thermophysical parameters depending on the temperature in the numerical heat transfer tests in the barrel wall of a 35 mm caliber cannon for a single shot and the sequence of shots for the chosen barrel steels. The idea is not to erroneously consider the phase transition effects on the selected metals twice, such as in thermal conductivity and specific heat.

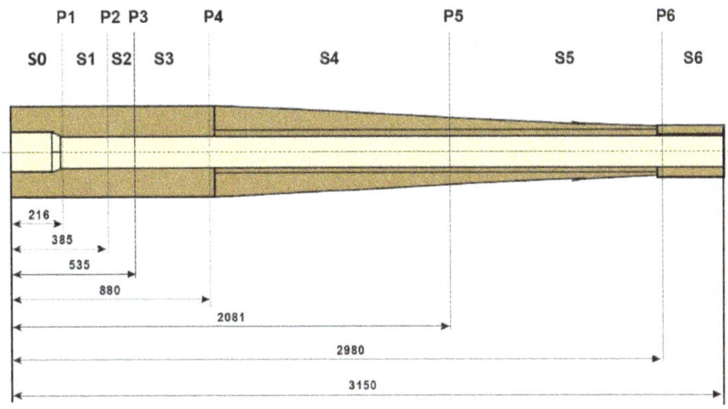

Figure 1. Heat transfer zones S1 to S6 of the 35 mm cannon barrel input to the calculations: S1: 0 ÷ 385 mm, r_{out} = 55.0 ÷ 55.0 mm; S2: 385 ÷ 535 mm, r_{out} = 55.0 ÷ 57.0 mm; S3: 535 ÷ 880 mm, r_{out} = 57.0 ÷ 59.5 mm; S4: 880 ÷ 2081 mm, r_{out} = 59.5 ÷ 44.07 mm; S5: 2081 ÷ 2980 mm, r_{out} = 44.07 ÷ 31.0 mm; S6: 2980 ÷ 3150 mm, r_{out} = 31.0 mm. The zone S1 includes the zone S0 of the cannon breech (reproduced with permission from [24], Military University of Technology, 2022)

1.1. Determination of the Heat Transfer Coefficient and Gas Temperature

The heat transfer coefficient can be calculated from a convective heat transfer correlation for a fully developed turbulent pipe flow, which expresses the Nusselt number Nu as a function of the Reynolds Re and Prandtl Pr numbers [25]:

$$Nu_D = 0.023\ Re_D^{0.8} Pr^{0.4} \tag{1}$$

For fluid flow in a pipe of circular cross section of diameter D, if the gas has a velocity w, density ρ, dynamic viscosity μ and thermal conductivity k_p, the definitions of the Nusselt and Reynolds numbers are, respectively:

$$Nu_D = \frac{hD}{k_p}\quad Re_D = \frac{\rho w D}{\mu} \tag{2}$$

By substituting Equation (2) into Equation (1), one can express h in the form:

$$h = \frac{0.023}{D^{0.2}} \cdot \frac{k_p}{\mu^{0.8}} Pr^{0.4} (\rho w)^{0.8} \tag{3}$$

The approximate value of the Prandtl number can be calculated using the simplified Eucken formula [23,25]:

$$Pr = \frac{4\gamma}{9\gamma - 5} \tag{4}$$

where γ is adiabatic index of the gunpowder gases. For γ = 1.20, we have $Pr^{0.4} \approx 0.93$.

Considering the weak temperature dependence of the $\frac{k_p}{\mu^{0.8}} \approx 285$ relation (for the average temperature of the gunpowder gases equal to 1000 °C), we have [25,26]:

$$h = \frac{6.1}{D^{0.2}} (\rho w)^{0.8}. \tag{5}$$

Since the density ρ and velocity w of the gunpowder gases are functions of time, we have different values of the time-dependent heat transfer coefficient h in the cross-section P1 to P6 of the 35 mm cannon barrel. In the adopted model of heat transfer in the gun barrel, we assume that the calculations ρ and w in the cross-section P1 to P6 are also valid in zones S1 to S6, respectively.

Density ρ, velocity w and bore gas temperature as a function of time $T_g(t)$ can be determined by solving the interior ballistic model, which is a model with lumped parameters [27–29]. The calculations took into account the phenomena occurring in the barrel until the projectile exits the barrel and the after muzzle period. The condition for completing the calculation is that the propellant pressure in the barrel drops to 0.18 MPa [30].

When the projectile is in the barrel, the model contains:

Energy conservation equation (the first law of thermodynamics):

$$dU = dQ - dW \tag{6}$$

Here, differential of internal energy dU taking into account mass fraction of burning propellant 'z_p' with respect to its initial mass m_p has the form:

$$dU = d(c_v m_p z_p T) = c_v m_p (T dz_p + z_p dT) \tag{7}$$

Amount of heat dQ release during burning of propellant of isochoric flame temperature T_1 and specific heat at constant volume c_v equals:

$$dQ = c_v T_1 m_p dz_p \tag{8}$$

Amount of sum of works of propellant gases dW taking into account coefficient of secondary works φ is given by:

$$dW = d\left(\varphi \frac{mv^2}{2}\right) = \varphi mv dv \tag{9}$$

Substituting Equations (7)–(9) into Equation (6) and replacing c_v by $c_v = \frac{R}{\gamma - 1}$ after some algebraic manipulations, we obtain:

$$\frac{d(RT)}{dt} = \frac{(f - RT) m_p \frac{dz_p}{dt} - (\gamma - 1)\varphi m v \frac{dv}{dt}}{m_p z_p} \tag{10}$$

where $f = RT_1$, $\gamma = c_p / c_v$.

Equation of state of propellant gases [27–29]:

$$p\left(V_0 + sl - \frac{m_p}{\rho_p}(1 - z_p) - \eta m_p z_p\right) = m_p z_p RT \tag{11}$$

Equation of mass fraction burning rate of the propellant (gas inflow) [27–29]:

$$\frac{dz_p}{dt} = \frac{S_1}{\Lambda_1}\sqrt{1 + 4\frac{\lambda_1}{\kappa_1} z_p} \cdot r_1 p \tag{12}$$

Equation of the projectile motion:

$$\varphi m \frac{dv}{dt} = ps \tag{13}$$

where $\varphi = K + \frac{1}{3}\frac{m_p}{m}$.

Definition of the projectile velocity:

$$\frac{dl}{dt} = v \tag{14}$$

Propellant gas density:

$$\rho = \frac{m_p z_p}{V_0 + sl - \frac{m_p}{\rho_p}(1 - z_p) - \eta m_p z_p} \tag{15}$$

Assuming a linear distribution of the velocity of the propellant gases in the barrel, we calculate the velocity w of gases in the considered cross-section $i = 1, \ldots, 6$, (i–a cross-section number from P1 to P6) of the barrel according to:

$$w = \frac{l_i}{l_0 + l} \cdot v \tag{16}$$

where: l_i—distance from the bottom of the chamber to the cross-section i of the barrel; l_0—length of the canon chamber, l—projectile travel inside the barrel.

In the period after the projectile muzzle, the model includes:

Energy conservation equation, taking into account the outflow of gases to the environment (through the muzzle of the barrel):

$$dU = dQ - dH \tag{17}$$

Considering that:

$$dU - d[c_v m_p (z_p - \zeta) T] = \frac{m_p R}{\gamma - 1}[T(dz_p - d\zeta) + (z_p - \zeta)dT] \tag{18}$$

$$dQ - c_v T_1 m_p dz_p = \frac{1}{\gamma - 1} f m_p dz_p \tag{19}$$

$$dH = c_p m_p T d\zeta = \frac{\gamma}{\gamma - 1} m_p RT d\zeta, \tag{20}$$

Equation (17) takes the form:

$$\frac{d(RT)}{dt} = \frac{(f - RT)\frac{dz_p}{dt} - (\gamma - 1)RT\frac{d\zeta}{dt}}{z_p - \zeta} \tag{21}$$

Equation of state of propellant gases [27–29]:

$$p\left(V_0 + sl_m - \frac{m_p}{\rho_p}(1 - z_p) - \eta m_p (z_p - \zeta)\right) = m_p (z_p - \zeta) RT \tag{22}$$

Propellant gas density:

$$\rho = \frac{m_p (z_p - \zeta)}{V_0 + sl_m - \frac{m_p}{\rho_p}(1 - z_p) - \eta m_p (z_p - \zeta)} \tag{23}$$

Rate of mass fraction of propellant gases flowing out of from the barrel (gas outflow):

$$\frac{d\zeta}{dt} = \frac{sp}{m_p \sqrt{RT}} \sqrt{\gamma \left(\frac{2}{\gamma + 1}\right)^{\frac{\gamma+1}{\gamma-1}}} \tag{24}$$

Assuming that the propellant gases flowing out of the barrel reach critical parameters, their velocity in the considered cross-section i of the barrel will be calculated according to:

$$w = \frac{l_i}{l_0 + l_m} \cdot w_{cr} \tag{25}$$

where $w_{cr} = \sqrt{\gamma R T_{cr}} = \sqrt{\frac{2\gamma}{\gamma+1} RT}$; w_{cr}, T_{cr}—critical velocity and critical temperature of propellant gases at the muzzle.

The initial conditions for calculations are the following:

$$t = 0,\ RT = RT_1 = f,\ z_p = 0.001,\ l = 0,\ v = 0,\ \zeta = 0.$$

It should be added that the variables $z_p(t)$, $l(t)$, $v(t)$, $T(t)$, $\zeta(t)$, $w(t)$, $\rho(t)$ and $p(t)$ are functions of time. The input data for the interior ballistic calculations are shown in Table 1.

Table 1. Input data to interior ballistics calculation.

Quantities and Units	Values
m, kg	0.380
m_p, kg	0.376
s, m^2	9.98×10^{-4}
V_0, m^3	373×10^{-6}
l_m, m	2.9342
K	1.04
f, J·kg^{-1}	1.071×10^6
η, m^3·kg^{-1}	1.064×10^{-3}
γ	1.2
R, J·kg^{-1}·K^{-1}	340
ρ_p, kg·m^{-3}	1600
r_1, m·Pa^{-1}·s^{-1}	0.597×10^{-9}
S_1, m^2	134.4×10^{-6}
Λ_1, m^3	75.2×10^{-9}
κ_1	0.755
λ_1	0.159
p_0, Pa	30×10^6

The calculation results of the heat transfer coefficient as a function of time $h_i(t)$ in the six cross-sections P1 to P6 and the gas temperature as a function of time $T_g(t)$ for the 35 mm anti-aircraft cannon barrel are shown in Figure 2, and so the values of $h_i(t)$ in the section P1 are valid in the zone S0 and S1, P2 in the zone S2, P3 in the zone S3, etc. In this paper, zone S1 includes the zone S0 of the cannon breech. Detailed and precise calculations of heat transfer in the S0 zone are not the subject of the study.

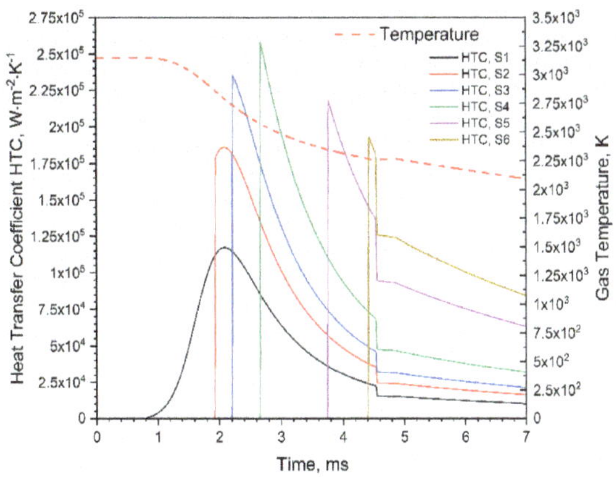

Figure 2. Heat transfer coefficient as a function of time $h_i(t)$ in the 6 cross-sections P1 to P6 and the gas temperature as a function of time $T_g(t)$ for the 35 mm anti-aircraft cannon barrel.

For t = 4.54 ms, we observe rapid drops of the heat transfer coefficient as a function of time $h_i(t)$ in each of the six cross-sections P1 to P6. This is the moment when the bullet leaves the barrel. The highest value is achieved by the heat transfer coefficient in the fourth zone. It has a slightly lower value in zone three.

1.2. Thermophysical Properties of Selected Barrel Steels

The thermophysical properties, i.e., thermal conductivity, specific heat and density as a function of temperature in the RT range up to 1000 °C, were adopted as a contribution to the initial boundary value problem of heat transfer in the barrel wall of a 35 mm caliber cannon, as shown in Figures 3–5 and in Tables 2–4.

For the selected steels, the experimental data on thermal conductivity was introduced in the form of Table 2. Data between measurement points were approximated in COMSOL software using cubic splines.

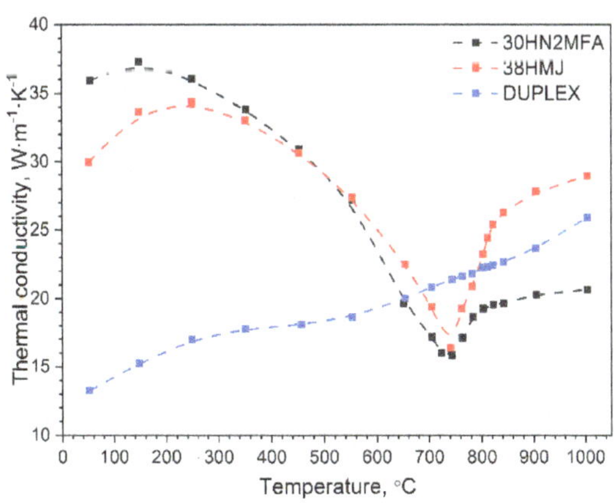

Figure 3. Thermal conductivity of selected barrel steels: 30HN2MFA, 38HMJ, DUPLEX [12].

Table 2. Data on thermal conductivity of selected barrel steels [12].

30HN2MFA		38HMJ		DUPLEX 2205	
T [°C]	k [$W \cdot m^{-1} \cdot K^{-1}$]	T [°C]	k [$W \cdot m^{-1} \cdot K^{-1}$]	T [°C]	k [$W \cdot m^{-1} \cdot K^{-1}$]
54.2	35.9	50.9	30.0	52.0	13.3
149.1	37.3	149.0	33.6	149.1	15.3
250.0	36.0	250.0	34.4	249.8	17.0
352.0	33.8	351.3	33.0	351.7	17.8
453.3	30.9	453.4	30.7	457.0	18.1
553.6	27.2	553.6	27.4	553.6	18.7
651.1	19.7	654.7	22.5	654.7	20.0
704.4	17.1	704.5	19.4	704.2	20.8
723.0	16.0	741.0	16.4	744.2	21.4
743.3	15.8	762.6	19.3	762.9	21.6
763.0	17.1	782.7	20.9	782.6	21.8
783.1	18.7	802.8	23.2	802.5	22.2
802.8	19.3	811.9	24.4	811.7	22.3
822.9	19.5	821.8	25.4	821.7	22.4
842.8	19.7	842.3	26.3	842.3	22.7
904.9	20.3	904.7	27.8	904.7	23.7
1004.3	20.6	1004.2	28.9	1004.1	25.9

The experimental specific heat data are presented in Table 3 and illustrated in Figure 4. Data between points were approximated in COMSOL using cubic splines.

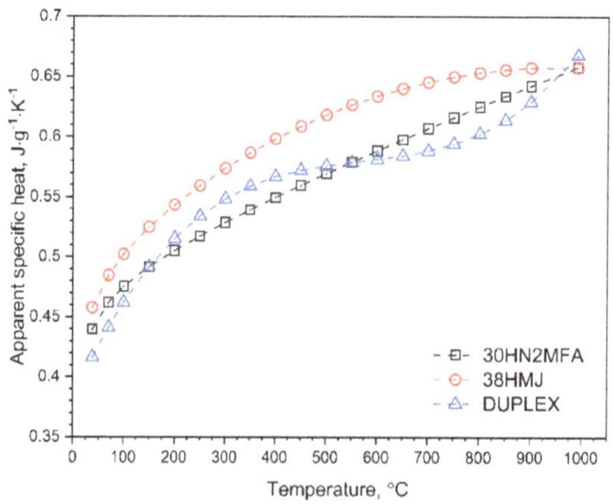

Figure 4. Apparent specific heat of chosen barrel steels: 30HN2MFA, 38HMJ, DUPLEX [12].

Table 3. Data on apparent specific heat of selected barrel steels [12].

	30HN2MFA	38HMJ	DUPLEX 2205
T [°C]	c_p [J·g^{-1}·K^{-1}]	c_p [J·g^{-1}·K^{-1}]	c_p [J·g^{-1}·K^{-1}]
38	0.440	0.458	0.417
70	0.462	0.485	0.442
100	0.475	0.502	0.462
150	0.492	0.525	0.492
200	0.505	0.543	0.515
250	0.517	0.559	0.534
300	0.528	0.574	0.548
350	0.539	0.587	0.559
400	0.550	0.598	0.567
450	0.560	0.609	0.572
500	0.569	0.618	0.576
550	0.579	0.626	0.579
600	0.589	0.634	0.582
650	0.598	0.640	0.584
700	0.607	0.645	0.588
750	0.616	0.650	0.594
800	0.625	0.653	0.602
850	0.634	0.656	0.614
900	0.642	0.657	0.629
991	0.658	0.658	0.668

The experimental density data are presented in Table 4 and illustrated in Figure 3. Data between points were approximated in COMSOL using cubic splines.

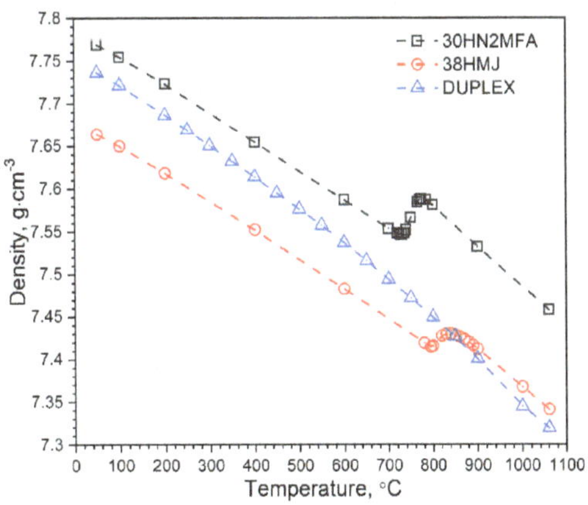

Figure 5. Density of chosen barrel steels: 30HN2MFA, 38HMJ, DUPLEX [12].

Table 4. Data on density of selected barrel steels [12].

30HN2MFA		38HMJ		DUPLEX 2205	
T [°C]	ρ [g·cm^{-3}]	T [°C]	ρ [g·cm^{-3}]	T [°C]	ρ [g·cm^{-3}]
50	7.77	50	7.66	50	7.74
100	7.75	100	7.65	100	7.72
200	7.72	200	7.62	200	7.69
400	7.65	400	7.55	250	7.67
600	7.59	600	7.48	300	7.65
700	7.55	780	7.42	350	7.63
720	7.55	795	7.41	400	7.61
725	7.55	800	7.42	450	7.60
730	7.55	820	7.43	500	7.58
735	7.55	830	7.43	550	7.56
740	7.55	840	7.43	600	7.54
750	7.57	850	7.43	650	7.52
765	7.58	860	7.43	700	7.49
770	7.59	870	7.42	750	7.47
775	7.59	880	7.42	800	7.45
785	7.59	890	7.42	850	7.43
800	7.58	900	7.41	900	7.40
900	7.53	1000	7.37	1000	7.34
1060	7.46	1060	7.34	1060	7.32

Our tests described in [12] showed that for the 38HMJ steel at about and 30HN2MFA at about 740 °C there was a ferrite–austenite phase transition, which was responsible for the material shrinkage. In numerical simulations of heat transfer in the cannon barrels, the energy related to the phase transition was included only in the material density and thermal conductivity, while in the specific heat this energy was ignored. Phase transition energy should not be taken into account multiple times, e.g., both in thermal conductivity and specific heat [12].

2. Initial Boundary Value Problem

The results of the transient heat transfer numerical simulations in the wall of a 35 mm cannon barrel for a single shot and for a sequence of shots has been presented in this paper. The initial temperature of the cannon was assumed as T_0 = 20 °C. The heat transfer on the barrel's outer surface was modeled as a boundary condition of the 3rd kind in a form $\dot{q} = h_{out} \cdot (T(t, r_z, z) - T_0)$. An equivalent heat transfer coefficient value of $h_{out} = 9.2\ \mathrm{W}/\left(\mathrm{m}^2 \cdot \mathrm{K}\right)$ was assumed to be the same on the entire outer surface of the barrel. The governing equation for nonlinear and axially symmetrical 2D IBVP is as follows:

$$\rho_s(T) c_s(T) \frac{\partial T}{\partial t} = \frac{1}{r} \frac{\partial}{\partial r}\left(k_s(T) r \frac{\partial T}{\partial r}\right) + \frac{\partial}{\partial z}\left(k_s(T) \frac{\partial T}{\partial z}\right) \tag{26}$$

with

$$r_{in} < r < r_{out}, 0 < z < l_m,\ t > 0, \tag{27}$$

where T is the temperature of the gun barrel, t is the time, r is the distance between node and the barrel axis line, ρ is the density of barrel material, and c is the specific heat of barrel material, with the initial condition:

$$T(0,r,z) = T_0 \text{ with } r_{in} < r < r_{out}\ 0 < z < l_m \text{ and } t = 0 \tag{28}$$

and the boundary conditions:

$$\dot{q}_i(t, r = r_{in},\ z) = h_i(t)\cdot(T(t, r_{in}, z) - T_g(t, r_{in}, z)),\ i = 1,\ \ldots\ ,6, \tag{29}$$

(i–a zone number from S1 to S6)

$$\dot{q} = h_{out}\cdot(T(t, r_{out}, z) - T_0), \tag{30}$$

where T_g is the gas temperature calculated by solving the internal ballistic model, $r_{in} = \frac{35}{2}$ mm, r_{out} dependent on the variable z–Figure 1.

The same IBVP was solved for the series of shots (27) to (30). The initial condition for the next shot was taken from the previous solution, i.e., $T(t_j, r, z) = T(0, r, z)$, with j standing for the number of shot. The boundary conditions remained unchanged during calculations. The calculations were made using FEM implemented in the COMSOL Multiphysics program. The number of mesh elements, including quad elements, is 26,200. Minimum element quality equals 0.8563. Duration of a single shot was 100 ms. A sequence of shots was adopted for the simulation of burst firing. The calculations were made on 6 sections of the barrel S1 to S6 (z in the middle of each zone). The numerical experiment was carried out on the DELL PRECISION TOWER 5610 workstation equipped with an Intel (R) Xeon (R) CPU ES-1620 v3 @ 3.50GHZ with 16 GB RAM under Windows 10 Operating System. The total computation time of the sixty shots was approximately 6 h. Mesh compaction near the inner surface was performed with a geometric sequence with length element ratio equaling 0.81 and the mesh between the zones compacted five times—Figure 6.

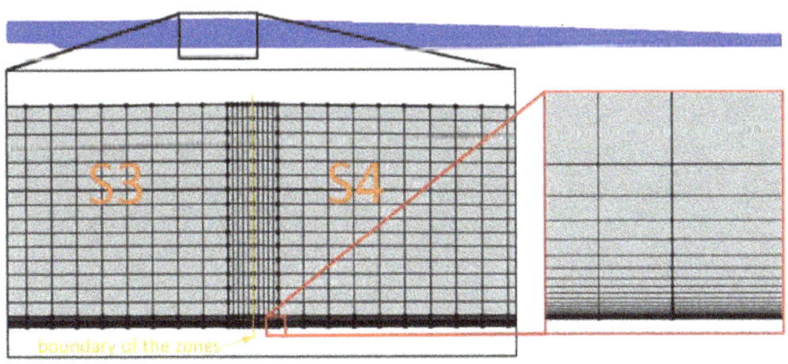

Figure 6. Meshed cell with quad elements of a barrel (shown in Figure 1).

2.1. Temperature Distibution in the Cannon Barrel for a Single Shot

For each of the selected steels, the temperature distributions $T_i(t, r_{in}, z)$ of the barrel's inner surface at the 6 zones S1 to S6 (z in the middle of each zone) for the single shot are shown separately in Figure 7. In each zone, the heat transfer coefficient as a function of time $h_i(t)$ is different—Figure 2. The dashed line on each Figure shows the time the bullet left the barrel (t = 4.54 ms).

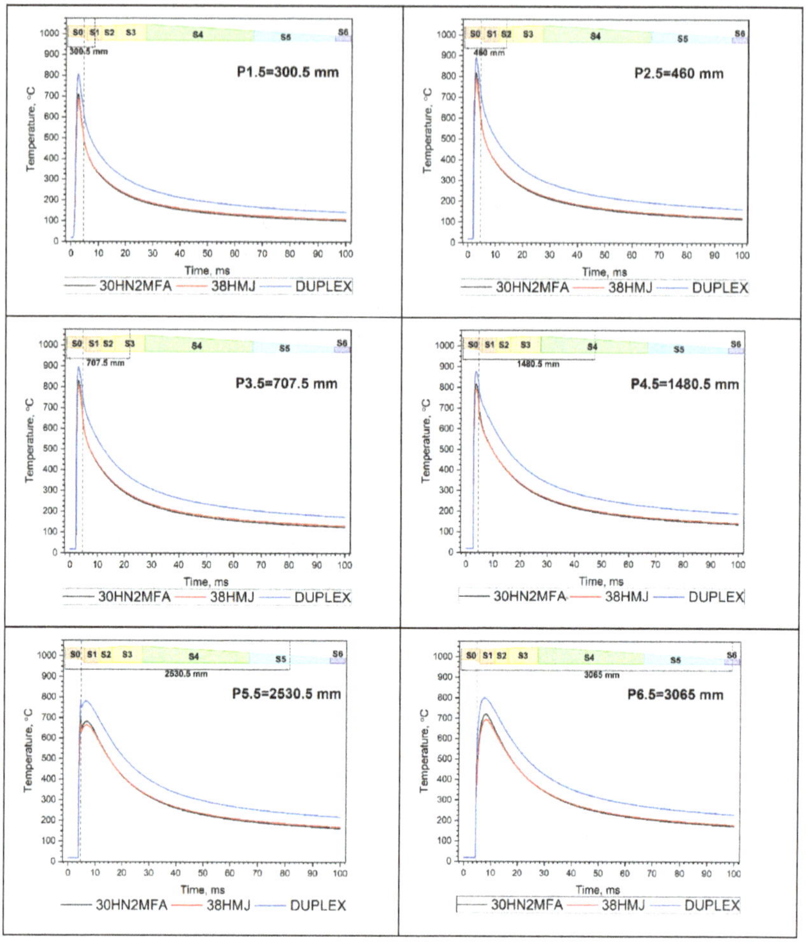

Figure 7. Temperature distribution $T_i(t, r_{in}, z)$ of the barrel's inner surface at the 6 zones S1 to S6 (z in the middle of each zone) for the single shot for the selected steels. The signs: P1.5—in the middle of the S1 zone, P2.5—in the middle of the S2 zone, etc.

The highest temperature, i.e., the so-called highest peak temperature occurs for DUPLEX steel. The 38HMJ and 30HN2 MFA steels behaved similarly, i.e., the temperature distribution $T_i(t, r_{in}, z)$ of the inner surface of the barrel in the six zones S1 to S6 (z in the middle of each zone) were practically the same for one shot. For each selected steel, zone S3 had the highest temperature (Figure 8). The disturbance of the temperature distribution $T_i(t, r_{in}, z)$ of the inner surface barrel in zone S5 was caused by a rapid decrease in the heat transfer coefficient $h_i(t)$ at the moment the bullet left the barrel—Figure 1. In zone S6, this effect did not occur because the bullet travelled there too briefly.

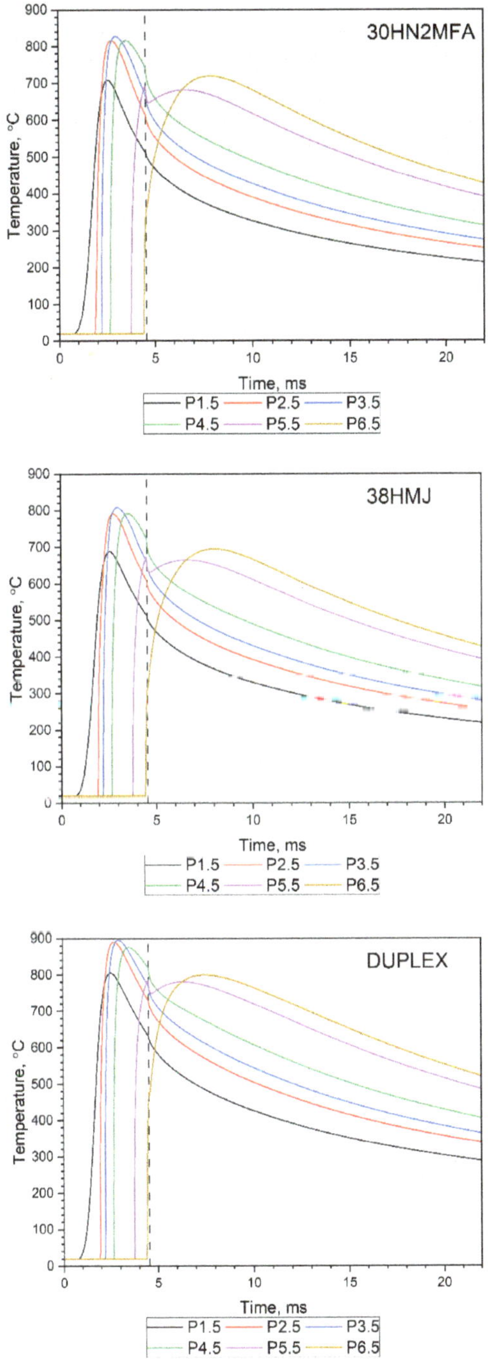

Figure 8. Temperature distribution, the so-called highest temperature $T_i(t, r_{in}, z)$ of the barrel's inner surface in the 6 zones S1 to S6 (z in the middle of each zone) for the single shot for each selected steel, separately. The signs: P1.5—in the middle of the S1 zone, P2.5—in the middle of the S2 zone, etc.

2.2. Temperature Distibution in the Cannon Barrel for a Series of Seven Shots

In all the presented calculations, we assume the time-dependent heat flux density on the inner surface of the barrel changes for the first and subsequent shots. This is because the temperature of the inner surface of the barrel changes. For the selected steels, the temperature distribution $T_i(t, r_{in}, z)$ of the barrel's inner surface at the six sections S1 to S6 (z in the middle of each zone) for the series of seven shots is shown in Figure 9.

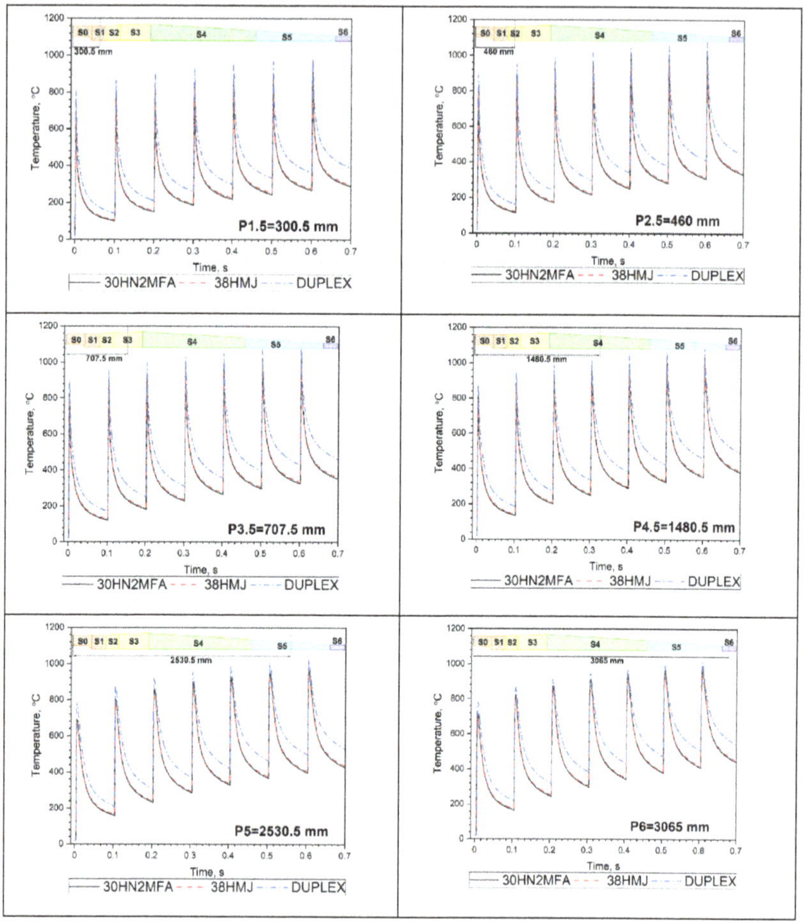

Figure 9. Temperature distribution $T_i(t, r_{in}, z)$ of the barrel's inner surface at the 6 zones S1 to S6 (z in the middle of each zone) for the sequence of seven shots for the selected steels. The signs: P1.5—in the middle of the S1 zone, P2.5—in the middle of the S2 zone, etc.

The lowest temperature, i.e., the lowest peak temperature, for 38HMJ and 30HN2MFA steel was the same for each shot in a series of seven shots. However, in the case of DUPLEX steel, this temperature was higher for each shot in a series of seven shots compared to the 38HMJ and 30HN2MFA steel.

2.3. *Temperature Distibution along the Barrel Thickness for a Series of Seven Shots*

For the selected steels, temperature distributions $T_i(t, r, z)$ along the barrel thickness for a sequence of seven shots in zone S6 (z in the middle of the sixth zone) and for the for the first, fourth and seventh shots in zone S6 are shown in Figure 10. In addition, the temperature distributions $T_i(t, r, z)$ along the barrel thickness for the selected steels for the first, fourth and seventh shots separately are illustrated in Figure 11.

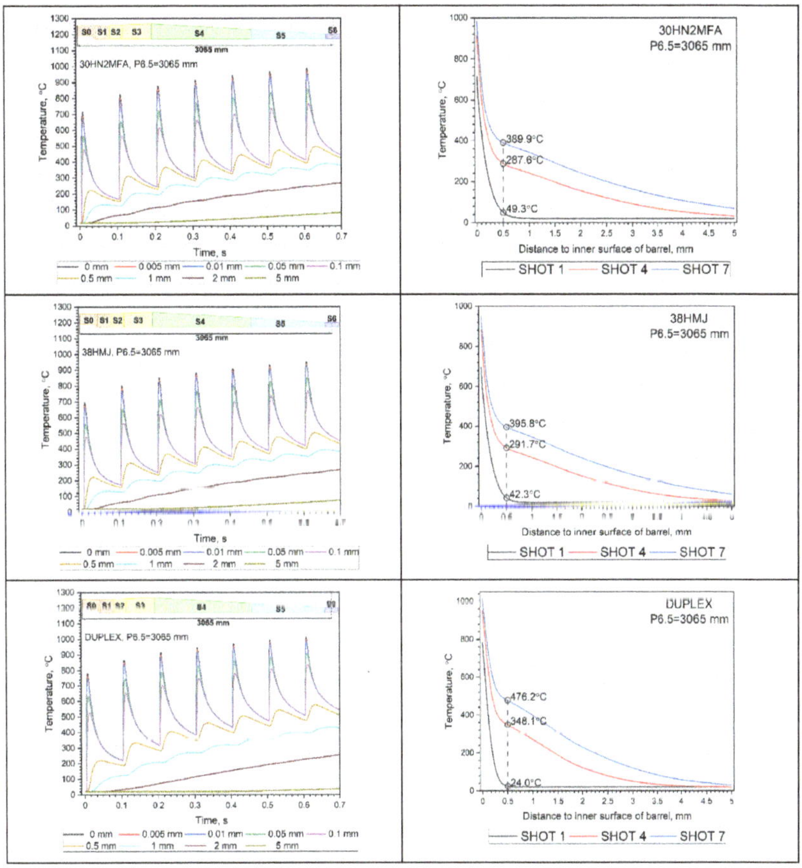

Figure 10. Temperature distribution $T_i(t, r, z)$ along the barrel thickness for selected steels for a sequence of seven shots: left side—z in the middle of the sixth zone S6 (color-coded for the distance from the inner surface of the barrel); right side—for the first, fourth and seventh shots. The sign: P6.5—in the middle of the S6 zone.

Figure 11 shows the temperature distributions $T_i(t, r, z)$ along the barrel thickness for a sequence of seven shots in zone S6 (z in the middle of the sixth zone) for all three selected steels: for shot 1—in the upper figure, for shot 4—in the middle figure, for shot 7—in the bottom drawing.

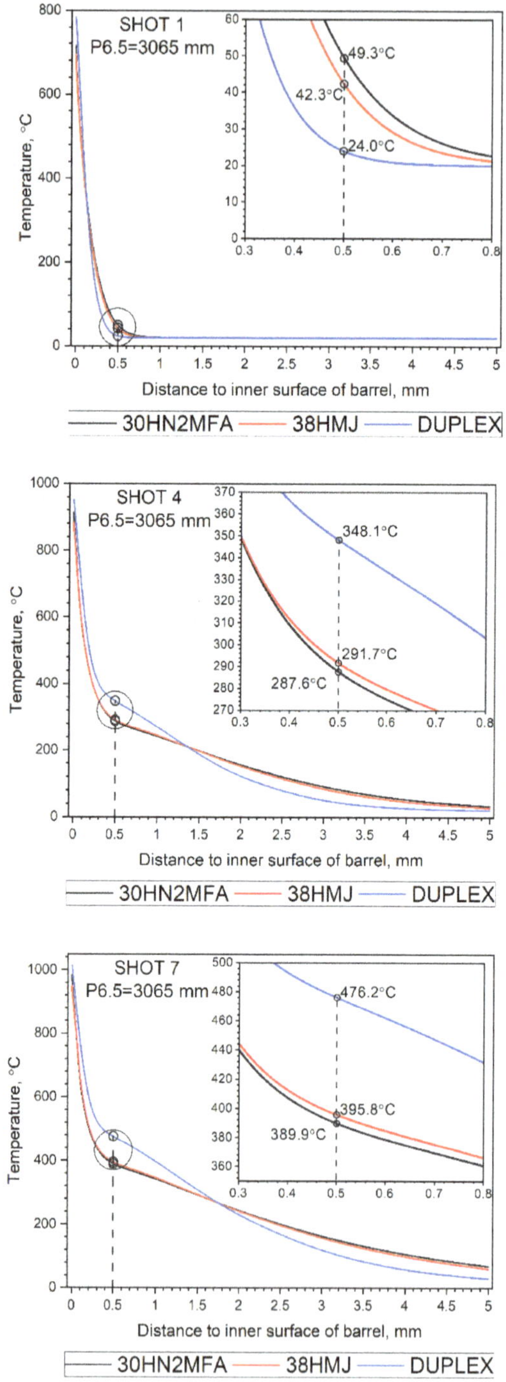

Figure 11. Temperature distributions $T_i(t, r, z)$ along the barrel thickness for selected steels for the first, fourth and seventh shots. The sign: P6.5—in the middle of the S6 zone.

2.4. Temperature Distibution in the Cannon Barrel for a Series of Sixty Shots

Thermophysical properties, i.e., thermal conductivity, specific heat and density as a function of temperature in the range of 1000 °C to 1300 °C, were obtained by the linear extrapolation of experimental data of the selected steels in the RT range up to 1000 °C. For the selected steels, temperature distributions $T_i(t, r, z)$ of the barrels inner surface and along the barrel thickness for a sequence of sixty shots in each zone S1 to S6 (z in the middle of each zone) are shown in Figure 12 for 30HN2MFA steel and Figure 13 for DUPLEX steel. The results for the 38HMJ steel are very similar to the results for the 30HN2MFA steel, therefore they are not shown in a separate drawing.

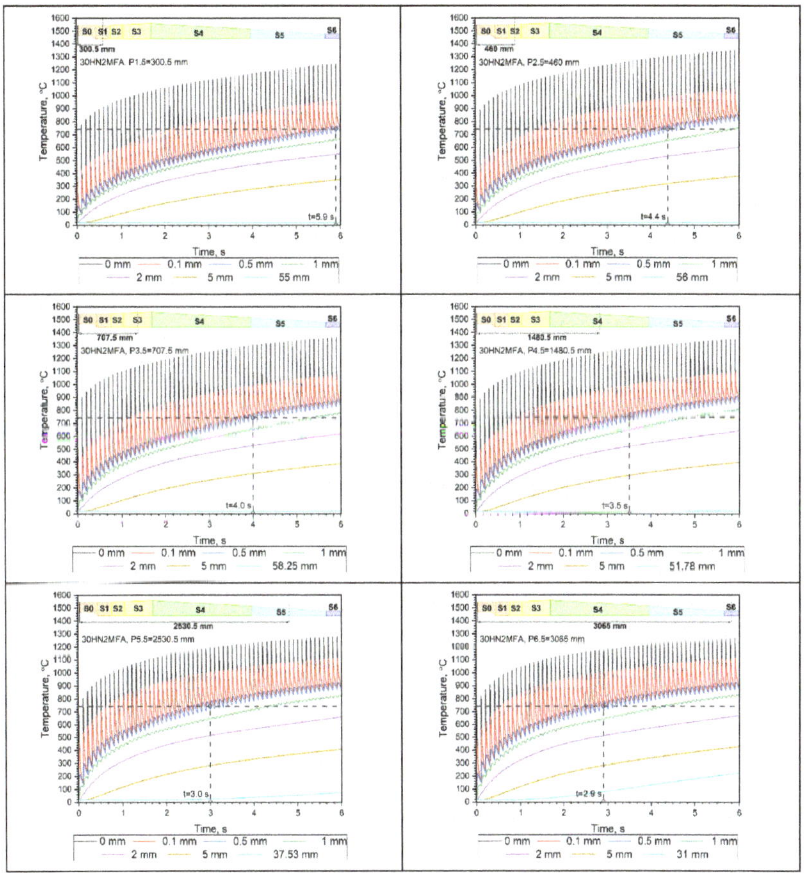

Figure 12. Temperature distribution $T_i(t, r_w, z)$ along the barrel thickness at the zones S1 to S6 (z in the middle of each zone) for the sequence of sixty shots, for the 30HN2MFA steel: black line—on the inner surface of the barrel, red line—0.1 mm below the inside surface, blue line—0.5 mm below the inside surface, green line—1 mm below the inside surface, violet line—2 mm under the inner surface, yellow line—5 mm under the inner surface, light blue line—on the outer surface of the barrel. The signs: P1.5—in the middle of the S1 zone, P2.5—in the middle of the S2 zone, etc.

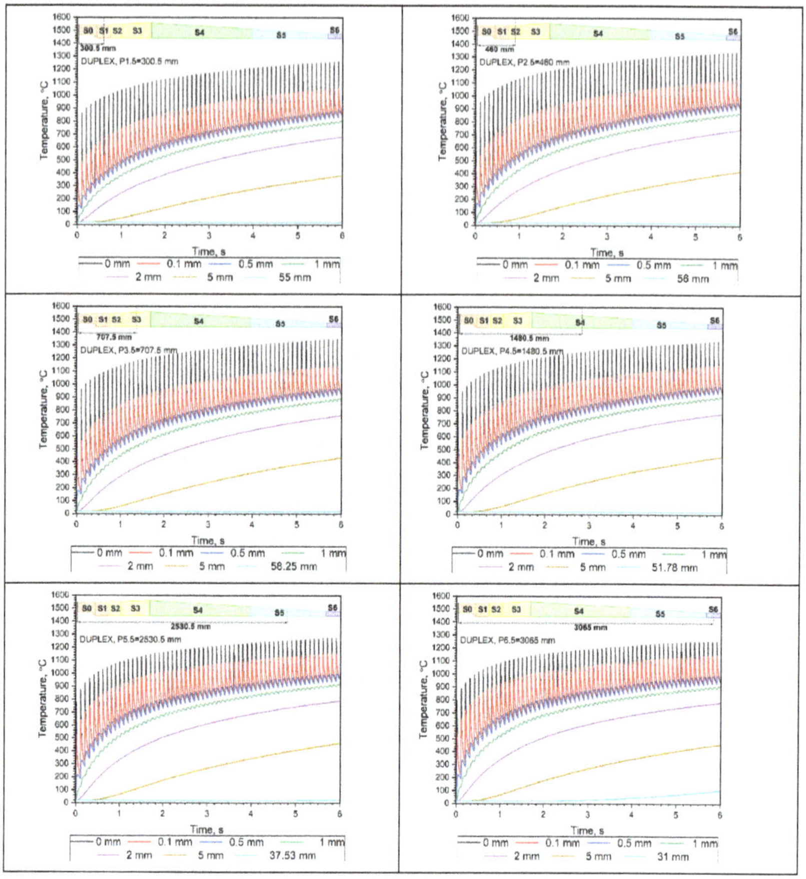

Figure 13. Temperature distribution $T_i(t, r_w, z)$ along the barrel thickness at the zones S1 to S6 (z in the middle of each zone) for the sequence of sixty shots, for the DUPLEX steel: black line—on the inner surface of the barrel, red line—0.1 mm below the inside surface, blue line—0.5 mm below the inside surface, green line—1 mm below the inside surface, violet line—2 mm under the inner surface, yellow line—5 mm under the inner surface, light blue line—on the outer surface of the barrel. The signs: P1.5—in the middle of the S1 zone, P2.5—in the middle of the S2 zone, etc.

Figure 14 shows the envelopes of the so-called highest peak temperatures and lowest peak base temperatures for 60 shots for all selected steels. For 38HMJ and 30HN2MFA steels, the lines match blue.

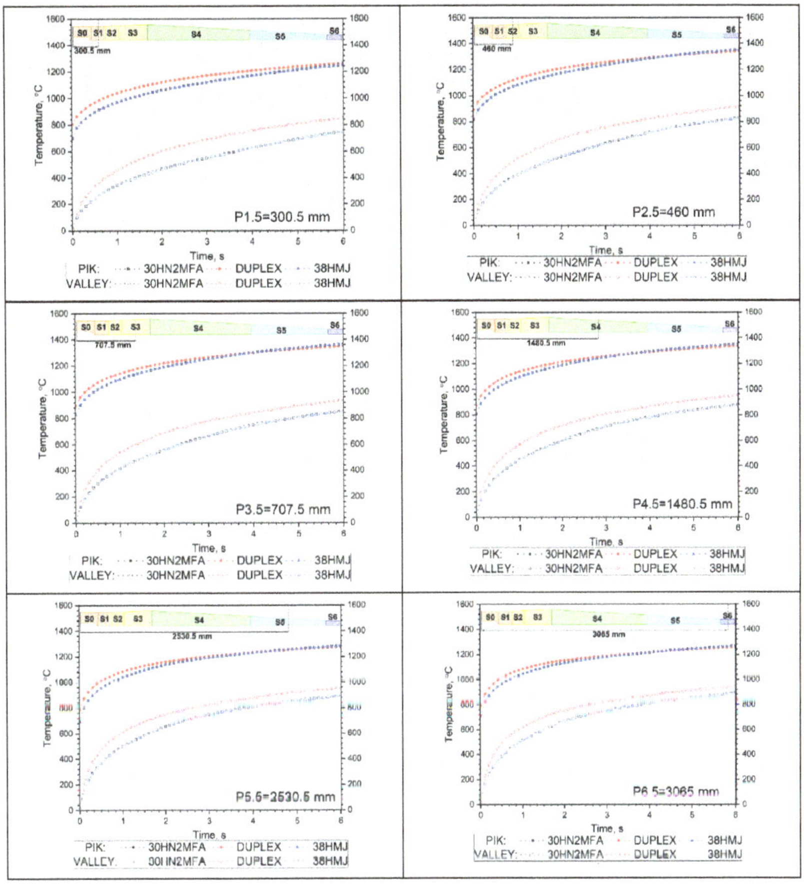

Figure 14. Envelope of the lowest and the highest temperature of the inner surface at the zones S1 to S6 (z in the middle of each zone) for the sequence of sixty shots, for chosen steels: 30HN2MFA, 38HMJ, DUPLEX. The signs: P1.5—in the middle of the S1 zone, P2.5—in the middle of the S2 zone, etc.

3. Discussion

The results of numerical tests of the heat transfer in the barrel of the 35 mm anti-aircraft gun made of three selected steel grades showed a similar nature of heat transfer in the 38HMJ and 30HN2MFA steels, but a different one in the Duplex steel. The heat transfer model is relatively simple and the obtained values of temperature fields on the inner surface of the barrel were not overestimated, as they were in the paper [24]. The division of the cannon into six zones S1 to S6 was agreed with the Polish weapons manufacturer. As numerical tests of heat transfer in the barrel are very time-consuming, such a division method reduces the calculation time to several hours for one steel.

In the case of a single shot—the temperature on the inner surface of the barrel:

In DUPLEX steel, the maximum temperature of the inner surface of the barrel, i.e., so-called highest peak temperature was about 87 °C higher than for the other two steels, and it dropped less than the other two. It results from a lower value of thermal diffusivity coefficient as a function of the Duplex steel temperature in relation to the other two. In each of the three selected steels, the maximum temperature of the inner surface of the barrel occurred in the third zone, S3. In the second, S2, and fourth, S4, zones, the temperatures were not much lower. In addition, the maximum temperatures on the inner surface of the barrel in the first four zones, S1 to S4, occurred before the exit of the bullet from the barrel, while the maximum temperatures in the fifth zone, S5, and the sixth zone, S6, occurred after the bullet exited the barrel.

In the case of the sequence of seven shots—temperature on the inner surface of the barrel:

In DUPLEX steel in the S3 zone, the highest temperature and the lowest temperature of the inner surface, i.e., the so-called highest peak temperature and lowest temperature of the peak base after the seven shots reached the values of 1088 °C and 462 °C, respectively—Figure 9. The difference between the highest and lowest inner surface temperature was maximum and equal to 626 °C in the S3 zone and minimum and equal to 468 °C in the S6 zone—Figure 9. In the 38HMJ and 30HN2MFA steels in the S3 zone, the lowest and the highest temperature of the inner surface after seven shots reached the values of 345 °C and 1039 °C for 30HN2MFA steel, and 355 °C and 991 °C for 38HMJ steel, respectively. The difference between the highest and lowest inner surface temperature for these steels was maximum and equal to 694 °C for 30HN2MFA steel and 636 °C for 38HMJ steel in the S3 zone and the minimum and equal to 552 °C for 30HN2MFA steel and 507 °C for 38HMJ steel in the S6 zone. For each of the selected steels, the lowest temperature reached its maximum in the S6 zone, and the increase in the lower internal surface temperature, i.e., in the lowest temperature of the peak base became an almost linear function of the number of shots.

In the case of the sequence of seven shots—the calculation of heat transfer along the barrel thickness:

On each curve of increasing temperature of the inner surface of the barrel during the shot, we could distinguish the so-called highest peak temperature and the lowest base temperature, which was in fact the temperature of the inner wall of the barrel. This temperature was practically identical to the temperature of the barrel wall at a depth of 0.5 mm below its inner surface—Figure 10. Therefore, it can be assumed that the temperature of the inner surface of the barrel during a series of shots is equal to the barrel temperature at a depth of 0.5 mm below its surface. Temperature distributions $T_i(t,r,z)$ along the barrel thickness for selected steels for the first, fourth and seventh shots are shown in Figure 11. At a depth of 0.5 mm, the greatest temperature difference occurred between 30HN2MFA, 38HMJ steels and DUPLEX steel. The difference increased with subsequent shots and after the seventh shot in the zone S6 it was about 86 °C—Figure 11 (lower drawing).

In the case of the sequence of sixty shots—the temperature along the barrel thickness:

After sixty shots, the highest internal surface temperature of the barrel occurred in the S3 zone and for all three steel grades, i.e., 30HN2MFA, 38 HMJ and DUPLEX steel, it was similar and amounted to approx. 1363 °C for 30HN2MFA and 38 HMJ steels, and 1348 °C for DUPLEX steel—Figures 12–14.

The lowest temperature of the internal surface in DUPLEX steel occurred in zones S1 and S2, i.e., around 849 °C in zone S1 and 916 °C in zone S2. For the remaining steels, the lowest temperature also occurred in zones S1 and S2, i.e., about 748 °C for 30HN2MFA and 38 HMJ steels in zone S1 and 827 °C for 30HN2MFA and 38 HMJ steels in zone S2. This is due to the fact that DUPLEX steel heats up to a higher temperature and cools down slowly as it has a lower thermal diffusivity coefficient than 30HN2MFA and 38HMJ steels. As it cools more slowly, the highest internal surface temperature after sixty shots is also lower than it would have been if this shielding effect, which is associated with an increase in inner wall temperature after each shot, was not observed in the heat flux density calculation. It should also be remembered that for 38HMJ and 30HN2MFA steels there is a shrinkage of the material and a phase change at a temperature of about 800 °C. The internal surface temperature of about 800 °C was achieved in 30HN2MFA and 38HMJ steels after about thirty shots in zone S5 (after 3.0 s) and S6 (after 2.9 s) and after about sixty shots in zone S1 (after 5.9 s)—Figure 12. It also means that the inner surface of the barrel in zones S5 and S6 will wear out the fastest. Due to the integral heat propagation effect in the steel, no changes were observed in the highest or lowest temperature of the inner surface of the barrel in the case of 30HN2MFA or 38HMJ steels specifically related to this shrinkage effect. After sixty shots, the maximum temperature of 30HN2MFA and 38HMJ steels and Duplex steel in the S2 to S4 zones was practically the same and was about 1363 °C for 30HN2MFA and 38 HMJ steels and 1348 °C for DUPLEX steel, while the lowest temperature in the 30HN2MFA and 38HMJ steels in the S5 and S6 zones was about 892°, and in DUPLEX steel it was about 955 °C in zone S5 and 944 °C in zone S6. After sixty shots, the outer surface of the barrel in zone S6 heated up to a temperature of about 226 °C for 30HN2MFA steel and 230 °C for 38 HMJ steel, and to 103 °C for DUPLEX steel–Figures 12 and 13. For selected steels, the envelopes of the highest and the lowest temperatures are shown in Figure 14. There were only differences between DUPLEX steel and the other steels, i.e., 30HN2MFA and 38HMJ.

4. Conclusions

The calculations of the heat transfer in the barrel of the 35 mm anti-aircraft gun were made for the temperature-dependent thermophysical parameters, i.e., thermal conductivity, specific heat and thermal expansion (in the RT range up to 1000 °C) of the selected barrel steels. The paper indicates that the energy of the phase transformation should not be taken into account multiple times, e.g., both in terms of thermal conductivity and specific heat.

The results of the numerical simulation of the heat transfer in the barrel of the 35 mm anti-aircraft cannon are summarized as follows:

(1) After the first shot, the maximum temperature on the inner surface of the barrel, the so-called highest temperature is the highest in DUPLEX steel—Figure 7. The temperature difference in relation to the other two steels is about 87 °C in zone S3 and decreases with successive shots, and after about 4 s and about 40 shots it is similar to the temperature of DUPLEX steel (in zone S3)—Figure 14. After sixty shots, the highest temperature of the 30HN2MFA and 38HMJ steels begins to exceed the highest temperature of the DUPLEX steel by about 15 °C, mostly in zone S3 and S4—Figure 14;

(2) After the first and subsequent shots, when the projectile leaves the barrel, instability appears in the calculations of $T_i(t, r_{in}, z)$ in zones S5 and S6—Figure 8. This is related to a sharp drop in the heat transfer coefficient $h_i(t)$ in these zones, much greater than in other zones—Figure 2;

(3) In Figure 9, for a series of 7 shots, it can be seen that the shape of $T_i(t, r_{in}, z)$ is the same in all zones from S1 to S6—Figure 9. In all zones, the so-called lowest temperature is highest for DUPLEX steels in each zone;

(4) The so-called lowest temperature on the inner surface of the barrel $T_i(t, r_{in}, z)$ plays a very important role in the analysis of heat transfer in the barrel, because it is related to the phase transition of the steel from which the barrel is made. It can be assumed that the temperature of the inner surface of the barrel during a series of shots is equal to the barrel temperature at a depth of 0.5 mm below its surface, i.e., $T_i(t, r = r_{in} - 0.5\text{ mm}, z)$ —Figures 10 and 11;

(5) For the 30HN2MFA and 38HMJ steels, for which the phase transition takes place, the temperature of 800 °C appears in different zones at different times, the fastest in zones S5 and S6. This means that zones S5 and S6 of the barrel will be exposed to the greatest wear. Already after about 3 s, i.e., after about thirty shots, these parts of the barrel will exceed the phase transition temperature—Figure 12;

(6) The so-called lowest temperature on the inner surface of the barrel $T_i(t, r_{in}, z)$ made of DUPLEX steel is always higher than the same temperature for a barrel made of 30HN2MFA or 38HMJ steel—Figure 14. In 2 s, i.e., after twenty-five shots, the difference between them in zones S2 and S3 is greatest at about 136 °C, after sixty shots it will drop in zone S6 to about 52 °C;

(7) Due to the lack of a phase transition, the DUPLEX steel can operate above the temperature of 800 °C. This steel does not have the material shrinkage effect and therefore repeatedly exceeding this temperature in the process of heating and cooling the barrel has no effect on the formation of cracks on the inner surface of the barrel.

Author Contributions: Conceptualization, M.Z., P.K. and Z.S.; methodology, P.K., M.Z. and Z.S.; software, M.Z., Z.S.; validation, J.Z. and M.P.; formal analysis, P.K., M.Z. and Z.S.; writing—original draft preparation, P.K., M.Z. and Z.S.; writing—review and editing, P.K., M.Z. and J.Z. All authors have read and agreed to the published version of the manuscript.

Funding: The research results reported in this work were obtained thanks to funding from the Polish National Centre for Research and Development 2012–2016 Scientific Fund, Project no. O ROB 0046 03 001.

Institutional Review Board Statement: Not applicable.

Informed Consent Statement: Not applicable.

Data Availability Statement: Not applicable.

Conflicts of Interest: The authors declare no conflict of interest.

Abbreviations

c_s	$J \cdot kg^{-1} \cdot K^{-1}$	specific heat of the barrel steel
c_p	$J \cdot kg^{-1} \cdot K^{-1}$	isobaric specific heat of the propellant gases
c_v	$J \cdot kg^{-1} \cdot K^{-1}$	isochoric specific heat of the propellant gases
f	$J \cdot kg^{-1}$	"force" of the propellant
H	J	enthalpy of the propellant gases flowing out from the barrel
K	-	constant of coefficient of secondary works
k_s	$W \cdot m^{-1} \cdot K^{-1}$	thermal conductivity of the barrel steel
k_p	$W \cdot m^{-1} \cdot K^{-1}$	thermal conductivity of propellant gases
l	m	travel of the projectile in the barrel
l_m	m	total distance travelled by the projectile along the barrel bore
m	kg	mass of the projectile
m_p	kg	mass of the propellant
p	Pa	pressure of propellant gases in the barrel
p_0	Pa	shot start pressure
Q	J	heat from combustion of the propellant
r_1	$m \cdot Pa^{-1} \cdot s^{-1}$	coefficient of linear law of burning rate
R	$J \cdot kg^{-1} \cdot K^{-1}$	gas constant of the propellant gases
s	m^2	cross-sectional area of the barrel bore
S_1	m^2	initial surface of grain of the propellant
t	s	time
T	K	temperature of propellant gases in the barrel
T_1	K	isochoric flame temperature of the propellant
U	J	internal energy of propellant gases in the barrel
v	$m \cdot s^{-1}$	velocity of the projectile
V_0	m^3	volume of the empty canon chamber
W	J	sum of works of the propellant gases
w	$m \cdot s^{-1}$	velocity of the gases
z_p	-	fraction of mass burned of the propellant
Greek letters		
γ	-	adiabatic index of the gunpowder gases
μ	$Pa \cdot s$	dynamic viscosity of the gunpowder gases
ζ	-	fraction of mass of the propellant which flowed out from the barrel
η	$m^3 \cdot kg^{-1}$	covolume of the propellant gases
κ_1, λ_1	-	shape coefficient of the propellant grain
Λ_1	m^3	initial volume of grain of the propellant
ρ_s	$kg \cdot m^{-3}$	density of the barrel steel
ρ	$kg \cdot m^{-3}$	density of propellant gases
ρ_p	$kg \cdot m^{-3}$	density of the propellant
φ	-	coefficient of the secondary works

References

1. Feng, G.-T.; Zhou, K.-D.; Zhang, Y.-Q.; He, L.; Li, J.-S.; Wang, J. The Study of Gun Barrel's Two-Dimensional Nonlinear Thermal Conduction. *Int. J. Thermophys.* **2019**, *40*, 37. [CrossRef]
2. Stiefel, L. (Ed.) *Gun Propulsion Technology*; American Institude of Aeronautics and Astronautics: Washington, WA, USA, 1988; ISBN 0930403207.
3. Cote, P.J.; Rickard, C. Gas–metal reaction products in the erosion of chromium-plated gun bores. *Wear* **2000**, *241*, 17–25. [CrossRef]
4. Sopok, S.; Rickard, C.; Dunn, S. Thermal–chemical–mechanical gun bore erosion of an advanced artillery system part one: Theories and mechanisms. *Wear* **2005**, *258*, 659–670. [CrossRef]
5. Sopok, S.; Rickard, C.; Dunn, S. Thermal–chemical–mechanical gun bore erosion of an advanced artillery system part two: Modeling and predictions. *Wear* **2005**, *258*, 671–683. [CrossRef]
6. Ahmad, I. The Problem of Gun Barrel Erosion: An Overview. In *Gun Propulsion Technology*; Stiefel, L., Ed.; American Inst. of Aeronautics and Astronautics: Washington, WA, USA, 1988; pp. 311–356, ISBN 0930403207.
7. Ebihara, W.T.; Rorabaugh, D.T. Mechanisms of Gun-Tube Erosion and Wear. In *Gun Propulsion Technology*; Stiefel, L., Ed.; American Inst. of Aeronautics and Astronautics: Washington, WA, USA, 1988; pp. 357–376, ISBN 0930403207.
8. Baracuti, A.J. Wear-Reduction Additives-Role of Propellant. In *Gun Propulsion Technology*; Stiefel, L., Ed.; American Inst. of Aeronautics and Astronautics: Washington, WA, USA, 1988; pp. 377–412, ISBN 0930403207.
9. Mishra, A.; Hameed, A.; Lawton, B. A Novel Scheme for Computing Gun Barrel Temperature History and Its Experimental Validation. *J. Press. Vessel Technol.* **2010**, *132*, 061202. [CrossRef]
10. Dębski, A.; Koniorczyk, P.; Leciejewski, Z.; Preiskorn, M.; Surma, Z.; Zmywaczyk, J. Analysis of Heat Transfer in a 35 mm Barrel of an Anti-Aircraft Cannon. *Probl. Mechatron. Armament Aviat. Saf. Eng.* **2016**, *7*, 71–86. [CrossRef]
11. Koniorczyk, P.; Sienkiewicz, J.; Zmywaczyk, J.; Dębski, A.; Zieliński, M.; Preiskorn, M. Effect of Microstructure on Thermophysical Properties of Heat-Treated Duplex Steel. *Materials* **2021**, *14*, 6043. [CrossRef] [PubMed]
12. Koniorczyk, P.; Zmywaczyk, J.; Dębski, A.; Zielinski, M.; Preiskorn, M.; Sienkiewicz, J. Investigation of Thermophysical Properties of Three Barrel Steels. *Metals* **2020**, *10*, 573. [CrossRef]
13. Koniorczyk, P.; Zmywaczyk, J.; Dębski, A.; Zieliński, M.; Cegła, M. (Eds.) Investigations of thermal diffusivity and thermal expansion for three types of the barrel steel. In Proceedings of the Thermophysics 2019: 24th International Meeting of Thermophysics and 20th Conference REFRA, Smolenice, Slovakia, 22–24 October 2019; AIP Publishing: Melville, NY, USA, 2019.
14. Zhen, W.; Jin, W. Heat Transfer Simulation of Large Caliber Gun Barrel. In *IOP Conference Series: Earth and Environmental Science*; IOP Publishing: Philadelphia, PA, USA, 2020; Volume 546, p. 42039.
15. Clutter, J.K.; Shyy, W. Computation of High-Speed Reacting Flow for Gun Propulsion Applications. *Numer. Heat Transf. Part A Appl.* **1997**, *31*, 355–374. [CrossRef]
16. Akçay, M.; Yükselen, M.A. Unsteady Thermal Studies of Gun Barrels During The Interior Unsteady Thermal Studies of Gun Barrels during The Interior Ballistic Cycle with Non-Homogenous Gun Barrel Material Thermal Characteristics. *J. Therm. Sci. Technol.* **2014**, *34*, 75–81.
17. Yong-Hai, W. Analysis of the Temperature Field of a Gun Tube Based on Thermal-Solid Coupling. *Res. J. Appl. Sci. Eng. Technol.* **2013**, *5*, 4110–4117. [CrossRef]
18. Hill, R.D.; Conner, J.M. Transient Heat Transfer Model of Machine Gun Barrels. *Mater. Manuf. Process.* **2012**, *27*, 840–845. [CrossRef]
19. Ryan, H.; Logan, M. Methodology for Transient Thermal Analysis of Machine Gun Barrels Subjected to Burst Firing Schedules. Available online: https://nts.com/content/uploads/2017/12/Methodology-for-Transient-Thermal-Analysis-of-Machine-Gun-Barrels-Subjected-to-Burst-Firing-Schedules.pdf (accessed on 28 February 2022).
20. Ding, C.; Liu, N.; Zhang, X. A mesh generation method for worn gun barrel and its application in projectile-barrel interaction analysis. *Finite Elem. Anal. Des.* **2017**, *124*, 22–32. [CrossRef]
21. Chen, H.; Yue, Z.; Ren, D.; Zeng, H.; Wei, T.; Zhao, K.; Yang, R.; Qiu, P.; Chen, L.; Shi, X. Thermal Conductivity during Phase Transitions. *Adv. Mater.* **2018**, *31*, 1806518. [CrossRef] [PubMed]
22. Yoon, J.; Park, J.; Park, J. Numerical Simulation and Design of a High-Temperature, High-Pressure Fluid Transport Pipe. *Appl. Sci.* **2020**, *10*, 5890. [CrossRef]
23. Sheu, T.W.H.; Lee, S.-M. Numerical Study of Two-Dimensional Solid-Gas Combustion through Granulated Propellants. *Numer. Heat Transf. Part A. Appl.* **1995**, *27*, 395–415. [CrossRef]
24. Leciejewski, Z.; Koniorczyk, P.; Dębski, A.; Preiskorn, M.; Surma, Z.; Zmywaczyk, J. Heat Transfer Calculations in Barrel Cover of 35 mm Naval Armament System Gun. *Probl. Mechatron. Armament Aviat. Saf. Eng.* **2018**, *9*, 53–70. [CrossRef]
25. Wiśniewski, S. ; *Wydawnictwo Naukowe PWN. Wymiana Ciepła*, 61st ed.; Wydawnictwo Naukowe PWN: Warszawa, Poland, 2017; ISBN 9788301194437.
26. Орлов, Б.В.; Мазинг, Г.Ю. *Термодинамические и Баллистические Основы Проектированя Ракетных Двигателей на Мвердом Мопливе*; Машиностроение: Москва, Россия, 1968. (In Russian)
27. Carlucci, D.E. *Ballistics: Theory and Design of Guns and Ammunition*, 2nd ed.; CRC Press: Hoboken, NJ, USA, 2013; ISBN 9781466564374.
28. Serebryakov, M.E. *Internal Ballistics of Gun Systems and Solid Rockets*; Oborongiz: Moscow, Russia, 1962.

29. John, C. *Theory of the Interior Ballistics of Guns*; John Wiley & Sons: New York, NY, USA, 1950.
30. Fikus, B.; Surma, Z.; Trebinski, R. Preliminary Application Correctness Assessment of Physical Burning Law in Interior Ballistics Phenomena Modeling in Small-Caliber Guns. In Proceedings of the 31st International Symposium on Ballistics, Hyderabad, India, 4–8 November 2019; DEStech Publications: Lancaster, UK, 2019; ISBN 978-1-60595-610-7.

energies

MDPI

Article

Numerical Study on Flow and Heat Transfer Characteristics of Supercritical CO_2 in Zigzag Microchannels

Yi Tu [1] and Yu Zeng [2,*]

[1] School of Mechanical Engineering, Hunan University of Arts and Science, Changde 415000, China; tuyi.huas@outlook.com
[2] School of Aeronautic Science and Engineering, Beihang University, Beijing 100191, China
* Correspondence: zengyu@buaa.edu.cn; Tel.: +86-186-1840-5545

Abstract: The zigzag channel is the uppermost channel type of an industrial printed circuit heat exchanger (PCHE). The effect of geometric properties on the flow and heat transfer performance of the channel is significant to the PCHE design and optimization. Numerical investigations were conducted on the flow and heat transfer characteristics of supercritical CO_2 (sCO_2) in semicircular zigzag channels by computational fluid dynamics method. The shear stress transfer (SST) k–ω model was used as turbulence model and the National Institute of Standards and Technology (NIST) real gas model with REFPROP database was used to evaluate the thermophysical parameters of sCO_2 in this numerical method. The effectiveness of the simulation method is verified by experimental data. Thermal hydraulic performance for zigzag channels with different pitch lengths, bending angles, and hydraulic diameters are studied comparatively based on this numerical method, with the boundary conditions which cover the pseudocritical point. The comparison results show that reducing the bending angle and pitch length will strengthen the effect of boundary layer separation on the leeward side of the wall and enhance the heat transfer performance, but the pressure drop of the channel will also increase, and the decrease of channel hydraulic diameter is beneficial to the heat transfer enhancement, but it is not as significant as that of the straight channel.

Keywords: supercritical CO_2; zigzag channel; micro channel; heat transfer; computational fluid dynamics

Citation: Tu, Y.; Zeng, Y. Numerical Study on Flow and Heat Transfer Characteristics of Supercritical CO_2 in Zigzag Microchannels. *Energies* **2022**, *15*, 2099. https://doi.org/10.3390/en15062099

Academic Editors: Abderrahmane Baïri, Angel A. Juan and Marcin Kamiński

Received: 10 February 2022
Accepted: 11 March 2022
Published: 13 March 2022

Publisher's Note: MDPI stays neutral with regard to jurisdictional claims in published maps and institutional affiliations.

1. Introduction

A printed circuit heat exchanger (PCHE) is a type of compact heat exchanger with high efficiency, high application pressure, and high application temperature. It was invented in Australia in 1980 and promoted for commercial application by Heatric. It has broad application prospects in the fields of ultra-high-temperature gas-cooled reactors, floating liquefied natural gas storage units, and other industrial energy [1]. PCHE typically employs diffusion-bonded arrays of plates where microchannels are formed by chemical etching [2]. The typical cross section shape is semicircular and the hydraulic diameter in a PCHE passage is between 700 μm and 1.5 mm [3]. The flow channel geometries can be designed as straight, zigzag, S-shape, and airfoil-finned channels [4]. However, the zigzag-type channel is more widely used in industrial applications. CO_2 is a nontoxic and inexpensive gas. It has excellent thermophysical properties (high specific heat, high thermal conductivity, and low viscosity) near the pseudocritical point, as shown in Figure 1, which can considerably enhance the heat transfer without sacrificing the hydraulic performance [5]. Consequently, the application of CO_2 in PCHE has become the focus of researchers.

Heat transfer and hydraulic characteristics are the basis of PCHE thermal design. Various experimental and numerical investigations have been performed to optimize the channel structures, fluid mediums, and operation conditions. Nikitin and his team first published the experimental results of the flow and heat transfer characteristics of sCO_2 in zigzag PCHE in 2016 and developed the correlations of Nu and f, while the correlations are only applicable to channels of the specific geometric parameters and Reynolds number range of those used in the experimental study [6]. Kruizenga et al. investigated the thermal–hydraulic performance of sCO_2 in a straight channel with semicircular cross section using both experimental and numerical methods, the analysis results showed that the commercial computational fluid dynamics (CFD) software can well predict the internal heat transfer characteristics of the PCHE channel [7]. Saeed and Kim also conducted the numerical analysis of an sCO_2 PCHE using ANSYS-CFX and validated the simulation results using published experimental data [8]. Tu and Zeng studied the flow and heat transfer performance in semicircular straight channels of sCO_2 fluid for both cooling and heating process using CFD method. A modified model based on Douglas A. Olson [9] correlation was proposed to predict the heat transfer performance of sCO_2 in semicircular channels for both heating and cooling conditions [10]. These literature conclusions fully confirm the feasibility of the numerical method.

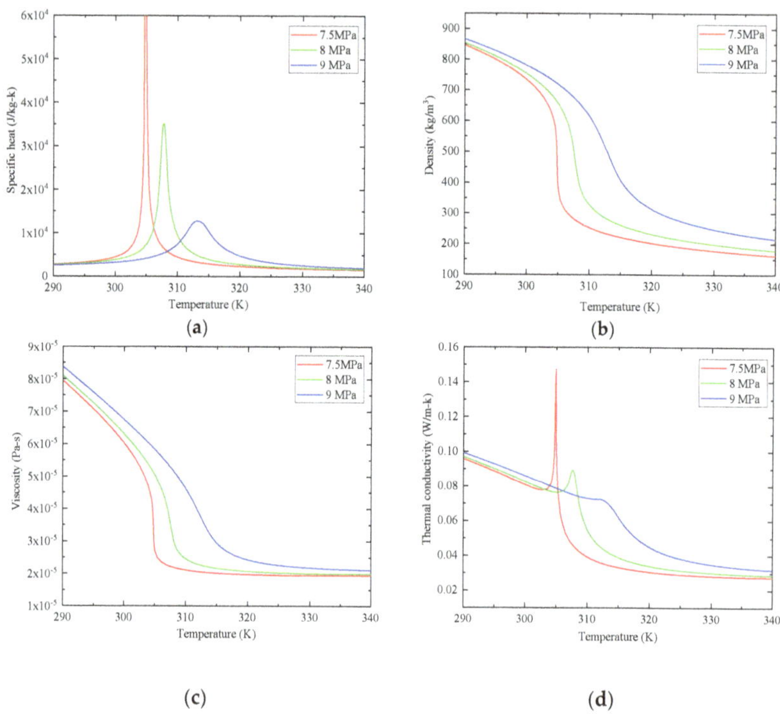

Figure 1. Thermophysical properties of supercritical CO_2 at different pressure: (**a**) specific heat; (**b**) density; (**c**) dynamic viscosity; (**d**) thermal conductivity.

Subsequently, a large number of studies focused on finding better channel types. Kim et al. compared the heat transfer and hydraulic performance of sCO_2 in PCHE with zigzag and airfoil-shaped fins. It was found that the thermal performance of the airfoil fin was close to that of zigzag, but the airfoil fin had lower pressure loss [11]. Mohammed et al. investigated the effect of channel shapes (zigzag, curve, and step) on the thermal and hydraulic performance of PCHE and found that the zigzag channels have the highest value of heat transfer coefficient and pressure drop [12]. Matsuo et al. conducted numerical simulations of three different channel types (zigzag, chamfered zigzag, airfoil) to study the geometrical effects on the local heat transfer coefficient and pressure drop for supercritical CO_2 in PCHE and developed new correlations for Nu of the zigzag channels [13]. In the research of [14–16], the PCHE with zigzag channel and discontinuous S-shaped fins were numerically and experimentally investigated, and it was found that the S-shaped channel can significantly improve the hydraulic performance while keeping almost equal heat transfer performance compared to the zigzag channels.

There are also studies focusing on thermal hydraulic characteristics of the other fluid media in PCHE channels. Dai et al. studied the flow and heat transfer performance of water in the semicircular zigzag passage experimentally [17]. Minghui Chen et al. investigated the thermal–hydraulic performance of a zigzag channel PCHE using helium as fluid media [18].

Most of the studies on the flow and heat transfer characteristics of PCHE channels use a specific geometric parameter channel or straight channel, or the comparison between zigzag channel and other types of channels such as S-type and discontinuous airfoil fin type. The experimental data and empirical correlations given in these studies are also limited to a certain type of channel, and the operating pressure, fluid bulk temperature, and Reynolds number are limited to a certain range. However, there are few studies on the effect of geometric parameters on the flow and heat transfer performance of a zigzag channel. This paper aims at modeling the forced convection heat transfer of CO_2 within the zigzag channels, which are the main channel type of PCHE, and studies the effects of its main geometric parameters (hydraulic diameter, pitch length, and bending angle) on its internal flow and heat transfer parameters, especially near the pseudocritical point. The numerical method and analysis results of this study can be used as a reference for PCHE industrial design and channel performance investigation.

2. Numerical Modeling

A numerical method for analyzing the steady-state flow and heat transfer properties of a zigzag channel is defined. In this method, ANSYS Fluent 2019 is used to solve the governing equations of the steady turbulent flow of sCO_2 in the zigzag channels. The NIST real gas model with REFPROP V9.1 database was used to evaluate the thermodynamics and transport of approximately of CO_2. Yoon et al. [19] and Ren et al. [20] conducted comparative studies using STD k–e, realizable k–e, and SST (shear stress transport) k–ω turbulence models to simulate the thermal–hydraulic performance of sCO_2 intube-flowing and found that the SST k–ω turbulence model gives the best quantitative prediction. The same conclusion was likewise reached in [21–24]. Therefore, the SST k–ω model is adopted for further analysis in this study. The pressure-based coupled algorithm was used to establish the coupling of velocity and pressure. The numerical simulation is considered convergent as all iterative residuals of the governing equations are less than 10^{-5}, and area-weighted average outlet temperature and area-weighted average inlet pressure are stable.

2.1. Geometry and Boundary Conditions

The flow and heat transfer performance of CO_2 in horizontal zigzag channels is investigated in this paper. Figure 2 shows a schematic diagram of the computational domain with the boundary condition adopted in this research. The study will consider the effects of different geometric factors, including hydraulic diameter, bending angle, and pitch length on the internal flow and heat transfer characteristics of the channel, as shown in Table 1. To check the independent effect of the geometric parameter, the comparative study only changes one geometric parameter at a time, and the rest remains unchanged. For example, for investigating the effect of bend angle θ on the channel flow and heat transfer performance, four types of bend angle, 100°, 115°, 140°, and 180° (straight), are considered for the geometric model, while L_p is fixed to 7.75 mm and d_h is fixed to 2 mm.

As shown in Table 2, the inlet temperature was changed from 280 K to 350 K to ensure the bulk temperature T_b covers the pseudocritical point of CO_2 for this analysis. The outlet pressure of CO_2 varies between 7.5 MPa and 9 MPa to keep its condition near the pseudocritical point. Constant wall heat flux (12 kW/m^2 for heating case and −12 kW/m^2 for cooling case) and mass flux 200 kg/m^2-s were adopted in this numerical simulation. The thermal properties of CO_2 were obtained from NIST Database (REFPROP V9.1).

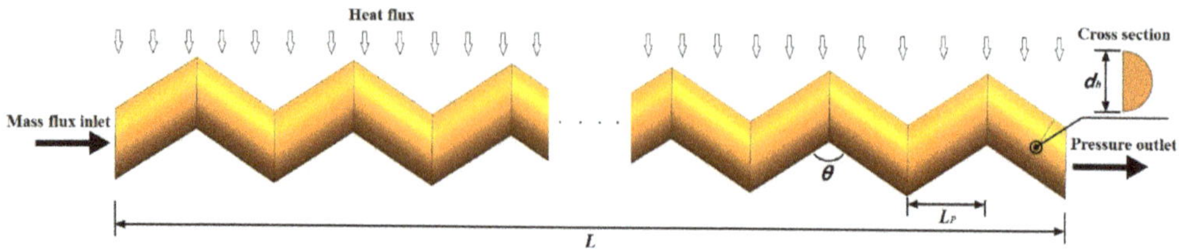

Figure 2. Physical model of zigzag channel.

Table 1. Geometric parameters.

Geometric Parameters	Values
Channel hydraulic diameters, d_h, mm	1.17 (experimental validation), 2, 4
Bending angle, θ, °	100, 115, 140, Straight
Channel pitch length, L_p, mm	3, 4.5, 6, 7.75
Channel total length, L, mm	500

Table 2. Boundary conditions in detail.

Inlet		Outlet	Wall
Temperature (K)	Mass flux (kg/m^2-s)	Pressure (MPa)	Constant heat flux (kW/m^2)
280~350	200	7.5, 8, 9	±12

2.2. Governing Equations

The governing equations regarding the continuity, momentum, and energy are expressed as Equations (1)–(3).

(1) Continuity equation:

$$\frac{\partial}{\partial x_i}(\rho u_i) = 0 \tag{1}$$

(2) Momentum equation [25]:

$$\frac{\partial}{\partial x_j}(\rho u_i u_j) = -\frac{\partial p}{\partial x_i} + \frac{\partial \tau_{ij}}{\partial x_j} + \rho g_i \tag{2}$$

(3) Energy equation:

$$\frac{\partial}{\partial x_i}(u_i(\rho E + p)) = \frac{\partial}{\partial x_i}\left(k_{eff}\frac{\partial T}{\partial x_i}\right) \tag{3}$$

where ρg_i is the gravitational body force, u_i is overall velocity vector, T is the temperature, ρ is the density, u_i is the velocity vector, E is the total energy, p is the static pressure, τ_{ij} is the stress tensor, and k_{eff} is the effective conductivity ($k_{eff} = k + k_t$, k_t is the turbulent thermal conductivity).

(4) Direct numerical simulation (DNS) of Navier–Stokes equations is the most accurate method for turbulence; however, it is not feasible in most situations to resolve the wide range of scales in time and space as the CPU requirements by far exceed the existing capacity. For this reason, averaging procedures such as the Reynolds method have to be applied to the Navier–Stokes equations to filter out the turbulent spectrum [26]. However, the averaging process introduces additional unknown terms into the transport equations that need to be provided by suitable turbulence models. The SST k–ω turbulence model is used in this paper and is described as follows.

The transport equations of the k–ω model are expressed as Equations (4) and (5):

$$\frac{\partial}{\partial x_i}(\rho k u_i) = \frac{\partial}{\partial x_j}\left(\Gamma_k \frac{\partial k}{\partial x_j}\right) + G_k - \rho\beta^* k\omega \quad (4)$$

$$\frac{\partial}{\partial x_i}(\rho \omega u_i) = \frac{\partial}{\partial x_j}\left(\Gamma_w \frac{\partial \omega}{\partial x_j}\right) + G_\omega - \rho\beta\omega^2 \quad (5)$$

where G_k is the generation of turbulence kinetic energy k due to mean velocity gradients, G_ω is the generation of ω, and Γ_k and Γ_w represent the effective diffusivity of k and ω calculated by Equations (6) and (7).

$$\Gamma_k = \mu + \mu_t\left(\frac{F_1}{\sigma_{k1}} + \frac{1-F_1}{\sigma_{k2}}\right) \quad (6)$$

$$\Gamma_\omega = \mu + \mu_t\left(\frac{F_1}{\sigma_{\omega 1}} + \frac{1-F_1}{\sigma_{\omega 2}}\right) \quad (7)$$

where σ_k and σ_ω are turbulent Prandtl numbers for k and ω, respectively, μ is the dynamic viscosity of the fluid, and F_1 is calculated as Equations (8)–(10).

$$F_1 = \tan\mathrm{h}\left(\phi_1^4\right) \quad (8)$$

$$\phi_1 = \min\left[\max\left(\frac{\sqrt{k}}{0.09\omega y}, \frac{500\mu}{\rho y^2 \omega}\right), \frac{4\rho k}{\sigma_{\omega 2} D_\omega y^2}\right] \quad (9)$$

$$D_\omega = 2(1-F_1)\rho\sigma_{\omega 2}\frac{1}{\omega}\frac{\partial k}{\partial x_j}\frac{\partial \omega}{\partial x_j} \quad (10)$$

The turbulent viscosity μ_t of the SST $k\omega$ model is calculated using Equations (11)–(15).

$$\mu_t = \frac{\rho k}{\omega}\frac{1}{\max\left(\frac{1}{a^*}, \frac{\sqrt{2S_{ij}}F_2}{a_1\omega}\right)} \quad (11)$$

$$S_{ij} = \frac{1}{2}\left(\frac{\partial u_i}{\partial x_j} + \frac{\partial u_j}{\partial x_i}\right) \quad (12)$$

$$F_2 = \tanh\left(\phi_2^2\right) \quad (13)$$

$$\phi_2 = \max\left(2\frac{\sqrt{k}}{0.09\omega y}, \frac{500\mu}{\rho y^2\omega}\right) \quad (14)$$

$$a^* = a^*_\infty\left(\frac{a_0^* + \frac{\rho k}{6\mu\omega}}{1 + \frac{\rho k}{6\mu\omega}}\right) \quad (15)$$

where μ_t is the turbulent viscosity, y is the wall distance, and the constants used in the SST model are as follows: $a^*_\infty = 1$, $a_1 = 0.31$, $\sigma_{k1} = 1.176$, $\sigma_{k2} = 1$, $\sigma_{\omega 1} = 2$, $\sigma_{\omega 2} = 1.168$, $a_0^* = 0.024$.

The second-order upwind scheme of Equation (16) is used to discretize the convective term of the above governing Equation [27].

$$\varphi_{f,sou} = \varphi + \nabla\varphi \cdot \vec{r} \quad (16)$$

where φ and $\nabla\varphi$ are the cell-centered value and its gradient in the upstream cell and $\vec{r}$ is the displacement vector from upstream cell centroid to the face centroid.

2.3. Data Reduction

The hydraulic diameter, d_h, was defined as Equation (17):

$$d_h = \frac{4A}{C_{wet}} \tag{17}$$

where A is the semicircular cross section area of the channel, and C_{wet} is the wet circumference of the cross section.

The average heat convection coefficient, h, was defined as Equation (18):

$$h = \frac{Q_w}{T_w - T_b} \tag{18}$$

where Q_w is the heat flux of the wall, T_w is the average wall temperature, and T_b is the fluid bulk temperature.

The channel total pressure drop, ΔP, was defined as Equation (19):

$$\Delta P = P_{in} - P_{out} \tag{19}$$

where P_{in} and P_{out} are area-weighted average pressure at the inlet and outlet of the channel, respectively.

2.4. Grid Independence and Model Validation

Meshes in this study are generated using ICEM CFD 2019, and the size of the first layer adjacent to the wall is less than 2×10^{-6} m to keep the wall $y^+ < 1$. Structured hexahedral cells are used in the whole computational domain, and the mesh is locally densified at the bend of the flow direction, as illustrated in Figure 3.

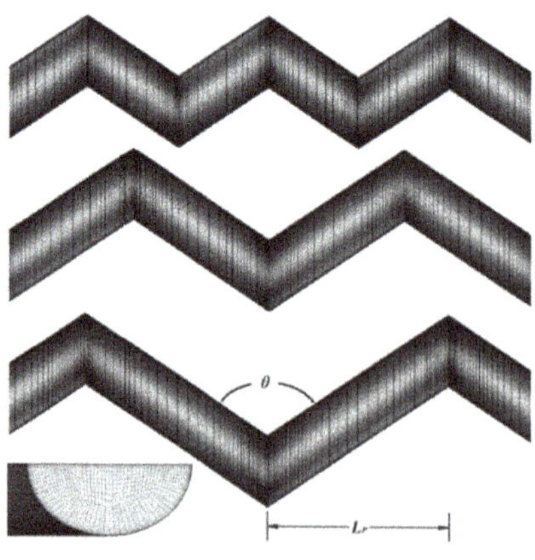

Figure 3. Mesh structure of the computational domain.

Mesh independence analysis was performed with five different mesh sizes of 91,656, 152,988, 233,508, 314,028, and 394,548. Percentage changes in physical variables h and ΔP were chosen as the basis for independence judgment. As the comparison result listed in Table 3, the relative error percentage of h changes from 11.01% to 1.17%, and the relative error percentage of ΔP changes from 19.78% to 0.59% with the mesh refinement. Consequently, the mesh size of 314,028 elements is considered sufficient, and 300,000 is used as the baseline for all the rest of the simulations.

Table 3. Mesh independence analysis.

No.	Number of Elements	h (W/m^2-K)	Error (%)	ΔP(Pa)	Error (%)
1	91,656	1655.298	11.01%	629.7	19.78%
2	152,988	1644.926	11.56%	639.9	21.72%
3	233,508	1737.778	6.57%	605.9	15.26%
4	314,028	1838.227	1.17%	528.8	0.59%
5	394,548	1860.027	0.00%	525.7	0.00%

2.5. Validation by Experimental Data

The experimental data in [28] were used to verify the accuracy of the numerical method. The experiments were carried out to investigate the thermal performance of sCO_2 in a straight channel with semicircular cross section. The hydraulic diameter and total length of the channel are 1.17 mm and 500 mm. The operating pressure, heat flux, and mass flux are 8.1 MPa, -20 kW/m^2, and 330 kg/m^2-s, respectively. As shown in Figure 4, the CFD simulation results and experimental data maintain a good consistency with the maximum relative error 17.1% over all analyzed T_b range, which covers the pseudocritical point. Thus, the numerical method adopted in this study for the flow and heat transfer performance of sCO_2 in the semicircular channel is reliable and comparatively accurate.

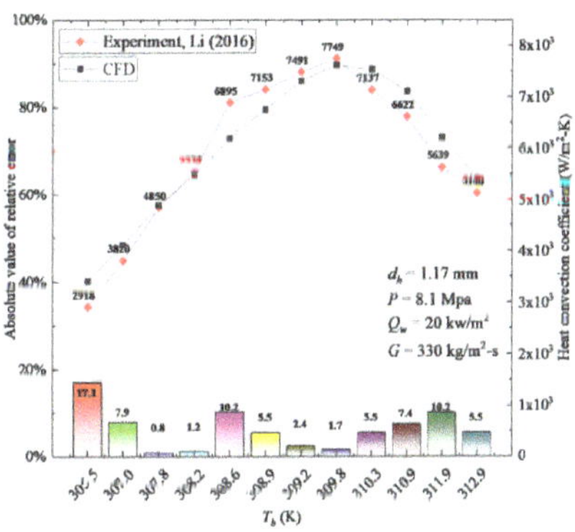

Figure 4. Validation with experimental data [28].

3. Results and Discussion

3.1. Effect of L_p on the Channel Flow and Heat Transfer Performance

To study the effect of L_p on thermal and hydraulic performance of zigzag channel, three different L_p (3, 4.5, and 6 mm) are considered for this comparative study. The other geometric factors d_h and θ take the valve 1.17 mm and 115°, respectively, and remain unchanged to avoid coupling effects. The channel has an inlet mass flux of G = 200 kg/m^2-s, an outlet pressure of P_{out} = 8 MPa, and a wall heat flux of Q_w = $\pm$12 kw/m^2-k. The bulk temperature T_b of CO_2 varies between 280 K and 360 K, covering the pseudocritical temperature T_m.

As shown in Figure 5, h of the three channels gradually increases and reaches the maximum value as the T_b of the fluid approaches T_m. This is due to the surge of the specific heat and thermal conductivity of CO_2 near the pseudocritical point. ΔP of the three types of channels decrease with the increase of T_b. This is mainly because the density of CO_2 decreases with the rising of T_b. It can be seen from the comparison results of the three channels that the heat convection coefficient h and pressure drop ΔP both decrease with the rising L_p.

Figure 6 shows the velocity vector along the zigzag channel with different L_p. The flow-field distribution possesses certain periodicity. A large velocity gradient occurs at the channel corner and the maximum velocity in the channel also appears in this area. Boundary layer separation occurs at the corner of the channel and the local velocity increases due to the appearance of vortex. As the velocity direction is different from the wall direction of the next pitch, it can strengthen the mixing of the mainstream and the fluid near the wall, which is conducive to the heat transfer enhancement. As can be seen from the partial enlarged view, the local velocity increases with the reduction of channel L_p, which means that the fluid at the boundary region is mixed with the fluid in the core region more sufficiently. As a result, the reduction of L_p enhances the channel heat transfer, and improves the channel total heat convection coefficient h. The local flow resistance ΔP also rises with the reduction of L_p as the wall separation increases.

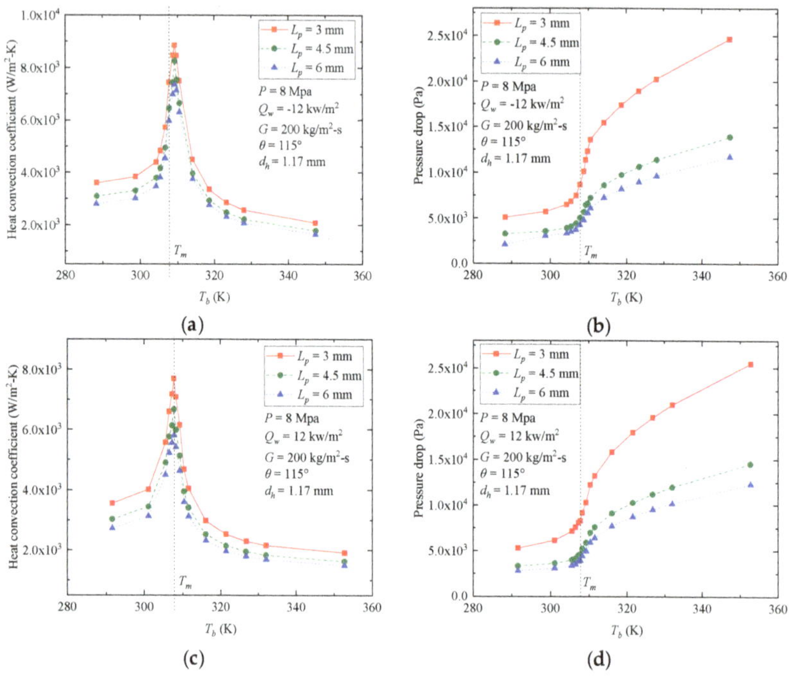

Figure 5. Effect of Lp on flow and heat transfer performance: (**a**) h of cooling case; (**b**) ΔP of cooling case; (**c**) h of heating case; (**d**) ΔP of heating case.

Figure 7 represents the local convective heat transfer coefficient in zigzag channel with different L_p. The local heat transfer coefficient increases significantly on the windward side of the corner area. It is because the boundary layer is locally thinner under the direct flushing of the incoming flow. As mentioned above, the local fluid velocity increases with the decrease of channel L_p, which also leads to the local heat transfer coefficient increasing.

3.2. Effect of θ on the Channel Flow and Heat Transfer Performance

In this part of the analysis, four different θ of the channel (100°, 115°, 140°, and straight) are considered for this comparative study with the inlet mass flux G = 200 kg/m^2-s, outlet pressure P_{out} = 8 MPa, and wall heat flux $Q_w = \pm 12$ kw/m^2-k. d_h and L_p of the channels remain unchanged with the values 2 mm and 7.75 mm, respectively. The bulk temperature T_b of the CO_2 varies between 280 K and 360 K to cover the pseudocritical temperature T_m.

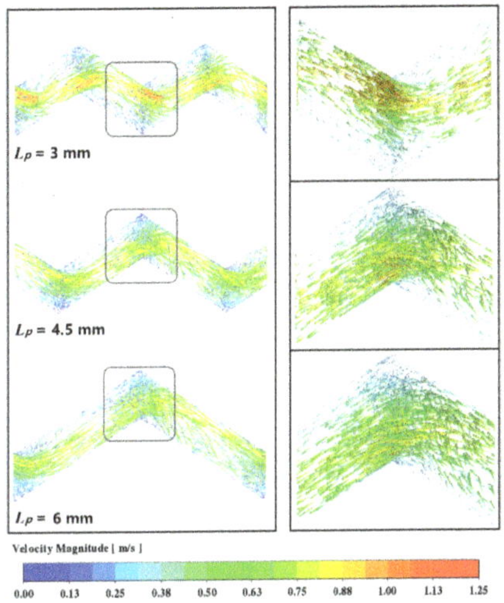

Figure 6. Velocity vector along the zigzag channel with L_p of 3 mm, 4.5 mm, and 6 mm.

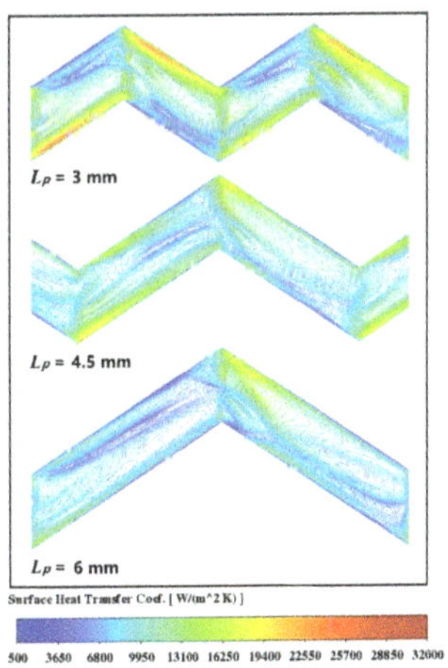

Figure 7. Local heat transfer coefficient of the zigzag channel with L_p of 3 mm, 4.5 mm, and 6 mm.

As can be seen from Figure 8, h and ΔP both decrease with the increase of θ, and better thermal performance for all of the zigzag channels is demonstrated, compared with the straight channel. The variation trend of h and ΔP of zigzag channel with T_b is the same as that of the straight channel. This provides an approach for defining the flow and heat transfer correlations in zigzag channels, as there have been several studies on the correlations of Nu of the sCO_2 semicircular straight channel [29,30].

Figure 9 shows the comparison of the velocity vector along the channel with different bend angles of the zigzag channel. A sharper bending angle will significantly increase the local fluid velocity at the turning position and aggravate the separation of the boundary layer, which will result in more violent mixing of fluid between the wall area and the core region. It means that the decrease of θ enhances the channel convective heat transfer under the geometric parameters of the current study. Therefore, h increases with the decrease of θ. As θ =180°, the channel becomes a straight channel, and h is smaller than any of the zigzag channels with bending angles.

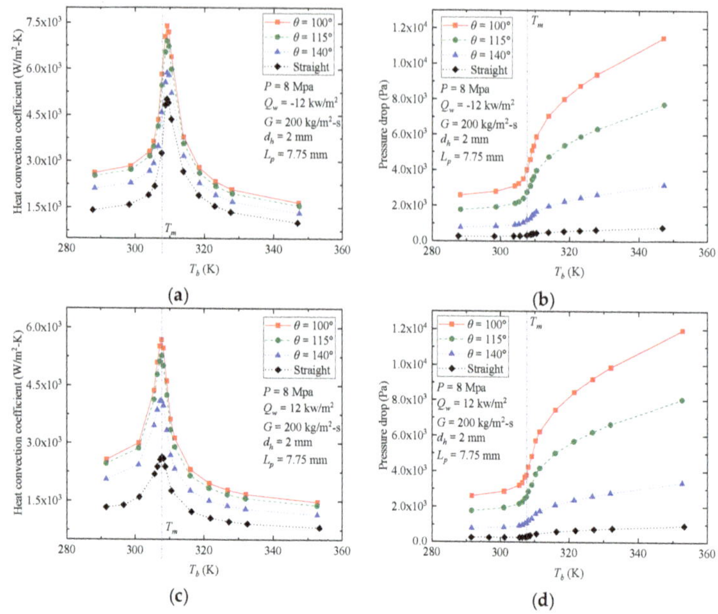

Figure 8. Effect of θ on flow and heat transfer performance: (**a**) h of cooling case; (**b**) ΔP of cooling case; (**c**) h of heating case; (**d**) ΔP of heating case.

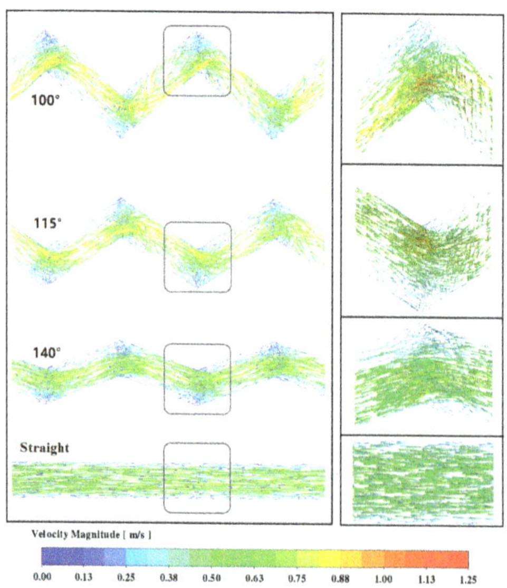

Figure 9. Velocity vector along the zigzag channel with θ of 100°, 115°, 140°, and straight.

Figure 10 shows the contour plots of local convective heat transfer coefficient in zigzag channel under different θ. It can be seen that the convective heat transfer coefficient of the wall surface of the zigzag channel is significantly higher than that of the straight channel. The region with the highest local convective heat transfer coefficient appears on the windward side of the turning angle of zigzag channel. It is because this area is washed by the mainstream and has a locally thinner boundary layer.

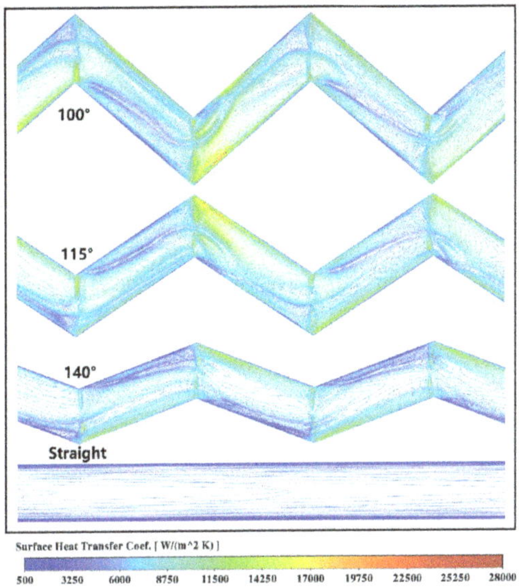

Figure 10. Local heat transfer coefficient of the zigzag channel with θ of 100°, 115°, 140°, and straight.

3.3. Effect of d_h on the Channel Flow and Heat Transfer Performance

In this comparative evaluation study, three different d_h of 1.17, 2, and 4 mm are used. The other geometric factors L_p and θ are set to 4.5 mm and 115°, respectively and remain unchanged. The channel has an inlet mass flux of G = 200 kg/m^2-s, an outlet pressure of P_{out} = 8 MPa, and a wall heat flux of $Q_w = \pm 12$ kw/m^2-k. The bulk temperature T_b of CO_2 varies between 280 K and 360 K, covering the pseudocritical temperature T_m.

With the reduction of channel d_h, the distance from the mainstream region to the wall also decreases, which is theoretically conducive to the heat transfer performance, and there are indeed such conclusions in the study on the thermal performance of the straight channel in [21,31] Nonetheless, for the zigzag channels, the heat convection coefficient h does not show an obvious increasing trend with the decrease of d_h. It can be seen from Figure 11 that h and ΔP increase significantly as d_h changes from 4 mm to 2 mm, especially in the heating cases. However, when d_h changes from 2 mm to 1.17 mm, neither h nor ΔP show significant change. This is different from the conclusion in the semicircular straight channel study.

Through the previous analysis cases, we found that the separation of boundary layer promotes the mixing and diffusion in the fluid and enhances the heat transfer performance of the zigzag channel. However, on the other hand, it will also reduce the effective heat transfer area of the wall, which is disadvantageous to the heat exchange. Figure 12 shows us another possible scenario. As for the d_h = 4 mm diameter case, the boundary layer separation area accounts for a large proportion of the total heat exchange area and the weakening effect of the separation of boundary layer on heat transfer becomes dominant. It can also be seen from Figure 13 that the local heat convective coefficient of the d_h = 4 mm channel has not been obviously enhanced on the windward side compared to the d_h = 1.17 mm and d_h = 2 mm channels.

As can be also seen from Figure 12, the boundary layer separation effect is weakened with the decrease of the d_h. In the d_h = 1.17 mm and d_h = 2 mm diameter cases, the boundary layer separation area will not account for as large a proportion of the total wall area as that presented in d_h = 4 mm case, which means that the boundary layer separation has a positive effect on the heat transfer performance of the 1.17 mm and 2 mm channels. When $L_p >> d_h$, this positive effect is enhanced with the increase of d_h. At the same time, there is an opposite influence whereby the heat transfer will be weakened with the increase of d_h due to the increasing distance between mainstream region and the wall. The combination of these two effects makes the convective heat transfer coefficient close for the 1.17 mm and 2 mm channels.

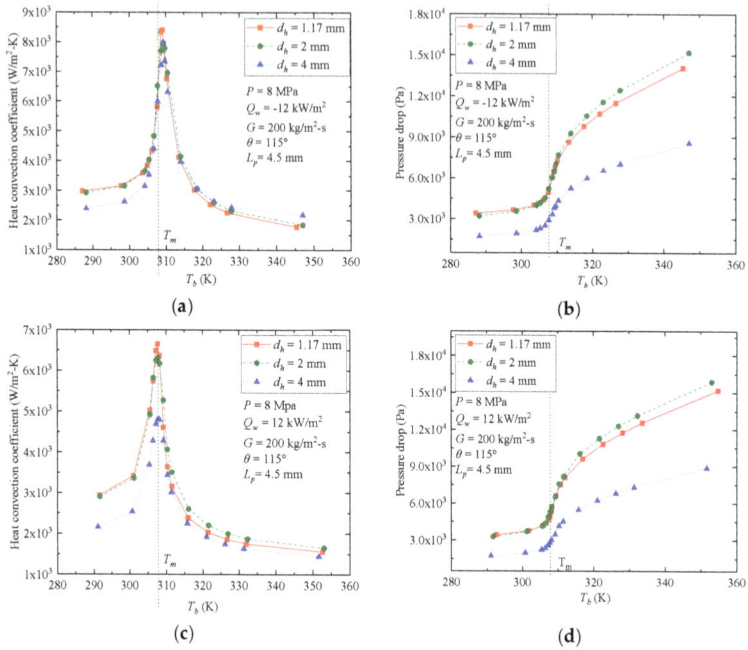

Figure 11. Effect of d_h on flow and heat transfer performance: (**a**) h of cooling case; (**b**) ΔP of cooling case; (**c**) h of heating case; (**d**) ΔP of heating case.

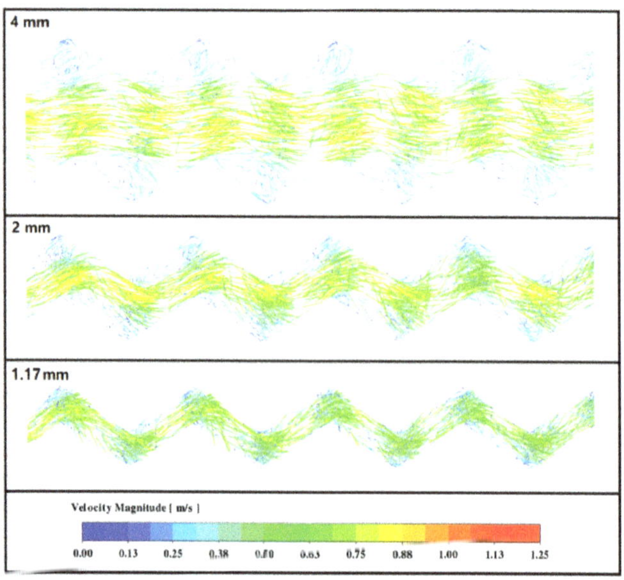

Figure 12. Velocity vector along the zigzag channel with d_h of 1.17 mm, 2 mm, and 4 mm.

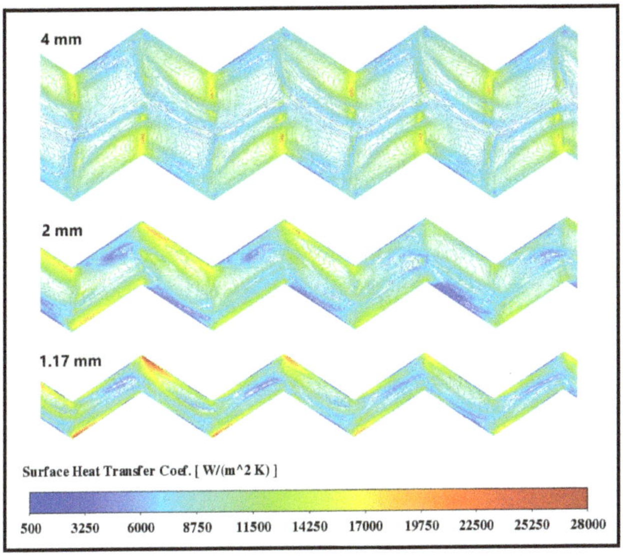

Figure 13. Local heat transfer coefficient of the zigzag channel with d_h of 1.17 mm, 2 mm, and 4 mm.

All three geometric parameters produce effects on the flow and heat transfer performance of the zigzag channel and have a certain regularity. When the size of d_h is close to L_p, the wall separation caused by channel turning will not strengthen the heat transfer performance. For industrial design, from the point of view of enhancing heat transfer, the L_p should be significantly larger than d_h for the zigzag channels.

4. Conclusions

The thermal and hydraulic performance of sCO_2 in zigzag channels of different pitch lengths (3 mm, 4.5 mm, 6 mm, 7.75 mm), bending angles (100°, 115°, 140°, straight), and hydraulic diameters (1.17 mm, 2 mm, 4 mm) are studied comparatively with the boundary condition covering the pseudocritical point using the CFD method. In this numerical method, the SST k–ω is adopted as the turbulence model and shows the quantitative prediction of the experiments' heat transfer data. The following conclusions were obtained:

(1) The drastic change of CO_2 thermophysical parameters has a significant effect on the hydraulic and heat transfer characteristics of the zigzag channel near the pseudocritical point, and its variation tendency with bulk temperature is the same as that of the straight channel.

(2) The reduction of pitch length enhances the effect of boundary layer separation behind the corner, which can improve the heat transfer performance. As a result, the heat convective coefficient and pressure drop of sCO_2 in the zigzag channel increase with the decrease of the pitch length.

(3) The decrease of channel bend angle can also increase the local velocity at the turning location and enhance the boundary layer separation effect. Therefore, the heat convective coefficient and pressure drop of sCO_2 in the zigzag channel both increase with the decrease of channel bend angle.

(4) The decrease of channel hydraulic diameter is conducive to the heat transfer of the zigzag channel, but it is not as significant as that of the straight channel, because the boundary layer separation effect will be weakened with the decrease of channel hydraulic diameter.

Author Contributions: Conceptualization, Y.T. and Y.Z.; methodology, Y.T.; software, Y.T.; validation, Y.T. and Y.Z.; formal analysis, Y.T.; investigation, Y.T.; resources, Y.Z.; data curation, Y.T.; writing—original draft preparation, Y.T.; writing—review and editing, Y.Z.; visualization, Y.T.; supervision, Y.Z.; project administration, Y.T.; funding acquisition, Y.T. All authors have read and agreed to the published version of the manuscript.

Funding: This research was funded by Natural Science project of Hunan Province, China, grant number 2020JJ5393 and Education Department of Hunan Province, China, grant number 21B0618.

Institutional Review Board Statement: Not applicable.

Informed Consent Statement: Not applicable.

Data Availability Statement: Not applicable.

Conflicts of Interest: The authors declare no conflict of interest.

Nomenclature

A	Cross section area [m^2]
C	Circumference [m]
C_p	Specific heat [J/kg-K]
d	Diameter [m]
f	Friction factor
G	Mass flux [kg/m^2-s]
h	Heat convection coefficient, [W/m^2-K]
k	Thermal conductivity [W/m-K], turbulent energy [J/kg]
L_P	Pitch length [m]
Nu	Nusselt number
P	Pressure [Pa]
Q	Heat flux [W/m^2]
Re	Reynolds number
T	Temperature [K]
u	Fluid velocity [m/s]
y	Wall distance [m]
ρ	Density [kg/m^3]
ΔP	Pressure drop [Pa]

Greek Symbols

α	Heat convection coefficient: [W/m^2-K]
ρ	Density [kg/m^3]
ω	Specific rate of turbulence dissipation [s^{-1}]
μ	Dynamic viscosity [kg/m-s]
y	Wall distance [m]
θ	Bend angle [°]

Subscripts

b	Bulk
h	Hydraulic
in	Inlet
m	Pseudocritical point
out	Outlet
w	Wall

References

1. Chen, M.; Sun, X.; Christensen, R.N.; Shi, S.; Skavdahl, I.; Utgikar, V.; Sabharwall, P. Experimental and Numerical Study of a Printed Circuit Heat Exchanger. *Ann. Nucl. Energy* **2016**, *97*, 221–231. [CrossRef]
2. Kim, W.; Baik, Y.J.; Jeon, S.; Jeon, D.; Byon, C. A Mathematical Correlation for Predicting the Thermal Performance of Cross, Parallel, and Counterflow PCHEs. *Int. J. Heat Mass Transf.* **2017**, *106*, 1294–1302. [CrossRef]
3. Pua, L.M.; Rumbold, S.O. Industrial Microchannel Devices—Where Are We Today? In *International Conference on Microchannels and Minichannels*; ASME: New York, NY, USA, 2003; Volume 1, pp. 773–780. [CrossRef]
4. Chen, M. Performance Testing and Modeling of Printed Circuit Heat Exchangers for Advanced Nuclear Reactor Applications. Ph.D. Thesis, University of Michigan, Ann Arbor, MI, USA, 2018.
5. Xu, X.Y.; Wang, Q.W.; Li, L.; Ekkad, S.V.; Ma, T. Thermal-Hydraulic Performance of Different Discontinuous Fins Used in a Printed Circuit Heat Exchanger for Supercritical CO_2. *Numer. Heat Transf. Part A Appl.* **2015**, *68*, 1067–1086. [CrossRef]
6. Nikitin, K.; Kato, Y.; Ngo, L. Printed Circuit Heat Exchanger Thermal-Hydraulic Performance in Supercritical CO_2 Experimental Loop. *Int. J. Refrig.* **2006**, *29*, 807–814. [CrossRef]
7. Kruizenga, A.; Anderson, M.; Fatima, R.; Corradini, M.; Towne, A.; Ranjan, D. Heat Transfer of Supercritical Carbon Dioxide in Printed Circuit Heat Exchanger Geometries. In Proceedings of the 14th International Heat Transfer Conference, IHTC 14, Washington, DC, USA, 8–13 August 2010; Volume 4, pp. 653–661. [CrossRef]
8. Saeed, M.; Kim, M.H. Thermal and Hydraulic Performance of SCO2 PCHE with Different Fin Configurations. *Appl. Therm. Eng.* **2017**, *127*, 975–985. [CrossRef]
9. Douglas, A.; Olson, D.A. *Heat Transfer in Turbulent Supercritical Carbon Dioxide Flowing in a Heated Horizontal Tube*; NIST Pubs: Gaithersburg, MD, USA, 1998.
10. Tu, Y.; Zeng, Y. Heat Transfer and Hydraulic Characteristics of Supercritical CO_2 in Cooled and Heated Horizontal Semicircular Channels. *J. Appl. Fluid Mech.* **2021**, *14*, 1351–1362. [CrossRef]
11. Kim, D.E.; Kim, M.H.; Cha, J.E.; Kim, S.O. Numerical Investigation on Thermal-Hydraulic Performance of New Printed Circuit Heat Exchanger Model. *Nucl. Eng. Des.* **2008**, *238*, 3269–3276. [CrossRef]
12. Mohammed, H.A.; Gunnasegaran, P.; Shuaib, N.H. Influence of Channel Shape on the Thermal and Hydraulic Performance of Microchannel Heat Sink. *Int. Commun. Heat Mass Transf.* **2011**, *38*, 474–480. [CrossRef]
13. Matsuo, B.K.Y.; Ranjan, D.; Anderson, M. Numerical Study of Compact Heat Exchanger Designs for Generation IV Supercritical Carbon Dioxide Power Conversion Cycles. *Nucl. Sci. Eng.* **2014**, *176*, 138–153. [CrossRef]
14. Tsuzuki, N.; Kato, Y.; Ishiduka, T. High Performance Printed Circuit Heat Exchanger. *Appl. Therm. Eng.* **2007**, *27*, 1702–1707. [CrossRef]
15. Ngo, T.L.; Kato, Y.; Nikitin, K.; Ishizuka, T. Heat Transfer and Pressure Drop Correlations of Microchannel Heat Exchangers with S-Shaped and Zigzag Fins for Carbon Dioxide Cycles. *Exp. Therm. Fluid Sci.* **2007**, *32*, 560–570. [CrossRef]
16. Wen, Z.X.; Lv, Y.G.; Li, Q. Comparative Study on Flow and Heat Transfer Characteristics of Sinusoidal and Zigzag Channel Printed Circuit Heat Exchangers. *Sci. China Technol. Sci.* **2020**, *63*, 655–667. [CrossRef]
17. Dai, Z.; Zheng, Z.; Fletcher, D.F.; Haynes, B.S. Experimental Study of Transient Behaviour of Laminar Flow in Zigzag Semi-Circular Microchannels. *Exp. Therm. Fluid Science* **2015**, *68*, 641–651. [CrossRef]
18. Chen, M.; Sun, X.; Christensen, R.N. Thermal-Hydraulic Performance of Printed Circuit Heat Exchangers with Zigzag Flow Channels. *Int. J. Heat Mass Transf.* **2019**, *130*, 356–367. [CrossRef]
19. Yoon, S.J.; O'Brien, J.; Chen, M.; Sabharwall, P.; Sun, X. Development and Validation of Nusselt Number and Friction Factor Correlations for Laminar Flow in Semi-Circular Zigzag Channel of Printed Circuit Heat Exchanger. *Appl. Therm. Eng.* **2017**, *123*, 1327–1344. [CrossRef]
20. Ren, Z.; Zhao, C.R.; Jiang, P.X.; Bo, H.L. Investigation on Local Convection Heat Transfer of Supercritical CO_2 during Cooling in Horizontal Semicircular Channels of Printed Circuit Heat Exchanger. *Appl. Therm. Eng.* **2019**, *157*, 113697. [CrossRef]
21. Li, H.; Kruizenga, A.; Anderson, M.; Corradini, M.; Luo, Y.; Wang, H.; Li, H. Development of a New Forced Convection Heat Transfer Correlation for CO_2 in Both Heating and Cooling Modes at Supercritical Pressures. *Int. J. Therm. Sci.* **2011**, *50*, 2430–2442. [CrossRef]
22. Xiang, M.; Guo, J.; Huai, X.; Cui, X. Thermal Analysis of Supercritical Pressure CO_2 in Horizontal Tubes under Cooling Condition. *J. Supercrit. Fluids* **2017**, *130*, 389–398. [CrossRef]
23. Liu, S.; Huang, Y.; Wang, J. Theoretical and Numerical Investigation on the Fin Effectiveness and the Fin Efficiency of Printed Circuit Heat Exchanger with Straight Channels. *Int. J. Therm. Sci.* **2018**, *132*, 558–566. [CrossRef]
24. Tu, Y.; Zeng, Y. Flow and Heat Transfer Characteristics Study of Supercritical CO_2 in Horizontal Semicircular Channel for Cooling Process. *Case Stud. Therm. Eng.* **2020**, *21*, 100691. [CrossRef]
25. Batchelor, C.K.; Batchelor, G.K. *An Introduction to Fluid Dynamics*; Cambridge University Press: Cambridge, UK, 2000; ISBN 0521663962.
26. Kamiński, M.; Ossowski, R.L. Navier-Stokes problems with random coefficients by the Weighted Least Squares Technique Stochastic Finite Volume Method. *Arch. Civ. Mech. Eng.* **2014**, *14*, 745–756. [CrossRef]
27. Barth, T.J.; Jespersen, D.C. The Design and Application of Upwind Schemes on Unstructured Meshes. In *Aiaa Aerospace Sciences Meeting*; AIAA: Reston, VA, USA, 1989; p. 0366.

28. Li, H.; Zhang, Y.; Zhang, L.; Yao, M.; Kruizenga, A.; Anderson, M. PDF-Based Modeling on the Turbulent Convection Heat Transfer of Supercritical CO_2 in the Printed Circuit Heat Exchangers for the Supercritical CO_2 Brayton Cycle. *Int. J. Heat Mass Transf.* **2016**, *98*, 204–218. [CrossRef]
29. Kruizenga, A.; Li, H.; Anderson, M.; Corradini, M. Supercritical Carbon Dioxide Heat Transfer in Horizontal Semicircular Channels. *J. Heat Transf.* **2012**, *134*, 081802. [CrossRef]
30. Jackson, J.D. Fluid Flow and Convective Heat Transfer to Fluids at Supercritical Pressure. *Nucl. Eng. Des.* **2013**, *264*, 24–40. [CrossRef]
31. Dang, C.; Hihara, E. In-Tube Cooling Heat Transfer of Supercritical Carbon Dioxide. Part 2. Comparison of Numerical Calculation with Different Turbulence Models. *Int. J. Refrig.* **2004**, *27*, 748–760. [CrossRef]

energies

MDPI

Article

Derivative Probes Signal Integration Techniques for High Energy Pulses Measurements

Adam Jóśko *, Bogdan Dziadak, Jacek Starzyński and Jan Sroka

Faculty of Electrical Engineering, Warsaw University of Technology, 00-661 Warsaw, Poland; bogdan.dziadak@pw.edu.pl (B.D.); jacek.starzynski@pw.edu.pl (J.S.); jan.sroka@pw.edu.pl (J.S.)
* Correspondence: adam.josko@pw.edu.pl

Abstract: The paper presents problems related to the processing of signals recorded with differential field probes E and H. The fundamental problem to which special attention has been paid is the result of the integration operation. Due to the presence of constant/slowly-varying components in the raw signal, there is a drift present in the outcome of integration. This line wander can be enormous. This is particularly evident if the integration is performed in a standard manner, uniformly over the entire recorded waveform. The paper contains the Authors' proposition to segment the signal and perform the integration independently in each of the sub-regions. This approach is based on the assumption of a local mean value instead of its global character for the recorded waveform. Although this leads to more complex signal processing, it gives significantly better results as it is suppressing the deterioration drift in the integrated signal more than 400 times. The results are presented on laboratory recordings and outdoor tests. In the first case, voltage pulses with durations of about 50 ns and rise times in the range of single ns were recorded. In the second case, high-energy electromagnetic pulse signals were used. It was formed by sinusoidal waveforms packets of 3 GHz frequency with a single packet duration of 5 μs and packet repetition frequency $f \leq 300$ Hz.

Keywords: electromagnetic field; signal processing; numerical integration; high speed field measurement

Citation: Jóśko, A.; Dziadak, B.; Starzyński, J.; Sroka, J. Derivative Probes Signal Integration Techniques for High Energy Pulses Measurements. *Energies* **2022**, *15*, 2244. https://doi.org/10.3390/en15062244

Academic Editors: Marcin Kamiński and Angel A. Juan

Received: 27 January 2022
Accepted: 14 March 2022
Published: 18 March 2022

1. Introduction

The measurement of high-energy current pulses is performed for lightning current measurements, measurement of partial discharges, measurements of the parameters of high voltage and high current generators. These pulses are generated for electromagnetic compatibility verification and testing in order to evaluate the system or equipment shielding effectiveness and its resistance to a high electromagnetic field [1,2]. These pulses are also generated and measured in magnetic flux compression generator tests where very high current values, up to 1 MA, are used to generate electromagnetic fields capable of damaging electronic devices [3,4]. The same is for Marx generators where very fast voltage pulses ranging up to 1 MV are generated, and the energy achieved allows for electronic equipment malfunction [5–7]. These high value pulses can be measured with the use of transducers utilizing the optical Faraday effect [8], Ampere's law by means of Rogowski coil and electromagnetic field probes [9].

In most cases mentioned above, both high voltage and high current measurements are performed indirectly by means of E and H field probes. This approach increases the safety of the measurement as there is a galvanic isolation of the measuring circuit and the tested circuit. On the other hand, it becomes necessary to perform additional conditioning or processing of the measurement signal. Among other popular methods used, there is the integration of measurement signals. It is performed when inductive or capacitive sensors are used to measure the field. The voltage induced at the coil terminals is directly proportional to the derivative of the magnetic field. For the capacitive sensors on the other hand, the current induced in the capacitor circuit is directly proportional to the derivative of the electric field. They require integration in both cases. The problems are presented in [10,11]. Moreover, in [12], Marconato et al. discuss the possibility of using different types of analogue and digital integrations in a circuit for the magnetic field measurement in a plasma machine. The proper selection of the integration interval plays a very important role, which was described in [13–15] and illustrated with an example of the Analog to Information (A2I) converter pre-integrator. On the other hand, an easy to implement algorithm using a second-order generalized integrator to control an induction motor is presented in [16].

Numerical integration brings the risk of accumulation of mean value present in the processed signal, which is manifested by the occurrence of a significant drift in the integrated output signal. The proposed methods described in the measurement instruments documentation work well in practice for periodic, stationary signals. For single pulse and in particular, floating signals, numerical integration with these methods often does not give good results.

The main goal of the work is to develop a method of numerical integration of signals which gives results comparable to analogue (hardware) integration (figures in the article). An additional goal is to develop a method not demanding computing power, so that it can be efficiently carried out directly on the oscilloscope (not always equipped with dedicated software and high computing power). For this reason, the starting point is the fundamental method of determining the mean value for the entire signal, the method commonly given in the documentation. For this method it is assumed that the mean value is constant all over the acquired signal. The Authors' proposition is to split the signal into segments (dependent on the signal form) and independently compute local mean values applied in the following signal processing. The digital filtering tool is also not excluded from the research field. An additional reason is the fact that digital filtering can also be used to remove slow varying signal frequency components closely related to the local mean values.

Thus, in the area of electromagnetic field measurement, the need to integrate a derivative signal is quite common, but implementing the appropriate integration method for a particular measurement case is not straightforward. Our paper focuses on discussing the basic methods of integrating the signal from E and H field probes with special emphasis on regions of averaging introducing significant differences in the case of numerical integration. The paper is composed as follows:

- In the introduction, we present the most common applications required for signal integration.
- The second chapter is devoted to the presentation of theoretical background for field probes: electric field (D-dot type) and magnetic field (B-dot type) and the possible signal integration methods for these probes. The problem of signal acquisition trigger configuration is presented.
- The third chapter presents two measurement setups for different signal generators. We explain our method of signal integration and discuss the defects of using an incorrect numerical integration algorithm approach.
- The fourth chapter contains discussion and comparison of different approaches to the integration aspect in the measurement of electromagnetic field.
- The fifth chapter contains summary of the achieved results where the proposed integration approach gives the effective cumulative integration drift attenuation. The obtained outcomes are characterized by the drift attenuation level of a range of 400.

2. Fundamentals of Field Probes and Integration Methods

2.1. Field Probes Functional Principle

The field probes used for measurements belong to a group of transmitters for which the signal (output voltage) is proportional to the rate of change of the measured quantity, i.e., to the derivative of the measured quantity. This applies both to the electric field probe, based on a capacitive transducer, and to the magnetic field probe using an inductive transducer.

The B-dot and D-dot probes are available in two versions: single ground type for fast alternating fields at the surface, and differential free field type for fast alternating fields in space. For the B-dot ground magnetic field probe, the output signal can be written with Equation (1). The output signal for the D-dot ground probe is given by Equation (2).

$$U(t) = Aeq\frac{dB(t)}{dt} = Aeq\cdot\mu_o\cdot\frac{dH(t)}{dt}, \tag{1}$$

$$U(t) = Rs\cdot Aeq\frac{dD(t)}{dt} = Rs\cdot Aeq\cdot\varepsilon_o\cdot\frac{dE(t)}{dt}, \tag{2}$$

where: Aeq is the equivalent area of the single sensor; B is the magnetic flux induction, H is the magnetic field strength; μ_o is the vacuum permeability. Rs is the impedance seen by a single channel of the sensor, D is electrical induction, E is electrical field strength; ε_o is vacuum permittivity.

As can be seen from Equations (1) and (2), the output signal is proportional to the physical dimensions of the probe, but most importantly it is proportional to the rate of change of the field—the derivative of the field. This forces the necessity of signal integration to obtain the value of measured field.

2.2. Signal Integration Methods

The following methods can be used to integrate the measurement signal:

- hardware (analogue) circuits;
- numerical methods.

Hardware integrators are built with RC circuits. The advantage of these integrators is the operational simplicity. This approach gives a signal directly at the output of the integrator that is proportional to the measured quantity, in this case the magnetic and electric fields. The output signal is not enormously lagged behind the raw signal before integration and can be directly recorded with an oscilloscope. This allows the operator for quick reading of the fundamental parameters of the measured field such as: its amplitude, frequency, rise and fall times or pulse length.

The condition for the correct integration of the signal is the preservation of time parameters of the signal and integrator. It should be remembered that the integration interval (0-t) should be shorter than the time constant τ = RC. This is a disadvantage of hardware methods, because the time parameters of the signal (field) being measured, must be known before the measurement. This makes it necessary to have a set of multiple integrators with different time constants ready when starting an experiment for which the frequency of the signal (field) is not known at all. The application of passive analogue integrators is relatively easy. Nevertheless, one should remember several practical aspects, which are already pointed out by the probe manufacturers themselves [17]. First, the integrator should be connected directly to the oscilloscope's input without any additional connecting cables. This is shown in Figure 1c (recommended connection). Laying the lead wires, one should remember to avoid, as far as possible, any bends in the cable. Manufacturers of probes do not recommend using e.g., angled BNC connections. It is also probably dictated by the fact that in the case of bent connections it is difficult to maintain constant geometry of the circuit and consequently impedance parameters. It is especially important at high frequencies. It should also be kept in mind that correct integration results are easier to be obtained when the entire measurement path is at a common ground reference potential. Therefore, a semi-rigid cable is commonly used in this type of measurements. However, it is not recommended to use passive analogue integrators in a measurement system with the optolink connections. This is mainly due to the low voltage range of the optoelectronic circuit and noticeable noise deteriorating the measurement signal. In this case, one should use numerical integration directly in the oscilloscope or perform that stage in the post-processing activity.

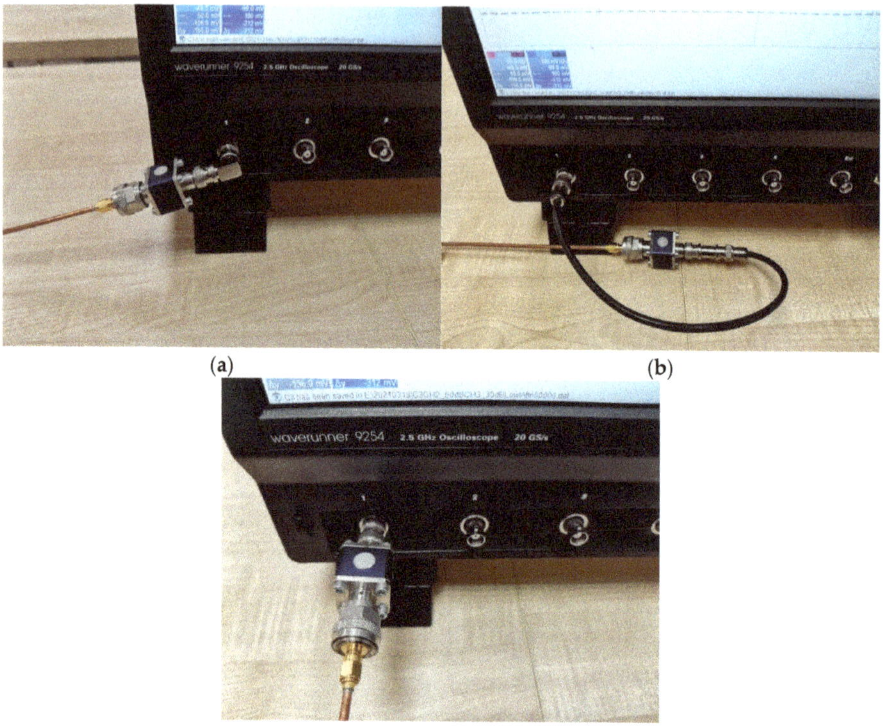

(**a**) (**b**) (**c**)

Figure 1. Probe manufacturer recommendations for the passive integrator connection: (**a**,**b**) not recommended, (**c**) recommended connection.

Numerical integration is the approximate calculation of definite integrals [18]. The methods approximate the integral by using the sum of the values of the function being integrated at several points. To obtain a more accurate approximation, the integration interval is divided into small fragments. The final result is the sum of the estimates of the integrals in each subinterval.

For the numerical integration of signals, the rectangle or trapezoid method can be used, but the latter is more accurate and popular.

In the trapezoid method, the approximation improves because one approximates each of the sub compartments linearly, which can be written as follows (3):

$$\int_{t0}^{tn} u(t)dt \approx \frac{h}{2}\sum_{i=0}^{n-1}(u(t_i) + u(t_{i+1})), \tag{3}$$

where n is the number of subintervals of length h.

The use of simple numerical methods is caused by the fact that in case of high sampling frequency of the signal (this is usually the case), the error of integration is relatively small (very narrow subintervals of integration). This gives the possibility of carrying out the integration process directly on oscilloscopes recording the waveforms from measurement equipment. The trapezoid method, though it can be considered basic (as compared for example to Simpson method), is commonly used as an integration formula in oscilloscopes.

Numerical post-processing provides the most tools, methods and opportunities that can be applied (if only necessary) into the integration process. In this case, the signal recorded on the oscilloscope is processed using signal processing dedicated software and powerful computers, after the completion of measurement experiments. A relatively long delay in obtaining results is a disadvantage of this procedure, but the certainty of the process correctness as well as the possibility of performing additional analysis, e.g., spectral or wavelet analysis and additional filtering often compensates for the mentioned disadvantage.

2.3. Practical Problems of the Signal Acquisition

By definition, the output signals of B-dot and D-dot probes do not contain a constant component. However, this component may appear in the conditioned measurement signal immediately before the functional integrator block. There may be several reasons for this condition. First of all, it can happen as a result of imbalance of the measurement path. Another reason may be the accumulation of electrostatic charges, especially in high-impedance lines (leads of the Programmable Gain Instrumentation Amplifier). In practice, however, a lot depends also on the selection of the oscilloscope recording time (period). Documentation dedicated to measurement instruments commonly gives the integration of a periodic, rectangular signal generated by oscilloscope built-in test generator as an example. In this case, as the signal occupies the entire recording period (window), and especially when the screen presents the whole number of signal periods (with significant amplitude), removing the DC component is an uncomplicated task (Figure 2). In manual mode (convenient for demonstration but impractical especially for a series of measurements), the average value is found using the oscilloscope knobs.

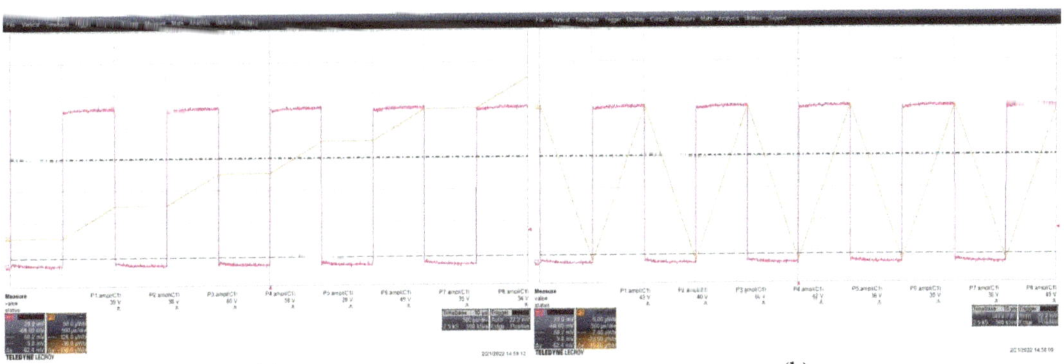

(a) (b)

Figure 2. Rectangular waveform integration process, (**a**) signal non-zero mean value (purple), integral signal (yellow), (**b**) signal with mean value extracted (purple), integral signal (yellow).

To automate the measurement, it is more convenient to determine the mean value using a dedicated function and subtract it from the samples of the recorded signal before integration. This technique works well for periodic and single shot signals under certain conditions.

For the single pulse signals, it is important to select the recording length as to record the entire phenomenon, possibly without an excessive "zero" space following the occurrence of the phenomenon. In each case, the trigger point is commonly set between the first and second oscilloscope display division of the time base (typical setting). For such a setting, the mean value before the trigger point (pre-trigger zone) for the background signal (zero would be ideal) can be determined. Depending on the approach, the mean value in the post-trigger region where the raw (not yet integrated) measurement signal (recorded phenomenon) is located, can be determined separately. This variant is especially helpful in cases where it is difficult to match the length of the registration window. Moreover, in the case when, apart from the constant component, there are slowly varying components in the signal, high-pass filtering, preceded by a spectral analysis of the signal, it turns out to be useful or even demanded.

3. Experiments Explanation and Results Discussion

3.1. Measurement Setup for Nanosecond Pulse

Experiments were performed in two independent configurations. The starting point was the laboratory configuration presented in the Figure 3, with the measurement of voltage and electric field in the neighborhood of the wire (plate-wire configuration) supplied by the kilovolts/nanoseconds pulse generator.

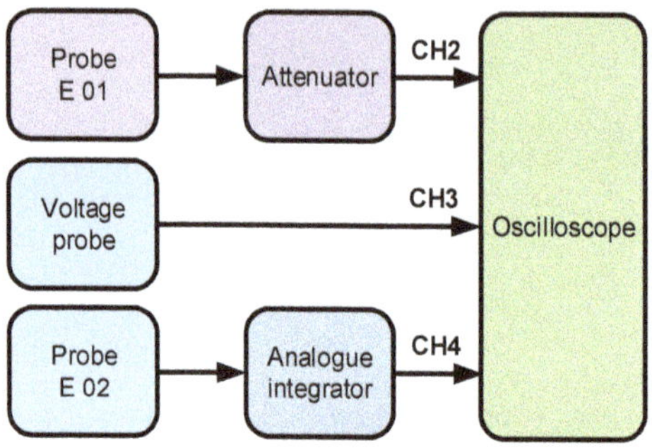

Figure 3. Laboratory setup for the electric field measurement. Probes E01 and E02—Montena SGE3-5G; Voltage probe—Tektronix P5100A; Attenuator—Montena attenuators: 10, 20, 30 dB, Analogue integrator: Montena ITR1-2U; Oscilloscope—LeCroy Waverunner 940Zi.

The results of various laboratory integration configurations will be presented in the example of measurement in the plate-wire system, used to estimate the voltage based on the value of the electric field. The measurement system consisted of three independent measurement paths. The first one was a voltage probe, the second was an electric field probe with analogue integration—a hardware, capacitive integrator and the third was an electric field probe identical to the second, but in this case the integration was performed numerically (Figure 4).

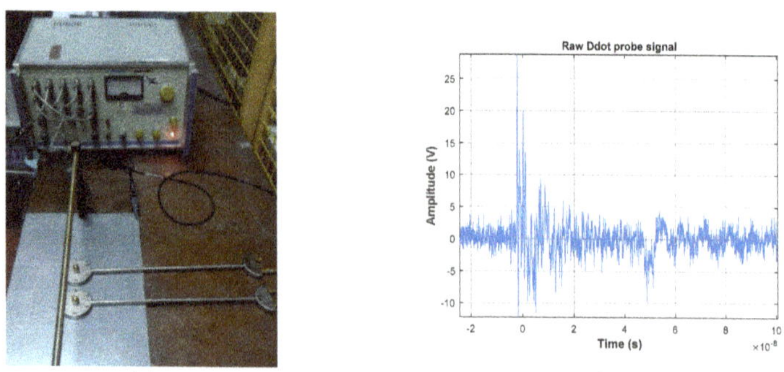

(**a**) (**b**)

Figure 4. Measurement setup (**a**), raw signal from electric field probes (**b**). Equipment used is the same as in the Figure 3 setup. Additionally, there is a pulse generator NOISE INS-420 shown in the picture. Figure 4b uses original oscilloscope time scaling. It's a convenient way to differentiate pre and post trigger signal regions.

Figure 5 presents the results of a series of measurements of a system powered by a pulse generator in the same manner as depicted above. The exemplary pulse was 2 kV amplitude of a 50 ns duration.

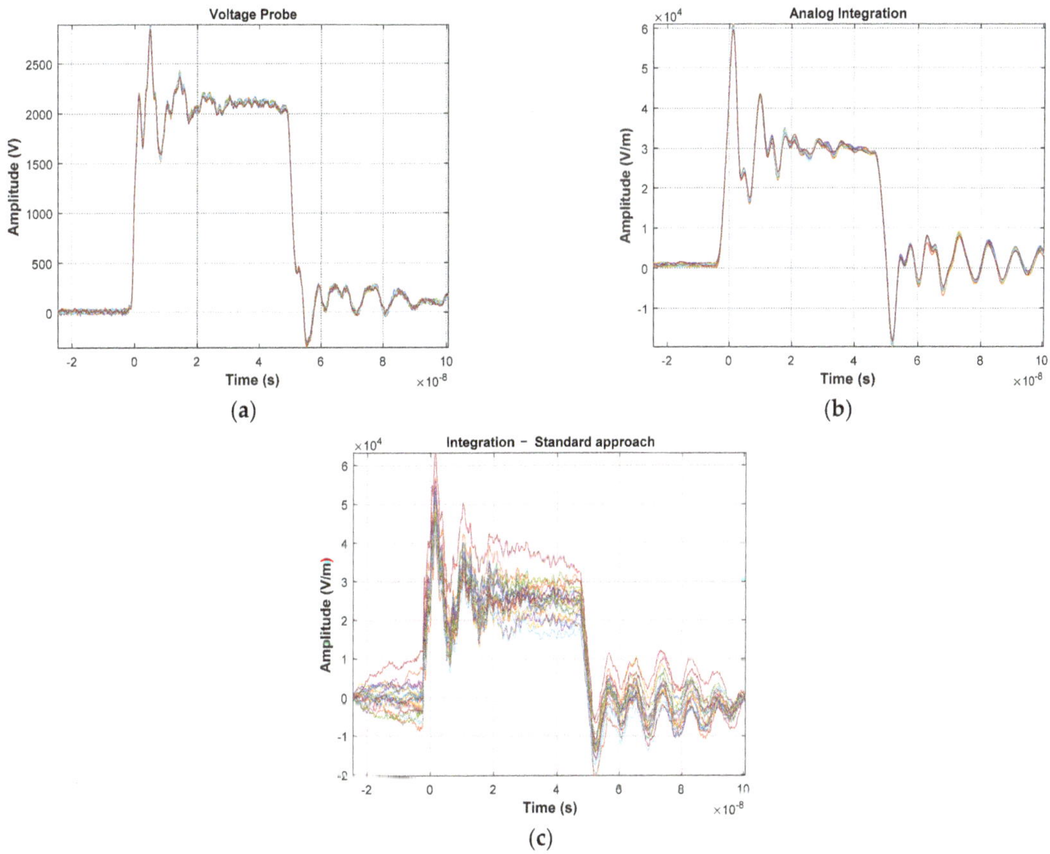

Figure 5. Measurement signals, (**a**) voltage probe, (**b**) electric field probe with analogue integration, (**c**) electric field probe with numerical integration.

In Figure 5, one can see the high repeatability and stability of the signal pulses when measured with voltage probe and ground plane field probe with hardware integration (Figure 5a,b). Unfortunately, it cannot be observed (and consequently confirmed) in the numerical integration case (Figure 5c). It is due the high sensitivity of the numerical integration to the presence of a DC and very low frequency components in the input signal. At first, in the case of numerical integration, the average value required for the proper integration process was determined for the entire recording window (range marked in red). The effect of accumulation of constant values can be seen already in the initial phase of recording, before the actual triggering ($t < 0$), which results in the appearance, instead of a zero signal, of rising or falling waveforms. As a result, the voltage impulse itself, when analyzing the measurement series, is characterized by a very large dispersion. Interpretation of the results in this case is difficult and leads to significant, unacceptable results. For this reason, a number of experiments were carried out to eliminate the above-mentioned undesirable effects. The first experiment assumed, as in the case of numerical integration carried out on an oscilloscope, that the constant component does not change in the recording window. This time, however, the value was determined and subtracted from the raw input only on the basis of the recorded background signal before the triggering of the measurement system ($t < 0$)—Figure 6.

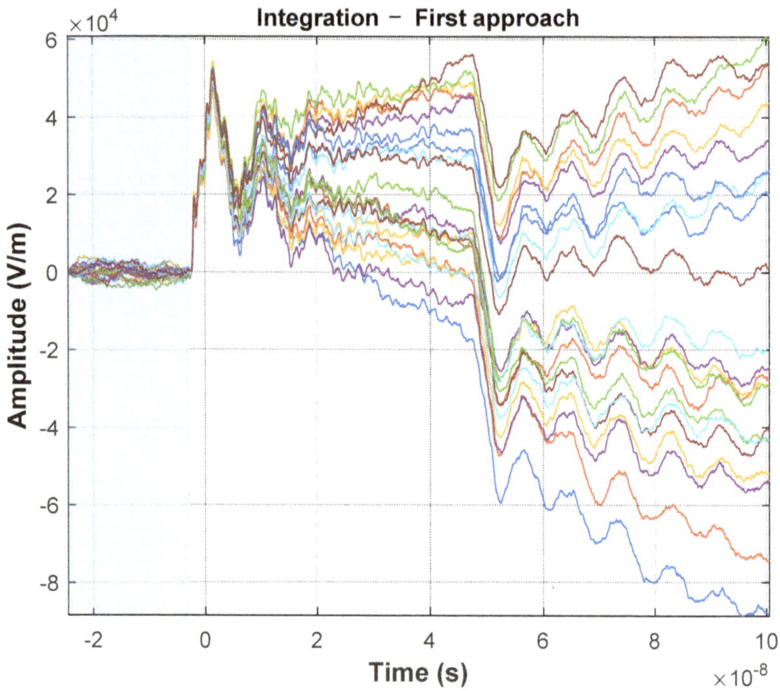

Figure 6. Integrated signal with mean value computed only for the pre-trigger region (blue region) and subtracted from signal only in that region.

The nature of the results of the first approach should be considered experimental (Figure 6). Although an improvement (signal stabilization) was achieved in the pre-trigger region, the final effect is much worse than in the case of the standard approach. This is mainly revealed in the enormous dispersion of the measurement series signals in the most important area, i.e., in the interval containing the measurement signal. Therefore, it was decided to modify the calculations so that the mean value determined in the pre-trigger interval was subtracted from the entire recorded signal (Figure 7).

As one can see in the second approach, the obtained results are better than in the first approach, but still much worse than the standard approach (Figure 5c). Nevertheless, the results obtained in the first and second approaches, related to the standard calculations, lead to the conclusion that the assumption that the constant component does not change in the recording window cannot be taken for granted. Therefore, subsequent experiments were carried out, fragmenting the recorded waveforms, determining the intervals in which only the background is visible and those in which the measurement signal was recorded.

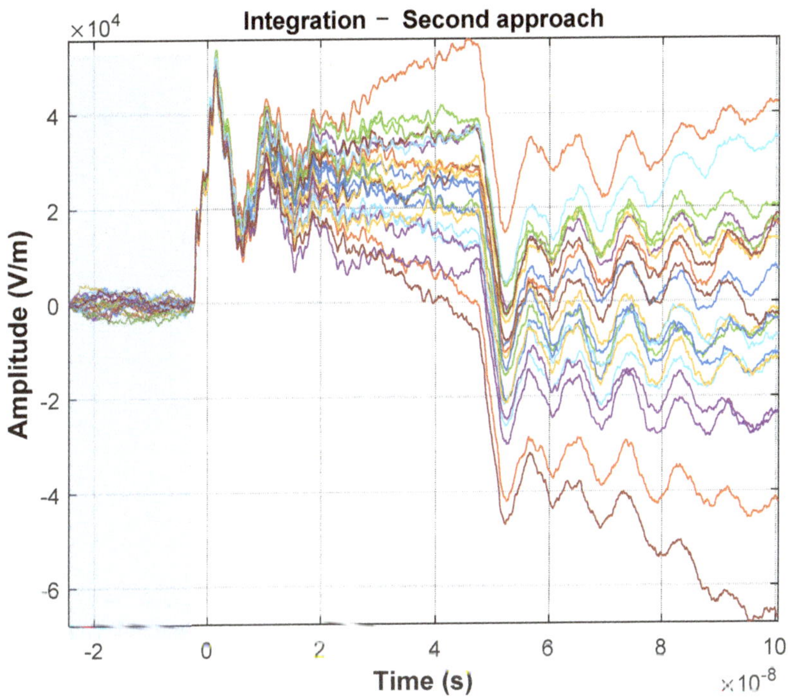

Figure 7. Integrated signal with mean value computed only for the pre-trigger region (blue region) and subtracted from all acquisition window signals.

Thus, in the third approach, mean values were determined in three intervals. Before the signal, during the signal–square pulse and after the signal. These values were subtracted independently in the respective regions. The results are shown in Figure 8, distinguishing the regions for which local mean values were determined and then used in the calculations. As can be observed, the assumption of local mean values significantly improved the obtained results. As before, the pre-trigger region does not show any trends. However, most importantly, the range in which the signal itself is located also does not show signs of rising or falling trends. It is also worth noting that the record fragments containing rising and falling edges obtained in this approach are characterized by a high repeatability in the series as compared one to another.

Comparing the results obtained in the third approach to the signal acquired with an analogue integrator, they are characterized by an even greater dispersion in the series. This is primarily due to the frequency properties of the analogue integrator and the raw numerical integration operation. This phenomenon can be minimized by averaging the results from a series of measurements, or by performing low-pass digital filtering (based on analysis of the signal spectrum), or by combining both techniques.

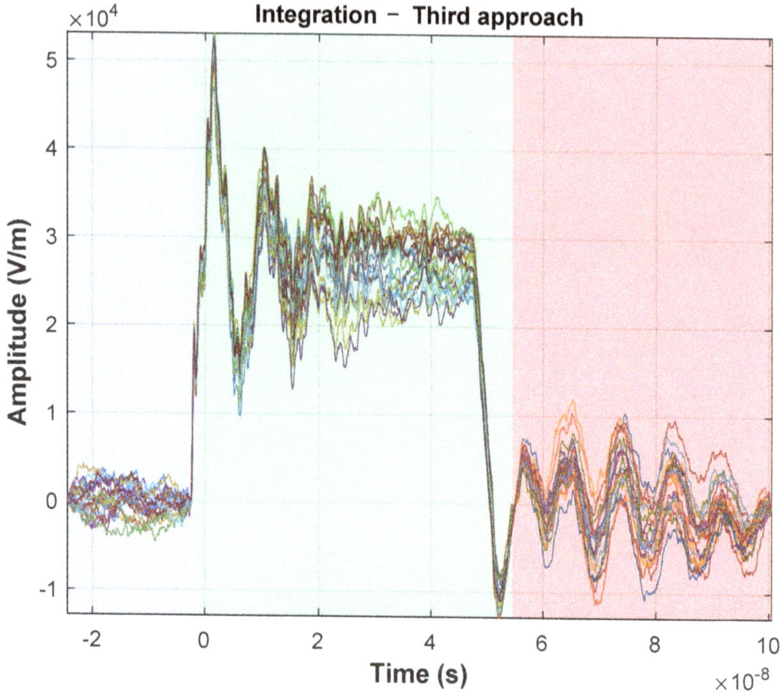

Figure 8. Integrated signal with mean value computed and subtracted from respective portions of signal (colored regions in the plot).

In order to meet the conditions of the experiment, another (fourth) approach of calculating the mean value was carried out. This time the mean value was calculated separately in pre-triggering and post-triggering intervals (Figure 9). The purpose of this test was to check how the introduction of computational simplifications would affect the final results. Though it represents much better performance compared to the first two cases, as it could be expected, the results obtained here are worse than in the third approach. The difference is especially visible in the intervals containing the rising and falling phases of the rectangular pulses. In all cases, the integration was also performed in the regions following the measurement signal. First of all, this activity made it possible to locate the end of the phenomenon, observe transients, and finally, possibly, detect wave phenomena. Summing up, the best results were achieved for the mean values calculated separately before, during and after the observed signal. Additionally in this case, the numerical low-pass filtration was carried out and the series of measurements were additionally averaged. Digital low-pass filtration parameters were selected upon the frequency spectrum of the measured square pulse signal (Figure 10) in order not to disturb the essential pulse properties. Duration of the observed pulses ranges within 50–55 ns. For this application, the low-pass filter cut off frequency was set to 400 MHz, which encompasses both a fundamental and significant number of harmonics. The obtained outcomes are presented in the Figure 11. Finally, a result very similar to the case with analogue integration was obtained. Therefore, a question can be asked about the advisability of all the above-mentioned measures. The answer is not complicated.

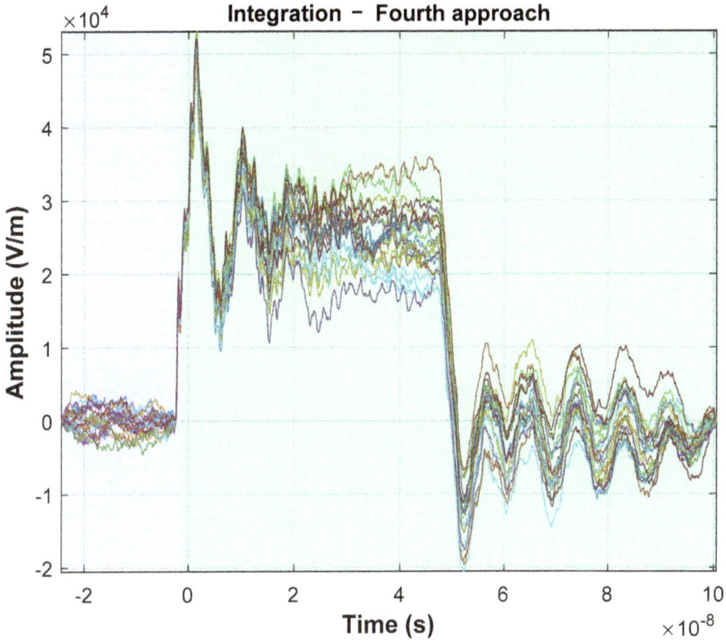

Figure 9. Integrated signal with mean value computed and subtracted from pre-trigger and post-trigger portions of signal (colored regions in the picture).

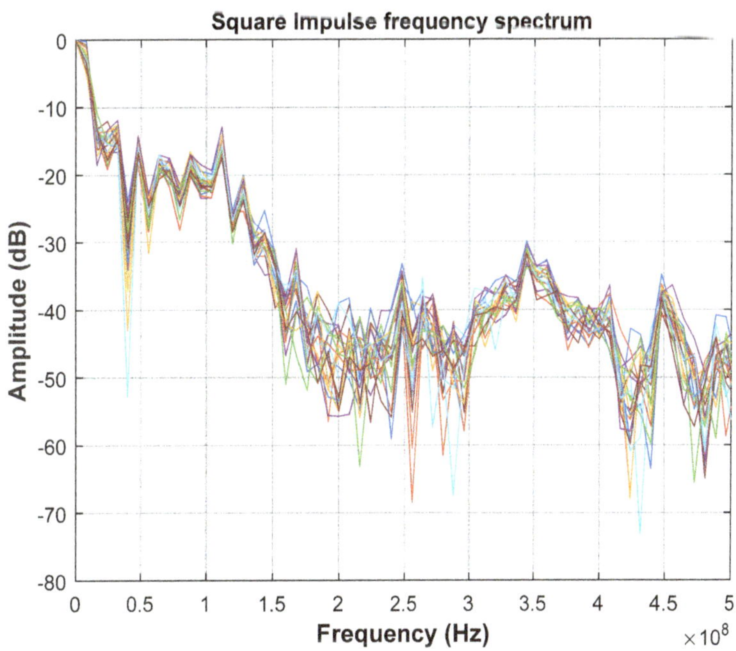

Figure 10. Frequency spectra set of measured signals.

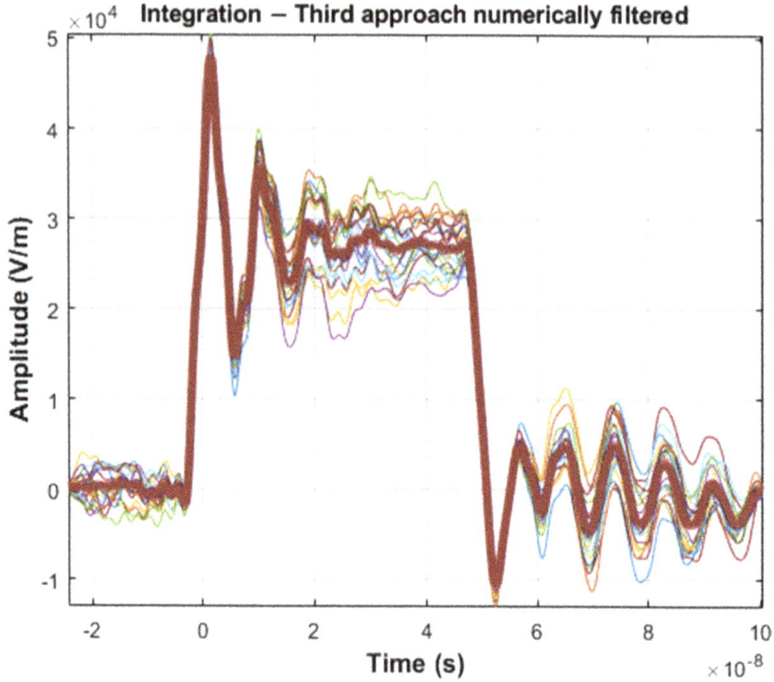

Figure 11. Digitally filtered integrated signal together with the averaged one based on the set of acquisitions.

The conducted experiments were carried out in conditions of relatively low electric field values and in a system in which the lead wires were not longer than 1 m, and the probes themselves were connected to the ground of the system.

These conditions may not always be met. In general, measurements may be performed for very large field exposure values with the requirement of the spatial distribution to be determined. In such a case, the probes will not have a galvanic reference point (ground), the recording devices will be located in special shielding boxes at a great distance from the signal source. The consequence of the last two conditions is the necessity to use optical links, ensuring galvanic isolation but also significantly limiting the range of operating voltages of the measurement setup. Under such conditions, the use of passive analogue integrators is limited.

3.2. Measurement Setup and Procedure for High Power Microwave—HPM Generator

The second, outdoor setup involved signal emitted from the HPM generator which has the form of a set of packets (pulse/sinus train) of a sinusoidal waveform with a frequency of 3 GHz. The duration of a single packet was approximately 5 μs and the repetition rate of the packets was adjustable up to 300 Hz. The total duration of one emission cycle was expressed in individual seconds. The measurement system setup is shown in Figure 12.

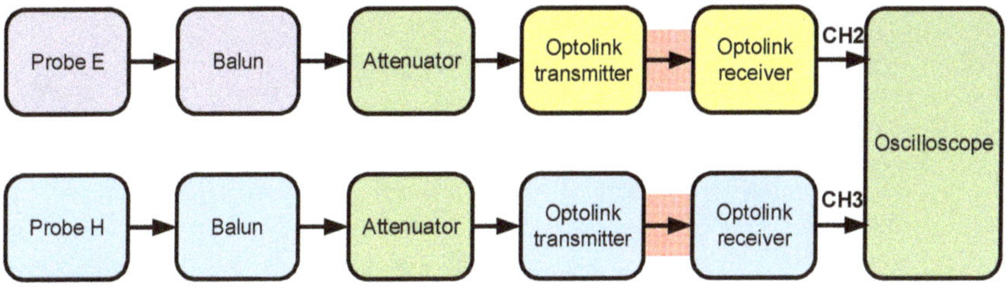

Figure 12. Measurement setup for the electric E and magnetic H fields. Probe E—Montena SGE3-5G; Probe H—Montena SGM2G; Balun—Montena BL3-5G; Optolink-Montena MOL3000 + FCLB100; Attenuator—Montena attenuators: 10, 20, 30 dB; Oscilloscope—LeCroy Waverunner 940Zi.

Field measurements with the HPM generator were made at distances of 10, 20 and 30 m from the signal source (parabolic antenna). Each time a set of a dozen or so sinusoidal packets was registered and the first of them was rejected due to its unspecified nature, which stems from the properties of the generator itself (Figure 13).

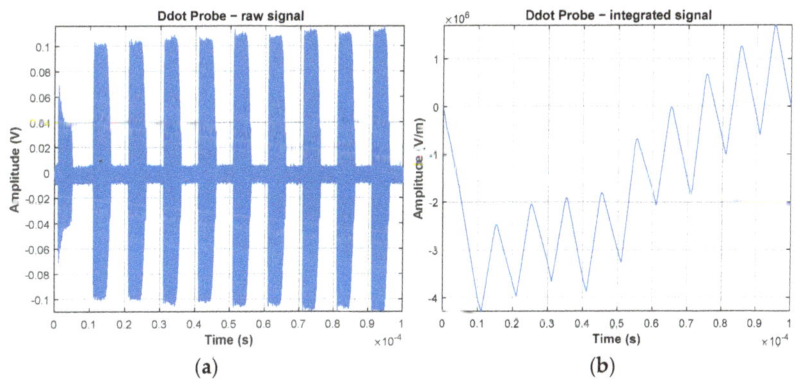

Figure 13. Sample HPM sinusoidal packets registration (**a**), together with initial integration (**b**)

The recording of fast-changing bursts of pulses repeated with a relatively low repetition frequency (GHz/kHz) requires an appropriate configuration of the recording device (oscilloscope), but thankfully it is typically available in devices operating in the Gigahertz bands.

Based on the acquired signal (Figure 13), initial integration was performed, but it was seriously disturbed. Integration of sinusoidal packets should result in sinusoidal wave form as well. Such an expectation cannot be found in the Figure 13.

Despite the differential nature of the probes used, the recorded signal showed noticeable low-frequency components (up to 2 MHz in Figure 14), which were the source of significant errors in the integration operation (Figure 13b). Thus, the traditional integration stage was additionally supplemented by high-pass filtering, with the cut-off frequency determined on the basis of the observed signal spectrum. The cut-off frequency of the filter was set to encompass the slow varying signal components—2 MHz region on Figure 14. Sample results are shown in Figure 15.

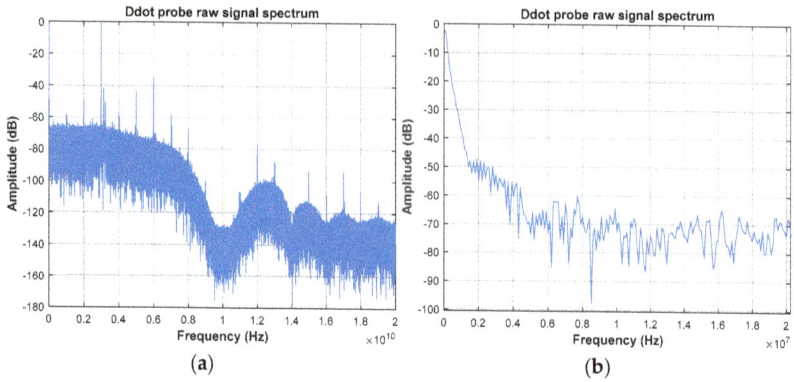

Figure 14. Electric field raw signal frequency spectrum, full bandwidth from 0 to 20 GHz (**a**), limited bandwidth 0 to 20 MHz (**b**).

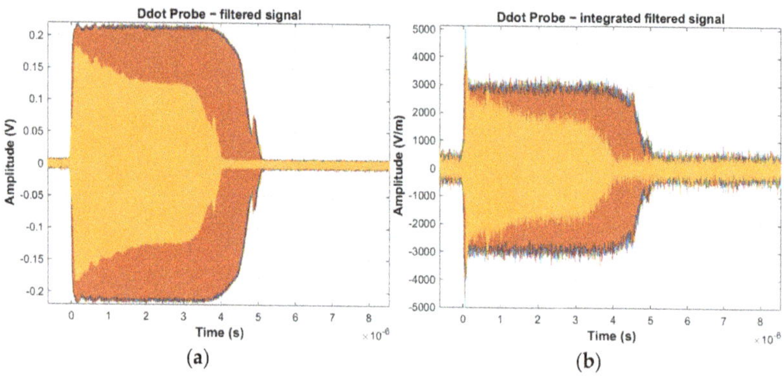

Figure 15. An example of electric field measurement signal, raw filtered signal from D-dot probe (**a**), integrated filtered signal from D-dot probe (**b**).

Although the electric field was the fundamental measurement parameter, it was also decided to register the magnetic field in the presented measurement system. This was primarily due to the intention to obtain as much information on the recorded phenomenon as possible. Independently, the reconstruction, re-alignment and configuration of the source and measurement object in the presented case is very complex and complicated. In practice, it becomes a one-time measurement observation opportunity. Registration of electric and magnetic fields allows for additional verification of correctness of the results by computation of the impedance of the medium, which in ideal conditions is 120π Ω. Based on the registration of fields in the presented system (Figure 16), the determined value of the medium impedance is 467 Ω +/− 26%, which is a satisfactory result because only the catalogue data of the measurement system component were taken into account when estimating the error, neglecting the imperfection of the geometric configuration of the measurement system.

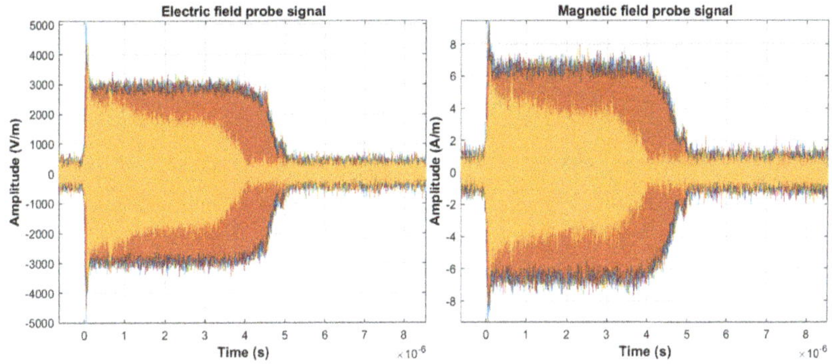

(a) (b)

Figure 16. Measurement results for the electric (**a**) and magnetic (**b**) fields measurement records in the outdoor tests.

Issues related to signal processing (integration operation) have the same course irrespective of whether they concern registration of electric or magnetic field. Therefore, the paper presents this issue only on the example of an electric field (most valuable parameter in the measurements performed).

4. Discussion and Comparison of Results

The necessary integration of the differential probes signal can be carried out in many ways. Hardware/analogue integrators give the possibility of direct integration, but their use is justified in a case where the signal frequency band is known or the measured signals have a relatively high amplitude and are grounded. However, these requirements cannot always be met. This is especially difficult in the case of spatial measurements (floating signals) and additionally high-energy EM fields. For safety reasons, the distances between the measurement point and the measurement instrumentation location are large. In such cases, fiber optic links are commonly used. Their basic feature, which is often a requirement, is galvanic insulation of the signal connection. However, these links limit the amplitude of the transmitted signals. In such systems (floating and low-amplitude signals), numerical integration is commonly used. A list of the different signal integration techniques is presented in Table 1.

In the work [19], passive RC integrators were used to integrate the signal from B-dot probes installed in the magnetically insulated transmission line—MITL. The authors get good results, but it should be noted that the probe is installed directly in the MITL line, where one is dealing with the reduction of interferences. In addition, the spatial configuration of the measurement system is constant and does not change during the measurements.

Yako at al. in the work [20] present the B-dot probe with internal integration (self-integration) obtained by the appropriate selection of the parameters of the measurement circuit. The system is tested with standard 8–20 µs pulses with a current amplitude ranging from 5 kA to 37 kA. As in the work [19], the spatial configuration of the system is constant, and the measurement circuit has a short signal path. In addition, the frequency parameters of the signal are known. The paper [21] presents the process of laboratory calibration of B-dot probes with pulses of a rise time from 4 to 400 ns. Integration is carried out numerically. Due to the stable parameters of the generated pulses, the standard method of eliminating the constant component (signal mean value) was used. The use of numerical integration and the elimination of the average value by means of low-pass FIR filters are presented in [22]. The authors carry out measurements with D-dot probes. Conditioning and signal processing is carried out using a dedicated (developed) measurement instrument instead of the oscilloscope.

Table 1. Integration methods comparison.

Integration Type	Method	Common Signal Parameter: Signal Rise Time	Requirements, Measurement Conditions	REF
Hardware	Passive integrator 1 μs or 5 μs	Magnetically insulated transmission line (MITL). t_{rise} = 96 ns	Directly in the transmission line, galvanic connection	[19]
Hardware	Self-integration probe selected frequency band.	Lightning current t_{rise} = 8 μs	Known signal parameters, unchanged measurement setup configuration, galvanic connection	[20]
Numerical	Mean value removal	Calibration testing signal t_{rise} = 4.2 ns	unchanged measurement setup configuration, galvanic connection	[21]
Numerical	FIR filter	High-power microwave (HPM) pulses t_{rise} = 3 ns	Self-developed measurement instrument	[22]
Numerical	FFT and FIR filter	HV pulses measured in the close neighborhood of the cable $t_{rise} \leq 1$ ns	Short connections, signal processing in Matlab	[23]
Numerical	Local Mean value (segmented signal) removal with an optional FFT and FIR filter	HV pulses, HPM pulses, $t_{rise} \leq 5$ ns	Floating signals, spatial, outdoor measurement. Numeric operation computed directly on oscilloscope	Current work

In turn, Huiscamp et al. [23] present a method of measurement of very fast voltage pulses (t_{rise} < 1 ns) with amplitudes up to 14 kV with D-dot probes mounted directly on the coaxial cable, with which the pulse is transmitted. The Authors propose to record the signal using an oscilloscope and then post-process it based on FFT analysis, elimination of the mean value component, taking into calculations the parameters of the transmission path and finally numerical integration. Signal processing is performed in the Matlab environment.

The method proposed in this article is supposed to be effective and require relatively simple numerical operations, although more complex operations such as FFT and filtration are not excluded. Compared to the methods listed above, the approach presented in the article is characterized by independent determination and elimination of the local mean values in signal segments. Its simplicity also makes it possible to be implemented directly on the oscilloscope. The measurement signal may contain variable frequency parameters and an average value that varies along the acquisition. Sensing of the EM field in space excludes the galvanic connection to the ground, which is guaranteed by the optical link. The spatial configuration of the measurement system can vary and the distance between the measurement instrument-oscilloscope location and the measurement probes does not matter.

The above features make it possible to use the method in the outdoor EM field measurements. In addition, the reliable value of the measured EM field is obtained right after registration, which in the case of EM field tests is often more important than a low measurement error.

5. Conclusions and Summary

Based on the waveforms recorded in the measurement grounded circuits, high repeatability of the waveforms can be observed (Figure 5a,b). The effectiveness of the proposed and used integration methods can be evidenced by the measure of the scatter of values, containing the residual "constants" after integration. Based on Figure 5a,b, it is reasonable to conclude that the recorded waveform in the final phase has zero value. However, in the first approach to the implementation of integration (Figure 6), it can be observed that this is not the case at all. The scatter of the final values in this case varies from −83 kV/m to 60 kV/m, i.e., the rate of changes is at the level of 143 kV/m. In the second approach (Figure 7), the respective value is noticeably smaller, but still 104 kV/m. In the third and fourth approaches (Figures 8 and 9), where the integration was performed segmented, these values are mutually comparable and reach only 0.3 kV/m, which proves high effectiveness of the applied modifications. The elimination of the trend in the integrated waveforms significantly facilitates or even enables a correct reading of the field parameters after integration.

The presented problem is common as measurement signals are acquired with the use of derivative nature probes. It extends the instrument (oscilloscope) user manuals procedure for which signal is being integrated and contains the DC component that is not varying along the acquisition buffer (window). In the practical conditioning procedure, it was assumed that the mean value of the signal was a variable along time in the recorded signal window. Based on that, the acquisition window was divided into pre and post trigger regions along with the signal and background noise content periods. Additionally, the measured signals frequency parameters were also taken into the account allowing for a proper selection of frequency of numerical filtration parameters. The latter technique promises to be a useful procedure in the integration computation. The presented HPM pulse examples, due to the nature of the measured signal, were not a demanding task and allowed for the elimination of slow-varying components (up to 5 MHz band). The filtration process is not constrained to such signals and can be applied in general as an integration technique. Each time, it should be adapted to the signals being measured, of course, so that it does not disturb the information of the observed phenomenon. Finally, as a result presented in the paper, it was possible to effectively determine the waveforms describing the changes in the electric and magnetic fields using the numerical integration operation. Removal of DC and additionally low-frequency components from the input raw signal, made it possible to avoid the accumulation of non-zero average values of the integrated waveform, which in turn gives the effect of saturation after integration.

Signal processing preceding the essential integration procedure assumes that it is performed under given conditions. First, the DC band components are not varying in time along the acquisition window (oscilloscope recording) and are relatively easy to investigate. In practice, it does not have to be fulfilled, thus instead of a precise mean value component one gets only an estimation. This, in turn, deteriorates the final results. The idea of mean values computed independently in different sub-periods of the acquisition window is also quite simple in terms of computational power requirements. On the other hand, the application of different procedures can significantly decrease the distortion of the measurement signal. Surely it can be a starting point to the automatic or at least semi-automatic processing procedure.

Author Contributions: Conceptualization, A.J., B.D., J.S. (Jacek Starzyński) and J.S. (Jan Sroka); methodology, A.J., B.D., J.S. (Jacek Starzyński) and J.S. (Jan Sroka); software, A.J.; validation, A.J., B.D., J.S. (Jacek Starzyński) and J.S. (Jan Sroka); formal analysis, A.J., B.D., J.S. (Jacek Starzyński) and J.S. (Jan Sroka); investigation, A.J., B.D. and J.S. (Jacek Starzyński); resources, A.J., B.D., J.S. (Jacek Starzyński) and J.S. (Jan Sroka); writing—original draft preparation, A.J., B.D. and J.S. (Jan Sroka); data curation, A.J.; writing—review and editing, A.J., B.D., J.S. (Jan Sroka) and J.S. (Jacek Starzyński); data curation, A.J.; visualization, A.J.; supervision, J.S. (Jacek Starzyński) and J.S. (Jan Sroka); project administration, J.S. (Jacek Starzyński); funding acquisition, J.S. (Jacek Starzyński). All authors have read and agreed to the published version of the manuscript.

Funding: The work was also supported by the CB POB within the project "High power and frequency electromagnetic impulse generator", "Generator wysokoenergetycznych, szybkozmiennych impulsów elektromagnetycznych (GWSIEM)", POB_182_42_Z01_POB7_2021.

Institutional Review Board Statement: Not applicable.

Informed Consent Statement: Not applicable.

Data Availability Statement: Not applicable.

Conflicts of Interest: The authors declare no conflict of interest.

References

1. Mariscotti, A. A Magnetic Field Probe with MHz Bandwidth and 7-Decade Dynamic Range. *IEEE Trans. Instrum. Meas.* **2009**, *58*, 2643–2652. [CrossRef]
2. Filik, K.; Hajder, S.; Masłowski, G. Multi-Stroke Lightning Interaction with Wiring Harness: Experimental Tests and Modelling. *Energies* **2021**, *14*, 2106. [CrossRef]
3. Novac, B.M.; Smith, I.R.; Rankin, D.F.; Hubbard, M. A Fast and Compact theta-Pinch Electromagnetic Flux-Compression Generator. *J. Phys. D Appl. Phys.* **2004**, *37*, 3041–3055. [CrossRef]
4. Lv, Q.-A.; Lei, B.; Gao, M.; Li, Z.-Y.; Chi, X.-P.; Li, H. Magnetic Flux Compression Generator as Future Military Pulsed Power Supply. *IEEE Trans. Magn.* **2009**, *45*, 545–549. [CrossRef]
5. Zhang, H.; Shu, T.; Liu, S.; Zhang, Z.; Song, L.; Zhang, H. A Compact Modular 5 GW Pulse PFN-Marx Generator for Driving HPM Source. *Electronics* **2021**, *10*, 545. [CrossRef]
6. Rąbkowski, J.; Łasica, A.; Zdanowski, M.; Wrona, G.; Starzyński, J. Portable DC Supply Based on SiC Power Devices for High-Voltage Marx Generator. *Electronics* **2021**, *10*, 313. [CrossRef]
7. Mucsi, V.; Ayub, A.S.; Muhammad-Sukki, F.; Zulkipli, M.; Muhtazaruddin, M.N.; Mohd Saudi, A.S.; Ardila-Rey, J.A. Lightning Protection Methods for Wind Turbine Blades: An Alternative Approach. *Appl. Sci.* **2020**, *10*, 2130. [CrossRef]
8. Albano, M.; Haddad, A.M.; Griffiths, H.; Coventry, P. Environmentally Friendly Compact Air-Insulated High-Voltage Substations. *Energies* **2018**, *11*, 2492. [CrossRef]
9. Li, Z.; Zhang, Q.; Zhang, L.; Liu, F.; Tan, X. Design of Rogowski Coil with external integrator for measurement of lightning current up to 400 kA. *Przegląd Elektrotechniczny* **2011**, *87*, 188–192.
10. Wang, H.; Fu, Z.; Wang, Y.; Tai, H.; Qin, S.; Liao, X. A Time-Domain Feedback Calibration Method for Air-Coil Magnetic Sensor. *Measurement* **2019**, *135*, 61–70. [CrossRef]
11. Norhisam, M.; Norrimah, A.; Wagiran, R.; Sidek, R.M.; Mariun, N.; Wakiwaka, H. Consideration of Theoretical Equation for Output Voltage of Linear Displacement Sensor Using Meander Coil and Pattern Guide. *Sens. Actuators A Phys.* **2008**, *147*, 470–473. [CrossRef]
12. Marconato, N.; Cavazzana, R.; Bettini, P.; Rigoni, A. Accurate Magnetic Sensor System Integrated Design. *Sensors* **2020**, *20*, 2929. [CrossRef] [PubMed]
13. Šaliga, J.; Kováč, O.; Andráš, I. Analog-to-Information Conversion with Random Interval Integration. *Sensors* **2021**, *21*, 3543. [CrossRef] [PubMed]
14. Murray, T.S.; Pouliquen, P.O.; Andreou, A.G. Design of a Parallel Sampling Encoder for Analog to Information (A2I) Converters: Theory, Architecture and CMOS Implementation. *Electronics* **2013**, *2*, 57–79. [CrossRef]
15. Silva, V.M.L.; Souza, C.P.; Freire, R.C.S.; Arruda, B.W.S.; Gurjão, E.C.; Reis, V.L. Novel IEEE-STD-1241-Based Test Methods for Analog-to-Information Converter. *IEEE Trans. Instrum. Meas.* **2020**, *69*, 1609–1619. [CrossRef]
16. Możdżyński, K. Simple Digital Integration Algorithm with Saturation and Drift Elimination Based Second-Order Generalized Integrator. In Proceedings of the 2015 9th International Conference on Compatibility and Power Electronics (CPE), Costa da Caparica, Portugal, 24–26 June 2015; pp. 312–316.
17. Integrator 1.2 µs Type ITR1-2U User's Manual. Montena, Rossens Switzerland 2015. Available online: www.montena.com (accessed on 15 January 2022).
18. Chapra, S.; Canale, R. *Numerical Methods for Engineers*, 8th ed.; MacGraw-Hill Education: New York, NY, USA, 2021.
19. Wei, B.; Guo, F.; Wang, Z.; Qing, Y.; Yuan, J.; Liang, J.; Xie, W. Frequency Response Properties of the B-Dot Sensors Employed on a High Current Pulsed Power Facility. *IEEE Sens. J.* **2021**, *21*, 17732–17737. [CrossRef]
20. Yao, C.; Xiao, Q.; Mi, Y.; Yuan, T.; Li, C.; Sima, W. Contactless Measurement of Lightning Current Using Self-Integrating B-Dot Probe. *IEEE Trans. Dielectr. Electr. Insul.* **2011**, *18*, 1323–1327. [CrossRef]
21. Agry, A.A.; Schill, R.A. Calibration of Electromagnetic Dot Sensor—Part 1: B-Dot Mode. *IEEE Sens. J.* **2014**, *14*, 3101–3110. [CrossRef]
22. Jakubowski, J.; Kuchta, M.; Kubacki, R. D-Dot Sensor Response Improvement in the Evaluation of High-Power Microwave Pulses. *Electronics* **2021**, *10*, 123. [CrossRef]
23. Huiskamp, T.; Beckers, F.J.C.M.; van Heesch, E.J.M.; Pemen, A.J.M. B-Dot and D-Dot Sensors for (Sub)Nanosecond High-Voltage and High-Current Pulse Measurements. *IEEE Sens. J.* **2016**, *16*, 3792–3801. [CrossRef]

energies

MDPI

Article

Numerical Investigation and Optimization of Cooling Flow Field Design for Proton Exchange Membrane Fuel Cell

Jiangnan Song [1], Ying Huang [1,*], Yi Liu [2], Zongpeng Ma [1], Lunjun Chen [1], Taike Li [1] and Xiang Zhang [1]

1 School of Mechanical Engineering, Guizhou University, Guiyang 550025, China; haitangguo233@163.com (J.S.); mazongpeng99@163.com (Z.M.); 17635133834@163.com (L.C.); Jacklee519240@163.com (T.L.); zx17315091761@163.com (X.Z.)

2 School of Data Science, Guizhou Institute of Technology, Guiyang 550003, China; 20140295@git.edu.cn

* Correspondence: yhuang3@gzu.edu.cn

Abstract: High temperatures and non-uniform temperatures both have a negative bearing on the performance of proton exchange membrane fuel cells. The temperature of proton exchange membrane fuel cells can be lowered by reasonably distributed cooling channels. The flow field distribution of five different cooling plates is designed, and the temperature uniformity, pressure drop and velocity of each cooling flow field are analyzed by computational fluid dynamics technology. The results show that while the pressure drop is high, the flow channel distribution of a multi-spiral flow field and honeycomb structure flow field contribute more to improving the temperature uniformity. As the coolant is blocked by the uniform plate, it is found that although the flow field channel with a uniform plate has poor performance in terms of temperature uniformity, its heat dissipation capacity is still better than that of the traditional serpentine flow field. The multi-spiral flow field has the strongest ability to maintain the temperature stability in the cooling plate when the heat flux increases. The increase in Reynolds number, although increasing the pressure drop, can reduce the maximum temperature and temperature difference of the flow field, ameliorate the temperature uniformity and improve the heat transfer capacity of the cooling plate.

Keywords: flow field design; structural optimization; honeycomb structure flow field; proton exchange membrane fuel cell; computational fluid dynamics

Citation: Song, J.; Huang, Y.; Liu, Y.; Ma, Z.; Chen, L.; Li, T.; Zhang, X. Numerical Investigation and Optimization of Cooling Flow Field Design for Proton Exchange Membrane Fuel Cell. *Energies* **2022**, *15*, 2609. https://doi.org/10.3390/en15072609

Academic Editor: Antonino S. Aricò

Received: 3 March 2022
Accepted: 30 March 2022
Published: 2 April 2022

1. Introduction

As one of the solutions to the global energy crisis and environmental problems, the proton exchange membrane fuel cell (PEMFC) has the advantages of near-zero emissions and high conversion efficiency [1–5]. However, the commercialization process of PEMFC still faces many challenges. Among them, the hydrothermal management of PEMFC also needs effective technical breakthroughs, which is the research focus of scholars today [6,7]. During the operation of a PEMFC, heat will be generated with the generation of electric energy. Fuel cells primarily generate heat from the entropic heat of reactions, the irreversibility of the electrochemical reactions, ohmic resistances and heat from the condensation of water vapors [8]. The increase in temperature in a certain range is conducive to improving the activity of the catalytic layer and accelerating the rate of the electrochemical reaction, but if the heat energy is not discharged in time, the overall temperature of the PEMFC will be too high and the local temperature distribution will be uneven, which will seriously degrade its performance [9–11].

A cooling plate is an indispensable structure of a fuel cell stack. It can reduce the temperature of the PEMFC and improve the temperature distribution in terms of non-uniformity [12,13]. Many studies have proven that a reasonably distributed flow channel can effectively improve the uniformity of temperature distribution during fuel cell operation, reduce the pressure drop of the cooling flow channel, avoid the occurrence of fluid blockage and cause the cooling liquid to circulate quickly.

Kurnia et al. [14] studied the heat transfer performance of parallel, serpentine, wavy, coiled and novel hybrid channels, and the coiled-base channel was discovered to be a desirable option, particularly in sensitive applications where cooling performance is crucial. Jeon [15] examined the cyclic and single cells and discovered that at high current densities, the cyclic cell's voltage was lowered due to increasing ohmic losses. The innovative serpentine channel exhibits the highest uniformity index of temperature distribution, power density and pressure drop, according to Atyabi et al. [16]. In comparison to other types, the design obtained the lowest temperature observed at the catalyst layer. The cooling field in serpentine channels had several passes and a high channel length, which allowed heat to be removed from the system but resulted in a substantial pressure drop across the system. Matian et al. [17] reported that increasing the size of the cooling channels resulted in a more uniform temperature distribution because more air could pass through the channels for a given pressure drop, allowing more thermal energy to be exchanged between the plate and cooling air. According to the research of Wilberforce et al. [18], a mixture of serpentine and parallel flow channels was intended to deliver better performance, owing to the prevalence of the serpentine channel portion, while still ensuring an overall lower pressure drop given the presence of parallel bypass channels, and the adapted serpentine designs with bypass channels presented a pressure drop 50 times lower than the classical serpentine design. Rahgoshay et al. [19] performed numerical analysis on two conventional cooling plates with serpentine and parallel flow fields, and found that modifying the rate of heat transfer has an effect on the performance of PEMFC and PEMFC with serpentine cooling flow fields compared to parallel cooling flow fields. In terms of effective physical parameters, the serpentine flow field offers greater cooling performance. According to the research of Yang et al. [20], operating temperatures have been shown to have significant effects on water distribution, and cells running at low temperatures have been shown to be more prone to severe water flooding, particularly downstream. Shian et al. [21] also discovered the essentiality of downstream water management; they investigated traditional straight channel cooling plates and innovative non-uniform flow channel designs, and the results showed that the downstream flow area improves the heat dissipation performance of the cooling plate. The results show that the optimum thermal, water, and gas management may be found in serpentine-based channel designs, and because of the substantially smaller pressure drop, the innovative hybrid parallel-serpentine-oblique-fin channel design generates the most net power. Sasmito et al. [22] evaluated numerically the performance of various gas and coolant channel designs simultaneously. Due to the existence of complex turns, Ravishankar et al. [23] presented four new designs and discovered that in comparison to serpentine, the pressure drop needed to accelerate the flow is higher in spiral and innovative designs. Castelain et al. [24] created an experimental device in order to characterize the chaotic geometries' thermal properties under consideration, and the measurements corroborated the simulated values, which indicate that for chaotic geometries, the interior convective heat transfer coefficient significantly increases when compared to the tube with no bends. Liu et al. [25] used the genetic algorithm with several objectives to optimize the operating condition, and then used the multi-objective genetic algorithm to optimize the PEMFC's channel design based on the ideal operating condition. The best channel produced through optimization was a tapered channel with heights of 0.3909 mm and 0.2042 mm at the inlet and outflow, respectively.

Innovative heat dissipation methods combined with a traditional cooling flow field are also being studied. Wen et al. [26] cut six pieces of heat conducting pyrolytic graphite into a channel shape, bound them to six central cathode airway plates and added forced convection; the results showed that this significantly reduced the volume, the temperature control system's weight and cooling capacity. Lin et al. [27] carried out a numerical analysis of a PEMFC stack with water cooling to determine the impact of configurations and cathode operating parameters on stack power density and efficiency of the system. The orthogonal analysis method has been shown to be reliable in obtaining the best with a confidence level nearing 95%, a mixture of setups and cathode operating conditions was discovered. Using graphite plates, Yin et al. [28] developed a new kW-scale air-cooled PEMFC stack. The experimental results confirmed that the stack with a channel on the edge performs better than the standard stack without edge channels. Because of the improved internal water balance, the counter-cross flow operation is better for stack performance than the co-cross flow operation. To improve the thermal management of a 10-cell air-cooled PEMFC stack. As heat spreaders, Zhao et al. [29] used five vapor chambers. The findings suggest that a high effective thermal conductivity can improve heat transfer and even out the temperature in the stack. Afshari et al. [30] compared the cooling performance of four different design methods, parallel flow field, serpentine flow field and metal foam porous medium flow field, among the models tested, a model with a porous metal foam flow field is the right alternative for decreasing the surface temperature difference, highest surface temperature, and average surface temperature. According to the simulation, Zhang et al. [31] investigated a novel method of cooling for a PEMFC stack; low membrane hydration is also caused by a higher temperature in the stack and, as a result, cell performance is limited, and the current density distribution is not uniform. The current cooling technique may be improved by boosting the heat transfer co-efficient between the stack and the coolant to minimize local overheating and improve the cell performance, according to the findings. To eliminate the need for a bulky humidifier and to lighten the cooling load of PEMFCs. Hwang et al. [32] used an external-mixing air-assist atomizer to build a cathode humidification and evaporative cooling system, and discovered that the humidification impact increased stack performance while the evaporative cooling effect decreased coolant temperature at the stack output. Saeedan et al. [33] proposed using water-CuO nanofluid as the coolant fluid and filling the flow field in the cooling plates with metal foam. The results showed that at low Reynolds numbers, the role of nanoparticles in improving temperature uniformity is more prominent. Furthermore, metal foam can lower the maximum temperature in the cooling channel by approximately 16.5 K and uniformize the temperature distribution, while the pressure drop increases only slightly. Asghari et al. [34] investigated the design of a cooling flow field as well as a thermal management sub-system of a 5 kW PEMFC system. The numerical simulation results show that a higher flow rate of coolant results in a more uniform temperature distribution, whereas a lower flow rate results in less pressure drop and parasitic losses. Ghasemi et al. [35] designed and simulated six cooling flow field designs. The results show that the spiral cooling flow field has the most uniform temperature distribution, but the pressure drop is large.

According to the literature created by predecessors, the design of a PEMFC cooling flow field shows a diversified trend, but there are still few field designs, especially for high-temperature PEMFCs, and most designs are lacking in innovation. This paper presents five innovative PEMFC cooling flow field designs, and analyzes the heat dissipation performance of the cooling plate by comparing the temperature and temperature uniformity, maximum temperature, pressure drop and cooling liquid velocity between the traditional serpentine cooling flow field and each new flow field. In addition, the operating conditions are optimized according to the numerical analysis.

2. Model Description

2.1. Computational Model

The fuel cell stack consists of multiple fuel cell units stacked together. The cooling plates are distributed at both ends of a single fuel cell and are in close contact with the bipolar plate. The heat generated during PEMFC operation enters the cooling plate through heat conduction in the bipolar plate, and then the heat is taken away by the coolant circulation in the cooling plate. Figure 1 shows the structure of the fuel cell stack.

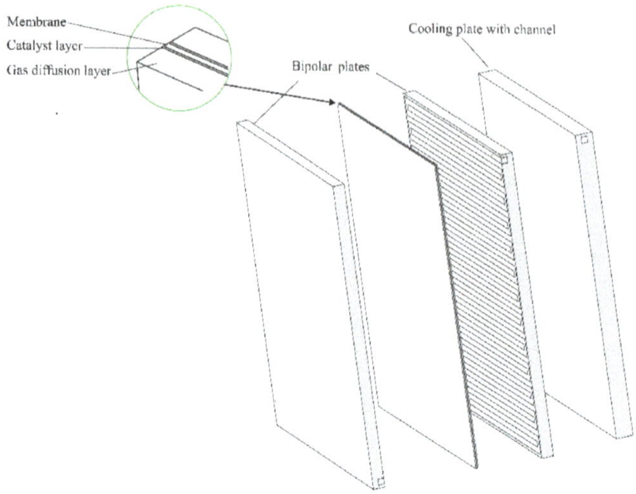

Figure 1. Single cell structure of PEMFC.

Figure 2 shows the cooling plate model to be calculated. Heat is transported from both sides of the cooling plate during its actual working process. The cooling plate is divided from the central plane according to the cooling plate's symmetry for ease of calculation, and the half model of the overall cooling plate is analyzed to simplify the calculation. The heat flux acts on the bottom, and the value is a fixed value of 5000 W/m^2, which is a common value encountered during typical PEMFC operation. The heat produced by PEMFCs is comparable to the output cell power (with PEMFCs with a rated power of 1 kW, around 1–1.5 kW of heat is produced) [36].

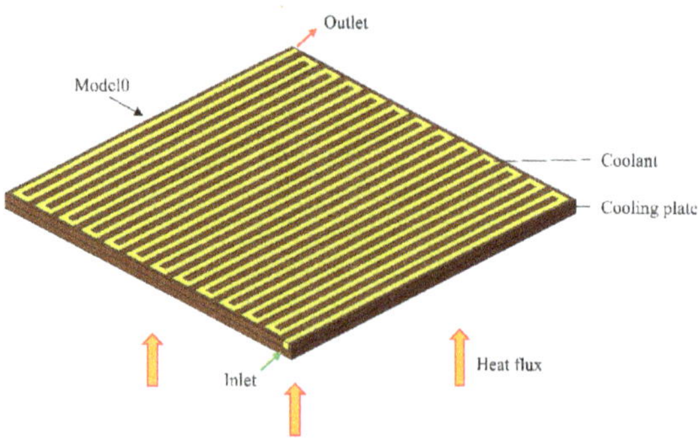

Figure 2. Calculation model of cooling plate.

Five different cooling channels are designed, as shown in Figure 3. Among them, model 1 is a multi-serpentine flow field, model 2 is a multi-turn flow field, model 3 is a multi-helical flow field, model 4 is a flow field with a uniform plate, and model 5 is a honeycomb structure flow field. The parameters of the geometric structure are shown in Table 1.

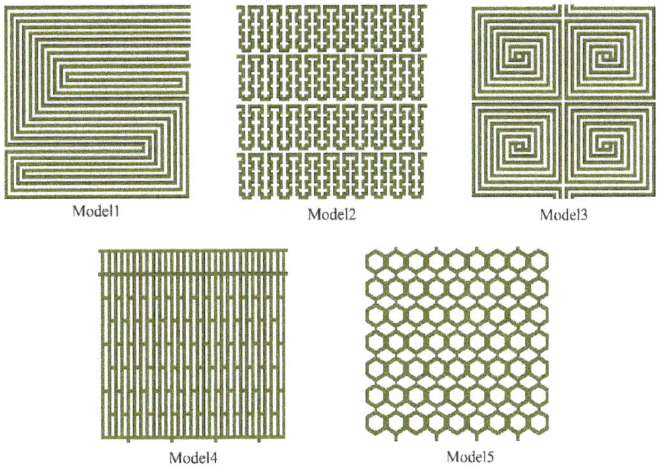

Figure 3. Design scheme of flow fields.

Table 1. Model parameters of flow fields.

Parameters	Values
Cooling area length	180 mm
Cooling area width	180 mm
Cooling area height	3 mm
Channel and rib width	3 mm
Channel depth	1 mm

The steady-state calculation formula for calculating the heat flow of a double cooling plate is as follows:

$$q = \frac{Q}{2A} \tag{1}$$

The cooling plate has two sides for heat transfer. For the n-cell stack with current I, when all the reaction enthalpies of the fuel cell are converted into electric energy and the aquatic product is water vapor,

$$Q = nI\left(-\Delta h_{\mathrm{f}}^{0}/2F - V\right) \tag{2}$$

where n is the number of cells, I is the cell current, V is the output voltage of the cell and A is the total area of the cell, $\Delta h_{\mathrm{f}}^{0}$ is the enthalpy of water formation, and F is the Faraday constant.

The regional uniformity index of the area-weighted variable γ_{a} is calculated using the following formula:

$$\gamma_{\mathrm{a}} = 1 - \frac{\sum_{\mathrm{i}=1}^{\mathrm{n}}\left[\left(\left|\phi_{\mathrm{i}} - \overline{\phi}_{\mathrm{a}}\right|\right)A_{\mathrm{i}}\right]}{2\left|\overline{\phi}_{\mathrm{a}}\right|\sum_{\mathrm{i}=1}^{\mathrm{n}} A_{\mathrm{i}}} \tag{3}$$

$\overline{\phi}_{\mathrm{a}}$ is the average of the variables across the surface:

$$\overline{\phi_{\mathrm{a}}} = \frac{\sum_{\mathrm{i}=1}^{\mathrm{n}} \phi_{\mathrm{i}} A_{\mathrm{i}}}{\sum_{\mathrm{i}=1}^{\mathrm{n}} A_{\mathrm{i}}} \tag{4}$$

where γ_a is the uniformity index, ϕ is variable across the surface, A is a superficial area, i is the mesh face index with n mesh faces, and n is the number of grids.

2.2. Model Assumptions

Although there is a temperature difference in the flow process of a cooling medium, it is within the allowable range of error. Therefore, it is considered that the density of the cooling medium is fixed. The simulation is carried out in an ideal situation to some extent. A homogeneous heat distribution over the active area of the cell is assumed. For the convenience of calculation, the following assumptions are made:

(a) The flow in the cooling channel is incompressible;
(b) The viscous loss between the fluid and the channel wall is not considered;
(c) The medium in the channel has the characteristics of a continuous medium;
(d) The boundary between fluid and solid is a non-slip boundary;
(e) The heat flux distribution at the bottom is uniform.

2.3. Governing Equations

Assuming that the flow of the cooling liquid in the channel is a three-dimensional steady laminar flow, the continuity equation, momentum equation and energy equation in the reaction process can be expressed as follows:

(a) continuity equation

$$\frac{\partial u_x}{\partial x} + \frac{\partial u_y}{\partial y} + \frac{\partial u_z}{\partial z} = 0 \tag{5}$$

(b) momentum equation

$$-\frac{1}{\rho}\frac{\partial p}{\partial x} + v\nabla^2 u_x = u_x\frac{\partial u_x}{\partial x} + u_y\frac{\partial u_x}{\partial y} + u_z\frac{\partial u_x}{\partial z} \tag{6}$$

$$-\frac{1}{\rho}\frac{\partial p}{\partial y} + v\nabla^2 u_y = u_x\frac{\partial u_y}{\partial x} + u_y\frac{\partial u_y}{\partial y} + u_z\frac{\partial u_y}{\partial z} \tag{7}$$

$$-\frac{1}{\rho}\frac{\partial p}{\partial z} + v\nabla^2 u_z = u_x\frac{\partial u_z}{\partial x} + u_y\frac{\partial u_z}{\partial y} + u_z\frac{\partial u_z}{\partial z} \tag{8}$$

(c) energy equation

$$u_x\frac{\partial t}{\partial x} + v\frac{\partial t}{\partial y} + w\frac{\partial t}{\partial z} = \frac{\lambda}{\rho c_p}\left(\frac{\partial^2 t}{\partial x^2} + \frac{\partial^2 t}{\partial y^2} + \frac{\partial^2 t}{\partial z^2}\right) \tag{9}$$

where u_x,u_y,u_z is the velocity component of fluid along the x, y and z axes; v is the kinematic viscosity; $\frac{\lambda}{\rho c_p}$ is the thermal diffusion coefficient.

2.4. Boundary Conditions and Convergence Criteria

Unlike other high-temperature-resistant materials, graphite does not soften as the temperature rises; in fact, its strength increases [37]. At the working temperature of a fuel cell, graphite has great thermal conductivity, allowing waste heat from the bipolar plate to be effectively transferred to the coolant. Because the volume of graphite varies little when the temperature changes quickly, it has good thermal shock resistance [38]. It possesses strong chemical stability and corrosion resistance at the same time [37,39]. Therefore, graphite is used as the material of the coolant and cooling plate. The model uses computational fluid dynamics software Fluent to analyze the heat transfer performance. The material of the cooling plate is graphite. The energy equation has been introduced and the SIMPLE algorithm is used to solve the continuity equation. The pressure term adopts the standard discrete format. The K-epsilon turbulence model is adopted for the flow of the coolant. A first-order slip boundary is used, the Navier-Stokes equations is used to calculate the flow iteratively, and the numerical simulation results are obtained. We set the inlet and outlet pressure, temperature and flow monitors to cooperate with the residual monitoring to determine that the solution is completed, and initialize with standard initialization. The residual errors of all parameters are below 10^{-4} as the iterative convergence judgment standard, and the calculated boundary conditions are shown in Table 2.

Table 2. Boundary conditions.

Parameters	Values
Cooling plate properties	
Material	graphite
Density	2250 kg/m^3
Specific heat	690 J/kg·K
Thermal conductivity	24.0 W/m·K
Coolant properties	
Density	992.2 kg/m^3
Specific heat	4179 J/kg·K
Thermal conductivity	0.62 W/m·K
Viscosity	0.000653 Pa·s
Operating conditions	
Heat flux	5000 W/m^2
Inlet coolant temperature	313 K
Inlet mass flow	0.002 kg/s

2.5. Grid Independence Verification

In order to verify that the numerical simulation results are not related to the number of grids, five grid numbers (234,149, 1,192,719, 1,457,725, 1,959,970 and 2,481,860) are selected for numerical simulation when the inlet mass flow is 0.002 kg/s. In Figure 4, we present a partial view of the grid of model 3. Hypermesh finite element meshing software and the hexahedral meshing method are used to encrypt the meshes to test the independence of meshes. The numerical simulation results show that when the grid number is 234,149, the numerical simulation results have the maximum deviation. Comparing the numerical simulation results of the models with the grid number of 1,959,970 and 2,481,860, it is found that the deviation between them is relatively small, and the numerical simulation results are very close, indicating that the grid number between 1,959,970 and 2,481,860 can be selected as the grid number of numerical simulation, but the larger the grid number is, the longer the calculation time will be. Considering the calculation accuracy and calculation time comprehensively, we select 1,959,970 here as the number of grids for numerical simulation. Table 3 shows the grid independence verification.

Figure 4. Local mesh of model 3.

Table 3. Grid independence verification.

Mesh	Element Number	Pressure Drop(Pa)	T_{max}(K)	T_{ave}(K)
Mesh1	234,149	15,254.47	318.64	316.49
Mesh2	1,192,719	17,013.06	319.71	317.74
Mesh3	1,457,725	17,113.01	318.73	317.74
Mesh4	1,959,970	17,105.10	318.76	317.74
Mesh5	2,481,860	17,105.63	318.79	317.74

2.6. Model Verification

In order to verify the reliability of the model, the research results of relevant materials are consulted, and the numerical simulation results are compared with the results of Baek's [40] research in Figure 5. In the numerical simulation, the Model F studied by Baek is used as the model, and the geometric structure and operating parameters (heat flux, inlet temperature, mass flow rate) were set to the same as the reference. It can be analyzed from the figure that when the inlet mass flow is 2×10^{-3} kg/s, the numerical simulation results in this paper are the lowest compared with those in the references. When the inlet mass flow rate is 6×10^{-3} kg/s, the numerical simulation results are the largest, approximately 10.1%. The results further verify the reliability of the numerical simulation method used in this study.

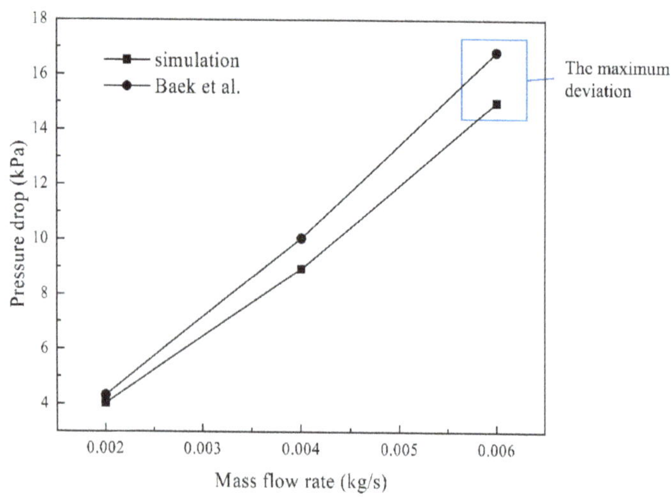

Figure 5. Model verification [36].

3. Simulation Results and Discussion

3.1. Temperature Distribution

Figure 6 shows the center plane temperature distribution of six different flow fields, and the cooling plate area of six different flow fields is 180 mm × 180 mm, where b, c, d, e, f are arranged with four inlets and four outlets, and the inlet mass flow is 0.002 kg/s. Figure 6a is a traditional single-channel serpentine flow field cooling plate. As can be seen from the figure, the heat dissipation performance of the single-channel flow field is the worst. The temperature distribution in the upstream of the flow channel in Figure 6e is below the overall average temperature, but the local temperature in the middle and downstream regions is high. Because the obstruction of the uniform plate leads to the low flow rate of the cooling liquid, the waste heat absorbed by the coolant from the bipolar plate cannot be discharged in time, resulting in the high local temperature of the cooling plate. Figure 7 shows the velocity distribution of the flow field. It can be seen that the velocity of this flow field is smaller than that of other flow fields due to the blockage of the uniform plate. In Figure 6b, due to the zigzag circling of a single channel, the local temperature distribution is uneven. Later, the optimization design will be carried out according to the design characteristics of the flow field. As can be seen from Figure 6c, the flow field temperature gradually increases from the left inlet to the right outlet. Figure 6f shows the temperature distribution of the honeycomb cooling flow field. It is observed that the overall temperature distribution upstream of the cooling plate is uniform and low, but the local temperature downstream is too high. Although the flow field of the honeycomb structure can make the coolant evenly distributed, it is still unable to avoid fluid blockage, resulting in a locally high temperature downstream. Figure 6d shows the temperature distribution of the multi-helical flow field. Due to the long length of the flow channel, there is an obvious temperature difference from inlet to outlet, but the overall situation is better than that of Figure 6a.

Figure 6. Temperature distribution.

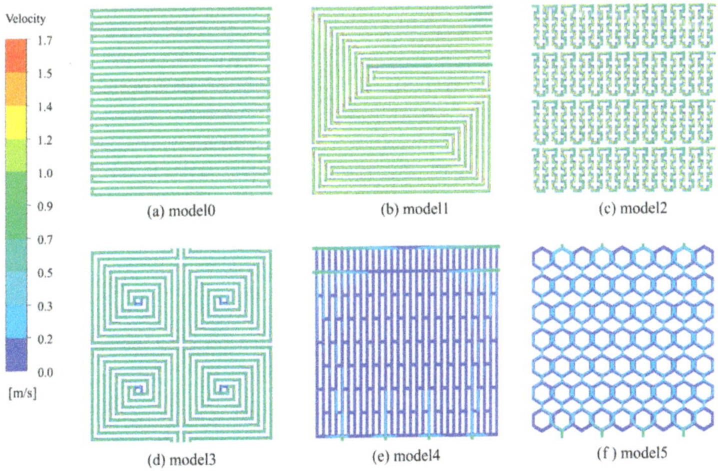

Figure 7. Velocity distribution.

Figure 6d shows the temperature distribution of the multi-helical flow field. It can be seen from the figure that the temperature at the corner of the multi-helical flow field is slightly higher than that of the surrounding environment. This is due to the reflux phenomenon of the fluid at the corner of the cooling channel. As shown in Figure 8, due to the reflux phenomenon, a small part of the fluid stays at the corner and cannot be discharged in time, while the heat of the cooling plate is continuously transmitted to the remaining coolant, resulting in a local temperature difference.

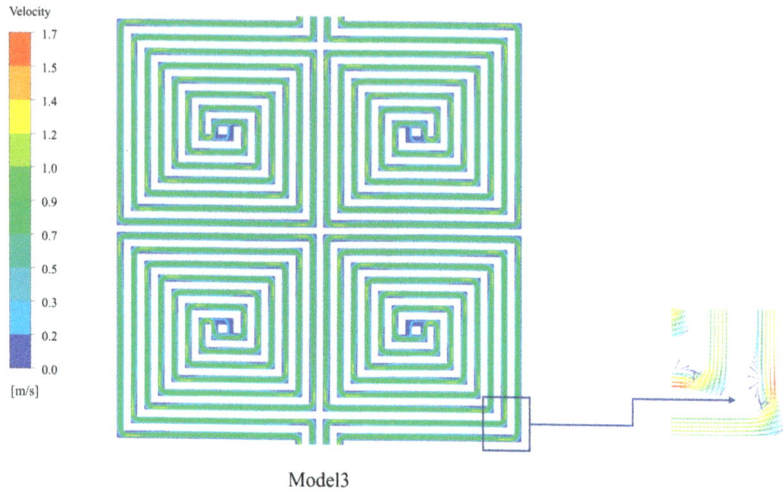

Figure 8. Local velocity of multi-helical flow field.

Table 4 shows and compares the parameters of six different cooling plates, including pressure drop, temperature difference, maximum temperature and temperature uniformity index. The temperature difference is the difference between the maximum temperature and the minimum temperature of the cooling plate in the simulation steady state. It can be seen from the table that the maximum temperature and temperature difference of the traditional single-channel serpentine cooling flow field are the maximum values of the six cooling channels, and the temperature is also the most uneven, showing inefficient performance. As can be seen from Figure 9c, the overall pressure of model 2 is high and the coolant is blocked seriously, which is reflected in Table 4 with the maximum pressure drop.

Table 4. Simulation results.

Case	ΔP (Pa)	ΔT (K)	T_{max} (K)	U_T
Model0	49,263.63	19.681	334.254	0.992421
Model1	19,242.26	7.1984	321.197	0.997850
Model2	79,753.15	7.1079	320.879	0.998066
Model3	17,105.10	5.1586	319.741	0.999358
Model4	1026.86	8.3532	322.542	0.997854
Model5	1593.00	9.2961	324.673	0.998077

The fluid of model 4 and model 5 has no obvious blockage, and the pressure drop of both is far less than model 0, model 1, model 2 and model 3. As can be seen from Figure 6, the flow rate of the coolant of model 4 and model 5 in the channel is small, in which the fluid uniform plate not only makes the coolant evenly distributed, but also hinders the transverse diffusion of the fluid body, making the flow rate of model 4 the minimum. It shows the highest temperature second only to the traditional single-channel serpentine flow field. The coolant flow rate of model 1, model 2 and model 3 in the channel is large and the pressure drop is high, but the higher flow rate promotes the discharge of waste heat, showing the minimum temperature difference and the minimum maximum temperature.

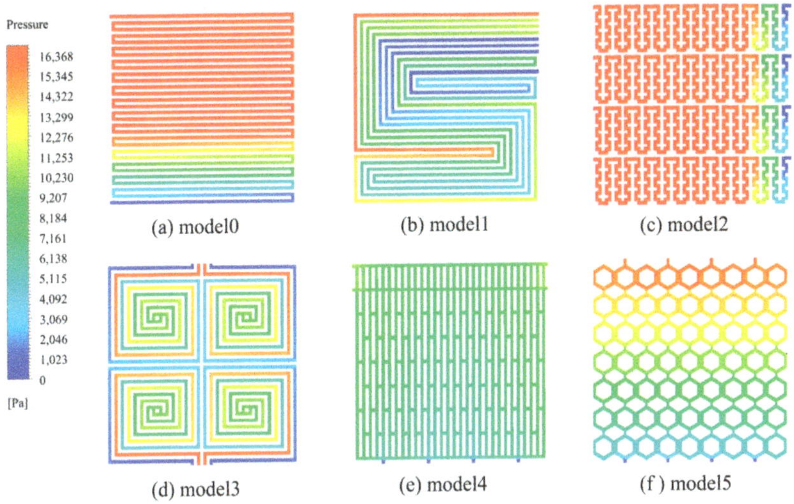

Figure 9. Pressure distribution.

3.2. Pressure Distribution

Figure 9 shows the pressure distribution of six different cooling channels, and the inlet mass flow is 0.002 kg/s. As can be seen from the figure, compared with other situations, the pressure distribution of model 4 and model 5 is more uniform. Model 0 and model 2 show the largest pressure difference in the reaction area, and the maximum pressure can reach 49,265.57 Pa and 79,226.62 Pa, respectively. The reason for the large pressure drop of model 0–model 3 is the long coolant transportation distance, while the coolant flow area of model 4 and model 5 is wide, the flow channels cross and connect with each other, and the pressure drop is reduced. The pressure loss produced by the long channel length is avoided due to the large number and small length of model 4 and model 5 channels. Model 1 has four inlets and four outlets in comparison to the serpentine flow field. It can be seen that the multi-inlet and multi-channel design helps to lessen the flow field's pressure loss. It can be summarized that the pressure drop can be effectively reduced by using a uniform plate flow field and honeycomb structure flow field.

3.3. Effect of Heat Flux

Figure 10 shows the effect of heat flux at the bottom of the cooling plate on the average temperature, maximum temperature difference, maximum temperature and temperature uniformity index of the cooling plate. It can be seen from Figure 10a–c that with the increase in bottom heat flux, the average temperature, maximum temperature difference and maximum temperature of the cooling plate increase significantly, among which the traditional single-channel serpentine flow field cooling plate increases the most. In Figure 10c, when the bottom heat flux is 4000 W/m^3, the serpentine flow field cooling plate represented by model 0 maintains a good temperature since the heat flux remains within model 0's heat exchange capacity. When the heat flux is increased to 5000 W/m^3, the temperature of model 0 rises significantly due to heat accumulation produced by the serpentine flow field's lengthy channel. For the maximum temperature difference, the effect of heat flux on the maximum temperature difference of model 2 and model 3 is slighter than that of other types of flow fields. In addition to the traditional serpentine cooling channel, the increase in heat flux has the same effect on the average temperature and maximum temperature of different types of cooling flow fields. For the new designed flow field structure, model 3 and model 4 show the highest temperature uniformity index, which shows that the deviation between the quantitatively measured surface temperature and the average temperature of the heat transfer surface of the flow channel structure is small, the temperature uniformity is high, and it has better heat dissipation performance. This is due to the uniform distribution of cooling channels and weaker blockage of the multi-helix flow field and honeycomb structure flow field.

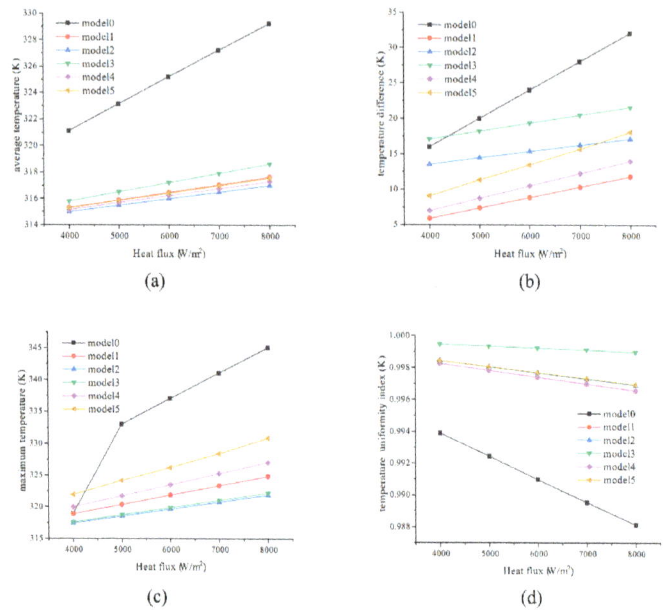

Figure 10. Effect of heat flux on heat transfer characteristics. (**a**) Average temperature, (**b**) temperature difference, (**c**) maximum temperature, (**d**) temperature uniformity index.

3.4. *Effect of Fluid Reynolds Number*

Figure 11a shows the maximum temperature of the cooling plate under different Reynolds numbers of the coolant. The boundary conditions of the numerical simulation are shown in Table 2, where the mass flow rate of the inlet is adjusted to achieve different Reynolds numbers. The results show that the maximum temperature of each type of cooling plate decreases with the increase in Reynolds number, because the larger mass flow at the inlet accelerates the heat dissipation. Figure 11b shows that the increase in Reynolds number will also increase the pressure drop in the channel due to the addition of more fluid flow. The rising trend of the Reynolds number of model 0 and model 2 is faster, because the fluid congestion in these two channels is more likely to occur.

Figure 12 shows the variation in the difference between the maximum temperature and the minimum temperature of each cooling flow field at different Reynolds numbers. The increase in the Reynolds number brings more flow of coolant, which alleviates the polarization of the working temperature of all types of cooling plates and improves the heat transfer capacity of the fuel cell cooling plates. Due to the multi-helical flow field structure with good heat dissipation performance, the temperature difference of model 3 always remains at a low value with the increase in Reynolds number.

The temperature uniformity index can present the temperature uniformity numerically. The closer the temperature uniformity index is to 1, the more uniform the temperature of the cooling flow field is. As can be seen from Figure 13, with the increase in Reynolds number, the temperature of all flow channels becomes more and more uniform. The traditional single-channel serpentine flow field maintains the lowest temperature uniformity, and the temperature uniformity of the multi-spiral flow field of model 3 is always the strongest. On the whole, increasing the Reynolds number can improve the heat transfer effect of the cooling plate.

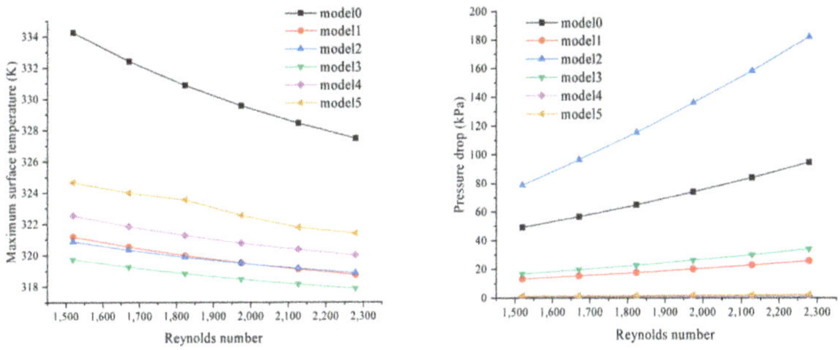

(a) (b)

Figure 11. Effect of Reynolds number on heat transfer characteristics. (**a**) Maximum surface temperature, (**b**) pressure drop.

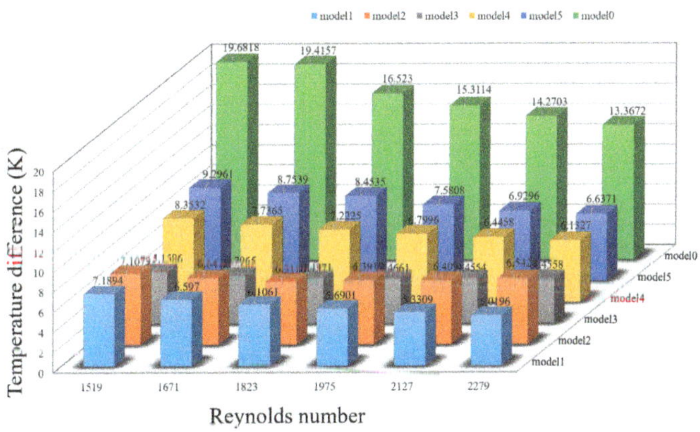

Figure 12. Effect of Reynolds number on temperature difference.

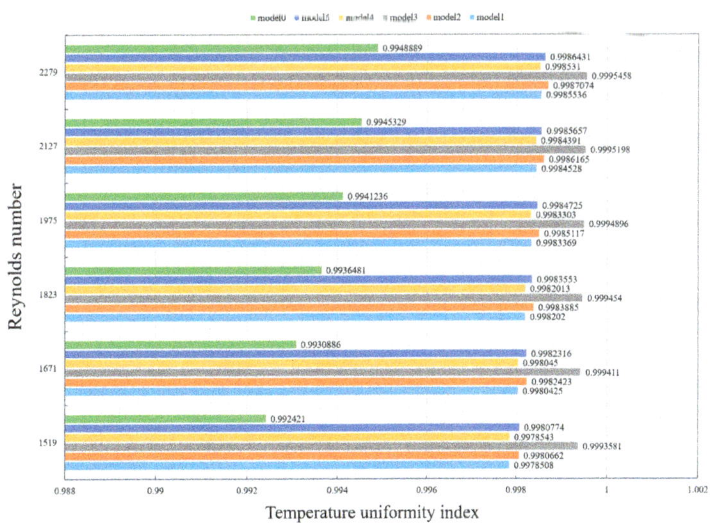

Figure 13. Effect of Reynolds number on temperature uniformity index.

3.5. Flow Distribution Improvement

It can be found from Figure 14a that the center temperature of the multi-serpentine cooling plate is high due to the transfer of heat from the inlet to the outlet and the winding of the cooling channel in the middle of the cooling plate. Therefore, the mass flow of the four inlets is redistributed with the total flow unchanged, as shown in Figure 14b, where half of the flow of the external cooling channel is distributed to the internal winding channel. The temperature uniformity at the bottom of the distributed cooling plate is improved, the uniformity index is increased from 0.9978508 to 0.9980883, the maximum temperature is reduced from 321.1978 K to 319.3245 K, the temperature difference is also reduced, and the average temperature is also reduced by 1.2096 K.

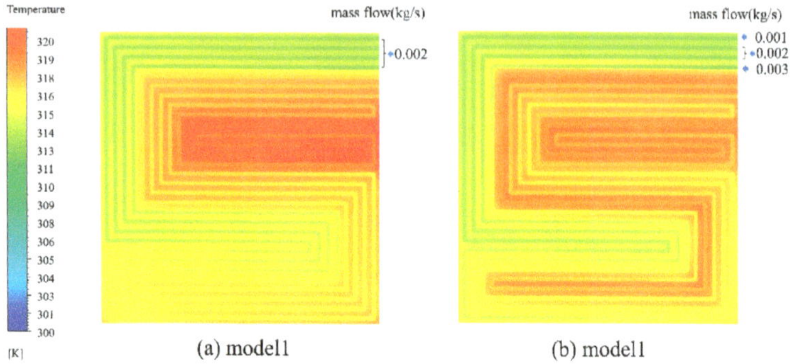

Figure 14. Effect of changing inlet flow on temperature distribution.

3.6. Effect of Bottom Non-Uniform Temperature Distribution

During the continuous operation of a PEMFC, the heat transmitted at the bottom of the cooling plate is not always uniform and constant. The temperature downstream of the coolant is always higher than the temperature upstream of the coolant due to heat exchange. After a lengthy period of operation, the temperature downstream of the cooling plate is higher than that upstream, and the temperature falls from high to low from downstream to upstream for cooling plates with a serpentine flow field, model 2, model 4 and model 5 cooling flow field distribution. To investigate the impact of non-uniform temperature on the heat transfer of the cooling plate, the uniform heat flow at the bottom is altered into a temperature gradient distribution from 324 K to 310 K. Figure 15 shows the temperature distribution results of the middle surface of the flow field.

As can be seen from Figure 15, the four models show similar temperature distributions in the case of non-uniform temperature distribution. The highest temperature of the four models is 323.99 K of model 5, and the lowest temperature is 323.9 K; the difference is not obvious. The lowest average temperature is 316.828 K of model 2 and the highest is 316.99 K of model 5. Due to the low temperature in the upstream, the heat exchange capacity of the coolant is small, and the heat exchange is mainly concentrated in the downstream region, which causes the serpentine flow field to avoid the heat accumulation generated by the longer flow channel, thus showing temperature performance similar to that of other flow channels.

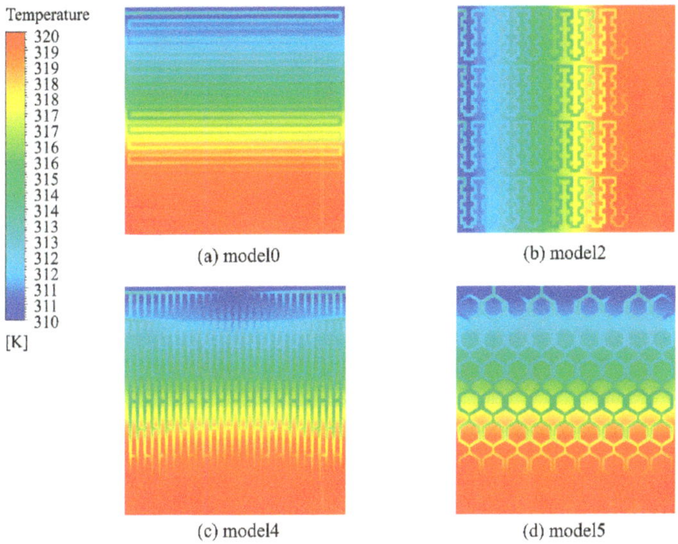

Figure 15. Effect of bottom non-uniform temperature distribution.

4. Conclusions

In order to improve the overheating problem caused by the low heat dissipation efficiency of the cooling plate during the operation of a PEMFC, five innovative cooling flow field channel designs are proposed. The heat dissipation capacity of these five flow fields under different working conditions is studied, and the following conclusions are obtained:

1. The flow channel distribution of a multi-spiral flow field and honeycomb structure flow field is more conducive to improving the temperature uniformity. The flow channel model 4 with a uniform plate has poor temperature uniformity because the coolant is blocked by the uniform plate, but the heat dissipation capacity is still stronger than the traditional serpentine flow field. Reasonable distribution of flow between different channels can effectively improve the heat dissipation capacity of the cooling plate.
2. The temperature distribution of a multi-spiral channel is uniform, but the pressure drop is large, and the pressure drop of model 2 is the largest, which is not conducive to pumping power, but the flow velocity in the channel is high and the heat dissipation capacity is strong. The flow channels are connected with each other, such as the uniform plate flow field and honeycomb structure flow field, which can make the pressure evenly distributed. Although the long flow passage can speed up the transmission of coolant, it can easily cause water congestion.
3. The multi-spiral flow field has the strongest ability to maintain the temperature stability in the cooling plate when the heat flux increases. The increase in the Reynolds number can reduce the maximum temperature and temperature difference of the flow field, improve the temperature uniformity and improve the heat transfer capacity of the cooling plate, but it will increase the pressure drop.

Author Contributions: Conceptualization, J.S. and Y.H.; Data curation, Y.L.; Funding acquisition, J.S.; Investigation, T.L. and X.Z.; Methodology, J.S. and L.C.; Project administration, J.S.; Software, Z.M.; Validation, Y.L.; Writing—review and editing, J.S. and Y.H. All authors have read and agreed to the published version of the manuscript.

Funding: This research was funded by the National Natural Science Foundation of China (Grant No.51805102) and the Guizhou Provincial Natural Science Foundation (Grant No. [2020]1Y238).

Institutional Review Board Statement: Not applicable.

Informed Consent Statement: Not applicable.

Data Availability Statement: Not applicable.

Acknowledgments: The authors would like to thank the anonymous reviewers and the editor for their valuable comments and suggestions.

Conflicts of Interest: The authors declare no conflict of interest.

References

1. Huang, Y.; Xiao, X.; Kang, H.; Lv, J.; Zeng, R.; Shen, J. Thermal management of polymer electrolyte membrane fuel cells: A critical review of heat transfer mechanisms, cooling approaches, and advanced cooling techniques analysis. *Energy Convers. Manag.* **2022**, *254*, 115221. [CrossRef]
2. Xu, Z.; Qiu, D.; Yi, P.; Peng, L.; Lai, X. Towards mass applications: A review on the challenges and developments in metallic bipolar plates for PEMFC. *Prog. Nat. Sci.* **2020**, *30*, 815–824. [CrossRef]
3. Kim, D.J.; Jo, M.J.; Nam, S.Y. A review of polymer–nanocomposite electrolyte membranes for fuel cell application. *J. Ind. Eng. Chem.* **2015**, *21*, 36–52. [CrossRef]
4. Tawfik, H.; Hung, Y.; Mahajan, D. Metal bipolar plates for PEM fuel cell—A review. *J. Power Sources* **2007**, *163*, 755–767. [CrossRef]
5. Dhimish, M.; Vieira, R.G.; Badran, G. Investigating the stability and degradation of hydrogen PEM fuel cell. *Int. J. Hydrog. Energy* **2021**, *46*, 37017–37028. [CrossRef]
6. Choi, E.J.; Hwang, S.H.; Park, J.Y.; Kim, M.S. Parametric analysis of simultaneous humidification and cooling for PEMFCs using direct water injection method. *Int. J. Hydrog. Energy* **2017**, *42*, 12531–12542. [CrossRef]
7. Rahimi-Esbo, M.; Rahgoshay, S.M.; Hassani, M.M.; Firouzjaei, K.D. Novel design and numerical evaluating of a cooling flow field in PEMFC with metallic bipolar plates. *Int. J. Hydrog. Energy* **2020**, *in press*. [CrossRef]
8. Mohamed, W.; Atan, R. Experimental thermal analysis on air cooling for closed-cathode Polymer Electrolyte Membrane fuel cells. *Int. J. Hydrog. Energy* **2015**, *40*, 10605–10626. [CrossRef]
9. Amirfazli, A.; Asghari, S.; Sarraf, M. An investigation into the effect of manifold geometry on uniformity of temperature dis-tribution in a PEMFC stack. *Energy* **2018**, *145*, 141–151. [CrossRef]
10. Barbir, F.; Yazıcı, S.; Yazici, S.; Yazici, M.S. Status and development of PEM fuel cell technology. *Int. J. Energy Res.* **2007**, *32*, 369–378. [CrossRef]
11. Shabani, B.; Andrews, J. An experimental investigation of a PEM fuel cell to supply both heat and power in a solar-hydrogen RAPS system. *Int. J. Hydrog. Energy* **2011**, *36*, 5442–5452. [CrossRef]
12. Li, H.; Tang, Y.; Wang, Z.; Shi, Z.; Wu, S.; Song, D.; Zhang, J.; Fatih, K.; Zhang, J.; Wang, H.; et al. A review of water flooding issues in the proton exchange membrane fuel cell. *J. Power Sources* **2008**, *178*, 103–117. [CrossRef]
13. Zakaria, I.; Azmi, W.H.; Mamat, A.M.I.; Mamat, R.; Saidur, R.; Abu Talib, S.A.; Mohamed, W.A.N.W. Thermal analysis of Al2O3–water ethylene glycol mixture nanofluid for single PEM fuel cell cooling plate: An experimental study. *Int. J. Hydrog. Energy* **2016**, *41*, 5096–5112. [CrossRef]
14. Kurnia, J.C.; Sasmito, A.P.; Mujumdar, A.S. Numerical investigation of laminar heat transfer performance of various cooling channel designs. *Appl. Therm. Eng.* **2011**, *31*, 1293–1304. [CrossRef]
15. Jeon, D.H. Numerical study of serpentine flow-field cooling plates on PEM fuel cells performance. *Int. J. Energy Res.* **2013**, *37*, 510–521. [CrossRef]
16. Soupremanien, U.; Le Person, S.; Favre-Marinet, M.; Bultel, Y. Tools for designing the cooling system of a proton exchange membrane fuel cell. *Appl. Therm. Eng.* **2012**, *40*, 161–173. [CrossRef]
17. Matian, M.; Marquis, A.; Brandon, N. Model based design and test of cooling plates for an air-cooled polymer electrolyte fuel cell stack—ScienceDirect. *Int. J. Hydrog. Energy* **2011**, *36*, 6051–6066. [CrossRef]
18. Wilberforce, T.; El-Hassan, Z.; Khatib, F.; Al Makky, A.; Mooney, J.; Barouaji, A.; Carton, J.G.; Olabi, A.G. Development of Bi-polar plate design of PEM fuel cell using CFD techniques. *Int. J. Hydrog. Energy* **2017**, *42*, 25663–25685. [CrossRef]
19. Rahgoshay, S.M.; Ranjbar, A.A.; Ramiar, A.; Alizadeh, E. Thermal investigation of a PEM fuel cell with cooling flow field. *Energy* **2017**, *134*, 61–73. [CrossRef]
20. Yang, X.G.; Qiang, Y.; Ping, C. Matching of water and temperature fields in proton exchange membrane fuel cells with non-uniform distributions. *Int. J. Hydrog. Energy* **2011**, *36*, 12524–12537. [CrossRef]
21. Shian, L.; Bengt, S. Numerical study on thermal performance of non-uniform flow channel designs for cooling plates of PEM fuel cells. *Numer. Heat. Tr. A-Appl.* **2018**, *74*, 917–930.
22. Sasmito, A.P.; Kurnia, J.C.; Mujumdar, A.S. Numerical evaluation of various gas and coolant channel designs for high performance liquid-cooled proton exchange membrane fuel cell stacks. *Energy* **2012**, *44*, 278–291. [CrossRef]
23. Ravishankar, S.; Prakash, K.A. Numerical studies on thermal performance of novel cooling plate designs in polymer electrolyte membrane fuel cell stacks. *Appl. Therm. Eng.* **2014**, *66*, 239–251. [CrossRef]
24. Castelain, C.; Lasbet, Y.; Auvity, B.; Peerhossaini, H. Experimental study of the thermal performance of chaotic geometries for their use in PEM fuel cells. *Int. J. Therm. Sci.* **2016**, *101*, 181–192. [CrossRef]

25. Liu, Z.; Zeng, X.; Ge, Y.; Shen, J.; Liu, W. Multi-objective optimization of operating conditions and channel structure for a proton exchange membrane fuel cell. *Int. J. Heat Mass Transf.* **2017**, *111*, 289–298. [CrossRef]
26. Wen, C.-Y.; Lin, Y.-S.; Lu, C.-H.; Luo, T.-W. Thermal management of a proton exchange membrane fuel cell stack with pyrolytic graphite sheets and fans combined. *Int. J. Hydrog. Energy* **2011**, *36*, 6082–6089. [CrossRef]
27. Lin, C.; Yan, X.; Wei, G.; Ke, C.; Shen, S.; Zhang, J. Optimization of configurations and cathode operating parameters on liquid-cooled proton exchange membrane fuel cell stacks by orthogonal method. *Appl. Energy* **2019**, *253*, 113496. [CrossRef]
28. Özden, E.; Tolj, I.; Barbir, F. Designing heat exchanger with spatially variable surface area for passive cooling of PEM fuel cell. *Appl. Therm. Eng.* **2013**, *51*, 1339–1344. [CrossRef]
29. Zhao, J.; Huang, Z.; Jian, B.; Bai, X.; Jian, Q. Thermal performance enhancement of air-cooled proton exchange membrane fuel cells by vapor chambers. *Energy Convers. Manag.* **2020**, *213*, 112830. [CrossRef]
30. Afshari, E.; Ziaei-Rad, M.; Shariati, Z. A study on using metal foam as coolant fluid distributor in the polymer electrolyte membrane fuel cell. *Int. J. Hydrog. Energy* **2016**, *41*, 1902–1912. [CrossRef]
31. Zhang, G.; Yuan, H.; Wang, Y.; Jiao, K. Three-dimensional simulation of a new cooling strategy for proton exchange membrane fuel cell stack using a non-isothermal multiphase model. *Appl. Energy* **2019**, *255*, 113865. [CrossRef]
32. Hwang, S.H.; Kim, M.S. An experimental study on the cathode humidification and evaporative cooling of polymer electrolyte membrane fuel cells using direct water injection method at high current densities. *Appl. Therm. Eng.* **2016**, *99*, 635–644. [CrossRef]
33. Saeedan, M.; Ziaei-Rad, M.; Afshari, E. Numerical thermal analysis of nanofluid flow through the cooling channels of a polymer electrolyte membrane fuel cell filled with metal foam. *Int. J. Energy Res.* **2020**, *44*, 5730–5748. [CrossRef]
34. Asghari, S.; Akhgar, H.; Imani, B.F. Design of thermal management subsystem for a 5kW polymer electrolyte membrane fuel cell system. *J. Power Sources* **2011**, *196*, 3141–3148. [CrossRef]
35. Ghasemi, M.; Ramiar, A.; Ranjbar, A.A.; Rahgoshay, S.M. A numerical study on thermal analysis and cooling flow fields effect on PEMFC performance. *Int. J. Hydrog. Energy* **2017**, *42*, 24319–24337. [CrossRef]
36. Yu, S.H.; Sohn, S.; Nam, J.H.; Kim, C.-J. Numerical study to examine the performance of multi-pass serpentine flow-fields for cooling plates in polymer electrolyte membrane fuel cells. *J. Power Sources* **2009**, *194*, 697–703. [CrossRef]
37. Inagaki, M.; Kaburagi, Y.; Hishiyama, Y. Thermal Management Material: Graphite. *Adv. Eng. Mater.* **2014**, *16*, 494–506. [CrossRef]
38. Fan, R.; Huang, Y.; Han, X.; Peng, X. High thermal conductivity and mechanical properties of Si@Graphite/Aluminum nitride/aluminum composites for high-efficiency thermal management. *J. Alloys Compd.* **2021**, *858*, 157630. [CrossRef]
39. Cao, J.; Ling, Z.; Lin, S.; He, Y.; Fang, X.; Zhang, Z. Thermochemical heat storage system for preventing battery thermal runaway propagation using sodium acetate trihydrate/expanded graphite. *Chem. Eng. J.* **2021**, *433*, 133536. [CrossRef]
40. Baek, S.M.; Yu, S.H.; Nam, J.H.; Kim, C.-J. A numerical study on uniform cooling of large-scale PEMFCs with different coolant flow field designs. *Appl. Therm. Eng.* **2011**, *31*, 1427–1434. [CrossRef]

energies

MDPI

Article

Numerical Analysis on the Flue Gas Temperature Maintenance System of a Solid Fuel-Fired Boiler Operating at Minimum Loads

Michalina Kurkus-Gruszecka *, Piotr Krawczyk and Janusz Lewandowski

Institute of Heat Engineering, Faculty of Power and Aeronautical Engineering, Warsaw University of Technology, Nowowiejska 21/25, 00-665 Warsaw, Poland; piotr.krawczyk@pw.edu.pl (P.K.); janusz.lewandowski@pw.edu.pl (J.L.)

* Correspondence: michalina.kurkus-gruszecka.dokt@pw.edu.pl; Tel.: +48-22-264-5299

Abstract: Currently, energy policy is associated with the increase in the share of renewable sources in systemic energy production. Due to this trend, coal-fired power units must increase their work flexibility. Adapting a coal power plant to work with a lower load often causes the issue of maintaining the temperature before the selective catalytic reduction (SCR) installation at a sufficiently high level. This paper presents a CFD analysis of the mixing area of two flue gas streams before the SCR installation with various methods for mixing flue gas streams. The novelty of the work is mixing the flue gas streams of different temperatures using a flap shape developed by the authors. A series of numerical simulations were performed to develop the location and method of introducing the higher temperature gas, obtaining a uniform distribution of the exhaust gas temperature. The simulation scheme was applied to a series of geometrical modifications of the boundary conditions. The tested solution using only a single, straight flap in the flue gas duct allows the amplitude to be reduced from 298 K to 144 K. As a result of the research, a mixing flap design was developed to reduce the initial temperature amplitude of the flue gas streams from 298 K to 43 K.

Keywords: flue gas bypass; flue gas mixing; flue gas temperature before SCR; low-load power boiler operation; power plant flexibility

Citation: Kurkus-Gruszecka, M.; Krawczyk, P.; Lewandowski, J. Numerical Analysis on the Flue Gas Temperature Maintenance System of a Solid Fuel-Fired Boiler Operating at Minimum Loads. *Energies* **2021**, *14*, 4420. https://doi.org/10.3390/en14154420

Academic Editor: Marcin Kamiński

Received: 26 June 2021
Accepted: 19 July 2021
Published: 22 July 2021

1. Introduction

Due to the increasing number of renewable energy sources with a share in energy systems, research is being conducted on a large scale to increase conventional power plant flexibility [1]. This aspect was addressed in [2], where the authors analyzed increased flexibility in systems with a high share of renewable sources. In [3], the flexibility and economic aspects of power plant operation in new low-carbon systems were analyzed. Increasing the flexibility of coal-fired power plant operation by activities related to the regulation of the steam cycle are presented in [4]. In [5,6], the cooperation of conventional power plants was analyzed in terms of the power grid flexibility. The works mentioned here are broadly related to increasing the power range flexibility to lower the coal unit minimum load [7]. At present, most coal-fired unit operating power fits the range of 50–100% of nominal capacity. In case of a significant power increase in the system due to the power produced by units with priority, e.g., renewables, the currently running conventional power plants reduce their operation [8]. If the power supplied to the electricity network still exceeds the demand, some conventional units have to be shut down and prepared for restart [9]. Shutting down and restarting coal-fired units is economically inefficient, shortens the unit's lifetime, and causes increased emissions of harmful substances [7]. Therefore, research to reduce the minimum power block output to values below 50% of the nominal load increases their stable operation under current conditions.

At the same time, the emission standards, concerning mainly dust, sulfur oxides, and nitrogen oxides emissions, have recently been stringent [3]. Selective catalytic reduction

(SCR) technology is the most frequently used for reducing nitrogen oxides in coal-fired power boilers, as indicated in [10,11]. Such installations require operation in a specific flue gas temperature range [11], between 585 K and 670 K, depending on the catalyst type. The required range is also indicated in [12] (the authors analyzed the installation and its impact on the quality of flue gases), and [13] concerns the installation's operation optimization. The issue that arises relatively often during attempts to increase the boiler operation flexibility is the insufficiently high flue gas temperature before the SCR installation, which results in its incorrect operation. One of the solutions for a too low temperature before the SCR issue is to connect the higher temperature flue gas from another part of the boiler to the main flue gas stream before the SCR installation. In the solution mentioned above, the key is to effectively mix the flue gas streams at different temperatures to obtain a uniform flue gas temperature field before the installation. The routing of an additional duct for transporting hot exhaust gases requires the consideration of design possibilities. In many modernized coal boilers, the SCR systems were installed additionally, so it is necessary to introduce hot flue gases from the top of the duct. There is a high risk of not mixing the hot flue gas stream with the main, cooler stream in such a configuration. The solution presented in this paper in the form of an adequately profiled turbulizing flap enables effective mixing of exhaust gas streams with the introduction of hot exhaust gas from the top of the duct and obtaining a temperature field with appropriate uniformity before the SCR installation.

If the elements regulating the flue gas flow installation, e.g., control vanes or flaps, are planned in an existing boiler, a key parameter that should be considered is the flue gas pressure drop caused by the installed element, especially in boiler operation with high loads. Any additional pressure drop in the flue gas ducts increases the flue gas fans' power consumption, and in some cases, it can cause fan inefficiency. Increased power consumption also negatively affects the overall power unit efficiency. The technology developed by the authors makes it possible to regulate the pressure drop caused by the additional turbulence flap, with the possibility to fold the flap during the boiler operation with the nominal load. Thus, the impact of the device on the flue gas pressure drop is reduced to a minimum.

With the increasing availability of computational power, computational fluid dynamics (CFD) is increasingly being applied to the calculation of power boilers [14–18], characterized by relatively large calculation volumes and multiple physical and chemical phenomena. CFD methods are used in power boiler calculations for many purposes. In [15], the CFD method was used to optimize nitrogen oxide removal from exhaust gases. The temperature distribution in the boiler, validated by acoustic measurements, was modeled in [16]. In several studies, the main objective was to determine the flue gas flow character in the boiler. In [17], the influence of the NOx control installation on the flue gas flow in a boiler was examined. The authors of [18] investigated heat transfer by conduction and radiation from the flue gases to the evaporator and boiler superheaters. The flue gas and air mix flow through the power boiler was analyzed in [19]. In [20], the exhaust gas recirculation performance was determined. Many studies have used CFD methods to calculate the distribution, formation and reduction of nitrogen oxides [21]. Many works also model sub-systems of power boilers, such as SCR reactors [10,22] or dedusting systems. In [23], the mixing of the flue gas stream with primary air was modeled to increase the flue gas temperature before the SCR installation. However, the authors did not present the geometry of the mixing system. Despite many works on numerical modeling of power boilers, there is a lack of models in the literature concerning the mixing of flue gas streams with different temperatures on a large scale. As the flow is non-reactive, without heat exchange with the environment, and is single phase. In terms of the computational model complexity, this type of numerical analysis has been carried out and verified many times over recent years. Nevertheless, there are always limitations and risks inherent in the use of such a calculation method. Today, models of this degree of complexity often allow the elimination of experimental confirmation in industrial applications. In addition, the model has been validated for the current flue geometry.

This article presents the selected results of the calculations that led to developing the final turbulence flap concept. The novelty of the work is the development of a device allowing for effective mixing of the flue gas streams while maintaining the following criteria:

- The hot flue gas stream is introduced from the top. Introducing the stream of hot flue gases from the bottom is impossible in terms of the boiler structure.
- The developed flap does not cause a significant pressure drop of exhaust gases during operation (40–60% of the nominal boiler load).
- The flap design allows it to be folded during boiler operation at nominal load so as to not interfere with the boiler operation.
- The device's design must be relatively simple and reliable because it is exposed to many hours of operation in high-temperature conditions and exhaust gas dustiness.

The developed shape of the flap allows for the flue gas stream to be mixed and obtain a uniform temperature field. Based on the analysis of the available literature, it is the first solution developed to mix the flue gas streams in the channel of a coal-fired boiler while maintaining the above criteria.

2. Model Description

2.1. Investigated Duct Location in the Boiler

The numerical model includes the flue gas flow through the external duct located downstream of the main boiler flue to the SCR installation, including introducing hot flue gases from the bypass duct into the main flue gas stream. A representative geometry of an OP-650 class coal-fired power boiler was chosen for the study. The analyzed boiler unit schematic with the key components highlighted is shown in Figure 1: the boiler outline, the SCR installation and the section of pipeline analyzed in this paper placed directly upstream of the SCR installation. In Figure 1, the flue gas flow path is also marked with blue arrows. The analyzed duct section is symmetrically divided on two sides of the boiler, which is well illustrated by the axonometric view located in the upper left corner of Figure 1.

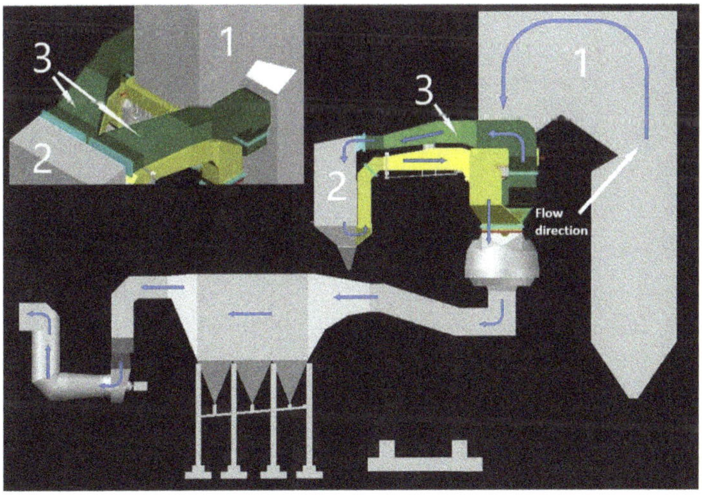

Figure 1. The analyzed boiler unit schematic with the key components: 1—boiler outline, 2—SCR installation, 3—analyzed duct section.

For further analyses, a section of the flue gas duct leading from the main boiler building to the SCR installation, marked in Figure 1 as number 3, was extracted from the presented geometry. As the analyzed duct section upstream of the SCR installation consists of two symmetrical parts, one of them was simulated in the numerical calculations using symmetry conditions.

2.2. The Developed Geometrical Variants

Four selected geometric options are presented in this paper, with the first three reflecting the progress of the fourth and final concept. As mentioned earlier, this study analyzed the bypass duct transporting higher temperature flue gases introduced from the top. The hot flue inlet configuration is the most difficult from the point of view of mixing the flue gas streams before the SCR system. The difficulty in mixing the flue gas streams is mainly due to buoyancy forces and relatively slow flue gas velocities resulting from low boiler load. To obtain a complete representation of the flue gas flow through the analyzed duct section, a full 3D geometry was implemented for the numerical calculations. A general schematic of the examined flue gas duct section is shown in Figure 2. The section shows the inlets of the flue gas streams and the flow direction towards the SCR reactor.

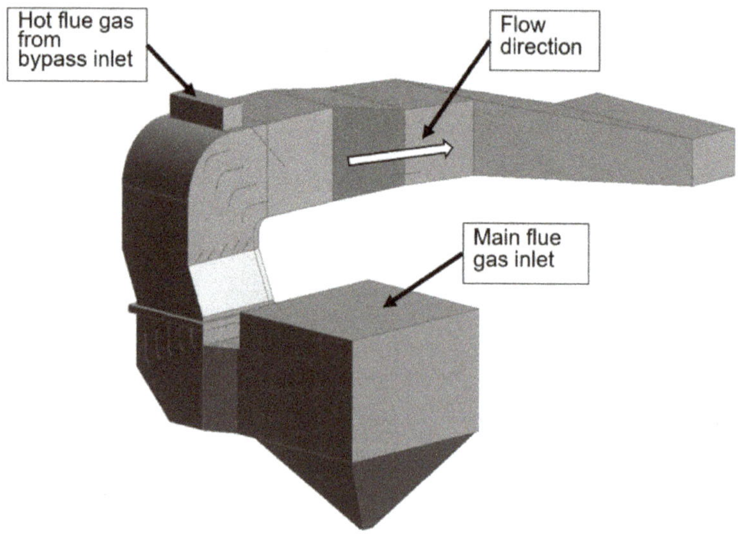

Figure 2. A general schematic of the examined flue gas duct section.

The geometric variants of the turbulence flap are shown in Figure 3. The geometries presented show the same bypass inlet location in each variant and the evolving geometry of the exhaust gas mixing elements. The other elements in the flue gas duct are fixed vanes which regulate the flue gas flow. The geometric variant G1 involves placing a single flap directly behind the hot flue gas inlet. The flap is inclined at an angle of 45 degrees and its length corresponds to covering half of the duct cross-section. A longer flap could not be used in this solution due to limitations on the maximum flue gas velocity, which increases as the flow cross-section area decreases.

In the geometric variant G2, three U-profiles were placed, with a total width of approximately two-thirds of the channel width and a length corresponding to covering half of the flow cross-section resulting from the velocity condition mentioned earlier. Geometric variations G3 and G4 are a combination of G1 and G2. They use a flat flap in the upper part and three U-profiles in the lower part. Both variants are constructed to cover half of the main duct cross-section. Variant G3 uses shorter but wider U-profiles with a total width of about the main duct of two-thirds. In variant G4, the profiles have a total width corresponding to half the main channel width. The designed geometries of the turbulence flaps, as seen from above, are shown in Figure 4.

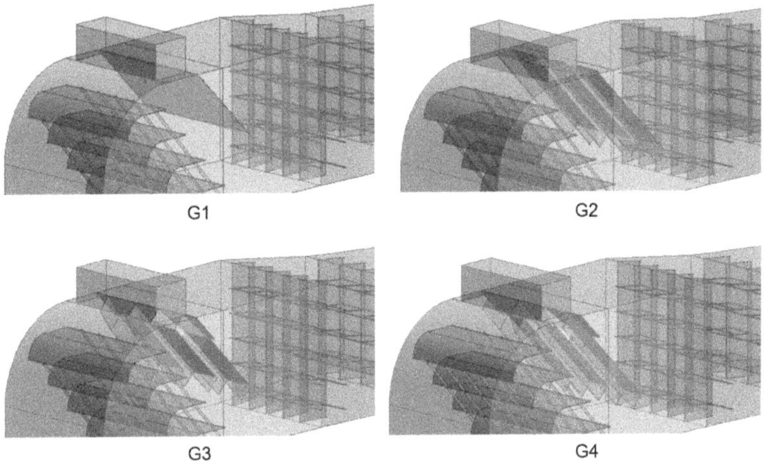

Figure 3. The four geometric variants developed, numbered from G1 to G4.

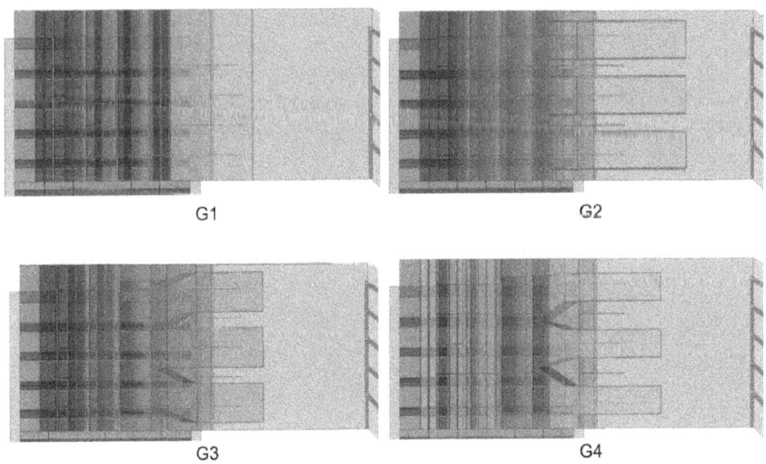

Figure 4. The four geometric variants seen from above, numbered from G1 to G4.

In order to adequately numerically reproduce the effects affecting the exhaust stream mixing, especially the buoyancy forces, the computational geometry was considered at a scale of 1:1. The basic geometrical dimensions of the analyzed channel section are shown in Table 1.

Table 1. The basic geometrical dimensions of the analyzed channel section.

Parameter	Value	Unit
Length of the analyzed channel section	32.10	m
Width of the analyzed channel section	17.35	m
Height of the analyzed channel section	18.13	m
Volume of the analyzed channel section	1094.5	m^3

2.3. Flow-Governing Equations and Model Assumptions

The main equations of fluid mechanics applied to numerical calculations of gas flow such as momentum, mass, energy and species conservation were used for the calculations.

They are widely described in many works, e.g., in [24]. Momentum conservation is represented by Equation (1):

$$\frac{\partial}{\partial x_i}(\rho u_i u_j) + \frac{\partial P}{\partial x_j} = \frac{\partial}{\partial x_i}\left\{\mu\left[\frac{\partial u_j}{\partial x_i} + \frac{\partial u_i}{\partial x_j} - \frac{2}{3}\delta_{ij}\frac{\partial u_i}{\partial x_i}\right]\right\} + \frac{\partial}{\partial x_i}(-\rho u_j u_i) - F_p, \quad (1)$$

Mass conservation (Equation (2)) is presented below:

$$\frac{\partial}{\partial x_i}(\rho u_i) = \sum_J S_j, \quad (2)$$

Equation (3) represents conservation of energy:

$$\frac{\partial}{\partial x_i}(u_i[\rho E + P]) = \frac{\partial}{\partial x_j}\left(\lambda_{eff}\frac{\partial T}{\partial x_j}\right) + S_j, \quad (3)$$

The species conservation is given by Equation (4):

$$\frac{\partial}{\partial x_i}(\rho u_j Y_k) = -\frac{\partial}{\partial x_j}\vec{J_k} + \dot{\omega}_k + S_k, \quad (4)$$

A realizable k-ε turbulence model was implemented for the calculations, with full buoyancy forces included. Detailed descriptions of the above equations and the k-epsilon turbulence model with experimental verification are presented in [24]. The k-ε realizable model was implemented since it is widely used to calculate free gas flows in relatively large domains, such as in power boilers [19,20]. In [25], this model was used to develop a flow in a large-scale coal-fired boiler. The analyzed channel geometry includes elements that can cause rotation, wall boundary layers and gas recirculation. According to [26], the applied turbulence model can provide improved numerical simulation results in the abovementioned phenomena. In the k-epsilon model, Reynolds stresses are supplemented by the Boussinesq relation according to Equation (5):

$$-\rho u_j u_i = \mu_t\left(\frac{\partial u_i}{\partial x_j} + \frac{\partial u_j}{\partial x_i}\right) - \frac{2}{3}\left(\rho k + \mu_t\frac{\partial u_k}{\partial x_k}\right)\delta_{ij}, \quad (5)$$

With the turbulent viscosity calculated from Equation (6):

$$\mu_t = \rho C_\mu k^2/\varepsilon, \quad (6)$$

Unlike the standard and RNG models, the value of C_μ is not constant in the k-epsilon realizable model. C_μ is a function of the mean strain and rotation velocities and the turbulence fields represented by k and epsilon. The effective thermal conductivity can be calculated from the following formula (Equation (7)):

$$\lambda_{eff} = \lambda + c_P\mu_t/Pr_t, \quad (7)$$

Based on the literature [27], the turbulent Prandtl number was assumed to be 0.85.

In keeping with the character of the flue gas flow passing through the duct in an industrial power boiler, the model adopts the simplifications and basic assumptions outlined below:

- Compressible single-phase gas flow;
- As there are particulate settlers in the boiler, the existence of fly ash particles is ignored;
- Gravity field is included with full buoyancy effects;
- The radiation effect is neglected;
- Flue gas composition assumed as a result of coal combustion with a relatively high calorific value.

The discrete form of the equations above and all assumptions were implemented in ANSYS Fluent (18.2, ANSYS, Inc., Canonsburg, PA, USA).

2.4. Meshes

As a full-scale 3D channel section simulation was analyzed, considering many elements installed in the channel, such as vanes and a turbulence flap, which require adequate calculation accuracy, so the implemented mesh is relatively large. The work performed a grid sensitivity analysis, examining grids with the following estimated number of elements: 5.5×10^6, 11×10^6, 17.3×10^6, 29×10^6, 46×10^6. The grid element count varies slightly between the analyzed cases, which is a direct result of the different turbulence flap geometries. In investigating the mesh sensitivity, several numerical simulations were performed analyzing parameters such as the final residual sum, mass, energy balance, maximum and minimum temperatures in the domain and pressure drop in the channel. The most reliable results were obtained for grids with 17.3, 29 and 46 million elements. Meshes with approximately 29 million elements were selected for further analysis because the parameters analyzed were highly reliable. The differences between the values obtained in the simulation with the 46 million grid did not exceed 1%. The chosen computational grid is shown in Figure 5.

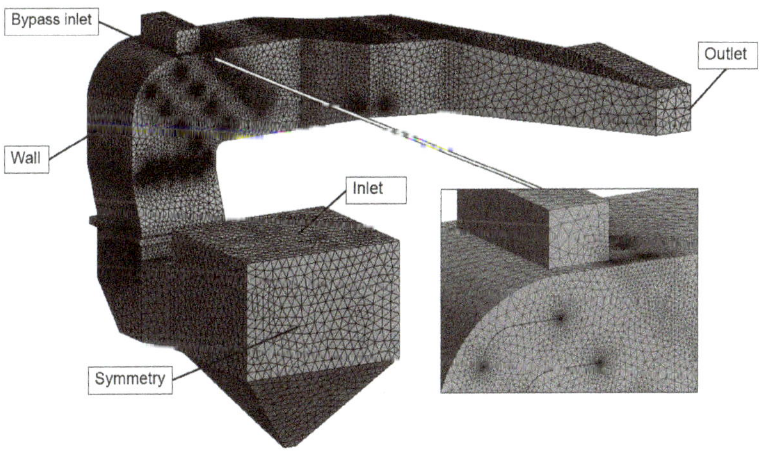

Figure 5. Computational grid of geometry G2 with a zoomed-in view and named selection marked.

As previously mentioned, the analyzed channel section contains many installed irregular-shaped flow control elements that significantly influence the simulation results. Therefore, an unstructured mesh was used in the computational domain, introducing the necessity of using more computing power. The mesh was given appropriately named selections corresponding to the boundary conditions described in the following subsection. The named regions are also shown in Figure 5.

2.5. Boundary Conditions and Simulations Settings

Each of the computational domains corresponding to the geometric variants was given homogeneous boundary conditions. The zones defined are inlet, bypass inlet, outlet, wall and symmetry, marked in Figure 5. The inlet boundary condition corresponds to a flow of 90% of the main exhaust stream at a temperature lower than that required for the efficient operation of the SCR reactor. The design inlet type was defined as a mass flow inlet. The main inlet turbulence was specified with the intensity ratio and the hydraulic diameter. Immediately upstream of the design inlet, the boiler has a heat exchanger covering the entire cross-section of the flue gas duct. Therefore, the flue gas flow upstream of the inlet is relatively uniform and regulated, making it possible to apply the uniform velocity field condition at the domain inlet.

The bypass inlet boundary condition corresponds to the higher temperature flue gases introduced into the main duct. These flue gases are led at 10% of the total amount from the higher temperature boiler part. Mixed with 90% of the flue gases from the main duct, they are supposed to ensure the safe operation of the SCR reactor in the appropriate temperature range. The design type of the bypass flue gas inlet is a mass flow inlet type with a uniform perpendicular velocity field. The uniform velocity field simplification was applied due to the relatively large dimensions of the duct, whose cross-section is almost four square meters. The flow is not laminar, and wall effects are negligible. The turbulence was specified with the intensity ratio and the inlet bypass duct hydraulic diameter.

The domain outlet located just upstream of the SCR reactor was defined as a pressure outlet. The appropriate conditions were applied, such as backflow temperature, exhaust composition and turbulence defined by the intensity and hydraulic outlet diameter.

The remaining boundary conditions are the symmetry condition and the wall condition. The symmetry condition was given on one surface, indicated in Figure 5, and it corresponds to the second, symmetrical part of the boiler, clearly visible in Figure 1. The wall condition was given on all other surfaces of the computational domain, i.e., the external surfaces of the duct as well as all surfaces corresponding to the flow control elements installed in the duct. All walls both inside and outside the channel were modeled as adiabatic. This approach was justified because the walls inside the duct, which are part of the flow control elements, are heated up to the temperature of the flue gases during the continuous boiler operation. Meanwhile, the external duct walls are well insulated, as indicated by modern temperature measurements installed within the examined boiler section.

The key chemical reactions affecting the flue gas composition no longer occur within the investigated boiler section, so the composition was assumed to be homogeneous for the inlets and the outlet. The flue gas composition and other boundary conditions are shown in Table 2. As symmetrical duct operation was simulated, the mass values refer to half of the flow.

Table 2. Flue gas composition and the main boundary conditions.

Parameter	Value	Unit
Oxygen volume fraction in the flue gas	0.033	-
Carbon dioxide volume fraction in the flue gas	0.137	-
Water vapor volume fraction in the flue gas	0.080	-
Nitrogen volume fraction in the flue gas	0.739	-
Other triatomic gas volume fraction in the flue gas	0.010	-
Main flow inlet temperature	567	K
Bypass inlet temperature	867	K
Outlet backflow temperature	597	K
Main inlet flow mass share	90	%
Bypass flow mass share	10	%
Main inlet mass flow	53.5473	kg/s
Bypass inlet mass flow	5.9497	kg/s

The key applied solver settings in ANSYS Fluent are coupled scheme with second order discretization for all parameters, pseudo-transient mode, convergence criteria: 10-4. In order to properly evaluate the simulation correctness, relevant parameters were monitored: outlet mass flow, mass-weighted outlet temperature, maximum and minimum temperature in the domain, pressure drop across the duct. The accuracy of the monitored parameters was obtained at a level below 0.1%. Simulations were carried out with a computing server and utilization of 60 cores. The time required to run a single simulation was approximately 8 h.

The numerical model was verified by comparing the current boiler geometry modeling results with the empirical values. The calculations were performed for several operational states of the boiler. The obtained results of temperatures, pressure drops and exhaust gas velocity distribution were compared with the current measurement data. The parameters calculated using the numerical model for the existing boiler structure were convergent with the measured parameters.

3. Results and Discussion

After calculating all geometric variants, and checking the results for correctness through appropriate monitors, the outcomes obtained were evaluated. The most important results testifying the effectiveness of mixing flue gas streams with different temperatures are the temperature fields generated by the calculations carried out. The flue gas temperature distribution for each geometric variant in the plane intersecting the design domain is shown in Figure 6. The right-hand side of Figure 6 also shows the temperature distribution on a plane perpendicular to the direction of flow, intersecting the mixing flap.

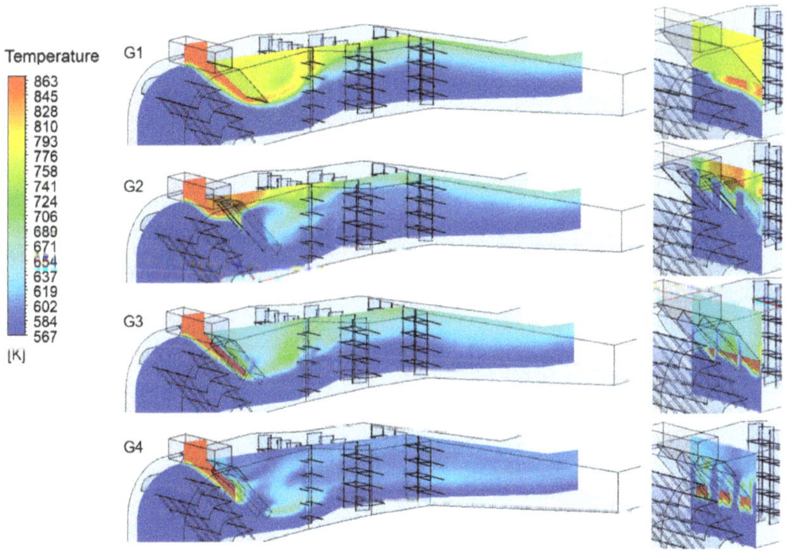

Figure 6. The flue gas temperature distribution for each geometric variant in the plane intersecting the computational domain (on the left) and in the plane perpendicular to the flow direction intersecting the mixing flap (on the right).

After analyzing the simulation results, it can be concluded that the most uniform temperature distribution was obtained for the G4 geometric variant. The simulation results of G1 variant indicate that the higher temperature exhaust gas is initially led to the lower part of the duct. However, immediately after the mixing flap, through buoyancy forces and the mass-dominant flow of the denser exhaust gas with a lower temperature, the hot exhaust gas is pushed to the upper part of the duct. They are then mixed to a small extent in the further duct section.

In variant G2, where U-profiles are used, mixing the flue gases is slightly better than in variant G1. In that case, however, most of the hot flue gases right after the bypass duct inlet are forced by the stream of denser and cooler flue gases into the spaces between the U-profiles and flush out the hot flue gases from further parts of the U-profiles. Therefore, the U-profiles installed in this way do not fulfill their intended role, not delivering the hot flue gases to the lower main duct section. Immediately after the mixing flap, the flue gases are directed upwards by buoyancy forces and mix to a small extent in the further section of the duct.

Variant G3 shows an improvement in the level of flue gas mixing compared to variants G1 and G2. The application of U-profiles with a flat section at the flap top allows for an appropriate hot flue gas distribution to the lower parts of the U-profiles. The initial flat section prevents hot flue gases from being washed out by the lower temperature main stream. However, as previously mentioned, the dimensions of each flap had to be adapted to the condition of maximum coverage of half the main duct cross-section. Therefore, U-profiles with a total width of two-thirds the width of the duct cannot be longer. Since the U-profile of variant G3 is wide but relatively short, the hot flue gases are not introduced deep enough to mix effectively with the cold flue gases.

The G4 variant represents the final concept developed, which represents a modification of the G3 variant. Similar to variant G3, a flat section is used in the upper flap section followed by three U-profiles. Variant G4 uses U-profiles that are narrower and longer than the profiles used in variant G3. As with G3, the flat section of the flap prevents the hot flue gases from being washed out in the upper duct section and ensures adequate hot flue gas distribution to the U-profiles. Suitably long profiles transport the hot flue gases to the lower part of the main duct. Then, due to the buoyancy forces, the hot flue gases are mixed with the main flue gas stream of higher density and lower temperature. Further downstream, the flue gas temperature is homogenized. Since the plane on which the temperature is displayed follows the curvature of the flue gas duct, clearly visible in Figure 1, the hot flue gas portion in the U-profile is cut off, so the observer cannot see the hot flue gas entering the end of the profile.

Figure 7 shows the temperature distributions at the computational domain outlet, corresponding to the SCR reactor exhaust inlet. The temperature scale has been narrowed to 100 K (from 570 to 670 K). The target temperature of the perfectly mixed exhaust gas is 597 K. The best degree of mixing of flue gases was obtained in the geometrical variant G4, as can be seen in Figure 7. In this case, the maximum flue gas temperature was 616 K, which is only 2.18% of the percentage deviation from the perfectly mixed flue gas temperature of 597 K. The minimum flue gas temperature, in this case, was 573.6, which is a deviation of 3.91% from the target temperature. In the cases G1–G3, the temperature amplitudes are considerably larger. All exceed values of 100 K. Simultaneously, in the lower section of the duct, flue gases with a low temperature (close to the initial temperature of the main stream) are observed, which indicates a complete lack of mixing of the lower layers of flue gases.

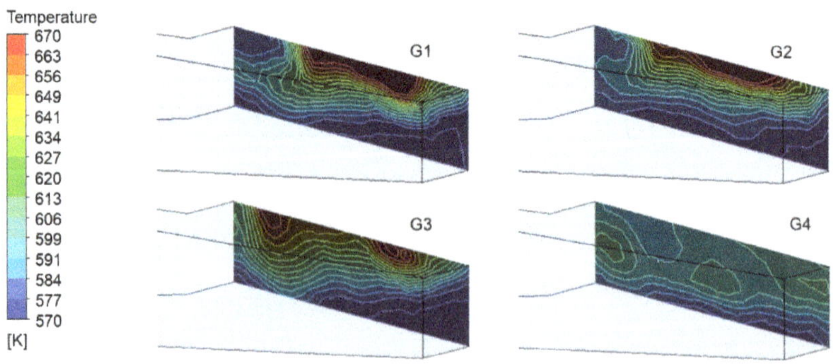

Figure 7. The temperature distributions at the computational domain outlet for each geometric variant.

Figure 8 shows a plot of the minimum and maximum temperatures found for each geometric variant at the outlet of the computational domain representing the inlet to the SCR reactor. The graph also shows the temperature amplitudes at the domain outlet, indicating the degree of exhaust gas stream mixing.

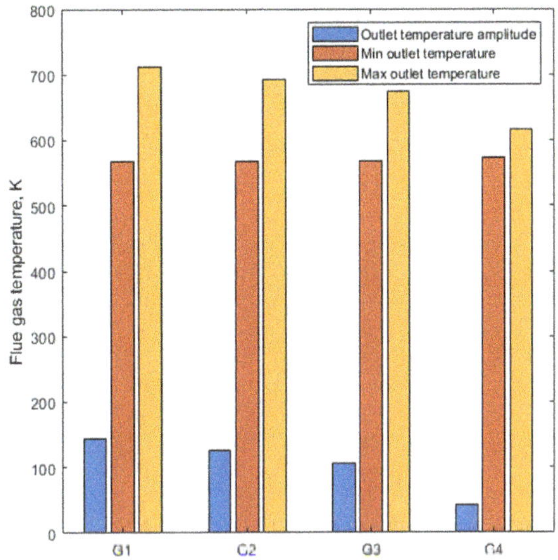

Figure 8. Plot of temperature and amplitude of flue gas temperature at duct outlet for each geometric variant.

The velocity vectors determined on the plane intersecting the computational domain are shown in Figure 9. It can be seen that for variant G1, the velocity of the main flue gas stream increases significantly in the area under the turbulizing flap. Meanwhile, a low-pressure field and backflows are created in the upper part behind the flap. In the G2 variant, the flue gases flow freely through the spaces between the turbulence flap's U-profiles, creating a slight swirl of gas behind the flap. The flow is then stabilized. As in the geometrical variant G1, in the variant G3 with its wide U-profile, the main exhaust flow velocity increases significantly in the area below the flap. Above the flap, a low-pressure field is created together with the backflow. The most uniform velocity field was obtained for variant G4, which is also the most effective in mixing the exhaust gas streams. The main exhaust stream flows gently through the relatively wide spaces between the flap U-profiles. Slight turbulence is created in the upper duct behind the flat part of the turbulence flap.

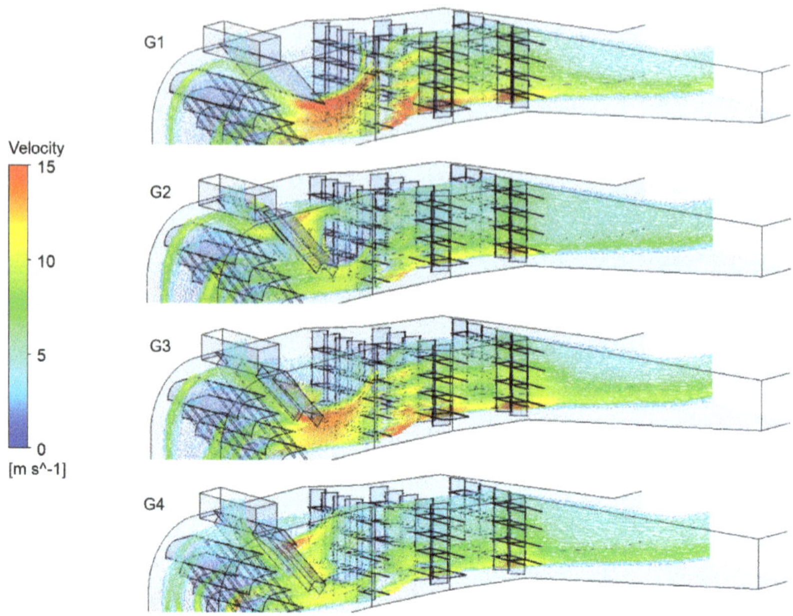

Figure 9. The flue gas velocity distribution for each geometric variant in the plane intersecting the computational domain.

4. Conclusions

This article presents an innovative method of mixing flue gas streams in a coal boiler using the designed mixing flap. The presented work is concerned with supporting the SCR system operation under low-load conditions of coal-fired boilers, contributing to the flexibility of the operation of these devices. The developed solution was exposed to CFD calculations, in which the distributions of temperature, velocity, density and other key thermodynamic parameters were examined. The results indicate that the invented flap works as intended, causing an adequate mixing of the exhaust gas streams. It results in a uniform gas temperature field before the inlet to the SCR system. The analyses showed that the mixing flap developed by the authors could lower the flue gas amplitude in the desired cross-section from 298 K to 43 K. In the intermediate solutions, amplitudes of 144, 125 and 106 K were obtained. By appropriate mixing, the maximum flue gas temperature was reduced by 251 K. In addition, the developed solution was subjected to computational analyses with regard to its functioning in the case of boiler operation with nominal load. The flap, as previously mentioned, can be folded towards the upper wall of the duct. It allows safe boiler operation in nominal conditions without significant pressure losses in the flue gas duct.

The developed solution entails investment costs and operating costs. However, due to the current energy policy and the need for coexistence of coal-fired boilers with renewable energy sources, such solutions are necessary for these facilities to function. As in the flue gas treatment installation, this type of modernization does not provide direct profits from the implementation but allows the facility to operate in new conditions of the energy system.

It is planned to create a construction design and then install the device on the OP-650 boiler in the longer term. Work will then be carried out to optimize the method. The next steps will involve the application of the method in coal boilers with different power ranges. Although the solution is dedicated to power boilers, it is possible to use the developed concept in other systems requiring mixing gases with different temperatures.

Author Contributions: Conceptualization, P.K., M.K.-G. and J.L.; final geometrical concept, P.K.; methodology, P.K. and M.K.-G.; numerical simulation, M.K.-G.; writing—original draft preparation, M.K.-G.; writing—review and editing, M.K.-G.; visualization, M.K.-G.; supervision, P.K. and J.L.; project administration, P.K. and J.L. All authors have read and agreed to the published version of the manuscript.

Funding: This research received no external funding.

Acknowledgments: This research is supported by the National Centre for Research and Development which is co-financed by the European Union in the framework of the Smart Growth Operational Programme and the Power Units 200+ Program. Innovative technology of changing the operating regime of 200 MWe power units.

Conflicts of Interest: The authors declare no conflict of interest.

Nomenclature

c_P	specific heat, J/(kg K)
E	fluid total energy, J/kg
F_p	pressure force, N
J	species mass fluxes, kg/s
k	turbulence kinetic energy, J/kg
P	fluid static pressure, Pa
S	mass source term, kg/(m^3 s)
S_h	energy source term, W/m^3
T	temperature, K
u	velocity, m/s
x	tensor length, m
Y	species mass fraction
Greek symbols	
ε	turbulent kinetic energy dissipation rate
$\dot{\omega}$	species production/destruction rate, kg/(m^3 s)
ρ	gas density, kg/m^3
λ	thermal conductivity, W/(m K)
δ	the Kronecker delta,
μ	viscosity, Pa s
Subscripts and superscripts	
eff	effective
i	tensor direction
j	tensor direction
k	species index
t	turbulent

References

1. Yoshiba, F.; Hanai, Y.; Watanabe, I.; Shirai, H. Methodology to evaluate contribution of thermal power plant flexibility to power system stability when increasing share of renewable energies: Classification and additional fuel cost of flexible operation. *Fuel* **2021**, *292*, 120352. [CrossRef]
2. Kubik, M.L.; Coker, P.J.; Barlow, J.F. Increasing thermal plant flexibility in a high renewables power system. *Appl. Energy* **2015**, *154*, 102–111. [CrossRef]
3. Brouwer, A.S.; van den Broek, M.; Seebregts, A.; Faaij, A. Operational flexibility and economics of power plants in future low-carbon power systems. *Appl. Energy* **2015**, *156*, 107–128. [CrossRef]
4. Zhao, Y.; Wang, C.; Liu, M.; Chong, D.; Yan, J. Improving operational flexibility by regulating extraction steam of high-pressure heaters on a 660 MW supercritical coal-fired power plant: A dynamic simulation. *Appl. Energy* **2018**, *212*, 1295–1309. [CrossRef]
5. Motalleb, M.; Thornton, M.; Reihani, E.; Ghorbani, R. Providing frequency regulation reserve services using demand response scheduling. *Energy Convers. Manag.* **2016**, *124*, 439–452. [CrossRef]
6. Denholm, P.; Hand, M. Grid flexibility and storage required to achieve very high penetration of variable renewable electricity. *Energy Policy* **2011**, *39*, 1817–1830. [CrossRef]
7. Oree, V.; Sayed Hassen, S.Z. A composite metric for assessing flexibility available in conventional generators of power systems. *Appl. Energy* **2016**, *177*, 683–691. [CrossRef]

8. Ulbig, A.; Andersson, G. Analyzing operational flexibility of electric power systems. *Int. J. Electr. Power Energy Syst.* **2015**, *72*, 155–164. [CrossRef]
9. Alizadeh, M.I.; Parsa Moghaddam, M.; Amjady, N.; Siano, P.; Sheikh-El-Eslami, M.K. Flexibility in future power systems with high renewable penetration: A review. *Renew. Sustain. Energy Rev.* **2016**, *57*, 1186–1193. [CrossRef]
10. Liu, X.; Tan, H.; Wang, Y.; Yang, F.; Mikulčić, H.; Vujanović, M.; Duić, N. Low NOx combustion and SCR flow field optimization in a low volatile coal fired boiler. *J. Environ. Manag.* **2018**, *220*, 30–35. [CrossRef]
11. Xiang, J.; Wang, P.; Su, S.; Zhang, L.; Cao, F.; Sun, Z.; Xiao, X.; Sun, L.; Hu, S. Control of NO and Hg0 emissions by SCR catalysts from coal-fired boiler. *Fuel Process. Technol.* **2015**, *135*, 168–173. [CrossRef]
12. Li, Z.; Jiang, J.; Ma, Z.; Wang, S.; Duan, L. Effect of selective catalytic reduction (SCR) on fine particle emission from two coal-fired power plants in China. *Atmos. Environ.* **2015**, *120*, 227–233. [CrossRef]
13. Pritchard, S.; DiFrancesco, C.; Kaneko, S.; Kobayashi, N.; Suyama, K.; Iida, K. Optimizing SCR Catalyst Design and Performance for Coal-Fired Boilers. In Proceedings of the EPRI/EPA 1995 Joint Symposium on Stationary Combustion, Kansas City, MO, USA, 16–19 May 1995.
14. Dal Secco, S.; Juan, O.; Louis-Louisy, M.; Lucas, J.Y.; Plion, P.; Porcheron, L. Using a genetic algorithm and CFD to identify low NOx configurations in an industrial boiler. *Fuel* **2015**, *158*, 672–683. [CrossRef]
15. Modliński, N.; Madejski, P.; Janda, T.; Szczepanek, K.; Kordylewski, W. A validation of computational fluid dynamics temperature distribution prediction in a pulverized coal boiler with acoustic temperature measurement. *Energy* **2015**, *92*, 77–86. [CrossRef]
16. Adamczyk, W.P.; Isaac, B.; Parra-Alvarez, J.; Smith, S.T.; Harris, D.; Thornock, J.N.; Zhou, M.; Smith, P.J.; Żmuda, R. Application of LES-CFD for predicting pulverized-coal working conditions after installation of NOx control system. *Energy* **2018**, *160*, 693–709. [CrossRef]
17. Madejski, P. Numerical study of a large-scale pulverized coal-fired boiler operation using CFD modeling based on the probability density function method. *Appl. Therm. Eng.* **2018**, *145*, 352–363. [CrossRef]
18. Laubscher, R.; Rousseau, P. CFD study of pulverized coal-fired boiler evaporator and radiant superheaters at varying loads. *Appl. Therm. Eng.* **2019**, *160*, 114057. [CrossRef]
19. Rajh, B.; Yin, C.; Samec, N.; Hriberšek, M.; Kokalj, F.; Zadravec, M. Advanced CFD modelling of air and recycled flue gas staging in a waste wood-fired grate boiler for higher combustion efficiency and greater environmental benefits. *J. Environ. Manag.* **2018**, *218*, 200–208. [CrossRef] [PubMed]
20. Gómez, M.A.; Martín, R.; Chapela, S.; Porteiro, J. Steady CFD combustion modeling for biomass boilers: An application to the study of the exhaust gas recirculation performance. *Energy Convers. Manag.* **2019**, *179*, 91–103. [CrossRef]
21. Kurkus-Gruszecka, M.; Krawczyk, P.; Badyda, K. Wpływ wybranych parametrów operacyjnych lancy wtryskowej na dystrybucję reagenta w komorze paleniskowej kotła energetycznego. *Rynek Energii* **2019**, *144*, 46–51.
22. Zeng, H.; Yuan, J.; Wang, J. Optimal design of a tower type SCR-deNOx facility for a 1000 MW coal-fired power plant based on CFD simulation and FMT validation. *Appl. Sci.* **2019**, *9*, 1012. [CrossRef]
23. Wang, G.; Zhang, L.; Ai, D.; Zhao, Y.; Zhou, Y. Research on Nox Formation and SCR Denitration System Control by Smoke Mixing under Low Load. *IOP Conf. Ser. Earth Environ. Sci.* **2020**, *440*, 042053. [CrossRef]
24. Shih, T.-H.; Liou, W.W.; Shabbir, A.; Yang, Z.; Zhu, J. A New k-ε Eddy Viscosity Model for High Reynolds Number Turbulent Flows. *Comput. Fluids* **1995**, *24*, 227–238. [CrossRef]
25. Xu, Y.; Zhang, Y.; Liu, F.; Shi, W.; Yuan, J. CFD analysis on the catalyst layer breakage failure of an SCR-DeNOx system for a 350 MW coal-fired power plant. *Comput. Chem. Eng.* **2014**, *69*, 119–127. [CrossRef]
26. ANSYS ANSYS FLUENT Theory Guide. *Knowl. Creat. Diffus. Util.* **2010**, *15317*, 724–746.
27. Weigand, B.; Ferguson, J.R.; Crawford, M.E. An extended Kays and Crawford turbulent Prandtl number model. *Int. J. Heat Mass Transf.* **1997**, *40*, 4191–4196. [CrossRef]

energies

Article

Analysis of Air Pollution around a CHP Plant: Real Measurements vs. Computer Simulations

Robert Cichowicz * and Maciej Dobrzański

Faculty of Civil Engineering, Architecture and Environmental Engineering, Lodz University of Technology, Al. Politechniki 6, 90-924 Lodz, Poland; maciej.dobrzanski@p.lodz.pl
* Correspondence: robert.cichowicz@p.lodz.pl

Abstract: This study examines the concentrations of air pollution in the vicinity of a combined heat and power plant (CHP) and a communication route, using computer modeling of pollutant dispersion and spatial analysis based on real measurements in the city of Łódź, Poland, Europe. The research takes into account the concentrations of particulate matter (PM_{10}, $PM_{2.5}$, $PM_{1.0}$) and gaseous pollutants (SO_2 and VOC) in winter and summer. The spatial distribution of pollutants is discussed, including the presence of areas with increased accumulations of pollutants. Because atmospheric air has no natural boundaries, when analyzing any location, not only local sources of pollution, but also background pollution, should be analyzed. A clear difference was observed between the concentrations of pollutants in the summer and winter seasons, with significantly higher concentrations in the winter (heating) period. The impacts of road transport, individual heating systems, and combined heat and power plants were also assessed. Computer calculations confirmed that road transport accounted for the largest share of both PM and SO_2 emissions. The CHP plant was responsible for the smallest percentage of dust emissions and was the next largest producer of SO_2 emissions. The share of the total emissions from the individual sources were compared with the results of detailed field tests. The numerical analysis of selected pollution sources in combination with the field analysis shows that the identified pollution sources included in the analysis represent only a part of the total observed pollutant concentrations (suggesting that other background sources account for the rest).

Keywords: dispersion of pollutants; air quality monitoring; SO_2; VOC; PM_{10}; $PM_{2.5}$; $PM_{1.0}$; 3D spatial analysis; outdoor air quality; air quality modeling

Citation: Cichowicz, R.; Dobrzański, M. Analysis of Air Pollution around a CHP Plant: Real Measurements vs. Computer Simulations. *Energies* **2022**, *15*, 553. https://doi.org/10.3390/en15020553

Academic Editors: Francesco Nocera and Robert H. Beach

Received: 25 November 2021
Accepted: 10 January 2022
Published: 13 January 2022

1. Introduction

According to data from the European Commission's Joint Research Center (JRS) [1], as much as 75% of the world's population lives in urban agglomerations. In Europe, the urbanization rate was 72% in 2015 [1]. Therefore, the state of air quality in large urban agglomerations is a matter of key concern. According to a European Environment Agency (EEA) report from 2020 [2], the most frequently analyzed pollutants are PM_{10}, $PM_{2.5}$, and SO_2. This is because large populations are exposed to these pollutants at concentrations higher than recommended by the EU and WHO. According to an EEA report [2], as much as 48% of the population living in urban agglomerations is exposed to concentrations of PM_{10} above the acceptable level of 20 $\mu g/m^3$ (average annual concentration) set by the WHO in 2005 [3], and 15% of the urban population in Europe is exposed to concentrations of PM_{10} above the EU standard of 40 $\mu g/m^3$ (average annual concentration of PM_{10}) [4]. Moreover, 74% of the urban population is exposed to average annual concentrations of $PM_{2.5}$ above the permissible level of 10 $\mu g/m^3$ established by the WHO, and 19% of people are exposed to an average daily concentration of SO_2 above the recommended limit of 20 $\mu g/m^3$. Using less restrictive EU standards, only 4% of the European population is exposed to levels of $PM_{2.5}$ beyond the permissible concentration of 25 $\mu g/m^3$ and less than 1% of the European population is exposed to SO_2 at levels above the recommended limit of 125 μg/m^3 (24-h limit). However, in 2021, the WHO [5] updated its statements regarding permissible levels of pollutants. For PM_{10} and $PM_{2.5}$, the permissible annual average concentrations were reduced by 25% and 50%, respectively, to 15 μg/m^3 and 5 μg/m^3. In the case of SO_2, the permissible level was increased by 100% from 20 μg/m^3 to 40 μg/m^3 (average daily SO_2 concentration), but this is still well below the limit permitted by the EU.

The main emitters of pollutants are the energy industry [6,7], agriculture, individual heating systems [8], and road transport [9,10]. According to the EEA [2], 41% of PM_{10} emissions are produced by secondary energy consumers (the commercial and public sectors, as well as private households), 10% by road transport, and 3% by the energy industry. The energy industry is responsible for as much as 47% of the emissions of gaseous pollutants, including SO_2. Other industries are responsible for 33% of gaseous pollutants, while households together with the service sector and trade sector contribute 15%. This information is based on statistical data collected by air quality monitoring systems situated in all European Union member states and varies between nations. The monitoring system consists of stationary ground stations that measure pollutant concentrations in a manual daily system and an automatic continuous system [11]. Due to the low density of air quality monitoring stations, the data they collect cannot be used for a detailed analysis of the impact of individual pollution sources on local air quality. For example, in Poland there are about 0.00062 stations/km^2 (in 2017, the number of PM_{10} measurement stations was 194). In Europe overall, the figure is about 0.00060 stations/km^2 (there were 2551 PM_{10} measurement stations in 2017) [12]. For this reason, air quality tests carried out with mobile measurement devices [13] or using numerical programs for calculating/simulating pollutant dispersion in a selected local area are very important. Mobile measuring equipment, such as unmanned aerial vehicles, can be used to transport measuring devices [14,15] or small stationary devices [16]. Numerical programs available include Aero 2010, Emitor, OPA03 [17], AERMOD [18], ENVI-met, and Austal 2000 [19,20].

In this study, we analyzed various anthropogenic sources of pollutants in a selected area, using numerical calculations and real measurements.

2. Methodology

2.1. Analyzed Area

The analysis was focused on an urban area in the city of Łódź. Łódź is the third largest city in Poland (central-eastern Europe) in terms of the number of inhabitants (population density: 2292.2 people/km^2, population: 672,185, area: 293.2 km^2). The area comprises a thoroughfare running from the west to the east along Pojezierska Street, on the intersection between Aleja Włókniarzy and Zgierska Street (Figure 1).

Figure 2 shows the selected fragment of the street (no. 1) is about 1.5 km long and runs through areas of different types and purposes. We distinguish between shopping areas with large-area stores (no. 2), green areas and parks (no. 3), single-family housing areas (no. 4), multi-family developments (no. 5) and industrial areas (no. 6). The gross development index in the area ranges from 0.5 to 1.0. The analyzed street plays an important role as a road transport route connecting two main streets in the city in the east–west system. It is both a local access route to residential and industrial areas and a transit route through the city. According to [21], the average traffic volume on this road section for every 15 min is between 500 and 750 vehicles (between 2000 and 3000 vehicles per hour). In the close vicinity, there is one of the two main heat and power plants in the city, called EC-3 (Figure 2). The EC-3 combustion installation includes 9 boilers: five coal-fired steam boilers, one steam boiler fired with light fuel oil, and three water boilers fired with heavy oil. The total thermal capacity is 804 MW, and the electrical capacity is 205.85 MW [22].

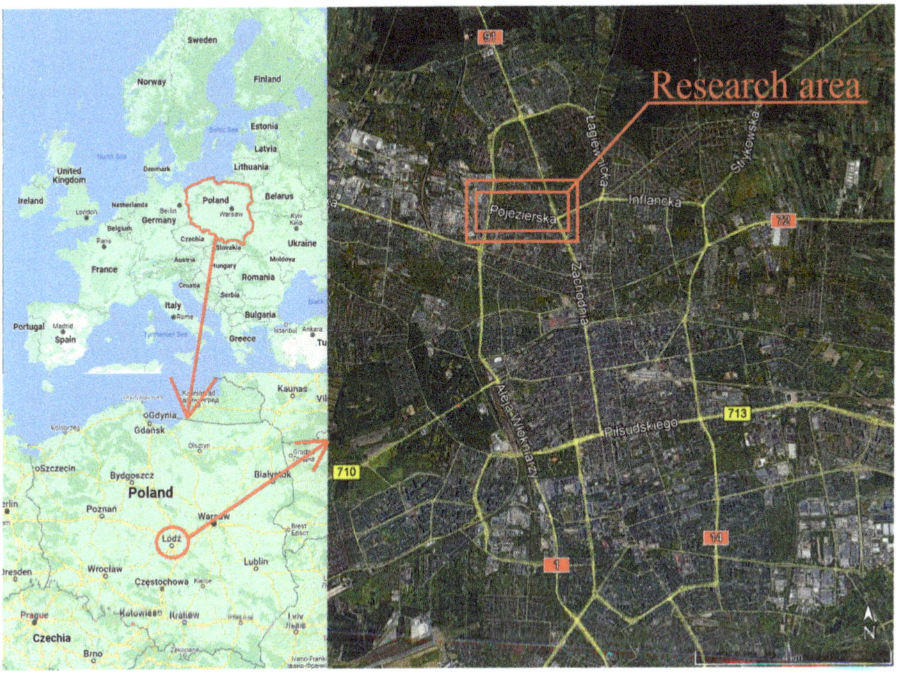

Figure 1. Location of the research area in the city of Łódź in Poland, Europe (photo background source: Google Earth Pro).

2.2. *Methodology of Analysis*

We used both actual measurements and numerical calculations of the dispersion of emissions from selected pollution sources. Based on analysis of the research area, three probable sources of air pollution were selected: EC3 heat and power plants fired with hard coal, light, and heavy fuel oil; road transport, and individual heating systems. The actual measurements were performed in the first quarter of the year, in the period from January to March 2021 (this is the winter heating season in central and eastern Europe), and in the third quarter of the year, from June to August 2021 (the summer period in Poland). Mobile measuring equipment was used, consisting of measuring and sampling devices installed on an unmanned aerial vehicle (UAV) and on a transport platform (TP). The use of the UAV allowed for measurements at heights from 5 m to 50 m above the ground. The TP was used for measurements at a height of about 2 m above the ground. The measuring apparatus was equipped with a laser-scattered (LS) sensor, which was used to measure PM_{10}, $PM_{2.5}$, and $PM_{1.0}$ (10,000 particles per second). It was also equipped with ElectroChemical (EC) sensors to measure H_2S (3 ppb–1 ppm), O_2 (0.20–100%), VOCs (Ethanol, Iso-Butane, 0–500 ppm, sensor type: MOS) and SO_2 (0.5–2000 ppm). Validation of the measurement data of particulate matter was performed on the basis of data from an accredited measuring station VIEP (the method equivalent to the reference method), while the gaseous pollutants were validated in relation to the VEGA-GC microchromatograph (equipped with a thermal conductivity detector TCD, minimum concentration of 500 ppb (0.005 ppm)). Numerical analyses of pollutant dispersion were carried out using the ArcGis [23] program, which was used to produce a graphical presentation of the actual measurement data, and the OPA03 program by Eko-Soft [24], which was used to simulate the concentrations of pollutants from selected pollution sources. Interpolation in ArcGis was carried out using the Empirical Bayesian Kriging 3D method. Both software programs are described in detail in [14,25]. The calculations performed in the OPA03 program are based on the legal acts in force in Poland [26] and the European Union [4]. The OPA03 software is based on the proprietary algorithm of the EKO-Soft company, in accordance with the methodology described in the Polish law [26]. Data on the wind rose in the analyzed period, emitter parameters (such as the number of chimneys and their height, speed of exhaust gases, mass concentration of pollutants emitted, average hourly number of vehicles, and type of fuel) were added to the program. Details for individual pollutant emitters are presented further in the article.

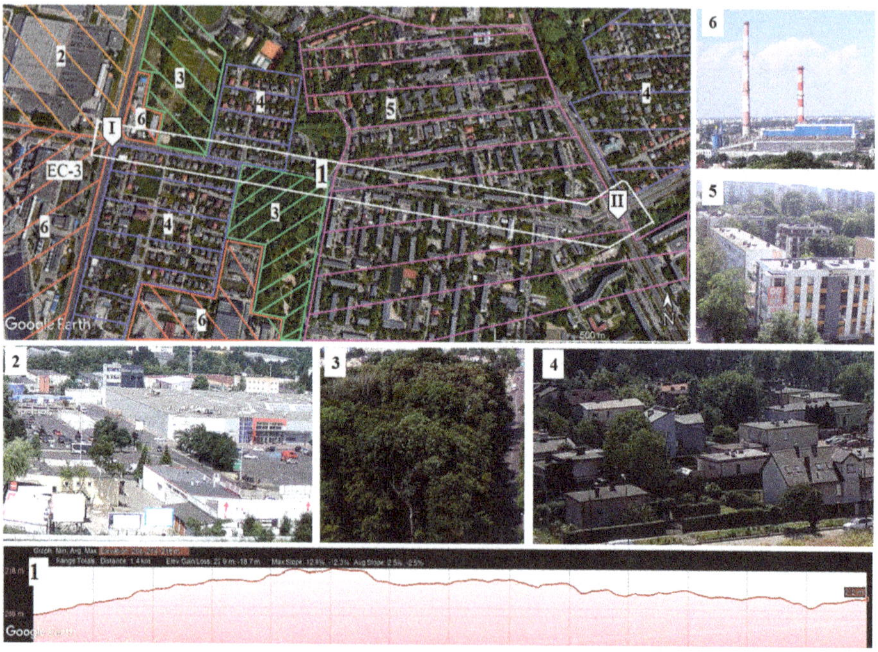

Figure 2. Map of the main areas affecting air quality: 1—analyzed area from the west intersection "I" to the east intersection "II"; 2—area of large-format stores; 3—green areas; 4—single-family houses; 5—multi-family houses; 6—industrial areas: warehouse, offices, small handicraft industries, and EC3 heat and power plant (photo background source: Google Earth Pro).

The input data for the calculation of pollutant emissions from the EC-3 CHP plant were provided for scientific purposes by Veolia Energia Łódź and are the actual measurements of emissions from the CHP plant taken during the analyzed period. According to annual data, the maximum recorded emissions of PM_{10}, $PM_{2.5}$, and SO_2 were 2.667 kg/h, 1.143 kg/h, and 128.81 kg/h, respectively. In accordance with the methodology presented in [27], the average volume of traffic measured during field measurements was adopted for the analysis. Different vehicle types and fuels were considered. According to [28], gasoline-powered passenger cars account for 55% of all vehicles using the analyzed communication artery, diesel-powered cars accounted for 30%, and LPG gas-powered cars for 15%. Vans were divided between those with diesel engines (75%) and those with gasoline engines (25%). Tractors and buses were 100% diesel, and 100% of motorcycles had gasoline engines (detailed data on pollutant emissions are provided later in this paper). Finally, we considered individual heating systems in single-family houses located in the immediate and close vicinity of the studied area. Individual heating systems are used for domestic hot water in summer and for heating in winter. It was assumed in the calculations that 70% of the buildings used hard coal as fuels, and 30% used natural gas.

In the numerical analysis in the OPA03 software, the simulation can be performed with or without the background level of pollution in the air. The background level of pollutions is understood as the concentration of pollutants in the air without the analyzed pollutant emitter. Background levels of pollution were not included in the numerical analyses, to illustrate the individual impact of pollution sources on the dispersion of air pollutants. A common level of 2 m above ground level was adopted for the analysis. Particulate matter pollutants PM_{10}, $PM_{2.5}$, and $PM_{1.0}$ were included in the field measurements, as well as gaseous SO_2 and VOCs. For the purposes of comparison, the numerical analysis was based on PM_{10} and SO_2 emissions.

2.3. Meteorological Conditions

Characteristic data for the winter (1st quarter of the year) and summer (3rd quarter of the year) periods in central Poland were selected for the analysis. The winter period was from January to March, which is the so-called the heating period because the outside air temperatures oscillate predominantly around 0 °C. For this reason, it was decided to choose two representative measurement series, A and B, for which the average air temperature was about 6 °C with a relative humidity of about 76% (Table 1). In the summer period, from June to August, average air temperatures above 18 °C predominate. Therefore, it was decided to choose two series, C and D, in which the average temperature was higher than 20 °C.

Table 1. Meteorological data for representative measurement series during the winter and summer periods (source: [29]).

Series	Date Y.M.D	Temperature [2 m Above Ground]			Relative Humidity [2 m Above Ground]			Wind Speed [10 m Above Ground]			Wind Direction
		°C			%			m/s			°
		Min	Mean	Max	Min	Mean	Max	Min	Mean	Max	Mean
A	22 January 2021	3.2	6	9.4	66	78	91	1	2.8	4	191
B	25 February 2021	−1.4	7	17.4	39	75	97	1	1.3	3	207
C	24 June 2021	17.2	22	28.3	61	81	100	1	2.1	5	190
D	7 July 2021	18.4	25	31.4	40	65	89	1	2.8	7	167

In the analysis of the dispersion of pollutants, another important parameter is the speed and direction of the wind. In the city of Łódź in 2021, winds from the west W (11%) and west–north WSW, and SW (9%) directions were prevailing, with wind speeds ranging from 0 m/s to 7.5 m/s (Figure 3). In the winter period from January to March, the average wind speed was 2.92 m/s (11% W). In the summer period from June to August, the average wind speed was 15% lower, amounting to 2.47 m/s (9% WSW).

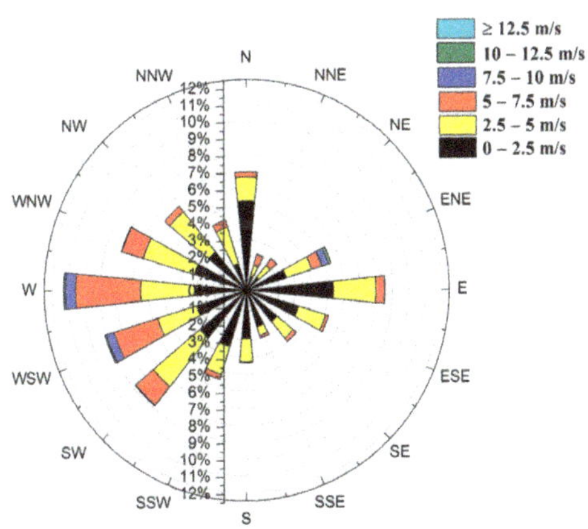

Figure 3. Wind rose for the city of Łódź in 2021 (own study based on data from source [29]).

3. Results

Based on the results of the field measurements, 3D maps were drawn using ArcGis software of the dispersion of pollution in the analyzed area. This form of 3D spatial analysis is an innovative approach, so the results are not comparable with the literature data. Due to the fact that dust pollution has similar field dispersion characteristics [14], PM_{10} pollution was selected for the graphic presentation. Figure 4 shows the results of PM_{10} dispersion for series A and B in the winter period, together with a longitudinal and vertical cross-section for series B to show changes in the altitude of the pollution.

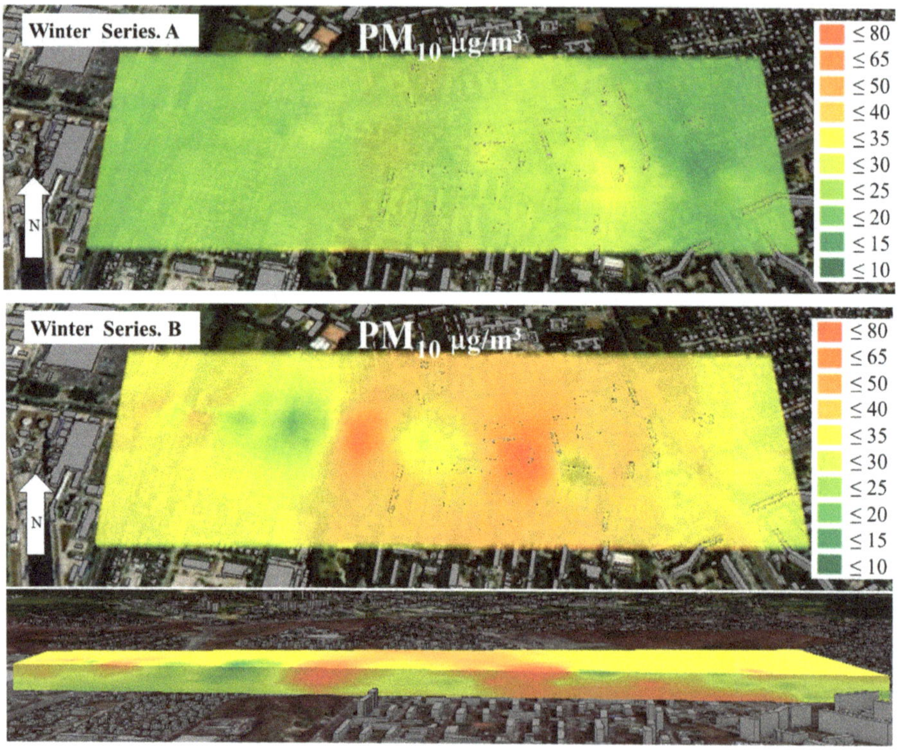

Figure 4. Spatial distribution of PM_{10} concentrations during the winter season in series A and B.

The selected series of representative measurements for the winter period show a variable concentration of PM_{10}. In series A, the average concentration of PM_{10} was 21.80 μg/m^3 and the maximum concentration was 42.40 μg/m^3. According to the air quality index adopted in Poland [30], the air quality of series A is classed as "Good" (limit of PM_{10} 20.1–50.0 μg/m^3). The spatial analysis shows that the entire area of analysis was characterized by an even concentration of PM_{10}. In comparison, series B showed double the concentrations of PM pollutants. The mean concentration of PM_{10} was 54.80 μg/m^3 and the maximum 77.60 μg/m^3. According to the air quality index in relation to PM_{10}, the air quality of series B is "Moderate" (50.1–80.0 μg/m^3). In series A, the concentration of PM_{10} did not exceed the level of 50 μg/m^3 allowed by EU standards, whereas in series B the EU limit was exceeded in many places by 55%. The increased concentration of particulate matter in series B can be explained by the fact that the average wind speed was less than half that in the series A. Tall buildings, with heights of 15–30 m, also contributed to the accumulation of pollution in the analyzed area. In series B, there are spaces with lower and higher PM_{10} concentrations. Elevated levels of $PM_{10} > 60$ μg/m^3 (red in Figure 4) occur at street crossings and in more densely built-up areas. Lower PM_{10} concentrations (green in Figure 4) relative to the mean value occur in the highest part of the analyzed area. This is probably related to the stronger ventilation. From the vertical cross-section view of the 3D dispersion, it can be concluded that concentrations above 40 $\mu g/m^3$ occur mainly close to the ground surface. At the intersections, the concentration of PM_{10} increases with height, which is probably related to the upward movement of pollutants and car exhaust fumes.

The concentrations of PM_{10} in series C and D in the summer period (Figure 5) were up to four times lower compared to the winter period. The mean concentrations of PM_{10} in series C and D were 8.20 $\mu g/m^3$ and 12.10 $\mu g/m^3$, respectively. In contrast to the winter period, during the summer period the concentration of PM_{10} was similar in the whole analyzed area. There were no areas with concentrations of particulate matter above the average value. Only in series D, during a period of high temperatures and low humidity, were PM_{10} concentrations observed exceeding 30 $\mu g/m^3$, as can be seen in the upper left area of Figure 5. The source was earthworks at a construction site. To sum up, during the summer period the permissible level PM_{10} of 50 $\mu g/m^3$ was not exceeded [4]. In the summer, the use of fuel for heating purposes in individual heating systems is reduced and the average speed of road transport increases. This contributes to lower emissions of particulate matter. To facilitate comparison of the 3D dispersion maps, further analysis of the air quality parameters was limited to two of the selected representative measurement series in order to facilitate the graphical reception and comparison of the results.

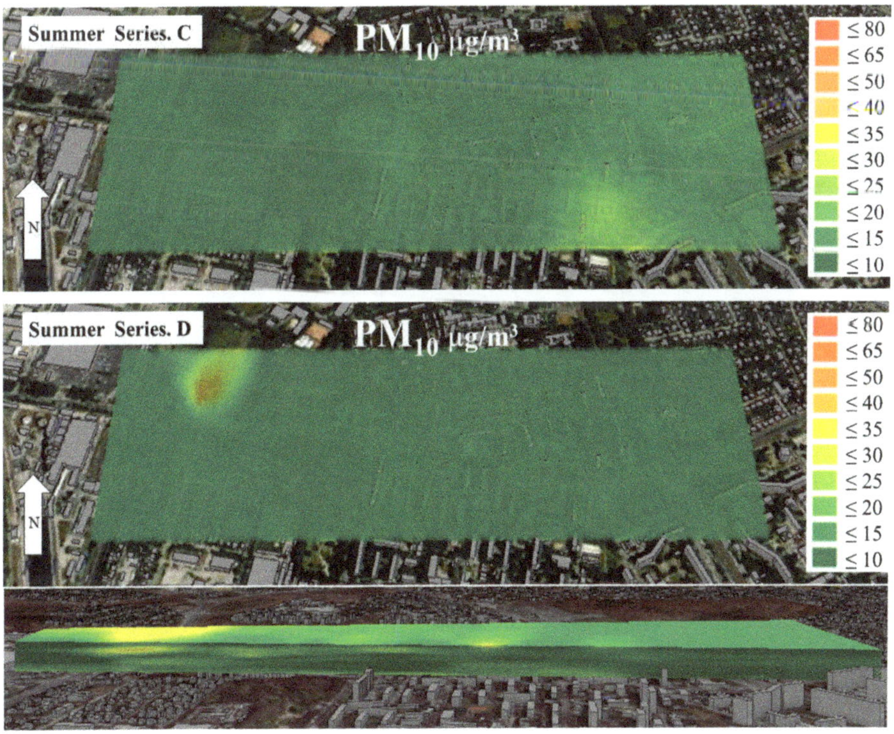

Figure 5. Spatial distribution of PM_{10} concentrations during the summer season in series C and D.

The emissions of pollutants selected in this study are mostly related to the combustion of fossil fuels. Therefore, SO_2, which is another of the products of the combustion of fuels used in motor vehicles, was also included in the analysis. In series A of the winter period, the concentration of SO_2 varied from 0.006 ppm to 0.346 ppm, i.e., from 20 $\mu g/m^3$

to 970 μg/m^3. Spatial analysis (Figure 6) showed the presence of an area with a high concentration of SO_2 above 0.24 ppm (>670 μg/m^3) at the sites of traffic jams before the eastern intersection. It may also be due to SO_2 being transported downwind from industrial emitters such as EC3. The second place with a high concentration of SO_2 was at the extreme western intersection. Concentrations of SO_2 below 0.16 ppm (<450 μg/m^3) were recorded only at a height of more than 30 m above ground level, in an area of low-rise single-family housing. This was probably due to the stronger ventilation in the area. According to the cross-section of the 3D dispersion map, the highest SO_2 concentrations above 0.24 ppm were measured at ground level. With increasing heights above ground level, the concentration of SO_2 decreased up to threefold. This suggests that the main sources of SO_2 were car exhaust fumes and exhaust fumes from individual heating systems (single-family buildings). According to the EU, 15% of SO_2 emissions are caused by individual heating systems [2]. Across the entire area, at a height of 2 m the permissible level of SO_2 (350 μg/m^3) according to EU standards [4] was exceeded by about 20–277%.

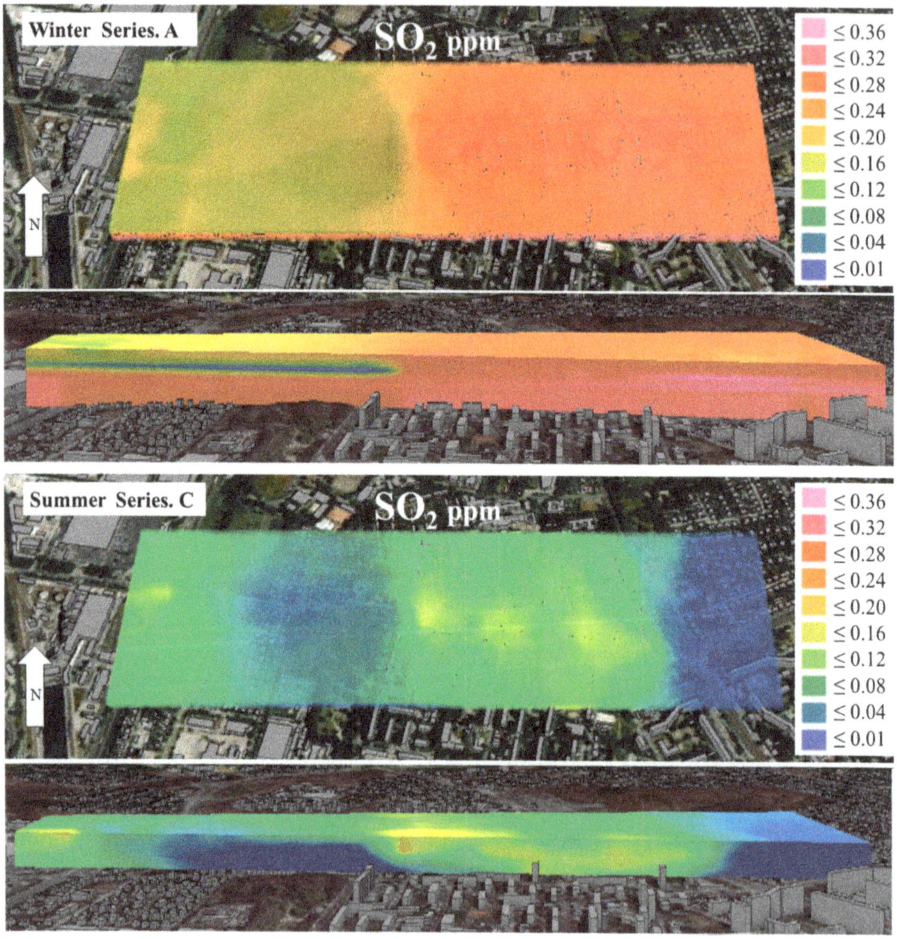

Figure 6. Spatial distribution of SO_2 concentrations during the winter season in series A and during the summer season in series C.

In the summer period, the SO_2 concentration decreased significantly, and was up to three times lower compared to the winter period. In series C (Figure 6), the concentration of SO_2 ranged from 0.001 ppm to 0.122 ppm (max 320 μg/m^3). Similar to the winter period, the spatial distribution showed the presence of areas with increased SO_2 concentrations at the intersections and the sites of traffic congestion. However, according to the cross-section of the pollution dispersion map, in summer the highest concentration of SO_2 was not at ground level, as it was in winter. This can be explained by the fact that there was no thermal inversion in the summer period. This prevented the accumulation of pollutants and enabled faster mixing (dilution) in the atmospheric air. The concentration of SO_2 was lowest at the highest point of the area of analysis and in the open space behind the crossing from the eastern side. This was probably related to the fact that these are zones of increased ventilation [31].

Finally, we considered the concentrations of Volatile Organic Compounds (Figure 7). In the winter and summer periods, the average VOCs concentration was about 20 μg/m^3 (0.005 ppm). However, in the winter period the VOCs concentration reached 0.09–0.12 ppm (310–420 μg/m^3), i.e., 53% higher than the maximum VOCs concentration in the summer period (0.023–0.079 ppm). This can be explained by a higher degree of photochemical reactions in the summer period, which reduce the concentration of VOCs. The cross-section of the pollution dispersion map for the winter months shows that the highest concentrations of VOCs were recorded close to the ground surface. As the altitude increased, the VOCs concentration quickly decreased to levels below 0.005 ppm (20 μg/m^3). In summer, the highest concentrations of VOCs pollution occurred in the area around Pojezierska Street and towards the western intersection, where the heat and power plant is located. Xu et al. similarly identified a heat and power plant as the main origin of VOCs [32].

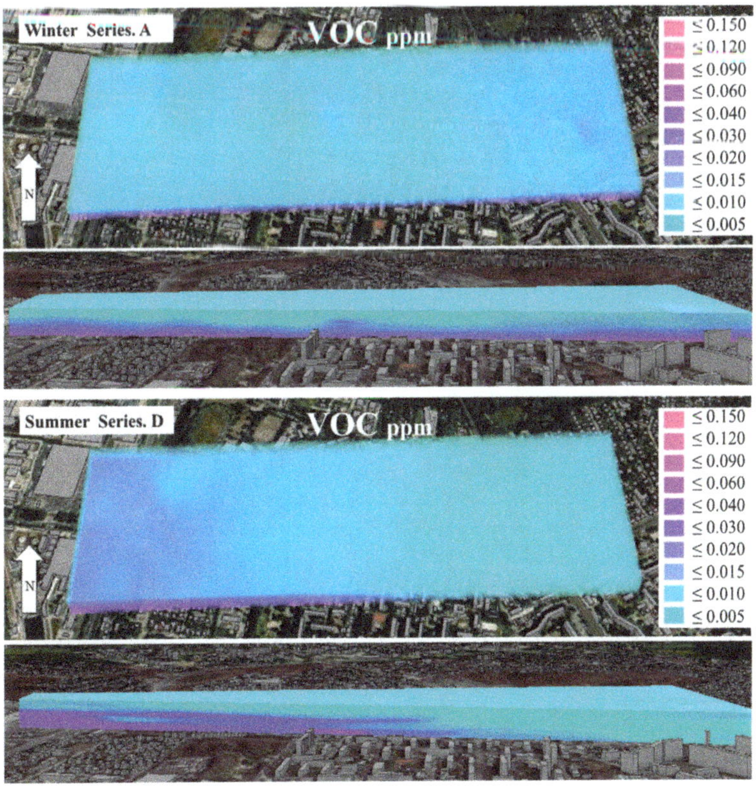

Figure 7. Spatial distribution of VOCs concentrations during the winter season in series A and during the summer season in series D.

Table 2 presents the results of actual measurements from the representative series (A–D) taken during the 3 months of research in the winter and summer periods. The data show that in the winter period the concentration of particulate matter was almost four times higher relative to the average value than in the summer period. The concentration of SO_2 was three times higher in the winter than in the summer. The average VOCs concentration remained at a similar level, regardless of the season.

Table 2. Measured concentrations of pollutants in a representative measurement series during the winter and summer periods in 2021.

		Winter		Summer	
Series		A	B	C	D
Date		22 January 2021	25 February 2021	24 June 2021	7 July 2021
PM_{10} $\mu g/m^3$	max	42.38	77.54	16.00	32.00
	mean	21.79	54.80	8.23	12.08
	min	11.28	41.69	3.30	8.60
$PM_{2.5}$ $\mu g/m^3$	max	36.60	65.40	15.00	30.00
	mean	14.98	38.62	5.22	10.77
	min	4.80	23.10	2.70	7.40
PM_1 $\mu g/m^3$	max	36.50	65.40	10.00	19.20
	mean	13.98	37.59	3.70	9.12
	min	3.80	22.10	1.10	6.40
VOCs ppm	max	0.090	0.122	0.023	0.079
	mean	0.0049	0.00598	0.005	0.022
	min	0.001	0.001	0.001	0.001
SO_2 ppm	max	0.346	0.269	0.164	0.122
	mean	0.248	0.131	0.059	0.075
	min	0.006	0.008	0.001	0.001

The next part of the analysis used numerical software to calculate the dispersion of selected pollutants in relation to their probable sources of emissions.

The area of interest includes a heat and power plant with a chimney 120 m tall, from which emissions are released. Data were obtained from Veolia Energia Łódź, comprising a collective measurement of emissions (kg/h) from the chimney after desulphurization and dedusting of flue gases from five boilers. As can be seen in Table 3, the emissions were mostly composed of SO_2 (despite the exhaust gas treatment systems). This suggests that the EC-3 CHP plant may be responsible for the high concentrations of SO_2 found in our analysis.

Table 3. Maximum hourly emissions of pollutants for the EC-3 CHP plant (own calculations based on data from Veolia Energia Łódź).

Emitter	Maximum Hourly Emission [kg/h]		
H120	PM_{10} 2.667	$PM_{2.5}$ 1.143	SO_2 128.81

Based on the parameters of the emitter and the amounts of pollutants, OPA03 software was used to simulate the dispersion of emissions from the EC-3 CHP plant. The results are shown in Figures 8–12. According to the simulation, in winter, the maximum concentration of PM_{10} emitted from EC-3 was 0.21 $\mu g/m^3$ (Figure 8).

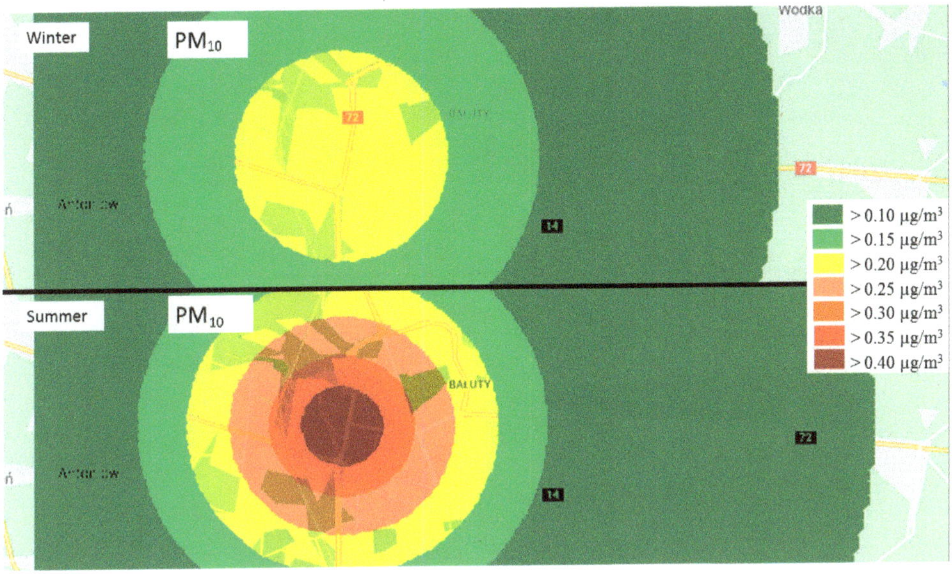

Figure 8. Dispersion diagram of the maximum 1-h concentrations of PM_{10} emitted in the summer and winter periods from EC-3.

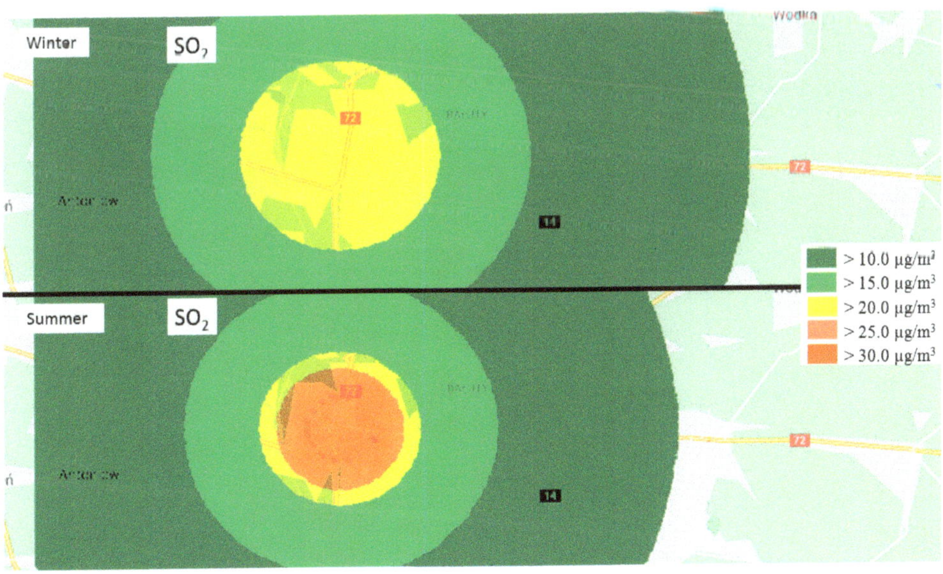

Figure 9. Dispersion diagram of the maximum 1-h concentrations of SO_2 emitted in the summer and winter periods from EC-3.

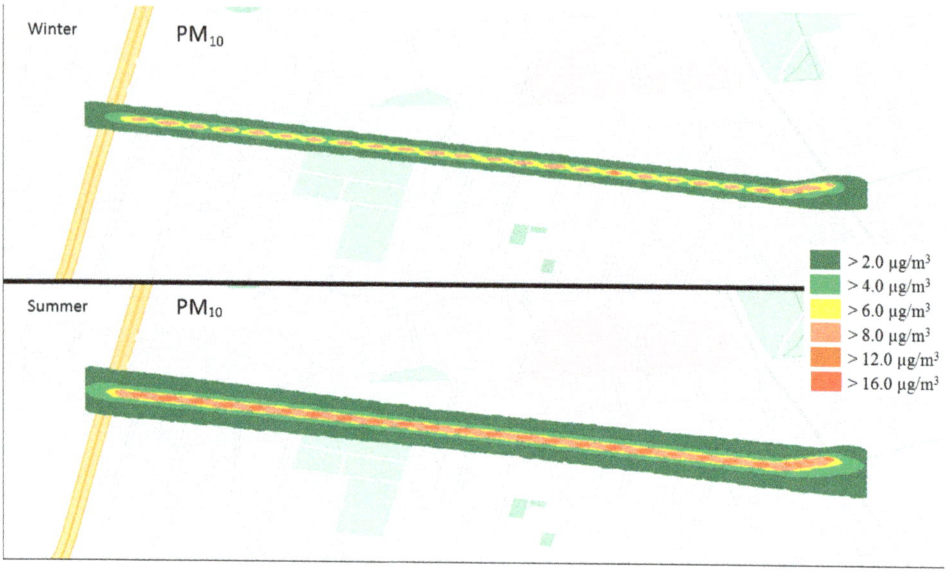

Figure 10. Dispersion diagram of the maximum 1-h concentrations of PM_{10} emitted in the summer and winter periods from road traffic.

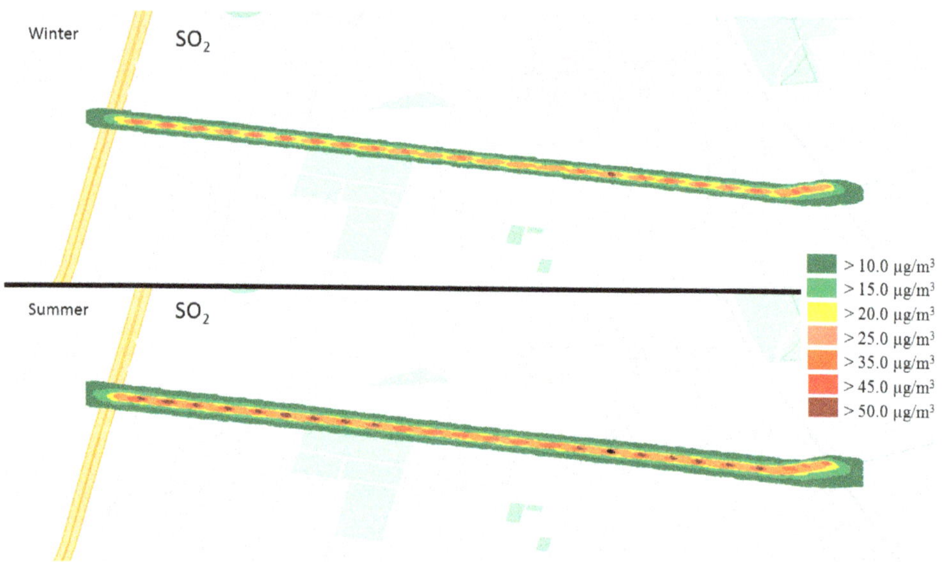

Figure 11. Dispersion diagram of the maximum 1-h SO_2 concentration in the summer and winter periods from road traffic.

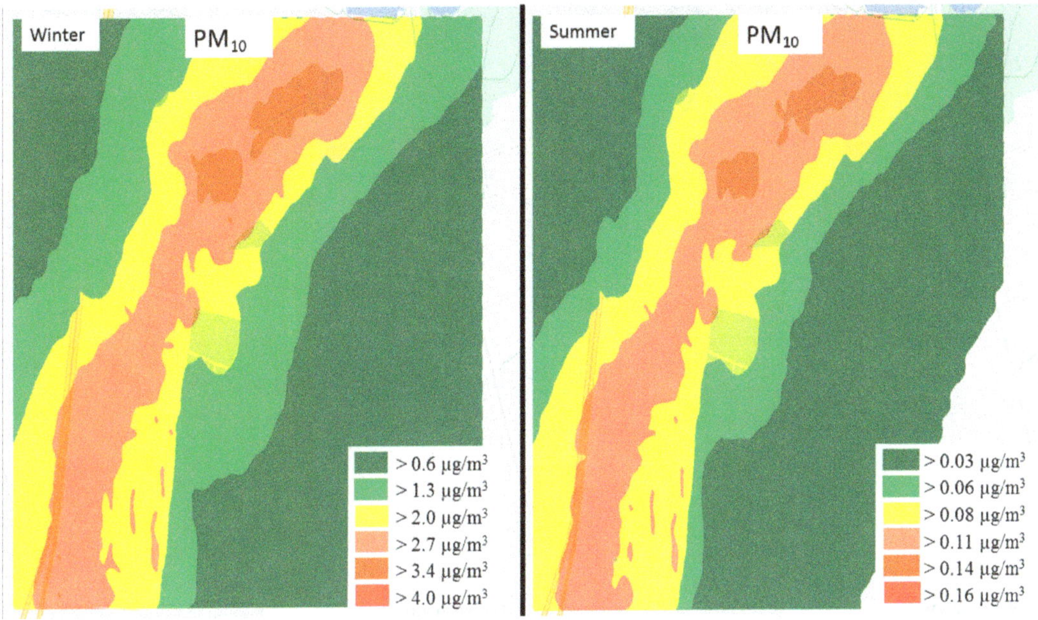

Figure 12. Dispersion diagram of the maximum 1-h PM_{10} concentrations of emissions from individual heating systems in the summer and winter periods.

In summer, the maximum concentration of PM_{10} according to our simulation was 0.42 µg/m^3, i.e., twice as high as in the winter period. This can be explained by the exhaust velocity from the chimney in the summer period, which at 5.24 m/s was three times lower than in the winter period (16.2 m/s). A slower exhaust outlet in the summer period allows for faster precipitation of pollutants, and this results in a higher concentration of dust pollutants in the vicinity of the heat and power plant. However, in both the winter and summer periods the concentration of PM_{10} caused by the emission from EC-3 did not exceed 0.5 µg/m^3 at a height of 2 m, which is less than 1% of the permissible value (50 µg/m^3).

The analysis shows that SO_2 was emitted from the CHP plant at a higher concentration than PM_{10} (Figure 9). In the winter period, the highest one-hour concentration according to the simulation was 20.35 µg/m^3. This value occurred in the immediate vicinity of EC-3, covering the entire area of the analyzed street. At a distance of about 2 km from the CHP plant, the concentration of SO_2 decreased to between 15 µg/m^3 and 20 µg/m^3. At a distance of about 6 km, it fell to below 15 µg/m^3. In the summer period, the scope of the EC-3′s environmental impact area was reduced by about 16%, which translated into a higher concentration than 25 µg/m^3 of SO_2 within a 1 km radius of EC-3. Based on computer simulations, Lee et al. [7] also observed higher SO_2 concentrations in the summer period, which were also explained by the lower outlet velocity in the summer period compared to the winter period. This resulted in a greater accumulation of pollution in the immediate vicinity of the heat and power plant.

The permissible maximum one-hour concentration of SO_2 in the air is 350 µg/m^3 [4]. The emissions of SO_2 from the combined heat and power plant amounted to only 8.9% of the limit value in the summer period and to 5.8% in the winter period.

According to traffic volume studies carried out during the air quality measurements, an average of 983 vehicles per hour traveled between the west and the east intersections in the winter period, at an average speed of 32 km/h. In the summer period, the intensity increased by 14% to 1118 vehicles per hour. The average vehicle speed increased to approximately 39 km/h. The analyzed street was used mainly by passenger cars, which accounted for 89% (summer period) and 91% (winter period) of the total number of vehicles. Light trucks accounted for 8% or 7% of the traffic in each period, trucks for 2% or 1%, and public buses for 1%. These results were used to create a numerical simulation in the OPA03 program of the dispersion of linear pollutants (Figures 10 and 11). Comparing the simulations of PM_{10} dispersion in the summer and winter periods (Figure 10), it can be observed that in the summer period there were higher concentrations of PM_{10} emissions. In the winter period, the maximum one-hour concentration was 12 $\mu g/m^3$, whereas in the summer period it was 17.7 $\mu g/m^3$. This was related to a 14% higher number of vehicles in the summer season, with a simultaneous increase in speed of only 7 km/h compared to the winter period. According to the simulation, the emissions from vehicle traffic had a small range of influence, as they were limited mainly to the immediate area of the street. This was due to the densely built-up area and the presence of tree stands (15–30 m tall trees). As Long et al. observed [27], local rough terrain has an impact on local meteorological conditions, especially in terms of wind direction and speed. Highly rough terrain contributes to protection against low windspeed and reduced airing, reducing the accumulation of pollutants. According to the simulation, the maximum concentration of PM_{10} was 35.4% of the permissible average daily concentration of 50 $\mu g/m^3$ [4].

The spatial distribution of SO_2 (Figure 11) according to the simulation was similar to the data for particulate matter. It was concentrated mainly in the road area and a small area of the surroundings (about 40 m). According to the simulations, the highest concentrations of SO_2 occurred within the lanes of the road, reaching 43.5 $\mu g/m^3$ in winter and 52.3 $\mu g/m^3$ in summer. In the area of the pedestrian sidewalks, the one-hour concentration decreased to below 15 $\mu g/m^3$. Road traffic emissions were at 12.4% of the maximum permissible level of 350 $\mu g/m^3$ stipulated by the EU [4] in winter and 14.9% of the maximum in summer.

In the immediate vicinity of the analyzed street, there are about 170 single-family houses with individual heating systems (70% coal fired and 30% natural gas). Based on detailed data in the literature on this source of emissions [33], presented in Table 4, calculations were made in the OPA03 program for point emitters located using the map of the analyzed area (Figure 2).

Table 4. Hourly emissions of pollutants from individual heating systems (source: [33]).

Source of Heat	Hourly Emission [g/GJ]	
5-years-old or older boiler, automatically powered by fine coal	PM_{10} 91.00	SO_2 343.00
Natural gas fired boiler	0.30	0.40

There was a visible difference between the summer and winter periods in terms of the concentrations of PM_{10} and SO_2 (Figures 12 and 13). Therefore, different scales were used in the figures to present the results. During the summer period, the PM_{10} concentration (hourly maximum) (Figure 12) fluctuated between 0.03 $\mu g/m^3$ and 0.161 $\mu g/m^3$, because the heating systems were used mainly for the purpose of preparing domestic hot water. In the winter period, the concentration of PM_{10} emitted from individual heating systems was higher than the highest value calculated in the summer period, ranging from 0.6 $\mu g/m^3$ to 4.0 $\mu g/m^3$. This can be explained by the increased combustion of fuels for the production of thermal energy to heat the buildings in winter. Kaczmarczyk et al. [8] and Specjał et al. [34] made similar observations.

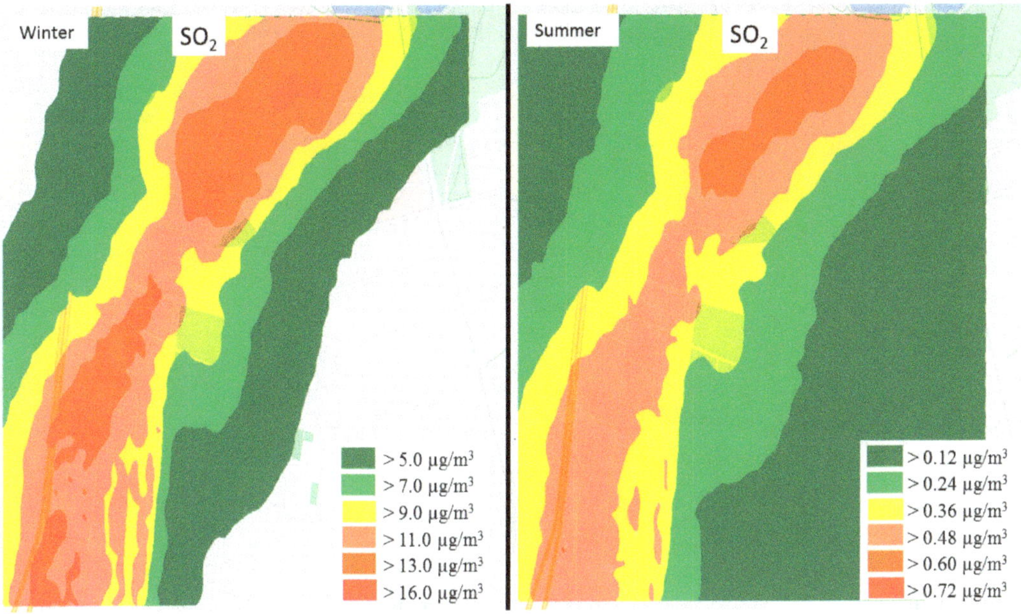

Figure 13. Dispersion diagram of the maximum 1 h SO_2 concentrations of emissions from individual heating systems in the summer and winter periods.

The concentration of SO_2 in the summer was more than 10 times lower than in the winter period, when there is increased production of heat energy. According to the results presented in Figure 13, in the summer period the maximum hourly SO_2 concentration varied in the range of 0.12–0.72 $\mu g/m^3$, whereas in the winter period it was in the range of 5.0–16.0 $\mu g/m^3$. The maximum value calculated in the summer period was 0.2% of the permissible value, and in the winter period it was 4.6% of the permissible value (350 $\mu g/m^3$).

The pollution from individual heating systems depended strongly on local factors, especially the wind direction. The highest concentrations of PM_{10} and SO_2 recorded in the axis of the location of the emitters, as the pollutants moved mainly in the direction of the WSW wind, which is dominant in the area. As a result, the emissions from individual heat sources did not affect the whole area of the analyzed street, but only the part in the direction of the wind.

4. Conclusions

In this study, we have compared the results of simulations performed using numerical software with data from actual field measurements. Maps were created of the distributions of air pollution in the vicinity of a heat and power plant and a communication route. For the numerical simulations, we assumed the highest concentrations of emissions from the selected pollution sources. According to the simulations, in the winter and summer periods, the maximum concentrations of PM_{10} were 16.22 $\mu g/m^3$ and 18.29 $\mu g/m^3$, respectively. According to our actual measurements, the maximum hourly concentration was in winter about 58.8 $\mu g/m^3$ and in summer 23.5 $\mu g/m^3$. The difference between the results of the simulation and the actual concentration of PM_{10} indicates the possibility of an additional source of dust pollution not included in the study, or the influence of background pollutants transported by the wind. There may also have been calculation errors associated with our method.

According to the simulation data shown in Figure 14, road transport accounted for the largest percentages of total PM_{10} emissions, at around 74% in winter and 96.9% in summer. The CHP was responsible for the smallest share of PM_{10} emissions, amounting to 1.3% or 2.3% of the total emissions according to the numerical calculations. This was related to the legal restrictions on dust emissions from power plants and the use of modern flue gas cleaning systems. The total maximum concentrations of SO_2 according to the numerical calculations were 81.0 $\mu g/m^3$ in winter and 84.0 $\mu g/m^3$ in summer. The concentration of SO_2 according to the actual measurements was about 350% higher than in the simulation for the winter period and about 140% higher than in the simulation for the summer period. Similar differences between real measurements and the results of simulations were reported by [7]. As in the case of PM_{10}, it can be explained by the high concentrations of pollutants transported by the air close to the ground surface, especially in winter during so-called thermal inversion. This causes the phenomenon of smog in the winter (poor air quality), as demonstrated by Wielgosiński et al. [35]. The vertical cross-sections through the dispersion maps of pollutants in winter (Figures 4, 6 and 7) showed the highest concentrations close to the ground level (approx. 2 m).

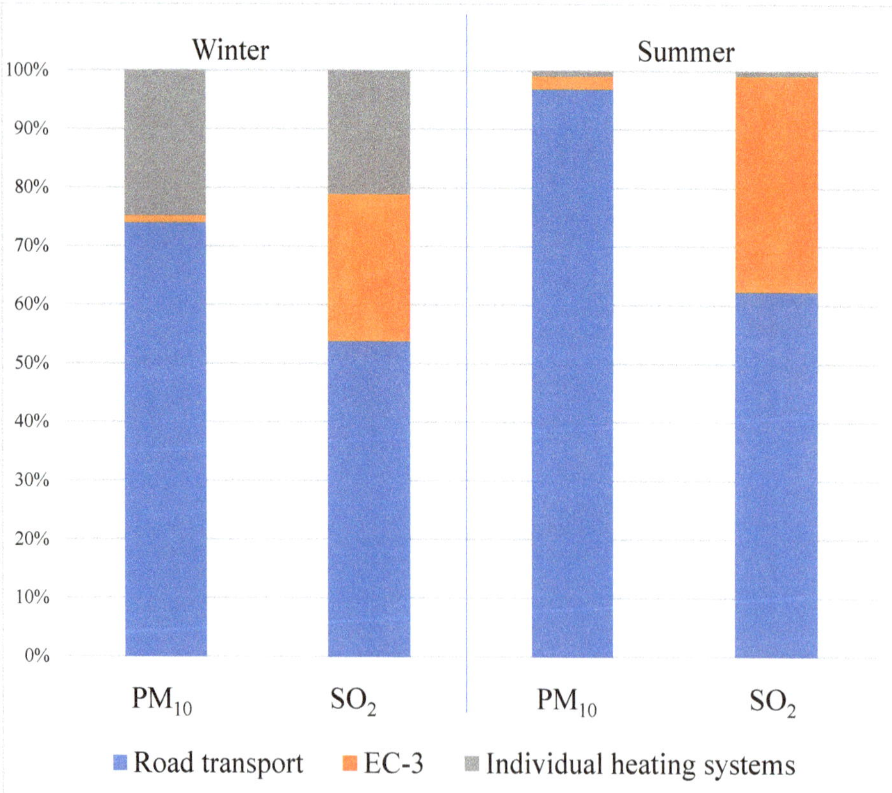

Figure 14. Percentage share of selected air pollution sources in the total maximum hourly concentrations of air pollutants in the summer and winter periods, based on numerical calculations.

According to the calculations performed by the OPA03 program (Figure 14), most emissions of SO_2 were caused by road transport, which was responsible for 53.8% and 62.2% of the total maximum concentrations in winter and summer, respectively. Road transport has a particularly strong impact on air quality in densely populated areas [36], where vehicles generate much higher concentrations of pollutants due to slow traffic and high vehicle aggregation with little airflow [37]. This is especially important in Poland where, according to comparative studies, the air quality is worse than in other European Union countries [38]. According to data from the European Union [2] and Poland [28], road transport is one of the main sources of PM and gas emissions. Individual heating systems were responsible for the smallest share of SO_2 emissions, amounting to 21.1% in winter and 0.8% of total emissions in summer. Similarly, Kaczmarczyk et al. [8] reported that individual heating systems were primarily responsible for the emission of particulate matter, especially when hard coal was used as fuel. Comparing the results from numerical calculations with the actual measurements shows the importance of using mobile measuring devices in air quality analyses, because simulations do not take into account all potential sources of air pollution or the correct level of background pollution. The presented research methodology can be implemented in any urban area, with a particular focus on local scale analysis.

Author Contributions: Conceptualization, R.C. and M.D.; methodology, R.C., M.D.; software, M.D., R.C.; writing—original draft, R.C., M.D.; review and editing, R.C. All authors have read and agreed to the published version of the manuscript.

Funding: This study was conducted as part of the research project entitled "Spatial analysis of air pollution changes in the Lodz agglomeration (in Polish: Analiza przestrzenna zmian stanu zanieczyszczenia powietrza w aglomeracji łódzkiej)", which was co-financed approx. 80% by the Provincial Fund for Environmental Protection and Water Management in Łódź (in Polish: Wojewódzki Fundusz Ochrony Środowiska i Gospodarki Wodnej w Łodzi).

Institutional Review Board Statement: Not applicable

Informed Consent Statement: Not applicable.

Data Availability Statement: Data available on request.

Conflicts of Interest: The authors declare no conflict of interest.

References

1. European Commission's Joint Research Centre (JRS). Available online: https://ghsl.jrc.ec.europa.eu/ (accessed on 12 September 2021).
2. Air Quality in Europe—2020 Report. Available online: https://www.eea.europa.eu/publications/air-quality-in-europe-2020-report (accessed on 12 September 2021).
3. World Health Organization. *WHO Air Quality Guidelines for Particulate Matter, Ozone, Nitrogen Dioxide and Sulfur Dioxide. Global Update 2005;* Summary of Risk Assessment; World Health Organization: Geneva, Switzerland, 2005; Available online: https://www.euro.who.int/en/health-topics/environment-and-health/air-quality/publications/pre2009/air-quality-guidelines.-global-update-2005.-particulate-matter,-ozone,-nitrogen-dioxide-and-sulfur-dioxide (accessed on 2 June 2021).
4. Legal Act of the European Union: Directive 2008/50/EC of the European Parliament and of the Council of 21 May 2008 on Ambient Air Quality and Cleaner Air for Europe OJ L 152; (BG, ES, CS, DA, DE, ET, EL, EN, FR, IT, LV, LT, HU, MT, NL, PL, PT, RO, SK, SL, FI, SV) Special edition in Croatian: 11 June 2008; 2008; Volume 29, Chapter 15, pp. 169–212. Available online: http://data.europa.eu/eli/dir/2008/50/oj (accessed on 2 August 2021).
5. World Health Organization. *WHO Global Air Quality Guidelines: Particulate Matter (PM2.5 and PM10), Ozone, Nitrogen Dioxide, Sulfur Dioxide and Carbon Monoxide;* World Health Organization: Geneva, Switzerland, 2021; Available online: https://apps.who.int/iris/handle/10665/345329 (accessed on 12 September 2021).
6. Meng, M.; Zhou, J. Has air pollution emission level in the Beijing–Tianjin–Hebei region peaked? A panel data analysis. *Ecol. Indic.* **2020**, *119*, 106875. [CrossRef] [PubMed]
7. Lee, H.; Yoo, J.; Kang, M.; Kang, J.; Jung, J.; Oh, K. Evaluation of concentrations and source contribution of PM 10 and SO 2 emitted from industrial complexes in Ulsan, Korea: Interfacing of the WRF–CALPUFF modeling tools. *Atmos. Pollut. Res.* **2014**, *5*, 664–676. [CrossRef]
8. Kaczmarczyk, M.; Sowiżdżał, A.; Tomaszewska, B. Energetic and Environmental Aspects of Individual Heat Generation for Sustainable Development at a Local Scale—A Case Study from Poland. *Energies* **2020**, *13*, 454. [CrossRef]
9. Batterman, S.; Ganguly, R.; Isakov, V.; Burke, J.; Arunachalam, S.; Snyder, M.; Robins, T.; Lewis, T. Dispersion Modeling of Traffic-Related Air Pollutant Exposures and Health Effects among Children with Asthma in Detroit, Michigan. *Transp. Res. Rec. J. Transp. Res. Board* **2014**, *2452*, 105–113. [CrossRef] [PubMed]
10. Tsai, D.H.; Wang, J.L.; Chuang, K.J.; Chan, C.C. Traffic-related air pollution and cardiovascular mortality in central Taiwan. *Sci. Total Environ.* **2010**, *408*, 1818–1823. [CrossRef] [PubMed]
11. Kuklinska, K.; Wolska, L.; Namiesnik, J. Air quality policy in the U.S. and the EU—A review. *Atmos. Pollut. Res.* **2015**, *6*, 129–137. [CrossRef]

12. Air Quality e-Reporting. Available online: https://www.eea.europa.eu/data-and-maps/data/aqereporting-9 (accessed on 12 September 2021).
13. Bossche, J.; Peters, J.; Verwaeren, J.; Botteldooren, D.; Theunis, J.; Baets, B. Mobile monitoring for mapping spatial variation in urban air quality: Development and validation of a methodology based on an extensive dataset. *Atmos. Environ.* **2015**, *105*, 148–161. [CrossRef]
14. Cichowicz, R.; Dobrzański, M. 3D Spatial Analysis of Particulate Matter (PM_{10}, $PM_{2.5}$ and $PM_{1.0}$) and Gaseous Pollutants (H_2S, SO_2 and VOC) in Urban Areas Surrounding a Large Heat and Power Plant. *Energies* **2021**, *14*, 4070. [CrossRef]
15. Jumaah, H.J.; Kalantar, B.; Halin, A.A.; Mansor, S.; Ueda, N.; Jumaah, S.J. Development of UAV-Based PM2.5 Monitoring System. *Drones* **2021**, *5*, 60. [CrossRef]
16. Kim, H.; Tae, S.; Zheng, P.; Kang, G.; Lee, H. Development of IoT-Based Particulate Matter Monitoring System for Construction Sites. *Int. J. Environ. Res. Public Health* **2021**, *18*, 11510. [CrossRef]
17. Łatuszyńska, M.; Strulak-Wójcikiewicz, R. A model for assessing the environmental impact of transport. *Oper. Res. Decis.* **2013**, *23*, 67–80. [CrossRef]
18. Abu-Allaban, M.; Abu-Qdais, H. Impact Assessment of Ambient Air Quality by Cement Industry: A Case Study in Jordan. *Aerosol Air Qual. Res.* **2011**, *11*, 802–810. [CrossRef]
19. Paas, B.; Schneider, C. A comparison of model performance between ENVI-met and Austal2000 for particulate matter. *Atmos. Environ.* **2016**, *145*, 392–404. [CrossRef]
20. Atamaleki, A.; Zarandi, S.M.; Fakhri, Y.; Mehrizi, E.A.; Hesam, G.; Faramarzi, M.; Darbandi, M. Estimation of air pollutants emission (PM10, CO, SO_2 and NOx) during development of the industry using AUSTAL 2000 model: A new method for sustainable development. *MethodsX* **2019**, *6*, 1581–1590. [CrossRef]
21. Kowalski, M.; Wiśniewski, S. Natężenie ruchu a zagospodarowanie Łodzi—zarys problematyki w świetle danych z Obszarowego Systemu Sterowania Ruchem. *Pr. Kom. Geogr. Komun. PTG* **2017**, *20*, 20–36. [CrossRef]
22. Technical Data of the EC-3 Heat and Power Plant. Available online: https://energiadlalodzi.pl/dane-kluczowe/dane-techniczne/ (accessed on 2 August 2021).
23. ArcGis Software for Creating Dispersion Maps. Available online: https://www.arcgis.com/index.html (accessed on 2 August 2021).
24. Calculation Software for Pollutant Concentration Analysis. Available online: http://www.eko-soft.com.pl/sysopa.htm (accessed on 2 June 2021).
25. Cichowicz, R.; Dobrzański, M. Modeling Pollutant Emissions: Influence of Two Heat and Power Plants on Urban Air Quality. *Energies* **2021**, *14*, 5218. [CrossRef]
26. Polish Legal Act. Rozporządzenie Ministra Środowiska z Dnia 26 Stycznia 2010 r. w Sprawie Wartości Odniesienia dla Niektórych Substancji w Powietrzu. Available online: http://isap.sejm.gov.pl/isap.nsf/DocDetails.xsp?id=wdu20100160087 (accessed on 2 June 2021).
27. Long, P.; Enjian, Y.; Yang, Y. Impact analysis of traffic-related air pollution based on real-time traffic and basic meteorological information. *J. Environ. Manag.* **2016**, *183*, 510–520. [CrossRef]
28. Centrum Badań i Edukacji Statystycznej GUS. *Development of the Methodology and Estimation of the External Costs of Air Pollution Emitted from Road Transport at National Level*; Final report; Centrum Badań i Edukacji Statystycznej GUS: Warszawa, Poland, 2018. Available online: http://stat.gov.pl (accessed on 12 August 2021).
29. Meteorological Data. Available online: https://danepubliczne.imgw.pl/ (accessed on 12 September 2021).
30. Polish Air Quality Index. Available online: https://powietrze.gios.gov.pl/pjp/current (accessed on 12 August 2021).
31. Badach, J.; Voordeckers, D.; Nyka, L.; Van Acker, M. A framework for Air Quality Management Zones—Useful GIS-based tool for urban planning: Case studies in Antwerp and Gdańsk. *Build. Environ.* **2020**, *174*, 106743. [CrossRef]
32. Xu, Y.; Yu, H.; Yan, Y.; Peng, L.; Li, R.; Wang, C.; Li, Z. Emission Characteristics of Volatile Organic Compounds from Typical Coal Utilization Sources: A Case Study in Shanxi of Northern China. *Aerosol Air Qual. Res.* **2021**, *21*, 210050. [CrossRef]
33. Instytut Chemicznej Przeróbki Węgla. Wskaźniki Emisji Zanieczyszczeń Powietrza Emitowanych z Indywidualnych Źródeł Ciepła—Raport. Available online: http://czysteogrzewanie.pl/wp-content/uploads/2013/02/Wska%C5%BAniki-emisji-zanieczyszcze%C5%84-powietrza-emitowanych-z-indywidualnych-%C5%BAr%C3%B3de%C5%82-ciep%C5%82a-Raport.pdf (accessed on 12 September 2021).
34. Specjał, A.; Lipczyńska, A.; Hurnik, M.; Król, M.; Palmowska, A.; Popiołek, Z. Case Study of Thermal Diagnostics of Single-Family House in Temperate Climate. *Energies* **2019**, *12*, 4549. [CrossRef]
35. Wielgosiński, G.; Czerwinska, J.; Namiecińska, O.; Cichowicz, R. Smog episodes in the Lodz agglomeration in the years 2014–2017. In *The E3S Web of Conferences*; EDP Sciences: Ulysse, France, 2018; p. 01039. [CrossRef]
36. Amirjamshidi, G.; Mostafa, T.S.; Misra, A.; Roorda, M.J. Integrated model for microsimulating vehicle emissions, pollutant dispersion and population expo-sure. *Transp. Res. Part D Transp. Environ.* **2013**, *18*, 16–24. [CrossRef]
37. Yao, E.; Song, Y. Study on eco-route planning algorithm and environmental impact assessment. *J. Intell. Transp. Syst. Technol. Plan. Oper.* **2013**, *17*, 42–53. [CrossRef]
38. Cichowicz, R.; Wielgosiński, G. Analysis of Variations in Air Pollution Fields in Selected Cities in Poland and Germany. *Ecol. Chem. Eng.* **2018**, *25*, 217–227. [CrossRef]

mathematics

Article

Designing a Solar Photovoltaic System for Generating Renewable Energy of a Hospital: Performance Analysis and Adjustment Based on RSM and ANFIS Approaches

Rami Alamoudi [1], Osman Taylan [1], Mehmet Azmi Aktacir [2] and Enrique Herrera-Viedma [3,4,*]

1 Department of Industrial Engineering, Faculty of Engineering, King Abdulaziz University, P.O. Box 80204, Jeddah 21589, Saudi Arabia; rami_alamodi@yahoo.com (R.A.); otaylan@kau.edu.sa (O.T.)
2 GAP Renewable Energy and Energy Efficiency Center, Department of Mechanical Engineering, Osmanbey Campus, Harran University, 63100 Sanliurfa, Turkey; aktacir@harran.edu.tr
3 Andalusian Research Institute in Data Science and Computational Intelligence, University of Granada, 18071 Granada, Spain
4 Department of Electrical and Computer Engineering, Faculty of Engineering, King Abdulaziz University, Jeddah 21589, Saudi Arabia
* Correspondence: viedma@decsai.ugr.es

Citation: Alamoudi, R.; Taylan, O.; Aktacir, M.A.; Herrera-Viedma, E. Designing a Solar Photovoltaic System for Generating Renewable Energy of a Hospital: Performance Analysis and Adjustment Based on RSM and ANFIS Approaches. *Mathematics* **2021**, *9*, 2929. https://doi.org/10.3390/math9222929

Academic Editors: Angel A. Juan and Marcin Kamiński

Received: 23 October 2021
Accepted: 15 November 2021
Published: 17 November 2021

Abstract: One of the most favorable renewable energy sources, solar photovoltaic (PV) can meet the electricity demand considerably. Sunlight is converted into electricity by the solar PV systems using cells containing semiconductor materials. A PV system is designed to meet the energy needs of King Abdulaziz University Hospital. A new method has been introduced to find optimal working capacity, and determine the self-consumption and sufficiency rates of the PV system. Response surface methodology (RSM) is used for determining the optimal working conditions of PV panels. Similarly, an adaptive neural network based fuzzy inference system (ANFIS) was employed to analyze the performance of solar PV panels. The outcomes of methods were compared to the actual outcomes available for testing the performance of models. Hence, for a 40 MW target PV system capacity, the RSM determined that approximately 33.96 MW electricity can be produced, when the radiation rate is 896.3 W/m^2, the module surface temperature is 41.4 °C, the outdoor temperature is 36.2 °C, the wind direction and speed are 305.6 and 6.7 m/s, respectively. The ANFIS model (with nine rules) gave the highest performance with lowest residual for the same design parameters. Hence, it was determined that the hourly electrical energy requirement of the hospital can be met by the PV system during the year.

Keywords: solar PV module; performance prediction; simulation; self-consumption model; RSM; ANFIS; hospital

1. Introduction

The energy planning systems have transformed from specific objectives with constraints to more complex approaches due to the insertion of multiple criteria, investors and needs of nations that are usually in conflict. Renewable and non-renewable energy sources are the basis of different energy systems. The world energy need is presently met mainly from fossil fuels (81%), renewable energy (14%), and nuclear sources (5%) [1]. Fossil fuels are disposable, and unsafe for the environment due to their impacts on climate and pollution rising. Similarly, nuclear sources and power reactors are deemed dangerous by some scientists as a result of their high capital costs, the power systems' control, opposing public opinion, nuclear waste management, and economies of the scale envisaged. However, they have many advantages such as lower emissions, higher security of supply and enabling of possible other technologies. The major direction of the world is to develop independent small nuclear units for energy generation that bring greater simplicity of design, short construction times, and reduced siting costs. On the other hand, small nuclear units are much more easily manageable investments whose costs often rival the capitalization of large plants. Renewable energy sources alleviate their downsides, and eventually cost less than fossil fuels that own useless production technologies. For instance, due to urgent environmental pollution and climate change issues, using a mix of fossil fuels and renewable energy sources, Italy carried out an 'energy transition' towards a more sustainable energy production and consumption system by adopting nuclear power to reduce the consumption of fossil fuels [2]. Solar photovoltaic (PV) as a favorable renewable energy source can meet the electricity demand of Saudi Arabia providing a 50 GW additional capacity. However, the aggregate global renewable energy capacity has reached 227 GW in recent times [3]. The average sunlight energy falling on Kingdom's land is about 2200 thermal kWh/m^2 per year which is acceptably higher when compared to some countries heavily investing in solar energy generation technologies. During the summer seasons, the electricity need reaches its peak load, which is twice higher than in the winter. Therefore, it is worthwhile to generate clean solar PV energy via sunlight [4]. In Saudi Arabia, the electricity consumption is estimated to exceed 40 GW nowadays and reach 120 GW per hour until the year 2028. The electricity consumption of industrial and service sectors is increasing about 6.9% per year mainly due to the investments and capacity expansions. This growth will require more fossil fuel consumption and eventually release a higher amount of CO_2 into the atmosphere. Although the Kingdom's annual solar irradiance is about 2000–2450 kWh/m^2, the availability of immense empty lands and ideal locations for solar installations and PV generation [4]; the renewable energy share of Kingdom is still less than 0.1%, compared to 14% share of the rest of the world [5]. In this context, Alnaser and Alnaser [6] claimed that only 0.1% of Kingdom's land is sufficient for the solar PV projects to meet the electricity demand estimated for 2050. Many countries are interested in reliable, sustainable, suitable, and diversified energy sources, and technologies due to the pros and cons of non-renewable energy sources and technologies. The challenging problem for a country is the determination of the proper energy sources and technologies for the public and private investments. Although Saudi Arabia has wind, and geothermal resources that can solve all energy demand in the future, the new PV technologies are more productive and can generate more energy efficiently. This study also aims to encourage government bodies and private organizations to invest in solar PV energy generation systems for achieving sustainable energy infrastructure.

A solar photovoltaic (PV) system aims to convert sunlight directly into electricity using PV cells. This system uses solar modules consisting of various solar cells containing semiconductor materials. Yildirim and Aktacir [7] investigated the efficiency of PV cells, the parameters affecting photovoltaic panel performance, and variabilities depending on PV technologies. Martin et al. [8] reported that the efficiency of converting solar energy into electrical energy is 9% using organic modules, which can reach 25% using crystalline modules. Monocrystalline, Multi-crystalline and thin film Silicone are broadly used in those PV technologies available which have the highest market share [7]. The most efficient PV modules are obtained from Monocrystalline technology, even highly more efficient than multi-crystalline technology are considered the leader of PV technologies [9] in industry. On the other hand, although solar radiation has the greatest influence on the power of the PV module [10] obtained, the module surface temperature affected by the wind speed and outdoor temperature are also important parameters. The wind speed and its direction have a cooling effect on the temperature of the PV module surface and significantly increase the electricity generation [11,12]. Kalledis et al. [10] have reported that the PV module surface temperature is reduced with rising wind speed. Although certain values of different parameters are considered as the ideal conditions, the reality is usually different, and the parameters do not represent the optimal field circumstances in which the PV panel operates [13].

Today, many studies in the literature related to renewable energy sources consider them as the alternative to fossil energy sources. Taylan et al. [1] used multi-criteria group decision making approaches for determining the attributes of energy sources, and selected technologies for PV energy generation. Lee [14] investigated the energy systems' essentials for the global economy to produce friendly new technologies for investment. Fan [15] stated that using energy more effectively results in energy efficient systems and reduces direct operating costs and initial investment costs. Tian et al. [16] built an energy evaluation procedure to integrate uncertain factors using stochastic models. Taylan et al. [1] used the experts' opinions and machine learning approaches to find out that solar PV was an attractive energy system for investment in the Kingdom. The regular daylight in the Kingdom is 12 h 8 min and 48 s on average, longer than several countries using solar PV systems extensively for energy generation. Akpolat et al. [17] investigated a PV system installed for a faculty building and found out that an 84.75-kWp grid- system can produce remarkable power and save about 90.298 kWh of energy annually for faculty buildings. Muteri et al. [18] summarized the current literature of life cycle assessment applied to different types of grid-connected PV systems to critically analyze the results related to energy and environmental impacts generated during the life cycle of PV technologies to provide information for future analyses. Yet, PV modules have 0.09 US$/kWh, however, diesel generators on average have 0.25 US$/kWh levelized electricity cost. Pradhan et al. [19] carried out a comparative analysis about different possible PV configurations in detail and found that the hybrid solar PV-wind energy system is the most suitable energy generation system. Almarshoud [20] examined the performance of a pilot PV system based on real time solar radiation data in 32 sites. Mittal et al. [21] used artificial neural networks (ANNs) to predict the PV Modules performance. Yahya-Khotbehsara, and Shahhoseini [22] merged the numerical and analytical approaches to determine the PV module parameters of Monocrystalline, Multi-crystalline and thin film technologies. Goverde et al. [23] investigated the PV module surface spatial temperature differences affected by wind. Goossens et al. [24] used wind tunnel experiments to investigate the influence of wind flow, and temperature patterns on the electrical performance of buildings integrated with PV modules. Curto et al. [25] investigated the economic impacts of feasibly generating energy from solar, wind and sea wave plants to achieve specific targets of decarbonization in Lampedusa, a small Italian island where currently the energy is supplied totally by diesel power plants. Awan et al. [26] determined that the northern province, Tabuk, is the most feasible region for a solar PV plant. Rani et al. [27] proposed a fuzzy TOPSIS approach for ranking the status of renewable energy sources. Daus et al. [28] calculated the unit cost of generated electric energy from solar PV for the utility sector, health facilities, housing, industrial enterprises, recreation areas and agricultural industries. Yoomak et al. [29] searched the location problem and its effect on the performance assessment of solar PV systems installed on the rooftop of residences in distinct regions of Thailand. Kassem et al. [30] analyzed the solar radiation of five distinct locations in Northern Cyprus statistically in addition to some meteorological parameters such as relative humidity, air temperature, sunshine, and solar radiation. Ascencio-Vásquez et al. [31] used the performance of PV systems to evaluate the risks occurring due to the diverse climate conditions for standardizing the evaluation criteria in regions. Zell et al. [32] believed that understanding the spatial and temporal variability requires considerably more data to optimize the planning and setting of solar energy power plants. Roy et al. [33] studied the features of perovskite solar cells and found them superior to the existing PV technologies for presenting the efficiency and various architectures used to date. Naderloo (2020) [34] predicted the solar radiation using ANN methods, ANFIS and RSM, carried out the sensitivity analysis, and found out that ANNs and RSM were superior to the ANFIS. Benmouiza and Cheknane (2019) [35] used fuzzy c-means (FCM), subtractive clustering, and grid partitioning algorithms to develop an ANFIS for forecasting solar radiation. The findings depicted that the ANFIS model developed with the FCM clustering algorithm gave the best results considering the RMSE approach of 112 W/m^2. Mohammadi et al. (2016) [36] developed and employed an ANFIS model to identify the solar radiation relevant parameters and predict the daily level of solar radiation. The results revealed that the climate conditions influence the solar radiation characteristic which is not identical for all locations. Aldair et al. (2018) [37] validated the effectiveness of ANFIS for tracking the maximum power point tracking (MPPT) approach in a stand-alone PV system. The results indicated that the ANFIS model controllers are more efficient and give better dynamic responses than the incremental conductance method and constant voltage method. Khosravi et al. (2020) [38] investigated the ANFIS and genetic algorithm combination and based on teaching-learning optimization algorithms and determined the optimum design parameters of different 100 MW solar power stations with a molten salt storage system.

PV systems generate cheaper and cleaner energy during the daytime and stop generating after the sun sets. So, these systems must be connected to the local electricity grid for transferring the excessively generated power to the grid and taking it from the grid back during the night. The disadvantage of these systems is that a self-balanced energy is needed for instantaneous energy consumption. The excessive power must be well-managed to avoid the problems. Hence, a well-established control system and restrictions of the energy generation for balancing the supply and demand level is required. This approach is called offsetting energy generation and consumption. This system is called an on grid photovoltaic system.

The design of grid photovoltaic systems requires detailed analysis by considering local parameters. Knowing the performance of PV panels under real operating conditions is extremely important. Solar panel manufacturers only give PV panel performance under standard test conditions (STC). Although STC defines solar radiation at 1000 W/m^2, surface temperature 25 °C and air mass (A.M.) 1.5 as ideal conditions, the reality is different; these parameters do not always represent the optimal field circumstances in which the PV panel operates [13]. In this study, to determine the optimal solar PV energy generating conditions and the panel performance, as a statistical and mathematical approach RSM was employed for modeling and analysis of this complex problem. As it was clearly stated, the response (the amount of solar PV energy generated) is affected by several factors. However, the response (PV generated) and the independent parameters' relations are not usually clearly known. On the other hand, the response cannot be formed well by linear approximations due to the complexity of problems, therefore higher degree polynomials might be employed.

This study aims to design a solar PV system for generating the electricity need of King Abdulaziz University (KAU) Hospital in Jeddah city. The hospital's energy demand is very high, and the energy consumption bill is around $1.5 million per month. Initially a detailed field work was conducted to determine the PV system performance for self-consumption and self-sufficiency models under real operating conditions. A two step work was carried out: in the first step, a 40 MW PV system was constructed to generate the electricity need of the KAU hospital. The second step includes determining the optimal operating conditions by RSM and ANFIS approaches. Both approaches were employed using the following parameters: surface temperature (°C) of modules, wind speed (m/s), radiation (W/m^2), outdoor temperature (°C), and wind direction. The RSM aimed to find out the optimal operating conditions of the solar PV panels and the factor space operating intervals required for the PV panel system. Our investigations depicted that generating maximum solar PV of 42.27 MW is possible for the KAU hospital, if the radiation level is about 896.3 W/m^2, the module surface temperature is 50.0 °C, the outdoor temperature is 40.3 °C, the wind direction is 305.6 and the wind speed is 6.7 m/s. On the other hand, the operation conditions of solar PV panels were simulated under different conditions, for instance, it was determined that obtaining a 33.96 MW solar PV system, the radiation should be 896.3, the module surface temperature should be 43.4 °C, the outdoor temperature should be 40.3 °C, the wind direction should be 305.9 and the wind speed should be 6.7 m/s.

The ANFIS intended to develop and analyze the solar PV modules by estimating the performance of them. The ANFIS models developed for the PV generation system can predict the performance of modules containing five, nine and eleven rules. Figure 1 presents the flow chart for this study including the solar power plant (SPP) design procedure and the applied methods.

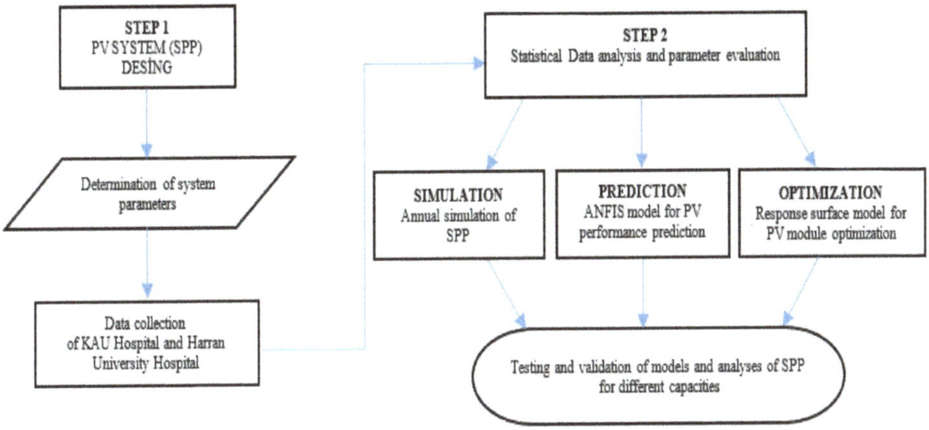

Figure 1. The solar PV panel system flow chart.

Thus, the design of this study is as follows; in Section 2, the solar PV system design is explained. Simulation of the solar PV system is discussed in Section 3. The data related to solar PV system parameters are analyzed, additionally, the performance prediction and optimization methods; the RSM and ANFIS approaches are given in Section 4. Section 5 covers the results, finding and discussions for the PV system. Section 5 is devoted to the conclusions.

2. Materials and Methods

2.1. Solar Energy Generation Design for KAU Hospital

The aim of this study is to construct a solar power plant (SPP) system to generate electricity for KAU Hospital. The hospital is in the KAU campus, the coordinates are [Lat/Lon] 21.290 and 39.130, as shown in Figure 2.

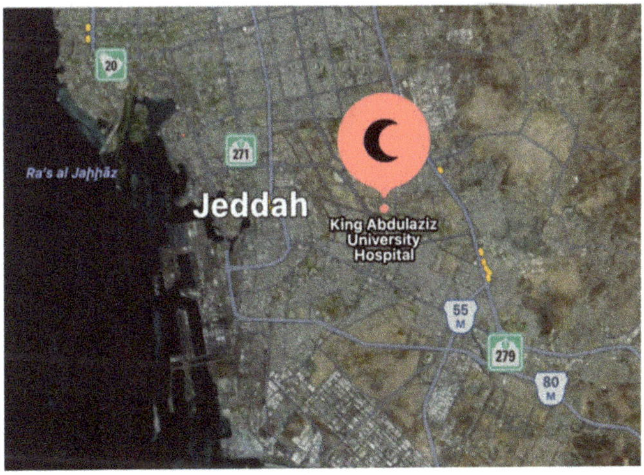

Figure 2. Location of the KAU hospital.

The hospital has a very high electricity consumption. Monthly electricity consumption data of KAU hospital for 2018 and 2019 are given in Figure 3. The maximum energy consumption of the hospital is during February, and the minimum consumption is in May.

When the data of 2019 are analyzed, the annual average hourly electricity need of KAU hospital is determined as 21.694 kWh.

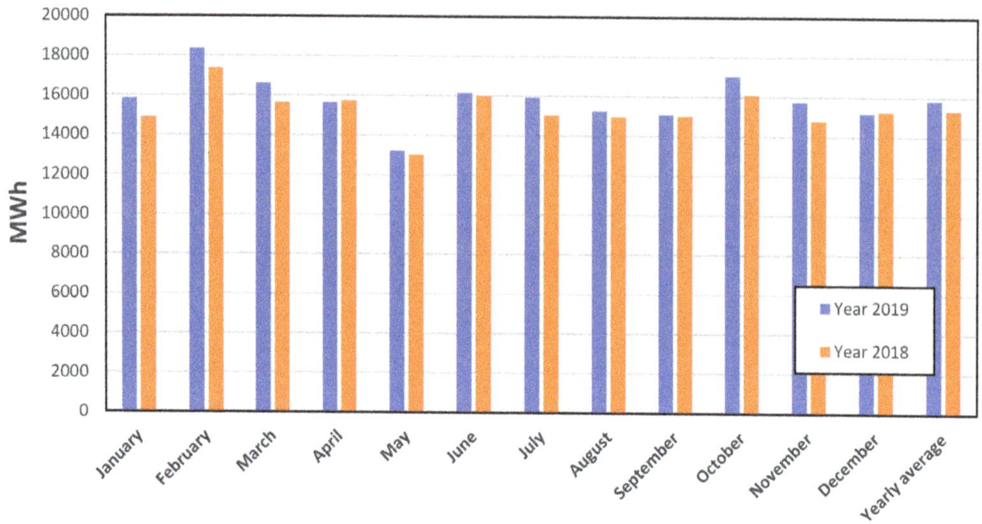

Figure 3. Monthly electricity consumption of KAU hospital.

2.2. The Solar Power Plant Types

The schematic picture of the PV solar system designed for the hospital is given in Figure 4. The system proposed for the hospital is an on grid PV system. While the sun is available during the day, the electricity need of the hospital will be met by generating electricity from solar energy. This model is known as a self-consumption model and was established to meet the electricity needs of a hospital. These models are called self-sufficient models. If the capacity of the system is well designed, which means greater than the energy consumption of the hospital, the excess energy can be supplied to the national grid during the daytime and reused at night.

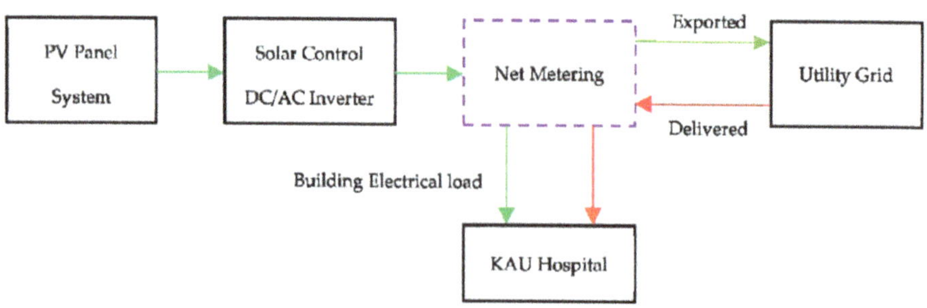

Figure 4. On grid solar power system for KAU hospital.

In this study, the PV system was designed according to the self-consumption model approach without storing the energy generated, and then the system's self-sufficiency values in different capacities were found. At the end of the study, the optimum capacity of the PV system was determined for different self-sufficiency rates.

2.3. PV System Design

This study aimed to find the hourly electricity consumption values by using the monthly respective data set of the KAU hospital. Additionally, the data obtained from

Harran University hospital (HUH) in Sanliurfa, Turkey, were employed for model building because the energy consumption of HUH is met by the SPP in accordance with the self-consumption model. In SPP of HUH, the electrical energy generation and consumption values of the hospital, and the local meteorological data are measured and recorded every 5 min. In this study, the electricity consumption (electricity load) profiles of both hospitals were considered equal by benchmarking the parameters. The PV system has been designed to perform the following steps:

2.3.1. Determining the Hourly Distribution of the Energy Consumption of the Harran University Hospital

Using electrical energy consumption of HUH between 1 January 2019 and 31 December 2019, hourly energy consumption was determined for an average day of the month. In Figure 5, according to the monthly and annual data of HUH, the distribution of electricity consumption for an average day is given. As can be seen from Figure 5.

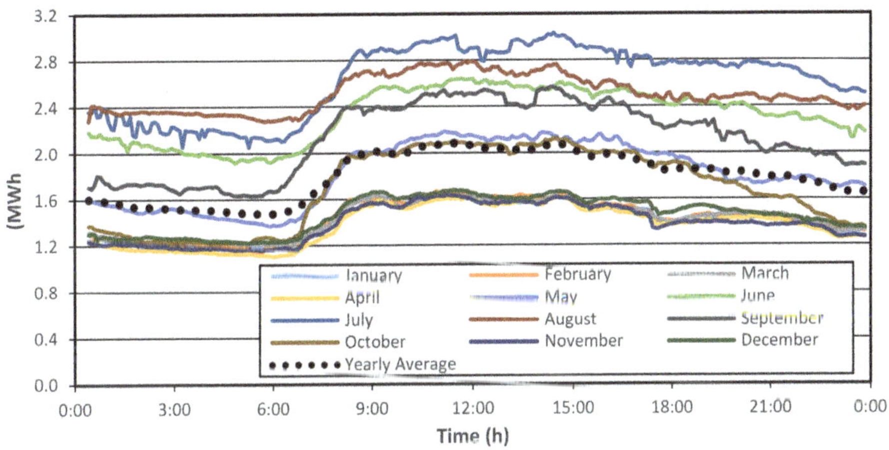

Figure 5. Monthly and yearly average distribution of the electricity consumption of Harran University hospital.

- The maximum energy consumption of HUH is in July.
- Electricity consumption is the highest in 4 months (summer period) from June to September,
- Electricity consumption is the lowest in the period of 6 months (winter period) from November to April,
- The electricity consumption profiles of an average day obtained for May and October are similar to the consumption profile obtained for an average day determined according to annual data.

2.3.2. Determining the Load Profile of the Energy Consumption of the Harran University Hospital

The electrical energy consumption load profile (LR) of HUH was calculated according to the following equation. In this equation, it shows hourly electrical energy consumption value with Q_{hour} and annual/monthly average hourly energy need with $Q_{average}$. According to the 2019 data of HUH, the daily average electrical energy consumption profile for 2019 is presented in Figure 6.

$$LR_{hour} = Q_{hour}/Q_{average} \tag{1}$$

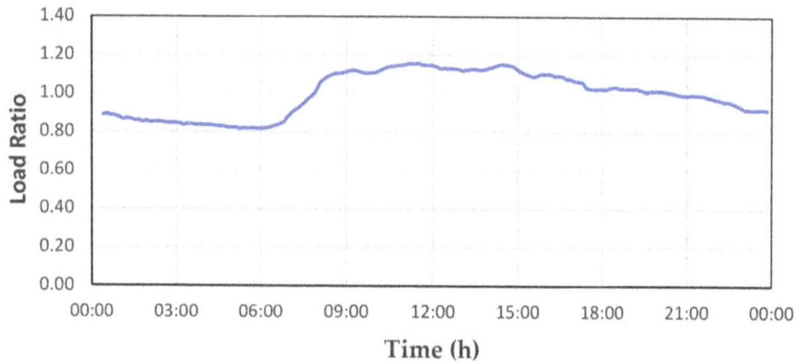

Figure 6. Average daily electrical energy consumption profile of Harran university hospital for 2019.

2.3.3. The Hourly Energy Consumption Distribution of the KAU Hospital

The electricity consumption profiles of two hospitals are considered similar. Considering the daily electricity consumption profile of HUH, and the hourly electricity consumption distribution profile, and the monthly total energy consumption values of KAU hospital, the average hourly energy requirement (Q_{hour}) of KAU hospital was calculated according to following equation:

$$Q_{hour} = LR_{hour} \cdot Q_{average} \tag{2}$$

According to the consumption data in 2019, the KAU hospital's (Figure 3) hourly electricity requirement is 21.694 kWh on average. The daily electricity consumption profile of the hospital is presented in Figure 7. This figure shows the maximum electricity requirement of KAU hospital which shows that it is 25.135 kWh at 11:30. If the PV system is designed according to the maximum electricity requirement of the KAU hospital, a PV system with 25 MW of capacity should be sufficient. However, in real operating conditions (local climatic conditions) PV panels perform with lower efficiency than their efficiency stated in the catalogue because of high temperature. PV panels are tested under 1000 W/m^2 solar radiation and 25 °C outdoor temperature conditions.

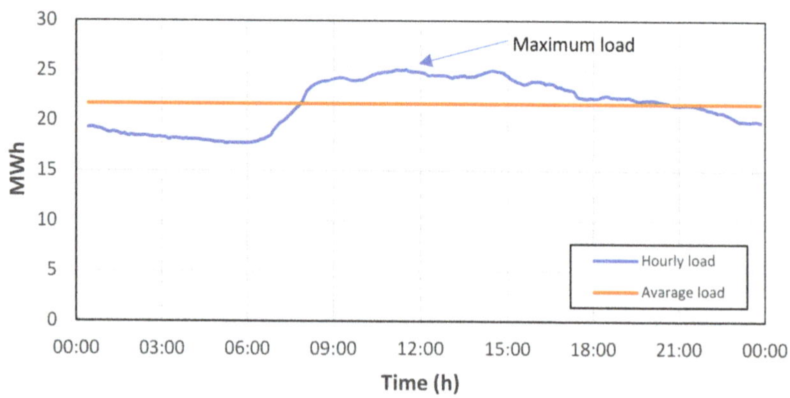

Figure 7. Daily average electrical energy consumption profile of KAU hospital.

PV system designing in accordance with the self consumption model (according to the hourly electricity consumption need) aims to meet the electricity needs of KAU hospital. To meet up the electricity needs of KAU hospital, an on-grid PV system of different capacities, ranging from 25 MW to 100 MW, was designed. Thus, performance evaluation of PV systems designed for different capacities was made easy. In all PV systems, crystalline silicon technology was used. PV panels are mounted and fixed in the open area to face them to the optimum tilt angle of the south direction. The optimum tilt angle for Jeddah is 22 degrees. Total losses of the PV system (inverter, cable, dust, etc.) were considered as 14%. In this study, all PV designs determined for KAU hospital were simulated under the local climate conditions of Jeddah and detailed analysis was carried out. For PV system simulation, the Solar-GIS program [39] was used. The PVGIS program [40] was used to validate the simulation results obtained from the Solar-GIS program which are the online ideal free tools that can be used for estimating electricity generation of the PV system. In Figure 8, the monthly electricity generation values obtained by both PVGIS and Solar-GIS programs of the PV system with 25 MW capacity are compared. The results obtained from both programs are very close to each other.

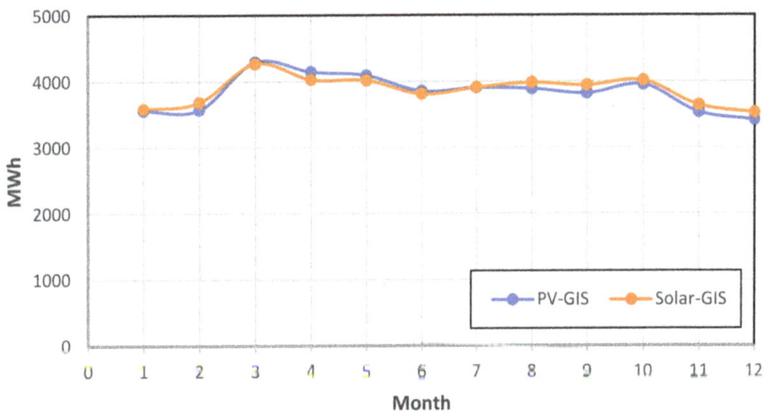

Figure 8. The comparison of monthly electricity generated from both PV-GIS and Solar-GIS programs for a 25 MW PV system.

3. Solar PV System Analysis and Performance Prediction

3.1. Data Collection and Analysis

Determining the optimal performance of the solar PV generation plant, precise and truthful parameters were ascertained, and related data were collected. The data employed in this study are for the time duration from January 2019 to December 2019 of radiation (W/m^2), module surface temperature (°C), wind speed (m/s), outdoor temperature (°C), and wind direction which were gathered from Harran University solar power plant located in the university campus. Wind direction measurement is expressed with an angle showing 0° of the north, 90° of the east, 180° of the south and 270° of the west. Historical data for the (37.158/39.007) [Lat/Lon] of variabilities of solar resources were obtained from monitoring stations located in Sanliurfa, Turkey. A comprehensive statistical analysis was conducted to determine the multicollinearity to show the intercorrelation between the independent factors. The findings showed that the module surface temperature and outdoor temperature are highly related to the remaining independent variables. The 'P, F, t and VIF' tests indicated the availability of redundant information among the independent variables, and weak linear relations, the interactions of predictors may be nonlinear, and the nonlinear relations can be dealt with RSM, ANFIS and simulation approaches.

Truly, there is often no unique 'best' set of independent variables that can be said to yield the most excellent outcomes. Different techniques do not all automatically lead to the same final prediction of related variables. As a result of the fact that the variable selection process is sometimes subjective, analysts may therefore need to emphasise their judgments on the pivotal areas of the problem. In this study, the highest coefficient of determination (R2) was found 0.946 for several combinations of sets of independent (input) variables. One interesting combination of the input variables was the radiation, module surface temperature and outdoor temperature. The other combination was the addition of all parameters for model development, both giving 0.946 coefficient of determination ratio. Therefore, we used all five parameters for ANFIS model development.

3.2. RSM for Optimization of Solar PV System

RSM is an optimization method used to determine the operating conditions of a process leading to achieving the best process performance [41]. RSM has extensive applications in semiconductors, electronics manufacturing, and machining. In most RSM problems, the form of relationships between independent factors and response is assumed unknown. When there are curvature relations between the factors in a system, a higher degree polynomial of process optimization approach can be employed, such as a second order model or above. Obviously, a polynomial model is unlikely to be a reasonable estimate of the true functional relationship over the entire domain of independent parameters, but for a relatively small region, the method works quite well. Figure 9 shows that there is no serious indication of the abnormality or excessive evidence of possible outliers. This plot also reveals nothing of unusual interest among the residuals, and the residual scatter does not appear more for the outcomes that show nonhomogeneous conditions. Therefore, the model is assumed to be adequate, the investigation of the normality assumption also approves the adequacy.

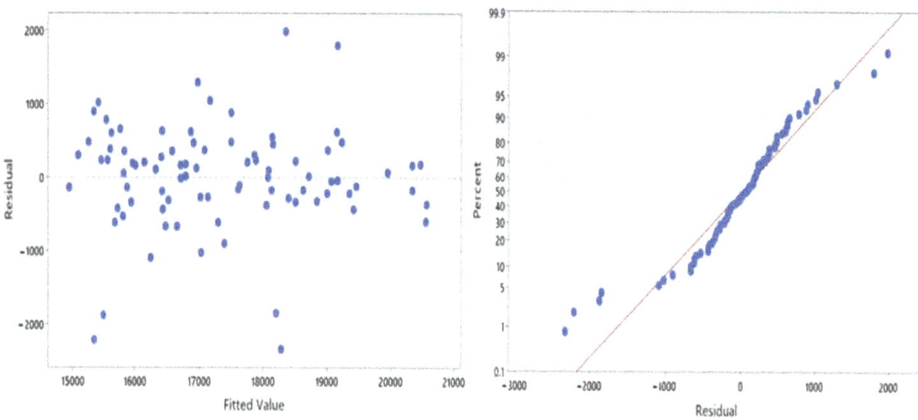

Figure 9. The probability plot of solar PV generation response, and the dispersion of residual.

The regression equation of solar PV generation where the factors are radiation (x_1), module surface temperature (x_2), outdoor temperature (x_3), wind direction (x_4) and wind speed (x_5) were established according to the following equation.

$$y_{ijk} = \beta_0 + \sum_{j=1}^{k} \beta_j x_j + \sum_{j=1}^{k} \beta_{jj} x_j^2 + \sum \sum_{i<j} \beta_{ij} x_i x_j + \in_{ijk} \quad (3)$$

where β_0, β_j, β_{jj}, and β_{ij} represent the overall mean effect, the effect of the j-th level of the row factor, the effect of the j-th level of column factor, and the effect of the interaction effect in the quadratic model, respectively. $\in_{ijk}$ is a random error component of a second order RSM, where y_{ijk} is the response and refers to the solar PV generation level in this study. x_i and x_j present the variables that are called factors. Dirnberger and Kraling (2013) [42] described the measurement procedure and uncertainty analysis which covers the complete daily calibration process of measurement devices in detail, the correction to standard testing conditions, and determination of electrical module parameters. They presented recent progress in reducing the measurement uncertainty for crystalline silicon and thin-film PV modules.

$$\text{Solar PV generation } (y_k)(\text{kWh}) = -13499 + 20.8x_1 + 752x_2 + 349x_3 - 8.1x_4 + 107x_5 + 0.52x_1x_2 + 0.12x_1x_3 + 0.1277x_1x_4 + 1.16x_1x_5 + 242x_2x_3 + 0.74x_2x_4 - 235x_2x_5 - 2.34x_3x_4 + 329x_3x_5 + 1.05x_4x_5 - 0.0389x_1^2 - 103x_2^2 - 165.6x_3^2 - 0.0275x_4^2 - 198x_5^2$$

The essential effects that arise from this analysis are the key impacts of x_1, x_2, x_3, x_4 and x_5. The interactions between the parameters x_1 x_2, x_1 x_3, ... are presented in the regression model with the coefficients presented above in the model.

3.3. ANFIS Approach for PV Efficiency Estimation and Analysis

The ANFIS model comprises ANNs and fuzzy logic to forecast the output data identified by input parameters. An ANFIS model is constituted by membership functions (MFs) [15]. Higher MFs numbers usually affect the outcomes optimality with lower accuracy [43], additional MFs cannot improve the effectiveness of a fuzzy model [44]. A fuzzy model's performance depends on efficiently selected system parameters, their complexity, and the type of training algorithm called the ANNs [45–48].

An ANFIS includes fuzzy implications presented in fuzzy 'If-Then' rules to represent the relations of fuzzy inputs-outputs parameters linguistically [15]. An efficient parameter control depends on the number of rules. In other words, an ANFIS is shaped by fuzzy rules and their term sets [46]. The rules are the backbone of an ANFIS system. When the parameters are nonlinear, Gaussian membership functions are used for identifying the fuzzy terms which will be used to forecast the PV generated. The aim of an ANFIS model is to forecast the performance of the solar PV module. The set of input–output data was split into three randomly selected parts: training data, testing, and validation data. Training data set includes 319 observations served for the ANFIS model building, and for testing and validation 100 data were employed, respectively. The designed ANFIS model consists of five nodes for input parameters with 25 Gauss membership function, five nodes in the hidden layer (H1~H5), and a node (P_k) to show the solar PV model outcome for the output layer. Hence, the ANFIS model has a total of sixty eight nodes arranged with thirty linear and fifty nonlinear parameters corresponding to the five input parameters.

The input parameters of ANNs are the radiation (W/m^2; x_1), module surface temperature (°C; x_2), outdoor temperature (°C; x_3), wind direction (x_4), and wind speed (m/s; x_5) and the outcome parameter of network is the PV generated (P_k). The input-hidden and hidden-output layers' coefficients called weights are presented by w_{ij} and w_{jk}, correspondingly. The following equation was used to calculate the k-th neuron's outcomes in the hidden layer.

$$net_k = \sum_{i=1}^{25} w_{ik} f_i \tag{4}$$

The input variables' MFs is shown by f_i, w_{ik}, depicts the weighting coefficient in the hidden layer. $p_k = f(net_k)$ shows the output MFs in the hidden layer and is found according to the following equation.

$$p_k = f(net_k) = \frac{1}{(1 + exp\ (-net_k))} \tag{5}$$

where $f(net)$ is the activation function in ANNs and the following equation was used to determine it.

$$net_k = \sum_{j=1}^{m} p_k w_{jk} \tag{6}$$

where m and w_{jk} show the number of neurons in a hidden layer and the weights, respectively. For the training process, input data were used, the outcomes of ANFIS model were determined and compared with the actual (A_k) outcomes presented in Equation (8). The learning constant value η was set up as 0.25, 0.50, and 0.70 as given in the following equation.

$$\Delta w_{ij} = -\eta \frac{\partial E}{\partial w_{ij}}, \; \Delta w_{jk} = -\eta \frac{\partial E}{\partial w_{jk}} \tag{7}$$

The best outcome of learning constant was obtained when η is equal to 0.70. The error of the p'th observation can be calculated according to the following equation.

$$E = \frac{1}{2}\sum_{p=1}^{N} E_p = \frac{1}{2}\sum_{p=1}^{N}\sum_{k=1}^{l} (A_k - P_k)_p^2 \tag{8}$$

The number of training data N, actual outcomes (A_k) and the predicted outcomes (P_k) are presented in the equation given above. The (E) shows the error estimator, is a squared error minimization function and called the Least-Squares Estimator (LSE). For specifying Gaussian membership functions (MFs), two parameters (c, σ) are used; the center 'c' of MFs and the width 'σ' of MFs are used for identifying the MFs.

The Gaussian MFs are shown in Figure 10 for the input parameters 'wind direction' and the 'module surface temperature', respectively. Their fuzzy linguistic term set can be stated as {very low, low, average, high, and very high}. The MF can be presented with a mathematical relation conforming to the following equation for the fuzzy linguistic term 'average' for the wind direction.

$$\text{Gaussian}\,(x,\,c,\,\sigma) = e^{-1/2\left(\frac{x-c}{\sigma}\right)^2} \tag{9}$$

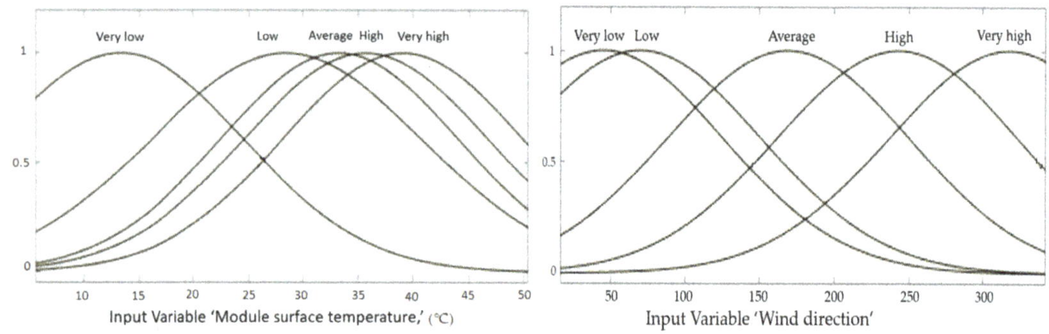

Figure 10. Gaussian MFs for wind direction and module surface temperature.

The fuzzy membership function of the fuzzy term 'average' used to identify the factor 'wind direction (x_4)'.

$$\mu(x_4) = f_{(x)} = \begin{cases} 0, & x < 15.75 \text{ and } x > 343.292 \\ e^{-\frac{1}{2}\left(\frac{x-178.812}{70}\right)^2}, & 15.75 \le x \le 343.292 \end{cases}$$

A neuro-fuzzy model is a set of fuzzy 'If-Then' rules [47]. Sugeno fuzzy modelling approach suggests an efficient way to produce fuzzy rules from the parameters data. In a Sugeno fuzzy model, fuzzy rules are usually constituted in the following form. In the following equation, B and C are the antecedent of the fuzzy term sets, whereas $y_n = f_n(x_1, x_2, \ldots, x_m)$ is the consequent part of the fuzzy rule. The input parameters ($x_1, x_2, \ldots, x_m$) are depicted as polynomial functions $f_n(x_1, x_2, \ldots, x_m)$, and r_n is the constant, presented as follows:

$$IF\ x_1\ is\ B\ and\ x_2\ is\ C\ldots\ldots\ THEN\ y_n = f_n(x_1, x_2, \ldots, x_m) = b_n x_1 + c_n x_2 + d_n x_3 + \ldots k_n x_m + r_n \quad (10)$$

The fuzzy reasoning procedure produces crisp outputs, 'y' shows the amount of PV generated under certain conditions by the modules. Thus, a fuzzy rule set of input–output parameters of a PV energy generation plant can be presented as follows.

Rule 1. *IF 'The radiation is 249 (W/m^2) and the module surface temperature is 28 °C AND the outdoor temperature is 31.2 °C AND the wind direction is 180. AND the wind speed is 2.92 m/s THEN The amount of PV energy generated is (kWh) = 4.575x_1 − 14.39x_2 + 14.13x_3 − 0.0469x_4 − 6.22x_5 + 339.4934 (1490 kWh).*

Rule 2. *IF 'The radiation is 336 (W/m^2) and the module surface temperature is 26.7 °C AND the outdoor temperature is 15.6 °C and the wind direction is 134. AND the wind speed is 3.22 m/s THEN The amount of PV energy generated is (kWh) = 6.785x_1 − 65.26x_2 + 25.35x_3 − 0.574x_4 − 67.35x_5 − 275.995 (363 kWh).*

The ANFIS model for the solar PV generation was developed using 319 data for training, 100 for testing, and 100 for the validation of the model. The training errors were determined for the observations by differencing the actual data (*At*) and the predicted data (*Pt*) obtained from the solar PV fuzzy inferencing model. The ANFIS model was optimized during the training process, and several factors were arranged to obtain the best outcomes. The optimization of ANFIS model and training process depend on certain factors such as the range of influence was set to 0.7, so the squash factor set to 1.25, the accept ratio set to 0.75 and the reject factor was set to 0.157 in this study. Additionally, the error tolerance limit was arranged as 0.001 and epochs as 3000. Consequently, the Root Mean Square Error (RMSE) achieved 66.98 for the training process of ANFIS model with nine rules, 113.5208 for ANFIS model with five rules, and 68.47 for the ANFIS model with eleven rules. On the other hand, the training error can be recorded as the mean squared error (*MSE*) for a trained ANFIS model. The *MSE* was calculated as follows:

$$MSE = \frac{1}{n}\sum\nolimits_{t=1}^{n}(A_t - P_t)^2 \quad (11)$$

To minimize the training process error, the gradient vector is obtained initially, calculated from the output layer by derivation of the findings and propagating backward until the input layer. In this work, three ANFIS models were developed including 5, 9 and 11 rules based on the sub clustering algorithm. Considering the training error and RMSE, the ANFIS model having 9 rules gave the best outcomes with minimum error for the solar PV generation model examined. The error (residual) was determined 0.5362% for the solar PV generation model of 9 rules ANFIS model, 1.26% for the ANFIS with 5 rules and 1.082% for the ANFIS model that has 11 rules. On the other hand, the performance of the ANFIS models was tested based on different rule-bases of the solar PV system. The findings are assessed and compared with the other models using the average prediction error approach. The following equation was employed for the calculation of the average prediction error.

$$Average\ prediction\ error = \frac{1}{n}\sum\nolimits_{k=1}^{n}\frac{|A_k - P_k|}{A_k} \times 100 \quad (12)$$

4. Results and Discussions for Solar PV System Findings

4.1. The Assessment of PV System Simulation

According to the results of the simulation of the PV system, yearly average values of PV electricity (AC) delivered by the total installed capacity of a PV system were found to be 1843 kWh/kWp. Figure 11 shows the distribution of hourly electricity production values of the designed PV systems by all months. As seen in Figure 11a, the system capacity is 25 MW and the maximum monthly electricity production is between 16 and 19 MWh. The maximum electrical energy requirement of KAU hospital will be approximately 25 MWh.

The energy generation amount of the PV system for a capacity of 25 MW was less than the hourly electricity requirement of the hospital. As seen in Figure 11b, when the system capacity is 35 MWh, the maximum electricity generation is approximately in the range of 23 to 26 MWh. Therefore, it cannot meet the hourly energy needs of the hospital in some months. Figure 11c shows that the system capacity is 45 MW and there is an exceeding production level of the hourly maximum electrical energy requirement of the hospital in all months. In case the electricity produced from the PV system is more than the electricity consumption of the hospital, the excess production is given to the local electricity grid (on grid PV system). When there is no production of the PV system, the electricity need of the hospital is met by the local electricity grid.

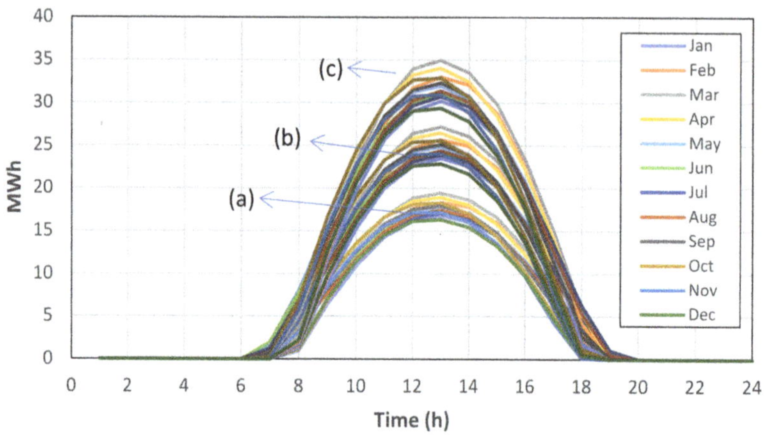

Figure 11. Average hourly profiles of total photovoltaic power output for; (**a**) 25 MW of PV capacity, (**b**) 35 MW of PV capacity, (**c**) 45 MW of PV capacity.

In all PV designs, the highest electrical energy production during the year was determined in March. The daily distribution of electrical energy production values of all PV systems in March are shown in Figure 12. In addition, the graphs show the hourly electrical energy consumption profile of the hospital for an average day of 2019.

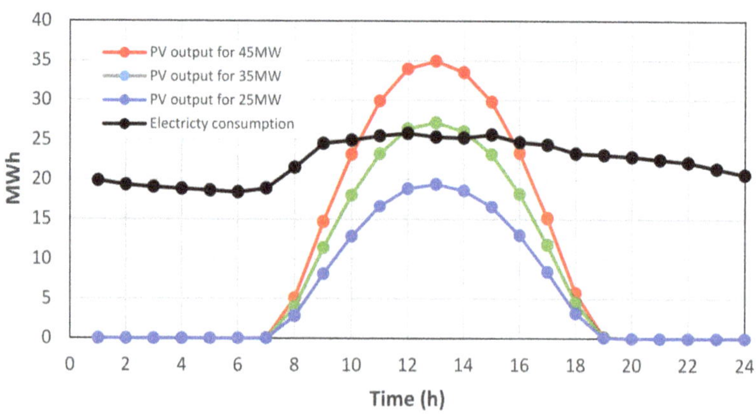

Figure 12. Average hourly profiles of total photovoltaic power output in March for 25 MW of PV capacity, 35 MW of PV capacity and 45 MW of PV capacity.

As seen in Figure 12, when the system capacity is 25 MW, the maximum electricity generation is approximately 20 MWh. The energy generation capacity of the PV system with 25 MW is below the hourly electricity requirement of the hospital. On the contrary, as it is seen in Figure 12 when the system capacity is 35 MW, the maximum electricity generation is approximately 27 MWh. The PV system produces the electrical energy needs of the hospital between 12:00 and 14:00 h. The PV system of 45 MW capacity can meet the electrical energy requirement of the hospital between 10:00 and 16:00 h, and some extra energy is produced.

Figure 13 shows the ratio of meeting the hourly electricity requirement of the hospital with energy generated from the PV system by all months. This ratio is called the self-sufficiency value of the PV system. For example, if the self-sufficiency ratio (SSR) is 30%, it means that 30% of the electrical energy requirement is produced from the PV system. On the other hand, self-consumption indicates that the entirety of the energy produced from the PV system is consumed instantly. This system does not have any storage units and are not fed to the local electricity grid. As it is seen in Figure 13, the self-sufficiency profile is similar in all capacities. Among the distribution of SSR data by month, the lowest performance was observed in February, but the highest performance was observed in May.

Table 1 presents the self-sufficiency ratio of PV systems for monthly and yearly periods. The highest performance was observed in May and this ratio was 31% for PV25, 37% for PV30, 43% for PV35, 50% for PV40, 56% for PV45, 62% for PV50, 93% for PV75 and 124% for PV100. According to the annual simulation results given in Table 1, the self-sufficiency ratio of the PV system for the KAU hospital is found as 24% for PV25, 29% for PV30, 34% for PV35, 39% for PV40, 44% for PV45, 48% for PV50, 73% for PV75 and 97% for PV100.

The annual total electricity consumption value of the KAU hospital for 2019 was 190.042.560 kWh. Figure 14 shows the annual electricity generation distribution of PV systems with different capacities for an average day.

Figure 15 presents the total annual electricity generation of the PV systems, and its comparison with the annual total electricity consumption of the KAU hospital. SSR is also given as a percentage in Figure 15. When the simulation results are analyzed, it is determined that the PV system capacity is 40 MW according to the self-consumption model for the KAU hospital. Based on this self-sufficiency model, the capacity of the PV system is considered 100 MW.

The Assessment of Solar PV Module Using RSM Approach

Figure 16a,b show the contour plots of solar PV plants under uncertain conditions. For instance, as depicted in Figure 16a, in case the wind speed is above 2 m per second, and the outdoor temperature is between 30 and 38 °C, the PV yield is 28 MWh. Similarly, Figure 16b shows the contour plots of the PV energy yield, when the wind speed is between 3 and 5.5 m per second and the radiation is above 820 W/m^2. Figure 16c,d shows the three-dimensional graph called response surface plot of solar PV energy generation versus wind speed, outdoor temperature, and radiation.

The difference of response is not the same at all levels of the factors in some problems. There is an interaction between the factors. Hence, the parallel lines in Figure 17, indicate, approximately, the factors' lack of interaction. Therefore, when Figure 17 is examined, the lines seem not to be parallel. This indicates interaction between the factors. In general, optimal solar PV generation is attained at average module surface temperature, high radiation, wind direction and wind speed level. Changing from low to high module surface temperature and outdoor temperature reduce the PV yield. Changing from intermediate to high degree module surface temperature, and outdoor temperature essentially reduces the PV generation. Figure 18 shows the individual effect of factors on the PV system. Hence, optimal PV generation levels of characteristics were determined and presented in Figure 18. Generating maximum PV of 42.27 MW is possible when the radiation level is 896.3 W/m^2, the module surface temperature is 50 °C, the outdoor temperature is 40.3 °C, the wind direction is 305.6 and the wind speed is 6.7 m/s.

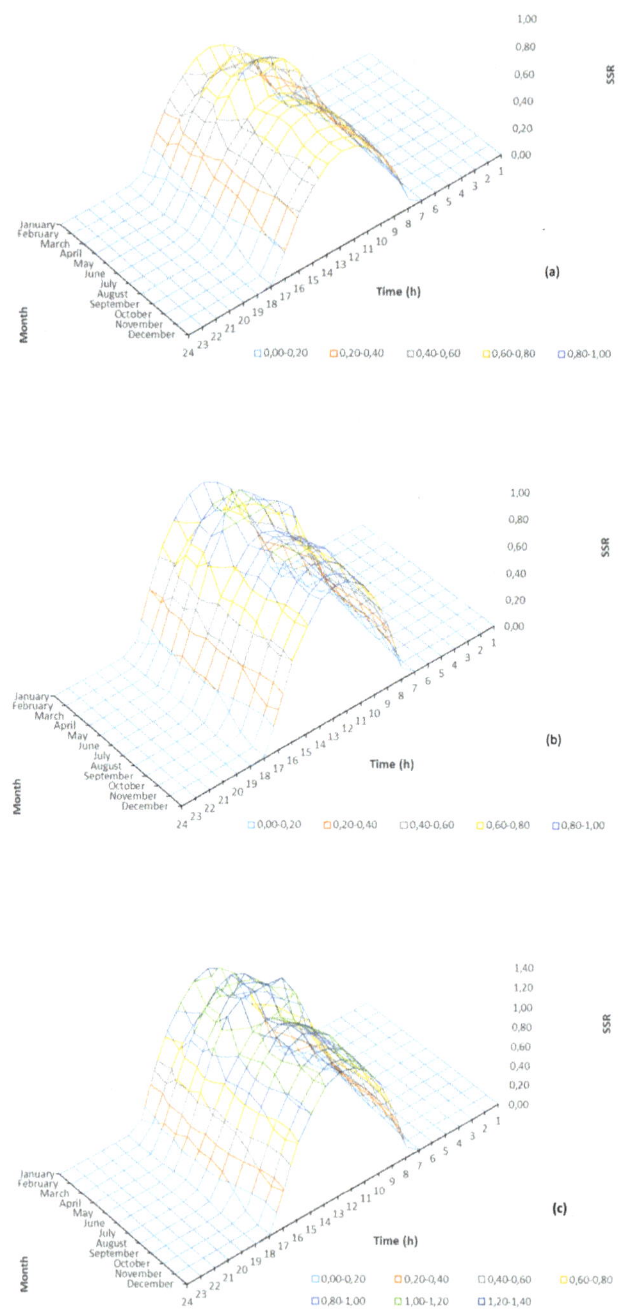

Figure 13. The ratio of PV systems meeting the hourly electricity need of the hospital (**a**) 25 MW of PV capacity, (**b**) 35 MW of PV capacity, (**c**) 45 MW of PV capacity.

Table 1. Self-sufficiency ratios of PV systems.

	PV25	PV30	PV35	PV40	PV45	PV50	PV75	PV100
January	0.22	0.27	0.31	0.36	0.40	0.45	0.67	0.90
February	0.19	0.23	0.27	0.31	0.35	0.39	0.58	0.78
March	0.26	0.31	0.36	0.41	0.47	0.52	0.78	1.03
April	0.27	0.32	0.37	0.42	0.48	0.53	0.80	1.06
May	0.31	0.37	0.43	0.50	0.56	0.62	0.93	1.24
June	0.24	0.29	0.33	0.38	0.43	0.48	0.72	0.96
July	0.25	0.29	0.34	0.39	0.44	0.49	0.74	0.98
August	0.26	0.31	0.36	0.41	0.46	0.51	0.77	1.02
September	0.25	0.30	0.36	0.41	0.46	0.51	0.76	1.01
October	0.23	0.28	0.33	0.37	0.42	0.46	0.70	0.93
November	0.22	0.27	0.31	0.36	0.40	0.45	0.67	0.90
December	0.23	0.27	0.32	0.36	0.41	0.45	0.68	0.90
Yearly	0.24	0.29	0.34	0.39	0.44	0.48	0.73	0.97

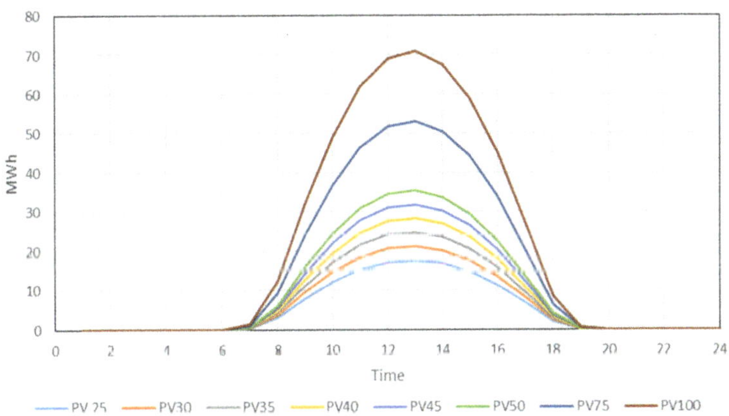

Figure 14. The annual distribution of electricity generation of PV systems for an average day.

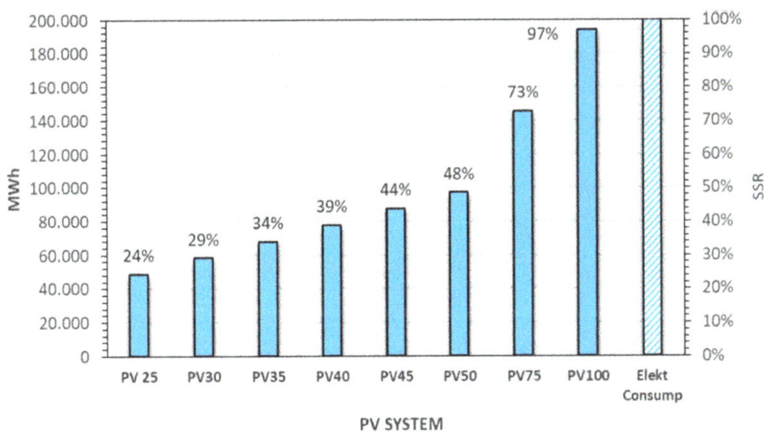

Figure 15. Total annual electricity generation of PV systems of different capacities.

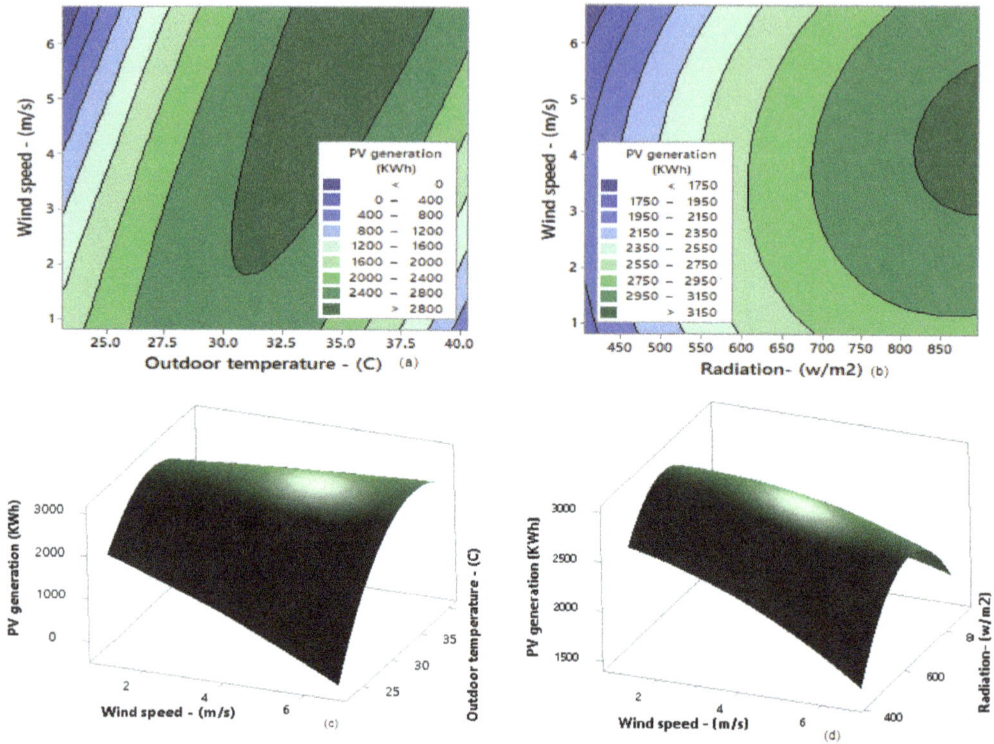

Figure 16. The contour plot of solar PV generation versus wind speed and outdoor temperature (**a**) and wind speed and radiation (**b**). The three-dimensional graph of solar PV energy generation versus wind speed, outdoor temperature (**c**), and wind speed radiation (**d**).

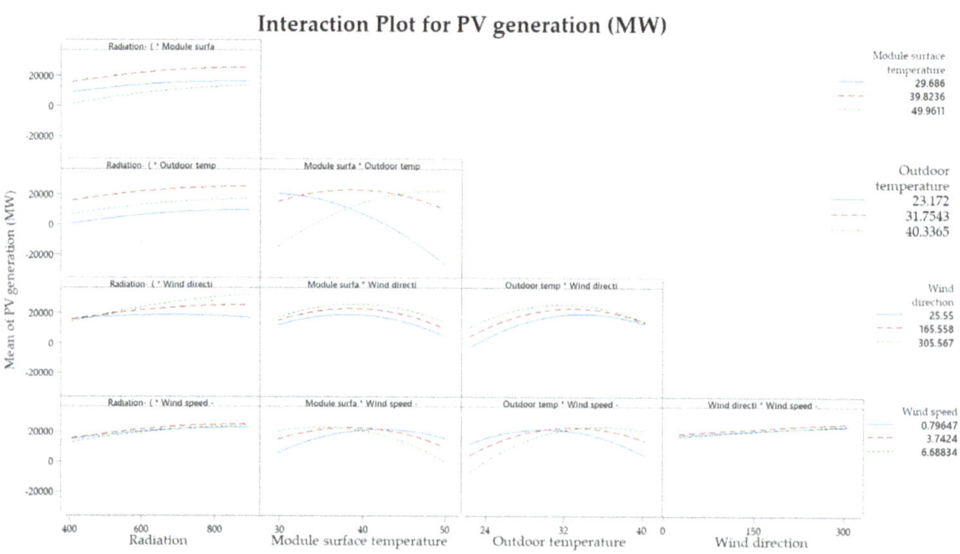

Figure 17. The plots of independent parameter interaction for solar PV generation.

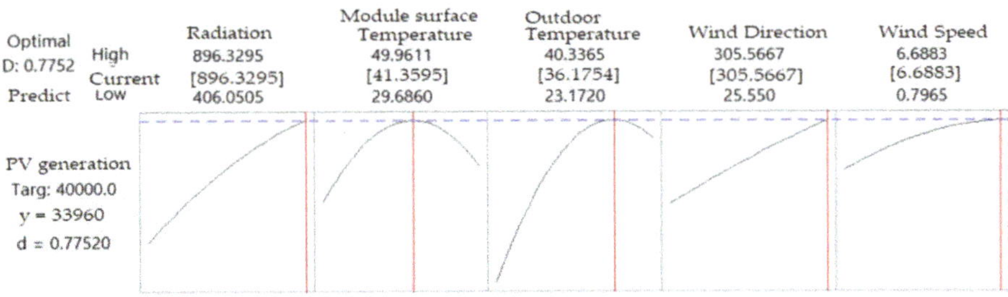

Figure 18. The individual effect of factors on solar PV generation system.

Figure 18 clearly shows that the intermediate module surface temperature, and outdoor temperature essentially increase the solar PV generation with high radiation, and wind speed. Hence, the optimal solar PV generation characteristics are determined and presented in Figure 18. When the operation conditions of solar PV are simulated under certain conditions, it was determined that the optimal solar PV of 33.96 MW is obtained if the radiation is 896.3, module surface temperature is 43.4 °C, outdoor temperature is 40.3 °C, wind direction is 305.9 and the wind speed is 6.7 m/s.

The effect analysis of the main factors x_1, x_2, x_3, x_4 and x_5 and the interactions x_1x_2, x_1x_3, x_1x_4 and etc are presented in the regression model. The effects of interactions and main factors showed that four factors positively affect the solar PV generation, only wind direction negatively affected it. Our investigation showed that the coefficients of x_1x_2, x_1, x_1x_2, $x_1{}^2$ and $x_1{}^2$ are very small, hence these interactions can be bounded. The effects of interactions and the main parameters are plotted in Figures 17 and 18, respectively. Four effects are positive in this equation, only wind direction has a negative effect. Hence all main effects are only considered to determine the optimal level and maximize the solar PV level.

4.2. The Assessment of Performance of Developed Models Using ANFIS Approach

For inferencing and obtaining the outcomes, fuzzy reasoning is used. As appears in Figure 19, fuzzy 'If-Then' rules are used for reasoning procedure, a nine rules ANFIS model was developed for the PV energy generation system. As appears in Figure 16, when the radiation is 249 W/m^2, the module surface temperature is 28 °C, the outdoor temperature is 31.2 °C, the wind direction is 180 and the wind speed is 2.92 m/s, then according to ANFIS approach, the PV module can generate 14.90 MW power.

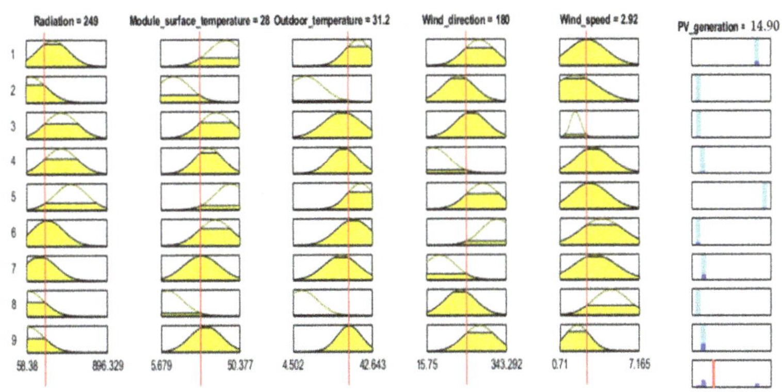

Figure 19. Fuzzy reasoning for PV energy generation system.

For testing the developed RSM and ANFIS models, the randomly selected input data were used to test the methods and to determine how perfectly they can generate and predict the consequences of the parameters. This step covers testing the performance of RSM and ANFIS approaches for the validation of the models. As appears in Table 2, a large amount of data set was utilized to identify the input–output interactions of the model. The findings of the RSM and ANFIS models for certain input factors are presented in Table 2.

Table 2. Actual and predicted solar PV generated for certain parameters.

Radiation-(W/m^2)	Module Surface Temperature-(°C)	Outdoor Temperature-(°C)	Wind Direction	Wind Speed-(m/s)	Actual PV (MW)	Predicted PV by ANFIS (MW)	Predicted PV by RSM (MW)
896.33	43.73	26.16	232.64	3.63	19.98	19.98	19.99
826.38	41.64	25.05	235.65	3.33	21.01	22.00	21.22
658.68	37.27	28.08	59.63	3.02	19.93	19.95	19.94
589.66	49.96	39.08	262.91	3.35	24.95	24.96	24.93
573.58	48.56	38.70	278.39	4.42	25.64	25.64	25.65
570.30	46.60	36.26	218.72	3.95	25.81	25.72	25.59
561.30	41.62	30.26	125.83	1.28	24.64	24.65	24.91
552.27	46.25	36.21	216.56	3.97	25.03	25.05	25.29
548.65	38.49	32.64	63.35	3.15	26.20	26.21	26.33
538.25	46.39	37.40	89.96	2.52	24.23	24.22	24.13
533.89	47.18	36.54	214.12	3.25	23.76	23.79	23.51
530.75	37.48	33.72	182.00	5.90	25.26	25.28	25.37
526.28	35.71	30.55	39.37	3.73	25.41	25.45	25.31
520.78	47.59	38.69	285.97	4.44	23.36	23.37	23.42

The results and findings showed that the average prediction error of the RSM model was found to be 1.743%. Similarly, the ANFIS models were evaluated with three different numbers of fuzzy rules: five, nine, and eleven rules. It was determined that the ANFIS model with five rules generated 1.96%, the one with nine rules had 0.75%, and the model with eleven rules had 1.16% error level on average. Figure 20 shows the actual solar PV versus predicted solar PV levels for real life data of certain parameters for the RSM and the ANFIS model with nine rules. The results and findings clearly depicted that these ANFIS models can be successfully employed for the performance prediction of solar PV modules. For instance, when the radiation is 573.58 W/m^2, the module surface temperature is 48.56 °C, the outdoor temperature is 38.70 °C, the wind direction is 278.39 and the wind speed is 4.42 m/s, the ANFIS model predicts the PV panels' performance to be 24.96 MW. Similarly, it is also predicted by the ANFIS approach that the PV module can generate 41.19 MW power when the radiation is 750 W/m^2, the module surface temperature is 25 °C, the outdoor temperature is 20 °C, the wind direction is 250 and the wind speed is 12.43 m/s.

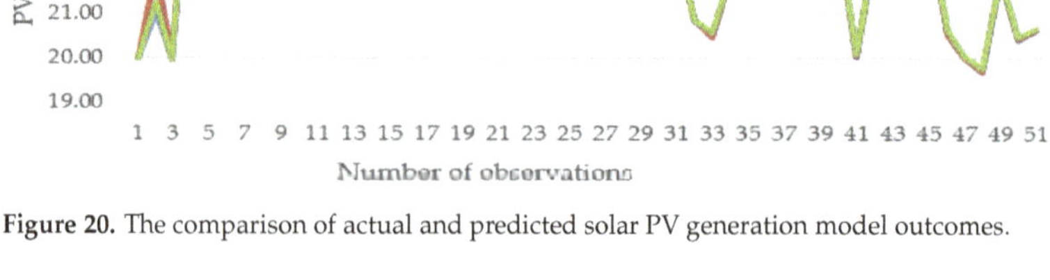

Figure 20. The comparison of actual and predicted solar PV generation model outcomes.

4.3. Comparison of the Results with the Cases Introduced by Other Works

Naderloo (2020) [34] developed a neural network and RSM methods to predict solar radiation and found out that RSM was superior to the ANFIS model in terms of performance, speed, and simplicity. The correlation coefficients and mean square errors of each method were considered for comparison of the ANFIS (0.993 and 0.0005), ANN (0.996 and 0.00029), and RSM (0.996 and 0.00027). Benmouiza et al. (2019) [35] analyzed the performance of the ANFIS model and found out that RMSE is 102.57 W/m^2 for 32 fuzzy rules and 129.13 for 243 fuzzy rules models, and the correlation coefficients were found to be 0.923 and 0.905 for these models, respectively. Mohammadi et al. (2016) [36] developed an ANFIS model for solar radiation based on RMSE during training and testing phases with 1, 2 and 3 fuzzy input parameters. They found that when the number of inputs is increased, the RMSE decreases, and the prediction accuracy enhances. Similarly, in our study, three ANFIS models were developed including five, nine and eleven fuzzy rules based on the sub clustering algorithm. The RMSE of ANFIS model with nine rules gave the best results with minimum error of solar PV generation. The results are presented in Table 3 for comparison. The RMSE was found to be 66.98 for the training process of ANFIS model with nine fuzzy rules, and RMSE was found at 113.52 for ANFIS model with nine rules, and 68.47 for the ANFIS model with eleven fuzzy rules. Aldair et al. (2018) [37] developed ANFIS controllers to determine the stand-alone PV system for which two input variables: the radiation and temperature were considered for the ANFIS model development. The difference between our model and Aldair's [37] model is that our model was established based on more variables.

Table 3. The PV power output comparison of ANFIS and RSM models.

	PV Model Power Output (Aldair et al.) [37]		Our PV Model Power Output	
Radiation	**Temperature (°C)**	**ANFIS (MW)**	**ANFIS (MW)**	**RSM (MW)**
500	0	33.36	46.14	48.50
500	25	27.72	34.78	35.23
500	50	22.58	32.02	30.61
750	0	51.4	56..12	52.98
750	25	43.6	47.78	41.19
750	50	35.98	36.86	34.53
1000	0	69.4	70.25	71.36
1000	25	59.1	58.17	60.88
1000	50	48.74	43.79	39.24

The ANFIS and RSM methods developed are highly efficient and effective under different weather conditions especially when the temperature is around 25 °C regardless of the radiation variation. In our study, all PV designs determined for KAU hospital were simulated under the local climate conditions of Jeddah and detailed analysis was carried out and presented in the previous sections of this work. For PV system simulation, the Solar-GIS program [43] and the PVGIS program [44] were used to validate the simulation results obtained from the Solar-GIS program. Figure 8 shows the comparison of monthly electricity generation obtained from both the PV-GIS and the Solar-GIS programs for a 25 MW PV system.

5. Conclusions

This study covers an on-grid PV system design in accordance with a self-consumption model developed for KAU Hospital. The solar PV system was simulated. In the design, the data of Harran university hospital, which produces electrical energy with the solar power plant, were used. The annual average PV electricity (AC) delivered by the total established capacity of the PV system was found to be 1843 kWh/kWp.

- A solar PV system with a capacity of 35 MW and/or more will be sufficient for the KAU hospital and meet the electrical energy demand of the hospital;
- For a PV system of 40 MW capacity, the maximum electricity generation is approximately between 26 and 31 MWh. Hence, the hourly maximum electrical energy requirement of the hospital between 11:00 and 15:00 h can be met by the PV system during all months;
- In all PV designs and simulation tests, the highest electrical energy production during the year was observed in March;
- The self-sufficiency ratio for March was 31% for PV25, 37% for PV30, 43% for PV35, 50% for PV40, 56% for PV45, 62% for PV50, 93% for PV75 and 124% for PV100;
- The self-sufficiency ratio for the yearly period was found as 24% for PV25, 29% for PV30, 34% for PV35, 39% for PV40, 44% for PV45, 48% for PV50, 73% for PV75 and 97% for PV100.

Additionally, the RSM and ANFIS models were developed to analyze the performance of the solar PV panels' energy generation system depending on uncertain parameter levels. The conclusions regarding the RSM approach showed that a polynomial model is rational for approximation and can be used for defining the relationships efficiently for the entire space of the independent parameters. Hence, Figure 9 showed the normality, and no extreme evidence pointing to possible outliers. Figure 16 examination showed that the parameters' lines are not parallel. This is the indication that an interaction exists between the factors. Hence, the optimal solar PV generation can be attained, at average module surface temperature, high radiation, wind direction and wind speed level. Changing from low to high module surface temperature and outdoor temperature reduces the solar PV yield. The optimal level of solar PV generation is achieved with average module surface temperature, high radiation, and high wind speed level. High surface temperature is not desired and can be reduced drastically with wind speed.

The conclusion demonstrated that the ANFIS model with nine rules gave the highest performance with the lowest residual. The ANFIS model can produce and predict the solar PV value for the output parameter regarding predetermined input parameters' intervals. The Gaussian MFs seems appropriate for defining the fuzzy linguistic terms used in fuzzy rules and in the inner loop of the model for fine-tuning the PV generation. Results and findings showed that the ANFIS model can successfully be utilized for the prediction of solar PV module performance.

As a result, meeting the electricity needs of KAU hospital is possible with a suitable capacity of PV system according to its economic resources. The PV systems' investment is particularly more attractive nowadays with the reducing PV system cost, and improved PV panel technologies (such as bifacial cell, hetero-junction solar cell). A 40 MW capacity PV system is recommended according to the self-consumption of KAU hospital. In addition, the capacity of the PV system for the self-sufficiency model should be 100 MW.

Author Contributions: The individual contribution of the authors was as follows: Conceptualization, O.T., M.A.A. and R.A.; together designed research, provide extensive advice throughout the study reading to research design, research methodology, data collection, and assessment of the results. Funding acquisition, E.H.-V.; writing—review and editing, R.A., O.T., M.A.A. and E.H.-V. All authors have read and agreed to the published version of the manuscript.

Funding: This work was funded by the Deanship of Scientific Research (DSR), King Abdulaziz University, Jeddah, under grant No. (D1441-135-626). The authors, therefore, acknowledge with thanks DSR technical and financial support.

Institutional Review Board Statement: Not applicable.

Informed Consent Statement: Not applicable.

Data Availability Statement: Data are contained within the article.

Acknowledgments: This work was funded by the Deanship of Scientific Research (DSR), King Abdulaziz University, Jeddah, under grant No. (D1441-135-626). The authors, therefore, acknowledge with thanks DSR for technical and financial support. In addition, the authors thank Harran University Presidency and GAPYENEV center for data supply and technical support.

Conflicts of Interest: The authors declare that they have no competing interests.

References

1. Taylan, O.; Alamoudi, R.; Kabli, M.; AlJifri, A.; Ramzi, F.; Herrera-Viedma, E. Assessment of Energy Systems Using Extended Fuzzy AHP. Fuzzy VIKOR. and TOPSIS Approaches to Manage Non-Cooperative Opinions. *Sustainability* **2020**, *12*, 2745. [CrossRef]
2. Bersano, A.; Segantin, S.; Falcone, N.; Panella, B.; Testoni, R. Evaluation of a potential reintroduction of nuclear energy in Italy to accelerate the energy transition. *Electr. J.* **2020**, *33*, 106813. [CrossRef]
3. Khan, M.M.A.; Asif, M.; Stach, E. Rooftop PV Potential in the Residential Sector of the Kingdom of Saudi Arabia. *Buildings* **2017**, *7*, 46. [CrossRef]
4. Almasoud, A.H.; Gandayh, H.M. Future of solar energy in Saudi Arabia. *J. King Saud Univ. Eng. Sci.* **2015**, *27*, 153–157. [CrossRef]
5. Belloumi, M.; Alshehry, A. Sustainable Energy Development in Saudi Arabia. *Sustainability* **2015**, *7*, 5153–5170. [CrossRef]
6. Alnaser, W.E.; Alnaser, N.W. The status of renewable energy in the GCC countries. *Renew. Sustain. Energy Rev.* **2011**, *15*, 3074–3098. [CrossRef]
7. Yıldırım, E.; Aktacir, M.A. Optimization of PV System and Technology in View of a Load Profile: Case of Public Building in Turkey. *Therm. Sci.* **2019**, *23*, 3567–3577. [CrossRef]
8. Martin, A.G.; Yoshihiro, H.; Wilhelm, W.; Ewan, D.D.; Dean, H.L.; Jochen, H.; Anita, W.H.H.B. Solar cell efficiency tables (version 50). *Prog. Photovolt. Res. Appl.* **2017**, *25*, 668–676.
9. Mehrabankhomartash, M.; Rayati, M.; Sheikhi, A.; Ranjbar, A.M. Practical battery size optimization of a PV system by considering individual customer damage function. *Renew. Sustain. Energy Rev.* **2017**, *67*, 36–50. [CrossRef]
10. Kaldellis, J.K.; Kapsali, M.; Kavadias, K.A. Temperature and wind speed impact on the efficiency of PV installations. Experience obtained from outdoor measurements in Greece. *Renew. Energy* **2014**, *66*, 612–624. [CrossRef]
11. Bai, A.; Popp, J.; Balogh, P.; Gabnai, Z.; Pályi, B.; Farkas, I.; Pintér, G.; Zsiborács, H. Technical and economic effects of cooling of monocrystalline photovoltaic modules under Hungarian conditions. *Renew. Sustain. Energy Rev.* **2016**, *60*, 1086–1099. [CrossRef]
12. Grubisic-Cabo, F.; Sandro, N.; Giuseppe, T. Photovoltaic panels: A review of the cooling techniques. *Trans. FAMENA* **2016**, *40*, 63–74.
13. Makrides, G.; Zinsser, B.; Norton, M.; Georghiou, G.E. Performance of Photovoltaics Under Actual Operating Conditions. In *Third Generation Photovoltaics*; Springer: Berlin/Heidelberg, Germany, 2012, ISBN 978-953-51-0304-2.
14. Lee, S.; Lee, H.; Yoon, B. Modeling and analyzing technology innovation in the energy sector: Patent-based HMM approach. *Comput. Ind. Eng.* **2012**, *63*, 564–577. [CrossRef]
15. Fan, Y. Energy Management and Economics. *Comput. Ind. Eng.* **2012**, *63*, 539–728. [CrossRef]
16. Tian, G.; Liu, Y.; Ke, H.; Chu, J. Energy evaluation method and its optimization models for process planning with stochastic characteristics: A case study in disassembly decision-making. *Comput. Ind. Eng.* **2012**, *63*, 553–563. [CrossRef]
17. Akpolat, A.N.; Dursun, E.; Kuzucuoğlu, A.E.; Yang, Y.; Blaabjerg, F.; Baba, A.F. Performance Analysis of a Grid-Connected Rooftop Solar Photovoltaic System. *Electronics* **2019**, *8*, 905. [CrossRef]
18. Muteri, V.; Cellura, M.; Curto, D.; Franzitta, V.; Longo, S.; Mistretta, M.; Parisi, M.L. Review on Life Cycle Assessment of Solar Photovoltaic Panels. *Energies* **2020**, *13*, 252. [CrossRef]
19. Pradhan, A.K.; Kar, S.K.; Mohanty, M.K. Grid Renewable Hybrid Power Generation System for a Public Health Centre in Rural Village. *Int. J. Renew. Energy Res.* **2016**, *6*, 282–288.
20. Almarshoud, A. Performance of solar resources in Saudi Arabia. *Renew. Sustain. Energy Rev.* **2016**, *66*, 694–701. [CrossRef]
21. Mittal, M.; Bora, B.; Saxena, S.; Gaur, A.M. Performance prediction of PV module using electrical equivalent model and artificial neural network. *Sol. Energy* **2018**, *176*, 104–117. [CrossRef]
22. Yahya-Khotbehsara, A.; Shahhoseini, A. A fast modeling of the double-diode model for PV modules using combined analytical and numerical approach. *Sol. Energy* **2018**, *162*, 403–409. [CrossRef]
23. Goverde, H.; Goossens, D.; Govaerts, J.; Catthoor, F.; Baert, K.; Poortmans, J.; Driesen, J. Spatial and temporal analysis of wind effects on PV modules: Consequences for electrical power evaluation. *Sol. Energy* **2017**, *147*, 292–299. [CrossRef]
24. Goossens, D.; Goverde, H.; Catthoor, F. Effect of wind on temperature patterns, electrical characteristics, and performance of building-integrated and building-applied inclined photovoltaic modules. *Sol. Energy* **2018**, *170*, 64–75. [CrossRef]
25. Curto, D.; Favuzza, S.; Franzitta, V.; Musca, R.; Navarro, M.A.N.; Zizz, G. Evaluation of the optimal renewable electricity mix for Lampedusa island: The adoption of a technical and economical methodology. *J. Clean. Prod.* **2020**, *263*, 121404. [CrossRef]
26. Awan, A.B.; Zubair, M.; Praveen, R.P.; Abokhalil, A.G. Solar Energy Resource Analysis and Evaluation of Photovoltaic System Performance in Various Regions of Saudi Arabia. *Sustainability* **2018**, *10*, 1129. [CrossRef]
27. Rani, P.; Mishra, A.R.; Pardasani, K.R.; Mardani, A.; Liao, H.; Streimikienef, D. A novel VIKOR approach based on entropy and divergence measures of Pythagorean fuzzy sets to evaluate renewable energy technologies in India. *J. Clean. Prod.* **2019**, *238*, 117936. [CrossRef]

28. Daus, Y.V.; Yudaev, I.V.; Stepanchuk, G.V. Reducing the Costs of Paying for Consumed Electric Energy by Utilizing Solar Energy. *Appl. Sol. Energy* **2018**, *54*, 139–143. [CrossRef]
29. Yoomak, Y.; Patcharoen, T.; Ngaopitakkul, A. Performance and Economic Evaluation of Solar Rooftop Systems in Different Regions of Thailand. *Sustainability* **2019**, *11*, 6647. [CrossRef]
30. Kassem, Y.; Camur, H.; Alhuoti, S.M.A. Solar Energy Technology for Northern Cyprus: Assessment, Statistical Analysis, and Feasibility Study. *Energies* **2020**, *13*, 940. [CrossRef]
31. Ascencio-Vásquez, J.; Brecl, K.; Topič, M. Methodology of Köppen-Geiger-Photovoltaic climate classification and implications to worldwide mapping of PV system performance. *Sol. Energy* **2019**, *191*, 672–685. [CrossRef]
32. Zell, E.; Gasim, S.; Wilcox, S.; Katamoura, S.; Stoffel, T.; Shibli, H.; Engel-Cox, J.; Al Subie, M. Assessment of solar radiation resources in Saudi Arabia. *Sol. Energy* **2015**, *119*, 422–438. [CrossRef]
33. Roy, P.; Sinha, N.K.; Tiwari, S.; Khare, A. A review on perovskite solar cells: Evolution of architecture, fabrication techniques, commercialization issues and status. *Sol. Energy* **2020**, *198*, 665–688. [CrossRef]
34. Naderloo, L. Prediction of solar radiation on the horizon using NN methods, ANFIS and RSM (Case study-Iran). *J. Earth Syst. Sci.* **2020**, *129*, 148.
35. Benmouiza, K.; Cheknane, A. Clustered ANFIS network using fuzzy c-means, subtractive clustering, and grid partitioning for hourly solar radiation forecasting. *Theor. Appl. Climatol.* **2019**, *137*, 31–43. [CrossRef]
36. Mohammadi, K.; Shamshirband, S.; Kamsin, A.; Lai, P.C.; Mansor, Z. Identifying the most significant input parameters for predicting global solar radiation using an ANFIS selection procedure. *Renew. Sustain. Energy Rev.* **2016**, *63*, 423–434. [CrossRef]
37. Aldair, A.A.; Obed, A.A.; Halihal, A.F. Design and implementation of ANFIS-reference model controller based MPPT using FPGA for photovoltaic system. *Renew. Sustain. Energy Rev.* **2018**, *82*, 2202–2217. [CrossRef]
38. Khosravi, A.; Malekan, M.; Pabon, J.J.G.; Zhao, X.; Assad, M.E.H. Design parameter modelling of solar power tower system using adaptive neuro-fuzzy inference system optimized with a combination of genetic algorithm and teaching learning-based optimization algorithm. *J. Clean. Prod.* **2020**, *244*, 118904. [CrossRef]
39. Solar-GIS. Available online: https://globalsolaratlas.info/map (accessed on 30 May 2020).
40. PVGIS. Available online: https://ec.europa.eu/jrc/en/pvgis (accessed on 30 May 2020).
41. Colak, N.S.; Sahin, E.; Dertli, E.; Yilmaz, M.T.; Taylan, O. Response surface methodology as optimization strategy for asymmetric bioreduction of acetophenone using whole cell of Lactobacillus senmaizukei. *Prep. Biochem. Biotechnol.* **2019**, *49*, 884–890. [CrossRef] [PubMed]
42. Dirnberger, D.; Kräling, U. Uncertainty in PV Module Measurement—Part I: Calibration of Crystalline and Thin-Film Modules. *IEEE J. Photovolt.* **2013**, *3*, 1016–1026. [CrossRef]
43. Taylan, O.; Darrab, I.A. Fuzzy control charts for process quality improvement and product assessment in tip shear carpet industry. *J. Manuf. Technol. Manag.* **2012**, *23*, 402–420. [CrossRef]
44. Taylan, O.; Taşkın, H. Fuzzy Modelling af A Production System. *J. Nav. Sci. Eng.* **2003**, *1*, 1–13.
45. Taylan, O.; Karagozoglu, B. An Adaptive Neuro-Fuzzy Model for Prediction of Student's Academic Performance. *Comput. Ind. Eng.* **2009**, *57*, 732–741. [CrossRef]
46. Taylan, O. Neural and fuzzy model performance evaluation of a dynamic production system. *Int. J. Prod. Res.* **2006**, *44*, 1093–1105. [CrossRef]
47. Taylan, O.; Darrab, I.A. Determining optimal quality distribution of latex weight using adaptive neuro-fuzzy modeling and control systems. *Comput. Ind. Eng.* **2011**, *61*, 686–696. [CrossRef]
48. Al-Ghamdi, K.; Taylan, O. A comparative study on modelling material removal rate by ANFIS and polynomial methods in electrical discharge machining process. *Comput. Ind. Eng.* **2015**, *79*, 27–41. [CrossRef]

energies

MDPI

Article

A Case Study: Sediment Erosion in Francis Turbines Operated at the San Francisco Hydropower Plant in Ecuador

Cristian Cruzatty [1,*], Darwin Jimenez [1], Esteban Valencia [1], Ivan Zambrano [1], Christian Mora [2], Xianwu Luo [3] and Edgar Cando [1,*]

[1] Departamento de Ingeniería Mecánica, Escuela Politécnica Nacional, Quito 170517, Ecuador; darwin.jimenez@epn.edu.ec (D.J.); esteban.valencia@epn.edu.ec (E.V.); ivan.zambrano@epn.edu.ec (I.Z.)

[2] Centro de Investigación y Recuperación de Turbinas Hidráulicas y Partes Industriales, CELEC EP, Baños de Agua Santa 180254, Ecuador; andres.mora@celec.gob.ec

[3] Department of Energy and Power Engineering, Tsinghua University, Beijing 100084, China; luoxw@mail.tsinghua.edu.cn

* Correspondence: cristian.cruzatty@epn.edu.ec (C.C.); edgar.cando@epn.edu.ec (E.C.)

Citation: Cruzatty, C.; Jimenez, D.; Valencia, E.; Zambrano, I.; Mora, C.; Luo, X.; Cando, E. A Case Study: Sediment Erosion in Francis turbines Operated at the San Francisco Hydropower Plant in Ecuador. *Energies* **2022**, *15*, 8. https://doi.org/10.3390/en15010008

Academic Editors: Marcin Kamiński and Angel A. Juan

Received: 18 September 2021
Accepted: 17 November 2021
Published: 21 December 2021

Abstract: The operation of various types of turbomachines is importantly affected by sediment erosion. Francis turbines used for power generation typically suffer said effects due to the fact that they are used in sediment-laden rivers and are usually operated disregarding the long-term effect of the erosion on turbine performance. This investigation seeks to study the erosion rate for the main components of the turbines located at San Francisco hydropower plant in Pastaza, Ecuador. A sediment characterization study was performed in order to determine the properties of the particles present in Pastaza River and accurately predict their effect on the turbine flow passages. A numerical approach combining liquid–solid two-phase flow simulation and an erosion model was used to analyze the erosion rates at different operating conditions and determine wear patterns in the components. As expected, the results indicated that an increase in the erosion rate was obtained for higher intake flows. However, a dramatic increase in the erosion rate was observed when the turbine was operated at near-full-load conditions, specifically when guide vane opening exceeded a 90% aperture.

Keywords: Francis turbine; sediment erosion; CFD; DPM

1. Introduction

Hydroelectric power is a renewable energy source and a significant component of worldwide electricity production. Around 17% of the total consumed electricity is produced through hydraulic energy sources [1,2], and almost 65% of the total electricity produced in Latin America is generated by hydroelectric power plants (around 709 TWh/y) [3,4]. However, most of the total technical hydraulic potential (2859 TWh/y) of the region is not harnessed by its installed hydropower capacity. Several large-scale hydropower projects are being currently studied and developed in the Andean region in the hopes of increasing the installed capacity and harnessing a larger portion of the available hydraulic potential. One of the most crucial factors that needs to be taken into consideration during the development of the aforementioned projects is the fact that hard particles are present in almost all rivers of the Andean and Himalayan region, causing considerable the erosion, mechanical wear, and failure of turbine components [3,5].

Sediments flowing through the river deposit in the dam's reservoir, reduce the reservoir's capacity, and increase the erosion wear of critical turbine components, such as: the spiral casing, guide vanes, runner, and draft tube. This phenomenon reduces the lifespan of the turbine and decreases its efficiency, which increases the cost of maintenance over time, leading to economic losses [6,7]. Erosion wear depends on several factors, including particle concentration, velocity, composition, size, and shape. Other variables, namely turbine materials and operating conditions, also have an effect on the erosion rate. Therefore, erosion reduction strategies can only work effectively after in-depth analyses making a holistic assessment of all the variables involved [8,9].

Extensive research has been conducted on erosion in Francis turbines. In 2013, Singh and Banerjee performed an analysis on the erosion of the runner blades, guide vanes, and labyrinth seals of the Maneri Bhali Stage-II hydroelectric power plant in India. Data collection of sediments at relevant locations and measurements of turbine efficiency were performed during three years to determine the effect of silt erosion on the efficiency of turbines [10]. In 2016, Koirala used a computational analysis coupled with field observations to determine the erosion patterns on the guide vanes of Kaligandaki hydroelectric power plant in Nepal and proposed erosion protection methods [11]. A year later, Masoodi and Harmain presented a detailed comparison of two sediment-laden rivers and their effect on the runner blades of Himalayan hydroelectric power plants in India. A new erosion model was proposed in this study [12]. Most recently, in 2020, Qian et al. executed a study on the erosion wear of the runner blades of a Francis turbine in Jhimruk Hydroelectric Center in Nepal using numerical simulations and comparing the results with the damage of the runners. He proposed changing the opening of the guide vanes to improve turbine efficiency and reduce the erosion rate [13]. Moreover, Noon and Kim discussed and analyzed the latest experimental and numerical techniques to determine sediment and cavitation erosion on different turbine components using baseline data from the Tarbela Dam hydroelectric project in Pakistan [14]. However, all the aforementioned studies were performed in Asia, and no research on the topic has been performed on South America, where similar erosion issues are found.

This study focuses on the analysis of sediment erosion in the Francis turbines of San Francisco hydroelectric power plant in Ecuador. The turbines of this power station suffer erosion wear damage, and to date, no effective strategies have been proposed to reduce the damage. A sediment characterization of the Pastaza River was conducted for this study in order to perform a numerical analysis of the turbines with sediment properties set as close as possible to the real conditions. Finally, a study on the erosion rate and pattern in different components of the turbine was carried out to better understand this phenomenon.

2. Case of Study: San Francisco Hydropower Plant

San Francisco hydro-power plant (SFH) is one of the largest energy generation centers in Ecuador, producing around 1140 GWh of electricity per annum, which represents 12% of the energy demand in the country. SFH is a 230 MW run-of-river hydropower plant located along Pastaza River, which consists of two vertical Francis turbines, each one running at 327.27 rpm under a net head of 213.4 m and a flow rate of 58 m^3/s. Since the plant began operations in 2007, it has suffered erosion problems, especially at the guide vanes and the outlet band of the runner. Figure 1 presents a georeference of the plant.

Figure 1. San Francisco hydroelectric power plant location.

2.1. *Sediment Characterization at Pastaza River*

The Pastaza River originates in the Andes mountains, where irregular geography and the presence of soft sediments due to high volcanic activity contribute to the high sediment content of South American rivers [15]. These sediments pass through the turbines of hydraulic power plants, resulting in sediment erosion on exposed turbine components. To tackle the problems derived from erosion wear, an analysis of the particulate matter that flows through each power plant becomes necessary for a proper assessment of the erosion in a particular station. On this basis, the samples for the analysis were collected from the following zones of the hydropower plant:

1. The reservoir after the desilting chamber;
2. The outlet of the discharge gate;
3. The outlet of the draft tube.

2.1.1. Sediment Analysis

In order to characterize the particles of the Pastaza River at San Francisco hydropower plant, the collected sediment samples were analyzed at the Soil Mechanics and Materials Testing Laboratory, Escuela Politecnica Nacional, performing a sieve and composition analysis. The results of this analysis were considered during the study.

2.1.2. Particle Size and Distribution

A similar approach as the one followed by Koirala et al. [11,16] was used for this study. The sieve analysis was carried out under the ASTM D422-63 (2007) standard. Five sieve measurements of 4.75 mm, 2.00 mm, 0.85 mm, 0.425 mm, and 0.075 mm were used on five 120 g sediment samples.

Additionally, since particle roundness (R) and sphericity (S) affect most macroscale mechanical properties of the particle such as strength, compressibility, and shear wave velocity, it is necessary to estimate these parameters to increase the fidelity of the simulation [17]. Roundness is described as the ratio between the average radius of curvature of the particle corners and the radius of the maximum inscribed circle, while sphericity is defined as the ratio of the particle width to particle length [18]. The sphericity (spherical shape factor) and roundness of the particles were estimated using the Krumbein–Sloss chart [19].

2.1.3. Mineral Composition Analysis

The mineral composition analysis for the study was performed through a particle count method using a D8 ADVANCE X-ray diffractometer and Diffrac plus software.

2.1.4. Sediment Concentration

Pastaza River is the third-largest river in Ecuador with an average annual flow 144.4 m^3/s and a precipitation of 3255 mm. Sediment concentration was determined based on data from San Francisco hydropower plant. The samples were collected daily 1 km upstream of the reservoir, in the reservoir itself, in the desilting chamber, and at the discharge during a month, as shown in Figure 2. Since heavier particles tend to deposit on the reservoir bed and mostly only suspended particles are drawn by the intake, water samples were taken at a constant depth of about 2 m from the surface. The average concentration was estimated considering daily values from all sampling points throughout the sampling period.

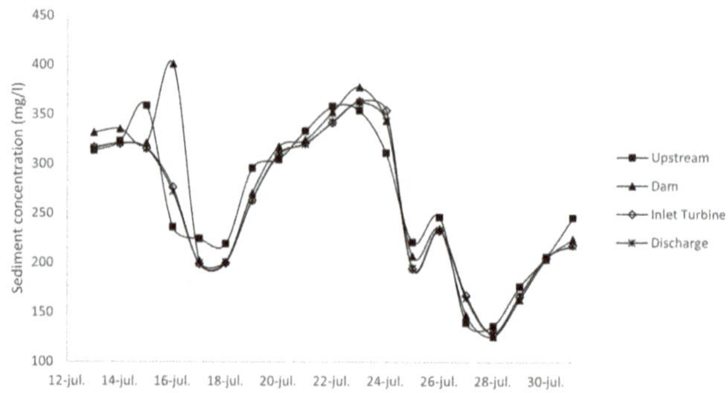

Figure 2. Sediment concentration in July 2010.

3. Numerical Analysis of the Erosion in Francis Turbines

3.1. Governing Equations

3.1.1. Liquid Phase Mathematical Model

Fluids were calculated using a Eulerian approach. The general form of the equations involved in the calculations is presented. The mass continuity equation has the following form:

$$\frac{\partial \rho}{\partial t} + \frac{\partial(\rho u_i)}{\partial x_i} = 0 \quad (1)$$

where:

- u = fluid phase velocity;
- ρ = fluid phase density.

The momentum conservation equation is shown in Equation (2).

$$\frac{\rho\partial(u_i)}{\partial t} + \frac{\rho\partial(u_i u_j)}{\partial x_j} = -\frac{\partial p}{\partial x_i} + \frac{\partial}{\partial x_j}\left[\mu\left(\frac{\partial u_i}{\partial x_j} + \frac{\partial u_j}{\partial x_i}\right)\right] + f_i \quad (2)$$

where:

- p = pressure;
- μ = dynamic viscosity;
- f_i = external forces.

3.1.2. Turbulence Model

A realizable k-ϵ turbulence model was selected for its ability to correctly capture the turbulent nature of the flow in Francis turbines [20–22]. This model was selected for its robustness and its improved boundary-layer-solving capacity under strong pressure gradients and flow separation compared to the standard k-ϵ model [23]. In addition, the k-ϵ turbulence model has a low computational expense when compared to k-ω SST. The transport equations for the realizable k-ϵ take the following form:

$$\frac{\partial(\rho k)}{\partial t} + \frac{\partial(\rho k u_j)}{\partial x_j} = \frac{\partial}{\partial x_j}\left[\left(\mu + \frac{\mu_t}{\sigma_k}\right)\frac{\partial k}{\partial x_j}\right] + G_k + G_b + \rho\epsilon - Y_M + S_k \quad (3)$$

$$\frac{\partial(\rho \epsilon)}{\partial t} + \frac{\partial(\rho \epsilon u_j)}{\partial x_j} = \frac{\partial}{\partial x_j}\left[\left(\mu + \frac{\mu_t}{\sigma_\epsilon}\right)\frac{\partial \epsilon}{\partial x_j}\right] + \rho C_1 S_\epsilon - \rho C_2 \frac{\epsilon^2}{k + \sqrt{v\epsilon}} + C_{1\epsilon}\frac{\epsilon}{k}C_{3\epsilon}G_b + S_\epsilon \quad (4)$$

$$C_1 = max\left[0.43, \frac{\sqrt{2S_{i,j}S_{i,j}\frac{k}{\epsilon}}}{\sqrt{2S_{i,j}S_{i,j}\frac{k}{\epsilon}} + 5}\right] \quad (5)$$

where:

- G_k = turbulent kinetic energy due to velocity gradients;
- G_b = turbulent kinetic energy due to buoyancy;
- Y_M = contribution of compressible fluctuations to the dissipation rate;
- $C_{1\epsilon}, C_2$ = constants;
- $\sigma_k, \sigma_\epsilon$ = Prandtl numbers;
- μ_t = Eddy dynamic viscosity;
- S_k, S_ϵ = user-defined terms.

The turbulence viscosity μ_t is computed by:

$$\mu_t = \rho C_\mu \frac{k^2}{\epsilon} \tag{6}$$

Model variable C_μ is defined by:

$$C_\mu = \frac{1}{4.04 + \sqrt{6}cos\phi \frac{kU^*}{\epsilon}} \tag{7}$$

$$\phi = \frac{1}{3}cos^{-1}(\sqrt{6}W) \tag{8}$$

$$W = \frac{S_{ij}S_{jk}S_{ki}}{\tilde{S}^3} \tag{9}$$

$$\tilde{S} = \sqrt{S_{ij}S_{ij}} \tag{10}$$

$$S_{ij} = \frac{1}{2}\left(\frac{\partial u_j}{\partial x_i} + \frac{\partial u_i}{x_j}\right) \tag{11}$$

$$U^* = \sqrt{S_{ij}S_{ij} + \tilde{\Omega}_{ij}\tilde{\Omega}_{ij}} \tag{12}$$

$$\tilde{\Omega}_{ij} = \Omega_{ij} - 2\epsilon_{ijk}\omega_k \tag{13}$$

$$\Omega_{ij} = \overline{\Omega_{ij}} - \epsilon_{ij}\omega_k \tag{14}$$

where $\overline{\Omega_{ij}}$ is the tensor for the mean rate of rotation in a reference frame rotating at an angular velocity ω_k.

3.1.3. Solid Phase Mathematical Model

Solid particles were simulated using a Lagrangian approach and were treated as if their volume fraction were low compared to that of the continuous phase. Equation (15) was derived from the force balance on the Lagrangian reference frame.

$$\frac{\partial(v_p)_i}{\partial t} = \frac{18\mu}{\rho_p d_p^2}\frac{C_D Re}{24} + \left(\frac{\rho}{\rho_p}\right)(v_p)_i\frac{\partial u_i}{\partial x_i} + \left(1 + \frac{\rho}{\rho_p}\right)g - \frac{1}{2}\frac{\rho}{\rho_p}\frac{\partial}{\partial t}(u_i - v_{pi}) + F_z \tag{15}$$

where:

- v_p = particle velocity;
- ρ_p = particle density;
- C_D = drag coefficient;
- Re = Reynolds number;
- F_z = other interaction forces per unit mass.

The term F_z activates force terms in situations in which multiple reference frames are used and frame or mesh rotation is activated. The drag coefficient was estimated using the equations for the nonspherical drag law shown in Equation (16).

$$C_D = \frac{24}{Re_{sph}}(1 + b_1 Re_{sph}^{b_2}) + \frac{b_3 Re_{sph}}{b_4 + Re_{sph}} \tag{16}$$

$$b_1 = exp(2.3288 + 6.4581\phi + 2.4486\phi^2) \tag{17}$$

$$b_2 = 0.0964 + 0.5565\phi \tag{18}$$

$$b_3 = exp(4.905 - 13.8944\phi + 18.4222\phi^2 - 10.2599\phi^3) \tag{19}$$

$$b_4 = exp(1.4681 + 12.2584\phi - 20.7322\phi^2 + 15.8855\phi^3) \tag{20}$$

where:

- Re_{sph} = Reynolds number of an equivalent sphere;
- ϕ = spherical shape factor.

Particle dispersion caused by turbulent flows can be estimated using the stochastic tracking model [24,25]. This method, also known as the discrete random walk model, takes into account the effect of turbulent velocity fluctuations on the trajectories of particles. Instantaneous fluid velocity, as shown in Equation (21), was used to integrate the particle trajectory equations along their path to predict the turbulent dispersion of particles. Random velocity fluctuations u' were determined through Equation (22), where ζ is a normally distributed random number. Particle diffusivity was estimated using Equation (23), where the integral time scale as defined in Equation (24) describes the time the particle remains in turbulent motion along a path ds.

$$u = \overline{u} + u'(t) \tag{21}$$

$$u' = \zeta\sqrt{2k/3} \tag{22}$$

$$D(t) = \overline{u_i' u_j'} T \tag{23}$$

$$T = \int_o^\infty \frac{v_p'(t) v_p'(t+s)}{\overline{v_p'^2}} ds \tag{24}$$

3.1.4. Erosion Model

The erosion model developed by Oka, Okamura, and Yoshida [26,27] was used to determine the erosion for the present case. This model is one of the most frequently used to determine the erosion in CFD analyses where solid particles suspended in a liquid medium are present [28–30]. The equation developed by Oka is the following:

$$E(\alpha) = g(\alpha) E_{90} \tag{25}$$

where:

- $E_{(\alpha)}$ = erosion damage in $mm^3 kg^{-1}$;
- $g(\alpha)$ = impact angle dependence of the normalized erosion;
- E_{90} = erosion damage at a normal angle.

and:

$$g(\alpha) = (sin\alpha)^{n1}(1 + Hv(1 - sin\alpha))^{n2} \tag{26}$$

$$E_{90} = K(aHv)^{k_1 b}\left(\frac{v}{v'}\right)^{k_2}\left(\frac{D}{D'}\right)^{k_3} \tag{27}$$

$$k_2 = 2.3(Hv)^{0.038} \tag{28}$$

$$n1, n2 = 2.3(Hv)^{0.038} \tag{29}$$

where Hv is the material Vickers hardness in GPa, k_2 is a velocity exponent, k_3 is a diameter exponent, and constants $n1$ and $n2$ are model exponents used to calculate the impact angle influence on the erosion rate. D' and v' are the reference diameter and velocity, respectively. The calibrated values of these parameters for the present case, in which sand particles and stainless steel were considered, are the ones presented in Table 1.

Table 1. Oka model parameters.

Parameter	Units	Value
k_1	-	−0.12
k_2	-	2.36
k_3	-	0.19
$n1$	-	0.78
$n2$	-	1.27
a	-	0.0221
b	-	0.45
E_{90}	$mm^3\ kg^{-1}$	3.53

3.2. Geometry and Conditions

Details of the general specifications of the turbine are presented in Table 2. In order to reduce the computational effort while using a more precise mesh for the numerical analysis, only one period of the turbine was simulated, which is comprises one stay vane, one guide vane, one runner blade, and an outlet domain representing the draft tube.

Table 2. Turbine specifications.

Parameter	Value
Runner inlet diameter (mm)	1530.8
Number of runner blades Z_b	13
Height of the guide vane (mm)	540.4
Number of guide vanes	20
Number of stay vanes	20

The computational domain is presented in Figure 3. The geometry was obtained performing a 3D scanning of the turbine. The obtained profiles were reconstructed using ANSYS BladeGen to obtain a smoother geometry optimized for mesh construction using TurboGrid.

3.3. Operating Conditions

Table 3 shows the operating conditions that were used to perform the simulations. These conditions were translated to mass flow inlet and pressure outlet boundary conditions. The atmospheric pressure from the region was used to define the outlet pressure.

Table 3. Operating conditions.

Parameter	Equation	Unit	Case 1	Case 2	Case 3	Case 4
Guide vane opening	-	%	55.17	77.91	89.92	93.46
Volumetric flow rate	-	$m^3\ s^{-1}$	33.2	50.8	59.7	62.4
Specific speed, n_{QE}	$nQ^{0.5}H^{-0.75}$	-	0.56	0.69	0.75	0.77
Discharge coefficient, Q_{nD}	$Qn^{-1}D^{-3}$	-	3.31	5.06	5.95	6.22
Energy coefficient, E_{nD}	$Hn^{-2}D^{-2}$	-	4.78	4.78	4.78	4.78
Speed factor, n_{ED}	$nDH^{-0.5}$	-	0.46	0.46	0.46	0.46

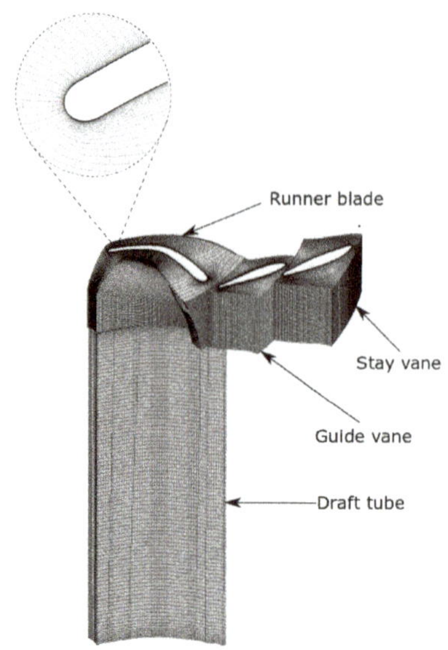

Figure 3. Computational domain of San Francisco's Francis turbine.

The characteristics of the sediments used for this study are shown in Table 4. Particle mass flow rate was calculated as a function of the volumetric water flow rate of each case using the average particle concentration.

Table 4. Sediment characteristics.

Characteristic	Unit	Value
Density	kg m^{-3}	2650
Size	µm	62
Average concentration	kg m^{-3}	0.334

3.4. Mesh

The mesh was generated using the Turbogrid module, which employs a high-fidelity hexahedric structured mesh with a uniform distribution. y^+ values were calculated for stay vanes, guide vanes, and runner blades through the following equation:

$$y^+ = \frac{u_t y}{v} \quad (30)$$

where u_T is the friction velocity, y is the distance to the nearest wall, and v is the kinematic viscosity. The first cell height of each domain was calculated to correctly compute the boundary layer with the selected turbulence model, as shown in Figure 3, by applying a locally refined region near the domain walls. The obtained y^+ values ranged between 45 and 125, which are considered appropriate for the selected turbulence model [31]. The quality of the mesh was also evaluated using the orthogonal quality model. The orthogonal quality of a cell was estimated as follows.

$$min\left(\frac{\vec{A}_i\vec{C}_i}{|A_i||C_i|}, \frac{\vec{A}_i\vec{f}_i}{|A_i||f_i|}\right) \quad (31)$$

where:

- A_i = face normal vector;
- f_i = vector from the centroid of the cell to the centroid of the face;

- C_i = vector from the centroid of the cell to the centroid of the adjacent cell.

A minimum orthogonal quality of 0.269 was obtained in 0.0000002% of mesh elements. The average orthogonal quality in all meshes was 0.93. The walls of the fully structured mesh are shown in Figure 4

Additionally, mesh independence studies were performed considering the pressure drop between the domain inlet and outlet. The structured mesh distribution was modified in all domain directions. Three different mesh resolutions were analyzed for each of the four individual operating conditions evaluated in the study. The results shown in Figure 5 indicate that the difference between the calculations of the fine and medium mesh resolutions is negligible.

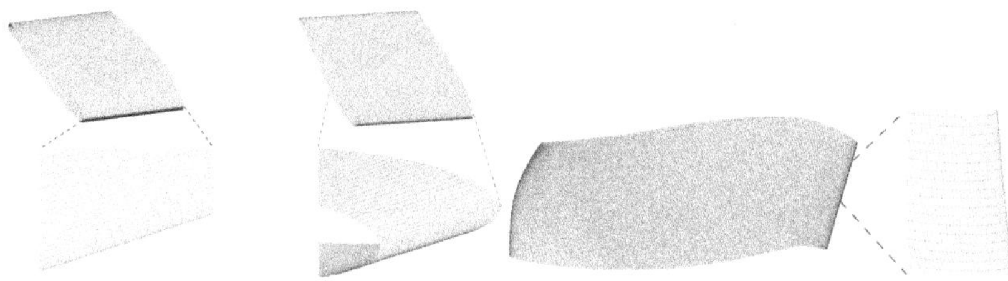

(a) Stay vane mesh **(b)** Guide vane mesh **(c)** Runner mesh

Figure 4. Mesh of the conceptual model.

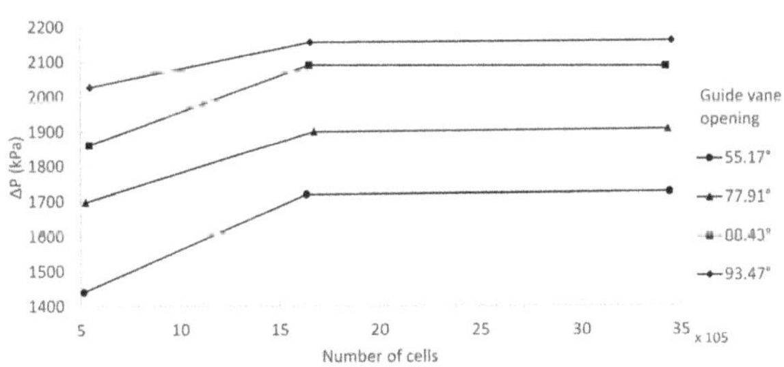

Figure 5. Mesh independence analysis.

3.5. Solver

The numerical simulation was performed using the commercial software ANSYS Fluent. The present simulation used a RANS approach for the liquid phase through a realizable $k-\epsilon$ model. The dispersed phase was estimated using the discrete phase model in the commercial CFD software ANSYS Fluent. The numerical simulation was performed coupling all the subdomains with the following imposed boundary conditions:

1. The total mass flow inlet was designated at the inlet of the stay vane and the nonoverlapping interfaces of the runner;
2. A rotating frame was applied for the runner domain, and other regions were considered to be in a stationary frame;
3. Periodic repeats interfaces were created between the stay vane outlet and guide vane inlet and between the outlet of the runner and the inlet of the outlet domain;
4. A standard interface was created between the guide vane outlet and the inlet of the runner;
5. The total pressure was designated at the outlet of the runner;
6. Solid walls were set as nonslip boundary conditions.

A setup used previously in [32] was used for the solid phase, where the injection was applied at the domain inlet and fully elastic collision was assumed at the walls. An analysis of the adequate number of particle injections was also carried out to generate a statistically meaningful sampling. One-hundred stochastic tracking tries were determined to be adequate to ensure that erosion on the walls of the turbine flow passage was independent of the number of injected particles.

The steady-state simulations were carried out using spatial derivatives discretized through a second-order upwind scheme. Full pressure–velocity coupling was enabled using the SIMPLE algorithm. Further, double precision was considered to improve the computational accuracy. A quantitative assessment of the discharge difference was made between the inlet and the outlet, which was lower than the order of 9×10^{-3}.

The postprocessing phase was carried out in ANSYS CFD-Post, obtaining estimations of the erosion rate on the surfaces of the studied components. Additionally, the pressure and velocity of the flow were determined. Turbine efficiency was calculated based on these results.

3.6. Validation

The study was validated by reproducing the numerical experiment of Nguyen [28], where a wet erosion test rig was used to discharge and project sand particles. A stainless steel plate specimen with a 196 Vickers' hardness was used for the experiment. The parameters of the experimental setup are shown in Table 5.

Table 5. Details of the experimental setup for the validation.

Parameter	Units	Value
Particle velocity	m s^{-1}	30
Particle diameter	µm	150
Nozzle diameter	mm	6.4
Plate dimensions	mm	$25 \times 25 \times 5$
Standoff distance	mm	12.7

The results shown in Figure 6 were obtained from the numerical assessment. A satisfactory agreement between the erosion pattern and the results of the experimental and computational tests was observed.

The chart shows the material removal in the specimen caused by sediment erosion, where the center of the chart is aligned with the center of the nozzle. An inverted "W" shape was obtained for the erosion pattern caused by an expected stagnation point in the zone directly below the nozzle. The highest erosion rate was observed right outside this stagnation zone.

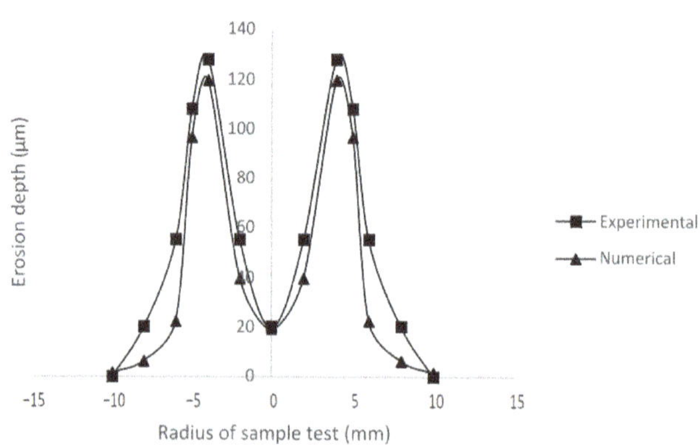

Figure 6. Numerical and experimental material removal in the test specimen (5 min impingement).

4. Results and Discussion

This section presents the results from the sediment analysis and the CFD analysis that were carried out to study the effect of sediment particles over the main components of SFH turbines when varying the guide vane opening. The simulation results were compared with actual site data.

4.1. Sediment Characterization

4.1.1. Particle Size

The analysis showed that 99.58% of the particles at the desilting basin were finer than 425 μm. In addition, the largest percentage (62.33%) of particles was finer than 75 μm. Figure 7 shows the particle size distribution of the sediment samples. The median grain size was determined as 9.28 μm. Furthermore, the characterization of the particle density was performed, obtaining a value of 2650 kg/m^3.

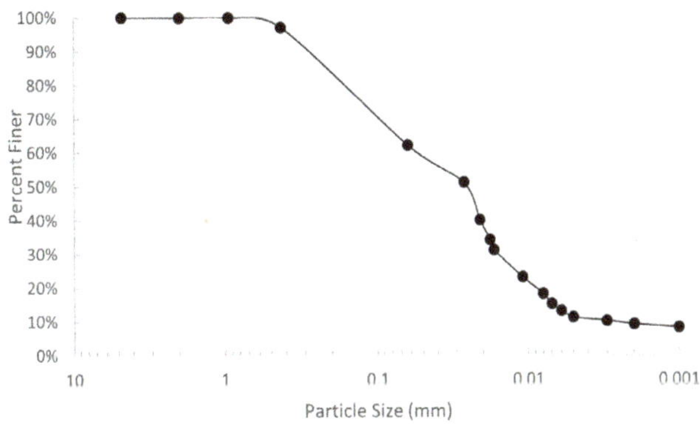

Figure 7. Sediment size distribution.

4.1.2. Mineral Composition

Figure 8 shows the proportion of the mineral content in sediment samples. The results showed that plagioclase minerals represented the highest proportion of sediments in the samples. The hardness values for this mineral group lies between 6.5 and 7.5 in the Mohs scale. When comparing this mineral composition to other reports, a difference in the proportion of quartz and plagioclase sediments was observed. Quartz is typically the predominant mineral found in most rivers, while in this study, plagioclase minerals composed the greatest part of the sediments found in Pastaza River. Nevertheless, the hardness values did not seem to differ significantly from other studies [10–12,14].

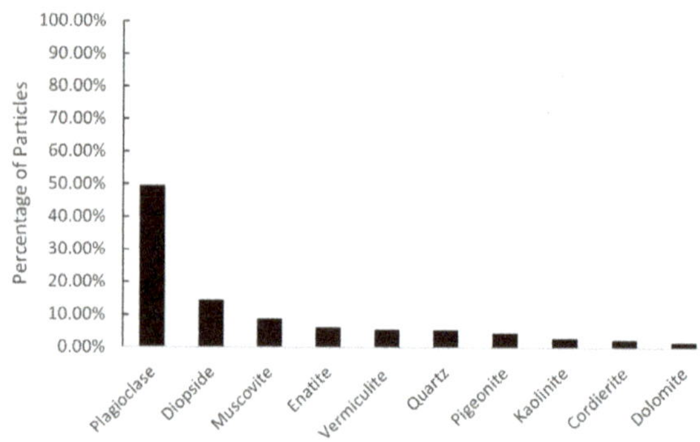

Figure 8. Sediment mineral composition.

4.1.3. Particle Shape

Figure 9 presents the shape of the sediments found in the samples. The analysis exhibited the sharp and slightly rounded edges of the sample particles, which are equivalent to angular and subangular particles based on IEC 62364 standards [33].

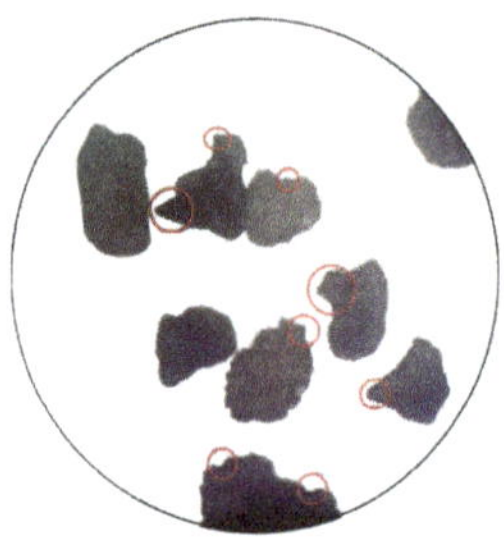

Figure 9. Shape of sediments found in Pastaza River.

Comparing the shape of the sediments with the sample chart, the sphericity and roundness were found to be $S = 0.7$ and $R = 0.3$, respectively.

4.1.4. Sediment Concentration

Table 6 shows particle concentration values in the river under normal conditions. The average concentration value was used to determine the particle mass flow rate.

Table 6. Particle concentration in Pastaza River (kg m^{-3}).

Maximum	Minimum	Average
0.436	0.125	0.334

4.2. Flow Field Prediction

Since erosion is governed by the velocity, incidence angle, and concentration of the solid particles at the time of collision, the erosion prediction depends on the solutions of these parameters. Figure 10 presents the flow field in the turbine, where the main parameters that influence the sediment flow field are the inlet flow and the guide vane opening. In this context, the highest velocity of the flow was observed on the pressure side near the leading edge for the stay vanes. On the other hand, guide vanes and runner blades presented higher flow velocity on the suction side and trailing edge

The efficiency of the turbine was calculated at four different operating points using the data from the flow numerical solution. These results were compared with the experimental data from SFH, as shown in Figure 11.

Satisfactory agreement between results was obtained, though a better prediction of the efficiency was obtained for higher flow rates.

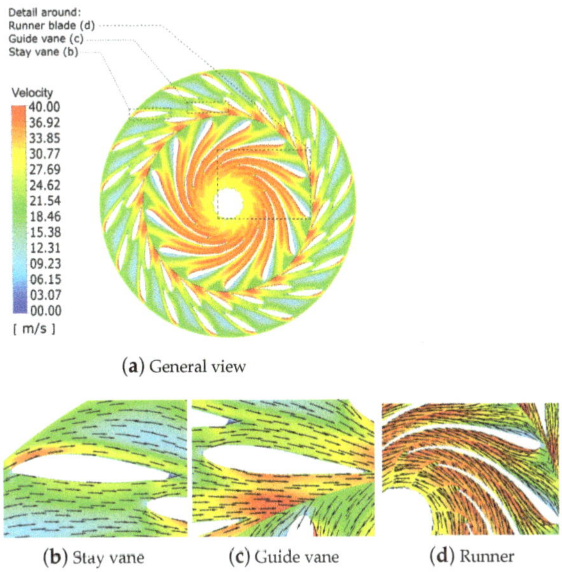

Figure 10. Velocity distribution in flow components at the best efficiency point.

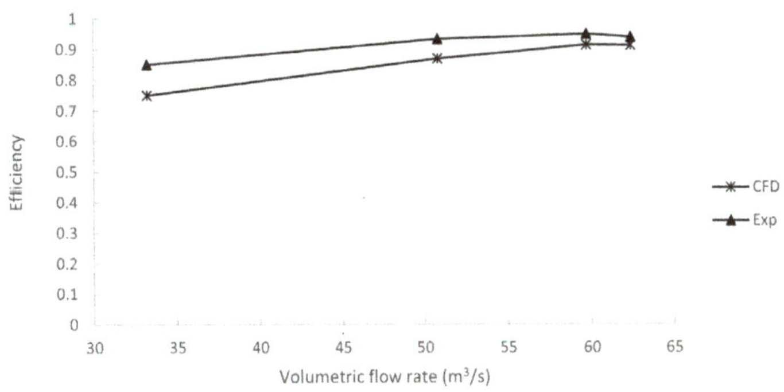

Figure 11. Numerical and experimental efficiency of the turbine.

4.3. Sediment Erosion Prediction

The sediment erosion patterns in critical turbine components are presented in Figure 12. As seen in Figure 12a, runner blades presented a higher erosion rate on the suction side near the trailing edge. In a similar manner, the guide vanes presented higher sediment erosion on the trailing edge of the suction side, as evidenced in Figure 12b. Comparing the flow field from Figure 10 with the eroded zones in Figure 12, it is evident that zones with the highest relative flow velocity experienced higher erosion rates, as expected.

4.3.1. Erosion Description: San Francisco Francis Turbines

This section compares actual site erosion damage on the turbine with the results from the CFD analysis. The images on the right of Figure 12 show the eroded components of a Francis turbine in SFH. Guide vanes presented a higher erosion rate near the clearance gap around the shaft and at both the leading and trailing edges of the vane since the inward flow accelerates near this region due to the decreasing net head pressure at the guide vane cascade. Regarding the runner, the most eroded areas were located at the leading edge and trailing edge of the blades due to the increase in particle velocity in these areas. Good agreement between numerical erosion results and site erosion was observed when comparing both components. The eroded areas of the runner blades coincided with the areas predicted by the numerical analysis. On the other hand, the eroded areas of the guide vanes did not match perfectly with the numerically predicted areas since the clearance gap near the hub and shroud that forces flow interaction with the shaft was not considered in this study.

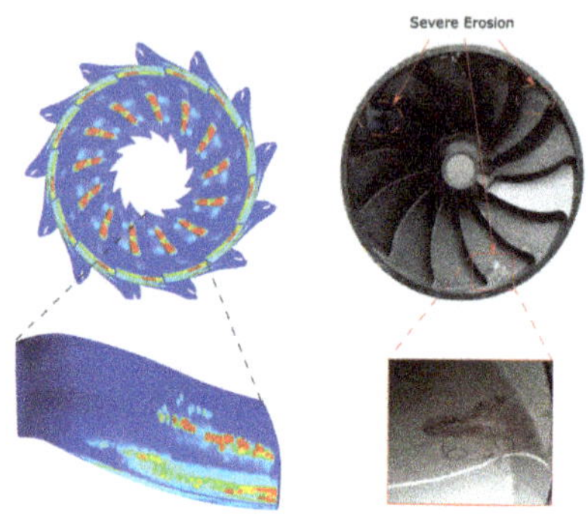

(**a**) Runner

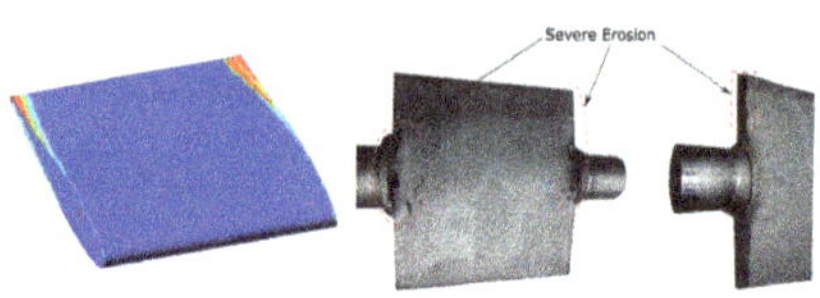

(**b**) Guide vane

Figure 12. Erosion profiles in turbine walls.

4.3.2. Effect of Operating Condition on the Erosion Rate

Figure 13 shows the influence of the guide vane opening and flow velocity on the erosion rate at the stay vanes, guide vanes, and runner. The erosion rate on the walls is calculated as:

$$Er = \frac{1}{A}\int Er_f dA \tag{32}$$

where Er_f is the facet value of the erosion rate and A is the cell area. The erosion increases when increasing guide vane opening since the velocity and the amount of particles impacting the walls is multiplied due to the rise in water flow. A dramatic increase in the erosion rate was observed for operating conditions with guide vane openings over 90%. The sudden increase in erosion rate observed past a certain operating point may be related to the increase in the intensity of turbulent vortices near the outlet of the blade. Previous works [34,35] have found a direct relation among turbulent flow, vortex formation, and accelerated erosion. Vortices and recirculation accelerate particles in the flow and change the impingement angle to critical values. Figure 14 shows the turbulence intensity of the flow surrounding the blade for the different operating conditions.

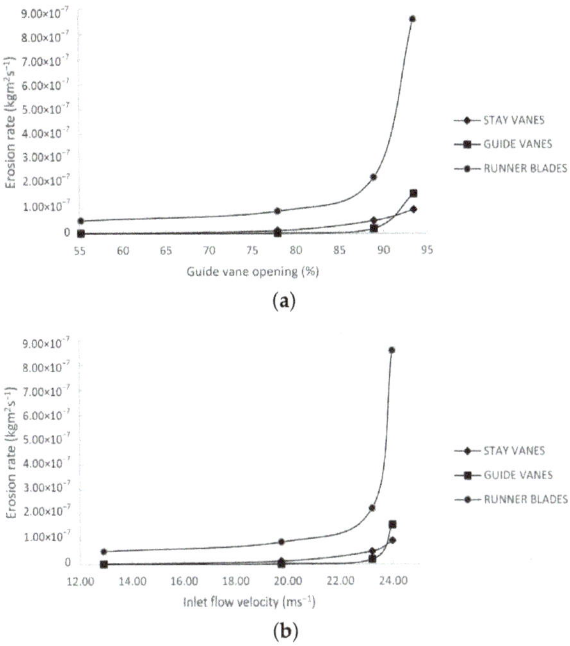

Figure 13. Erosion rate as a function of (**a**) guide vane opening and (**b**) inlet velocity.

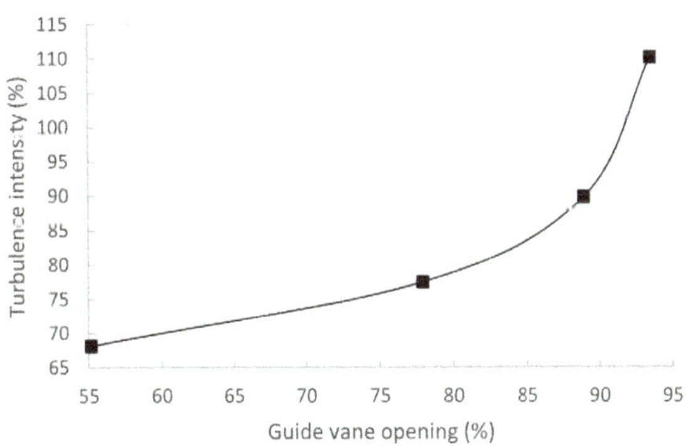

Figure 14. Flow turbulence intensity for different operating conditions.

5. Conclusions

A CFD study replicating the operating conditions of the Francis turbines of San Francisco hydropower plant in Pastaza, Ecuador, was carried out. Flow conditions and erosion patterns were studied for different performance points, obtaining a detailed prediction of wear damage in different turbine components. From the results of the numerical analysis, the following can be concluded

Erosion damage increases significantly for higher flow rates, when the opening of the guide vane exceeds an 85% aperture considering the closed position as a reference.

Operating the turbines at the previously mentioned conditions would result in unnecessary and accelerated erosion wear since the best performance point was obtained at a lower flow rate.

The operation of Francis turbines in sediment-laden rivers should be carried out with particular consideration of the effect that guide vane opening has on the formation of turbulent flow and vorticity. This situation can lead to accelerated erosion rates since vortices and recirculation can accelerate particles in the flow and change the impingement angle to critical values.

CFD is a powerful tool that can be used to prevent such occurrences and analyze the operating conditions in hydropower plants that best harness the available power without sacrificing mechanical integrity.

This study was conducted with the aim of contributing to the creation of a clear and cost-effective strategy to prevent and reduce erosion in existing hydropower plants and proposing an effective erosion-based operating procedure for Francis turbines in the Andean region.

Author Contributions: Conceptualization, E.C.; methodology, E.C. and E.V.; software, C.C.; validation, C.C.; formal analysis, C.C. and D.J.; investigation, C.C. and D.J.; resources, E.C., C.M. and E.V.; data curation, E.V.; writing—original draft preparation, C.C. and D.J.; writing—review and editing, C.C., E.C., E.V. and X.L.; visualization, C.C. and D.J.; supervision, E.C. and I.Z.; project administration, E.C. and I.Z.; funding acquisition, E.C. All authors have read and agreed to the published version of the manuscript.

Funding: This research was funded by Escuela Politécnica Nacional (PIS 19-06).

Institutional Review Board Statement: Not applicable.

Informed Consent Statement: Not applicable.

Acknowledgments: The authors gratefully acknowledge the financial support provided by Escuela Politécnica Nacional through the project PIS 19-06.

Conflicts of Interest: The authors declare no conflict of interest.

References

1. Gernaat, D.E.; Bogaart, P.W.; van Vuuren, D.P.; Biemans, H.; Niessink, R. High-resolution assessment of global technical and economic hydropower potential. *Nat. Energy* **2017**, *2*, 821–828. [CrossRef]
2. Sipahutar, R.; Bernas, S.M.; Imanuddin, M.S. Renewable energy and hydropower utilization tendency worldwide. *Renew. Sustain. Energy Rev.* **2013**, *17*, 213–215.
3. Killingtveit, Å. 15-Hydroelectric Power. In *Future Energy*, 3rd ed.; Letcher, T.M., Ed.; Elsevier: Amsterdam, The Netherlands, 2020; pp. 315–330. [CrossRef]
4. Hoes, O.A.; Meijer, L.J.; Van Der Ent, R.J.; Van De Giesen, N.C. Systematic high-resolution assessment of global hydropower potential. *PLoS ONE* **2017**, *12*, e0171844. [CrossRef]
5. Koirala, R.; Zhu, B.; Neopane, H.P. Effect of guide vane clearance gap on Francis turbine performance. *Energies* **2016**, *9*, 275. [CrossRef]
6. Noon, A.A.; Kim, M.H. Erosion wear on Francis turbine components due to sediment flow. *Wear* **2017**, *378*, 126–135. [CrossRef]
7. Levy, A.V. The solid particle erosion behavior of steel as a function of microstructure. *Wear* **1981**, *68*, 269–287. [CrossRef]
8. Thapa, B.S.; Thapa, B.; Dahlhaug, O.G. Empirical modelling of sediment erosion in Francis turbines. *Energy* **2012**, *41*, 386–391. [CrossRef]
9. Thapa, B.S.; Gjosater, K.; Eltvik, M.; Dahlhaug, O.G.; Thapa, B. Effects of turbine design parameters on sediment erosion of Francis runner. In Proceedings of the 2nd International Conference on the Developments in Renewable Energy Technology (ICDRET 2012), Dhaka, Bangladesh, 5–7 January 2012; pp. 1–5.
10. Singh, M.; Banerjee, J.; Patel, P.; Tiwari, H. Effect of silt erosion on Francis turbine: A case study of Maneri Bhali Stage-II, Uttarakhand, India. *ISH J. Hydraul. Eng.* **2013**, *19*, 1–10. [CrossRef]
11. Koirala, R.; Thapa, B.; Neopane, H.P.; Zhu, B.; Chhetry, B. Sediment erosion in guide vanes of Francis turbine: A case study of Kaligandaki Hydropower Plant, Nepal. *Wear* **2016**, *362*, 53–60. [CrossRef]
12. Masoodi, J.; Harmain, G. Sediment erosion of Francis turbine runners in the Himalayan region of India. *Int. J. Hydropower Dams* **2017**, *24*, 82–89.
13. Qian, Z.; Zhao, Z.; Guo, Z.; Thapa, B.S.; Thapa, B. Erosion wear on runner of Francis turbine in Jhimruk Hydroelectric Center. *J. Fluids Eng.* **2020**, *142*, 094502. [CrossRef]

14. Noon, A.A.; Kim, M.H. Sediment and Cavitation Erosion in Francis Turbines—Review of Latest Experimental and Numerical Techniques. *Energies* **2021**, *14*, 1516. [CrossRef]
15. Laraque, A.; Bernal, C.; Bourrel, L.; Darrozes, J.; Christophoul, F.; Armijos, E.; Fraizy, P.; Pombosa, R.; Guyot, J.L. Sediment budget of the Napo river, Amazon basin, Ecuador and Peru. *Hydrol. Process. Int. J.* **2009**, *23*, 3509–3524. [CrossRef]
16. Koirala, R.; Chitrakar, S.; Regmi, S.N.; Khadka, M.; Thapa, B.; Neopane, H.P. Analysis of sediment samples and erosion potential: A case study of Upper Tamakoshi Hydroelectric Project. *Hydro Nepal* **2015**, *16*, 28–31. [CrossRef]
17. Cruz-Matías, I.; Ayala, D.; Hiller, D.; Gutsch, S.; Zacharias, M.; Estradé, S.; Peiró, F. Sphericity and roundness computation for particles using the extreme vertices model. *J. Comput. Sci.* **2019**, *30*, 28–40. [CrossRef]
18. Hryciw, R.D.; Zheng, J.; Shetler, K. Particle roundness and sphericity from images of assemblies by chart estimates and computer methods. *J. Geotech. Geoenviron. Eng.* **2016**, *142*, 04016038. [CrossRef]
19. Krumbein, W.C.; Sloss, L.L. *Stratigraphy and Sedimentation*; W.H. Freeman & Co.: San Francisco, CA, USA,1951; pp. 114–128.
20. Stoessel, L.; Nilsson, H. Steady and unsteady numerical simulations of the flow in the Tokke Francis turbine model, at three operating conditions. *J. Phys. Conf. Ser.* **2015**, *579*, 012011. [CrossRef]
21. Iovănel, R.; Bucur, D.; Cervantes, M. Study on the Accuracy of RANS Modelling of the Turbulent Flow Developed in a Kaplan Turbine Operated at BEP. Part 1—Velocity Field. *J. Appl. Fluid Mech.* **2019**, *12*, 1449–1461. [CrossRef]
22. Liu, H.L.; Liu, M.M.; Dong, L.; Ren, Y.; Du, H. Effects of computational grids and turbulence models on numerical simulation of centrifugal pump with CFD. *IOP Conf. Ser. Earth Environ. Sci.* **2012**, *15*, 062005. [CrossRef]
23. ANSYS Inc. *ANSYS Fluent User's Guide, R2014, Section 4.4.3*; ANSYS, Inc.: Canonsburg, PA, USA, 2014.
24. ANSYS Inc. *ANSYS Fluent User's Guide, R2014, Section 15.2.2*; ANSYS, Inc.: Canonsburg, PA, USA, 2014.
25. Huilier, D.G.F. An Overview of the Lagrangian Dispersion Modeling of Heavy Particles in Homogeneous Isotropic Turbulence and Considerations on Related LES Simulations. *Fluids* **2021**, *6*, 145. [CrossRef]
26. Oka, Y.; Yoshida, T.; Okamura, K. Practical estimation of erosion damage caused by solid particle impact, Part 1: Effects of impact parameters on a predictive equation. *Wear* **2005**, *259*, 95–101. [CrossRef]
27. Oka, Y.; Yoshida, T. Practical estimation of erosion damage caused by solid particle impact Part 2: Mechanical properties of materials directly associated with erosion damage. *Wear* **2005**, *259*, 102–109. [CrossRef]
28. Nguyen, V.; Nguyen, Q.; Liu, Z.; Wan, S.; Lim, C.; Zhang, Y. A combined numerical–experimental study on the effect of surface evolution on the water–sand multiphase flow characteristics and the material erosion behavior. *Wear* **2014**, *319*, 96–109. [CrossRef]
29. Pereira, G.; de Souza, F.; de Moro Martins, D. Numerical prediction of the erosion due to particles in elbows. *Powder Technol.* **2014**, *261*, 105–117. [CrossRef]
30. Messa, G.; Wang, Y. Importance of accounting for finite particle size in CFD based erosion prediction. *Powder Technol.* **2014**, *261*, 105–117.
31. Cando, E.; Yu, A.; Zhu, L.; Liu, J.; Lu, L.; Hidalgo, V.; Luo, X.W. Unsteady numerical analysis of the liquid–solid two-phase flow around a step using Eulerian-Lagrangian and the filter-based RANS method. *J. Mech. Sci. Technol.* **2017**, *31*, 2781–2790. [CrossRef]
32. Cando, E.; Huan, R.F.; Valencia, E.; Luo, X.W. Sediment Erosion Prediction for a Francis Turbine Based on Liquid-Solid Flow Simulation Using Modified PANS. In Proceedings of the 4th World Congress on Mechanical, Chemical, and Material Engineering, Madrid, Spain, 16–18 August 2018.
33. Hydraulic Machines-Guidelines for Dealing with Hydro-Abrasive Erosion in Kaplan, Francis, and Pelton Turbines, IEC 62634. 2019. Available online: https://webstore.iec.ch/preview/info_iec62364%7Bed2.0.RLV%7Den.pdf (accessed on 10 August 2021)
34. Chen, Y.; Li, R.; Han, W.; Guo, T.; Su, M.; Wei, S. Sediment Erosion Characteristics and Mechanism on Guide Vane End-Clearance of Hydro Turbine. *Appl. Sci.* **2019**, *9*, 4137. [CrossRef]
35. Neopane, H.P.; Dahlhaug, O.G.; Cervantes, M. The effect of sediment characteristics for predicting erosion on Francis turbines blades. *Int. J. Hydropower Dams* **2012**, *19*, 79–83.

MDPI
St. Alban-Anlage 66
4052 Basel
Switzerland
www.mdpi.com

MDPI Books Editorial Office
E-mail: books@mdpi.com
www.mdpi.com/books

www.ingramcontent.com/pod-product-compliance
Lightning Source LLC
Chambersburg PA
CBHW041932260926
51850CB00018B/56
* 9 7 8 3 0 3 6 5 9 2 0 0 8 *